# CHINA IN WESTERN LITERATURE

*A Continuation of Cordier's Bibliotheca Sinica*

*Compiled by*

TUNG-LI YUAN 袁同禮

*Far Eastern Publications  Yale University  New Haven Conn.  1958*

# FOREWORD

The first volume of Henri Cordier's *Bibliotheca Sinica* appeared in 1878. The final volume was printed in 1924. For several decades students throughout the world have been hoping for a continuation of Cordier's exhaustive work -- one that would record, as his did, all known books and monographs on China in the major languages of the West. Thanks to years of selfless labor on the part of Dr. T. L. Yuan, who from 1926 to 1948 was Director of the National Library of Peiping, these hopes have now been realized. Instead of being restricted to sporadic and incomplete lists, treating only special periods or subjects, students of Chinese affairs now have for ready reference a record of virtually all books concerning China published in English, French and German between the years 1921 and 1957. It is of more than passing interest that this Continuation appears on the Eightieth Anniversary of the publication of Cordier's first volume.

Highly competent in the techniques of library science, and widely read in the literature of his country, both in Chinese and in Western languages, Dr. Yuan was uniquely qualified to bring to completion this heavy task. The 18,000 works which he describes were not copied from other sources but were in nearly every instance examined by him personally to assure accuracy in all details. To provide against important omissions he visited most of the great Oriental libraries, first in the United States and then in Europe, gaining information and suggestions from bibliographers in all these centers. The consequence is that his Continuation embodies, for the period and for the languages treated, more works on China than are to be found in any single library, or in any catalog.

During his years as Director of China's greatest library, and in the course of his wide travels, Dr. Yuan had the opportunity to meet personally most of the writers of this generation whose books he describes. This is especially true of that growing number of Chinese scholars and men of letters who, fortunately for the West, have chosen to write about their country in English, French, or German. Acquaintance with these writers and knowledge of his own language enabled Dr. Yuan to assign the proper characters to their names, even though the title pages commonly omit them. Librarians, and students who read the Chinese language, will find their research lightened. For making this typographically possible, credit is due to Professor George A. Kennedy of Yale University.

The appearance of this work, despite the mental barriers that temporarily divide the world, testifies that China lives -- and will continue to live -- in the imagination of the West. One needs only to open the pages of this book to perceive what a broad and liberal spirit of intellectual cooperation pervades the world.

Arthur W. Hummel

Washington, D. C.

# PREFACE

The first edition of Henri Cordier's monumental *Bibliotheca Sinica*, published in two volumes between the years 1878 and 1885, represents the first systematic attempt to record western publications on China from the sixteenth century to the eighties of the nineteenth century. A supplement published in 1895 lists such literature to the end of 1894. That Cordier's work filled a substantial need is attested by the fact that within a few years the first edition was exhausted. Considerably enlarged and revised, a second edition in four volumes was published between 1904 and 1908; and a supplementary volume appeared in 1924.

The need for a continuation of Cordier's bibliography is obvious -- all the more so because there has been a vast output of sinological studies, in recent decades, studies often unknown even to specialists. The present work is intended to fill this need.

The scope of this continuation is limited in several respects: it is restricted to the period from 1921 to 1957; it does not include articles in periodicals unless they were issued subsequently as independent monographs; it comprises only works in English, French and German, an exception being made for Portuguese, a language rich in works on Macao. Chinese texts with added titles in western languages, such as the Harvard-Yenching Sinological Index series, are generally excluded. Maps and charts are omitted because they require special treatment. Notwithstanding these limitations, the bibliography represents a comprehensive survey of all types of writings on China, with no attempt to select or reject, but rather, to record and describe.

It would have been a great help to investigators had it been possible to list articles in journals, for these are fugitive in character and often appear in unexpected places. Indeed, an effort was made in this direction, the labor being apportioned between my friend the late Dr. Cheuk-woon Taam and myself. While I was concentrating on monographic publications, he recorded articles in journals. Furthermore, we adopted a similar classification with a view to publishing the two bibliographies simultaneously. But Dr. Taam's untimely death on October 20, 1956 not only deprived me of his valued collaboration, but also prevented the carrying out of our plan. It is now my earnest hope that support may be found to bring his labors to fruition.

In the past thirty-five years, an increasing number of Chinese authors have written about China in western languages. But since their names do not generally appear on the title pages in Chinese characters, it is often very hard to identify them. The difficulty is increased by the natural desire of Chinese authors to romanize their names according to the sounds in their own local dialects. Furthermore, those who studied in France or Germany frequently adopted the French or German systems of romanization. To overcome this difficulty, efforts have been made to make a clear identification of all Chinese names, irrespective of the way they happen to be spelled. This is done by inserting the Chinese characters beside the romanized form. It is hoped that this more precise identification will be of help to students of Chinese studies and to librarians for the years to come.

In the catalogs of American and English libraries, Chinese names are usually romanized according to the Wade-Giles system as established in H. A. Giles' *Chinese-English Dictionary*. But since this system seems to many

Chinese authors not to represent properly the pronunciation of their names, the forms adopted by the authors themselves are accepted for the main entry in the present work. Any readers, however, who have access to the printed catalog cards of the Library of Congress will find there the names of these authors with the Wade-Giles romanization added in parentheses.

However great the debt we owe to the labors of Cordier, it has long been recognized that his scheme of classification was far from satisfactory. Hence, on the advice of a number of scholars, I have arranged the titles under broader subject groups in the hope that readers may find more readily the items desired. The geographical divisions, designed as they are for convenience, should not be taken too literally. For example, works on archaeological discoveries at Tunhuang are grouped with those under Sinkiang rather than under Kansu. It stands to reason that such classifications must be arbitrary, hence it is not expected that every reader will fully agree with them.

The bibliographical data comprising this work were collected at the Library of Congress and at twenty other leading libraries in the United States. Subsequently, search was made in London, Oxford, Cambridge, Paris, Frankfurt, Marburg, Munich, Zurich, Berne, Brussels, Leyden, and The Hague. The cordial assistance which I received from librarians of these institutions promoted the fulfillment of my task, and will always be remembered with gratitude. Titles not found in the above-mentioned depositories were culled from various national bibliographies. In particular, the National Union Catalog at Washington was a continual help, and greatly facilitated the work of checking.

Efforts have been made to render the entries complete in every detail, only the dimensions of the books have been omitted. In a work of this range and detail, omissions and misprints are inevitable. Despite every effort to be inclusive for the years treated, titles unknown to the compiler will doubtless be found. Any corrections and additions will be gratefully received, for it is hoped that important omissions may appear in a supplementary volume. The present work is to be regarded as no more than the first step in an unfulfilled task and a modest contribution toward a more thorough and systematic study of China.

Obviously, a work of this magnitude could not have been brought to completion without the help of many scholars. It is with sincere appreciation that I express my gratitude to Dr. Arthur W. Hummel and Dr. Hu Shih for their inspiration, guidance and continuing interest. I am indebted to Dr. Horace I. Poleman, Chief of the Orientalia Division, and Dr. Edwin G. Beal, Head of the Chinese Section in the Library of Congress, for their advice and constructive criticism. Grateful acknowledgement is due to Dr. L. Quincy Mumford, Librarian of Congress, and Mr. Verner W. Clapp, President of the Council on Library Resources, Inc. for their encouragement. In particular, I wish to record my indebtedness to Dr. A. Kaiming Chiu, Librarian of the Chinese-Japanese Library at Harvard University; Miss Gussie Gaskill, Curator of the Wason Collection at Cornell University; Miss Ruth Lapham Butler, Custodian of the Newberry Library; Dr. Rudolf Löwenthal of Georgetown University; and F. W. Paar of the New York Public Library; who generously verified many bibliographical details. I must express my gratitude also to Mr. Beverley H. Brown, Dr. J. M. Coopersmith, Mr. Nathan K. Kaganoff, Mr. Russell Le Gaer, Dr. Walter H. Maurer, Mrs. Grace E. M. May, Mr. Peter Petcoff, and Dr. K. T. Wu, my colleague at the Library of Congress, for their invariable and generous assistance. For help in identifying Chinese authors, I wish to express my appreciation to Professor

Chen Chou-Yi of the Claremont Graduate School; Professor Franklin L. Ho of Columbia University; Dr. Tch'en Hiong-Fei of the Chinese Embassy, Paris; Mr. Frank Tao of the Chinese News Service; Mr. Tao Pung-Fei of Los Altos, California; and Mr. Chia-pi Hsu of the East Asiatic Library at Columbia University.

In the course of my researches in Europe, I incurred obligations to Professor Walter Simon of the School of Oriental and African Studies, University of London; Mr. A. F. L. Beeston of the Bodleian Library; Professor Charles R. Boxer of the King's College, University of London; Professor Paul Demiéville of the Collège de France; Madame Marie R. Guignard of the Bibliothèque nationale; Madame Collette Meuvret of the Ecole nationale des langues orientales vivantes; Dr. W. Seuberlich of the Westdeutsche Bibliothek; Dr. Walter Heissig of the Universität Göttingen; Dr. Wolfgang Franke of the Universität Hamburg; Dr. A. F. P. Hulsewé of the Sinologisch Instituut at Leyden; and Dr. Gosta Montell of the Statens Etnografiska Museum at Stockholm, who responded cheerfully to my inquiries and requests. They saved me from many errors and their counsel and encouragement materially lightened my work.

My acknowledgements would be incomplete if I did not mention the assistance I received from the Osterreichische Nationalbibliothek, the Bibliothèque royal de Belgique; the National Library of Canada; the Commonwealth National Library at Canberra; the Raffles Library at Singapore, the National Library of India, the National Library of Philippines; the National Central Library at Taipei; the National Diet Library at Tokyo and the Library of the University of Hong Kong. To their directors and staff, I extend my hearty thanks.

To the Rockefeller Foundation, I am under a great debt of gratitude for the generous support which enabled me to spend a year in Europe. The China Foundation furthered the completion of this work by several grants; to the Trustees of that Foundation, I express my grateful appreciation.

My obligation is great to Professor Serge Elisséeff, Director of the Harvard-Yenching Institute, and to Dr. Chang Chi-yun, Minister of Education, Republic of China, for substantial help in securing a subsidy toward the cost of printing.

A special word of acknowledgement is due to Professor George A. Kennedy, Director of Far Eastern Publications, Yale University, who took pains to see the bibliography through the press. In particular I wish to express my heartfelt thanks to Mr. and Mrs. Toshio Kono for their constant and invaluable service in expediting the production of this volume. To Mrs. Patricia Fleischer and Mr. George C. Hatch, Jr., I owe a special debt for their help in typing and reading proof. Mention should also be made of the assistance of my son, Cheng Yuan, who from time to time made valuable suggestions.

Finally, I must acknowledge the forbearance of my wife, Hui-Hsi Yuan, who saw me through the more difficult stages of research and who rendered valuable assistance in the preparation of the Index. Without her understanding help, this bibliography could hardly have been completed.

Tung-Li Yuan

# ABBREVIATIONS

| | | | |
|---|---|---|---|
| Abh. | Abhandlung | introd. | introduction |
| abp. | archbishop | Jahrg. | Jahrgang |
| arr. | arranged | Jr. | Junior |
| Aufl. | Auflage | l. | leaf, leaves |
| augm. | augmented | ltd. | limited |
| Ausg. | Ausgabe | ms., mss. | manuscript(s) |
| b. | birth | Mitt. | Mitteilungen |
| Bd. | Band | n. d. | no date (of publication) |
| Bde | Bände | n. p. | no place (of publication) |
| bearb. | bearbeitet | n. s. | new series |
| BEFEO | Bulletin de l'École fran- | no. | number(s), numéro |
| | caise d'Extrême-Orient | nouv. | nouveau, nouvelle |
| Bl. | Blatt | nr. | numer |
| BMFEA | Bulletin of the Museum of | numb. | numbered |
| | Far Eastern Antiquities | off. | office |
| bp. | bishop | p. | page(s) |
| Buchdr. | Buchdrucker, Buchdruck- | p. l. | preliminary leaf (leaves) |
| | erei | pl. | plate(s) |
| bull. | bulletin | port, ports. | portrait(s) |
| c. | copyright | pref. | preface |
| ca. | circa | préf. | préface |
| cf. | compare | print. | printing |
| ch. | chapter | priv. print. | privately printed |
| Cie. | Compagnie | pseud. | pseudonym |
| cm. | centimeter | pt., pts. | part(s), parte |
| Co. | Company | pub. | publishing |
| col. | colored | publ. | publication(s) |
| comp. | compile, compiler | rev. | revised |
| corr. | corrected | ser. | series |
| d. | death | sér. | série |
| diagr.(s) | diagram(s) | suppl. | supplement |
| Diss. | Dissertation | t. | tome |
| ed. | edited, editor, edition | t. p. | title page |
| éd. | édition | tab. | table(s) |
| Eng. | England | tr. | translator, translated, trans- |
| enl. | enlarged | | lation |
| et al | et alii | übers. | übersetzt |
| evang. | evangelistic | univ. | university |
| facsim.(s) | facsimile(s) | ungez. | ungezeichnet |
| fasc. | fascicle | v., vol., vols. | volume(s) |
| fl. | flourished | verb. | verbesserte |
| fold. | folded, folding | | |
| front.(s) | frontispiece(s) | | |
| geb. | gebunden | | |
| gez. | gezeichnet | | |
| govt. | government | | |
| Govt. | Government Printing | | |
| Print. Off. | Office | | |
| hdgrs. | headquarters | | |
| HJAS | Harvard Journal of | | |
| | Asiatic Studies | | |
| hrsg. | herausgegeben | | |
| illus. | illustration(s), illustrated | | |
| impr. | imprimerie | | |
| inc. | incorporated | | |
| incl. | including | | |

TABLE OF CONTENTS

# I. BIBLIOGRAPHY AND REFERENCE

## General Bibliographies

[AUSTRALIA. Joint Service Staff, Washington, D.C.] China; handbook of selected reference material. [Washington] 1949- 12 pts.
———. Supplement. no. 1. 1 v. (unpaged).

BATES, MINER SEARLE, 1897- An introduction to Oriental journals in western languages, with an annotated bibliography of representative articles. Nanking, Institute of Chinese Cultural Studies, the University of Nanking. 1933. 65 p. (Publications [of the Institute of Chinese cultural studies] ser. B).

BULLETIN of Far Eastern Bibliography, ed. by E.H. Pritchard. v.1-5, February 1936-40. Washington, Committee on Far Eastern Studies, American Council of Learned Societies, 1936-40. 5 v.

CHAO, KUO-CHÜN, 趙國鈞 1918- Selected works in English for a topical study of modern China, 1840-1952. Cambridge, Regional Studies Program on East Asia, Harvard University, 1952. 38 p.

CHINA. Bureau of International Exchange. List of Chinese government publications. [Shanghai] Pub. by Academia Sinica.Bureau of International Exchange, 1930. 67 p.

CLAREMONT COLLEGE, Claremont, Calif. Library. Materials on the Pacific area, in selected libraries of the Los Angeles region. Claremont, Calif., Claremont Colleges Library, 1943-44. 3 pts.

CORDIER, HENRI, 1849-1925. Bibliotheca Sinica. Dictionnaire bibliographique des ouvrages relatifs à l'Empire chinois. 2. éd., rev., cor.et considérablement augm. Paris, E. Guilmoto, 1904-08. 4 v.
———. Supplément et index. Paris, P. Geuthner, 1922-24. 4 v. in 1.
———. Same; Reprint ed. Peking, 1938. 5 v.
———. Author index to the Bibliotheca Sinica of Henri Cordier (2nd edition, 4 v. Paris, 1904-08. Suppl. 1 v. Paris, 1924), compiled, issued and distributed by the East Asiatic Library, Columbia University Libraries. New York, 1953. iv, 84 p.

FAIRBANK, JOHN KING, 1907- Modern China; a bibliographical guide to Chinese works, 1898-1937, by John King Fairbank and Kwang-ching Liu, 劉廣京 . Cambridge, Harvard University Press, 1950. xviii, 608 p. (Harvard-Yenching Institute studies, v. 1).
———. Japanese studies of modern China; a bibliographical guide to historical and social-science research on the 19th and 20th centuries, by John King Fairbank and Masataka Banno. Rutland, Vt., Published for the Harvard-Yenching Institute [by] C.E. Tuttle Co., 1955. xviii, 331 p.

FAR EASTERN bibliography. 1941-date. Ithaca, N.Y., Pub. for the Far Eastern Assn. by Cornell Univ. Press, 1941-date.

HANKOW CLUB, Library. Hankow. Bibliography of China, being a rough index to Cordier's "Bibliotheca Sinica." Volumes 1-4428. [Hankow] 1926. 14 p. (Its "China Class." Appendix vii. 1926).

INSTITUTE OF PACIFIC RELATIONS. American Council. Far Eastern bibliographies, 1947. New York [1947] [19] l.

JOHNSEN, JULIA EMILY, comp. Selected articles on China yesterday and today, with an introduction by Ping-wen Kuo, 郭秉文 . New York, H.W. Wilson, 1928. lxxviii, [5]-362 p. fold. map, fold. tab. (The handbook series. Ser. II, v. 3).

KERNER, ROBERT JOSEPH, 1887-1956. Northeastern Asia, a selected bibliography; contributions to the bibliography of the relations of China, Russia,
and Japan, with special reference to Korea, Manchuria, Mongolia, and eastern Siberia, in oriental and European languages. Berkeley, University of
California Press, 1939. 2 v. [Publications of the Northeastern Asia seminar
of the University of California].

KYOTO. UNIVERSITY. Research Institute of Humanistic Sciences. Annual bibliography of oriental studies for 1946-50. Compiled by J. Kurata [and] Y. Ka-
wakatsu. Kyoto, 1952. x, 157, 118 p.

LÖWENTHAL RUDOLF, 1904- Bibliography of Russian literature on China and
adjacent countries, 1931-36. Cambridge, 1949. iii, 93 l.

———. Works on the Far East and Central Asia published in the U.S.S.R., 1937-
47. Ithaca, 1949. [12] p. Reprinted from Far Eastern Quarterly 8:2.

MARUZEN CO. Tokyo. A selected and classified catalogue of books written in
European languages originally published in Japan and China. Tokyo, Maruzen Co., [1936] 89, [3] p.

PEKING. NATIONAL LIBRARY. Selected Chinese books, 1933-37, edited and
published by the National library of Peiping through the generosity of the
Rockefeller foundation, New York. [Peiping, The National Library of Pei-
ping] 1940. vi, 214 p.

PROBSTHAIN, ARTHUR. Encyclopaedia of books on China. London, A. Probsthain (late Probsthain and Co.) 1927. [3]-283 (i.e. 289) p. plates.

QUARTERLY bulletin of Chinese bibliography. English ed. v. 1-4, 1934-37;n.s.
v. 1-8, 1940-48. Edited by the National Library of Peiping. Peiping, Kunming, Chungking, 1934-48.

TÊNG, SSÜ-YÜ, 鄧嗣禹, 1906- An annotated bibliography of selected Chinese
reference works. Rev. ed. Compiled by Ssü-yü Têng and Knight Biggerstaff.
Cambridge, Harvard University Press, 1950. x 326 p. (Harvard-Yenching
Institute studies, v. 2).

U.S. Dept. of State. Office of Intelligence Research. Research on China, completed and in progress. Compiled and distributed by External Research Staff.
Washington, 1953-57. 8 v. (Its External research list, 2.1-2.8).

———. Library of Congress. China: a selected list of references on contemporary economic and industrial development with special emphasis on post-
war reconstruction. Comp. by Helen F. Conover. Rev. ed. Washington,
1946. 118 p. 1st ed. 1945.

WALKER, RICHARD LOUIS, 1922- Western language periodicals on China; a
selective list. New Haven, Far Eastern Publications, Yale University, 1949.
i, 30 p.

WOO, KANG, 吳康, 1896- Histoire de la bibliographie chinoise. Paris, E.
Leroux, 1938. [vii]-viii, 127 p. (Bibliothéque de l'Institut des hautes études
chinoises. v. 5).

## Reading Lists

AYSCOUGH, FLORENCE (WHEELOCK), 1878-1942. Friendly books on far Cathay, (being a bibliography for the student) and a synopsis of Chinese history. Shanghai, Commercial Press, 1921. cover-title, 58 p.

BENTLEY, WILDER, 1900- comp. Culture of the Far East in northern California; a check list of books and pamphlets available to students of inter-cul-
tural relations. With a supplementary list of books on Japanese culture in
the William Dallam Armes collection of Japanese prints, comp. by Chiura
Obata. Stockton, Calif., Stockton Junior College, 1947. cover-title, 14 l.

CHINA INSTITUTE IN AMERICA. One hundred selected books on China (rev.
list) New York, China Institute in America [1928?] cover-title, 16 p. (Bull.
6).

[———.] China; a brief list of introductory readings. [New York, 1939?]      25

numb. 1.
——. China's changing civilization; a selected bibliography of books in the
English language, by Loo Lai-han, 盧麗嫺. New York, China Institute in
America [c1935] 35 p.
EAST AND WEST ASSOCIATION, New York. A miscellaneous [6] list of sour-
ces in the metropolitan area for teaching materials on China and India. [New
York] East and West Association, c1943. cover-title, 6 numb. 1.
——. What to read about China. New York, East and West Association, 1945-
17 p. 1st ed. 1942.
HEIMERS, LILI, 1881- China; broadsides, charts and maps, exhibits, films,
music-songs-games, pictures, publications, and recordings. Montclair in-
stitute and workshop on China for elementary and secondary school teachers,
Dr. Bangnee A. Liu, 劉彭年, director, June 26-July 8, 1944. [Upper Mont-
clair, N.J., 1944] 4 numb. 1.
HORTON, MARION LOUISE. China, books for children and young people. Chi-
cago, American Library Association [1942] folder (6 p.) "Reprinted from
the Booklist, March 1, 1942."
HUMMEL, ARTHUR WILLIAM, 1884- Toward understanding China. Chicago,
American Library Association, 1942. folder (6 p.) "Reprinted from the
Booklist, January 1, 1942."
INSTITUTE OF PACIFIC RELATIONS. San Francisco Bay Region Division. Pre-
liminary checklist of publications of the Institute of Pacific relations rela-
ting to China. San Francisco, Institute of Pacific Relations, San Francisco
Bay Region Division, 1944. cover-title, 8 p.
ROBSON, HARRIET HARDISON, comp. Books for the traveller or sojourner in
China, a selective bibliography, with introductory notes by Ruth Earnshaw.
New York, American Council, Institute of Pacific Relations [c1937] 24 p.
THOMAS, S.B. Recent books on China, 1945-51. 1948-51 compiled by S. B.
Thomas. 1945-47 compiled by Knight Biggerstaff. New York, American In-
stitute of Pacific Relations, 1951. cover-title, 16 1.
U.S. Central Intelligence Agency. Chinese book list. No. 1-    1955. [Wash-
ington] 1955-
——. Library of Congress. What one should know about China; an annotated
list of some dependable books. [n.p., 1942?] [4] p. "Reprinted from Wilson
library bulletin, September 1942."
——. Office of Strategic Services. Research and Analysis Branch. Check-list
of books on northwest China. [Washington] 1944. 7 1. (Its R and A 1846).
WILLIAMS, FREDERICK WELLS, 1857-1928. The best hundred books on China;
a finding list of books in English, selected and annotated, by Frederick Wells
Williams and the Rev. Frank W. Price. New Haven, Yale University Library, 1924. 20 p.

## Yearbooks

The CHINA annual. 1944. Shanghai, The Asia Statistics Co. [1944] 1234 p. maps.
CHINA handbook. 1937/43, 1937/44, 1937/45, 1950, 1951, 1952/53, 1953/54,
1954/55, 1956/57. 9 v. illus., fold. maps. Compiled 1937/43-37/45 by the
Chinese Ministry of Information; 1950-   by the China Handbook Editorial
Board. Imprint varies: 1937/43-37/44, Chungking.    — 1937/43, 1937/45,
New York, Macmillan. — 1950, New York, Rockport Press. — 1951-
Taipei. Issues of 1937-43 ed. published in Chungking and New York.
The CHINA year book. 1912-39. London, G. Routledge; New York, E.P. Dut-
ton, 1912-19; Peking and Tientsin, Tientsin Press, 1921-39. 20 v. fold.
maps.
The CHINESE year book. 1st-5th issue; 1935/36-1940/41. Shanghai, Commer-
cial Press, [1935-41] 5 v. fold. map, tables (part fold.) diagrs.

Almanacs and Calendars

CHINESE ASSOCIATION FOR THE UNITED NATIONS. A symposium on the
  World clanedar: 1. The Chinese and the world's ancient calendars by Tung
  Tso-pin, 董作賓. 2. On the so-called world calendar by Kao Ping-tze, 高
  平子 . Taipei, 1951. 29 p.
HSÜEH, CHUNG-SAN, 薛仲三. A Sino-western calendar for two thousand years
  1-2000 A.D., by Hsüeh, Chung-san and Ouyang, Yi, 歐陽頤. Changsha,
  Commercial Press, 1940. xx, 438 p.
100 YEARS Chinese-English calendar, 1864-1963. [Penang, Chee Chin Chong,
  1950. 100 p.
KOEHN, ALFRED. comp. A year of the Horse. Peking, Lotus Court, 1943. iii,
  45 p.
——. A year of the Ram. Peiping, Lotus Court, 1943. iii. 43 p.
——. A year of the Cock. Peiping, Lotus Court, 1945. [3] 12 p.
——. A year of the Dog. Peking, Lotus Court, 1946. 46 p.
——. A year of the Pig. Peiping, Lotus Court, 1947. 46 p.
——. A year of the Rat. Peiping, Lotus Court, 1948. 57 p.
TAN, PONG-GUAN, 陳邦元 . Sixty years Anglo-Chinese calendar, 1876-1935.
  Singapore, Union Times Press Co., 1925. 126 p.
——. Eighty years Anglo-Chinese calendar, 1876-1955. Singapore, Hong
  Cheong Press, 1935. 168 p.
WELCH, WINDON CHANDLER. Chinese-American calendar for the 102 Chinese
  years commencing January 24, 1849, and ending February 5, 1951. Wash-
  ington, Govt. Print. Off., 1928. vii, 102 p.
——. Chinese-American calendar for the 40th through the 89th year of the Chi-
  nese Republic, February 6, 1951 to January 23, 2001. [Supplement] Washington, Administrative Division, Immigration and Naturalization Service, 1953.
  vii, 102 p.

Libraries
Surveys (a) Chinese Libraries

CHEKIANG, (PROVINCE) PROVINCIAL LIBRARY, Hangchow. A brief guide to
  the Provincial library of Chekiang. Hangchow, 1926. folder ([1], 5 p.) illus.
LIBRARY ASSOCIATION OF CHINA. Libraries in China. Peiping, Library Association of China, 1929. iii numb. l., 43 p. illus., plates.
——. Libraries in China; papers prepared on the occasion of the tenth anniver-
  sary of the Library Association of China. Peiping, Library Association of
  China, 1935. 132 p. map.
PEKING. NATIONAL LIBRARY. Metropolitan library competition. [Peking,
  1927] cover-title, 49 p. incl. illus., plans.
——. A short sketch of the National library of Peiping. Peiping, National li-
  brary of Peiping, 1931. cover-title, 9 p. fold. plates (plans).
——. The report of the building committee of the National library of Peiping.
  Peiping, The China Foundation for the Promotion of Education and Culture,
  1933. cover-title, 10, [13] p.
——. The National library of Peiping and its activities. Peiping, National library of Peiping, 1934. cover-title, 16 p. plates, plans.
——. La Bibliothèque nationale de Peiping et ses activités. [Peiping] La Bibliothèque nationale de Peiping, 1931. cover-title, 16 p. plates.
——. Some facts about the National library of Peiping. Peiping, National library of Peiping, 1934. 7 p.
SHANGHAI. ORIENTAL LIBRARY. A description of the Oriental library before
  and after the destruction by Japanese on February 1, 1932, prepared and
  published by the Board of directors of the Oriental library. Shanghai, 1932.
  29, [1] p. plates, ports.

SHAW, CHARLES BUNSEN, 1894- The libraries of the Christian colleges of
China; a report of a survey made in 1947-48. New York, United Board for
Christian Colleges in China, 1948. 87 1.

TAAM, CHEUK-WOON, 譚卓垣 (T'an Cho-yüan] 1900-56. The development of
Chinese libraries under the Ch'ing dynasty, 1644-1911. Shanghai, Commercial Press, 1935. ix, 107 p.

WONG, VI-LIEN, 黃維廉 . The Low library-a history. Shanghai, St. John's University [1924] cover-title, 12 p. incl. tables, diagr. plates. (Stamped on cover:
Bulletin no. 17). "Reprinted from'The St. John's echo,'February, 1924. "

WU, KWANG-TSING, 吳光清 1905- Scholarship, book production and libraries
in China, 618-1644. Chicago, 1944. vii, 291 1. Thesis-University of Chicago.

## Surveys (b) Libraries outside of China

ELISSÉEF, SERGE, 1889- The Chinese-Japanese Library of the Harvard-Yenching Institute. Cambridge, 1956. [20] p. Reprinted from Harvard Library
Bulletin 10:1.

HARVARD UNIVERSITY. Library. Harvard college library, Chinese-Japanese
collection. Outline of classification and index to classes. Cambridge, 1930.
25 1.

————. Index arranged by the four corners of the first character, according to
Wong's "Revised four-corner numeral system." [Cambridge, 1930] 12 1.

————. Library. Chinese-Japanese Library. A guide to the Chinese-Japanese library of Harvard university, under the auspices of the Harvard-Yenching Institute. Cambridge, 1932. 24 p.

JOINT COMMITTEE OF THE FAR EASTERN ASSOCIATION AND THE AMERI-
CAN LIBRARY ASSOCIATION. Oriental collections, U. S. A. and abroad; minutes and discussions, sectional meeting, Far Eastern Association, Ann Arbor, Michigan, April 12, 1950. Ames, Iowa, Office of the Chairman [1950]
25 1.

LAUFER, BERTHOLD, 1871-1934. The Gest Chinese research library at Mc-
Gill University, Montreal [Montreal, 1929] 8 p. illus.

RÉSILLAC-ROESE, ROBERT DE. The Gest Chinese research library, McGill
university, Montreal, Canada. [Montreal] 1931. 2-10 numb. 1.

TOKYO, TOYO BUNKO. Rough history and description of the Oriental library
(Toyo Bunko) Tokyo, The Oriental Library, 1926. 14 p. plate, port. 1st ed.
1924.

————. The Toyo Bunko of the Oriental library of Japan, the Morrison collection,
by Emil S. Fischer. Tientsin, 1934. 12 p. Reprinted from the 'Osaka maini-
chi' and 'The Tokio Nichi-Nichi' of Sept. 7-8, 1934, and the 'Peking and Tientsin Times' of Sept. 18, 1934.

## Catalogs (a) Chinese Libraries

CANTON. SUN YAT-SEN UNIVERSITY. Library. Sun Yat-sen University library
catalogue. [Canton] 1930. 345 p. (Western series no. 1).

CHINA. General Staff. Library. Classified catalog of the General Staff Office Library. [n. p. , 1936] [12], 134 p.

————. Geological Survey. Library. Catalogue of the library of the National Geological Survey of China. Publication series, December 1927. [Peking, Peking Leader Press, 1927] cover-title, ii, 44 p., plates.

————. Ministry of Foreign Affairs. Library. Library catalogue, part I. Collection in western languages. Nanking, 1929. viii, 90 numb. 1.

————. Supplement to the Library catalogue (Western languages section) no. 1-
June-July 1929- [Nanking, 1929-

————. Ministry of Foreign Affairs. Library. Catalogue of books in foreign languages. [Nanking] 1935. vii, 382 p.

HANKOW CLUB, Library. Hankow. "China class." [Hankow] 1922. cover-title, [2] 176 p.
———. 1st Supplement. 1923. 63 p.
———. 2d Supplement. 1924. 139 p.
———. 3rd Supplement. 1924. [140]-162 p.
———. 4th Supplement. 1925. 31 p.
NANKING. NATIONAL CENTRAL UNIVERSITY. Library. Southeastern University Library catalogue April 1924; class list and author index. Nanking, National Southeastern University Library, 1924. cover-title, 4 l., 86 p., 1 l., 87-136 p.
———. Library. Classified catalog. Nanking, National Central University Library, 1929-36. 2 v.
NANKING. UNIVERSITY. Library. Loan books for rural workers in the University of Nanking library. [Nanking] Issued by the College of Agriculture and Forestry, 1926. 11 p. (Publications of the University of Nanking, College of agriculture and forestry, Nanking, China. Bulletin no. 16).
———. Library. The checklist of serials and periodicals. July 1934. Nanking, University of Nanking Library [1934] cover-title, iii, 128 numb. l.
———. Library. Books on China in the University of Nanking library; a classified list. Nanking, University of Nanking library, 1937. 129 numb. l.
PEKING. COLLEGE OF CHINESE STUDIES, Library. Books on China. Peiping, 1931. 359 p.
———. Supplement 1. 1934. 86 p.
PEKING. NATIONAL LIBRARY, ed. Union catalogue of books in European languages in Peiping libraries, edited by the National Library of Peiping. Peiping, Published by the National Library of Peiping and the National Academy of Peiping, 1931. 4 v.
———. A classified catalogue of the Möllendorff collection deposited in the library by Mr. Chu Chi-chien,朱啓鈐 . Peiping, 1932. 285 p., 1 l., 65 p. port.
———. A classified list of reference books in the reading rooms of the National library of Peiping, 1932. Peiping, 1932. 353, 74 p.
———. Catalogue du fonds français de la Bibliothèque nationale de Peiping (par ordre d'auteurs) Peiping, Bibliothèque nationale de Peiping, 1934. 192 p.
———. A classified list of serial publications in the National library of Peiping. Peiping, 1936. 41 p.
PEKING. NATIONAL TSING HUA UNIVERSITY. Library. Classified catalog of the Tsing Hua college library. Peking, Tsing Hua College, 1927. xiii p., 1482 (i. e. 1484) p., plates.
PEKING. NATIONAL UNIVERSITY. Library. List of serials. [Peiping, Printed by the University Press, The National University of Peking] 1936. cover-title, 189 p.
PEKING. PEI-T'ANG LIBRARY. Catalogue of the Pei-t'ang Library. Peking, Lazarist Mission Press, 1944-48. 3 v. (1206 columns) facsims.
SHANGHAI. CHIAO-TUNG UNIVERSITY. Library. Library catalogue [Foreign books department] reclassified and compiled by Wolfe S. Hwang, 黃惠孚 . [Siccawei, Shanghai, Printed by Ming Chong Press] 1928. xxiv, 380 p., plates, ports.
———. Library. Library catalog, compiled by Tswen-hsuin Tsien, 錢存訓. Shanghai, Chiao-tung University Library, 1934. 9 v. in 1.
SHANGHAI. CUSTOMS REFERENCE LIBRARY. Complete catalogue of books in European languages (correct up to December 31, 1933) Shanghai, Commercial Press, 1934. cover-title, 108 p.
SHANGHAI. SCIENCE SOCIETY OF CHINA. Library. Catalogue of the Science Society of China Library. Shanghai, 1939. xvi, 496 p.
SHANGHAI. SHANGHAI CLUB. Library. Catalogue of the non-fiction books, to 1st October, 1932. [Shanghai] Shanghai Times, 1932. 608 p.

SHANGHAI. SHANGHAI SCIENCE INSTITUTE. Library. List of scientific peri-
odicals in the library of the Shanghai Science Institute. [Shanghai] 1934. cov-
er-title, 83 p.
———. Library. Classified catalogue of books and periodicals in the Shanghai
Science Institute. [Shanghai] 1937 . [814] p.
———. Supplement 1-     [Shanghai, 1939-    1 v. (various pagings).
SOOCHOW. UNIVERSITY. Comparative Law School of China, Shanghai. Library.
Library catalogue. Shanghai, Soochow University Law School, 1937. iii-iv,
218, ii, 84, ii, 85-160 p. 1933 ed. 30, 74 p.
TIENTSIN. NANKAI UNIVERSITY. Library. Library catalog 1925-      v. 1-
Tientsin and Peking, Printed by Kuang Hua Press, [1926]. 556 p.   illus.
(incl. plans).
WUCHANG. NATIONAL WU-HAN UNIVERSITY. Library. A classified catalogue
of the National Wu-han University Library, 1928-34. v. 1.   Wuchang, Nation-
al Wu-han Univ. Press, 1935-     1332 p.

### Catalogs (b) Libraries outside of China

ÉCOLE FRANÇAISE D'EXTRÊME-ORIENT, Hanoi. Bibliothèque. Inventaire du
fonds chinois de la bibliothèque de l'École française d'Extrême-Orient. Hanoi, Imp. d'Extrême-Orient, 1929-54. 5 v.
ESSEX INSTITUTE, Salem, Mass. Library. Catalog of books on China in the
Essex Institute, compiled by Louise Marion Taylor. Salem, Mass., The Essex Institute, 1926. ix, 392 p.
GARDNER, CHARLES SIDNEY, 1900-  A union list of selected Chinese books in
American libraries. Washington, D. C. , American Council of Learned Societies,   1932. cover-title,  iii,  50 p.
———. comp. A union list of selected western books on China in American libraries. 2d ed., rev. and enl. Compiled by Charles S. Gardner. Washington, D. C. , Committee on Chinese studies, American Council of Learned Societies [c1938] xi, 111 p. 1st ed. 1932.
HARVARD UNIVERSITY. Library. Chinese-Japanese Library. A classified catalogue of Chinese books in the Chinese-Japanese library of the Harvard-Yenching Institute at Harvard University, compiled by A. Kaiming Chiu. Cambridge, Harvard-Yenching Institute, 1938-40. 3 v.
HERVOUET, J. Catalogue des monographies locales chinoises dans les biblio-
thèques d'Europe. La Haye, Mouton, 1956. 100 p. (Bibliographie scientifiques, 1).
SOUTH MANCHURIA RAILWAY COMPANY. Library. Dairen. Classified catalogue of books in European languages in the Dairen library of the South Manchuria Railway Co. Far East. [Dairen] The Dairen Library, 1937. vi p.,
265 l.
———. Library, Mukden. Explanatory notes on some books and mss. of the Mukden library, prepared for the honourable members of Commission of Enquiry
from League of Nations, by Toshiwo Etôh, librarian of the Mukden Library,
South Manchuria Railway Co. Mukden, Manchuria, 1932. cover-title, 20, 8
p., plates.
TOKYO. TÔYÔ BUNKO. Catalogue of the Asiatic library of Dr. G. E. Morrison,
now a part of the Oriental Library, Tokyo, Japan. Tokyo, Published by the
Oriental Library, 1924. 2 v.
———. Index of a classified catalogue of books in European languages in the Toyo Bunko. Authors, 1917-36. Tokyo, 1951. 2 v.

### Librarianship

CH'IU, ALFRED K'AI-MING,裘開明 , 1898-   comp. A classification scheme for
Chinese and Japanese books, by A. K'ai-ming ch'iu, with the assistance of

H.Y. Fêng, 馮漢驥 [and] Zunvair Yue, 于振寰 . Washington, D.C., Committees of Far Eastern Studies, American Council of Learned Societies,1943. xxiv, 361 (i.e. 362) numb. l.

DOO, DING U., 杜定友 , 1898- Book classification. Shanghai, Shanghai Library Association, 1925. [3]-19, 130, vi, 212, 63 p.

HUANG, MO-LING, 陳黃嘉陵 . Uniform headings for Chinese anonymous classics, for Course LS426. Urbana, University of Illinois Library School,1949. Microfilm copy of typewritten manuscript. Negative. Collation of the original, as determined from the film: 36 l.

KUEI, CHIH-BER, 桂質柏 , 1900- Bibliographical and administrative problems arising from the incorporation of Chinese books in American libraries. Peiping, The Leader Press, 1931. ix, 138 p. Thesis - Univ. of Chicago.

MATTICE, HAROLD ALLISON, 1879- English-Chinese-Japanese lexicon of bibliographical, cataloguing and library terms. New York, New York Public Library, 1944. 38 p. "Reprinted from the Bulletin of the New York public library of May-June 1944."

PEKING. NATIONAL LIBRARY. Chinese catalogue cards and how to order and use them. Peiping, National Library, 1936. ii, 12 p. illus.

PI, KAO-PING, 皮高品 . Chinese decimal classification and relative index. Wuchang, Boone Library School, 1934. [578] p. 130 p. (Boone library school ser.).

SUN, TS'UNG-T'IEN, 孫從添 . Bookman's manual (Ts'ang-shu chi-yao) 藏書紀要, translated by Achilles Fang,方志彤. Cambridge, 1951. 45 p. Reprinted from HJAS, 14:1-2, June 1951.

TAI, TSE-CHIEN, 戴志騫 , 1888- Professional education for librarianship, with an introduction by John Boynton Kaiser. New York, H.W. Wilson, 1925. x, 259 p.

U.S. Library of Congress. Catalog division. Classification of Chinese books based on the Imperial catalogue, Ssu k'u ch'üan shu tsung mu, 四庫全書總目, completed 1772-82, by Chi Yün, 紀昀 , and a commission of scholars under the supervision of the Emperor Ch'ien Lung. Prepared and photographed in the office of the chairman of the Library committee, U.S.Department of agriculture. Washington, D.C., November, 1916. Revised March, 1922. [Washington, 1922] 5 numb. l., 22 l.

WOOD, MARY ELIZABETH, 1861-1931. comp. The Boxer indemnity and the library movement in China. A collection of official documents pertaining to the Boxer indemnity and public libraries in China. Hankow, Printed by the Central China Post [1924?] cover-title, 38, [10] p. plates.

YEH, TE-HUI, 葉德輝 , 1864-1927. Bookman's decalogue (Ts'ang-shu shih-yueh) 藏書十約, translated by Achilles Fang, 方志彤 . Cambridge, 1950. 41 p. Reprinted from HJAS, 13:1-2, June 1950.

## Printing and Paper

CARTER, THOMAS FRANCIS, 1882-1925. The invention of printing in China and its spread westward. New York, Columbia University Press [1931] xxvi p., 282 p. plates, fold. map, facsims., fold. tab.

———. The same. Rev. by L. Carrington Goodrich. 2d ed. New York, Ronald Press [1955] xxiv, 293 p. illus., port., facsims.

CHIN, CHIEN, 金簡 , d. 1795. A Chinese printing manual, 1776. 武英殿聚珍版程式 Translated from the Chinese with notes and introd. by Richard C. Rudolph. Los Angeles, Printed by the W. Ritchie Press for members of the Typophiles, 1954. xxvi, 20 p. 1 mounted col. illus., 16 plates. (Typophile chap books, 29).

GUPPY, HENRY, 1861-1948. Stepping-stones to the art of typography. With fourteen facsimiles. Manchester, The University Press; London, New York [etc.] Longmans, Green, 1928. 45 p. facsims.

HÜLLE, HERMANN, 1870-1940. Über den alten chinesischen Typendruck und seine Entwickelung un den Ländern des Fernen Ostens. [Berlin] Gedruckt auf Veranlassung der H. Berthold Messinglinienfabrik und Schriftgiesserei a.-g., 1923. 15 p. facsim.

HUNTER, DARD, 1883- Old papermaking in China and Japan. Chillicothe, O., Mountain House Press, 1932. 71 p. incl. front., illus. (part mounted; part col.; incl. map) plates (part mounted col. fold.) facsim., mounted samples (part fold.).

———. A papermaking pilgrimage to Japan, Korea and China. New York, Pynson Printers, 1936. 148, [2] p., front., illus., plates.

———. Chinese ceremonial paper; a monograph relating to the fabrication of paper and tin foil and the use of paper in Chinese rites and religious ceremonies. [Chillicothe, O.] The Mountain House Press, 1937. [9]-79, [3] p. front., illus., plates, samples.

KELLING, RUDOLF. Zum chinesischen Stempel-und Holztafeldruck, nebst vermischten Beiträgen aus dem Gesamtgebiete der Schrift-und Buchgeschichte, von Rudolf Kelling, Johannes Schubert und Otto Fischer. Leipzig, O. Harrassowitz, 1940. 142 p. plates (Buch und Schrift, Neue Folge, 3).

LAUFER, BERTHOLD, 1874-1934. Paper and printing in ancient China. Chicago, Printed for the Caxton Club, 1931. 33, [1] p.

P'AN, FRANCIS K., 潘光迴 [P'an Kuang-chiung] 1904- One year of rehabilitation of the Commercial Press. [Shanghai] 1933. 26 p. 1 illus., plates, ports.

PELLIOT, PAUL, 1878-1945. Les débuts de l'imprimerie en Chine. Paris, Impr. Nationale, Librairie d'Amérique et d'Orient, 1953. viii, 138 p. (His Œuvres posthumes, 4).

PRUSSIA. Staatsbibliothek, Berlin. Das Buch in China und das Buch über China; Buch-Austellung veranstaltet von der Preussischen Staatsbibliothek und dem China-Institut. Frankfurt a.M., 1928. xiii, 152 p.

RENKER, ARMIN, 1891- Papier und Druck im Fernen Osten. Mainz, Gutenberg-Gesellschaft, 1936. 7-55, [1] p. incl. plates, facsims. [Kleiner Druck der Gutenberg-Gesellschaft, 25].

RÜHL, INGEBORG. Die Papierwirtschaft in China, Japan und Mandschukuo. Erlangen, 1942. vi, 185 l. Diss.-Univ. Erlangen.

RUPPEL, ALOYS LEONHARD, 1882- Haben die Chinesen und Koreaner die Buchdruckerkunst erfunden? Mainz, Verlag der Gutenberg-Gesellschaft, 1954. 11 p. illus. (Kleiner Druck der Gutenberg-Gesellschaft, 56).

TSCHICHOLD, JAN, 1902- Der Erfinder des Papiers, Ts'ai Lun, in einer alten chinesischen Darstellung (Neujahrsgabe). Überreicht von der Züricher Papierfabrik an der Sihl. Zürich, 1955. 6 p. plate.

U.S. Bureau of Foreign and Domestic Commerce (Dept. of Commerce). Paper and Paper products in China. Comp. from special reports of consular officers of the Department of State and representatives of the Department of Commerce. Washington, Govt. Print. Off., 1925. ii, 19 p. incl. tables. (Trade information bulletin, 309).

WU, KUANG-TSING, 吳光清, 1905- Ming printing and printers. Cambridge, 1943. [57] p. plates. Reprinted from HJAS, 7:3, February, 1943.

———. Chinese printing under four alien dynasties (916-1368 A.D.) Cambridge, 1950. [76] p. plates. Reprinted from HJAS 13:3-4, December 1950.

## Journalism and the Press

BRITTON, ROSWELL SESSOMS, 1897-1951. The Chinese periodical press,1800-1912. Shanghai [etc.] Kelly and Walsh, 1933. vi, 151 p. 24 plates (facsim.) on 18 l.

CHAO, THOMAS MING-HENG, 趙敏恆, 1904- The foreign press in China, a preliminary paper prepared for the fourth biennial conference of the Institute of Pacific relations. Shanghai, China Institute of Pacific relations,1931.

114 p. illus. (ports.), table.

CHINA COMMERCIAL ADVERTISING AGENCY, Shanghai. China publishers'directory; a practical guide to newspapers and periodicals for China adverti-
sers. Shanghai, China Commercial Advertising Agency, 1934. 123, 4 p.
port., maps (1 fold.).

CROW, CARL, INC., Shanghai. Newspaper directory of China (including Hongkong) with check list of newspapers and periodicals published in Japan, Chosen, Java, Sumatra, Borneo, Siam, Singapore and Federated Malay states,
1931-        Shanghai, C. Crow, 1931. 52 p.

————. Newspaper directory of China (including Hongkong). Shanghai, C. Crow,
1935. 201 p.

LIANG, CH'I-CH'AO, 梁啓超, 1873-1929. Comments on journalism. Translated by James C.Y. Shen, 沈承怡. Columbia, Mo., Press of the Crippled
Turtle, 1953. 7 p. (Oldtime comments on journalism, no. 4).

LIN, MOUSHENG, 林俸聖, 1906- A guide to leading Chinese periodicals. New
York, China Institute in America [c1936] 30, [4] p.

LIN, SHU-SHEN, 林素珊. Histoire du journalisme en Chine. Avesnes-sur-
Helpe, Éditions de "L'Observateur," 1937. 164 p.Thèse - Univ. de Lille.

LIN, YU-T'ANG, 林玉堂, 1895- A history of the press and public opinion in
China. Shanghai [etc.] Pub. for China Institute of Pacific Relations by Kelly
and Walsh, 1936; Chicago, University of Chicago Press, 1936. 179 p., 1 illus.

LÖWENTHAL, RUDOLF, 1904- The religious periodical press in China, with
7 maps and 16 charts by Rudolf Löwenthal, with the assistance of Ch'en Hung-
shun, 陳鴻舜, Ku T'ing-ch'ang, 古廷昌, and William W.Y. Liang, 梁允
彝. Peking, The Synodal Commission in China, 1940. vi, 294 p. incl. maps,
tables.

[NORTH-CHINA DAILY NEWS AND HERALD]. China's attempt to muzzle the
foreign press; an account of the endeavours of Nanking to suppress the truth
about affairs in China. [Shanghai, North-China Daily News and Herald, 1929]
30, [2] p.

PATTERSON, DON DENHAM. The journalism of China. Columbia, Mo., 1922.
89 p. incl. 2 illus. (facsim.) plates. (The University of Missouri bulletin.
v. 23, no. 34. Journalism series, no. 26).

TONG, HOLLINGTON KONG, 董顯光, 1887- Dateline: China; the beginning of
China's press relations with the world. New York, Rockport Press, 1950.
xiii, 269 p.

WOODHEAD, HENRY GEORGE WANDESFORDE, 1883- Adventures in Far Eastern journalism; a record of thirty-three years' experience. Far Eastern ed.
with revisions. Tokyo, Hokuseido Press, 1935. ix p., 266 p. front., illus.
(coat of arms) plates, ports., facsims. (part fold.).

YALE UNIVERSITY. Institute of Far Eastern Languages. Chinese newspaper
manual. New Haven, 1952. xxiv, 262 p. (Mirror series A, 15).

YENCHING UNIVERSITY, Peking. Dept. of Journalism. Directory of Peking
daily papers, compiled and published by the Department of Journalism, Yenching University. Peking, 1925. cover-title, v, 27 p.

YUI, CHIEN-HSUIN, 余建勛. Das alte chinesische Nachrichtenwesen und die
chinesische Staatspresse. Berlin, Fährmannverlag, 1934. [3]-86, 4 p.

## II. GENERAL WORKS

### China: General Surveys

ABENSOUR, LÉON, 1889-  La Chine. Paris, Éditions de "Sciences et voyages," 1928. 96. illus. (incl. maps).

AMERICAN ACADEMY OF POLITICAL AND SOCIAL SCIENCE, Philadelphia. China, edited by Henry F. James.  Philadelphia, 1930. v, [1], 431 p., plates, maps, diagrs. (The annals of the American academy of political and social science. v. 152, November, 1930).

AMERICAN UNIVERSITY CLUB OF CHINA. Lectures 1921/22. Shanghai, Commercial Press, 1923.  v. illus., plates, ports.

AUSTRALIAN INSTITUTE OF INTERNATIONAL AFFAIRS, Victorian Branch. China to-day.  Melbourne, 194-  . 47 p. maps, tables, (World affairs papers, 4).

AUXION DE RUFFÉ, REGINALD D', baron, 1875-  Chine et Chinois d'aujourd'hui; le nouveau péril jaune.  Paris, Berger-Levrault, 1926. xiii, 494 p., front., plates.

———. Is China mad? Translated from the French by R.T. Peyton-Griffin. Shanghai, Kelly and Walsh, 1928.   xiv, 358, [xvi]-xvii, v p. incl. front. plates, ports.

BALL, JAMES DYER, 1847-1919. Things Chinese; or, Notes connected with China. 5th ed. Revised by E. Chalmers Werner.  Shanghai [etc.] Kelly and Walsh, 1925; London, John Murray, 1926. iv, 766 p.

[BIBLIOGRAPHISCHES INSTITUT, Leipzig]. Schlag nach über China, Japan, und Mandschukuo, wissenswerte Tatsachen, übersichten und tabellen nebst einer vielfarbigen Übersichtskarte von China und Japan. [Leipzig, 1940] cover-title, 31, [1] p. fold. map.

BLAND, JOHN OTWAY PERCY, 1863-1945.  China, Japan and Korea. London, W. Heinemann, 1921. x, 327 p. plates.

———. China: the pity of it.  Garden City, N.Y., Doubleday, Doran; London, Heinemann, 1932. 358 p.

[BRITISH UNITED AID TO CHINA, London]. What do you know about China? [London, 1946] 12 (i.e. 23), [3] p. illus.

BUNKER, FRANK FOREST, 1873-  China and Japan.  Philadelphia, London and Chicago, J.B. Lippincott [c1928]    viii, 253 p. illus. (Lands and peoples).

CHIN, LI-TSE. China-the prey? The social, economic and political background of the Chinese people by Chin Li-tse and George F. Green.  London, International Publishing Co., 1938. 47 p. plates, map.

CLAPP, FREDERICK MORTIMER. A series of ten radio talks on China today (with select bibliography) by Frederick Mortimer Clapp, Lloyd P. Horsfall, William L. Nunn, [and] Benjamin H. Williams. [Pittsburgh] 1928. 5-96 p. (University of Pittsburgh. Radio publication no. 44).

CORDIER, HENRI, 1849-1925. La Chine. Paris, Payot, 1921. 138 p. fold. map. (Collection Payot. [8]).

DEKOBRA, MAURICE, 1885- Confucius in a tail-coat; ancient China in modern costume, translated from "Confucius en pullover" by Metcalfe Wood. London, T.W. Laurie [1935] 7-217, [1] p. front., plates, ports.

DONOVAN, JOHN PATRICK. Yesterday and to-day in China. London, Drane's [1924] 237 p. xxix pl.(incl. front., ports.).

DRIESCH, HANS ADOLF EDUARD, 1867-1941. Fern-Ost als gäste Jungchinas. Leipzig, F.A. Brockhaus, 1925. [5]-314 p., front., illus. (map, plan) plates (part col.) ports.

ETHERTON, PERCY THOMAS, 1879- China, the facts. London, E. Benn, 1927. vii-xiii,[1] p., 17-259 p. front.,plates,ports., fold. map.

EICHHORN, WERNER. China; gestern, heute, morgen. Mit einer Einführung von Eduard Erkes. Leipzig, Hesse and Becker, 1929. 215 p. (Prometheus-Bücher).

GEORGE, SIR ANTHONY HASTINGS, 1886-1944. China - an international address at Washington: 1943. A Newcomen address, 1943. [Princeton, Princeton University Press, 1944] 40 p. illus.

GOODNOW, FRANK JOHNSON, 1859-1939. China; an analysis. Baltimore, Johns Hopkins Press, 1926. viii, 279 p.

GORDON, EDWARD. China in pictures, edited by Edward Gordon; foreword by His Excellency V. K. Wellington Koo. London, Williams and Norgate, 1942. 23, [1] p. illus. (incl. ports., map).

GRAYBILL, HENRY BLAIR. The new China; a civics reader for middle-school students, by Henry Blair Graybill and You-kuang Chu, 朱有光. A revision of Graybill's "Modern China." Boston, New York [etc.] Ginn [c1930] xi, [1], 361 p. col. front., illus. (incl. ports., maps) 1st ed. 1925.

GT. BRIT. Dept. of Overseas Trade. China. Notes on some aspects of life in China for the information of business visitors. London, H. M. Stationery Off., 1934. viii, 32 p.

GULL, EDWARD MANICO, 1883- Facets of the Chinese question. London, E. Benn, [1931] xxi, 198 p. incl. front., illus. (maps, music) plates.

HALL, RONALD ACOTT, 1892- Eminent authorities on China. London, G. Allen and Unwin, 1931. viii, 275 p. plates, 2 port.

HARVARD UNIVERSITY. Committee on Regional Studies. Papers on China from the East Asia regional studies seminar. Cambridge, 1947-55. 9 v.

HIGH, STANLEY, 1895- China's place in the sun. New York, Macmillan, 1922. xxix, 3-212 p. front., plates.

HODGKIN, HENRY THEODORE, 1877-1933. Living issues in China. New York, Friendship Press [c1932] viii, 215 p.

HOUSTOUN, JOHN FLEMING. China. Edinburgh and London, Oliver and Boyd, 1953. [4], 92 p. illus. tables, (One approach geography-history ser.).

HOVELAQUE, ÉMILE LUCIEN, 1865- China, tr. by Mrs. Laurence Binyon. London and Toronto, J. M. Dent; New York, E. P. Dutton, 1923. xxii, 272 p. French ed. Paris, E. Flammarion, 1920.

HU, SHIH, 胡適, 1891- China's own critics, a selection of essays by Hu Shih and Lin Yu-tang, 林玉堂, with Commentaries by Wang Ching-wei, 汪精衛. Peiping, China United Press [1931] vii, [11]-166 p. (Half-title: China United Press series [3] ).

HUGHES, ERNEST RICHARD, 1883-1956, ed. China, body and soul; contributions by Laurence Binyon, Roger Fry, E. R. Hughes [and others]. Edited by E. R. Hughes. London, Secker and Warburg [1938] 166 p.

HUNDHAUSEN, VINCENZ, 1878-1955. Schlaglichter auf China; überlegungen eines unbefangenen Chinadeutschen aus den Jahren 1925 bis 1932. Peiping, Verlag der Pappelinsel-Werkstatt, 193-     211 p.

HUTCHINSON, PAUL, 1890-1956. China's real revolution. New York, Missionary Education Movement of the United States and Canada [c1924] x, 182 p. front., plates, ports.

JOHNSON, EMORY RICHARD, 1864- Interpretations. New York and London, D. Appleton, 1928. 3-223, [1] p. front. (4 port.).

KEIM, JEAN ALPHONSE, 1904- Panorama de la Chine. [Paris] Hachette [1951] 269 p. illus. (Le Tour du monde).

KERVYN, LOUIS MARIE. L'empire chinois et les barbares. Pékin, La Politique de Pékin, 1929. 74 numb. 1. (Collection de la "Politique de Pékin").

LAMOTT, WILLIS, 1893- Look again at China. New York, Friendship Press, c1948. 64 p. illus., ports., map.

LEE, TENG-HWEE, 李登輝, 1872-1947, ed. Vital factors in China's problems; readings in current literature. Shanghai, Commercial Press, 1928. x(i. e. ix), 440 p.

LIU, YUAN-LUNG. The Far East is not very far; letters from Liu Yuan-lung
and Wang Shou-ming [pseud.] edited by Anna Melissa Graves. [Baltimore]
Priv. print. [by the Waverly Press ] 1942. xx, 317 p. incl. front. ports.

MACNAIR, HARLEY FARNSWORTH, 1891-1947. China's new nationalism and
other essays. Shanghai, Commercial Press, 1925. [v]-xi, 398 p.

———. ed. Voices from unoccupied China, by Liu Nai-chen, 劉迺誠 , [and oth-
ers]. Edited by Harley Farnsworth MacNair. Chicago, University of Chicago Press [1944] 1v, 106, [1] p.

———. China. Berkeley and Los Angeles, University of California Press, 1946.
ix-xxix, [6], 573, [1] p. illus. (incl. maps) plates, ports. [The United nations series].

MARTIN, WILLIAM, 1888-1934. Il faut comprendre la Chine. 2e éd. Paris, Librarie Académique Perrin, 1935. iv, iv, viii, 271 p. plates, map.

———. Understand the Chinese, translated from the French by E. W. Dickes;
with an introduction by Sir Arthur Salter. New York, Harper, London, Methuen, 1934. xiii p., 249, [1] p. front., plates.

MONROE, PAUL, 1869-1947. China: a nation in evolution. Chautauqua, N.Y.,
Chautauqua Press, 1927; New York, Macmillan, 1928. xv, [1], 447 p. front,
plates (1 fold.) ports., double maps.

MORGAN, EVAN, 1860- A new mind, and other essays. Shanghai, Kelly and
Walsh [pref. 1930] 244 p.

NEW DELHI. Indian Institute of International Affairs. China. New Delhi, I.I.I.
A., 1945. 24 p.

PERNITZSCH, MAX GERHARD, 1882- China. 2., erweiterte Aufl. Berlin,
Junker und Dünnhaupt, 1943. 156 p. fold. map. (Half-title: Kleine auslandskunde, hrsg. von prof. dr. F.A. Six... Bd.4/5). 1. Aufl. 1940.

ROWE, DAVID NELSON, 1905- ed. China: an area manual, v. 1, by Chih-tsing
Hsia, 夏志清 [and others] Edited by David Nelson Rowe and Willmoore Kendall. Chevy Chase, Md., Operations Research Office, Johns Hopkins University [1954-   257 p. maps (1 fold. col. in pocket)( Johns Hopkins University. Operations Research Office. Project POWOW. Technical memorandum
ORO-T-229).

ROXBY, PERCY MAUDE, 1880-1947. China. [London, New York, etc.] Oxford University Press, 1942. 32 p. (Oxford pamphlets on world affairs, 54).

———. La Chine. London, New York, etc. Oxford University Press, 1944. 32
p. maps (Études internationales, collection Oxford).

SHEN, YI, 沈怡, 1901- China und sein Weltprogram von Shen Yi und Heinrich
Stadelmann. Dresden, F. M. Gutewort [1925] 164 p. front., plates, ports,
facsims.

SMITH, JOHN NIND. China's hour. London, M. Hopkinson, 1930. 176 p. fold.
map.

STANFORD UNIVERSITY. China Project. North China. New Haven, Human Relation Area Files, 1956. 2 v. maps (HRAF Subcontractor's monog. HRAF-27,
Stanford-1).

———. China Project. Central South China. New Haven, Human Relation Area
Files [1956] 2 v. maps (HRAF Subcontractor's monog. HRAF-28, Stanford 2).

———. China Project. East China. New Haven, Human Relation Area Files, 1956.
2 v. maps (HRAF Subcontractor's monog. HRAF-29, Stanford-3).

———. China Project. Southwest China. New Haven, Human Relation Area Files,
1956. 2 v. illus. maps (HRAF Subcontractor's monog. HRAF-30, Stanford-4).

STRAWN, SILAS HARDY, 1866-1946. China's problems: address at Tsinghua.
China's problems internal not external. [Tientsin] Tientsin Press [1926?]
6 p.

T'ANG, LEANG-LI,湯良禮 , 1901- The foundations of modern China, with a
preface by Wang Ching-wei. London, N. Douglas [1928] x, 290 p.

———. ed. China facts and fancies. Shanghai, China United Press, 1936. x, 296
p. (Half-title: "China to-day" series. [7]).

THAT untravell'd world, an elementary introduction to the study of China. Groton, Mass., Groton School [c1928] viii, [2], 181, [1] p. incl. front., illus. (incl. map).

TAYLOR, GEORGE EDWARD, 1905- Changing China, edited by Maxwell S. Stewart; cover by LaVerne Riess. A cooperative project between American council, Institute of Pacific Relations, and Webster Publishing Company. St. Louis, Dallas [etc., 1942] 94 p. illus. (incl. ports., maps).

THOMAS, W.J. China, what you want to know. Sydney, N.S.W., Bookstall Co., 1942. 63, [1] p.

VAN BERGEN, ROBERT. The story of China. New York, Cincinnati [etc.] American Book Co. [c1922] 236 p. front. (map) illus.

WALTER, WILHELM P.O. Das China von heute, 中國近況 . Frankfurt am Main, Societäts-Verlag, 1932. 119, [1] p. 112 plates on 56 l.

WASHINGTON (STATE) UNIVERSITY. Far Eastern and Russian Institute. A general handbook of China. Seattle, 1956. 2 v. tables. (HRAF Subcontractor's monog. HRAF-55.Wash. 4).

———. Far Eastern and Russian Institute. A regional handbook on Northeast China. Seattle, 1956. 1v, 561 p. maps, tables (HRAF-61. Wash. 9).

———. Far Eastern and Russian Institute. A regional handbook on Northwest China. Seattle, 1956. 2 v. maps, tables, (HRAF-59. Wash.-5).

WEGENER, GEORG, 1863-1939. China, ein Zukunftsproblem; sechs Vorträge. Berlin, A. Scherl, [c1925] 77, [1] p., (Flugschriften des "Tag." 19).

———. China, eine Landes- und Volkskunde. Leipzig und Berlin, B.G.Teubner, 1930. 233 p. illus. (maps) xvi plates (incl. ports.) on 8 l.

WENLEY, ARCHIBALD GIBSON, 1898- China, by A.G. Wenley and John A. Pope. Washington, Smithsonian Institution, 1944. v, 85 p. illus., 25 plates on 13 l., maps (part fold.) (Smithsonian institution. War background studies, 20).

WERNER, EDWARD THEODORE CHALMERS, 1864- Autumn leaves; an autobiography with a sheaf of papers, sociological and sinological, philosophical and metaphysical. Shanghai [etc.] Kelly and Walsh, 1928. 747, [1] p. front., plates, ports., map, facsim.

WHYMANT, A. NEVILLE JOHN, 1894- ed. A China manual. London, Chinese Govt. Information Off. [1949?] 352 p. illus., port.

WIEGER, LÉON, 1856-1933. ed. and tr. Chine moderne. Hien-hien, Impr. de [Hien-hien] 1920-32. 10 v illus.

WILLIAMS, EDWARD THOMAS, 1854-1944. China yesterday and to-day. 5th ed., rev. New York, Thomas Y. Crowell, [c1932] London, G.G. Harrap and Co., 1933. xxiv, 743 (i.e. 765) p. front., plates, ports., fold. map (in pocket) fold. plan. 1st ed. 1923.

WILSON, SADIE MAI. What do you know about China?. A source book of materials. Nashville, Tenn., Cokesbury Press, 1929. 266 p. illus. (incl. music) plates, diagr.

WINFIELD, GERALD FREEMAN, 1908- China: the land and the people. Rev. ed. New York, Sloane [1950] vii, 431 p. illus., maps. 1st ed. 1948.

WINN, VIOLA SCHULDT. A new China, a course for junior high school groups. New York, Friendship Press [1948] 126 p.

WRIGHT, ARTHUR F. 1913- China; a background essay for one in a series of film-discussion programs on international understanding. [Pasadena? California, 1952] 9 p.

YANG, YUNG-CH'ING, 楊永清 , 1892-1956. China's modern aspirations and achievements. Honolulu,University of Hawaii, 1935. 13 p. (University of Hawaii. Occasional papers, 27).

YAUKEY, GRACE (SYDENSTRICKER) 1899- Let's read about China, by Cornelia Spencer [pseud.] Grand Rapids, Fideler Co. [c1955]    128 p. illus. ("Let's read about" books). 1st ed. 1948.

YEH, GEORGE, 葉公超 , 1904- Introducing China, by George Yeh and C. P.

Fitzgerald.  London,  I.  Pitman [1948] xvi,  116 p.  illus. ,  maps.
ZAU,  FI-DAUNG, 卲帝棠 ,  1897-  Glimpses into the problems of China; a ser-
ies of letters by a Chinese contributor to the foreign press of Shanghai, by
F.D.Z.  Shanghai, Kelly and Walsh,  1930-33.  3 v.

### Civilization and Culture

ABEGG,  LILY,  1901- Ostasien denkt anders; Versuch einer Analyse des west-
östlichen Gegensatzes.  [Zürich] Atlantis Verlag [1949] 425 p.
────.  The mind of East Asia.  London, New York, Thames and Hudson [1952]
344 p.  illus.
AMANN,  GUSTAV,  1882-  Im spiegel Chinas, vom Zusammenstoss unserer
westlichen mit asiatischer Kultur und Bolschewismus.  Berlin-Grunewald,
K.  Vowinckel,  1925.  198 p.
BARKER,  ALDRED FARRER,  1868-  China and the Chinese.  With a "foreword"
by His Excellency the Chinese minister to Australia (Dr.  Hsu Mo, 徐謨 )
[Melbourne, Robertson and Mullens,  1944] cover-title,  52 p.
BECKMANN,  JOHANNES,  1901-  Altes und neues China, vom Glanz und Schatten seiner Kultur.  Luzern, Räber,  1944.  176 p.  plates.
BODDE,  DERK,  1909-  China's gifts to the West.  Washington, American Coun-
cil on Education,  1942.  vi,  40 p.,  illus.  ([American council on education.
Committee on Asiatic studies in American education] Asiatic studies in A-
merican education,  1).
────.  Chinese ideas in the West, prepared for the Committee on Asiatic Stud-
ies in American Education.  Washington, American Council on Education
[1948] viii,  42 p.  illus.  (Asiatic studies in American education,  3).
CARVER,  SAXON ROWE.  Carved on our hearts.  Nashville, Tenn. , Broadman
Press [1946] 90 p.  illus.
CHATLEY,  HERBERT,  1885-  The origin and diffusion of Chinese culture.  London, China Society [1948] cover-title,  6 p.
CHÊNG,  CHE-YU, 鄭啓愚 , Oriental and occidental cultures contrasted: an introduction to "culturology."  Berkeley, Gillick Press,  1943.  v,  [1],  158 p.
illus. (map) diagrs.
CHINESISCH-DEUTSCHER Almanach,  1927-28,  1928-29,  1930,  1931,  1932,
1933,  1934,  1935.  Frankfurt am Main, China-Institut,  1927-35.  8 v.  illus.
CHU,  FINLAY M. , 朱鳳鳴 ,  1919-  China's old culture and new order; a study
of the Chinese revolutions in the light of the social movement theory.  Madison,  1955.  v.  731 1.  Thesis - Univ. of Wisconsin.
CLARK,  GROVER,  1891-1938.  The great wall crumbles.  New York, Macmillan,  1935.  xvii,  406 p.  illus.(incl. maps).
────.  China am Ende?  Fünf Jahrtausende chinesische Kultur, Gesellschaft,
Religion, Politik und Wirtschaft.  Ins Deutsche übertragen von [Alb. Otto]
van Bebber.  Leipzig, [etc. ] W. Goldmann [1936] 336 p.  illus.
CLAUDEL,  PAUL,  1868-1954.  Sous le signe du dragon.  Avec un port. de l'au-
teur gravé sur bois par Gilbert Poilliot.  [Paris] Table ronde [1948] 241 p.
port. (Le Choix, 7).  Nouv. éd. Paris, Gallimard, 1957.
DANTON,  GEORGE HENRY,  1880- The Chinese people, new problems and old
backgrounds.  Boston, Marshall Jones,  1938.  iii-vi,  312 p.
DECAUX,  JACQUES.  Orient and Occident; se rencontreront-ils jamais?  Paris,
J. Susse [1945] 181 p.
DICKINSON,  GOLDSWORTHY LOWES,  1862-1932.  An essay on the civilizations
of India, China and Japan.  New York, Doubleday Page, 1926.  85 p. 1st ed. ,
1913.
────.  Indien, China und Japan; aus dem Englischen übers. von Albert Malata.
Heidelberg, Niels Kampmann,  1927.  72 p.
────.  Briefe eines chinesischen Gelehrten.  Aus dem Englischen ins Deutsche
übertragen von Albert Malata.  Celle, Niels Kampmann,  1925.  58 p. English

ed.: Letters from John Chinaman, London, 1901; Letters from a Chinese official, New York, 1903.

[———.] Hands off China! The letters of a Chinese official. New York, William Faro, 1932. 9-75, [1] p.

———. Letters from John Chinaman. London, G. Allen and Unwin [1939] 3-62, [2] p. 1st ed. 1901.

———. Letters from John Chinaman and other essays, with an introduction by E. M. Forster. London, G. Allen and Unwin [1946] 216 p.

DUBS, HOMER HASENPFLUG, 1892- China, the land of humanistic scholarship; an inaugural lecture delivered before the University of Oxford on 23 February 1948. Oxford, Clarendon Press, 1949. 24 p.

EAST AND WEST ASSOCIATION, New York. The people of China; who they are, how they live, what they like, why they are fighting. [New York] 1943. cover-title, 20 p. illus. (map). 1st ed. 1942.

ESTERER, MAXIMILIAN. Chinas natürliche Ordnung und die Maschine. Stuttgart und Berlin, Cotta [c1929] 175 p. plates. (Wege der technik).

FLEWELLING, RALPH TYLER, 1871- Reflections on the basic ideas of East and West; a study in cultural contrasts. Peiping, College of Chinese Studies, California College in China, 1935. cover-title, ix, 114 p.

FORMAN, HARRISON, 1904- Changing China; with 250 photos. by the author. New York, Crown Publishers [1948] 337 p. illus., ports., maps.

FORSTER, LANCELOT, 1882- The new culture in China, with an introduction by Sir Michael E. Sadler. London, G. Allen and Unwin [1936] 240 p.

FRANKE, OTTO, 1863-1946. Aus Kultur und Geschichte Chinas. Vorträge und Abhandlungen aus den Jahren 1902-42. Peking, Deutschland-Institut, 1945. viii, 405 p.

GALBRAITH, WINIFRED. The Chinese. Harmondsworth, Middlesex, Eng., New York, Penguin Books; Cairo, W.J. Eady [1943] Melbourne, Lothian, 1943. 147 p. incl. front. (port.) (Pelican books).

GOULD, RANDALL. China in the sun. Garden City, N.Y., Doubleday, 1946. ix-xi, [2], 403 p.

GROUSSET, RENÉ, 1885-1952. Les civilisations de l'Orient. Paris, G. Crès et Cie, 1929-30. 4 v. illus. (incl. ports.) t. 3: Chine.

———. The civilizations of the East, translated from the French by Catherine Alison Philips. New York, London, A.A. Knopf [1931-34]; London, H. Hamilton, 1931-34. 4 v. illus. v. 3: China.

HARVEY, EDWIN DEEKS, 1880- The mind of China. New Haven, Yale University Press; London, H. Milford, Oxford University Press, 1933. x, 321 p.

HONGKONG. UNIVERSITY. Institute of Oriental Studies. Radio talks on Chinese civilization, delivered under the auspices of the Institute of Oriental Studies and edited by F.S. Drake. Hong Kong, University Press, 1954. 6, 173 p. table.

HSIAO, CH'IEN, 蕭乾 , 1911- ed. A harp with a thousand strings (a Chinese anthology in six parts). London, Pilot Press [1944] xxiv, 536 p. illus.(incl. facsims.) fold. tab.

———. The dragon beards versus the blueprints (meditations on post-war culture) by Hsiao Ch'ien. London, The Pilot Press [1944] viii, 34, [1]p. incl. front.

HSU, FRANCIS L.K., 許烺光 , 1909- Americans and Chinese: two ways of life. New York, H. Schuman [1953] 457 p.

HU SHIH, 胡適 , 1891- The Chinese renaissance. Chicago, University of Chicago Press [1934] xi, 110 p. (The Haskell lectures in comparative religion [1933]).

HUGHES, ERNEST RICHARD, 1883-1956. The invasion of China by the western world. London, A. and C. Black, 1937; New York, Macmillan, 1938. xvi, 323, [1] p. fold. front., maps (part fold.) (The pioneer histories).

———. L'invasion de la Chine par l'Occident. Traduit par Suzanne Le Quesne.

Paris, Payot, 1938. 288 p. maps (Bibliothèque historique).

KELLY, HOWARD. Dragon doodles, from fantasy to fact. London, Watts [1946] vii, 80 p. front., illus, (incl. plans) plates, port., diagrs.

KIANG, KANG-HU, 江亢虎, 1883-1946. On Chinese studies. Shanghai, Commercial Press, 1934. vi, 403 p.

———. Chinese civilization; an introduction to sinology. Shanghai, Chung Hwa Book Co., 1935, xxx, 676 p.

KOO, TS-ZUNG, 顧子仁, 1887- Basic values in Chinese culture; syllabus by T. Z. Koo. Iowa City, 1950. 86 p. Mimeographed.

KU, HUNG-MING, 辜鴻銘, 1857-1928. Chinas Verteidigung gegen europäischen Ideen: kritische Aufsätze. Übers. von Richard Wilhelm. Hrsg. mit einem Vorwort von Alfons Paquet. Jena, E. Diederichs, 1921. xiv p., 148 p. 1st ed. 1911.

———. The spirit of the Chinese people. With an essay on civilization and anarchy. 2nd ed. Peking, Commercial Press, 1922. 4, x, 160 p. 1st ed. 1915.

———. Der Geist des chinesischen Volkes. 2. ed. Jena, E. Diederichs, 1924. 181, [1] p. 1. ed., 1916.

———. L'esprit du peuple chinois. Traduit de l'anglais par P. Rival. Paris, Stock, 1927. viii, 180, [3] p.

———. Papers from a viceroy's yamen; a Chinese plea for the cause of good government and true civilization in China. [2nd ed. ] Peking, North China Standard, 1923. 162 p. port. 1st ed., 1901.

KÜHN, HERBERT, 1895- Tat und Versenkung; Europa und Asien. Mainz / Rhein, Verlag Kirchheim, 1948. 161 p. 32 plates.

LATOURETTE, KENNETH SCOTT, 1884- The China that is to be. Eugene, Oregon State System of Higher Education, 1949. ix, 56 p. (Condon lectures).

LEE, SHAO-CH'ANG, 李紹昌, 1891- The development of Chinese culture, a synoptic chart and bibliography. Honolulu, Hawaii, Advertiser Publishing Co., 1926. 18 p. double map, fold. tab. (University of Hawaii, Occasional papers, 4).

———. A brief interpretative outline for the study of Chinese culture. Preliminary paper for the second general session of the Institute of Pacific Relations, July 15-29, 1927. Honolulu, 1927. 58 p.

———. China's cultural development. 2d rev. ed. [East Lansing] Michigan State College Press, c1952. sheet.

LEGENDRE, AIMÉ FRANÇOIS, 1867- La civilisation chinoise moderne. Paris, Payot, 1926. [7]-298 p., plates. (Collection d'études, de documents et de témoignages pour servir à l'histoire de notre temps).

———. Modern Chinese civilization. Translated from the French by Elsie Martin Jones. London, J. Cape [1929] vii-xxiii, 7-295 p.

MALRAUX, ANDRÉ, 1895- La tentation de l'Occident. Paris, B. Grasset, 1951 (c1926); Genève, Skira, 1945. 205 p.

MAURER, HERRYMON, 1914- Collision of East and West; with an introd. by Hu Shih. Chicago, H. Regnery Co., 1951. xvi, 352 p.

NAVILLE, PIERRE. La Chine future. [Paris] Éditions de Minuit [1952] 237 p. (Documents).

NEEDHAM, JOSEPH, 1900- Some thoughts about China; report of an address. London, The China Society [1946] cover-title, 4 p.

———. Science and society in ancient China. London, Watts [1947] 20 p. illus. (Conway memorial lecture).

NORTHROP, FILMER STUART CUCKOW, 1893- The meeting of East and West, an inquiry concerning world understanding. New York, Macmillan, 1946; London, Macmillan, 1948. xxii, 531 p. col. front., xvi plates (incl. plan) on 8 l., diagrs.

NOTT, STANLEY CHARLES, 1902- Voices from the Flowery Kingdom; being an illustrated descriptive record of the beginnings of Chinese cultural existence, incorporating a complete survey of the numerous emblematic forces selected from nature by the ritualistic leaders of the Chinese throughout the ages, with an introduction by Byron E. Eldred. New York, Chinese Culture Study Group of America, 1947. xxv, 278 p. illus., plates (part col.).

PARK, NO-YONG, 鮑訥榮, 1899- An Oriental view of American civilization. Boston and New York, Hale, Cushman and Flint, c1934. 128 p.

PEFFER, NATHANIEL, 1890- China: the collapse of a civilization. New York, John Day, 1930. viii, 3-306 p.

PIPER, HARTMUT, 1878- Der gesetzmässige Lebenslauf der Völker Chinas und Japans. Leipzig, T. Weicher, 1929. xv, 110 p.

PORAK, RENÉ. L'âme chinoise. Paris, Flammarion [1950] 284 p. (Bibliothèque de philosophie scientifique).

PRATT, HELEN GAY, 1889- China and her unfinished revolution. [New York] American Council, Institute of Pacific Relations, 1937. ix, 173 p. maps, (Her Peoples of the Pacific: I).

RATTENBURY, HAROLD BURGOYNE. Face to face with China, with 45 photographs by Cecil Beaton and 15 pictorial charts in colour designed by the Isotype Institute. London, Toronto [etc.] G.G. Harrap, [1945] 144 p. plates (part double) port., maps, diagrs.

——. Through Chinese eyes. London, Edingburgh House Press, 1945. 152 p.

——. This is China. London, F. Muller [1949] 254 p. plates, map (on lining papers).

ROBERTS, STEPHEN HENRY, 1901- The gifts of the old China to the new. Canberra, Australian Institute of Anatomy, 1939. 16 p. (George Ernest Morrison lectures).

RODES, JEAN. Les Chinois; essai de psychologie ethnographique. Paris, F.Alcan, 1923. iii, 232 p. (On cover: Bibliothèque d'histoire contemporaine).

SANTAYANA, SILVIO GEORGE, 1899- China. Minneapolis, Burgess, c1944. ii, 67 numb. l.

SAUNDERS, J. ROSCOE, 1873- The Chinese as they are. New York, Chicago [etc.] Fleming H. Revell [c1921] 176 p. front., plates, ports., fold. map.

SAUNDERS, KENNETH JAMES, 1883-1937. Whither Asia? A study of three leaders [Mahatma Gandhi, Hu Shih and Kagawa]. New York, Macmillan, 1933. 221 p.

——. The ideals of East and West. New York, Macmillan; Cambridge, Eng., The University Press, 1934. xxiii, 246, [2] p.

——. A pageant of Asia; a study of three civilizations. London, Oxford University Press, 1934. xii, 452 p. front., illus. (incl. plans) plates, ports.

SIÉ, C.K., 謝壽康, 1894- Est-Ouest, reflets croisés. Préfaces: Paul Hymans, Gustave van Zype. Paris, Maison du livre français; Bruxelles, Éditions "Labor" [1932] 9-213 p.

——. L'esprit chinois en face du problème des races. Paris, Plon [1939] 9-44 p.

SOONG, MAY-LINC,蔣宋美齡, 1897- This is our China. New York and London, Harper [c1940] 312 p., front., plates, ports.

——. China in peace and war. Preface by Charlotte Haldane. 3d impression. London, Hurst and Blackett, 1940. 255, [1] p. front., ports.

——. Unser China. Deutsche Übertragung von Dagmar Juul. Zürich, Rascher Verlag [1943] iv, 272 p.

——. China shall rise again. Including ten official statements of China's present progress. New York and London, Harper [c1941] xv, 356 p., incl. tables. 3 maps on 1 l.

——. The same. Preface by Generalissimo Chiang Kai-shek. 2nd impression. London, Hurst and Blackett, 1941. xii, 15-256 p. incl. 3 maps on 1 l., tables.

SPALDING, H.N., 1877-1953. Civilization in East and West; an introduction to the study of human progress. London, Oxford University Press, 1939. xv, 334 p.

The SPIRIT of China. Contributors: Christopher Dawson, P. Fitzgerald, C.S. Wang, 王承緒 [and others]. [London, Changing World Publications, 1942] 23, [1] p. illus. (incl. port., map) (The Changing world).

T'AO, PUNG-FAI, 陶鵬飛. Chinas Geist und Kraft, mit einem Vorwort von E. Rousselle. Breslau, Priebatsch, 1935. 250 p. front., illus., plates, ports.

THERE is another China [essays and articles for Chang Poling of Nankai] New York, King's Crown Press, 1948. viii, 178 p. port.

TIMPERLEY, HAROLD JOHN, 1898- Some contrasts between China and Japan in the light of history. London, The China Society (associated with the China Institute) [1941] cover-title, 10 p.

TITIEV, MISCHA, 1901- Chinese elements in Japanese culture. Canberra, Australian National University, 1954. 20 p. (George Ernest Morrison lectures).

[TOURRIER, THEODORE]. A Chinaman's opinion of us and of his own people (as expressed in letters from Australia to his friend in China) written by Hwuy-ung, translated by J.A. Makepeace. New York, Frederick A. Stokes Co.; London, Chatto and Windus, 1927. x, 322 p.

TSCHARNER, EDUARD HORST VON, 1901- Chinesischer Kulturgeist. Bern, F. Pochon-Jent AG, 1939. iv, 16 p.

TUNG, TSO-PIN, 董作賓, 1895- An interpretation of the ancient Chinese civilization. Taipei, Chinese Association for the United Nations, 1952. 34 p. (Unachina publications, ser. I, 9).

VISSERING, CARL EMMO. China. 12 Vorträge über Geschichte, Kultur und Kunst. Tientsin, Peiyang Press, 1943. 191 p. plates, map.

WEI, CHO-MIN, 韋卓民, 1888- The spirit of Chinese culture. New York, C. Scribner, 1947. xii, 186 p. (Hewett lectures, 1946).

WERNER, EDWARD THEODORE CHALMERS, 1864- A history of Chinese civilization, v. 1. Shanghai, Shanghai Times, 1940. 448 p. col. front., plates (part col.) maps.

WESTHARP, ALFRED. "Hsin Tao," version française "Moralité naturelle." Réinterprétation des anciennes idées chinois du point de vue de la science naturelle moderne. Pékin, A. Nachbaur, 1924. 10 p.

——. Esquisse d'une psychologie de collaboration entire l'Extrême-Occident et l'Extrême-Orient. Pékin, Impr. de la "Politique de Pékin," 1926. 46 p. (Collection de la "Politique de Pékin").

WHITE, VAUGHAN. Our neighbors, the Chinese. New York, Toronto, Rinehart, [1946] xiv, 267 p.

WILHELM, HELLMUT, 1905- Gesellschaft und Staat in China, acht Vorträge. Peking, H. Vetch [1944] 175 p.

WILHELM, RICHARD, 1873- 1930. Ostasien. Werden und Wandel des chinesischen Kulturkreises. Potsdam, Müller and Kiepenheuer; Zürich, Orell Füssli, 1928.219 p.incl. map (Das Weltbild; Bücher des lebendigen Wissen. 5).

[YAUKEY, GRACE (SYDENSTRICKER)] 1899- China, by Cornelia Spencer [pseud.] Illustrated by Rafaello Busoni. [New York] Holiday House [1944] 25 p. col. front., col. illus.

——. Made in China; the story of China's expression by Cornelia Spencer [pseud.] Foreword by Lin Yutang, illustrated by Kurt Wiese. [2d ed., rev.] New York, Knopf; London, Harrap; Toronto, Ryerson Press, 1952. 258 p. illus. 1st ed. 1943.

## Chinese Culture and the West

AMANN, GUSTAV, 1882- Kulturgegensätze zwischen Europa und China; ein verständigungs Versuch. Berlin, M. Krayn, 1921. 50 p.

AMBROSE, EDNA. Studying China in American elementary schools, prepared by Edna Ambrose and Kay Grimshaw at the Harvard workshop in social studies for the Committee on Asiatic Studies, American council on education, at the  request of United China Relief.  New York, N.Y. [United China Relief, 1943] cover-title, 16 p. illus. (ports.).

AMERICAN COUNCIL OF LEARNED SOCIETIES. Committee on the Promotion of Chinese Studies. Progress of Chinese studies in the United States of A - merica: a report recommended by the American Council of the Institute of Pacific Relations for reference in connection with the conference to be held at Hangchow, China, October, 1931. 102 p. (Its Bulletin, 1).

————. Committee on the Promotion of Chinese Studies. Careers for students of Chinese language and civilization, edited for the Committee on the Promotion of Chinese Studies of the American Council of Learned Societies by Lewis Hodous, in collaboration with Esson M. Gale and Kenneth S. Latourette. Chicago, Pub. for the American  Council, Institute of Pacific Relations, by the University of Chicago Press [c1933] ix, 65 p.

APPLETON, WILLIAM WORTHEN. A cycle of Cathay; the Chinese vogue in England during the seventeenth and eighteenth centuries. New York, Columbia University Press, 1951. xii, 182 p. illus., ports., map.

AURICH, URSULA. "China im Spiegel der deutschen Literatur des 18. Jahrhunderts." Berlin, E. Ebering, 1935. 174 p. (Germanische studien, 169).

BERNARD, HENRI, 1897-  La Chine en France durant la renaissance.  Shanghai, Impr. de T'ou-sè-wè, 1940. cover-title, 14 p. "Extrait du Bulletin de l'Université l'Aurore déc. 1940."

BODDE, DERK, 1909-  Tolstoy and China, by Derk Bodde with the collaboration of Galia Speshneff Bodde.  Princeton, Princeton University Press, 1950. v, 110 p. (History of ideas series, 4).

CARTER, EDWARD CLARK, 1878-1954. ed. China and Japan in our university curricula, with a special section on the University of Hawaii.  Chicago, University of Chicago Press [1930] 191 p.

CENTRE D'ÉTUDES SINOLOGIQUES DE PÉKIN. Mélanges sinologiques.  Pékin, 1951. 103 p.

CENTRE FRANCO-CHINOIS D'ÉTUDES SINOLOGIQUES, Peking. Deux siècles de sinologie française.  Pékin, Centre franco-chinois d'études sinologiques, 1943. xii, 74 p., illus. (facsims.) double plates.

CHANG, CH'I-YUN, 張其昀 , 1901-  The centenary celebration of Sino-American intellectual friendship.  Taipei, China Culture Pub. Foundation, 1953. 13 p. (Pamphlet on Chinese affairs).

CHANG, HSIN-CHANG, 張心滄. Allegory and courtesy in Spenser; a Chinese view.  Edinburgh, University Press, 1955. x, 227 p. (Edinburgh University publications; language and literature, 8).

CH'EN, CH'UAN, 陳銓, 1905-  Die chinesische schöne Literatur im deutschen Schrifttum. [Glückstadt und Hamburg, Druck von J.J. Augustin, 1933] 108, [6], 12 p. Diss. - Univ. Kiel.

CH'EN, SOPHIA H., 任陳衡哲. The outstanding cultural assets of the Chinese people. The Chinese point of view of the so-called material civilization of the West. Honolulu, Institute of Pacific Relations, 1927. 16 p.

————. Symposium on Chinese culture.  Shanghai, China Institute of Pacific Relations, 1931. 373 p. illus.

CH'EN, SHOU-I, 陳受頤 , 1899-  The influence of China on English culture during the eighteenth century.  Chicago, 1928. iii-xvi, 218, 7 l. Thesis - Univ. of Chicago.

CHINESISCH-SCHWEIZERISCHE GESELLSCHAFT. Reden und Vorträge gehalten an der Gründungsversammlung, Luzern 6 März, 1945. [Luzern, 1945] 52 p.

DANTON, GEORGE HENRY, 1880-  The culture contacts of the United States and China; the earliest Sino-American culture contacts, 1784-1844. New York, Columbia University Press, 1931. 133 p.

DEMIÉVILLE, PAUL, 1894-  Le réorganisation des études orientales en Grande-Bretagne, communication faité à la Société Asiatique le 18 Nov. 1949, par

Paul Demiéville et J. Sauvaget. Paris, Société Asiatique, 1950. 11 p.
DUBS, HOMER HASENPFLUG, 1892- A Roman city in ancient China. London,
China Society, 1957. 4, 48 p. map. (China Society sinological ser., 5).
DUYVENDAK, JAN JULIUS LODEWIJK, 1889-1954. A bird's eye view of Euro-
pean sinology. New York, China Institute in America, [1931?] 11 p.
———. Holland's contribution to Chinese studies. London, China Society, 1950.
23 p. illus.
ÉCOLE FRANÇAISE D'EXTRÊME-ORIENT, Hanoi. Études asiatiques, publiées
à l'occasion du vingt-cinquième anniversaire de l'École française d'Extrême-
Orient par ses membres et ses collaborateurs. [Paris] G. Van Oest, 1925.
2 v. illus. (incl. plans) plates, maps (part fold.) (Publications de l'École
française d'Extrême-Orient. [Vol. 19-20]).
ENGEMANN, WALTER, 1898- Voltaire und China: ein Beitrag sur Geschichte
der Völkerkunde und zur Geschichte der Geschichts-schreibung sowie zu ihr-
en gegenseitigen Beziehungen. Leipzig, 1932. 155 p. Diss.-Univ. Leipzig.
ERKES, EDUARD, 1891- China und Europa; Kontrast und Ausgleich zweier
Weltkulturen. Leipzig, Volk und Buch Verlag [1947] 79 p. illus. (Die Hum-
boldt-Bücherei, 1).
EUCKEN, RUDOLF CHRISTOF, 1846-1926. Das Lebensproblem in China und in
Europa, von Rudolf Eucken und Carsun Chang, 張嘉森. Leipzig, Quelle and
Meyer, 1922. viii, 200 p.
FAN, TS'UN-CHUNG, 范存忠, 1904- Dr. Johnson and Chinese culture. [Lec-
ture delivered before the China Society on 15th December, 1944] London,
China Society, 1945. 19, [1] p. illus., facsim. (China Society occasional pa-
pers. New series, 6).
FENN, WILLIAM PURVIANCE, 1902- Ah Sin and his brethren in American lit-
erature; delivered before the convocation of the College of Chinese Studies,
June 1933. Peiping, College of Chinese Studies [1933] x, 131, xli p.
FOSTER, JOHN B., 1911- China and the Chinese in American literature 1850-
1950. Mankato, Minn., 1952. 641 l. Thesis - Mankato State Teachers College.
FRANKE, HERBERT, 1914- Europa in der ostasiatischen Geschichts-schreibung des 13. und 14. Jahrhunderts. München, 1951. 10 p. (Saeculum II, 1).
———. Sinologie. Bern, A. Francke, 1953. 216 p. (Orientalistik, 1. T.) Wissenschaftliche Forschungsberichte. Geisteswissenschaftliche Reihe, Bd. 19).
FRANKE, WOLFGANG, 1912- Titelverzeichnis chinesischer Übersetzungen
deutscher Werke, zusammengestellt von Wolfgang Franke unter Mitwirkung
von Dsang Schau-dien, 張紹典. Peking, 1942. viii, 53 p. (Peking. Deutschland Institute. Bibliographische Reihe, 1.).
GOETHE, JOHANN WOLFGANG VON, 1749-1832. Chinesisch-deutsche Jahrs-
und Tageszeiten. Mit einem Nachwort von Luitgard Albrecht-Natorp. Kre-
feld, Scherpe-Verlag, 1947. 23 p.
HARTMANN, HORST. Die Erweiterung der europäischen Chinakenntnis durch
die "Description de la Chine" des Jesuitenpaters Du Halde. Ein Beitrag zur
Würdigung der Verdienste des Jesuitenmissionare um die kulturelle Er-
schliessung des chinesischen Reiches und die kulturvermittlung zwischen
China und Europa. Göttingen, 1949. 129 l. Diss. - Univ. Göttingen.
HUDSON, GEOFFREY FRANCIS, 1903- Europe and China; a survey of their
relation from the earliest times to 1800. London, E. Arnold [1931] viii, 9-
336 p. incl. maps, diagrs.
HUNG, CHENG-FU, 洪申黻. Un siècle d'influence chinoise sur la littérature
française (1815-1930). Paris, F. Loviton, 1934. 280 p. Thèse - Univ. de
Paris.
LACH, DONALD FREDERICK, 1917- Contributions of China to German civili-
zation, 1648-1740. Chicago, 1941. 165 l. Thesis - University of Chicago.
LEW, TIMOTHY TINGFANG, 劉廷芳, 1894-1947. China in American school
text-books, a problem of education in international understanding and world-

wide brotherhood. Peking, Chinese Social and Political Science Association [1923]    154 p. "Special supplement of the Chinese social and political
science review, July 1923."
LÜTHI, KARL JACOB. Chinesisch in der Schweiz. Vortrag gehalten von K. J.
    Lüthi, an der Jahresversammlung des Vereins Schweizer. Gutenberg-mu-
    seum in Bern. 4 März 1934. Bern, Bücher und Co., 1934. iv, 31 p. illus.
    plates.
MALLERET, LOUIS, ed. Le cinquantenaire de l'École française d'Extrême-
    Orient. Paris, E. de Boccard; en vente à la Librairie A. Maisonneuve,
    1953. 176 p. plates, ports., facsims.
MARKEL, RUDOLF FRANZ. Leibniz und China. Berlin, Walter de Gruyter,
    1952. 38 p. (Leibniz zu seinem 300 Geburtstag, 1646-1946. Lfg. 8). Diss.-
    Univ. Marburg.
MASON, MARY GERTRUDE, 1900-   Western concepts of China and the Chinese,
    1840-76. New York [Printed, The Seeman Printery] 1939. xv, 288 p.
MAVERICK, LEWIS ADAMS, 1891-  Chinese influences upon Quesnay and Tur-
    got. Claremont, Calif., 1942. 12 p. (Claremont Oriental Studies, 4).
————. China, a model for Europe. San Antonio, Tex., Paul Anderson, c1946.
    xi, [1], 334 p.
NOTES on Far Eastern studies in America. no. 1-12. June 1937-42. Washing-
    ton, D. C., Committees on Chinese and Japanese studies, American Coun-
    cil of Learned Societies [1937-42] 12 nos. semiannual.
PINOT, VIRGILE. La Chine et la formation de l'esprit philosophique en France
    (1640-1740). Paris, P. Geuthner, 1932. [9]-480 p.
————. ed. Documents inédits relatifs à la connaissance de la Chine en France
    de 1685 à 1740. Paris, P. Geuthner, 1932. 130 p.
PITKIN, VICTOR ELLSWORTH, 1907-   Studying China in American  high
    schools, prepared by Victor Pitkin and Wilson Colvin at the Harvard work-
    shop in social studies for the Committee on Asiatic studies, American coun-
    cil on education, at the request of United China Relief. New York [United
    China Relief, 1943] cover-title, 5-16 p. illus. (map).
POUZYNA, I. V. La Chine, l'Italie et les débuts de la renaissance (XIIIe-XIVe
    siècles) Paris, Les Éditions d'art et d'histoire, 1935. 102 p., plates.
REICHWEIN, ADOLF, 1898- 1945. China und Europa. Geistige und Künstleri-
    sche Beziehungen in 18. Jahrhundert. Berlin, Oesterheld and Co., 1923.
    179 p. illus. (plan), plates.
————. China and Europe; intellectual and artistic contacts in the eighteenth cen-
    tury. Translated by J. C. Powell. New York, A. A. Knopf; London, Kegan
    Paul, 1925. vii, 174 p. illus., plates. (The history of civilization. [Modern
    history]).
RIDGE, WILLIAM SHELDON, 1875-1946. When the West came to the East,  a
    lecture delivered at the College of Chinese Studies, Peiping. Peiping, Col-
    lege of Chinese Studies, 1935. 32 p.
SCHORER, EDGAR. L'influence de la Chine sur la genèse et le développement
    de la doctrine physiocratique. Paris, Éditions F. Loviton et Cie, 1938. 192
    p. Thèse - Univ. de Fribourg (Suisse).
SCHULER, P. BERTRAM. Altes Erbe des neuen China. Ein Beitrag zur Ver-
    ständigung von West und Ost. Paderborn, F. Schöningh; Wien, R. Fürlinger;
    Zürich, B. Götschmann, 1937. iv, 319 p. illus.
SCHULTHEIS, FREDERIC DWIGHT. The growth of the knowledge of China in
    the West; a lecture delivered at the College of Chinese Studies, Peking. Pe-
    king, College of Chinese Studies, 1938. cover-title, 23 p.
SELDEN, ELIZABETH S. 1888-  China in German poetry from 1773 to 1883.
    Berkeley and Los Angeles, University of California Press, 1942. ix, 141-
    316 p. front. (University of California publications in modern philology, 25:3).
SWISHER, EARL, 1902- Asiatic studies program at the University of Colorado;
    report of activities of the Institute of Asiatic Affairs over the period 1944 to

1949. [Boulder] University of Colorado, 1950. 110 p.

TING, TCHAO-TSING, 丁肇青. Les descriptions de la Chine par les français (1650-1750). Paris, P. Geuthner, 1928. 112 p.

TSCHARNER, EDUARD HORST VON, 1901- China in der deutschen Dichtung bis zur Klassik. München, E. Reinhardt, 1939. iv, 126, [2] p., illus. plates.

———. Die Chinakunde als Wissenschaft; Antrittsvorlesung gehalten an der Universität Bern am 17. Juni 1939, in erweiterter Gestalt. St. Gallen, H.Tschudy, 1940. 24 p.

VENNE, PETER. China und die Chinesen in der neuren englischen und amerikanischen Literatur. Zürich, Juris Verlag, 1951. 85 p. Diss. - Univ. Zürich.

WINTERS, LEE E., JR., 1922- The relationship of Chinese poetry to British and American poetry of the twentieth century. Berkeley, 1956. 165 l.

WYLIE, ALEXANDER, 1815-87. Chinese researches. Shanghai, 1897. [London, K. Paul, Trench, Trubner and co., 1937] [549] p. front. (port.) illus., plates.

YIAN, TSOUAN-LIN, 閻宗齡. Essai sur le Père Du Halde et sa description de la Chine. Fribourg, Fraguière frères, 1937. 119 p. Thèse - Univ. Fribourg.

ZACH, ERWIN VON, 1872-1942. Sinologische Beiträge (Grammatik, Lexikographie, Übersetzungen). Batavia, Druckerei Tong Ah, 1930- 3 v.

# III. GEOGRAPHY AND TRAVEL

## Historical Geography and Early Travels
### General Works

AL-MARWAZĪ, fl. 1056-1120. Sharaf al-Zamān Ṭāhir Marvazī on China, the Turks and India; Arabic text (circa A.D. 1120) with an English translation and commentary by V. Minorsky. London, Royal Asiatic Society, 1942. 170 p.; [1], 53 p. (James G. Forlong fund, vol. XXII).

BERNARD, AUGUSTIN, 1865- La mappemonde Ricci du Musée historique de Pékin. Pékin, Impr. de la "Politique de Pékin," 1928. [3], 13 p. port. fold. facsim. (Collection de la "Politique de Pékin").

BOURDON, LÉON, Une description inédite de la baie de Canton à la fin du XVIe siècle. Lisbonne, 1950. 28 p. map. "Breve informacão sobre algũas cousas das ilhas da China (texte)": p. 21-28.

CHANG, KUEI-SHENG, 張桂生 1921- Chinese great explorers: their effect upon Chinese geographic knowledge prior to 1600. Ann Arbor, University Microfilms [1955] ([University Microfilms, Ann Arbor, Mich.] Publication no. 12, 550). vi, 439 l. illus., maps. Thesis-Univ. of Michigan.

CHOU, TA-KUAN, 周達觀, fl. 1297. Mémoires sur les coutumes du Cambodge de Tcheou Ta-kouan. Version nouvelle, suivie d'un commentaire inachevé [par Paul Pelliot] Paris, Librairie d'Amérique et d'Orient, 1951. 178 p. (Œuvres posthumes de Paul Pelliot, 3).

COUVREUR, SÉRAPHIN, 1835-1919. Géographie ancienne et moderne de la Chine. Sien Hsien, Impr. de la mission catholique, 1934. 426 p. maps. 1st ed. 1917.

DUYVENDAK, JAN JULIUS LODEWIJK, 1889-1954. Ma Huan, 馬觀, re-examined. Amsterdam, Noord-Hollandsche uitgeversmaatschappij, 1933. 74 p. (Verhandelingen der Koninklijke akademie van wetenschappen te Amsterdam. Afdeeling letterkunde. Nieuwe reeks, deel XXXII, no. 2 [i.e. 3]).

——. China's discovery of Africa; lectures given at the University of London on January 22 and 23, 1947. London, A. Probsthain, 1949. 35 p. plates, map.

FERRAND, GABRIEL, 1864-1935. ed. Le pilote des mers de l'Inde, de la Chine et de l'Indonésie par Sulaymān al-Mahrī et Sīhāb Ad-Dīn Ahmad bin Mājid. Text arabe. (reproduction phototypique de MS de la Bibliothèque Nationale de Paris). Paris, P. Geuthner, 1921-23. 2 v. plates, (Instructions nautiques et routiers arabs et portugais des 15e et 16e siècles, 2).

FROGER, FRANÇOIS, b. 1676- Relation du premier voyage des Francois à la Chine fait en 1698, 1699 et 1700 sur le vaisseau "L'Amphitrite," hrsg. von E.A. Voretzsch. Leipzig, Verlag der Asia Major, 1926. [iii]-xvi, 187 p.

FUCHS, WALTER, 1902- Der Jesuiten Atlas der Kanghsi Zeit; China und die Aussenländer. Peking, Verlegt bei der Katholischen Universität, 1941. cover-title, 35 folded maps (in portfolio) (Monumenta Serica. Monog. ser. 3).

——. Der Jesuiten-Atlas der Kanghsi-Zeit, seine Entstehungsgeschichte nebst Namens-vindices für die Karten der Mandjurei, Mongolei, Ostturkestan und Tibet, mit Wiedergabe der Jesuiten-Karten in originalgrösse. Peking, Fu-Jen Universität, 1943. iii, 414 p. maps, Atlas. (Monumenta Serica, Monog. ser. 4).

——. The "Mongol atlas" of China, by Chu-Ssu-pen, 朱思本, and the Kuang yü-t'u, 廣興圖. With 48 facsimile maps dating from about 1555. Peiping, Fu Jen Univ., 1946. 32 p. maps. (Monumenta Serica. Monog. ser. 8 ).

GOODRICH, LUTHER CARRINGTON, 1894- China's first knowledge of the Americas, address before the convocation of the College of Chinese Studies, May 1937. Peking, College of Chinese Studies, California College in China, 1938. 18 p. 1 illus., fold. map.

ḤASAN IBN YAZĪD, ABŪ ZAID, al-Sīrāfī. Voyage du marchand arabe Sulaymân en Inde et en Chine, rédigé en 851, suivi de remarques par Abû Zayd Ḥasan (vers 916) Traduit de l'arabe avec introd., glossaire et index, par Gabriel Ferrand. Bois dessinés et gravés par Andrée Karpelès. Paris, Éditions Bossard, 1922. 155 p. illus. (Les Classiques de l'Orient, v. 7).

———. Aḫbār aṣ-Ṣīn wa l-Hind. Relation de la Chine et de l'Inde rédigée en 851. Text établi, traduit et commenté par Jean Sauvaget. Paris, Belles Lettres, 1948. xli, 27, 27, [28]-79 p. maps (Collection arabe). In part, opposite pages numbered in duplicate. In 2 books, the first said to be taken down from statements made by a merchant named Sulaimān, the second a continuation of the first, by Ḥasan. "Table bibliographique": p. ix-xiv.

HERRMANN, ALBERT, 1886- Die Verkehrswege zwischen China, Indien und Rom um 100 nach Chr. Geb. Leipzig, J.C. Hinrichs, 1922. 8 p. map (Leipzig. Universität. Forschungsinstitut für vergleichende Religionsgeschichte. Veröffentlichungen, 7).

———. Historical and commercial atlas of China. Cambridge, Mass., Harvard University Press, 1935. 5-112 p., incl. 119 maps (part col.) diagr. (Harvard-Yenching institute. Monograph series, v. 1).

———. Das Land der Seide und Tibet im lichte der Antike. Leipzig, K.F.Koehlers antiquarium, 1938. ix, 178 p., ix plates (incl. fold. maps) (Quellen und forschungen zur geschichte der geographie und völkerunde...hrsg. von dr. Albert Herrmann...[bd. 1]).

HU, SHIH, 1891- A note on Ch'üan Tsu-wang, 全祖望, Chao I-ch'ing, 趙一清 and Tai Chên, 戴震; a study of independent convergence in research as illustrated in their works on the Shui-ching chu. Washington, 1944. cover-title, 970-982 p. "Reprinted from the biographical dictionary, Eminent Chinese of the Ch'ing period, Vol.II."

IBN BATUTA, 1304-77. Travels in Asia and Africa, 1325-54, translated and selected by H.A.R. Gibb, with an introduction and notes. London, G. Routledge and sons; New York, R.M. McBride and Co., 1929. vii, 398 p.front., plates, maps. (The Broadway travellers, ed. by Sir E. Denison Ross and Eileen Power). 1957 ed. 4 v. (Publications Hakluyt Soc.).

KAMMERER, ALBERT, 1875- La découverte de la Chine par les Portugais au XVIème siècle et la cartographie des portulans. Avec des notes de toponymie chinoise, par Paul Pelliot. Leiden, E.J. Brill, 1944. ix, 260 p. plates, maps. (T'oung pao; archives concernant l'histoire, les langues, la géographie, l'ethnographie et les arts de l'Asie orientale. Suppl. au vol. 39).

LATTIMORE, OWEN, 1900- Inner Asian frontiers of China. [2d ed.] Irvington-on-Hudson, N.Y., Capitol Pub. Co., and American Geographical Society, New York, 1951. lxi, 585 p. maps. (American Geographical Society [of New York] Research series no. 21) 1st ed. New York and London, 1940.

LAUFER, BERTHOLD, 1874-1934. China and the discovery of America. New York, China Institute in America [1931?] 7 p.

MENDES PINTO, FERNÃO, b. 1509. À propos des Voyages aventureux de Fernand Mendez Pinto; notes de A.J.H. Charignon, recueillies et complétées par M. Médard. Pékin, Impr. des Lazaristes, 1935 [i. e. 1936] [v]-xviii, 417, [2] p. front. (port.) plates, fold. maps.

ODORICO DA PORDENONE, 1286-1331. De Venise à Pékin au moyen age. Récit adapté en français moderne par Henriette Demoulin. Paris, P. Téqui, 1938. 126 p. map, (Collection Les beaux voyages d'autrefois).

ROBERTS, FRANCES MARKLEY. Western travellers to China. A personalized story of China's relations with the West in religion, commerce, diplomacy and culture, during eleven centuries. Shanghai [etc.] Kelly and Walsh, 1932. iii, 178 p. front. (map) illus.

SCHOFF, WILFRED HARVEY, 1874-  Early communication between China and
the Mediterranean; a paper submitted at the general meeting of the American philosophical society held at Philadelphia April 21, 1921 by Wilfred H.
Schoff. [Philadelphia, Pa., 1921] 9, [1] p.

SELLMAN, ROGER RAYMOND. An outline atlas of Eastern history. London, E.
Arnold [1954] 63 p. (p. 5-56 maps).

SHERWOOD, MERRIAM, 1892-  The road to Cathay, by Merriam Sherwood and
Elmer Mantz; decorations by William Siegel. New York, Macmillan, 1928.
xii, 251 p. col. front., double maps.

SHUI CHING CHU, 水經注. Northern India according to the Shui-ching-chu.
Translated and edited by Luciano Petech. Roma, Istituto italiano per il
Medio ed Estremo Orient. 1950. viii, 89 p. (Série Orientale Roma, 2).

SINAÏSKI, VASILLI IVANOVICH, 1876-  Rome et Chine dans quelques rapproche-
ments (juridiques, économiques, religieux, chronologiques, astrologiques,
totémiques et folkloristiques) Rīgā, 1936. 1 v.

SYKES, SIR PERCY MOLESWORTH, 1867-1945. The quest for Cathay. London,
A. and C. Black, 1936. xii, 279, [1] p. col. front., illus., plates, maps.

————. À la recherche du Cathay; découverte de la Chine par l'Europe et de l'Occident par la Chine. Traduit par Robert Godet. Paris, Payot, 1938. 240 p.
illus., plates, maps.

————. Europa sucht China. [Ins Deutsche Übertragen von van Bebber] Leipzig,
W. Goldmann [1938] 189 p. plates, maps (part fold.)

YAMADA, KENTARO. A short history of ambergris by the Arabs and Chinese
in the Indian ocean. Kinki, Institute of World Economics, Kinki University,
1955. 26 p. (Kinki. University. Institute of World Economics, Report 8).

Marco Polo

POLO, MARCO, 1254-1323? The Book of Ser Marco Polo, the Venetian, concerning the kingdoms and marvels of the east. Translated and edited, with
notes, by Colonel Sir Henry Yule, 3d. ed., revised throughout in the light of
recent discoveries by Henri Cordier. With a memoir of Henry Yule by his
daughter, Amy Frances Yule. London, John Murray, 1921; New York, C.
Scribner, 1926. 2 v. illus. fold. plates. fold. maps. facsims.

————. Trois chapitres de Marco Polo. Pékin, A. Nachbaur, 1921. 14 l.

————. Le livre de Marco Polo; traduit en français moderne et annoté d'après
les sources chinoises par A. J. H. Charignon. Pékin, A. Nachbaur, 1924-
28. 3 v.

————. The travels of Marco Polo. New York, J. H. Sears [1926] xii, 303 p.
(The Royal blue library).

————. The travels of Marco Polo, the Venetian, with an introduction by John
Masefield. Fully illustrated with twenty drawings in pen and ink by Adrian
De Friston and eleven photogravure plates. London and Toronto, J. M. Dent;
New York, E. P. Dutton, 1926. xviii, 461, [1] p. front., illus., plates, ports.,
fold. map, plan.

————. The travels of Marco Polo [the Venetian] Revised from Marsden's translation and edited with introduction by Manuel Komroff. New York, Boni and
Liveright [c1926]; London, J. Cape [1928] xxxii, 369 p. illus.

————. The book of Ser Marco Polo, the Venetion, concerning the kingdoms and
marvels of the East; edited with an introduction by George B. Parks. New
York, Macmillan, 1929; N. Y. Book League of America, 1929. xxxiii p., 392
p. incl. front. 2 maps (1 fold.) (The modern readers' series) 1st ed. 1927.

————. The same. Translated and edited, with notes, by Colonel Sir Henry Yule,
3d ed., revised throughout in the light of recent discoveries by Henri Cordier, with a  memoir of Henry Yule by his daughter, Amy Frances Yule.
London, J. Murray [1929] 2 v. fronts., illus. (incl. coats of arms) plates
(part col., part fold.) ports., maps (part fold.) plans, facsims. (part fold.)

"Third edition (reprinted) September 1929."

——. Les merveilleux voyages de Marco Polo dans l'Asie du XIII$^e$ siècle, pub. par Maurice Turpaud. Paris, "Éditions Spes," 1929. 214 p. plates ("Des fleurs et des fruits").

——. The travels of Marco Polo [the Venetian] edited with introduction by Manuel Komroff, illustrations by Witold Gordon. The Kublai Khan ed. New York, H. Liveright [c1930] Garden City, N.Y., Garden City Pub. Co. [1935] xxxii p., 3-370 p. front., illus., plates.

——. The travels of Marco Polo, translated into English from the text of L.F. Benedetto by Professor Aldo Ricci, with an introduction and index by Sir E. Denison Ross. London, G. Routledge [1931] New York, Viking Press, 1931. xviii, 439 p. illus., IV plates.(incl. front., facsim.) 4 double maps. (The Broadway travellers, edited by Sir E. Denison Ross and Eileen Power).

——. The same. Introduction by Carl Van Doren. New York, Literary Guild of America, 193? xvii, 340 p. (The Guild classics).

——. The same. New York, Grosset and Dunlap [1931] xvii, 340 p. (Universal library).

——. The same. Revised from Marsden's translation and edited with an introduction by Manuel Komroff. New York, The Modern Library [1931] xxxi, 351 p. (The modern library of the world's best books) "First Modern library edition."

——. Le livre de Marco Polo, gentilhomme venitien, 1271-95. Eaux fortes de Mariette Lydis. [Paris] Les Cent vue, 1932. 200 p. incl. col. front., col. plates.

——. The travels of Marco Polo. London, J.M. Dent. New York, E.P. Dutton [1932] xvi, 461, [1] p. (Everyman's library, ed. by Ernest Rhys. Travel and topography. [no. 306]) "First published in this edition 1908. Reprinted...1923. Reset 1932."

——. The same. The Marsden translation revised and edited with an introduction by Manuel Komroff; decorated by W.A. Dwiggins. Rochester, N.Y., The Printing House of Leo Hart, 1933. xxxvii, [1], 414 p. illus. (part col.).

——. The same. Revised and edited with an introduction by Manuel Komroff; illustrations by Nikolai Fyodorovitch Lapshin. New York, Printed for the members of the Limited Editions Club, 1934. 2 v. col. illus.

——. Der mitteldeutsche Marco Polo, nach der Admonter Handschrift herausgegeben von Ed. Horst von Tscharner. Berlin, Weidmann, 1935. lii, 102 p. facsim., diagrs. (Deutsche texte des mittelalters, hrsg. von der Preussischen akademie der wissenschaften. bd. XL).

——. The most noble and famous travels of Marco Polo, together with the travels of Nicolò de' Conti, edited from the Elizabethan translation of John Frampton, with introduction, notes and appendices by N.M. Penzer, M.A. 2d ed. London, A. and C. Black, 1937. lxiv, 381 p. maps (1 fold.) facsim. "First published 1929 by the Argonaut press in an edition limited to 1050 copies. Second edition, enlarged, 1937."

——. The description of the world [translated and annotated by] A.C. Moule and Paul Pelliot. London, G. Routledge and sons, limited, 1938. 2 v. fronts. (ports., 1 col.) illus. (incl. plan) plates, facsims., geneal. tables (1 fold.).

——. Die Reisen des Marco Polo. Seinen Aufzeichungen nacherzählt von Rudolf Eger. Schutzumschlag von Willi Schnabel. Aarau, H.R. Sauerländer and Co., 1944. iv, 219 p.

——. The adventures of Marco Polo, as dictated in prison to a scribe in the year 1298; what he experienced and heard during his twenty-four years spent in travel through Asia and at the court of Kublai-Khan. Ed. for the modern reader by Richard J. Walsh, with an introd. by Pearl S. Buck. Illus. by Cyrus Le Roy Baldridge. New York, John Day, 1948. xi, 193 p. illus., col. plates, col. maps. (An Asia book).

——. The travels of Marco Polo. the Venetian; tr. and ed. by William Mars-

den, re-ed. by Thomas Wright. Illus. by Jon Carbino.  Garden City, N. Y.,
Doubleday; N.Y. Book League of America, c1948. 344 p. illus. (part col.)
map (on lining-papers) (Doubleday limited editions).

――――. Am Hofe des Grosskhans, bearb. von Albert Herrmann. Neue Ausg.
Leipzig, F.A. Brockhaus, 1949 [c1924] 166 p. illus. 1. Aufl. 1924; 2. Aufl.
1926.

――――. Itinerarium, Antverpiae, 1485. Reproduced in phototype from the original edition in possession of the Toyo Bunko (Oriental Library) by the National Diet Library, Tokyo, Japan. Tokyo, 1949. facsim. ([147] p.), [1] p. Title from colophon of reprint. The original has no imprint, but is generally
assigned to the press of Gerardus Leeu, at Antwerp (or Gouda) ca. 1485. Cf.
Campbell, Annales, 1434; Stillwell. 2d census, P822.

――――. The travels of Marco Polo; rev. and ed., with an introduction, by Manuel Komroff. Illustrated by Nikolai Fyodorovitch Lapshin. New York, Heritage Press, 1950. xxix, 477 p. col. illus.

――――. Die Weltreise des Marco Polo. [Nach den Originalberichten seiner Ent-
deckungsfahrten; bearb. von] Richard Euringer. Stuttgart, Verlag deutsche
Volksbücher [1953] 326 p. maps.

――――. Le livre de Marco Polo; ou, Le devisement du monde. Texte intégral,
mis en français moderne et commenté par A. t'Serstevens. Paris, A. Michel [1955] 346 p. illus., map.

――――. La description du monde. Texte intégral en Francais moderne, avec introduction et notes par Louis Hambis. Paris, C. Klincksieck, 1955. xvii,
433 p. col. plates, fold. map.

## Works About Marco Polo

BONVALOT, GABRIEL, 1853-1933. Voyages. Les chercheurs de routes. Mar-
co Polo. Paris, G. Crès et cie, 1924. 251 p., plates, maps (part fold.).
BRADHAM, C.M. Marco Polo. Exeter, A. Wheaton, 1937. 40 p. incl. front.,
illus. (map). (Makers of history, 14).
CHARIGNON, ANTOINE JOSEPH HENRI, 1872-1930. La grande Java de Marco
Polo en Cochinchine; étude de géographie historique d'après les sources chinoises et arabes. [Saigon, 1930] 159 p.
COLLIS, MAURICE, 1889- Marco Polo. London, Faber and Faber [1950] ix,
190 p. illus., map.
DIEU, LÉON. Marco Polo chez le Grand Khan. Namur, Grands Lacs, 1947.
174 p. illus. map, (Collection Lavigerie, 14).
DRUTMAN, IRVING. Marco Polo; story by Irving Drutman and Jerry Felsheim,
illustrations by Harrison Moore. Prepared and edited by developing new reading materials [and] conducted under the auspices of the U.S. Works progress
administration. New York, Board of Education of the City of New York, 1939.
26 l. illus.
FINGER, CHARLES J. The travels of Marco Polo. Girard, Kan., Haldeman-
Julius Co. [c1924] 64 p. (Little blue book, no. 513, ed. by E. Haldeman-Julius ).
HART, HENRY HERSCH, 1886- Venetian adventurer, being an account of the
life and times and of the book of Messer Marco Polo. Stanford, Stanford U-
niv. Press [1947] xiv, 286 p. illus., maps, facsims. "Third edition." 1st
ed. 1942, 2d ed. 1943.
HOFFMANN, AGNES. Untersuchungen zu den altdeutschen Marco Polo-Texten.
Ohlau i. Schlesien, H. Eschenhagen kg., 1936. x, 87 p. illus. (facsims.)
(Freiburger forschungen zur kunst- und literaturgeschichte, 4). Diss.-Frei-
burg i. Br.
IWAMURA, SHINOBU. Manuscripts and printed editions of Marco Polo's travels
Tokyo, National Diet Library, 1949. cover-title, 23 p.
KOMROFF, MANUEL, 1890- Marco Polo; illustrated by Edgard Cirlin.  New

York, Messner [1952] 171 p. illus.

MOULE, ARTHUR CHRISTOPHER, 1873-1957. Quinsai, with other notes on Marco Polo. Cambridge [Eng.] University Press, 1957. xii, 92 p. front. (port.), illus. plates, (incl. map), plan.

OLSCHKI, LEONARDO, 1885- Marco Polo's precursors, with a map of Asia. Baltimore, Johns Hopkins Press, 1943. ix, 100 p. fold. map.

[RAPISARDA, ANTONIO] 1900- Vie et aventures de Marco Polo. 4. éd. Paris, Mercure de France, 1937. 306 p.

RIVERAIN, JEAN. Marco Polo à travers l'Asie inconnue. Paris, Larousse, 1954. 208 p. illus. col. plate (Contes et gestes historiques).

SCOTT, SIR JAMES GEORGE, 1851- Marco Polo. With twelve full-page illustrations, four of them in colour. London, A. and C. Black, 1927. v, [1], 89, [1] p. front. (port.) illus. (map) plates (part col.) (Peeps at great explorers).

SHKLOVSKIĬ, VIKTOR BORISOVICH, 1893- Le voyage de Marco Polo. Traduit du russe par Marc Slonim. Introduction de K. Kounine. Paris, Payot, 1948. 246 p. illus. map, (Bibliothèque géographique) 1er éd., 1938.

WALRAET, MARCEL. Sur les traces de Marco Polo. Bruxelles, Office de publicité, 1948. 98 p. illus., fold. map. (Collection Lebègue, 8. sér., no 93).

WALSH, RICHARD JOHN, 1886- Adventures and discoveries of Marco Polo; illustrated by Cyrus Le Roy Baldridge. New York, Random House [1953] 183 p. illus. (World landmark books, W-3).

## Modern Geography

BUXTON, LEONARD HALFORD DUDLEY, 1889-1939. China, the land and the people; a human geography, with a chapter on the climate by W. G. Kendrew. Oxford, The Clarendon Press, 1929. xiii, [5], 333, [1] p. illus. (maps) xvi plates (incl front.) diagrs.

CHAO, SUNG-CHIAO, 趙松橋, 1919- Geographical regions of China. Worcester, 1948. 164 p. Thesis - Clark University.

CHU, CHI-JUNG, 朱繼榮, 1918- Jūnggwo dìlǐ gāngyàu. A sketch of Chinese geography in Yale romanization. New Haven, Far Eastern Publications, Yale University, 1954. x, 218 p. maps. (Mirror series A, 17).

COOLE, ARTHUR BRADDAN. A commercial geography of China for middle schools. [Tientsin, Chihli Press, 1931] viii, 110 p. diagr. tables, illus. 2 fold. maps.

CRESSEY, GEORGE BABCOCK, 1896- China's geographic foundations, a survey of the land and its people. New York and London, McGraw-Hill; Shanghai, United Book and Stationery Co., 1934. xvii, 436 p. illus., maps ( 1 fold.) tables (1 fold.) diagrs.

———. Géographie humaine et économique de la Chine. Préface et traduction de Charles Mourey. Paris, Payot, 1939. 471 p. plates, maps (Bibliothèque géographique ).

———. Asia's lands and peoples; a geography of one-third the earth and two-thirds its people. 2d ed. New York, McGraw-Hill, 1951. London, McGraw-Hill, 1952. x, 597 p. illus., maps. (McGraw-Hill series in geography).

———. Land of the 500 million; a geography of China. New York and London, McGraw-Hill, 1955. xv, 387 p. illus., maps, tables. (McGraw-Hill series in geography).

ENGLAENDER, A. L. The origin and growth of deserts and the encroachment of the desert on North China. [n. p.] 1928. 32 numb. l.

FURZHOLZER, EDMUND. China. Land und Volk. Frankfurt a M., Limpert, 1954. 191 p. illus. (Limpert-Bild-Tschenbücher).

FUSON, CHESTER GARFIELD. The new geography of China, a senior middle school textbook. Shanghai, Commercial Press, [1933] xii, 273, 2 p., plates, fold. map.

GT. BRIT. Naval Staff. Naval Intelligence Division. Geographical Handbook :
  China proper, [edited by P. M. Roxby and T. W. Freeman] London, 1944-
  45. 3 v. illus., maps (Geographical Handbook ser. B. R. 530).
HANDEL-MAZZETTI, HEINRICH RAPHAEL EDUARD, FREIHERR VON, 1882-
  Kartenaufnahmen in Hunan und ihre geographischen Ergebnisse. (In Akadem-
  ie der wissenschaften in Wien. Mathematisch-natur-wissenschaftliche klasse. Denkschriften. Wien, 1928. 101. bd., p. [195]-212. 2 maps (1 fold.) ).
HAWKINS, HORATIO B. Commercial press geography of China. Rev. 13th ed.
  Shanghai, Commercial Press, 1923. viii, 86, ix p., illus. maps (part
  fold.).
HOSIE, ALEXANDER, 1853-1925. China, geographical, commercial, industrial. A handbook to Philip's Commercial map of China. London, G. Philip
  and Son, 1922. 24 p. fold. map.
JOÜON, RENÉ. Géographie de la Chine. 3e éd. [Shanghai, Impr. de l'Orpheli-
  nat] 1932. cover-title, iv, 82 p. illus., maps, diagrs.
——. Géographie commerciale de la Chine. 4e éd. Shanghai, Impr. de l'Orphelinat, 1937. 11, [2], 91 [i.e. 140] p. incl. illus. (1 col.), maps, col.
  diagrs.
LEHMANN, OTTO, 1884- Die geographischen Ergebnisse der Reise durch
  Guidschou (Kweitschou). (In Akademie der wissenschaften. Vienna. Mathematisch-natur-wissenschaftliche klasse. Denkschriften. Wien, 1926. 100.
  bd., p. [77]-99. plates., fold. map, diagrs.).
LOBB, HENRY BROUGHAM. A short regional geography of China, by H. B.
  Lobb and Llewelyn Tipping. Calcutta, London [etc.] Macmillan, 1926. 55 p.
  illus. (maps).
MENZ, GERHARD, 1885- China. Berlin, Zentral Verlag, 1930. 88 p. incl. ta-
  bles, illus. (maps) (Weltpolitische Bücherei, 17).
U. S. Army Language School, Monterey, Calif. Geography of China. [Presidio
  of Monterey] Army Language School, Chinese-Cantonese Dept., 1953. 54 p.
  illus.
——. The same; character text. [Presidio of Monterey] Army Language School,
  Chinese-Cantonese Dept., 1953. 27 l.
VAN DEN BOSCH, JEAN. Capitales en Chine. Anvers, Le Papegay, 1953. 56 p.

## Land and Soil

CHANG, CH'I-YÜN, 張其昀 , 1901-    The natural resources of China. New
  York, Sino-international Economic Research Center [1945]  71 p.  illus.
  (maps) (Sino-international economic pamphlets: no. 1).
CHU, L. T., 朱蓮青. A reconnaissance soil survey of Ch'êngtu area, Szech'uan.
  Nanking, National Geological Survey of China [1937] 86, 53, 2 p., incl. maps,
  tables, diagrs. front., VIII plates. (Soil bulletin, 18, February 1937).
HOENIGFELD, ARLINE G. A comparison between the agricultural geography of
  the Szechwan Basin and the Yunnan Plateau. [n. p.] 1949. Microfilm copy of
  typescript. Negative. Collation of the original, as determined from the film:
  165 l. illus., maps. Thesis - University of Maryland.
HOU, KUANG-CH'IUNG, 侯光烱 , 1905- A soil survey of Tinghsien, Hopei
  province, by K. C. Hou, L. C. Chu, 朱蓮青, and L. C. Li, 李連捷. Peiping, The National Geological Survey of China, 1935. 76, 57, 3 p., IX plates,
  maps (1 fold.) tables (1 fold.) fold. profile. (Soil bulletin, 13).
LI, LIEN-CHIEH, 李連捷, 1909- Soils of Yungning, Kwangsi. Nanking, National Geological Survey of China [1936] 90, 58, 2 p. incl. illus., tables,
  diagrs. VI plates, fold. map (in pocket) (Soil bulletin, 16, October 1936).
LIU, HAI-P'ÊNG, 劉海逢 . Soils of Chengtu and Hwayang area, Szechuan. Pehpei, Chungking, [1941] 34, 3 p., fold. map, tables, fold. diagr. (Soil bulletin, 23).
LOWDERMILK, WALTER CLAY, 1888- History of soil use in the Wu t'ai shan

area, by W.C. Lowdermilk and Dean R. Wickes. [Shanghai, Printed by Kelly and Walsh, 1938] cover-title, 31 p. plates, maps (1 fold.).

MA, Y.T., 馬溶之. Soils of northwestern Kansu. Changsha [1938] 8, 82, 2 p., plates, map (in pocket) tables (1 fold.) (Soil bulletin, 19).

MOYER, RAYMOND TYSON, 1899- Soils of Shansi province. Peiping, The National Geological Survey of China [1935] 60 p.; 6 p. illus. (incl. maps) plates, fold. tables. (Soil bulletin, 10, April 1935).

PENDLETON, ROBERT LARIMORE, 1890- A reconnaissance soil survey of the Harbin region, by Robert L. Pendleton, L.C. Ch'ang, 常隆慶, W. Chen, 陳偉, and K.C. Hou, 侯光炯. Peiping, Published by the National Geological Survey of China [1935] 134, 20 p., incl. tables. X plates, fold. map. (Soil bulletin, 11, July 1935).

RICHARDSON, H.L. Soils and agriculture of Szechuan. Chungking, National Agricultural Research Bureau, 1942. 162 p. (Special Bulletin, 27).

——. Grasslands of South China. Washington, 1945. 13 l. (United Nations Interim Commission on Food and Agriculture. Pam Misc., 14).

THORP, JAMES, 1896- A reconnaissance investigation of the saline delta soils of eastern Kiangsu, by James Thorp and K.C. Hou. Peiping, The Geological Survey of China [1934] 94, [48] p., incl. tables, diagrs. VI plates, fold. col. map (in pocket) (Soil bulletin, 7, May 1934).

——. Soils of northern and northwestern China, by James Thorp and K.C. Hou. Peiping, National Geological Survey of China [1935] 154, 34 p., incl. tables. XX plates, 2 fold. maps. (Soil bulletin, 12. July 1935).

——. Geography of the soils of China. Published by the National Geological Survey of China. Nanking, China, 1936. xv, [1], 552 p. incl. illus.,, charts, tables (1 fold.) diagrs. 96 plates on 49 l., maps (1 fold.).

——. Notes on Shantung, by James Thorp and T.Y. Tschau. Nanking, National Geological Survey of China [1936] 130, 50, 3 p., illus. XIII plates, 2 fold. col. maps, tables (part fold.) diagrs. (Soil bulletin, 14, May 1936).

——. Thirty-four representative soils of China. Nanking, National Geological Survey of China, 1936. 56 p.

TSCHAU, T.Y., 周昌雲, 1903- [Chou, Ch'ang-yün]. Bericht über die Bodenkartierung im bezirk Chüyung, Kiangsu, von T.Y. Tschau, L.C. Li, 李連捷, und E.F. Chen, 陳恩鳳. Peiping, The National Geological Survey of China [1934] 54, [48] p., incl. illus., tables, diagrs. fold. col. map (in pocket) (Soil bulletin, 8. August 1934).

——. Bericht über die Bodenkartierung des Weiho-Tales, Shensi, China, von T.Y. Tschau, N.F. Chang, K.C. Hou, 侯光炯, W. Chen, 陳偉, [und] L.C. Li, 李連捷. Peiping, The National Geological Survey of China [1935] 51, 35 p., incl. tables, diagr. fold. col. map (in pocket) (Soil bulletin, 9, April 1935).

——. Die Böden der kreise Changsha, Hsiangt'an, Hsianghsiang und Hengshan, Hunan, China. Nanking, The National Geological Survey of China [1937] 113, 72, 3 p., illus. tables (1 fold. in pocket) (Soil bulletin, 17).

## Mountains and Rivers

BAKER, DWIGHT CONDO. T'ai Shan, an account of the sacred eastern peak of China. Shanghai, Commercial Press, 1925. xx, 225 p. front., illus. (incl. maps) plates.

DRANSMANN, FRANZ. T'aishan-Küfow guide. Yenchowfu, Catholic Mission Press, 1934. vi, 368 p. incl. plates, ports, facsims, col. front. added t-p: Täschan-Tchüfu Führer.

FISCHER, EMIL SIGMUND, 1865-1945. The sacred Wu Tai Shan, in connection with modern travel from Tai Yuan Fu viâ Mount Wu Tai to the Mongolian border. Shanghai, Kelly and Walsh, 1925. 37 p. front., plates (1 fold.) fold. map. Reprinted from the Journal of the Royal Asiatic society of Great Brit-

ain and Ireland. North China branch, Shanghai, v. 54, 1923.
GEIL, WILLIAM EDGAR, 1865-1925. The sacred 5 of China. London, The C.
   W. Daniel Co. [1926], Boston, Houghton Mifflin, 1926. xix, 355 p. front.,
   illus., plates.
STÜBEL, HANS, 1885- Der Wu-i-schan. Tôkyô, Deutsche Gesellschaft für Na-
   tur- und Völkerkunde Ostasiens, 1937. 41 p., plates. (Added t.-p.: "Mitteilungen" der Deutschen gesellschaft für natur- und völkerkunde Ostasiens.
   bd. xxx, t.D).

## Yellow River

ASIA DEVELOPMENT COMPANY, LTD. Turning the Whang Ho, Shantung, China. [Shanghai? 1923] 44 p.; 21 p. illus.
CHINA. Public Works Commission. Studies on Yellow River project. Publication no. 1-12. Nanking, 1947-   12 v.
HU, CHANG-TU, 胡長度, 1920- The Yellow River administration in the Ch'ing
   dynasty. Ann Arbor, University Microfilms [1954] ([University Microfilms,
   Ann Arbor, Mich.] Publication no. 8351). Collation of the original: vi, 273 1.
   illus. ( part mounted) maps. Thesis - University of Washington.
KÖHLER, GÜNTHER. Der Hwang-ho, eine Physiogeographie. Gotha, J. Perthes,
   1929. 104 p. illus., plates (1 fold.) fold. map. (Ergänzungsheft nr. 203 zu
   "Petermanns mitteilungen").
LIU, DSE-MING, 劉子明, 1911- Die wirtschaftliche Bedeutung der Regulier-
   ung des Huang-Ho. Münster i W., H. Buschmann, 1937. 120 p. illus. Diss.
   Univ. Münster.
SHEN, YI, 沈怡, 1901- Der Flussbau in China. Dresden, 1925. 134 1. Diss.
   Dresden Tech. Hochschule.
TÊNG, TZǓ-HUI, 鄧子恢, 1897- Report on the multiple-purpose plan for per-
   manently controlling the Yellow River and exploiting its water resources, de-
   livered on July 18, 1955, at the second session of the First National People's
   Congress. Peking, Foreign Languages Press, 1955. 48 p. illus.

## Yangtze River

AYSCOUGH, MRS. FLORENCE (WHEELOCK) 1878- Der Yangtse Kiang; Chinas
   grosser Strom, seine Legende und seine Poesie. Tôkyô, Deutsche Gesellschaft für Natur- und Völkerkunde Ostasiens, 1937. 18 p. 2 plates, map.
   ("Mitteilungen" der Deutschen gesellschaft für natur- und völkerunde Ostasiens...bd. XXXIX, t.E).
BARBOUR, GEORGE BROWN, 1890- Physiographic history of the Yangtze (with
   24 text figures, 1 plate and 1 frontispiece). Peiping, The National Geological Survey of China, 1935. 112 p; 1, 24 p. front., illus., tab., fold. plates.
   (Geological memoirs, ser. A, 14).
"CHARON," pseud. comp. "Excelsior," being an inadequate description of the
   upper Yangtze. Shanghai, North-China Daily News and Herald, 1934. 50 p.
   front., illus.
CHINA. Yangtse River Commission. Technical Committee. Annual report. 1922-
   26. [Peking, 1923-27] 5 v. plates, tables, diagrs. (part. fold.) charts.[Pub-
   lication, no. 1-5].
———. Inspectorate General of Customs. Handbook for the guidance of shipmasters on the Ichang-Chungking section of the Yangtze River, by S.C. Plant. 2d
   issue, rev. and enl. by R.G. Everest. Shanghai, Statistical Dept. of the Inspectorate General of Customs; sold by Kelly and Walsh, 1932. x, 102 p. illus., fold. col. map, charts. (China. [Inspectorate General of Customs] The
   maritime customs. 2. Special series, no. 34).
———. Inspectorate General of Customs. Anchorages in general use on the Upper Yangtze. Addenda to the Handbook for the guidance of shipmasters on the

Ichang-Chungking section of the Yangtze River [by S.C. Plant] Shanghai,Statistical Dept. of the Inspectorate General of Customs, 1936. Microfilm copy made by the Interdepartmental Committee for Acquisition of Foreign Publications. Negative. Collation of the original, as determined from the film: 17 p.

———. Whangpoo Conservancy Board. General series. Report. no. 1-15? [Shanghai] 1911-36.    no. illus., maps (part fold., part col.) diagrs.

FITKIN, GRETCHEN MAE. The great river; the story of a voyage on the Yangtze Kiang, with an introduction by Arthur de Carle Sowerby, illustrated with photographs by Donald Mennie. Shanghai, North-China Daily News and Herald, Kelly and Walsh, 1922. iii, v, 153 p. front., plates, port.

GT. BRIT. Hydrographic Office. Ch'ang chiang pilot, comprising the Ch'ang chiang from Wu-sung bar to the head of navigation; also P'o-yang hu and the rivers flowing into it, Han chiang, Tung-t'ing hu and the rivers flowing into it, Chia-ling chiang and Min chiang. [Prepared by F.N. Shearme] 3d ed. London, 1954. xlix, 394 p. illus., charts. 2d. ed., 1928.

MENNIE, DONALD. The grandeur of the gorges; fifty photographic studies, with descriptive notes, of China's great waterways, the Yangtze Kiang, including twelve hand-coloured prints, from photographs. Shanghai, A. S. Watson, 1926. 9 l. illus., mounted plates (part col.).

MEURVILLE, R. DE, d. 1946? La Chine du Yang-tsé; Shanghai, les villes du Han, le moyen fleuve, I-chang, le haut fleuve, Chungking. Préface de René Grousset. Avec treize cartes et plans. Paris, Payot, 1946. 157 p., illus. (incl. maps, plan) diagrs. (Bibliothèque géographique).

PLANT, CORNELL. Glimpses of the Yangtze gorges. Numerous illus. and drawings in black and white by Ivon A. Donnelly. 2d ed. Shanghai, Kelly and Walsh, 1936. xv, 86 p. illus., maps.

SAVAGE, JOHN LUCIEN, 1879- Preliminary report on Yangtse Gorge project. Preliminary report on Ta-Tu-Ho and Ma-Ping-Ho projects, Upper Ming-Kiang and Kwan-Hsien projects, Lung-Chi-Ho projects, Tang-Lang-Chuan projects. Chungking, National Resources Commission, 1944. 98, viii, 238 l. tables, charts.

WANG, CHUNG-CHI, 王鍾麒, 1898- La navigation du Yan Tseu. Paris, Les Presses Modernes, 1932. 315 p. fig., maps. Thèse - Univ. de Paris.

WOODHEAD, HENRY GEORGE WANDESFORDE, 1883- The Yangtsze and its problems. [Shanghai] Printed by the Mercury Press, 1931. 150 p. plates(1 fold.).

## Other Rivers

CHATLEY, HERBERT, 1885- Report on the inspection of the Huai river project. Shanghai, 1933. 12, 14 p. 2 maps.

CHINA. Chihli River Commission. Public statement No. 1-5. Tientsin, 1918-25. 5 v. illus. map.

———. General report No. 1-3. Tientsin, 1921-24. 3 v.

———. Final report and grand scheme. 1918-25. Tientsin, Printed by the Hua Pei Press [1926?] 56 p. plates, fold. maps, fold. plans, fold. charts, tables, diagrs.

———. Directorate-general for Repairing of Yung Ting Ho Dyke Breaches. General report of the Directorate-general for the repairing of the Yung Ting Ho dyke breaches of 1924. Peking, 1926. [130] p. plates, ports., 2 plans ( 1 fold.) tables (part fold.) fold. diagr.

———. Hai-Ho Conservancy Commission. Report, 1914-    Tientsin, 1915- irregular.

———. Huai River Commission. Projects of the flood control, navigation, and irrigation for the Huai river system (a translation). Huaiyin, 1930. [252] p. incl. tables. fold. plates, port., fold. maps, diagrs.(part fold.)(Its Official

technical report no. 1).
———. Min River Conservancy Board. Annual report, 1920-    Shanghai, 1920-
FAWCETT, PHILIP NORRISON. Conservancy works on the Liao river, North
    China. London, The Institution of Civil Engineers, 1930. 17, [1] p. incl. tab.,
    diagrs. fold. plates. (The Institution of civil engineers. Selected engineering
    papers, 100).
KWANGTUNG. Board of Conservancy Works. The Sunglung flood prevention pro-
    ject. Canton, 1928. 25 p. map.
———. River Conservancy Commission. Annual report No. 1-13. Canton, 1916-
    35. 12 v. Nos. 1-10 published under the name of Board of Conservancy Works.
LI, HSIEH, 李協, 1882-194-. Report on the Wei-Pei irrigation work, Shensi.
    Peking, Peking Leader Press, 1923. 19 p. maps, plan, plates, ports, tables.
OKAZAKI, BUNKICHI, 1872- Records of the Upper Liao river conservancy
    works. [Dairen, South Manchuria Railway Co., 1940] iv, 332 (i.e. 335) p.,
    incl. tables, forms. plates, fold. plans, diagrs. (part fold.).
SZECHWAN. Bureau of Hydraulic Engineering. A note on the Tukiangyien, 都
    江堰, irrigation system. [Chengtu] 1943. 17, 35 p. illus. maps. (Szechwan
    hydraulic publication series, v. 1, no. 6).

## Description and Travel - 1921-48

ANDERSON, JOHAN GUNNAR, 1874- Der Drache und die fremden Teufel. Leip-
    zig, F.A. Brockhaus, 1927. 390 p. illus. ports. maps.
———. The dragon and the foreign devils; translated from the Swedish by Charles
    Wharton Stork. Boston, Little, Brown, 1928. xi, 341 p. front., plates,
    ports.
ARNHOLD, ERNA, 1881- Was ich in China sah. Breslau, F. Hirt, 1927. 30,
    [1] p. plates. (Her Draussen in fernen ländern).
AUXION DE RUFFÉ, REGINALD D', baron, 1875- In the shadow of the pago-
    das. Shanghai, Kelly and Walsh, 1926. 301 p.
BEATON, CECIL WALTER HARDY, 1904- Far East. London, B.T. Batsford,
    [1945] vi, 110, [1] p. col. front., illus. (incl. ports.) plates.
———. Chinese album. [London] B. T. Batsford, [1946] 77, [1] p. of illus. (incl.
    ports.).
BIGLAND, EILEEN. Into China. New York, Macmillan, [c1940]; London, Col-
    lins, 1940. 298 p. illus. (map) plates.
BLASCO IBÁÑEZ, VICENTE, 1867-1928. Chine; traduit de l'espagnol par Renée
    Lafont. Avec quatre planches hors-texte tirées en héliogravurs. Paris,
    Flammarion, [1932] 126, [2] p. front., illus. (map), plates.
BONNARD, ABEL, 1883- En Chine (1920-21) Paris, A. Fayard, c1924. 362 p.
———. In China, 1920-21, translated by Veronica Lucas. London, G. Routledge,
    1926; New York, E. P. Dutton, 1927. ix, 361 p.
BORNAND, JEANNE. En Chine. Tisons arrachés du feu, par Jeanne Bornand et
    Gustave Bornand. Bâle, Librairie des Missions; Lausanne, Édition La Con-
    corde [1925] iv, 173 p.
BRADFORD, RUTH. "Maskee!" The journal and letters of Ruth Bradford, 1861-
    72. Hartford, Prospect Press, 1938. [3]-162 p., illus., port.
BUXTON, LEONARD HALFORD DUDLEY. The eastern road. With 19 full-page
    plates. London, K. Paul; New York, E. P. Dutton, 1924. xii, 268 p. XIX
    plates (incl. front.) on 10 l.
CARPENTER, FRANK GEORGE, 1855-1924. China, with 105 illustrations from
    original photographs. Garden City, N.Y., Doubleday, Page, 1925. xiv,
    310 p. front., plates. (Carpenter's world travels).
CARR, HARRY, 1877-1936. Riding the tiger; an American newspaper man in
    the Orient. Boston and New York, Houghton Mifflin, 1934. 262 p.
CARY, MELBERT BRINKERHOFF, 1892- The estivation of two mao tzu; being
    an informal and occasionally frivolous account of our vacation in China dur-

ing the summer of 1934. New York, Priv. print., The Press of the Woolly
Whale, 1935. 124 (i.e. 126) numb. l., double front., illus. (map).
CASTELL, WULF DIETHER, GRAF ZU. Chinaflug. Berlin, Zürich, Atlantis-
Verlag[1938] 192 p. incl. plates, ports.
CATLEEN, ELLEN. Peking studies. Shanghai, Kelly and Walsh, 1934. 87,[1]
p. illus. (part col.; incl. col. plan).
CHADOURNE, MARC, 1895- Extrême Orient. Paris, Plon [1935] v, 249 p.
(His Tour de la terre. [11]).
———. Ostasiatische Reise. [Einzig berechtigte Übersetzung von Vivian Rode-
wald-Grebin] Berlin, D. Reimer, 1936. 256 p.
CHAUVELOT, ROBERT, 1879- Visions d'Extrême-Orient; Corée - Chine - In-
dochine - Siam - Birmanie; avec un portrait de l'auteur, 27 ornements et
lettrines et 80 photographies. Paris, Berger-Levrault, 1928. xii, 224 p.,
front., plates, ports.
CHESTERTON, ADA ELIZABETH (JONES) "MRS. CECIL CHESTERTON,"
1888- Young China and new Japan. Philadelphia, J.B. Lippincott; London,
G.G. Harrap, 1933. 310, [1] p. front., plates, ports., fold. map.
CLAYTON, EDWARD HYERS, 1886- Heaven below. New York, Prentice-Hall,
1944. v, [1], 282 p. illus. (maps).
CLUNE, FRANK, 1894- Sky high to Shanghai, an account of my Oriental travels in the spring of 1938, with side glances at the history, geography and pol-
itics of the Asiatic littoral. Sydney, Angus and Robertson, 1947. xiv, 379 p.
plates, ports. 1st ed. 1939.
COLLINS, GILBERT, 1890- Far Eastern jaunts, with sixteen illustrations and
a map. London, Methuen, [1924] vii, 282 p., front., plates, map.
———. Extreme oriental mixture, with twenty illustrations and a map. London,
Methuen, ltd. [1925] xiii, 266 p. front., plates, map.
COLLINS, GRACE. Chin takes and talks, an absurd travel diary. Chicago, A.
Kroch, 1943. 126 p. front. (port.) plates.
COLOMBAN, EUDORE DE. Grisailles. (1er - 3e série). Pékin, Impr. de la
"Politique de Pékin," 1924-25. 3 v. illus. port. (Collection de la "Politique
de Pékin").
———. Esquisses jaunes. Pékin, Impr. de la "Politique de Pékin," 1928. 153
p. (Collection de la "Politique de Pékin").
COMITÉ NATIONAL D'ÉTUDES SOCIALES ET POLITIQUES, Paris. Impres-
sions de voyages en Chine et au Japon. Boulogne-sur-Seine, Impr. d'études
sociales et politiques, 1929. 21 p.
CONSTANT, CHARLES SAMUEL DE, 1762-1835. Récit de trois voyages à la
Chine (1779-93); passages choisis et annotés par Philippe de Vargas. Pékin,
Yenching University, 1939. 58 p. front.(port.), illus. plates. (Petit collec-
tion "Chine-France," 3).
CORDES, ERNST, 1908- Kleines Volk-grosses Volk; Japàn-China. Eine Gegen-
überstellung japanischer und chinesischer Wesensart in Erlebnisberichten.
Berlin, Safari-verlag [c1939] 268 p. plates, port.
———. Die Lotoslaterne; Erlebnisse in China. Stuttgart, Rowohlt [1948] 285 p.
CORMIER, GEORGES. Le raid Pékin-Paris. Paris, Éditions "Publi-Inter"
[1954] 110 p. illus.
CRESSY-MARCKS, VIOLET OLIVIA (RUTLEY). Journey into China. London,
Hodder and Stoughton [1940]; New York, E.P. Dutton, 1942. 324 p. front.,
plates, ports., maps, facsims.
CROISSET, FRANCIS DE, 1877- Le dragon blessé. Paris, B. Grasset [1936]
277 p.
———. The wounded dragon, translated from the French by Paul Selver. Lon-
don, Geoffrey Bles, 1937. 215 p.
CROW, CARL, 1883-1945. Handbook for China (including Hongkong). With six
maps and plans. 5th ed. Hong Kong [etc.] Kelly and Walsh, 1933. v, 390,
[11] p. fold. map, fold. plans.

CURTIS, CLAUDE H., 1912- A marine along the idols. Grand Rapids, Zonder-
vin Pub. House, 1949. 79 p.
DAVID-NEEL, ALEXANDRA, 1874- Sous des nuées d'orages [récit de voyage]
Paris, Plon [1940] iii, 279 p. fold. map.
DAVIS, ROBERT HOBART, 1869- Oriental odyssey; people behind the sun, by
Bob Davis; with forty-seven illustrations from photographs by the author and
others. New York, Frederick A. Stokes, 1937. xii, 266 p. front., plates.
DAYE, PIERRE, 1892- La Chine est un pays charmant. Paris, Les Éditions
de France, c1927. 211 p.
DIGBY, GEORGE. Down wind. New York, E. P. Dutton, [c1939] viii, 311 p.
DINGLE, EDWIN JOHN. Borderlands of eternity, embracing "Across China on
foot." Los Angeles, Calif., Distributed by the Institute of Mental Physics
[1939] 560 p. plates, ports.
DIXON, BENJAMIN FRANKLIN, 1892- Seeing China through a porthole; the run-
ning mate to "Seeing the world through a porthole": a year and a half in Chi-
na with the U. S. S. Asheville; more pictures and stories for the folks at home.
Manila, P. I., Mission Press, 1924. 137 p. plates, ports., map, facsims.
DOBSON, RICHARD PORTWAY. China cycle. London, Macmillan, 1946. vi,
216, [1] p. front., plates.
DONNELLY, IVON A. The China coast. With verse by Joan Power. [Tientsin]
Tientsin Press, 1931. 71, [1] p. illus. col. plates, maps, plans.
DONOVAN, JOHN PATRICK. Yesterday and to-day in China. London, Drane's,
[1924] 237 p. plates, port.
DREVET, CAMILLE. La Chine de Sun Yatsen; trois mois en Chine, 1927-28.
Paris, l'auteur, 1928. 63 p.
EIGNER, JULIUS. Gelbe Mitte, goldener Kreis; ein Chinabuch. Hattingen, Hundt-
Verlag [c1951] 327 p.
ENDERS, MRS. ELIZABETH CRUMP. Swinging lanterns. New York, London,
D. Appleton, 1923. xiv, [1], 358, [1] p. front., plates, port., map.
———. Temple bells and silver sails. New York, London, D. Appleton, 1925.
xii p., 337 p. front., plates.
ESTCOURT, DORIS. Maiden voyage; travel letters of a girl who ran away. Ed-
inburgh and London, W. Blackwood, 1930. vii, 182, [1] p. 2 plates.
FARRÈRE, CLAUDE, 1876- Jonques et sampans, par Claude Farrère et
Charles Fouqueray. Paris, Horizons de France, 1945. 158 p.
FILCHNER, WILHELM, 1877-1957. Tschung-kue, das Reich der Mitte. Alt-
China vor dem Zusammenbruch. Berlin, Deutsche Buch-gemeinschaft
[c1925] vii, [1], 360 p. illus. (incl. maps, plans) plates.
FIRMINGER, F. E. Action and counteraction in China. [Tokyo, Bunka Johokyo-
ku] 1939. unpaged. illus.
FISCHER, EMIL SIGMUND, 1865-1945. Travels through Japan, Korea and Chi-
na. Tientsin, Tientsin Press, 1928. 42 p. 2 plates, fold. map.
———. From Shanghai to Changsha in an automobile; interesting account of a
test journey by Emil Fischer who accompanied Miss A. Viola Smith as her
pilot. Shanghai [1935] 23 p. illus.
———. Travels in China, 1894-1940. Tientsin, Tientsin Press, 1941. xviii,
340 p. incl. illus., plates, ports., maps. front., plates, fold. map (in pocket).
FISCHER, FRIEDA (BARTDORFF). Chinesisches Tagebuch; Lehr- und Wander-
jahre. München, F. Bruckmann [c1942] 214 p. front., plates, ports., facsim.
FISCHER, OTTO, 1886-1948. Wanderfahrten eines Kunstfreundes in China und
Japan. Stuttgart [etc.] Deutsche Verlags-Anstalt [c1939] 507 p. front.,
plates.
FLEMING, PETER, 1907- One's company; a journey to China; illustrated with
photographs taken by the author. New York, C. Scribner, 1934. London, J.
Cape, 1934. 319 p. incl. front. plates, port., double map. 1950 ed., Cape,
287 p. [Traveller's Library].

FLEMING, PETER, 1907- A forgotten journey. London, R. Hart-Davis, 1952. 189 p. illus.

FORTUNE, ROBERT, 1813-80. Three years' wanderings in the northern provinces of China, including a visit to the tea, silk, and cotton countries; with an account of the agriculture and horticulture of the Chinese. New plants, etc. 2d. ed. London, J. Murray, 1847. Reprint ed. Shanghai, 1935. xxiv, 420 p. illus., map.

FOUQUET, GAËTAN. À pied en Birmanie et en Chine. Paris, J. Susse, 1946. 195 p. plates, illus.

FRANCK, HARRY ALVERSON, 1881- Wandering in northern China, illustrated with 171 unusual photographs by the author, with a map showing his route. New York, Century, [c1923] xx, 502 p. front., plates, fold. map.

————. Wandering in China; illus. with 171 unusual photos. by the author, with a map showing his route. London, T.F. Unwin, 1924. xx, 502 p. plates, ports., fold. col. map.

————. Roving through southern China, illustrated with 171 unusual photographs by the author, with a map showing his route. New York and London, Century [c1925] London, Fisher Unwin, 1926. xxi, 649 p. incl. front. plates, fold. map.

————. Marco Polo, junior; the true story of an imaginary American boy's travel-adventures all over China, illustrated with 11 photographs taken by the author and with a map showing the routes. New York and London, Century [c1929] xi, 293 p. front., plates.

————. China; a geographical reader; with many illustrations, largely from photographs by the author. Rev. 1935. Dansville, N.Y., F.A. Owen [c1935] 256 p. illus. (His Travels in many lands).

FRANCK, RACHEL (LATTA). I married a vagabond; the story of the family of the writing vagabond; drawings by Charles Child. New York, London, D. Appleton-Century, 1939. 241 p. illus.

FREUDMANN, W. Tschi-lai!--Erhebet euch! Erlebnisse eines Arztes in China und Burma, 1939-45. Linz, Verlag Neue Zeit, 1947. 219 p.

FRISCH, MAX, 1911- Bin; order, Die Reise nach Peking. Zürich, Atlantis Verlag [1945] 111 p.

FUNG, KWOK-YING, 馮國英, 1905- China; photographs arranged and edited by Fritz Henle. New York, H. Holt [1943] 192 p. incl. front., illus.

GARDINER, JAMES. In and out of China cities. Sydney, Donald F. Peltigrew, 1947-49. 2 v. illus. plates, ports.

GAUTIER, JULES. Jonques et pagodas. La Chine illustrée. Paris, 1934. 228 p.

GEORGE, MARIAN M., 1865- A little journey to China and Japan. Chicago, A. Flanagan, 1928. 3-166 p. illus. (Library of travel).

GERVAIS, ALBERT, 1892- AEsculape en Chine. 7. éd. [Paris] Gallimard [c1933] [7]-251 p.

————. A surgeon's China, translated from the French by Vincent Sheean. London, Hamilton [1934] 9-302, [1] p. front. (port.) illus.

————. Medicine man in China, translated from the French by Vincent Sheean. New York, Frederick A. Stokes, 1934. 336 p. illus.

————. Ein Arzt erlebt China. [Aus dem Französischen übertragen von Albert Freiherr von Bodman] Berlin, Wegweiser Verlag, 1935; Leipzig, W. Goldmann [1944] 235 p. illus. Translation of AEsculape en Chine.

————. The same. Neuausgabe. München, W. Goldmann, 1950. 236 p.

GIELGUD, L.E. About it and about; leaves from a diary of travel. Edinburgh and London, W. Blackwood, 1928. xxiii, 310 p. front. (facsim.).

GILBERT DE VOISINS, AUGUSTE, comte, 1877- Voyages; écrit en Chine. Paris, G. Crès, 1923. 2 v. 21 plates (incl. port.).

GOEKE, GERTRUD. Schwingende Laternen; China-Erlebnisse. Hamburg, Broschek [c1944] 247 p. illus.

GOERGER, ANDRÉ. En marge de la croisière jaune; de Moscou en Chine - de

Beyrouth à Srinagar - le "tour du monde" - trois mois en Chine. Avec 121 gravures et une carte hors-texte. Paris, Rieder, 1935. [vii]-viii, 310 p., XLIX plates (incl. front.) on 25 l., fold. map.

GROSCH, EBERHARD. China. 6 Bilder zusammengestellt und beschrieben nach einem Aufenthalt in Ostasien, 1935-39. Frankfurt a. M. Ernst Grosch, Tee Import, 1952. 8 p. (Gross-Tee-Sammelbilder 1:3).

GROSSE, ERNST, 1877-1927. Ostasiatische Erinnerungen eines kolonial- und ausland-Deutschen. München, Neuer Filser-Verlag; inhaber: dr. Benno Filser, 1938. viii, 328 p. plates, fold. map.

GUNNING, ROBERT. China, by Robert and Mary Gunning. [Columbus, O., New York, American Education Press, c1939] cover-title, 32 p. illus. (incl. map) (Unit study book, 611).

HALDANE, MRS. CHARLOTTE, 1894- Deux mois en Chine. Paris, Association française "Les Amis du Peuple Chinois," 1939. 23 p.

HAYES, MRS. EVA FATIMA (MORRIS). If you were in China; a plan book for junior high school groups; drawings by Emily Jean Baer. New York, Friendship Press [c1940] 45, [3] p. illus. (incl. map).

HEATH, ARTHUR HAROLD, 1862- Sketches of vanishing China. London, T. Butterworth [1927] 184, [4] p. incl. col. mounted front., illus., col. mounted plates.

HEDIN, SVEN ANDERS, 1865-1952. Von Peking nach Moskau. 4. Aufl. Leipzig, F. A. Brockhaus, 1925. 321 p. incl. map, front., plates, ports.

HELFRITZ, HANS, 1902- Ewigkeit und Wandel im Fernen Osten; mit einer Einleitung von Dagobert von Mikusch. Berlin, Deutsche Verlagsgesellschaft [c1936] 111 p. incl. 96 plates (incl. 2 maps) on 48 l.

HENSLEY, MRS. MATIE MANARD. Oceanic interlude. San Antonio, Tex., The Naylor Co., 1941. ix, 192 p. front., plates, ports., fold. map, facsims.

HERRMANN, WILHELM KARL. Ein Ritt für Deutschland. Mit 1 Titelbild und 228 Abbildungen nach eigenen Aufnahmen des Verfassers, 14 Zeichnungen im Text und 6 Karten. Berlin-Leipzig, Nibelungen-Verlag, 1940. 591 p. front., illus., plates (1 fold.) ports., facsims., fold. map.

HERVÉ, GUY. Au pays des pagodes et des jonques. Paris, Jacques Lanore, 1937. 91 p.

HOMER, JOY. Dawn watch in China. Boston, Houghton Mifflin, 1941; London, Collins, 1941. 340 p.

HOPPENOT, HÉLÈNE. Chine; texte de Paul Claudel, photographies d'Hélène Hoppenot. [Genève] A. Skira [1946] [19] p., 81 plates.

HOROSE, S. La muraille de Pékin à Paris. Paris, Éditions Argo [1929] 220 p. (Collection univers).

HOSIE, DOROTHEA (SOOTHILL) lady, 1885- Brave new China. London, Hodder and Stoughton [1938] xii, 251 p. front. (group port.) plates.

HSU, SUZANNE. Le vin nouveau dans la vieille outre. (ou, Propos sur la Chine et les chinois) Pékin, Impr. de la "Politique de Pékin," 1933. 138 p. (Collection de la "Politique de Pékin").

HUC, ÉVARISTE RÉGIS, 1813-60. Une invraisemblable traversée de la Chine. Paris, Flammarion, 1934. 96 p. (Collection Bonnes Lectures).

HURST, IDA. Typist in China. London, J. Long [1941] 256 p. front., plates.

JACQUES, NORBERT, 1880- Auf dem chinesischen Fluss; Reisebuch von Norbert Jacques, mit Bildern nach Aufnahmen des Verfassers. Berlin, S. Fischer, 1921. 11-265, [3] p., plates.

JAPAN. Dept. of Railways. Guide to China, with land and sea routes between the American and European continents. 2d (rev.) ed. Issued by the Japanese government railways, Tokyo, Japan. Tokyo, 1924. xvi, iii, iii a-b, iv-cxxiv, 448 p., front., illus. (incl. plans) maps (part fold., 1 in pocket) (Official guide-books issued by the Japanese government railways. [Official series. vol. D]).

JOHNSTON, LENA E. China and her peoples. London, United Council for Missionary Education, 1923. 136 p. front., illus. (map) plates.

JOSEPH, BERTHA COBLENS. China. Developed in grade III, Commodore Sloat school, San Francisco, California. New York, Teachers college, Columbia University [c1932] 20 p. ([Columbia university. Teachers college] Teachers' lesson unit series. no. 36).

JOUGLET, RENÉ, 1884- Dans le sillage des jonques; orné de 15 pages en héliogravure. Paris, B. Grasset [1935]    ix, [13]-252 p., front., plates.

KATZ, RICHARD. Funkelnder Ferner Osten! Erlebtes in China - Korea - Japan. Berlin, Ullstein [c1931] 298, [1] p., front., plates, fold. map.

KERBY, PHILIP. Beyond the Bund. New York, Payson and Clarke [c1927] 272 p.

KING, PAUL HENRY, 1853- ed. Voyaging to China in 1855 and 1904; a contrast in travel, edited by Paul King. London, Heath, Cranton, 1936. 187 p. front., plates.

KNAUSS, ROBERT, 1892- Im Grossflugzeug nach Peking; der erste Weltflug der Deutschen Luft-Hansa. Berlin, Union deutsche Verlagsgesellschaft 1927] 176 p. front. (port.) illus., fold. map.

KOLLBRUNNER, ULRICH. Meine Reise nach Sumatra, den Philippinen und Südchina. Zürich, J. Rügg Söhne, 1929. iv, 184 p. illus. plates.

KÖRBER, LILI. Adventures in the East. London, John Lane [1937] 7-347 p.

KRUG, HANS JOACHIM, 1893- Wanderungen und Wandlungen in China. Berlin, Scherl [c1941] 326 p. illus., maps, plans.

LALOY, LOUIS, 1874-1944. Miroir de la Chine; présages, images, mirages. Paris, Desclée, de Brouwer [c1933] 340 p. (Les îles).

――――. Mirror of China. New York, A.A. Knopf, 1936. viii, [1] p., 3-307, [1] p.

LAMONT, FLORENCE HASKELL (CORLISS), 1873- Far Eastern diary, 1920. New York, Horizon Press, 1951. 95 p.

LANDENBERGER, EMIL, 1882- Ostasien im Zick-Zack, mit einem Bildnis des Verfassers. Stuttgart, E. Landenberger, 1931. 155 p. port.

LAY, ARTHUR CROALL HYDE, 1900- Four generations in China, Japan, and Korea. Edinburgh, Oliver and Boyd, 1952. 241 p. illus.

LEWIS, CECIL, 1898- Sagittarius rising. London, P. Davies [1936] vii-viii, 331, [1] p.

――――. Schütze im Aufstieg; eine autobiographische Erzählung, Deutsch von Hans Reisiger. Berlin, Rowohlt [1937] 324, [1] p.

LEWISOHN, WILLIAM. China's wild west; a round trip of five thousand miles in a motor car. Shanghai, North-China Daily News and Herald, 1937. ix, 61 p. illus., map.

LINCOLN, IGNATIUS TIMOTHY TREBICH, 1879-1943. Der grösste Abenteurer des XX. Jahrhunderts!? Die Wahrheit über mein Leben. Leipzig [etc.] Amalthea-Verlag [c1931] 290 p. front., plates, ports., facsims., fold. map.

――――. The autobiography of an adventurer; translated from the German by Emile Burns. London, L. Stein, 1931. New York, H. Holt [c1932] 3-291 p.

LÖHNDORFF, ERNST FRIEDRICH, 1899- Unheimliches China, ein Reisebericht. Bremen, C. Schünemann [1940, c1939] 262 p. 1953 ed. 211 p.

LONDRES, ALBERT. La Chine en folie. Paris, A. Michel [c1925] 254 p.

LYAUTEY, PIERRE. Chine ou Japon (1932-33) Paris, Plon [1933] 246 p.

LYTTELTON, HON. MRS. EDITH SOPHY (BALFOUR), 1865-1948. Travelling days, by Edith Lyttelton. London, G. Bles, 1933. 239, [1] p.

MACKIE, E.F. Chinese adventure. Sydney, Clarendon Pub. Co., 1944. 66 p.

MCMAHON, THOMAS J. The Orient I found; with 62 illustrations. New York, D. Appleton, London, Duckworth, 1926. 223 p. front., plates, ports., map.

MADER, FRIEDRICH WILHELM, 1866- Von Hankow bis zum Kukunor. Kapitän Münchhausens Abenteurer auf einen Reise durch China nach Tibet. Erzählung. Stuttgart, Union, 1930. 301 p. illus. (Fahrten und Abenteuer in aller Welt).

――――. Im Banne des goldenen Drachen. Abenteuer-Erzählung. Neubearb. von G. Bröhl. Düsseldorf, Deutsche Buchvertriebs. und Verlag-Ges., 1952.

215 p.

MAGRINI, LUCIANO, 1885-   China von heute und gestern; aus dem Italienischen übertragen von hofrat Franz Latterer-Lintenburg. Tübingen, F. F. Heine, 1934. viii, 232 p. front., plates.

MARSH, JAMES REID. The charm of the Middle kingdom. Boston, Little, Brown, 1922. xvi, 245 p. front., plates, ports.

MAURETTE, FERNAND, 1878-   Tour de Pacifique. [Paris[ Hachette [1934] 224 p.

MAY, KARL, 1842-1912. Der blaurote Methusalem; eine lustige Studentenfahrt nach China. Radebeul bei Dresden, Karl May Verlag [1929] 569 p. (Gesammelte Werke, 40).

MENON, KUMARA PADMANABHA SIVASANKARA, 1898-   Delhi-Chungking, a travel diary. Foreword by Jowaharlal Nehru. [Bombay, New York] Indian Branch, Oxford University Press [1947] viii, 257 p. illus., 2 fold. maps (in pocket).

MONTMOLLIN, ERIC DE. Empire du Ciel. Neuchâtel, La Baconniere, 1941. iv, 225 p. illus.

——. Image de la Chine. Neuchâtel, La Baconniere, 1942. 139 p. illus.

——. Das Gesicht Chinas. Zürich/New-York, Oprecht [1943] 11-130, [6] p., incl. mounted front., mounted plates (part double).

MOORE, V. ELIZABETH. We go to China with Lady Cripps on a vivid and exciting tour of the new republic. Edited by Hector Hutt. London, P. J. Press, 1948. 243 p. ports.

MUTIUS, GERHARD VON, 1865-   Ostasiatische Pilgerfahrt. Aus dem Tagebuch einer Reise nach China und Japan, 1908-09. Berlin, G. Stilke, 1921. 75 p. (Preussische Jahrbücher. Schriftenreihe, 2).

NACHBAUR, ALBERT, -1933. Pékinades, avec un préface de Jean Bouchot. Pékin, A. Nachbaur, 1921. 164, [2] p. illus.

——. Encor des pékinades. Pékin, A. Nachbaur, 1924. 170, [2] p.

NELSON, DANIEL, 1902-48. Journey to Chungking. Minneapolis, Augsburg Publishing House [1945] 154 p. 8 front. (incl. port.) on 4 l.

NEWMAN, MRS. LUCY WHEELER. Along the Yangtze river and stories retold. Boston, Christopher Publishing House [c1937] vii, 9-62 p.

NOURSE, MARY AUGUSTA. China, country of contrasts, by Mary A. Nourse and Delia Goetz. New York, Harcourt, Brace, [1944] x, 229 p. incl. front., illus. (incl. map).

NYBERG, RAGNAR. On the dragon seas; a sailor's adventures in the Far East, by Ragnar Nyberg and Alvar Zacke; translated from the Swedish by Edith M. Nielson. 2d impression. London, Hurst and Blackett [1935] 7-287 p. front., plates, ports.

NYE, JEAN PALMER. Ricsha rambles. Boston, R. G. Badger [c1930] 238 p. front., plates.

ORTMAN, MRS. BLANCHE SELLERS. New York to Peking. San Francisco, Priv. print., 1921. 146 p. front., plates.

OSSENDOWSKI, FERDYNAND ANTONI, 1876-1944. Hinter Chinas Mauer. [Übertragen von Otto Marbach] Dresden, C. Reissner, 1929. 311 p.

PAUL, CHARLES. Campagne en Chine. Paris, Stock (Delamain et Boutelleau) 1939. [9]-580 p., fold. maps, fold. plans.

PAYNE, JESSIE. What China looks like; illustrated by Bessie Darling Inglis. London, T. Nelson, 1933. iv, 5-94 p. illus. (Ready Practice, 93).

PECK, GRAHAM, 1914-   Through China's wall, with illustrations by the author. Boston, Houghton Mifflin, 1940. London, Collins, 1941. 371 p. illus. (incl. maps, plan) plates.

PELKA, OTTO, 1875-   Ostasiatische Reisebilder im Kunstgewerbe des 18. Jahrhunderts. Leipzig, K. W. Hiersemann, 1924. 58 p., 87 plates.

PERCKHAMMER, HEINZ VON. Von China und Chinesen. Zürich-Leipzig, Orell Fussli, 1930. iv, 16 p. plates. (Schaubücher, 28).

————. China and the Chinese. London, G. Routledge [1931] xvi p. 63 plates on 32 l. (1 double). (Seen by the camera. [2]).

PEYERIMHOFF DE FONTENELLE, HENRI DE, 1871-  Impressions de voyage en Chine et au Japon. Boulogne-sur-Seine, Impr. d'études sociales et politiques, 1929. 23 p. (Comité national d'études sociales et politiques, séance du 3 juin 1929, fasc. 399).

PIERROT, GEORGE FRANCIS, 1898-  The vagabond trail; around the world in 100 days; foreword by Lowell Thomas; illustrations by Robert M. Brinkerhoff. New York, London, D. Appleton-Century, 1935.   xiv, 248 p. incl. front., illus.

PURCELL, VICTOR WILLIAM WILLIAMS SAUNDERS, 1896-  Chinese evergreen. London, M. Joseph [1938] 286, [1] p.

PYKE, RICHARD LIONEL, 1899-  The green edge of Asia. London, G. Allen and Unwin [1937] 151, [1] p. front., plates.

"RANGER," pseud. Up and down the China coast by "Ranger," [pseud.] with a foreword by L. E. O. Charlton. London, D. Archer, 1936. 286 p. front. plates, ports.

RATTENBURY, HAROLD BURGOYNE. China, my China. London, F. Muller ltd. [1944] 271 p. plates.

————. China-Burma vagabond. London, F. Muller ltd. [1946] 279 p. plates.

————. Let my people know! Being an account of a visit paid to Burma and China, by H. B. Rattenbury and Hilda M. Porter. London, Methodist Missionary Society, 1947. 135 p. illus. maps.

RAUCAT, THOMAS. De Shang-haï à Canton. Paris, Émile-Paul frères, 1927. 3-83, [1] p., front. (Ceinture du monde. [1]).

REIN, ELISABETH MARIA, 1897-  Das Schmetterlingshaus. Heilbronn, E. Salzer, 1941; Stuttgart, Spemann, 1949. 277 p.

RODES, JEAN. À travers la Chine actuelle. Paris, Fasquelle [c1932] 194 p., front., plates, port.

ROSS, RALPH COLIN, 1923-41. Von Chicago nach Chungking; einem jungen Deutschen erschliesst sich die Welt, mit einem Vorwort von Colin Ross. Berlin, Verlag Die Heimbücherei, J. Jahr [c1941] 251, [1] p. front. (port.) plates.

LE ROY LIBERGE, G. Le Chine encore chinoise. La Chapelle-Montligeon (Orne), Impr. de Montligeon, 1926. 164 p.

RUPPRECHT, crown prince of Bavaria, 1869-  Reise-erinnerungen aus Ostasien. München, J. Kösel and F. Pustet, 1923. xii, 501 p. plates.

SALZMANN, ERICH VON, 1876-1941. China siegt; Gedanken und Reiseeindrücke über das revolutionäre Reich der Mitte. Hamburg [etc.] Hanseatische Verlagsanstalt [1929] 197 p.

SARRAT, PIERRE. Impressions sur la Chine. Paris, Mariage, 1944. 40 p. illus.

SCHMITTHENNER, HEINRICH, 1887-  Chinesische Landschaften und Städte. Stuttgart, Strecker und Schröder, 1925. x, 303 p. front. illus. maps, plans, plates.

————. China im Profil, mit 11 Karten im Text und einer farbigen Übersichtskarte. Leipzig, Bibliographisches Institut ag, 1934. 129 p. illus. (plans) maps (1 fold.).

SCHOLZ, OSKAR. China, unter Mitwirkung von Werner Vogel. Berlin, C. Heymanns Verlag, 1928. xi, 383 p. (Handbücher des Weltverkehrs. 2).

SCOTT, ERASTUS HOWARD, 1855-1928. Travel letters from the Orient. [Chicago, Scott, Foresman, c1922] 3-84 p. illus. (incl. map).

SEWELL, WILLIAM GAWAN. The land and life of China. London, Edinburgh House Press, 1933. 144 p. front., illus., plates, fold. map. [The "land and life" ser., I].

SHOR, JEAN BOWIE. After you, Marco Polo. New York, McGraw-Hill [1955] 294 p. illus.

———. The trail of Marco Polo. London, Muller, 1956. 251 p. plates (incl. ports) maps.

SITWELL, OSBERT, 1892-   Escape with me! An Oriental sketch-book. London, Macmillan, 1939; New York, Harrison-Hilton books, 1940. xv, 339, [1] p. front., 15 plates.

SMEDLEY, AGNES, 1890-1950. Chinese destinies; sketches of present-day China. New York, Vanguard Press [c1933] viii, 315 p. front., plates.

———. Chinesische Schicksale, Skizzen aus dem China von heute. [Autorisierte Übertragung aus dem Amerikanischem von Julian Gumperz und Willi Schulz] Moskau, Verlagsgenossenschaft Ausländischer Arbeiter in der UdSSR, 1934. 116 p.

SPEAKMAN, HAROLD, 1888-   Beyond Shanghai, with eight illustrations in full color from paintings by the author. New York, Cincinnati, The Abingdon Press [c1922] 198 p. col. front., col. plates.

STEELE, JAMES KING. Wandering feet along well-known highways and unfrequented byways of China and Japan; a collection of travel sketches. San Francisco, A. Carlisle and Co., 1923. 301 p. plates.

STEINLE, MICH. Mit der Nord-China Expedition; Reiseerlebnisse, Sitten und Gebräuche der Chinesen und Mongolen. Hamburg, Weltbund Verlag [1922] 158 p. front. fig., plates.

STEVENS, HERBERT. Through deep defiles to Tibetan uplands; the travels of a naturalist from the Irrawaddy to the Yangtse. London, H. F. and G. Witherby [1934] 250 p. front., plates, fold. map, plan.

SUES, ILONA RALF. Shark's fins and millet. Boston, Little, Brown, 1944. x, 331 p. plates, ports.

TANG, SHENG, 唐笙. The long way home. With an introduction by S. I. Hsiung, 熊式一, and 35 illus. by Deh Lan, 德蘭. London, New York, Hutchinson [1949] 191 p. illus.

THAI, VINH. Ancestral voices: recollections of Chungking, August-December 1943. Translated from the French [manuscript] by James Kirkup. London, Collins, 1956. 192 p.

THOMAS, JAMES A. A pioneer tobacco merchant in the Orient. Durham, N. C., Duke University Press, 1928. 3-339 p. col. front., plates, ports., facsims. (Duke university publications).

THOMAS, WILLIAM HERBERT EVANS. Vanished China: Far Eastern banking memoirs. London, Thorsons, 1956. 350 p.

THORPE, CARLYLE. A journey to the walnut sections of Europe and Asia. Los Angeles, Priv. print., 1923. 101 p. plates.

TICHY, HERBERT, 1912-   China ohne Mauer. Mit 56 Bildern nach Zeichnungen des Pekinger Malers Chen Chih-nung. Wien, L. W. Seidel, 1954 [c1948] 199 p. illus.

TIETJENS, EUNICE (HAMMOND), 1884-   China, edited by Burton Holmes; text by Eunice Tietjens and Louise Strong Hammond, illustrations by Burton Holmes. Chicago, Ill., Wheeler Pub. Co. [c1940] ix, [1], 420 p. illus. (The Burton Holmes travel stories).

TING, SING-WU, 丁星吾, ed. China the beautiful, edited by Ting Sing Wu. Translated by Liang Shih Chiu, 梁實秋, rev. by Wu Cha Chen, 伍稼青. [Hong Kong, International Culture Press, 1955] 216 p. (chiefly illus., col. plates, maps).

TINLING, CHRISTINE ISABEL, 1869-   Bits of China, travel-sketches in the Orient, introduction by Anna A. Gordon. New York, Chicago [etc.] Fleming H. Revell [c1925] 222 p. front., plates.

TOYNBEE, ARNOLD JOSEPH, 1889-   A journey to China; or, Things which are seen. London, Constable, 1931. x, 345 p. fold. map.

TRACY, JANE ALLYN (FOOTE). See China with me. Boston, Mass., Stratford [c1930] xiii, 216 p. incl. front., illus., ports.

TWEEDIE, ETHEL BRILLIANA (HARLEY) "MRS. ALEC TWEEDIE." An adventurous journey (Russia - Siberia - China) with four water colour sketches by the author, two maps and sixty-six other illustrations. London, Hutchinson [1926] viii, 397 p., col. front., plates (part col.) ports., maps (1 fold.) facsim.

UKERS, WILLIAM HARRISON, 1873- A trip to China. New York, Tea and Coffee Trade Journal Co., 1926. 43 p. incl. diagrs. table, illus. (Little Journey ser.).

U.S. Army Service Forces. Special Service Division. A pocket guide to China. Washington, War and Navy Depts. [1944] 64 p.

——. Navy. Pacific Fleet and Pacific Ocean Areas. Information bulletin. The coasts of North China, Manchuria and Korea. [n.p.] 1945. 2 v. (226 p.)illus., col. maps (part fold.) (Its Cincpac-Cincpoa bulletin, 48-45).

——. Navy. Pacific Fleet and Pacific Ocean Areas. Information bulletin. Shantung peninsula. [n.p.] 1945. cover-title, 114, [2] p. incl. illus. (part fold.; incl. maps, charts) tables. (Its Cincpac-Cincpoa bulletin, 119-45).

VANLANDE, RENÉ, 1886- Comptoirs en Chine. Paris, J. Peyronnet [c1935] [9]-206 p., front. (port.) (Collection "Outre mer").

VOGEL, HANS, 1887- China ohne Maske; 20000 km mit der schweizerischen Film-expedition. Mit 120 photographischen Aufnahmen auf 80 Kunstdrucktafeln. Zürich und Leipzig, A. Müller [c1937] 178, [2] p. plates.

WADE, MRS. MARY HAZELTON (BLANCHARD), 1860- Twin travelers in China and Japan, with a frontispiece in color and eight illustrations from photographs. New York, Frederick A. Stokes [1922] 3-179, [1] p. col. front., plates.

WAMPLER, ERNEST MICHAEL, 1885- China suffers; or, My six years of work during the incident. Elgin, Ill., Brethren Pub. House [1945] 277 p. illus. (incl. ports.).

WARD, HON. EDWARD HENRY HAROLD, 1905- Chinese crackers. [London] J. Lane [1947] 187 p. plates.

WARNER, LANGDON, 1881-1955. The long old road in China, with illustrations from photographs. Garden City, N.Y., Doubleday, Page, 1926. viii p., 168 p. front., illus. (map, plans) plates.

WELLS, CARVETH, 1887- North of Singapore. London, Jarrolds [1941] 256 p. illus. (map) plates, port.

WHEATCROFT, RACHEL. Siam and Cambodia in pen and pastel, with excursions in China and Burmah. London, Constable, 1928. x, 296 p. col. front., illus., plates (part col.) fold. map.

WHITE, HERBERT CLARENCE, 1896- Romantic China; an album containing thirty-two photographic studies of China's historic monuments and charming beauty spots complete with descriptive and historical notes, by the White brothers. Shanghai, Browhite Arts [c1930] [95] p. incl. front., illus., 41 plates.

WILHELM, RICHARD, 1873-1930. Die Seele Chinas; mit 36 Abbildungen. Berlin, R. Hobbing [c1926] 356 p. front., plates, ports.

——. The soul of China; the text translated by John Holroyd Reece; the poems by Arthur Waley. New York, Harcourt, Brace [c1928] 382 p.

[WILKINSON, IRIS GUIVER]. Dragon rampant [by] Robin Hyde [pseud.] 2d impression. London, Hurst and Blackett [1939] 317, [1] p.

WILLIS, BAILEY, 1857-1949. Friendly China; two thousand miles afoot among the Chinese. Stanford, Stanford University Press [1949] xviii, 312 p. illus., maps.

WINGATE, ALFRED WOODROW STANLEY, 1861-1938. A cavalier in China, with a foreword by Sir Francis Younghusband. London, Grayson and Grayson [1940] 5-327 p. front. (port.) plates.

WITTE, JOHANNES, 1877- Sommer-sonnentage in Japan und China; Reise-erlebnisse in Ostasien im Jahre 1924. Von missiondirektor d. dr. J. Witte. Göttingen, Vandenhoeck and Ruprecht, 1925. 217,[1]p. 16 plates on 8 l.

WOLF, RICHARD. Umgang mit Chinesen. 2 Aufl. Nürnberg, Luken and Luken, 1949. 31 p. (Umgang mit Völkern, 6). 1. Aufl., Berlin, 1943.

[WOLLSCHLÄGER, ALFRED], 1901-  Kulis, Kapitäne und Kopfjäger; Fahrten und Erlebnisse zwischen Peking und der Timor-see, von A. E. Johann[pseud] Berlin, Ullstein [1936] 269, [1] p., plates, ports.

WOMEN'S INTERNATIONAL LEAGUE FOR PEACE AND FREEDOM. Report of the W. I. L. P. F. delegation to China, by Camile Drevet and Edith M. Pye. Genève, Women's International League for Peace and Freedom, 1928. 50 p.

YORKE, GERALD, 1901-  China changes. London, J. Cape [1935] New York, C. Scribner's sons, 1936. 7-334 p. front., plates, fold. map.

ZÖRNER, HANS, 1895-1937. "Briefe aus China," etc. Berlin, Parey, 1937. 79 p. illus. plates.


1949 -


ALL-CHINA CONGRESS OF TRADE UNIONS, 7th. Glimpses of People's China. Peking, Foreign Languages Press, 1954. 93 p. ports.

AUSTRALIA-CHINA SOCIETY. New South Wales Branch. Report on China by members of the Australian Cultural delegation, May-June, 1956. Sydney, the Society, 1956. 56 p. illus.

BARTEL, KURT. Osten erglüht [von] Kuba [pseud. Berlin] Verlag Neues Leben, 1954. 261 p. illus.

BEAUVOIR, SIMONE DE, 1908-  La longue marche; essai sur la Chine. [Paris] Gallimard [1957] 484 p.

BERLIOUX, MONIQUE. Mon séjour chez Mao Tsé-toung. Paris, Flammarion, 1955. 236 p.

BING, GEOFFREY H. C., 1909-  M. P. in new China. London, Britain-China Friendship Association, 1953. 16 p.

BODDE, DERK, 1909-  Peking diary, a year of revolution. New York, Schuman [1950]; London, J. Cape, [1951] xxi, 292 p. illus., ports.

————. Peking Tagebuch. Ein Jahr  Revolution in China. Übertragen aus dem A-merikanischen. Wiesbaden, F. A. Brockhaus, 1952. 335 p. illus.

BRITONS in China, report of the first British delegation to visit new China, with a foreword by Sydney Silverman, M. P. London, Britain-China Friendship Association, 1952. 34 p.

BRULLER, JEAN, 1902-  Les divagations d'un français en Chine [par] Vercors [pseud.] 70 dessins et 14 photochromes de l'auteur. Paris, A. Michel [1956] 307 p. illus.

CAMERON, JAMES, 1911-  Mandarin red; a journey behind the "Bamboo Curtain." London, M. Joseph [1955]; New York, Rinehart [1955] 287 p. illus.

CAMPBELL, ERNEST WALTER. People's victory in China. Sydney, Current Book Distributors, 1948. 31 p.

CASSON, SIR HUGH MAXWELL, 1910-  Red lacquer days; an illustrated journal describing a recent visit to Peking. London, Lion and Unicorn Press, 1956. 1 v. (unpaged) illus., facsims.

CHAUDHRY, RAHMATULLAH. A Pakistani in New China. [Lahore? 1955?] 50 p. illus.

CHINA. Erlebt von deutschen Künstlern. Ein Reisebericht in Studienarbeiten von Fritz Cremer, Bernhard Kretzschmar, Bert Heller und Werner Klemke. Red. und Gestaltung, Gerhard Pommeranz-Liedtke. Berlin, Deutsche Akademie der Kunste, 1955. 28 p. illus.

CHINA im Bild. 1956. Peking, Verlag für fremdsprachige Literatur, 1956. 40 p.

CHINA PICTORIAL. New China. [Edited by the China Pictorial. 2d ed.] Peking, Foreign Languages Press, 1953. 1 v. (unpaged, chiefly illus. (part col.) ).

————. Neues China. Peking, Verlag für fremdsprachige Literatur, 1953. 69 p. illus.

CLUNE, FRANK, 1894-  Ashes of Hiroshima; a post-war trip to Japan and China. Sydney, Angus and Robertson [1950] xviii, 299, [2] p. plates, ports., maps.

COCTEAU, JEAN, 1889-  Aux confins de la Chine. Illustrés par Lou Albert-Lasard. Paris, Lasard, 1955. 1 v. illus.

DEKKERS, RENÉ. Lettres de Chine. Bruxelles, Éditions de la librairie encyclopédique, 1956. 136 p. illus.

DUCHROW, ALFRED. China - eine Riese ist erwacht. Ein Reisebericht einmal anders. Berlin, Zentralkomitee der SED, Abteilung Agitation und Presse/ Rundfunk, 1956. 63 p. illus.

ELEVEN visit China. London, Britain-China Friendship Association, 1951. 8 p.

FARGE, YVES, 1899-  Von Peking bis Phjöngjang. Reportage. Berlin, Volk und Welt, 1953. 204 p. illus.

FRANCE. Direction de la documentation. La Chine. [Paris, Documentation française, 1954?] 1 v. (chiefly illus.).

FRÉDÉRIX, PIERRE, 1897-  Une ports s'ouvre sur la Chine. [Paris] Hachette [1955] 256 p. illus. (Choses vues, aventures vécues).

FREUNDSCHAFTSBESUCH einer Delegation der Regierung der Deutschen Demokratischen Republik in der Volksrepublik China, in der Koreanischen Volksdemokratischen Republik und in der Mongolischen Volksrepublik vom 8 bis 28 Dezember, 1955. Hrsg. vom Presseamt beim Minister-präsidenten d. DDR. Berlin, Deutscher Zentralverlag, 1956. 95 p. illus.

GALE, GEORGE STAFFORD. No flies in China. London, Allen and Unwin [1955]; New York, Morrow [1955] 166 p.

GARLAND, MARGARET. Journey to new China. With a foreword by Ormond Wilson. Christchurch [N. Z.] Caxton Press, 1954. 200 p. illus.

GASCAR, PIERRE, 1916-  Chine ouverte. Photos d'Ergy Landau. [Paris] Gallimard [1955] 183 p. illus.

———. Aujourd'hui la Chine. Texte de Pierre Gascar. Photos d'Ergy Landau. Ouverture de Claude Roy. Lausanne, Guilde du livre [1955] 163 p. illus.

GATTI, ARMAND. Chine. Paris, Éditions du Seuil, 1957. 192 p. illus.(Petite planète, 12).

GERVAIS, ALBERT, 1892-  AEsculape dans la Chine en révolte. [Paris] Gallimard [1953] 317 p.

———. Morgenröte über China. Ein Arzt erlebt China zwischen Vergangenheit und Zukunft. Ins Deutsche Übertragen von Werner von Grünau. München, Goldmann, 1954. 262 p.

GESELLSCHAFT FÜR DEUTSCH-SOWJETISCHE FREUNDSCHAFT, Berlin. China - ohne Mauer. Ein Bericht von Peking nach Kanton. Fotos: G. Kiesling. Text: E. von Kügelgen. Berlin, 1957. 19 p. (Erläuterungsheft zum Bildband, 88).

GIGON, FERNAND. Chine en casquette. Paris, Del Duca, 1956. 317 p. plates, illus (photos).

GLIMPSES of People's China. [1st ed.] Peking, Foreign Languages Press[1954] 93 p.

GORAL, ANDRÉ. Où va la Chine? Paris, Laoste, 1956. 208 p. (Les Grands problèms humains).

GRISAR, ELISABETH. Retour de Chine. Lyon, Écrivains réunis, 1954. 376 p. illus.

GRÜMM, HANS. China heute; sechs Wochen im neuen China. Aus einem Reisetagebuch. Wien, Globus Verlag, 1951. 133 p. illus.

HERMLIN, STEPHAN. Ferne Nähe. Berlin, Aufbau-Verlag, 1954. 132 p. illus.

HOGARTH, PAUL, 1917-  Looking at China: the journal of an artist. Drawings of a nation in transition. London, Lawrence and Wishart, 1956. 96 p. illus.

HYDE, DOUGLAS. The mind behind new China. London, Phoenix House [1956] 36 p. (A background book).

IM neuen China. Ein Reisebericht eines Schweizer Kulturdelegation 1955 (So sahen wir China von Hugo Kramer, Rene Mauroux, Margrit Lobsiger-Dellenbach, Max Winiger). Zürich, Verlagsvereinigung "Zeitdienst," 1956.

124 p. illus. plates.

JAIN, JAGDISH CHANDRA. Amidst the Chinese people. With a prefaratory[sic] letter by Mulk Raj Anand. Delhi, Atma Ram, 1955. 152 p. illus.

KENNEN Sie China? (Auswahlangebot) Leipzig, Leipziger Kommisions-und Grossbuchhandel, 1956. 24 p. illus.

KÖNIG, JOHANNES. Befreites China; Bilddokumente vom Kampf und Sieg und von der Aufbauarbeit des chinesischen Volkes. Dresden, Sachsenverlag [1951] 35 p. illus.

KYAW MIN, U, 1899- Through the Iron Curtain via the back door. Rangoon, Printed by Burmese Advertising Press [1952?] London, E. Benn, 1953(287 p.) 291 p. illus.

LABOULAYE, ÉDOUARD DE, 1885- Images d'une Chine défunte; souvenirs. Paris [Se trouve à la Maison du livre, 1953] 136 p.

LANDMAN, LYNN. Profile of Red China, by Lynn and Amos Landman. New York, Simon and Schuster [1951] x, 245 p.

LERICHE, FERNAND. Through People's China in a friendship train. Pref. by Louis Saillant. [London] W.F.T.U. Publications [1953] 63 p. illus.

LLEWELLYN, BERNARD, 1919- I left my roots in China. New York, Oxford University Press, London, Allen and Unwin, 1953. 175 p. illus.

LORENTZ, ANNA. China in Bewegung. Kleine Erlebnisse einer Frau. Berlin, Allgemeiner Deutscher Verlag, 1949. 143 p. (Berliner Reihe, 5).

MAGNIEN, MARIUS. Au pays de Mao-Tsé-Toung. Préf. de Marcel Cachin. Paris, Éditions sociales [1952] 351 p.

MALLESON, MILES, 1886- An actor visits China. London, Britain-China Friendship Association, 1953. 12 p.

MATTHIAS, LEO L. China auf eigenen Wegen. Ergebnis einer Reise. Hamburg, Rowohly, 1957. 240 p. map.

MONMOUSSEAU, GASTON. La Chine selon Jean Brécot. Paris, Éditeurs français réunis [1956] 176 p. illus., map.

MUJEEB, M.A. Glimpses of new China. Delhi, Maktaba Jamia, 1953. 96 p.

MUKHERJEE, SAILAKUMAR. A visit to new China. Calcutta, A. Mukherjee and Co., 1956. 147 p. illus.

PALMER, HELEN GWYNNETH. Australian teacher in China. Sydney, Teachers' Sponsoring Committee, 1953. ii, 50 p. ports, map.

PAYNE, PIERRE STEPHEN ROBERT, 1911- Journey to red China. London, W. Heinemann [1947] vi, 198 p. map (on lining-papers).

———. Journal de Chine; traduit de l'anglais par Henri Morisset. Paris, Delamain et Boutelleau, 1950. 350 p. map (Aspects du monde).

PECK, GRAHAM, 1914- Two kinds of time; illustrated by the author. Boston, Houghton, Mifflin, 1950. viii, 725 p. illus., maps.

PEN portaits from new China. Peking, Foreign Languages Press, 1956. 115 p.

PEOPLE'S China as we saw it [by Sudhindra Pramanik and others] Peking, Foreign Languages Press, 1955. 39 p. illus.

PHILLIPS, MORGAN, 1885- East meets West, a pictorial story of the Labour Party Delegation to the Soviet Union and China. With a foreword by C.R. Attlee. [1st ed.] London, Lincolns-Prager [1954] 96 p. illus.

ROBINSON, JOAN, 1903- Letters from a visitor to China. Cambridge [Eng.] Students' Bookshops, 1954. 35 p.

SANTHISTAN, VARKEY. New China at a glance. Kottayam, News India Publications [1952] 52 p.

SCHLEINITZ, KARL HEINZ. Reisebilder aus China. Berlin, Kongress-Verlag 1956. 190 p. illus.

SEGONZAC, ADALBERT DE, 1912- Visa pour Pékin. Paris, Gallimard[1956 291 p. illus. (L'Air du temps).

———. Visa for Peking. [Translated from the French by the author with the cooperation of Marion Barwick] London, Heinemann [1956] xiv, 205 p. illus.

SHASTRI, BRAJKISHORE. From my China diary. Delhi, Siddhartha Publica-

tions [1954] 55 p.
SOHONI, SHANKAR VINAYEK. Ceylon, Burma, China and Russia. Poona, Venus Book Stall [1951] 64 p. illus.
STAROBIN, JOSEPH ROBERT, 1913- Paris to Peking. New York, Cameron Associates [1955] 280 p.
SUNDARLAL. China today; an account of the Indian Goodwill Mission to China, September-October 1951. Allahabad, Hindustani Culture Society [1952] xxi, 701 p. plates, group ports., fold. map.
UHSE, BODO, 1904- Tagebuch aus China. Mit Bildern von Werner Klemke. Berlin, Aufbau-Verlag, 1956. 174 p. illus.
VAIKUNTHAVASAN, K. Three months in new China and Soviet Union. With a foreword by J.D. Bernal. Colombo, Ceylon, People's Press [1953] 147 p. illus.
VASSILIEFF, ELIZABETH (SUTTON). Peking Moscow letters; about a four months' journey, to and from Vienna, by way of People's China and the Soviet Union. Melbourne, Australian Book Society, 1953. 295 p. illus.
VIDAL, NICOLE. Voyage en Chine. Paris, Lacoste, 1955. 200 p. (Voyages).
WRIGHT, THOMAS. Australian's visit to People's China: report on the first Australian trade union delegation to People's China. Sydney, Sheet Metal Working, Agricultural Implement and Stove-making Industrial Union of Australia, 1952. 30 p. illus. ports.

Regions - North China
Peking, Tientsin and Jehol

ADAM, MAURICE, 1889-1932. tr. Description sommaire de 25 districts des environs de Pékin d'après le Je sīa kieou wen k'ao, 日下舊聞考. Ch. CVIII à CXLIV. Pékin, Impr. des Lazaristes, 1928. vii, 135 p. front. plates.
ARLINGTON, LEWIS CHARLES, 1859-1942. In search of old Peking, by L.C. Arlington and William Lewisohn. Peking, H. Vetch, 1935. vi, [6], 382 p. front., illus. (incl. maps) plates (part fold.) ports., plans (part fold.).
BOUCHOT, JEAN. Scènes de la vie des Hutungs, croquis des moeurs pékinoises. 3e éd. Pékin, A. Nachbaur, 1926. ii, 127 p. plates.
BOUILLARD, GEORGES, 1862-1930. Pékin et ses environs, série 1-15? Pékin, A. Nachbaur, 1922-24. 15 v. ? illus. plates, fold. maps (in pockets) plans.
———. Les tombeaux impériaux: Ming et Tsing. historique, cartes, plans. Pékin, A. Nachbaur, 1931. 225 p. plates, (part fold., part col.) fold. plans, fold. maps.
BREDON, JULIET. Peking, a historical and intimate description of its chief places of interest. [3d ed., rev. and enl.] Shanghai, Kelly and Walsh, 1931. xvi, 571 p. plates, fold. maps, plans. 2nd ed. 1922, 522 p.
CASSEVILLE, HENRY. Pékin, ville éternelle. Paris, Fasquelle [1934] [9]-185 p.
CHAO, LILIAN, 趙麗蓮. A souvenir of Peking. Peiping, Hung Y. Hsiao, 1946. 128 p. illus. map.
CORDES, ERNST, 1908- Peking, der leere Thron. Erlebnisbericht aus Nordchina. Berlin, Rowolt, 1937. 223 p. plates.
DANBY, HOPE. The garden of perfect brightness; the history of the Yüan Ming Yüan and of the emperors who lived there. Introductory note by Sir John T. Pratt. London, Williams and Norgate [1950]; Chicago, H. Regnery Co. 1950. 239 p. illus., ports., map (on lining papers).
DEVARANNE, THEODOR, 1880- Von Tsingtau bis Peking; Streifzüge durch Nordchina, von Pfarrer Devaranne. Die Umschlagzeichnung wurde von Herrn Kunstmaler O. Delling...hergestellt. Berlin, Allgemeiner evangelisch-protestanischer Missionsverein, 1927. 35 p. plates.
ECKSTEIN, OSKAR, 1879- Sonne über Peking. Erlenbach-Zürich, Rotapfel-

Verlag [1942] 197 p. plates.

FISCHER, EMIL SIGMUND, 1865-1945. Guide to Peking and its environs near and far, by Fei-Shi [pseud.] Fully rev. ed. Tientsin, Tientsin Press, 1924. 237 p. illus.

——. The mausolea of the Manchu dynasty (1644-1912 A.D.) with particular reference to the desecrated Tung Ling, north-east of Peking. Tientsin, Tientsin Press, 1929. 4 p. illus. plates.

——. The Tung Ling, 東陵, and the Hsi Ling, 西陵; or, The eastern and western Manchu mausolea in China, revisited in 1936. Also reprint of "A journey along the east coast of China," China travels of Emil S. Fischer 1894-1936. Tientsin, Tientsin Press, 1936. 24 p. incl. table. illus. plates.

——. Souvenir of the sights of Jehol's capital. Tientsin, Tientsin Press, 1936. 12 p.

——. My third journey to the capital of Jehol in 1938. Tientsin, Tientsin Press, 1938. 12 p. illus. (incl. plan, ports.).

GESELLSCHAFT FÜR DEUTSCH-SOWJETISCHE FREUNDSCHAFT, Berlin. Peking, die Hauptstadt d. Volksrepublik China. Fotos: G. Kiesling. Text: E. von Kügelgen. Berlin, 1957. 16 p. (Erläuterungsheft zum Bildband, 87).

GRANTHAM, ALEXANDRA ETHELDRED (VON HERDER), 1867-  The temple of heaven: a short study. Peking, Peking Institute of Fine Arts, 192? 40 p.

HEDIN, SVEN ANDERS, 1865-1952. Jehol, die Kaiserstadt; mit 78 Abbildungen nach Handzeichnungen des Verfassers und photographischen Aufnahmen von dr. Gösta Montell sowie einem Lageplan. Leipzig, F.A. Brockhaus, 1932. 211, [1] p. front., illus. (incl. plan) plates, ports.

——. Jehol, city of emperors, translated from the Swedish by E.G. Nash. New York, E.P. Dutton, 1933. xiv, 278 p. incl. plates. front., plates, ports, map.

HU, CHIA, 胡茄. Peking today and yesterday. Peking, Foreign Languages Press, 1956. 122 p. illus.

HUBRECHT, ALPHONSE. Grandeur et suprématie de Péking. Péking, Impr. des Lazaristes, 1928. xi, [5], 607 p. illus., plates, ports., maps, facsims., plans.

KATES, GEORGE NORBERT, 1895-  The years that were fat; Peking, 1933-40; with photos. by Hedda Hammer Morrison. New York, Harper [1952] 268 p. illus.

KO, LING. 格林 My three years in Peking. Translated by T. H. Yang. Delhi, Siddhartha, 195? 146 p.

LEWISOHN, WILLIAM. The western hills of Peking; a route book and map. Peking, French Bookstore, 1933. 57 p. fold. map (in pocket).

LIN, CH'ING, 麟慶, 1791-1846. Extraits des carnets de Lin K'ing. Sites de Pékin et des environs, vus par un lettré chinois, avec 26 bois reproduits de l'édition chinoise originale, par Jean R. Baylin. Réédités par Albert Nachbaur. Peiping, 1929. [26] p. illus.

——. Visite aux temples de Pékin; extraits du carnet de voyage de Lin K'ing, traduit par Jean R. Baylin. Pékin, La "Politique de Pékin," 1921. 78 p. illus. port. (Collection de la "Politique de Pékin").

MALONE, CARROLL BROWN, 1886-  History of the Peking summer palaces under the Ch'ing dynasty. [Urbana] University of Illinois, 1934. 247 p. illus. (incl. port., map, plans) ([Illinois. University] Illinois studies in the social sciences. Vol. XIX, no. 1-2).

MENNIE, DONALD. The pageant of Peking, comprising sixty-six Vandyck photogravures of Peking and environs from photographs by Donald Mennie, with an introduction by Putnam Weale [pseud.] descriptive notes by S. Couling. Shanghai, A.S. Watson, 1922. 40 p., 66 mounted plates.

MONTELL, GÖSTA, 1899-  The Chinese lama temple, Potala of Jehol; exhibition of historical and ethnographical collections made by Dr. Gösta Montell, member of Dr. Sven Hedin's expeditions, and donated by Vincent Bendix.

New York, New York World's Fair 1939 [c1939] 65, [1] p. incl. front.(port.) illus. plates.

THE PEIPING CHRONICLE. Guide to "Peking." Peiping, Peiping Chronicle, 1933. v, 88 p. plates, 3 maps on fold. 1. 1st ed. 1931.

PEKING. COLLEGE OF CHINESE STUDIES. Library. A bibliography of readings on Peiping for tourists, compiled by the Library of the College of Chinese Studies cooperating with California College in China. Peiping, China, 1936. 6 p.

PEKING Utility Book, published by the Mothers' Club of Peking, the Peking Friday study club, the Peking American college women's club. Peking, 1921-40. ? v. [Later published by Peking International Women's Club].

PERCKHAMMER, HEINZ VON. Peking; Geleitwort von Arthur Holitscher. Berlin, Albertus-Verlag [c1928] xx, 200 p. of illus. plan. (Das gesicht der städte).

QUENNELL, PETER, 1905- A superficial journey through Tokyo and Peking. London, Faber and Faber [1932] 250 p. front., plates, ports.

RASMUSSEN, OTTO DURHAM, 1888- Tientsin; an illustrated outline history. [Tientsin] The Tientsin Press, 1925. 320, xvi p. plates, ports., fold. plans, facsims.

SEKINO, TADASHI, 1868-1935. Summer palace and lama temples in Jehol. Tokyo, Kokusai bunka shinkokai (The Society for international cultural relations) 1935. 16, 2 p., mounted col. front., illus. (plan) plates [Kokusai bunka shinkokai. Publications, series - B., 9].

SIAO, EVA. Peking; Eindrücke und Begegnungen. Eingeleitet von Bodo Uhse. Dresden, Sachsenverlag, 1956 [c1955] 34 p. illus. (part col.) ports. (part col.).

THOS. COOK AND SON. Peking, North China, South Manchuria and Korea, with maps, plans and illustrations. 5th ed. Peking, Thos. Cook and Son, 1924. 143 p. front. (fold. map) illus. fold. plan.

TSOU, PAO-CHÜN, 鄒豹君. A regional study of Shantung and its significance in the life of North China. Chungking, 1943. Microfilm copy. (negative) of typescript. Collation of the original: 244 l., diagrs., maps, tables.

WHITE, HERBERT CLARENCE, 1896- Peking the beautiful; comprising seventy photographic studies of the celebrated monuments of China's northern capital and its environs complete with descriptive and historical notes, introduction by Hu Shih. Shanghai, Commercial Press [c1927] 154, [1] p. mounted front., mounted illus. (part col.).

## Northwest China

ALDRICH, RICHARD LEWIS, 1897- Tun-Huang: The rise of the Kansu port in the T'ang dynasty. Ann Arbor, 1942. 186 l. plates. Thesis - University of Michigan.

BOHLIN, BIRGER, 1898- Notes on the hydrography of western Kansu. Stockholm [Tryckeri aktiebolaget Thule ] 1940. 54 p. illus., plates, maps (part fold.) (Reports from the scientific expedition to the north-western provinces of China under the leadership of Dr. Sven Hedin. The Sino-Swedish expedition. Publication 10. III. Geology. 3).

CLARK, LEONARD FRANCIS. The marching wind. New York, Funk and Wagnalls, 1954. London, Hutchinson, 1955. 368 p. illus.

FARRER, REGINALD JOHN, 1880-1920. The rainbow bridge. London, E. Arnold, 1921. xi, 383 p. front., plates, fold. map. A continuation of his On the caves of the world.

KAN-SU, zwischen Gletscher und Wüste, hrsg. von einem Freundeskreis. Wien-Mödling, Missionsdruckerei St. Gabriel [1939] 120 p. plates, fold. map.

KAO, CHONG RWEN, 高鍾潤, 1914- Geographic influences upon the economic activities of the Kansu corridor of northwest China. Iowa City, 1949. v,

109 p. Thesis - State University of Iowa.

YANG, CHI, 楊紀 . China's great northwest, translated and published by the International Department, Ministry of Information, Nanking, 1946. 48 1.

## East China
## Nanking and Soochow

HOFFMANN, ALFRED, 1911-  Nanking. Shanghai; Max Nössler, 1945. 254 p. photos.

KWOK, K. W., 郭錫麒 . The splendours of historic Nanking. Eighty photographic studies, with descriptive notes of ancient and modern Nanking. Shanghai, Kelly and Walsh, 1933. 12 p. 80 plates.

MA, CH'AO-CHÜN, 馬超俊, 1886-  Nanking's development 1927-37; report on the activities of the municipality of Nanking, 1937. 137 p.

NANCE, FLORENCE RUSH. Soochow, the Garden City. Shanghai, Kelly and Walsh, 1936. 76 p. plates, fold. maps.

## Shanghai

ALL about Shanghai and environs; a standard guide book; historical and contemporary facts and statistics. Shanghai, The University Press [1934-    ? v. front., illus. (incl. ports.) fold. plans. annual.

ALMANAC-SHANGHAI, 1946/47. Ed. by Ossi Lewin. [Shanghai] "Shanghai Echo" Pub. Co. 1 v. illus., ports.

[ARDENNE DE TIZAC, ANDRÉE FRANÇOISE CAROLINE D'] 1878-  Changhai et le destin de la Chine, par Andrée Viollis, pseud. Introduction par Henri Rohrer. Paris, R. A. Corrêa, 1933. [9]-258, [1] p. incl. plates, map. (Faits et gestes).

LE CURIEUX Changhai; traduit par Ting Oueng. Pékin, Impr. de la "Politique de Pékin," 1936. 45 l. illus. (Collection de la "Politique de Pékin").

DAY. RUTH. Shanghai: 1935. Claremont, Calif., The Saunders Studio Press, 1936. 86 p.

FEETHAM, RICHARD, 1874-  Report of the Hon. Richard Feetham, to the Shanghai Municipal council. Shanghai, North-China Daily News and Herald, 1931-    2 v. fold. map, 3 fold. plans, tables (1 fold.) fold. diagrs.

HAUSER, ERNEST O., 1910-  Shanghai: city for sale. New York, Harcourt, Brace [c1940] 3-323 p.

————. Blancs et jaunes à Chang-Haï, tr. de l'anglais par Maurice Beerblock. Paris, La Nouvelle édition [1945] 273 p. fold. map. (Collection diplomatique and politique internationale).

KARNS, MAURINE. Shanghai; high lights, low lights, tael lights. By Maurine Karns and Pat Patterson. Shanghai, The Tridon Press [1936] 52 p. front., illus.

KOUNIN, I. I. ed. The diamond jubilee of the International settlement of Shanghai. I. I. Kounin, managing editor; Alex Yaron, art editor. Shanghai, Post Mercury Co., designed and executed by Adcraft studios [1940] 270, [9] p. illus. (incl. ports.) mounted plates (1 fold.) mounted fold. facsim.

LANNING, GEORGE, 1852-1920. The history of Shanghai, by G. Lanning - S. Couling. Shanghai [etc.] For the Shanghai Municipal Council by Kelly and Walsh, 1921-23. 2 v. fold. front., plates (part fold.) ports. (1 fold.) fold. map, fold. plans.

MILLER, G. E., pseud. Shanghai, the paradise of adventurers. New York, Orsay Pub. House, 1937. 307 p.

POTT, FRANCIS LISTER HAWKS, 1864-1947. A short history of Shanghai, being an account of the growth and development of the international settlement. Shanghai [etc.] Kelly and Walsh, 1928.    [ix]-xii, 336 p. fold. front., plates, fold. plan.

SECKER, FRITZ. Schen 甲; Studien aus einer chinesischen Weltstadt. 2. Aufl.
Schanghai, Max Nössler, 1932. [6] 1., 130 p. plates.
SHANGHAI, photographed and depicted by Ellen Thorbecke with sketches by
Scheff. Shanghai, North China Daily News and Herald, 1941. 82 p. illus.
U. S. Navy. Pacific Fleet and Pacific Ocean Areas. Information bulletin. Shang-
hai-Yin-hsien (Ningpo). [n.p.] 1945. cover-title, ii, 181 (i. e. 190), [2] p.
incl. plates, maps, charts, tables. (Its Cincpac-Cincpoa bulletin no. 30-45).
WILKINSON, EDWARD SHELDON, 1883-  Shanghai country walks. 2nd ed.
Shanghai, North China Daily News and Herald, 1934. 149, [1] p. incl. front.
illus. maps (part fold.).
YUAN, L. Z. Sightlights on Shanghai. Shanghai, Mercury Press [1934] 142 p.
illus.

### Chekiang

BIRD, GEORGE E. Hangchow holidays. "Where to go and what to see." Shanghai, Millington, 1948. vii, 90 p. illus. plates, fold. map.
CROW, CARL, 1883-1945. Chekiang highways. Shanghai [etc.] Kelly and Walsh,
1937. 173 p. illus. (part double, incl. maps, plan, facsim.).
FITCH, ROBERT FERRIS, 1873-  Hangchow-Chekiang itineraries. 4th rev. and
enl. ed. Shanghai, Kelly and Walsh, 1935. vii, 132 p. chart. front. illus.
plans, port. plates. 1st ed. 1918, 2nd ed. 1922, 3rd ed. 1929.
———. Pootoo itineraries; describing the chief places of interest with a special
trip to Lo-chia-shan. Shanghai, Kelly and Walsh, 1929.  xx,  90 p. front.
plates, fold. maps, plans.

### Kiangsi

STONE, ALBERT H. Historic Lushan: the Kuling mountains; edited at the direction of the Kuling Council by Albert H. Stone and J. Hammond Reed. Hankow, Arthington Press, for the Religious Tract Society, 1921. 106 p. plates,
map.
WEGENER, GEORG, 1863-1939. Im innersten China; eine Forschungsreise
durch die Provinz Kiang-si. Berlin, A. Scherl, 1926. xi, [1], 409, [1] p.
front., illus., plates, ports., map. and atlas of IV fold. maps.

### Fukien

ANTI-COBWEB CLUB, Foochow. Fukien; a study of a province in China. Shanghai, Presbyterian Mission Press, 1925. ii, 113 p. col. front., plates, fold.
map.
———. Fukien, arts and industries; papers by members of the Anti-cobweb society, Foochow, Fukien, China. Foochow, Christian Herald Industrial Mission Press, 1933. 310 p. col. front., illus., plates.
HURLBUT, FLOY, 1888-  The Fukienese; a study in human geography. [Mun-
cie? Ind., The author, c1939] xxiii, 143 p. incl. front., illus. (incl. maps)
diagrs. Thesis - University of Nebraska.

### Central and South China

BOŬINAIS, A. P. A. The Lungchow region; its frontier rivers, roads, towns and
marts. Shanghai, Statistical Department, Inspectorate General of Customs,
1923. 33 p. illus. maps (China. Maritime Customs, II. Special ser., 39).
CAILLARD, GASTON FÉLIX. L'Indochine, géographie, histoire, mise en valeur. Kouang-Tchéou-Wan. Paris, Édition Notre domaine colonial [1922]
124, [4] p. illus. (incl. maps) (Notre domaine colonial, VIII).
CANTON, China. "Progressive Canton." Issued by the Canton Municipality.

[Canton, The Novelty Print. Co.] 1921. 35 p. plates.

——. Advertising and Commission Agency. Canton; its port, industries and trade. Canton, 1932. x, 250 p. illus. maps.

CENTRAL CHINA RAILWAY COMPANY. Guide-book for central China. Central China calls. Rev. ed. Shanghai, Central China Railways, 1942. 75, [1] p. illus. (incl. port., maps).

LEE, EDWARD BING-SHUEY, 李炳瑞, 1903-56. Modern Canton. Shanghai, Mercury Press, 1936. xv, [1], 176, [5] p. incl. front. (map) illus. plates, ports., fold. plans, diagrs. (part fold.).

McCLURE, FLOYD ALONZO, 1897- Notes on the island of Hainan. [Canton, 1922] [1], 66-79 p. plates, fold. map. "Reprinted from the Lingnaam agricultural review, vol. 1, no. 1."

MOULY. Haï-Nan; l'île aux cent visages. Paris, P. Lethielleux [1946] 134 p. illus., maps (part fold.).

NG, YONG-SANG, 伍陽生. Canton, city of the rams; a general description and a brief historical survey. With four stories from popular Cantonese folklore. Canton, M.S. Cheung, 1936. vii, 138 p. illus.

RAPPORT sur la situation administrative économique et financière du Territoire de Kouang-Tchéou-Wan durant la période 1931-32. Hanoi, Impr. G. Taupin et Cie, 1932. 43 p. (Gouvernement géneral de l'Indochine. Territoire de Kouang-Tchéou-Wan).

SAVINA, F.M., 1876- Monographie de Hainan. Conférence fait le 10 decembre à la société de géographie de Hanoi. Hanoi, 1929. p. (Cahiers de la société de géographie de Hanoi, 1929).

U.S. Office of Strategic Services. Research and Analysis Branch. Psychology Division. Short guide to South China. [Washington] 1942. 17 p. (R and A 654).

WEISKOPF, FRANZ CARL, 1900- Die Reise nach Kanton; Bericht, Erzählung, Poesie und weitere Bedeutung. Berlin, Dietz, 1953 [c1952] 149 p. (His Ausgewählte Werke in Einzelausgaben).

## Southwest China

CORDIER, GEORGES, -1936. Un voyage in Yunnansen; guide. 2. éd. Hanoi, Impr. d'Extrême-Orient, 1923. 117 p. diag. maps. 1er éd. 1911.

——. La province du Yunnan. Hanoi, Impr. Mac-Dinh-Tu, 1928. 573 p. incl. tables.

DESSIRIER, JEAN LOUIS, d. 1915. A travers les marches révoltées; ouest-chinois: Yun Nan-Se-Tchouen-Marches Thibétaines; avec 61 gravures hors texte. Paris, Plon-Nourrit [1923] vii, 316 p. plates, ports.

DYMOND, MRS. M.M. Yunnan. London, Marshall Bros. 1929. 95 p.

CHINA INFORMATION COMMITTEE. A guide to Chungking; the city of double celebration. Chungking, The China Information Committee [1939] 65 p. tables, diagrs.

FISCHER, EMIL SIGMUND, 1865-1945. Journey to the sacred Mount Omei in western Szechuan. Tientsin, Tientsin Press, 1937. 19 p. illus. (incl.port.).

HUANG, SHOU-FU, 黃綬芙. A new edition of the Omei illustrated guide book, by Huang Shou-fu and T'an Chung-yo, 譚鍾嶽, A.D. 1887-91. With an English translation by Dryden Linsley Phelps, pictures redrawn from the original plates by Yü Tzu-tan, 俞子丹. Cheng-tu, Jih Hsing Yin Shua Kung Yeh Shê, 1936. [454] p. illus. (West China union university. Harvard-Yenching institute series ).

KINGDON-WARD, FRANCIS, 1885-1958. From China to Hkamti Long. London, E. Arnold, 1924. 317 p. front., 1 illus., plates, fold. map.

LÉCORCHÉ, MAURICE. Vingt-cinq ans d'Indochine et de Yunnan; souvenirs 1919-43. Toulouse, É. Privat [1950] 286 p. illus., fold. maps (1 col.).

LE ROUX, P. Un pèlerinage bouddhique en Chine: Le Mont Omi. Changhai?,

1925. 57 p. plates.

MOWLL, HOWARD KILVINTON WEST, 1890-  West China as seen through the eyes of the westerner. Canberra, Australian Institute of Anatomy, 1940. 20 p. (George Ernest Morrison lectures).

OESTERHELT, OTTO, 1883-  Routenaufnahmen in West-Szetschwan; die Sifangebirge im chinesisch-tibetischen Grenzgebiet nach den topographischen Ergebnissen der Stötznerschen Expedition 1914. Mit einem Geleitwort von Sven Hedin. Gotha, J. Perthes, 1938. 156 p. incl. tables. plates, maps (part fold.) diagrs. (part fold.) (Ergänzungsheft nr. 235 zu ''Petermanns mitteilungen'').

REITLINGER, GERALD, 1900-  South of the clouds; a winter ride through Yünnan. London, Faber and Faber [1939] 9-327 p. front., plates, fold. map.

SCHULZE, DIETER. Das politisch-geographische und geopolitische Kräfteverhältnis zwischen den drei chinesischen Südwest-Provinzen [Jun-nan, Kwangsi, Kwang-tung], Britisch-Birma und Französisch-Indochina im Spiegel der Geschichte. Heidelberg, Heidelberger Verlag-Anstalt und Druckerei, 1940. 213 p. map. Diss.- Univ. München.

TAO, FRANK, 陶啓湘. Chungking--China's war capital. Chungking, Chinese Ministry of information, 1943. 30 p. (China Handbook ser., 21).

VASSAL, MME. GABRIELLE M. In and round Yunnan Fou. London, W. Heinemann, 1922. x, 187 p. front., plates, port., map.

———. Mon séjour au Tonkin et au Yunnan. Avant-propos de Charles Richet. Paris, P. Roger, 1928. 248 p. 16 plates, fold. map. (Voyages de jadis et d'aujourd'hui).

WIENS, HEROLD JACOB, 1912-  The Shu Tao; or, The road to Szechuan. A study of the development and significance of Shensi-Szechuan road communication in west China. Ann Arbor, Mich., 1948. Microfilm copy of typewritten ms. Made in 1949 by University Microfilms (Publication no. 1122) Positive. Collation of the original: 200 l. illus., maps (part fold.) Thesis-Univ. of Michigan.

WISSMANN, HERMANN VON, 1895-  Süd-Yünnan als teilraum Südostasiens. Heidelberg [etc.] K. Vowinckel, 1943. 30 p., illus. (incl. maps, diagr.) plates. (Schriften zur geopolitik, hft. 22).

YÜN-NAN PIEN TI WEN T'I YEN CHIU.   雲南邊地問題研究 . Territoires et populations des confins du Yunnan, traduit du chinois par J. Siguret. Peiping, Chine, H. Vetch [1937-40] 2 v. fold. maps.


## Burma Road

BRADLEY, NEVILLE. The old Burma road, a journey on foot and muleback from the diary, notes and reminiscences of Doctor Neville Bradley, for many years a medical missionary in China, with a foreword by Lady Erskine Crum. London, Toronto, W. Heinemann [1945] vii, [1], 138 p. front. plates.

EPSTEIN, SAMUEL and BERYL (WILLIAMS). The Burma road; story by Douglas Coe, illustrations by Winfield Scott Hoskins. New York, J. Messner inc. [1946] 192 p. incl. front. (map) illus.

FRIBERG, HANS DANIEL, 1908-  West China and the Burma road. Minneapolis, Augsburg Publishing House [c1941] 174 p. front., illus.(maps) plates.

LONG, FRANK ANTHONY. The old Burma road, by Frank Anthony Long [and] Gertrude Joyce Long. Kansas City, Mo., Burton Pub. Co. [1942] 7-293 p.

LOWE, CHUAN-HUA, 駱傳華 , 1902-  The Yunnan-Burma highway. Chungking, China Information Pub. Co. [1940] cover-title, 18 p. map (Chungking pamphlets, 5).

METFORD, BEATRIX. Where China meets Burma; life and travel in the Burma-China border lands. London and Glasgow, Blackie [1935] viii, 231 p. front. (ports.) plates, fold. map.

SAMSON, GERALD. The Burma Road; report of an address. London, China

Society [1946] cover-title, 8 p.

SLATER, ROBERT HENRY LAWSON. Guns through Arcady; Burma and the Burma road, with illustrations by the author. Sydney, London, Angus and Robertson, ltd., 1941.    x,  239, [2] p. incl. illus., map. front.

SMITH, NICOL. Burma road, with illustrations from photographs by the author. Garden City, N.Y., Garden City Pub. Co. [1942] 333 p. plates. 1st ed. 1940.

T'AN, PEI-YING, 譚伯英, 1896-  The building of the Burma road. New York, London, Whittlesey House, McGraw-Hill [1945] 200 p. plates, double map.

U.S. Army. Y-force Operations Staff. Reconstruction of the Burma road, operational, logistical and historical data current to October 24, 1944 on the rebuilding of the land supply route to isolated China by China's Yunnan-Burma highway engineering administration, the United States Army's Burma road engineers [and] Y-force operations staff, United States Army. Prepared and distributed by public relations officer, Y-force Operations Staff. New York [1944?] 19 numb. 1. fold. plates. Reproduced from type-written copy.

# IV. HISTORY

## Historiography

BIELENSTEIN, HANS. The restoration of the Han dynasty; with prolegomena on the historiography of the Hou Han shu. [Stockholm, 1953] 209 p. fold. maps, diagrs., geneal. tables. Diss.-Stockholm.

CHU, SHIH-CHIA, 朱士嘉, 1905- Chang Hsüeh-ch'êng, 章學誠, his contributions to Chinese local historiography. Ann Arbor, University Microfilms, 1950. ([University Microfilms, Ann Arbor, Mich.] Publication no. 1644). Collation of the original: v, 225 l. 2 fold. tables.

FRANKE, OTTO, 1863-1946. Das Tse tschi t'ung kien, 資治通鑑, und das T'ung kien kang mu, 通鑑總目, ihr Wesen, ihr Verhältnis zueinander und ihr Quellenwart. Berlin, Verlag der Akademie der Wissenschaften, 1930. 46 p. (Preussische Akademie der Wissenschaften zu Berlin. Sitzungbericht. Phil.-hist. Kl. 1930).

GARDNER, CHARLES SIDNEY, 1900- Chinese traditional historiography. Cambridge, Harvard University Press, 1938. xi, 3-120 p. (Harvard historical monographs. 11).

HAN, YU-SHAN, 韓玉珊, 1899- Elements of Chinese historiography. Hollywood, Calif., W.M. Hawley, 1955. 246 p. ports., facsims.

HUFF, ELIZABETH. Shih hsüeh. Cambridge, 1947. 229 l.

[KU, CHIEH-KANG] 顧頡剛, 1893- The autobiography of a Chinese historian, being the preface to a symposium on ancient Chinese history (Ku shih pien) translated and annotated by Arthur W. Hummel. Leyden, E.J. Brill, 1931. [v]-xliii, 199, [1] p. (Sinica leidensia edidit Institutum sinologicum Lugduno-Batavum, I).

LATOURETTE, KENNETH SCOTT, 1884- Chinese historical studies during the past seven years. [New York, 1921] cover-title, p. 703-716. "Reprinted from the American historical review, Vol.XXVI, no. 4, July, 1921."

LO, TCHEN-YING, 羅振英, [Lo Chên-ying]. Les formes et les méthodes historiques en Chine. Une famille d'historiens et son œuvre. Paris, P. Geuthner, 1931. 116 p. (Université de Lyon. Bibliotheca franco-sinica lugdunensis. Études et documents publiés par l'Institut franco-chinois de Lyon, t. IX).

NIVISON, DAVID SHEPHERD, 1923- The literary and historical thought of Chang Hsüeh-ch'eng 1738-1801; a study of his life and writing, with translations of six essays from the Wen-shih t'ung-i, 文史通義. Cambridge, 1953. 397 l. Thesis - Harvard University.

SSŬ-MA, CH'IEN, 司馬遷, ca. 145-ca. 86 B.C. Ssŭ-ma Ch'ien's historiographical attitude as reflected in four late warring states biographies. By Frank Algerton Kierman, Jr. Ann Arbor, University Microfilms [1953] ([University Microfilms, Ann Arbor, Mich.] Publication 6415). Collation of the original: lviii, 228, [7] l. map.

SWINGLE, WALTER TENNYSON, 1871-1952. Chinese historical sources. [New York, 1921] cover-title, 717-725 p. "Reprinted from the American historical review. Vol. XXVI, no. 4. July, 1921."

TEGGART, FREDERICK JOHN, 1870-1946. Rome and China; a study of correlations in historical events. Berkeley, University of California Press, 1939. xvii, 283 p. maps (1 fold.).

## Chronology

AKIYAMA, AISABURŌ. A chronological list of Japan and China. Tokyo, 1930.

42 p.

CHAIT, RALPH MILTON, 1892-  comp. A chronological arrangement of the names of all the Chinese emperors and the dates of their reign together with lists of Chinese seal, character and symbolic marks. New York, Priv. print. [c1928] 47, [1] p. illus.

MOULE, ARTHUR CHRISTOPHER, 1873-1957. The rulers of China, 221 B.C. - A.D. 1949; chronological tables. With an introductory section on the earlier rulers C. 2100-249 B.C. by W. Perceval Yetts. London, Routledge and K. Paul [1957] xxiii, 131 p.

SUSKI, PETER MARIE, 1875-  The year names of China and Japan. Los Angeles, The Science Society; London, K. Paul, c1931. cover-title, 40 p.

### Outlines, Study and Teaching

[AMERICAN HISTORICAL ASSOCIATION. Historical Service Board]. Our Chinese ally. [Madison, Wis., USAFI, 1944] cover-title, 61 p. incl. illus. (incl. ports., maps) tab., diagr. ([U.S.] War dept. Education manual EM 42. G I roundtable series).

BIGGERSTAFF, KNIGHT, 1906-  China: revolutionary changes in an ancient civilization. Ithaca, N.Y., Cornell University Press, 1945. 78 p. (Cornell university curriculum series in world history. No. 4).

CHANG, P'ÊNG-CH'UN, 張彭春, 1892-1957. China: whence and whither? An outline of a high school unit of study. A preliminary draft for experimental use in the senior high schools of the territory of Hawaii. Honolulu, T.H., Institute of Pacific Relations, 1934. 130 p. illus. (incl. maps).

————. China at the crossroads; the Chinese situation in perspective, with a foreword by Professor Eileen Power. London, Evans Brothers [1936] 179, [1] p. illus. (incl. maps).

CHESNEAUX, JEAN. L'Extrême-Orient de 1840 à 1941, Chine et Japon. Paris, Centre de documentation universitaire [1955] 82 p. (Les Cours de Sorbonne).

FENN, HENRY COURTENAY, 1894-  Jŭnggwo lìshř gāngyàu. A sketch of Chinese history. New Haven, Institute of Far Eastern Languages, Yale University, 1952. 2 v. illus., maps (Mirror series A, 10-11 ).

GALE, ESSON McDOWELL, 1884-  Basics of the Chinese civilization; a topical survey in outline, with readings. Shanghai, Kelly and Walsh, 1934. v-xi, 112 p.

GOODRICH, LUTHER CARRINGTON, 1894-  A syllabus of the history of Chinese civilization and culture. 5th ed. [rev.] By L.C. Goodrich [and] H.C. Fenn. [New York, China Society of America, 1950] 55 p. illus. 1st ed. 1929.

JOHNSEN, JULIA EMILY, comp. China and Japan; a study outline. New York, H.W. Wilson [1922] cover-title, 51 p. (The reference shelf. v. 1, no. 2).

LEE, SHAO-CH'ANG, 李紹昌, 1891-  China: ancient and modern. [Honolulu, 1937] cover-title, 31 p. illus. (maps) fold. tab. (University of Hawaii. Occasional papers. no. 33). Rev. ed. 1940. 28 p. (University of Hawaii Bull. 19: 7 ).

LATOURETTE, KENNETH SCOTT, 1884-  China under the republic. [New York, Institute of International Education] 1921. 23 p. (Institute of international education. International relations clubs, syllabus, IX ).

ROBERTSON, JAMES ALEXANDER, 1873-  The Far East, with special reference to China, its culture, civilization and history, an outline for individual and group study. Chapel Hill, N.C., University of North Carolina Press [c1931] 87 p. ([North Carolina. University. University extension division] University of North Carolina extension bulletin. Vol. XI, no. 2 ).

### General Works

CHANG, CH'I-YUN, 張其昀 , 1901-  China of the fifty centuries. Taipei, China Culture Pub. Foundation, 1953. 25 p. illus. maps (Pamphlet on Chinese Affairs ).

COLLIS, MAURICE, 1889-  The Great within. London, Faber and Faber[1941] 349 p. illus. (maps) plates, ports., fold. plan.

——. La cité interdite, traduit de l'anglais par Marc et Francois Laugier. Paris, Calmann-Lévy [1946] 389 p. plates, plans.

DE FRANCIS, JOHN FRANCIS, 1911-  Talks on Chinese history, by John De Francis and Elizabeth Jen Young,楊任永甯. New Haven, Institute of Far Eastern Languages, Yale University, 1952. 2 v.

DOUGLAS, SIR ROBERT KENNAWAY, 1838-1913. China, with special article: Late events and present conditions, by Jeremiah W. Jenks. [Memorial ed.] New York, P.F. Collier [c1936] xiii, 366 p. front., illus. (maps) plates (1 col.) port. (The history of nations. Vol. VI ).

EBERHARD, WOLFRAM, 1909-  Chinas Geschichte. Bern, A. Franck[c1948] 403 p. plates, maps. (Bibliotheca sinica; chinesische Philosophie, Literatur, Kunst, Geschichte, Bd. 1 ).

——. A history of China [translated by E.W. Dickes] Berkeley, University of California Press, 1950. xvi, 374 p. illus., maps. Eng. ed.: London, Routledge and K. Paul, 1950. 368 p.

——. Histoire de la Chine des origines à nos jours. Traduction de George Deniker. Paris, Payot, 1952. 351 p. maps, illus. (Bibliothèque historique ).

ELWELL-SUTTON, ALBERT SIGISMUND, 1878-  The Chinese people; their past, present, and future, with a foreword by J. Percy Bruce. London, I. Nicholson and Watson, 1934. 264 p. (The university extension library ).

ERKES, EDUARD, 1891-  Die Entwicklung der chinesischen Gesellschaft von der Urzeit bis zur Gegenwart. Berlin, Akademie Verlag, 1953. 30 p.(Sächs Akademie der Wissenschaften zu Leipzig. Bericht über die Verhandgn. Philhist. Kl. Bd. 100, Heft 4 ).

——. Geschichte Chinas von den Anfängen bis zum Eindringen des ausländischen Kapitals. Berlin, Akademie-Verlag, 1956. 155 p. illus.

——. The same. 2. durchges Aufl. Berlin, Akademie Verlag, 1957. 153 p. illus. maps (Best u. Verl., 5172 ).

ESCARRA, JEAN, 1885-1955. La Chine; passé et présent. Paris, A. Colin, 1937. Nouv. éd. 1949. 213, [1] p. incl. double map. (Collection Armand Colin no 202 ).

——. China then and now. [Translated by C.C. Langhorne and W. Sheldon Ridge] Peking, H. Vetch, 1940. viii p., 289 p. front., plates, ports.

FITZGERALD, CHARLES PATRICK, 1902-  China; a short cultural history; edited by Professor C.G. Seligman. London, Cresset Press, 1935; New York, D. Appleton-Century, 1938. xviii, [2], 615 p. front., illus. (incl. plans) plates, maps (1 fold.). Rev. ed. 1950.

——. The same. [4th rev. ed.] New York, Praeger; London, Cresset Press, 1954. xviii, 621 p. illus., maps (1 fold.).

FRANKE, OTTO, 1863-1946. Geschichte des chinesischen Reiches; eines Darstellung seiner Entsyehung, seines Wessens und seiner Entwicklung bis zur neuesten Zeit. Berlin, W. de Gruyter, 1930-52. 5 v. fold. map.

FRANKEL, HANS H., 1916-  Catalogue of translations from the Chinese dynastic histories for the period 220-960. Berkeley, University of California Press, 1957. 295 p. (China dynastic histories translations: Supplement 1 ).

GOODRICH, LUTHER CARRINGTON, 1894-  A short history of the Chinese people. New York, London, Harper [1943]; London, Allen and Unwin, 1948. xv p., 260 p. illus. (maps) plates.

——. The same. Rev. ed. New York, Harper [1951] xv, 288 p. illus., maps.

——. History of China, a self-teaching course, based on "A short history of the Chinese people." [Madison, Wis.] Pub. for the United States Armed Forces Institute by Harper [1944] ix, 320 p. incl. illus. (incl. maps (1 double) ) forms. ([U.S.] War dept. Education manual EM 209 ).

GOWEN, HERBERT HENRY, 1864-  An outline history of China, with a thorough account of the republican era interpreted in its historical perspective, by Herbert H. Gowen and Josef Washington Hall.  New York, London, D. Appleton, 1926. xxviii p., 542 p. fold. map. 1st ed. 1913.

GRANET, MARCEL, 1884-1940. La civilisation chinoise; la vie publique et la vie privée; avec 5 cartes et 2 figures dans le texte et 10 planches hors texte. Paris, La Renaissance du livre, 1929.    xxi, 523, [1] p. illus. (incl. maps) x plates. (L'Évolution de l'humanité, synthèse collective. [1. section. xxv] ).

———. The same.  Paris, A. Michel, 1948 [c1929] xxi, 523 p. illus., maps (part fold. ) (L'Évolution de l'humanité; synthèse collective. 1. section, 25 ).

———. Chinese civilization. Translated by Kathleen E. Innes and Mabel R. Brailsford.  London, Kegan Paul; New York, A. A. Knopf, 1930. xxiii, 444 p. front. 1 illus., plates, maps. (History of civilization).

———. The same. [Translated by Kathleen E. Innes and Mabel R. Brailsford ] New York, Barnes and Noble, 1951. xxiii, 444 p. illus., maps.

GRANTHAM, ALEXANDRA ETHELDRED (VON HERDER), 1867-  Hills of blue, a picture-roll of Chinese history from far beginnings to the death of Ch'ien Lung, A. D. 1799, with 19 portraits and a map.  London, Methuen [1927] xi, 643, [1] p. front., ports.

GROOT, JAN JAKOB MARIA DE, 1854-1921, ed. and tr. Chinesische Urkunden zur Geschichte Asiens... in vollständiger Zusammenfassung übersetzt und erläutert von J. J. M. de Groot, mit Unterstützung durch die Preussische Akademie der Wissenschaften.  Berlin und Leipzig, W. de Gruyter, 1921-26. 2 v. Vol. 1 was published in 1921 under title: Die Hunnen der vorchristlichen zeit; chinesische urkunden zur geschichte Asiens, 1. teil. Vol. 2, "aus dem nachlass des verfassers herausgegeben von O. Franke."

GROUSSET, RENÉ, 1885-1952. Histoire de la Chine.  Paris, A. Fayard [1947, c1942] 428 p. maps. (Les Grandes études historiques ).

———. The rise and splendour of the Chinese Empire. [Translated by Anthony Watson-Gandy and Terence Gordon. 1st American ed. ] Berkeley, University of California Press, 1953. London, G. Bles, 1952. 312 p. illus., port., maps.

HAENISCH, ERICH, 1880-  Chinas Weg vom Lehnsreich zum Einheitsstaat. Vorgetragen am 6. Juni, 1947.  München, Verlag der Bayerischen Akademie der Wissenschaften, 1948. 23 p. (Sitzungsberichte der Bayerischen Akademie der Wissenschaften, Phil-hist. Kl., Jahrg. 1947, Heft 3 ).

HALOUN, GUSTAV, 1898-1951. Seit wann kannten die Chinesen die Tocharer oder Indogermanen überhaupt  von Gustav Haloun.  Leipzig, Verlag der Asia Major, 1926-  207 p. diagrs.

HERMANNS, MATTHIAS. Vom Urmenschen zur Hochkultur; Chinas Ursprung und Entwicklung. Bd. 1.  Yenchowfu, Missionsdruckerei, 1935. 1 v. charts, col. front. plates, ports.

JAEGER-STUX, G. Histoire de la Chine.  Paris, Richard-Masse, 1947 [c1946] 125, [3] p. illus., ports. (Collection Triptyque. Histoire, 3 ).

JONES, FRANCIS CLIFFORD. China.  [London] Arrowsmith [1937] 2 v. (Modern states series. No. XIII-XIV ).

KEETON, GEORGE WILLIAMS, 1902-  China, the Far East and the future. 2d ed.  London, Stevens, 1949. xi, 511 p. fold. col. map. (Library of world affairs, no. 6 ).

KRAUSE, FRIEDRICH ERNST AUGUST, 1879-  Geschichte Ostasiens. Göttingen, Vandenhoeck and Ruprecht, 1925. 2 v. illus. (maps).

KUO, SHIEN-YEN, 郭先彦, 1905-  4600 Jahre China. Seine politischen, wirtschaftlichen und kulturellen Verhältnisse. Von Kuo Shien-yen und Karl Hinkel. Nebst einer Vorbemerkung über die chinesische Sprache und Schrift. Von Gu Bau-tschang, 顧葆常.  Göttingen, Verlag "Offentliches Leben," 1930. viii, 133 p. fold. map. (Öffentliches leben. Neue folge. 7 ).

LAMB, GENE. A tabloid Chinese history. Introduction by Chiang Ch'ao-tsung,

江朝宗. Tientsin, Peiyang Press, 1936. 71, vi p. plates, maps, port.,
fold. facsim., fold. table.

LANE, JOHN E. ed. Researches in the social sciences on China; essays and abstracts by graduates of the East Asian Institute, Columbia University. New
York, Reproduced for private distribution by the East Asian Institute of Columbia University, 1957. vi, 89 p. (Columbia University. [East Asian Insti-
tute] East Asian Institute studies, 3 ).

LATOURETTE, KENNETH SCOTT, 1884-   The development of China. 6th ed.,
rev. Boston, New York, Houghton Mifflin, 1946. xi, [1] p., 343, [1] p. 1st
ed. 1917.

————. The Chinese, their history and culture. 3d ed., rev. New York, Macmillan, 1946. xvi, 847 p. maps (1 fold.) 1st ed. 1934; 2nd ed. 1943.

LATTIMORE, ELEANOR (HOLGATE), 1895-   China yesterday and today; edi-
ted by Marguerite Ann Stewart. A cooperative project between American
Council, Institute of Pacific Relations and Webster Pub. Co. St. Louis, New
York [etc., 1946] 111 p. illus. (incl. port., maps).

LÉGER, FRANÇOIS. Les influences occidentales dans la révolution de l'Orient:
Inde, Malaisie, Chine, 1850-1950. Paris, Plon [1955] 2 v. maps. (Civilisations d'hier et d'aujourd'hui ).

LI, CHIEN-NUNG. 李劍農. The political history of China, 1840-1928. Translated and edited by Ssu-yu Teng, 鄧嗣禹, and Jeremy Ingalls. Princeton, N.
J., D. Van Nostrand; London, Macmillan [1956] 545 p.

LIANG, YÜN-LI, 梁鋆立, 1900-   China, by Y.L. Liang and Neville Whymant.
London, Macdonald [1946] xi, 13-192 p. (Cross-roads series.).

LOUZON, ROBERT. La Chine; ses trois millénaires d'histoire, ses cinquante
ans de révolution. Cannes, Impr. Aegitna, 1954. 158 p. illus., ports.,
maps. (Collection de la révolution prolétarienne, 3 ).

LYALL, LEONARD ARTHUR, 1867-1940. China; with a foreword by H.A.L.
Fisher. New York, C. Scribner, 1934. London, E. Benn, 1934. 7-383, [1]
p. [The modern world; a survey of historical forces].

MASPÉRO, GEORGES, 1872-   La Chine. Nouv. éd. mise à jour. Préface
d'André Duboscq. Paris, Delagrave, 1925. 2 v. (Bibliothèque d'histoire et
de politique ) 1er éd., 1918.

MASPERO, HENRI, 1883-1945. Les institutions de la Chine; essai historique
[par] Henri Maspero [et] Jean Escarra. Préf. de Paul Demiéville. [1. éd.]
Paris, Presses universitaires de France, 1952. 174 p. maps.

————. La Chine antique. Nouv. éd. révisée d'après les corrections et additions
laissées par l'auteur et pourvue de caractères chinois. Paris, Impr. nationale, 1955. xxiv, 519 p. fold. maps. 1er éd., 1927.

LA MAZELIÈRE, ANTOINE ROUS, marquis de, 1864-   Quelques notes sur
l'histoire de Chine. Paris, Librairie Plon, 1938. 98 p. illus. fold. map.
1er éd. 1901.

MENZ, GERHARD, 1885-   Der Kampf um Nordchina. Leipzig, W. Goldmann
[c1936] 91 p. map (on lining paper) (Weltgeschehen).

NOURSE, MARY AUGUSTA. The four hundred million; a short history of the
Chinese. Indianapolis, New York, Bobbs-Merrill [c1935] 375 p. front., illus.,
plates, maps, facsim., diagr.

————. The same. 3d ed. New York, The New Home Library [1943] 17-413 p.

————. 400 millions d'hommes. Histoire des chinois. Paris, Payot, 1936. 351
p. maps (Bibliothèque historique ).

————. 400 [i. e. Vierhundert] Millionen, die Geschichte der Chinesen. Mit einem Schlusskapitel über letzte Zeit und Gegenwart von Lin Tsiu-sen, 林秋生 ·
Berlin, A. Metzner, 1936. 405 p. illus.

PERCHERON, MAURICE, 1891-   La Chine. Illus. en couleurs de Zenker. Paris, F. Nathan, 1952 [c1935]; Neuchâtel, Delachaux et Niestle, 1946. 159 p.
illus. (part col.) (Collection "Pays et cités d'arts") 1er éd., 1935.

POTT, FRANCIS LISTER HAWKS, 1864-1947. A sketch of Chinese history. 5th rev. ed. Shanghai, Kelly and Walsh, 1936. x, 305 p. fold. maps. 1st ed. 1903.

PULLEYBLANK, E.G., 1922- Chinese history and world history; an inaugural lecture. Cambridge [Eng.] University Press [1955] 35 p.

ROSTHORN, ARTHUR VON, 1862-1945. Geschichte Chinas. Stuttgart-Gotha, F.A. Perthes, 1923. 226 p. (Weltgeschichte in gemienverständlicher Darstellung, 10 ).

ROY, CLAUDE, 1915- Clefs pour la Chine. [Paris] Gallimard [1953] 353 p. illus.

——. Into China. Translated from the French by Mervyn Savill. [1st ed.] New York, McBride [1956] 420 p. illus.

——. Schlüssel zu China. Aus dem Französisch übers. von Lore Krüger. Berlin, Aufbau Verlag, 1956. 513 p.

SEEGER, ELIZABETH, 1889- The pageant of Chinese history, illustrated by Bernard Watkins. 3d ed. New York, Toronto, Longmans, Green, 1947. xvi, 414 (i.e. 418) p. illus. (incl. maps). 1st ed. 1934; 2nd ed. 1944.

[SIMPSON, BERTRAM LENOX] 1877-1930. The vanished empire, by B.L. Putnam Weale [pseud.] London, Macmillan, 1926. ix, 379 p. front. (ports.) plates, 2 maps, 2 facsim.

SOOTHILL, WILLIAM EDWARD, 1861-1935. A history of China. With a supplementary chapter by G.F. Hudson. [Rev. ed.] London, E. Benn [1950]; New York, Contemporary Books, 1951. 127 p. map (on lining papers) 1st ed. 1928.

SOULIÉ, CHARLES GEORGES, 1878- Histoire de la Chine de l'antiquité jusqu' en 1929, par George Soulié de Morant. Paris, Payot, 1929. [7]-539 p. illus. (maps) (Bibliothèque historique ).

TOMKINSON, LEONARD. Studies in the theory and practice of peace and war in Chinese history and literature. [Shanghai] Published for the Friends' Centre, by Christian Literature Society, 1940. viii, 208 p.

TS'UI, CHI, 崔驥, 1902-50. A short history of Chinese civilization, with a preface by Laurence Binyon. London, Gollancz, 1942; New York, G.P. Putnam [1943] xix, 388 p. front., illus. (incl. maps).

——. Histoire de la Chine et de la civilisation chinois. Traduit d'après la 4ᵉ édition par George Deniker. Paris, Payot, 1949. 336 p. illus. maps. (Bibliothèque historique ).

——. Geschichte Chinas und seiner Kultur, mit einem Vorwort von E.H. v. Tscharner, zahlreichen Karten und Anhang. Zürich, Pan-verlag [1945] xix, 492 p. front., illus. (incl. maps).

WALTZ, EMELYN. Far Eastern history. [Rev. ed.] Boston, Christopher Pub. House [1953] 578 p. illus.

WIEGER, LÉON, 1856-1933. La Chine à travers les âges. Précis. Index biographique. Index bibliographique. 2. éd. Hien-Hien, Impr. de Hien-Hien, 1924. 531 p. 1er ed., 1920.

——. China throughout the ages. Translated by Edward Chalmers Werner. [Hsien-hsien] Hsien Press, 1928. 508 p. illus. (incl. port.).

——. Textes historiques; histoire politique de la Chine depuis l'origine, jusqu' en 1929. 3. éd. rev. et complétée. [Hsien-hsien] Impr. de Hien-hien, 1929. 2 v. (2103 p.) illus.

WILHELM, HELLMUT, 1905- Chinas Geschichte, zehn einführende Vorträge. Peking, H. Vetch [1942] 208 p.

——. Geschichte der chinesischen Kultur. Mit einer Farbigen und 33 schwarzen Tafeln. München, F. Bruckmann a.g. [c1928] 300 p. illus., plates ( 1 col. mounted ).

——. A short history of Chinese civilization; translated by Joan Joshua. With an introduction by Lionel Giles. London [etc.] G.G. Harrap [1929]; New

York, Viking Press, 1929. 283, [1] p. illus., 33 plates (incl. col. front. ).
────. Histoire de la civilisation chinoise. Traduction française de G. Lepage.
Paris, Payot, 1931. 303 p. (Bibliothèque historique ).
WILLIAMS, EDWARD THOMAS, 1854-1944. A short history of China. New
York and London, Harper, 1928. xviii, 670 p. front., plates, ports., maps.
(Harper's historical series ).
WILLIAMSON, HENRY RAYMOND. China among the nations. London, Student
Christian Movement Press [1943] 125 p. front. (group port.).
WINGATE, LITITIA BERYL (TUCKER) "MRS. ALFRED WINGATE." China
through the ages. London, C. Lockwood, 1932. 3-252 p. front. (map ).
YANG, LIEN-SHÊNG, 楊聯陞, 1914- Topics in Chinese history. Cambridge,
Harvard University Press, 1950, London, Oxford University Press, 1950.
vii, 57 p. (Harvard-Yenching Institute studies, 4 ).
YAO, SHAN-YU, 姚善友, 1912- The chronological and seasonal distribution
of floods and droughts in Chinese history, 206 B.C.-A.D. 1911. Philadelphia, 1942. 273-312 p. inc. tables. "Reprinted from HJAS, vol. 7."
[YAUKEY, GRACE (SYDENSTRICKER) ] 1899- The land of the Chinese people,
by Cornelia Spencer [pseud. ] London, Museum Press [1947] viii, 136 p.
plates, ports., fold. map. (Portraits of the nations series ).
────. The same. Photos. by courtesy of Asia and World outlook. Rev. ed.
Philadelphia, Lippincott [1951] 120 p. illus. (Portraits of the nations series)
1st ed. 1945.


Ancient
Earliest - 219


BAUER, WOLFGANG, 1930- Chang Liang, 張良, und Ch'en P'ing, 陳平,
zwei Politiker aus der Gründungszeit der Han-Dynastie. München, 1953.
133 1. mounted illus., mounted map. Diss.-Univ. Munich.
BIELENSTEIN, HANS. Emperor Kuang-Wu, 光武, A.D. 25-57, and the Northern barbarians; the seventeenth George Ernest Morrison lecture in ethnology
Wednesday, 2 November, 1955. Canberra, Australian National University,
1956. 23 p. (George Ernest Morrison lectures ).
BODDE, DERK, 1909- China's first unifier; a study of the Ch'in dynasty as
seen in the life of Li Ssŭ, 李斯 (280?-208 B.C.). Leiden, E.J. Brill, 1938.
viii, 270 p. front. (facsim.) (Sinica leidensia, 3 ).
BRITTON, ROSWELL SESSOMS, 1897-1951. Chinese interstate intercourse before 700 B.C. (In American journal of international law. Concord, H.H.,
1935. v. 29, p. 616-635 ).
DEBNICHI, ALEKSY. The Chu-shu-chi-nien, 竹書紀年, as a source to the so-
cial history of ancient China. Warszawa, Państwowe Wydawn. Naukowe,
1956. 101 p. (Prace orientalistyczne, t. 3 ). At head of title: Polska Akade-
mia Nauk. Komitet Orientalistyczny.
DEBON, GÜNTHER, 1921- Die Kapitel 101 und 102 (die Biographien des Yüan
Ang, 袁盎, und Ch'ao Ts'oh,晁錯, Chang Shih-chi, 張釋之, und Feng
T'ang, 馮唐) aus Szema Ts'iens Shi-ki 史記. München, 1953. 116 1.
Diss.-Univ. Munich.
ERKES, EDUARD, 1891- Neue Beiträge zur Geschichte des Choukönigs Yu.
Berlin, Akademie Verlag, 1954. 44 p. (Sächsische Akademie der Wissen-
schaften zu Leipzig. Bericht über die Verhandlungen. Phil-hist. Kl. Bd.101:
3 ).
GRANET, MARCEL, 1884-1940. La féodalité chinoise. Oslo, Ascheoug; Cam-
bridge, Harvard University Press, 1952. 227 p. (Instituttet for sammenlign-
ende kulturforskning. Ser.A : Forelesninger, 22 ).
HIRTH, FRIEDRICH, 1845-1927. The ancient history of China to the end of the
Ch'ou dynasty. New York, Columbia University Press, 1923. xx, 383 p.

map. 1st ed. 1908.

LÜ, PU-WEI, 呂不韋, -235 B.C. Frühling und Herbst des Lü Bu We; aus dem Chinesischen verdeutscht und erläutert von Richard Wilhelm. Jena, E. Diederichs, 1928. xii, 541 [1] p.

OLSVANGER, IMMANUEL, 1888- Fû-Hsî, 伏羲, the sage of ancient China. Jerusalem, Massadah, 1948. 16 p.

PAN, KU, 班固, 32-92. The history of the former Han dynasty. A critical translation, with annotations, by Homer H. Dubs, with the collaboration of Jen T'ai, 任泰, and P'an Lo-chi, 潘洛基. Baltimore, Waverly Press,1938-49. 3 v. fold. map.

[————.] Die Monographie über Wang Mang, 王莽, Ts'ien-Han-shu kap. 99) kritisch bearbeitet, übersetzt und erklärt von Hans O. H. Stange. Leipzig, Deutsche morgenländische Gesellschaft, in Kommission bei F. A. Brockhaus, 1939. xli, 336 p. (Abhandlungen für die kunde des Morgenlandes, mit unterstützung der Deutschen forschungsgemeinschaft, hrsg. von der Deutschen morgenländischen gesellschaft. XXII [i. e. XXIII] 3 ).

[————.] Wang Mang; a translation of the official account of his rise to power as given in the History of the former Han dynasty, with introd. and notes [by ] Clyde Bailey Sargent. [Shanghai, Graphic Art Book Co., pref. 1947] 206 p. geneal. tables.

PO HU T'UNG, 白虎通. Po hu t'ung; the comprehensive discussions in the White Tiger Hall, a contribution to the history of classical studies in the Han period, by Tjan Tjoe Som, 曾珠森. Leiden, E. J. Brill, 1949. 2 v. (Sinica leidensia, 6 ).

POHL, HERBERT. Schi Ki Kapitel 128. [ 龜策列傳 ] Ein Beitrag zur altchinesische Divination. Hamburg, 1948. ii, 62 l. Diss.-Univ. Hamburg.

RUDOLPH, RICHARD CASPER, 1909- Wu Tzŭ-hsü, 伍子胥, his life and posthumous cult: a critical study of Shih-chi 66. Berkeley, 1942. iv, 142 l.

SJÖQUIST, KARL OSKAR. Das Feng-chien-Wesen [ 封建 ] der chinesische Feudalismus nach Abhandlungen aus verschiedenen Dynastien. Berlin, 1938. 56 p. Diss.-Univ. Berlin.

[SSŬ-MA, CH'IEN] ca. 145-ca. 86 B.C. Statesman, patriot, and general in ancient China; three Shih chi biographies of the Ch'in dynasty (225-206 B.C.) translated and discussed by Derk Bodde. New Haven, American Oriental Society, 1940. xi, 75 p. front. (American oriental series, v. 17 ).

STANGE, HANS OTTO HEINRICH, 1903- Leben, Persönlichkeit und Werk Wang Mang's 王莽 dargestellt nach dem 99. Kapitel der Han-annalen. Erlangen-Bruck, Krahl, 1934. 98 p. Diss.-Univ. Berlin.

TSCHEPE, ALBERT, 1844- Histoire du Royaume de Ts'in (777-207 av. J.C.). 2e éd. Changhai, Impr. de la Mission catholique, 1923. ii, 2, 379, 19 p. fold. map. (Variétés sinologiques, 27 ). 1er éd. 1909.

WILBUR, CLARENCE MARTIN, 1908- Slavery in China during the Former Han dynasty, 206 B.C.-A.D. 25. [Chicago, 1943] 490 p. plates, fold. map. (Field museum of natural history. Publication 525 ).

220-617

CHIN SHU, 晉書. English. Selections. Biography of Ku K'ai-chih, 顧愷之 [Chin shu 92. 21a-22a] Translated and annotated by Chen Shih-hsiang, 陳世驤. Berkeley, University of California Press, 1953. Cambridge, Univ. Press, 1953. 31 p. (Institute of East Asiatic studies, University of California. Chinese dynastic histories translations, 2 ).

————. Account of the T'ŭ-yü-hún, 吐谷渾, in the history of the Chin dynasty [Chin shu 97. 4a-7b] Translated and annotated by Thomas D. Carroll, Berkeley, University of California Press, 1953. 47 p. (Institute of East Asiatic Studies, University of California. Chinese dynastic histories translations, 4).

————. The rise of the former Ch'in 前秦 state and its spread under Fu Chien,

符堅 , through 370 A.D. based on Chin shu 113, translated and edited by
Michael C. Rogers. Berkeley, 1953. iv, 393 l. maps, diagr. Thesis - University of California.

CHOU SHU. English. Selections. Biography of Su Ch'o [ 蘇綽 ] [Chou shu, chüan
23] Translated and annotated by Chauncey S. Goodrich. Berkeley, University
of California Press, 1953. 116 p. (Institute of East Asiatic Studies, University of California. Chinese dynastic histories translations, 3 ).

EBERHARD, WOLFRAM, 1909- Das Toba-Reich Nordchinas; eine soziologische Untersuchung. Leiden, E.J. Brill, 1949. viii, 395 p.

IMBERT, HENRI. L'empereur Yang-ti, 煬帝 . (Le Sardanapale chinois). Pékin, Impr. de la "Politique de Pékin," 1922. 14 p. (Collection de la "Politique de Pékin").

SCHREIBER, GERHARD, 1911- The history of the Former Yen 燕 dynasty,
285-370. Ann Arbor, University Microfilms [1955] ([University Microfilms,
Ann Arbor, Mich.] Publication no. 11,469 ). Collation of the original: viii,
361 l. fold. maps, tables. Thesis - Columbia University.

SCOTT, MARGARET INVER. A study of the Ch'iang [ 羌 ] with special reference to their settlements in China from the second to the fifth century A.D.
Cambridge, Eng., 1953. 208, 94 p. Thesis - University of Cambridge.

SSŬ-MA, KUANG, 司馬光 , 1019-86. The chronicle of the Three Kingdoms(220-
265) Chapters 69-78 from the Tzŭ chih t'ung chien, 資治通鑑 , translated
and annotated by Achilles Fang, 方志彤; edited by Glen W. Baxter. v. 1.
Cambridge, Harvard University Press, 1952- 698 p. (Harvard-Yenching
Institute studies, 6 ).

WENLEY, ARCHIBALD GIBSON, 1898- The Grand Empress Dowager Wên
Ming, 文明皇后, and the Northern Wei necropolis at Fang Shan, 方山.
Washington, 1947. 28 p. illus., port., maps. (Freer Gallery of Art, Wash-
ington, D.C. Occasional papers, 1:1 ).

## Medieval
### 618 -1276

BINGHAM, WOODBRIDGE, 1901- The founding of the T'ang dynasty; the fall of
Sui and rise of T'ang, a preliminary survey. Baltimore, Waverly Press,
1941. xiv, 183, [1] p. incl. geneal. tab. front. (port.) fold. maps. [Ameri-
can council of learned societies devoted to humanistic studies. Studies in Chinese and related civilizations, 4 ].

BURIKS PIETER. Fan Chung-yens, 范仲淹 , Versuch einer Reform des chinesischen Beamtenstaates in den Jahren 1043/44. Göttingen, 1954. 75 l.Diss.-
Göttingen.

FITZGERALD, CHARLES PATRICK, 1902- Son of Heaven, a biography of Li
Shih-min [ 李世民 ], founder of the T'ang dynasty. Cambridge [Eng.] The
University Press, 1933. ix, 232 p. incl. illus.(maps, plans) geneal. table,
front.(port.) III plates.

———. Li Che-min, unificateur de la Chine 600 à 649. Avant-propos et traduction de G. Lepage. Paris, Payot, 1935. 247 p. illus. (maps, geneal. table).
(Bibliothèque historique ).

———. The Empress Wu. Melbourne, Cheshire for the Australian National University, 1955. London, Cresset Press, 1956. 252 p. illus.

FRANKE, OTTO, 1863-1946. Der Bericht Wang Ngan-schis [ 王安石 ] von 1058
über Reform des Beamtentmus. Berlin, W. de Gruyter, 1932. 51, x p.
(Preussische Akademie der Wissenschaften zu Berlin. Sitzungbericht. Phil-
hist. Kl. 1932 ).

FU, LO-HUAN, 傅樂煥 . "Nat Pat" and "Ordos" (camps and tents). A study of
the way of life and military organization of the Khitan emperors and their
people. London, 1950. vii, 229 l. plates. Thesis - University of London,
School of Oriental and African Studies.

HAENISCH, ERICH, 1880-   Die Ehreninschrift für den Rebellengeneral Ts'ui
Lih, 崔立 , im Licht der konfuzianischen Moral, ein Episode aus dem 13.
Jahrhundert.  Berlin, In Kommission bei W. de Gruyter, 1944. 79 p.facsim.
(Abhandlungen der Preussischen Akademie der Wissenschaften, Jahrg.1944.
Phil-hist. Kl. Nr. 4 ).

HAN, YÜ, 韓愈 , 768-824. The veritable record of the T'ang emperor Shun-
tsung, February 28, 805-August 31, 805. Han Yü's Shun-tsung shih-lu, translated with introd. and notes by Bernard S. Solomon.  Cambridge, Harvard U-
niversity Press, London, Oxford University Press, 1955. xxxi, 82 p. (Harvard-Yenching Institute studies, 13 ).

HSIN T'ANG SHU.  Le traité des examens, traduit de la Nouvelle histoire des
T'ang (chap. XLIV, XLV ) par Robert Des Rotours.  Paris, E. Leroux, 1932.
[v]-viii, 414, [2] p. (Bibliothèque de l'Institut des hautes études chinoises.
Vol. II ).

——. Traité des fonctionnaires et Traité de l'armée, tr. de la Nouvelle histoire des T'ang (chap. XLVI-L ) par Robert Des Rotours.  Leyde, E.J. Brill,
1947-48. 2 v. 9 maps (part fold.) (Bibliothèque de l'Institut des hautes études
chinoises, v. 6 ).

——. Biography of Huang Ch'ao, 黃巢 , translated and annotated by Howard S.
Levy.  Berkeley, University of California Press, London, Cambridge Uni-
versity Press, 1955. 144 p. fold. maps (in pocket). (California. University.
Institute of East Asiatic Studies. Chinese dynastic histories translations, 5 ).

[HUC, ÉVARISTE RÉGIS] 1813-60. Communism in China in the XI century, with
an introduction by F. R. Martin.  London [E. Ingham] 1927. 20 p.

KRACKE, EDWARD A., Jr., 1908-   Civil service in early Sung China, 960-
1067; with particular emphasis on the development of controlled sponsorship
to foster administrative responsibility.  Cambridge, Harvard University
Press, 1953. xv, 262 p. diagrs. (Harvard-Yenching Institute. Monograph
series, v. 13 )

[LI, PO-YÜEH ] 李百藥 565-648. Nachrichten aus der Geschichte der nördlich-
en Thsi. Von dr. August Pfizmaier. (In K. Akademie der wissenschaften, Vienna. Phil-hist. Kl. Denkschriften.  Wien, 1884. 34. bd., 1. abth., p. 1-96 ).

PARKER, EDWARD HARPER, 1849-1926. A thousand years of the Tartars. 2d
ed., rev. and reset. New York, A.A. Knopf; London, Kegan Paul, 1924.
[xi]-xii, 288 p. front., plates, double maps. (History of civilization ).

PULLEYBLANK. EDWIN GEORGE, 1922-   The background of the rebellion of
An Lu-shan, 安祿山 .  London and New York, Oxford University Press,1955.
x, 264 p. plates, col. fold. maps, tables. (London. University. School of
Oriental and African Studies.  London Oriental ser., 4 ).

SCHAFER, EDWARD H. Jr., 1913-   The reign of Liu Ch'ang, 劉鋹 , first emperor of southern Han: a critical translation of the text of Wu-tai-shih, with
special inquiries into relevant phases of contemporary Chinese civilization.
Berkeley, 1947. xvi, 199 l. map.

——. The empire of Min. Rutland, Vt. Published for the Harvard-Yenching
Institute, by C.E. Tuttle, 1954. xii, 146 p.

SIU, SIANG-TCH'OU 徐象樞 [Hsü, Hsiang-shu]. L'oeuvre de T'ang T'ai-tsong,
唐太宗 .  Zi-ka-wei près Chang-hai, Impr. de l'Orphelinat de T'ou-sè-wè,
1924. v, 77, 77 p. Thèse - Université l'Aurore.

TCHEOU, HOAN, 周暉 . Le prêt sur récolte institué en Chine au XIe siècle par
le ministre novateur Wang Ngan-che, 王安石 .  Paris, Jouve et Cie, 1930.
150 p. Thèse - Univ. de Paris.

WILLIAMSON, HENRY RAYMOND. Wang An Shih, 王安石 , a Chinese statesman and educationalist of the Sung dynasty.  London, A. Probsthain, 1935-
37. 2 v. (Probsthain's Oriental series, vol. XXI-XXII ).

WITTFOGEL, KARL AUGUST, 1896-   History of Chinese society: Liao, 907-
1125 [by] Karl A. Wittfogel and Fêng Chia-shêng, 馮家昇 , with the assistance of John DeFrancis [and others]  Philadelphia, American Philosophical

Society; distributed by Macmillan Co., New York, 1949. xv, 752 p. illus.,
maps (1 fold.) "Issued as Transactions of the American Philosophical Society, volume 36 (1946)."

### 1277-1643
### (See also Mongolia - History)

BOXER, CHARLES RALPH, 1904-  ed. South China in the sixteenth century,
being the narratives of Galeote Pereira, Fr. Gaspar da Cruz, O. P. [and] Fr.
Martin de Rada, O. E. S. A. (1550-75) London, Printed for the Hakluyt Society, 1953. xci, 388 p. illus., maps (part fold.) facsim. (Works issued by
the Hakluyt Society, 2d ser., no. 106 ).

CHAN, ALBERT, 陳綸緒 , 1915-  The decline and fall of the Ming dynasty; a
study of the internal factors. Cambridge, 1954. 296 l. Thesis - Harvard U-
niversity.

CHAN, DAVID B., 陳少岳 , 1927-  The usurpation of the Prince of Yen, 1398-
1402. Berkeley, 1956. 321 l. Thesis - Univ. of California.

CHANG, YU-CH'UAN, 張煜全 , 1880-  Wang Shou-jên, 王守仁 , as a statesman. Peking, Chinese Social and Political Science Association, 1940. iv,
[2], 31-99, [155]-252, [319]-374, 473-517, [3] p. Reprinted from the Review,
v. 23 ).

FRANKE, OTTO, 1863-1946. Li Tschi, 李贄 , ein Beitrag zur Geschichte der
chinesischen Geisteskämpfe im 16. jahrhundert. Berlin, Akademie der Wissenschaften, in kommission bei W. de Gruyter u. co., 1938. 62 p. (Abhandlungen der Preussischen akademie der wissenschaften. Jahrg. 1937. Phil -
hist. Kl., 10 ).

————. Li Tschi und Matteo Ricci. Berlin, Akademie der Wissenschaften, in
kommission bei W. de Gruyter u. co., 1939. 24 p. (Abhandlungen der Preussischen akademie der wissenschaften. Jahrg. 1938. Phil-hist. Kl., 5 ).

FRANKE, WOLFGANG, 1912-  Preliminary notes on the important Chinese literary sources for the history of the Ming dynasty, (1368-1644). Chengtu,
Chinese Cultural Studies Research Institute, West China Union University,
1948. 118 p. (Studia serica. monographs. ser. a., 2 ).

HUCKER, CHARLES OSCAR, 1919-  The Chinese Censorate of the Ming dynasty, including an analysis of its activities during the decade, 1424-34. Chicago, 1950. 381 l. Thesis - Univ. of Chicago.

MacSHERRY, CHARLES W. Impairment of the Ming tributary system as exhibited in trade involving Fukien. Berkeley, 1956. 347 l. Thesis - University
of California.

PARSONS, JAMES B., 1921-  The rebellion of Chang Hsien-chung, 張獻忠 ,
as an example of the internal disturbances in China during the late Ming dynasty. Berkeley, 1954. 316 l. Thesis - University of California.

PELLIOT, PAUL. Le Hôja et le Sayyid Ḥussain de l'histoire des Ming. Leiden,
E. J. Brill, 1948. 81-292 p. Reprinted from T'oung Pao, 38: 2-5.

PENG, TSUN-SZE, 彭遵泗 . Shu Pi, 蜀碧 , das kostbare Heldenblut von Shu.
Erstmalig übertragen aus dem chinesischen Urtexte von Fritz Weiss. Berlin, Carl Heymann, 1929. vii, 106 p. map.

ROUSE, UTA M., 1912-  Hu k'ou yu sheng 虎口餘生記 :1642. A translation with
socio-historical annotation. New Haven, 1945. 132 l. plates. Thesis - Yale
University.

TRIGAULT, NICOLAS, 1577-1628. The China that was; China as discovered by
the Jesuits at the close of the sixteenth century [by] L. J. Gallagher, S. J.,
from the Latin of Nicholas Trigault, S. J. Milwaukee, The Bruce Pub. Co.
[1942] xx, 199 p. front., ports., fold. map.

YANG, YÜ, 楊瑀 , 1285-1361. Beiträge zur Kulturgeschichte Chinas unter der
Mongolenherrschaft: das Shan-kü sin-hua 山居新語 des Yang Yü, von
Herbert Franke. Wiesbaden, F. Steiner, 1956. 160 p. (Abhandlungen für

die Kunde des Morgenlandes, XXXII, 2 ).

## Modern: Manchu Dynasty
### 1644 - 1800

BOUVET, JOACHIM, 1656-1730. The history of Cang-hy, 康熙, the present emperour of China, presented to the most Christian king, by Father J. Bouvet. London, Printed for F. Coggan, MDCXIX. [Washington, 1937] 61 1. Print from microfilm negative of original in the New York Public library.

HIBBERT, ELOISE TALCOTT. K'ang Hsi, emperor of China. London, Kegan Paul [1940]    x,   3-298 p. front., plates, ports.

————. Jesuit adventure in China: during the reign of K'ang Hsi. New York, E. P. Dutton [1941]    x,   3-298 p. front., plates, ports.

HUANG CH'ING K'AI KUO FANG LÜEH,   皇清開國方略. Huang ts'ing k'ai kuo fang lüeh. Die Grüdung des mandschurischen Kaiserreiches, übers. und erklärt von Erich Hauer. Berlin and Leipzig, W. de Gruyter, 1926. xxv, 710 p. fold. map.

MICHAEL, FRANZ, 1907- The origin of Manchu rule in China; frontier and bureaucracy as interacting forces in the Chinese empire, by Franz Michael. Baltimore, The Johns Hopkins press, 1942. viii, 127 p. fold. map.

ORLÉANS, PIERRE JOSEPH D', 1641-98. History of the two Tartar conquerors of China, including the two journeys into Tartary of Father Ferdinand Verbiest, in the suite of the Emperor Kang-Hi: from the French of Père Pierre Joseph d'Orléans. To which is added Father Pereira's journey into Tartary in the suite of the same emperor, from the Dutch of Nicolaas Witsen. Tr. and ed. by the Earl of Ellesmere. With an introduction by R. H. Major. London, Printed for the Hakluyt society, 1854; Reprint ed., Tientsin, 1940. xv, vi, 153 p. (Works issued by the Hakluyt society. [no. XVII] ).

WANG, HSIU-CH'U, 王秀楚, fl. 1645. A ten day's massacre in Yangchow. Rendered into English by Lucien Mao,毛如升. Shanghai, Hsi Feng Chê, 1930. 65 p.

### 1801-1861

CHIANG, SIANG-TSEH, 蔣湘澤. The Nien Rebellion. Seattle, University of Washington Press, 1954. xvi, 159 p. maps. (University of Washington publications on Asia ).

COLLIS, MAURICE, 1889- Foreign mud, being an account of the opium imbroglio at Canton in the 1830's and the Anglo-Chinese war that followed. London, Faber and Faber [1946] New York, A. A. Knopf, 1947. 318 p. plates, ports., maps.

————. La guerre de l'opium (Foreign mud) Tr. de l'anglais par Marc et François Laugier. Paris, Calmann-Lévy [1948] 335 p. illus., ports., maps. (Nouvelle collection historique ).

GRANTHAM, ALEXANDRA ETHELDRED (VON HERDER), 1867- A Manchu monarch; an interpretation of Chia Ch'ing. London, G. Allen and Unwin [1934] 223, [1] p. front. (port.).

KINDLER, OTTO, 1905- Opiumkrieg in China. Berlin, O. Uhlmann [1940] 47, [1] p. illus. (Weltpirat England, 8 ).

KUO, PIN-CHIA, 郭斌佳, 1908- A critical study of the first Anglo-Chinese war, with documents. Shanghai, Commercial Press, 1935. 315 p.

PALIKAO, CHARLES GUILLAUME MARIE APOLLINAIRE ANTOINE COUSIN DE MONTAUBAN, comte de, 1796-1878. L'expédition de Chine de 1860; souvenirs du général Cousin de Montauban, comte de Palikao, publiés par son petit-fils, le comte de Palikao; avec 8 gravures hors texte et une carte. Paris, Plon [1932] viii, 450 p. front.(port.) plates, fold. map, plan.

SMITH, DAVID BONNER-, 1890-1950, ed. The second China war, 1856-60. Ed-

ited by D. Bonner-Smith and E. W. R. Lumby. [London] Printed for the Navy Records Society, 1954. xxii, 413 p. maps. (Publications of the Navy Records Society, 95 ).
TÊNG, SSŬ-YŬ, 鄧嗣禹 , 1906-   Chang Hsi, 張喜 , and the treaty of Nanking,
1842. Chicago, University of Chicago Press [1944] xi, 191 p. illus.(map ).

T'ai p'ing t'ien kuo

BOARDMAN, EUGENE POWERS, 1910-  Christian influence upon the ideology
of the Taiping Rebellion, 1851-64. Madison, University of Wisconsin Press,
1952. xi, 188 p. map (on cover) facsim. A revision of the author's thesis,
Harvard University.
CHENG, JAMES CHESTER, 鄭吉士 . Some aspects of the Taiping rebellion in
China. Cambridge, Eng., 1950. 310 p. Thesis - University of Cambridge.
CORNELSSEN, LUCY. Tai ping tien guo. Rebellen unterm Kreuz; ein Tatsachenbericht über die grosse chinesische Revolution, 1849-64. Berlin, Brunnen-
verlag, W. Bischoff [1938] 318, [4] p. 2 maps on 1 l.
HAMBERG, THEODORE. The visions of Hung-Siu-tshuen, 洪秀全 , and origin
of the Kwang-si insurrection. Hongkong, Printed at the China Mail office,
1854. [Peiping, Reprinted by Yenching University Library, 1935] [iii]-v, 63
p.; 30 numb. l.
LAAI, YI-FAAI, 賴義輝 . The part played by the pirates of Kwangtung and
Kwangsi provinces in the Taiping Insurrection. Berkeley, 1950.  l. Thesis-
Univ. of California.
MARX, KARL, 1818-83. Marx on China, 1853-60; articles from the New York
daily tribune. With an introd. and notes by Dona Torr. London, Lawrence
and Wishart, 1951. xxiii, 98 p.
———. Über China; das Eindringen des englischen Kapitalismus in China. [Arti-
kel aus der New York Daily tribune] Besorgt vom Marx-Engels-Lenin-Stalin-
Institut beim ZK der SED. [1.Aufl.] Berlin, Dietz, 1955. 156 p. (Bücherei
des Marxismus-Leninismus, Bd. 46 ).
MEADOWS, THOMAS TAYLOR. The Chinese and their rebellions, viewed in
connection with their national philosophy, ethics, legislation, and administration. To which is added, an essay on civilization and its present state in
the East and West. Stanford, Calif., Academic Reprints [1953] lx, 656 p.
maps (part fold.). Reprinted from the 1856 ed.
MORSE, HOSEA BALLOU, 1855-1934. In the days of the Taipings, being the
recollections of Ting Kienchang, otherwise Meisun, sometime scoutmaster
and captain in the ever-victorious army and interpreter-in-chief to General
Ward and General Gordon; an historical retrospect, by H. B. Morse. Salem,
Mass., The Essex institute, 1927. xii, 434 p. front., plates, ports., map.
OEHLER, WILHELM. Die Taiping-Bewegung. Geschichte eines chinesisch-
christlichen Gottesreichs. Gütersloh, Bertelsmann, 1923. 175 p. (Beiträge
zur Förderung christlichen Theologie, Bd. 28, 2 ).
SHIH, TA-K'AI, 石達開 , 1831-63. "Le journal de Che Ta-kai," épisodes de la
guerre des Tai-ping; traduit par Li Choen. Pékin, Impr. de la "Politique
de Pékin," 1927. 182 p. plates. (Collection de la "Politique de Pékin" ).
TÊNG, SSŬ-YŬ, 鄧嗣禹 , 1906-  New light on the history of the Taiping Rebellion. Cambridge, Harvard University Press, 1950. ii, 132 p.

1862-1911

CAMERON, MERIBETH ELLIOTT, 1905-  The reform movement in China,1898-
1912. Stanford, Stanford University Press; London, H. Milford, Oxford U-
niversity Press, 1931. 223 p. (Stanford university publications. University
series. History, economics, and political science. 3:1 ).
CHEN, CHANGBIN, 陳翔冰. La presse française et les questions chinoises

(1894-1901) Étude sur la rivalité des puissances étrangères en Chine. Paris, Impr. R. Foulon, 1941. [7]-208 p. Thèse-Univ. de Paris.

CH'EN, TIEH-MING, 陳鐵民 , 1906- The Sino-Japanese war, 1894-95: its origin, development and diplomatic background. Berkeley, 1944. 288 1. Thesis-Univ. of California.

CHING-SHAN, 景善 , 1823-1900. The diary of His Excellency Ching-shan; being a Chinese account of the Boxer troubles. Published and translated by J. J. L. Duyvendak. Lugduni Batavorum, E. J. Brill, 1924. cover-title, viii, 85, 48 p.

————. The case of the Ching Shan diary by Ch'êng Ming-chou, 程明洲 . ii, 7 p. (Occasional papers by the scholars, fellows and their advisers in Chinese studies at Yenching University, 2 ).

CHOU, HSIANG-KUANG, 周祥光 . Modern History of China. Delhi, Metropolitan Book Co. [1952] vii, 167 p. fold. map.

CLEGG, ARTHUR. The birth of new China; a sketch of one hundred years, 1842-1942. London, Lawrence and Wishart [1943]; Allahabad, Kitab Mahal, 1943. 144 p. illus. (maps).

DER LING, princess, 德齡公主 , d. 1944. Son of Heaven. New York, London, D. Appleton-Century, 1935. xi, 248 p. front., plates, ports.

DUBARBIER, GEORGES, 1888- Histoire de la Chine moderne. Paris, Presses universitaires de France, 1949. 126, [2] p. map. ("Que sais-je?" Le point des connaissances actuelles, 308 ).

DUCHESNE, ALBERT. Quand les Belges devaient partir pour la Chine. Un projet d'expédition contre les Boxers, 1900. Bruxelles, Éditions L'Avenir [1949?] 48 p. (Collection d'histoire militaire belge ).

FAIRBANK, JOHN KING, 1907- ed. Ch'ing documents: an introductory syllabus, compiled by John King Fairbank for use in the seminar in modern Chinese history at Harvard University. Cambridge, Published with the assistance of the Harvard-Yenching Institute and distributed by Harvard University Press, 1952. 2 v.

FRANKE, WOLFGANG, 1912- Die Staatspolitischen Reformversuche K'ang Yu-weis, 康有爲 , und seiner Schule. Ein Beitrag zur geistigen Auseinandersetzung Chinas mit dem Abendlande. Berlin, 1935. 89 p. incl. facsims.

JULLIAN, ÉLIE ALPHONSE, 1859- Souvenirs de l'expédition de Chine, 1900-02, avec deux croquis. Paris, J. Peyronnet, 1928. [7]-106 p., incl. maps. (Collection Les clochers de France. [nᵒ 26] ).

KENT, PERCY HORACE BRAUND, 1876- The twentieth century in the Far East; a perspective of events, cultural influences and policies. London, E. Arnold [1937] 390 p.

MA, TE-CHIH, 麥德智 . Le mouvement réformiste et les événements de la cour de Pékin en 1898. Lyon, Bosc frères, M. and L. Riou, 1934. 125 p. Thèse-Univ. de Lyon.

MANNIX, WILLIAM FRANCIS. Memoirs of Li Hung Chang, by William Francis Mannix, with the story of a literary forgery, by Ralph D. Paine. Boston and New York, Houghton Mifflin, 1923. lxxxii, 298 p. front. (port. group ).

RATTENBURY, HAROLD BURGOYNE. Understanding China. London, F. Muller [1942] 127 p. illus. (map).

REID, JOHN GILBERT, 1899- The Manchu abdication and the powers, 1908-12; an episode in pre-war diplomacy; a study of the rôle of foreign diplomacy during the reign of Hsüan-T'ung. Berkeley, Calif., University of California Press, 1935. xiii, 497 p. front. (ports.) fold. map.

SIMPSON, BERTRAM LENOX, 1877-1930. Indiscreet letters from Peking; being the notes of an eye-witness, which set forth in some detail, from day to day, the real story of the siege and sack of a distressed capital in 1900--the year of great tribulation; edited by B. L. Putnam Weale [pseud.]. New York, Dodd, Mead, 1922. vii, 447 p. plan.

SO, KWAN-WAI, 蘇均煒 , 1919- Western influences and the Chinese reform movement of 1898. Madison, 1950. i, 269 l. Thesis-Univ. of Wisconsin.

SPECTOR, STANLEY, 1924-  Li Hung-chang and the Huai-chūn. Ann Arbor, University Microfilms [1954] ([University Microfilms, Ann Arbor, Mich.] Publication 7200 ). Collation of the original: xi, 641 l. illus., maps.Thesis-University of Washington.

STEIGER, GEORGE NYE, 1883-  China and the Occident; the origin and development of the Boxer movement. New Haven, Yale University Press; London, H. Milford, Oxford University Press, 1927. xix, 349 p. map.

TAN, CHESTER C., 譚春霖 [T'an, Ch'un-lin ]. The Boxer catastrophe. New York, Columbia University Press; London, Oxford University Press, 1955. ix, 276 p. (Columbia studies in the social sciences, 583 ).

T'AN, YÜN-SHAN, 譚雲山, 1901-  Modern China, a short history, political, economic and social. [Rev. and enl. ed.] Allahabad, Kitabistan [1944] 122 p. (Andhra University ser. 19 ).

THOMSON, HARRY CRAUFUIRD. The case for China. New York, C. Scribner; London, G. Allen and Unwin, 1933. 322 p. illus. (maps).

TYLER, WILLIAM FERDINAND, 1865-  Pulling strings in China. London, Constable, 1929. x, 310 p. front. (port.) illus.(music) fold. maps.

VOSKAMP, C.J. ed. Chinesische Gegensätze, mit einer Vorbemerkung und Randbemerkungen von Fritz Wertheimer. Berlin, Buchhandlung der Berliner Missions-Gesellschaft, 1924. 71 p.

WAITE, CARLETON FREDERICK. Some elements of international military cooperation in the suppression of the 1900 antiforeign rising in China with special reference to the forces of the United States. Los Angeles, University of Southern California Press, 1935. 52 p. (University of Southern California. School of research studies, 12 ).

WANG, S.T. L'histoire anecdotique chinois--sous les Tsing. Pékin, Impr. de la "Politique de Pékin," 1924. 236 p. illus. (Collection de la "Politique de Pékin").

WASHINGTON (STATE) UNIVERSITY. Far Eastern and Russian Institute.Guide to the memorials of seven leading officials of nineteenth-century China. Prepared by the staff of the Modern Chinese History Project. Edited by Chung-li Chang, 張仲禮, and Stanley Spector. Translators: Mort Bobrow [and others] Foreword by Franz Michael. Seattle, University of Washington Press, 1955. xv, 457 p. (University of Washington publication on Asia ).

WRIGHT, MARY CLABAUGH. The T'ung-chih restoration. Cambridge, 195- 589 l. Thesis - Radcliffe College.

———. The last stand of Chinese conservatism; the T'ung-chih restoration, 1862- 74. Stanford, Stanford University Press [1957] x, 426 p. (Stanford studies in history, economics, and political science, 13 ).

Republic
1912-1936

BAKER, JOHN EARL, 1880-1957. Explaining China. London, A.M, Philpot, 1927. xviii, 312 p. incl. tables. front., plates, ports., maps (part double).

BERTRAM, JAMES M. Crisis in China; the story of the Sian mutiny. London, Macmillan, 1937. xxii, 318 p. front., plates, ports.

———. First act in China; the story of the Sian mutiny. New York, Viking Press, 1938. xviii p., 3-284 p. plates, ports.

CASSEVILLE, HENRY. De Chiang Kai Shek à Mao Tse Tung (Chine 1927-50 ). Paris, Charles-Lavauzelle [1950] 191 p. 3 fold. maps.

CHANG, PO-HSÜN, 張伯訓, 1910-  China's revolution, 1911-12, and its foreign relations; a study of the fall of the Manchu Empire and the founding of the Chinese Republic. Washington, 1948. vi, 376 l. Thesis-Georgetown University.

CHEN, FOU-CHOEN, 沈福順 [Shen Fu-shūn]. La révolution chinoise. Paris,

F. Alcan, 1929. 183 p. Thèse-Univ. de Paris.
CHINA. Ministry of Information. A Chinese chronology, 1931-46. London, U.K. office, Chinese Ministry of Information, 1946. 38 p.
THE CHINA PRESS, Shanghai. The silver jubilee of the Republic of China. 1911-October 10, 1936. With the 25th anniversary supplement of the China Press. Shanghai, [China Press, 1936] cover-title, 204 p. illus. (incl ports., map, facsims.) diagrs.
CROW, CARL, 1883-1945. China takes her place. New York and London, Harper [1944] xxi, 282 p.
FINCH, PERCY. Shanghai and beyond. New York, Scribner, 1953. 357 p.
FOSTER, JOHN. Chinese realities. London, Edinburgh House Press, 1928. 240 p. diagr.
GANNES, HARRY, 1900-41. When China unites; an interpretive history of the Chinese revolution. New York, A.A. Knopf, 1937. 3-293, xiii, [1] p. maps (1 fold.).
——. The same; a history of China's struggle for national independence. London, J.M. Dent, 1938. 276 p. including maps.
GANNETT, LEWIS STILES, 1891- Young China. Rev. ed. New York, The Nation [c1927] viii, 55 p. illus.
GILES, HERBERT ALLEN, 1845-1935. Chaos in China. Cambridge [Eng.] W. Heffer, 1924. 43, [1] p.
GLICK, CARL, 1890- Double ten, Captain O'Banion's story of the Chinese revolution. London, New York, Whittlesey House, McGraw-Hill [1945] 3-281 p. front., ports.
GREEN, OWEN MORTIMER. The story of China's revolution. London, New York [etc.] Hutchinson [1945] 240 p. front., plates, ports.
HALL, JOSEF WASHINGTON, 1894- In the land of the laughing Buddha; the adventures of an American barbarian in China, by Upton Close (Josef Washington Hall). New York and London, G.P. Putnam, 1924. xxiii, 359 p. front., plates, port.
HUTCHINSON, PAUL, 1890-1956. What and why in China. Chicago, Willett, Clark and Colby, 1928. 134 p. illus. (maps).
JOHNSTON, SIR REGINALD FLEMING, 1874-1938. Twilight in the Forbidden city. With a preface by the Emperor. London, V. Gollancz, 1934. 486 p. front., illus., plates (part fold.) ports., plans (1 fold.) facsims., geneal. tab.
KOTENEV, ANATOL M. New lamps for old; an interpretation of events in modern China and whither they lead. Shanghai, North-China Daily News and Herald, 1931. 371, [7] p.
KRARUP-NIELSEN, AAGE. The dragon awakes. Authorized translation from the Danish. London, John Lane; New York, Dodd, Mead [1928] xvi, 208 p. front., plates, ports., fold. map.
LA FARGUE, THOMAS EDWARD. China and the world war. Stanford, Stanford University Press; London, H. Milford, Oxford University Press, 1937. x, 278 p. illus. (map) (Hoover war library publications, 12 ).
LATOURETTE, KENNETH SCOTT, 1884- A history of modern China. London, Baltimore, Penguin Books [1954] 233 p. illus. (Pelican books, A302 ).
LATTIMORE, OWEN, 1900- China, a short history, by Owen and Eleanor Lattimore. New York, W.W. Norton [1947] London, Pelican Books. 218 p., illus. (maps).
——. The making of modern China, a short history by Owen and Eleanor Lattimore. Washington, The Infantry Journal [1944] 7-178 p. illus. (maps) (Fighting forces series ).
——. The same. New York, W.W. Norton [1944] 212 p. illus. (maps).
——. The same. London, G. Allen and Unwin [1945] 7-212 p., illus. (maps).
——. La genèse de la Chine moderne, par Owen et Eleanor Lattimore. Paris, Payot, 1946. 156 p. map.(Bibliothèque géographique ).

LOH, PICHON PEI-YUNG, 陸品清. The popular upsurge in China: Nationalism and westernization, 1919-27. Chicago, 1955. 362 l. Thesis-Univ. of Chicago.

MARQUÈS-RIVIÈRE, JEAN. La Chine dans le monde, la révolution chinoise de 1912 à 1935; préface du rév. P.J. de Reviers de Mauny, S.J.; avec dixsept croquis. Paris, Payot, 1935. [7]-284 p. illus. (incl. maps) (Collection d'études, de documents et de témoignages pour servir à l'histoire de notre temps ).

MINKNER-CANTON, EDMUND. Ganz China unter dem Sonnenbanner des Südens. Die Lage im heutigen China. Berlin, Schlieffen-Verlag, 1928. 126 p. illus.

MISSELWITZ, HENRY FRANCIS, 1900- The dragon stirs; an intimate sketchbook of China's Kuomintang revolution, 1927-29. New York, Harbinger House [c1941] 293 p. front.

MOWRER, EDGAR ANSEL, 1892- Mowrer in China, by Edgar Ansel Mowrer; with six maps by Marthe Rajchman. Harmondsworth, Middlesex, Eng., Penguin Books [1938] ix, 11-216 p. illus. (maps).

———. The dragon wakes, a report from China. New York, W. Morrow, 1939. v, [1], 242 p. illus. (maps).

PARK, NO YONG, 鮑納燊, 1899- Making a new China; with an introduction by Honorable Henrik Shipstead. Boston, Stratford Co. [c1929] vii, 308 p.

QUIGLEY, HAROLD SCOTT, 1889- China today, by Harold S. Quigley. Chinese-American collaboration and economic development in China, by Chang Kia-ngau. A talk on Russia, by Eric A. Johnston. The Pope's way to peace, by the Reverend John A. O'Brien. New York, Carnegie Endowment for International Peace, Division of Intercourse and Education [1944] 589-663 p. (Interantional conciliation, October, 1944, no. 404 ).

RASMUSSEN, ALBERT HENRY. Return to the sea. London, Canstable [1956] 207 p. illus.

RODES, JEAN. La Chine nationaliste, 1912-30. Paris, F. Alcan, 1931. v, 193 p. (Les Questions du temps présent ).

ROYAL INSTITUTE OF INTERNATIONAL AFFAIRS. Information dept. Chronology of events in China, 1911-27; with a foreword by Sir Frederick Whyte. London, Association for International Understanding [1928] 46 p.

STANTON, EDWIN F., 1901- Brief authority; excursions of a common man in an uncommon world. New York, Harper [1956] 290 p. illus.

STRONG, ANNA LOUISE, 1885- China's millions. New York, Coward-McCann, 1928. xiv, 413 p. front., plates, ports.

———. The same; the revolutionary struggles from 1927 to 1935, introduction by John Cournos. New York, Knight publishing co., 1935; London, V. Gollancz, 1936. vi, ix-xviii, 457 p. 1st ed. 1928.

———. China-Reise; mit Borodin durch China und die Mongolei aus dem Amerikanischen von Lucie Hecht. Berlin, Neuer Deutscher Verlag, 1928. 214,[2] p. plates, ports.

SÜHL, MARGA. Die Grossmächte und die chinesische Revolution bis zum Ausbruch des ersten Weltkrieges. Kiel, 1944. 115 p. illus. Diss.-Univ. Kiel.

T'ANG, LEANG-LI, 湯良禮, 1901- The inner history of the Chinese revolution. London, G. Routledge, 1930. xv, 391 p.

TÉRY, SIMONE. Fièvre jaune (la Chine convulsée). Paris, E. Flammarion [1928] xii p., [15]-294 p.

TSE, TSAN-TAI, 謝纘泰, 1872-193? The Chinese republic; secret history of the revolution. Hong Kong, South China Morning Post, 1924. ii, 30 p. port.

TYLER, WILLIAM FERDINAND, 1865- Pulling strings in China. London, Constable, 1929. x, 310 p. front.(port.) illus. (music) fold. maps.

VAIDYA, KESHAV BALKRISHNA, 1896- Reflections of the recent Canton revolt and after. Canton, K.B. Vaidya for National Pub. Ltd. [1936] 34, 36 p. plates, ports., facsims.

VALENTIN, FERDINAND. L'avènement d'une république; luttes intérieures de la Chine de 1911 à 1923. Paris, Perrin et Cie, 1926. ii, 316 p.

VAN DORN, HAROLD ARCHER, 1896-  Twenty years of the Chinese republic;
two decades of progress. New York, A.A. Knopf, 1932. xiv, 309, vii,[1] p.
plates, map, diagr.
VANLANDE, RENÉ. Souvenirs de la révolution chinoise. Paris, J. Peyronnet,
1928. 64 p. (Collection Les clochers de France, [24] ).
WOODHEAD, HENRY GEORGE WANDESFORDE, 1883-  The truth about the
Chinese Republic. London, Hurst and Blackett [1925] 287 p. front. (port.).

1937-

ABEGG, LILY, 1901-  Chinas Erneuerung, der Raum als Waffe.  Frankfurt a.
M., Societäts-Verlag [c1940] 481, [3] p. 32 plates (incl. ports.) on 16 l., 2
maps on fold. 1. (in pocket ).
ALCOTT, CARROLL DUARD, 1901-  My war with Japan. New York, H. Holt
[1943] 368 p.
ANDERSSON, JOHAN GUNNAR, 1874-  China fights for the world. London, K.
Paul, Trench, Trubner and co. ltd. [1939] xiii, 272 p. illus., XVI plates
(incl. front.(port.) ) fold. map.
AUDEN, WYSTAN HUGH, 1907-  Journey to a war, by W.H. Auden and Christopher Isherwood. New York, Random House [c1939] 13-301 p. front. plates,
ports.
BERTRAM, JAMES M. North China front. London, Macmillan, 1939. xvi, 514
p. front., plates, ports.
———. Unconquered. Journal of a year's adventures among the fighting peasants
of north China. New York, John Day [c1939]  ix,  3-340 p. front. (port.)
plates.
BISSON, THOMAS ARTHUR, 1900-  Japan in China. New York, Macmillan,
1938. 417 p. plates, ports., maps (incl. fold. front.).
BISWAS, RAMNATH. China defies death. [Calcutta, Madhabendra Mitter, for
the Paryatak Prakasana Bhawan, 1944] 176 p.
BOOKER, EDNA LEE. News is my job; a correspondent in war-torn China. New
York, Macmillan, 1940.  xii,  375 p. front., plates, ports.
———. Flight from China, by Edna Lee Booker, in collaboration with John S.
Potter. Decorations by Peggy Bacon. New York, Macmillan, 1945. x p.,
236 p. incl. front., illus.
CARLSON, EVANS FORDYCE, 1896-  Twin stars of China, a behind-the-scenes
story of China's valiant struggle for existence, by a U.S. marine who lived
and moved with the people; illustrated from photographs taken by the author.
New York, Dodd, Mead, 1940.  xiv,  331 p. front., plates, ports.
CHESTER, WILFRED L. China at bay. Shanghai [etc. ] Kelly and Walsh, 1938.
214 p.
CHIANG, NEWTON, 蔣翼振, 1900-  On foot to freedom; a diary of experiences
during the Sino-Japanese war. With an introduction by Douglas N. Sargent.
New York, Friendship Press [1945] 48 p. front. (group port.) illus., map.
CHINA INFORMATION COMMITTEE. China after four years of war, prepared
under the auspices of the China information committee, Chungking.  Chung-
king, The China Pub. Co., 1941. iv, [2], 182 p.
CHINA. Consulate. San Francisco. Pacific coast press opinion of the fifth anniversary of China's war with Japan. Compiled by the consulate-general of the
Republic of China, San Francisco, California, U.S.A. [San Francisco, 1942]
63 p. illus. (incl. port.).
———. Ministry of Information. China after five years of war. Prepared under
the auspices of the Ministry of information of the Republic of China. New
York, Chinese News Service [1942] iv, 233, v-vii p.
———. The same; with a preface by Dr. V.K. Wellington Koo. London, V. Gol-
lancz, 1943. 230 p. illus. (map) plates, port., 2 fold. maps.
———. China after five years of war series. [Chungking, China Pub. Co., 1942]

19 nos.

———. China's fifth war anniversary, a collection of articles, messages, speeches and comments. Chungking, 1942. cover-title, iv, 86 p.

———. China after seven years of war. Chungking, Chinese Ministry of Information [1944] 157 p.

———. The same, by Hawthorne Cheng, 鄭鈞, Samuel M. Chao, 趙敏求, Chu Fu-sung, 朱撫松 [and others]; edited by Hollington K. Tong, 董顯光. New York, Macmillan, 1945. 246 p. plates.

———. Into the eighth year; messages and articles commemorating seven years of China's continuous resistance to aggression. With a foreword by V.K. Wellington Koo. London, Chinese Ministry of Information, 1945. 78 p. illus.

THE CHINA PRESS, Shanghai. China today, a special supplement issued on the occasion of the 28th anniversary of the founding of the Republic of China. Shanghai, 1939. cover-title, 66 p. incl. illus., ports.

EKINS, HERBERT ROSLYN, 1901-   China fights for her life, by H.R. Ekins and Theon Wright. New York, London, Whittlesey House, McGraw-Hill Book Co. [c1938] xix, 335 p. plates, ports.

EPSTEIN, ISRAEL, 1915-   The people's war; with six full-page woodcuts carved specially for this book by Chen Yin-chiao. London, V. Gollancz, 1939. 384 p. incl. front., illus.

FARMER, FRANCIS RHODES. Shanghai harvest, a diary of three years in the China war. London, Museum Press [1945] 294 p. illus. (map) plates, ports.

FITCH, GERALDINE. Blunder out of China; a commentary on the White-Jacoby book. [New York, American China Policy Assn., 1947?] 32 p.

GOULD, RANDALL. Chungking today. Shanghai, The Mercury Press, 1941. 11-97 p. plates, group port.

HALL, RONALD OWEN, bp., 1895-   China's fight for freedom. [London, Odhams Press, 1943?] cover-title, 48 p. illus. (incl. ports., maps).

HANSON, HALDORE E. "Humane endeavour"; the story of the China war. New York, Toronto, Farrar and Rinehart [c1939] x, 390 p. front. illus. (map).

HSIAO, CH'IEN, 蕭乾, 1911-   China but not Cathay. London, Pilot Press [1942] viii, 135, [1] p. incl. front., illus. fold. map.

I-FENG, 易風, pseud. Give back my rivers and hills!   還我河山. Translated from the Chinese by Innes Jackson. London, Macmillan, 1945. xviii, 135, [1] p. front., plates.

K'UNG, HSIANG-HSI, 孔祥熙, 1881-   China's wartime progress. Chungking, The China Information Committee, 1939. cover-title, 18 p.

LAMOTT, WILLIS, 1893-   The amazing Chinese. New York, Friendship Press, c1940. 48, [1] p. front., illus.

LEONARD, ROYAL. I flew for China. Garden City, N.Y., Doubleday, Doran, 1942. xx, 295 p.

LIN, ADET, 林無雙, 1923-   Dawn over Chungking [by] Adet, Anor, 林如斯, and Meimei Lin, 林相如. New York, John Day [c1941] 3-240 p.

LIN, YU-T'ANG, 林玉堂, 1895-   The vigil of a nation. New York, John Day [1944]; Toronto, Longmans, Green, 1945; London, Heinemann, 1946. vii, [2], 262 p. illus. (map) plates, ports.

MAURER, HERRYMON, 1914-   The end is not yet; China at war. New York, Robert M. McBride [c1941]; London, Toronto, W Heinemann, 1942. 11-321 p.

MUNDAY, MADELEINE CONSTANCE. Rice bowl broken. London, New York [etc.] Hutchinson [1945?] 139 p. front., plates.

NOLDE, ANDRÉ. La Chine de Chiang Kaï Chek. Paris, Corrêa [1946] [7]-196 p., 2 l. incl. front. (map).

ON KIN, U. China as a Burman saw it. Rangoon, American Baptist Mission Press, 1939. vii, 63 p. illus. (incl. group port.).

PAYNE, PIERRE STEPHEN ROBERT, 1911-   China awake. New York, Dodd, Mead [1947] ix, 424 p. map (on lining-papers).

PRICE, FRANCIS WILSON, 1895-   China, twilight or dawn?  New York, Friend-

ship Press [1948] vi, 184 p. fold. col. map.
SAMSON, GERALD. Warning lights of Asia. London, R. Hale [1940] 317 p.
front., illus. (maps) plates, ports.
——. The Far East ablaze. [London] H. Joseph [1945] 183 p. illus. (maps )
plates, ports.
SANDISON, ALEXANDER, 1885-   Escape into activities. The flight into nor-
mality. Discipline and leadership. China under war conditions. [By] Drs. A.
Sandison, R. Hargreaves, H. Crichton-Miller, and F. M. Edwards. October,
1940. London, C. W. Daniel [1940] 47, [1] p. (Individual psychology medi-
cal pamphlets, 22 ).
SCHENKE, WOLF. Reise an der gelben Front; Beobachtungen eines deutschen
Kriegsberichterstatters in China, mit 24 Abbildungen auf Kunstdrucktafeln
nach Aufnahmen des Verfassers sowie 2 Karten. Oldenburg i. O., G. Stalling
.[1940] 336 p. illus., ports., maps (on lining papers).
SMEDLEY, AGNES, 1890-1950. Battle hymn of China. New York, A. A. Knopf,
London, V. Gollancz, 1944. 7-365 p. fold. map.
SNOW, EDGAR, 1905-  Scorched earth. London, V. Gollancz, 1941. 396 p.
——. The battle for Asia. New York, Random House [c1941] xii, 431 p. illus.
(map) plates, ports.
——. The same. Cleveland and New York, The World Pub. Co. [1942] ix, 431 p.
SOUTH MANCHURIA RAILWAY COMPANY. Information and Publicity Dept.
North China in transition. [Tokyo? 1938] cover-title, 23 p. plates. (China
incident series, 6 ).
STEWART, MAXWELL SLUTZ, 1900-  War-time China. New York, San Fran-
cisco [etc.] American Council, Institute of Pacific Relations, 1944. 63 p.
illus. (incl. ports., maps). (I. P. R. pamphlets, 10 ).
STRONG, ANNA LOUISE, 1885-  One-fifth of mankind. New York, Modern Age
Books [c1938] 215 p. incl. front. (map).
——. China fights for freedom. [London] L. Drummond [1939] viii, [2], 231 p.
incl. front. (map) 1 illus.
SUBILIA, JEAN DANIEL. La Chine qui bouillonne. Genève, Éditions "Labor,"
1941. iv, xx, 272 p. plates, illus. map.
——. Gärendes China. Übersetzung von Guy Sylwan und Karl Huber. Zürich,
Verlag der Ostasienmission, 1943. 216, [2] p. plates.
TAYLOR, GEORGE EDWARD, 1905-  The struggle for north China. New York,
International Secretariat, Institute of Pacific Relations, 1940. xiv, 250 p.
illus. (map) diagr. (I. P. R. inquiry series).
TONG, HOLLINGTON KONG, 董顯光 , 1887-  China and the world press. [n. p.,
1948] 282 p.
UNITED SERVICE TO CHINA. What Li Wen saw. New York, United China re-
lief [1941?] 31, [1] p. illus., diagr.
URACH, ALBRECHT, fürst, 1903-  Ostasien, Kampf um das kommende Gross-
reich. Berlin, Steiniger-Verlage; Verlagsabteilung R. Hobbing [1940] 191,
[5] p. illus. (maps) plates, ports.
UTLEY, FREDA. China at war. London, Faber and Faber [1939] xv, 306 p.
incl. front. (port.) plates, ports., fold. map.
VAIDYA, KESHAV BALKRISHNA, 1896-  The secret of China's resistance. Ka-
rachi, Educational Pub. Co., 1943. 2, 164 p. [His The Un-Pacific series, 2].
WARTIME China, as seen by westerners. Chungking, China Pub. Co. [pref.
1942] iv, [2], 319 p. diagrs.
WHITE, THEODORE HAROLD, 1915-  Thunder out of China [by] Theodore H.
White and Annalee Jacoby. New York, William Sloane Associates [1946];
London, V. Gollancz, 1947. xvi, 331 p. maps.
——. Donner aus China, von Theodore White und Annalee Jacoby. Aus dem A-
merikanischen von Barbara Doyle-Reck. Stuttgart, Hamburg, Baden-Baden,
Rowohlt Verlag; Zürich, Wien, Europa Verlag, 1949. 373 p.

# V. BIOGRAPHY

## General

ALLAN, CHARLES WILFRID, 1870-   Makers of Cathay, 3rd ed.   Shanghai, Kelly and Walsh, 1936. vi p., 363 p. 1st ed. 1909; 2d ed. 1925.

AMERICAN UNIVERSITY CLUB OF SHANGHAI. American university men in China, published by the American University Club of Shanghai. Shanghai, Comacrib Press, 1936. iii-xii, 233 p. plates.

CHINA. Ministry of Information. Chinese Who's Who. Chungking, Chinese Ministry of Information, 1943. cover-title, 75 p. (China Handbook ser. 23 ).

The CHINA who's who (foreign). ed. by Carroll Lunt. A biographical dictionary 1922-   Shanghai, Union Printing and Service Agency, 1922-   v. ports. annual.

COMMERCIAL PRESS. Chung-kuo jen-ming ta tz'u-tien. (Indexes) A romanized index to the surnames in the Chinese biographical dictionary. Chung-kuo jen-ming ta tz'u-tien, compiled by M. Jean Gates. Washington, D.C., Priv. print., 1942. cover-title, 32 p.

GILLIS, IRVIN VAN GORDER, 1875-1948. comp. Supplementary index to Giles' "Chinese biographical dictionary," compiled by I.V. Gillis and Yü Ping-yüeh, 于炳耀 . Peiping, 1936. [88] p.

The GREAT international golden book of Peiping; a unique collection of portraits of well-known members of the diplomatic corps, administrators, military and navy officers [and others] Peiping, A. Yourieff, 1933. 1 v. (unpaged ) ports.

HARVARD UNIVERSITY. Committee on International and Regional Studies. Biographies of Kuomintang leaders. Cambridge, Mass., 1948. 3 v. Mimeographed.

KUO, HELENA, 郭鏡秋. Giants of China; illustrated by Woodi Ishmael. New York, E.P. Dutton, 1944. 254 p. illus.

LLEWELLYN, BERNARD, 1919-   China's courts and concubines: some people in Chinese history; illustrated by Pauline Diana Baynes. London, G. Allen and Unwin, 1956. 214 p. illus.

LY HOI-SANG, 黎海生 , 1870-1944. Illustrious prime ministers of China, their ancient manners, customs and philosophies, a symphony of the spheres, by Ly Hoi Sang and Richard Alexander. [New York, Printed by Manger, Hughes and Manger, c1928] [vii]-xii, 13-108 numb. 1., 6 1. incl. illus., ports. front.

MARTIN, BERNARD, 1897-   The strain of harmony; men and women in the history of China. London, W. Heinemann [1948] xii, 187 p. plates, ports.

MAYERS, WILLIAM FREDERICK, 1831-78. The Chinese reader's manual; a handbook of biographical, historical, mythological, and general literary reference. Reprinted from the original edition. Shanghai, Presbyterian Mission Press, 1924. xvi, 444 p. 1st ed. 1874. First reprint ed. 1910.

NELLIST, GEORGE FERGUSON MITCHELL, 1889-   ed. Men of Shanghai and North China; a standard biographical reference work. Shanghai, Oriental Press, 1933. 516 p. incl. ports.

NORTH, ROBERT CARVER, 1914-   Kuomintang and Chinese communist elites, by Robert C. North with the collaboration of Ithiel de Sola Pool. Introd. by John K. Fairbank. [Stanford] Stanford University Press, 1952. vii, 130 p. maps, tables. (Hoover Institute studies. Series B: Elite studies, 8).

PANKING. Les chevaliers chinois. Pékin, Impr. de la "Politique de Pékin,"

1922. 220 p. (Collection de la "Politique de Pékin").

PERLEBERG, MAX, 1900-  Who's who in modern China (from the beginning of the Chinese Republic to the end of 1953) Over 2000 detailed biographies of the most important men who took part in the great struggle for China, including detailed histories of the political parties, government organisations, a glossary of new terms used in contemporary Chinese together with a double index in Chinese and English and two charts.  Hong Kong, Ye Olde Printerie, 1954. xii, 428 p. col. illus., 2 diagrs.

U.S. Library of Congress. Orientalia division.  Some eminent Chinese of the seventeenth century; twenty-two biographies from a proposed dictionary of Ch'ing dynasty biography; Arthur W. Hummel, editor.  Baltimore, Md., Waverly Press, 1936. vi, 21 p.

————. Eminent Chinese of the Ch'ing period (1644-1912) Edited by Arthur W. Hummel. Washington, Govt. Print. Off., 1943-44. 2 v.

WALKER, MERLE R. Contemporary Chinese leaders, brief sketches.  New York, China Society of America (inc.) 1922. 31 p. (China society pamphlets, 3 ).

WEIG, JOHANN. Die chinesischen Familiennamen nach dem Büchlein. [Bei dja sing, 百家姓 ] nebst Anhang enthaltend Angaben über berühmte Persönlichkeiten der chinesischen Geschichte. Tsingtau, Missionsdruckerei, 1931.[v]- x, 285 p. illus., 2 port. on 1 l.

WHO'S Who in China. Shanghai, China Weekly Review, 1918-50. 1st ed. 1918; 2d. ed. 1920; 3d. ed. 1926; Supplement, 1928; 4th ed. 1931; Supplement,1933; 5th ed., 1936; Supplement, 1940; 6th ed., 1950.

WU, EUGENE, 吳文津, 1922-  Leaders of twentieth entury China; an annotated bibliography of selected Chinese biographical works in the Hoover Library. Stanford, Stanford University Press, 1956. vii, 106 p. (Hoover Institute and Library. Bibliographical series, 4 ).

## Special
## 19th Century

BALES, WILLIAM LESLIE, 1893-  Tso Tsung-t'ang, 左宗棠, soldier and statesman of old China.  Shanghai, Kelly and Walsh, 1937. xvi, 436 p.front., illus. (maps), ports.

CHEN, GIDEON, 陳其田. [Ch'en, Ch'i-t'ien]  Lin Tse-hsü, 林則徐, pioneer promoter of the adoption of western means of maritime defense in China. Peiping, Department of Economics, Yenching University, 1934. vi, 65 p. front. (port.), illus., plates. (Modern industrial technique in China: part 1 ).

————. Tseng Kuo-fan, 曾國藩, pioneer promoter of the steamship in China. Peiping, Department of Economics, Yenching University, 1935. 98 p. front. illus., plates, ports., facsims. (Modern industrial technique in China: part 2 ).

————. Tso Tsung-t'ang, 左宗棠, pioneer promoter of the modern dockyard and the woollen mill in China.  Peiping, Department of Economics, Yenching University [1938] v, 93 p. front., illus., plates, ports. (Modern industrial technique in China : part 3 ).

HAIL, WILLIAM JAMES. Tsêng Kuo-fan and the Taiping rebellion, with a short sketch of his later career.  New Haven, Yale University Press; London, H. Milford, Oxford University Press, 1927. xvii, 422 p. maps. (Yale historical publications. Miscellany, XVIII ).

## Tz'ŭ-Hsi

BLAND, JOHN OTWAY PERCY, 1863-1945. comp. China under the empress dowager, being the history of the life and times of Tz'ŭ hsi, compiled from state papers and the private diary of the comptroller of her household, by J.

O. P. Bland and E. Backhouse. Peking, H. Vetch, 1939. xxiii, [2], 470 p., front., plates (1 col.) ports., 2 fold. maps, 2 facsim. (1 col.).

BACKHOUSE, SIR EDMUND TRELAWNEY, 1873-1944. Les empereurs Mandchous; mémoires de la cour de Pékin. Traduction de L. M. Mitchell. Préface de m. Henri Maspero. Paris, Payot, 1934. [7]-329, [1] p. (Bibliothèque historique ).

CABANEL, FERNANDE. La dernière impératrice; vie de l'impératrice de Chine, Tseu-hi (1835-1909) Paris, La Nouvelle société d'édition[1936] [7]-219 p.

COLLIS, MAURICE, 1889- New sources for the life of the Empress Dowager Tz'ŭ Hsi; a lecture delivered before the China Society on March 21st, 1944. London, China Society, 1944. cover-title, 8 p.

DER LING, 德齡公主, princess. Old Buddha. New York, Dodd, Mead, 1928. xviii, 347 p. front., plates, ports.

——. Imperial incense; illustrations by Bertha Lumm. New York, Dodd, Mead, 1933. ix p., 267 p. col. front., illus., col. plates.

HUSSEY, HARRY, 1882- Venerable ancestor; the life and times of Tz'ŭ hsi, 1835-1908, Empress of China. Garden City, N. Y., Doubleday, 1949. xix, 354 p. illus.

VARÈ, DANIELE, 1880-1956. The last of the empresses and the passing from the old China to the new. London, J. Murray [1936] xiii, 258 p. front.(port.) illus. (incl. plan) plates.

——. The last empress. New York, Doubleday, Doran, 1936. xvii, 320 p. front. (port.) illus. (incl. plan) plates.

——. The same. Garden City, N. Y., The Sun Dial Press [1938, c1936] xvi, 320 p. front., illus. (incl. plan) plates, port.

——. Die latzte Kaiserin. Vom alten zum neuen China. Übers. aus dem Englischen. Wien, Erasmus-Verlag, 1952. 264 p.

WU, YUNG, 吳永. The flight of an empress, told by Wu Yung, whose other name is Yü-ch'uan,漁川 ; transcribed by Liu K'un, 劉昆; translated and edited by Ida Pruitt; introduction by Kenneth Scott Latourette. New Haven, Yale University Press, 1936. xxiii, 222 p. plates, port., map.

## 20th Century
## Sun Yat-sen

AMANN, GUSTAV, 1882- Sun Yatsens Vermächtnis; Geschichte der chinesischen Revolution; mit Vorworten von Karl Haushofer und Engelbert Krebs. Berlin-Grunewald, K. Vowinckel, 1928. xxvi, 270, [1] p. front., plates, ports., 2 maps.

——. The legacy of Sun Yatsen; a history of the Chinese revolution; with prefaces by Karl Haushofer and Engelbert Krebs, translated from the German by Frederick Philip Grove. New York and Montreal, L. Carrier [c1929] xii, 302 p. front., plates, ports.

BAKER, NINA (BROWN), 1888- Sun Yat-sen. Ilustrations by Jeanyee Wong,黃 如珍 . New York, Vanguard Press [1946] 247 p. illus.

BUCK, PEARL (SYDENSTRICKER), 1892- The man who changed China: the story of Sun Yat-sen; illustrated by Fred Castellon. New York, Random House [1953] 185 p. illus. (World landmark books, W-9 ).

BURCHETT, GEORGE HAROLD. Building China's republic: epic of vision, valour, victory. Father of the republic Dr. Sun Yat-sen, man of vision and action, by George Harold Burchett and Winston Harold Burchett. Melbourne, Australia-China Cooperation Association, 1943. cover-title, 16 p.

CHAN, WILHELM, 1906- Der Einfluss der Gedankengänge von dr. Sun Yat Sen auf die Entwicklung der Sozialpolitik Chinas. Berlin-Charlottenburg, Gebrüder Hoffmann, 1931. 89, [1] p.

CHEN, STEPHEN, 程錫藩 . Sun Yat-sen, a portrait by Stephen Chen and Robert Payne. New York, John Day [1946] 242 p. front. (port.).

CHIANG, MONLIN, 蔣夢麟, 1886- Sun Yatsen on international cooperation: On international development of China by Chiang Monlin. On Sino-Japanese relations, by Hollington K. Tong. Taipei, Cultural Pub. Foundation, 1953. 15 p. (Pamphlet on Chinese affairs ).

CHU, CHI-HSIEN, 朱啓賢, 1911- A study of the development of Sun Yat-sen's philosophical ideas. Ann Arbor, University Microfilms, 1950. ([University Microfilms, Ann Arbor, Mich.] Publication no. 1837 ). Collation of the original: 233, 12, [3] 1. Thesis-Columbia University.

HALL, JOSEF WASHINGTON, 1894- Eminent Asians; six great personalities of the new East, by "Upton Close." Portrait drawings of Orré Nobles. New York and London, D. Appleton, 1929. 3-510, [1] p. incl. ports. front.

HERRFAHRDT, HEINRICH, 1890- Sun Yatsen; der Vater des neuen China; ein Beispiel westöstlicher Begegnung. Hamburg, Drei-Türme-Verlag [c1948 ] 239 p.

HUNG JAIR. Les idées économiques de Sun Yat Sen. Toulouse, Impr. F. Boisseau, 1934. 197, [2] p. diagrs. Thèse-Univ. de Toulouse.

JAHN, WERNER. Der Einfluss Sun Yatsens auf die verfassungsrechtliche Entwicklung Chinas. Marburg, 1948. vi, 58 l. Diss.-Univ. Marburg.

JANSEN, MARIUS B. The Japanese and Sun Yat-sen. Cambridge, Harvard University Press, 1954; London, Oxford University Press, 1955. viii, 274 p. group port., facsims. (Harvard historical monographs, 27 ).

[KUO MIN TANG]. Dr. Sun Yat-sen, his life and achievements; published under the auspices of the Publicity department of the Central Executive Committee. [Shanghai] Shanghai Mercury [192- ] [3]-71 p. plates, ports.

LEE, EDWARD BING-SHUEY, 李炳瑞, 1903-56. Dr. Sun Yat-sen's life and principles. Peiping, Leader Press [1931] vii, 43 p. incl. plates, port.

LI, CHAO-WEI, 李肇偉. La souveraineté nationale d'après la doctrine politique de Sun-Yet-sin. Dijon, Impr. du Palais, M. Pornon, 1934. [5]-153, [1] p. Thèse-Univ. de Dijon.

LI, TI-TSUN, 李迪俊, 1901- The political and economic theories of Sun Yat-sen. Madison, Wis., 1929. 203 p., 25 numb. l. Thesis-University of Wisconsin.

LINEBARGER, PAUL MYRON ANTHONY, 1913- The political doctrines of Sun Yat-sen; an exposition of the San min chu i. Baltimore, The Johns Hopkins Press, 1937. xiv, 278 p. (Johns Hopkins university studies in historical and political science. Extra volumes. New ser., 24 ).

LINEBARGER, PAUL MYRON WENTWORTH, 1871-1939. Sun Yat Sen and the Chinese republic. New York and London, Century [c1925] xviii, 371 p.front., plates, ports.

———. The gospel of Chung Shan, according to Paul Linebarger, edited with introduction and comment by Paul Myron Anthony Linebarger. Paris, Comité général executif du Kuomintang en Europe. For sale at Brentano's, 1932. 263, [1] p. illus. (incl. ports., facsims.).

———. Gegensätze und Aehnlichkeiten zwischen Sun Yat Sens "San min chi i" und dem deutschen National-Sozialismus, mit Anekdoten von Sun Yat Sen. Washington, D. C., Éditions Mid-nation [1937] 39 p.

———. The ocean men; an allegory of the Sun Yat-sen revolutions; edited with an introduction by P. M. Anthony Linebarger. Washington, D. C., Mid-nation editions, c1937. 67 p.

———. La Chine et la Judée, trop vieilles pour mourir; une esquisse des révolutions de Sun Yat-sen. Washington, D. C., Éditions Mid-nation [1937] 64 p.

———. Livret-questionnaire pour les étudiants sur les doctrines politiques de Sun Yat-sen, d'après The political dictrines of Sun Yat-sen - an expostition of the San min chu i. Washington, D. C., Éditions Mid-nation [1937] 30 p.

———. Mes mémoires abrégés sur les révolutions de Sun Yat-sen. Paris, Éditions Mid-nation, 1938. 201, [1] p., port.

MARTIN, BERNARD, 1897- Strange vigour, a biography of Sun Yat-sen. London, W. Heinemann [1944] xii, 248 p. port.

RESTARICK, HENRY BOND, bp., 1854-1933. Sun Yat Sen, liberator of China, with a preface by Kenneth Scott Latourette. New Haven, Yale University Press; London, H. Milford, Oxford University Press, 1931. xvii, 167 p. front., plates, ports.

————. Sun Yat-sen, libérateur de la Chine. Traduction de R. -Ch. Duval. Paris, Payot, 1932. 198 p. (Bibliothèque historique ).

"SAGGITARIUS," pseud. The strange apotheosis of Sun Yat-sen. London,Heath, Cranton [1939] 189, [2] p.

SHARMAN, LYON, 1872-  Sun Yat-sen, his life and its meaning; a critical biography. New York, John Day [c1934] xvii, 418 p. front. (port.).

SOULIÉ, CHARLES GEORGES, 1878-  Soun Iat-Sènn, par George Soulié de Morant. Paris, Gallimard [1931] 223, [1] p. incl. front. (port.).

SUN, YAT-SEN, 孫中山 , 1866-1925. Memoirs of a Chinese revolutionary, a programme of national reconstruction for China, with a frontispiece portrait of the author. London, Hutchinson [1927] 254 p. front.(port.) 1st ed. 1918.

————. The same. Taipei, China Cultural Service, 1953. ix, 206 p.

————. Souvenirs d'un révolutionnaire chinois. Préf. de H.G. Chiu, 丘漢興 , adapté du chinois par E. Dalter. [Paris ] Éditions de la Nouvelle revue critique [1933] 221 p.

————. Aufzeichnungen eines chinesischen Revolutionärs, hrsg. und eingeleitet durch eine Darstellung der Entwicklung Sun Yat Sens und des Sun-Yat-Senismus von K.A. Wittfogel. Wien, Agis-Verlag [1927?] 344 p.

————. 30 Jahre chinesische Revolution, ins deutsche Übertragen von Tsan Wan, 萬燦 . Berlin, Schlieffen-Verlag, 1927. 88 p.

————. Sun Yat-sen, his political and social ideals; a source book, compiled, translated and annotated by Leonard Shihlien Hsü, 許仕廉 . Los Angeles, University of Southern California Press [c1933] xxiii, 505 p. incl. front.(port.) diagrs.

————. The teachings of Sun Yat-sen; selections from his writings, compiled and introduced by Professor N. Gangulee. Foreword by Dr. V.K. Wellington Koo. London, Sylvan Press [1945] ix-xl, 132 p., incl. front.(port.) 1 illus.,diagr.

————. 10 letters of Sun Yat-sen, 1914-16. Stanford, Stanford University Libraries, 1942. 58 p. front. (port.).

————. Sun Yat-sen: commemorative album. Peking, 1956. 17 p. port. plates.

TAI, CHI-T'AO, 戴季陶 , 1890-1949. Die geistigen Grundlagen des Sun Yat Senismus, mit einer Systemtabelle der Philosophie des Volkslebens. Berlin, Lankwitz, Würfel Verlag, 1931. 93 p. table.

TCHENG, CHAO-YUEN, 陳紹源 [Ch'en, Shao-yüan]. L'évolution de la vie constitutionelle de la Chine, sous l'influence de Sun Yat Sen et de sa doctrine (1885-1937). Paris, Librairie générale de droit et de jurisprudence, 1937. 190 p. diagrs. Thèse-Univ. de Dijon.

TSUI, SHU-CHIN, 崔書琴 , 1906-57. Influence of the Canton-Moscow entente upon Sun Yat-sen's political philosophy. Cambridge, 1933. 292 1. Thesis - Harvard University.

WILLIAM, MAURICE. Sun Yat-sen versus communism; new evidence establishing China's right to the support of democratic nations. Baltimore, Williams and Wilkins, 1932. xx, 232 p. diagr.

WOU, SAO-FONG, 吳秀峯 , 1898-  Sun Yat-sen, sa vie et sa doctrine; étude historique, philosophique, juridique, politique, économique et sociale. Paris, Les Presses universitaires de France, 1929. 219 p.

ZOLOTOW, MAURICE, 1913-  Maurice William and Sun Yat-sen. London, R. Hale [1948] 128 p. ports.

## Chiang Kai-shek

AMANN, GUSTAV, 1882-  Chiang Kaishek und die Regierung der Kuomintang in

China. II., vom verfasser ergänzte Aufl. Heidelberg, K. Vowinckel, 1939.
viii, 240 p. incl. front. (facsim.) illus. plates, ports., fold. map. (His Geschichte Chinas in neuester zeit, bd. II ). 1. Aufl. 1936.

————. Bauernkrieg in China; Chiang Kaisheks Kampf gegen den Aufstand, 1932-
35. Heidelberg, K. Vowinckel, 1939. 157, [1] p. plates, port. maps (1 fold.).
(His Geschichte Chinas in neuester zeit. Bd. III ).

BERKOV, ROBERT. Strong man of China; the story of Chiang Kai-shek. Boston, Houghton Mifflin, 1938. xv, 288 p. front., ports.

The BIG four: Churchill, Roosevelt, Stalin [and] Chiang Kai-shek, by Vernon
Bartlett, Emil Ludwig, Marshal Voroshilov and S. I. Hsiung, 熊式一. London,
Practical Press [1943] 32 p. (To-day's booklets, ed. by M. Grindea ).

BURBIDGE, WILLIAM FRANK. Rising China; a brief history of China and a biographical sketch of Generalissimo and Madame Chiang Kai-shek. [Bognor
Regis, London, J. Crowther, 1943 ] 40 p. front. (group port.).

CHANG, HSIN-HAI, 張歆海, 1898-  Chiang Kai-shek, Asia's man of destiny.
Garden City, New York, Doubleday, Doran, 1944. xv, 357 p. ports.

————. Tschiang Kai Schek, Chinas grosser mann. "Aus dem Englischen übersetzt von N. O. Scarpi [pseud. ]" [Zürich, Büchergilde Gutenberg, 1945]
360 p. plates, ports.

CH'EN, PU-LAI, 陳布雷, 1890-1948. Chronology of President Chiang Kai-shek,
edited by Ch'en Pu-lai [and] Tang Cheng-chu, 唐振楚. Translated by Sampson C. Shen, 沈錡. Taipei, Chinese Cultural Service, 1954. 82 p. (Pamphlet on Kuomintang affairs ).

CH'EN, TSUNG-HSI, 陳宗熙. General Chiang Kai-shek: the builder of new China, by Chen Tsung-hsi, Wang An-tsiang, 王鸞祥, and Wang I-ting, 王翼廷.
Shanghai, Commercial Press, 1929. x, [3]-107 p. front., ports., map,
facsim.

CLARK, ELMER TALMAGE, 1886-  The Chiangs of China. New York, Abingdon-Cokesbury Press [1943] 123 p. front., plates, ports., facsim.

HAHN, EMILY, 1905-  Chiang Kai-shek, an unauthorized biography. [1st ed. ]
Garden City, N. Y., Doubleday, 1955. 382 p.

HEDIN, SVEN ANDERS,1865-1952.Chiang Kai-shek, marshal of China, translated
from the Swedish by Bernard Norbelie. New York, John Day [c1940] xiv,
290 p. illus. (map) plates, ports.

L'HOMME providentiel de la Chine. [Chungking, Le Correspondant chinois,
1940] cover-title, 7, [1] p. ports.

HSIUNG, SHIH-I, 熊式一, 1902-  The life of Chiang Kai-shek. London, P. Davies [1948] xvii, 398 p. illus., ports., maps (on lining papers).

LIN, TSIU-SEN,     . Chiang Kai-shek, Erneuerer und Einiger Chinas.
Zürich, Chinas Kulturdienst, 1943. iv, 54 p. (Schriften des chinesischen
Kultur-Dienstes ).

MARBACH, OTTO, 1901-  Marschall Chiang Kai-shek und Frau, zwei Führer-
gestalten im Fernen Osten. Bern, P. Haupt, 1938. 112 p.

MATHEWS, BASEL JOSEPH, 1879-  Wings over China (Generalissimo and Madame Chiang Kai-shek). New York, Friendship Press, 1940. Melbourne,
Book Depot, 1942. 20 p. (Eagle books, 25 ).

MILLER, BASIL WILLIAM, 1897-  Generalissimo and Madame Chiang Kai-
shek, Christian liberators of China. Grand Rapids, Mich., Zondervan Pub.
House [1943] 157 p.

OWEN, FRANK, 1905-  Our ally China, the story of a great people and its man
of destiny, Chiang Kai-shek. London, W. H. Allen, 1942. 63 p.

PANETH, PHILIP. The Generalissimo Chiang Kai-shek. London, J. Bale and
Staples [c1943] [7]-79 p.

————. Chiang Kai-shek carries on. London, Alliance Press [1944] 155, [1] p.
incl. front. (port.).

REASON, JOYCE, 1894-  Chiang Kai-shek and the unity of China. London, Edinburgh House Press, 1943. 79, [1] p. illus. (map).

REYNOLDS, ERNEST EDWIN, 1894-  Four modern statesmen, Winston Churchill, Franklin D. Roosevelt, Joseph Stalin, Chiang Kai-shek. Oxford University Press, 1944. 132 p. (Living names).

SIÉ, CHÉOU-KANG, 謝壽康 [Hsieh, Shou-k'ang] 1894-  Le maréchal Chiang
Kai Shek: son enfance, sa jeunesse. [3. éd. Paris] Presses universitaires
de France, 1947. 257 p. illus., ports. 1er éd. Paris-Bruxelles, 1941; 2e
éd., Genève, 1942.

———. President Chiang Kai-shek: his childhood and youth. Taipei, China Cultural Service [1954] 131 p. illus.

SOONG, MAYLING, 蔣宋美齡 , 1897-  Sian: a coup d'état, by Mayling Soong
Chiang (Madame Chiang Kai-shek). A fortnight in Sian: extracts from a diary by Chiang Kai-shek. Shanghai, The China Pub. Co., 1937. x, 119 p.

———. General Chiang Kai-shek; the account of the fortnight in Sian when the
fate of China hung in the balance, by General and Madame Chiang Kai-shek.
Garden City, N.Y., Doubleday, Doran, 1937. xi p., 187 p.

———. China at the crossroads; an account of the fortnight in Sian, when the
fate of China hung in the balance, by General and Madame Chiang Kai-shek.
London, Faber and Faber [1937] 7-232 p.

———. Les origines du drame chinois, par Tchang Kai-chek et Soong Mayling.
Traduit de l'anglais par Robert Delle Donne. Paris, Gallimard [1938] xxii,
[7]-205 p.

———. Gefangen in Sian, von Chiang Kai-shek und Chiang Soong May-ling. Mit
einer Einführung von Tsiang Pa-lie, 蔣百里. [Diese deutsche Aufl. hat Lin
Tsiu-sen, 林秋生 , besorgt ] München, F. Bruckmann [1938] 118 p. front.
ports. (fold.), facsim. (Schriften des chinesischen Kultur-Dienstes ).

———. The same. (Das Tagebuch des Marshalls und die Niederschriften seiner
Gattin. Chinesisch geschrieben [und mit] einer Einführung von Tsiang Pa-lie.
Deutsche Ausgabe besorgt von Lin Tsiu-sen. 2 Aufl. Erlenbach-Zürich, E.
Rentsch Verlag, 1943. iv, 128 p. (Schriften des chinesischen Kultur-Dien-
stes ).

TONG, HOLLINGTON KONG, 董顯光 , 1887-  Chiang Kai-shek, soldier and
statesman; authorized biography. Shanghai, China Pub. Co., 1937. 2 v.
fronts., ports., fold. map.

———. Chiang Kai-shek. [Rev. ed. Taipei] China Pub. Co. [c1953] 562 p.

———. Abridged biography of President Chiang. Taipei, China Cultural Service [1954] 29 p. (Pamphlets on Kuomintang affairs ).

## Soong Mayling

BRIGHT, JAGAT S. Madame Chiang Kai Shek (a biographical memoir). Lahore,
The Hero Publications, 1943. [13]-142 p.

GARRETT, EVELYN. The four queens. London, MacDonald [1944] xi, 13-224 p.

HAHN, EMILY, 1905-  The Soong sisters. London, R. Hale [1943]; Garden
City, N.Y., Doubleday, Doran, 1943. xx, 287 p. front., ports., map. 1st
American ed. 1941.

———. Chinas drei grosse Schwestern, die Schwestern Soong: Frau Chiang Kai-
shek, Frau Sun Yat-sen, Frau Kung. [7. Aufl. Bern] A. Scherz [1942] 317
p. ports.

HULL, HELEN ROSE. Mayling Soong Chiang. New York, Coward-McCann, inc.
[1943] 32 p.

NICOLAY, HELEN, 1866-  China's first lady. New York, London, D. Appleton-Century [1944] ix, 224 p. front., ports.

SOONG, MAYLING, 1897-  Madame Chiang Kai-shek's trip through the United
States and Canada. [San Francisco, The Chinese Nationalist Daily, 1944?]
cover-title, 3-150, [1] p. incl. illus., ports.

[THOMAS, HARRY J.] The first lady of China; the historic wartime visit of
Mme. Chiang Kai-shek to the United States in 1943. [New York, Internation-

al Business Machines Corporation, c1943] [197] p. illus. (incl. ports.).

[YAUKEY, GRACE (SYDENSTRICKER) ] 1899-  Three sisters; the story of the Soong family of China, by Cornelia Spencer [pseud.] Illustrated by Kurt Wiese. New York, John Day [1939] viii, 279 p. incl. front., illus.

## Others

BATE, DON. Wang Ching Wei, 汪精衛: puppet or patriot. Chicago, R.F. Seymour, 1941. 187 p.

BORREY, FRANCIS. Une sage chinois, Kou Hong Ming, 辜鴻銘; notes biographiques. Paris, M. Rivière, 1930. 105 p. front. (port.).

CHÊNG, T'IEN-HSI, 鄭天錫, 1884-  East and West; episodes in a sixty years' journey. London, New York, Hutchincon [1951] 247 p. illus.

CHIANG, MONLIN, 蔣夢麟, 1886-  Tides from the West, a Chinese autobiography. New Haven, Yale Univ. Press, 1947. vi, 282 p.

LEVENSON, JOSEPH RICHMOND, 1920-  Liang Ch'i-ch'ao, 梁啓超, and the mind of modern China. Cambridge, Harvard University Press, 1953. xii, 256 p. (Harvard historical monographs, 26 ).

LI, EDWARD S.G. The life of Li Yuan-hung, 黎元洪 [1864-1928]. Tientsin, Tientsin Press[1925] 111 p. ports.

McALEAVY, H. Wang T'ao (1828?-90), the life and writings of a displaced person; with a translation of Mei-li hsiao chuan [ 媚黎小傳], a short story by Wang T'ao. London, China Society, 1953. 40 p. illus.

NING LAO T'AI-T'AI, 甯老太太, 1867-  A daughter of Han; the autobiography of a Chinese working woman, by Ida Pruitt, from the story told her by Ning Lao T'ai-t'ai. New Haven, Yale University Press; London, H. Milford, Oxford University Press, 1945. viii p., 249, [1] p. illus. (map, plan) ports.

———. Eine Tochter chinas. Das Leben Ning Lao T'ai-t'ai, einer Frau aus dem Volke. Erzählt von ihr selbst und aufgeschrieben von Ida Pruitt. Deutsche übertragen von Magda H. Larsen. Zürich, Rotapfel Verlag, 1949. 279 p.

SHEN, JAMES CHENG-YEE, 沈成怡, 1920-  Liang Chi-chao and his times. Ann Arbor, University Microfilms [1954] ([University Microfilms, Ann Arbor, Mich.] Publication no. 7589). Collation of the original: x, 372 l. illus., ports. Thesis-University of Missouri.

SIMON, PAUL. Deux personalitiés de la Chine contemporaine: Wu Pei-fu, 吳佩孚, et Wang Ching-wei, 汪精衛. Vervièrs, Leens, 1939. 7 p.

T'ANG, LIANG-LI, 湯良禮, 1901-  Wang Ching-wei, a political biography. Peiping, China United Press [1931] ix, [11]-223 p. (China united press series, [2] ).

TRET'ÍAKOV, SERGEĬ MIKHAĬLOVICH, 1892-  Den Schi-chua, 鄧惜華, ein junger Chinese erzählt sein Leben; Biointerview. Berlin, Malik-Verlag [1932] 9-507, [2] p.

———. A Chinese testament; the autobiography of Tan Shih-hua, 鄧熙華, as told to S. Tretiakov. New York, Simon and Schuster, 1934. London, Gollancz, 1934. ix p., 3-316 p.

VERBRUGGE, RAPHAËL, 1872-  Yuan Che-k'ai, 袁世凱; sa vie, son temps. Paris, P. Geuthner, 1934. [7]-242 p., XVIII plates (incl. ports.) on 9 l. (Les grandes figures de l'Orient, IV ).

WANG, CHAO-MING, 汪兆銘, 1883-1944. À la mémoire de M. Tsen Tsonming, 曾仲鳴. Hanoi, Impr. d'Extrême-Orient, 1939. 12 p. port.

## Mao Tse-tung

BOGDANOV, NIKOLAĬ. Erzählungen über Mao Tse-tung. [Deutsch von Veronica Ensslen] Berlin, Verlag Kultur und Fortschritt, 1952. 134 p. illus.

FROMENTIN, PIERRE, 1914-  Mao Tsê Tung, le dragon rouge. Paris, Éditions Médicis [1949] 211 p. port. (Grandes vies, grandes destinées ).

MAO, TSE-T'UNG, 1893- The autobiography of Mao Tse-tung [dictated by Edgar Snow, annotated by Tang Szu-chen, 唐思眞 ] 2nd ed. Canton, Truth Book Co., 1949 (c1938). 51 p.
————. Mao Tse-t'ung: Kurzbiographie. Aus dem Englischen. 2 Aufl. Berlin, Dietz, 1954. 20 p.
PAYNE, PIERRE STEPHEN ROBERT, 1911- Mao Tsê-tung, ruler of Red China. New York, Schuman [1950]; London, Secker and Warburg, 1951. xvii, 303 p. ports., maps.
————. Mao Tsé Toung. Avec trois poèmes par Mao Tsé Toung. Traduit de l'anglais par Janine Mitaud. Paris, P. Seghers [1949] 38 p. port. (Poésie 49.17).
————. Mao Tse-tung. Übers. von Franziska Meister-Weidner. Hamburg, Krüger, 1951. 385 p.
ROY, CLAUDE, 1915- Premières clefs pour la Chine; une vie de Mao Tse Toung. Paris, Éditeurs français réunis [1950] 84 p.
SIAO, EMI, 蕭三. Mao Tse-tung: his childhood and youth. Bombay, People's Publishing House, 1953. 76 p.
————. Kindheit und Jugend Mao Tse-tung. Deutsche Fassung mit Nachwort und Anmerkungen von Alex. Wedding. Berlin, Verlag Neues Leben, 1953. 124 p. illus. port.
STRONG, ANNA LOUISE, 1885- The thought of Mao Tse-tung. Chefoo, Chefoo News [1947] 28 p.

### Other Communists

BATLIWALA, S.S. Makers of new China; 2nd and rev. ed. Bombay, People's Pub. House, 1944. vi, 189, viii p. photos, map. 1st ed. 1943.
ELEGANT, ROBERT S. China's Red masters; political biographies of the Chinese Communist leaders. New York, Twayne Publishers [1951]; London, The Bodley Head, 1952. 264 p. ports.
————. Chinas rote Herren. Die politischen Biographien der Kommunistischen Führer Chinas. Übers. von Michael Kogon. Frankfurt a.M., Verlag d. Frankfurter Helfte, 1952. 269 p. illus.
GT. BRIT. Foreign Office. Research Dept. List of aliases and alternative versions of the names of leading Chinese communists and fellow travellers. London, 1952. 11 p. (LR 22/42).
SMEDLEY, AGNES, 1890-1950. The great road; the life and times of Chu Teh, 朱德. New York, Monthly Review Press, 1956. 461 p. illus.
SNOW, HELEN (FOSTER) 1907- Red dust; autobiographies of Chinese Communists, as told to Nym Wales [pseud.] With an introduction by Robert Carver North. Stanford, Stanford University Press [1952] 238 p. illus., ports. map (on lining papers).
U.S. Dept. of State. Office of Intelligence Research. Leaders of Communist China. Washington, 1950. 280 p. (OIR Report 5126).
WEI CHEN, pseud. Who's who in communist China, a study of Russian domination. New York, Free Trade Union Committee, American Federation of Labor, 1954. 14 p.

### Westerners associated with China
(See also Christianity and Foreign Missions-Lives of Missionaries)

### Gordon and his Contemporaries

ABEND, HALLETT EDWARD, 1884-1955. The god from the West; a biography of Frederick Townsend Ward. Garden City, N.Y., Doubleday, 1947. xv, 304 p. map (on lining-papers).
ALLEN, BERNARD MEREDITH, 1864- Gordon in China. London, Macmillan, 1933. ix, 222 p. front., plates, ports., maps (1 fold.) plan.
CAHILL, HOLGER. A Yankee adventurer; the story of Ward and the Taiping

rebellion. New York, The Macaulay Co., 1930. 11-296 p. front., illus.(incl. map) plates, ports.

CHACK, PAUL, 1876-1945. Courbet, le vainqueur de Fou-Tchéou. Paris, Amiot-Dumont [1949] 163 p.

CHEN, LYEN-TCHE, 沈鍊之. Rôle du général Charles-George Gordon dans la répression de l'insurrection des Thai-Phing (Mars 1863-juin 1864). Lyon, Bosc frères, 1933. 115 p. fold. map. (Lyon. Université. Bibliotheca francosinica lugdunensis. Étude et documents publiés par l'Institut franco-chinois de Lyon, 5 ).

HANSON, LAWRENCE. Gordon, the story of a hero [by] Lawrence and Elisabeth Hanson. London, P. Davies [1953] 256 p. illus.

————. Chinese Gordon: the story of a hero [by] Lawrence and Elisabeth Hanson. New York, Funk and Wagnalls Co., 1954. 256 p. illus.

MORISON, JOHN LYLE, 1875-  The eighth Earl of Elgin; a chapter in nineteenth-century imperial history. [London] Hodder and Stoughton, 1928. 317, [1] p. front., plates (part col.) ports.

YEAGER, CARL FRANCIS, 1923-  Anson Burlingame; his mission to China and the first Chinese mission to western nations. Washington, 1950. 112 l. illus. Thesis-Georgetown University.

## Diplomats and Officials

ARLINGTON, LEWIS CHARLES, 1859-1942. Through the dragon's eyes; fifty years' experiences of a foreigner in the Chinese government service, with a foreword by E. Alabaster. London, Constable, 1931. lvii, 348 p. col. front., plates (part col.) ports., fold. map.

BOWER, LEON M. Willard D. Straight and the American policy in China, 1906-13. Boulder, Colo., 195-  247 l. Thesis-University of Colorado.

CHENNAULT, CLAIRE LEE, 1890-  Way of a fighter; the memoirs of Claire Lee Chennault; ed. by Robert Hotz. New York, G. P. Putnam [1949] xxii, 375 p. illus., ports., maps.

CLUNE, FRANK, 1894-  Chinese Morrison. Melbourne, The Bread and Cheese Club, 1941. 88 p., front. (port.).

HEWLETT, SIR WILLIAM MEYRICK, 1876-1944. Forty years in China. London, Macmillan, 1943. ix, 261, [1] p. illus. (plans) fold. map.

KING, PAUL HENRY, 1853-1938. In the Chinese customs service; a personal record of forty-seven years. London, T.F. Unwin [1924] 307, [1] p. illus. (facsims.) ports.

LOHBECK, DON, 1917-  Patrick J. Hurley: a biography. Chicago, H. Regnery Co., 1956. 513 p.

OUDENDIJK, WILLEM JACOBUS, 1874-1953. Ways and by-ways in diplomacy. London, P. Davies [1939] xi, 386 p. front., plates, ports.

PANIKKAR, KAVALAM MADHAVA, 1896-  In two Chinas, memoirs of a diplomat. London, G. Allen and Unwin [1955] 183 p.

————. Botschafter in beiden China. Mit ein Rede von Jawaharlal Pandit Nehru und eine Einführung von A.C.N. Nambiar. Übertragen von Arthur Seiffhart. Frankfurt a.M., Scheffler, 1956. 243 p. illus.

PAYNE, PIERRE STEPHEN ROBERT, 1911-  The Marshall story; a biography of General George C. Marshall. [1st ed.] New York, Prentice-Hall [1951] xii, 344 p. ports.

————. General Marshall; a study in loyalties. London, Heinemann [1952] 335 p. illus.

REINSCH, PAUL SAMUEL, 1869-1923. An American diplomat in China. Garden City, N.Y., and Toronto, Doubleday, Page, 1922. xii p., 396 p.

SELLE, EARL ALBERT, 1906-  Donald of China. Sydney, Invincible Press [c1948] 376 p. port., map (on lining-paper).

STUART, JOHN LEIGHTON, 1876-  Fifty years in China; the memoirs of John

Leighton Stuart, missionary and ambassador. New York, Random House [1954] 346 p. illus.

VARÈ, DANIELE, 1880-1956. Laughing diplomat. New York, Doubleday, Doran, 1938; London, J. Murray, 1938. xii, 448 p. front. (port.).

——. Der lachende Diplomat. Übers. von Annie Polzer. Berlin [etc.] P. Zsolnay, 1938. 547 p., front. (port.).

VARG, PAUL A. Open door diplomat; the life of W. W. Rockhill. Urbana, University of Illinois Press, 1952. ix, 141 p. port. (Illinois studies in the social sciences, v. 33, no. 4 ).

WRIGHT, STANLEY FOWLER, 1873- Hart and the Chinese customs. Belfast, Published for the Queen's University [by] W. Mullan, 1950. xvi, 949 p. illus., ports.

WU, LIEN-TEH, 伍連德, 1879- Reminiscences of George E. Morrison; and Chinese abroad. Canberra, Australian Institute of Anatomy, 1936. 19 p. (George Ernest Morrison lectures ).

## Journalists and Lawyers

ABEND, HALLETT EDWARD, 1884-1955. My life in China, 1926-41. New York, Harcourt, Brace [1943] viii, 396 p.

——. My years in China, 1926-41. London, John Lane [1944] 3-395 p.

——. Mes années en Chine (1928 [i. e. 1926]-41) traduit de l'anglais par Jeanne Fournier-Pargoire. Paris, J. Tallandier [1946] [7]-318 p. (Témoignages sur notre temps ).

ALLMAN, NORWOOD FRANCIS, 1893- Shanghai lawyer. New York, London, Whittlesey House, McGraw-Hill Book Co. [1943] 3-283 p.

POWELL, JOHN BENJAMIN, 1888-1947. My twenty-five years in China. New York, Macmillan, 1945. 436 p.

WOODHEAD, HENRY GEORGE WANDESFORDE, 1883- A journalist in China, with eight illustrations. London, Hurst and Blackett [1934] ix, 13-281 p. front., illus. (coat of arms) plates, ports.

——. Leaves from an editor's scrap book. Peking, 193- . 129 p.

## Sinologues

CORDIER, HENRI, 1849-1925. Bibliographie des oeuvres de Henri Cordier. Paris, P. Geuthner, 1924. vii, 151 p.

JÄGER, FRITZ, 1886-1957. Otto Franke, 1863-1946. Wiesbaden, 1950. [18] p. port. Reprinted from Zeitschrift der Deutschen Morgenländischen Gesellschaft, Bd. 100, Hft. 1.

LATOURETTE, KENNETH SCOTT, 1884- Biographical memoir of Berthold Laufer, 1874-1934. Presented to the academy at the autumn meeting, 1936. [Washington, National Academy of Sciences, 1937] p. 43-68. front. (port.) (National academy of sciences. Biographical memoirs. vol. XVIII- 3d memoir ).

PELLIOT, PAUL, 1878-1945. Henri Cordier: Nécrologie. Extrait du T'oung-pao, vol. XXIV, n⁰ 1, année 1925/26. Leide, E. J. Brill, 1925. cover-title, 15 p. port.

REISCHAUER, EDWIN OLDFATHER, 1910- Serge Elisséef [a biography] Cambridge, 1957. 35 p. port. Reprinted from HJAS 20: 1-2.

RENOU, LOUIS. Notice sur la vie et les travaux de Paul Pelliot, lut dans la séance de 21 Avril 1950. Dijon, Impr. Darantière, 1950. 19 p. port. (Institut de France. Publications, 1950. 4 ).

RICHTHOFEN, FERDINAND PAUL WILHELM, freiherr VON, 1833-1905. Meister und Schüler; Ferdinand freiherr von Richthofen an Sven Hedin, mit einer Einleitung und Erläuterungen von Sven Hedin. Zur 100. Wiederkehr des Geburtstages von Ferdinand von Richthofen im namen des im Ferdinand von

Richthofentag vereinigten Schülerkreises, hrsg. von Ernst Tiessen.    Berlin, D. Reimer, 1933. 148 p. 5 port., double facsim.

————. Ferdinand von Richthofen; ansprachen Anlässlich der Gedächtnisfeier zu seinem 100. Geburtstage an der Universität Berlin.   Stuttgart, Kommissions-verlag von J. Engelhorns nachf., 1933. 17 p. front. (port.) (Berliner geographische arbeiten. hft. 5 ).

SOCIÉTÉ ASIATIQUE, Paris. Paul Pelliot [par Georges Salles et al.   Paris ] 1946 [i. e. 1947] 79 p. port.

WERNER, EDWARD THEODORE CHALMERS, 1864-   Memorigrams.   Shanghai, Shanghai Times, 1940. 160 p. ports.

WILHELM, SALOME (BLUMHARDT). Richard Wilhelm. Der geistige Mittler zwischen China und Europa, mit einer Einleitung von Walter F. Otto. Düsseldorff, E. Diederichs [1956] 392 p. port.

# VI. POLITICS AND GOVERNMENT

## Political History

CHOU, HSIANG-KUANG, 周祥光. Political thought of China. Foreword by S. Radhakrishnan. Delhi, S. Chand, 1954. iii, 244 p.

GRIMM, TILEMANN. Das Neiko der Ming-Zeit (1368-1643). Seine Entstehung, Konsolidierung und Bedeutung für die gesellschaftliche Entwicklung im China des 15. Jahrhunderts. Hamburg, 1953. ix, 104 p. Diss.-Univ. Hamburg.

HAENISCH, ERICH, 1880- Politische Systeme und Kämpfe im alten China. Berlin, W. de Gruyter, 1951. 27 p.

————. Fürst und Volk, Soldat und Beamter in Staatsnot; Betrachtungen aus der Geschichte Chinas. München, Verlag der Bayerischen Akademie der Wissenschaften, 1953. 40 p. fold. facsim. (Sitzungsberichte der Bayerischen Akademie der Wissenschaften. Phil-hist. Kl. Jahrg. 1952, Heft 6 ).

HSIAO, KUNG-CH'ÜAN, 蕭公權, 1897- China's contribution to world peace. Chungking, China Institute of Pacific Relations, 1945. iv, 52 p. (China council series, 1 ).

HSIEH, PAO-CHAO, 謝保樵, 1896- The government of China(1644-1911). Baltimore, Johns Hopkins Press, 1925. 414 p. (Johns Hopkins university studies in historical and political science. Extra volumes. New ser., 3 ).

HUANG, TSUNG-HSI, 黃宗羲, 1610-95. A plan for the Prince: the Ming-i taifang lu, 明夷待訪錄, of Huang Tsung-hsi; translated and explained [by] William Theodore De Bary. Ann Arbor, University Microfilms [1954] ([University Microfilms, Ann Arbor, Mich.] Publication 6599 ). vi, 455 l.

KUHN, FRANZ, 1889- Chinesische Staatsweisheit. Darmstadt, O. Reichl. 1923; Bremen, Storm, 1947. xxiv, 184, [2] p.

————. Altchinesische Staatsweisheit. [3. veränderte Aufl.] Zürich, Verlag Die Waage [1954] 198 p. illus.

LI, HSIUNG-FEI, 李雄飛. Les censeurs sous la dynastie mandchoue (1616-1911) en Chine. Paris, Impr. Les Presses modernes, 1936. 144, [5] p.

LIANG, CH'I-CH'AO, 梁啓超, 1873-1929. History of Chinese political thought during the early Tsin period, with two portraits. New York, Harcourt, Brace, London, K. Paul, 1930. viii, 210 p. 2 port. (incl. front.) diagr.(International library of psychology, philosophy and scientific method ).

————. La conception de la loi et les théories des légistes à la veille des Ts'in. Extrait de l'Histoire des théories politiques à la veille des Ts'in. Traduction, introduction et notes par Jean Escarra [et] Robert Germain. Préface de Georges Padoux. Pékin, China Booksellers, 1926. xxxvii, 82 p.

LIEM, CHANNING. The influence of Western political thought upon China. Ann Arbor, University Microfilms [1952] ([University Microfilms, Ann Arbor, Mich.] Publication no. 2997 ). Collation of the original: 229, 9 l. Thesis - Princeton University

LIN, MOU-SHÊNG, 林佺聖, 1906- Men and ideas, an informal history of Chinese political thought; introduction by Pearl S. Buck. New York, John Day [1942] xiv, 256 p.

POTT, WILLIAM SUMNER, APPLETON, 1893- Chinese political philosophy. New York, A.A. Knopf, 1925. xi, 110 p. (Political science classics).

SIAO, KING-FANG, 蕭金芳 [Hsiao Chin-fang] 1902- La Chine, inspiratrice du despotisme éclairé. Paris, Les Presses universitaires de France [1939] cover-title, 19, [1] p.

TALBOTT, NATHAN M., 1917- Intellectual origins and aspects of political thought in the Jen Hsueh, 仁學, of T'an Ssu-t'ung, 譚嗣同, martyr of the 1898 reform. Seattle, 1956. 388 l. Thesis - Univ. of Washington

TEWKSBURY, DONALD GEORGE, 1894- Source book on Far Eastern political ideologies. 1. Modern period. China [and] Japan. New York, 1949. 189 p.

TEZUKA, R. Chūn Ch'en Tao, 君臣道, Studien über das von Konfucius vertretene Tao von Herrscher und Untertan. Berlin, Würfel Verlag, 1930. 55 p. illus.

THEUNISSEN, PETER, 1906- Su Ts'in, 蘇秦, und die Politik der Längs-und Quer-Achse (Tsung-Heng Schule) in chinesischen Altertum. Breslau, Antonius Verlag, 1938. 87 p. Diss.-Univ. Berlin.

THOMAS, ELBERT DUNCAN, 1883-1953. Chinese political thought; a study based upon the theories of the principal thinkers of the Chou period; foreword by Edward Thomas Williams. New York, Prentice-Hall, 1927. xvi p., 317 p.

TSENG, YU-HAO, 曾友豪, 1900- Modern Chinese legal and political philosophy. Shanghai, Commercial Press, 1930. 320 p.

WALKER, RICHARD LOUIS, 1922- The multi-state system of ancient China. Hamden, Conn., Shoe String Press [1954, c1953] xii, 135 p. maps.

WIST, HANS, 1904- Das chinesische Zensorat. Hamburg, J.J. Augustin, 1932. 45, [1] p. Diss.-Univ. Hamburg.

WOO, KANG, 吳康, 1896- Les trois théories politiques du Tch'ouen ts'ieou interprétées par Tong Tchong-chou, 董仲舒, d'après les principes de l'école de Kong-yang. Paris, E. Leroux, 1932. iii, 254 p.

WU, KUO-CHENG, 吳國禎, 1903- Ancient Chinese political theories. Shanghai, Commercial Press, 1928. 340 p.

ZIAH, C.F. Philosophie-politique de la Chine ancienne 700-221 av. J.-C. Paris, L. Rodstein, 1934. 189 p. Thèse-Univ. de Paris.

## General Surveys - 1912-1927

ABEND, HALLETT EDWARD, 1884-1955. Canton now; notes on what the Canton leaders are trying to do, spring and summer, 1926. Peking, Peking Leader Press, 1926. 41 p. (Peking leader reprints, 23).

BAKER, JOHN EARL, 1880-1957. Peace, unification and representative government. Peking, The Leader Press, 1925. 14 p. (Peking Leader reprints, 7).

BAU, MINGCHIEN JOSHUA, 鮑明鈐 [Pao Ming-ch'ien] 1894- Modern democracy in China. Shanghai, Commercial Press, 1923. x, 467 p.

BROWDER, EARL RUSSELL, 1891- Civil war in nationalistic China. Chicago, Labor Unity Pub. Association, 1927. 57 p.

CHEN, WAN-LI, 鄭文禮 [Chêng Wen-li]. Les développements des institutions politiques de la Chine depuis l'établissement de la république (1912) jusqu'à nos jours (1925) (étude d'histoire constitutionelle et de droit comparé) Paris, Jouve et cie, 1926. 182 p.

CLARK, ELMER TALMAGE, 1886- What's the matter in China? Nashville, Tenn., Board of Missions; Methodist Episcopal Church, South [c1927] 96 p. (The world parish series, edited by E. T. Clark).

CLARK, GROVER, 1891-1938. In perspective; a review of the politico-military situation in China in the summer of 1927. Peking, The Leader Press, 1927. 69 p. (Peking Leader reprint, 32).

———. China in 1927; a summary of the main events and tendencies in one of China's most eventful years. Peking, The Leader Press, 1928. 59 p.

COMITÉ NATIONALE D'ÉTUDES SOCIALES ET POLITIQUES, Paris. L'état politique actuel de la Chine. Conférence de M. André Duboscq. Boulogne-sur-Seine, Impr. d'études sociales et politiques, 1922. 27 p.

DUBARBIER, GEORGES, 1888- La Chine contemporaine et économique. Paris, P. Geuthner, 1926. [vii]-viii, 373 p. 2 fold. maps.

DUBOSCQ, ANDRÉ, 1876- L'évolution de la Chine; politique et tendances(1911-

21) avec carte hors texte. Paris, Éditions Bossard, 1921. 194 p. fold. map.

ETHERTON, PERCY THOMAS, 1879-   China: the facts. London, Benn, 1927.
    259 p.  illus.

———. The crisis in China. Boston, Little, Brown, 1927. vii-xiv,  17-259 p.
    front., plates, ports., fold. map.

FOREIGN POLICY ASSOCIATION, New York. Forward or backward in China?
    discussed by Dr. Hu Shih, Mr. Grover Clark and Dr. Stanley K. Hornbeck;
    a stenographic report of the  96th New York luncheon discussion, February
    26, 1927, of the Foreign policy association.  New York [1927] 34 p. ([F. P. A]
    Pamphlet, 43, series 1926-27 ).

GRIGGS, DAVID THURSTON, 1916-   The anti-imperialist theme in Chinese
    nationalism, 1919-26.  Cambridge, 1952. 2 v. Thesis-Harvard University.

HORNBECK, STANLEY KUHL, 1883-   China to-day: political. Boston, World
    Peace Foundation [1927]p. [417]-566. (World peace foundation. Pamphlets 10:5).

———. The situation in China. New York, The China Society of America, 1927.
    23 p.

HU, HAN-MIN, 胡漢民 , 1879-1936. Government headquarters declarations.
    Canton, 1925. [1], 10 p.

———. Selected documents and addresses.  Canton, Ministry of Foreign Affairs,
    1925. 49 p.

KING, LOUIS MAGRATH, 1886-   China in turmoil, studies in personality. Lon-
    don, Heath, Cranton, 1927. 11-233 p. front., plates, ports.

LAO-P'ONG-YO, pseud. La Chine nouvelle. Le double dragon chinois, jaune ou
    rouge? Paris, J. Peyronnet et c$^{ie}$, 1927. [9]-382 p. (Éditions coloniales ).

McELROY, ROBERT McNUTT, 1872-   The American constitution and the Chi-
    nese republic. 2d ed. New York, China Society of America (inc.) 1922. 15,
    [1] p. (China society pamphlets, II ).

MALONE, CECIL L'ESTRANGE, 1890-   New China; report of an investigation.
    London, Independent Labour Party Publication Department [1926-   2 v. illus.
    (incl. map) plates.

———. Das neue China und seine sozialen Kämpfe. Übersetzung und historisch-
    politische Einleitung von Franz Joseph Furtwängler. Berlin, Verlagsgesell-
    schaft des Allgemeinen Deutschen Gewerkschaftsbundes, 1928. 158 p.

PYE, LUCIAN WILMOT, 1921-   The politics of Tuchunism in North China, 1920-
    27. An aspect of political and social change in modern China. New Haven,
    1941. 305 l. Thesis-Yale University.

RANSOME, ARTHUR, 1884-   The Chinese puzzle, with a foreword by the Rt.
    Hon. David Lloyd George, M. P.  London, G. Allen and Unwin [1927] [9]-189
    p. illus. (plan).

[RINE, VICTOR] 1884-   Letters from China; how the red sun dried up the  red
    herring, by the Wandering eye [pseud. ]; with a series of genial essayettes on
    the art of reading news. New York, Raimond and Bart, 1928. 5-71 p. front.
    plates.

RUSSELL, BERTRAND RUSSELL, 3d earl, 1872-   The problem of China. Lon-
    don, G. Allen and Unwin ltd.; New York, Century, 1922. 7-260 p.

———. China und das Problem des Fernen Ostens, mit einer Einführung von
    Karl Haushofer. München, Drei Masken Verlag, 1925. vii, 224 p.

SIÉ, TON-FA, 謝東發. La situation actuelle de la Chine. Conférence de M.Sié
    Ton-fa. Boulogne-sur-Seine, Impr. d'études sociales et politique, 1925. 47
    p. (Comité national d'études sociales et politiques, séance du 10 juillet 1925,
    fasc. 290 ).

TYAU, MIN-CH'IEN TUK ZUNG,  刁敏謙 , 1888-   China awakened. New York,
    Macmillan, 1922.  xvi, 475 p. front., plates, ports., double map.

WANG, CHUNG-HUI, 王寵惠,1882-1958. La Chine. Conférence de M. Wang Chung-
    hui. Boulogne-sur-Seine, Impr. d'études sociales et politiques, 1923. 21 p.

    (Comité national d'études sociales et politiques, Séance du 5 Novembre 1923,
    fasc. 233 ).

WHAT about China? Pertinent facts concerning the present situation in that country (questions and answers) Pittsburgh, Pa., Chinese Students' Club, 1927.
12 p.
WILLOUGHBY, WESTEL WOODBURY, 1867-1945. Constitutional government in
China, present conditions and prostpects. Washington, Carnegie Endowment,
1922. viii, 61 p. (Pamphlet series of the Carnegie endowment for international peace. Division of international law, 47 ).
WITTFOGEL, KARL AUGUST, 1896-  Das erwachende China, ein Abriss der
Geschichte und der gegenwärtigen Probleme Chinas. Wien, Agis-Verlag,
1926. 174 p.
————. Schanghai-Kanton. Berlin, Internationaler Arbeiter-Verlag, 1927. 29 p.

1927-1937

ABEND, HALLETT EDWARD, 1884-1955. Tortured China. New York, I. Wash-
burn, 1930; London, Allen and Unwin, 1931. xiii, 305 p. front., plates.
————. Can China survive? [By] Hallett Abend and Anthony J. Billingham. New
York, I. Washburn [c1936]   ix,  317 p. front., plates.
————. Chaos in Asia. New York, I. Washburn [c1939] 313 p. illus. (map).
ANGELICO. Mélanges chronologiques chinois. Pékin, Impr. de la "Politique
de Pékin," 1929-31. 3 v. in 1. (Collection de la "Politique de Pékin").
FOREIGN POLICY ASSOCIATION, New York. Nationalist China, discussed by
William Hung, 洪業, Arthur N. Holcombe, David Z. T. Yui, 余日章; 113th
New York luncheon discussion, February 2, 1929. New York, Foreign Poli-
cy Association [1929] 23 p. ( [F. P. A.] Pamphlet, 54. Series 1928-29. March,
1929 ).
GRANET, MARCEL, 1884-1940. Le droite et la gauche en Chine. Paris, 1934.
32 p. (Bulletin de l'Institut français de sociologie, Fasc. 111 ).
HOLCOMBE, ARTHUR NORMAN, 1884-   The spirit of the Chinese revolution;
Lowell Institute lectures, 1930. New York, A. A. Knopf, 1930. 3-185, vi p.
————. The Chinese revolution; a phase in the regeneration of a world power.
Cambridge, Harvard University Press, 1931. xiii, 401 p. incl. diagr.
HOU, YONG-LING, 朗永齡. La vie politique et constitutionnelle en Chine. Pé-
kin, Impr. de la "Politique de Pékin," 1935. 62 p. (Collection de la "Poli-
tique de Pékin").
KAO, KOUEI-FEN, 高桂芳. Politique intérieure et extérieure de la Chine de-
puis 1926 jusqu'à nos jours. Nancy, Impr. Grandville, 1935. 160 p. Thèse-
Univ. de Nancy.
KLOCKE, EDUARD. Was geht in China vor? Ein Führer durch die Wirrnisse in
Ostasien. Hannover, A. Sponholtz, 1928? 15 p.
KUO MIN TANG. Nationalist China. Published by the Secretariat, the Kuomin-
tang of China, the Central Political Council, the Canton branch. Canton
[1927] cover-title, [3]-38 p. port.
LEE, EDWARD BING-SHUEY, 李炳瑞, 1903-56. China in 1930. Peiping, Lead-
er Press, 1930. 50 p.
LI, SHÊNG-WU, 李聖五, 1900-   International law as applied to civil war, by
F. S. Li. Shanghai, Commercial Press, 1933. vi, 223 p.
LIANG, HUBERT S., 梁士純, [Liang Shih-chūn] 1903-   China and her national
crisis; a comprehensive and timely analysis and interpretation of some of
the most pressing issues, domestic and foreign, facing the Chinese nation
to-day. Shanghai, China Weekly Review, 1936. 34 p.
LINEBARGER, PAUL MYRON WENTWORTH, 1871-1939. La Chine navrée.
[Paris, Impr. Dubois and Bauer, 1931] cover-title, 39 p. port.
LINEBARGER, PAUL MYRON ANTHONY, 1913-   Government in republican
China; foreword by Fritz Morstein Marx. New York and London, McGraw-
Hill, 1938. xv, 203 p. (McGraw-Hill studies in political science ).
LYNN, JERMYN CHI-HUNG, 凌啓鴻, [Ling, Ch'i-hung] Political parties in

China, with a foreword by J.C. Ferguson. Peiping, H. Vetch [1930] 255,[1] p.

MacNAIR, HARLEY FARNSWORTH, 1891-1947. China in revolution; an analysis of politics and militarism under the republic. Chicago, University of Chicago Press [c1931] xi, 244 p. front.

MÄNCHEN-HELFEN, OTTO, 1894- Drittel der Menschheit; ein Ostasienbuch. Berlin, Der Bücherkreis, c1932. 193 p.

MINKNER, EDMUND. Ganz China unter dem Sonnenbanner des Südens; die Lage im heutigen China. Im Anhang, eine chinesische Gedenkschrift zum dritten Todestage Sun Yat-sens, übers. vom Verfasser. Berlin, Schlieffen Verlag, 1928. 126 p. front. ports., plates.

MONESTIER, ALPHONSE, 1881-1955. À travers la crise nationaliste chinoise. Pékin, Impr. de la "Politique de Pékin," 1928-35. 18 v. (Collection de la "Politique de Pékin").

QUIGLEY, HAROLD SCOTT, 1889- Chinese politics today. [Minneapolis] University of Minnesota Press [c1934] 31 p. illus. (map) (The day and hour series of the University of Minnesota, 8 ).

RIBEIRO, EUGENIO. The nationalist movement in China. Washington, D.C. c1928. 54 numb. l. maps.

SFORZA, CARLO, conte, 1872-1952. L'énigme chinoise. Paris, Payot, 1928. [7]-208 p. (Bibliothèque politique et économique ).

TCHANG, PI-KAI. Die Bodenzersplitterung in China. Freiburg, V.B., Schillinger, 1934. 65 p. Diss.-Univ. Freiburg.

TCHEOU, SOU-YUN, 周蜀雲 [Chou Shu-yun]. L'évolution de l'opinion publique depuis la révolution de 1911 et l'organisation des parties politiques actuels en Chine. Nancy, 1931. 192 p. Thèse-Univ. de Nancy.

TCHOU, LOUIS NGAO-SIANG, 朱鶴翔 [Chu Ho-hsiang] 1891- La Chine d'aujourd'hui. Conférence faite à l'Institut Belge des hautes études chinoises le 26 Févr. 1937. Bruxelles, Musée royaux d'art et d'histoire, 1937. 16 p.

TSEN, TSONMING, 曾仲鳴 [Tseng Chung-ming] 1896-1939. La Chine qui lutte. Pékin, A. Nachbaur, 1930. 184 p.

TYAU, MIN-CH'IEN TUK ZUNG, 刁敏謙, 1888- ed. Two years of nationalist China. Shanghai, Kelly and Walsh, 1930. 3-523 p. front., plates (2 col., 1 fold.) ports., maps (1 fold.) facsims., tables, diagrs. (part fold.).

VANDERVELDE, ÉMILE, 1866-1938. À travers la révolution chinoise; soviets et Kuomintang. Paris, Alcan; Bruxelles, L'Églantine, 1931. [9]-240 p., plates, ports.

WANG, CHAO-MING, 汪兆銘, 1884-1944. The Chinese national revolution; essays and documents, by Wang Ching-wei and others. Peiping, China United Press [1931] xi, [1], [15]-188 p. (China united press series, [1] ).

———. China's problems and their solution, by Wang Ching-wei. Shanghai, China United Press, 1934. xxii, 199 p. port. ("China to-day" series, [2] ).

———. Problèmes chinois et leurs solutions; cet ouvrage traduit de l'anglais par J.Em. Lemière et précédé d'une esquisse biographique de l'auteur par T'ang Leang-li. Shanghai, China United Press, 1935. 237 p. port. [La Chine d'aujourd'hui. 2 ].

———. China's leaders and their policies; messages to the Chinese people by Wang Ching-wei and Chiang Kai-shek. Supplement to the People's tribune. Shanghai, China United Press, 1935. cover-title, 18. 19-36 p. (China reconstruction series, 2 ).

———. À la jeunesse et au peuple chinois. Discours par Wang Ching-wei et Chiang Kai-shek. Paris, Agence Chekiai, 1936. 32 p. (La Chine d'aujourd'hui, 3 ).

WHYTE, SIR FREDERICK, 1883- La révolution chinoise et l'éveil politique de l'Asie. Bruxelles, Impr. médicale et scientifique, 1928. cover-title, 20 p. "Supplément de la Revue de l'Université de Bruxelles, nᵒ 3, février-mars-avril."

WU, CHAO-CHU, 伍朝樞 , 1886-1934. The Nationalist program for China. New
Haven, Yale University Press; London, H. Milford, Oxford University Press,
1929. iv, 112 p.
WU, CHEW-CHONG, 吳超滄 . L'évolution politique de la République chinoise.
Paris, Presses modernes, 1936. 147 p. illus. Thèse-Univ. de Paris.
YOUNG, C. KUNGSON, 楊光洭 , 1900-42. Nationalist China in retrospect(1926-
30). Paris, Central Executive Committee of Kuomintang in Europe [1930] 35,
[1] p.
————. L'œuvre du Gouvernement national, édité en français. Paris, Agence
Chekiai, 1935 [c1934] 108 p. (La Chine d'aujourd'hui, 2 ).

1937-

BISSON, THOMAS ARTHUR, 1900-  China's national front; problems and poli-
cies. New York, Foreign Policy Association [1941] p. [105]-124. illus.(map)
(Foreign policy reports, 17:9. July 15, 1941 ).
CHANG, CARSEN, 張嘉森 , 1886-  The third force in China. New York, Book-
man Associates [c1952] 345 p. illus.
CH'ÉN, CH'ÊNG, 陳誠 , 1896-  The road to security and peace. Taipei, 1951.
22 p.
————. Premier Chen Cheng speaks; a supplement to China handbook 1951. Tai-
pei, Office of the Govt. Spokesman, 1951. 56 p.
————. Report on Free China. Taipei, 1952. 51 p. fold. map.
————. An oral report on Free China to the second session of the First National
Assembly on March 4, 1954. [Taipei] Govt. Information Bureau, 1954. 23 p.;
17 p.
————. Report on Free China; as submitted to the second session of the First National Assembly on March 4, 1954. Taipei, Govt. Information Bureau, 1954.
60 p.
CHEN, PAKY, 陳伯驥 . Theory and practice of Chinese democracy. London,
1939. ii, 247, 6, 29 l. Thesis-London School of Economics.
CHIANG KAI-SHEK, 蔣介石 , 1886-  Manifesto to the people. [Shanghai, Commercial Press, 1927] cover-title, 14 p.
————. Ausgewählte Reden des Marschalls Chiang Kaishek; aus dem Chinesisch-
en übertragen von Tao Pung Fai, 陶鵬飛 . Geleitwort von Tai Chi-tao, 戴
季陶 . Heidelberg-Berlin, K. Vowinckel, 1936. 105, [1] p. front., plates,
ports., fold. facsim.
————. General Chiang Kai-shek and the communist crisis; Madame Chiang
Kai-shek on the New life movement. Shanghai, China Weekly Review Press
[1937?] viii, 86 p. incl. ports. front., port.
————.China's struggle for freedom; Generalissimo Chiang Kai-shek's wartime
messages to the nation. Hankow, China Information Committee [1937?] cov-
er-title, 29 p.
————. Chinas Kampf; Reden aus Frieden und Krieg, hrsg. von Konrad Frantz.
Luzern, Vita Nova Verlag, 1940. 102 p. map. (Männer und Völker, eine
Schriftenreihe, 4 ).
————. Resisting external aggression and regenerating the Chinese nation. Han-
kow, The China Information Committee [1938?] 54 p.
————. Generalissimo Chiang speaks. Hong Kong, The Pacific Pub. Co.[1939]
cover-title, iii, [2], 219, [1] p.
————. A philosophy of action; or, What I mean by action, by Generalissimo
Chiang Kai-shek; translated into English with a foreword and notes in the na-
ture of a discursive commentary. Chungking, China Information Committee,
1940. cover-title, 28 p.
————. La philosophie de l'action. Chungking, Le Correspondant chinois, 1940.
cover-title, 32 p.
————. China fights on; war messages of Chiang Kai-shek, translated by Frank

Wilson Price. Chungking, China Pub. Co. [1941?- 2 v. front. (port.).

——. All we are and all we have; speeches and messages since Pearl harbor [by] Generalissimo Chiang Kai-shek, December 9, 1941-November 17, 1942. New York, Chinese News Service [1942?]; New York, John Day Co., 1943. 61 p. illus. (port.).

——. Resistance and reconstruction; messages during China's six years of war, 1937-43. New York and London, Harper [1943] xxiv, 322 p.

——. Generalissimo Chiang Kai-shek's war speeches, July, 1937-January, 1944. Chungking, Chinese Ministry of Information [1944] 129 p. port.

——. The voice of China; speeches of Generalissimo and Madame Chiang Kai-shek between December 7, 1941, and October 10, 1943, including some recent messages to British leaders and the British people. With a foreword by V.K. Wellington Koo. London, New York [etc.] Published on behalf of the London Office, Chinese Ministry of Information by Hutchinson [1944] 112 p. incl. front.

——. Before final victory, speeches by Generalissimo Chiang Kai-shek, 1943-44. New York, Chinese News Service [1945] 80 p.

——. The collected wartime messages of Generalissimo Chiang Kai-shek, 1937-45, compiled by Chinese Ministry of Information. New York, John Day [1946] 2 v. ports., facsims.

——. China's destiny; authorized translation by Wang Chung-hui, with an introduction by Lin Yutang. New York, Macmillan, 1947; Taipei, China Cultural Service, 1953. xi, 260 p. "First edition (in Chinese), Chungking, March 1943. First English edition, New York, 1947."

——. The destiny of China. 1st ed. Translated and published by Wang Sheng-chih. [Singapore? 194- ] 141 p.

——. China's destiny and Chinese economic theory, by Chiang Kai-shek, with notes and commentary by Philip Jaffe. New York, Roy Publishers [1947] 347 p.

——. Destin de la Chine [et La théorie économique chinoise] Présenté et commenté par Philip Jaffe. Tr. de l'américain par S.T. Vincenot et Francine Péris. Paris, Amiot-Dumont [1949] 293 p. fold. map. (Archives d'histoire contemporaine).

——. Selected speeches and messages, 1937-45. Taipei, China Cultural Service [195?] 279 p.

——. Selected speeches and messages, 1949-50. Taipei, Office of the Govt. Spokesman, 1950. 52 p.

——. Selected speeches and messages, 1949-52. [Taipei] Off. of the Govt. Spokesman [1952] 104 p.

——. Selected speeches and messages in 1954. Taipei, Govt. Information Bureau, 1954. 30, 24 p.

——. Address at the opening of the second session of the First National Assembly on February 19, 1954. [Taipei?] Govt. Information Bureau [1954] 16 p.; 15 p.

——. Messages, October 10, 1954-February 14, 1955. Taipei, Fourth Dept., Central Committee of the Kuomintang [1955] cover-title, 63 p.

——. Selected speeches and messages in 1955. [Taipei?] Govt. Information Office [1955] 65 p.

CH'IEN, TUAN-SHÊNG, 錢端升, 1900- China's national unification; some political and administrative aspects. Prepared for the 1939 study meeting of the Institute of Pacific Relations, Virginia Beach, Virginia, November, 1939. Kowloon, H.K., China Institute of Pacific Relations, 1939. 16 numb. l.

CHINA. Government Information Office. Why the Government bans the Democratic League? Nanking, Government Information Office, 1947. 30 p.

——. National Assembly. 1954. Free China's National Assembly: its second session, February 1954. Taipei, Fourth Department, Central Committee of the Kuomintang, 1955. 46 p.

CHINA NEWS PRESS. Free China in five years. Taipei, 1955. 30 p. illus. ports.
    maps.
FIELD, FREDERICK VANDERBILT, 1905-  China's greatest crisis.  New York,
    New Century [1945] 32 p. illus. (incl. ports.).
FORMAN, HARRISON, 1904-  Blunder in Asia.  New York, Didier [1950] 190 p.
GODDARD, WILLIAM G. The Ming sheng, 民生 : a study of Chinese democracy.
    Canberra, Australian Institute of Anatomy, 1941. 24 p. (George Ernest Mor-
    rison lectures ).
———. Two Chinas?  Wellington, N. Z. Chinese Anti-Communist Union [1955]
    15 p.
GUSE, FELIX. China; Ereignisse und Zustände; Eine Skizze. Berlin, G. Stilke,
    1937. 77 p. maps. (Schriftenreihe der Preussischen Jahrbücher, 40 ).
HAO, CHIH-HSIANG, 郝志翔 , 1904-  China belongs to the Chinese people. With
    forewords by J. Leighton Stuart and Victor W. Odlum.  Shanghai, Commer-
    cial Press, 1948. xxxiv, 518 p. illus.
L'INDÉPENDANCE BELGE. La Chine moderne [Special number of the Indepen-
    dance Belge].  Bruxelles, L'Indépendance Belge, 1937. 24 p. illus.
LACY, CREIGHTON. Is China a democracy?  New York, John Day [1943] 154 p.
LIN, MOU-SHENG, 林倅聖 , 1906-  Chungking dialogues.  New York, John Day
    [1945] x, 149 p.
LINEBARGER, PAUL MYRON ANTHONY, 1913-  The China of Chiang K'ai-
    shek: a political study.  Boston, World Peace Foundation, 1941. xi, 449 p.
    front., 2 ports. (incl. front.) diagrs. (part fold.).
MALOOF, LOUIS JOSEPH. Truth about China's crisis. Huntington, Ind., Our
    Sunday Visitor Press [1949?] 143 p.
MARTIN, R. ORMSBY. Tradition and transition in Chinese politics. Sydney,
    Australian Institute of International Affairs, 1943. 31, [1] p. (Australia in a
    new world, 3 ).
OU va la Chine? Saigon, A. Portail, 1939. 178 p. (Amicale des citoyens fran-
    çais d'origine chinois).
POLITICAL CONSULTATIVE CONFERENCE, Chungking, 1946. Political Con-
    sultative Conference. With relevant documents and references. [Shanghai]
    International Publishers [1946-   1 v.
PRINGLE, JOHN MARTIN DOUGLAS, 1912-  China struggles for unity, by J.
    M. D. Pringle; with 24 maps by Marthe Rajchman. Harmondsworth, Middle-
    dex, Eng., Penguin Books [1939] x, 11-182 p. incl. front.(map) illus.(maps).
QUIGLEY, HAROLD SCOTT, 1889-  Free China. New York, Carnegie Endow-
    ment for International Peace, Division of Intercourse and Education [1940]
    131-180 p. (International conciliation. April, 1940, no. 359 ).
RANNEY, JOHN CALYER. The major foreign powers: the governments of Great
    Britain, France, the Soviet Union and China [by] John C. Ranney [and] Gwen-
    dolen M. Carter, under the general editorship of Benjamin F. Wright. New
    York, Harcourt, Brace, 1949. xxix, 865, [xxxi]-cxlii p. maps, diagrs.
ROSINGER, LAWRENCE KAELTER, 1915-  Deadlock in China. San Francisco,
    New York [etc.] American Council, Institute of Pacific Relations, 1940. 32 p.
    illus. (maps).
———. China's wartime politics, 1937-44.  Princeton, Princeton University
    Press, 1945. viii p., 3-133 p.
———. China's crisis. New York, A. A. Knopf, 1945. xii, 259, xiii, [1]p. fold.
    map.
———. China in ferment. New York, N. Y., Foreign Policy Association [1947]
    243-251, [1] p. (Foreign policy reports, 22:20. January 1, 1947 ).
SCHENKE, WOLF. China im Sturm; von Chiang Kai-shek zu Mao Tse-tung.
    Hamburg, H. H. Nölke, 1949. 326 p. illus., ports.
SHEN, SHIH-HUA, 沈士華 , 1901-  Chinese unity. London, Oxford University
    Press, Indian Branch [1943] 19 p. (The Russell lecture, 1943 ).
SOONG, MAYLING, 蔣宋美齡 , 1897-  War messages and other selections.

[Hankow, China Information Committee, 1938] iv p., 381 p.

————. We Chinese women; speeches and writings during the first United nations year, February 12, 1942-November 16, 1942. New York, John Day [1943] v, 55 p.

STEWART, MAXWELL SLUTZ, 1900-  Divided China. [Toronto, Canadian Association for Adult Education and the Canadian Institute of International Affairs, 1946] cover-title, 20 p. illus. (map) (Behind the headlines. 6:5).

SUN, FO, 孫科, 1891-  China looks forward. London, G. Allen and Unwin [1944] 260 p.

————. The same; with an introduction by Lin Yutang. New York, John Day [1944] xvi, 276 p. illus.(map).

————. La Chine de demain. Paris, Nagel [1946]  iii,  403, [4] p. (Écrits politiques).

TAO, PUNG-FAI,  陶鵬飛. Die Volksführung im heutigen China. Berlin, 1941. 141 l. Diss.-Univ. Berlin.

TSÊNG, HSÜ-PAI, 曾虛白, 1894-  A new China emerges. [Translated and published by MSA/JCRR Information Office. n.p., 1952] 13, 11 p.

WANG, CHENGTING T., 王正廷, 1882-  Democratic China; an address delivered before the Philadelphia Board of trade, October 21, 1937. [Philadelphia? 1937] 5 numb. l.

WANG, EUGENE H.C., 王漢中. Free China during 1950, by Eugene H.C. Wang and others. Taipei, China Cultural Service, 1951. 52 p.

YIH, DACHIN, 葉達卿, 1911-  The information of Chinese bureaucracy. Cambridge, 1946. 422 l. Thesis-Harvard University.


## Central Government


[BISSON, THOMAS ARTHUR] 1900-  The Nanking government. New York [Foreign Policy Association, 1929] p.[295]-312. illus.(map)(Foreign policy association. Information service. 5:17. October 30, 1929 ).

CHANG, HUI-WEN, 張匯文, 1907-  The development of the civil service examination system in China since 1911. Stanford, 1932. xii, 526 l. fold. table. Thesis-Stanford University.

CH'IEN, TUAN-SHENG, 錢端升, 1900-  The government and politics of China. Cambridge, Harvard University Press, 1950. xviii, 526 p. fold. map, diagrs.

CHINA. Government Information Office. The Chinese government--its work and policy. Toward a better understanding of the Chinese situation by Wu Techen, 吳鐵城. Nanking, Government Information Office, 1947. 18 p.

HOUN, FRANKLIN W., 侯服五[Hou Fu-wu] 1920-  Central government of China 1912-28 an institutional study. Madison, University of Wisconsin Press, 1957. ix, 246 p.

JOBEZ, ROBERT, ed. and tr. Organisation du gouvernement nationaliste d'après les textes législatifs. Traduction de Robert Jobez. Sienhsien, Impr. de la Mission [1929?] 175 p.

LO, KORCH HUANG,  羅篁, 1897-  The civil service system of China. Taipei, China Cultural Service [1954?] 35 p.

LUM, KALFRED DIP, 林蚕 , 1899-  Chinese government. Shanghai, Mercury Press, 1934. ix, 177 p. diagr.

OUANG, T.T., 王治纛, 1893-  Le gouvernement de la Chine moderne. Essai sur la réglementation des pouvoirs publics et sur les rapports entre le gouvernement central et le gouvernement des provinces. Paris, Jouve, 1923. 186 p. Thèse-Univ. de Paris.

PEN, LY-TOAN, 彭禮端. Étude historique et critique sur l'organisation administrative de la Chine depuis 1912 jusqu'à 1931. Lyon, Bosc-Riou, 1931. 129 p. Thèse-Univ. de Lyon.

SHEN, JAMES, 沈劍虹. Chinese government structure. Chungking, Chinese Ministry of Information, 1943. 52 p. (China Handbook ser., 3 ).

WU, CHIH-FANG, 吳芷芳. Chinese government and politics, with a foreword by His Excellency Sun Fo. Shanghai, Commercial Press, 1934. xv, 473 p.

## Provincial and Local Governments

CHANG, CH'UN-MING, 張純明, 1904-  A new government for rural China: the political aspect of rural reconstruction. Preliminary paper prepared for the sixth conference of the Institute of Pacific relations held at Yosemite, California, August 15-29, 1936. [Shanghai] China Institute of Pacific Relations, 1936. 51 p. (Papers presented at the sixth conference of the Institute of Pacific relations, Yosemite national park, California, August 15 to 29, 1936. 4:4 ).

CHANG, YU-SING, 張又新? L'autonomie locale en Chine. Nancy, Impr. Grandville, 1933. 123 p. Thèse-Univ. de Nancy.

CH'ÊN, HAN-MING, 陳漢民. New life for Kiangsi. By C. W. H. Young [pseud.] Shanghai, [China Pub. Co.] 1935. xii, 196 p. illus., plates (part col.), ports., facsims.

GNIEU, HIS. Le régime administratif de la Chine; les rapports juridiques entre le gouvernement central et les gouvernement provinciaux. Paris, Jouve, 1923. 161 p. Thèse-Univ. de Paris.

HSU, HAN-HAO, 徐漢豪, 1907-  L'administration provinciale en Chine. Nancy, Impr. de Grandville, 1931. 134 p. Thèse-Univ. de Nancy.

KOU, KI-YONG, 顧繼榮 [Ku Chi-yung]. La sous-préfecture chinoise, étude de son administration actuelle, origine-organisation-services (thèse pour le doctorat en droit - 1926) par Jean Kou Ki-yong. Zi-ka-wei-Chang-hai, Impr. de l'Orphelinat de T'ou-sè-wè, 1930. 134 p.

TUNG, MONG-SHENG, 童蒙聖. L'administration locale en France et en Chine. Nancy, Impr. Vagner, 1937. 140 p. Thèse-Univ. de Nancy.

WANG, KAN-YÜ, 王贛愚, 1906-  The local government of China; a study of the administrative nature of local units. Chungking, China Institute of Pacific Relations, 1945. iii, 50 p. tables. (China council series, 6 ).

YAO, TING-CHEN, 姚定塵. Le gouvernement central et les gouvernements locaux en Chine. Paris, A. Pedone, 1933. ii, 170 p. Thèse-Univ. de Grenoble.

## Nationalist Party: Kuo min tang

CHANG, CH'I-YÜN, 張其昀, 1901-  The Kuomintang on the march; translated by Michael Tung. Taipei, China Cultural Service, 1954. 33 p. (Pamphlet on Kuomintang affairs ).

———. The rebirth of the Kuomintang; the Seventh National Congress. Translated into English by Nee Yuan-ching, 倪元卿. Rev. and edited by Tsao Wen-yen, 曹文彥. Taipei, China Cultural Service [195-] 123 p.

CH'ÊN, CHIH-MAI, 陳之邁, 1908-  Kuomintang-Communist relations; a historical survey. [Washington? D.C., 1949] 38 l.

CHIANG KAI-SHEK, 1886-  Declaration to Kuomintang members, April, 1927. [Shanghai, Commercial Press, 1927] cover-title, 2, 19, [1] p. 2 port.

———. The reform of the Kuomintang. A resolution introduced by President Chiang Kai-shek and adopted at a meeting of the standing committee of the Central Executive Committee held on July 22, 1950. Taipei, 1950. 13 l.

———. Statement to all members of the Kuomintang, September, 1949; with Chinese text. Taipei, China Cultural Service [1954] 29 p. (Pamphlets on Kuomintang affairs ).

———. Message on KMT's 60th anniversary, November 12, 1954; with Chinese text. Taipei, China Cultural Service [1954] 14 p. (Pamphlets on Kuomintang affairs ).

CHINA INFORMATION COMMITTEE. An outline of the organization of the Kuomintang and the Chinese government. Chungking, The China Information Committee, 1940. 14 p.

FOREIGN POLICY ASSOCIATION, New York. The rise of the Kuomintang, a survey of government in China since 1911. [New York, Foreign Policy Association, 1928] p. [156]-186. illus. (map) (Information service. 4:8. June 22, 1928 ).

KOUANG, SIOU-WENG, 鄺修文 [Kwan Hsiu-wen]. Étude sur les rapports entre le gouvernement National et le Kuomintang. Nancy, Impr. Grandville, 1933. 120 p. Thèse-Univ. de Nancy.

KUO-MIN-TANG. The Kuomintang manifesto and platform. Adopted by the Seventh National Convention, October, 1952. Taipei, Fourth Dept., Central Committee, Kuomintang [1952?] cover-title, 11 p.

——. The same. Adopted by the Seventh National Convention, October 20, 1952. Taipei, China Cultural Service [1954] 35 p. (Pamphlets on Kuomintang affairs ).

PARIS. Parti de la Jeune Chine. Combattre l'expansion de la terreur rouge, c'est non seulement pour défendre l'intégrité du territoire de la Chine, mais encore pour assurer la paix mondiale. Fontenay-aux-Roses, Impr. Louis Bellenand et fils, 1929. 1 v.

——. Le mouvement nationaliste et le Parti de Jeune Chine. Fontenay-aux-Roses, Impr. Louis Bellenand et fils, 1930. 8 p.

SHEN, JAMES, 沈劍虹. Kuomintang--China's ruling party. Chungking, Chinese Ministry of Information, 1943. 45 p. (China Handbook ser., 2 ).

SUN, YAT-SEN, 1866-1925. The three principles, by Sun Yat-sen; known to the Chinese as the "San min chu i"; translated from the original Chinese by a well-known sinologue with notes by an independent commentator. Shanghai, North China Daily News and Herald, 1927. 106 p.

——. San min chu i, The three principles of the people, by Dr. Sun Yat-sen. Translated into English, by Frank W. Price; edited by L. T. Chen, 陳立廷. Shanghai, China Committee, Institute of Pacific Relations, 1927. xvii, [3]-514 p. incl. front. (port.) diagrs. (International understanding series ).

——. The same; translated by Frank W. Price; edited by L. T. Chen, under the auspices of China Committee, Institute of Pacific Relations. Chungking, Ministry of Information, 1943. xvii, [3]-514 p. incl. front. (port.) diagrs. (International understanding series ).

——. The same. Translated into English by Frank W. Price, edited by L. T. Chen. [Calcutta] Calcutta Office, Chinese Ministry of Information, 1942[i.e. 1944] xvii, 317 p. port.

——. The same. Translated into English by Frank W. Price; abridged and edited by the Commission for the Compilation of the History of the Kuomintang. Taipei, China Cultural Service, 1953. xiv, 213 p.

——. The triple demism of Sun Yat-sen, translated from the Chinese, annotated and appraised by Paschal M. d'Elia, S. J. with introduction and index. English ed. Wuchang, The Franciscan Press, 1931. 747 p. incl. front.(port) illus. (1 col.) diagrs. (1 fold.).

——. Die drei nationalen Grundlehren. Berlin, Schlieffen-Verlag, 1927- 1 v. front. (port.) facsim. CONTENTS-I. Die Grundlehren von dem Volkstum, übertragen von Tsan Wan, 萬燦 .

——. The principle of nationalism. [With Chinese text] Translated into English by Frank W. Price, abridged and edited by the Commission for the Compilation of the History of the Kuomintang. Taipei, China Cultural Service [pref. 1953] 69 p.

——. The principle of democracy. [With Chinese text] Translated into English by Frank W. Price; abridged and edited by the Commission for the Compilation of the History of the Kuomintang. Taipei, China Cultural Service [pref. 1953] 142 p.

——. The principle of livelihood. [With Chinese text] Translated into English

by Frank W. Price; abridged and edited by the Commission for the Compila-
tion of the History of the Kuomintang. Taipei, China Cultural Service [pref.
1953] 89 p.
——. The cult of Dr. Sun; Sun Wen hsueh shu, 孫文學說. Translation by Wei
Yung, 韋榮. Shanghai, The Independent Weekly, 1931. ii, 230, xx p.
TSEN, TSONMING, 曾仲鳴, 1896-1939. La Chine et le Kuomintang. Shanghai,
Librairie franco-chinoise [1930] [7]-121 p.
WANG, CHÉNG, 王政. The Kuomintang; a sociological study of demoralization.
Stanford, Calif., 1953. iii, 179 p. Thesis-Stanford University.
WANG, CHI-WEN. The Chinese nationalist party (Kuomintang), imperialism and
the two great internationals after the anti-communistic movement; translated
by Tang Chung-tzu, 唐崇慈. Hankow, 1928. cover-title, 39, [34] p.
WHITE, THEODORE HAROLD, 1915- [Articles on the Kuomintang and the Chinese Communist Party and the reply of Dr. Liang Han-chao, 梁寒操, to the
article on the Kuomintang. n.p., 1943?] Microfilm copy of typescript. 1 v.
(various pagings ).
WOO, THOMAS TZE CHUNG, 吳之椿, [Wu Chih-chun] 1893- The Kuomintang
and the future of the Chinese revolution. London, G. Allen and Unwin[1928]
9-278 p.

## Communist Party: Kung Ch'an tang
### Bibliographies

CHAO, KUO-CHŪN, 趙國鈞, 1918- comp. Draft survey of materials relating
to communism in China 1927-34, collected by Harold R. Isaacs. Stanford,
Hoover Institute and Library, 1948. 57 1.
FAIRBANK, JOHN KING, 1907- Chinese Communist publications: an annotated
bibliography of material in the Chinese Library at Harvard University, edited by J.K. Fairbank and E-tu Zen Sun for the Russian Research Center and
mimeographed for private distribution. Cambridge, Russian Research Center, Harvard University, 1949. iv, 122 1.
QUAN, LAU KING, 關魯敬, 1906- A survey of material from Communist China in the Library of Congress and a pilot study on Chinese communist statements on the United States. Washington, Library of Congress, 1951. 113 p.
SHIRATO, ICHIRŌ. Japanese sources on the history of the Chinese Communist
movement; an annotated bibliography of materials in the East Asiatic Library
of Columbia University and the Division of Orientalia, Library of Congress.
Edited by C. Martin Wilbur. New York, Reproduced for private distribution
by the East Asian Institute of Columbia University, 1953. viii, 69 p.(Columbia University. [East Asian Institute] East Asian Institute studies, 2 ).
WILBUR, CLARENCE MARTIN, 1908- Chinese sources on the history of the
Chinese Communist movement; an annotated bibliography of materials in the
East Asiatic Library of Columbia University, edited by C. Martin Wilbur,
with the assistance of Joan J. Feldman and Sophie Lou. New York, Repro-
diced for private distribution by the East Asian Institute of Columbia University, 1950. 56 p. (Columbia University. [East Asian Institute] East Asian
Institute studies, 1 ).
WRITINGS of the members of the Central Committee of Chinese Communist Party. New York, Columbia University East Asiatic Library, 1952. 41 p.

### Ideology

CH'ÊN, PO-TA, 陳伯達, 1905- Mao Tse-tung on the Chinese revolution; written in commemoration of the 30th anniversary of the Communist Party of China. Peking, Foreign Languages Press, 1953. 86 p.
——.La théorie de Mao Tsé-toung sur la révolution chinoise. En commémora-
tion du xxxe anniversaire du Parti communiste chinois. Pékin, Éditions en

langues étrangères, 1953. 81 p.

——. Mao Tse-tung über die chinesische Revolution; zum 30. Jahrestag der Kommunistischen Partei Chinas [von] Tschen Bo-da. [Übers. von Siegfried Behrsing] Berlin, Dietz, 1953. 72 p.

——. Stalin and the Chinese revolution, in celebration of Stalin's seventieth birthday. Peking, Foreign Languages Press, 1953. 55 p.

LIU, SHAO-CH'I, 劉少奇, 1900-   May day address. (April 29, 1950) Peking, 1950. 10 p.

——. Adresse du premier mai. Pékin, Éditions en langues étrangères, 1950. 33 p.

——. On inner-party struggle. A lecture delivered on July 2, 1941 at the party school for Central China. Peking, Foreign Languages Press [1950?]; Bombay, People's Pub. House, 1951. (64 p.) 92 p. port.

——. On the party. [3d ed.] Peking, Foreign Languages Press, 1951; Bombay, People's Pub. House, 1951. 190 p. port.

——. Über die Partei; Referat über die Abänderung des Parteistatuts auf dem VII. Parteitag der Kommunistischen Partei Chinas im Mai 1945. Berlin, Dietz, 1954. 176 p.

——. Internationalism and nationalism. [4th ed.] Peking, Foreign Languages Press, 1954. 50 p.

——. L'internationalisme et le nationalisme [par] Liou Chao-chi. [1.ed.] Pékin, Éditions en langues étrangères [1951] 56 p. illus.

——. How to be a good Communist. [2d rev. ed.] Peking, Foreign Languages Press [1952]; New York, New Century, 1952. 1st ed. 1951.

——. Pour être un bon communist par Liou Chao-tchi. Traduction de Paul Jamati. Paris, Éditions sociales, 1955. 120 p.

LU, TING-I, 陸定一, 1907-   "Let flowers of many kinds blossom, divers schools of thought contend!", a speech on the policy of the Communist Party of China on art, literature and science delivered on May 26, 1956. Peking, Foreign Languages Press, 1957. 39 p.

MAO, TSÊ-TUNG, 毛澤東, 1893-   Selected works. New York, International Publishers [1954-56] 5 v.

——. The same. London, Lawrence and Wishart, 1954-57. 5 v. illus.

——. The same. Bombay, People's Pub. House, 1954. 4 v. illus.

——. Oeuvres choises. Paris, Éditions sociales, 1955-57. 4 v.

——. Ausgewahlte Schriften. Übers. aus dem Russischen von Leon Nebenzahl. Berlin, Dietz, 1956. 4 v.

——. Three important writings: China's new democracy, the Dictatorship of People's democracy, Chinese revolution and the Communist Party of China. Bombay, People's Pub. House, 1950. 86 p.

——. New life in new China, by Mao Tse-tung and others. Calcutta, Purabi Publishers, 1945 (c1937). iv, 163 p.

——. The new stage. Report to the sixth enlarged plenum of the Central Committee of the Communist Party of China. Chungking, New China Information Committee [1938?] cover-title, 76 p.

——. China's strategy for victory. Bombay, People's Pub. House [1945] xxix, 116 p.

——. The fight for a new China. New York, New Century [1945] 80 p.

——. On coalition government; report to the 7th congress of the Chinese Communist Party of Yenan, September, 1945. Chungking, New China News Agency, 1945. 94 p.

——. On coalition government. Peking, Foreign Languages Press, 1955. 118 p. illus.

——. The way out of China's civil war; a report on coalition government delivered to the 7th national congress of the Chinese Communist Party. Bombay, People's Pub. House [1946] iv, 84 p.

——. China's new democracy; with an introduction by Earl Browder. Bombay,

People's Pub. House, 1944;  New York, New Century [1945] 72 p. port.

———, Mao Tse-tung's "democracy," a digest of the bible of Chinese communism, commentary by Lin Yutang, with expurgated passages restored. [New York, Chinese News Service, 1947] 23 p.

———. Turning point in China.  New York, New Century, 1948. 24 p.

———. New democracy; basis of social, political and economic structure of new China.  Shanghai, Chinese-American Pub. Co. [1949] 83 p.

———. La nouvelle démocratie.  Paris, Éditions sociales, 1951. 207 p.

———. On new democracy.  Peking, Foreign Languages Press, 1954. 84 p. illus.

———. On people's democratic dictatorship, and Speech at the preparatory meeting of the new PCC.  Peking, English Language Service, New China News Agency, 1949. cover-title, 27 p. port.

———. People's democratic dictatorship.  London, Lawrence and Wishart, 1950. 40 p.

———. On people's democratic rule.  [New York, New Century, 1950] cover-title. 24 p. (Marxist pamphlets, 5 ).

———. The dictatorship of people's democracy.  Articles written for the 28th anniversary (July 1, 1949) of the Communist Party of China.  Bombay, People's Pub. House, 1950. 13 p.

———. On people's democratic dictatorship, together with his two speeches delivered at the preparatory committee meeting and the first plenary session of the Chinese People's Political Consultative Conference. [3d ed. ] Peking, Foreign Languages Press, 1950. 45 p. port.

———. La dictature de la démocratie populaire avec les deux discours prononcés à la réunion préparatoire et à la première session plénière de la Conférence consultative politique du peuple chinois.  Pékin, Éditions en langues étrangères, 1949. 38 p. port.

———. Über die Diktatur der Volksdemokratie.  Peking, Verlag für Fremdsprachige Literatur, 1950. 25 p. port.

———. The same.  Berlin, Dietz, 1952. 21 p. (Kleine Bücherei des Marxismus-Leninismus ).

———. The dictatorship of the people's democracy; edited by Tien-yi Li, 李田意. New Haven, Far Eastern Publications, Yale University, 1951. 13 p., 21 p. ( [Yale University. Dept. of Oriental Studies]  Mirror series C, 5 ).

———. Lessons of the Chinese Revolution [by] Mao Tse-tung and Liu Shao-chi. [1st Indian ed. Bombay, Published by J. Bhatt for People's Pub. House, 1950] 31 p.

———. La stratégie de la guerre révolutionnaire en Chine.  Paris, Éditions sociales, 1950. 118 p.  maps.

———. Strategic problems of China's revolutionary war. [1st Indian ed. ] Bombay, People's Pub. House [1951] 82 p. maps.

———. The same.  Peking, Foreign Languages Press, 1954. 132 p. illus.

———. Strategische Fragen des revolutionären Krieges in China.  Berlin, Dietz, 1955. 115 p.

———. On practice; on the relation between knowledge and practice - between knowing and doing.  Peking, 1951. 23 p. illus.

———. Concerning practice; on the connection between cognition and practice - the connection between knowledge and deeds.  Bombay, People's Pub. House, 1951;  London, Labour Monthly, 1951. 16 p.

———. Über die Praxis. Über den Zusammenhang von Erkenntnis über Praxis, von Wissen und Handeln.  Berlin, Dietz, 1952. 26 p. (Kleine Bücherei des Marxismus-Leninismus).

———. On contradiction.  Peking, Foreign Languages Press, 1952. 2d ed. 1953. 71 p. illus.

———. The same.  New York, International Publishers [1953] 61 p.

———. Über den Widerspruch. [4. Aufl. ] Berlin, Dietz, 1956. 60 p. (Kleine Bücherei des Marxismus-Leninismus ).

————. Introductory remarks to "The Communist." Peking, Foreign Languages Press, 1953. 23 p.

————. Pour la parution de "La Communist." Pékin, Édition en langues étrangères, 1953. 24 p.

————. Einleitung zur Zeitschrift "Der Kommunist." Peking, Verlag für Fremdsprachige Literatur, 1953. 25 p. (Kleine Bücherei des Marxismus-Leninismus ).

————. On the rectification of incorrect ideas in the Party. Peking, Foreign Languages Press, 1953. 19 p.

————. A single spark can start a prairie fire. Peking, Foreign Languages Press, 1953. 22 p.

————. Why can China's red political power exist? Peking, Foreign Languages Press, 1953. 17 p.

————. Contre le libéralisme. Pékin, Édition en langues étrangères, 1954. 6 p.

————. On the protracted war. Peking, Foreign Languages Press, 1954. 140 p. illus.

————. The question of independence and autonomy within the united front. Peking, Foreign Languages Press, 1954. 9 p.

————. Problems of war and strategy. Peking, Foreign Languages Press, 1954. 30 p.

————. On methods of leadership. Peking, Foreign Languages Press, 1955. 10 p.

————. Oppose the Party "eight-legged essay." Peking, Foreign Languages Press, 1955. 27 p.

————. Our study and the current situation. Appendix: Resolution on some questions in the history of our Party. Peking, Foreign Languages Press, 1955. 116 p. port.

————. Preface and postscript to "rural survey." Peking, Foreign Languages Press, 1955. 9 p.

————. Reform our study. Peking, Foreign Languages Press, 1955. 13 p.

————. Analysis of the classes in Chinese society. Peking, Foreign Languages Press, 1956. 17 p.

————. On the correct handling of contradictions among the people. [Peking, 1957] 26 p.

————. The same; text of a speech made on February 27, 1957, at the eleventh session (enlarged) of the Supreme State Conference. London, Communist Party, 1957. 15 p.

————. Maoism, a sourcebook; selections from the writings of Mao Tse-tung. Introduced and edited by H. Arthur Steiner. [Los Angeles] University of California at Los Angeles, 1952. 142 p.

PEOPLE'S DAILY, Peking. On the historical experience of the dictatorship of the proletariat. This article was written by the Editorial Department of the People's Daily on the basis of the discussion which took place at an enlarged meeting of the Political Bureau of the Central Committee of the Communist Party of China. Peking, Foreign Languages Press, 1956. 20 p.

————. More on the historical experience of the dictatorship of the proletariat. Peking, Foreign Languages Press, 1957. 43 p.

————. Nochmals über die historischen Erfahrungen der Diktatur des Proletariats. Artikel der Zeitung "Schenminschipao" vom 29. Dezember, 1956. Moskau, Verlag für fremdsprachige Literatur, 1957. 48 p.

WANG, CHIA-HSIANG, 王稼祥 , 1907-  Communists and the Three People's Principles by Wang Chia-hsiang, Chen Po-ta and Lo-fu, 洛甫 (Chang Wen-tien, 張聞天 ). Chungking, New China Information Committee, 1940. 76 p. (Its Bull., 16 ).

## Organization

CHINA. Government Information Office. Chinese communist organizations and activities shown in graphic charts. Taipei, 1956. cover-title, [1] l. 1 map, 21 charts.

The COMMUNIST PARTY, leader of the Chinese revolution. Peking, Foreign Languages Press, 1951. 41 p. illus.

COMMUNIST PARTY. CHINA. Documents of the National Conference of the Communist Party of China, March 1955. Peking, Foreign Languages Press, 1955. 63 p

——. National Congress, 1956. The political report of the Central Committee of the Communist Party of China to the Eighth National Congress of the Party. Delivered on Sept. 15, 1956 [by] Lui Shao-chi. Peking, Foreign Languages Press, 1956. 100 p.

——. The same; 57 p. (Hsinhua News Agency release. Supplement.).

——. Full text of a political report by Liu Shao-ch'i, delivered on the opening day of the Congress in Peking on September 15, 1956. Singapore, 1956. 40 p. (Radio Malaya monitoring digest, 216 ).

——. Rapport politique du Comité central du Parti communiste chinois au 8e Congrès [presenté par] Liou Chao-chi [suivi de] Résolution du 8e Congrès sur le rapport politique. Pékin, Éditions en langues étrangères, 1956. 134 p

——. Rechenschaftsbericht des Zentralkomitees der Kommunistischen Partei Chinas an den 8. Parteitag, von Liu Shao-chi. Berlin, Dietz, 1956. 63 p.

——. Report on revision of the Constitution of the Communist Party of China, by Teng Hsiao-ping, 鄧小平, on behalf of the Central Committee delivered on the opening day of the Congress in Peking on September 15, 1956. [Peking, 1956] 24 p. Issued also as a special supplement to Radio Malaya monitoring digest, 218.

——. Statuts du parti communiste chinois [suivi de] Rapport sur les modifications des statuts du Parti [par] Teng Siao-ping. Pékin, Édition en langues étrangères, 1956. 111 p.

——. The Constitution of the Communist Party of China. Report on the revision of the Constitution of the Communist Party of China [by] Teng Hsiao-ping. Peking, Foreign Languages Press, 1956. 109 p.

——. Über die Veränderungen im Statut der Kommunistischen Partei Chinas von Dõng Ssjau-ping, 鄧小平. Berlin, Dietz, 1956. 31 p. (Material vom 8. Parteitag der Kommunistischen Partei Chinas ).

——. Eighth National Congress of the Communist Party of China. Peking, Foreign Languages Press, 1956. 3 v.

——. Der 8. Parteitag der Kommunistischen Partei Chinas. Dokumente. Peking, Verlag für fremdsprachige Literatur, 1956. 3 v.

——. Recueil de documents. Paris, 1957. 255 p. illus. (Les cahiers du communisme, numéro spécial. Janv., 1957).

DEMOCRATIC centralism in China; party rule and its disguise. [London, 1955] 15 p.

FANG, SHU, 方叔. Campaign of party-expansion of the Chinese Communist Party in 1952. Kowloon, H.K., Union Research Institute [1954] cover-title, 38 p. (Communist China problem research series [EC1] ).

HU, CH'IAO-MU, 胡喬木, 1905-  Thirty years of the Communist Party of China. Peking, Foreign Languages Press, 1952. 93 p. 1951 ed.: London, Lawrence and Wishart, 1951. 95 p.

——. Les trente années du Parti communiste chinois, par Hou Kiao-mou. Pékin, Éditions en langues étrangères, 1952. 117 p.

——. 30 [i.e. Dreissig] Jahre Geschichte der Kommunistischen Partei Chinas von Hu Tschiau-mu. [Übersetzt von Fritz Jensen] Berlin, Dietz, 1954. 111 p

GOEL, SITA RAM. Communist Party in China: a study in treason. Calcutta, Society for Defence of Freedom in Asia [1953] 106 p. (Inside Communist Slave-Empire series, no. 5 ).

MAO, TSE-TUNG, 1893-  Report to the Central Committee of the Chinese Communist Party, December 25, 1947; broadcast from North Shensi on January 1, 1948. New York, 1948. 12 l.

———. The Chinese revolution and the Chinese Communist Party; published in
Chinese, November 15, 1939, translated into English March 22, 1949 by
Huang Li. Shanghai, China Digest, 1949. 19 1.

———. The Chinese revolution and the Communist Party of China. New York,
Committee for a Democratic Far Eastern Policy, 1949. 20 p.

———. Chinese revolution and the Communist Party of China. [Bombay] People's Pub. House [1950] 30 p.

———. La révolution chinoise et le Parti communiste chinois. Pékin, Édition
en langues étrangères, 1953. 58 p.

———. The Chinese revolution and the Chinese Communist Party. Peking, Foreign Languages Press, 1954. 56 p. port.

———. The role of the Chinese Communist Party in the national war. Peking,
Foreign Languages Press, 1956. 33 p.

———. The tasks of the Chinese Communist Party in the period of resistance to
Japan. Peking, Foreign Languages Press, 1956. 44 p.

MAO'S China; party reform documents, 1942-44. Translation and introd. by Boyd
Compton. Seattle, University of Washington Press, 1952. lii, 278 p. map
(University of Washington publications on Asia).

MĪF, PAVEL ALEKSANDROVĪCH, 1901-  Heroic China, fifteen years of the
Communist Party of China. New York, Workers Library Publishers [1937]
96 p. illus. (map).

———. Pour une Chine libre et forte. Quinze années de lutte heroique du Parti
communist de Chine. Paris, Bureau d'éditions, de diffusion et de publicité,
1937. 60 p. illus.

RESOLUTIONS and telegrams of the six Plenum of the Central Committee, Communist Party of China, November 6, 1938. Hong Kong, New China Information Committee, 1938. 22 p.


General Works: 1921-1948


AMANN, GUSTAV, 1882-  Bauernkrieg in China; Chiang Kaisheks Kampf gegen
den Aufstand, 1932-35. Heidelberg [etc.] Vowinckel, 1939. 157,[1] p. plates,
port., maps (1 fold.) (His Geschichte Chinas in neuester zeit. Bd. III ).

BAND, CLAIRE. Dragon fangs; two years with Chinese guerrillas, by Claire
and William Band. London, G. Allen and Unwin [1947] xii, 347 p. illus.
ports., maps.

———. Two years with the Chinese Communists, by Claire and William Band.
New Haven, Yale University Press, 1948. xii, 347 p. illus., ports., maps.

[BISSON, THOMAS ARTHUR] 1900-  The communist movement in China. New
York, Foreign Policy Association [1933] p. [37]-44. illus. (map) (Foreign
policy reports. 9:4. April 26, 1933 ).

BROWDER, EARL RUSSELL, 1891-  Why America is interested in the Chinese
Communists, [an address made before the Shanghai tiffin club, New York city. March 13, 1945] New York, New Century [1945] 16 p. illus. (incl. group
port.).

BUKHARIN, NIKOLAI IVANOVICH, 1888-1938. Les problèmes de la révolution
chinoise. Paris, Bureau d'éditions, de diffusion et de publicité, 1927. 61 p.

———. Die Probleme der chinesischen Revolution. Hamburg, C. Hoym Nachfolger, 1927. 63 p.

CHAPMAN, HERBERT OWEN. The Chinese revolution, 1926-27; a record of the
period under communist control as seen from the nationalist capital, Hankow.
London, Constable, 1928. xvii, 310 p. fold. map.

CH'ÊN, PO-TA, 陳伯達, 1905-  Critique of "China's destiny,"review of Marshal
Chiang Kai-shek's book, by Chen Pai-ta. Bombay, People's Pub. House
[1944] 49 p.

———. Notes on ten years of civil war, 1927-36. Peking, Foreign Languages
Press, 1954. 108 p.

CHIANG, KAI-SHEK, 1886-  Generalissimo Chiang's speech on the communist question delivered at the People's Political Council, Chungking, March 6, 1941.  Chungking, The China Information Committee [1941] 7, [1] p.

CHINA. Government Information Office, Montreal. China's twenty-five year struggle against communism.  Montreal, 1948. 32 p. (Pamphlet, 1 ).

CHINA: the march toward unity,  by Mao Tse-tung, Wang Ming, 王明, Georgi Dimitroff [and others]  New York, Workers Library Publishers [1937] 7-125 p.

ÜBER die antijapanische nationale Einheitsfront in China. [Articles by G. Demitrov, Wan Min, Mao Tse-tung and others]. Moskau, Verlagsgenossenschaft ausländischer Arbeiter in der UdSSR, 1937. 126 p.

CHINA'S democracy on the march. [Cheefoo] Cheefoo News [1947] cover-title, 47 p. Contents - At this decisive moment in our heroic struggle, let us resolutely meet the impending high tide of democracy, by Jao Su-shih, 饒漱石. Explanation of several basic questions concerning the post-war international situation, by Lu Ting-yi, 陸定一.

CHINA'S resistance in its sixth year. [n.p.] 1943. 85 p.

COLLINS, EDWARD MATTHEW, 1917-  American communist support of communism in China, 1920-41.  Washington, 1956. 238 l. Thesis-Georgetown University.

DOCUMENTS on the problem of the Chinese Communist Party, presented at the People's Political Council in March 1941, and the eleventh plenary session of the Central Executive Committee of the Kuomintang in October 1943. With appendices.  Chungking, Secretariat of the Supreme National Defense Council, 1944. 70, 48 p. plates.

DRIDZO, SOLOMON ABRAMOVICH, 1878-  Revolution und Konterrevolution in China, von A. Lozovski [pseud.]  Moskau, Rote Gewerkschafts-Internationale, 1928. 79 p. incl. tables.

EPSTEIN, ISRAEL, 1915-  I visit Yenan. Bombay, People's Pub. House, 1945. 96 p.

————. The unfinished revolution in China.  Boston, Little, Brown, 1947. viii, 442 p. illus. (maps).

————. China. Von Sun Jat-sen zu Mao Tse-tung. Aus dem Amerikanischen übers. von Hanna Köditz.  Berlin, Volk and Welt, 1950. 594 p.

FORMAN, HARRISON, 1904-  Report from Red China.  New York, H. Holt and company [1945] iv, [2], 250 p. plates, ports., maps.

————. The same.  London, R. Hale limited, 1946. vii, 247, [1] p. front., plates, ports.

————. Ce que j'ai vue en Chine rouge. Traduit par Sabine Bernard-Derosne. Paris, P. Seghers, 1946. 274 p. illus. fold. map.

GAUTIER, JULES. La Chine brûle, sera-t-elle bolchevisée?  Paris, Éditions d'Art, 1927. 273 p.

GELDER, GEORGE STUART, ed. The Chinese communists.  London, V. Gollancz ltd., 1946. xlii, 290 p. incl. front., 1 illus.

HO, OWEN, 何墌. L'évolution du socialisme en Chine.  Nancy, Impr. G. Thomas, 1935. [5]-156 p. Thèse-Univ. de Nancy.

INTERNATIONAL ANTI-COMMUNIST ENTENTE. Bolshevism in China.  Geneva, International Entente against the Third International, 1932. 27 p. fold. map.

————. Le bolchévisme en Chine.  Genève, Entente internationale contre la IIIe Internationale, 1932. 27 p. fold. map.

ISAACS, HAROLD ROBERT, 1910-  The tragedy of the Chinese revolution. [Rev. ed.]  Stanford, Stanford University Press [1951]; London, Oxford University Press, 1951. xv, 382 p. map (on lining papers). 1st ed., London, Secker and Warburg, 1938. 501 p.

KE, HAN. The Shansi-Hopei-Honan border region; report for 1937-39. Pt. 1. Chungking, New China Information Committee [1940] 34 p. fold. map. (Its bulletin, 15 ).

[KISSELEFF] comp. A history of communism in China; formation and activities of the Communist Party. Valuable reports among Peking Soviet documents. Tientsin, Tientsin Press, 1927. cover-title, 67 p.

KUMARAMANGALAM, MOHAN, ed. Who threatens China's unity? Bombay, People's Pub. House [1944] 52 p.

KUOMINTANG Communist negotiations. [Yenan] New China News Agency, 1945. cover-title, 1, 2, 195 p. (on double leaves) (Liberated China series).

The LIBERATED regions of China behind the enemy lines. v. 1; Mar. 1945. [n.p.] 59 p.

LINDSAY, MICHAEL, 1909- North China front. With a preface by Lord Listowel. [London, China Campaign Committee, 1944?] 23 p. plates, port.

MAO, TSÉ-TUNG, 1893- Red China; being the report on the progress and achievements of the Chinese Soviet Republic, delivered by the president, Mao Tse-tung, at the second Chinese national soviet congress, at Juikin, Kiangsi, January 22, 1934. London, M. Lawrence, limited [1934]; New York, International Publishers, 1934. 34 p. illus.(map).

MÖLLER, HEINZ. Von Kanton bis Schanghai, 1926-27, von Asiatics, [pseud.]. Wien-Berlin, Agis Verlag, c1928. viii, 352 p.

NEW CHINA INFORMATION COMMITTEE. Friction aids Japan; documents concerning instances of friction, 1939-40. Chungking, New China Information Committee, 1940. 70 p. (Its Bull., 14 ).

NORTH-CHINA DAILY NEWS, Shanghai. A bolshevized China-the world's greatest peril; also Nationalists' deliberate policy attacking all missions; Chinese pastor stoned to death at Yochow, Hunan, and other reprints from the "North-China daily news" and the "China press." Shanghai, E. E. Strother [1927] 23, [1] p. illus. (incl. port.).

[NOSAKA, SANZŌ]. The war in the Far East and the tasks of the Communists in the struggle against imperialist war and military intervention; report of Comrade Okano [pseud.] at the XIIth Plenum of the Executive Committee of the Communist International. New York, Workers' Library Publishers [1932?] 51 p. ("Twelfth Plenum" series ).

OTSUKA, REIZO. The red influence in China. Prepared for the sixth conference of the Institute of Pacific Relations to be held at Yosemite, California, August 15th to 29th, 1936. Tokyo, Japanese Council, Institute of Pacific Relations, 1936. ii, 5-97 p. (Japanese council papers, 17 ).

OUR task in 1945. [Yenan?] 1945. cover-title, 49 p.

PADOUX, GEORGES, 1867- L'échec du communisme en Chine. Commucation faité le 2 Novembre 1939 à l'Académie diplomatique internationale, Paris. Paris, A. Pedone, 1940. 15 p.

RÄTE-China, Dokumente der Chinesischen Revolution. Moskau, Verlagsgenossenschaft Ausländischer Arbeiter in der UdSSR, 1934. 730 p. fold. maps (part col., in pocket).

ROY, MANABENDRA NATH, 1893- 1954. Revolution und Konterrevolution in China. Übers. aus dem Englischen manuskript von Paul Frölich. [Berlin] Soziologische Verlagsanstalt [c1930] 9-478, [2] p. illus. (map).

——. Revolution and counter-revolution in China. Calcutta, Renaissance Publishers [1946] viii, 689 p.

——. My experiences in China. 2nd ed. Calcutta, Renaissance publishers, 1946. 70 p. 1st ed. 1938.

SCHMITZ, PETER. Der Bolschewismus in China. [Wien] 1931. 84 p. (Veröffentlichungen des Akademischen Missionsvereins, Wien, 6 ).

SENG, SIN-FU. China; a survey of the historical and economic forces behind the nationalist revolution. London, Communist Party of Great Britain, 1927. 104 p.

The SHENSI-Kansu-Ninghsia border region. Hong Kong, New China Information Committee, 1941. 17 p. ports.

——, Annual report, delivered by Chairman Lin Tsŭ-han, 林祖涵 , in the

fourth  meeting of the Border Region government on June 6, 1944. Yenan,
1944. 1 v.
———. Laws and regulations.  Yenan? 1945. 72 p.
———. Survey of Shensi-Kansu-Ninghsia border region, by Hsu Yung-ying, 徐
永瑛. New York, International Secretariat, Institute of Pacific Relations,
1945. 97 p.
[SIMON, PAUL]. Le mouvement communiste en Chine.  Verviers, Éditions
Leens [1938] 2 v. (Faits et nouvelles d'Extrême-Orient, no. 3-4 ).
———. Le mouvement communiste en Chine des origines à nos jours.  Paris,
Recueil Sirey [1939] 253 p.
[SIMPSON, BERTRAM LENOX] 1877-1930. Why China sees red, by Putnam
Weale [pseud.] New York, Dodd, Mead, 1925. xii, 337 p. front., plates,
ports., maps.
———. Chang Tso-lin's struggle against the communist menace. By Putnam
Weale [pseud.] Shanghai, Kelly and Walsh, 1927. vii, 167 p. front.(port.).
SMEDLEY, AGNES, 1890-1950. Red flood over China.  Moscow, Cooperative
Pub. Society of Foreign Workers in the USSR, 1934. 391 p.
———. China blutet. Vom Sterben des alten China. London, Malik Verlag; Mos-
kau and Leningrad, Verlagsgenossenschaft Ausländ, 1936; 2. Aufl. Berlin,
Dietz, 1953. 313 p.
———. China's Red army marches.  New York, Vanguard Press, International
Publishers, 1934. London, Lawrence and Wishart, 1936. xxi, 311 p. illus.
(music) double map.
———. La Chine rouge en marche. Traduits et adaptés, de l'anglais par Renaud
de Jouvenel. Paris, Editions sociales internationales, 1937. 320 p. map.
(Collection Ciment).
———. China fights back; an American woman with the Eighth route army.  New
York, Vanguard Press [c1938] London, V. Gollancz, 1938 [286 p.] xxii,282
p. plates, ports.
———. China kämpft. Vom Werden des neuen China.  London, Malik Verlag;
Moskau and Leningrad, Verlagsgenossenschaft, Ausländ, 1936; 2. Aufl. Ber-
lin, Dietz, 1953. 397 p.
SNOW, EDGAR, 1905-  Red star over China.  London, V. Gollancz, Toronto,
Macmillan, 1937. 464 p.
———. The same.  New York, Random House [c1938] xiv, 474 p. plates, ports.
———. The same.  Rev. ed.  New York, Garden City Pub. Co. [1939] xiv, 520 p.
plates, ports.
———. The same.  New York, Modern library [1944] xiii, 529 p. (The Modern
library of the world's best books ).
[SNOW, HELEN (FOSTER) ] 1907-  Inside red China, by Nym Wales.  New
York, Doubleday, Doran, 1939. xxiv, 356 p. plates, ports.
———. New China, by Nym Wales.  Calcutta, Eagle Publishers, 1944. x, ii,
234 (i. e. 238) p. plates, ports.
STEIN, GUENTHER. The challenge of red China.  New York, London, Whittlesey House, McGraw-Hill Book Co. [1945]; London, Pilot Press, 1945 [388
p.] x, 490 p. illus., plates, ports., maps (1 fold.).
———. La Chine rouge; traduit de l'anglais par André Stivène.  Genève, Jeheber [1947] 424 p.
STRONG, ANNA LOUISE, 1885-  The Kuomintang-communist crisis in China;
a first-hand account of one of the most critical periods in Far Eastern history.  [New York? 1941] 15 p. "Reprinted from 'Amerasia,' March 1941."
———. China's new crisis, with other authentic documents. [London] Fore Publications [1942?] 62 p. (Key books, no. 14 ).
———. Tomorrow's China.  New York, Committee for a Democratic Far Eastern Policy [1948] 128 p. map (on cover) "Published in India, under the title, 'Dawn out of China.' "
———. The Chinese conquer China.  Garden City, N.Y., Doubleday, 1949. xii,

275 p.

————. J'ai vu la Chine nouvelle; traduit par René Latour. Paris, Hier et Aujourd'hui, 1949. 340 p. map. (Essais et documents).

SUMMARY of conversations between the Chinese government and the representatives of the Chinese Communist Party. Shanghai, International Publishers,
1945. 12 p.

TAN, PING-SHAN, 譚平山, 1887-  Entwicklungswege der chinesischen Revolution. Mit einem Vorwort von Karl A. Wittfogel und einem Nachwort von Ras-
kolnikow. Hamburg, Carl Hoym Nachfolger [1927] 35 p.

T'ANG, LIANG-LI, 湯良禮, 1901-  ed. Suppressing communist-banditry in
China. [Rev. ed.] Shanghai, China United Press, 1934. xiii, 131 p. plates,
ports. ("China to-day" series, 1 ).

————. Chinas Kampf gegen den Kommunismis. Shanghai, Verlag China United
Press, 1935. xviii, 92 p. plates, ports. (Schriften-Reihe "China von heute,"
1 ).

THOMAS, JAMES. Die Kantoner Kommune und der Kampf gegen den weissen
Terror in den Kolonien und Halbkolonien. Zürich, Mopr. Verlag, 1933. 15 p.

TUNG, PI-WU, 董必武, 1886-  Memorandum on China's liberated areas; a factual report on Chinese areas liberated from Japanese occupation. San Francisco, May 18, 1945. [San Francisco, 1945] 31, [1] p. illus. (map).

U. S. Office of Strategic Services. Research and Analysis Branch. News trans-
mitted from communist China beamed to North America. Washington, 1945.
v 1., 30 p. fold. tables. (Its R and A no. 2986).

UTLEY, FREDA, 1898-  Last chance in China. Indianapolis, Bobbs-Merrill
Co. [1947] 408 p. map (on lining-papers).

VERS la fin du communisme et du banditisme en Chine. Édité en français par C.
Kuangson Young, 楊光烓 .  Paris, Agence Chekiai, 1934. 140 p. (Coll. de la
Chine d'aujourd'hui).

WAN, YAH-KANG, 萬亞康 , 1909-  The rise of communism in China, 1920-50.
Edited by C. S. Kwei, 桂中樞. Hongkong, Chung Shu Pub. Co. [1952] 77 p.

WANG, MING, 王明 [Ch'en, Shao-yu, 陳紹禹], 1907-  Revolutionary China
today; speeches by Wang Ming and Kang Sin, 康生 [趙容]. Moscow [etc. ] Co-
operative Pub. Society of Foreign Workers in the U. S. S. R. , 1934; New
York, Workers' Library Publishers, 1934. 126, [1] p. At head of title: Thirteenth plenum of the Executive committee of the Communist International, December, 1933.

————. Das revolutionäre China von heute. Moskau-Leningrad, Verlagsgenossenschaft ausländischer Arbeiter in der UdSSR, 1934. 93, [1] p.

————. Le front unique dans le pays coloniaux, par Van Min. Paris, Bureau
d'Éditions, 1935. 48 p.

————. The revolutionary movement in the colonial countries; speech, revised
and augmented, delivered August 7, 1935. New York, Workers' Library Publishers, 1935. 64 p. At head of title: Seventh world congress of the Communist International.

————. Im zeichen der chinesischen Sowjets; die revolutionäre Bewegung in den
kolonialen und halbkolonialen Ländern und die Taktik der kommunistischen
Parteien. Umgearbeitetes und ergänztes Stenogramm der Rede in der 23
Sitzung des Kongresses (7. August 1935). Strassburg, Promethens Verlag,
1935. 61 p. map.

WEST MEETS EAST COMMITTEE. The truth about communism in China. Foreword by Dr. Harry McNeill. New York, West meets East Committee [1939]
32 p.

YANG, CHIEN, 揚銓 , 1893-1936. The communist situation in China. Nanking,
1931. 11 p.

[YOUNG COMMUNIST INTERNATIONAL]. La jeunesse avec la révolution chinoise. Paris, Bureau d'éditions, de diffusion et de publicité, 1927. 60 p.
illus.

1949-

ABBAS, KHWAJA AHMAD. In the image of Mao Tse-tung. Bombay, People's
    Pub. House, 1953. 105 p. illus.
ABEGG, LILY. Im neuen China. [Zürich] Atlantis Verlag [1957] 285 p. illus.
ALLEN, STEWART, 1899-   China under Communist control. [Toronto, Cana-
    dian Institute of International Affairs, 1954. 16 p. (Behind the headlines, v.
    14, no. 1 ).
ALLEY, REWI, 1897-   Yo banfa! (We have a way!) Edited by Shirley Barton.
    Foreword by Joseph Needham. Shanghai, China Monthly Review, 1952. 193
    p. illus.
———. The people have strength. [1st ed.] Peking, 1954. 281 p. illus. Sequel
    to Yo banfa! (We have a way!).
AMERICAN ACADEMY OF POLITICAL AND SOCIAL SCIENCE, Philadelphia.
    Report on China, edited by H. Arthur Steiner. Philadelphia, 1951. ix, 291 p.
    map. (Its Annals, v. 277).
AMERICAN CONSULATE GENERAL, Hong Kong. Developments in Communist
    China: the documentary record (1950-52). Hong Kong, 1952. 15 p. (A list-
    ing of the Current Background ser., Nos. 1-200).
AMERICAN FEDERATION OF LABOR. Free Trade Union Committee. Sun Yat-
    sen vs. Stalin; the truth about life in Communist China. New York, Free
    Trade Union Committee, American Federation of Labor, 1951? 24 p.
ASTAFYEV, G. China from a semi-colony to a people's democracy. Bombay,
    People's Publishing House, 1950. 69 p.
BALL, WILLIAM MACMAHON, 1901-   Notes on nationalism and communism in
    the Far East. Submitted by the IPR International Secretariat as a preparato-
    y paper for the Eleventh Conference of the Institute of Pacific Relations to be
    held at Lucknow in Oct. 1950. New York, International Secretariat, Insti-
    tute of Pacific Relations, 1950. 41 p. (Secretariat paper, 7 ).
———. Nationalism and communism in East Asia. [Carlton] Melbourne Univer-
    sity Press; Cambridge [Eng.] University Press, 1952. 2nd ed. 1955. 210 p.
    illus.
BARNETT, A. Doak, 1921-   Profile of Red China. New York, Published by the
    Foreign Policy Association in cooperation with the American Institute of Pa-
    cific Relations, 1950. [230]-243 p. (Foreign policy reports, 25:19 ).
BARTLETT, VERNON, 1894-   China, by Vernon Bartlett and George Vine.
    London, News Chronicle, 1951. 20 p. illus. map.
BELDEN, JACK, 1910-   China shakes the world. New York, Harper [1949]
    London, V. Gollancz, 1950. vii, 524 p.
———. La Chine ébranle le monde. Traduction de l'américan par Pierre Singer.
    Paris, Gallimard, 1951. 569 p.
———. China erschüttert die Welt. Einzig berechtigte deutsche Übersetzung von
    Hans L. du Mont. Braunschweig, O. E. Kleine, 1951. 382 p.
BLOFELD, JOHN EATON CALTHORPE, 1913-   Red China in perspective. Lon-
    don, A. Wingate [1951] 242 p.
BRANDT, CONRAD, 1920-   A documentary history of Chinese communism, by
    Conrad Brandt, Benjamin Schwartz and John K. Fairbank. London, Allen
    and Unwin [1952] 552 p.
———. Der Kommunismus in China; eine Dokumentar-Geschichte. Bearb. von
    Conrad Brandt, Benjamin Schwartz und John K. Fairbank. [Aus dem Ameri-
    kanischen übertragen von Margaret Montgelas] Mit einer Einführung von Rob-
    ert Borchardt. München, R. Oldenbourg, 1955. 392 p.
BRIEUX, JEAN JACQUES, 1921-   La Chine du nationalism au communisme.
    Paris, Éditions du Seuil [1951, c1950] 445 p. maps (1 fold.) diagrs. (Collec-
    tions Esprit. "Frontière ouverte").
BROWDER, EARL RUSSELL, 1891-   Chinese lessons for American Marxists;
    a lecture delivered before the discussion circle at the Woodstock Hotel, New

York City, January 17, 1949. New York, 1949. 48 p.

BUNZEL, RUTH. An anthropological approach to Chinese communism, by Ruth Bunzel and John Hast Weakland. New York, Research in contemporary cultures, Columbia University, 1952. 249 p. (U.S. Dept. of State, External research staff, Ser. 1 (143) ).

BURCHETT, WILFRED GRAHAM, 1911-　China's feet unbound. London, Lawrence and Wishart, 1952. 190 p.

——. The same. Melbourne, World Unity Publications, 1952. 190 p.

——. China verändert sich; übers. von Anni Seipel und Gottfried Lessing. Berlin, Verlag, Volk und Welt, 1952. 443 p.

CHAO, KUO-CHÜN, 趙國鈞, 1918-　Thirty years of the communist movement in China--a chronology of major developments, 1920-50. Cambridge, Russian Research Centre, Harvard University, 1950. 32, 5 l.

——. The mass organizations in Communist China. [Cambridge] Center for International Studies, Massachusetts Institute of Technology, 1953 [i. e. 1954] 157 l.

——. Some current political developments in Communist China. Cambridge, Center for International Studies, Massachusetts Institute of Technology, 1954. 52 p.

CHASSIN, LIONEL MAX, 1902-　La conquête de la Chine par Mao Tse-tung, 1945-49. Paris, Payot, 1952. 244 p. 12 maps. (Collection de mémoires, études et documents pour servir à l'histoire de la guerre ).

——. L'ascension de Mao Tsé-tung, 1921-45. Paris, Payot, 1953. 216 p. 8 maps. (Collection de mémoires, études et documents pour servir à l'histoire de la guerre ).

CH'ÊN, THEODORE HSI-EN, 陳錫恩, 1902-　Chinese communism and the proletarian-socialist revolution. Los Angeles, University of Southern California Press, 1955. 36 p.

——. The Chinese communist regime; a documentary study. Los Angeles, 1956. 2 v. (380 p.).

CHENG, HSUEH-CHIA, 鄭學稼. An interpretation of the purge of Kao [Kang] and Jao [Shu-shih] in Chinese Communist Party. Taipei, Asian People's Anti-communist League, 1955. cover-title, 20 p.

CHINA fights for peace. Peking, Foreign Languages Press, 1950. iv, 64 p. illus., ports.

CHINA'S revolutionary wars. Peking, Foreign Languages Press, 1951. 47 p. illus.

CHINAS revolutionäre Kriege. Zum 30. Jahrestag des Gründung des Kommunistische Partei Chinas am 1. Juli 1951. Berlin, Diet-Verlag, 1953. 47 p. (Internationale Schriftenreihe, 19 ).

CHINE nouvelle. Paris, Démocratie nouvelle, 1950. 336 p.

CHIU, SIN-MING, 趙善鳴 [Chao Shan-ming]. Some basic conceptions and rules of conduct of Chinese Communism; initial collation towards the conceptual and operational code of Chinese Communist leaders. Lackland Air Force Base, Tex., Air Force Personnel and Training Research Center, Air Research and Development Command, 1955. xi, 39 p. ( [U.S.] Human Resources Research Institute. Research memorandum, no. 34 ).

CHOU, EN-LAI, 周恩來, 1898-　The first year of the People's China. Bombay, People's Pub. House, 1950. 39 p.

——. The first year of victory. [Reports submitted by Chou En-lai and others to the National Committee of the People's Political Consultative Conference in commemoration of the first anniversary of the founding of the People's Republic of China] Peking, Foreign Languages Press, 1950. 95 p. map.

——. Première année de victoire de la Chine nouvelle. Luttons pour la consolidation et le développement de la victoire du peuple chinois. Pékin, Éditions en langues étrangères, 1950. 32 p.

——. China advances; a report to a meeting of the People's Political Consultative Conference held in commemoration of the founding of the People's Republic of China. [Reprint ed.] London, Britain-China Friendship Association, 1950. 19 p.

——. Report on the work of the government, made at the first session of the First National People's Congress of the People's Republic of China, September 23, 1954. Peking, Foreign Languages Press, 1954. 55 p. illus.

——. Bericht über die von der Regierung der Volksrepublik China geleistete Arbeit. Peking, Verlag für fremdsprachige Literatur, 1954. 70 p. front. (port.).

——. Political report, delivered at the second session of the second national committee of the Chinese People's Political Consultative Conference on January 30, 1956. Peking, Foreign Languages Press, 1956. 47 p.

——. On present international situation, China's foreign policy, and the liberation of Taiwan, delivered at the third session of the First National People's Congress on June 28, 1956. Peking, Foreign Languages Press, 1956. 31 p.

CHUNG, WÊN-HUI, 陳鍾文惠, 1903-  Chinese Communist anti-Americanism and the resist-America aid-Korea campaign. Lackland Air Force Base, Tex., Air Force Personnel and Training Research Center, Air Research and Development Command, 1955. xiii, 22 p. ( [U.S.] Human Resources Research Institute. Research memorandum, no. 36 ).

——. Wartime "mass" campaigns in communist China; official country-wide "mass movements" in professed support of the Korean War.  Lackland Air Force Base, Tex., Air Force Personnel and Training Research Center, Air Research and Development Command, 1955. xiv, 84 p. map. ( [U.S.] Human Resources Research Institute. Research memorandum no. 43 ).

CLEGG, ARTHUR. Neues China--neue Welt. Berlin, Dietz Verlag, 1951.91 p. map.

COMPLETE and consolidate the victory. Peking, Foreign Languages Press, 1950. 48 p. (New China library series, 1 ).

CORDES, ERNST, 1908-  China; Revolution innerhalb einer Revolution. Berlin, Safari-Verlag [c1951] 154 p. illus.

COURTEDO, PIERRE. "La nouvelle Chine est à nous (Mao Tse-toung).  Paris, L'humanité, 1953. 79 p.

DAI, SHEN-YU, 戴盛虞, 1921-  Mao Tse-tung and confucianism.  Philadelphia, 1953. 416 l. Thesis-Univ. of Pennsylvania.

DAVIDSON, BASIL, 1914-  Daybreak in China. London, Cape [1953] 191 p. illus.

DEVERALL, RICHARD LAWRENCE-GRACE, 1911-  The communist gospel of peace according to Marz, Mao Tze-tung, Lenin, and Stalin. Tokyo, 1952. 28 p. illus.

——. The great seduction; Red China's drive to bring free Japan behind the Iron Curtain. Tokyo, Printed by International Literature Print Co., 1953. 427 p. illus.

DUMONT, RENÉ. Révolution dans les campagnes chinoises. Paris, Éditions du Seuil, 1957. 464 p. (Coll. Esprit).

DUNLAP, ALBERT MENZO, 1884-  Behind the Bamboo Curtain: the experiences of an American doctor in China. Foreword by Daniel T. MacDougal; introd. by John Leighton Stuart. Illus. by Eva Wyman Dunlap. Washington, Public Affairs Press [1956] 208 p. illus.

ENDICOTT, MARY AUSTIN. Five stars over China. [The story of our return to new China. 1st Canadian ed.  Toronto, privately printed, 1953] 464 p. illus.

——. Fünf Sterne über China. Berlin, Union Verlag, 1956. xvi, 392 p. map, (Bibliothek d. CDU, 7 ).

EPSTEIN, ISRAEL, 1915-  From opium war to liberation. Peking, New World Press, 1956. 146 p.

ERMASHEV, I.I. Morgenröte über Asien. Berlin, Dietz, 1951. 280 p.

FACTS about communist rule in China. London, 1956. 34 p.

FALCONER, ALUN. New China, friend or foe? Foreword by Joseph Needham. London, Naldrett Press [1950] 127 p. illus., map. (Books that matter series).

————. I saw new China. Preface by Joseph Needham. [London, Britain-China Friendship Association, 1954] 14 p.

FAURE, EDGAR, 1908- Le serpent et la Tortue. Les problèmes de la Chine populaire. Paris, Julliard, Sequana, 1957. 239 p.

FITZGERALD, CHARLES PATRICK, 1902- The revolutionary tradition in China. Canberra, Australian National University, 1951. 22 p. (George Ernest Morrison lectures).

————. Revolution in China. London, Cresset Press, New York, Praeger, 1952. 289 p. illus.

————. The same. Übers. von Joseph Kalmer. Frankfurt a. M., Europäische Verlag-Anst., 1955; Büchergilde Gutenberg, 1957. 286 p.

FREI DEUTSCHE JUGEND. Was weisst du über die Volksrepublik China? Hrsg. vom Zentralrat der FDJ, Abteilung Agitation/Propaganda. Berlin, Verlag Junge Welt, 1954. 11 p.

GERMANY (Deutsche Republic, 1949- ) Ministerium für Volksbildung. Handreichungen für Aussprachen, Rezitationen und Feierstunden aus Anlass des Nationalfeiertages der Volksrepublik China am 1 Oktober. Hrsg. vom Ministerium für Volksbildung, Abteilung Gesamtdeutsche und Internationale Beziehungen. Berlin, Volk und Wissen, 1955. 45 p.

GOEL, SITA RAM. The China debate, whom shall we believe? Calcutta, Society for Defence of Freedom in Asia [1953] 48 p. (Inside Communist Slave-Empire ser., 1 ).

————. Mind-murder in Mao-land. [2d ed.] Calcutta, Society for Defence of Freedom in Asia [1953] 67 p. (Inside Communist Slave-Empire ser., 2 ).

————. Red brother or yellow slave. Calcutta, Society for Defence of Freedom in Asia [1953] 82 p. (Inside Communist Slave-Empire ser., 4 ).

————. Conquest of China, by Mao Tse-tung, commentary by Sita Ram Goel. Calcutta, Society for Defence of Freedom in Asia [1954] 276 p. illus. (World communism ser., 2 ).

GOSSET, PIERRE ET RENÉE. Chine rouge, an vii. Photos de Jean Philippe Charbonnier. Paris, R. Julliard, 1956. vii, 288 p. illus. (Terrifiante Asie, 2 ).

GOURLAY, WALTER E., 1921- The Chinese communist cadre; key to political control. Cambridge, Mass., Russian Research Center, Harvard University, 1952. iv, 122 p. Mimeographed.

GUETTIER, JEAN. Terreur sur le monde. Paris, Nouvelles éditions latines, 1956. 256 p.

A GUIDE to new China. 3rd. ed. Peking, Foreign Languages Press, 1953. iv, 124 p. plates, port. fold. tables. 1st ed. 1951

GUILLAIN, ROBERT, 1908- Revolution in China. Bombay, Hind Kitabs [1952] 39 p.

————. 600 [i. e. Six cent] millions de Chinois sous le drapeau rouge. Paris, R. Julliard [1956] 290 p.

————. The blue ants: 600 million Chinese under the red flag; translated by Mervyn Savill. London, Secker and Warburg, 1957. ix, 259 p. map.

————. 600 million Chinese. Translated by Mervyn Savill. New York, Criterion Books [1957] 310 p. German ed.: 600 millionen Chinesen. 1957. 256 p.

HAN, SUSAN SU-CHIN, 韓素珊, 1926- The concept of the proletariat in Chinese communism. Chicago, 1955. 156 l. Thesis-Univ. of Chicago.

HANDBOOK on People's China. Peking, Foreign Languages Press, 1957. 235 p. 3 col. illus. (1 mounted) tables.

HENDERSON, HORACE WRIGHT. The truth about China. Glasgow, J. S. Burns [1955] 39 p.

HO, CHEN-YUN, 何振榮. Communist China, 1955. Kowloon, Hong Kong, Union Research Institute, 1956. xlii, 198 p. (Communist China problem research ser., 15 ).

HSIA, ZOH-TSUNG, 夏淑貞 [Hsia Shu-chên]. Unbreakable China. Singapore, Low Phay Hock [1949?] 141 p. illus.

HU, CH'IU-YÜAN, 胡秋原, 1910-  China: from cultural vacuum to Communism. Hongkong, Institute for the Study of Chinese Problems, 1950. 46 p.

HUTHEESING, GUNOTTAM PURUSHOTTAM. Window on China, by Raja Hutheesing. London, D. Verschoyle [1953]; Bombay, Casement Publications, 1953. 191 p.

――――. The great peace; an Asian's candid report on Red China. New York, Harper [1953] 246 p.

JACQUEMYNS, GUILLAUME. Paix ou guerre? La politique des États-Unis et de l'U.R.S.S. La reconnaissance du governement de la Chine communiste. Bruxelles, Institut universitaire d'information sociale et économique, 1955. 60 p. (Institut universitaire. "Insoc" 2-3).

JEFREMOV, J.K. Land der Vulkane. Ins deutsche Übertragen von Bruno Tutenberg. Berlin, Neues Leben, 1953. 354 p.

JENKINS, ALFRED LE SESNE, 1916-  China and the Communist "peace offensive." [Washington] Dept. of State [1954] 9 p. ( [U.S.] Dept. of State. Public Services Division. Series S, 28 ).

JENSEN, FRITZ. China siegt. Mit 12 chinesischen Originalholzschnitten, 28 Tiefdruckbildern nach Aufnahmen des Verfassers. [2. Aufl., neu durchgesehen und ergänzt] Berlin, Dietz, 1950. 333 p. illus.

JOBEZ, ROBERT. De Confucius à Lénine; la montée au pouvoir du parti communiste chinois. Saigon, "France-Asie," 1951. 224 p.

――――. L'expérience communiste en Chine. De Confucius à la nouvelle démocratie [par] Robert Magenoz [pseud.] Paris, Iles d'or [1954] 306 p.

JOHNSON, HEWLETT, 1874-  I Appeal. London, Britain-China Friendship Association, 1952. 16 p.

――――. China's new creative age. With drawings and maps by Nowell Johnson. London, Lawrence and Wishart; New York, International Publishers, 1953. 199 p. illus.

――――. Ein Viertel der Menschheit. Chinas neues schöpferisches Zeitalter. Wien, Globus Verlag, 1954. 261 p. illus.

KEESING, DONALD B. Use of top-level personnel by the Chinese Communist Government, 1949-53. Cambridge, Center for International Studies, Massachusetts Institute of Technology, 1954. vi, 73 l.

KARANJIA, RUSTOM KHURSHEDJI, 1912-  China stands up and Wolves of the wild West. Bombay, People's Pub. House, 1952. 256 p. illus.

KIERMAN, FRANK ALGERTON, 1914-  The Chinese Communists in the light of Chinese history. Cambridge, Center for International Studies, Massachusetts Institute of Technology, 1954. 44 p.

――――. The Chinese intelligentsia and the Communists. Cambridge, Center for International Studies, Massachusetts Institute of Technology, 1954. 24 p.

KNIGHT, MARY, 1899-  Red blight. Los Angeles, L.L. Morrison [1951] 208 p. illus., ports.

KOVALEV, EVGENIĬ FEDOROVICH. Über die demokratischen Umgestaltungen in der Chinesischen Volksrepublik. [n.p., 1951?] 24 p. (Materialien für Propagandisten und Agitatoren, Heft 2 ).

KUO, PIN-CHIA, 郭斌佳, 1908-  China: new age and new outlook. New York, Knopf, London, Gollancz, 1956. 231 p.

LIAO, KAI-LUNG, 廖蓋隆. From Yenan to Peking; the Chinese People's War of Liberation, from reconstruction to first five-year plan. Peking, Foreign Languages Press, 1954. 187 p.

LINDSAY, MICHAEL, 1909-  China and the West. Canberra, Australian National University, 1953. 28 p. (George Ernest Morrison lectures).

――――. China and the cold war; a study in international politics. [Carlton] Melbourne University Press, London, Cambridge University Press [1955] 286 p.

LIU, SHAO-T'ANG, 劉紹唐, 1921-  Out of Red China; translated from the Chinese by Jack Chia and Henry Walter. Introd. by Hu Shih. New York, Duell, Sloan and Pearce [1953] 269 p.

———. Ich komme aus Rot-China. Übertr. aus dem Englischen. Wien, Holzner, 1955. 289 p.

McCONAUGHY, WALTER P. China in the shadow of communism. [Washington] Dept. of State [1954] 9 p. ( [U.S.] Dept. of State. Publication 5383. Far Eastern series, 63 ).

MARTINSON, HAROLD H., 1905-  Red Dragon over China. Minneapolis, Augsburg Pub. House [1956] 328 p. illus.

MASSACHUSETTS INSTITUTE OF TECHNOLOGY. Center for International Studies. Essays on communism in Asia; papers from the CENIS China project. Cambridge, 1955 [i.e. 1956] 1 v. (various pagings).

MEHTA, ASOKA, 1911-  China: the pathfinder. Bombay, Socialist Party, 1949. 9 p.

MONSTERLEET, JEAN, 1912-  Vu en Chine [par] Louis Dransard [pseud.] Paris, P. Téqui [1952] 122 p.

———. L'empire de Mao Tsetung, 1949-54. Lille, S.I.L.I.C. [1954] 222 p. illus.

———. Wird der Gelbe Mann rot; Politik, Wirtschaft und Gesellschaft im kommunistischen China. [Ins deutsche Übertragen von Eduard Thomas Sauer] Freiburg, Herder, 1956. viii, 328 p. illus. maps.

MOORAD, GEORGE, 1908-  Lost peace in China. New York, E.P. Dutton, 1949. 262 p.

MORAES, FRANCIS ROBERT, 1907-  Report on Mao's China. New York and London, Macmillan, 1953. 212 p.

———. Behind the Bamboo Curtain. London, Phoenix House, 1956. 40 p. (Background books).

NIKIFOROV, V.N. Die Volksrevolution in China von V. Nikiforov, G. Erenburg und M. Jufev. Übers. von Leon Nebenzahl. Berlin, Dietz, 1952. 150 p.

PAYNE, PIERRE STEPHEN ROBERT, 1911-  The Changing face of China. London, Bureau of Current Affairs, 1949. 20 p. (Current Affairs No. 73 ).

———. Red storm over Asia. New York, Macmillan, 1951. xiii, 309 p. col. map (on lining paper).

PROBLEMS of Red China. Hong Kong, Free Life Pub. House; London, Bailey and Swinfen, 1954. 123 p. tables.

REPORT on communist China; an NBC radio discussion by Derk Bodde, Albert Ravenholt and Phillips Talbot. Chicago, 1950. 16 p. (University of Chicago Round Table, 654 ).

ROSTOW, WALT WHITMAN, 1916-  The prospects for Chinese communist society [by] W.W. Rostow in collaboration with Richard W. Hatch, Frank A. Kierman, Jr. [and] Alexander Eckstein, and with the assistance of others at the Center for International Studies. Cambridge, Center for International Studies, Massachusetts Institute of Technology, 1954. 2 v. (xiii, 400, xiic (i.e. xcii) p.).

———. The prospects for Communist China [by] W.W. Rostow in collaboration with Richard W. Hatch, Frank A. Kierman, Jr., Alexander Eckstein and with the assistance of others at the Center for International Studies, Massachusetts Institute of Technology. [Cambridge ] Technology Press of Massachusetts Institute of Technology [1954] New York, John Wiley, 1954. London, Chapman and Hall, 1955. xx, 379 p. map. (Technology Press books in the social sciences).

———. A comparison of Russian and Chinese societies under communism. Cambridge, Center for International Studies, Massachusetts Institute of Technology, 1955. 25 p.

SCHUMAN, JULIAN. Assignment China. New York, Whittier Books; Toronto, Burns and MacEachern, 1956. 253 p.

SCHWARTZ, BENJAMIN ISADORE, 1916-   Communism in China until the rise
of Mao Tse-tung. Microfilm copy of typescript. Collation of the original: 5,
301, 14 l. Thesis-Harvard University.
———. Chinese communism and the rise of Mao.   Cambridge, Harvard University Press, 1951. 258 p. (Russian Research Center studies, 4 ).
———. China and the Soviet theory of "peoples democracy" [by] Benjamin Isadore Schwartz. Summary [by CENIS staff] Cambridge, Center for International Studies, Massachusetts Institute of Technology [1954] 17 p.
SHAH, KHUSHAL TALAKSI. The promise that is new China.  Bombay, Vora
[1953] 342 p. illus.
THE SHANGHAI NEWS. Special supplement issued in celebration of the 1st anniversary of the founding of the People's Republic of China. Shanghai, 1950.
40 p. illus., ports., map.
SHEPHERD, CHARLES REGINALD, 1885-   A nation betrayed; the story of communism in China.  New York, Exposition Press [1954] 179 p.
SHERIDAN, WILLIAM JOHN, 1873-   Watching the Chinese Curtain fall.  [Van-
couver, Mitchell] c1954. 126 p.
SIMONOV, KONSTANTIN MIKHAĬLOVICH, 1915-   Das kämpfende China. [Ü-
bersetzung von A.E. Thoss] Berlin, Verlag Kultur und Fortschritt [1950]
157 p.
SOONG, CHING-LING,  孫宋慶齡 , 1890-   The struggle for new China.  Peking
Foreign Languages Press, 1952. 398 p.
SOZIALISTISCHE EINHEITSPARTEI DEUTSCHLANDS.  Zentralkomitee. Tatsachen über die Volksrepublik China, die jeder wissen soll; Material für Agitatoren und Referenten. [n.p., 1954] 24 p. illus.
STAHMER, HANS GEORG, 1892-   Japans Niederlage-Asiens Sieg. Aufstieg eines grösseren Ostasien.  Bielefeld, Deutscher Heimat-Verlag, 1952. 318 p.
illus.
STALIN, IOSIF, 1879-1953. Stalin on China; a collection of five writings of Comrade Stalin on the Chinese question.  Bombay, People's Pub. House [1951]
106 p.
———. Über die Perspektiven der Revolution in China. Rede in der Chinesischen Kommission des EKKI 30. November 1926. Fragen der chinesischen
Revolution, Thesen für Propagandisten, gebilligt vom ZK der KPdSU(B).
Moskau, Verlag für Fremdsprachlige Literatur [1955?] 66 p.
STEINER, H. ARTHUR, 1905-  ed. Chinese communism in action. [Los An-
geles] Political Science 159, University of California at Los Angeles, 1953.
3 v. (xxiii, 313 l.).
SUIGO, CARLO. In the land of Mao Tse-tung. Translated from the Italian by
Muriel Currey and edited by Clifford Witting.  London, G. Allen and Unwin
[1953] 311 p. plates, port. map.
TANG, PETER SHÊNG-HAO,   唐盛鎬 . Communist China today; domestic and
foreign policies.  New York, F.A. Praeger [1957] xvi, 536 p. map(on lining
papers) [Praeger publications in Russian history and world communism, 35].
TENNIEN, MARK A., 1900-  No secret is safe behind the bamboo curtain.
New York, Farrar, Straus and Young [1952] 270 p. illus.
———. Kein Geheimnis ist sicher hinter dem Bambus Vorhang. Einführung von
Kardinal Spellman. Übertr. von Emil K. Pohl.  Salzburg, Otto Müller, 1954.
266 p. illus.
THOMAS, S.B., Government and administration in Communist China. Rev. [i.e.
2d] ed. New York, International Secretariat, Institute of Pacific Relations
[1955] iii, 196 p. 1st ed. 1953.
TOWNSEND, PETER, 1919-  In China now. With an introduction by Basil Da-
vidson. [London, Union of Democratic Control, 1953] 31 p.
———. China phoenix; the revolution in China. With an introduction by S. Radhakrishnan.  London, Cape [1955] 406 p. illus.
TRULLINGER, O.O. Red banners over Asia. Oxford, Pen-in-Hand [1950] xi,

212 p.

UNION RESEARCH INSTITUTE. Index to the material on Communist China held by the Union Research Institute. Kowloon, Hong Kong [1957] xii, 250 p.

U.S. CENTRAL INTELLIGENCE AGENCY. Administrative divisions of China. [Washington] 1949. 128 p. illus.

U.S. Congress. House. Committee on Foreign Affairs. The strategy and tactics of world communism. Report of Subcommittee No. 5, National and International Movements. Supplement 3, Country studies; C. Communism in China. Washington, Govt. Print. Off., 1949. 106 p. (81st Cong., 1st sess. House Document, 154 Pt. 3 ).

————. Congress. Senate. Committee on the Judiciary. Nature of communism in occupied China; a documentary from the record of the Subcommittee to Investigate the Administration of the Internal Security Act and Other Internal Security Laws of the Committee on the Judiciary, United States Senate, Eighty-fifth Congress, first session. Washington, Govt. Print. Off., 1957. iv, 48 p. (chiefly illus., maps).

VAIDYA, KESHAV BALKRISHNA, 1896-  Southward Mao; will Communism spread to Eastern regions? Bombay, Popular Book Depot [1950] 94 p.

VAN DER SPRENKEL, OTTO P.N.B., 1906-  New China; three views by Otto B. Van der Sprenkel, Robert Guillain [and] Michael Lindsay. Edited by Otto B. Van der Sprenkel, with an introd. by Kingsley Martin. London, Turnstile Press [1950] xv, 241 p. illus.

WALKER, RICHARD LOUIS, 1922-  China under communism, the first five years. New Haven, Yale University Press; London, G. Allen and Unwin, 1955. xv, 403 p. illus.

————. China unter dem Kommunismus. Die ersten fünf Jahre. Übers. von Eugene Ort. Stuttgart, Vorwerk, 1956. 452 p. illus.

WANG, CHARLES KILORD ATHEN, 王徽葵, 1904-  Reactions in Communist China; an analysis of letters to newspaper editors. Lackland, Air Force Base, Texas. Air Force personnel and training research center, 1955. 115 p. (Air University. Maxwell field, Ala. Human Resources institute. Technical research report, 33 ).

WEI, HENRY, 韋文起, 1909-  State and government in Communist China: their ideological basis and statutory pattern to the spring of 1953. Lackland Air Force Base, Tex., Air Force Personnel and Training Research Center, Air Research and Development Command, 1955. xvi, 56 p. map. ( [U.S.] Human Resources Research Institute. Research memorandum, 38 ).

WHAT choice do we have in China; a NBC radio discussion by Herrlee G. Creel, Knight Biggerstaff and David N. Rowe. Chicago, 1950. 16 p. (University of Chicago Round Table, 618 ).

YÜ, FREDERICK T.C., 喻德基, 1921-  The strategy and tactics of Chinese Communist propaganda as of 1952. Lackland Air Force Base, Tex., Air Force Personnel and Training Research Center, Air Research and Development Command, 1955. xv, 70 p. map. ( [U.S.] Human Resources Research Institute. Research memorandum no. 39 ).

————. The propaganda machine in Communist China, with special reference to ideology, policy, and regulations, as of 1952. Lackland Air Force Base, Tex., Air Force Personnel and Training Research Center, Air Research and Development Command, 1955. xiii, 79 p. map. ( [U.S.] Human Resources Research Institute. Research memorandum no. 37 ).

## Counter Movements

ASIAN PEOPLES' ANTI-COMMUNIST LEAGUE. The international communist conspiracy in Asia. Taipei, 1954. 30 p.

————. All roads lead to freedom; report. 1st-    Taipei, China [1955?-    v. illus.

――――. Communist tyranny and people's resistance on the Chinese aminland during 1954. Taipei, 1955. 82 p.

――――. The current strategy and tactics of international communism. [n. p.] 1955. 32 p.

――――. How to combat communism. Taipei, 1955. 38 p.

――――. How to save Asia from communist menace by Tetsuzo Watanabe. Taipei, 1955. 22 p.

――――. Nehru's illusions. Taipei, 1955. 38 p.

――――. Provisional record of the forum on the anti-communist movement of Asia. Taipei, 1955. 28 p.

――――. Provisional record of the forum on international situation and communist peace offensive. Taipei, 1955. 16 p.

――――. A study of the Communist "peaceful co-existence" conspiracy. Taipei, 1955. cover-title, 54 p.

――――. Charts about Chinese communists on the mainland. Taipei, 1955-56. 2 v.

――――. Development of the Chinese People's anti-communist movement; report on the work of the Asian People's Anti-communist League, Republic of China. Taipei, 1956. 62 p.

――――. Important documents of the second Asian Peoples' Anti-Communist Conference. Taipei, 1956. 33 p.

――――. Communist menace to Asia. [Taipei] 1957. 45 p.

――――. Documents of the Asian Peoples' Anti-Communist League. [Taipei,1957] 39 p.

――――. How China fights Communsim. [Taipei, 1957] 49 p.

――――. The overseas united front of the Chinese Communists. [Taipei, 1957] 70 p.

CHINESE WOMEN'S ANTI-AGGRESSION LEAGUE, Taipei. A pictorial report of the work of the Chinese women's anti-aggression league. Taipei, 1951. 66 p. illus.

FREE CHINA COMMITTEE FOR AIDING ANTI-COMMUNIST CHINESE POWS IN KOREA, Taipei. How we helped the anti-communist Chinese POWs regain freedom. Taipei, 1954. 29 p. plates.

GODDARD, WILLIAM G. Peaceful co-existence? Melbourne, Victorian Chinese National Salvation Association, 1955. 16 p.

LIANG, YOU-MING. True stories of anti-communist Chinese heroines. Taipei, Chinese Women's Anti-aggression League, 1955. 40 p.

SHIH, CH'ÊNG-CHIH, 史誠之. People's resistance in mainland China, 1950-55. Hong Kong, Union Research Institute [1956] v, 116 p. (Communist China problem research series EC 17 ).

WANG, TSUN-MING, 王俊明, 1926- Wang Tsun-ming, anti-Communist: an autobiographical account of Chinese Communist thought reform. Washington, Psychological Warfare Division, Human Resources Research Office, George Washington University, 1954. xi, 64 l. ( [George Washington University, Washington, D. C. Psychological Warfare Division] Staff memorandum).

WU, TE-CHEN, 吳鐵城, 1888-1953. An appeal for the formation of an Asiatic peoples' anti-communist front. Hong Kong, Chinese People's Foreign Relations Association, 1949. 12 p.

## Intervention in Korean War

ALL-CHINA ASSOCIATION OF THE FINE ARTS WORKERS. The paper-tiger; a collection of anti-aggression cartoons. Peking, Cultural Press, 1951. 82 p. (p. 13-82 illus.).

BRAZDA, JAROSLAV JAN, 1924- The Korean armistice agreement: a comparative study. Gainsville, Florida, 1956. 323 l. Thesis-Univ. of Florida.

BURCHETT, WILFRED GRAHAM, 1911- Koje unscreened, by Wilfred Bur-

chett and Alan Winnington. [1st ed.] Peking [1953] 171 p. illus.
———. The same. London, Britain-China Friendship Association [1953?] 111 p.
illus.
CHANG, TAO-LI. Why China helps Korea. Bombay, People's Pub. House [1951]
43 p.
CHINESE PEOPLE'S COMMITTEE FOR WORLD PEACE. Exhibition on bacter-
iological war crimes committed by the Government of the United States of A-
merica. [Peking, 1952] 51 p. illus.
———. Report of the Joint Interrogation Group of Korean and Chinese Specialists and Newspaper Correspondents on the interrogation of war prisoners E-
noch and Quinn; with supplementary material. Peking, 1952. 32 p.
———. Shall brothers be; an account, written by American and British prisoners of war, of their treatment at the hands of the Chinese people's volunteers and Korean people's army in P.O.W. camps in Korea. Peking, 1952.
81 p. illus.
———. Statements by two American Air Force officers, Kenneth Lloyd Enoch
and John Quinn, admitting their participation in germ warfare in Korea, and
other documents. [Peking?, 1952] 16 p. illus.
———. Aussagen von zwei gefangenen U.S. Luft-Waffen-Offizieren über ihre Be-
teiligung an der bakteriologischen Kriegführung in Korea, mit vollstandiger
Wiedergabe ihrer Niederschriften in Faksimile. In deutsche Sprache hrsg.
vom Deutschen Friedenskomitee. Peking, 1952. 95 p. illus.
———. Stop U.S. germ warfare! Peking, 1952. 5 pt. illus.
———. Documents and materials on the Korean armistice negotiations, with
special reference to item 4 of the agenda dealing with the question of prison
ers of war. Peking, 1952. 2 v.
———. The realization of the armistice in Korea. Peking, 1953. 95 p. illus.
maps.
———. The struggle for peace in Korea; selected documents. Rev. ed. Peking,
1953. 76 p.
———. The struggle for the armistice in Korea; selected documents. Peking,
1953. 148 p.
———. United Nations P.O.W.'s in Korea. Peking, 1953. 92 p. illus.
CHOU, EN-LAI, 1898-  Statements at the Geneva Conference. [Peking?] 1954.
15 p. "Supplement to 'People's China,' July 1, 1954."
CLEWS, JOHN. The Communists' new weapon: germ warfare. Foreword by A.
V. Hill. London, Lincolns Prager, 1953. 32 p.
DEPOSITIONS of nineteen captured U.S. airmen on their participation in germ
warfare in Korea. [Peking? 1953] 67 p. illus. "Supplement to 'People's
China,' December 1, 1953."
FARGE, YVES, 1899-  Témoignage sur la Chine et la Corée. Paris, Éditeurs
français réunis [1952] 160 p. illus., ports.
FRIENDSHIP for peace. Peking, Foreign Languages Press [1953] ii, 66 p. illus.
port.
GENEVA. CONFERENCE, 1954. Documents relating to the discussion of Korea
and Indo-China at the Geneva Conference, April 27-June 15, 1954. London,
H.M. Stationery Off. [1954] vii, 168 p. ( [Gt. Brit. Foreign Office] Miscel-
laneous, 1954, no. 16 ).
GT. BRIT. Foreign Office. Further summary of events relating to Korea, October 1950 to May 1951, with annexes. London, H.M. Stationery Off., 1951.
65 p. ( [Gt. Brit. Foreign Office] Korea, 1951, no. 2 ).
———. Korea; the Indian proposal for resolving the prisoners of war problem.
London, H.M. Stationery Off. [1952] 19 p. (Its Korea, 1952, no. 2 ).
———. Korea; a summary of developments in the armistice negotiations and the
prisoner of war camps, June 1951-May 1952. London, H.M. Stationery Off.,
1952. 27 p. (Its Korea, 1952, no. 1 ).
———. Korea; a summary of further developments in the military situation,

armistice negotiations, and prisoner of war camps up to January 1953. London, H. M. Stationery Off. [1953] 31 p. (Its Korea, 1953, no. 1 ).

HUNTER, EDWARD, journalist. Brainwashing; the story of men who defied it.
New York, Farrar, Straus and Cudahy [1956] 310 p.

INTERNATIONAL SCIENTIFIC COMMISSION FOR THE INVESTIGATION OF
THE FACTS CONCERNING BACTERIAL WARFARE IN KOREA AND CHINA.
Report. [Prague? 1952] cover-title, 63 p. facsim.

———. Report (with appendices). Peking, 1952. 665 p. illus. map, tables.

JEBB, SIR GLADWYN, 1900-  Korea. United Nations resolution on Chinese intervention in Korea, passed by the General Assembly of the United Nations
on 1st February, 1951. Speeches of Sir Gladwyn Jebb, United Kingdom permanent representative to the United Nations, between 18th January and 1st
February, 1951 and statement by the Prime Minister in the House of Commons on 1st February, 1951. London, H. M. Stationery Off. [1951] 23 p.
( [Gt. Brit. Foreign Office] Korea, 1951, no. 1 ).

JOY, CHARLES TURNER, 1895-1956. How Communists negotiate. With a foreword by Matthew B. Ridgway. New York, Macmillan, 1955. 178 p.

KOREA (People's Democratic Republic, 1948-  ). Department of Cultural Relations with Foreign Countries. Documents on the Geneva Conference. [n. p.]
Department of Cultural Relations with Foreign Countries, Ministry of Culture and Propaganda, PDRK, 1954. 80 p.

PASLEY, VIRGINIA (SCHMITZ) 1905-   21 stayed; the story of the American
GI's who chose Communist China: who they were and why they stayed. With
a prefatory note by Carl Sandburg. New York, Farrar, Straus and Cudahy
[1955] 248 p. illus.

———. 22 stayed. London, W. H. Allen, 1955. 224 p. illus.

PRATT, SIR JOHN THOMAS, 1876-  Korea, the lie that led to war. [London]
Britain China Freindship Association [1951] [8] p.

RACING towards victory; stories from the Korean front. [1st ed.] Peking, Foreign Languages Press, 1954. 184 p.

RILEY, JOHN W. The Reds take a city; the Communist occupation of Seoul, with
eyewitness accounts. By John W. Riley, Jr. and Wilbur Schramm. Narratives [by eminent Koreans] translated by Hugh Heung-wu Cynn. New Brunswick, Rutgers University Press [1951] 210 p.

SHIH CHIEH CHIH SHIH, 世界知識. A chronicle of principal events relating
to the Korean question, 1945-54. Edited and published by Shihchieh chihshih
(World culture) Peking, 1954. 93 p. "Translated from a special supplement
to the April 20, 1954 issue (No. 8) of Shihchieh chihshih (World culture). "

UNITED NATIONS COMMAND. Special report of the Unified Command on the
Korean armistice agreement signed at Panmunjom on July 27, 1953. London, H. M. Stationery Off., 1953. 35 p. ( [Gt. Brit. Foreign Office] Korea,
1953, no. 2 ).

———. Military armistice in Korea and Temporary supplementary agreement,
signed at Panmunjom, Korea, July 27, 1953, entered into force July 27,
1953. [Washington, Govt. Print. Off., 1953] iii, 127 p. (U. S. Dept. of
State. Publication 5197. Treaties and other international acts series, 2782).

U. S. Dept. of State. The Korean problem at the Geneva Conference, April 26-
June 15, 1954. [Washington, Govt. Print. Off., 1954] vii, 193 p. (Its Publication 5609. International organization and conference series II (Far Eastern), 4 ).

———. Dept. of the Army. Communist interrogation, indoctrination, and exploitation of prisoners of war. Washington, 1956. 71 p. illus. (Its Pamphlet no.
30-101).

VIEWS of Chinese scientists on U. S. bacterial warfare. Peking, Chinese Medical Association, 1952. 65 p. (Chinese medical journal. Suppl. v. 70 ).

WINNINGTON, ALAN. Plain perfidy. [The plot to wreck Korean peace, by] Alan
Winnington [and] Wilfred Burchett. Peking [1954] 238 p. illus., ports.

—————. The same.    London,  **Britain-China** Friendship Association [1954] 179 p.
    illus.

# VII. ARMY, NAVY AND AIR FORCE

## Military History

SADLER, A.L. Three military classics of China. Sydney, Australiasian Medical Pub. Co., 1944. 55, 23 p.

SUN TZŬ, 孫子 , 6th cent. B.C. The principles of war; a new translation from a revised text. Ceylon, Royal Air Force, 1943. x, 77, [1] p.

————. The art of war; the oldest military treatise in the world, translated from the Chinese by Lionel Giles; introduction and notes by Thomas R. Phillips. Harrisburg, Pa., Military Service Pub. Co., 1944. 99 p. (Military classics).

————. The same; military manual written cir. B.C. 510, the original Chinese text appended; translated, with an introduction, by Cheng Lin, 鄭麐 . Chungking, World Encyclopedia Institute, China Section [1945] v, [3], 59 p.; 6,18 p. (Ancient Chinese classics series ).

————. Sun Tse et les anciens chinois. Ou Tse, 吳子 , et Se-ma Fa, 司馬法 (Ve au llle siècle avant J-C). Présentés et annotés par L. Nachin. Paris, Berger-Levrault, 1948. xix, 184 p. (Les Classiques de l'art militaire).

## Dictionaries

CONSTANT, SAMUEL VICTOR, 1894-  Chinese military terms; English-Chinese, Chinese-English. Peking, China Booksellers [1927] 122 p.

DAVIDSON-HOUSTON, JAMES VIVIAN, 1901-  Chinese and English modern military dictionary; 5,500 army, navy, air, technical terms, compiled by Captain J. V. Davidson-Houston [and] Lieutenant R. V. Dewar-Durie. Issued under the patronage of H. E. Marshal Chang Hsüeh-liang. Peiping, H. Vetch [1935] 410 p., front.(facsim.) illus. (part col.).

————. The same; 6,500 army, navy, air, technical terms, compiled by Captain J. V. Davidson-Houston [and] Lieutenant R. V. Dewar-Durie. With appendices, revised by Major R. V. Dewar-Durie. Calcutta, Calcutta General Printing Co., 1942. [470] p. illus. (part col.).

GERR, STANLEY. Japanese-Chinese-English dictionary of aeronautical and meteorological terms, including aero- and hydrodynamics, airplane construction and stress analysis, propeller theory, internal combustion engines, airports and ground installations [and] meteorology, with a section in kana. New York, G. E. Stechert [1945] vi, 439 p.

LANZ, JOHN E. Lanz aviation dictionary in nine languages: English, Spanish, Portuguese, French, Italian, German, Russian, Chinese [and] Japanese. South Pasadena, Calif., P. D. and Ione Perkins, 1944. x, 430 p. illus.

U. S. Army Language School, Monterey, Calif. A glossary of Chinese military terms, prepared by Chinese Mandarin Dept. Presidio of Monterey, 1951. 126 p.

————. Military terminology (conversation) [Monterey] Army Language School, Far Eastern Lanuage Division, Chinese-Cantonese Language Dept. [1951] 52 l.

————. War Dept. Chinese military dictionary. Washington, Govt. Print. Off., 1945. x, 415 p. (War Dept. Technical manual TM30-533).

## Army and Navy

BRISSAUD-DESMAILLET, GEORGE HENRI, 1869-  L'armée chinois, le problème des troupes en excédent; armée nationale de défense, armée nationale de gendarmerie; armée nationale du travail.  Paris, Charles-Lavanzelle et Cie, 1927. 86 p. tables.

CARLSON, EVANS FORDYCE, 1896-  The Chinese army, its organization and military efficiency.  New York, International Secretariat, Institute of Pacific Relations, 1940. ix, 3-142 p.   illus.(map) (I.P.R. inquiry series ).

CH'ÊN, HSIAO-WEI, 陳孝威, 1892-  Present military problems in China; a reply to Major-General Walter S. Grant and other American military officers in Manila.  Hong Kong, The Observatory, 1940. cover-title, vi, 82, [2] p.

CHINA INFORMATION COMMITTEE.  China's guerilla fighters.  Hankow, China Information Committee, 1938. 27 p.

DAVIS, GEORGE THOMPSON BROWN, 1873-  China's Christian army, a story of Marshal Feng and his soldiers; introduction by Charles Gallaudet Trumbull.  New York, Christian Alliance Pub. Co., c1925. 136 p. front., plates, ports.

IMPEY, LAWRENCE.  The Chinese army as a military force. 2d and enl. ed.; illustrated with two sketch maps and many photographs taken by the author.  Tientsin, Tientsin Press, 1926. 56 p. plates, ports., maps.

KAO, GEORGE, 高克毅, 1912-  ed. How China trains her soldiers and civilians.  New York, Trans-Pacific News Service, 1941. 29 p.(China reference ser.).

KOTENEV, ANATOL M. 1882-  The Chinese soldier; basic principles, spirit, science of war, and heroes of the Chinese armies.  Shanghai, Kelly and Walsh, 1937. xiii, 173 p.  front., 1 illus., plates, ports.

LIU, FREDERICK FU,   劉馥 . A military history of modern China, 1924-49.  Princeton, Princeton University Press, 1956. 312 p.  illus.

POWELL, RALPH LORIN, 1917-  The modernization and control of the Chinese armies, 1894-1912.  Cambridge, 1953. 2 v. Thesis-Harvard University.

————.  The rise of Chinese military power, 1895-1912.  Princeton, N.J., Princeton University Press, 1955. x, 383 p.  map.

ROWE, DAVID NELSON, 1905-  China's military potential and the enforcement of peace.  New Haven, Conn., 1943. 19 numb. 1. (Yale institute of international studies. [Memorandum, 4 ]).

U.S. Chinese-American Training Center, Ramgarh, Bihar, India. Ramgarh; a pictorial story of the Chinese-American training center in India where the soldiers of two great nations have combined their efforts to mould the means of defeating the common enemy. "Now it can be told." [Ranchi, Printed at the Catholic Press, 1945?] [5]-219 (i.e. 223), [3] p. illus. (incl. ports.).

————. Congress. House. Committee on Foreign Affairs. Assist China to modernize her armed forces. Report. [To accompany H.R. 6795] [Washington, Govt. Print. Off., 1946] 5 p. ( [U.S.] 79th Cong., 2d sess. House. Rept. 2361 ).

————. Congress. House. Committee on Naval Affairs. Providing assistance to the Republic of China in augmenting and maintaining a naval establishment, and for other purposes. Report. [To accompany H.R. 5356] [Washington, Govt. Print. Off., 1946] 5 p. ( [U.S.] 79th Cong., 2d sess. House. Rept. 1529 ).

————. Congress. Senate. Committee on Naval Affairs. Miscellaneous bills. Hearing before the Committee on naval affairs, United States Senate, Seventy-ninth Congress, second session. April 11, 1946. Washington, Govt. Print. Off., 1946. iii, 9 p.

WIDLER, ELLY. Six months prisoner of the Szechwan military. With 25 photographs of the Szechwan military, etc., and sketch showing the grand retreat from Chungking on 16th. October 1923. [Shanghai] China Press, 1924. 25-170 p., plates, ports.


## Army, Communist

BASIC agreement for military reorganization and for the integration of the com-

munist forces into the National Army. Signed Feb. 25, 1946. With Chinese
text. Shanghai, International Publishers, 1946. 9, 9 p.

BELDEN, JACK, 1910-   The New Fourth Army.  Shanghai, Shanghai Evening
Post and Mercury, 1940. 66 p. illus. port.

The CHINESE PEOPLE'S LIBERATION ARMY.    Peking, Foreign Languages
Press, 1950. 61 p. illus., ports.

L'ARMÉE POPULAIRE DE LIBÉRATION DE CHINE.    Pékin, Éditions en langues
étrangères, 1950. 71 p. plates.

Die CHINESISCHE VOLKSBEFREIUNGS ARMEE.   Peking, Verlag für Fremdsprachige Literatur, 1951. 71 p.

———.  Berlin, Kongress-Verlag, 1950. 63 p.

CHU, TÊ, 朱德 , 1886?-  On the battlefronts of the liberated areas.   Peking,
Foreign Languages Press, 1952. 91 p.

HANRAHAN, GENE Z. comp. Chinese communist guerrilla tactics, July 1952;
a source book. [New York, Columbia University Press, 1952] 134 p.  illus.

HSIANG, YING, 項英 , 1897-1947. The Eighth Route and New Fourth Armies,
by Hsiang Ying and Yeh T'ing, 葉挺.  Chungking, New China Information
Committee, 1939. 39 p. (Its Bull., 10 ).

LINDSAY, MICHAEL, 1909-   The military prospects in a Chinese civil war.
New York, Institute of Pacific Relations, 1946. 14 numb. l.

NEW CHINA INFORMATION COMMITTEE. How the eighth route army fights in
North China.  Hongkong [1939?] cover-title, 33 p.

PENG, TEH-HUEI, 彭德懷, 1900-   Unity and the defence of North China.
Chungking, New China Information Committee, 1940. 41 p. illus. maps (Its
Bull., 13 ).

POOL, ITHIEL DE SOLA, 1917-  Satellite generals; a study of military elites
in the Soviet sphere, by Ithiel de Sola Pool with the collaboration of George
K. Schueller [and others] Stanford, Stanford University Press [1955] vi, 165
p. (Hoover Institute studies, Series B: Elites, 5 ).

RIGG, ROBERT B. Red China's fighting hordes, a realistic account of the Chinese Communist army by a U.S. Army officer. Harrisburg, Pa., Military
Service Pub. Co. [1951] xiv, 378 p. illus., ports., map.

TING, LI, 丁勵 . Militia of Communist China.  Kowloon, H.K., Union Research
Institute [1954] 145 p. (Communist China problem research series, EC7 ).

U.S. Office of Strategic Services. Research and Analysis. Branch. The guerrilla front in north China.  [Washington] 1943. iv l., 22 p. fold. map. (Its R.
and A. no. 892 ).

YEH, CHIEN-YING, 葉劍英, 1902-  Report on the general military situation of
the Chinese communist party in the war of resistance.  [Yenan?] 1944. cover-
title, 48 p. fold. tab.

———.  A general introduction to the Chinese Communist Party's war of resistance: an address to the Sino-Foreign Press Mission to Yenan, on 22 June
1944. Translated by O.W.I. Chungking, [U.S.] Office of War Information,
1944. Microfilm copy (positive) of typescript. Collation of the original: 29 l.
fold. table.


## Police

JAO, HOUA-SON, 饒華孫. La police administrative en Chine.   Bordeaux, Impr.
E. Castera, 1939. [5]-138 p.

YEE, FRANK KICHUN, 余秀豪 , 1904-  Police in modern China.  Berkeley,
1942. 486 l. Thesis-University of California.


## Air Force

FLYING TIGERS (American Volunteer Group, Chinese Air Force), Inc. Bill of
rights requesting veteran recognition by Congress for the original Flying

Tigers, American volunteer group, Chinese Air Force, 1941-42, presented by Flying Tigers (AVG), Inc. New York [1945] 33 p.

GRAND CENTRAL ART GALLERIES, New York. Americans valiant and glorious, on exhibition, Grand Central Art Galleries. New York, N.Y. July 2nd-July 13th, 1945. [New York, 1945] 75, [1] p. illus. (ports.).

GREENLAW, OLGA (SOWERS). The lady and the Tigers. New York, E.P. Dutton, 1943. 11-317 p. front., plates, ports., facsims.

HAGER, ALICE (ROGERS) 1894- Wings for the dragon; the air war in Asia. New York, Dodd, Mead, 1945. xvi, 307 p. plates, ports., maps.

HOTZ, ROBERT B. With General Chennault; the story of the Flying tigers. New York, Coward-McCann, inc. [1943] x, 276 p. plates, ports.

LIANG, YU-MING, 梁又銘, 1906- Air combats, illustrated; Chinese Air Force. [Shanghai, Chen Chi Publisher, 1947] [4] 1., 24 [i.e. 31] col. plates (incl. ports.), [1] 1.

U.S. Air Force. Air Matériel Command. A chronicle of foreign nationals utilized as U.S. Army auxiliary military police in China, 1946-47. [n.p.,1952] cover-title. 1 v. (various pagings) photos.

WHELAN, RUSSELL, 1901- The Flying tigers; the story of the American volunteer group. Garden City, N.Y., Garden City Pub. Co.[1944] 224 p. plates, ports.

# VIII. LAW AND LEGISLATION

## Bibliographies and Dictionaries

[CHANG, CH'UNG-ÊN] 張崇恩 , comp. Anglo-Chinese law dictionary. [Tien-tsin? 1936?] 2 v.

CHAO, MING-KAO, 趙明高 , 1892- A dictionary of words and phrases of government, law, commerce, and education in English and Chinese. Pei Ling, Mukden, Sin Hua Press, 1930. [vii]-viii, [2], 231, [2] p. front. (port.).

CHINA. Ministry of Foreign Affairs. Dictionary of words and phrases of international law and diplomacy in English and French, with Chinese translations. [Peking, pref. 1925] 1 v. (various pagings).

PADOUX, GEORGES, 1867- List of English and French translations of modern Chinese laws and regulations. [Peking, 1936] [567]-644, 8 p. "Reprinted from the Chinese social and political science review, 19:4, Jan. 1936."

U.S. Bureau of Foreign and Domestic Commerce. "Finding list," bibliography of modern Chinese law in Library of Congress. Comp. and ed. July-Dec. 1944 by China Legal Section, Far Eastern Unit, Bureau of Foreign and Domestic Commerce, Dept. of Commerce. [Washington] Mimeographed by the China American Council of Commerce and Industry [1944?] 48 l.

———. Dept. of the Army. Army Library. Bibliography on foreign law of China, Japan, Korea, Philippine Islands, and USSR. Washington, Law Branch, Army Library, 1953. 9 l.

## Legal History

BÜCKLING, GERHARD, 1883- Han Fe-dsi, 韓非子 , in seinen Beziehungen zur chinesischen Rechtsschule und zum Kaisergedanken der Tsindynastie. Mayen [Buchdr. L. Schreder] 1948. 96, xxi p.

BÜNGER, KARL, 1903- Quellen zur Rechtsgeschichte der T'ang-Zeit. Peiping, Catholic Univ., 1946. xv, 311 p. (Monumenta serica. Monog. ser. 9 ).

———. ed. Religiöse Bindungen in frühen und in orientalischen Rechten, hrsg. von Karl Bünger und Hermann Trimborn. Wiesbaden, O. Harrassowitz, 1952. 69 p.

CHINA. Laws, statutes, etc. Manuel du Code chinois, par le P. Gui Boulais. Chang-Hai, 1923-24. 2 v. (Variétés sinologiques, 55 ).

ESCARRA, JEAN, 1885-1955. Le droit chinois; conception et évolution, institutions législatives et judiciaires, science et enseignement. Pékin, Éditions H. Vetch; Paris, Librairie du Recueil Sirey, 1936. xii, 559, [5] p.

———. Chinese law; conception and evolution, legislative and judicial institutions, science and teaching. Translated from the French by Gertrude R. Browne, for Work Projects Administration, W. P. 2799, University of Washington, Seattle. Seattle, 193? 696 l.

HAN, FEI, 韓非 , d. 233 B.C. The complete works of Han Fei tzǔ, a classic of Chinese legalism; translated from the Chinese with introduction, notes, glossary, and index by W.K. Liao, 廖文奎 . v. 1. London, A. Probsthain, 1939-xxxiii, 310 p. (Probsthain's oriental series. vol. 25 ).

The "HSI yüan lu", 洗冤錄 , or, "Instructions to coroners", tr. from the Chinese by Herbert A. Giles. London, J. Bale and Danielsson, 1924. 49 p. illus. "Reprinted from the Proceedings of the Royal society of medicine, 1924, vol. 17."

HU, YAN-MUNG, 胡養蒙 . Étude philosophique et juridique de la conception de "ming" et de "fen" dans le droit chinois. Préface de Jean Escarra. Paris,

Les éditions Domat-Montchrestien, 1932. xvii, [7]-139 p. fold. facsim. (É-
tudes de sociologie et d'ethnologie juridiques, 7 ).

HULSEWÉ, ANTHONY FRANÇOIS PAULUS, 1910-   Remnants of Han law. v.1.
Leiden, E.J. Brill, 1955-   455 p. (Sinica Leidensia, v.9 ). Vol. 1 issued
also as thesis, Leyden.

KROKER, EDUARD JOSEF, 1913-   Der Gedanke der Macht im Shang-kün-shu,
商君書. Mödling, 1951. 71 p. Thesis-Univ. Zürich.

————. The same. Mödling, Missionsdruckerei St. Gabriel Verlag, 1951. 280 p.
(St. Gabrieler Studien, Bd. 12 ).

KUEI, WAN-JUNG, 桂萬榮. T'ang-yin-pi-shih, 棠陰比事. Parallel cases
from under the peartree; a 13th century manual of jurisprudence and detec-
tion. Translated from the original Chinese with an introd. and notes by R.H.
van Gulik. Leiden, E.J. Brill, 1956. xiv, 198 p. facsims. (Sinica Leidensia, 10 ).

KUNG-SUN YANG, 公孫鞅, d. 338 B.C. The book of Lord Shang, 商君書, a
classic of the Chinese school of law; translated from the Chinese with introduction and notes by Dr. J.J.L. Duyvendak. London, A. Probsthain, 1928.
xiv, 346 p.   (Probsthain's oriental ser. vol.17 ).

LI, SIN-YANG. Doctrines du droit public en Chine antique, specialement dans
l'école légiste du VIIIe siècle avant J.C. Pars, les Presses modernes, 193?
114 p.

OU, KOEI-HING, 吳冠英. La peine d'après le Code des T'ang; étude de droit
pénal chinois ancien. Shanghai, Université l'Aurore, 1935. ii, 116 p. Thèse-
Univ. l'Aurore.

PHAM-QUANG-BACH. Essai sur l'idée de la loi dans le Code Gia-Long. Paris,
Picart, 1935. 299 p. Thèse-Univ. de Paris.

PHAN-VAN-TRUONG. Le droit pénal à travers l'ancienne législation chinoise.
Étude comparée sur le Code Gia-Long. Paris, E. Sagot, 1922. 190, [4] p.

RATCHNEVSKY, PAUL. Essai sur la codification et la législation à l'époque
des Yuan. Paris, E. Leroux, 1937. [v]-xcic, [1] p. Thèse complémentaire-
Univ. de Paris.

————. ed. and tr. Un code des Yuan. Paris, E. Leroux, 1937. 4, 348 p.(Bibliothèque de l'Institut des hautes études chinoise, 4 ).

SIAO, KING-FANG, 蕭金芳, [Hsiao Chin-fang] 1902-   Les conceptions fondamentales du droit public dans la Chine antique, par Siao King-fang. Paris,
Recueil Sirey, 1940. [xi]-xii, 101 p. (Bibliothèque d'histoire politique et constitutionelle. IV ).

SIÉ, KUAN-SHENG, 謝冠生, 1897-   Esquisse d'une histoire du droit chinois,
1: De l'origine jusqu'à la fin de l'époque féodale, par Sié Cheou-tchang, 謝
壽昌. Paris, Jouve, 1924. 198 p.

SIU, TCHOAN-PAO, 徐傳保, [Hsu Ch'uan-pao] 1901-   Le droit des gens et la
Chine antique. Préface de M. Yves de la Brière. Paris, Jouve et cie, 1926,
[i.e. 1927] -   181 p. illus.

TS'AO, WÊN-YEN, 曹文彥, 1908-   The development of Chinese law. Rev. ed.
Taipei, China Culture Pub. Foundation, 1953. 18 p. (Pamphlets on Chinese
affairs ).

WONG, HAO-HSIANG, 王孝祥. L'esprit de la loi et l'esprit du monde dans la
philosophie de Han Fei tseu. Paris, Impr., R. Foulon, 1941. [5]-142 p.
Thèse-Univ. de Paris.


General Works


CHÜ, CHENG, 居正, 1876-1951. On the reconstruction of the Chinese system
of law, translated by Chang Chi-tai, 張企泰. Nanking, 1947. 32 p.

ESCARRA, JEAN, 1885-1955. Les problèmes généraux de la codification du
droit privé chinois. Pékin, Impr. de la "Politique de Pékin," 1922. vii, 30
p. (Collection de la "Politique de Pékin."

——. Chinese law and comparative jurisprudence. Tientsin, La Librairie française, 1926. 35, [1] p.

——. L'enseignement et la science du droit en Chine. [Paris] Institut international de coopération intellectuelle, 1936. vi, [9]-103 p.

HAAS, OTTO. Gewohnheitsrechtliche Vertragstypen in China. Bonn, 1941. 811. plate. Diss.-Univ. Bonn.

HOLMES, OLIVER WENDELL, 1841-1935. Justice Holmes to Doctor Wu; an intimate correspondence, 1921-32. New York, Central Book Co. [1947?] 58 p. port.

NEEDHAM, JOSEPH, 1900- Human law and the laws of nature in China and the West. London, Oxford University Press, 1951. 44 p. (L. T. Hobhouse memorial trust lecture, 20 ).

POUND, ROSCOE, 1870- Law and the administration of justice, three lectures. Nanking, Sino-American Cultural Service, 1947. 2, 113 p.

RUETE, HANS HELLMUTH. Der Einfluss des abendländischen Rechtes auf die Rechtsgestaltung in Japan und China. Bonn a. Rh., L. Röhrscheid [1940] xxii, 122 p. (Rechtsvergleichende untersuchungen zur gesamten strafrechtswissenschaft, 12. hft.). Issued also as inaugural dissertation, Marburg.

STERN, JACQUES, 1876- Naturrecht und Weltrecht im Lichte der Rechtsentwicklung Japans und Chinas; Vortrag gehalten am 12. september 1927 in Tokio von dr. Jacques Stern. Tokio, Japanisch-deutsches Kulturinstitut; Berlin, Japaninstitut, 1927. 24 p.

SUN, T.C., 孫祖基. Anglo-American law maxims [compiled and translated into Chinese by T. C. Sun] Taipei, 1955. 77 p.

TCHANG, KIEN, 章劍. Le régime de ngan-tche, 安置制度, formule d'une variété de peine réadaptative, avec notes historiques comparatives sur la France et la Chine. Lyon, Bosc frères M. et L. Riou, 1941. 194 p. Thèse-Lyon.

TCHOU, KAO-YONG, 朱高融, [Chu Kao-jung]. De l'indivision sous ses deux principales formes en droit chinois comparé avec le droit étranger. Shanghai, Université l'Aurore; Paris, Librairie du Recueil Sirey; [etc., etc.] 1934. 64 p. Thèse-Université l'Aurore.

WU, JOHN C.H., 吳經熊, [Wu Ching-hsiung] 1899- Juridical essays and studies. Shanghai, Commercial Press, 1928. xvi, 267 p.

——. Legal systems of old and new China, a comparison; one of a series of lectures given at the Northwestern university law school in January 1930 under the auspices of the Rosenthal foundation lectureship. Chicago, 1930. 14 p.

——. The art of law and other essays juridical and literary. Shanghai, Commercial Press, 1936. xxi, 221 p.

——. comp. Essays in jurisprudence and legal philosophy, selected by John C. H. Wu and M. C. Liang. [Shanghai] Soochow University Law School [1938] [732] p.

——. Fountain of justice; a study in the natural law. New York, Sheed and Ward, 1955. 287 p.

YÜ, WEI, 呂渭, [Lü Wei]. Le statut des fonctionnaires en Chine depuis la révolution de 1926 à nos jours. Nancy, Impr. Vagner, 1937. 138 p. Thèse - Univ. de Nancy.

## Constitution

CHENG, YEN-CHENG. Les principaux mouvements constitutionnels en Chine de 1897 à 1935. Lyon, Impr. P. Ferréol, 1936. [7]-156 p. Thèse - Univ. de Dijon.

CHIANG, HAI-CHÁO, 江海潮. Die Wandlungen im chinesischen Verfassungsrecht seit dem Zusammenbruch der Mandschu-dynastie unter besonderer Berücksichtigung der rechtlichen Stellung des Staatshauptes. Berlin, C. Heymann, 1937. x, 306 p. (Institut für ausländisches öffentliches recht und völkerrecht. Beiträge zum ausländischen öffentlichen recht und völkerrecht, 23).

CHINA. Commission on Extraterritoriality. Constitution and supplementary laws and documents of the Republic of China. Tr. and pub. by the Commission on Extraterritoriality. Peking, 1924. 198 p.

——. Constitution. Constitution of the Republic of China. English translation with Chinese text. [Peking, 1924] 34, [16] p. English and Chinese.Translated and published by the Commission on Extraterritoriality.

——. Organic law of the National government of the Republic of China. Nanking, 1928. cover-title, 12, 14 p. 2 fold. tab.

——. The same. Zi-ka-wei, Impr. de T'ou-sè-wè, 1928. cover-title, 12,[14] p. fold. tables.

——. The same. New York, China Institute in America [1929?] 8 p. fold. diagr.

——. Constitution provisoire et lois organiques de la République chinoise. Traduction officielle. Shanghai, La Presse orientale, 1932. 120 p.

——. First draft of the permanent constitution of China. Drafted by John C. H. Wu, 吳經熊 , translated by Yui Ming, 余銘 . Shanghai [China Press] 1933. 17 p. illus. Reprinted from the China Press, August 17, 1933.

——. Draft of the constitution of the Republic of China. Projet de constitution de la republique de Chine. Progetto di constituzione della repubblica della Cina. [n. p., 1936] 53 p. Chinese, English, French and Italian in parallel columns.

——. China's constitutions: permanent and provisional. Chungking, Chinese Ministry of Information, 1945. cover-title, 16 p.

——. The organic law of the Republic of China [and] The final draft constitution of the Republic of China. New York, Chinese News Service [1945] 24 p.

-——. China's draft constitution, the full text of two important documents in the evolution of Chinese democracy: Organic law of the National government of the Republic of China. Final draft of the Constitution of the Republic of China. [New York, 1945] 30 p.

——. The Constitution of the Republic of China. New York, Chinese News Service [1947] cover-title, 25 p.

——. The same (with Chinese text) adopted by the National Assembly. Taipei, China Culture Pub. Foundation, 1954. 46 p. (Pamphlets on Chinese affairs).

HO, JEN CHING, 何任清 . Histoire constitutionelle de la Chine. Toulouse, C. Dirion, G. Labadie, successeur, 1936. 190 p. Thèse - Univ. de Toulouse.

HSÜ, DAU-LIN, 徐道鄰, 1906- Die Verfassungswandlung. Berlin und Leipzig, W. de Gruyter and co., 1932. 182 p. (Beiträge zum ausländischen öffentlichen rect und völkerrecht, 15 ).

KONG, CHIN TSONG, 孔慶宗 , 1898- La constitution des cinq pouvoirs, théorie-application. Étude sur une doctrine nouvelle du droit public chinois et les institutions politiques de la Chine moderne. Paris, M. Rivière, 1932. iii, [7]-380 p., diagrs.

LO, HOAI, 羅懷, 1895- La nouvelle législation chinoise; ses fondements -ses tendances. Préface de m. le baron Silvercruys. Paris, A. Pedone, 1932. iii, 189 p.

PAN, WEI-TUNG, 潘維東 , 1915- The Chinese constitution; a study of forty years of constitution-making in China. Washington, The Catholic University of America Press, 1945. xi, 327 p. (The Catholic university of America. Studies in politics, government and international law, vol. 3 ). Thesis-Catholic university of America.

SIAO, KING-FANG, 蕭金芳, 1902- L'évolution constitutionnelle de la Chine moderne. Bruxelles, 1938. 528 l. Thèse - Univ. Libre de Bruxelles.

——. Exposé historique et analytique de la théorie des cinq pouvoirs en Chine. Bruxelles, Impr. medicale et scientifique, 1939. cover-title, 13 p.

SIÉ, KUAN-SHENG, 謝冠生 , 1897- A brief survey of the Chinese Constitution. Taipei, China Cultural Service [1954] 80 p. diagrs. (Pamphlets on Kuomintang affairs ).

SIÉ, YING-CHOW,    謝瀛洲, 1893-  Le fédéralisme en Chine; étude sur quelques constitutions provinciales.  Paris, H. d'Arthez, 1924. 237 p.

SIU, QUI, 徐基. Le pouvoir de contrôle en Chine. Nancy, Impr. Vagner, 1937. 141, [1] p. Thèse-Univ. Nancy.

SONG, YUEN-ZOU, 宋淵如, [Sung Yüan-ju]. Le mouvement de la Constitution chinoise; étude du projet de Constitution du Yuan législatif du 16 octobre 1934. Nancy, Impr. Grnadville, 1935. [7]-264 p. Thèse-Univ. Nancy.

TCH'EN, HIONG-FEI, 陳雄飛, [Ch'en Hsiung-fei] 1912-  Essai de droit constitutionnel chinois. Les cinq pouvoirs. Shanghai, Université l'Aurore;[etc., etc.] 1933. iv, 186 p. Thèse-Univ. l'Aurore.

TCHENG, SOUMAY, 鄭毓秀, [Cheng, Yu-hsiu] 1894-  Le mouvement constitutionnel en Chine: étude de droit comparé. Paris, Recueil Sirey, 1925. 157 p. Thèse-Univ. de Paris.

TSAO, WEN-YEN, 曹文彥, 1908-  The constitutional structure of modern China.  [Melbourne] Melbourne Univ. Press [1947] xvii, 304 p. illus., ports.
────. The main features of the permanent Constitution of the Republic of China. Taipei, China Culture Pub. Foundation, 1953. 12 p. (Pamphlets on Chinese affairs).

TSI, TCHOU-SHENG, 漆竹生. Étude sur le projet de Constitution de la République chinoise du 5 mai 1936. Paris, Domat-Montchrestien, 1940. 242 p. Thèse - Univ. Paris.

TSU, DJENCHOW. Historique de l'évolution des constitutions chinoises (1905-31). Paris, Les Éditions Domat Montchrestien, Loviton et Cie, 1934. 196 p. illus. Thèse-Univ. de Paris.

WOO, JAMES, 吳凱聲, [Wu K'ai-sheng] 1900-  Le problème constitutionnel chinois; la constitution du 10 octobre 1923, avec une table de transcription des mots chinois par Maurice Courant, et une préface par Edouard Lambert. Paris, M. Giard, 1925. [vii]-xiii, [6], 150 p. (Bibliothèque de l'Institut de droit comparé de Lyon. Études et documents. t. 11 ).

WOU, KACK-TCHENG, 何克誠, [Ho Ke-chêng]. L'évolution du droit dans les institutions fondamentales de la Chine depuis l'antiquité jusqu'à la révolution de 1911. Nancy, Société d'impressions typographiques, 1938. [9]-160 p. Thèse-Univ. Nancy.

WU, FRIEDRICH C., 吳騏, [Wu chi]. La nouvelle Chine et le gouvernement national: étude sur la loi organique du 10 Octobre 1928 et les organisations des pouvoirs publics dans le gouvernement national. Préface de Jean Escarra. Paris, Marcel Rivière, 1929. vi, 216 p.

## Civil Law

BRYAN, ROBERT THOMAS, 1892-  An outline of Chinese civil law. Shanghai, Commercial Press, 1925. vi, 92 p.

CHANG, CHU KUING, 張祖庚. Essai sur la nationalité chinoise.  La Varenne Saint-Hilaire (Seine) Impr. M. and G. Durand, 1941. 152 p. Thèse-Univ. de Paris.

CHEN TSEN I, PIERRE CLAVER, 沈曾怡. De la responsabilité civile en droit chinois. Paris, Domat-Montchrestien, 1934. 142 p. fold. facsim. Thèse - Univ. de Paris.

CHINA. Laws, statutes, etc. The regulations relating to civil procedure of the Republic of China. Published by the Commission on Extraterritoriality. Peking, 1923. cover-title, iii, [3], 189 p.
────. Règlement de procédure civile de la République de Chine, promulgué le 22 juillet, 1921. Suivi du règlement d'exécution du même jour, et du règlement sur les voies d'exécution en matière civile du 3 août, 1920. Publié par la Commission de l'exterritorialité. Pékin, Impr. du Pei-t'ang, 1924. xxi, 259 p.
────. Revised law of nationality. Detailed rules for the application of Revised

law of nationality. Rules for the application of laws (with Chinese text) Translated and published by the Commission on Extraterritoriality. Peking, 1925. cover-title, 21, [12] p.

————. Draft Chinese Civil code. Presented by the Ministry of Justice to the chief executive of the Republic of China for promulgation on the 23rd day of the 11th month of the 14th year of the Republic (Nov. 23rd, 1925) Book 1. General principles, English and Chinese. Translated and published by the Commission of Extraterritoriality. Peking, 1926. 56, 36 p.

————. The Civil code of the Republic of China. Translated into English by Ching-lin Hsia, 夏晉麟, James L. E. Chow, 周福慶, Liu Chieh, 劉鍇 [and] Yu-kon Chang, 張與公. Introduction by the Hon. Foo Ping-sheung, 傅秉常. Shanghai [etc.] Kelly and Walsh, 1931. xxxii, 382 p.

————. The same. Preface by Hu Han-min. Introduction by Foo Ping-sheung. Shanghai [etc.] Kelly and Walsh, limited, 1930-31. 2 v.

————. Code civil de la République de Chine. Traduits du chinois par Ho Tchong-chan, 何崇善. Introduction de Foo Ping-sheung. Préface de son exc. Hu Han-min, Zi-Ka-Wei, près. Changhai, Impr. de l'Orphelinat de T'ou-Sè-Wè; Paris, Recueil Sirey (scoiété anonyme) 1930-31. 2 v.

————. Code de procédure civile (26 décembre 1930 et 3 février 1931) et Loi sur la conciliation en matière civile (20 janvier 1930) Texte chinois et traduction française par François Théry, S.J. Tientsin, Hautes études, 1932. ii, 111, 111, 18, [3] p. (Le droit chinois moderne, 15 ).

————. Commentaries on the Chinese Civil code, by Boyer P.H. Chu, 朱寶賢. Shanghai, Shanghai, Law Books Pub. Society, 1935-     v.

————. Code de procédure civile (révisé) de la République chinoise (1er juillet 1935); texte chinois et traduction française rev. et mise à jour à la date de promulgation du nouveau code, par C.M. Ricard. Tientsin, Hautes études; [etc., etc.] 1936. [1], 125, 125, 19, [4] p. (Le droit chinois moderne, 25 ).

————. The law of compulsory execution of the Republic of China. Translated from Chinese by N. M. Shoolingin. Tientsin, International Law Office, 1946. v, 26 p.

————. Civil code of the Republic of China. Taipei, Law School of Soochow University, 1953. cover-title, 154 l.

CODEX juris civilis Reipublicae Sinicae. Tsinanfu, typis missionis catholicae, 1934. vii, 212 p.

ESCARRA, JEAN, 1885-1955. La codification du droit de la famille et du droit des successions (livres IV et V du Code civil de la République chinoise) Rapport présenté au Conseil législatif du gouvernement national. Shanghai,Impr. de l'Orphelinat de T'ou-Sè-Wè, 1931. ii, 87 p.

HO, TCHONG-CHAN, 何崇善, ed. and tr. Règlement provisoire relatif au notariat du 30 juillet 1935; règlement d'application et tarif du 14 février 1936; formules. Texte chinois et traduction française. Tientsin, Hautes études; [etc., etc.] 1936. [1], 44, 44 p. (Le droit chinois moderne, 27 ).

HOU, YOU-ING, 胡毓寶. Étude sur la parenté en droit chinois. Paris, Les Éditions Domat-Montchrestien, 1933. 254 p., diagrs., facsim.

JAMIESON, GEORGE, 1843-1920. Chinese family and commercial law. Shanghai [etc.] Kelly and Walsh, 1921. ii, 188 p.

LO, CHE-TSI, 羅時濟. La succession "ab intestat" dans le code civil chinois. Toulouse, Impr. Touloise, 1932. [7]-115, [1] p. Thèse-Univ. de Nancy.

MÖLLENDORFF, PAUL GEORG VON, 1848-1901. The family law of the Chinese. Translated from the German by Mrs. S.M. Broadbent. Rangoon, Supdt. Government Print. and Stationery, 1925. 43 p. 1st ed. Shanghai, 1879.

RÎAZANOVSKÎĬ, VALENTÎN ALEKSANDROVICH, 1884-   Fundamental institutions of Chinese civil law. Harbin, Chinese Eastern Railway, 1926. 74 p. [Condensed from the author's Modern Civil Law of China].

————. The modern civil law of China. Harbin, Printed by "Zaria," 1927-28.

2 v.

――――. Chinese civil law. Tientsin, 1938. 310 p.

RICARD, C. M. ed. and tr. Règlement de détail pour l'application de la Loi sur l'état-civil; texte chinois et traduction française par C. M. Ricard et m. ph. Kou Cheou-hi, 顧守熙. Tientsin, Hautes études, 1934. 8, 8 p. (Le droit chinois moderne, 20-a).

SHIH, HUNG-SHUN, 施宏勛. Le testament dans le nouveau Code civil chinois. Nancy, Impr. G. Thomas, 1936. [5]-115, [1] p. Thèse-Univ. de Nancy.

SIAO, T'ONG, 蕭桐, [Hsiao T'ung]. De la succession et de l'adoption en droit chinois. ZI-Ka-Wei-Chang-Hai, Impr. de l'Orphelinat de T'ou-Sè-Wè, 1927. 112 p. Thèse-Université l'Aurore.

SUN, SI-FONG, 孫璽鳳. Du rôle des décisions d'interprétation (Kiai che li) comme source du droit chinois, principalement en matière de fiançailles. Paris, E. Duchemin, L. Chauny et L. Quinsac, successeurs, 1932. 179, [1] p. At head of title: Georges Sun.

TCH'EN, SI-TAN, 陳錫潭. L'adoption en droit chinois. Zi-ka-wei, Chang-Hai, Impr. de l'Orphelinat de T'ou-sè-wè, 1924. 84 p. Thèse-Université l'Aurore.

THÉRY, FRANÇOIS, 1890- ed. and tr. Code civil de la République de Chine. Livre IV: De la famille et livre V: De la succession, et lois d'application de ces deux livres. Texte chinois et traduction française. Tientsin, Procure de la Mission de Sienhsien, 1931. vii, [1], 43, 43, [2] p. [Le droit chinois moderne, 10 ].

――――. Code foncier de la République de Chine. Texte chinois et traduction française. Tientsin, Procure de la Mission de Sienhsien, 1931. 80, 80, [5] p. [Le droit chinois moderne, 11 ].

――――. Loi sur l'état-civil, promulguée le 12 décembre 1931, entrée en vigueur le 1 juillet 1934. Texte chinois et traduction française, par François Théry, S. J. et Hoang Jou-hsiang, 黃汝祥. Tientsin, Hautes études; [etc., etc.] 1934. ii, 32, 32, [2] p. (Le droit chinois moderne, 20 ).

――――. Interprétations du Yuan judiciaire en matière civile [1929- Texte chinois et traduction française. Tientsin, Hautes études, 1936- 3 v. (Le droit chinois moderne. 26, 31, 35 ).

――――. Éléments de droit civil chinois (livres I à III du Code civil). Tientsin, Hautes études, 1939-[42] 1233, [1] p. (Le droit chinois moderne, 33 ).

VALK, MARIUS HENDRIKUS VAN DER., 1908- An outline of modern Chinese family law. Peking, H. Vetch, 1939. 219 p. (Monumenta serica. Monograph series, 2 ).

――――. Conservatism in modern Chinese family law. Leiden, E. J. Brill, 1956. 90 p. (Studia et documenta, ad iura Orientis antiqui pertinentia, 4 ).

WOO, SOO. L'antichrèse en droit comparé (Chine, Angleterre et France). Dijon, Impr. du Palais, M. Pornon, 1936. [9]-157 p. Thèse-Univ. de Dijon.

YU, TCHEN-P'ONG, 于振鵬. L'hypothèque dans le droit coutumier chinois. Lyon, Bosc frères, M. et L. Riou, 1940. 114 p. Thèse-Univ. de Lyon.

### Criminal Law

AN, YÜ-KUN, 安裕琨. Reform von Vermögensverbrechen im deutschen, chinesischen und japanischen Strafrecht. Berlin, 1940. 80 p. Diss.-Univ. Berlin.

CHANG, CHUNG-KONG, 張仲絳, 1908- Unrechtsausschliessungsgründe im deutschen und chinesischen Recht. Marburg a. d. Lahn, Hessischer Verlag K. Euker, 1938. 47, [1] p. Diss.-Univ. Marburg.

CH'EN, SHU-CHIUNG, 陳叔絅, 1910- Die Strafzumessung im chinesischen und deutschen Recht. Eine rechtsvergleichende Studie. Zenlenroda, Sporn, 1937. 40 p. Diss.-Univ. Jena.

CHINA. Laws, statutes, etc. The provisional Criminal code of the Republic of China, embodying presidential mandates, the provisional Criminal code amendment act, the revised draft of the Law on offences relating to morphine, revised regulations governing military criminal cases, regulations governing naval criminal cases. Published by the Commission on Extraterritoriality. Peking, 1923. 2, 8, 2, 190 p.

——. Code pénal provisoire de la République de Chine, du 30 mars 1912. Suivi de l'acte modificatif du 24 décembre, 1914, du Code des contraventions, et des règlements sur la répression du trafic de la morphine et de la corruption des fonctionnaires publics. Publié par la Commission de l'exterritorialité. Pékin, Impr. du Pei-t'ang, 1923. x, 152 p.

——. The regulations relating to criminal procedure of the Republic of China (promulgated on Nov. 14, 1921) embodying presidential mandates, regulations relating to the enforcement of the regulations relating to criminal procedure, regulations relating to summary criminal procedure, and provisional regulations relating to sentence by order. Published by the Commission on Extraterritoriality. Peking, 1923. v, 131, 4, 3, 4, [2] p.

——. Règlement de procédure pénale de la République de Chine du 14 novembre. Suivi du Règlement d'exécution, du Règlement sur le décret pénal et du Règlement sur la procédure pénale sommaire. Publié par la Commission de l'exterritorialité. Pékin, Impr. du Pei-t'ang, 1923. xiii, 142 p.

——. The Chinese Criminal code (promulgated by the Chinese nationalist government) translated by Yu Tinn-hugh, 余天休. Shanghai, The International Pub. Co., 1928. [iii]-xii, 293 p.

——. The Criminal code of the Republic of China. (Promulgated on 10th March, 1928, by the National government). Translated into English by S. L. Burdett in collaboration with Judge Lone Liang, 梁龍. Shanghai, Despatch Print. Co., 1928? 103 numb. l.

——. Code pénal de la République de Chine, traduction française par Tch'en Hiong-fei, 陳雄飛. Zi-Ka-Wei près Chang-hai, Impr. de l'Orphelinat de T'ou-Sè-Wè, 1929. 2 p., 2 l., 87 p.

——. Code pénal de la République de Chine, promulgué le 10 mars 1928, entré en vigueur le 1er septembre 1928. Traduit du chinois, avec une introduction, des notes et une suite de textes complémentaires et de documents annexes, par Jean Escarra. Paris, M. Giard, 1930. lxxx, 214 p., 1 l. incl. geneal. tables. (Bibliothèque de l'Institut de droit comparé de Lyon. Série de criminologie et de droit pénal comparé. t. II (1. ptie.) ).

——. The Criminal code of the Republic of China, embodying the Law governing the application of the Criminal code and the Penal code of army, navy, and air forces of the Republic of China. Translated into English by Chao-yuen C. Chang, 張肇元, foreword by the Hon. Sun Fo. Shanghai, Kelly and Walsh, 1935. 184 p.

——. The Chinese Criminal code and special criminal and administrative laws, translated and annotated by the Legal department of the Shanghai Municipal council. Shanghai, Commercial Press, 1935. [1], v-xi, v-xi, 178, 178, 179-216 p.

——. Code pénal de la République chinoise; texte chinois accompagné d'une traduction française par C. M. Ricard et me. ph. Kou Cheou-hi, 顧守熙, P.C. Leblanc, et Wang Tse-sin, 王自新. Tientsin, Hautes études, 1935. 98, 98, 10, [3] p. (Le droit chinois moderne, 21 ).

——. Code pénal de la République de Chine. Promulgué de 1er janvier 1935, entré en vigueur le 1er juillet 1935. Traduit du chinois avec une introduction et des notes, par Ho Tchong-chan, 何崇善. Préface de Wang Yung-pin, 王用賓. Zi-Ka-Wei, Impr. de l'Orphelinat de T'ou-Sè-Wè; Paris, Librairie du Recueil Sirey, 1935. xxv, 110 p.

——. Code de procédure pénale de la République chinoise. Texte chinois accompagné d'une traduction française, par le Bureau de traductions des Services de police de la concession française de Shanghai, sous la direction de P.C. Leblanc. Tientsin, Hautes études, 1935. [1], 114, 114, 12 p. (Le droit chinois moderne, 23 ).

————. The Code of criminal procedure of the Republic of China and the Court agreement relating to the Chinese courts in the international settlement of Shanghai, China, translated by the Legal department of the Shanghai Municipal council. Shanghai, Commercial Press, 1936. vii, 140, 140, 141-239 p.

————. Das chinesische Strafgesetzbuch vom 1. januar 1935, übersetzt von dr. Chang Chungkong, 張仲絳, und dr. H. Herrfahrdt. Bonn a.Rh., L. Röhrscheid, 1938. vi, 86 p. (Rechtsvergleichende untersuchungen zur gesamten strafrechtswissenschaft, hrsg, von dr. Erich Schwinge. 9, hft. ).

KENNEDY, GEORGE ALEXANDER, 1901- Die Rolle des Geständnisses im chinesischen Gesetz. Berlin, 1939. 74 p. Diss. -Univ. Berlin.

KING, SHIH-DING, 金世鼎. Étude comparée de la justice pénale en Chine et en France. [Paris] Recueil Sirey [1945] 166 p. (Nouvelle collection de l'Institut de criminologie de l'Université de Paris, publiée sous la direction de mm. Hugueney et Donnedieu de Vabres. IV ).

MEIJER, MARINUS JOHAN. The introduction of modern criminal law in China. Batavia, 1950. 214 p. (Sinica Indonesiana, v. 2 ). Proefschrift - Universiteit van Indonesie.

## Commercial Law

ALLMAN, NORWOOD FRANCIS, 1893- Handbook on the protection of trademarks, patents, copyrights, and trade-names in China. Shanghai, Kelly and Walsh, 1924. iii, 207, [5] p. incl. forms.

————. tr. Chinese trade-mark law, regulations and classification of merchandise. Shanghai, The China Law Journal, 1931. cover-title, 19 numb. l.

————. tr. Revised Chinese trade-mark law, regulations and classification of merchandise. Shanghai, Allman and Co., 1936. cover-title, [1], 20, [20, [1] p.].

BAYLIN, J.R. Loi chinois sur les effets du commerce. Pékin, Impr. de la ''Politique de Pékin,'' 1930. 32 p.

BRITISH CHAMBER OF COMMERCE, Shanghai. The Nanking government's laws and regulations affecting trade, commerce, finance, etc. v. 1-15; Oct. 9, 1929-35. Shanghai, Issued by the British Chamber of Commerce, 1929-36. 15 v. Mimeographed.

————. Nanking laws and regulations. Index. Volumes I to XI. 7 numb. l., 1 l., 8-14 numb. l.

————. The same. Volumes I to XV. 9 numb. l., 1 l., 10-17 numb. l.

————. The Insurance enterprise law (revised and promulgated by the National government of the Republic of China, 11th January, 1937.) Regulations governing the enforcement of the Insurance enterprise law (passed by the Legislative yuan, 27th November, 1936, and promulgated by the National government of the Republic of China, 11th January, 1937.) Shanghai, British Chamber of Commerce, 1937. 17, 3 numb. l.

BÜNGER, KARL, 1903- Zivil- und handelsgesetzbuch sowie Wichsel- und Scheckgesetz von China. Marburg in Hessen, N.G.Elwert, 1934. 318 p.(Arbeiten zum handels- , gewerbe- und landwirtschaftsrecht, 73 ).

CHANG, YUKON, 張興公, tr. The Bankruptcy law of the Republic of China, promulgated 1935; translated into English by Yukon Chang, and Lily C.Yung; introduction by the Hon. Foo Ping-sheung, 傅秉常. Shanghai, Kelly and Walsh, 1936. xvii, 53 p.

CHEN, THEODORE, 鄭希陶, comp. The modern commercial legislation of China, translated and compiled by Theodore Chen and Norwood F. Allman. Shanghai, 1926. 152, [92] p.

CHINA. Laws, statutes, etc. Trade mark law, and detailed regulations. Published by the Commission on Extraterritoriality. Peking, 1923. cover-title, 33 p.

————. Regulations relating to commerce. I. Ordinance for the general regulations of traders. II. Commercial associations' ordinance. III. Regulations of the Arbitration court of commerce. IV. Detailed regulations relating to the administration of the Arbitration court of commerce. V. The law of chambers of commerce. Published by the Commission on Extraterritoriality. Peking, 1923. cover-title, 126 p.

———. Législation commerciale de la République de Chine. (Textes mis à jour au 1er octobre, 1923) Publié par la Commission de l'exterritorialité. Pékin, Impr. Nashbaur, 1924. x, [9], 213 p.

———. Copyright law of China, National government regulations promulgated May 23, 1928, translated by Norwood F. Allman. Shanghai [1928] cover-title, 12 p.

———. Company law. [Promulgated by the National Government on the 26th December, 1929] Translated into English by H. K. Shih. Shanghai, Bureau of Industrial and Commercial Information, Ministry of Industry, Commerce and Labor [1929] cover-title, 41 p.

———. The Chinese insurance business act (promulgated by the National government on July 5, 1935) Translated by Wei Wen Han, 魏文瀚 , and Samuel H. Chang, 張似旭. Shanghai, Mercury Press [1935?] 28 p.

———. The company law of China, promulgated 12th April, 1946. English tr. by Chao-yuen C. Chang, 張肇元. Foreword by the Hon. Sun Fo. 2d ed., rev. Shanghai, Kelly and Walsh, 1946. 103 p.

———. The same. Rev. 1946. [Translation by Chao-yuen C. Chang] [New York, Chinese News Service] 1946. 58 p.

———. Loi sur les sociétés du 12 avril 1946. Traduction française par André Bonnichon et P. Suen Li-che, 孫立時. Tientsin, Hautes études, 1946. 102 p. (Collection "Le droit chinois moderne").

———. Loi révisée sur les sociétés, traduit par Jean Escarra and Wei Tenglin, 魏登臨. Paris, Librairie du Recueil Sirey pour Office d'Information du gouvernement chinois, 1948. vii, 82 p.

———. The company law of China, promulgated 12 April, 1946. English translation by Chao-yuan C. Chang. Foreword by Wang Chung-hui. Taipei, Law School of Soochow University, 1953. 59 numb. l.

ESCARRA, JEAN, 1885-1955. ed. and tr. Loi sur les effets de commerce du 30 octobre 1929. Texte chinois et traduction française, introduction et notes. Loi d'application de la Loi sur les effets de commerce. Tientsin, Hautes études; [etc., etc.] 1934. viii, 34, 34 p. (Le droit chinois moderne, 7-bis ).

HUNG, WILLIAM SHIH-HAO, 洪士豪. Commercial law of China. [Shanghai?] 1932. xix, [3]-307 p.

———. Outlines of modern Chinese law; legal history, contracts, agency, sales, bailments and carriers, partnership, property, domestic relations, succession, private corporations, negotiable instruments, criminal law, including list of prevailing laws and table of degrees of punishment. [Shanghai? 1934] xxv, 317 p.

KIRFEL, HARALD WILLIBALD, 1914- Das Gewohnheitsrecht bei Kauf und Verkauf von Immobilien in China und Mandschukuo. [Bonn] 1940. 62 p. Diss.-Univ. Bonn.

LIU, SHIH-FANG FRANCIS, 劉士芳 , 1901- tr. The Negotiable instrument law of the Republic of China; translation by S. Francis Liu, Boyer P. H. Chu, 朱寶賢 , and Lin-chong Chen, 陳令莊. Shanghai, 1930. vii, 40, 40 p.

McNEILL, JOHN, ed. and tr. Code of maritime law (promulgated the 30th December, 18th year (1929), and enforced the 1st January, 20th year (1931) of the republic) Chinese text with English translation, translated and edited by John McNeill and Dr. Wei Wen-han, 魏文瀚. Shanghai, China Law Journal (1931) [1], 41, 41, 42-49, [1] p.

SUN, HAO-HSUAN, 孫浩煊, 1898- tr. The Chinese law on negotiable instruments (promulgated by the National government of China on the thirtieth of

October, 1929). Shanghai, Kelly and Walsh, 1930. viii, 78 p.

THÉRY, FRANÇOIS, 1890-  Les sociétés de commerce en Chine.  Tientsin, Société française de librairie et d'édition, 1929. 437 p. Thèse-Univ. de Louvain.

——. ed. and tr. La Loi du 26 décembre 1929 sur les sociétés commerciales,
traduction française.  Pékin, Impr. de la Politique de Pékin, 1930. 47 p.
(Collection de la "Politique de Pékin").

——. ed. and tr. Loi sur les assurances, promulguée le 30 décembre 1929.
Traduite du Se-fa kong pao du 18 janvier 1930.  Zi-Ka-Wei près Chang-hai,
Impr. de l'Orphelinat de T'ou-Sè-Wè, 1930. 28 p.

——. ed. and tr. Loi sur le commerce maritime, promulguée le 30 décembre
1929. Traduite du Se-fa kong pao du 25 janvier et du 1er février 1930.  Zi-
Ka-Wei près Shanghai, Impr. de l'Orphelinat de T'ou-Sè-Wè, 1930. 47 p.

——. ed. and tr. Loi sur les navires (4 décembre 1930) et Loi sur l'enrégis-
trement des navires (5 décembre 1930) Texte chinois et traduction française.
Tientsin, Hautes études, 1931. 25, 25 p. (Le droit chinois moderne, 12 ).

——. ed. and tr. Loi sur la faillite, promulguée le 17 juillet 1935, entre en
vigueur le 1 octobre 1935. Texte chinois, et traduction française.  Tientsin,
Hautes études, 1935. iii, 31, 31 p. (Le droit chinois moderne, 24 ).

WEI, TAO-MING, 魏道明 , 1898-  Le chèque en Chine.  Paris, Recueil Sirey,
1925. 138 p. Thèse - Univ. de Paris.

WOLFE, ARCHIBALD JOHN, 1878-  Protesting drafts in China.  Washington,
Govt. Print. Off., 1923. ii, 28 p. (U.S. Bureau of foreign and domestic commerce Trade information bull., 142 ).

### Municipal Law

CH'EN, KYI-TSUNG, 陳繼貞. Le système municipal en Chine.  Gembloux
(Belg.) Impr. J. Duculot, 1937. viii, 178 p. (Université de Louvain. Faculté de droit. École des sciences politiques et sociales. Collection ).

JAO, DAIN-HOUA, 饒詹華. La Loi municipale chinoise du 20 mai 1930.  Bordeaux, Impr. E. Castera, 1939. [5]-146 p. Thèse-Univ. de Bordeaux.

LOO, KON-TUNG, 盧幹東. La vie municipale et l'urbanisme en Chine.  Lyon,
Bosc frères, M. et L. Riou, 1934. 172 p. Thèse-Univ. de Lyon.

SHANGHAI (French Concession). Compte-rendu de le gestion pour l'exercise
1910-33.  Changhai, Impr. Municipale, 1911-34. 23 v. ?

TCHANG, TENG-TI, 張登棣 , [Chang Têng-ti]. Les titres de location perpétu-
elle sur les concessions de Shanghai.  Tientsin, Hautes études, 1940. 178 p.
incl. maps, facsims. (Le droit chinois moderne, 34 ).

TIENTSIN. (British Municipal Council) Ordinances, etc. Building and sanitary
by-laws. 1936. [Tientsin] Tientsin Press [1937] xxiii, 76 (i. e. 92) p. plates.

——. Municipal by-laws. 1936. [Tientsin] Tientsin Press [1937] 14, [2], 19 p.

——. (French Concession) Ordinances, etc. Ordonnances, rapports et documents. Gestion financière de l'exercice.  Tientsin, 1938-41. 4 v. ?

### Administration of Justice

CHINA. Commission on Extraterritoriality. A general statement of the present
conditions of the Chinese judiciary. Pub. by the Commission on Extraterritoriality.  Peking, 1925. cover-title, 19 p.

——. General and particular tables showing estimated amount of ordinary judicial expenditures under the control of the Ministry of Justice for Peking
and various provinces for the 12th year of the Republic of China and General
and particular tables showing actual amount of ordinary judicial expenditures
under the control of the Ministry of Justice for Peking and various provinces
for the 12th year of the Republic of China.  Peking, 1925. cover-title, 31 p.,

incl. tables.

———. Tables showing the qualifications of the judicial officers of China and tables showing the length of service of the judicial officers of China. (Made in September, 1925). Peking, 1926. cover-title, 12, 11 p.

———. Tables showing the dates of the establishment of the courts of China, their localities, and the regions within their jurisdiction (with maps showing the locality of the various courts). Peking, 1926. cover-title, [1], 13 p. 22 maps.

———. Laws, statutes, etc. Laws, ordinances, regulations and rules relating to the judicial administration of the Republic of China. Translated and published by the Commission on Extraterritoriality. Peking, 1923. 364 p.

———. Ministry of Justice. Rules for the application of laws (translation) Peking, The Ministry of Justice, 1921. cover-title, 7 p.

———. Judicial statistics of the third to the tenth year of the Republic of China comp. by the Ministry of Justice. Pub. by the Commission on Extraterritoriality. Peking, 1925. 2 v.

———. Supreme Court. The Chinese Supreme Court decisions. (Relating to general principles of civil law, obligations, and commercial law.) Translated by F. T. Cheng, 鄭天錫 . Published by the Commission on Extraterritoriality. Peking, 1923. ix, 6 p., 2 1., 229 p.

———. Recueil des sommaires de la jurisprudence de la Cour suprême de la République de Chine en matière civile et commerciale (1912-18) Publié par la Commission de l'Exterritorialité. Chang-Hai, Impr. de la Mission catholique, Orphelinat de T'ou-Sè-Wè, 1924-25. xxii, 258, [6], 259-528 p. fold. tables.

———. Tables of comparative statistics relating to civil and criminal cases in the Supreme Court from year I to year X of the Republic of China. Comp. by the Secretarial office of the Supreme Court. Tr. and pub. by the Commission on Extraterritoriality. Peking, 1925. cover-title, 25 p.

———. Supreme Court (Nanking). L'année judiciaire chinoise. Jurisprudence de la Cour suprême de Nanking. 1.- année; 1928- Affaires civiles, traduction par François Théry. Affaires pénales, traduction par Robert Jobez. Tientsin, Hautes études; Paris, Librairie du Recueil Sirey, 1933- 3 v. (Le droit chinois moderne, nᵒ 16, 18, 19 ).

———. Supreme Court. Interpretations of the Supreme Court at Peking, years 1915 and 1916; translations, notes and introd. by M. H. van der Valk. Batavia, Sinological Institute, Faculty of Arts; University of Indonesia [1949] 382 p. (Sinica Indonesiana, 1 ).

HOU TS'OUEI, CHOU-YEN, 胡崔淑言 . L'œuvre de la Cour suprême de Pékin (Ta li yuan) et le droit chinois des obligations. Paris, Librairie technique et économique, 1938. 200 p. Thèse-Univ. de Paris.

KING, SHIH-DING, 金世鼎 , 1908- Le recrutement de la magistrature en Chine. Paris, Librairie sociale et économique, 1940. 194, [2] p.

THÉRY, FRANÇOIS, 1890- tr. Loi d'organisation des tribunaux (28 octobre 1932). Loi d'organisation de la Cour administrative (17 novembre 1932). Loi sur les procès administratifs (17 novembre 1932). Loi sur les recours (en matière administrative) (24 mars 1930). Texte chinois et traduction française, par François Théry, S. J. Tientsin, Hautes études; Shanghai, Université l'Aurore, 1933. 38, [1] p. (Le droit chinois moderne, 17).

WANG, MING-YANG, 王明揚 . La responsabilité civile des fonctionnaires envers les particuliers en droit chinois. Paris, 1953. 201 l. Thèse-Univ. de Paris.

YEN, KU-WEI, 嚴可爲 . Le droit administratif local en Chine. Nancy, Impr. G. Thomas, 1935. [7]-227 p. Thèse-Univ. de Nancy.

## Extraterritoriality

AMERICAN CHAMBER OF COMMERCE OF TIENTSIN. Memorandum of the American Chamber of Commerce of Tientsin, relative to extraterritoriality in China. Tientsin, December, 1925. [Tientsin, Tientsin Press, 1925?] 62 p.

BAU, MINGCHIEN JOSHUA, 鮑明鈐, 1894-  Relinquishment of extraterritoriality in China. Kyoto, 1929. 28 p.

CHINA. Commission on Extraterritoriality. Summary and recommendations of the report of the Commission on Extraterritoriality in China, Peking, September 16, 1926. (In American journal of international law. Concord, N. H., 1927. v. 21, suppl., p. 58-66 ).

CITIZENS' LEAGUE, Nanking. Syllabus on extraterritoriality in China. [Nanking] Pub. under the auspices of the Committee on the Abolition of Extraterritoriality in China [1929] 132 p.

COMMISSION ON EXTRATERRITORIAL JURISDICTION IN CHINA. Report of the Commission on Extraterritoriality in China, Peking, September 16, 1926, being the report to the governments of the commission appointed in pursuance to Resolution v of the Conference on the Limitation of Armaments, together with a brief summary thereof. Washington, Govt. Print. Off., 1926. xiv, 156 p. incl. tables.

———. Report of the Commission on Extraterritoriality in China. Presented by the secretary of state for foreign affairs to Parliament by command of His Majesty. London, H. M. Stationery Off., 1926. 130 p. ( [Gt. Brit. Foreign office] China, no. 3 (1926) ).

———. Declaration and memoranda by the Chinese commissioner. Presented to the Commission on Extraterritoriality in China [In continuation of "China no. 3 (1926)" (Cmd. 2774+) ] London, H. M. Stationery Off., 1927. 15 p. ( [Gt. Brit. Foreign office] China, no. 1 (1927) ).

ESCARRA, JEAN, 1885-1955. The extra-territoriality problem; being a memorandum presented to the Commission for extra-territoriality. Peking, La Librairie française, 1923. cover-title, 30 p. "Reprinted from the Peking leader, June, 1923."

———. Droits et intérêts étrangers en Chine; préface de S. Exc. Dr. Wang Chung-hui, ministre de la justice du gouvernement national de la République chinoise. Paris, Librairie du Recueil Sirey, 1928. xxviii, 88 p.

———. Le régime des concessions étrangères en Chine. (In Hague. Academy of international law. Recueil des cours, 1929, II. Paris, 1930. v. 27, p. [1]=140. port.).

FISHEL, WESLEY R. The end of extraterritoriality in China. Berkeley, University of California Press, 1952. xi, 318 p.

FOREIGN POLICY ASSOCIATION, New York. Extraterritoriality in China. [New York, Foreign Policy Association, 1925] 9 numb. 1. (Editorial information service. Series 1925-26. 1:6. December 18, 1925).

———. The conflict of policies in China, exterritoriality, customs autonomy, treaty revision, discussed by Dr.Ping Wen Kuo, 郭秉文, [and] Mr. Charles C. Batchelder. Mr. James G. McDonald, chairman. 82nd luncheon discussion, Hotel Astor, New York, December 5, 1925, of the Foreign Policy Association. New York [1925?] 29 p. (F. P. A. Pamphlet, 36. Series of 1925-26 ).

FRANKE, OTTO, 1863-1946. Zur Geschichte der Exterritorialität in China. Berlin, Verlag der Akademie der Wissenschaften in Kommission bei Walter de Gruyter u. co., 1935. 63 p. (Sitzungbericht der Preussischen Akademie der Wissenschaften, Phil-Hist. Kl. 1935. XXXI ).

GT. BRIT. Foreign Office. Chinese mandate of December 28, 1929, regarding extraterritorial rights in China and correspondence between His Majesty's government in the United Kingdom and the Chinese government in connexion therewith. Presented by the Secretary of state for foreign affairs to Parliament by command of His Majesty. London, H. M. Stationery Off., 1930. 6 p. (China no. 1 (1930) ).

KEETON, GEORGE WILLIAMS, 1902-   The development of extraterritoriality in China. London, New York, Longmans, Green and co., 1928. 2 v.

KIANG YONG-TCHANG, 姜榮章. De la juridiction consulaire en Chine. Paris, Éditions de "La Vie universitaire," 1922. 120 p. Thèse-Univ. de Paris.

KOUO, KIN YAO, 郭錦堯. La Chine et les capitulations. Nancy, Impr. G. Thomas, 1938. 171 p. Thèse-Univ. Nancy.

LI TZU-HYUNG, ed. Abolition of extraterritoriality in China. With an introduction by Wei Tao-ming, 魏道明. (Published under the auspices of the International Relations Committee) [Nanking, China, 1929?] iv, 86 p. (International relations series).

LIU, SHIH-SHUN, 劉師舜, 1900- Extraterritoriality: its rise and its decline. New York, Columbia University, 1925. 235 p. (Studies in history, economics and public law, vol. CXVIII, no. 2; whole no. 263 ).

MAH, NGUI-WING, 馬如榮, 1893- Foreign jurisdiction in China. [New York, 1924] p. 676-695. Thesis-University of California, 1921. Reprint from the American journal of international law, 18: 4, October, 1924.

MARCHAND, MARCEL G. Dir Konsulargerichtsbarkeit unter besonderer Berücksichtigen der schweizerischen Konsularjurisdiktion in China. Bern, 1947. 112 p. Thesis-Univ. Bern.

MICKEL, HEINZ, 1912- Die Frage der Exterritorialität in China nach ihrem heutigen Stande. Giessen, Glagow, 1934. 83 p. Diss.-Univ. Giessen.

MILLARD, THOMAS FRANKLIN FAIRFAX, 1868-1942. The end of exterritoriality in China. Shanghai, A.B.C. Press, 1931. [3]-278 p.

OUANG, ROLAND HIAO-HI, 汪孝熙, 1904- Essai sur le régime des capitulations en Chine. Préface de m. Georges Scelle. Paris, Librairie du Recueil Sirey, 1933. [vii]-xvi, 419 p. Issued also as the author's thesis, Univ. de Genève.

PADOUX, GEORGES, 1867- La loi chinoise du 5 août 1918 sur l'application des lois étrangères en Chine. 2e éd. rev. et augm. Pékin, Impr. de la "Politique de Pékin," 1933. 116 p. (Collection de la "Politique de Pékin").

RICH, RAYMOND THOMAS. Extraterritoriality and tariff autonomy in China. Shanghai, China Committee of the Institute of Pacific Relations [1925?] iv, 95 p. (International understanding series).

RIEGE, HEINZ, 1907- Die Gebietshoheit Chinas und ihre Einschränkungen. Breslau, 1933. xii, 101 p. Diss.-Univ. Breslau.

SHOTWELL, JAMES THOMSON, 1874- Extraterritoriality in China. Preliminary paper prepared for the third general session of the Institute of Pacific relations to be held at Kyoto, Japan, October 28th to November 9th, 1929. [New York] American Council, Institute of Pacific Relations, 1929. 24 p.

SONG, KOUO TCHOU, 宋國樞. L'administration de la justice aux étrangers en Chine. Paris, Les Presses modernes, 1929. 144 p. Thèse-Univ. de Paris.

SOULIE, CHARLES GEORGES, 1878- Exterritorialité et intérêts étrangers en Chine, par Georges Soulié de Morant; préface par M. Stéphen Pichon. Paris, P. Geuthner, 1925. xvi, 508 p.

TAN, RAYMOND SHEN-CHI, 譚顯揖. La condition juridique des étrangers et particulièrement des sociétés commerciales françaises en Chine. Préface de m. P. Ravier du Magny. Paris, Librairie du Recueil Sirey, 1932. iv p., [7]-139, [1] p.

TSENG, JU-PAI, 曾如柏. Entwicklung und Abbau der extraterritorial-Jurisdiktion in China. Bonn a. Rh., L. Röhrscheid [1940] viii, 94 p. (Rechtsvergleichende untersuchungen zur gesamten strafrechtswissenschaft. 13. hft.) Issued also as Diss., Univ. Marburg.

WANG, CHIN-CHUAN, 王金泉. Essai historique et critique sur la question de l'abolition de l'exterritorialité en Chine. Paris, Impr. centrale de l'est, 1934. 118 p. Thèse-Univ. de Nancy.

WANG, CHING-CH'UN, 王景春, 1883- Extraterritoriality in China, a monograph. New York, China Institute in America [1931] 19, [1] p.

WANG, TIEH-YAI, 王鐵崖. The status of aliens and foreign enterprise in China.

Chungking, China Institute of Pacific Relations, 1945. viii, 61 p. (China council series, 4 ).

WILLOUGHBY, WESTEL WOODBURY, 1867-1945. Foreign rights and interests
in China. Rev. and enl. ed. Baltimore, Johns Hopkins Press, 1927. 2 v.
(Semicentennial publications of the Johns Hopkins university, 1876-1926).

WOODHEAD, HENRY GEORGE WANDESFORDE, 1883-  Extraterritoriality in
China, the case against abolition. Tientsin, Tientsin Press [1929] 72 p. illus.
"Reprinted from the Peking and Tientsin times, September and October,
1929."

WRIGHT, QUINCY, 1890-  Some legal consequences if extraterritoriality is a-
bolished in China. (In American journal of international law. Concord, N. H.,
1930. v. 24, p. 217-227 ).

## Extraterritorial Courts

CHINA. Commission on Extraterritoriality. Documents relating to procedure in
trials of mixed cases and tables showing the number of such cases. Tr. and
pub. by the Commission on Extraterritoriality. Peking, 1925. cover-title,
8, 2-5 p. incl. fold. tables.
———. Laws, statutes, etc. Provisional regulations governing lawyers of non-
exterritorial powers. [Pekin?] The Ministry of Justice, 1921. cover-title,
2 p.
———. Regulations and tables relating to cases involving subjects of non-extra-
territorial powers of the Republic of China. Translated and published by the
Commission on Extraterritoriality. Peking, 1925. cover-title, 12 p., 2 l.,
64, 25 p.

JOHNSTONE, WILLIAM CRANE, 1901-  The Shanghai problem. Stanford University, Calif., Stanford University Press; London, H. Milford, Oxford U-
niversity Press [c1937] xi, 326 p. fold. map. [Stanford books in world poli-
tics].

KOTENEV, ANATOL M. Shanghai: its Mixed court and Council; material relating to the history of the Shanghai Municipal Council and the history, practice
and statistics of the International mixed court. Chinese modern law and Shanghai municipal land regulations and bye-laws governing the life in the settlement. Shanghai, North-China Daily News and Herald, 1925. xxvi, 588 p.
———. Shanghai: its municipality and the Chinese; being the history of the Shanghai Municipal council and its relations with the Chinese, the practice of the
International mixed court, and the inauguration and constitution of the Shanghai Provisional court. A companion volume to "Shanghai: its Mixed court and
Council" by the same author. Shanghai, North-China Daily News and Herald,
1927. [xv]-xvii, 548 (i.e.554) p., illus.(plan) fold.plan.

NANKING. CONFERENCE ON REORGANIZATION OF THE SHANGHAI PROVI-
SIONAL COURT, Dec. 9, 1929-Feb. 17, 1930. Chinese courts in the International settlement at Shanghai. Agreement by diplomatic representatives in
China of the United States of America, Brazil, France, Great Britain, Netherlands, and Norway, with the minister for foreign affairs of China, with at-
tached notes and a unilateral declaration. Signed February 17, 1930. Washington, Govt. Print. Off., 1932. 9 p. ( [U.S. Dept. of state. Publication, no.
362] Executive agreement series, 37 ).
———. The same. Agreement extending the duration of the agreement and at-
tached notes of February 17, 1930, by diplomatic representatives in China of
the United States of America, Brazil, France, Great Britain, Netherlands,
and Norway, with the minister for foreign affairs of China. Effected by exchange of notes signed February 8, 11, and 12, 1933. And Unilateral declaration renewing the unilateral declaration of February 17, 1930. Signed February 8, 1933. Washington, Govt. Print. Off., 1933. 5 p. ( [U.S. Dept. of
state. Publication, no.501] Executive agreement series, 45 ).

———. Exchanges of notes between the governments of the United Kingdom, Brazil, France, Netherlands, Norway and the United States and the Chinese government renewing the agreement and exchange of notes of February 17, 1930 relating to the Chinese courts in the International settlement at Shanghai. [With declaration] Nanking, February 8 to 12, 1933. London, H. M. Stationery Off., 1933. 6 p. ( [Gt. Brit. Foreign office] Treaty series, no.20 (1933) ) At head of title: Chinese courts at Shanghai. [Gt. Brit. ] Parliament. Papers by command. Cmd. 4348.

TCHEN, YAOTONG, 陳耀東 . De la disparition de la juridiction consulaire dans certains pays d'Orient. Paris, Les Presses modernes, 1931 [i. e. 1932]- 186 p. Thèse-Univ. de Paris.

THOMSON, JOHN SEABURY, 1921-  The government of the International Settlement at Shanghai; a study in the politics of an international area. Ann Arbor, University Microfilms [1954] ( [University Microfilms, Ann Arbor, Mich. ] Publication 6722). Collation of the original: xii, 401 l. Thesis-Columbia University.

U. S. Consulate, Nanking. Manual of probate procedure in American consular courts in China. John K. Davis, American consul and Walter E. Smith, American vice consul. 1923. Washington, Govt. Print. Off., 1923. vii, 32 p. incl. forms.

———. Court for China. Rules of procedure for the United States Court for China. [Shanghai, A. R. Hager] 1939. xiv, 132, 3, 133-136 p.

———. The same. Extraterritorial cases. Including the decisions of the United States Court for China from its beginning, those reviewing the same by the Court of Appeals and the leading cases decided by other courts on questions of extraterritoriality. Compiled and edited by Charles Sumner Lobingier. Manila, Bureau of Printing, 1920-28. 2 v.

## Laws of Communist China

BONNICHON, ANDRÉ. Le droit de la Chine communist, par André Bonnichon. Les droits de l'accusé, un témoignage, par Louis Watine. La Haye, Commission Internationale de Juristes, 1955. 2 v.

———. Law in communist China. [The Hague, International Commission of Jurists, 1956] 35 p.

CHAO, KUO-CHÜN, 趙國鈞 , 1918-  Basic level elections and the 1954 national constitution of mainland China. Cambridge, Center for International Studies, Massachusetts Institute of Technology, 1954. 54 p.

CHINA. (People's Republic of China, 1949-  ) All-China People's Congress. Documents of the first session of the first Natioanl People's Congress of the People's Republic of China. Peking, Foreign Languages Press, 1955. 231 p.

———. Constitution. The draft Constitution of the People's Republic of China. [Peking? 1954] 15 p. (Supplement to People's China, July 1, 1954.).

———. Constitution. [Peking? 1954] cover-title, 27 p.

———. Constitution of the People's Republic of China, adopted on September 20, 1954 by the first National People's Congress of the People's Republic of China, at its first session. Peking, Foreign Languages Press, 1954. 57 p.

———. The same. Peking, 1954. 63 p. (on double leaves) 2 col. plates.

———. Verfassung der Volksrepublik China. Berlin-Karlshorst, Botschaft die Volksrepublik China in die DDR, 1954. 20 p.

———. Laws, statutes, etc. The marriage law. [Peking?] All-China Democratic Women's Federation [1950?] 12 p.

———. The marriage law of the People's Republic of China, together with other relevant articles. Peking, Foreign Languages Press, 1950. iv, 41 p.

———. La Loi sur le mariage de la République populaire de Chine suivie de deux autres documents. Pékin, Éditions en langues étrangères, 1950. 52 p.

———. The electoral law for the All-China People's Congress and local People's

Congresses of all levels, with an explanation. [1st ed.] Peking, Foreign
Languages Press, 1953. 48 p.

——. Electoral law for the All-China People's Congress and local people's
congresses of all levels, and An explanation of the Electoral law, by Vice-
Premier Teng Hsiao-ping, 鄧小平. [Peking? 1953] 15 p. "Supplement to
'People's China' April 1, 1953."

CHINESE SOVIET REPUBLIC. Laws, statutes, etc. Fundamental laws of the
Chinese Soviet Republic, with an introduction by Bela Kun. London, M. Lawrence [1934] New York, International Publishers [1934] 87, [5] p. illus.
(map) diagrs.

——. Constitution de la Chine soviétique; recueil des lois fondamentales du
gouvernement soviétique chinois. Préface de Bela Kun. Paris, Bureau d'é-
ditions, de diffusion et de publicité, 1935. 101 p.

——. Die grundgesetze der Chinesischen Räterepublik. Moskau-Leningrad,
Verlagsgenossenschaft ausländischer Arbeiter in der UdSSR, 1934. 96 p.
diagrs.

CHUNG KUO-JÊN-MIN-CHÊNG-CHIH-HSIEH-SHANG-HUI-I,          中國人民政治
協商會議 . The important documents of the first plenary session of the Chinese People's Political Consulative Conference. Peking, Foreign Languages
Press, 1949. 44 p.

——. Documents importants de la première session plénière de la Conférence
consultative politique du peuple chinois. Pékin, Éditions en langues étrangères, 1949. 49 p.

——. The common program and other documents of the first plenary session of
the Chinese People's Political Consultative Conference. Peking, Foreign
Languages Press, 1950. 44 p.

——. Das gemeinsame Programm und andere Dokumente der politischen Kon-
sultativ-Conferenz des chinesische Volkes. Peking, Verlag für fremdsprachige Literatur, 1952. 48 p.

——. New China forges ahead; important documents of the third session of the
First National Committee of the Chinese People's Political Consultative Conference. Peking, Foreign Languages Press, 1952. 78 p. illus.

DEUTSCHES INSTITUT FÜR RECHTSWISSENSCHAFT. Die Verfassungen der a-
siatischen Länder der Volksdemokratie. [Übers. und bearb. von einem Kol-
lektiv der Deutschen Akademie für Staats- und Rechtswissenschaft Walter Ul-
bricht, Potsdam-Babelsberg, unter verantwortlicher Redaktion von Heinz
Engelbert] Berlin, Deutscher Zentralverlag [1955] 101 p.

LIU, SHAO-CH'I, 1900-  Report on the draft constitution of the People's Republic of China. Constitution of the People's Republic of China. [Adopted on September 20, 1954 by the First National People's Congress at its first session]
Peking, Foreign Languages Press, 1954. 101 p. port.

——. Bericht über den Verfassungsentwurf der Volksrepublik China. Die Verfassung der Volksrepublik China. [Von] Liu Schao-tschi. Peking, Verlag für
Fremdsprachige Literatur, 1954. 121 p. port.

## IX. FOREIGN RELATIONS

### General Works

ALFONSI, MARC. Les cessions à bail en Chine; histoire diplomatique et de droit international public. Paris, Domat-Montchrestien, 1940. [vii]-xxxiv, 154 p.

BAU, MINGCHIEN JOSHUA, 鮑明鈐, 1894- The foreign relations of China: a history and a survey. Rev. and enl. ed. New York, Chicago, Fleming H. Revell, 1922. v-xii, 541 p.

———. China and world peace; studies in Chinese international relations. New York, Chicago, Fleming H. Revell [c1928] 7-194 p.

———. Foreign navigation in Chinese waters. Preliminary paper prepared for the fourth biennial conference of the Institute of Pacific Relations to be held at Hangchow, from Oct. 21 to Nov. 4, 1931. Shanghai, China Institute of Pacific Relations [1931] cover-title, 29 p. incl. tables.

[BISSON, THOMAS ARTHUR] 1900- The dismemberment of China. New York, Foreign Policy Association [1934] p. [41]-52. illus. (map) (Foreign policy reports. 10:4. April 25, 1934 ).

———. Struggle of the powers in China. New York, Foreign Policy Association [1936] p. [121]-132. (Foreign policy reports. 12:10. August 1, 1936 ).

BLAKESLEE, GEORGE HUBBARD, 1871-1954. Oriental affairs in the light of the Kyoto conference, discussed by George H. Blakeslee and James G. McDonald. 119th New York luncheon discussion, December 7, 1929. New York, Foreign Policy Associaton [1929] 27, [1] p. [Foreign policy association. Pamphlet no. 62. Series 1929-30. January, 1930].

CHAN, CHUNG-SING, 陳宗城, 1900- Les concessions en Chine. Paris, Les presses universitaires de France, 1925. 149 p. Thèse-Univ. de Paris.

CHANG, CHUNG-TAO, 張忠道. Les traités inégaux de la Chine et l'attitude des puissances. 中國之不平等條約及各國之態度 Paris, M. Rivière, 1929. [7]-216 p.

CHAO, CHIN-YUNG, 趙金鏞. A brief history of Chinese foreign relations. Taipei, China Cultural Service [195?] 62 p.

———. Foreign advisers and the diplomacy of the Manchu empire. Taipei, China Culture Pub. Foundation, 1954. 49 p.

———. Chinese diplomatic practice and treaty relations, 1842-1943, with special reference to the period of Ch'ing Dynasty. Taipei, China Cultural Service, 1955. 65 p.

CHAO, MING-KAO, 趙明高, 1892- Essays on Chinese and foreigners, with Chinese notes. Pei Ling, Mukden, Sin Hua Press, 1930. vii-xii, 125 p. front., illus., ports.

CHAO, TSUN-SHIN, 趙俊欣. Essai d'analyse juridique du problème de la révision des traités; un appel à la révision des traités inégaux entre la Chine et les pays étrangers. Paris, Domat-Montchrestien, 1937. 9-221 p.

CH'EN, WU-WO, 陳無我. True facts about the Lincheng incident. 臨案紀實 Peking, Peking Express Press, 1924. 26, 31 p.

CHEN, YAO-SHENG, 陳堯聖. The International Settlement at Shanghai. London, 1939. iv, 3, 526 l. Thesis-London School of Economics.

CHU, CHAO-HSIN, 朱兆莘, 1880-1933. Revision of unequal treaties. China appeals to the League of Nations. Official text of the speeches of Mr. Chao-Hsin Chu, and press comments thereon. [2d ed.] [London, Printed by the London Caledonian Press, 1926] 48 p. front. (port.).

CHU, HUNG-TI, 朱鴻題, 1908- China and the League of Nations. Urbana,

1937. 399 l. Thesis-University of Illinois.

CURTIS, LIONEL, 1872-1955. The capital question of China. London, Macmillan, 1932. xix, 322 p. 4 fold. maps.

DUBOSCQ, ANDRÉ, 1876- La Chine en face des puissances. Paris, Delagrave, 1926. 127, [1] p. illus.(map) (Bibliothèque d'histoire et de politique).

DUNCAN, ROBERT MOORE. Peiping municipality and the diplomatic quarter. Peiping, Department of Political Science, Yenching University, 1933. vii, 146 p. fold. plans, tables (1 fold.).

ESCARRA, JEAN, 1885-1955. La Chine et le droit internationale, préface de m. Marcel Sibert. Paris, A. Pedone, 1931. xx, 419, [7] p. fold. map. (Publications de la Revue générale de droit international public, 4 ).

FARRÈRE, CLAUDE, 1876- L'Europe en Asie. Paris, Flammarion [1939] 101 p.

FOREIGN POLICY ASSOCIATION, New York, Foreign interests in China. [New York, Foreign Policy Association, 1927] p. [303]-317 incl. tables. (Information service. 2:25. February 16, 1927).

——. Treaty revision in China. [New York, Foreign Policy Association, 1928] p.[297]-320. (Information service. 4:15. September 28, 1928).

FOX, CHARLES JAMES, 1877- The protocol of 1901, charter of Peking's diplomatocracy. Tientsin, North China Star, 1926. 57 p. fold. tables.

FU, LO-SHU, 傅樂淑, 1920- Sino-western relations during the K'ang-hsi period, 1661-1722. Chicago, 1952. 363 l. Thesis-Univ. of Chicago.

GILBERT, RODNEY YONKERS, 1889- What's wrong with China. New York, Frederick A. Stokes [1926] 315 p.

——. The unequal treaties; China and the foreigner. London, J. Murray [1929] v, vii-xi, 248 p.

GODSHALL, WILSON LEON, 1895- Tsingtau under three flags. Shanghai, Commercial Press, 1929. xi, [3]-580 p. fold. front., plates, maps (part fold.).

GREEN, OWEN MORTIMER. The foreigner in China. London, New York, Hutchinson [1943] 7-190 p. front., plates, ports.

HINZELMANN, HANS HEINZ, 1889- Chinesen und fremde Teufel; der Roman von den fünftausendjährigen Geheimnissen in China. Hamm, G. Grote [1950] 241 p.

HODGKIN, HENRY THEODORE, 1877-1933. China in the family of nations. London, G. Allen and Unwin ltd. [1923] 9-267 p. (Selly Oak colleges publications, no. 4 ).

HSIA, CHIN-LIN, 夏晉麟, 1896- Studies in Chinese diplomatic history. Shanghai, Commercial Press, 1925. xii, 226 p.

——. The status of Shanghai; a historical review of the international settlement. Its future development and possibilities through Sino-foreign co-operation. [Under the auspices of the China Council of the Institute of Pacific Relations] Shanghai, Kelly and Walsh, 1929. xiv, 202 p. (International understanding series ).

HSU, EMMANUEL C.Y., 徐中約, 1923- China's entrance into the family of nations. Cambridge, 195- 280 p. Thesis-Harvard University.

HSÜ, SHU-HSI, 徐淑希, 1892- China and her political entity (a study of China's foreign relations with reference to Korea, Manchuria and Mongolia) New York, London [etc.] Oxford University Press, 1926. xxiv, 438 p.

——. An introduction to Sino-foreign relations. Prepared under the auspices of the Council of international affairs, Chunking. Shanghai, Kelly and Walsh, 1941. 165 p. ( [Council of international affairs] Political and economic studies, 14 ).

HU, SHÊNG, 胡繩. Imperialism and Chinese politics. Peking, Foreign Languages Press, 1955. 308 p.

HU, SHIH, 胡適, 1891- Two papers on post-war China. 1. Requirements for a joint peace in the Pacific. 2. Asia and universal world order. Chungking, China Council, Institute of Pacific Relations [1942] 13 numb. l. (China Council papers, 1.).

HU, TAO-WEI, 胡道維. The case for China; abolition of special foreign privileges and immunities. [Peking] Peking Express Press [1926] 2 v.

JOSEPH, PHILIP, 1901-   Foreign diplomacy in China, 1894-1900; a study in political and economic relations with China. With an introduction by Sir A. Frederick Whyte. London, G. Allen and Unwin [1928] [9]-458 p. illus.(maps) (Studies in economics and political science, no. 93 in the series of monographs by writers connected with the London school of economics and political science).

KAO, LOU, 高魯, 1881-1947. Conception d'une fédération mondiale. Paris, Librairie du Recueil Sirey, 1930. 116 p. (Bibliothèque de l'Académie diplomatique internationale. I ).

KEETON, GEORGE WILLIAMS, 1902-   Some factors in a Far Eastern peace settlement. Submitted by the International secretariat of the Institute of Pacific Relations as a document for the eighth conference of the IPR to be held in December 1942. New York, International Secretariat, Institute of Pacific Relations [1942] 30 (i.e. 29) numb. 1. (Secretariat paper, 6 ).

KING, WUNSZ, 金問泗 1892-   ed. V.K. Wellington Koo's foreign policy, some selected documents. Shanghai, Kelly and Walsh, 1931. xii p., 1 1., 141 p., 1 1., 6, 153 p. front. (ports.).

KING-HALL, STEPHEN, 1893-   The China of to-day. London, L.and V.Woolf, 1927. 44, [2] p.

KU, DJAO-FING. Essai sur les idées pacifistes et le droit international en Chine (après la révolution de 1911). Nancy, Impr. Grandville, 1933. 160 p. Thèse-Univ. de Nancy.

KUO, SHUN-P'ING, 郭舜平, 1908-   Chinese reaction to foreign encroachment, with special reference to the first Sino-Japanese War and its immediate aftermath. Ann Arbor, University Microfilms [1954] 323, 3 1. ( [University Microfilms, Ann Arbor, Mich.] Publication 6652). Thesis-Columbia University.

LEVI, WERNER, 1912-   Modern China's foreign policy. Minneapolis, University of Minnesota Press [1953] 399 p. map.

LIAU, HAN-SIN. Die ungleichen Verträge und die chinesische Revolution. Berlin, Vertretung der Kuo-Min-Tang, 1927. 39 p. port., map.

LIN, TSIU-SEN, 林秋生. Organismus und Organisation; ein chinesicher Beitrag zur Ordnung der Welt. Erlenbach-Zürich, E. Rentsch [1944] v. 48 p. (Schriften des chinesischen Kultur-Dienstes ).

LIU, PINGHOU C., 劉平侯, 1903-   Chinese foreign affairs - organization and control. [New York] Pub. under the auspices of the Graduate School of New York University [c1937] v, [1], 27 p. diagrs. Abridgment of thesis-New York university.

MacNAIR, HARLEY FARNSWORTH, 1891-1947. ed. Modern Chinese history; selected readings; a collection of extracts from various sources chosen to illustrate some of the chief phases of China's international relations during the past hundred years. Shanghai, Commercial Press, 1937 (c1923). xxxvii, 910 p. front., illus. (incl. ports., plan). 1st ed. 1923.

———. China's international relations and other essays. Shanghai, Commercial Press, 1926. [v]-vii, 326 p.

MAO, YEE-HANG, 毛以亨, 1896-   Les relations politiques et économiques entre la Chine et les puissances de 1842 à 1860. Lyon, Impr. Bosc frères et Riou, 1923. 215 p. Thèse-Univ. de Paris.

MENG, SSŬ-MING, 蒙思明, 1908-   The organization and functions of the Tsungli Yamen. Cambridge, 1949. iii, 188 1. Thesis-Harvard University.

MENZ, GERHARD, 1885-   Flutwende; die Entwicklung der Beziehungen Chinas zum Abendlande in den letzten 100 Jahren. Leipzig, J.C. Hinrichs, 1926. 163, [1] p. fold. map.

MILLARD, THOMAS FRANKLIN FAIRFAX, 1868-1942. China, where it is to-day and why.  New York, Harcourt, Brace [c1928] vi,  3-350 p.

THE NORTH-CHINA DAILY NEWS, Shanghai.  China in chaos; a brief outline of
the foreign concessions, with examples of China's disruption and failure to
observe her obligations due to civil war, Bolshevist propaganda and mob law.
[Shanghai, North-China Daily News and Herald, 1927] cover-title, 56 p. illus.

NORTON, HENRY KITTREDGE, 1884-   China and the powers.  New York, John
Day, 1927.  London, G. Allen and Unwin, 1927. xi, 264 p., 1 l. incl. front.,
maps.

PARIS.  École Libre des Sciences Politiques.  Société des anciens élèves et é-
lèves chinois.  La Chine et le monde, étude des questions politiques, diplomatiques, économiques, juridiques et sociales; publiée avec la collaboration des
anciens élèves et élèves chinois de l'École libre des sciences politiques de
Paris.  Paris, Les Presses universitaires de France, 1925-   3 v.

PERGAMENT, MIKHAIL ÎAKOVLEVICH, 1866-1932. The diplomatic quarter in
Peking, its juristic nature.  Peking, China Booksellers, 1927. 133 p.

PHAN, YUNG-KING, 潘瀛江.  La politique extérieure de la Chine de 1842 à nos
jours.  Nancy, Impr. Grandville, 1932. 126 p. Thèse-Univ. de Nancy.

PARK, NO-YONG, 鮑訥榮, 1899-   China in the League of Nations, a chapter
on China's foreign relations.  Cambridge, 1932. 299 p. Thesis-Harvard University.

POLLARD, ROBERT THOMAS, 1897-1939. China's foreign relations, 1917-31.
New York, Macmillan, 1933. x,  416 p. Thesis-University of Minnesota.

PRATT, SIR JOHN THOMAS, 1876-   The expansion of Europe into the Far East.
London, Sylvan Press [1947] 218 p. maps.

————.  War and politics in China.  London, J. Cape [1943] 9-289, [1] p. fold.
maps.

The PRESENT situation in China.  Tokyo, Philip Dodge International Study Club
of Tokyo, 1925. 14 p.

QUAN, LAU-KING, 關魯敬, 1906-   China's relations with the League of Nations, 1919-36.  [Hong Kong, The Asiatic Litho. Printing Press] 1939. xiii
(i.e. xviii), 414 p. diagrs.

QUIGLEY, HAROLD SCOTT, 1889-   Chinese politics and foreign powers.  Syllabus on recent Chinese politics and diplomacy.  New York, Carnegie Endowment for International Peace, Division of Intercourse and Education [1927]
46 p. (International conciliation, 227 ).

RASMUSSEN, OTTO DURHAM, 1888-   What's right with China; an answer to
foreign criticisms.  Shanghai, Commercial Press, 1927. xx, 249 p., [251]-
255 p.

REID, GILBERT, 1857-1927. China, captive or free? A study of China's entanglements.  New York, Dodd, Mead, 1921. vii,  332 p.

————.  Der Kampf um Chinas Freiheit; eine Darstellung der politischen Ver-
wickelungen Chinas, übers. von W. E. Peters.  Leipzig, K. F. Koehler, 1923.
xvi, 279 p.

SEE, CHONG SU, 施宗樹, 1892-   The Chinese question; the underlying cause
of the present crisis in China.  Manila, The Bulletin Pub. Co., 1925. [7]-
32 p.

————.  The same.  [Oxford, Bridge and Co., 1926] cover-title, 40 p.

SHEN, WEI-TAI, 沈惟泰, 1906-   China's foreign policy, 1839-60.  New York,
1932. v-vii, 9-197, [1] p. Thesis-Columbia university.

SOOTHILL, WILLIAM EDWARD, 1861-1935. China and the West, a sketch of
their intercourse.  London, Oxford University Press, H. Milford, 1925. viii,
216 p. front., fold. map.

SÜHL, MARGA.  Die Grossmächte und die chinesische Revolution bis zum Ausbruch des ersten Weltkriegs.  Kiel, 1944. 115 l. Diss.-Univ. Kiel

SWEN, WEN-MING, 孫文明, [Sun Wên-ming].  Étude sur les traités politiques
sino-étrangers; la politique de la révision des traités inégaux du gouvernement national de Chine.  Paris, P. Bossuet, 1937. 255 p.

SUN, YAT-SEN, 孫中山, 1866-1925. The vital problem of China. Taipei, China Cultural Service [1953] 174 p.

SZE, SAO-KE ALFRED, 施肇基, 1877-1958. Addresses. Baltimore, Johns Hopkins Press, 1926. ix, 131 p.

———. China and the treaty powers; an address. Washington, 1927. 17 p.

SZE, TSUNG-YU, 施宗嶽, 1900-  China and the most-favored-nation clause. New York, Chicago, Fleming H. Revell [c1925] 267 p.

TAI, SIEOU TSIN, 戴修駿, 1894-  Le pacifisme de la Chine de la Conférence de la Haye à la Société des Nations. Paris, Éditions de "La vie universitaire," 1922. 206 p. Thesis-Univ. de Paris.

T'ANG, LIANG-LI, 湯良禮, 1901-  China in revolt; how a civilisation became a nation; foreword by Dr. Tsai Yuan-pei, 蔡元培, preface by the Hon. Bertrand Russell. London, N. Douglas [1927] xvii, 19-176 p.

———. China in Aufruhr. Deutsch von Else Baronin Werkmann. Leipzig, C. Weller and Co., 1927. 349 p. map.

TCHAI, HENRI TSOUN-TCHUN, 翟俊千, [Chai Chün-ch'ien] 1893-  Essai historique et analytique sur la situation internationale de la Chine; conséquences des traités sino-étrangers. Paris, P. Geuthner, 1929. 235 p. (Bibliotheca Franco-Sinica Lugdunensis. Études et documents publiés par l'Institut franco-chinois de Lyon, t. 3 ).

TCHAO, TCHUN-TCH'EOU, 趙春卅, [Chao Chun-chou]. Évolution des relations diplomatiques de la Chine avec les puissances (1587-1929). Paris, A. Pedone, 1931. 207 p. Thèse-Univ. de Paris.

TEICHMAN, SIR ERIC, 1884-1944. Affairs of China; a survey of the recent history and present circumstances of the Republic of China. With three maps. London, Methuen [1938] 3-311, [1] p. illus. (maps).

TÊNG, SSŬ-YŬ, 鄧嗣禹, 1906-  China's response to the West; a documentary survey, 1839-1923 [by] Ssŭ-yü Têng [and] John K. Fairbank, with E-tu Zen Sun, 孫任以都, Chaoying Fang, 房兆楹, and others. [Prepared in coöperation with the International Secretariat of the Institute of Pacific Relations] Cambridge, Harvard University Press, 1954. vi, 296 p.

———. Research guide [by] Ssŭ-yü Têng [and] John K. Fairbank, with the collaboration of E-tu Zen Sun, Chaoying Fang, and others. Cambridge, Harvard University Press, 1954. 84 p.

TROUCHE, MARCEL. Le quartier diplomatique de Pékin; étude historique et juridique. Rodez, Impr. G. Subervie [1935] 208 p. fold. plans. Thèse-Univ. de Paris.

TSENG, YU-HAO, 曾友豪, 1900-  The termination of unequal treaties in international law; studies in comparative jurisprudence and conventional law of nations. Shanghai, Commercial Press, 1931. 549 p.

TUAN, MAO-LAN, 段茂瀾, 1899-  Le situation internationale actuelle de la République chinoise. Exposé fait à l'Académie diplomatique internationale à Paris, le 21 mai 1952. Paris, Grou-Radenez, 1952. 16 p.

TUNG, LIN, 董霖, 1907-  China and some phases of international law. With a foreword by Quincy Wright. Issued under the auspices of the China Institute of Pacific Relations. London and New York, Oxford University Press, 1940. xiv, 210 p.

TYAU, MIN-CH'IEN TUK ZUNG, 刁敏謙, 1888-  China's diplomatic relations 1931-32; a survey. Preliminary paper prepared for the fifth biennial conference of the Institute of Pacific Relations to be held at Banff, Canada, August 14 to 28, 1933. Shanghai, China Institute of Pacific Relations, 1933. 57 p.

UNION OF CHINESE ASSOCIATIONS IN GREAT BRITAIN. China's case by Lo Wen-kan, 羅文幹, V. K. Ting, 丁文江, Hu Shih, 胡適, and H. L. Yen, 顏鶴齡. London, Caledonian Press, 1925. 7, [1] p.

WALKER, RICHARD LOUIS, 1922-  ed. China and the West: cultural collision; selected documents. [New Haven] Far Eastern Publications, Yale University, 1956. 254 p.

WANG, CHAO-MING, 汪兆銘, 1884-1944. China and the nations; being the draft
of the report on international problems prepared for the International problems committee of the People's conference of delegates at Peking in April,
1925. Rendered in English, and edited with an introduction, explanatory foot-
notes and a map, by I-sen Teng and John Nind Smith. New York, Frederick
A. Stokes, 1927. xxiv, 141, [1] p. fold. map.
———. La Chine et les Nations; traduction française de C. Heywood d'après la
version anglais de I-sen Teng et John Nind Smith. Paris, Gallimard, 1928.
222 p. map. (Collection "Documents bleus").
WANG, CHUNG-HUI, 王寵惠, 1882-1958. Peaceful means of settling international
disputes. Peking, Peking Leader Press, 1927. cover-title, 6 p. (Peking
Leader reprints, 19 ).
———. Ten years of China's foreign relations. Readjustment of Sino-foreign relations through diplomatic channels. Nanking, Chinese League of Nations U-
nion, 1937. 10 p.
WARE, EDITH ELLEN, 1882- Business and politics in the Far East. New Haven, Pub. for the Carnegie Endowment for International Peace by Yale University Press; London, H. Milford, Oxford University Press, 1932. x, 250 p.
illus. (maps) diagrs. (The Carnegie endowment for international peace. World
economic problems).
WHYTE, SIR FREDERICK, 1883- China and foreign powers, an historicl review of their relations. Published under the auspices of the Royal Institute of
International Affairs. 2d and rev. ed. London, Oxford University Press
[1928] viii, 93 p.
———. Der Ferne Osten, von England aus gesehen. Stuttgart [etc.] Deutsche
Verlag-Anstalt [1936] 68, [1] p. (Weltwende; eine schriftenreihe, hrsg. von
Hermann Stegemann).
WOO, JAMES K'AI-SHÊNG, 吳凱聲, 1900- La politique étrangère du gouvernement national de Chine et la revision des traités inégaux. Préface par Édouard Lambert. Paris, M.Giard, 1931. 112 p. (Bibliothèque de l'Institut de
droit comparé de Lyon. Études et documents. t. 28 ).
WOU, KIENPANG, 吳建邦. La Chine et les grandes puissances; étude d'histoire
diplomatique contemporaine. Gand, Impr. S. Hussein, 1926. ix, 414 p.(Collection de l'École des sciences politiques et sociales de l'Université de Louvain).
WOU, P., 吳本中, [Wu Pên-chung] 1904- Histoire diplomatique de la Chine
depuis 1919; la révision des traités sino-étrangers. Paris, Rousseau et cie,
1932. xx, 334 p.
YANG, LÉON, 楊柳風, [Yang Liu-feng] Les territoires à bail en Chine; étude
d'histoire diplomatique et de droit international. Paris, Presses universitaires de France, 1929. viii, 215 p. Thèse-Univ. de Paris.
YEH, GEORGE K.C., 葉公超, 1904- Foreign policy speeches, 1955. [Taipei,
Ministry of Foreign Affairs, 1956] 52 p.

## General Treaties

CARNEGIE ENDOWMENT FOR INTERNATIONAL PEACE. Division of International Law. Treaties and agreements with and concerning China, 1919-29.
Washington, Carnegie Endowment for International Peace, 1929. xiv, 282 p.
(Pamphlet series of the Carnegie endowment for international peace, Division
of international law, 50 ).
CH'ÊN, YIN-CHING, 陳英競, 1907- ed. Treaties and agreements between the
Republic of China and other powers, 1929-54; together with certain international documents affecting the interests of the Republic of China, compiled
and edited by Yin Ching Chen. Washington, Sino-American Pub. Service,
1957. xiii, 491 p.
CHINA. Treaties, etc., 1901. Final protocol between China and the powers rep-

resented at Peking. Settlement of matters growing out of the Boxer uprising in 1900. Signed at Peking, September 7, 1901. Washington, Govt. Print. Off., 1924. 29 p. incl. tables. ( [U.S.] Treaties, etc. Treaty series, 397 ).
————. 1925. Treaties between China and other countries, other than Japan, Great Britain, United States, France, and Russia. Tokyo, Treaty Bureau, Department of Foreign Affairs, 1926. 2000 p.
————. 1928. Sino-foreign treaties 1928. Nanking, Intelligence and Publicity Dept., Ministry of Foreign Affairs, Republic of China [1929] vi, vi, 90, 90 p. ports.
————. 1928. Sino-foreign treaties of 1928; texts of the documents which lay the new foundations for Sino-foreign relations. Peking, Peking Leader Press, 1929. 3-52 p. fold. tables. (Peking leader reprints, 43 ).
————. 1929? The Sino-foreign treaties. Shanghai, British Chamber of Commerce [1929?]-38. 4 v.
MacMURRAY, JOHN VAN ANTWERP, 1881-   ed. Treaties and agreements with and concerning China, 1894-1919; a collection of state papers, private agreements, and other documents, in reference to the rights and obligations of the Chinese government in relation to foreign powers, and in reference to the interrelation of those powers in respect to China, during the period from the Sino-Japanese war to the conclusion of the world war of 1914-19, comp. and ed. by John V.A. MacMurray. New York [etc.] Oxford University Press, 1921. 2 v. front., fold. maps, double plan. (Publications of the Carnegie endowment for international peace. Division of international law, Washington).

## Washington Conference

BUELL, RAYMOND LESLIE, 1896-1946. The Washington conference. New York, London, D. Appleton, 1922. xiii, 461 p. fold. map.
CANADA. Delegate to the Conference on the Limitation of Armament Washington, D.C., 1921-22. Conference on the limitation of armament held at Washington November 12, 1921, to February 6, 1922. Report of the Canadian delegate including treaties and resolutions. Ottawa, F.A. Acland, printer, 1922. 222 p. ( [Parliament] 1922. Sessional paper, no. 47 ).
COUNCIL ON FOREIGN RELATIONS. Conference of the Council on foreign relations, Hotel Astor, New York City, February 17, 1922. Subject: comments upon the Conference on the limitation of armaments and Far Eastern questions, presiding, Hon. John W. Davis; speaker, Hon. Norman H. Davis; discussion led by Mr. Paul D. Cravath. [New York? 1922] 48 p.
FRANCE, Ministère des Affaires Etrangères. Documents diplomatiques. Conférence de Washington. Juillet 1921-février 1922. Paris, Impr. Nationale, 1923. xi, 208 p.
ICHIHASHI, YAMATO. The Washington conference and after; a historical survey. Stanford, Calif., Stanford University Press, 1928. xii, 443 p.
JACQUEMART, ANDRÉ. La Conférence de Washington (11 novembre 1921- 6 février 1922) Le désarmement naval, l'accord du Pacifique. Paris, Jouve, 1923. 144 p.
KANE, ALBERT ELI, 1901-   China, the powers and the Washington conference. [Shanghai, Commercial Press, 1937] vi, 233, [1] p. Thesis-Columiba University.
TOMIMAS, SHUTARO. The Nine-power treaty and the Kellogg-Briand treaty (review of Secretary Stimson's position) [n.p.] 1932. 37 p.
U.S. President, 1921-23 (Harding). Conference on the limitation  of armament. Address of the President of the United States submitting the treaties and resolutions approved and adopted by the Conference on the limitation of armament together with the Report of the American delegation of the proceedings of the Conference on the limitation of armament, submitted to the President February 9, 1922. Washington, Govt. Print. Off., 1922. xiii, 132 p. (67th

Cong., 2d sess. Senate. Doc. 125).

WANG, T. L., 王祖廉 . Introduction to China and the Washington Conference. Chicago, Chinese Students Alliance in the U.S.A. [1921] 32 p. (Series on China and the Washington Conference, 1 ).

WASHINGTON, D.C. CONFERENCE ON THE LIMITATION OF ARMAMENT, 1921-22. Washington Conference on the limitation of armaments. New York, American Association for International Conciliation [1921-22] xxxiii, 382 p. 2 v. (International conciliation, pub. monthly by the American association for international conciliation. December, 1921, no. 169, March, 1922, no. 172 ).

――――. Conference on the limitation of armament, Washington, November 12, 1921-February 6, 1922. Conférence de la limitation des armements, Washington, 12 novembre 1921-6 février 1922. Washington, Govt. Print. Off., 1922. 1757 p.

――――. Conference on limitation of armament. Washington, 1921-22. (Treaties, resolutions, etc.) London, Printed and pub. by H. M. Stationery Off., 1922. 88 p. ( [Gt. Brit. Foreign office] Miscellaneous, no. 1 (1922) ).

――――. Conference on the limitation of armament. Subcommittees. Washington, November 12, 1921-February 6, 1922. Conférence de la limitation des armaments. Sous-commissions. Washington, 12 novembre 1921- 6 février 1922. Washington, Govt. Print. Off., 1922. 747 p. incl. tables.

――――. Resolutions adopted by the Conference on the limitation of armament in the discussions of Pacific and Far Eastern questions. [Peking? 1922? cover-title, [56] p.

――――. Armament conference treaties. Treaties and resolutions approved and adopted by the Conference on the limitation of armament submitted by the President of the United States to the Senate for advice and consent to their ratification. Washington, Govt. Print. Off., 1922. 44 p. ( [U.S.] 67th Cong., 2d sess. Senate. Doc. 124 ).

――――. Treaties and resolutions of the Conference on the limitation of armament as ratified by the United States Senate; facts and tables. New York and Washington, Federal Trade Information Service, c1922. 60 p. incl. tables.

――――. Nine powers treaty on China. Treaty, submitted by the President of the United States, between the United States, Belgium, the British empire, China, France, Italy, Japan, the Netherlands, and Portugal, relating to principles and policies to be followed in matters concerning China. Washington, Govt. Print. Off., 1922. 11 p. ( [U.S.] 67th Cong., 2d sess. Senate. Executive P ).

――――. Treaty between all nine powers relating to principles and policies to be followed in matters concerning China. Traité entre les neuf puissances relatif aux principes et politiques à suivre dans les addaires concernant la Chine. [Peking, 1922?] cover-title, 13, 13, [14] p.

――――. Treaty between the United States, Belgium, the British Empire, China, France, Italy, Japan, the Netherlands, and Portugal. Regarding principles and policies to be followed in matters concerning China. Signed at Washington, February 6, 1922. Washington, Govt. Print. Off., 1925. 10 p. ( [U.S. Treaties, etc.] Treaty series, no. 723).

――――. The same. Relating to the revision of the Chinese customs tariff. Signed at Washington, February 6, 1922. Washington, Govt. Print. Off., 1925. 11 p ( [U.S. Treaties, etc.] Treaty series, no. 724).

――――. Treaty between the United States of America, Belgium, the British Empire, China, France, France, Italy, Japan, the Netherlands and Portugal, relating to principles and policies to be followed in matters concerning China. Washington, February 6, 1922. [Ratifications deposited at Washington, August 5, 1925.] London, H. M. Stationery Off., 1925. 6 p. ( [Gt. Brit. Foreign office] Treaty series, 1925, 42 ). Gt. Brit. Parliament. Papers by command. Cmd. 2517.

―――― .] Treaty between the United States of America, Belgium, the British Empire, China, France, Italy, Japan, the Netherlands and Portugal, relating to the Chinese customs tariff. Washington, February 6, 1922. [Ratification deposited at Washington, August 5, 1925.] London, H. M. Stationery Off., 1925. 7 p. (Foreign Office. Treaty series, 43 ).

——. Principles and policies to be followed in matters concerning China. Trea ty between the United States of America, Belgium, the British empire, China, France, Italy, Japan, the Netherlands, and Portugal (Nine power treaty) Signed at Washington, February, 1922. And Procès verbal of deposit of ratifications. Washington, Govt. Print. Off., 1937. 11 p. ( [U.S. Treaties, etc.] Treaty series, no. 723 ).

WILLOUGHBY, WESTEL WOODBURY, 1867-1945. China at the conference; a report. Baltimore, Johns Hopkins Press, 1922. xvi, 419 p.

## Relations with Asiatic Countries
## China and Asia

BARNES, JOSEPH, 1907-  ed. Empire in the East. Contributors, Owen Lattimore, John E. Orchard, Joseph Barnes, Grover Clark, Frederick V. Field, H. Foster Bain, Carl L. Alsberg, Pearl S. Buck, Tyler Dennett, Nathaniel Peffer. Garden City, N. Y., Doubleday, Doran, 1934. vii, 3-322 p.

CAMERON, MERIBETH ELLIOTT, 1905-  China, Japan, and the powers, by Meribeth E. Cameron, Thomas H. D. Mahoney [and] George E. McReynolds. With a foreword by Kenneth Scott Latourette. New York, Ronald Press [1952] xiii, 682 p. maps.

CHOW, S. R., 周鯁生 , 1889-  Winning the peace in the Pacific; a Chinese view of Far Eastern postwar plans and requirements for a stable security system in the Pacific area, with a foreword by Hu Shih. Published in cooperation with the International Secretariat, Institute of Pacific Relations. New York, Macmillan, 1944. xi, 98 p.

——. The Far East in a new world order. Chungking, China Institute of Pacific Relations, 1945. iii, 35 p. (China council series, 7 ).

CHOW, TEH-KAO, 周德高 . Postwar historical events and foreign policies of the great powers in the Far East. Peiping, Printed by St. James Cooperative Print. Society, 1937. 98 p.

CLYDE, PAUL HIBBERT, 1896-  A history of the modern and contemporary Far East; a survey of western contacts with eastern Asia during the nineteenth and twentieth centuries. New York, Prentice-Hall, 1937. xix, 858 p. incl. front., illus. (incl. ports.) maps (1 fold. in pocket) (Prentice-Hall history series ).

——. The Far East; a history of the impact of the West on eastern Asia. 2d ed. New York, Prentice-Hall [1952] 942 p. illus. 1st ed. 1948.

DAVID, HEINRICH, 1902-  Zur Politik der Grossmächte im Fernen Osten 1894-1902; eine Studie zur Erklärung der Vorgänge der Gegenwart. Zürich, Rascher, 1932. 73, [2] p.

DEWEY, JOHN, 1859-1952. China, Japan and the U. S. A.; present-day conditions in the Far East and their bearing on the Washington conference. New York, Republic Pub. Co., 1921. 64 p. (New republic pamphlet, I ).

DUBOSCQ, ANDRÉ, 1876-  La Chine et le Pacifique. Paris, A. Fayard [c1931] [11]-204 p.

FRANKE, OTTO, 1863-1946. Die Grossmächte in Ostasien von 1894 bis 1914; ein Beitrag zur Vorgeschichte des Krieges, hrsg. mit Unterstützung der Hamburgischen Wissenschaftlichen Stiftung. Braunschweig und Hamburg, G. Westermann, 1923. xxiv, 407, [1] p. (Hamburgische forschungen; wirtschaftl. u. politische studien aus hanseatischem interessengebiet, 10.).

GODDARD, WILLIAM G. The new order in Asia; an essay on the future of civilisation. [Sydney, Epworth Press, 1940] 56 p. incl. front., illus. (ports., facsims.).

HOU, YONG LING, 胡永齡, [Hu Yung-ling]. Condition de paix en Extrême-Orient (Japon-Chine-Société des Nations) Plan Henri-Demont de 1908 proposé
  aux alliés en 1918.  Paris, Union universelle "Pour supprimer ce crime: la
  guerre," 1936. 290 p. front. (port.) fold. tab.
HUDSON, GEOFFREY FRANCIS, 1903-   The Far East in world politics, a stud-
  y in recent history. 2d ed.  London, Oxford University Press, H. Milford,
  1939. vii, [2], 276, [5] p. front., plates, ports. 1st ed. 1937.
────.  An atlas of Far Eastern politics, by G. F. Hudson and Marthe Rajchman.
  Enl. ed., with a supplement for the years 1938 to 1942 by George E. Taylor
  and additional maps by Marthe Rajchman.  New York, Issued under the au-
  spices of the International Secretariat, Institute of Pacific Relations, by John
  Day, 1942. 7-207 p. illus. (maps) 1st ed. 1938.
────.  Questions of East and West; studies in current history.  London, Odhams
  Press [1953] 191 p.
KIRBY, EDWARDS STUART, 1909-   Some political aspects of Far Eastern eco-
  nomic development.  New York, International Secretariat, Institute of Paci-
  fic Relations, 1950. 55 p. (Secretariat paper, 4 ).
LATOURETTE, KENNETH SCOTT, 1884-   A short history of the Far East.
  Rev. ed.  New York, Macmillan [1951] xiv, 730 p. maps (1 fold.) 1st ed.
  1946.
────.  The American record in the Far East, 1945-51. New York, Macmillan,
  1952. 208 p.
LATTIMORE, OWEN, 1900-   Solution in Asia.  Boston, Little, Brown; London,
  Cresset, 1945. 214 p. illus. (map) (Fighting forces series).
────.  The situation in Asia.  Boston, Little, Brown, 1949. 244 p.  map (on lin-
  ing papers).
LÉVY, ROGER, 1887-   Extrême-Orient et Pacifique.  Paris, A. Colin, 1935.
  [5]-220 p. illus. (maps) (Collection Armand Colin (Section de géographie ),
  184 ).
────.  Regards sur l'Asie: Chine, Japon, Corée, Viet Nam, Haute-Asie.  Par-
  is, A. Colin, 1952. 230 p. illus. (Collection "Sciences politiques").
────.  Situations en Extrême-Orient. Avec une introd. de Pierre Gourou et une
  carte originale de Joseph Hackin.  Paris [Centre d'études de politique étran-
  gère] 1954. 18, [15] p. map.
LINEBARGER, PAUL MYRON ANTHONY, 1913-   Far Eastern governments and
  politics: China and Japan [by] Paul M. A. Linebarger, Djang Chu, 章楚, [and]
  Ardath W. Burks. 2d ed.  Princeton, Van Nostrand [1956] 643 p. illus. (Van
  Nostrand political science series ) 1st ed. 1954.
MacNAIR, HARLEY FARNSWORTH, 1891-1947. Modern Far Eastern interna-
  tional relations, by Harley Farnsworth MacNair and Donald F. Lach.  New
  York, Van Nostrand [1950] London, Macmillan, 1950. xi, 681 p. illus.,
  ports., maps (part col.).
MAKI, JOHN McGILVREY, 1909-   comp. Selected documents, Far Eastern in-
  ternational relations (1689-1951) [Seattle] University of Washington, 1951.
  ii, 333 l.
MATHEWS, BASIL JOSEPH, 1879-1951. World tides in the Far East.  London,
  Edinburgh House Press, 1933; New York, Friendship Press, 1934. 160 p.
  illus. (map).
MICHAEL, FRANZ H., 1907-   The Far East in the modern world [by] Franz H.
  Michael [and] George E. Taylor.  New York, Holt; London, Methuen [1956]
  724 p.
MOGI, SOBEI. The problem of the Far East, by Sobei Mogi and H. Vere Red-
  man.  Philadelphia, J. B. Lippincott; London, Gollancz; Toronto, Ryerson
  Press [1935] 348 p. diagrs.
MORLEY, FELIX. Our Far Eastern assignment, with an introduction by the
  Honorable Henry Morganthau.  Council of Christian Associations.  New York,
  Association Press, 1926. vii-viii, ix-xiv, 185 p. illus. (maps) plates, diagr.

MORSE, HOSEA BALLOU, 1855-1934. Far Eastern international relations, by
    Hosea Ballou Morse and Harley Farnsworth MacNair. Boston, New York
    [etc.] Houghton Mifflin [c1931]   xvi, [3]-846 p. front., maps (part double)
    1st ed. Shanghai, 1928.
NEXT step in Asia [by] John K. Fairbank [and others. Cambridge] Harvard Uni-
    versity Press, 1949. 90 p.
NOURSE, MARY AUGUSTA. Gärung in Fern-ost. Übers. von Helen Scherer.
    Frankfurt a.M., Wolfgang Metzner, 1951. 316 p. map.
OSTWALD, PAUL, 1884-  Ostasien und die Weltpolitik. Bonn, K. Schroeder,
    1928. 186 p.
PARK, NO-YONG, 鮑訥榮, 1899-  Retreat of the West; the white man's adven-
    ture in eastern Asia. Boston, Hale, Cushman and Flint [c1937] xiv, 336 p.
PEFFER, NATHANIEL, 1890-  Must we fight in Asia? New York and London,
    Harper, 1935.   v, 244 p.
QUIGLEY, HAROLD SCOTT, 1889-  The Far East, an international survey, by
    Harold S. Quigley and George H. Blakeslee. Boston, World Peace Founda-
    tion, 1938. x, 353 p. fold. maps.
REINHARD, ERNST. Die imperialistische Politik im Fernen Osten. Bern und
    Leipzig, E. Bircher, 1926. 237 p. fig. maps.
ROYAL INSTITUTE OF INTERNATIONAL AFFIARS. Problems of the post-war
    settlement in the Far East; interim report by a group of members of the Roy-
    al Institute of International Affairs. London, Royal Institute of International
    Affairs [1942] 7 v. (United Kingdom paper, 1 ).
————. British reactions to the war in the Far East, 1941/2; interim report by
    a group of members of the Royal Institute of International Affairs. London,
    Royal Institute of International Affairs [1942] 6 numb. l. (United Kingdom pa-
    per, 4 ).
SCHMITT, ERICH, 1893-  Ostasien in der Weltpolitik. Bonn, Bonner Univbuch-
    dr., 1940. 24 p. (Kriegsvorträge der Rheinischen Friedrich-Wilhelms-Univ.
    Bonn.[a.Rh.] Heft 6 ).
SCHNEE, HEINRICH, 1871-  Völker und Mächte im Fernen Osten; Eindrücke
    von der Reise mit der Mandschurei-kommission. Berlin, Deutsche Buch-
    Gemeinschaft [c1933] 365, [1] p., illus. (maps) plates, ports., diagrs.
SOYESHIMA, MICHIMASA. Oriental interpretations of the Far Eastern problem.
    [Lectures on the Harris foundation, 1925] by Michimasa Soyeshima [and P.W.
    Kuo, 郭秉文. Chicago, University of Chicago Press [c1925] ix, 219,[1] p.
STRAELEN, HENRICUS VAN, 1903-  New diplomacy in the Far East, a blue-
    print for the training of future diplomats. With an introduction by Professor
    Dr.J.A. Veraart. London, Luzac [1944] 40 p.
————. The Far East must be understood. With a preface by Djang Tsukung, 張
    資拱 . London, Luzac [1945] 151 p.
TONG, HOLLINGTON KONG, 董顯光, 1887-  Problems and personalities in
    the Far East. Shanghai, China Press [1933] cover-title, 157 p. illus.(incl.
    ports., maps).
————. Men and events in the Far East. Shanghai, The Joint Publication Co.
    [1933] 158 p. illus.(incl.ports., maps) (Contemporary history series, 2 ).
TŌYŌ BUNKO. Tokyo. Seminar on Modern China, ed. List of the Blue Books
    concerning the Far East in the libraries of Tōyō Bunko and Hitotsubashi Uni-
    versity. Tokyo, 1956. 94 p.
TREAT, PAYSON JACKSON, 1879-  The Far East; a political and diplomatic
    history. Rev. ed. New York and London, Harper [c1935] xi, 563 p. fold.
    front., maps. [Harper's historical series] 1st ed. 1928.
U.S. Congress. Senate. Committee on Armed Services. Military situation in the
    Far East. Hearings before the Committee on Armed Services and the Com-
    mittee on Foreign Relations, United States Senate, Eighty-second Congress,
    first session, to conduct an inquiry into the military situation in the Far East
    and the facts surrounding the relief of General of the Army MacArthur from

his assignments in that area. Washington, Govt. Print.Off., 1951. 5 pts.
(iii, 3691 p.).

VINACKE, HAROLD MONK, 1893-  A history of the Far East in modern times.
5th ed. New York, Appleton-Century-Crofts [1950] xix, 785 p. maps (part
fold., 1 col.). 1st ed. 1928.

———. Far eastern politics in the postwar period. New York, Appleton-Century-Crofts; London, G. Allen and Unwin, 1956. 497 p. illus.

WHYTE, SIR FREDERICK, 1883-   The future of East and West; an essay in sur-
mise. London, Sidgwick and Jackson [1932] 180 p. (World problems of to-
day ).

———. A British view of Pacific affairs in 1936. Prepared for the sixth conference of the Institute of Pacific Relations held at Yosemite, California, from
August 15th to 29th, 1936. London, Royal Institute of International Affairs,
1936. 29 p. (United Kingdom papers, 5 ).

WOODHEAD, HENRY GEORGE WANDESFORDE, 1883-   Occidental interpreta-
tions of the Far Eastern problem. Lectures on the Harris Foundation, 1925.
By H.G.W.Woodhead, Julean Arnold [and] Henry Kittredge Norton. Chicago,
University of Chicago Press, 1926. ix, 252 p.

## China and India

BAGCHI, PRABODH CHANDRA, 1898-1956. India and China; a thousand years
of cultural relations. 2d ed., rev. and enl. Bombay, Hind Kitabs [1950]
New York, Philosophical Library, 1950. vi, 234 p. fold. map.

CHANG, CARSUN, 張嘉森 , 1886-   China and Gandhian India. Edited by D.Kal-
idas Nag. Allahabad, Indo-Chinese Literature Publications, 1956. xiii, 318 p.

CHOU EN-LAI in India, a souvenir. Delhi, People's Pub. House, 1954. 52 p.
illus. ports.

DIKSHITAR, V.R. RAMACHANDRA. Southern India and China. Madras, 1945.
28 p. (Madras. University. Endowment lecture).

FEER, MARK CECIL ISELIN, 1928-   India's China policy, 1949-54. Medford,
The Fletcher School of Law and Diplomacy, 1954. 283 l. Thesis-Fletcher
School of Law and Diplomacy.

FISHER, MARGARET WELPLEY, 1903-   Indian views of Sino-Indian relations
[by] Margaret W. Fisher [and] Joan V. Bondurant. Berkeley [Institute of International Studies] University of California, 1956. 163, xxix p. (Indian
press digests. Monograph series, 1 ).

INDIA. Ministry of Education. Exhibition of Professor Raghu Vira's collection
of Chinese, Tibetan, Mongolian, Manchurian and Hsi Hsia literatures, paintings, estampages of inscriptions, colored movies and slides, illustrative of
the interflow of culture between India and High and East Asia. Exhibition
court of Eastern court, New Delhi, from 29th September to 6th October, 1955.
New Delhi, 1955. 2 p. plates.

"INDIA'S heart is one with China"; Generalissimo and Madame Chiang Kai-
shek's visit; comradeship-in-arms of two great countries, a turning point in
history. [Bombay, Times of India Press, 1943?] 34 p. illus.(incl. ports.).

The INDIAN CULTURAL DELEGATION in China, 1955. Peking, Foreign Languages Press, 1955. 103 p. illus.

KHAN, SIR MUHAMMAD ZAFRULLA, 1893-   India and China. Allahabad, Kitabistan [1944] 34 p. (The Indian Institute of International Affairs, New Delhi.
[Publications] 17 ).

LOHIA, RAM MANOHAR. India on China; foreword by Jawaharlal Nehru. Allahabad, Kitabistan, 1938. 52 p. (All India Congress Committee. Political
economic ser., 9 ).

MOTHER INDIA. The folly of recognising Red China. Bombay, 1950. 28 p.

MUKERJI, PRABHAT KUMAR. Indian literature abroad (China) Calcutta, Calcutta Oriental Press [1928] ii, 98 p. (Calcutta Oriental ser. 22, E 14 ).

―――. Indian literature in China and the Far East. Calcutta, Greater Indian Society, 1932. iv, 334, 18, 4 p.

NAIR, V.G. Short studies on China and India (Reproduced from the Indian journals). Madras [Sino-Indian Cultural Society in India] printed at Thompson and Co., 1949. 164 p.

PANIKKAR, KAVALAM MADHAVA, 1896-  India and China: a study of cultural relations. Bombay, Asia Pub. House, London, Luzac, 1957. 107 p.

RADHAKRISHNAN, SIR SARVEPALLI, 1888-  India and China, lectures delivered in China in May 1944. Bombay, Hind kitabs [1944] 3rd ed. 1954.168 p.

SOONG, CHING-LING, 孫宋慶齡, 1890-  Good neighbours meet, speeches in India, Burma and Pakistan, 1955-56. Peking, Foreign Languages Press, 1956. 86 p. illus.

TAGORE, SIR RABINDRANATH, 1861-1941. Talks in China; lectures delivered in April and May, 1924. Calcutta, Visva-Bharati Book Shop, 1925. 157, iii p.

―――. China and India. Santiniketan, Sino-Indian Cultural Society, 1938. 16 p.

TAI, CHI-T'AO, 戴季陶, 1890-1949. On cultural relations between China and India; with a biographical introduction by Tan Yun-shan, 譚雲山. Santiniketan, Sino-Indian Cultural Society in India, 1947. vii, 15 p. (Sino-Indian pamphlet, 8 ).

―――. Goodwill message to India, with a biographical introduction by Tan Yun-shan. Santiniketan, Sino-Indian Cultural Society in India, 1948. 14 p. (Sino-Indian pamphlet, 11 ).

TAN, YUN-SHAN, 譚雲山, 1901-  Cultural interchange between India and China. Santiniketan, Sino-Indian Cultural Society in India, 1937. 16 p.

―――. India's contributions to Chinese culture and Chinese studies in India. Santiniketan, Sino-Indian Cultural Society of India, 1942. 19 p.

―――. China, India and the war. Calcutta, China Press [pref. 1944. 74 p. group port.

―――. The Visva-Bharati Cheena-Bhavana and the Sino -Indian Cultural Society Santiniketan, Sino-Indian Cultural Society of India, 1944. 25 p.

―――. China's civilization and the spirit of Indian and Chinese cultures. Santiniketan, Sino-Indian Cultural Society of India, 1949. 26 p.

―――. Ahimsa in Sino-Indian culture. Santiniketan, Sino-Indian Cultural Society of India, 1949. 22 p.

―――. Inter-Asian cultural co-operation and the union of Asia. Santiniketan, Sino-Indian Cultural Society of India, 1949. 19 p.

―――. An appeal to conscience and Sino-Indian relationship. Santiniketan, Sino-Indian Cultural Society of India, 1950. 23 p.

## China and Japan
### Treaties, Documents, etc.

CARNEGIE ENDOWMENT FOR INTERNATIONAL PEACE. Division of International Law. The Sino-Japanese negotiations of 1915; Japanese and Chinese documents and Chinese official statement. Washington, The Endowment, 1921. viii, 76 p. (Pamphlet series of the Carnegie endowment for international peace. Division of international law, 45 ).

CHINA. Delegation to the Conference on the Limitation of Armament, Washington, D.C., 1921-22. Conversations between the Chinese and Japanese representatives in regard to the Shantung question. Treaty for the settlement of outstanding questions relative to Shantung. Agreed terms of understanding recorded in the Minutes of the Chinese and Japanese delegations concerning the conclusion of the treaty for the settlement of outstanding questions relative to Shantung. Prepared by the Chinese delegation. Washington, Govt. Print. Off., 1923. vi, 74 p.

―――. Treaties, etc., 1922. Treaty between China and Japan for the settlement of outstanding questions relating to Shantung - with an agreement supplemen-

tary thereto. Concluded at Washington on February 4, 1922. Washington,
Govt. Print.Off., 1922. 14 p. ( [U.S.] 67th Cong., 2d sess. Senate.Doc.166).
————. Treaty for the settlement of outstanding questions relative to Shantung.
[Peking? 1922?] cover-title, 16, 4, 6, [22] p.
————. Agreement concerning the exchange of correspondence between the Re-
public of China and the Empire of Japan. [Peking? 1922?] cover-title,[30] p.
————. Agreement concerning the exchange of insured letters and boxes between
the Republic of China and the Empire of Japan. [Peking? 1922?] cover-title,
[20] p.
————. Agreement concerning the exchange of money orders between the Republic of China and the Empire of Japan. [Peking? 1922?] cover-title, [46] p.
incl. forms.
————. Agreement concerning the exchange of postal parcels between the Republic of China and the Empire of Japan. [Peking? 1922] cover-title, [46] p.
————. 1915. Les 21 demands et les traités et accords du 25 mai 1915 entre la
Chine et le Japon. Textes et documents. Paris, Impr. de Vangirard, 1931.
48 p.
CHINA. Treaties, etc., 1952. Treaty of peace between the Republic of China
and Japan. [Taipei? 1952?] 1 v. (unpaged).

JAPAN. Delegation to the Conference on the Limitation of Armament, Washington, D.C., 1921-22. Conversations between the Chinese and Japanese representatives in regard to the Shantung question. Treaty for the settlement of
outstanding questions relative to Shangtung. Agreed terms of understanding
recorded in the Minutes of the Japanese and Chinese delegations concerning
the conclusion of the treaty for the settlement of outstanding questions relative to Shantung. Minutes prepared by the Japanese delegation. Washington,
Govt. Print. Off., 1922. iii, 396 p.

## General Works

AMERICA'S position on the Shantung question as indicated in public speeches,
by President Harding, ex-President Wilson, Senator Lodge, etc., and in official hearings and state papers. [Washington,D.C., Press of Ransdell Inc.,
1921?] 40 p. "Published by the Weekly review of the Far East, Shanghai,
China."
[ASADA, KEIICHI]. Expenditures of the Sino-Japanese war, by Giicho Ono.
New York [etc.] Oxford University Press, 1922. xv, 330 p. incl. tables.
(Publications of the Carnegie endowment for international peace. Division of
economics and history.).
ASSOCIATION FOR THE STUDY OF JAPANESE AFFAIRS, Nanking. Anti-Chi-
nese and anti-foreign teachings in new textbooks and publications of Japan.
Nanking, 193-    52, 52 p.
BAU, MINGCHIEN JOSHUA, 1894-   The Shantung question. Edited by the Eng-
lish editorial committee for the Washington conference of the Chinese students' alliance. [Chicago] Chinese Students' Alliance in the United States of
America [c1921] 47 p. (Series on China and the Washington conference, 2 ).
CASSEVILLE, HENRY. Nankin contre Tokyo (Chine 1928-33) 2 portraits et 2
cartes hors texte. Paris, Éditions Berger-Levrault, 1934. xv, 224 p.ports.,
fold. maps.
CHALLAYE, FÉLICIEN, 1875-   La Chine et le Japon politiques. Paris, F.Al-
can, 1921. viii, 323, [1] p. (Les questions actuelles, études de culture générale, pub. sous la direction de Émile Borel et Georges Dumas ).
CHANG, CHÛN, 張羣, 1889-   Sino-Japanese relations and America. Taipei,
Off. of the Govt. Spokesman, 1952. cover-title, 58 p.
CHINESE CONSOLIDATED BENEVOLENT ASSOCIATION, New York. Free China protests peace conference exclusion. Earned equal participation on record of resisting Japanese aggression for twenty years at staggering cost and

ruinous sacrifice. National government's fight against glaring injustice supported and urged by free Chinese the world over. New York, 1951. 28 p.

DOTSON, LILLIAN YOTA, 1921-  Sino-Japanese war of 1894-95. New Haven, 1951. 2-205 l. ii-xii, ii-xxxv l. Thesis-Yale University

GODSHALL, WILSON LEON, 1895-  The international aspects of the Shantung question. Philadelphia, 1923. 172 p. Thesis-University of Pennsylvania.

HARVIN, HARRY L., JR., 1923-  The Far East in the Peace Conference of 1919. Durham, N.C., Duke University, 1956. 2 v. Thesis-Duke University.

HO, YING-CHIN, 何應欽, 1889-  Report on the acceptance of the Japanese surrender. Nanking, Ministry of Information [1946] 12 numb. l.

HSÜ, SHU-HSI, 徐淑希, 1892-  The treaties and notes of 1915. Peiping, 1932. 30 p. Reprinted from Chinese Social and Political Science Review, April 1932.

HUNTER, EDWARD. The France and Germany of Asia. Chicago, Esquire-Coronet, inc. [c1938] 17, [1] p. 1 illus.

KAWAKAMI, KIYOSHI KARL, 1875-  Japan's Pacific policy, especially in relation to China, the Far East, and the Washington conference. New York, E.P. Dutton [c1922] xiv, 3-380 p.

KWONG, TSE-WING, 鄺子榮 . The Shantung settlement. Los Angeles, University of Southern California, 1923. 30, [1] l.

LÉVY, ROGER, 1887-  Relations de la Chine et du Japon. Paris, Paul Hartmann, éditeur, 1938. [11]-135, [1] p. incl. map. (Centre d'études de politique étrangère. Section d'information. Publication, 8 ).

LU, ALBERT T., 魯鐘平. Hirota's three principles vis-à-vis China. Nanking, Council of International Affairs, 1936. 32 p. Reprinted from Information Bulletin, Nanking, 1:7).

MAH, NGUI WING, 馬如榮, 1893-  Sino-Japanese relations since the Tangku truce, May 31, 1933. A brief historical survey by N. Wing Mah [and] C. F. Chang, 張忠黻. [New York? 1936] 20 numb. l. (Papers presented at the sixth conference of the Institute of Pacific relations, Yosemite national park, California, August 15 to 29, 1936. 11:2).

MILLARD, THOMAS FRANKLIN FAIRFAX, 1868-1942. The A B C's of the twenty-one demands. Shanghai, Weekly Review of the Far East, 1921. 12 p.

———. The same. N[ew] Y[ork] Chinese Students' Committee on Washington Conference, 1921. 15 p. "Reprinted with the consent of the Weekly review of the Far East."

———. The Shantung case at the conference. 2nd ed. Shanghai, Millard's Review of the Far East, 1921. 76 p. illus. (map, facsim.).

OSAKA. Chamber of Commerce and Industry. Résumé des relations politiques et économiques entre le Japon et la Chine établi par la chambre du commerce et de l'industrie d'Osaka. Quels sont les intérêts et les privilèges du Japon en Chine? Comment la Chine a-t-elle violé les droits que le Japon tient des traités? Osaka, Société d'impr. Hamada, 1931. cover-title, 11 p.

———. Fédération économique sur les Problèmes de Chine d'Osaka. Ensignements anti-étrangers. Osaka, 1931. iv, 128 p. plates.

OSBORNE, SIDNEY. The new Japanese peril. New York, Macmillan, 1921. viii, 184 p.

OZAKI, HOTSUMI. Recent developments in Sino-Japanese relations. Prepared for the sixth conference of the Institute of Pacific Relations to be held at Yosemite, California, August 15th to 29th, 1936. Tokyo, Japanese Council, Institute of Pacific Relations, 1936. 22 p. (Japanese council papers, 14 ).

PIPPON, ANTON, 1909-  Wo stehen heute China und Japan? Kevelaer, Butzon und Bercker [1949] 80 p. maps.

RINE, VICTOR, 1884-  Machiavelli of Nippon; Japan's plan of world conquest, willed by Emperor Meiji, developed by Premier Tanaka; "Tanaka memorial" proven genuine by Victor Rine. New York, The Wandering eye, 1932. [5]-111 p. front. (port.) map.

ROYAL INSTITUTE OF INTERNATIONAL AFFAIRS. China and Japan. 3d. ed.

London, Royal Institute of International Affairs;  New York, Toronto [etc.]
Oxford University Press [1941] xi, 163 p. maps (1 fold.) (Chatham house information papers, 21a).

SHIGEMITSU, MAMORU, 1887-1957. Revolutionary foreign policy of China; a report submitted to the Japanese Government. [Tokyo?] 1931. 151 p.

STRUNK, ROLAND. Achtung! Asien marschiert! Ein Tatsachenbericht, von Roland Strunk und Martin Rikli.  Berlin, Drei Masken Verlag a.g. [1934] 221, [1] p. illus. (maps) plates, ports., facsims.

SUN, YAT-SEN, 1866-1925. China and Japan: natural friends - unnatural enemies; a guide for China's foreign policy. With a foreword by President Wang Ching-wei. Edited by T'ang Leang-li.  Shanghai, China United Press, 1941. vii-xx, 182 p. illus. (facsim.).

TANAKA, GIICHI, baron, 1863-1929. Tanaka memorial: Japanese imperialism stripped. The secret memorandum of Tanaka, Premier of Japan.  New York, Workers Library Publishers [1927] 37 p.

———. Japan's positive policy in Machuria. [n.p., 1931] cover-title, 30 p. incl. map. Caption title: Memorial presented to His Majesty the Emperor of Japan by Premier Tanaka, outlining the positive policy in Manchuria.

———. The memorial of Premier Tanaka; or, A Japanese secret design for the conquest of China as well as the United States and the rest of the world. N[ew] Y[ork] World Peace Movement [1931?] 44 p.

———. Tanaka's secret memorial to the Japanese emperor.  Peiping, Northeastern Affairs Research Society [1932] 55 p.

———. Eingabe an den japanischen Kaiser über positive Politik gegen die Mandschurei und Mongolei, eingereicht am 25 Juli 1927 vom Premierminister Tanaka. Übersetz vom I-Djiu-Bund. Schanghai-Woosung, Tung chi Universität, 1932. 78 p. map.

———. Secret memorial concerning Manchuria, Mongolia, China, U.S.A. and the world, submitted by General Tanaka (the then premier of Japan) to the Japanese emperor in 1927. 11th ed.  Shanghai, The China Critic [1932] cover-title, ii, 42 p. "Reprinted from the China Critic, 4:39, Sept. 24, 1931."

———. Die Kriegsziele des japanischen Imperialismus; das geheime Memorandum des japanischen Ministerpräsidenten Tanaka über die japanische Politik in der Mandschurei. Mit einem Vorwort, einem einleitenden Artikel und einer Übersichtskarte der Mandschurei.  Hamburg-Berlin, C. Hoym nachf.[c1932] 39, [1] p. illus. (double map).

———. Le brigandage japonais en Mandchourie; mémorandum présenté par le président du conseil japonais à l'empereur du Japon.  Paris, Bureau d'éditions, 1932. 54 p.

———. The Tanaka memorial; an outline presented to the Japanese emperor on July 25, 1927 by Premier Tanaka for the Japanese conquest of China and other nations. With introduction by V. Kwonglee Kwong, 鄺兆縈. [San Francisco, T.W. Chinn, 1937?] cover-title, 14 p.

———. Japan to use "blood and iron" policy on China. Japan must first crush the United States to accomplish the "blood and iron" policy.  Marysville, Calif., Chinese Patriotic Society, 1937. 24 p.

———. Le mémoire Tanaka; le plan prémédité de l'aggression japonaise.  Genève, Le Bureau de presse de la Délégation chinoise, 1938. 47 p. map. (China. Delegation to the League of Nations. Press Bureau publications, 11 ).

———. Japanese imperialism exposed, the secret Tanaka document.  New York, International Publishers [1942] 47 p.

———. Japan's dream of world empire; the Tanaka memorial. Edited, with an introduction, by Carl Crow.  New York, London, Harper [1942] 118 p.

———. The same.  London. G. Allen and Unwin [1943] 68 p.

TCHEN, HOSHIEN, 陳和銑, 1894-  Les relations diplomatiques entre la Chine et le Japon de 1871 à nos jours; traités, conventions, échange de lettres, etc., avec une carte de la Chine et du Japon.  Paris, Éditions de "La Vie universitaire,'' 1921. 328 p. fold. map.

TS'AO, YUN-HSIANG, 曹雲祥, 1881-  comp. Symposium concerning Japan's
Far Eastern policy. Compiled by Y.S. Tsao and J.S. Tow, 屠汝涑 . Shanghai, China Institute of International Relations, 1934. iii, [1], 44 p.

[TSINAN Affair]. The facts and circumstances of the collision between Japanese
and Chinese troops at Tsinan. [Osaka] The Osaka Chamber of Commerce
and Industry [1928] cover-title, 11, 9 p.

TSINAN affair; sixty-two photographs showing effect of indiscriminate bombardment at Tsinan and results of wanton murders of Chinese by Japanese troops
in Shantung as well as documents concerning Japanese military action, with
English translation. Shanghai, International Relations Committee, 1928. 1 v.

The TSINAN case and the League of nations. [n. p., 1928] cover-title, 18 p.

TSINAN incident, 1928. [Edited by] Shinichiro Kato. Tsingtao, 1928. cover-title,
30 p. plates, fold. plans.

The TSINANFU crisis, published by the faculty and students of Tsing Hua university, Peking. [Peking, 1928] cover-title, 5, 58 p. port., maps.

TSUNODA, RYŪSAKU, 1877-  tr. Japan in the Chinese dynastic histories: Later
Han through Ming dynasties. Editor: L. Carrington Goodrich. South Pasaden-
a [Calif.] P.D. and I. Perkins, 1951. vii, 187 l. maps. (Perkins Asiatic monographs, no. 2 ).

U.S. Congress. Senate. Committee on Foreign Relations. Payment to government of Japan for proposed deportation of enemy aliens from China during
the world war. Report. [To accompany S. 1607] [Washington, Govt. Print. Off.,
1937] 5 p. (75th Cong., 1st sess. Senate. Rept. 384 ).

VERNON, YVONNE. Chine, Japon, Stamboul. Préface de Charles Diehl. Paris,
A. Tolmer, 1925. 157 p.

VOICE of the Chinese people regarding Sino-Japanese questions. Shanghai, 1928.
78 p.

WANG, I-T'UNG, 王伊同, 1914-  Official relations between China and Japan,
1368-1549. Cambridge, Harvard University Press, 1953; London, Oxford
University Press, 1953. xi, 128 p. (Harvard-Yenching Institute studies, 9 ).

WERMANN, ERNST. Die Schantung-frage. Leipzig, R. Noske, 1931. viii, 95 p.,
1 l. incl. maps. (Abhandlungen des Instituts für politik, ausländisches öffentliches recht und völkerrecht an der Universität Leipzig. hft. 12 ).

WOOD, GE-ZAY, 何傑才, 1897-  The twenty-one demands, Japan versus China. New York, Chicago [etc.] Fleming H. Revell [c1921] [7]-178 p.

———. The Chino-Japanese treaties of May 25, 1915. New York, Chicago [etc.]
Fleming H. Revell [c1921] 151 p.

———. The Shantung question; a study in diplomacy and world politics. New York,
Chicago [etc.] Fleming H. Revell [c1922] [5]-372 p.

———. China, the United States, and the Anglo-Japanese alliance. New York,
Chicago [etc.] Fleming H. Revell [c1921] viii, [2], 11-176 p.

WOODRUFF, GEORGE, 1881-  What of China and Japan? [Chicago] The Illinois
Chamber of Commerce, 1921. 36 p.

YONG, THADDÉE ANN-YUEN,     楊安然. Chine et Japon à la Conférence de la
paix. Lophem-lez-Bruges [Belgique] Abbaye de Saint-André, 1934. viii, 304
p. fold. map. (École des sciences politiques et sociales de l'Université catholique de Louvain. [Bibliothèque] ).


Japan's Invasion, 1931 (including attack on Shanghai)
( See also Northeastern  Provinces )


AKAGI, ROY HIDEMICHI, 1892-  Manchuria, discudded by Roy H. Akagi, T.Z.
Koo, 顧子仁, [and] Joseph P. Chamberlain, January 23, 1932. New York
luncheon discussion. New York, Foreign Policy Association [1932] 27 p. [For-
eign policy association. Pamphlet, 79. Series 1931-32. March, 1932].

ALBRECHT, DIETGER. Der chinesisch-japanische Konflikt und das Völkerrecht.

Leipzig, R. Noske, 1933. v-vi, 164 p. map. (Frankfurter Abhandlungen zum modernen Völkerrecht, 41 ).

AMERICAN COMMITTEE FOR JUSTICE TO CHINA. The case for China; a summary of recent events in Manchuria. [New York] American Committee for Justice to China, 1933. 34 p.

AMOY. University. A manifesto on the Japanese invasion of Manchuria, issued by the faculty and staff of the Univeristy of Amoy. [Amoy] 1931. cover-title, 1 v. (various pagings) illus.

BASSETT, REGINALD, 1901-   Democracy and foreign policy; a case history, the Sino-Japanese dispute, 1931-33. London, London School of Economics and Political Science, University of London; New York, Longmans, Green [1952] xxiii, 654 p. (Publications of the London School of Economics).

BALET, JEAN CYPRIEN, 1867-   Le drame de l'Extrême-Orient. Que veut le Japon? Que veut la Chine? Préface de Georges Leygues; fac-similé d'un autographe du général Nogi. Paris, Éditions du "Temps présent" [1931] 189 p. 1 l. incl. facsim. fold. map.

CUTLACK, FREDERIC MORLEY, 1886-   The Manchurian arena; an Australian view of the Far Eastern conflict. Sydney, Angus and Robertson, 1934. viii, 76 p., 1 l. incl. front.(map).

DIETRICH, PAUL R. La guerre en Chine. Paris, Bureau d'éditions, 1932. 44 p.

FRÊNE, VICTOR. The meaning of the Manchurian crisis. [Shanghai, Shameen Print. Press, 1931] 24 p.

GOTHEIN, GEORG, 1857-   China and Japan: a world coalition against Japan. London, Hamilton Press [1934] 32 p.

HALL, HENRY. War in the Far East. New York, International Pamphlets [c1930] 31 p. (International pamphlets, 2 ).

HISHIDA, SEIJI GEORGE, 1874-   Comments on John Bassett Moore's discussion with reference to Manchurian incident, embargo and neutrality, "aggressor," Kellogg pact, League, American "birthright," etc. 2d ed. including additional considerations on the boycott. Tokyo [The Maruzen Co.] 1934. ix, 21, [1], [21]-69 p., port.

HOLMES, WALTER M. An eye-witness in Manchuria. London, M. Lawrence [1932] 60 p. map.

HOSTILE activities of Japanese troops in the northeastern provinces of China. (From September 18, 1931 to November 7, 1931 ). Nanking, 1931. cover-title, 18 p.

HSU, DAU-LIN, 徐道鄰, 1906-   Chronik der chinesisch-japanischen Beziehungen; eine Materialsammlung; für die Liga für Vaterlands-verteidigung der Chinesen in Deutschland, von Hsu Dau-lin und Chu Chi, 朱偰. Berlin, O. Elsner, 1931. 54 p. fold. map.

HSÜ, SHU-HSI, 徐淑希, 1892-   The Manchurian question. Rev. ed. Peiping, 1931. iii, 120 p. 1st ed. 1929.

———. The Manchurian dilemma; force or pacific settlement by Shu-hsi Hsu and Robert Moore Duncan. Shanghai, China Council, Institute of Pacific Relations, 1931. 88 p.

———. Questions relating to Manchuria. Prepared for the fourth general session of the Institute of Pacific Relations to be held at Hangchow, October 21 to November 3, 1931. Shanghai, 1931. 30 p.

———. Manchuria at Hangchow. Peiping, 1931. cover-title, 16 p.

———. A reply to Mr. Matsuoka. 3rd ed. Peiping, The Leader Press, 1932. 24 p. 1st ed. 1930.

———. Background of the Manchurian situation. Peiping, 1932. 43 p.

———. Essays on the Manchurian problem. Shanghai, China Council, Institute of Pacific Relations, 1932. v-xxii, 349 p.

———. Japan's fifty-four cases. Peiping, 1932. 63 p.

HSU, TUN-CHANG, 徐敦璋, 1905-   ed. Secret documents relating to the Japanese policy toward Manchuria and Mongolia. Peiping [China Institute of

International Affairs] 1932. cover-title, viii, 80 p. maps. (China institute of international affairs. Studies on matters of current international interest, 2 ).

Les INCIDENTS sino-japonais en Mandchourie. Paris, Éditions internationales, 1932. 167 p.

INSTITUTE OF PACIFIC RELATIONS. American Council. Conflict in the Far East, 1931-32. New York, 1932. 47 p.

——. The conflict around Manchuria and America's part in it; a study course in six parts for American women. New York, American Council, Institute of Pacific Relations, 1933. 65 numb. l.

INTERNATIONAL RELATIONS COMMITTEE. One year of Japanese occupation of Manchuria. Nanking, International Relations Committee [1932] iv, [2], 118 p.

JAPANESE ASSOCIATION IN CHINA, Shanghai. Presenting Japan's side of the case. Shanghai, Japanese Association in China, 1931. cover-title, 77 p.

JAPANESE CHAMBER OF COMMERCE, New York. Background of the Manchurian trouble; a companion pamphlet to the ''Background of the Shanghai trouble'' New York, Bureau of Information, Japanese Chamber of Commerce [1932] 29 p. map.

JOHNSEN, JULIA EMILY, comp. Chinese-Japanese war. New York, H. W. Wilson Co., 1933. 196 p. (The reference shelf, 8:8 ).

KATSUKI, Z. The Manchurian incident: inforamtion on its causes and status. n. p. [1931] 20 p. map.

KAWAKAMI, KIYOSHI KARL, 1875-  Japan speaks on the Sino-Japanese crisis, with an introduction by Tsuyoshi Inukai. New York, Macmillan, 1932. xvi, 184 p. fold. map.

——. Japan spricht! Der chinesisch-japanische Konflikt. Mit einer Einführung von Tsuyoshi Inukai. [Autorisierte Übersetzung von Else Baronin Werkmann] Wien, W. Braumüller, 1933. 175 p. map.

KUEI, CHUNG-SHU, 桂中樞, 1897-  Plain speaking on Japan; a collection of articles on the Sino-Japanese conflict, originally published in the ''Shanghai evening post and mercury'' under the column, ''As a Chinese sees it.'' Shanghai, Commercial Press, 1933. 229 p.

K'UNG, T. P., 冀德柏, 1891-  The tragic death of Chang Tso-lin, 張作霖; a documentary survey of a prelude to the Japanese invasion of Manchuria. Peiping, 1932. 39 p.

KUO MIN TANG. Central Executive Committee. Publicity Dept. The Japanese invasion of Manchuria. Shanghai, 1932. cover-title, 135 l.

LEE, EDWARD BING-SHUEY, 李炳瑞, 1903-56. One year of the Japan-China undeclared war and the attitude of the powers, with forewords by Sun Fo, Hu Han-min [and others] Shanghai [Mercury Press] 1933. xxi, 587 p. plates, ports., maps (1 double) plans, facsim.

——. Two years of the Japan-China undeclared war and the attitude of the powers, with forewords by Sun Fo, Hu Han-min [and others] and introduction to second edition by Eugene Chen. Shanghai, [Mercury Press] 1933. xxv, [3], 613 p. front., plates, ports., maps ( 1 double ) plans, facsim.

LEI, K.N., 雷國能, 1896-  ed. Information and opinion concerning the Japanese invasion of Manchuria and Shanghai, from sources other than Chinese. Shanghai, Shanghai Bar Association, 1932. xi, 445 p.

LÉVY, ROGER, 1887-  A qui la Mandchourie? Paris, A. Pedone, 1932. 294 p 2 maps (1 fold.) (Le droit international et l'actualité).

LI, TSI-GZIOU, 李濟歐, 1908-  La défense passive des populations civiles contre la guerre aéro-chimique en Chine. Lyon, Bosc et Riou, 1933. 59 p. illus. (Lyons. Université. Faculté de médicine et de pharmacie. Section de médicine. Thèse, 351 ).

LIANG, YUN-LI, 梁鋆立, 1900-  Rechtsprobleme des Mandschureikonflikts. Breslau, J. U. Kerns, 1935. 14 p.

LING, CHONG-YUN, 林崇墉. La position et les droits du Japon en Mandchourie.

Préface de m. Marcel Sibert. Paris, A. Pedone, 1933. ii, 464 p. fold. map. (Publications de la Revue générale de droit international public, 7 ).

LYON. Université. Institut franco-chinois. A qui le bon droit: Chine ou Japon? Opinion mondiale sur le conflit sino-japonais. Publié par les étudients de l'Institut franco-chinois de Lyon. Lyon, Impr. M. Camus, 1932. 63 p.

MARK, FUNG CHAU, 麥逢秋. Le conflit sino-japonais en Mandchourie et le droit international. Nancy, Société d'impressions typographiques, 1933. [5]-131 p. Thèse-Univ. de Nancy.

MEMORANDUM on the disturbances in Tientsin of November 1931. Submitted by the people of Tientsin, the twenty-first year of the Republic of China. [Tientsin, 1932] 16 p. incl. map.

MEMORANDUM submitted to the Commission of inquiry of the League of nations, by professors and administrators of the educational and cultural institutions of Peiping. [Peiping] 1932. 39 p.

MENG, CHIH, 孟治, 1900- China speaks on the conflict between China and Japan, with an introduction by W. W. Yen. New York, Macmillan, 1932. xx, 211 p. illus., mounted fold. map.

——. China spricht, der Streitfall zwischen China und Japan; mit einer Einleitung von W. W. Yen. Berlin, Sektion der Kuomintang in Deutschland, 1933. 150 p.

MÊNG, G., 孟鞠如, [Mêng Chū-ju] 1910- La position juridique du Japon en Mandchourie; avec une carte en couleurs hors-texte des chemins de fer en Mandchourie. Paris, A. Pedone, 1933. 263 (i. e. 265) p. fold. map.

MERCIER, DÉSIRÉ FÉLICIEN FRANÇOIS JOSEPH, cardinal, 1851-1926. L'invasion et l'occupation de la Mandchourie jugées à la lumière de la doctrine catholique par les écrits du cardinal Mercier, publiés par dom P. C. Lou Tseng-tsiang, 陸徵祥. Paris, Les Éditions du Foyer [1934?] 36 p. front., plates, port.

MICHAEL, FRANZ, 1907- Der Streit um die Mandschurei; die chinesisch-japanischen Rechtsbeziehungen in den "drei östlichen Provinzen" Chinas vor Ausbruch des Konfliktes im september 1931. Leipzig, R. Noske, 1933. viii, 101 p. illus. (map) (Abhandlungen des Instituts für politik, ausländisches öffentliches recht und völkerrecht an der Universität Leipzig, 29 ).

MUELLER, HANS JOACHIM, 1911- Die Rechtslage im chinesisch-japanischen Konflikt 1931-33. Marburg, 1933. 74 p. Diss.-Univ. Marburg.

NORTHEASTERN AFFAIRS RESEARCH INSTITUTE, Peiping. Japan's aggressive policy carried on in the name of the Mikado by the military party, based on material from Japanese sources. Peiping, The Northeastern Affairs Research Institute, 1932. 22 p.

——. Japan's deceitful diplomacy. Peiping, The Northeastern Affairs Research Institute, 1932. cover-title, 22 p.

——. Japan's responsibility for banditry in the three eastern provinces (Manchuria). Peiping, The North-Eastern Affairs Research Institute, 1932. cover-title, 11 p.

PEPING-LIAONING RAILWAY. Peping Liaoning railway and Japanese occupation of Manchuria. Prepared by the Peping-Liaoning railway administration for the Commission of Inquiry of the League of Nations. Tientsin, Tientsin Press, 1932. vi, 92 p. fold. maps, diagr.

PENLINGTON, JOHN N. The Mukden mandate; acts and aims in Manchuria. Tokio, Maruzen, 1932. ii, 264, vi p. port. plates.

The PRESS UNION, Shanghai. The Sino-Japanese conflict: the situation reviewed by American and British editors in China. Shanghai, Press Union [1932] cover-title, 32 p.

RASMUSSEN, OTTO DURHAM, 1888- The China-Japan war. Tonbridge, The author, 1932. cover-title, 24 p.

REA, GEORGE BRONSON, 1869-1938. The highway to hostilities in the Far East. Shanghai, Japanese Association in China, 1932. 35 p.

SAINT-PIERRE, RENÉ. La guerre en Extrême-Orient: est-elle prochaine? est-elle fatale? Exposé de R. Saint-Pierre et J.C. Balet. Paris, Le Redressement français [1935] 83 p. map.

SALCEDO, A. Kuramoto plot exposed. Shanghai, 1934. 51 p. illus.

SATO, YASUNOSUKE. Sino-Japanese problems. Tokyo, Japan Council, Institute of Pacific Relations, 1931. 48 p. (Institute of Pacific Relations. 4th Conference. Documents, v. 2 ).

SAUZEY, J.A., 1896- La guerre en fourrures; notes de campagne. Paris, Les Éditions de France, c1933. ii, 294 p., 1 illus., fold. map.

SCELLE, GEORGES, 1878- Le conflit sino-japonais. Le droit dans le conflit sino-japonais par Georges Scelle; Le conflit sino-japonais et l'opinion publique par Louis de Brouckère. Glaris, Impr. Rod. Tschudy, 1932. 20 p. (Série en langue française des brochures de l'Association suisse pour la Société des Nations, 8 ).

SHANGHAI. Chamber of Commerce. An open letter to the League of Nations commission of inquiry into the Manchurian situation; accompanied by the article "A refutal of Japanese misrepresentations with regard to the causes leading to the Sino-Japanese crisis." Shanghai, The Mercury Press, 1932. 42 p.

――――. Manchurian Refugees' Relief Association. Japanese brutalities in Manchuria. The seven death penalties. The Fushun massacre. Shanghai, 1932. 8 p.

SINO-SCOTTISH SOCIETY, Edinburgh. Appeal from the Chinese Government. [Statement issued in Edinburgh on February 13th, 1932] Geneva, 1932. [3] l.

SMITH, SARA RECTOR, 1890- The Manchurian crisis, 1931-32; a tragedy in international relations. New York, Columbia Univ. Press; London, Oxford University Press, 1948. ix, 281 p. map.

SNOW, EDGAR, 1905- Far Eastern front. New York, H. Smith and R. Haas [c1933] xv, 336 p. front., plates, ports., map.

SORGE, WOLFGANG, 1891- Krieg entbrennt am Pazifik. Berlin, Scherl [c1934] 228, [1] p. plates, 3 fold. maps.

SOUTH MANCHURIA RAILWAY COMPANY SERVANTS' SOCIETY. Declaration on Sino-Japanese clashes issue, by the Servants' Society of the South Manchuria Railway Company. Dairen, 1931. cover-title, 16 p.

STEWART, RAY. War in China. New York, International Pamphlets [1932] cover-title, 31 p. incl. map. (International pamphlets, 19 ).

STIMSON, HENRY LEWIS, 1867-1950. The Far Eastern crisis; recollections and observations. New York, London, Pub. for the Council on Foreign Relations by Harper, 1936. xii, 293 (i.e. 295) p. front., illus. (maps) plates, ports.

STORY, RUSSELL McCULLOCH, 1883-1942. The struggle for Manchuria. An address before the convocation of the North China Union Language School, Nov. 24, 1931. Peiping, North China Union Language School [1932] cover-title, 19 p.

――――. The present situation in China, an address. Peiping, North China Union Language School, 1932. 13 p.

SZE, SAO-KE ALFRED, 施肇基, 1877-1958. The broader issues of the Sino-Japanese question. [An address given before the Chicago Council on Foreign Relations, November 10, 1932] New York, Chinese Cultural Society [1933] 15 p.

――――. Some questions answered; address before the Richmond College Club, Richmond, Va., February 14, 1933. New York, Chinese Cultural Society [1933] 9 p.

――――. Some plain speaking with regard to the Chinese-Japanese situation. Baltimore, J.H. Furst [1933]; Nanking, Waichiaopu, 1933. 15 p.

UNGERN-STERNBERG, LEONIE VON. Krieg in China, der Bürgerkrieg in China und der chinesisch-japanische Konflikt. Berlin, Junker und Dünnhaupt,

1933. 116 p. (Fachschriften zur Politik und staatsbürgerlichen Erziehung ).

U.S. Library of Congress. A list of recent references on the Sino-Japanese dispute, with special reference to the action of the League of nations. [Prepared by the Reading room of the Library of Congress, Study room reference service, James T. Ruby] May 20th, 1933. [Washington, D.C., 1933] 2-22(i.e. 23) numb. l.

WHAT the Japanese have done in northeast China (Manchuria) since September 18, 1931; a report prepared by the refugees from northeast China in consequence of Japanese invasion and presented to the Commission of Inquiry appointed by the League of Nations. Peiping, 1932. 57 p.

WHYMANT, A. NEVILLE JOHN, 1894-   The Chinese-Japanese puzzle; a study of origins, causes and effects. London, V. Gollancz, 1932. 158, [1] p.

WOODHEAD, HENRY GEORGE WANDESFORDE, 1883-   Current comment on events in China; the Sino-Japanese crisis. [Dairen?] South Manchuria Railway Co. [1932?] 99 p. ''Reprint of a selection of articles appearing in 'The Shanghai Evening Post and Mercury,' Oct. 1931-June 1932.''

WRIGHT, QUINCY, 1890-   Some legal aspects of the Far Eastern situation.(In American journal of international law. Concord, N.H., 1933. v. 27, p. 509-516 ).

[WU, HERBERT HAN-TAO],   吳翰濤, 1898-   Japan's acts of treaty violation and encroachment upon the sovereign rights of China in the north-eastern provinces (Manchuria) Peiping, North-eastern Affairs Research Institute, 1932. cover-title, 208 p.

——. A legal study. Japan's acts of treaty violation and encroachment upon the sovereign rights of China in the north-eastern provinces (Manchuria). Peiping, North-eastern Affairs Research Institute, 1932. 208 p.

YONG, THADDÉE ANN-YUEN, 楊安然, 1905-   Aux origines du conflit mandchou: Chine, Japon, paix de Versailles. Honoré d'une préface de son exc.le dʳ V.K. Wellington Koo. Paris, P. Geuthner, 1934. vii, [1], 304 p. fold. map.

YU, JOSEPH, 俞佑世. Memoirs of Kupeikow; a photographic story of the fighting in North China. Shanghai, Liang Yu Publishing Co., 1933. 93 p. illus. maps.

ZUMOTO, MOTOSADA, 1862-   ed. Sino-Japanese entanglements, 1931-32 (a military record) Tokyo, Herald Press [1932] iii, iii, 335 p., 1 l.incl. illus. (maps) plates. fold. maps.

——. ed. Die Chinesisch-japanischen Schwierigkeiten, 1931-32; übersetzt von Jacob Fischer. [Tokyo, Printed by M. Kobayashi and co.] 1932. v, iv, v, 315 p., [317]-384 p., 1 l. incl. illus. (maps) plates.


## Japan's Attack on Shanghai, 1932


CHANG, CHIH-CHUNG, 張治中, 1891-   The fifth army in the Shanghai war. Shanghai, 1932. [122], 68, 4 p. illus. (incl. maps), ports.

JAPAN. Consulate. Shanghai. The Shanghai incident; communiques. [Shanghai, 1932-   1 v.

——. Ministry of Foreign Affairs. Appeal of the Chinese Government. Statement by the Japanese Government. Feb. 7, 1932. Geneva, 1932. 4 l.   Referring to the despatch of expeditionary force to Shanghai occasioned by the presence of the Chinese 19th Army.

——. The same. Communication from the Japanese Delegation. February 1, 1932. Incidents at Shanghai. [Official telegram received by the Japanese Delegation] Geneva, 1932. [3] l.

——. The same. Communication from the Chinese Delegation dated February 14th. Shanghai incidents. Official telegram received by the Japanese Delegation. Geneva, 1932. [1] l.

——. The same. Communication from the Japanese Delegation. Incidents at

Shanghai. Substance of a telegram dated Tokio, March 8th from Mr. Yoshizawa, Minister for Foreign Affairs. Geneva, 1932. [1] 1.

——. Navy Dept. The Shanghai incident and the imperial Japanese navy. Tokyo, Navy Dept., 1932. cover-title, 2, 36 p.

JAPAN'S military aggression in Shanghai as seen by neutral observers; four reports by the Committee of Enquiry set up at Shanghai under article XV, paragraph 1, of the Covenant of the League of Nations. Nanking, Department of Intelligence and Publicity, Waichiaopu, 1933. 20 p. (China. Ministry of Foreign Affairs. Information Bull., 2 ).

JAPANESE CHAMBER OF COMMERCE, Los Angeles. The present situation in Manchuria and Shanghai. The reason why Japan decided to dispatch a portion of her army to Shanghai. Los Angeles, 1932. 30 p.

——. Shanghai. Aspects of anti-Japanese movements in China; situation after the conclusion of the agreement on the cessation of hostilities around Shanghai. Shanghai, Japanese Chamber of Commerce, 1932. cover-title, 28 p.

KEY, SARGENT, ed. Eighty-eight years of commercial progress ruined; Shanghai shelled and bombed; a collection of editorials and reports written by impartial foreign observers on the local war situation for leading American and British papers including ''The Shanghai evening post and mercury,'' ''The China press,'' ''North China daily news,'' etc.; compiled and edited by Sargent Key. Shanghai, 1932. ix, 162 p. plates.

LEAGUE OF NATIONS. Reports of the Committee of Enquiry set up at Shanghai under article 15, paragraph 1, of the Covenant. [Geneva] 1932. 10 p. (A. [Extr.] 3. 1932. VII ).

——. Correspondence and resolutions respecting events in Shanghai and neighbourhood, February-March 1932. [In continuation of ''Miscellaneous no. 4 (1932)'' ] London, H. M. Stationery Off., 1932. 15 p. ( [Gt. Brit. Foreign office] Miscellaneous no. 5 (1932) ).

——. Consular Committee to Report on Events at Shanghai. Reports to the League of Nations by the committee of representatives at Shanghai of certain states members of the League Council appointed to report on events in Shanghai and neighbourhood, Shanghai, February 6 and 12, 1932. London, H. M. Stationery Off., 1932. 10 p. ( [Gt. Brit. Foreign office] Miscellaneous no. 4 (1932) ).

——. Special Assembly, 1932- Cessation of hostilities in Shanghai and neighbourhood and withdrawal of Japanese forces. Resolution adopted by the Special Assembly of the League of Nations, Geneva, April 30, 1932. and Agreement concluded between the Chinese and Japanese representatives with the assistance of representatives of friendly powers, Shanghai, May 5, 1932. London, H. M. Stationery Off., 1932. 6 p. ( [Gt. Brit. Foreign office] China no. 1 (1932) ).

LOWE, CHUAN-HUA, 駱傳華, 1902- comp. Official documents relating to Japan's undeclared war in Shanghai. Shanghai, Chinese Chamber of Commerce, 1932. 77 p.

NATIONAL CRISIS SALVATION ASSOCIATION OF CHINA. Appeal from the Chinese Government. Communication from the Chinese Delegation. [Telegram, dated the 2nd of March] Geneva, 1932. [1] 1.

——. The same. [Telegram] Mar. 4, 1932. Geneva, 1932. [1] 1.

——. The same. [Telegram from the Hon. Mr. Wen Tsung-yao, 温宗堯, representing the National Crisis Salvation Association] Nov. 22, 1932. Geneva, 1932. [1] 1.

The PRESS UNION, Shanghai. The Shanghai incident. Shanghai, Press Union [1932] cover-title, 45 p.

——, Shanghai. The Shanghai incident misrepresented. Shanghai editors draw attention to incorrect reports in American newspapers. Shanghai, Union [1932] 10 p. illus. (facsim.).

SHANGHAI. Secretariat. Japanese invasion of Shanghai (January 28-March 7,

1932) A record of facts. Secretariat, City Government of Greater Shanghai.
[Shanghai? 1932] 11, [1] p.

SHINOBU, JUMPEI. International law in the Shanghai conflict. Tokyo, Maruzen,
1933. iv, vi, 267 p.

SYMPOSIUM on Japan's undeclared war in Shanghai. Contributors: Kwei Chung-
shu, 桂中樞, Y. S. Tsao, 曹雲祥, Stewart Yui, 余日宣, [and ten others]
Shanghai, Chinese Chamber of Commerce [1932] 207, [1], xv, [1] p. illus.,
plates, fold. map, facsim.

WONG, CHI-YUEN, 王志遠, ed. The Japanese invasion and China's defence; a
symposium edited by Wong Chi-yuen and T'ang Leang-li. Shanghai, Publicity department of the 19th Route Army; distributing agents: China United
Press [1932] 72 p. illus.(map) plates, ports.

WRIGHT, QUINCY, 1890-  Responsibility for losses in Shanghai.  (In American
journal of international law.  Concord, N. H.,  1932. v. 26, p. 586-590 ).

ZUMOTO, MOTOSADA, 1862-  Fightings around Shanghai.  Tokyo, Herald
Press, 1932. 39 p. 3 fold. maps. (Herald of Asia library of contemporary
history, 8 ).

### Japan's Invasion and the League of Nations
### Documents

CHINA. Appeal by the Chinese Government under article 11 of the Covenant.
Text[s] of cablegram[s] received by the Chinese Delegation, from Nanking.
Nos. 1-94, Sept. 21-Oct. 31, 1931.  Geneva, 1931. 94 pts. in 34.
——— . Appeal from the Chinese Government. Statement communicated by the
Chinese Delegation in conformity with article 15, paragraph 2, of the Cove-
nant of the League of Nations. [Geneva, 1931] 48 p. fold. map.
——— . Appeal from the Chinese Government under article 15 of the Covenant.
Statement communicated by the Chinese Delegation in conformity with article
15, paragraph 2. [Geneva] 1932. 48 p. fold. map. (League of Nations. Series
of publications. VII. Political. 1932. VII. 3 ).
——— . Document. no. 1-29.  Peiping [etc.] 1932-   29 nos. maps. Memoran-
da presented to the League of Nations.
——— . Assessor to the Commission of Enquiry into Sino-Japanese Dispute.
[Memoranda presented to the Lytton Commission] Doc. no. 1-29.  Peiping,
1932. 29 nos. maps.
——— . Memoranda submitted April-August 1932.  Nanking, Waichiaopu [1932]
xxxviii, 661 p. illus., col. maps.
——— . Memoranda presented to the Lytton Commission by V. K. Wellington Koo,
assessor. New York, Chinese Cultural Society [1932-33] 3 v.  maps.
——— . Delegation to the League of Nations. The Sino-Japanese dispute from
September 18, 1931 to February 22, 1932. Statement of the case with all the
relevant facts submitted by the Chinese delegation to the League Council in
conformity with article XV, paragraph 2 of the Covenant of the League of Nations. Nanking, Waichiaopu, The Intelligence and publicity department [1933]
69 p. fold. map. (China. Ministry of foreign affairs. Information Bull., 1 ).
——— . China's reply to Japan's observations on the Lytton report. Communication from the Chinese delegation to the members of the Council and of the
League. Nanking, Waichiaopu, The Intelligence and publicity department
[1933] [3]-50 p. (China. Ministry of foreign affairs. Information Bull., 4 ).
——— . Ministry of Foreign Affairs. Appeal from the Chinese Government. Preliminary statement [dated February 9th] forwarded by the Chinese representative in compliance with Article XV (paragraph 2) of the Covenant and with
the notes exchanged with the Secretary-General on the subject of this statement. Geneva, 1932. 5 1.

JAPAN. Appeal by the Chinese government. Observations of the Japanese government on the report of the Commission of enquiry. [Geneva, 1932] 40 p.

At head of title: [Communicated to the Council and the members of the League]
Official no.: C.775. M.366. 1932. VII. Geneva, November 19th, 1932.
League of nations.

———. Observations of the Japanese government on the Report of the Commission of enquiry, appointed by the resolution of December 10, 1931, of the Council of the League of Nations. [Tokyo] League of Nations Association of Japan, 1932. 63, [82] p.

———. Delegation to the League of Nations. Appeal from the Chinese government in virtue of article 15 of the Covenant. Explanatory note communicated by the Japanese government. [Geneva] 1932. 13 p. map.

———. The Manchurian question; Japan's case in the Sino-Japanese dispute as presented before the League of Nations. Geneva, Japanese delegation to the League of Nations, 1933. 167, [1] p.

———. Supplement to The Manchurian question; Japan's case in the Sino-Japanese dispute as presented before the League of Nations. Geneva, Japanese delegation to the League of nations, 1933. 19 p.

———. Japan's case as presented before the Special session of the Assembly of the League of nations. Geneva, Japanese delegation to the League of Nations, 1933. 47, [1] p.

———. Japan's case in the Sino-Japanese dispute as presented before the Special session of the Assembly of the League of nations. Geneva, Japanese delegation to the League of nations, 1933. 64 p.

———. Ministry of Foreign Affairs. Appeal of the Chinese Government under Article 11 of the Covenant. Communication from the Japanese Government, October 7th. Geneva, 1931. [1] l.

———. The same. Reply from the Japanese Government, dated October 9th, to the Chinese note of October 5th. Geneva, 1931. [1] l.

———. The same. Communication from the Japanese Government. Memorandum. Oct. 9. Geneva, 1931. 2 l.

———. The same. Communication by the Japanese Government. Reply to the telegram of the President of the Council dated October 9th. Geneva, 1931. 4 l.

———. The same. Official telegram received by the Japanese Delegation, Tokio, October 11th, 1931. Geneva, 1931. 4 l.

———. The same. [Note concerning certain facts mentioned in Marshal Chang Hsuehliang's circular telegram dated Nov. 9, 1931, handed by Japanese Minister in China to Chinese Foreign Office, Nov. 13, 1931. Paris, 1931] 4 l.

———. The same. Communication from the Japanese Delegation concerning the incidents at Tientsin. Protest made by [the] Japanese Minister in China, to the Minister of Foreign Affairs at Nanking. [Nov. 28, 1931] Paris, 1931. 2 l.

———. The same. Communication from the Japanese Delegation. Declaration made by the Japanese Government on December 27th, 1931. Geneva, 1931. 3 l.

———. Appeal from the Chinese Government. [Note] Feb. 23, 1932. Geneva, 1932. 6 l.

———. The present condition of China, with reference to circumstances affecting international relations and the good understanding between nations upon which peace depends. [n.p.] 1932. xi, 142 p. (Document A).

———. La situation actuelle en Chine, en tant qu'elle effecte les relations internationales et la bonne entente entre les nations, dont la paix dépend. [n.p., 1932] xii, [747] p. incl. tables. fold. map. (Document A).

———. Appeal from the Chinese Government. Communication from the Japanese Delegation. February 24th, 1933. Statement of the Japanese Government in virtue of paragraph 5 of article 15 of the Covenant of the League. Geneva, 1933. 16 l.

LEAGUE OF NATIONS. Appeal from the Chinese government in virtue of article 15 of the Covenant. Report of the Secretary-General on the action taken by the League on the Sino-Japanese dispute. [Geneva] 1932. 30 p. ( A. (Extr.)

**4.** 1932. VII ).

——. Commission of Enquiry into the Sino-Japanese Dispute. Preliminary report on conditions in Manchuria from the Commission of Enquiry appointed by the Council of the League of Nations. Mukden, April 30, 1932. London, H. M. Stationery Off., 1932. 6 p. ( [Gt. Brit. Foreign office] China no. 2 ).

——. Appeal by the Chinese Government. Report of the Commission of Enquiry signed by the members of the commission on September 4th, 1932, at Peiping. [Geneva, 1932] 148 p. (Series of League of Nations publications: VII. Political. 1932. VII. 12).

——. Report. [n. p.] 1932. 291, 16 p.

——. Appeal by the Chinese Government. Supplementary documents to the Report of the Commission of Enquiry. [Geneva, 1932] 280 p. fold. map. (Series of League of Nations publications: VII. Political. 1932. VII. 14 ).

——. Appel du gouvernement chinois. Rapport de la Commission d'étude. Genève, 1932. 160 p. (c663. M. 320. 1932, VI ).

——. Documents annexés au Rapport de la Commission d'étude. Genève, 1932. 300 p. (C663. M320. 1932, VII ).

——. The report of the Commission of Inquiry into the Sino-Japanese dispute. Tokyo, 1932. cover-title, 129 p. Reprinted from Japan Advertiser, Oct. 6, 1932.

——. The report of the Commission of Enquiry into the Sino-Japanese Dispute. [Tokyo?] League of Nations Assn. of Japan [1932] 245 p.; 307 p.

——. Der Lytton-Bericht; Bericht der Untersuchungskommission des Völkerbundes über den chinesisch-japanischen Streit in der Mandschurei mit Schlussbericht der Völkerbundversammlung vom 24. Februar 1933 und Anhängen; übersetzt nach den englischen Original. Mit einer Karte der Mandschurei. Leipzig, B. Tauchnitz, 1933. xv, 276 p. fold. map. (Urkunden und Forschungen zum internationalen Recht, hrsg. von Mitgliedern der Hamburgischen Juristen-Fakultät, 1 ).

——. Delegation from China. Appeal from the Chinese Government. Communication from the Chinese Government. Apr. 21, 1932. The puppet Government of Manchuria. Geneva, 1932. 12 (i. e. 13) 1.

——. The same. Communication from the Chinese Delegation. [Geneva, 1932] 34 p. (League of Nations. Series of publications. VII. Political 1932. VII. 16) Official no.: A(Extr.) A. 155. 1932. VII. "Chinese comments on the 'Observations of the Japanese Government on the report of the Commission of Enquiry' and on the statements made by the Japanese representative on the Council."-p. [5].

——. The same. Communication from the Chinese Delegation. Apr. 13, 1932. [Memorandum concerning measures taken by the Chinese Government in compliance with the Council resolutions of September 30 and December 10, 1931] Geneva, 1932. 13 1.

——. The same. Communication from the Chinese Delegation. 26th April. A memorandum on the Japanese occupation of Manchuria. Geneva, 1932. 21 1. Official no.: A(Extr.)106. 1932. VII. Legal recapitulation of the Chinese case, with summary of events. Supplements memorandum of April 21 (A. (Extr.) 105. 1932. VII).

——. Non-recognition of "Manchukuo." Letter dated May 1, 1934 [from the Chinese Delegation] Geneva, 1934. 2 p. Official no.: C. 188. M. 77. 1934. VII. Concerning measures proposed by the Assembly's Advisory Committee in circular letter (official no.: C. L. 117(a)1933. VII) with particular reference to narcotic drugs.

——. Appeal from the Chinese Government. Communication from the Chinese Delegation [Note, dated September 17th, addressed by the Chinese delegate to the President of the Extraordinary Assembly] Geneva, 1932. 3 1. Official no.: C. 654. M. 317. 1932. VII. [A. (Extr.)140. 1932. VII] Concerns legal aspect of Japanese recognition of Man-chu-kuo.

————. The same. Communication from the Chinese Delegation. Dec. 26th, 1932. Geneva, 1932. 16 1. Official no.: C. 859. M. 401. 1932. VII. Chinese comments on the Japanese delegate's memorandum of Nov. 28, 1932, and statements in the Special Assembly of Dec. 6 and 8, 1932.

————. Delegation from Japan. Japan's case as presented before the special session of the Assembly of the League of Nations. [Addresses delivered by Yosuke Matsuoka, chief Japanese delegate, before the ninth and fourteenth plenary meetings, December, 1932] Geneva, 1932. 47 p.

————. Japan's case in the Sino-Japanese dispute as presented before the Special session of the Assembly of the League of Nations. Geneva, 1933. 64 p.

————. The Manchurian question; Japan's case in the Sino-Japanese dispute as presented before the League of Nations. Geneva, 1933. 167 p.

————. Supplement to The Manchurian question; Japan's case in the Sino-Japanese dispute as presented before the League of Nations. Geneva, 1933. 19 p.

————. Secretariat. Information Section. Summary of the Report of the Commission of enquiry into the Sino-Japanese dispute. [Geneva, 1932] 15 p.

————. Übersicht über den Bericht der Studien-kommission für den chinesisch-japanischen Konflikt. Hrsg. von der Informationsabteilung des Völkerbundes, Genf. 1933. 24 p. (Genf. Sekretariat des Völkerbundes, 1933).

————. Special Assembly, 1932-33. Records of the Special session of the Assembly convened in virtue of Article 15 of the Covenant at the request of the Chinese Government. Geneva, 1932. 5 v. (Official Journal. Special Suppl. No. 101-102, 111-113).

————. Actes de la session extraordinaire de l'Assemblée convoquée en vertu de l'article 15 du Pacte sur la demande du gouvernement chinois. Genève, 1932. 5 v. (Journal Officiel. Supplement spécial. No. 101-102, 111-113 ).

————. Appeal of the Chinese government. Draft of the report provided for in article 15, paragraph 4, of the Covenant. (Submitted by the Special committee of the Assembly in execution of part III (paragraph 5) of the resolution of March 11th, 1932.) [Geneva] 1933. 27 p. (A. (Extr.) 22. 1933. VII).

————. The League's verdict on the Sino-Japanese dispute. Report on the Sino-Japanese dispute unanimously adopted by the Special Assembly of the League of nations on February 24, 1933, under article 15, paragraph 4, of the Covenant. Nanking, Waichiaopu, The Intelligence and Publicity Department [1933] [3]-50 p. ( [China. Ministry of foreign affairs] Information bulletin, 5.).

————. Assembly report on the Sino-Japanese dispute, adopted on February 24th, 1933. [Geneva, 1933] 22 p.

————. Sino-Japanese dispute; report adopted on February 24, 1933, by the Assembly of the League of Nations. Washington, Govt. Print. Off., 1933. 22 p. ( [U.S.] Dept. of state. [Publication, no. 449] ).

————. The verdict of the League; China and Japan in Manchuria; the official documents, with notes and an introduction by Manley O. Hudson. Boston, World Peace Foundation, 1933. 102, iv p. [World peace foundation publications].

————. Report of the League Assembly on the Manchurian dispute. Nanking, International Relations Committee [1933] iii, 88 p.

## General Works

BLAKESLEE, GEORGE HUBBARD, 1871-1954. The Lytton report, discussed by Dr. George H. Blakeslee [and] Nathaniel Peffer, November 5, 1932. New York luncheon discussion. New York, Foreign Policy Association [1932] 26 p. [Foreign policy association. Pamphlet, 86. Series 1932-33. December, 1932].

BRETSCHER, WILLY, 1897- Der chinesisch-japanische Konflikt vor dem Völkerbund-Die Genfer Ratstagung im Januar und Februar 1932 - die ausserordentliche Versammlung im März 1932, von W. Bretscher und Walther Weibel.

Zürich, SA. aus der Neuen Züricher Zeitung, 1932. 137 p.

[BUELL, RAYMOND LESLIE] 1896-1946. International action on the Lytton report. New York, Foreign Policy Association [1932] p. [207]-218. (Foreign policy reports. 8:18. November 9, 1932).

ESCARRA, JEAN, 1885-1955. Cours sténographié de m. le professeur Jean Escarra. La Société des nations et le conflit sino-japonais, jeudi 12 janvier 1933-[jeudi 23 février 1933. Paris, Centre européen de la Dotation Carnegie, 1933] 190 p. [Carniegie endowment for international peace. Division of intercourse and education. European center. Cours de 1932/33].

————. Jean Escarra: Le conflit sino-japonais et la Société des nations. Jean Ray: La position, l'œuvre et la politique du Japon en Mandchourie. Paris, Publications de la Conciliation internationale [1933] 3-278 p., fold. map. ( [Conciliation internationale] Bulletin n⁰ 3-4 - 1933 ).

The FAR EASTERN problem; official texts and summary of the Lytton report. New York, Carnegie Endowment for International Peace, Division of Intercourse and Education [1933] 91 p. (International conciliation, 286. January, 1933).

GENEVA RESEARCH CENTER. The League and Manchuria; the first-third phase of the Chinese-Japanese conflict, September 18 - December 31, 1931. Geneva, Geneva Research Information Committee, 1931. 34, 60, 91 p. (Geneva special studies, 2:10-12, October-December 1931).

————. The League and Shanghai; the fourth phase of the Chinese-Japanese conflict, January 1-April 30, 1932. Geneva, Geneva Research Center [1932] 104 p. (Geneva special studies, 3:5, May 1932).

————. The League and the Lytton report; the fifth phase of the Chinese-Japanese conflict (May 1-December 31, 1932) Geneva, Geneva Research Center [1932] 36 p. (Geneva special studies, 3:10, 1932).

————. The League and "Manchukuo"; the sixth phase of the Chinese-Japanese conflict, January 1, 1933-August 1, 1934. Geneva, Geneva Research Center [1934] 40 p. (Geneva special studies. 5:3, 1934).

HERALD OF ASIA. The Lytton report and Japanese reaction. Tokyo, Herald Press [1932?] cover-title, 22 p. (Its history of contemporary history, 10 ).

————. Le rapport Lytton et la réaction japonaise. Traduit de l'anglais. Tokyo, Herald Press, 1932. cover-title, 22 p. (Its Bibliothèque d'histoire contemporaine).

HSU, TUN-CHANG, 徐敦璋, 1905-  The League of nations and the Manchurian crisis. Peiping, 1931. cover-title, iii, 45 p. (China institute of international affairs. Studies on matters of current international interest, 1 ).

INTERNATIONAL ASSOCIATION OF JAPAN. Les conclusions logiques du rapport Lytton. [Genève] Association japonaise pour la Société des nations [1932?] 23, [1] p.

INTERNATIONAL RELATIONS COMMITTEE, Nanking. Public opinion towards the report of the League enquiry commission on Sino-Japanese dispute. Nanking, International Relations Committee [1932] vi, 105 p.

ISHII, KIKUJIRO, 1866-1945. The League of Nations and the Chinese problem. Tokyo, The League of Nations Association, 1932. 14 p.

JOHNSON, GRACE ALLEN (FITCH) "MRS. LEWIS JEROME JOHNSON," 1871- The case of China and Japan before the League of nations; a dramatization of the events of 1931-33, by Mrs. Lewis Jerome Johnson and Sir Herbert B. Ames, kt. [Boston? 1933] x, 50 p. front.(ports.) diagrs.

KOBAYASHI, JUNICHIRO. Le conflit sino-japonais et la Société des nations. The Sino-Japanese dispute and the League of Nations. Genève, Kundig, 1932.[1], 3-35, 3-35, [2] p.

KOO, VI KYUIN WELLINGTON,    顧維鈞 , 1888-  A statement of the views of the Chinese government on the report of the Commission of enquiry of the League of Nations. Geneva, Chinese Delegation to the League of Nations, 1932. 46 p.

——. Views of the Chinese government on the Lytton report. Statement by V.K. Wellington Koo, China's representative on the Council of the League of Nations. Nanking, Waichiaopu, The Intelligence and Publicity Department [1933] [3]-42 p. (China. Ministry of foreign affairs. Information Bull., 3 ).

LO, WÊN-KAN, 羅文幹 , 1888-1942. Appeal from the Chinese Government. Communication from the Chinese Delegation. [ Text of a speech on August 29th] Geneva, 1932. 7 l.

LYTTON, VICTOR ALEXANDER GEORGE ROBERT BULWER-LYTTON, 2nd earl of, 1876-1947. An address: [broadcast from Geneva, November 20,1932] concerning the work of the Commission of Inquiry sent to Manchuria by the League of Nations. New York, China Institute in America, 1932. 6 p.

——. The Lytton report and after. London, League of Nations Union, 1933. 79 p.

——. The League, the Far East and ourselves. The Ludwig Mond lecture in the University of Manchester, delivered on May 17, 1934, and published by the League of Nations Union with the permission of the University. London, League of Nations Union, 1934. 15, 1 p. front. (port.).

——. The Far Eastern problem and world peace. New York, Chinese Cultural Society, 1935. 14 p.

MARTIN, WILLIAM, 1888-1934. Le Japon contre la Société des nations. [Genève] Impr. du ''Journal de Genève,'' 1932. 158 p.

MATSUOKA, YOSUKE, 1880-1946. Japan's case in the Sino-Japanese dispute, as presented before the assembly of the League of Nations, at the final meeting on the subject. New York, Japanese Chamber of Commerce,Inc., 1933. 19 p.

SAITO, HIROSI, 1886-1939. Manchuria and the Lytton report: an address at the American Academy of Political and Social Science, Philadelphia, Nov. 28, 1932. [Washington] 1932. 12 p.

SOKOLSKY, GEORGE EPHRAIM, 1893-  The Lytton report; an address before the League of Nations Association at New York, October 13, 1932. New York, League of Nations Association [1932] [11] p.

[SUN, JUI-CHIN], 孫瑞芹, 1898-  ed. and tr. Welcome to the League of Nations inquiry commission. What leading Chinese papers in Peiping and Tientsin think of your mission and the Manchurian question. Peiping, 1932. 45 p.

——. comp. Chinese public opinion as reflected in leading North China newspapers concerning League Commission of Inquiry. Peiping, Northeastern Affairs Research Institute, 1932. 45 p.

TSURUMI, YUSUKE, 1885-  Le conflit sino-japonais. I.Japon et Société des nations. II.La question de Mandchourie. III. Le boycottage anti-japonais en Chine. Paris, Librairie du Recueil Sirey, 1932. 60 p.

TULLIÉ, A.R. La Mandchourie et le conflit sino-japonais devant la Société des nations. Paris, Librairie du Recueil Sirey, 1935. 379 p. fold. map, diagrs. Thèse-Univ. de Toulouse.

WEIBEL, WALTHER, 1882-  Völkerbundsversammlung: die Tagungen von 1932 und 1933. Zürich, Neue Züricher Zeitung, 1933. 350 p.

WILLOUGHBY, WESTEL WOODBURY, 1867-1945. The Sino-Japanese controversy and the League of Nations. Baltimore, Johns Hopkins Press, 1935. xxv, 733 p.

[YOSHIDA, ISABURO] 1878-  Notes et informations présentées par l'assesseur japonais à la commission d'étude de la société des nations. Tokio, 1932. 6 v. illus. (incl. map, facsims), tables (part fold.).

ZUMOTO, MOTOSADA, 1862-  Lytton commission on China and Manchuria. Tokyo, Herald Press, 1932. cover-title, ii, 19 p. (Herald of Asia library of contemporary history, 9 ).

——. Lytton report and Japanese reaction. Tokyo, Herald Press, 1932. cover-title, 22 p. (Herald of Asia library of contemporary history, 10 ).

Japan's Invasion, 1937
Documents

BRUSSELS. NINE-POWER CONFERENCE, 1937. The Conference of Brussels,
November 3-24, 1937, convened in virtue of article 7 of the Nine-power trea-
ty of Washington of 1922. Washington, Govt. Print. Off., 1938. iv, 82 p.
[U.S. Dept. of state. Publication 1232. Conference series 37 ]
———. Report of the Conference dated November 24th, 1937. Brussels, Printed
by A. Lesigne [1938?] 32 p.
CHINA. Delegation to the Nine-Power Conference, Brussels, 1937. Japanese
aggression and the Nine-Power Conference at Brussels. Brussels, Pub. by
the Press Bureau of the Chinese Delegation, Hotel Astoria [1937] 2 v.
———. Ministry of Information. Chronology of major events in Sino-Japanese
War. Chungking, 1943. cover-title, 14 p.
CHINA INFORMATION COMMITTEE. Japanese actions in contravention of the
Nine-power pact since the Mukden incident. Hankow, China Information Com-
mittee [1937?] cover-title, 58 p. illus.(maps).
———. Can China win? Hankow, Publ. by the China Information Committee
[Hong Kong, Printed by the South China Morning Post, ltd., 1938] 18 p.
———. Documentary evidence of Japan's national policy; authentic expositions of
Japan's imperialistic designs on the Asiatic continent and elsewhere her ten-
tacles can reach. Hankow, China Information Committee [1938?] cover-title,
72 p.
———. Japan's invasion engulfs China in horror and sorrow. The world has
known no greater historical tragedy than that now being wrought by Japan upon the 450,000,000 peaceful people of China and their cultural and economic
regeneration into a modern state. Hankow, China Information Committee
[1938] cover-title, 38 p. illus.
———. Japanese propaganda in the mirror of events. Hankow, China Informa
tion Committee [1938] cover-title, 14 p.
———. Japanese trample on foreign rights in China. Hankow, Publ. by the China Information Committee [Hong Kong, Printed by South China Morning Post,
1938] 16 p.
———. Air raids upon Chungking; Japan's policy of terrorism. Chungking, China Information Committee, 1939. 13 p.
———. China's spiritual mobilization; outline of the plan. Chungking, China In-
formation Committee, 1939. 18 p.
CHINA PUBLISHING COMPANY. China fights back. [Chungking, etc., The China Pub. Co., 1941?] 58, [2] p. illus.(incl. ports.).
GT. BRIT. Ministry of Information. The war in China. [London, 1945] 9 p.
JAPAN. Ministry of Foreign Affairs. Appeal of the Chinese Government. Japanese Government's reply to the invitation addressed to it by the Council. Tele-
gram, Tokyo, September 22nd, 1938. Geneva, 1938. [1] l. Official no.:
C:326.M.193.1938.VII.
LEAGUE OF NATIONS. Sino-Japanese conflict. Appeal by the Chinese government. Geneva, 1937. 59 p. (League of nations. Official journal. Special sup-
plement no. 177 ).
———. Assembly. Far East Advisory Committee. First[-Second] report of the
sub-committee of the Far East Advisory committee adopted by the Committee on October 5th, 1937. [Geneva] 1937. 2 v. (A.78.1937.VII; A.80.1937.
VII ).
———. Council. The League of Nations resolution and report on the Sino-Japan-
ese dispute adopted in September, 1938. [Geneva?] 1938. 3 p.; 4 p.
———. Delegation from China. Japanese aggression and world opinion, July 7 to
October 7, 1937. Geneva, Press Bureau of the Chinese Delegation [1937]
127 p.
———. ———. Japanese aggression and the League of Nations. 1937-39/40. Ge-

neva, Press Bureau of the Chinese Delegation [1937-40] 8 v.

——. ——. L'agression japonaise et la Société des Nations, 1937. Genève, Bureau de presse de la Délégation chinoise [1937] 2 v.

——. ——. Communication from the Chinese Delegation. Mar. 1, 1939. Geneva, 1939. 12 p. Official no.: C. 86. M. 46. 1939. VII. [Concerns Japanese bombings of open cities, also continues day-by-day account of the war.]

——. ——. The same. July 1st, 1939. [Some facts concerning the indiscriminate bombardment and killing of Chinese non-combatants and the destruction of non-military objectives by the Japanese forces, January-May, 1939] Geneva, 1939. 19 p. Official no.: C. 205. M. 133. 1939. VII.

——. Delegation from New Zealand. Sino-Japanese conflict: report on proceedings at the League of Nations and "Nine Power" Conference. [Wellington, E. V. Paul, Govt. Printer, 1938] 4 p.

U. S. Congress. House. Committee on Foreign Affairs. Requesting the President of the United States to furnish certain information to the House of Representatives relative to the conflict between Japan and China. Adverse report. [To accompany H. Res. 364] [Washington, Govt. Print. Off., 1937] 19 p. incl. tables. (75th Cong., 2d sess. House. Rept. 1651).

——. Dept. of State. American diplomacy in the Far East; official press releases of the U. S. Department of State on the Sino-Japanese situation during 1938-41, 1942-44, edited by K. C. Li, 李國欽 . New York, 1942, 1946. 2 v.

——. ——. Japan: 1931-41. Washington, Govt. Print. Off., 1943. 2 v. (Its Foreign relations of the United States: diplomatic papers).

——. Office of Strategic Services. Research and Analysis Branch. A decade of Japanese aggression. [Washington] 1941. 5 l. (Its R and A no. 109).

——. ——. Bombing objectives in Canton, China. Interview with Mr. L. K. Little, by Mr. R. D. Wolcott. [Washington] 1942. 2 l. (Its Interview no. 5 ).

## General Works

ACCOUNT of the Japanese atrocities at Nanking during the winter of 1937-38. With an introductory note by John LeRoy Christian. Washington, D. C., 1942. iii, 21 numb. l.

ALL-CHINA UNION OF NATIONAL LIBERATION ASSOCIATION. All-China Union fighting for national liberty and world peace. Paris, Asie-Asia-Shudian] 1937? cover-title, 37 p.

AMERICAN COMMITTEE FOR NON-PARTICIPATION IN JAPANESE AGGRESSION. America's share in Japan's war guilt. New York, American Committee for Non-Participation in Japanese Aggression [1938] 80 p.

[——.] Shall America stop arming Japan? [New York, 1940] 40 p. illus. (incl. maps) diagrs.

AMERICAN INFORMATION COMMITTEE, Shanghai. After three years of war in China. "Europe capitulates - China fights on for liberty, democracy, independence!" Shanghai, American Information Committee [1940] cover-title, 23 p. [Its Publications, 12].

AUXION DE RUFFÉ, REGINALD D', baron, 1875-  Chine et Japon 1938; les coulisses du drame. Avec, hors texte, 31 reproductions photographiques et 2 cartes. Paris, Éditions Berger-Levrault, 1939. xii, 421 p. front., plates, ports., 2 maps (1 col., fold.).

[BALET, JEAN CYPRIEN] 1867-  L'économie et les finances du Japon dans le conflit avec la Chine. [Paris, Société parisienne d'imprimerie, c1938] 37 p.

BOMBS on China. War letters from missionaries. London, Livingston Press, 1938. 30 p. (On the Spot booklet, 2).

BONCHON, HENRY. Le redoutable drame d'Extrême-Asie. Hanoi, G. Taupin et Cie, 1938. 63 p. (Éditions de la Volonté indochinoise, numéro spécial du 8 juillet, 1939).

BORREY, FRANCIS. L'aggression japonaise à la Chine. Paris, L. Rodstein,

1938. 39 p.

[BRATTER, HERBERT MAX] 1900-   The cases for Japan and China. Frank arguments for both sides. [Tokyo] The Foreign Affairs Association of Japan [1938] cover-title, 26 p.

BRUECHER, MAX. China und Japan; Gegensätze und Gemeinsames. Hrsg. vom Luftwaffenführungsstab IC/VIII. Leipzig, Schwartzhäupter-Verlag [1942?] 70 p.

BUSS, CLAUDE ALBERT, 1893-   War and diplomacy in eastern Asia. New York, Macmillan, 1941. xi, 570 p. fold. maps.

CANDELON, RENÉ. La politique aggressive du Japon en Chine depuis l'affaire de Formose (1874) jusqu'à nos jours. Hanoi, Impr. du Trung-Bac Tan-Van, 1938. vii, 91 p.

CANTON COMMITTEE FOR JUSTICE TO CHINA. The bombing of Canton, published by the Canton Committee for Justice to China. [Canton, 1938] [28] p. illus.(incl. map).

CHALLAYE, FÉLICIEN, 1875-   La Chine, le Japon et les puissances. Paris, Éditions Rieder, 1938. 95, [1] p. (Préoccupations de notre temps).

CHALUX, pseud. Autour du conflit sino-japonais. Bruxelles, Office de publicité, 1938. 241 p. illus.

CHAMBERLIN, WILLIAM HENRY, 1897-   Japan in China. London, Duckworth [1940] 143 p.

CH'EN CHENG, 陳誠, 1896-   A study of fundamental aspects of two years of China's war of resistance. Chungking, People's Foreign Relations Association of China, 1939. [2], 6 p. port.

CH'EN, LIN, 陳霖. China's fight for national liberation. New York, Workers Library Publishers, 1938. 62 p.

———. Chine héroïque; la lutte du peuple chinois contre l'aggresseur japonais par Tchen Lin. Paris, Bureau d'éditions, 1938. 87 p.

CHIANG, KAI-SHEK, 1886-   Generalissimo Chiang assails Konoye's statement. Chungking, China Information Committee, 1939. 16 p.

———. Generalissimo Chiang Kai-shek's message to the Japanese people, July 7, 1940. Chungking, China Information Committee, 1940. cover-title, 14 p.

[CHINA CAMPAIGN COMMITTEE, London] China. The world's oldest civilisation fighting against Japanese aggression. [London, Lawrence and Wishart, 1938?] 8 l. illus. (incl. ports.).

CHINA im Kampf für Sammelband über den imperialistischen Einfall Japans in China. Hrsg. unter der Redaktion von G. Friedrich und F. Lang. Strassbourg, Éditions Prométhée, 1937. 190 p.

CHINA WEEKLY REVIEW. Japan's war in China. Shanghai, China Weekly Review Press [1938-40] 5 v. maps (part fold.).

CHINA'S air raid experiences, a symposium by U Tun Hla Oung [and others] [Calcutta] Calcutta Office, Chinese Ministry of Information, 1942. cover-title, 23 p. (Pamphlet, 2).

CHINESE CONSOLIDATED BENEVOLENT ASSOCIATION, Los Angeles. True facts of Japanese aggression in China. Los Angeles, Chinese Consolidated Benevolent Association, 1937. 16 p.

———. Rhode Island. The Sino-Japanese undeclared war. Providence, R.I., the Association, 1938. cover-title, 15 p.

———. San Francisco. Japan in China, a symposium of authoritative statements and world opinion. Editor: Victor K. Kwong, 鄺兆榮. San Francisco, the Association, 1937. cover-title, 3-34 p. illus. (incl. ports., map).

———. ———. Analyses of the Sino-Japanese conflict, edited by Churchill T. Chiu, 趙九疇. San Francisco, the Association, 1938. cover-title, 3-31 p. illus.

CHINESE INSTITUTE OF INTERNATIONAL RELATIONS, Shanghai. Communication from the Chinese Delegation. [Telegraphic message to the Assembly from Dr. W.W. Yen, President of the Chinese Institute of International Relations] Geneva, 1937. [1] p.

CHOW, S.R., 周鯁生, 1889-  China's relations with Japan since 1931, by S.R. Chow and P.C.Kuo, 郭斌佳. Kowloon, China Institute of Pacific Relations, 1939. 48 1.

CHRÉTIEN, MAXIME. La "guerre totale" du Japon en Chine. Paris, A. Pedone, 1939. iv, 75 p.

CLAVERY, ÉDOUARD, 1867-  L'anarchie en Chine et le rôle du Japon. Paris, Presses modernes, 1938. 100 p.

CROW, CARL, 1883-1945. I speak for the Chinese. New York and London, Harper, 1937. viii, 84 p.

DIFFENDORFER, RALPH EUGENE, 1879-  China and Japan? New York, The Methodist Book Concern [c1938] 59 p. diagrs.

DOUGLAS, HENRY HULBERT. Japan's record. [n.p., 1940?] 16 numb. 1.

EAGLETON, CLYDE, 1891-  The Far Eastern crisis. Dallas, Tex., Southern Methodist University, 1938. 34 p. (Arnold foundation studies in public affairs. 7:2. Autumn, 1938).

ESCARRA, JEAN, 1885-1955. L'honorable paix japonaise. Paris, B. Grasset [1938] 238 p.

————. Réflexions sur la politique du Japon à l'égard de la Chine et sur quelques aspects juridiques du conflit actuel. [Perpignan? 1938?] cover-title, 27 p.

FARRÈRE, CLAUDE, 1876-  Le grand drame de l'Asie. Paris, Flammarion [1938] 197 p.

FEDERATION OF CHINESE CULTURAL ASSOCIATIONS. The Sino-Japanese conflict; a chronicle of important events from Sept. 18, 1931 to Sept. 18, 1937. Shanghai, Federation of Chinese Cultural Association [1938?] 19 p. illus. (maps).

————. Overseas Chinese rally to aid of fatherland. Shanghai, Federation of Chinese Cultural Associations, 1938. 9 p.

La FERMETURE aux navires chinois des ports chinois. Genève, Bureau du Japon pour les conférences internationales, 1937. 15 p.

FIELD, FREDERICK VANDERBILT, 1905-  China's capacity for resistance. New York [etc.] American Council, Institute of Pacific Relations [c1937] 20 p.

FOREIGN AFFAIRS ASSOCIATION OF JAPAN. How the North China affair arose. [Tokyo, H. Toyoshima, Foreign Affairs Association of Japan, 1937] cover-title, 52 p. illus., plates, maps (part fold.).

————. The Sino-Japanese conflict: a short survey. [Tokyo, H.Toyoshima, Foreign Affairs Association of Japan, 1937] cover-title, 10 p. plates.

[————.] The Sino-Japanese conflict and financial resources, a symposium. [Tokyo, 1937] 37 p. diagrs.

FRY, VARIAN. War in China; America's role in the Far East; with maps and charts by Henry Adams Grant. [New York] Foreign Policy Association [c1938] 95, [1] p. illus. (maps) diagrs. (Headline books, 13).

GOETTE, JOHN ANDREW, 1896-  Japan fights for Asia. New York, Harcourt, Brace [1943] 3-248 p.

————. The same. London, MacDonald [1945] v, 7-190 p.

GREEN, OWEN MORTIMER. China's struggle with the dictators; foreword by H.E. the Chinese ambassador. London and Melbourne, Hutchinson [1942] 283 p. plates, ports.

HANNICH, GUSTAV. Krieg und Flüchtlingsnot in China. Stuttgart, Basel, Evang. Missionsverlag, 1939. 16 p. (Mission und Gemeinde, 52 ).

HARCOURT-SMITH, SIMON. Japanese frenzy. London, H.Hamilton [1942] ix, [1], 217, [1] p. fold. map.

————. Fire in the Pacific. New York, A.A.Knopf, 1942. xv, 236 p. fold. map.

HSÜ, SHIH-YING, 許世英, 1872-  Sino-Japanese relation in prospect. Hankow, Chinese League of Nations Union [1938] cover-title, 6 p. (Special publication series, 12 ).

HSÜ, SHU-HSI, 徐淑希, 1892-  The North China problem. Shanghai [etc.] Kelly and Walsh, 1937. 112 p. ([Council of international affairs] Political and economic studies, 1).

————. How the Far Eastern war was begun. Shanghai [etc.] Kelly and Walsh, 1938. 97 p. ( [Council of international affairs, Hankow] Political and economic studies, 2 ).

————. The war conduct of the Japanese. Shanghai [etc.] Kelly and Walsh, 1938. 217 p. ( [Council of international affairs, Hankow] Political and economic studies, 3 ).

————. Three weeks of Canton bombings. Shanghai [etc.] Kelly and Walsh, 1939. ( [Council of international affairs] Political and economic studies, 5 ).

————. comp. A digest of Japanese war conduct. Shanghai [etc.] Kelly and Walsh, 1939. 102 p. ( [Council of international affairs] Political and economic studies, 6 ).

————. ed. Documents of the Nanking safety zone. Shanghai [etc.] Kelly and Walsh, 1939. 167, [1] p. ( [Council of international affairs] Political and economic studies, 7 ).

————. Japan and the third powers. Shanghai [etc.] Kelly and Walsh, 1941. 4 v. ( [Council of international affairs] Political and economic studies, 10-13 ).

————. comp. A new digest of Japanese war conduct. Shanghai [etc.] Kelly and Walsh, 1941. xii, 273 p. ( [Council of international affairs] Political and economic studies, 15 ).

————. Whither Japan. Shanghai [etc.] Kelly and Walsh, 1941-    2 v. ( [Council of international affairs] Political and economic studies, 16 ).

HU, SHIH, 胡適, 1891-  The issues behind the Far Eastern conflict. ''An address delivered before Foreign Policy Association, New York, November 13, 1937.'' [New York, China Institute in America, 1937] 8 p.

————. China, too, is fighting to defend a way of life, an address delivered at Washington, D.C., March 23, 1942. [San Francisco, Grabhorn Press, 1942] 17, [1] p.

————. China's place in the present world struggle. A Howard Crawley memorial lecture delivered before the faculty and students, Wharton school of finance and commerce, University of Pennsylvania, April 20, 1942. Philadelphia, University of Pennsylvania Press, 1942. 14 p.

INAHARA, KATSUJI. Japan's continental policy. [Tokyo, Foreign Affairs Association of Japan, 1938] 51, [1] p.

INUI, KIYO SUE. The United States and Japan in Asia, address delivered at Commonwealth Club of California April 26, 1940. San Francisco, Japanese Chamber of Commerce [1940] 17 p.

JAP beast and his plot to rape the world, uncensored photos. [Louisville, Ky., C.T. Dearing Printing Co., 1942] cover-title, 3-66 p. illus. (incl. ports., maps).

JAPAN FOREIGN TRADE FEDERATION. Official view of the Sino-Japanese conflict. [Tokyo] Japan Foreign Trade Federation [ 1937?] 25 p.

JAPAN in East Asia. [Bristol] Printed for private distribution [by Western Printing Services, 1939] 152 p.

THE JAPAN TIMES AND MAIL. The truth behind the Sino-Japanese crisis. Japan acts to keep Eastern civilization safe for the world. Tokyo, The Japan Times and Mail, 1937. 104 p. 1 illus., plates, ports., map.

JAPANESE ASSOCIATION OF AMERICA, San Francisco. What is Japan fighting for? The truth about the Sino-Japanese conflict. [San Francisco, 1937?] cover-title, 8 p.

JAPANESE CHAMBER OF COMMERCE, New York. The Sino-Japanese crisis, 1937; first comprehensive, authentic, factual statement, with official American and Japanese documents. New York, Japanese Chamber of Commerce of New York [1937] cover-title, 91, [1] p.

————. Seattle. The undeclared Sino-Japanese war: questions and answers. What does Japan want in China? What of Japan's overpopulation? Will communism save China? Why was Manchukuo born? Who are the most misruled people on earth? etc. Seattle, Japanese Chamber of Commerce and Japanese Association of North America, 1937. 13 p.

JEN, TAI, 任泰, 1904-  comp. Documents illustrative of Japan's national policy. Nanking, Council of International Affairs, 1937. 62 p.

JOHNSEN, JULIA EMILY, comp. Chinese-Japanese war, 1937-   New York, H. W. Wilson, 1938. 257 p. (The reference shelf. 11:9).

JONES, ELI STANLEY, 1884-  An open letter to the people of Japan.  Nanking, Reprinted by the Chinese League of Nations Union [1937] 12 p. (Chinese League of Nations Union, Sino-Japanese issue series, 3 ).

KANAI, KIYOSHI. A few thoughts and facts on the Sino-Japanese conflict of 1937-38, by "Tiger" Kiyoshi Kanai. Shanghai [South Pasadena, Calif., Perkins Oriental Books] 1938. 16 p.

KAWAI, TATSUO, 1889-  The goal of Japanese expansion. Tokyo, Hokuseido Press, 1938. viii, 9-120 p. front.(port.) fold. map.

KAWAKAMI, KIYOSHI KARL, 1875-  Japan in China, her motives and aims, with introductory notes by the Right Hon. Sir John Tilley and Captain the Right Hon. Lord Sempill and a foreword by Viscount Ishii. London, J. Murray [1938] xix, 188 p. illus. (map).

———. Le Japon en Chine, ses mobiles et ses buts.  Paris, B. Grasset [1938] [7]-296 p.

KING, WENSZ, 金問泗, 1892-  Development of the crisis in the Far East in the last six years brought about by continuous Japanese aggressions against China.  Brussels, The Press Bureau of the Chinese delegation, 1937. 44 p. tables.

KUNMING. NATIONAL SOUTHWEST ASSOCIATED UNIVERSITY. Library. Japan's aggression and public opinion, compiled and published by the National Southwest Associated University Library, Kunming. [Kunming, 1938] vii, 498 p. tables.

KUO MIN TANG. La presse chinoise en le conflit sino-japonais, 1937. Japanese aggression and Chinese opinion. Par le Bureau du Kouomintang en Europe (Paris) Paris, Éditions A. Pedone, 1938. 156 p.

KYOTO. BUSINESS MEN OF KYOTO. The Sino-Japanese conflict. Kyoto, Business men of Kyoto [1937] 24 p. illus.

LAVES, WALTER HERMAN CARL, 1902-  A radio discussion of crisis in the Orient by Walter Laves, Clifton Utley and Quincy Wright.   Chicago, 1939. 28 p. (University of Chicago. Round table, 69 ).

LIANG, HUBERT S., 梁士純, 1903-  China fights; a collection of timely and outspoken articles dealing with the Sino-Japanese struggle. Shanghai, China Weekly Review [1938?] 59 p.

LIANG, LONE, 梁龍, 1894-  China muss· siegen, drei Vorträge. Mit einer Kundgebung des Generalissimus Tschiang Kaischek und Geleitworten von Sun Fo, Quo Tai-chi [und] Tsien-Tai. [Prag, H. Mercy Sohn, 1938?] 115 p. map.

———. Warum China kämpft; sechs Vörtrage. Prag, H. Mercy Sohn, 1938. 11 p. map.

———. La guerre d'idéologie en Extrême-Orient (cinq conférences faites en 1940) Lisbonne [Composta e impresso na "Gráfica lisbonense"] 1942. 219 p.

LIN, MOUSHÊNG, 林傪聖, 1906-  American press opinion on the Sino-Japanese conflict.  New York, Chinese Cultural Society [ 1937] 36 p.

———. International law and the undeclared war.  New York, Chinese Cultural Society [1937] 23 p.

———. ed. Facts and figures concerning the Far Eastern situation.  New York, China Institute in America [1940] 47 p. illus.(map).

LIN, TSIU-SEN, 林秋生. China und Japan im Spiegel der Geschichte.  Erlenbach-Zürich, E. Rentsch [1944-46] 2 v. maps (2 fold.) geneal. tables.(Schriften des chinesischen kulturdienstes).

LIN, YU-T'ANG, 林語堂, 1895-  The birth of a new China, a personal story of the Sino-Japanese war. New York, John Day [c1939] [xviii]-xix, 349-421 p.

MA, CHIH-CHÊN, 馬志振. Controverses et conventions internationales au regard de la guerre sino-japonaise. Paris, Recueil Sirey, 1941. 218 p. Thèse-Univ. de Paris.

MacNAIR, HARLEY FARNSWORTH, 1891-1947. The real conflict between China and Japan; an analysis of opposing ideologies. Chicago, University of Chicago Press [1938] xvi, 215, [1] p.

MAO, TSE-TUNG, 毛澤東, 1893-  Aspects of China's anti-Japanese struggle. Bombay, People's Pub. House, 1948. 80 p.

――――. On the tactics of fighting Japanese imperialism. Peking, Foreign Languages Press, 1953. 47 p.

――――. Strategic problems in the anti-Japanese guerrilla war. Peking, Foreign Languages Press, 1954. 65 p. illus.

――――. Questions of tactics in the present anti-Japanese united front. On Policy. Peking, Foreign Languages Press, 1954. 36 p.

――――. The policies, measures and perspectives of combating Japanese invasion. Peking, Foreign Languages Press, 1954. 14 p.

――――. Economic and financial problems during the anti-Japanese war and other articles. Peking, Foreign Languages Press, 1955. 64 p. front.(port.).

――――. The situation and tasks in the anti-Japanese war after the fall of Shanghai and Taiyuan. Peking, Foreign Languages Press, 1956. 25 p.

MIKI, KIYOSHI, 1897-1945. Introductory studies on the Sino-Japanese conflict, by Kiyoshi Miki and Karoku Hosokawa. Tokyo, Japanese Council, Institute of Pacific Relations, 1941. xiv, 104 p. ("Far Eastern conflict" series [I] ).

MOSSDORF, OTTO, 1882-  Der Krieg in Ostasien. Bd. 1. Der chinesisch-japanische Konflikt. 3. und weitere Aufl. von "Der Krieg in Fernost." Leipzig, W. Conrad [1943, c1941] 298 p. maps.

MUKHERJEE, HIREN. China calling. Calcutta, Anti-Fascist People's Union, 1942. viii, 90 p. photo, map.

NEHRU, JAWAHARLAL, 1889-  China, Spain and the war: essays and writings. Allahabad, Kitabistan, 1940. 269 p. front. photos.

NOËL, PERCY. When Japan fights. [Tokyo] The Hokuseido Press, 1937. x,249 p.

OLIVER, FRANK. Special undeclared war. With an introduction by Peter Fleming. London, J. Cape [1939] 368 p. front., plates, ports., fold. maps.

OSAKA. CHAMBER OF COMMERCE AND INDUSTRY. Bushido and Chinese military leaders, differences in racial traits between Japanese and Chinese manifested in China emergency. [Osaka] The Investigation committee on Chinese affairs of the Osaka Chamber of Commerce and Industry, 1938. cover-title, 26 p. illus.

――――. Japan's righteous course; right will prevail in the end. [Osaka] The Investigation committee on Chinese affairs of the Osaka Chamber of Commerce and Industry, 1938. cover-title, 11, [1] p. plates.

P'AN, STEPHEN CHAO-YING, 潘朝英, 1908-  China fights on, an inside story of China's long struggle against our common enemies. New York, London [etc.] Fleming H. Revell [1945] 188 p. front., plates, ports.

PRATT, SIR JOHN THOMAS, 1876-  China and Japan. [London] Pub. for the Historical Association by P.S. King, 1944. cover-title, 30 p. (Historical association pamphlet, 129 ).

The PULSE of Japan; that ideals and aims behind Japanese action in east Asia may be better perceived. Tokyo, Tokyo Information Bureau [1938?] 133 p. plates.

QUIGLEY, HAROLD SCOTT, 1889-  Far Eastern war, 1937-41. Boston, World Peace Foundation, 1942. xi, 369 p. 2 fold. maps.

RAYNAUD, JEAN. Le Maréchal Tchang Kaï-chek devant le Prince Konoye; conférence donnée au Théâtre des Ambassadeurs, le 2 décembre, 1938. Dinard, Braun et Liorit, 1939. 32 p.

————. Guerre en Asie. Dinard, Braun et Liorit [1939] 256 p.

RUBINOW, EDWARD SAUL, 1914-   Sino-Japanese warfare and the League of nations. [Geneva, Geneva Research Centre, 1938] cover-title, 93 p. (Geneva studies, 9:3, May, 1938 ).

SCHLESINGER, RUDOLF, 1901-   Ein Volk kämpft für seine Freiheit. Ursachen, Verlauf und Aussichten des Krieges in China. Prag, A. Werner, 1939. 204 p. map.

SCIZE, PIERRE, Le conflit sino-japonais; conférence faité par Pierre Scize à son retour de Chine. Paris, Agence Chekiai, 1938. 15 p.

SEKINE, GUMPEI, 1886-   The open door under new order. [Tokyo] To-a Kensetsu Kyokai [1939] cover-title, iii, 53 p.

SHEPHERD, CHARLES REGINALD, 1885-   The case against Japan; a concise survey of the historical antecedents of the present far eastern imbroglio. New York, D. Ryerson; London, Jarrold [c1938] viii, 242 p.

SIEN, FOON. comp. Three years' resistance; a comprehensive review of events in the Sino-Japanese war. [Vancouver, 1940] 26 p. illus.

SIMON, PAUL. Les atrocités japonaises en Chine? Vervièrs, Leens, 1938. 16 p. (Faits et nouvelles d'Extrême-Orient).

————. Bombardement aériens. Vervièrs, Leens, 1938. 16 p. illus. (Faits et nouvelles d'Extrême-Orient).

————. Le démembrement de la Chine: Condition de paix. Vervièrs, Leens, 1938. 8 p. (Faits et nouvelles d'Extrême-Orient).

————. La guerre en Extrême-Orient. Réponse à Mgr. Paul Yu-pin. Vervièrs, Leens, 1938. 64 p. illus.

————. Pourquoi la guerre de Chine se prolonge-t-elle? Fays-Polleur, 1940. 11 p.

SIU, KING-YUAN, 徐鏡遠 , [Hsü Ching-yüan] 1905-   Le règlement des différends internationaux et le conflit sino-japonais. Louvain, Belgique, R. Fonteyn, 1934. vii, 351 p. [Bibliothèque de l'École des sciences politiques et sociales de l'Université de Louvain].

SNOW, HELEN (FOSTER), 1907-   China resists. Calcutta, Modern Publishers, 1944. vi, 178 p.

SOUTH MANCHURIA RAILWAY COMPANY. China incident and Japan. [Tokyo, Printed at the Herald Press, 1937] cover-title, 43 p. (China incident series-No. 3 ).

SUMA, YAKICHIRO, 1892-   Where Japan stands; addresses delivered in America on the Sino-Japanese conflict. Tokyo, Hokuseido Press, 1940. vii, 237 p. front. (port.).

TAI, ERH-CHING, 戴爾卿. British opinion of the Sino-Japanese war, 1937-41. London, 1952. iv, 240 p. Thesis-London School of Economics.

TAKAISHI, SHINGORO, 1878-   Japan speaks out. [Tokyo] Hokuseido Press [1938] viii, 173 p. front., port.

[TAMAI, KATSUNORI]. Barley and soldiers, by Ashihei Hino [pseud.] Translated by K. and L:W: Bush. Tokyo, Kenkyusha, 1939; Rev. ed. 1941. ii, 207 p. map.

[————.] Mud and soldiers, by Ashihei Hino [pseud.] Translated by Lewis Bush. Tokyo, Kenkyusha, 1939. iii, 160 p.

[————.] Wheat and soldiers, by Corporal Ashihei Hino [pseud.] translated by Baroness Shidzué Ishimoto. New York [etc.] Farrar and Rinehart [c1939] xii, 191 p.

[————.] Weizen und Soldaten, Kriegbriefe, Aufzeichnungen und Tagebücher eines japanischen Unteroffiziers von Ashihei Hino. Aus dem Japanischen von A. von Choinatzky und Teisuke Kosima. Stuttgart, Cotta, 1940. [11]-494 p. fold. map.

[————.] War and soldier, by Ashihei Hino [pseud.] translated from the Japanese by Lewis Bush. London, Putnam [1940] vi, 3-579 p. illus. (maps).

[————.] Flower and soldiers, by Ashihei Hino [pseud.] Translated by Lewis

Bush. Tokyo, Kenkyusha [1940] ii, 213 p.

——. ] Sea and soldiers, by Ashihei Hino [pseud.] Translated by Lewis Bush. Tokyo, Kenkyusha [1940] 172 p. Third edition.

TANIGUCHI, MASARU. The soldiers log: 10,000 miles of battle, translated by R. Toombs Fincher and Yoshi Okada. [Tokyo] The Hokuseido Press [1940] xi, 176 p. front.(port.).

TCHENG, KIA-KAN, 陳家幹, [Ch'en Chia-kan] Le conflit sino-japonais et l'équilibre des puissances en Extrême-Orient. Dijon, Impr. Bernigaud et Privat, 1938. 190 p. Thèse-Univ. de Dijon.

THOMAS, ANDREW FRANK, 1896-  Sino-Japanese conflict: What history says. [Tokyo, 1939] 98 p.

THORMAGNE, WERNER. La bataille pour l'Asie; l'heure du Japon. Neuchâtel et Paris, V. Attinger, 1939. vi, 275 p. incl. table, illus.(map).

TIMPERLEY, HAROLD JOHN, 1898-  ed. What war means: the Japanese terror in China; a documentary record. London, V. Gollancz, 1938. 288 p. illus.(plan).

——. ed. Japanese terror in China. New York, Modern Age Books [c1938] 220 p. illus.(map).

——. ed. The same. Calcutta, Thacker, Spink [c1938] 222 p. illus. (map).

——. ed. La guerre telle qu'elle est: la terreur japonaise en Chine; compte rendu documentaire. Paris, A. Pedone, 1939. 278, [2] p. illus. (map).

TWINEM, MARY (FINE). A message to the West from a former westerner [by] (Mrs. Paul D.) Mary Fine Twinem. Nanking, Chinese League of Nations Union, 1937. 5 p. (Chinese League of Nations Union. Sino-Japanese issue ser. 2 ).

UTLEY, FREDA, 1898-  Japan can be stopped! by Freda Utley and David Wills. London, The "News Chronicle" publications department [1937] 63, [1] p.

——. On peut arrêter le Japon! par Freda Utley et David Wills. Traduction de l'anglais et publié en français par le Bureau de presse de la Délégation chinoise, Genève. Bruxelles, M. Weissenbruch, 1937. 64 p. tables. (China. Delegation to the League of Nations. Press Bureau publications, 6 ).

——. Japan's feet of clay. New York, W.W. Norton [1937] 393 p. incl.tables.

——. Japan's gamble in China. [London] Secker and Warburg, 1938. x, 302 p. map.

VIATTE, AUGUSTE. La Chine, le Japon et la justice internationale. Paris, Les Éditions du Cerf, 1938. iv, 49 p.

WALSH, TOM. The Sino-Japanese conflict. Sydney and London, Angus and Robertson, 1939. 111, [1] p.

WANG, CHÊNG-T'ING T., 王正廷, 1882-  Japan's aggressions upon China. Address at the Armistice eve banquet of the International good-will congress, November 10, 1937, Boston, Massachusetts. [Boston? 1937] 6 numb. l.

——. Selected statements and addresses concerning the Sino-Japanese conflict. [n.p.] 1938. cover-title, 12 p.

WANG, CHING-CH'UN, 王景春 1883-  Japan's continental adventure, with an introduction by the Right Hon. Viscount Cecil of Chelwood, P.C. London, G.Allen and Unwin [1941] [9]-224 p.

WANG, MING, 王明, 1907-  China can win; The new stage in the aggression of Japanese imperialism and the new period in the struggle of the Chinese people. New York, Workers Library Publishers, 1937. 47 p. illus. map.

——. Pour comprendre l'agression du Japon contre la Chine, par Van Min. Paris, Bureau d'éditions, 1937. 61, [1] p.

——. Old intrigues in new clothing, by Chen Shao-yu (Wang Ming) On the development, the difficulties and the future of the national anti-Japanese united front, by Chin Po-ku, 秦博古. [Hongkong, 1939] cover-title, 31 [1] p. (Bulletin, New China information committee, 7 ).

WEI, HENRY, 韋文起, 1909-  The Sino-Japanese hostilities and international law. [Chicago, University of Chicago libraries, Dept. of photographic reproduction,

1945] Film copy of type-written manuscript. Collation of the original: 8, 220-241, 245-253 numb. l.

WILLIAMS, FREDERICK VINCENT. Behind the news in China. New York, Nelson Hughes [1938] vii, 122 p.

WILLOUGHBY, WESTEL WOODBURY, 1867-1945. Japan's case examined, with supplementary chapters on the Far Eastern policies of the United States, and the significance to the world of the conflict in the Far East. Baltimore, Johns Hopkins Press, 1940. x, 237 p.

WRIGHT, QUINCY, 1890- The existing legal situation as it relates to the conflict in the Far East. New York, International Secretariat, Institute of Pacific Relations, 1939. vii, [1], 3-129 p. (I. P. R. Inquiry series).

————. Legal problems in the Far Eastern conflict. Part I. The legal background in the Far East, by Quincy Wright. Part II. The problem of non-recognition, by H. Lauterpacht, Edwin M. Borchard and Phoebe Morrison. New York, International Secretariat, Institute of Pacific Relations, 1941. xi, 211 p. (I. P. R. inquiry series).

YAMAMOTO, S. Le point de vue catholique sur la conflit sino-japonais. Tokyo, 1937. 16 p.

YAMATO, TAKIO. Considération sur le conflit sino-japonais. Point de vue d'un Japonais. Bruxelles, Impr. Van Buggenhoudt, 1938. 58 p. map.

YOUNG, ARTHUR A. ed. China faces Japan. New York, Chinese Students' Christian Association in North America, 1937. 80 p. illus.

YOUNG, ARTHUR MORGAN, 1874- Japan's war on China. [London, Fact, 1937] cover-title, [3]-97, [1] p. illus.(maps) (Fact, a monograph a month, 9 ).

YOUNG, C. KUANGSON, 楊光姓 , 1900-42. ed. The Sino-Japanese conflict and the League of nations, 1937; speeches, documents, press comments. Geneva, Press bureau of the Chinese delegation [1937] 250 p.

YOUNG, STONELAKE Y. P., 楊陸溥, 1898- A few vital data concerning the economic aspects of the Sino-Japanese conflict. Geneva, Chinese delegation to the League of Nations, 1937. 39 p. tables.

YÜ, PIN, bp., 于斌, 1901- La guerre en Extrême-Orient. Un problème psychique international; appel aux hommes de bonne foi, aux hommes de bonne volonté, par mgr. Paul Yu-Pin. Bruxelles, Éditions de la Cité chrétienne, 1937. 36 p.

————. The war in the Far East, by Paul Yu-pin. Oxford, Catholic Social Guild, 1938. 32 p.


## Japan's Attack on Shanghai, 1937

AUXION DE RUFFÉ, REGINALD D', baron, 1875- La bataille de Shanghaï. Les mauvais bergers. Avec, en hors texte, le fac-similé d'une étiquette d'emballage d'un paquet d'opium et, dans le texte, une carte des concessions internationales. Paris, Berger-Levrault, 1938. vii, [1], 258 p. illus.(map) facsim.

BRUCE, GEORGE C. Shanghai's undeclared war. [An illustrated factual recording of the Shanghai hostilities, 1937] Shanghai, Mercury Press [1937] 88 p., 116 p. of illus.

FOREIGN AFFAIRS ASSOCIATION OF JAPAN. Japan's case in the Shanghai hostilities. [Tokyo] Foreign Affairs Association of Japan [1937] cover-title, 13, [1] p.

————. Why Japan had to fight in Shanghai. [Tokyo, Hiromu Toyoshima, Foreign Affairs Association of Japan, 1937] 54 p. plates (1 fold.) maps (2 fold.).

————. Why the fighting in Shanghai. [Tokyo, H. Toyoshima, Foreign Affairs Association of Japan, 1937] 54 p. plates (1 fold.) maps (2 fold).

HSÜ, SHU-HSI, 1892- Japan and Shanghai. Shanghai, Kelly and Walsh, 1938. 104 p. ( [Council of international affairs] Political and economic studies, 4).

JAPANESE CHAMBER OF COMMERCE, Los Angeles. Japan's position in the

Shanghai and North China hostilities; issued by the Japanese chamber of commerce of Los Angeles to present true facts concerning the present Orient conflict. Los Angeles, 1937. 21, [2] p.

[POLLEY, CLAD ELMER] ed. U.S.S.Augusta under fire; Sino-Japanese incident, 1937-38, Shanghai, China. [Shanghai, North China Daily News, 1938] 136 p. illus.(incl. ports.).

SHANGHAI CITIZEN'S LEAGUE. Shanghai's refugee problem. Shanghai, Shanghai Citizen's League [1937?] cover-title, 15 p. incl. plates.

WOODHEAD, HENRY GEORGE WANDESFORDE, 1883-   My experiences in the Japanese occupation of Shanghai. London, China Society, 1943. 17 p. (China Society occasional papers, n.s., 4).

## Japan's Puppet Governments

CENTRAL China in motion. Asiatic echoes, ed. by F.E. Firminger. [Tokyo, F.E.Firminger, 1939?] cover-title, iii, 70 p. plates, ports.

CHIANG, KAI-SHEK, 1886-   Generalissimo Chiang's statements following the publication of Wang Ching-wei's secret agreement with Japan. Chungking, China Information Committee, 1940. 32 p.

CHINA. Ministry of Information. Agreements between Wang Ching-wei, 汪精衞, and Japan. Chungking, Chinese Ministry of information, 1943. cover-title, 16 p.

_____. (New Reformed Government of the Republic of China). China-Japan. Treaty concerning basic relations and protocol annexed thereto. Signed at Nanking, November 30, 1940. (In American journal of international law. Concord, N.H., 1941. v. 35, suppl., p. 125-128).

_____. Fundamental points for readjustment of Sino-Japanese relations [An agreement signed 30 December 1939 between Japan and the New Reformed Government of the  Republic of China of Wang Ching-wei] Nanking, 1940. 8 p.

_____. The National Government of China, organization and personnel, October 1941. Nanking, Compilation Bureau, International Publicity Board [1941] 1 v. unpaged. illus.

FOREIGN AFFAIRS ASSOCIATION OF JAPAN. Japanese relief work in the occupied areas. Tokyo, Foreign Affairs Association of Japan [1938?] 22,[2] p. incl. map. plates (incl. ports.).

GT. BRIT. Ministry of Information. Economic developments in Japan and Japanese-controlled territory from September 1944 to the time of her collapse. [London, 1945] 36 p.

_____. Treaties, etc., 1936-52 (George VI). Arrangement between His Majesty's government in the United Kingdom and the Japanese government relating to local issues at Tientsin, June 19, 1940. London, H.M. Stationery Off., 1940. 3 p. ([Foreign office] China no. 1 (1940)) Cmd. 6212.

ITŌ, TAKEO, 1895-   Problems in the Japanese occupied areas in China. Tokyo, Japanese Council, Institute of Pacific Relations, 1941. 102 p. ("Far Eastern conflict" series, 4).

KUO MIN TANG. Publicity Board. Documents concerning the secret agreement between Wang Ching-wei and Japan on December 30, 1939, containing the full text of the agreement and Generalissimo Chiang Kai-shek's message to peoples of friendly powers. Chungking, Central Executive Committee of Kuomintang, 1940. 20 p. illus.

_____. Secret agreements and contracts between the "Nanking Reformed Government" and Japan, originally signed in 1938; subsequently acknowledged by Wang Ching-wei. Chungking, Central Executive Committee of Kuomintang, 1940. 15 p.

MOTE, FREDERICK W., 1922-   Japanese-sponsored governments in China, 1937-45; an annotated bibliography compiled from materials in the Chinese

collection of the Hoover Library. Stanford, Stanford University Press, 1954.
viii, 68 p. (Hoover Institute and Library. Bibliographical series, 3 ).

STATISTICAL data on Japanese and Far Eastern occupied cities and towns.
[Washington, 1945?] vi numb. l., 152 p. incl. maps.

U.S. Office of Strategic Services. Research and Analysis Branch. Financial
programs of Japan in and occupied areas. Assemblage #44. Rev. ed.
Honolulu, 1944. 2 v. in 1 (263 p.) (Its R and A 2629).

————. Biographical intelligence on former puppet China. Honolulu, T.H., 1945.
262 l. (Its R and A 3363).

————. The puppet governmental bodies of occupied North China. [Washington]
1945. iii l., 16 p. (Its R and A 3075).

————. Personnel of the North China Political Council. Washington, 1945. xi,
30 p. diagrs. (Its R and A 3102).

————. Structure and personnel of the Nanking puppet government and Hong Kong
administration. [Washington] 1945. iii, 84 l. (Its R and A 2565).

————. Japanese attempts at indoctrination of youth in occupied areas. [Wash-
ington] 1945 7 l. (Its Current intelligence study, 3 ).

————. Japanese-controlled firms in occupied China and inner Mongolia. Washington, 1945. ii l., 32 p. (Its R and A no. 3109).

————. Programs of Japan in China: central coastal provinces, with biographies.
Assemblage #49. Honolulu, 1945. vi, 222 l. (Its R and A 2896).

————. The same. Part II. Southern coast, with biographies. Assemblage #51.
Washington, 1945. viii l., 262 p. (Its R and A 2896. 1).

————. The same. Part III. Northern coast, with biographies. Assemblage #52.
Honolulu, 1945. vii l., 262 p. (Its R and A 3049).

————. The Japanese occupation of the southeast China coast. [Washington] 1945.
7 l. (Its R and A 2659S).

WARD, ROBERT SPENCER, 1906-  Asia for the Asiatics? The techniques of
Japanese occupation. Introduction by Laurence Salisbury. Chicago, University of Chicago Press [1945] xiv, 204, [1] p.

## China and other Asiatic Countries

BEYER, HENRY OTLEY, 1883-  Early history of Philippine relations with foreign countries, especially China. Manila, National printing co., 1948. 17 p.

BURMA (UNION). Dept. of Information and Broadcasting. Kuomintang aggression against Burma. [Rangoon] Ministry of Information, Government of the
Union of Burma, 1953. 221 p. illus. facsims. maps.

CHINA and the Asian-African Conference; documents. Peking, Foreign Languages Press, 1955. 80 p. illus.

HOONTRAKUL, LIKHIT, 雲茂倫. The historical records of the Siamese-Chi-
nese relations commencing from ancient times up to the time when the Siamese people formed themselves into a State called Siam with the town of Suk-
hotai as capital. 中暹兩族關係史    Bangkok, C. Limsaro, 1953. 137 p.
maps, illus.

JAIN, GIRILAL C. Chinese "Panchsheela" in Burma. Bombay, Democratic Research Service, 1956. 45 p.

NAIR, V.G. China and Burma interpreted. Madras, [Sino-Indian Cultural Society in India] printed at Thompson and Co., 1947. 139 p.

MAUNG MAUNG, U. Grim war against Kuomintang. With a foreword by U. Thant.
Rangoon, Nu Yin Press, 1953. iv, 86 p. illus.

RHEE, SYNGMAN, 1875-  Syngman Rhee's state visit to China; a collection of
statements and remarks on Free China. Edited by Eugene H. C. Wang, 王廣
中. Taipei, China Culture Pub. Foundation, 1953. 28 p. illus. (Pamphlets
on Chinese affairs).

THOMAS, S.B. Communist China and her neighbors. [Toronto] Canadian Institute of International Affairs, 1955. 16 p. (Behind the headlines, 15:2 ).

Relations with Western Countries
China and Australia and New Zealand

BAKHAP, THOMAS JEROME KINGSTON. Trade between the commonwealth [of Australia] and China. Report by Senator Thomas J.K. Bakhap. [Melbourne] Printed and pub. for the government of the Commonwealth of Australia [1922] 15 p.

BURCHETT, GEORGE HAROLD. China the senior partner. Melbourne, Australian-China Cooperation Association, 1943. 16 p.

———. China and the White Australia policy. [Melbourne] Australia-China Cooperation Association, 1944. 47 p.

CH'EN, WEI-PING, 陳維屏. The objects of the foundation of the Lectureship, and a review of Dr. Morrison's life in China. Canberra, Australian Institute of Anatomy, 1932. 11 p. (George Ernest Morrison lectures).

FOCUS on China: toward the understanding of one of Australia's Pacific neighbours. Sydney, Church Missionary Society, 1944. 100 p. plates.

LOCKWOOD, RUPERT ERNEST. China our neighbour. Sydney, Current Book Distributors, 1951. 15 p.

MATHEWS, PHILIP. China and New Zealand; a talk on the cultural, political and economic importance of China to New Zealand. Auckland, Chinese Bookshop, 1949. 15 p.

MELBOURNE, ALEXANDER CLIFFORD VERNON. Report on Australian intercourse with Japan and China, submitted to the Senate of the University of Queensland by A.C.V. Melbourne. Brisbane, F. Phillips, Government Printer, 1932. ix, [1], 159, [1] p.

MILNER, IAN FRANK GEORGE. New Zealand's interests and policies in the Far East. New York, International Secretariat, Institute of Pacific Relations, 1940. xi, 131 p. (I.P.R. inquiry series).

SHEPHERD, JACK. Australia's interests and policies in the Far East. New York, International Secretariat, Institute of Pacific Relations, 1940. xiv, 212 p. (I.P.R. inquiry series).

TSAO, WEN-YEN, 曹文彥, 1908- Two Pacific democracies: China and Australia. Introduction by R.M. Crawford. Melbourne, F.W. Cheshire pty., 1941. xvii, 157, [1] p. front., plates, ports.

China and Belgium and Netherlands

CHINA. Ministry of Foreign Affairs. Statements of the Chinese government and other official documents relating to the negotiation for the termination of the Sino-Belgian treaty of amity, commerce and navigation of November 2, 1865. With the said treaty as an appendix. Peking, Wai Chiao Pu, 1926. cover-title, [3], 54 p.

DUYVENDAK, J.J.L., 1889-1954. The last Dutch embassy to the Chinese court, 1794-95. Leiden, E.J. Brill, 1938. 137 p. plates, map, tables. Reprinted from T'oung Pao, vol. 34.

ELST, LÉON GEORGES JOSEPH MARIE PHILOMÈNE, baron VAN DER, 1856- Léopold II et la Chine. Bruxelles, A. Dewit, 1924. cover-title, 55 p. Reprinted from Revue Générale, Avr.-mai, 1924.

FROCHISSE, J.M. La Belgique et la Chine; relations diplomatiques et économiques (1839-1909) Bruxelles, L'Édition universelle [1936] [9]-459 p. [Bibliothèque de l'École des sciences politiques et sociales de l'Université de Louvain].

HAGUE. PERMANENT COURT OF INTERNATIONAL JUSTICE. Affaire relative à la dénonciation du traité sino-belge du 2 novembre 1865. Denunciation of the treaty of November 2nd, 1865, between China and Belgium. Leyde, Société d'édtions A.W. Sijthoff, 1927. 15, 4-15 p. (Publications. Sér. A, no. 8).

------. The same. Ordonnance du 21 février 1928. Denunciation of the treaty of
   November 2nd, 1865, between China and Belgium. Order of February 21st,
   1928. Leyde, Société d'éditions A. W. Sijthoff, 1928. 7, [4]-7 p. (Publica-
   tions. Sér. A, no. 14 ).
------. The same. Ordonnance du 13 août 1928. Denunciation of the treaty of No-
   vember 2nd, 1865, between China and Belgium. Order of August 13th, 1928.
   Leyde, Société d'éditions A. W Sijthoff, 1928. 7,[4]-7 p. (Publications. Sér.
   A, no. 16 ).
------. Affaire relative à la denonciation du traité sino-belge du 2 novembre 1865.
   Affaire relative à l'usine de Chorzów (Indemnités) Ordonnances du 25 mai
   1929. Denunciation of the treaty of November 2nd, 1865, between China and
   Belgium. Case concerning the factory at Chorzów (Indemnities) Orders of
   May 25th, 1929. Leyde, Société d'éditions A. W. Sijthoff, 1929. 15, [4]-8,
   [11]-15 p. (Publications. Sér. A. no. 18/19).
MELOTTE DE LAVAUX, ADRIEN DE, 1874-  Les derniers jours d'une léga-
   tion. Liège, Impr. nationales des militaires mutilés et invalides de la
   guerre, 1925. 87 p.
WANG, KING-KY, 王景岐, 1882-1941. La voix de la Chine; addresses, discours, déclarations, lettres, interviews. 2e éd. Préfaces de m. Jules Des-
   trée et de m. Paul Gille. Bruxelles, Office de publicité, 1929. [7]-241 p.
   1st ed. 1927.


## China and Canada

ANGUS, HENRY FORBES, 1891-  Canada and the Far East, 1940-53. [Toron-
   to] University of Toronto Press, 1953. 129 p.
CANADA. Dept. of Trade and Commerce. The trade of Canada with Japan and
   China. Ottawa, 1931. 17 numb. 1. incl. tables.
------. Treaties, etc., 1944. Treaty between the government of Canada and the
   government of the Republic of China concerning the relinquishment of extra-
   territorial rights and the regulation of related matters (with exchange of
   notes) Ottawa, 14th April, 1944. [Ratifications exchanged at Chungking, 3rd
   April, 1945] London, H. M. Stationery Off. [1946] 5 p. ( [Gt. Brit. Foreign
   office] Treaty series no. 43 (1946) ) Gt. Brit. Parliament. Papers by command. Cmd. 6948.
GARDNER, D. H. Canadian interests and policies in the Far East since World
   War II. Submitted by the Canadian Institute of International Affairs as a preparatory paper for the Eleventh Conference of the Institute of Pacific Relations to be held at Lucknow in October 1950. Toronto, Canadian Institute of
   International Affairs; distributed by International Secretariat, Institute of
   Pacific Relations, New York, 1950. 15 l. (Canadian paper, 1 ).
LOWER, ARTHUR REGINALD MARSDEN, 1889-  Canada and the Far East -
   1940. New York, International Secretariat, Institute of Pacific Relations,
   1940. ix, 3-152 p. incl. tables. (I. P. R. inquiry series).
STRANGE, WILLIAM. Canada, the Pacific and war. Toronto, New York [etc. ]
   T. Nelson [c1937] ix, 220 p. front. (fold. map) illus. (International affairs,
   1 ).
WOODSWORTH, CHARLES JAMES, 1909-  Canadian policies in Asia. Prepared for the Twelfth Conference of the Institute of Pacific Relations to be
   held at Kyoto, Japan, in September 1954. Toronto, Canadian Institute of
   International Affairs, 1954. i, 44 p. tables. (Canadian Institute of International Affairs. Canadian paper, 1 ).


## China and France

BONIFACY, AUGUSTE LOUIS M. À propos d'une collection de peintures chinoises représentant divers épisodes de la guerre franco-chinoise de 1884-

85 et conservées à l'École française d'Extrême-Orient. Hanoi, Impr. d'Extrême-Orient, 1931. 43 p. map, fold. plates.

BONNINGUE, ALFRED EDMOND VICTOR. La France à Kouang-Tchéou-Wan. Préface de M. A. Silvestre. Paris, Berger-Levrault, 1931. x, 70 p. maps, plates.

BURTON, WILBUR. The French strangle-hold on Yunnan; a first-hand survey. Shanghai, China Weekly Review [1933?] 46 p. illus. (map).

CHANG, YEN-SHEN T. H., 張雁深. Essays on Sino-French relations. Peking, sold at Yenching University Bookstore, 1940. 64 p.

CHO, HUAN-LAI, 卓還來, 1912-42. Les origines du conflit franco-chinois à propos du Tonkin jusqu'en 1883. Paris, Jouve et cie, 1935. 228 p. Thèse - Univ. de Paris.

DES COURTILS, LOUIS. La concession française de Changhaï. Paris, Recueil Sirey, 1934. 230 p. fold. plan.

FREDET, JEAN, 1879-1948. Les Français en Chine, Charles de Montigny, créateur de la concession française de Changhai, d'après des documents inédits. Changhai, 1923. 16 p.

——. Quand la Chine s'ouvrait; Charles de Montigny, consul de France. Shanghai, Impr. de T'ou-sè-wè [1943] iv, 310 p. front., plates (1 fold.) ports., map, facsim.

——. The same. Paris, Société de l'histoire des colonies françaises; en vente: Librairie Larose, 1953. xv, 292 p. illus., ports., map. (Bibliothèque d'histoire coloniale, nouv. sér.).

GROSSE-ASCHHOFF, ANGELUS FRANCIS J., 1910- The negotiations between Ch'i-ying and Lagrené, 1844-46. St. Bonaventure, N. Y., Franciscan Institute, 1950. vii, 196 p. (Franciscan Institute publications. Missiology series, 2 ). Thesis-Columbia University.

LÉVY, ROGER, 1887- La politique française en Extrême-Orient, 1936-38. Paris, Paul Hartmann, 1939. 181 p. (Centre d'études de politique étrangère. Section d'information. Publication no. 13-1939).

——. French interests and policies in the Far East. Part. I. A century of French Far Eastern affairs, by Roger Lévy, with a supplement by Guy Lacam: The economic relations of Indo-China with southern China. Part II. French Indo-China in transition, by Andrew Roth. New York, International Secretariat, Institute of Pacific Relations, 1941. xi, 209 p. illus. (map) (I. P. R. Inquiry series).

MAYBON, CHARLES B., 1872- La concession française d'autrefois. B. Edan, Chancelier et consul de France à Changhai (1850-61) Conférence faite par Charles B. Maybon. Pékin, A. Nachbaur, 1924. 58 p. map.

——. Histoire de la concession française de Changhai, publiée sous le haut patronage de s. e. m. le ministre des affaires étrangères, du Conseil d'administration municipale de la concession française et de la Chambre de commerce française de Chine. Paris, Plon [1929] vii, 458 p. plates (1 fold.) ports., maps (1 double) plans (part double).

PAINLEVÉ, PAUL, 1863-1933. La Mission Painlevé en Chine, édité par Alphonse Monestier. Pékin, La "Politique de Pékin," 1921. 150 p. illus. plates, ports., (Collection de la "Politique de Pékin").

PALIKAO, CHARLES GUILLAUME MARIE APOLLINAIRE ANTOINE COUSIN DE MONTAUBAN, comte DE, 1796-1878. L'expédition de Chine de 1860; souvenirs du général Cousin de Montauban, comte de Palikao, publiés par son petit-fils, le comte de Palikao; avec 8 gravures hors texte et une carte. Paris, Plon [1932] viii, 450 p. front. (port. ) plates, fold. map, plan.

PELLIOT, PAUL, 1878-1945. L'origine des relations de la France avec la Chine: Le premier voyage de "l'Amphitrite" en Chine. Paris, P. Geuthner, 1930. 78 p.

TCHENG, TSE-SIO, 鄭子修. Les relations de Lyon avec la Chine; étude d'histoire et de géographie économiques. Paris, L. Rodstein [1937] 17-182 p.

incl. illus., maps (1 fold.) diagrs. (Bibliothèque de l'Institut de géographie
de l'Université de Lyon et des "Études rhodaniennes").

VERBRUGGE, RAPHAËL, 1872-   La belle route maritime de France en Chine
(Marseille-Changhai). Bruxelles, A. Dewit, 1926. 211 p. illus. incl. maps.
Reprinted from Bull. de la Société royale de géographie d'Anvers.

## China and Germany

BEE, BENJAMIN MING-CHÜ, 皮名舉, 1908-   The leasing of Kiaochow; a study
in diplomacy and imperialism. Cambridge, 1935. 450 l. Thesis-Harvard
University.

BLOCH, KURT. German interests and policies in the Far East. New York, International Secretariat, Institute of Pacific Relations, 1940. xiv, 75 p. (I. P.
R. inquiry series).

CHINA. Treaties, etc., 1921. L'accord sino-allemand et les documents annexés.
Signed in Peking, May 20, 1921. [Pékin, 1921?] cover-title, [56] p.

EHLERS, OTTO E. Im Osten Asiens. 7. Aufl. mit einem Nachtrag: Tsingtau im
Weltkrieg. Neu-Finkenkrug bei Berlin, Hermann Paetel [1924] viii, 184 p.
plates, maps.(Sammlung belchrender Unterhaltungs-schriften, 2 ).

DJANG, FENG-DJEN, 張鳳楨, [Chang Feng-chên] 1902-   The diplomatic relations between China and Germany since 1898. Shanghai, Commercial Press,
1936. iii-iv, 281, [1] p. Thesis-Johns Hopkins University.

FISCHER, OTTO, 1886-1948. China und Deutschland, ein Versuch. Münster in
Westfalen, Aschendorff, 1927. 110 p. (Deutschtum und Ausland, Heft 12 ).

HEYKING, ELISABETH (VON FLEMMING) baronin VON, 1861-1925. Tagebücher aus vier Weltteilen 1886/1904, hrsg. von Grete Litzmann. Leipzig, Koehler und Amelang [1926] 413 p. front.(port.).

KLEHMET, OBERST D. Tsingtau; Rückblick auf die Geschichte, besonders der
Belagerung und des Falles der Festung, mit kritischen Betrachtungen. Berlin, G. Bath, 1931. 46 p. incl. table, maps, plates.

LINEBARGER, PAUL MYRON WENTWORTH, 1871-1939. Deutschlands gegenwärtige Gelegenheiten in China. Brüssel (Belgien) [Impr. aux Presses Til-
bury, L. Flas et fils] 1936. 55 p.

NOREM, RALPH AUGUSTINE, 1897-   Kiaochow leased territory. [Berkeley,
University of California Press, 1936] 150 p. 3 maps (1 fold.) (Publications
of the University of California at Los Angeles in social sciences. 6:1).

RADOWITZ, JOSEPH MARIA FRIEDRICH WILHELM LUDWIG VON, 1839-1912.
Briefe aus Ostasien, hrsg. von Hajo Holborn. Stuttgart, Berlin [etc.] Deutsche Verlags-Anstalt, 1926. vi, [1], 123, [1] p.

SCHOEN, WALTER VON. Auf Vorposten für Deutschland; unsere Kolonien im
Weltkrieg. Berlin, Ullstein, c1935. 250, [1] p. illus.(maps), plates, ports.,
facsim.

U.S. Office of Coordinator of Information. Research and Analysis Branch. Far
Eastern Section. German-Chinese relations, 1933-41. Washington [1942?]
18 l. (Its Memorandum no. 11 ).

WALDERSEE, ALFRED HEINRICH KARL LUDWIG, graf VON, 1832-1904.Denk-
würdigkeiten des General-Feldmarschalls Alfred grafen von Waldersee; auf
Veranlassung des Generalleutnants Georg grafen von Waldersee bearb. und
hrsg. von Heinrich Otto Meisner. Stuttgart und Berlin, Deutsche Verlags-
Anstalt, 1923-25. 3 v. front. (port.).

———. A field-marshal's memoirs: from the diary, correspondence, and reminiscences of Alfred, count von Waldersee. Condensed and translated by Frederic Whyte. London, Hutchinson and co., 1924. xxi, 22-286 p. front.(port.).

WOOD, CARLTON LEROY, 1911-   Die Beziehungen Deutschlands zu China.
Eine historische Betrachtung in politischer und ökonomischer Hinsicht vom
19. Jahrhundert bis zum Jahre 1934. [München, Gebrüder Giehrl Bücher,
1936] 110 p. incl. tables. Diss.-Univ. Heidelburg.

China and Great Britain
Treaties, Documents, etc.

CHINA. Courts: Mixed Court, Shanghai. Trial of rioters at the Mixed Court, Shanghai. A verbatim report of the trial of the Chinese arrested during the riot of May 30, 1925, at the International Mixed Court, Shanghai, on June 2, 3, 9, 10 and 11 from the Mixed Court Register. Shanghai, North China Daily News and Herald, 1925. 24 p.

————. Ministry of Foreign Affairs. [A collection of notes exchanged concerning the Shameen massacre in Canton] Peking, 1925. 29, 59 p.

————. Treaties, etc., 1943. Sino-British treaty for the abolition of extraterritoriality and related rights in China. [Chungking, 1943] cover-title, 19 p.; cover-title, 21 p.

GT. BRIT. Colonial Office. Weihaiwei. Report for 1902-29. London, H. M. Stationery Off., 1920-30. 28 v. (Colonial Reports. Annual ser.).

————. Foreign Office. Papers respecting the first firing in the Shameen affair of June 23, 1925. Presented by the Secretary of state for foreign affairs to Parliament by command of His Majesty. London, H. M. Stationery Off., 1926. 15 p. (China no. 1 (1926) ) (Parliament. Papers by command. Cmd. 2636).

————. Report of the advisory committee together with other documents respecting the China indemnity. Presented by the Secretary of state for foreign affairs to Parliament by command of His Majesty. London, H. M. Stationery Off., 1926. 197 p. incl. tables. ( [Foreign office] China, no. 2 (1926) ) (Parliament. Papers by command. Cmd. 2766).

————. Papers respecting the agreements relative to the British concessions at Hankow and Kiukiang. Presented by the Secretary of state for foreign affairs to Parliament by command of His Majesty. London, H. M. Stationery Off., 1927. 14 p. (China no. 3 (1927) ) (Parliament. Papers by command. Cmd. 2869).

————. Papers relating to the Nanking incident of March 24 and 25, 1927. Presented by the Secretary of state for foreign affairs to Parliament by command of His Majesty. London, H. M. Stationery Off., 1927. 31 p. (China no. 4 (1927) ).

————. Papers relating to the settlement of the Nanking incident of March 24, 1927. Presented by the Secretary of state for foreign affairs to Parliament by command of His Majesty. London, H. M. Stationery Off., 1928. 6 p. (China no. 1 (1928) ).

————. Exchange of notes between His Majesty's government in the United Kingdom and the Chinese government regarding the rendition of the British concession at Chinkiang. Nanking, October 31, 1929. London, H. M. Stationery Off., 1930. 4 p. (Treaty series, 1930, no. 3 ).

————. Exchange of notes between His Majesty's government in the United Kingdom and the Chinese government regarding claims for losses sustained by British subjects at Chinkiang in 1927. Nanking, November 9, 1929. London, H. M. Stationery Off., 1930. 4 p. (Treaty series, 1930, no. 4 ).

————. Exchange of notes between His Majesty's government in the United Kingdom and the Chinese government regarding the rendition of the British concession at Amoy. Nanking, September 17, 1930. London, H. M. Stationery Off., 1930. 3 p. (Treaty series, 1930, no. 44 ).

————. Papers regarding the disposal of the British share of the China indemnity of 1901. September 19-November 14, 1930. Presented by the Secretary of state for foreign affairs to Parliament by command of His Majesty. London, H. M. Stationery Off., 1930. 15 p. (China no. 3 (1930) ).

————. Exchange of notes between His Majesty's government in the United Kingdom and the Chinese government regarding the disposal of the British share of the China indemnity of 1901. Nanking, September 19 and 22, 1930. London, H. M. Stationery Off., 1931. 9 p. (Treaty series, no. 18 (1931) ).

———. Legation. China. Exchange of notes (December 20, 1928) relative to the renunciation of the rights of His Majesty's government in Canada to benefit by the provisions of existing treaties limiting the right of China to settle her national customs tariffs or to impose tonnage dues. Ottawa, F. A Acland, 1930. 8 p. (Canada. [Treaties, etc.] Treaty series, 1929, no. 5 ).

———. Treasury. China. Copy of Treasury minutes, dated the 7th December 1927, relative to the leases of His Majesty's government in the British concessions in China. London, H. M. Stationery Off., 1927. 3 p.

———. Treaties, etc. List of treaties, etc., between Great Britain and China (1842-1922), including international treaties, and treaties between Great Britain and foreign powers relating to China. London, H. M. Stationery Off., 1925. 113 p. ( [Foreign office] Treaty series, 1925, no. 34 ).

———. Treaties, etc. 1910-36 (George V). Agreement between the British and German governments relating to German debts and property in China. Signed at London, April 5, 1923. London, H. M. Stationery Off., 1923. 7 p. ( [Foreign office] Treaty series, 1923, no. 8 ).

———. Treaty between His Majesty and the President of the Chinese Republic together with other documents relating to the Chinese customs tariff, etc. Nanking, December 20, 1928. [Ratifications exchanged at London, March 14, 1929] London, H. M. Stationery Off., 1929. 12 p. ( [Foreign office] Treaty series, 1929, no. 10 ).

———. Agreement between His Majesty's government in the United Kingdom and the Brazilian, Netherlands, Norwegian, and United States governments and the Chinese government relating to the Chinese courts in the International settlement at Shanghai, with relative exchange of notes and declaration. Nanking, February 17, 1930. London, H. M. Stationery Off., 1930. 9 p. ( [Foreign office] Treaty series, 1930, no. 20 ).

———. Convention between His Majesty and the President of the national government of the Republic of China for the rendition of Weihaiwei and Agreement regarding certain facilities for His Majesty's navy after rendition. Nanking, April 18, 1930. [The Convention and Agreement have not been ratified by His Majesty] Presented by the Secretary of state for foreign affairs to Parliament by command of His Majesty. London, H. M. Stationery Off., 1930. 10 p. (Foreign office. China no. 2 (1930) ).

———. The same. [With map and two plans] Nanking, April 18, 1930. [Ratifications exchanged at Nanking, October 1, 1930] London, H. M. Stationery Off., 1930. 10 p. fold. map., fold. plans. ( [Gt. Brit. Foreign office] Treaty series, 1930, no. 50 ).

———. Exchange of notes between His Majesty's government in the United Kingdom and the government of India and the Chinese government regarding the establishment of a commission to determine the southern section of the boundary between Burma and Yunnan. Nanking, April 9, 1935. London, H. M. Stationery Off., 1935. 4 p. ( [Foreign office] Treaty series, no. 15 (1935) ).

———. Treaties, etc., 1936-52 (George VI). Exchange of notes between His Majesty's government in the United Kingdom and the Chinese government regarding air services over China. Hankow, December 18, 1937. London, H. M. Stationery Off., 1938. 3 p. ( [Foreign office] Treaty series no. 28 (1938) ).

———. Exchange of notes between the government of the United Kingdom and the Chinese government regarding the air service between south-west China and British ports. Chungking, January 24, 1939. London, H. M. Stationery Off., 1939. 3 p. ( [Foreign office] Treaty series no. 52 (1939) ).

———. Treaty between His Majesty in respect of the United Kingdom and India and His Excellency the President of the National Government of the Republic of China for the relinquishment of extra-territorial rights in China and the regulation of related matters (with Exchange of notes and Agreed minute) Chungking, January 11, 1943. [The treaty has not yet been ratified by His

Majesty]  London, H. M. Stationery Off., 1943. 8 p. ( [Gt. Brit. Foreign office]  China no. 1 (1943) ).

————. The same. Ratifications exchanged at Chungking May 20, 1943. London, H. M. Stationery Off., 1943. 32 p. ( [Gt. Brit. Foreign Office] Treaty series, 1943, no. 2 ).

————. Air transport agreement between the Government of the United Kingdom of Great Britain and Northern Ireland and the Government of the Republic of China, with exchanges of notes, Nanking, 23rd July, 1947. London, H. M. Stationery Off. [1947] 37 p.([Gt. Brit. Foreign Office] Treaty series, 1947, no. 71 ).

————. Exchanges of notes between His Majesty's Government in the United Kingdom and the Government of Burma, and the National Government of the Republic of China concerning the Burma-Yunnan boundary, Chungking, 18th June, 1941. London, H. M. Stationery Off. [1947]  17 p. fold. maps. ( [Gt. Brit. Foreign Office] Treaty series, 1947, no. 80) [Gt. Brit. Parliament. Papers by command] Cmd. 7246.

————. Exchange of notes constituting an agreement between the Government of the United Kingdom and the Government of the Republic of China for the transfer of certain British naval vessels to China and the mutual waiver of claims in respect of the loss of other vessels, with annex, London, 18th May, 1948. London, H. M. Stationery Off. [1948] 4 p. ( [Gt. Brit. Foreign Office] Treaty series, 1948, no. 39 ) [Gt. Brit. Parliament. Papers by command] Cmd. 7457.

————. Exchanges of notes between His Majesty's Government in the United Kingdom of Great Britain and Northern Ireland and the Government of the Chinese Republic for the prevention of smuggling between Hong Kong and Chinese ports, with annexes and maps, Nanking, 12th January and 18th October 1948. London, H. M. Stationery Off. [1949] 18 p. fold. maps ( [Gt. Brit. Foreign Office] Treaty series, 1949, no. 9 ).

————. Exchanges of notes between His Majesty's Government in the United Kingdom and the Government of Burma, and the National Government of the Republic of China concerning the Burma-Yunnan boundary, Chungking, 18th June 1941. London, H. M. Stationery Off., 1956. 16 p. fold. col. maps (1 in pocket) ( [Gt. Brit. Foreign Office] Treaty series, 1956, no. 48 ).

INTERNATIONAL COMMISSION OF JUDGES, 1925. A report of the proceedings of the International commission of judges. [Shanghai? 1925?] [211] p.

WEI-HAI-WEI. Commissioner. Commissioner's speech at the Government offices, Weihaiwei. Weihaiwei, 1930. 24 p.

## General Works

BLOFELD, JOHN EATON CALTHORPE, 1913-  Sino-British cultural relations; report of an address. London, China Society [1946] cover-title, 9 p.

BRITISH imperialism in east Asia - its invasion and retreat. [n.p., 194-] (Pamphlets on the world freedom, no. 5 ). Microfilm. Positive. Collation of the original, as determined from the film: 52 p.

BURNS, ELINOR. British imperialism in China. London, 1926. 64 p. fold. map. (The Colonial series of the Labour Research Department, 1926, v. 3 ).

COMMUNIST PARTY OF GREAT BRITAIN. Murder! An indictment of British imperialism in China. London, Communist Party of Great Britain [1925] cover-title, 18 p.

COSTIN, WILLIAM CONRAD. Great Britain and China, 1833-60. Oxford, The Clarendon Press, 1937. vi, [2], 362 p. fold. maps.

EARL, LAWRENCE. Yangtse incident; the story of H. M. S. Amethyst, April 20, 1949 to July 31, 1949. With a foreword by J. S. Kerans. London, Harrap [1950]; New York, Knopf, 1951; London, Hamilton, 1956. 240 p. illus., ports., maps.

FEETHAM, RICHARD, 1874-   Great Britain and China; the future of Shanghai.
    London, China Association, 1931. 23 p.
FORD, JULIA ELLSWORTH (SHAW) 1859-   Peace depends on Great Britain.
    [Rye, N.Y., The Rye Chronicle Press, 1921] 11 p.
FOX, GRACE ESTELLE, 1899-   British admirals and Chinese pirates, 1832-
    69.  London, K. Paul [1940] xiv, 227 p. front., plates, fold. map, fac-
    sims. Issued also as thesis, Columbia University.
[FRIEDMAN, IRVING SIGMUND] 1915-   The relations of Great Britain with Chi-
    na: 1933-39.  New York, International Secretariat, Institute of Pacific Rela-
    tions, 1939. 141 numb. l.
HALL, RONALD OWEN, bp., 1895-   China and Britain.  London, Edinburgh
    House Press, 1927. 175 p.
HAUSHOFER, ALBRECHT, 1903-   Englands Einbruch in China.  Berlin, Junker
    und Dünnhaupt, 1940. 52, [2] p. (Das Britische reich in der weltpolitik, hft.
    31 ).
HODGKIN, HENRY THEODORE, 1877-1933. Recent events in China.  London,
    Friends' Bookshop, 1925. 15 p.
HSIA, CHIN-LIN, 夏晉麟 1896-   British Far Eastern policy, 1937-40.  Chung-
    king, Published by the China Information Pub. Co. [1940] cover-title, 25 p.
    (Chungking pamphlets, 1 ).
[HUBBARD, GILBERT ERNEST] 1885-   British Far Eastern policy.  London,
    Royal Institute of International Affairs [1939] v, 53 p. maps (Information de-
    partment papers, 24 ).
———. The same.  London, Royal Institute of International Affairs [1942] 52 numb.
    l. ( United Kingdom paper, 2 ).
———. The same.  New York, International Secretariat, Institute of Pacific Re-
    lations, 1943. xi, 97 p. (I.P.R. Inquiry series).
KIERNAN, E. VICTOR GORDON. British diplomacy in China, 1880 to 1885.
    Cambridge [Eng.] The University Press, 1939. xi, 327 p.
McCORDOCK, ROBERT STANLEY, 1897-   British Far Eastern policy, 1894-
    1900. New York, Columbia University Press; London, P.S. King, 1931.
    376 p. (Studies in history, economics and public law, 346 ). Published also
    as thesis, Columbia University.
PELCOVITS, NATHAN ALBERT, 1912-   Old China hands and the Foreign Of-
    fice. New York, Pub. under the auspices of American Institute of Pacific
    Relations by the King's Crown Press, 1948. xi, 349 p.
PHILLIPS, CECIL ERNEST LUCAS, 1898-   Escape of the Amethyst, by C.E.
    Lucas Phillips with the co-operation of J.S. Kerans. London, Heinemann
    [1957] 274 p. illus.
PRATT, SIR JOHN THOMAS, 1876-   Great Britain and China. [London, New
    York, etc.] Oxford University Press, 1942. 32 p. (Oxford pamphlets on
    world affairs, 58 ).
———. China and Britain. London, Collins [1944] 126, [2] p. col. front., illus.,
    col. plates, maps. (The Nations and Britain).
PRITCHARD, EARL HAMPTON, 1907-   Anglo-Chinese relations during the
    seventeenth and eighteenth centuries. Urbana, University of Illinois [1930?]
    244 p. illus.(map) fold. tables, diagrs. (University of Illinois studies in the
    social sciences. vol. XVII, no. 1-2).
———. The crucial years of early Anglo-Chinese relations, 1750-1800. Pull-
    man, Wash., [1937?] [95]-442 p. illus.(map) diagrs. (Research studies of
    the State college of Washington. 4:3-4).
ROLOFSON, WILLIAM M. Relations between the Chinese and the British Gov-
    ernment of Malaya up to 1942. Microfilm copy of typescript. Collation of
    the original, as determined from the film: iv, 181 l. Thesis-University of
    Chicago.
SMITH, EDWARD GEORGE, 1874-   Britain in China. London, National Coun-
    cil for Prevention of War [1927?] 7, [1] p.

SMITH, RENNIE, 1888-  Peace with China. London, National Council for Pre-
vention of War [1927] 11, [1] p.
SOOTHILL, WILLIAM EDWARD, 1861-1935. China and England. London, Ox-
ford University Press, H. Milford, 1928. 228 p.
TANG, LI, 趙唐理. Anglo-Chinese diplomatic relations 1858-70. London, 1951.
Thesis-London School of Economics. x, 404, 31 l.
TOYNBEE, ARNOLD JOSEPH, 1889-  British interests in the Far East. [Not-
tingham Citizen Press, 1938] cover-title, [2], 16 p. (University college, Not-
tingham. Cust foundation lecture, 1938).
WAI. La crise nationaliste chinoise; les incidents de Shanghai. Pékin, A. Nach-
baur, 1925.  99 p.
WANG, SHÊN-TSU, 王繩祖. The Margary affair and the Chefoo agreement.
London, New York [etc.] Oxford University Press, 1940. viii, 138 p. 2 fold.
maps.

## China and Italy

TAMAGNA, FRANK M., 1910-  Italy's interests and policies in the Far East.
New York, International Secretariat, Institute of Pacific Relations, 1941.
xiii, 91 p. incl. tables. (I. P. R. inquiry series).

## China and Russia
### Treaties, Documents, etc.

CHINA. Treaties, etc., 1924. Agreements between the Republic of China and
the Union of Soviet Socialist Republics and annexes [May 31, 1924] (In American journal of international law. Concord, N.H., 1925. v. 19, suppl., p. 53-
63 ).
———. (National Government of the Republic of China) Treaties, etc. Treaty of
friendship and alliance between the Republic of China and Union of Soviet Socialist Republics, concluded at Moscow, August 14, 1945. [Shanghai] International Publishers, 1946. 18, 17 p.
———. (People's Republic of China, 1949-   ) Treaties, etc., 1950. Sino-Soviet
treaty and agreements, signed in Moscow on February 14, 1950. Peking,
Foreign Languages Press, 1950. 25 p.
RUSSIA. Treaties, etc., 1950. Treaty and agreements between Soviet Union and
the Chinese People's Republic concluded February 14, 1950. Moscow, New
Times, 1950. 8 p.

## General Works

ARSEN'EV, VLADIMIR KLAVDIEVICH, 1872-1930. Russen und Chinesen in
Ostsibirien, übersetzt von Franz Daniel. Berlin, A. Scherl [1926] 228 p.
illus. fold. map.
CAHEN, GASTON. Some early Russo-Chinese relations. Translated and edited
by W. Sheldon Ridge. Shanghai, "The National Review" office, 1914. [Pei-
ping, Wên-tien-ko shu-chuang, 1936] 128 p.
CH'ÊNG, T'IEN-FANG, 程天放, 1899-  A history of Sino-Russian relations.
Introd. by John Leighton Stuart. Washington, Public Affairs Press [1957]
viii, 389 p.
CHINA. Ministry of Foreign Affairs. Documents with reference to the Sino-Russian dispute, 1929. Nanking, The Far Eastern Information Bureau [1929]
66 p. illus.
DALLIN, DAVID J., 1889-  Soviet Russia and the Far East. New Haven, Yale
Univ. Press, 1948. vii, 398 p. maps (1 fold.).
———. The rise of Russia in Asia. New Haven, Yale Univ. Press, 1949; Lon-
don, Hollis and Carter, 1950. xi, 293 p. maps.

[DEAN, MRS. VERA (MICHELES) ]. Russia and China in Manchuria. New York
[Foreign Policy Association , 1929] p. [193]-202. illus.(map) (Foreign policy association. Information service. 5:11. August 7, 1929).

DUDGEON, JOHN HEPBURN. Historical sketch of the ecclesiastical, political,
and commercial relations of Russia with China, drawn chiefly from original
sources. ["Anastic edition"] Peking, 1872. [Peking, Wen tien ko, 1940] iii,
8, 53, 23 p.

EVANS, JACK EARL, 1925-  Russia on the Amur, 1643-89. Washington, 1952.
196 l. illus. Thesis-Georgetown University.

FREEMAN, ALWYN VERNON, 1910-  Status of Dairen under the Sino-Soviet
agreement of August 14, 1945. (In American journal of international law.
Lancaster, Pa., 1948. v. 42, p. 142-148).

INTERNATIONAL RELATIONS COMMITTEE. The Sino-Russian crisis; the actual facts brought to light. Nanking, The International Relations Committee
[1929] 105 p. illus.(incl. facsims.) plates.

KORFF, SERGIEĬ ALEKSANDROVICH, baron, 1876-   Russia in the Far East.
Washington, Carnegie Endowment for International Peace, 1921. vi, 50 p.
(Carnegie Endowment. Division of International Law. Pamphlets. Confiden-
tial print. 4 ).

KRAKOWSKI, ÉDOUARD, 1896-  Chine et Russie; l'Orient contre la civilisation occidentale. Paris, La Colombe [1957] 412 p. facsims.

LEW, DANIEL H., 劉毓棠, [Liu Yü-tang]. Manchurian booty and international
law. (In American journal of international law. Concord, N.H., 1946. v. 40,
p. 584-591).

LIPMAN, NATAN DAVIDOVICH. Mit der roten Armee im Fernen Osten, Aufzeichnungen eines Rotarmisten.   Moskau, Verlagsgenossenschaft ausländischer Arbeiter in der UdSSR, 1932. 244 p. front.(port.). "Russischer titel:
Записки красноармейца. Berechtige übersetzung aus dem russischen Josef
Kagan."

LOBANOV-ROSTOVSKY, ANDREI, 1892-  Russia and Asia. New York, Macmillan, 1933. viii, 334 p. incl. maps.
———. The same. Ann Arbor, G. Wahr Pub. Co., 1951. 342 p. illus.

MANDEL, WILLIAM, comp. Soviet source materials on USSR relations with
East Asia, 1945-50. With an Introductory survey of Soviet Far Eastern policy since Yalta, by Max Beloff. Prelim. ed. New York, International Secretariat, Institute of Pacific Relations [1950] 289 p.

MOORE, HARRIET LUCY, 1912-  A record of Soviet Far Eastern relations,
1931-42. Submitted as a document for the eighth conference of the IPR. New
York, International Secretariat, Institute of Pacific Relations [1942] 92 1.
(Secretariat paper, 4 ).
———. Soviet Far Eastern policy, 1931-45. Princeton, N.J., Princeton University Press, 1945. xv, 284 p. [Institute of Pacific relations. I.P.R. inquiry
series].

PARRY, ALBERT, 1901-  Russian (Greek orthodox) missionaries in China,
1689-1917; their cultural, political and economic role. Chicago, 1938. 140 1.
Thesis-Univ. of Chicago.

PASVOLSKY, LEO, 1893-1953. Russia in the Far East. New York, Macmillan,
1922. ix, 181 p.

PAVLOVSKY, MICHEL N. Chinese-Russian relations. New York, Philosophical Library [1949] viii, 194 p. fold. maps.

PETROV, VICTOR P., 1907-  Manchuria as an objective of Russian foreign
policy. Washington, 1954. 373 1. Thesis-American University.

ROMANOV, BORIS ALEKSANDROVICH, 1889-  Russia in Manchuria, 1892-
1906. Translated from the Russian by Susan Wilbur Jones. Ann Arbor, Published for American Council of Learned Societies by J.W. Edwards [1952]
x, 549 p. (Russian Translation Project series of the American Council of
Learned Societies, 15 ).

ROY, MANABENDRA NATH, 1893-1954. Sino-Soviet treaty. Calcutta, Renais-
sance Publishers [1945] cover-title, 50 p.
SUMNER, BENEDICT HUMPHREY, 1893-1951. Tsardom and imperialism in the
Far East and middle East, 1880-1914. London, H. Milford [1942] 43, [1] p.
(The Raleigh lecture on history. British academy, 1940). "From the Pro-
ceedings of the British academy. Volume xxvii."
TANG, PETER S. H., 唐盛鎬. Russian and soviet policy in Manchuria and Outer
Mongolia, 1911-31. New York, 1954. 589 l. Thesis-Columbia University.
TSAI, WEI-PING, 蔡維屏, 1911- The Russo-Japanese conflict in the Far East.
Urbana, 1938. 264 l. Thesis-University of Illinois.
U.S. Office of Strategic Services. Research and Analysis Branch. Russo-Chi-
nese relations and potential Soviet contributions to China's postwar economic
development. Washington, 1945. 37 p. (Its R and A No. 3331).
WEIGH, KEN-SHEN, 魏良聲, 1899- Russo-Chinese diplomacy. Shanghai, Com-
mercial Press, 1928. xxi, [3]-382 p. Published also as thesis, Johns Hop-
kins University.
WU, AITCHEN K., 吳藹辰, 1892- Aspects of Sino-Soviet relations. London,
1950. 617 l. Thesis-London School of Economics.
———. China and the Soviet Union, a study of Sino-Soviet relations. London,
Methuen; New York, John Day, 1950. xvi, 434 p.
YAKHONTOFF, VICTOR A., 1881- Russia and the Soviet Union in the Far East.
New York, Coward-McCann, inc. [c1931] London, G. Allen and Unwin, 1932.
xxii, 454 p. 2 fold. maps.

### Moscow and Chinese Communists

ASIAN PEOPLES' ANTI-COMMUNIST LEAGUE. "Asia First" in Soviet Russia's
strategy for world conquest. Taipei, 1956. cover-title, 37 p.
———. Intrigues of Soviet imperialists and Chinese Communists. [Taipei] 1956.
cover-title, 73 p.
———. Mao Tse-tung can never be a Tito. [Taipei] 1957. 61 p.
Die ASIENPOLITIK der UdSSR, 1939-51. Bonn, 1952. 111 p.
BELOFF, MAX, 1913- Soviet Far Eastern policy since Yalta. Submitted by the
IPR International Secretariat as a preparatory paper for the Eleventh IPR
Conference to be held at Lucknow in October 1950. New York, International
Secretariat, Institute of Pacific Relations, 1950. 36 p. (Secretariat paper, 2 ).
———. Soviet policy in the Far East, 1944-51. London, New York, Oxford Uni-
versity Press, 1953. vi, 278 p.
BOORMAN, HOWARD L., 1920- Moscow-Peking axis: strengths and strains,
by Howard L. Boorman [and others] Foreword by Arthur H. Dean. New York,
Published for the Council on Foreign Relations by Harper, 1957. xxi, 227 p.
tables. (Publications of the Council on Foreign Relations).
BRANDT, CONRAD, 1920- Soviet failure in China, 1920-27. Cambridge, 1956.
181 l. Thesis-Harvard University.
CHIANG, KAI-SHEK, 1886- Soviet Russia in China; a summing-up at seventy,
Chiang Chung-cheng. New York, Farrar, Straus and Cudahy, Toronto, Am-
bassador Books, 1957. London, Harrap, 1957. 392 p.
CHINESE ASSOCIATION FOR THE UNITED NATIONS. Can Mao Tse-tung become
a Tito? [Taipeh] 1950. 36 p. (Its Unachina publications, ser. I, 3 ).
CHINESE communism and its relation to Soviet communism. [n. p., 1951] 131 p.
COLONNA di Stigliano, Ferdinand Joseph, principe d'Altora, 1871- Les Sovi-
ets en Chine (pour comprendre le drame chinois). Paris-Bruges, Desclée de
Brouwer, 1930. 114 p.
COMMUNIST INTERNATIONAL (Monthly). China at bay; [special supplement to
the Communist International] London, Modern Books, 1936. 79, [1] p. map.
———. [La Chine soviétique]; numero spécial de l'Internationale Communiste,

organe mensuel du Comité exécutif de l'Internationale Communiste. Paris, Bureau d'éditions de diffusion et de publicité, 1936. 119 p.

——. Executive Committee. China in revolt; [a reprint of some of the speeches made during the consideration of the Chinese question by the Executive Committee of the Comintern at its 7th plenary session] Chicago?, 1927. 64 p.

——. Die chinesische Frage auf dem 8 Plenum der Exekutive der Kommunistischen Internationale, Mai, 1927. Hamburg, C. Hoym Nachfolger [c1927] 160 p.

CREEL, GEORGE, 1876-1955. Russia's race for Asia. Indianapolis, Bobbs-Merrill Co. [1949] 264 p.

DAI, SHEN-YU, 戴盛虞, 1921- Peking, Moscow, and the communist parties of colonial Asia. Cambridge, Center for International Studies, Massachusetts Institute of Technology, 1954. 167 l.

ECKSTEIN, ALEXANDER, 1915- Moscow-Peking axis; the economic pattern. [Rev. November 1, 1956]. Cambridge, Mass., 1956. 64 p.

EUDIN, XENIA JOUKOFF. Soviet Russia and the East, 1920-27; a documentary survey, by Xenia Joukoff Eudin and Robert C. North. Stanford, Stanford University Press, 1957. xviii, 478 p. illus. (The Hoover Library on War, Revolution, and Peace. Publication, 25 ).

FAHNE DES KOMMUNISMUS. Der Kampf um die Kommunistische Internationale; dokumente der russischen Opposition nicht veröffentlicht vom Stalin'schen ZK. Veröffentlicht vom Verlag der "Fahne des Kommunismus." Berlin, Druckerei für Arbeiter-Literatur Willy Iszdonat, 1928. 176 p.

FUSE, KATSUJI. Soviet policy in the Orient. East Peking, Enjinsha, 1927. 5, 2, 409 p. illus., ports.

GILBERT, RODNEY YONKERS, 1889- Competitive coexistence: the new Soviet challenge. New York, Distributed by the Bookmailer [1956] 182 p.

HIDAKA, NOBORU, comp. The Comintern's intrigues in Manchoukuo. [Dairen?] Manchuria Daily News, 1940. 64 p.

HUDSON, GEOFFREY FRANCIS, 1903- Soviet Chinese relations, 1917-27. Oxford, St. Antony's College, 1954. 12 l. (St. Antony's papers on Soviet affairs).

JAMES, MAURICE. Soviet China, by M.James and R. Doonping. New York, International Pamphlets [1932] cover-title, 31 p. incl. 1 illus., map. (International pamphlets, 20 ).

KREITNER, GUSTAV, RITTER VON. Hinter China steht Moskau. Berlin, E.S. S. Mittler, 1932. vii, [1], 144, [3] p. illus.(maps, 1 double).

LEUNG, SHAU-YAN, 梁受欣, 1910- The sino-soviet relations, 1919-29. Washington, D.C., 1943. 313 l. Thesis-Georgetown University.

The MANCHURIA DAILY NEWS. The Comintern's activity in Manchuria; a general survey. Hsinking, 1940. 49 p.

MARTIN, PAUL. De quoi comprendre les événements d'Extrême-Orient; les menées du Komintern. Paris, Éditions Baudinière [1937] cover-title, 22, [1] p. fold. map.

MĪTAREVSKIĬ, N. World wide Soviet plots. As disclosed by hitherto unpublished documents seized at the U.S.S.R. embassy in Peking. Tientsin, The Tientsin Press [1927] 203 p. plates, fold. map, fold. facsim., diagrs. (part fold.)

MÖDLHAMMER, FRANZ LUDWIG. Moskaus Hand im Fernen Osten; hrsg. im Auftrage der Anti-Komintern. Mit einem Geleitwort seiner Exzellenz des kaiserlich japanischen ausserordentlichen und bevollmächtigten Botschafters in Berlin, graf Mushakoji, und einer Erklärung des ausserordentlichen und b bevollmächtigten Botschafters des deutschen Reiches, Joachim von Ribbentrop. Berlin-Leipzig, Nibelungen-verlag, 1937. xvi, 186 p. illus. (maps) plates, ports. (Schwertbücher, schriften über Ostprobleme und bolschewismus. bd. III ).

——. Moscow's hand in the Far East; translated from German. Tokyo, Nippon

Dempo Tsushinsha [1938] 202 p., plates, ports.

NEUT, ÉDOUARD. Le Bolchevisme russe et la jeunesse intellectuelle chinoise. Rapport présenté par Dom Édouard Neut. Louvain, Semaine de missiologie, 1927. 15 p.

NORTH, ROBERT CARVER, 1914-  Moscow and Chinese Communists.  Stanford, Stanford University Press [1953] ix, 306 p. (Hoover Institute studies. Special studies).

NORTH CHINA DAILY NEWS, Shanghai. The Soviets in China unmasked; documents revealing bolshevistic plans and methods seized in the USSR embassy, Peking, April 6, 1927. Shanghai, North-China Daily News and Herald, 1927. 48 p. Reprinted from North-China Daily News, May 11, 1927.

PEKING AND TIENTSIN TIMES, Tientsin. Bolshevik activities in China; some documents seized in the Soviet military attachës office at Peking on April 6, 1927. [Tientsin, 1927] 13 p. illus.(incl. facsims.).

PICK, EUGENE, pseud. China in the grip of the Reds; sketches of the extravagant effort made by Soviet Russia to set up and control a red regime in China, with strong light upon the ruthless character of Borodin and his agents, by Captain Eugene Pick, late of the Red army intelligence service in China. Shanghai, North-China Daily News and Herald, 1927. 46, [2] p. port.

The PROCESS of the USSR's bolshevization of China until the conclusion of the Sino-Soviet pact. Tokyo, The Times Publishing Co., 1937. 32 p.

"RED" hands on China. London, Bemrose, 1927. 79 p.

700 MILLIONS for peace and democracy. Peking, Foreign Languages Press, 1950. ii, 82 p. illus., ports.

SOUTH MANCHURIA RAILWAY COMPANY. Information and Publicity Dept. Communist plottings in the Far East. [Tokyo? 1938] 22 p. fold. map, diagrs. (China incident series, no. 5).

SOVIET intrigues in China; mischievous interference in internal affairs. Hong Kong, Publicity Bureau for South China [1927?] xxiii, 96 p.

SOVIET plot in China. no. I-VI (Documents 1-32 inclusive) Peking, Metropolitan Police Headquarters, 1927. 6 no. in 1 v. illus.(facsims.).

SOWJETCHINA in Gefahr! Moskau-Leningrad, Verlagsgenossenschaft ausländischer Arbeiter der UdSSR, 1933. 38, [1] p. illus.

STARLINGER, WILHELM. Hinter Russland China. Würzburg, Marienburg-Verlag, 1957. 141 p.

STEINER, H. ARTHUR, 1905-  Mainsprings of Chinese communist foreign policy. New York, 1950. 100 p. Reprinted from American J. of International Law, January 1950.

SWANK, EMORY C., 1922-  The Moscow-Peking axis: an interpretation based primarily on Communist source materials, 1949-February 1953. [Washington] External Research Staff, Office of Intelligence Research, Dept. of State [1953] ii, 39 p.

TELLKAMP, A. Hammer und Sichel über China. Siegburg, F. Schmitt [1949] 208 p.

THOMPSON, ELIZABETH M. Chinese-Soviet relations. Washington, 1952. 16 p. (Editorial research reports, 11 ).

TROŤSKIĬ, LEV, 1879-1940. The draft program of the Communist International, a criticism of fundamentals. Introduction by James P. Cannon. New York, "The Militant," 1929. xi, 139, [1] p.

——. L'Internationale communiste après Lénine (le grand organisateur de la défaite) Paris, Rieder, 1930. 438 p.

——. Problems of the Chinese revolution, with appendices by Zinoviev, Vuyovitch, Nassunov and others. Translated with an introduction by Max Shachtman. New York, Pioneer Publishers, 1932. 432, [15] p.

TSÚ, JOHN BING-MIN, 祖炳民, 1914-  Sino-Soviet relations 1946-52. New York, 1953. 2 v. Thesis-Fordham University.

[URBAHNS, HUGO]. ed. Wie die chinesische Revolution zugrunde gerichtet wur-

de; Brief aus Schanghai gerichtet an das Executiv-Komitee der Kommunistischen Internationale, von Stalin unterschlagen. Berlin, Verlag der "Fahne
des Kommunismus," 1927. 32 p.

VAIDYA, KESHAV BALKRISHNA, 1896-  And now China: inside story of Soviet
designs on China. Bombay, Thacker, 1945. vi, 125 p. (His :The Un-Pacific
ser., 3 ).

WALTERS, EDISON KERMIT. Communism in China and its effect on Sino-Soviet
foreign relations. Washington, 1948. 71 l. Thesis-Georgetown University.

WEI, HENRY, 韋文起, 1909-  Mao Tse-tung's "lean-to-one-side" policy.
Lackland Air Force Base, Tex., Air Force Personnel and Training Research
Center, Air Research and Development Command, 1955. 52 p. (Human Re-
sources Research Institute. Research memorandum, 40 ).

——. China and Soviet Russia; with an introduction by Quincy Wright. Princeton, N.J., Van Nostrand [1956] xvi, 379 p. maps.

WHITING, ALLEN SUESS, 1926-  Soviet policy in China, 1917-24. Ann Arbor,
University Microfilms, 1953. ( [University Microfilms, Ann Arbor, Mich.]
Publication 5213 ). Collation of the original: 2, viii, 314 l. Thesis-Columbia
University.

——. Soviet policies in China, 1917-24. New York, Columbia University
Press, 1954. x, 350 p. (Studies of the Russian Institute of Columbia University).

WILBUR, CLARENCE MARTIN, 1908-  ed. Documents on communism, nationalism, and Soviet advisers in China, 1918-27; papers seized in the 1927 Peking raid. Edited, with introductory essays, by C. Martin Wilbur and Julie
Lien-ying How, 夏連蔭. New York, Columbia University Press, 1956.xviii,
617 p. facsims.

YAKHONTOFF, VICTOR A., 1881-  The Chinese soviets. New York, Coward-
McCann, 1934. xiv, 296 p.

### China and the United States
### Treaties, Documents, etc.

CHIAO, MING-SHUN, 喬明顺. The beginning of American-Chinese diplomatic
relations: the Cushing mission and the Treaty of Wanghia of 1844. Notre
Dame, Ind., 1954. xii, 289 l.

CHINA. Treaties, etc., 1943. Treaty between the Republic of China and the U-
nited States of America for the relinquishment of extra-territorial rights in
China and the regulation of related matters. [Chungking, Ministry of Foreign Affairs, 1943. 13 p.; cover-title, 12 p.

U.S. Congress. House. Committee on Foreign Affairs. Chinese indemnity.
Hearings before the Committee on Foreign Affairs, House of Representatives, Sixty-eighth Congress, first session, on H.J. Res. 201, to provide
for the remission of further payments of the annual installments of the Chinese indemnity. March 31 and April 1 and 2, 1924. Washington, Govt.Print.
Off., 1924. ii, 98 p.

——. Revision of treaties with China. Report. [To accompany H.Con.Res. 46]
[Washington, Govt. Print. Off., 1927] 15 p. (69th Cong., 2d sess. House.
Rept. 1891).

——. Amending the China aid act of 1948. Report to accompany H.R. 3830.
[Washington, Govt. Print. Off., 1949] 6 p. ( [U.S.] 81st Cong., 1st sess.,
1949. House. Report no. 329 ).

——. Foreign policy of the United States in the Far East [Formosa] report to
accompany H.Res. 452. Washington, Govt. Print. Off., 1950. 7 p. (81st
Cong., 2nd sess., 1950. House. Report 1619).

——. Denial of passports by Department of State to correspondents wishing
to visit Communist China. Hearing before the Subcommittee on the Far East
and the Pacific of the Committee on Foreign Affairs, House of Representa-

tives, Eighty-fifth Congress, first session. March 28, 1957. Washington, Govt. Print. Off., 1957. v, 37 p.

U. S. Congress. Senate. Committee on Appropriations. United States aid to Formosa. Staff report of the special committee on Foreign economic cooperation of the Senate appropriation commitee, August 7, 1951. Washington, Govt. Print. Off., 1951. 8 p.

———. Congress. Senate. Committee on Foreign Relations. Remission of Chinese indemnity. Report. [To accompany H. J. Res. 248] [Washington, Govt. Print. Off., 1924] 8 p. (68th Cong., 1st sess. Senate. Rept. 518).

———. Friendship, commerce, and navigation with China. Hearing before a subcommittee of the Committee on Foreign Relations, United States Senate, Eightieth Congress, second session, on a Treaty of friendship, commerce, and navigation between the United States of America and the Republic of China, together with a protocol thereto, signed at Nanking on November 4, 1946. Apr. 26, 1948. Washington, Govt. Print. Off., 1948. iii, 82 p.

———. Aid to China. Report on S. 2393, a bill to promote the general welfare, national interest, and foreign policy of the United States by providing aid to China. Washington, Govt. Print. Off., 1948. iii, 20 p. fold. map. ( [U.S.] 80th Cong., 2d sess., 1948. Senate. Report no. 1026).

———. Authorizing the President to employ the Armed Forces of the United States for protecting the security of Formosa, the Pescadores, and related positions and territories of that area. Report of the Committee on Foreign Relations and the Committee on Armed Services on S. J. Res. 28. Washington, Govt. Print. Off., 1955. ii, 9 p. map. (84th Cong., 1st sess. Senate. Report no. 13 ).

———. Mutual defense treaty with China; report on Executive A, Eighty-fourth Congress, first session. Washington, Govt. Print. Off., 1955. iii, 15 p. fold. map. (84th Cong., 1st sess. Senate. Executive report no. 2 ).

U. S. Dept. of State. List of treaties, conventions, exchanges of notes, and other international agreements in force between the United States and China, and between the United States and other powers in relation to China. Submitted in pursuance of article I of the resolution (no. XI) regarding existing commitments of China or with respect to China, adopted by the Conference on the Limitation of Armament, February 1, 1922. Washington, Govt. Print. Off., 1925. ii, 7 p.

———. Text of letter from the Secretary of State, the Honorable Henry L. Stimson, to the Honorable William E. Borah, chairman, Committee on Foreign Relations, United States Senate. February 23, 1932. Washington, Govt. Print. Off., 1932. 7 p. [Publication, no. 296].

———. Text of proposed China aid bill and background information on economic assistance program for China, submitted to the Committee on Foreign Affairs. Feb. 20, 1948. Washington, Govt. Print. Off., 1948. iii, 54 p.

———. Report on the operations of the Department of State. Message from the President of the United States transmitting a report by the Secretary of State. [Washington, Govt. Print. Off., 1948] 15 p. ( [U.S.] 80th Cong., 2d sess., 1948. House. Document no. 562 ). Relates to executive agreements establishing the United States Educational Foundation in China and the United States Educational Foundation in Burma.

———. A summary of American-Chinese relations; letter from the Secretary of State [Dean Acheson] to the President transmitting the record of United States relations with China. [Washington, 1949] 16 p. (Its Publication 3608. Far Eastern series, 31 ).

———. United States relations with China, with special reference to the period 1944-49, based on the files of the Department of State. [Washington, Govt. Print. Off., 1949] xli, 1054 p. fold. col. map. (Its Publication 3573. Far Eastern series, 30 ).

———. Transcript of round table discussion on American policy toward China,

held in the Department of State October 6, 7 and 8, 1949. [Reported by E. Moyer and E. Voce. Washington, 1949] 1 v.(various pagings).
———. The China problem and U.S. policy. [Washington] Dept. of State [1954] 20 p. (U.S. Dept. of State. Publication 5460. Far Eastern series, 64 ).
———. The Far East. Washington, Govt. Print. Off., 1954. 1008 p. (Its Foreign relations of the United States: diplomatic papers 1937. v. 3 ).
———. Renunciation of force; U.S. and Chinese communist positions. [Washington, 1956] 15 p. (Its Publication 6280. General foreign policy series, 107 ).
———. China, 1942-    Washington, Govt. Print. Off., 1956-    v. (v. 1: 782 p.) (Its Foreign relations of the United States: diplomatic papers ).
U. S.  Economic Cooperation Administration. Economic aid to China under the China aid act of 1948. Washington, 1949. 129 p maps.
———. U.S. economic assistance to Formosa, 1 January to 31 December 1950. [Washington, 1951] 46 p. illus., maps.
U. S.  Office of Coordinator of Information. Research and Analysis Branch. American aid to China. [Washington, 1941?] 74 1. (Its Far Eastern study no. 21 ).
U. S.  President, 1945-53 (Truman). Aid to China. Message transmitting recommendation that the Congress authorize a program for aid to China in the amount of $570,000,000 to provide assistance until June 30, 1948. [Washington, Govt. Print. Off., 1948] 4 p. ( [U.S.] 80th Cong., 2d sess., 1948. House. Document no. 536 ).
———. The same. Message transmitting a proposed program of aid to China. [Washington, Govt. Print. Off., 1948] 4 p. ( [U.S.] 80th Cong., 2d sess., 1948. Senate. Document no. 120 ).
U. S.  Treaties, etc., 1913-21 (Wilson). Treaty between the United States and China. Confirming the application of a five per cent ad valorem rate of duty to importations of goods into China by citizens of the United States. Signed at Washington, October 20, 1920. Washington, Govt. Print. Off., 1922. 19 p. (Treaty series, 657 ).
U. S.  Treaties, etc., 1923-29 (Coolidge). Treaty between the United States and China. Regulating tariff. relations. Signed at Peiping, July 25, 1928. Washington, Govt. Print. Off., 1929. 2 p. (Treaty series, 773 ).
U. S.  Treaties, etc., 1929-33 (Hoover). Arbitration. Treaty between the United States of America and China. Signed at Washington, June 27, 1930. Washington, Govt. Print. Off., 1933. 15 p. (Treaty series, no. 857 ).
U. S.  Treaties, etc., 1933-45 (Franklin D. Roosevelt). Principles applying to mutual aid in the prosecution of the war against aggression. Preliminary agreement between the United States of America and China, signed at Washington June 2, 1942, effective June 2, 1942. Washington, Govt. Print. Off., 1942. 3 p. ( [U.S. Dept. of State. Publication 1766] Executive agreement series 251 ).
———. Relinquishment of extraterritorial rights in China and the regulation of related matters. Treaty and an accompanying exchange of notes between the United States of America and China, signed at Washington January 11, 1943. Proclaimed by the President of the United States May 24, 1943. Washington, Govt. Print. Off., 1943. 35 p. ( [U.S. Treaties, etc.] Treaty series 984 ).
———. Jurisdiction over criminal offenses committed by armed forces. Agreement between the United States of America and China, effected by exchange of notes signed at Chungking, May 21, 1943, effective May 21, 1943. Washington, Govt. Print. Off., 1944. 14 p. ( [U.S. Dept. of state. Publication 2071] Executive agreement series 360 ).
———. Military service. Agreement between the United States of America and China, effected by exchanges of notes, signed at Washington November 6, 1943 and May 11 and June 13, 1944. Washington, Govt. Print. Off., 1945. 4 p. ( [U.S. Dept. of state. Publication 2262 ] Executive agreement series 426 ).

U. S. Treaties, etc., 1945-53 (Truman). Disposition of lend-lease supplies in the United States. Agreement between the United States of America and China, signed at Washington June 14, 1946. Effective from September 2, 1945. [Washington, Govt. Print. Off., 1946] 6 p. ( [U.S. Dept. of state. Publication 2605] Treaties and other international acts series 1533 ).

———. Air transport services. Agreement and accompanying exchange of notes between the United States of America and China signed at Nanking December 20, 1946, entered into force December 20, 1946. [Washington, Govt. Print. Off., 1947] iii, 34 p. ( [U.S.] Dept. of State. Publication 2855. Treaties and other international acts series, 1609 ).

———. Mutual aid. Agreement between the United States of America and China, implementing preliminary agreement of June 2, 1942, signed at Washington June 28, 1946, entered into force June 28, 1946. [Washington, Govt. Print. Off., 1948] 3 p. (U.S. Dept. of State. Publication 3186. Treaties and other international acts series, 1746 ).

———. United States armed forces in China. Agreement between the United States of America and China effected by exchange of notes signed at Nanking August 29 and September 3, 1947, entered into force September 3, 1947. [Washington, Govt. Print. Off., 1948] 8 p. (U.S. Dept. of State. Publication 3095. Treaties and other international acts series, 1715 ).

———. Claims resulting from activities of United States military forces in China. Agreement between the United States of America and China, effected by exchange of notes dated at Nanking October 13, 1947 and March 17, 1948, entered into force March 17, 1948. [Washington, Govt. Print. Off., 1948] 10 p. (U.S. Dept. of State. Publication 3258. Treaties and other international acts series, 1776 ).

———. Relief assistance. Agreement and exchange of notes between the United States of America and China, signed at Nanking October 27, 1947, entered into force October 27, 1947. [Washington, Govt. Print. Off., 1948] iii, 43 p. ( [U.S.] Dept. of State. Publication 3026. Treaties and other international acts series, 1674 ).

———. United States Educational Foundation in China. Agreement between the United States of America and China signed at Nanking November 10, 1947, entered into force November 10, 1947. [Washington, Govt. Print. Off., 1948] iii, 25 p. ( U.S. Dept. of State. Publication 3050. Treaties and other international acts series, 1687 ).

———. Transfer of United States naval vessels and equipment to the Chinese Government. Agreement and accompanying notes between the United States of America and China signed at Nanking December 8, 1947, entered into force December 8, 1947. [Washington, Govt. Print. Off., 1948] iii, 35 p. (U.S. Dept. of State. Publication 3069 Treaties and other international acts series, 1691).

———. Friendship, commerce and navigation. Treaty and protocol between the United States of America and China signed at Nanking, November 4, 1946. Proclaimed by the President of the United States of America January 12,1949, entered into force November 30, 1948, and exchange of notes signed at Nanking November 29, 1948. [Washington, Govt. Print. Off., 1949] iii, 107 p. ( [U.S.] Dept. of State. Publication 3425. Treaties and other international acts series, 1871 ).

———. Trade, application of most-favored-nation treatment to areas under occupation or control. Agreement between the United States of America and China effected by exchange of notes signed at Nanking July 3, 1948, entered into force July 3, 1948. [Washington, Govt. Print. Off., 1949] 14 p. (U.S. Dept. of State. Publication 3372. Treaties and other international acts series, 1839 ).

———. Economic cooperation with China under Public law 472, 80th Congress. Agreement between the United States of America and China, signed at Nanking July 3, 1948, entered into force July 3, 1948. [Washington, Govt. Print.

Off., 1949] 42 p. (U.S. Dept. of State. Publication 3375. Treaties and other international acts series, 1837 ).

———. The same. Agreement between the United States of America and China amending Agreement of July 3, 1948 effected by exchange of notes signed at Canton March 26 and 31, 1949, entered into force March 31, 1949. [Washington, Govt. Print. Off., 1949] 5 p. (U.S. Dept. of State. Publication 3545. Treaties and other international acts series, 1923 ).

———. Joint Commission on Rural Reconstruction in China. Agreement between the United States of America and China effected by exchange of notes signed at Nanking August 3 and 5, 1948, entered into force August 5, 1948. [Washington, Govt. Print. Off., 1949] 19 p. (U.S. Dept. of State. Publication 3389. Treaties and other international acts series, 1848 ).

———. The same. Agreement between the United States of America and China extending and modifying Agreement of August 5, 1948, effected by exchange of notes signed at Canton June 27, 1949, entered into force June 27, 1949. [Washington, Govt. Print. Off., 1949] 2 p. (U.S. Dept. of State. Publication 3678).

———. Air transport services. Agreement between the United States of America and China, extending and amending Agreement of December 20, 1946, effected by exchange of notes dated at Washington December 1 and 19, 1950, entered into force December 20, 1950. [Washington, Govt. Print. Off., 1951] 3 p. (U.S. Dept. of State. Publication 4118. Treaties and other international acts series 2184 ).

———. Mutual defense assistance. Agreement between the United States of America and China effected by exchange of notes signed at Taipai January 30 and February 9, 1951, entered into force February 9, 1951. [Washington, Govt. Print. Off., 1951] 9 p. (U.S. Dept. of State. Publication 4350. Treaties and other international acts series, 2293).

———. Mutual security, assurances under Mutual security act of 1951. Agreement between the United States of America and China effected by exchange of notes signed at Taipei December 29, 1951, and January 2, 1952, entered into force January 2, 1952. [Washington, Govt. Print. Off., 1953] 11 p. (U.S. Dept. of State. Publication 4891. Treaties and other international acts series, 2604 ).

———. Mutual defense assistance. Agreement between the United States of America and China, amending Agreement of January 30 and February 9, 1951, effected by exchange of notes signed at Taipei October 23 and November 1, 1952, entered into force November 1, 1952. [Washington, Govt. Print. Off., 1953] 15 p. (U.S. Dept. of State. Publication 5064. Treaties and other international acts series, 2712 ).

———. Economic cooperation, guaranties under Public law 472, 80th Congress, as amended. Agreement between the United States of America and China, effected by exchange of notes signed at Taipei June 25, 1952, entered into force June 25, 1952. [Washington, Govt. Print. Off., 1953] 10 p. (U.S. Dept. of State. Publication 4936. Treaties and other international acts series, 2657).

———. Economic cooperation with China, under Public law 472, 80th Congress. Agreement between the United States of America and China, amending Agreement of July 3, 1948, as amended, effected by exchange of notes, signed at Taipei January 21 and 31, 1950, entered into force January 31, 1950; operative retroactively December 31, 1949. [Washington, Govt. Print. Off., 1955] 9 p. (U.S. Dept. of State. Publication 5808. Treaties and other international acts series, 3077 ).

———. Relief supplies and packages; reimbursement of ocean freight charges. Agreement between the United States of America and China effected by exchange of notes dated at Taipei Ocotober 20 and December 12, 1952, entered into force December 12, 1952; operative retroactively July 1, 1952. [Washington, Govt. Print. Off., 1954] 10 p. (U.S. Dept. of State. Publication 5168. Treaties and other international acts series, 2749 ).

U. S.   Treaties, etc., 1953-   (Eisenhower). Relief supplies and packages; postal charges. Agreement between the United States of America and China, a-
mending Agreement of November 5 and 18, 1948, as amended, effected by
exchange of notes dated at Taipei July 12 and October 26, 1954, entered into
force October 26, 1954. [Washington, Govt. Print. Off., 1955] 5 p. (U.S.
Dept. of State. Publication 5822. Treaties and other international acts series,
3151 ).
————. Defense; loan of vessels to China. Agreement between the United States
of America and China, effected by exchange of notes signed at Taipei January
13, 1954, entered into force January 13, 1954. [Washington, Govt. Print.
Off., 1955] 11 p. (U.S. Dept. of State. Publication 5406. Treaties and other
international acts series, 2916 ).
————. Defense; loan of vessels and small craft to China.  Agreement between
the United States of America and China, effected by exchange of notes signed
at Taipei May 14, 1954, entered into force May 14, 1954. [Washington, Govt.
Print. Off., 1955] 14 p. (U.S. Dept. of State. Publication 5543. Treaties and
other international acts series, 2979 ).
————. Atomic energy, cooperation for civil uses. Agreement between the United States of America and China signed at Washington July 18, 1955. [Wash-
ington, Govt. Print. Off., 1955] 6 p. (U.S. Dept. of State. Publication 5962.
Treaties and other international acts series, 3307 ).
————. Mutual defense treaty between the United States of America, and the Republic of China signed at Washington, December 2,1954, and Exchange of notes
signed at Washington December 10, 1954. [Washington, Govt. Print. Off.,
1956] 24 p. (U.S. Dept. of State. Publication 5850. Treaties and other international acts series, 3178 ).
————. Air transport services. Agreement between the United States of America
and China amending Agreement of December 20, 1946, as extended and amended, effected by exchange of notes dated at Washington February 7 and April
15, 1955. [Washington, Govt. Print. Off., 1956] 2 p. (U.S. Dept. of State.
Publication 6121. Treaties and other international acts series, 3347 ).
————. Defense; loan of vessels and small craft to China.  Agreement between
the United States of America and China, amending Agreement of May 14, 1954,
effected by exchange of notes signed at Taipei March 22 and 31, 1955. [Wash-
ington, Govt. Print. Off., 1956] 5 p. (U.S. Dept. of State. Publication 6143.
Treaties and other international acts series, 3215 ).
————. The same. Agreement between the United States of America and China
amending Agreement of May 14, 1954, as amended, effected by exchange of
notes dated at Taipei  June 18, 1955. [Washington, Govt. Print. Off., 1956]
5 p. (U.S. Dept. of State. Publication 6119. Treaties and other international
acts series, 3346 ).
————. The same. Agreement between the United States of America and China,
amending Agreement of May 14, 1954, as amended, effected by exchange of
notes dated at Taipei October 16 and 20, 1956. [Washington, Govt. Print.
Off., 1956] 6 p. (Treaties and other international acts series, 3676 ).
————. Establishment of United States Navy Medical Research Center at Taipei,
Taiwan. Agreement between the United States of America and China, effec-
ted by exchanges of notes dated at Taipei March 30, April 26, and October
14, 1955. [Washington, Govt. Print. Off., 1956] 20 p. (Treaties and other
international acts series, 3493 ).
————. Passport visas. Agreement between the United States of America and
China effected by exchange of notes dated at Taipei December 20, 1955, and
February 20, 1956. [Washington, Govt. Print. Off., 1956] 12 p. (Treaties
and other international acts series, 3539 ).
————. Mutual defense assistance: disposition of equipment and materials. A-
greement between the United States of America and China effected by exchange of notes signed at Taipei April 3, 1956. [Washington, Govt. Print.

Off., 1956] 8 p. (Treaties and other international acts series, 3571 ).
――――. Surplus agricultural commodities. Agreement and exchange of notes between the United States of America and China signed at Taipei, August 14, 1956. [Washington, Govt. Print. Off., 1956] 20 p. (Treaties and other international acts series, 3666 ).
――――. The same. Agreement between the United States of America and China amending article I, paragraph 1, of Agreement of August 14, 1956, effected by exchange of notes signed at Taipei October 5 and 12, 1956. [Washington, Govt. Print. Off., 1957] 4 p. (Treaties and other international acts series, 3718 ).
――――. Mutual defense assistance; construction of military installations and facilities. Agreement between the United States of America and China effected by exchange of notes signed at Taipei November 21, 1956. [Washington, Govt. Print. Off., 1957] 16 p. (Treaties and other international acts series, 3713 ).
――――. United States Navy Medical Research Center at Taipei, Taiwan. Agreement between the United States of America and China amending Agreement of October 14, 1955, effected by exchange of notes signed at Taipei December 27, 1956. [Washington, Govt. Print. Off., 1957] 7 p. (Treaties and other international acts series, 3720 ).
――――. Mutual security: investment guaranties. Agreement between the United States of America and China amending Agreement of June 25, 1952, effected by exchange of notes signed at Taipei May 3, 1957. [Washington, Govt. Print. Off., 1957] 8 p. (Treaties and other international acts series, 3831 ).
――――. Defense: loan of vessels and small craft to China. Agreement between the United States of America and China amending annex to Agreement of May 14, 1954, effected by exchange of notes dated at Taipei May 16, 1957. [Washington, Govt. Print. Off., 1957] 6 p. (Treaties and other international acts series, 3837 ).

## General Works

ALLEN, WILLIAM DANGAIX, 1904-   American enlightened imperialism, and essays on our cultural relations with India, Philippines, China. Peking, San Yu Press, 1933. iii, 168 p. plates, facsim.
AMERICAN COUNCIL OF LEARNED SOCIETIES. Directory of organizations in America concerned with China. Prepared and published by the American Council of Learned Societies. Washington, D. C., 1942. 116, [7] p.
ARNOLD, JULEAN HERBERT, 1875-1946. comp. China through the American window. Shanghai, American Chamber of Commerce, 1932. 85 p. illus. (incl. map) diagrs.
――――. China's fate and America's future. Washington, 1939. 3-14 p.
BARNETT, ROBERT W., 1911-   China, America's ally. New York, American Council, Institute of Pacific Relations, 1942. 48 p. illus. (maps) (Far Eastern pamphlets, 5 ).
BAU, MINGCHIEN JOSHUA, 1894-   The open door doctrine in relation to China. New York, Macmillan, 1923. xxviii, 245 p. (Knights of Columbus historical series ).
BISSON, THOMAS ARTHUR, 1900-   Showdown in the Orient. New York, N. Y., Foreign Policy Association [1940] 48 p. illus. (map) (World affairs pamphlets. [New series], 8, April 1940 ).
――――. American policy in the Far East, 1931-41. Rev. ed., with a supplementary chapter by Miriam S. Farley. New York, International Secretariat, Institute of Pacific Relations, 1941. xiii, 206 p. (I. P. R. Inquiry series ). 1st ed. 1939.
――――. America's Far Eastern policy. New York, International Secretariat, Institute of Pacific Relations, distributed by Macmillan, New York, 1945. xiii, 235 p. (I. P. R. Inquiry series ).

BORG, DOROTHY, 1902-    American policy and the Chinese revolution, 1925-
    28. New York, American Institute of Pacific Relations, Macmillan, 1947.
    x, 440 p. Issued also as thesis, Columbia University.
BULLITT, WILLIAM CHRISTIAN, 1891-    Report to the Joint Committee on
    Foreign Economic Cooperation concerning China, pursuant to section 124 of
    Public law 472, 80th Congress. Washington, Govt. Print. Off., 1948. ii, 13 p.
CHINA and America; a chronicle of cultural relations. v. 1-2, no. 3; Mar. 1948-
    June 1949. [New York] China Institute in America. 2 v. in 1. ports.
CHOU, I-KUA, 周宜适, 1916-    The American policy in China, 1929-39. [Med-
    ford, Mass.] 1949. 7 p. ([Fletcher School of Law and Diplomacy, Medford,
    Mass.] Thesis abstract, 1949, no. 2 ).
CH'OU PAN I WU SHIH MO. 籌辦夷務始末. China's management of the Ameri-
    can barbarians; a study of Sino-American relations, 1841-61, with documents.
    By Earl Swisher. New Haven, Published for the Far Eastern Association by
    Far Eastern Publications, Yale University [1953] xxi, 844 p. (Far Eastern
    Association. Monograph, 2 ).
CHRISTOPHER, JAMES WILLIAM. Conflict in the Far East; American diploma-
    cy in China from 1928-33. Leiden, E.J. Brill, 1950. xiv, 335 p. fold. maps.
CHU, CHARLES CHIA-HWEI, 朱家恢, 1920-    The China policy of the Taft-
    Knox administration, 1909-13. Chicago, 1956. 565 l. Thesis-University of
    Chicago.
CLYDE, PAUL HIBBERT, 1896-    ed. United States policy toward China; dip-
    lomatic and public documents, 1839-1939. Durham, N.C., Duke Univ. Press,
    1940. xv, 321 p. incl. front. (facsim.) (Duke University publications ).
CONFERENCE ON AMERICAN RELATIONS WITH CHINA, Baltimore, 1925. A-
    merican relations with China; a report of the Conference held at Johns Hop-
    kins University, September 17-20, 1925, with supplementary materials, and
    arranged to be of use to discussion groups, current events clubs, and univer-
    sity classes. Published for the Conference on American Relations with China.
    Baltimore, Johns Hopkins Press, 1925. 198 p.
CURRY, ROY WATSON. Woodrow Wilson and Far Eastern policy, 1913-21. New
    York, Bookman Associates [c1957] 411 p. (Bookman monograph ser.).
DENNETT, TYLER, 1883-1949. Americans in eastern Asia; a critical study of
    the policy of the United States with reference to China, Japan and Korea in
    the 19th century. New York, Barnes and Noble, 1941. xviii, 725 p. illus.
    (maps) [A reprint of 1922 ed. published by Macmillan].
DULLES, FOSTER RHEA, 1900-    China and America; the story of their rela-
    tions since 1784. Princeton, N.J., Princeton Univ. Press, 1946. vii, 277 p.
FAIRBANK, JOHN KING, 1907-    The United States and China. Cambridge,
    Harvard Univ. Press, 1948. xiv, 384 p. maps (part col.) (The American
    foreign policy library ).
FARLEY, MIRIAM SOUTHWELL, ed. American Far Eastern policy and the Sino-
    Japanese war; a report of seven discussion conferences held under the auspi-
    ces of the American Council, Institute of Pacific Relations, March to May,
    1938. New York, American Council, Institute of Pacific Relations [c1938]
    viii, 71 p. (Studies of the Pacific, I ).
FEIS, HERBERT, 1893-    The China tangle; the American effort in China from
    Pearl Harbor to the Marshall mission. Princeton, Princeton Univ. Press,
    1953. x, 445 p. maps.
FIFIELD, RUSSELL HUNT, 1914-    Woodrow Wilson and the Far East; the di-
    plomacy of the Shantung question. New York, Crowell [1952] xv, 383 p. map
    (on lining papers).
GAING, OHN, 1923-    American policy in China, 1922-27. Washington, D.C.,
    1953. 388 l. Thesis-Georgetown University.
GANDHI, SHANTI SWARUP, 1915-    United States diplomatic relations with Chi-
    na, 1869-82. Washington, D.C., 1953. 479 l. Thesis-Georgetown University.
GOETZ, DELIA. The dragon and the eagle; America looks at China. Pictures by

Thomas Handforth. [New York] Foreign Policy Association, distributed through the Vanguard Press [1945] 61, [1] p. incl. col. front., col. illus. (incl. map).

GRIGGS, DAVID THURSTON, 1916-  Americans in China: some Chinese views. Washington, Foundation for Foreign Affairs, 1948. 59 p. (Foundation pamphlet, 5 ).

GRISWOLD, ALFRED WHITNEY, 1906-  The Far Eastern policy of the United States. New York, Harcourt, Brace [c1938] 3-530 p. double map.

HANSON, HALDORE E., 1912-  America's need for understanding China. Washington, Govt. Print. Off., 1944. 14 p. [U.S. Dept. of State. Publication 2230. Far Eastern series 7].

HAWKINS, EVERETT DAY, 1906-  America's role in China. New York, American Council, Institute of Pacific Relations, 1947. 64 p. illus., ports. (I. P. R. pamphlets, 26 ).

HORNBECK, STANLEY KUHL, 1883-  China and American foreign policy. [Washington, 1928] 18 l.

———. Address on American policy and the Chinese-Russian dispute, at Williamstown institute of politics on Aug. 27, 1929. Washington, Dept. of State, 1929. 13 l. (Dept. of State. Press Release, Aug. 29, 1929).

———. The United States and the Far East: certain fundamentals of policy. [Boston] World Peace Foundation, 1942. vi, 100 p.

JOHNSTONE, WILLIAM CRANE, 1901-  Memorandum on the efforts of the Sino-Japanese conflict on American rights and interests in China. New York, American Council, Institute of Pacific Relations [1939] 53 numb. l.

JUDD, WALTER H., 1898-  Our ally China; a speech made in the United States Congress. Shanghai, International Publishers, 1945. 13, 14 p.

KARIG, WALTER, 1898-  Asia's good neighbor; we were once...can we be again? Indianapolis, Bobbs-Merrill [c1937] 308 p. fold. map.

KOO, VI KYUIN WELLINGTON, 顧維鈞, 1888-  The open door policy and world peace; given under the auspices of the Dunford House Cobden memorial association in London on 28 June 1939, the Rt. Hon. the Earl of Lytton, in the chair. London, New York [etc.] Oxford University Press, 1939. 24 p. (Richard Cobden lecture. 11th ).

LI, T'IEN-I, 李田意, 1915-  The United States and the recognition of the Chinese Republic. Peiping, National Peking Univ. Press, 1948. 43 p. (National Peking University. College of Arts, Semicentennial papers, 17.).

———. Woodrow Wilson's China policy, 1913-17. [Kansas City, Mo.] Univ. of Kansas City Press; [distributed by] Twayne Publishers, New York, 1952. 268 p.

LIN, CHING-JÜN, 林景潤, 1898-1947. The "open door" in China. New York, Chinese Students Committee on Washington Conference, 1921. 16 p.

LINEBARGER, PAUL MYRON WENTWORTH, 1871-1939. Our common cause with China against imperialism and communism. Los Angeles, Kuomin-tang (Chinese Nationalist party) [1927] 30, [2] p. ("Chinese politics made easy" series ).

LOCKWOOD, WILLIAM WIRT, 1906-  America and the Far Eastern war. New York, American Council, Institute of Pacific Relations [c1937] 20 p.

MA, WÊN-HUAN, 馬文煥, 1900-  American policy toward China as revealed in the debates of Congress. Shanghai, Kelly and Walsh [1934] x, 293, [4] p.

MILLARD, THOMAS FRANKLIN FAIRFAX, 1868-1942. The A B C's of the Hay doctrine. Shanghai, Weekly Review of the Far East, 1921. cover-title, 10 p.

NORTH, JOSEPH. What are we doing in China? New York, New Century Publishers [1945] 23 p. illus.

PECK, WILLYS RUGGLES, 1882-1952. State department aid to cultural exchange with China. Washington, Govt. Print. Off., 1944. 20 p. [U.S. Dept. of State. Publication 2159. Far Eastern series 6].

REA, GEORGE BRONSON, 1869-1936. The highway to hostilities in the Far East.

Shanghai, The Japanese Association in China, 1932. cover-title, 35 p.

ROBINSON, GEROID TANQUARY. Asia's American problem; a diffident discussion of the project sometimes called the new international Chinese consortium, and of certain other combustible matters pertaining thereto. New York, B. W. Huebsch, 1921. 3-27 p. (The Freeman pamphlets).

SHEN, YUN-KUNG, 沈允公, 1909-  American official attitudes toward governments in China, 1898-1947. Madison, 1948. i, 217 1. Thesis-Univ. of Wisconsin.

SHERRY, JOHN C., 1909-  Aspects of American policy regarding the unification of the Chinese nationalistic government, 1944-48. New York, 1956. 270 1. Thesis-Fordham University.

SOONG, MAY-LING, 蔣宋美齡, 1897-  Addresses delivered before the House of Representatives and the Senate of the United States, February 18, 1943. Stamford, Conn., The Overbrook Press, 1943. 15, [1] p. illus.

————. Addresses delivered before the Senate of the United States and the House of Representatives on February 18, 1943, together with other addresses delivered during her visit to the United States. Washington, 1943. 26 p.

————. China, as told by Madame Chiang Kai-shek in a series of addresses in New York, San Francisco, Chicago and in Ottawa, Canada, in behalf of the Chinese relief and of the Chinese government. York, Pa., The Maple Press Co., 1944. 47, [1] p. col. illus.

T'ANG, LIANG-LI, 湯良禮, 1901-  American imperialism in China. Shanghai, China United Press, 1943. x, 208 p. ("Tribune" monographs, 1.).

TORREGROSA, MANUEL FRANCIS, 1924-  U.S. dollar diplomacy in China, 1909-13. Washington, 1951. iv, 366 1. Thesis-Georgetown University.

UHLMANN, GEORGES. La Chine, nouvelle Amérique. Pékin, Impr. de la "Politique de Pékin," 1935. 60 p. map. (Collection de la "Politique de Pékin").

U.S. policy toward China with general foreign and Far Eastern policy statements, letters and speeches by Harry S. Truman, James F. Byrnes and John Carter Vincent. With Chinese translation. Shanghai, International Publishers, 1946. 20, 18 p.

U.S. Commissioner to China, 1900-01. Affairs in China. Report of William W. Rockhill, late commissioner to China, with accompanying documents. [n. p] Reprinted in China, 1941. 391 p. Issued in 1901 as U.S. 57th Cong. 1st sess., Senate doc. 67, with title: Report of William W. Rockhill, late commissioner to China.

————. Executive Headquarters, Peiping. History of the Executive headquarters, January 1946 to February 1947. Peiping, 1947. 42 p.

————. Judge-Advocate-General's Dept. (Army). Report of the judge advocate, United States Forces, China Theater, United States Army Forces China, Nanking Headquarters Command, and Army Advisory Group China, 1 January 1945 to 10 June 1947. [Washington, 1948] iii, iv-vi, 128 p.

WALLACE, HENRY AGARD, 1888-  Soviet Asia mission. New York, Reynal and Hitchcock [1946] 254 p. plates (incl. ports., map).

————. Ma mission en Asie soviétique, tr. de l'américain. Introd. de Philippe Soupault. Paris, R. Julliard [1947] 266 p. fold. map. (Sequana).

————. Sondermission in Sowjet-Asien und China. [Autorisierte Übertragung von William G. Frank] Zürich, Steinberg [1947] 216 p. map.

WANG, SAMUEL HSUAN, 王瑄, 1914-  The Sino-Japanese war and the American Far Eastern policy, 1931-41. Ithaca, 1947. [7], 373 1. Thesis-Cornell University.

WHITAKER, URBAN G., JR., 1924-  American and Chinese political problems 1912-23. Seattle, 1954. 415 1. Thesis-Univ. of Washington.

WILLIAMS, BENJAMIN HARRISON, 1889-  The protection of American citizens in China. [New York, 1923] 2 pt. Thesis-Univ. of California, 1921. Reprinted from the American journal of international law, 16:1, January, 1922 and 17:3, July, 1923.

WILLOUGHBY, WESTEL WOODBURY, 1867-1945. Far Eastern policies of the
    United States. (In American journal of international law. Concord, N.H.,
    1940. v. 34., p. 193-207 ).
YEN, EN-TSUNG, 嚴恩椿 . The open door policy. Boston, The Stratford Co.,
    1923. 191 p.


1949-


ACHESON, DEAN GOODERHAM, 1893-    United States policy toward Asia; ad-
    dress. [Washington, 1950] 16 p. (Dept. of State. Publication 3817. Far Eas-
    tern series, 33 ).
————. Crisis in Asia, an examination of U.S. policy; remarks. [Washington]
    Office of Public Affairs, Dept. of State [1950] 111-118 p. (Dept. of State.
    Publication 3747. Far Eastern series, 32) "Reprinted from the Department
    of State bulletin of January 23, 1950."
————. Our Far Eastern policy; debate, decision and action. Address [delivered
    before the Women's National Press Club, Washington, D.C.] April 18, 1951.
    [Washington] Dept. of State [Division of Publications, Office of Public Affairs,
    1951] 11 p. (Dept. of State. Publication 4201. Far Eastern series, 41 ).
————. American policy toward China, statement before a Joint Senate Commit-
    tee June 4, 1951. [Washington, Govt. Print. Off., 1951] 49 p. (Dept. of
    State. Publication 4255. Far Eastern series 43 ).
ALLISON, JOHN M., 1905-    Our Far Eastern policy. [Washington, Govt.Print.
    Off., 1952] 652-657 p. (Department of State publication 4595. Far Eastern se-
    ries, 56 ). "Reprinted from the Department of State bulletin of April 28,
    1952."
BABCOCK, FENTON, 1926-    Issues of China policy before Congress, Septem-
    ber 1945 to September 1955. New Haven, 1956. ii-ix, 152, iv l. Thesis-
    Yale University.
CHANG, YU-NAN, 張煜南 , 1920-    American security problems in the Far
    East, 1950-52. Seattle, 1954. 342 l. Thesis-Univ. of Washington.
CHEN, LI-FU, 陳立夫 , 1899-    Chinese-American relations as affected by
    Communist conspiracy in recent years. New York, 1953. 22 p.
CHINESE ASSOCIATION FOR THE UNITED NATIONS. The Sino-American trea-
    ty of mutual defense. Taipei, 1955. 40 p.
COUNCIL ON FOREIGN RELATIONS. American policy toward China; a report
    on the views of leading citizens in twenty-three cities, edited by Joseph Bar-
    ber. New York [1950] iv, 49 p. (Its Publications).
DINWIDDIE, JOSEPH. Aid to Nationalist China. New York, Vantage Press
    [1957] 177 p.
DODGE, DOROTHY RAE, 1927-    Recognition of the Central people's govern-
    ment of the People's Republic of China: legal and political aspects, an analy-
    sis of United States recognition policy as seen in the China case. Minneapol-
    is, 1955. ii, 634 l. Thesis-Univ. of Minnesota.
DULLES, JOHN FOSTER, 1888-    The threat of a Red Asia. [Text of speech
    before the Overseas Press Club of America, New York, N.Y., March 29,
    1954. Washington] Dept. of State [1954] 10 p. ( [U.S.] Dept. of State. Public
    Services Division. Series S, no. 13 ).
FLYNN, JOHN THOMAS, 1883-    While you slept; our tragedy in Asia and who
    made it. New York, Devin-Adair, 1951. 192 p. illus.
GULICK, LUTHER HALSEY, 1892-    A new American policy in China. [An In-
    ternational Committee report. Washington, National Planning Assn., 1949]
    vi, 35 p. (Planning pamphlets, 68 ).
HILLIS, DICK, 1913-    Dare we recognize Red China?  Grand Rapids, Zonder-
    van Pub. House [1956] 32 p.
HUANG, WILLIAM YUNG-NIEN, 黃永年 , 1917-    China's role with respect to
    major political and security questions under consideration by the United

States. Ann Arbor, 1953. 826 1. Thesis-University of Michigan.

KAMP, JOSEPH PETER, 1900-  America betrayed; the tragic consequences of Reds on the Government payroll! New York, Constitutional Educational League, c1950. 63 p.

LINDBECK, JOHN M.H., 1915-  Communist China and American Far Eastern policy; [based on an address made at Ohio State University on July 21, 1955. Washington] Dept. of State [1955] 21 p. ( [U.S.] Dept. of State. Publication 6198. Far Eastern series, 70 ).

LIU, TA-NIEN, 劉大年. Geschichte der amerikanischen Aggression in China [von] Lju Da-njän. [Aus dem Russischen übersetzt von Nikolai Stscherbina] Berlin, Dietz, 1956. 352 p.

LUCE, CLARE (BOOTHE) 1903-  The mystery of American policy in China; an address at testimonial dinner honoring the Most Reverend Paul Yu-Pin, D.D., Archbishop of Nanking, New York, June 14, 1949. [New York, Plain Talk, 1949] 34 p.

MID-WEST DEBATE BUREAU. Debate handbook: Recognition of communist China. Resolved: That the United States should extend diplomatic recognition to the communistic government of China. Normal, Ill. [1954] ii, 198 p.

MOY, EARNEST K., 梅其駒 ,1895-1958. Why not recognize red China even now? New York, The author, 1952. 15 p.

NEW CHINA NEWS AGENCY. The Truman doctrine in China. Hong Kong, New China News Agency, 1949. 39 p.

————. La doctrine Truman en Chine. Hong Kong, New China News Agency, 1949. 40 p.

NIXON, RICHARD MILHOUS, 1913-  US Vice-President Nixon's state visit to Free China; a collection of speeches and remarks on Free China. Edited by Eugene H.C. Wang, 王漢中. Taipei, China Culture Pub. Foundation, 1953. 33 p. illus. (Pamphlets on Chinese affairs ).

REISCHAUER, EDWIN OLDFATHER, 1910-  Toward a new Far Eastern policy [by] Edwin O. Reischauer. The economic task in Asia [by] Howard C. Gary. [New York, Foreign Policy Association, 1950] 61 p. illus., maps. (Headline series, no. 84 ).

————. Wanted: an Asian policy. New York, Knopf, 1955. 276 p.

RUSK, DEAN, 1909-  The underlying principles of Far Eastern policy. Address before the World Council, Seattle, Wash., on Nov. 6. Washington, Division of Publications, Office of Public Affairs, 1951] 821-824 p. (U.S. Dept. of State. Publication 4417. Far Eastern series, 52 ). "Reprinted from the Department of State bulletin of November 19, 1951."

TOMPKINS, ELON FARNSWORTH, 1887-  Disaster in Asia; a series of articles revealing how American Far Eastern policy became a program for communist mastery of Asia, reprinted from New York Journal American. [n.p., 1950] folder (7 p.).

UTLEY, FREDA, 1898-  The China story. Chicago, H. Regnery Co., 1951. xiii, 274 p.

VALEO, FRANCIS RALPH, 1916-  The China white paper; a summary with commentary of the Department of State's "United States relations with China." Washington, 1949. iii, 57 p. (Public affairs bulletin, 77 ).

VINACKE, HAROLD MONK, 1893-  The United States and the Far East. Submitted by the American Institute of Pacific Relations as a preparatory paper for the Eleventh Conference of the Institute of Pacific Relations to be held at Lucknow, India, in October 1950. New York, American Institute of Pacific Relations [1950] 53 p. (United States paper, 1 ).

————. The United States and the Far East, 1945-51. Stanford, Stanford University Press, 1952. vi, 144 p.

WALCH, JOHN WESTON, 1902-  Complete handbook on recognition of communist China. Portland, Me., c1954. 192 p.

WINFIELD, GERALD FREEMAN, 1908-  What can the United States do in China? New York, Foreign Policy Assn., 1949. 12 p. (Foreign policy reports, 25:1 ).

WU, HSIU-CH'ÜAN, 伍修權, 1909-   China accuses! Speeches of the Special Representative of the Central People's Government of the People's Republic of China at the United Nations. Peking, Foreign Languages Press [1951] 107 p. illus.

――――. La Chine accuse! Discours de l'envoyé spécial du Gouvernement populaire central de la République populaire de Chine à l'Organisation des Nations Unies. Pékin, Éditions en langues étrangères, 1951. 120 p. illus.

YEN, HSI-SHAN, 閻錫山, 1883-   Comments on the White Paper on China, a speech delivered to the members of the Chinese anti-aggression league. Canton, 1949. 16 p.

## China and other Western Countries

CHINA. Ministry of Foreign Affairs. Exchange of notes between China and Mexico embodying an agreement for the provisional modification of the Sino-Mexican treaty of 1899. [Peking? 1921?] cover-title, 11, 13, [16] p.

――――. Treaties, etc., 1940. Treaty of amity between the Republic of China and the Dominican Republic. [n. p., 1941] cover-title, 8 p.; 4 p.

――――. Treaties, etc., 1937. Treaty of amity between the Republic of China and the Republic of Estonia, London, 1937. [London, 1938?] cover-title, 3 p.; cover-title, 4 p.

EGYPT. Treaties, etc., 1917-   (Fuad I). Accord commercial provisoire entre l'Égypte et la Chine le 23 avril 1930. (Extrait du "Journal officiel" no. 61 du 26 juin 1930) Le Caire, Impr. Nationale, 1930. [2], [4] p.

## China and World War II

AMERICAN IRON AND STEEL INSTITUTE, New York. Steel products manual; packaging, loading and shipping methods for China Defense Supplies, inc. New York, American Iron and Steel Institute, 1942. cover-title, 25 p. illus.

BELDEN, JACK, 1910-   Still time to die. New York and London, Harper [1944] ix, 322 p.

――――. Il est toujours temps de mourir. Adapté de l'anglais par Julien Blanc. Paris, La Jeune Parque, 1946. 251 p. (Fenêtres sur le monde, 6 ).

――――. Zum Sterben ist immer noch Zeit. Aus dem Englischen übertragen von Leonhard Kolb. Zürich, Büchergilde Gutenberg, 1945. 1v, 448 p. illus. maps.

BURR, SAMUEL ENGLE. China A. P. O.: more than experience; a story of the China theater, 1944-45. [1st ed.] Washington, 1952-   v.

CALDWELL, JOHN COPE, 1913-   American agent [by] Mark Gayn and John Caldwell. New York, H. Holt [1947] 220 p.

CHANG, CH'I-YUN, 張其昀, 1901-   Record of the Cairo conference. Taipei, China Culture Pub. Foundation, 1953. 16 p. port. (Pamphlet on Chinese affairs).

CHATTOPADHYAYA, KAMALADEVI, 1903-   In war-torn China. [3d ed.] Bombay, Padma Publications [1944] xvi, 74 p. (Current topics series, no. 1 ).

CHINA. Ministry of Information. Inside wartime China. [Chungking, Printed by the Prabasi Press, 1943] cover-title, [100] p. illus. (incl. ports.).

DOMEI TSUSHINSHA. The greater east Asia war, its cause and aims, with Shanghai proclamations. Shanghai, Domei News Agency [1942?] 60 p.

ELDRIDGE, FRED. Wrath in Burma; the uncensored story of General Stilwell and international maneuvers in the Far East. Garden City, N.Y., Doubleday, 1946. 320 p. plates, ports.

HO, YUNG-CHI, 何永佶, 1902-   The big circle. New York, Exposition Press [1948] 152 p. group port., maps.

KARAKA, DOSOO FRAMJEE, 1911-   Chungking diary, with a foreword by Edgar Snow. Bombay, Thacker, 1944. viii, 223 p. 1st ed. 1942.

LEE, KUNG-SAM, 李公三. The secrets of China's victory. [Shanghai, 1946]
    viii, 169 p. illus.

LIN, YU-T'ANG, 林語堂, 1895-   Between tears and laughter. New York, John
    Day [1943]; London, Dorothy Crisp, 1945. 216 p.

McROBERTS, DUNCAN. While China bleeds; introduction by H.A. Ironside.
    Grand Rapids, Mich., Zondervan Pub. House [c1943] 162, [3] p.

MAO, TSE-TUNG, 1893-   China and the second imperialist world war. Chung-
    king, New China Information Committee, 1939. 50 p. (Its Bull., 9 ).

MORRIS, DAVID ELWYN, 1920-   China changed my mind. London, Cassell
    [1948]; Boston, Houghton, Mifflin [1949] 202 p. plates.

PAYNE, PIERRE STEPHEN ROBERT, 1911-   Chungking diary. London, Toron-
    to, W. Heinemann [1945] vi, 526 p. front.

———. Forever China. New York, Dodd, Mead [1945] ix, 573 p.

ROMANUS, CHARLES F. Stilwell's mission to China, by Charles F. Romanus
    and Riley Sunderland. Washington, Office of the Chief of Military History,
    Dept. of the Army, 1953 [c1952] xix, 441 p. illus., ports., maps (3 fold.col.
    in pocket) (United States Army in World War II: China-Burma-India theater).

———. Stilwell's command problems, by Charles F. Romanus and Riley Sunder-
    land. Washington, Office of the Chief of Military History, Dept. of the Army,
    1956 [c1955] xviii, 518 p. illus., ports., maps (4 fold. col., 2 in pocket )
    diagrs., tables. (United States Army in World War II: China-Burma-India
    theater ).

ROSINGER, LAWRENCE KAELTER, 1915-   Strategy of the war in Asia. New
    York, Foreign Policy Association [1943] [25]-35, [1] p. illus.(map) (Foreign
    policy reports, 19:3, April 15, 1943 ).

SNOW, EDGAR, 1905-   People on our side. New York, Random House [1944]
    xii, 324 p. illus.(maps) plates, ports.

———. Glory and bondage. London, V. Gollancz ltd., 1945. 263 p.

———. The same. Sydney, Angus and Robertson, 1946. ix, 257, [1] p.

STILWELL, JOSEPH WARREN, 1883-1946. The Stilwell papers, arr. and ed.
    by Theodore H. White. New York, W. Sloane Associates [1948]; London,
    Macdonald, 1949. xvi, 357 p. illus., ports., maps, facsims.

———. L'aventure chinoise 1941-44. Traduction de l'américain par F. Veillet-
    Lavallée. Neuchâtel, La Baconniere, 1949. 322 p. (Histoire et société d'au-
    jourd'hui).

STRATTON, ROY OLIN. SACO, the rice paddy navy. Pleasantville, N.Y.] C.S.
    Palmer Pub. Co., 1950. xvi, 408 p. illus., ports., maps.

TAMURA, KOHSAKU. Genesis of the Pacific war. Tokyo, The Foreign Affairs
    Association of Japan. 73 p.

TIPTON, LAURANCE, 1909-   Chinese escapade. London, Macmillan, 1949.
    vii, 247 p. plates, maps.

TSUJI, MASANOBU, 1902-   Underground escape; a translation from the Japan-
    ese. Tokyo, R. Booth and T. Fukuda [c1952] 298 p. illus.

U.S. Army. Forces in the Far East. Army operations in China; prepared by
    Headquarters, USAFFE and Eighth U.S. Army (Rear) [Tokyo?] Distributed
    by Office of the Chief of Military History, Dept. of the Army [1956] 2 v. maps,
    plans. (Japanese monograph no. 71-72 ).

———. South China area operations record, 1937-41. Prepared by Military His-
    tory Section. [n.p.] Distributed by Office of the Chief of Military History,
    Dept. of the Army [1956] cover-title, 139 p. maps, tables. (Japanese mono-
    graph no. 180 ).

———. National Archives. Preliminary inventory of the records of the Ameri-
    can War Production Mission in China (Record group 220) Compiled by John
    E. Maddox. Washington, 1955. v, 10 p. (Its Publication no. 56-6. Prelimi-
    nary inventories, no. 88 ).

WHITE, MARY CULLER, 1875-   I was there when it happened in China. Nashville, Abingdon-Cokesbury Press [1947] 123 p.

## China and the United Nations

BROOK, DAVID. The U.N. and the China dilemma. New York, Vantage Press
[1956] 87 p.

BROWN, BENJAMIN HOUSTON, 1915-    Chinese representation; a case study
in United Nations political affairs. Pt. 1 [by] Benjamin H. Brown, pt. 2 [by]
Fred Greene. New York, Woodrow Wilson Foundation, 1955. 52 p.

BRYAN, D.H. DEREK. The United Nations need China. London, Britain-China
Friendship Association, 1953. 12 p.

CHINA. News Service. China at U.N. Assembly, October 23 to December 16,
1946. Selected documents [presented by the Chinese Delegation] [New York,
1946] cover-title, 40 p. group ports. (on cover).

GREW, JOSEPH CLARK, 1880-    Invasion alert! The Red China drive for a UN
seat. Baltimore, Maran Publishers [1956] 81 p.

SMITH, ROBERT AURA, 1899-    Should the UN admit Red China; with Chinese
translation. Taipei, China Culture Pub. Foundation, 1954. 18 p. (Pamphlets
on Chinese affairs ).

TSIANG, TINGFU F., 蔣廷黻, 1895-    The charter of the United Nations and
the package deal. New York, Chinese Delegation to the United Nations, 1955.
37 p.

UNITED NATIONS. Delegation from China. China presents her case to the Uni-
Nations. New York, 1949. cover-title, 79 p.

――――. China fights for peace and freedom. New York, 1951. 99 p.

――――. General Assembly. Political and Security Committee. Threats to the political independence and territorial integrity of China and to the peace of the
Far East, resulting from Soviet violations of the Sino-Soviet treaty and of the
charter of United Nations. Lake Success, 1949. 20 p. (A/C. 1/sR. 338 ).

U.S. Congress. House. Committee on Foreign Affairs. Opposing the admission
of Communist China to membership in the United Nations. Washington, Govt.
Print. Off., 1951. 1 p. (82nd Cong. 1st sess. House. Report 463 ).

――――. Reiterating the opposition of the House of Representatives to the seating
of the communist regime in China in the United Nations. Report to accompany
H.Res. 627. Washington, Govt. Print. Off., 1954. 6 p. (83d Cong. 2d sess.
House. Report 2213 ).

――――. Expressions by the House of Representatives, the Senate, and the Committee on Foreign Affairs that the Chinese Communists are not entitled to and
should not be recognized to represent China in the United Nations. 84th Congress, 2d session, Committee on Foreign Affairs, House of Representatives.
[Washington, Govt. Print. Off., 1956] 8 p.

# X. ECONOMICS, INDUSTRY AND COMMERCE

## Bibliographies and Dictionaries

CHIANG, NAI-YUNG, 蔣乃鏞, 1913-    Anglo-Chinese dictionary of textile terms. [Enl. 3d ed. Shanghai, Tso chê shu shê, 1950] 8, 214 p.

HO, SHIH-FANG, 何士芳. A dictionary of economic terms. Shanghai, Commercial Press, 1934. xi, 349 p.

KYOTO. UNIVERSITY. Dept. of Economics. Bibliography on the industry and mining in China in European languages. [Kyoto] 3rd Section, Sina-Keizai-Kanko-Tyosabu, Dept. of Economics, Kyoto Imperial University, 1940. 2 v.

PAAUW, DOUGLAS SEYMOUR, 1921-    Bibliographical guide to Modern China: works in Western languages. Section 5: Economic; compiled by Douglas S. Paauw and John K. Fairbank. Cambridge, 1952. 50 p.

YÜAN, T'UNG-LI, 袁同禮, 1895-    Economic and social development of modern China: a bibliographical guide. New Haven, Human Relations Area Files, 1956. viii, 130, v, 87 p. (Behavior science bibliographies).

## Economic History

BALAZS, ÉTIENNE, 1905-    Études sur la société et l'économie de la Chine médiévale. Leiden, E.J. Brill, 1953-54. 3 v. fold. tables. (Bibliothèque de l'institut des hautes études, 9 ).

———. Beiträge zur Wirtschaftsgeschichte der T'ang-Zeit (618-906). Berlin, 1931-32. 92, 73 p. (Berlin. Universität. Seminar für orientalische Sprachen. Mitteil. Bd. 34-35, Abt. 1 ).

BÖHME, KARL, 1882-    Wirtschaftsanschauungen chinesischer Klassiker. Hamburg, Ackermann und Wulff, 1926. iii, 76 p. Diss.-Univ. Tübingen.

CHANG, T'IEN-TSÊ, 張天澤. Sino-Portuguese trade from 1514 to 1644; a synthesis of Portuguese and Chinese sources. Leyden, E.J. Brill, 1934. [v]-viii, 157 p.

CHEN, CHIH-JANG, 陳志讓. The state economic policies of the Ch'ing dynasty, 1840-95. London, 1956. 478 l. Thesis-School of Oriental and African Studies, University of London.

CHI, CH'AO-TING, 冀朝鼎, 1903-    Key economic areas in Chinese history, as revealed in the development of public works for water-control. London, G. Allen and Unwin [1936] xxiii, 168 p. front.(map) plans. Thesis-Columbia University.

ENCHES, EVELYN LESLIE. The economic principles of the Confucian school. [Pasadena, Calif.] 1935. 29 numb. l.

FAIRBANK, JOHN KING, 1907-    Factors of change in the Chinese economy of the late Ch'ing period by John K. Fairbank, A. Eckstein and L.S. Yang, 楊聯陞 . Cambridge, Chinese Economic and Political Studies, Harvard University, 1956. 46 p. (1956 Conference on the Chinese economy. Conference paper.).

FRANKE, HERBERT, 1914-    Geld und Wirtschaft in China unter der Mongolen-Herrschaft; Beiträge zur Wirtschaftsgeschichte der Yüan-Zeit. Leipzig, O. Harrassowitz, 1949. 171 p. fold. map (inserted) (Das Mongolische Weltreich; Quellen und Forschungen, 3 ).

FRANKE, OTTO, 1863-1946. Staatssozialistische Versuche im alten und mittelalterlichen China. Berlin, 1931. 27 p. (Sitzungbericht der Preussian Akademie der Wissenschaften. Phil. hist. Kl., 1931 ).

HINTON, HAROLD C., 1924-    The grain tribute system of China, 1845-1911.

Cambridge, Chinese Economic and Political Studies, Harvard University; distributed by Harvard University Press, 1956. 163 p. (Chinese Economic and Political Studies. Special series ).

HUAN K'UAN, 桓寬. Discourses on salt and iron, 鹽鐵論, a debate on state control of commerce and industry in ancient China, chapters I-XIX, translated from the Chinese of Huan K'uan, with introduction and notes, by Esson M. Gale. Leyden, E.J. Brill, 1931. lvi, 165 p. (Sinica leidensia edidit Institutum sinologicum Lugduno-Batavum. vol. II ).

——. The genesis and meaning of Huan K'uan's "Discourses on salt and iron" by Chün-ming Chang, 張純明. Peiping, printed by San Yu press, 1934. 52 p. incl. tables. "Reprinted from the Chinese Social and Political Science Review, April 1934."

KIRBY, E[DWARD] STUART, 1909- Introduction to the economic history of China. London, Allen and Unwin [1954] 202 p.

——. Einführung in die Wirtschafts-und Sozial-geschichte Chinas, übers. von G. Felten unter Mitwirkung von Walter Stromeyer. München, R.Oldenbourg, 1955. 239 p.

KUAN, CHUNG, 管仲, d. 645 B.C. Les doctrines juridique et économique de Koan-tse, par Chen Kia-i, 沈家詒. Zi-Ka-Wei-Chang-Hai, Impr. de l'Orphelinat de T'ou-Sè-Wè, 1928. 70 p. Thèse-Université l'Aurore.

——. Kuan-tse, das Leben und Wirken eines altchinesischen Staatsmannes, von Ernst Victor Zenker. Wien, Hölder-Pichler-Tempsky, 1941. 32 p. (Akademie der Wissenschaften in Wien. Phil.-hist. Klasse. Sitzungsberichte, 219. Bd., 5. Abhandlung ).

——. Economic dialogues in ancient China; selections from the Kuan-tzŭ, a book written probably three centuries before Christ. Translators: T'an Pofu, 檀伯孚, and Wen Kung-wen, 溫孔文, (Adam K.W. Wen) Expert critic: Hsiao Kung-chüan, 蕭公權. The enterprise directed, the book edited and published by Lewis Maverick. [Carbondale, Ill.] 1954. x, 470 p.

LEE, MABEL PING-HUA, 李美步, 1897- The economic history of China, with special reference to agriculture. New York, Columbia University, 1921. 461 p. fold. tables. (Studies in history, economics and public law, vol.XCIC, no.1).

LIANG, FANG-CHUNG, 梁方仲. The single-whip method (I-t'iao-pien fa) 一條鞭法, of taxation in China; translated from the Chinese by Wang Yü-ch'uan, 王毓銓. Cambridge, Chinese Economic and Political Studies, Harvard University; distributed by Harvard University Press, 1956. 71 p. ( [Harvard University] Chinese Economic and Political Studies, Special series ).

LÜ, LIEN-TCHING, 呂濂敬. Les greniers publics de prévoyance sous la dynastie des Ts'ing. Paris, Jouve et Cie, 1932. 212 p.

PAN, KU, 班固, 32-92. Food and money in ancient China; the earliest economic history of China to A.D. 25, Han shu 24, with related texts, Han shu 91 and Shih-chi 129. Translated and annotated by Nancy Lee Swann. Princeton, Princeton Univ. Press, 1950. xiii, 482, [79] p. illus., maps (1 fold.).

SCHÖPPLEIN, MARIANNE (RIEGER). Die Entwicklung der Grundlasten unter der Ming Dynastie 1368-1643. Eine Beitrag zur Finanzgeschichte Chinas. Frankfurt a.M., 1942. 111 p. Diss.-Univ. Frankfurt.

[SUNG, LIEN], 宋濂, 1310-81. Economic structure of the Yüan dynasty; translation of chapters 93 and 94 of the Yüan shih, by Herbert Franz Schurmann. Cambridge, Harvard Univ. Press, 1956. xviii, 251 p. 3 maps. (Harvard-Yenching Institute studies, 16 ).

TING, WEN-TSI, 丁文治, 1911- Die geschichtliche Entwicklung der chinesischen Landwirtschaftspolitik von der Chou-Dynastie (1134-247 v.Chr.) bis zum Ch'ing-Dynstie (1644-1911). Stradtroda, E. und E. Richter, 1940. 70 p. Diss.-Univ. Jena.

TWITCHETT, DENIS CRISPIN. Financial administration under the T'ang dynasty. Cambridge, Eng., 1955. 324 l. Thesis-University of Cambridge.

YANG, LIEN-SHENG, 楊聯陞, 1914- Notes on the economic history of the

Chin dynasty. Cambridge, 1946. 145 p. Thesis-Harvard University.

———. Money and credit in China, a short history. Cambridge, Harvard Univ. Press, 1952. 143 p. (Harvard-Yenching Institute. Monograph series, 12 ).

## Statistics

CHINA. Directorate General of Budgets, Accounts and Statistics. Statistical abstract of the Republic of China, 1935, 1940, 1945. Chuugking [sic] 3 v.

———. Statistical abstracts of the Republic of China, 1955-    Taipei, 1955- v.

———. The Directorate General of Budgets, Accounts and Statistics: its establishment, structure, powers and duties, personnel and work. Prepared by the Directorate General of Budgets, Accounts and Statistics of the National government of the Republic of China. [Chungking?] 1946. cover-title, 36 p.

HWANG TSONG, 黃鍾 , 1904-    Methode und Ergebnisse der neuesten Bevölkerungsstatistik Chinas. Leipzig und Berlin, B.G. Teubner, 1933. 77 p. incl. tables. fold. map. (Ergänzungsheft zum Deutschen statistischen zentralblatt, hft. 13 ).

LIEU, D.K., 劉大鈞 , [Liu Ta-chün]  1890-    Statistical work in China. Shanghai, 1930.  41 p. At head of title: XIX^e session de l'Institut international de statistique, Tokio, 1930.

LIN, PETER WEI, 林暐 , 1894-    A statistical study of the personnel of Chinese National government (for the year 1929). Shanghai, 1930. 76 p.

WANG, C.Y. JOHN, 王仲武. Statistical terms translated into Chinese. Shanghai, Commercial Press, 1930. iii, [3], ii, 34 p.

## National Income

LIU, TA-CHUNG, 劉大中 , 1914-    China's national income, 1931-36, an exploratory study. Washington, D.C., Brookings Institution, 1946. xii, 91 p.

OU, PAO-SAN, 巫寶三, 1905-    National income of China; 1933, 1936 and 1946. Nanking, Institute of Social Sciences, Academia Sinica, 1947. 26 p. (Academia Sinica. Institute of Social Sciences. Social science study papers, 1 ).

———. Capital formation and consumers' outlay in China. Cambridge, 1949. 219 l. Thesis-Harvard University.

## General Surveys

AMERICAN BANKERS' ASSOCIATION. China, an economic survey, 1923. [New York] American Bankers Association [1923] cover-title, 40 p. diagr.

ARNOLD, JULEAN HERBERT, 1875-1946. Changes in the economic life of the Chinese people. Washington, Govt. Print. Off., 1922. 25 p. incl. tables. (Bureau of foreign and domestic commerce. Trade information bull., 5 ).

———. China, a commercial and industrial handbook. Washington, Govt. Print. Off., 1926. xvi, 818 p. incl. illus., tables, diagrs. 2 fold. maps. (Bureau of foreign and domestic commerce. Trade promotion ser., 38 ).

———. Some bigger issues in China's problems. Shanghai, Commercial Press, 1928. iv, 11 p.; 5, 10 p. fold. map, 2 fold. diagr.

ASSOCIATION NATIONALE DES CHAMBRES DE COMMERCE DE CHINE. La Chine d'aujourd'hui; rapport sur la situation économique en Chine. Paris, 1929. 76 p.

AUXION DE RUFFÉ, REGINALD D', baron, 1875-    Les grands problèms actuels de politique en Chine envisagés aux points de vue démographiques et économiques. Communication faité à la Société de Statistique de Paris, le 27 avril, 1927. Nancy, Berger-Levrault, 1927. ii, 11 p.

CHAI, HAY-TSOU, 翟海舟 , 1894-    La situation économique et politique de la

Chine et ses perspectives d'avenir. Louvain, Impr. F. Ceuterick, 1921. vii, 69 (i.e. 169) p. (Collection de l'École des sciences politiques et sociales (de Louvain] ).

[CH'I, CH'AO-TING, 冀朝鼎, 1903-   ]. Wartime economic development of China. New York, International Secretariat, Institute of Pacific Relations [1940] 149 numb. l. maps, diagrs.

CHING, PETER, 荆磐石, [Ching P'an-shih]. China's wartime economics. With a foreword by Edward Bing-Shuey Lee, 李炳瑞. Chungking, People's Foreign Relations Assn. of China [1941] 29 p.

CLARK, GROVER, 1891-1938. Economic rivalries in China. New Haven, Yale Univ. Press; London, H. Milford, Oxford Univ. Press, 1932. [3]-132 p. tables (part fold.) iv diagr. (The Carnegie endowment for international peace. World economic problems ).

CONDLIFFE, JOHN BELL, 1891-   China to-day: economic. Boston, World Peace Foundation, 1932. 214 p. 3 maps on 1 fold. l., diagr.

DOLSEN, JAMES H. The awakening of China. [Chicago, The Daily Worker Pub. Co., c1926] 267, [1] p. illus.

ECONOMIC conditions in China, January 1934-March 1935; a brief review. Shanghai, Chinese Workers Correspondence, 1935. cover-title, 48 p.

FREYN, HUBERT, 1897-   China's progress in 1940. Chungking [etc.] China Pub. Co. [1941?] ii, 41 p.

———. Free China's new deal. New York, Macmillan, 1943. xviii, 277 p. incl. tables.

GENERAL MOTORS CORPORATION. Economic survey of China. [New York, foreword 1943] 192 p. maps (part fold.).

HELLAUER, JOSEF, 1871-   ed. China, Wirtschaft und Wirtschaftsgrundlagen, von K. Blickle [et.al.] Berlin, W. de Gruyter, 1921. 281 p.

HSÜ, YUNG YING, 徐永瑛, 1902-   comp. Chinese views of wartime economic difficulties, translated from the Chinese press. New York, International Secretariat, Institute of Pacific Relations [1942] 30 numb. l. (Secretariat paper, 8 ).

INSTITUTE OF PACIFIC RELATIONS. Economic preparedness in China and Japan. New York [etc.] American Council, Institute of Pacific Relations [c1937] 32 p.

K'O, SIANG-FENG, 柯象峯. L'organisation de la production, du crédit et de l'échange en Chine de 1894 à 1914. Lyon, Impr. Bosc frères et Riou, 1929. iv, 202 p. chart. Thèse-Univ. de Lyon.

KUO, SHIEN-YEN, 郭先彥, 1905-   Kapitalismus und Grundeigentum in China. [Gelnhausen, O. Wetig, 1930] 80 p. Diss.-Frankfurt am Main.

LACHIN, MAURICE. La Chine capitaliste. Paris, Gallimard [c1938] [11]-303, [1] p. maps (1 fold.) (Problèmes et documents).

LEVY, MARION JOSEPH, 1918-   The rise of the modern Chinese business class; two introductory essays. New York, International Secretariat, Institute of Pacific Relations, 1949. iii, 64 p.

———. Some problems of modernization in China. New York, International Secretariat, Institute of Pacific Relations, 1949. 35 l.

LI, BANGHAN, 李邦漢, 1896-   Die chinesische Volkswirtschaft unter dem Einfluss der fremden Mächte. Borna-Leipzig, 1926. Diss.-Univ. Frankfurt

LIANG, CHIANG, 梁強. Die chinesische Wirtschafts-und Sozialverfassung zwischen Freiheit und Bindung. Ein Überblick bis zum Jahre 1937. Wurzburg, Triltsch, 1938. vi, 121 p. Diss.-Univ. Jena.

LIANG, SSU-MU, 梁師目. Die Wirtschaftsstruktur Chinas und die Wirtschtspolitik der Nanking-Regierung. Frankfurt, 1934. 29 p. Diss.-Univ. Frankfurt.

MORSE, HOSEA BALLOU, 1855-1934. The trade and administration of the Chinese empire. 3rd rev. ed. London and New York, Longmans, Green, 1921.

xi, 451 p. incl. tables, plates, fold. maps, diagrs. 1st ed. 1908. Rev. ed.
1913.

MURRAY, JOHN LOVELL, 1874-    China today and tomorrow. Statement on the
cultural life of China by Dr. V. K. Wellington Koo. Foreword by Dr. George
Yeh. London, Great Britain and the East [1943] 64 p. ports., maps.

NAGANO, AKIRA. Development of capitalism in China. Prepared for the fourth
bi-annual conference of the Institute of Pacific Relations to be held at Hangchow from Oct. 21 to Nov. 4, 1931. Tokyo, Japan Council, Institute of Pacific Relations [1931] 139 p.

NEARING, SCOTT, 1883-    Whither China? An economic interpretation of recent events in the Far East. New York, International Publishers [c1927] vi,
9-225 p. incl. maps.

NELSON, JOHN H. Changing factors in the economic life of China. Washington,
Govt. Print. Off., 1925. ii, 21 p. incl. tables. (Bureau of foreign and domestic commerce. Trade information bull., 312 ).

OEHLER, WILHELM, 1877-    Chinas Erwachen auf dem nationalen, wirtschaftlichen, sozialen, geistigen und religiosen Gebiet. Erlebtes und Erforschtes.
Wernigerode, Verlag "Die Aue," c1925. 137 p.

OTTE, FRIEDRICH W. K. China; wirtschaftspolitische Landeskunde, mit 1 Karte, 6 Diagrammen und einer Vorrede von Carsun Chang, 張嘉森. Gotha, J.
Perthes, 1927. xi, [1], 111 p. fold. map, diagrs. (Ergänzungsheft nr. 194
zu "Petermanns mitteilungen").

REMER, CHARLES FREDERICK, 1889-    ed. Readings in economics for China,
selected materials with explanatory introductions. Shanghai, Commercial
Press, 1933 (c1922). x, 685 p. diagrs.

ROWE, DAVID NELSON, 1905-    China among the powers. New York, Harcourt, Brace [1945] x, 205 p. illus. (map).

SIÉ, TSO-TCHÉOU, 謝作舟. La révolution économique dans la Chine contemporaine, 1840-1929. Paris, Albert Mechelinck, 1930. 180 p.

TCHANG, PI-KAI, 張丕介. Die Bodenzersplitterung in China. Freiburg v. B.,
Schillinger, 1934. 65 p. Diss.-Univ. Freiburg.

UNITED NATIONS. Economic Commission for Asia and the Far East. Report on
the first session held at Shanghai, 16-25 June 1947. [Lake Success] 1947.
24 p. (United Nations. [Document] E/452 ).

U. S. Industrial College of the Armed Forces. Committee on Foreign Resources.
The economic war potential of China; report. Industrial mobilization course,
Jan.-June 1946. Washington [1946] 84 p.

————. Office of Strategic Services. Research and Analysis Branch. Current
food, coal and transportation situation prevailing in China. Washington, 1946.
24, xxxvi p. fold. maps. ( Its R and A No. 3433 ).

WILHELM, RICHARD, 187.-1930. Chinesische wirtschaftspsychologie. Leipzig, Deutsche Wissentschaftliche Buchhandlung, 1930. 120 p. fold. map.
(Schriften des Weltwirtschafts-Instituts der Handelshochschule, Leipzig, 5).

————. Chinese economic psychology, tr. from the German by Bruno Lasker.
New York, International Secretariat, Institute of Pacific Relations, 1947.
64 l.

WITTFOGEL, KARL AUGUST, 1896-    New light on Chinese society; an investigation of China's socio-economic structure. New York, International Secretariat, Institute of Pacific Relations, 1938. 41 p.

YANG, SUEH-CHANG, 楊雪章, 1918-    China's depression and subsequent re-
covery, 1931-36; an inquiry into the applicability of the modern income-de-
termination theory. Cambridge, 1950. 265 l. Thesis-Harvard University.

## Regional Surveys

BARNETT, ROBERT W., 1911-    Economic Shanghai: hostage to politics, 1937-
41. New York, International Secretariat, Institute of Pacific Relations, 1941.

xiii, [1], 210 p. front., plates, fold. map, plans. (I.P.R. inquiry series ).
CHINA. Bureau of Foreign Trade. China industrial handbooks. Kiangsu. First
series of the reports by the national industrial investigation. Compiled and
published by Bureau of Foreign Trade, Ministry of Industry. Shanghai, 1933.
xxv, 1083, [3] p. fold. map, tables (1 fold.).
——. The same. Chekiang. Second series of the reports by the national industry investigation. Compiled and published by Bureau of Foreign Trade, Ministry of Industry. Shanghai, 1935. xx, 954 p. incl. tables.
GAUSS, CLARENCE EDWARD, 1887-    Economic development of Shantung Province, 1912-21. Excerpts from advance copy of Decennial report of the Tsingtau customs. Washington, Govt. Print. Off., 1922. 20 p. incl. tables. (Bureau of foreign and domestic commerce. Trade information bull., 70 ).
HINDER, ELEANOR M. Social and industrial problems of Shanghai, with special
reference to the administrative and regulatory work of the Shanghai Municipal Council. New York, International Secretariat, Institute of Pacific Relations, 1942. v, 74 numb. l. incl. map. (I.P.R. International research series ).
HOSIE, SIR ALEXANDER, 1853-1925. Szechwan, its products, industries and
resources. Shanghai, Kelly and Walsh, 1922. 185, vii p. fold. maps.
KYI, ZUH-TSING, 季厚眘 . Tsingtao; a historical, political and economic survey. Tsingtao, Catholic Mission Press, 1930. xvi, 125 p. incl. 2 front. ( 5
port.) illus.
KWANGTUNG. Drafting Committee of the Five-Year Reconstruction Plan. Outline of the five-year reconstruction plan of Kwangtung Province. [Canton]
1947. 1 v. (unpaged).
KWANGTUNG RECONSTRUCTION RESEARCH COMMITTEE. Post-war Kwangtung; reconstruction and prospects. [Canton] 1947. cover-title, 108 p. plates,
port., fold. map.
LI, TEH, 李德, 1913-    Hankau und sein Wirtschaftsleben. Charlottenburg,
Druck: K.u.R. Hoffmann [1938] 69 p. illus.(maps). Diss.-Univ. Berlin.
LOH, S.Y., 陸世宜, [Lu Shih-i]. The forerunner in the reconstruction of China. [n.p.] 1921. 13p.; 8 p.
MURPHEY, [WILLIAM] RHOADS, 1919-    Shanghai, key to modern China. Cambridge, Harvard University Press, 1953. London, Geoffrey Cumberlege,
1954. xii, 232 p. illus., maps.
REVIEW of Tsingtao, 1928-29. Tsingtao, "The Tsingtao times," 1928. 44 p.
illus., ports., 2 fold. maps (in pocket).
TIEFENSEE, FRANZ WILHELM. Die provinz Dschi-li nebst Djing-dschau in
wirtschafts-geographischer Betrachtung. Rastenburg, Sack, 1928. 76 p.
Diss.-Univ. Königsburg.
U.S. Bureau of Foreign and Domestic Commerce (Dept. of Commerce). Plan for
industrial development of Szechwan Province, China. With related information. Washington, Govt. Print. Off., 1922. ii, 10 p. incl. tables. (Trade information bull., 62 ).

## Money and Banking
### Currency

ARAKI, MITSUTARŌ, 1894-    Report on the currency system of China, pre-
pared for the Fourth Bi-annual Conference of the Institute of Pacific Rela-
tions to be held at Hangchow from Oct. 21st-Nov. 4th, 1931. Tokyo, Japan
Council of the Institute of Pacific Relations [1931] 94 p.
BOULEAU, MARCEL. Étude practique des opérations de change en Extrême-
Orient. Pékin, A. Nachbaur, 1923. 180 p. forms, illus., tables.
——, Practical guide to Far Eastern exchanges. Peking, La Librairie Fran-
çaise, 1923. xii, 148 p. incl. tables.
BUSCH, MANFRED VON. Der Silberkrieg in Ostasien. Berlin, Duncker und

Humblot, 1942. 143, [1] p. illus.(map).

CHANG, LIANG-ZUNG, 張樑任, 1908-   Die Shanghaier Goldbörse. Ihre Währungspolitische und weltwirtschaftliche Bedeutung. Berlin, 193? 85 p. Diss.-Univ. Berlin.

CHAO, PAO-CHUAN, 趙葆全, 1900-   Silver. Ithaca, N.Y., 1936. 277 p. tables, diagrs. Thesis-Cornell University.

CHEN, CHIN-TAO, 陳錦濤, 1871-1939. The silver situation in China: A memorandum presented to the American Economic Mission to China. Nanking, 1935. 24 p. charts.

CHENG, SHAO-TEH, 程紹德. Étude sur le marché monétaire de Changhai. Paris, L. Rodstein, 1932. 494 p. incl. tables.

CHINA. Commission of Financial Experts. Memorandum on certain matters relating to the currency, submitted to the National Government through the Minister of finance, on March 27, 1929. [Shanghai, 1929] 6 numb. l.

———. Memorandum on the withdrawal of copper coins from circulation. [Shanghai, 1929] 21 numb. l.

———. Project of law for the gradual introduction of a gold-standard currency system in China, together with a report in support thereof. Submitted to the Minister of finance by the Commission of Financial Experts on November 11, 1929. [Nanking? 1929?] v numb. l., 206 numb. l. maps, tables (1 fold.) fold. diagr.

———. L'étalon or en Chine. Projet de loi remis au Ministère des finances par la mission Kemmerer le 11 novembre 1929, et exposé des motifs justifiant son adoption. Traduction française par J.R.B. Nouv. éd., avec le texte chinois. Tientsin, Hautes études; Shanghai, Université l'Aurore, 1934. 68, [68] p. (Le droit chinois moderne, 8 ).

———. Currency Reserve Board. The new monetary policy of China. Currency Reserve Board, Shanghai, January 15, 1936. [Shanghai, 1936] cover-title, 20 p.

———. Ministry of Industry. Silver and prices in China; report of the Committee for the study of silver values and commodity prices, Ministry of industries. Shanghai, Commercial Press, 1935. xxi, 245 p. incl. maps, diagrs. tables (part fold.).

CHINA NEWS SERVICE, New York. Temporary foreign exchange regulations and temporary foreign trade regulations of the National Government of China. New York, Chinese News Service, 1946. 16 p.

CH'U HUI-EN, 褚會恩. Exchange control and intervention. Tientsin, Hautes études, 1941. 40 p. (Tientsin. Institut des hautes études industrieles et commerciales. Economic studies, 17 ).

CHUNG, MONG SOO, 鍾夢甦. L'ancien régime et les dernières réformes monetaires de la Chine. Dijon, Impr. du Palais-M. Pornon, 1935. [7]-145 p. Thèse-Univ. de Dijon.

DSCHANG, KOWEI, 張果爲, [Chang Kuo-wei] 1901-   Die chinesische Geldverfassung. Berlin, W. Christians, 1930. 127, [1] p. incl. fold. tables, diagrs. (Christians volkswirtschaftliche bücherei, 15 ).

GT. BRIT. Treasury. Chinese currency. Arrangements proposed in regard to the Chinese currency stabilisation fund. Presented to Parliament by the financial secretary to the Treasury by command of His Majesty, March, 1939. London, H.M. Stationery Off., 1939. 3 p. ( [Parliament. Papers by command] Cmd. 5963 ).

GUREVICH, M.S. China and the silver problem. Translated by I. Epstein. Tientsin, A.J. Serebrennikoff and Co., 1935. 64 p.

HOU, TSEU-KIANG, 胡自強, [Hu Tzŭ-chiang]. Le cours du change extérieur en Chine depuis 1912. Nancy, Impr. G. Thomas, 1936. [5]-192 p. incl. tables, diagrs. Thèse-Univ. de Nancy.

HU, HSIEN-CHIN, 胡先塏, 1915-   Inflation and inflation control in China, 1937-47. Urbana, 1950. 22 p. Abstract of thesis-University of Illinois.

KANN, EDUARD, 1880-    The currencies of China; an investigation of gold and silver transactions affecting China, with a section on copper; foreword by Julean Arnold, with six illustrations.  Shanghai, Kelly and Walsh, 1926. xviii, 374, [375]-540, [xxi]-xlviii p. col. front., plates, fold. tables.

KOH, TSO-FAN, 谷春帆, [Ku Chūn-fan]. Silver at work, with special reference to China.  Shanghai, Finance and Commerce, 1935. 51 p.

KUO, SUNG-CHUAN, 郭松泉. Paper money.  Tientsin, Hautes études, 1938. 81 p. (Tientsin. Institut des hautes études industrieles et commerciales. Economic studies, 10 ).

LAI, KWOK-KO, 趙國高. Études sur le marché du change de Changaï et ses relations avec la balance des comptes de la Chine.  Lyon, Bosc frères, M. et L. Riou, 1935. [ix]-xi, 191, [1] p. Thèse-Univ. de Lyon.

LEE, FREDERIC EDWARD. Currency, banking, and finance in China.  Washington, Govt. Print. Off., 1926. x, 220 p. incl. tables. (Bureau of foreign and domestic commerce. Trade promotion series, 27 ).

LEE, JEAN,李鴻一. La crise économique et la réforme monétaire en Chine (1935).  Paris, A. Pedone, 1936. 118 p. Thèse-Univ. de Paris.

LIAO, BAO-SEING, 廖寶賢. Die Bedeutung des Silberproblems für die Entwicklung der chinesischen Währungsverhältnisse.  Berlin, Duncker und Humblot, 1939. viii, 144 p. (Neue reihe staatswissenschaftlicher arbeiten, 6. hft. ).

LIN, WEI-YING, 林維英, 1908-    China under depreciated silver, 1926-31.  Shanghai, Commercial Press, 1935. xiii, 230 p. fold. tables, fold. diagrs. (The Foreign trade association of China. Monograph, 1 ). Thesis-Columbia University.

———. The new monetary system of China; a personal interpretation.  Shanghai [etc.] Kelly and Walsh, 1936 [i.e. 1937] 175 p. incl. tables (1 fold.).

LIU, SIEN-WEI, 劉先緯. Les problèmes monétaires et financiers de la Chine avant et depuis les hostilités sino-japonaises.  Paris, Domat-Montchrestien, 1940. 200 p. Thèse-Univ. de Paris.

LIU, SING-CHEN, 劉星晨. La dépréciation actuelle de l'argent en Chine et ses remèdes.  Nancy, Poncelet, 1931. cover-title, 146 p. Thèse-Univ. de Nancy.

MEI, YUNG-MOU, 梅遑讓. La crise de l'argent en Chine et la réforme monétaire du 4 novembre 1935.  Nancy, Impr. G. Thomas, 1936. [5]-178 p. diagrs. (1 fold.) Thèse-Univ. de Nancy.

MONETARY AND ECONOMIC CONFERENCE, London, 1933. Silver. Memorandum of agreement between the United States of America, Australia, Canada, China, India, Mexico, Peru and Spain. With supplementary undertakings. Signed at London, July 22, 24, and 26, 1933. Effective April 24, 1934. Washington, Govt. Print. Off., 1934. 12 p. ( [Dept. of State. Publication no.613] Executive agreement series no. 63 ).

———. Silver agreement between the governments of Canada, the commonwealth of Australia, India, China, Mexico, Peru, Spain and the United States, with supplementary undertakings signed July 24 and 26, 1933, London, July 22, 1933. [Ratifications deposited at Washington by His Majesty's governments in Canada and the commonwealth of Australia and the government of India, March 28, February 16 and March 21, 1934, respectively] London, H. M. Stationery Off., 1934. 13 p. ( [Gt. Brit. Foreign office] Treaty series, no. 24 (1934) ).

NEW exchange rules and revised temporary trade regulations of the Republic of China, August 1947. Shanghai, North China Daily News and Herald, 1947. 10 p.

PINNICK, ALFRED WILLIAM. Silver and China; an investigation of the monetary principles governing China's trade and prosperity. Shanghai, Kelly and Walsh, 1930. xvii, 90 p.

REVISED temporary regulations with regard to trade and foreign exchange transactions. Shanghai, China Daily Tribune Pub. Co., 1947. 40 p.

SALTER, JAMES ARTHUR, 1881-1939. China and silver.  New York, Economic

Forum, 1934. [3]-117 p.

———. China and the depression; impressions of a three months visit. Shanghai, National Economic Council, 1934. 149 p. (National Economic Council.
Special ser., 3 ).

SHEN, LIN-YU, 沈麟玉, 1902-    China's currency reform; a historical survey.
Shanghai, Mercury Press, 1941. xiv, 184 p. plates, tables.

T'ANG, LIANG-LI, 湯良禮, 1901-    China's new currency system. Shanghai,
China United Press, 1936. ix, 138 p. port. ("China to-day" series. [8] ).

TSON, HAUIN-KIO, 曾還九. Le système monétaire en Chine. Nancy, Impr.
Grandville, 1934. 149 p. Thèse-Univ. de Nancy.

U.S. Office of Coordinator of Information. Research and Analysis Branch. Stabilization and silver in American aid to China. [Washington, 1941] 26 p. (Its
Memorandum no. B.R.6 ).

———. Office of Strategic Services. Research and Analysis Branch. Inflation in
free China. [Washington, 1945] 8 l. (Its Current intelligence study, 36 ).

WU, CHI-YUEN, 伍啓元, 1912-    Currency, exchange and prices in wartime
China, July 1937 to June 1944. [Preliminary report] Chungking, China Institute of Pacific Relations, 1945. i, 111 l.

YĂN, TJING-HSI, 1910-    Die Silberentwertung im Rahmen der chinesischen
Geldverfassung. Jena, Gedruckt in der Buchdruck-werkstätte, g.m.b.h.,
1933. 102 p. Diss.-Univ. Jena.

YEN, CHI-CHIN, 顏飢金. Le problème de la monnaie chinoise. Paris, L. Rodstein, 1933. 166 p., tables. Thèse-Univ. de Caen.

## Banking

BANK OF CHINA. An analysis of the accounts of the principal Chinese banks,
1921-31. Compiled and published by the Research Department, Bank of China, Shanghai. [Shanghai, 1933] x, 353 p., 1 l. incl. illus., tables (part fold)
diagrs. fold. maps.

BUREAU, ANDRÉ. La crise bancaire en 1921-23 (Banque industrielle de Chine,
Banca di sconto, Landmandsbank, Andresens og Bergens kreditbank) Étude
juridique et politique de l'intervention de l'État. Paris, Société anonyme de
publications périodiques, 1923. 144 p.

CHĔN, CHIA-TSŬN, 陳家駿. Das chinesische Bankwesen, unter besonderer
Berücksichtigung der neuen chinesischen Banken. Berlin-Wien-Zürich, Österreichischer Wirtschaftsverlag, Kommanditgesellschaft Payer und co.,
1938. viii, 104 p. incl. tables. (Bank- und kreditwirtschaft; betriebswirt-
schaftliche abhandlungen, hft. 1 ).

CHEN, SHIH-CHEN, 陳世振, 1913-    A proposed banking system for China:
with special reference to the system of the United States. Ann Arbor, University Microfilms [1955] ( [University Microfilms, Ann Arbor, Mich.] Publication no. 13,463 ). Collation of the original: vi, 256 l. Thesis-University
of Illinois.

CHINA. Commission of Financial Experts. Project of a general banking law, together with a report in support thereof. Submitted to the National Government
through the Minister of finance on December 10, 1929. [Shanghai, 1929] 68
numb. l.

———. Project of law for the creation of the Central reserve bank of China, together with a report in support thereof. Submitted to the National Government
through the Minister of finance on December 10, 1929. [Shanghai, 1929] 142
numb. l.

———. Directorate General of Postal Remittances and Savings Banks. Report on
the postal remittances and savings banks. 1930-36. First-6th issue. Shanghai [1931-36] 6 v. tables.

———. Directorate General of Posts. Report on the working of the Chinese post
office savings bank. 1919-20. Shanghai, 1920-21. 2 v. tables. ([Publications]

II. Public series: S. B. no. 1 ).

DZEN, TIEN-YUE, 曾天宇, 1889-   Das Bankwesen in China, ein Beitrag zur Organisation und den Problemen der inländischen und ausländischen Banken in China. Berlin, W. Christian Verlag, 1927. 143 p. incl. tables, diagrs. (Christians Volkswirtschaftliche Bücherei, 3 ).

HALL, RAY OVID, 1891-   The Chinese national banks, from their founding to the moratorium. Berlin, privately printed, 1921. 291 p. Thesis-Columbia University.

HO, FENG-SHAN, 何鳳山, 1903-   Das Bankwesen in China und seine Probleme. Murnau Obby, Fürst, 1932. vi, 194 p. fold. tables. Diss.-Univ. München.

HSIA, CHIN-HSIUNG, 夏晉熊, 1908-   La reconstruction monétaire et bancaire de la Chine contemporaine. Paris, Librairie technique et économique, 1938. [7]-162 p.

HSU, WEI-CHU, 徐維初. Die Tätigkeit des ausländischen Bankwesens in China insbesondere in Hinsicht auf die ''Deutsch-Asiatische Bank.'' München, 1941. 177 l. Diss.-Univ. München.

KAO, MONG-TSANG, 高莽蒼. Die Bedeutung von Schanghai für die chinesische Volkswirtschaft unter besonderer Berücksichtigung des Bankwesens. Berlin, 1938. xix, 289 p. Diss.-Univ. Berlin.

KU, SUI-LU, 顧綏祿. Die Form bankmässiger Transaktionen im inneren chinesischen Verkehr, mit besonderer Berücksichtigung des Notengeschäfts. Hamburg, Kommissionsverlag L. Friederichsen, 1926. vi, 77 p. illus.(facsims.) (Veröffentlichungen des Seminars für Sprache und Kultur Chinas an der Hamburgischen universität, 1 ).

LEE, BAEN ELMER, 李培恩, [Li P'ei-ên] 1889-   Modern banking reforms in China [1842-1941] Ann Arbor, University Microfilms, 1941 [i. e. 1951] ( [University Microfilms, Ann Arbor, Mich.] Publication no. 2349 ). Collation of the original: xi, 266 l. tables. Thesis-Columbia University.

LEE, TUH-YUEH, 李德燿. The evolution of banking in China. New Brunswick, N.J., Rutgers University, 1952. 60 l. Thesis-Rutgers University.

LI, CHIEN-MING, 李建名. The accounting system of native banks in Peking and Tientsin. Tientsin, Hautes études, 1941. xiv, 301 p. (Tientsin. Institut des hautes études industrieles et commerciales. Economic studies, 19 ).

PU, SHOU-HAI, 浦壽海, 1920-   Banking reform in China. Cambridge, 1946. 239 p. Thesis-Harvard University.

SHEN, KI-FEIN, 沈其蕃. Essai sur l'origine et l'évolution des banques en Chine. Paris, Domat-Montchrestien, 1936. vii, 261 p. Thèse-Univ. de Caen.

TAMAGNA, FRANK M., 1910-   Banking and finance in China, with a preface by T. V. Soong. New York, International Secretariat, Institute of Pacific Relations, 1942. xxi, 400 p. incl. tables, diagr. (I. P. R. inquiry series ).

TCHEN, TSOU-SIANG, 鄭祖驤. La circulation fiduciaire et les banques d'émission centrale en Chine. Nancy, Impr. G. Thomas, 1931. [7]-159 p. Thèse-Univ. de Nancy.

YUEN, TSE-KIEN, 袁子健, 1908-   Étude sur les établissements de crédit en Chine. Paris, Au commerce des idées, 1929. 135 p. Thèse-Univ. de Grenoble, 1929.

## Public Finance and Taxation
### Public Finance

BANK OF CHINA. Research Department. Chinese government loan issues and obligations, compiled and edited by the Research Department, Bank of China. Shanghai, Bank of China, 1930. 109, 5, 7 p. charts (part fold.) and fold. tables.

BAYLIN, J.R. Chinese internal loans [by] J.R. Baylin [and] E.Kann. [Peiping] A. Nachbaur by arrangement with the Bureau of Industrail and Commercial

Information, 1929. 3-38 [i. e. 52] p. fold. diagrs.

――――. Emprunts intérieurs chinois (caractéristiques et tables d'amortissement) par J. R. Baylin. Memorandum de T. V. Soong sur la situation financière du gouvernement national (janvier 1929). Pékin, A. Nachbaur [1929] 28 p. incl. tables, charts. (Encyclopédie des questions chinoises ).

CHANG, YING-HUA, 張英華, 1886- The financial reconstruction of China. Peking, 1923. 49 p. incl. tables.

CH'EN, P'ING-TSANG, 陳炳章, 1899- Recent financial developments in China, 1934-36. [Shanghai, 1937] Reprinted from the Chinese Year Book, 1936-37, p. 548-778.

CHINA. Commission of Financial Experts. Report on revenue policy. Submitted to the National government through the Minister of finance by the Commission of financial experts on December 10, 1929. [Shanghai, 1929] [2], 14 p. Manifold copy.

――――. Project of an organic law setting up a department of national debt within the Ministry of Finance, together with a report therof and regulations governing the organization of the department. Submitted to the National government through the Minister of finance on June 14, 1929. [Shanghai, 1929] 18 numb. l.

――――. Projects of law dealing with financial planning, budget, preparation, budget enforcement, accounting, fiscal control, supervisory inspection and audit; together with reports in support thereof. Submitted to the National government through the Minister of finance on December 10, 1929. [Nanking? 1929?] 2 v. tables, diagrs. (4 fold.).

――――. Project of a public credit rehabilitation law, together with a report on the national debt of China and the rehabilitation of China's credit. Submitted to the National government through the Minister of finance on December 10,1929. [Nanking? 1929?] 2 v. tables (part fold.) diagr.

――――. Ministry of Finance. Report on progress in Chinese finances. Nanking, August 5, 1932. [Geneva, Printed by Sonor, 1932] 20 p. incl. tables.

CHU, CHI, 朱儗 1907- Hauptproblems der Finanzreform Chinas. Peiping, Universitätsverlag, 1932. v, 258, 6 p. incl. tables. Diss.-Univ. Berlin.

CHU, PAKONG, 朱伯康. Der staatshaushalt und das finanzsystem Chinas. Leipzig, H. Buske, 1937. 133 p. (Frankfurter wirtschaftswissenschaftliche studien, 2 ).

La DETTE chinoise. Emprunts intérieurs et emprunts extérieurs. Tables d'amortissements. Pékin, A. Nachbaur, 1925. 21 tables, fo (Encyclopédie des questions chinoises ).

DUNG, BI, 董璧, 1909- Eine Studie über die chinesische Finanzwirtschaft mit besonderer Berücksichtigung ihrer gegenwärtigen Neuordnung. Hamburg, E. Korff, 1934. 171 l. Diss.-Univ. Hamburg.

FINANCE and commerce year book. 1921/22-29// Shanghai, China, "Finance and commerce" [etc.] 1921-  7 v.

KANN, EDUARD, 1880- The history of China's internal loan issues. Shanghai, 'Finance and Commerce,' 1934. 104 p. tables (part fold.).

LEAGUE OF NATIONS. Delegation from China. The financial situation in China and Japan. Geneva, Press Bureau of the Chinese Delegation [1933?] 44 p.

LEE, CHOU-YING, 李超英, 1901- The system of Chinese public finance; a comparative study. London, P. S. King, 1936. xiii, 256 p. diagr.

LI, CHUAN SHIH, 李權時, 1895- Central and local finance in China; a study of the fiscal relations between the central, the provincial, and the local governments. New York, Columbia University, 1922. 187 p. (Studies in history, economics and public law, whole no. 226 ).

LONG, YIN, 龍吟. Le contrôle du budget en Chine, comparaison avec les systèmes anglais et français. Lyon, Impr. générale lyonnaise, 1943. cover-title, 196 p.

PAAUW, DOUGLAS SEYMOUR, 1921- Chinese public finance during the Nanking government period.  Cambridge, 1950. 389 p. Thesis-Harvard University.

PADOUX, GEORGES, 1867-    The financial reconstruction of China and the consolidation of China's present indebtedness. 3d printing.  Peking, La Librairie française [1924?] 22 p. incl. tables.

———. The consolidation of China's unsecured indebtedness and the creation of a Chinese consolidated budget, memorandum for the Commission for the Readjustment of Finance.  Tientsin, Librairie française, 1925. 28 p.

PEKING. AMERICAN CHAMBER OF COMMERCE. Chinese government finances; a study made by a committee of the American Chamber of Commerce, Peking. [Peking, 1923] cover-title, 20 p. fold. tables.

SHAW, KINN WEI, 壽景偉, [Shou Ching-wei] 1891-    Democracy and finance in China; a study in the development of fiscal systems and ideals.  New York, Columbia University Press, 1926. 215 p. (Studies in history, economics, and public law. No. 282 ).

TAY, MING-CHUNG, 戴鳴鍾, 1914-    Das Finanz- und Steuerwesen Chinas unter besonderer Berücksichtigung der Einkommensteuer.  Jena, G. Fischer, 1940. viii, 98 p. (Forschungen zur finanzwissenschaft, schriften des Instituts für finanzwesen der Wirtschaftshochschule Berlin, 4 ).

TCHÉOU, JEUNGENS, 周鴻鈞. Des dettes publiques chinoises.  Lyon, Bosc frères et Riou, 1927. 107 p. incl. tables.

UCHIDA, KATSUSKI. The problem of China's loan adjustment. Prepared for the fourth bi-annual conference of the Institute of Pacific Relations to be held at Hangchow from Oct. 21 to Nov. 4, 1931.  Tokyo, Japan Council, Institute of Pacific Relations, 1931. [4], 15 p. tables.

YIN, WEN-CHING, 尹文敬. Le système fiscal de la Chine.  Paris, Impr. du Montpanasse et de Persan-Beaumont, 1929. 212 p. Thèse-Univ. de Paris.

YOUNG, ARTHUR NICHOLS, 1890-    China's financial progress.  New York, Foreign Policy Association [1938] p. [25]-36. (Foreign policy reports. 14:3. April 15, 1938 ).

———. China's economic and financial reconstruction. [New York] 1947. cover-title, 81 p. (Papers submitted to the Committee on International Economic Policy by its Advisory Committee on Economics. 13 ).

## Tariff and Taxation

BAU, MINGCHIEN JOSHUA, 鮑明鈐, 1894-    Tariff autonomy of China.  Kyoto, 1929. 12 p.

BEAL, EDWIN GEORGE, 1913-    The origin of likin.  Ann Arbor, University Microfilms, 1950. ( [University Microfilms, Ann Arbor, Mich.] Publication no. 1739 ). Collation of the original: xiii, 324 l. diagrs. Thesis-Columbia University.

BUSS, CLAUDE ALBERT, 1893-    The relation of tariff autonomy to the political situation in China.  Philadelphia, 1927. 141 l. illus.(map) diagrs. Thesis-Univ. of Pennsylvania.

CHAU, YAU-PIK, 周有壁, [Chou You-pi] 1905-    The taxation reforms of the Chinese national government in the decade 1927-37.  Chicago, 1945. 316-363 p. Part of thesis-University of Chicago.

CHINA. Central Salt Administration. Accounts. Issue 1-18; 1913-29.  Shanghai, 1915-31. 16 v. ?

———. Statistical review of the work of the inspectorate, 1913-33, with special attention given to the evaluation of results achieved during the last five years, prepared by F.A. Cleveland.  Shanghai, 1934. iii, 240 f. incl. charts, tables.

CHINA. Commission of Financial Experts. Project of law for a documentary stamp tax, together with a report in support thereof. Submitted to the Minister of finance on November 18, 1929. [Shanghai, 1929] 27 numb. l.

———. Project of law for a special consumption tax on Portland cement. Submitted to the National government through the Minister of finance on December 10, 1929. [Shanghai, 1929] 16 numb. l.

———. Project of law for increasing the customs revenue from import duties, for simplifying import duties, and for the eventual abolition of customs duties levied upon the internal trade of China, together with a report thereof. Submitted to the National government through the Minister of finance on December 10, 1929. [Shanghai, 1929] 12 numb. l.

———. Project of law for placing customs duties on imports from abroad upon a gold basis. Submitted to the National government through the Minister of finance on December 10, 1929. [Shanghai, 1929] 11 numb. l.

———. Project of tariff law, together with a report in support thereof. Submitted to the National government through the Minister of finance on December 10, 1929. [Shanghai, 1929] 103 numb. l.

CHINA. Inspectorate General of Customs. General tariff of import and export duties, including the lists of duty-free goods and of articles which are contraband or subject to special regulation. Shanghai, Statistical Dept., Inspectorate General of Customs, 1929. 72 p. (Its Imperial maritime customs III. Miscellaneous series, no. 8 ).

———. Customs export tariff of the Republic of China. (1931). Promulgated by the National government on 7th May, 1931 and showing rates effective from 1st June 1931. Shanghai, Statistical Dept., Inspectorate General of Customs, 1931. iv, 37 p.

———. Guide to the metric edition of the export tariff ( 1931) and classification of returns: effective from the 1st February, 1934. English version. Shanghai, Statistical Dept., Inspectorate General of Customs, 1934. 138 p. (Maritime customs. III. Miscellaneous series: 41 ).

———. Customs export tariff of the Republic of China, 1934, showing rates effective from 21st June 1934. Shanghai, Statistical Dept., Inspectorate General of Customs, 1934. iv, 39 p.

———. The same. Rev. Sept. 1945. Shanghai, Statistical Dept., Inspectorate General of Customs, 1946. iv, 30 p.

———. Customs import tariff of the Republic of China (1931) Promulgated by the National government on 29th December 1930 and showing rates effective from 1st January 1931. Shanghai, Statistical Dept., Inspectorate General of Customs, 1932. vi, 105 p. incl. tables.

———. Guide to the import tariff (1931) and classification of returns. English version. Shanghai, Statistical Dept., Inspectorate General of Customs, 1933. 212 p. (Maritime customs. III. Miscellaneous series: 40 ).

———. Customs import tariff of the Republic of China, 1934, showing rates effective from July 1934. Shanghai, Statistical Dept., Inspectorate General of Customs, 1934. vi, 106 p.

———. The same. Rev. Sept. 1945. Shanghai, Statistical Dept., Inspectorate General of Customs, 1946. vi, 79 p.

———. Code of customs regulations and procedure. 2d ed.: rev. and enl. Shanghai, Statistical Dept., Inspectorate General of Customs, 1935. xii, 463 p. incl. forms (part fold.) (Maritime customs. III. Miscellaneous series: 44 ).

———. Documents illustrative of the origin, development and activities of the Chinese Customs Service. Shanghai, Statistical Dept., Inspectorate General of Customs, 1937-40. 7 v. (Its The maritime customs. IV: Service series, 69 ).

CHINA. Laws, statutes, etc. The income tax law of the Republic of China (promulgated by the President on December 23, 1955 and enforced on January 1, 1956) Taipei, Ministry of Finance, 1956. 54 p.

———. The income tax law of the Republic of China (1956). Taipei, Bank of China, 1956. 40 p.

———. Ministry of Finance. Direct tax laws and regulations, translated into English and published by the Direct tax administration of the Ministry of Fi-

nance at Chingking, July 1, 1943. Washington, China-American Council of
Commerce and Industry, 1944. 30 p. tables.

CHOW, LIANG-DONG, 周良棟. L'impôt du sel en Chine. Nancy, Impr. G. Thomas, 1936. [7]-119 p. Thèse-Univ. de Nancy.

FOREIGN POLICY ASSOCIATION, New York. The Chinese tariff conference -
October 26, 1925. [New York, Foreign Policy Association, 1925] 11 numb.
l. (Editorial information service. Series 1925-26. 1:2. October 24, 1925).

FU, CH'UAN-PO, 符傳鉢. Étude historique et critique sur le régime douanier
de la Chine. Paris, P. Geuthner, 1930. 155, [1] p. diagr. (Université de
Lyon. Bibliothèque franco-sinica lugdunensis. Études et documents publiés
par l'Institut franco-chinois de Lyon. t. VIII ).

HOU, HON-CHUN, 胡鴻鈞. Histoire douanière de la Chine de 1842 à 1911. Paris, Les Presses modernes, 1929. 222 p. Thèse-Univ. de Paris.

LEE, EDWARD BING-SHUEY, 李炳瑞, 1903-56. China's struggle for tariff autonomy, with an introduction by Chengting T. Wang and a preface by T. V.
Soong. [Shanghai? 1929] xiii, 90 p. (International relations series ).

LI, PAO-CH'EN, 李寶霙. Income tax in China. Tientsin, Hautes études, 1937.
105 l. Appendix, 15 l. (Tientsin. Institut des hautes études industrieles et
commerciales. Economic studies, 7 ).

LIU, T'ING-MIEN, 劉廷冕, 1897-  Modern tariff policies with special reference to China. New York, Alliance Print. Corp., 1924. ix, 140 p. Thesis-
Columbia University.

LU, WELLINGTON T.Y., 陸東亞, 1910-  comp. Current Chinese industrial
and commercial tax laws and regulations. [Taipei, Taxes Affairs Publication, 1952. xi, 136 p. ports.

MAO, CHO-TING, 毛卓亭, 1926-  Taxation and accelerated industrialization,
with special reference to the Chinese tax system during 1928-36. Ann Arbor,
University Microfilms [1954] ( [University Microfilms, Ann Arbor, Mich.]
Publication no. 10,308 ) Collation of the original: xi, 334 l. illus. Thesis-
Northwestern University.

PEKING. SPECIAL CONFERENCE ON THE CHINESE CUSTOMS TARIFF, Oct.
1925-April, 1926. The Special conference on the Chinese customs tariff (October 1925-April 1926) Peking, 1928. iv, 629 p.

SIAO, STÉPHANE, 蕭子風. Les régimes douaniers de la Chine. 中國關稅制度
Paris, P. Bossuet [1931?] 230 p.

SUN, I-SHUAN, 孫義宣, 1920-  Salt taxation in China. Madison, 1953. ii,
230 l. Thesis-Univ. of Wisconsin.

T'AO, ALFRED C., [T'ao Chieh-ching] 1911-  A study of the tax
structure in China, with some recommendations for the post-war period.
陶潔卿
Peiping, National Peking University, 1946. 75 p.

TING, TSO-CHAO, 丁作韶. La douane chinoise. Paris, P. Geuthner, 1931.
214 p.

[U.S. Office of Coordinator of Information. Research and Analysis Branch] The
importance of salt in the economy of the Sino-Japanese struggle. June 17,
1942. [Washington, 1942] 4 p. (Office of Strategic Services. Far Eastern
Section. Situation report, 11 ).

WANG, KAI-HUA, 王開化. Die Bedeutung der listischen Lehre für China.
Shanghai, Lo-chun Book Co., 1929. v, 153 p. Diss.-Univ. Tübingen.

WRIGHT, STANLEY FOWLER, 1873-  The collection and disposal of the maritime and native customs revenue since the revolution of 1911, with an account of the loan services administered by the Inspector General of Customs.
Second ed. rev. and enl. Shanghai, Statistical Dept., Inspectorate General
of Customs, 1927. 276 p. incl. tables, fold. diagr. (China. Inspectorate general of customs. The maritime customs. II. - Special series: no. 41 ).

——, China's customs revenue since the revolution of 1911. 3d ed., rev. and
enl. Shanghai, Statistical Dept., Inspectorate General of Customs, 1935.
[iii]-iv, 674 p. incl. tables. fold. diagr. (China Inspectorate general of cus-

toms. The Maritime customs. II. - Special series: no. 41 ).
————. China's struggle for tariff autonomy: 1843-1938. Shanghai, Kelly and
Walsh, 1938. xi, 775 p.
————. The origin and development of the Chinese customs service 1843-1911;
an historical outline. Shanghai, privately printed, 1939. 147 p.
YU, TSUNG-FAN, 余宗范. L'impôt foncier en Chine depuis 1912. Paris, Impr.
J. Delalain, 1939. [7]-104, [6] p. Thèse-Univ. de Paris.

### Prices - Index Numbers

BANK OF CHINA. Research Dept. An analysis of Shanghai commodity prices,
1923-32. Shanghai, 1933. v, 352 p. diagrs. tables.
CHINA. Bureau of Markets. The index number of customs import prices in
Shanghai. 上海輸入貨物關價指數表, by T. Sheng, 盛俊. Shanghai, 1925.
cover-title, 6, 2, [1], 24, 18, 2 p. incl. tables.
————. Index numbers of supplementary import prices in Shanghai. By T. Sheng.
Shanghai, 1925. 63 p. incl. tables.
————. Remarks on revision of the tables of prices in Shanghai. Explanations of
the index numbers of import and export prices in Shanghai. Shanghai, 1925.
110 p. incl. tables.
————. The Shanghai wholesale price index number.     上海物價指數論叢 Ed.
by T. Sheng. Shanghai, 1925. cover-title, 3 l., 55, 75, [4] p.
————. Monthly report on prices and price indexes in Shanghai. 上海物價月報
October, 1925-June 1928. Vol.1-Vol.4, no. 6. Shanghai [1925-28] 4 v. ta-
bles, diagrs.
————. Prices and price indexes in Shanghai,     上海物價月報, July 1928-June
1940. Shanghai, 1928-40. 13 v. tables, diagrs. From April 1929 to June
1940, issued under the name of the National Tariff Commission.
CHINA. National Tariff Commission. The Shanghai market prices report. Jan.-
March, 1923 [-Oct.-Dec.1933] Shanghai [1923-34?] 40 v. in 6. quarterly.
————. The cost of living index number in Shanghai. Shanghai, 1930. cover-ti-
tle, 28 p. incl. tables, diagr. (Bulletin. Statistical series, no.IV ).
————. The revision of the price index numbers. By T. Sheng. (With appendices)
Shanghai, 1931. cover-title, iii, 22, 30 p. incl. tables, diagrs. (Bulletin.
Statistical series, VI ).
————. Basic prices of commodities in the index numbers of the wholesale, ex-
port and import prices of Shanghai. Shanghai, 1934. 15 p. (Its Statistical se-
ries, 10 ).
————. Price index numbers in Shanghai ending December 1933. Shanghai, 1934.
ii, 15 p. charts.
————. A report on the revision of the index numbers of import prices in Shang-
hai. Shanghai, 1934. [2], 10 p.
————. Annual report of Shanghai commodity prices 上海物價年刊, 1934-38.
Shanghai, 1935-39. 4 v. tables, diagrs.
HO, FRANKLIN LIEN, 何廉, 1895-   comp. Wholesale prices and price index
numbers in North China, 1913 to 1929. Tientsin, Nankai University Commit-
tee on Social and Economic Research, 1929. 145 p. (Its Bull. Price Ser., 1 ).
————. Index numbers of the quantities and prices of imports and exports and of
the barter terms of trade in China, 1867-1928. Tientsin, Nankai University
Committee on Sociel and Economic Research, 1930. 24 p. (Its Bull. Price
Ser., 4 ).
INSTITUTE OF SOCIAL RESEARCH. Peiping. Monthly index numbers of the
cost of living in Peiping. v. 1-9. Peiping, China [1929-Je 1937] 9 v. diagrs.
monthly.
NANKAI UNIVERSITY. Nankai Institute of Economics. Bulletin. Price series.
no. 1-   May 1929-Je. 1930// Tientsin, Printed by China Press, 1929-

2 v. tables, diagrs. annual.

————. Nankai index numbers, 1934-36 (of commodity-prices at wholesale, cost of living, foreign exchange rates, and quantities and prices of imports and exports) Tientsin, Nankai Institute of Economics, Nankai University, 1935-37. 3 v. diagrs.

YANG, SIMON, 楊西孟. An index of the cost of living in Peiping. Peiping, [Institute of Social Research] 1928. 16 p. incl. tables, diagrs. (Institute of Social Research, Bull., 1).

————. A study of the standard of living of working families in Shanghai, by Simon Yang and L. K. T'ao, 陶孟和. Peiping, Institute of Social Research, 1931. 86, lvi p. tables. (Social Research Publ. Monog. 3).

The YENCHING index numbers. v. 1-2. Jan. 1940-Aug. 1941. Peking, Dept. of Economics, Yenching Univ. 2 v. tables. monthly.

## Modern Industries and Industrialization
### Textile Industries

BARKER, ALDRED FARRER, 1868-    The textile industries of China, their present position and future possibilities, by Aldred Farrer Barker and Kenneth Crookes Barker. A report presented to Chiao-tung University with particular reference to the proposed institution of a school of textile industries. Shanghai, 1934. iv, 224 p. illus.

BLANCHARD, FESSENDEN SEAVER, 1888-    The textile industries of China and Japan; post-war opportunities and problems for America. New York, Textile Research Institute [1944] v, 71 p.

CHIN, CHIEN-YIN, 金建寅. Wool industry and trade in China. Tientsin, Hautes Études, 1937. a-h, 152 p. diagrs. (Hautes Études industrielles et commerciales. Economic studies, 6).

CHIN, ROCKWOOD QUOCK-PING, 陳國平, [Ch'en Kuo-ping] 1911-    Cotton mills, Japan's economic spearhead in China, a study in international competition. New Haven, 1937. 371 l. Thesis-Yale University.

CHINA. Cotton Industry Commission. The organization and activities of the Central Bureau of Cotton Anti-adulteration. Shanghai, 1937. 23 p. plates.

————. A preliminary report of the classification of Chinese cotton in China. Shanghai, 1936. 32 p. (Special report, 4).

————. Tentative cotton standards. Rev. ed. Shanghai, 1936. 58 p. illus. plates.

CHINA CORPORATION, New York. A review of the cotton textile industry of China, prepared by China Corporation in association with William Hunt and Company. [New York, 1944] cover-title, v, 52 numb. l. incl. tables.

CHÜ, T.S., 曲直生. Marketing of cotton in Hopei province by T.S. Chü and T. Chin, 秦瓚. Peiping, Institute of Social Research, 1930. 54 p. (Its Bull., 3).

FONG, H.D., 方顯庭, 1902-    Cotton industry and trade in China. Tientsin, Chihli Press, 1932. 2 v. illus.(map) fold. tables, diagrs., fold. form.(Nankai institute of economics. Industry series. Bull., 4).

————. Terminal marketing of Tientsin cotton. Tientsin, Chihli Press, 1934. 47 p. map, tables.

GT. BRIT. Cotton Mission. Report of the Cotton Mission. London, H. M. Stationery Off., 1931. 96 p.

HUANG, CHIH-YAO, 黃植堯. Die Bedeutung der Baumwolle in der chinesischen Volkswirtschaft. Marburg/Lahn, Gleiser, 1941. 69 p. Diss.-Univ. Marburg.

KING, S.T., 金秀清. China's cotton industry. A statistical study of ownership of capital, output, and labor conditions, by Miss S. T. King and D.K. Lieu. [Shanghai?] 1929. cover-title, 51 p. In vol. XXII "Documents of the third conference, Institute of Pacific relations, Kyoto, Japan, 1929."

LEVY, BENAS. Baumwolle und Baumwollindustrie in Ostindien, Japan und Chi-

na. Berlin, L. Schöttlander, 1930. 48 p. illus.
LIANG, LELAND SUNG, 梁勳, 1920-    Problems of the cotton manufacturer in
    China. Philadelphia, 1955. 202 1. Thesis-Univ. of Pennsylvania.
MOSER, CHARLES KROTH, 1877-    The cotton textile industry of Far Eastern
    countries. Boston, Pepperell Manufacturing Co., 1930. 144 p. plates.
PEASE, ARNO S., 1872-    The cotton industry of Japan and China, being the
    report of the journey to Japan and China, February-April 1929. Manchester,
    International Federation of Master Cotton Spinners' and Manufacturers' As-
    sociations, 1929. vi, 51, 52-254 p. front. illus.
SCHWEIGER, KARL-HEINZ. Strukturwandlungen auf dem Gebiet der Textilwirt-
    schaft in überseeischen Ländern, gezeigt an den Beispielen China und Indien
    in den Jahren 1938-47. Hamburg, 1948. x, 128 1. tables. Diss.-Univ. Ham-
    burg.
TCHAO, KAUANG-TCHEN, 趙光宸, [Chao Kuang-chēn]. Textile raw materials.
    Tientsin, Hautes études, 1935. 3 v. (Tientsin. Institut des hautes études in-
    dustrieles et commerciales. Economic studies, 2 ).
TING, LEONARD G., 丁佶, 1909-43. Recent development in China's cotton in-
    dustry. Shanghai, China Institute of Pacific Relations, 1936. 43 p.
WANG, TING-HSIEN, 王庭顯. Research on raw cotton and its trade in Tientsin.
    Tientsin, Hautes études, 1935. iii, 97 p. (Tientsin. Institut des hautes études
    industrieles et commerciales. Economic studies, 4 ).

## Electrical Industries

BOARD OF ARBITRATION IN THE ARBITRATION CASE BETWEEN RADIO COR-
    PORATION OF AMERICA VERSUS THE NATIONAL GOVERNMENT OF THE
    REPUBLIC OF CHINA, April 11-13, 1935. Decision in the arbitration case
    between Radio Corporation of America versus the National government of the
    Republic of China. The Hague, 1935. 22 numb. 1.
CHAO, TSÊNG-CHIO, 趙曾鈺, 1901-    The public utilities of Shanghai, 1946-
    47 [by] T. C. Tsao. [Shanghai, 1948?] ix, 122 p. port., diagrs.
CHINA. National Construction Commission. Electrification of the lower Yangtze
    area, Schedule 1. Nanking, 1930. 14 p. map.
_____. National Resources Commission. Central electrical manufacturing works,
    National Resources Commission, Republic of China. New York, 1944. 19 p.
MANGOLD, RUDOLF. Die elektrotechnische Industrie und der chinesische Markt,
    hrsg. von der Chinastudien-Gesellschaft für deutsch-chinesische wirtschaft-
    liche Zusammenarbeit unter Mitwirkung der Wirtschaftsgruppe Elektroindus-
    trie. Berlin, Leipzig, W. de Gruyter, 1935. 154 p. fold. map, tables (part
    fold.).
YEH, KUNG-CHIA, 葉孔嘉, 1924-    Electric power development in mainland
    China: prewar and postwar. Santa Monica, Rand Corp., 1956. 119 p. tables.
    (Rand research memorandum-1821).
ZEPPERNICK, GÜNTHER. Die bergwirtschaftliche Bedeutung der chinesischen
    Kohlenverkommen für die Gestaltung der Kraftstoffwirtschaft Chinas. Frei-
    berg, 1942. 119 1. illus. map. Diss.-Univ. Freiberg.

## Handicrafts

FONG, H.D., 方顯庭, 1902-    Tientsin carpet industry. Tientsin, Printed by
    the Chihli Press, 1929. 77, [1] p. incl. tables. (Nankai university Committee
    on social and economic research. Industry ser. Bull., 1 ).
_____. Rayon and cotton weaving in Tientsin. Tientsin, Chihli Press, 1930. 79,
    [1] p. (Nankai Univ. Committee on social and economic research. Industry
    ser., Bull., 2 ).
_____. Hosiery knitting in Tientsin. Tientsin, Chihli Press, 1930. 76 p. (Nan-
    kai Univ. Committee on social and economic research. Industry ser. Bull., 3).

―――. Rural industries in China, by H. D. Fong, with the assistance of Chih Wu, 吳知. Tientsin, Chihli Press, 1933. 68 p. tables. (Nankai Institute of Economics. Industry ser. Bull., 5 ).

―――. Rural weaving and the merchant employers in a North China district. Tientsin, Chihli Press, 1935. 80 p. map, diagrs. (Nankai Institute of Economics. Industry ser., Bull., 7 ).

―――. The growth and decline of rural industrial enterprises in North China, by H. D. Fong with the assistance of H. H. Pi, 畢相輝. Tientsin, Chihli Press, 1936. 83 p. incl. maps, tables. (Nankai Institute of Economics, Industry ser., Bull., 8 ).

HERMAN, THEODORE, 1913-   An analysis of China's export handicraft industries to 1930. Ann Arbor, University Microfilms [1954] ( [University Microfilms, Ann Arbor, Mich.] Publication no. 8348 ). Collation of the original: 270 l. illus., maps. Thesis-University of Washington.

HOMMEL, RUDOLF P. China at work; an illustrated record of the primitive industries of China's masses, whose life is toil, and thus an account of Chinese civilization. New York, John Day [c1937] x, 366 p. illus.

LI, P'U-LUNG, 李步龍. The brick industry in Tientsin and the problems of its modernization. Tientsin, Hautes études, 1940. 42 p. (Tientsin. Institut des hautes études industrieles et commerciales. Economic studies, 15 ).

SWIRE, G. WARREN. The coast and river trade of China. London, Royal Institute of International Affairs, 1931. [24] l. incl. tables. (Prepared for the 4th biennial conference of the Institute of Pacific Relations, Hangchow, 1931 ).

WOIDT, HANNA. Chinese handicrafts, a picture book. Peking, 1944. 51 p. plates (part col.).


## Industrial Cooperatives

ALLEY, REWI, 1897-   The Chinese industrial co-operatives. Chungking, China Information Pub. Co.[1940] cover-title, 25 p. (Chungking pamphlets, 4 ).

―――. Two years of Indusco. Hong Kong, Chinese Industrial Cooperatives, Hong Kong Promotion Committee, 1940. 25 p. plates, ports., tables.

BURCHETT, GEORGE HAROLD. China's cooperative societies; their genesis and development [and other articles] Melbourne, Australia-China Cooperation Association, 1941. cover-title, 9 p. ports.

CHAND, MAHESH. Co-operation in China and Japan, by Maheshchand. Foreword by H. L. Kaji. Bombay, Vora [1946] 75 p.

CH'ÊN, FRANCIS J.,      陳鵬. Cooperative enterprises in Fukien province. Translated by R. S. Ward. Foochow, 1940. 31 numb. l.

CH'ÊN, HAN-SHÊNG, 陳翰笙, 1897-   Gung ho! The story of the Chinese cooperatives. New York, American Institute of Pacific Relations, 1947. 63 p. illus., double map. (I. P. R. pamphlets, 24 ).

CH'ÊN, JACK, 陳伊範. Progress of China's industrial cooperatives; a series of twenty drawings. New York, Indusco, 194? 20 p. illus.

CH'ÊN, KUO-FU, 陳果夫, 1892-1951. The co-operative movement in China. Shanghai, China Co-operators' Union, 1933; 2nd ed. 1947. 48 p. map, tables, diagrs.

CHINA. Ministry of Social Affairs. Central Cooperative Administration. The Chinese cooperative movement. Nanking, 1947. 48 p.

CHINESE INDUSTRIAL COOPERATIVES. General report. [Hong Kong, 1938-41] 3 v.

―――. Chinese industrial cooperatives; for a new economic offensive, for prolonged resistance, for productive relief, for the salvation of China's industry, for victorious peacetime reconstruction. [Hong Kong, 1938] 64 p. illus. fold. map.

―――. The people strike back! Or, The story of Chinese industrial cooperatives. [Hongkong, Hongkong-Shanghai Industrial Cooperatives Promotion

Committee, 1938] 68 p. illus., fold. map.
———. China's industrial reconstruction; the story of the Chinese industrial co-operatives. [Hongkong, Hongkong-Shanghai Industrial Cooperatives Promotion Committee, 1939] 68 p. illus., map.
———. Appeal, Chinese industrial co-operatives. [Hongkong, Printed by S. C. M. post, 1939] cover-title, 15 p. illus., plates.
———. A nation rebuilds; the story of the Chinese industrial cooperatives. [New York? 1943?] cover-title, 32 p. illus. (incl. ports.).
———. Shantan Bailie School, 1948, technical training school of the Chinese Industrial Cooperatives. Shanghai, International Committee for Chinese Industrial Cooperatives, 1948. 49 p.
———. Chengtu Depot. Report. 1940-    [Hongkong] Chinese Industrial Cooperatives, Hongkong Promotion Committee. 1 v. illus.
———. Northwest headquarters. Reports, prepared by the staff of the Northwest headquarters. [1938/39-40] [Hongkong] Chinese Industrial Cooperatives, Hongkong Promotion Committee, 1940-41. 2 v. illus., plates, ports., diagrs.
DZUNG, KYI-UNG, 陳繼恩, [Ch'en Chi-ên] 1914-    The Chinese industrial co-operative movement. Ann Arbor, University Microfilms [1952] ([University Microfilms, Ann Arbor, Mich.] Publication no. 2940 ) Collation of the original: 1 v. (various pagings) diagrs., tables. Thesis-Princeton University.
GOULLART, PETER. Report on the industrial cooperatives of Likiang, Yunnan. New York, 1945. 7 l.
HOGG, GEORGE AYLWIN. I see a new China. Boston, Little, Brown, 1944. London, V. Gollancz, 1945. xv, 210, [1] p. front.(port.).
HSU, YAN-KEE. Le mouvement coopératif en Chine. Paris, L. Rodstein, 1933. 183 p. incl. tables. Thèse-Univ. de Caen.
[SNOW, HELEN (FOSTER) ] 1907-    China builds for democracy; a story of co-operative industry, by Nym Wales [pseud.] New York, Modern Age Books, 1941. Allahabad, Kitabistan, 1942. xv, 310 p. incl. illus.(map) tables ( 1 fold.) plates, ports.
STEVENS, WAYNE MACKENZIE, 1893-    Cooperative organization and management with special references to China. [n. p. 1936?] 2 v. illus., tables (part fold.) diagrs.

## Industrialization

ALLEN, GEORGE CYRIL, 1900-    Western enterprise in Far Eastern economic development, China and Japan, by G. C. Allen and Audrey G. Donnithorne. London, Allen and Unwin, 1954; New York, Macmillan, 1954. 291 p. maps.
BARNETT, ROBERT W., 1911-    ed. Factors in Chinese economic reconstruction, a summary of discussions organized by the Washington office of the IPR. This study is submitted by the American council as a document of the eighth conference of the IPR to be held in December, 1942. New York, American Council, Institute of Pacific Relations [1942] 12 numb. 1. (American council paper, 8 ).
CHEN, GIDEON, 陳其田. Chinese government economic planning and reconstruction since 1927. Shanghai, China Institute of Pacific Relations, 1933. 56 p.
CHIANG, KAI-SHEK, 1886-    China's post-war economic reconstruction, by Chiang Kai-shek and T. V. Soong. With English translation. Shanghai, International Publishers [1945] 16, 13 p.
CHINA. National Construction Commission. The National Construction Commission of the National Government. [Nanking] 1930. cover-title, 16 p. fold. diagr.
———. National Economic Council. The National Economic Council: history, organization, and activities. Chin Fen, 秦汾, Secretary-General. Nanking, 1935. cover-title, 3 numb. 1., 79, 34 p. incl. tables, diagr.

————. Annual report. 1935-36. Nanking, 1936-37. 2 v. plates, ports., tables, diagrs. (part fold.).

CHINA-AMERICAN COUNCIL OF COMMERCE AND INDUSTRY. Guide to the industrialization of China. 2d ed. [New York] 1945. 3 v. v. 1. Mining and metallurgy by Guy C. Riddel. - v. 2. Chemicals and basic processing by Ralph C. Lamis. - v. 3. Power report by Robert F. Hamilton.

CHUNG, AN-MIN, 鍾安民, 1921-    The development of modern manufacturing industry in China, 1928-1949. Philadelphia, 1953. 301 l. Thesis-Univ. of Pennsylvania.

CLEMENTS, JULIUS MORGAN, 1869-    Cement industry of China. Washington, Govt. Print. Off., 1922. ii, 8 p. incl. tables. (Bureau of foreign and domestic commerce. Trade information bull., 7 ).

FONG, H. D., 1902-    Industrialization and labor in Hopei, with special reference to Tientsin. Shanghai, National Christian Council, 1931. 17 l.

————. China's industrialization; a statistical survey. Preliminary paper prepared for the fourth biennial conference of the Institute of Pacific Relations, to be held in Hangchow, from October 21st to November 4th, 1931. Shanghai, China Institute of Pacific Relations [1931] 46 p., 1 l. incl. tables (part fold.) fold. diagrs.

————. Toward economic control in China. [Shanghai] China Institute of Pacific Relations, 1936. 91 p. fold. map. (Papers presented at the sixth conference of the Institute of Pacific Relations, Yosemite national park, California. 4:3).

————. Industrial organization in China. [Tientsin, Printed by Chihli Press, 1937] 88 p.(Nankai institute of economics. Industry series. Bull., 10).

————. Problems of economic reconstruction in China, by H. D. Fong, K. Y. Yin, 尹國墉 and Tso-fan Koh, 谷春帆. (Pt. 1. Principles of post-war economic reconstruction in China. Pt. 11. Capital stock in China. Chungking, China Council, Institute of Pacific Relations, 1942. 38 l. incl. tables. (China Council paper, 2 ).

————. The post-war industrialization of China. [Washington, National Planning Association, 1942] iii, [1], 92 p. illus.(map) (Planning pamphlets, 12 and 13 ).

GULL, EDWARD MANICO, 1883-    China's economic reconstruction; an outline of its determining factors and predictable trends, constituting part I of a larger I. P. R. research report on the same subject. Submitted by the Royal Institute of International Affairs as a document for the Ninth Conference of the I. P. R. to be held in January 1945. London, Royal Institute of International Affairs [1945] 22 numb. l. (United Kingdom paper, 2 ).

————. Essentials of reconstruction in China. Constitutes part of a larger IPR research report. Submitted by the Royal Institute of International Affairs as a document for the Tenth Conference of the IPR to be held at Stratford-upon-Avon, England, September 1947. London, Royal Institute of International Affairs, 1947. 63 l. (United Kingdom paper, 2 ).

HAN, KWEI-CHANG, 韓貴章. Die Beziehungen zwischen Industrieaufbau und Verkehrsgestaltung im modernen China. Leipzig, 1942. ii, 192 l. illus. Diss.-Univ. Leipzig.

HO, FRANKLIN LIEN, 何廉, 1895-    Extent and effects of industrialization in China, by Franklin L. Ho and Hsien Ding Fong. A data paper submitted to the biennial conference of the Institute of Pacific relations, October 1929. [Tientsin, 1929] cover-title, 34 p. incl. tables.

————. Industrialization in China; a study of conditions in Tientsin, by Franklin L. Ho and H. D. Fong. [Tientsin] 1929. cover-title, 30 p. incl. forms.

HSU, IH-SEN, 徐益生, 1921-    A study of possible factors affecting the acceleration of industrial development in China. Ann Arbor, University Microfilms [1954] ([University Microfilms, Ann Arbor, Mich.] Publication no. 10, 218 ). Collation of the original: vii, 317 l. maps, diagr., tables. Thesis-State University of Iowa.

HUBBARD, GILBERT ERNEST, 1885-    comp. Eastern industrialization and its
    effect on the West; with a conclusion by Professor T. E. Gregory. London,
    Oxford University Press, H. Milford, 1938. xx, 418 p. "First published Oc-
    tober 1935; 2d ed. enl. and rev., July 1938."
KIRBY, E. STUART, 1909-    Some political aspects of Far Eastern economic
    development. New York, Institute of Pacific Relations, 1950. 55 p. (Its Sec-
    retariat paper, 4 ).
LIEU, D. K., 劉大鈞, [Liu Ta-chün] 1890-    China's industries and finance, be-
    ing a series of studies in Chinese industrial and financial questions. Peking
    [etc.] The Chinese Government Bureau of Economic Information [1927] xiv,
    238 p. incl. tables. port., diagr.
———. A preliminary report on Shanghai industrialization. Shanghai, 1933. cov-
    er-title, 68 p. incl. tables (part fold.) (The China institute of economic and
    statistical research, 1:1 ).
———. The growth and industrialization of Shanghai. Shanghai, China Institute
    of Pacific Relations, 1936. ix, 473 p. incl. tables (part fold.) diagrs.
———. International aspects of China's economic reconstruction. Shanghai, Chi-
    na Institute of Pacific Relations, 1947. 32 l. (Institute of Pacific Relations,
    10th conference, Stratford-upon-Avon, 1947, China paper, 2 ).
———. China's economic stabilization and reconstruction. New Brunswick, Rut-
    gers Univ. Press, 1948. x, 159 p. map.
LOH, ARTHUR TSUNG-YUAN, 陸宗源, 1923-    The theory of economic devel-
    opment and planning in an underdeveloped country, as applicable to China.
    Urbana, 1952. 8 p. Abstract of thesis-University of Illinois.
MA, TSIE, 馬節. Eine Untersuchung über die Grundlagen der Industrialisierung
    Chinas. München, 1941. 131 l. Diss.-Univ. München.
NIEH, C. L., 聶其焜. China's industrial development: its problems and pros-
    pect. Shanghai, China Institute of Pacific Relations, 1933. 53 p. (Institute
    of Pacific Relations. 5th Conference, Banff, 1933. Documents, 10:2 ).
RECONSTRUCTION in China; a record of progress and achievement in facts and
    figures. Shanghai, China United Press, 1935. xiv, 401 p. plates, ports.,
    maps (part fold.). "China to-day ser. [3] ).
RISCHE, BERNO, 1897-    Stand und Entwicklung der chinesischen Industrie,
    mit besonderer Berücksichtigung der Absatzmöglichkeiten für ausländische
    Maschinen. Berlin, Maschinenbau-Verlag [1931] 176, [2] p. incl. tables.
ROSEN, GEORGE, 1920-    Patterns of Far Eastern industrial development, with
    special reference to their influence on foreign trade in the Far East. New
    York, Institute of Pacific Relations, 1950. 32 l. (Secretariat paper, 5 ).
SUN, YAT-SEN, 1866-1925. The international development of China. New York
    and London, G. P. Putnam's sons, 1929. xvi, 265 p. plates (2 plans) 17 maps
    (1 fold. in pocket). 1st ed., 1922.
———. The same. Reprinted from the second ed. Chungking, China Pub. Co.,
    1941. xv, 265 p. plates (2 plans) 17  maps (1 fold.).
———. The same. Reprinted from the 2d ed. [Calcutta] Calcutta office, Chinese
    Ministry of Information, 1942. xiii, 191 p. plates (2 plans) maps (1 fold.).
———. The same. Reprinted from the 2d ed. Chungking, Ministry of Informa-
    tion, 1943. xiii, 191 p. plates ( 2 plans) maps (1 fold.).
———. The same. London, New York [etc.] Pub. on behalf of the London office,
    Chinese Ministry of Information, by Hutchinson [1945?] 176 p. plates (2 plans)
    maps (1 fold.).
———. The same. Nanking, Ministry of Information, 1947; Taipei, China Cul-
    tural Service, 1953. 233 p. illus. maps.
———. The same. [With Chinese text, New ed,] Taipei, China Cultural Service
    [1953] 330 p. illus.
———. Fundamentals of national reconstruction. Chungking and Calcutta, Chi-
    nese Ministry of Information [1945] iv, 96, [1] p. incl. facsim., diagrs.,
    front. (port.) "Translator's preface" signed: Z. B. Toong, 董壽彭.

————. The same. [With Chinese text. Taipei] China Cultural Service [1953] vii, 266 p. port., diagrs., facsim.

————. Dr. Sun Yatsen's principles of industrial development of China, abridged and annotated by Ling Ping, 凌冰. Shanghai, The New Age Pub. Co., 1928. 4, 63 p.

SZE, SAO-KE ALFRED, 施肇基, 1877-1958. Reconstruction in China. New York, Chinese Cultural Society [1934?] cover-title, 15 p.

TAMAGNA, FRANK M., 1910-   Politics and economics in Far Eastern reconstruction. New York, Institute of Pacific Relations [1947] 22 l. (Secretariat paper, 5).

TAO, SIU, 陶秀. L'œuvre du Conseil national économique chinois. Nancy, Impr. G. Thomas, 1936. [5]-175 p. Thèse-Univ. de Nancy.

TAYLOR, GEORGE EDWARD, 1905-   The reconstruction movement in China. Submitted as a preparatory paper for the Sixth Conference of the Institute of Pacific Relations held at Yosemite, California, August 1936. London, Royal Institute of International Affairs, 1936. 2-35 numb. l. (United Kingdom papers, 6).

TAYLOR, JOHN BERNARD, 1878-   Farm and factory in China: aspects of the industrial revolution. London, Student Christian Movement, 1928. 106, [1] p.

TING, CHEN, 丁忱, 1919-   Industrialization, capital formation and internal savings, with special reference to the post-war industrialization of China. Cambridge, 1945. 256 l. Thesis-Harvard University.

U.S. Foreign Economic Administration. Guide to the industrialization of China, edited by Alexander Taube. Washington, D.C., Foreign Economic Administration, 1945. 10 v. 3400 l. Typescript.

VINACKE, HAROLD MONK, 1893-   Problems of industrial development in China; a preliminary study. Princeton, Princeton University Press, 1926. ix, 205 p.

WANG, FOH-SHEN, 汪馥蓀. China's industrial production 1931-46. Nanking, Institute of Social Sciences, Academia Sinica, 1948. 17 p. diagr. tables. (Academia Sinica. Institute of Social Sciences. Social Science study papers, 2).

WANG, YAO-T'IEN, 汪堯田. China's economic reconstruction. [Shanghai, Longmans Book] 1948. v, 108 p.

WHAT the Chinese think about post-war reconstruction: Internal economic development, by Ching-chao Wu, 吳景超; China in world economy, by Chohming Li, 李卓敏; Post-war foreign policy by Yuan Chen, 陳源. New York, Foreign Policy Association [1943] [213]-228 p. (Foreign policy reports, 19: 16, November 1, 1943).

WONG, WÊN-HAO, 翁文灏, 1889-   China's economic development. [Hankow, Chinese League of Nations Union, 1938] 5 p. (Special publications series, 13).

————. Report on economic affairs. Nanking, The International Department, Ministry of Information [1946] 16 l.

WU, CHI-YUEN, 伍超元, 1912-   China's social environment and her economic future. Shanghai, China Institute of Pacific Relations, 1947. 19 l. (China paper, 3).

WU, CHING-CH'AO, 吳景超, 1901-   Industrial planning in China. Chungking, China Institute of Pacific Relations, 1945. iii, 41 p. (China council series, 3).

WU, DING-CHANG, 吳鼎昌, 1884-1950. International economic co-operation in China. Peping, 1929. 14 p.

WU, HSI-YUNG, 吳希庸. L'industrialisation de la Chine et l'économie nationale chinoise. Nancy, Poncelot, 1931. [9]-182 p. Thèse-Univ. de Nancy.

WU, TAO-KUN, 吳道昆, 1907-   Mathematisch statistische Untersuchung zur chinesischen Industrie. Jena, 1937. 65 p. Diss.-Univ. Berlin.

WU, YUANLI, 吳元黎, 1920-   Capital formation and the economic order: an analytical study with special reference to the case of a poor country [China] London, 1945. iv, 548 l. Thesis-London School of Economics.

————. China's economic policy; planning or free enterprise? New York, Sino-International Economic Research Center [1946] 60 p. incl. tables. (Sino-international economic pamphlets, 4 ).

————. China's international economic position. Shanghai, China Institute of Pacific Relations, 1947. 28 1. (China paper, 1 ).

Foreign Trade
General Works

ABEND, HALLETT EDWARD, 1884-1955. Treaty ports. Garden City, Doubleday, Doran, 1944. viii, [2], 271 p. illus.(map).

AHLERS, JOHN. Western interests under fire. Chungking, The China Information Pub. Co. [1940] cover-title, 28 p. (Chungking pamphlets, 3 ).

————. Japan closing the "open door" in China. Prepared under the auspices of the Council of International Affairs, Chungking. Shanghai, Kelly and Walsh, 1940. viii, 140 p. ( [Council of international affairs] Political and economic studies, 8 ).

CHANG, HSIAO-MEI, 張肖梅, 1906-    The position of China as a producer of raw materials and a consumer of manufactured products. Preliminary paper prepared for the Fifth Biennial Conference of the Institute of Pacific Relations, to be held at Banff, August 14 to 28, 1933. [Shanghai] China Institute of Pacific Relations, 1933. 45 p. of diagrs., tables.

CHANG, YU-SHIN, 張與新? Die Entwicklungstendenzen des chinesischen Aussenhandels nach dem Weltkriege (eine Untersuchung über die internationale Wirtschaftsverflechtung Chinas). Gelnhausen, Dissertations-druck von F. W. Kalbfleisch, 1936. 93 p. Diss.-Univ. Frankfurt.

CHAO, ZOO BIANG, 趙祖邦. Étude sur le commerce extérieur de la Chine de 1864 à 1932. Lyon, Impr. franco-suisse [1935] 176 p. Thèse-Univ. de Paris.

CHÊNG, YU-KWEI, 鄭友揆, 1909-    Foreign trade and industrial development of China, an historical and integrated analysis through 1948. Washington, University Press of Washington, D.C. [1956] xi, 278 p. map, diagrs.,tables.

CHINA. Inspectorate General of Customs. Dangerous and hazardous cargo usually imported into China: its nature and treatment. 3d ed., rev. Shanghai, Statistical Dept., Inspectorate General of Customs, 1940. ix, 27 1. (Its Maritime customs II. Special series, no. 40 ).

CHINA WEEKLY REVIEW. Japan's war on foreign business. Shanghai, China Weekly Review Press [1938?] 74 p.

CHOW, KWONG-SHU, 周光庶. A handbook of Chinese trade customs. Shanghai, Far Eastern Press, 1933. 3-236 p.

FAIRBANK, JOHN KING, 1907-    Trade and diplomacy on the China coast; the opening of the treaty ports, 1842-54. Cambridge, Harvard University Press; London, Oxford University Press, 1953. 2 v. port., maps. (Harvard historical studies, v.62-63 ).

FENG, CHAOI, 馮兆異, 1894-    [Der Aussenhandel Chinas von 1913-23] Leipzig, Fickers-Verlag [1926] 56 p. Diss.-Univ. Leipzig.

HO, PING-YIN, 何炳賢, 1903-    The foreign trade of China. Shanghai, Commercial Press, 1935. xvi, 826 p. tables (part fold.).

HSU, OSCAR T., 徐則駿. Handel und Handelpolitik Chinas. Hamburg, 1934. 54 p. incl. charts, tables. Diss.-Univ. Hamburg.

HUNTER, WILLIAM C., 1812-91. The 'fan kwae' at Canton before treaty days, 1825-44, by an old resident (William C. Hunter). [Reprint ed.] Shanghai, The Oriental Affairs [1938] 97, [1] p. fold. plan. First published in 1882.

LAU, CHUNG-HIM, 劉仲謙, [Liu, Chung-ch'ien]. Names of commodities and other appellatives in Chinese and English, edited by Lau Chung-him and Yao Yuan-lum, 姚元綸. Hong Kong, Lau Chung-him, 1955. 479 p.

LI, CHEN-NAN, 李振南, 1898-    Factors affecting China's foreign trade. Shanghai, Chiao-tung University Research Institute, 1938. 54 p.

LIEU, D.K., 劉大鈞, 1890-    Notes on China's foreign trade and trade policy. New York, Institute of Pacific Relations, 1945. 34 numb. l. incl. tables.(Institute of Pacific Relations, Secretariat paper, 5 ).

MORSE, HOSEA BALLOU, 1855-1934. The guilds of China, with an account of the guild merchant or Co-hong of Canton. 2d ed.  London, New York, Longmans, Green, 1932. ix, 111 p. plates (incl. front.). 1st ed. 1909.

[MOSER, CHARLES KROTH] 1877-    Where China buys and sells. Washington, Govt. Print. Off., 1935. iv, 57 p. incl. tables. (U.S. Bureau of foreign and domestic commerce. Trade information bull., 827 ).

PRATIQUE commerciale en Chine, d'après Berliner. 2. éd., rev. et. cor.par J.R. Baylin.  Pékin, A. Nachbaur, 1928. 179 p.incl. tables. plates (part col.) maps, diagrs. (Encyclopédie des questions chinoises).

REMER, CHARLES FREDERICK, 1889-    The foreign trade of China. Shanghai, Commercial Press, 1926. [v]-xii, 269 p. diagrs.

ROSINGER, LAWRENCE KAELTER, 1915-    China as a post-war market. New York, Foreign Policy Association [1945] 251-263, [1] p. incl. tables. (Foreign policy reports. 20:20. January 1, 1945 ).

THEOPHILE, HANS. Der Überseeverkehr Chinas. Ein Beitrag zu den östasiatischen Schiffahrtsproblemen. Hamburg, 1942. ix, 251 l. Diss.-Univ. Hamburg.

TSANG, CHIH, 章植. China's postwar markets. New York, International Secretariat, Institute of Pacific Relations, distributed by Macmillan, 1945. xi, 239 p.

U.S. Bureau of Foreign and Domestic Commerce. China trade facts, by Julean Arnold. Washington, Govt. Print. Off., 1925. 12 p.

——. Sales territories in China, by Charles K. Moser. Washington, Govt. Print. Off., 1929. 50 p. incl. map.

WANG, SHAO-CHENG, 王紹成, 1906-    Aussenhandel und Zollproblem Chinas. Berlin, Funk, 1935. 73 p. Diss.-Univ. Berlin.

WATSON, ERNEST. The principal articles of Chinese commerce (import and export) with a description of the origin, appearance, characteristics, and general properties of each commodity; an account of the methods of preparation or manufacture together with various tests, etc., by means of which the different products may be readily identified. 2d ed. Shanghai, Statistical Dept., Inspectorate General of Customs, 1930. ix, 630 p. illus. (The Maritime customs. II. Special series, no. 38 ). 1st ed. 1923.

WILLIAMS, CHARLES ALFRED SPEED, 1884-    Manual of Chinese products. Peiping, Printed at Kwang Yuen Press, 1933. vii-x, 256 p. front.

WU, CHAO-CHANG, 吳兆璋. Trade in bristles. Tientsin, Hautes études,1938. v, vi, 108 p. incl. diagrs. illus. (charts) (Tientsin. Institut des hautes études industrieles et commerciales. Economic studies, 13 ).

ZIMMERMANN, EDWIN. Chinas wirtschaftliche Verhältnisse und seine Beziehungen zur schweizerischen Export-Industrie. St. Gallen, J. Zehnder,1923. vi, 119 p. fold. tables. Thèse-Univ. de Neuchatel.

### Statistics

BANK OF CHINA. Research Dept. Statistics of China's foreign trade, 1912-30. With complete texts of tariff regulations, compiled and edited by the Research Department, Bank of China. Shanghai, Bank of China, 1931. viii, 133 p.incl. charts, tables.

——. Statistics of China's foreign trade, 1930-33, compiled and edited by the Research Department, Bank of China. Shanghai, Bank of China, 1934. 111 p. 1 l. incl. tables, diagrs.

——. Supplement, Jan.-Nov. 1934. Shanghai, 1934. 14 p. incl. tables.

CHENG, MING-JU, 鄭名儒. The statistical comparisons of the foreign trade of China before and after the great war. Fribourg, 1936. ii, vii, iii, 123 p.

Thèse-Univ. de Fribourg (Suisse).

CHINA. Custom-House, Antung. Antung customs monthly returns. 1922-28.
[Antung, 1923-29] 8 v.

———. Inspectorate General of Customs. Quarterly returns of trade, 華洋貿易
統計册季刊 . Shanghai, 1869-1931.    v. (The maritime customs. I.-Sta-
tistical series: no. 2 ). Title varies: 1869-1913, Customs gazette. 1914-
Quarterly returns of trade.

———. Annual trade report and returns, 1920-31,    華洋貿易統計年刊 . Shanghai, 1921-32. 12 v. fold. map, fold. plan, tables. (The maritime customs.
I.-Statistical series: nos. 3 to 5 ).

———. Decennial reports on the trade, navigation, industries, etc., of the ports
open to foreign commerce in China and Corea, and on the condition and development of the treaty port provinces [1892-1901, 1902-11, 1912-21, 1922-31]
Shanghai, 1904-33. 6 v. plates, maps, plans, tables, diagrs. profile (China.
Imperial maritime customs. 1. Statistical ser. 6 ).

———. Foreign trade of China, 1920-31. Shanghai, 1921-32. 36 v. fold. map,
tables, diagrs. (part col., part fold.).

———. The trade of China, 1932-46. Shanghai, 1933-47.  15 v. fold. map, tables, diagrs. (part fold.) (The maritime customs. I-Statistical series: no.1).

———. The trade of China, 1935-40. Introductory survey with tables for revenue,
value, treasure, and shipping. Shanghai, 1936-41. 6 v. tables.

———. Monthly returns of the foreign trade of China, 海關進出口貿易統計月報.
Nov. 1931-49? [Shanghai]     v. in  (Its Chinese maritime customs. I. Statistical series: no. 8). Publication suspended May 1943?-June 1946.

———. Shanghai monthly returns of foreign trade, 1932-42. Shanghai, 1932-43//
10 v. tables.

———. Shanghai annual returns of foreign trade, 1936-40. Analysis of imports
and exports. Published by order of the inspector general of customs. Shanghai, Statistical Department of the Inspectorate General of Customs, 1937-41.
v. tables. (The maritime customs. I.-Statistical series: no. 2 ).

CHINA. Ministry of Industry. Foreign trade of China; statistical series, Nos. 1-
V. Nanking, Ministry of Industry, Commerce and Labor, 1929. 5 v. tables,
diagrs. 1. Value of the export of Chinese goods, 1912-18.  2. Value of the
import of foreign goods, 1912-18.  3. Statistics of the export of silk, silk
materials and products, 1912-18.  4. Statistics of the export of tea, 1912-18.
5. Statistics of the export of beans and peas, 1912-18.

CHUN, Y.S., 陳伯莊. Statistics of commodity flow of Chinese maritime customs and railways, 1912-36, 中國海關鐵路主要商品流通概况, by Y.S. Chun
and Y.L. Huang, 黃蔭萊. Shanghai [Chiao-Tung University, Research In-
stitute] 1937. 430 p. (Chiao-Tung University Research Institute. Special ser.
7:1 ).

TS'AI, CH'IEN, 蔡謙, 1908-  Trend and character of China's foreign trade,
1912-31; a statistical analysis of exports and imports by country as well as
by products, by Chien Tsai and Kwan-wai Chan, 陳君慧. Rev. ed. [Shang-
hai] China Institute of Pacific Relations, 1933. 52 p. incl. tables, diagrs.

———. Statistics of foreign trade of different Chinese ports with various countries (1919, 1927-31) [by] Chien Tsai and Yu-kwei Cheng, 鄭友揆. Shanghai, Commercial Press, 1936. xii, 427 p. (Institute of social sciences, Academia sinica. Studies and reports, 5 ).

U.S. Bureau of Foreign and Domestic Commerce. Monthly trade report, China.
[Shanghai, etc., 1922-40]   v. in    maps, tables, diagrs. irregular.

YANG, TUAN-LIU, 楊端六, 1885-  Statistics of China's foreign trade during
the last sixty-five years [by] C. Yang, H.B. Hau, 侯厚培, and others. [Nan-
king?] 1931. xxiv, xiv, 189 p. diagrs., tables. (Academia Sinica, National
Research Institute of Social Sciences. Monog., 4 ).

Trade with Germany

BARTSCH, KARIN. Hamburgs Handelsbeziehungen mit China und Britisch Ostindien, 1842-67. Hamburg, 1956. iii, 165 l. Diss.-Univ. Hamburg.
BEUTLER, HEINZ. Hundert Jahre Carlowitz und Co., Hamburg und China. Ein
Beitrag zur wirtschaftsgeschichtliche Entwicklung des deutsche China-Han-
dels. Hamburg, 1946. 182 l. plate, map. Diss.-Univ. Hamburg.
REICHSVERBAND der deutschen Industrie. Bericht der China-Studien-Kommis-
sion. Berlin, Selbstverlag des Reichsverbandes der deutschen Industrie,1930.
191, [1] p. fold. front. illus., maps. (Veröffentlichungen des Reichsverban-
des der deutschen Industrie, 57 ).
RÖSER, WALTER. Deutsch-Chinesische Wirtschaftsbeziehungen. Buckeburg,
H. Prinz, 1935. 163 p. incl. tables. Diss.-Univ. Frankfurt a.M.
WIDMANN, EDUARD. Gegenwartsprobleme des deutschen Aussenhandels mit
China unter besonderer Berücksichtigung der deutschen Einfuhrorganisation
in China. Heidelberg, Heidelberg Verlag-Anst, 1935. 143 p. Diss.-Univ.
Heidelberg.

## Trade with Great Britain

GT. BRIT. Dept. of Overseas Trade. Report on economic and commercial con-
ditions in China. 1919-37. London, H.M. Stationery Off., 1920-37. 17 v.
———.Economic Mission to the Far East. Report of the British Economic Mis-
sion to the Far East. 1930-31. London, H.M. Stationery Off., 1931. 156 p.
incl. tables.
———. Trade Mission to China. Report, October to December, 1946. London,
H.M. Stationery Off., 1948. 231 p. fold. col. maps.
GREENBERG, MICHAEL. British trade and the opening of China, 1800-42.
Cambridge [Eng.] University Press, 1951. xii, 238 p. (Cambridge studies
in economic history ).
GULL, EDWARD MANICO, 1883-    The future of British economic interests in
the Far East. London, The Royal Institute of International Affairs [1942] 20
numb. l. (United Kingdom paper, 3 ).
———. British economic interests in the Far East. Prepared as a report in the
International research series of the Institute of Pacific Relations. Issued un-
der the auspices of the Royal Institute of International Affairs. London, Ox-
ford University Press, H. Milford; New York, International Secretariat, In-
stitute of Pacific Relations, 1943. vii, 272 p.
JONES, SIR CLEMENT WAKEFIELD, 1880-    Chief officer in China, 1840-53.
Liverpool, C. Birchall [1955] 119 p. illus.
KUO, CHUNG-YING, 仉郭冲頴 1912-    British trade in China, 1894-1914. Mad-
ison, 1947. iii, 288 l. Thesis-Univ. of Wisconsin.
LUBBOCK, ALFRED BASIL, 1876-1944. The China clippers. 5th ed. Glasgow,
J. Brown, 1922. xv, 388, xxxvi p. front., plates, ports., map. 1st ed.1914.
MORSE, HOSEA BALLOU, 1855-1934. The chronicles of the East India compa-
by, trading to China, 1635-1834. Cambridge, Harvard University Press;
Oxford, The Clarendon Press, 1926-29. 5 v. fronts., plates, ports., fold.
maps, 2 plans. (Vol. v supplementary, 1742-74 ).

## Trade with Japan

CHEN, TSUNG-CHING, 陳宗經. Les relations commerciales entre la Chine et
le Japon depuis l'avènement de la République chinoise à nos jours. Paris,
P. Bossuet, 1936. ix, 331 p., 1 l. incl. tables, diagrs. Thèse-Univ.de Paris.
ITANI, ZENICHI, 1899-    The export of Japanese capital to China. Prepared for
the 4th bi-annual conference of the Institute of Pacific Relations to be held at
Hangchow, 1931. Tokyo, Japan Council of the Institute of Pacific Relations,
1931. 36 p. incl. tables.
JENZOWSKI, SIEGFRIED. Die chinesisch-japanischen Boykottfälle als völker-

rechtliches Problem. Köhn, 1939. 61 p. Diss.-Univ. Köhn.

LOWE, CHUAN-HUA, 駱傳華, 1902-   Japan's economic offensive in China; introduction by Professor Paul H. Douglas. London, G. Allen and Unwin [1930] 179, [1] p. front., plates, fold. maps, diagr.

NATIONAL INDUSTRIAL CONFERENCE BOARD. Economic aspects of Sino-Japanese relations. [New York] National Industrial Conference Board, 1933. 21 numb. 1. incl. tables, diagrs. (Conference board information service: Foreign affairs. Memorandum, 3 ).

OSAKA. CHAMBER OF COMMERCE AND INDUSTRY. A synopsis of the boycott in China. The Chinese government encourages and directs the anti-Japanese boycott. The anti-Japanese boycott by China is tantamount to an act of war. [Osaka] 1932. 9, [1] p.

PRESS UNION, Shanghai. The anti-Japanese boycott movement in China (from October, 1931 to January, 1932) [Shanghai, 1932] cover-title, 66 p. diagr.

REMER, CHARLES FREDERICK, 1889-   A study of Chinese boycotts, with special reference to their economic effectiveness [by] C.F. Remer with the assistance of William B. Palmer. Baltimore, Johns Hopkins Press, 1933. xii, 306 p. double diagrs.

TSHA, T.Y., 蔡正雅, [Ts'ai Chêng-ya]. Statistics of Sino-Japanese trade [by] T.Y. Tsha, Z.L. Chen, 陳善林, and others.   [Shanghai] Sino-Japanese Trade Research Institute, The Chinese Economic Society, 1933. xvi, 222, 110 p. incl. tables, diagrs.

## Trade with United States

AUGUR, HELEN. Tall ships to Cathay. Garden City, N.Y., Doubleday [1951] 255 p. illus., ports.

BROWN, DONALD MACKENZIE, 1908-   ed. China trade days in California; selected letters from the Thompson papers, 1832-63. Berkeley, Univ. of California Press, 1947. xvii, 94 p. ports.

CAMPBELL, CHARLES SOUTTER, 1911-   Special business interests and the open door policy. New Haven, Yale University Press, 1951. 88 p. (Yale historical publications. Miscellany, 53 ). Thesis-Yale University.

CHAO, TSI-CHING, 趙梓慶. Les relations économiques sino-américaines. Paris, L. Rodstein, 1933. 243 p. fold. tables. Thèse-Univ. de Paris.

DIETRICH, ETHEL BARBARA, 1891-   Far Eastern trade of the United States. New York, International Secretariat, Institute of Pacific Relations, 1940. xii, 116 p. incl. tables, diagrs. (I.P.R. inquiry series).

DULLES, FOSTER RHEA, 1900-   The old China trade. Boston and New York, Houghton Mifflin, 1930. 228 p. front., plates, ports., facsim., diagr.

GREENBIE, SYDNEY, 1889-   Gold of Ophir; the China trade in the making of America, by Sydney Greenbie and Marjorie Barstow Greenbie. Rev. ed. with introduction by Rufus Rockwell Wilson. New York, Wilson-Erickson, 1937. xix, 330 p. front., plates, ports. 1st ed. N.Y., Doubleday, Page, 1925

GRIFFIN, ELDON, 1895-   Clippers and consuls; American consular and commercial relations with eastern Asia, 1845-60. Ann Arbor, Mich., Edwards Brothers, 1938. xxii, 533 p. incl. front., illus., plates, maps, facsims.( 1 fold.) tables.

HENDERSON, DANIEL MacINTYRE, 1880- Yankee ships in China seas; adventures of pioneer Americans in the troubled Far East. New York, Hastings House [1946] xiv, 274 p. plates, 2 port.(incl. front.).

HEWES, AGNES (DANFORTH). Two oceans to Canton; the story of the old China trade; illustrated by Harry Roth. New York, A.A. Knopf, 1944. [3]-184,[1], vii p. illus., double maps.

KEARNY, THOMAS. Commodore Lawrence Kearny and the open door and most favored nation policy in China in 1842-43, an American viewpoint, based on newly discovered Chinese documents. Newark, N.J., New Jersey Historical

Society, 1932. [28] p.

LATOURETTE, KENNETH SCOTT, 1884-    Voyages of American ships to China, 1784-1844. New Haven, Connecticut Academy of Arts and Sciences [1927] p. [237]-271. (Transactions of the Connecticut academy of arts and sciences, v. 28 [art. iv] ).

LIN, LIN, 林霖, 1906-    American imports from China, prior to and immediately following the Sino-Japanese war, 1932-38. New York, Research Department, Trans-Pacific News Service, 1940. 2-9 numb. l. tables, diagr. (China economic information bull., 1 ).

LOINES, ELMA, 1882-    ed. The China trade post-bag of the Seth Low family of Salem and New York, 1829-73. Manchester, Me., Falmouth Pub. House, 1953. ix, 324 p. illus., ports., maps, facsims.

MALIN, MORTON V., 1922-    American economic interests in China, 1900-08. [College Park, Md.] 1954. iv, 183 l. Thesis-University of Maryland.

MILNAR, ANTHONY LEE, 1910-    Chinese-American relations with especial reference to the imposition of the boycott, 1905-06. Washington, 1948 [i.e. 1949] iv, 307 l. Thesis-Georgetown University.

NEW YORK. METROPOLITAN MUSEUM OF ART. The China trade and its influences. New York [Printed by the Harbor Press ] 1941. xi, 21 p. 101 plates on 30 l.

PAN, SHŪ-LUN, 潘序倫, 1895-    The trade of the United States with China. New York, China Trade Bureau [c1924] vii-xix, 367 p. diagr. Thesis-Columbia University.

REA, GEORGE BRONSON, 1869-1936. What American[s] don't know about ''the open door.'' Shanghai, The Japanese Association in China, 1932. 3-40 p.

SHEWAN, ANDREW. The great days of sail, some reminiscences of a tea-clipper captain, edited by Rex Clements. Boston, Houghton Mifflin, 1927. 240 p. front., plates, ports.

TSAI, WILLIAM WEI-LIN, 蔡蔚林, 1922-    China's foreign exchange position and export trade to the United States, 1937-48. Ann Arbor, University Microfilms [1953] ([University Microfilms, Ann Arbor, Mich.] Publication no. 5911 ). vii, 326 l. illus. map, tables. Thesis-Univ. of Washington.

U.S. Bureau of Foreign and Domestic Commerce (Dept of Commerce). Trade of the United States with China, Hongkong and Kwangtung. 1937-    [Washington, 1938-    v. tables, diagrs.

———. China trade act, 1922, with regulations and forms. Edition of 1935, with amendments as of February 26, 1925, and June 25, 1938. Washington, Govt. Print. Off., 1940. ii, 29 p. incl. tables, forms.

U. S. Congress. House. Committee on the Judiciary. Incorporation of companies to promote trade in China. Report. [To accompany H.R. 4810] [Washington, Govt. Print. Off., 1921] 7 p. (67th Cong., 1st sess. House. Rept.13).

U. S. Congress. Senate. Committee on Commerce. To amend the China trade act of 1922. Report. [To accompany H.R. 7190] [Washington, Govt. Print. Off., 1925] 20 p. (68th Cong., 2d sess. Senate. Rept. 1205 ).

U. S. Congress. Senate. Committee on Foreign Relations. Study of treaties of United States and other governments affecting our commerce and trade with China. Report. [To accompany S.Res. 256] [Washington, Govt. Print. Off., 1930] 2 p. (71st Cong., 2d sess. Senate. Rept. 719 ).

———. Commercial relations with China. Hearings before a subcommittee of the Committee on Foreign Relations, United States Senate, Seventy-first Congress, second[-third] session, pursuant to S. Res. 256, a resolution authorizing an examination and study of stipulations relating to commerce in existing treaties of the United States and other governments with the Republic of China, and conditions that may affect our commerce and trade with China. Printed for the use of the Committee on Foreign Relations. Washington, Govt. Print. Off., 1930-31. 4 pt. tables, diagrs.

———. Commercial relations with China. Partial report. [Pursuant to S.Res.

256]  [Washington, Govt. Print. Off., 1931] 26 p. incl. tables. (71st Cong., 3d sess. Senate. Rept. 1600 ).

————. Commercial relations with China. Report. [To accompany S.Res. 442] [Washington, Govt. Print. Off., 1931] 28 p. (71st Cong., 3d sess. Senate. Rept. 1716 ).

————. Treaty of friendship, commerce, and navigation with China. Report to accompany Executive J, Eightieth Congress, first session. [Washington, Govt. Print. Off., 1948] 8 p.  ( [U.S.] 80th Cong., 2d sess., 1948. Senate. Executive rep[or]t no. 8 ).

U. S. Congress. Senate. Committee on Government Operations. Control of trade with the Soviet bloc. Interim report of the Committee on Government Operations made by its Senate Permanent Subcommittee on Investigations pursuant to S. res. 40, a resolution authorizing the Committee on Government Operations to employ temporary additional personnel and increasing the limit of expenditures. Washington, Govt. Print. Off., 1953. iv, 57 p.tables. (83d Cong., 1st sess. Senate. Report no. 606 ).

————. East-West trade. Hearings before the Permanent Subcommittee on Investigations. Eighty-fourth Congress, second session. Washington, Govt. Print. Off., 1956. 3 v.

U. S. Congress. Senate. Committee on Interstate and Foreign Commerce. Export controls and policies in the Far East; special report of the Subcommittee on Export Controls and Policies of the Committee on Interstate and Foreign Commerce pursuant to S. Res. 365, 81st Congress, continued by S. Res. 56, 82d Congress, a resolution authorizing ths study and investigation of export policies and control regulations. Washington, Govt. Print. Off., 1951. iii, 66 p.

————. Investigation of shipments to Communist China. Hearings before a subcommittee of the Committee on Interstate and Foreign Commerce, United States Senate, Eighty-first Congress, second session [-Eighty-second Congress, second session] on investigation of shipments of strategic materials to Communist China. Washington, Govt. Print. Off., 1951. 3 pts. facsims.

U. S. Congress. Senate. Committee on the Judiciary. Promotion of trade in China. Hearing before a subcommittee of the Committee on the Judiciary, United States Senate, Sixty-seventh Congress, first session, on H.R. 4810, a bill to authorize the incorporation of companies to promote trade in China. May 10, 1921. Washington, Govt. Print. Off., 1921. 72 p.

U. S. Office of Strategic Services. Research and Analysis Branch. North American trade with China and Japan. Prelim. [Washington] 1945. iii, 19, [12] l. tables. (Its R and A no. 2839 ).

U. S. Tariff Commission. An analysis of the trade between China and the United States. Prepared in response to Senate resolution 334, 72d Congress, 2d session. February 1934.  [Washington, 1934] cover-title, 29 l. tables (part fold.).

————. United States imports from China, an analysis of the prewar trade. Washington, 1945. cover-title, vi, 241 (i.e. 243) p. incl. tables.

VALEO, FRANCIS RALPH, 1916-    Far eastern economic development and the west coast economy, by Francis R. Valeo and Jean C. Curtis. Washington, 1950. 83 p. diagrs. (Public affairs bull., 84 ).

VEVIER, CHARLES, 1924-    The United States and China, 1906-13; a study of finance and diplomacy. New Brunswick,N.J., Rutgers University Press, 1955. ix, 229 p. map.

VINCE, ANDRÉ. La doctrine américaine de la porte ouverte en Chine et son application dans la politique internationale. Besançon, Impr. Jacques et Demontrond, 1946. 148 p.

WRIGHT, PHILIP GREEN, 1861-1934. The American tariff and oriental trade. Chicago, Pub. for the American Council, Institute of Pacific Relations, by the University of Chicago Press [c1931] [5]-177 p. incl.tables, diagrs.

## Opium Trade

ASIAN PEOPLES' ANTI-COMMUNIST LEAGUE. The illicit narcotic trade of the
Chinese Communists. [Taipei, 1957] 28 p.

AUXION DE RUFFÉ, REGINALD D', 1875-   La farce de l'opium. Paris, Berger-Levrault, 1939. 72 p. plates.

CHINA. Cultivation and trade of opium in China: situation in the Province of Hupeh. Geneva, 1934. 4 p. ''Translation of an extract from the 'Gazette of the
Ministry of the Interior,' series 6, no. 52, dated 29th December, 1933'': p.
1-3. ''Extract from 'Peking and Tientsin Times' of 8th January 1934'': p. 4.

————. Committee for the Investigation of the Chinese Communist Narcotic Traffic. Chinese communists' world-wide narcotic. [Taipei] 1956. [194] p.

CHINA. Inspectorate General of Customs. Second conference on opium. Letter to
the Secretary-General [of the League of Nations] transmitting the observations
of the Chinese customs authorities on certain questions connected with the traffic in opium and other drugs. Geneva, 1924. [4] l.

————. Circular issued by the Inspector-General of Customs in China in regard
to the use of the registered letter post for smuggling drugs into China. Geneva, 1926. 8 l.

————. Narcotics. Geneva, 1928. [5] l.

CHINA. Laws, statutes, etc. Regulations of the Nanking Government concerning
opium. Amendment of the law for the suppression of opium. Geneva, 1928.
4 l.

————. Text of a law on the prohibition of opium and regulations thereunder, promulgated on September 17th, 1928, by the National Government of the Chinese Republic. Geneva, 1929. 9 l.

CHINA. Ministry of Finance. A scheme for the prohibition within three years of
the illicit use of opium, submitted by the Ministry of Finance to the Central
Political Council. Circulated at the request of Mr. Lyall. [Geneva, 1927]
4 l.

CHINA. National Opium Suppression Commission. Traffic in opium and other
dangerous drugs. Annual report. 1928-36. Nanking, 1929-37. 8 v.

————. The same. Important regulations, rules and instructions promulgated by
the Chinese government in recent years. [Nanking, 1934] 37 p.

DEVERALL, RICHARD LAWRENCE-GRACE, 1911-   Mao Tze-tung: stop this
dirty opium business! How Red China is selling opium and heroin to produce
revenue for China's war machine. Tokyo, Printed by Toyoh Print. and Book-
binding Co., 1954. 85 p. illus.

————. Red China's dirty drug war; the story of the opium, heroin, morphine and
philopon traffic. With introductions by Masamutsu Nagahama and Matthew
Woll. [3d ed.] Tokyo, 1954 [i.e. 1955] ix, 220 p. illus.

GAVIT, JOHN PALMER, 1868-   ''Opium.'' London, Routledge and sons, ltd.,
1925; New York, Brentano, 1927. xi, 308 p.

GILES, HERBERT ALLEN, 1845-1935. Some truths about opium. Cambridge
[Eng.] W. Heffer, 1923. 40 p.

GOLDSMITH, MARGARET LELAND, 1894-   The trail of opium, the eleventh
plague. London, R. Hale, 1939. 9-286 p. front., plates.

GT. BRIT. Foreign Office. Correspondence respecting the cultivation of opium
in China. [In continuation of ''China no. 2 (1913)'' [Cd. 6876] ] London, H.
M. Stationery Off., 1921. iv, 117 p. (China no. 1 (1921) ).

HOIJER, OLOF. Le trafic de l'opium et d'autres stupéfiants; étude de droit international et d'histoire diplomatique. Paris, ''Éditions Spes,'' 1925. 300 p.

INTERNATIONAL ANTI-OPIUM ASSOCIATION, Peking. The war against opium.
The International Anti-Opium Association, Peking. Tientsin, Tientsin Press,
1922. xiv, 238, 239-250 p. front. (port.) plates, facsims.

JAPAN. Ministry of Foreign Affairs. Ordinance for the purpose of regulating
traffic in drugs by Japanese subjects in China. Geneva, 1928. 7 l.

LO, REN YEN, 羅運炎, 1890-  The opium problem in the Far East.  Shanghai, Commercial Press, 1933.  [iii]-iv, 146 p.

LUBBOCK, ALFRED BASIL, 1876-1944. The opium clippers.  Boston, Charles E. Lauriat, 1933.  xiv, 392 p. front., 1 illus., plates (1 col., 1 fold.) ports., maps (part fold.).

OWEN, DAVID EDWARD, 1898-  British opium policy in China and India.  New Haven, Yale University Press; London, H. Milford, Oxford University Press, 1934.  ix, 399 p. (Yale historical publications. Studies. VIII ).

STACKPOLE, EDOUARD A., 1905-  Captain Prescott and the opium smugglers. With illus. of the Chinese scene and period of 1840-50, together with famous ship-masters and ships which made history on the China coast.  Mystic, Conn. Marine Historical Association, 1954.  78 p. illus. ports., facsim. (Marine Historical Association, Mystic, Conn. [Publication] 26 ).

STELLE, CHARLES CLARKSON, 1910-  American trade in opium in the nineteenth century.  Berkeley, 1941. Part of thesis-Univ. of Chicago. "Reprinted from the Pacific historical review, v. 9 (1940) p. 425-444 and v.10(1941) p. 57-74."

SZE, SAO-KE ALFRED, 施肇基, 1877-1958. comp. Geneva opium conferences; statements of the Chinese delegation.  Baltimore, Johns Hopkins Press,1926. vii, 163 p.

U.S. Congress. Senate. Committee on the Judiciary. Communist China and illicit narcotic traffic.  Hearings before the Subcommittee to Investigate the Administration of the Internal Security Act and Other Internal Security Laws of the Committee on the Judiciary, United States Senate, Eighty-fourth Congress, first session.  Washington, Govt. Print. Off., 1955.  v, 100 p. illus., port.

WANG, KING KY, 王景岐, 1882-1941. China and the problem of narcotics before the League of Nations; views exposed during the 12th sitting of the Opium committee at Geneva.  Brussels, "Ligue anti-opium d'outremer," 1929. 23 p.
———. La Chine et le problème des stupéfiants devant la Société des Nations. Vues exposées au cours de la XIIme session de la Commission d'Opium à Genève.  Bruxelles, "Ligne anti-opium d'outremer," 1929. 20 p.

WANG, ADINE, 王亞徽 . La Chine et le problème de l'opium.  Paris, A. Pedone, 1933.  244 p.

WU, WEN-TSAO, 吳文藻, 1902-  The Chinese opium question in British opinion and action.  New York, Academy Press, 1928. 192 p. Thesis-Columbia University.

## Directories

AMERICANS and American firms in China; directory. 1946.  [Shanghai] Shanghai Evening Post and Mercury.  170 p.

CHINA. Bureau of Foreign Trade. China importers and exporters directory. Shanghai [1936] 700 p. illus.

The CHINA directory; annual publication.  Hongkong [China Mail Office]    v.

CHINA Hong List. General and business directory for Shanghai and the principal ports and cities of China. 1932-      Shanghai, 1932-      v.

CHINA-AMERICA COUNCIL OF COMMERCE AND INDUSTRY. Directory of the China-America Council of Commerce and Industry; a guide to nearly 400 American companies interested in developing trade between China and the U. S. A.  New York, 1946.  359 p.

CHINA, JAPAN AND SOUTH AMERICA TRADING CO., LTD. Private code of China, Japan and South America trading co., ltd. for use between South and Central America, London, Manchester and the Far East and New York-New Orleans-San Francisco.  Comp. and printed by American Code Co.(inc.) New York, c1921.  [1], iv, 80, a-c, 212, [3] p.

CHINESE-AMERICAN trade; annual and directory. English section. 1937. New York, The Chinese Chamber of Commerce of New York, 1937. 291 p.

illus., diagrs.

COMACRIB directory of China, combined Chinese-foreign commercial and classified directory of China and Hong Kong. v. 1-     Shanghai, Commercial Credit Information Bureau, c1925-     v. Title varies.

CREDIT Men's business directory of China (with which is amalgamated the Rosenstock's Business Directory of China) 徵信工商行名錄. Shanghai, Bankers' Cooperative Credit Service, 1934, 1935. 2 v.

The DIRECTORY and chronicle for China, Japan, Corea, Indo-China, Straits Settlement, Malay States, etc. 1864-1941. Hong Kong and London, Hong Kong Daily Press, 1864-1941.     v.

DIRECTORY of China; official, business and residential directory for the principal ports and cities of China, 中國行名簿, 1947, 1948. Shanghai section. Shanghai, China Daily Tribune Pub. Co., 1947-48. 2 v.

DIRECTORY of firms and institutions in Peking and Tientsin, including a residential list. Peking, The Peking chronicle.     v. annual.

DOLLAR directory, 上海行名錄, 1943-48. Shanghai, Park Mercantile Co., 1943-48. 6 v.

FOREIGN TRADE ASSOCIATION OF CHINA. Directory of importers and exporters in China. Shanghai, 1948. 1 v.

———. Handbook of Chinese manufacturers. Shanghai, Foreign Trade Association, 1949. 528 p.

IMPORTERS AND EXPORTERS ASSOCIATION OF TIENTSIN. Directory of members. Tientsin.     v.

JAPANESE trade directory of Shanghai. 1st-     ed.; 1940-     Shanghai, Japanese Chamber of Commerce [1940-     v. illus. (ports.).

The NORTH-CHINA desk hong list; a general and business directory for Shanghai and the northern and river ports, etc. Shanghai, North-China Daily News and Herald [etc.]     v. Title varies.

The NORTH CHINA hong list. Tientsin, Tientsin Press, 1923-27.     v.

PHILIPPINE-CHINESE business guide and pictorial directory. Cebu City, D. Ingco.     v. illus., ports., maps.

ROSENSTOCK'S directory of China and Manila, commercial, industrial, residential, 1913-29. Manila, P.L. Rosenstock Pub. Co., 1913-29. 16 v.

The SHANGHAI directory. 1939. 字林報行名簿. Shanghai, North-China Daily News and Herald, 1939. ? v.

SHANGHAI dollar directory, 1929-38. Shanghai, Mercury Press, 1930-39.     v.

## International Economic Relations
### Foreign Investments and Technical Cooperation

BANK OF CHINA. Research Department. Chinese government foreign loan obligations, compiled and published by the Research Department, Bank of China. Shanghai, 1935. 95, 191 p. fold. tables, diagrs.

BAYLIN, J.R. comp. Foreign loan obligations of China; a compendium of such secured external loan obligations of China as are provided with regular amortization tables, compiled and edited by J.R. Baylin. Tientsin, La Librairie française, 1925. viii, 96 p. fold. tables. (Special series of the Chinese government bureau of economic information, no. 1 (2d ed.) ).

CAMPBELL, WILLIAM KENNETH HUNTER, 1886-     Technical collaboration with China. Co-operation for economically underdeveloped countries. [Geneva, 1938] 103 p.

CARNEGIE ENDOWMENT FOR INTERNATIONAL PEACE. Division of International Law. The consortium; the official text of the four-power agreement for a loan to China and relevant documents. Washington, The Endowment, 1921. ix, 76 p. (Pamphlet series of the Carnegie endowment for international peace. Division of international law, 40 ).

CHINA. Commission for the Readjustment of Finance. Tables of inadequately secured foreign loans of the Ministry of Finance. Peking, 1925. cover-title, 5 p., 24 tables.

COONS, ARTHUR GARDINER, 1900-    The foreign public debt of China. Philadelphia, University of Pennsylvania Press; London, H. Milford, Oxford University Press, 1930. v-xi, 251 p. tables (part fold.).

ELLIS, HOWARD SYLVESTER, 1898-    French and German investments in China. Honolulu, Institute of Pacific Relations, 1929. 5-20 p. incl. tables ( 2 fold.).

FIELD, FREDERICK VANDERBILT, 1905-    American participation in the China consortiums. Chicago, Pub. for the American Council, Institute of Pacific Relations by the University of Chicago Press [1931] vii-ix, 198 p.

GAUSS, CLARENCE EDWARD, 1887-    U.S. loan to trade with China, by Clarence E. Gauss and Cornell Franklin. With Chinese translation. Shanghai, International Publishers, 1946. 10, 8 p.

GOODFRIEND, ARTHUR. The only war we seek; with a foreword by Chester Bowles. [New York] Published for Americans for Democratic Action by Farrar, Straus and Young [1951] 128 p. illus.

GT. BRIT. Foreign Office. Correspondence respecting the new financial consortium in China. London, H. M. Stationery Off., 1921. iv, [5]-56 p. (Miscellaneous, no. 9, 1921 ).

HOE, Y.C., 何永佶, 1902-    The program of technical cooperation between China and the League of Nations. Shanghai, 1933. 30 numb. 1. (Institute of Pacific Relations, 5th conference, Banff, 1933, Documents, v. 15 ).

HOU, CHI-MING, 侯繼明 , 1924-    Foreign capital in China's economic development, 1895-1937. Ann Arbor, University Microfilms [1954] ( [University Microfilms, Ann Arbor, Mich.] Publication no. 10,267 ). Collation of the original: v, 373 1. tables. Thesis-Columbia University.

JONES, FRANCIS CLIFFORD. Shanghai and Tientsin, with special reference to foreign interests, with the co-operation of certain members of the Royal Institute of International Affairs. Prepared as a report in the International research series of the Institute of Pacific Relations. London, Oxford University Press, H. Milford; New York, American Council, Institute of Pacific Relations, 1940. x, 182 p. incl. tables. fold. plans.

KAO, PING-SHU, 高平叔 . Foreign loans to China. New York, N. Y., Sino-international Economic Research Center [1946] 62 p. (Sino-international economic pamphlets, 2 ).

LEAGUE OF NATIONS. Council. Committee on Technical Collaboration with China. Report to the Council of its technical delegate on his mission in China from date of appointment until April 1, 1934. Shanghai, North-China Daily News and Herald, 1934. 51 p.

――――. Report of the technical agent of the Council on his mission in China from the date of his appointment until April 1st, 1934. [Geneva, 1934] 72 p. (Series of League of Nations publications. General. 1934.1 ).

――――. Rapport du délégé technique du Conseil sur sa mission en Chine depuis la date de sa nomination jusqu'au 1er avril 1934. Genève, 1934. iv, 78 p. (Série de publications de la Société des Nations. Questions générales. 1934. 1 ).

――――. Report on technical co-operation between the League of Nations and China, by Ludwig Rajchman, technical expert of the League of Nations. Peiping, Peiping Chronicle, 1934. 84 p. (China chronicle, 7 ).

LIEU, D.K., 劉大鈞, 1890-    Foreign investments in China. A cooperative research study made under the joint auspices of the Institute of Pacific Relations (Honolulu, H.I.), Social Science Research Council (New York), Brookings Institute of Economics and Chinese Government Bureau of Statistics (Nanking). [Shanghai?] 1929. cover-title, 131 p. incl. tables.

LIN, WEI-YING, 林維英 , 1908-    China and foreign capital. Chungking, China Institute of Pacific Relations, 1945. iii, 50 p.(China council series, 2 ).

MILLARD, THOMAS FRANKLIN FAIRFAX, 1868-1942. China, America and international financial readjustment. Shanghai, The Weekly Review of the Far East, 1921. cover-title, 11 p.

P'U, YU-SHU, 蒲友書, 1918- The consortium reorganization loan to China, 1911-14; an episode in pre-war diplomacy and international finance. Ann Arbor, University Microfilms, 1950 [i. e. 1951] ( [University Microfilms, Ann Arbor, Mich.] Publication no. 2446 ). Collation of the original: xxi, 671 l. Thesis-University of Michigan.

REMER, CHARLES FREDERICK, 1889- American investments in China. Honolulu, Institute of Pacific Relations, 1929. 5-39 p.

————. Foreign investments in China. New York, Macmillan, 1933. xxi, 708 p. illus.(maps) diagrs.

STANLEY, CHARLES JOHNSON, 1914- Hu Kuang-yung, 胡先墉, and China's early foreign loans. Cambridge, 1951. 164 p.

## Relief and Rehabilitation

BARNETT, IRVING. UNRRA in China; a case study in financial assistance for economic development (with emphasis on agricultural programs). New York, 1955. vi, 338 l. Thesis-Columbia University.

CHINA. Relief and rehabilitation in China; a report by Tingfu F. Tsiang, 蔣廷黻 . Washington, 1944. ii, iii-iv l., 37 p. incl. tables.

————. National Relief and Rehabilitation Administration. Opening address of Tingfu F. Tsiang at the National conference of CNRRA regional and field directors. Shanghai, 1946. 14 p.

————. National Relief Commission. China war relief; a special pictorial illustrating the activities of the National Relief Commission and National Red Cross Society of China during the Sino-Japanese hostilities. Chungking, 1940. 32 l. illus.

CHINA LIBERATED AREAS RELIEF ASSOCIATION. Information Department. UNRRA relief for the Chinese people; a report. Shanghai, 1947. 41 p.

NATIONAL PLANNING ASSOCIATION. China's relief needs. [Washington] National Planning Association [1945] cover-title, 52 p. (Planning pamphlets, 40 ).

RAY, JEFFERSON FRANKLIN, 1905- UNRRA in China; a case study of the interplay of interests in a program of international aid to an undeveloped country. New York, International Secretariat, Institute of Pacific Relations [1947] 64 l. (Secretariat paper, 6 ).

RED CROSS. China. Red Cross Society of China. Disaster strikes the Tachens; [report of an investigation into crimes committed by Chiang Kai-shek's troops, instigated and protected by the United States, during their withdrawal from the Tachens and other islands. Peking, 1955] 44 p. illus.

TAI, PAO-LIU, 戴寶鎏, 1907- Summary report on UNRRA activities in China. Brief notes prepared on behalf of UNRRA headquarters for the use of the Round Tables at the Tenth Conference of the I. P. R. at Stratford-upon-Avon. New York, International Secretariat, Institute of Pacific Relations [1947] 8 l.

UNITED NATIONS RELIEF AND REHABILITATION ADMINISTRATION. Anhwei weekly report for Office of the Economic and Financial Advisor. Report no. 1- 1946-

————. Chekiang-Fukien weekly report for Office of the Economic and Financial Advisor. Report no. [1] - Mar. 16, 1946-May 9, 1946.

————. China Office monthly report. July 1946-May 1947.

————. CNRRA-UNRRA news. No.1-118. Shanghai, 1946-47.

————. Honan weekly report for Office of the Economic and Financial Advisor. Report no. 1- Mar. 25, 1946-Oct. 21, 1946.

————. Hopei-Jehol weekly report for Office of the Economic and Financial Advisor. Report no. 1- Mar. 18, 1946-Oct. 1946.

————. Hunan weekly report for Office of the Economic and Financial Advisor.
Report no. 1-    Apr. 27, 1946-Sept. 1946.
————. Kiangsi weekly report for Office of the Economic and Financial Advisor.
Report no. 1-    Apr. 27, 1946-Aug. 1946.
————. Kiangsu-Nanking weekly report for Office of the Economic and Financial
Advisor. Report no. 1-10. Apr. 28-Oct. 14, 1946. [Nanking] 1946.
————. Kwangtung weekly report for Office of the Economic and Financial Advi-
sor. Report no. 1-    Nov. 1945-July 1946.
————. Northeast Regional Office weekly report for Office of the Economic and
Financial Advisor. Report no. 1-13. May 8-Sept. 15, 1946.
————. Shanghai weekly report for Office of the Economic and Financial Advisor.
Report no. 1-10. June 12-Aug. 31, 1946. Shanghai, 1946.
————. Taiwan weekly report. no. 1-    May 26, 1946-
UNTED SERVICE TO CHINA. Purposes and program of United China relief.
[New York, 1942?] cover-title, [6] p.

### Transportation and Communication
### Transportation

CHEN, CHIH-HWA, 陳澤華. Verkehrentwicklung und Verkehrsplanung in China
und ihre Auswirkung auf die Volkswirtschaft. Wien, 1941. iv, 192, vii p.
Diss.-Univ. Wien.
CH'EN, HO-SEN, 陳鶴聲. Entwicklung und Ausbaumöglichkeiten des chinesi-
schen Transportwesens unter dem Gesichtspunkte der Industrialisierung.
Jena, Fischer, 1937. [42] p. (Weltwirtschaftl. Archiv, 45 ).
CHENG, MING-JU, 鄭名儒. The influence of communications, internal and ex-
ternal, upon the economic future of China. London, G. Routledge, 1930.
xiii, 177 p. 2 maps (1 fold.).
CRAWFORD, WALLACE. Transportation in wartime China. Chungking, China
Information Pub. Co. [1940] cover-title, 23 p. illus.(maps) (Chungking
pamphlets, 8 ).
FLIEGNER, EBERHARD. Das Verkehrsbild im chinesischen Güterverkehr des
letzten Jahrzehntes. Stuttgart, 1940. 79 l. illus. map. Diss. - Stuttgart
Tech. Hochs.
U.S. Office of Strategic Services. Research and Analysis Branch. Transport
facilities of the North China coast. [Washington] 1945. [6] l. (Its R and A
no. 2899 ).
————. Transportation conditions and routes in eastern Suiyuan and southern
Chahar. Washington, 1945.  17 p. (Its R and A no. 3335 ).
————. Transportation in northwest China. Washington, 1945. 40 p. fold. col.
maps. (Its R and A no. 3088 ).

### Railways

CHANG, KIA-NGAU, 張嘉璈. [Chang, Chia-ao] 1888-    China's struggle for
railroad development. New York, John Day [1943] vii, 340 p. incl. illus.
(maps) tables. plates.
CHAO, YUNG-SEEN, 趙永新. Les chemins de fer chinois; étude historique,
politique, économique et financière. Paris, Librairie technique et économique [1939] 272 p. illus.(map) Thèse-Univ. de Paris.
————. Railways in Communist China. Kowloon, H.K., Union Research Institute [1955] 101, 3 p. fold. map. (Communist China problem research series, EC10 ).
CHEN, LAWRENCE M., 陳文通. Chinese national railways and reconstruction.
Nanking, 1936. 18 p. plates. (Council of International Affairs, Information
bull.).
CHENG, LIN, 鄭麐. The Chinese railways, past and present. Shanghai, China

United Press [1937] xii, 332 p. fold. map, diagr. (China to-day series) "Revised and enlarged edition." First published 1935 under title: The Chinese railways; a historical survey. 214 p.

CHINA. Commission of Financial Experts. Report on railway finance. Submitted to the National government through the Minister of Finance on December 10, 1929. [Shanghai, 1929] cover-title, 54 numb. l. illus. maps.

——. Ministry of Communications. Statistics of government railways. 1915-22. Peking, 1916-23//? 7 v. fold. map, diagrs.

——. Chinese government railways. Store accounts manual. Prescribed by Ministry of Communications, October, 1921. [Peking, 1921] ii, 48 p.

——. Annual report 1920/21-    Peking, 1922-      v. tables (part fold.), diagrs.

——. Railway loan agreements of China. 2nd ed. Peking, 1922. 2 v. 1st ed., 1916.

——. Minutes of the standing committee on the unification of railway accounts and statistics. (first to tenth conference) Peking, 1925. [3], 591, 9 p. forms.

——. Outstanding debts. [Peking? 1925] cover-title, 34 p.

CHINA'S railways; a story of heroic reconstruction. Peking, Foreign Languages Press [1950?] 45 p. ports., fold. map.

CHU-KE, LING, 諸葛林, 1919-    China's railway rolling stock; a study of postwar purchase. [Seattle, Pub. for the College of Economics and Business by the University of Washington Press, 1946] x, 110 p. incl. tables.

DSCHOU, FANG-SCHI, 周芳世, 1903-    Das Eisenbahnwesen in China. Charlottenburg, Studentenhaus-Dr., 1934. 87 p. Diss.-Tech. Hoch. Berlin.

GRIFFIN, ELDON, 1895-    China's railways as a market for Pacific Northwest products; a study of a phase of the external relations of the region. Seattle, Bureau of Business Research, College of Economics and Business, University of Washington, 1946. xii, 78 numb. l. front., plates, tables (2 fold.) maps on 2 fold. l.

INVESTMENT values of Chinese railway bonds. [Tientsin] La Librairie française, 1923. cover-title, 70 p. maps (1 fold.) tables (1 fold.).

LAYNG, CHARLES. Report on Chinese railways. Chicago, Economic Warfare Section, Dept. of Justice, 1944. unpaged. illus.

LING, HUNG-HSÜN, 凌鴻勛, 1894-    Canton-Hankow railway; difficult work over middle section in full progress, entire line to be completed by end of 1936. [Hengchow, Hunan, 1935] 28 p. incl. illus., map.

LOCHOW, H.J. VON. China's national railways; historical survey and postwar planning. Peiping, 1948. 162 p. illus.

SIAO, WUISIN, 蕭偉信, 1898-    Die Entwicklung des Eisenbahnwesens in China. Berlin, J. Springer, 1927. 102 p. map. Diss.-Univ. Basel.

STRINGER, HAROLD. The Chinese railway system. Shanghai [etc.] Kelly and Walsh, 1922. 216 p. plates, fold. map, tables, diagrs.

——. China, a new aspect. London, H.F. and G. Witherby [1929] 240 p. map.

TING, V.K., 丁文江, 1887-1936. A reconnaissance survey of a railway line from Chungching to Kuangchouwan, by V.K. Ting and S.Y. Tseng, 曾世英. Peiping, National Geological Survey of China [1930?] 14, 86, 6 p. incl. illus., tables, plates (incl. fold. maps, fold. profiles) (China. Geological survey. Memoirs, ser. B, no. 4).

ULLENS DE SCHOOTEN, JEAN. Les chemins de fer chinois: étude historique, économique et financière. Bruxelles, Maurice Lamertin, 1928. 266 p. map.

U.S. Bureau of Foreign and Domestic Commerce. Railway transportation in occupied China, prepared in Far Eastern Unit, Bureau of Foreign and Domestic Commerce. [Washington] 1943-    2 v. illus., fold. maps, diagrs.

——. Office of Strategic Services. Research and Analysis Branch. Free China railways; recent aspects of their construction, operation, and maintenance. Washington, 1943. 21 p. map. (Its R and A no. 1008).

[——.] Canton-Hankow Railway. [n.p., 194-]. Typescript.

[———.] Report on the Kowloon-Canton Railway. [n. p., 194-]. Typescript.
WALKER, GUY MORRISON, 1870-    Some China. New York, A.L. Fowle, 1922.
    cover-title, 74 p.
ZEN, I-TU, 孫任以都 1921-    Chinese railways and British interests, 1898-1911.
    New York, King's Crown Press, Columbia University, 1954. viii, 230 p. 2
    maps.
            (See also Northeastern Provinces-Railways)

## Water Transportation

CHI, HENAN, 祁仍奚. The port of Hulutao (an international trade link in Chi-
    na's economic program). Shanghai, Commercial Press, 1930. ii, vi, 53 p.
    plates (part fold.) ports., fold. map, plans (1 fold.).
CHINA. Inspectorate General of Customs. The coastwise lights of China; an il-
    lustrated account of the Chinese maritime customs lights service. [Shanghai,
    Statistical Dept., Inspectorate General of Customs, 1932?] xviii, 243 p.
    illus., maps.
———. List of lighthouses, light-vessels, buoys, beacons, etc., on the coast
    and rivers of China, 1947. Corr. to 1st Dec. 1946. Shanghai, Statistical
    Dept., Inspectorate General of Customs, 1948. 162 p. illus.(part col.) fold.
    col. map. (Chinese maritime customs. III. Miscellaneous series, 6 ).
———. Marine Dept. Report. 1933-36. Shanghai, Statistical Dept., Inspectorate
    General of Customs, 1934-37. 4 v. in    illus., maps (part fold.) annual.
    (The maritime customs. III. Miscellaneous series, no. 38 ).
DONNELLY, IVON ARTHUR, 1890-    Chinese junks and other native craft. 3d
    ed. [Shanghai] Kelly and Walsh, 1939 (c1925). 3-142 p. incl. col. mounted
    front., illus., plates (part col. mounted ).
DSCHU, GWENG-TZAM, 朱光贊, [Chu Kuang-tsan]. Die Binnenschiffahrt auf
    dem Jangtse-Kiang seit 1900. Berlin-Wilmersdorf, R. Mannheim, 1933.[1],
    vi, 95 p.
HUNT (WILLIAM) AND COMPANY. Review of pre-war merchant shipping in Far
    Eastern waters. Chungking, in association with the China Corporation, New
    York. [New York] China Corporation, c1944. 1 v. maps, charts, tables,
    diagrs.
JARDINE, MATHESON AND COMPANY, LTD. The China shipping manual, 1937-
    38. [Shanghai?] Published for private distribution [1937?] 228 p. illus.(part
    col.) fold. maps.
LEAGUE OF NATIONS. Committee for Communications and Transit. Committee
    of Experts on Hydraulic and Road Questions in China. Co-operation between
    the Organisation for Communications and Transit of the League of Nations and
    the National Government of China; report. [Geneva, 1936] 213 p. diagrs.(Se-
    ries of League of Nations publications. VIII. Transit. 1936. VIII. 4 ).
LIU, KWANG-CHING, 劉廣京, 1921-    Two steamship companies in China, 1862-
    77. Cambridge, 1956. 206 l. Thesis-Harvard University.
TS'EIN, SIANG-SUEN, 錢翔孫. Le port de Changhai; étude économique. Lyon,
    Bosc frères, M. et L. Riou, 1934. 164 p. incl. tables.
U.S. Office of Strategic Services. Research and Analysis Branch. Studies on se-
    lected Chinese ports. [Washington] 1945. 5 l. (Its R and A no. 3006 ).
WORCESTER, G.R.G. Junks and sampans of the Upper Yangtze. Shanghai, 1940.
    x, 96 p. plates (part col.) map. (China. Inspectorate General of Customs.
    The maritime customs. III. Miscellaneous series, 51 ).
———. The junks and sampans of the Yangtze; a study in Chinese nautical re-
    search. Shanghai, Statistical Dept., Inspectorate General of Customs, 1947-
    48. 2 v. illus., fold. col. map. (The maritime customs. III. Miscellaneous
    series, 54 ).

## Highways

CHINA. Bureau of Public Roads. The new Shanghai Hangchow highway. Nanking, National Economic Council, 1932. 9 p. plates (1 fold.) maps (part fold.) fold. tables.

————. The Nanking-Wuhu and Süancheng-Changhing highways upon the occasion of their opening to traffic. Nanking, National Economic Council, 1933. 18, [24] p. plates (1 fold.) fold. maps.

————. The Soochow-Kashing highway upon the occasion of its opening to traffic. Nanking, National Economic Council, 1933. 15, [18] p. plates, 2 fold. maps, tables (1 fold.).

————. Highways in China; tables, charts and maps. Nanking, National Economic Council, 1935. [13] p. maps, tables, diagrs.

CLEMENTS, JULIUS MORGAN, 1869-   China: automotive conditions and the good roads movement. Washington, Govt. Print. Off., 1922. 21 p. ( [U.S.] Bureau of foreign and domestic commerce. Trade information bull., 2 ).

SMITH, A. VIOLA, 1893-   Motor roads in China. Washington, Govt. Print. Off., 1931. v, 132 p. incl. illus., tables. fold. map. (U.S. Bureau of foreign and domestic commerce. Trade promotion ser., 120 ).

## Postal Service

CHINA. Directorate General of Posts. Report on the working of the Chinese post office. (English and Chinese texts) 1904-38. Shanghai, 1905-39.    v. fold. maps.

————. International parcel tariff (Provisional issue)  Shanghai, Supply department of the Directorate General of Posts, 1922. cover-title, [18] p.

————. International parcel tariff [15th issue] Published for the use of the postal service and the information of the public. Shanghai, The Supply department of the Directorate General of Posts, 1931. 208 p. incl. tables. ( [Publications] II. -Public series, 19 ).

————. China postal atlas, showing the postal establishments and postal routes in each province. [3d ed.] Nanking, Directorate General of Posts, 1933. 12, 3 p. 40 col. maps on [1], 29 numb. 1. (part double, part fold.).

————. The postal law. English version. Rev. ed. Taipei, 1956. 28 p. (Public ser. II, 2 ).

————. Postal regulations. English version. Rev. ed. Taipei, 1956. 110 p. (Public series 11, 3 ).

————. Ministry of Communications. Statistics of international communications of China. Post. 1928-29. Shanghai, 1930-   1 v. tables.

————. A brief statistical report of communications, June 1931. Nanking, 1931. 68 p. tables.

CHU, CHIA-HUA, 朱家驊, 1893-   The Ministry of communications in 1934. Shanghai, China United Press, 1935. cover-title, 18 p. [China reconstruction ser. 1 ].

————. China's postal and other communication services. Shanghai, China United Press [1937] ix, 259 p. port. diagrs.("China to-day" ser. 9 ).

STARR, JAMES. The Chinese air-post, 1920-35, by James Starr and Samuel J. Mills. De luxe ed. [Philadelphia] The authors, 1937. 112 p. illus.(incl. maps).

## Postage Stamps

AKAGI, ROY HIDEMICHI, 1892-   The postage stamps of Manchoukuo. New York, 1941. 3-101 p. illus.

CHINA Reconstructs. Postage stamps of the People's Republic of China, 1949-54. Shanghai, 1955. 46 p.

LIVINGSTON, LYONS F. The postage stamps of China. Baltimore, L.F.Livingston, Inc., 1951-52. 2 v.

————. Classical China. Baltimore, Livingston and Martin, c1956. 1 v. (loose-
    leaf).
LISSINK, KALENIK. Notes of the Russian revolutionary stamps, 1920-22. Mon-
    golia-its stamps, 1924-27, compiled and arranged by John L. Stroub. [New
    York, 1927] 16 p. illus. (facsims.).
MA, ZUNG-SUNG, 馬潤生. Ma's illustrated catalogue of the stamps of China.
    Compiled, supplemented and translated by Ma Ren-chuen, 馬任全. With 700
    illustrations. Shanghai, Shun Chang, 1947. 568 p. illus. port.
MANCHOUKUO POSTAL SOCIETY. Postage stamps of Manchoukuo, 1940. Hsin-
    king, Published by the Manchoukuo Postal Society [1940] 60 p. plates (part
    col.).
The POSTAGE stamp catalogue of People's Republic of China. Hong Kong, Wah
    Nan Stamp Service, 1955. 214 p. illus.
ROSENBERG, WILLIAM. Local post of China: history-description-prices; a
    study based upon private collections. Shanghai [The Willow Pattern Press,
    1940] 141, [1] p. illus., col. plates, map, facsims.
STANDARD catalogue; People's posts of China. 1952-        Hongkong, Universal
    Stamp Service, 1952. 282 p. illus.

## Telegraphy

CHINA. Ministry of Communications. Rules and regulations for the acceptance
    and transmission of press telegrams. [Peking? 1922] cover-title, 6, [6] p.
————. Statistics of international communications of China. Telegraph. 1928-29.
    Shanghai, 1930-      1 v. tables.
————. Communications of China. A brief statistical report January-June, 1932.
    Nanking, Ministry of Communications, 1932? iv, 83 p., 1 l. incl. tables (1
    fold.).
————. The selected statistics of transportation and communication in China.
    Nanking, 1948. 10 p.

## Weights and Measures

CHINA. National Bureau of Standard Weights and Measures. Unification of
    weights and measures in China, by Chenlott C. Wu, 吳承洛, with Message
    from Kung P. Chin, 陳公博, Minister of industries, and notice to importers,
    dealers and manufacturers of commercial commodities. Nanking, 1934. cov-
    er-title, 2, 4, 46 p. plates, tables (1 fold.) diagrs.
CHOU, HSI-SAN, 周錫三. Standards of weights and measures. Shanghai, Com-
    mercial Press, 1935. 91 p.
LIU, CHIN-YU, 劉晉鈺. L'unification des mesures chinoises, par Liu Chin-yu
    et M. Vittrant. Changhai, Impr. Tou-sè-wè. 1927. 24 p.
RIGGS, SYDNEY C. Weights and measurements of cargo exported from Shanghai
    and North China. 1931 rev. ed. Shanghai, Official Measurer's Off., 1931.
    165 p.

## Miscellaneous

CHINA stock and share handbook. Shanghai, The North-China Daily News and
    Herald, 1925-29.      v. tables, forms.
DUNG, YIEN, 鄧賢. Life insurance in China: a study of the factors hindering
    its development. Philadelphia, 1928. 124 p. Thesis-Univ. of Pennsylvania.

## Economy of Communist China

ABBAS, KHWAJA AHMAD. China can make it; eye witness account of the amaz-
    ing industrial progress in New China. Bombay, People's Pub. House, 1951.
    16 p.

ADLER, SOLOMON. The Chinese economy. New York, Monthly Review Press, 1957; London, Routledge and K. Paul, 1957. xi, 276 p. maps (on lining papers) tables.

ASIAN PEOPLES' ANTI-COMMUNIST LEAGUE. An analysis of Japan's trade with the Chinese communists. Taipei, 1955. 34 p.

——. First five-year plan of the Chinese communists. Taipei, 1956. cover-title, 46 p.

BRITISH COUNCIL FOR THE PROMOTION OF INTERNATIONAL TRADE, London. China's foreign trade: an analysis and guide for the British businessmen. London, 1954. 67, 2 p.

CHAO, KUO-CHUN, 趙國鈞, 1918-   Source materials from Communist China. Cambridge, Mass., 1952. 3 v.

CHENG, CHO-YÜAN, 鄭竹園. Monetary affairs of Communist China. Kowloon, H.K., Union Research Institute [1954] cover-title, 160 p. (Communist China problem research series, EC5 ).

——. The China mainland market under communist control. Kowloon, Hong Kong, Union Research Institute [1956] cover-title, 96 p. (Communist China problem research series, EC14 ).

CHINA. (People's Republic of China, 1949-   ). Customs import/export tariff. Provisional regulations effective from 16th May 1951. [unofficial translation] Hong Kong, O.K. Print. Press, 1951. 57, 31 p.

——. First five-year plan for development of the national economy of the People's Republic of China in 1953-57. Peking, Foreign Languages Press, 1956. 1 v. ( chiefly illus.).

——. Le premier plan quinquennal pour le développement de l'économie nationale de la République populaire de Chine (1953-57). Pékin, Éditions en langues étrangères, 1956. 1 v. (chiefly illus.).

——. First five-year plan for development of the national economy of the People's Republic of China in 1953-57, adopted on July 30, 1955 by the first National People's Congress at its second session. Peking, Foreign Languages Press, 1956. 232 p.

——. All-China People's Congress. New China advances to socialism; a selection of speeches delivered at the third session of the First National People's Congress. Peking, Foreign Languages Press, 1956. 199 p.

——. State Statistical Bureau. Report on national economic development and fulfilment of the State plan in 1954. Peking, Foreign Languages Press, 1956. 48 p.

——. Report on fulfilment of the national economic plan of the People's Republic of China in 1955, with statistical summary. Peking, Foreign Languages Press, 1956. 57 p.

CHINA COMMITTEE FOR THE PROMOTION OF INTERNATIONAL TRADE. New China's economic achievements 1949-52. Peking, 1952. 285 p.

——. Réalisations économiques de la Chine nouvelle, 1949-52. Pékin, Éditions en langues étrangères, 1953. 156 p.

——. Die wirtschaftlichen Errungenschaften des neuen China 1949-52. Berlin, Verlag die Wirtschaft, 1953. 238 p.

CHINA RECONSTRUCTS. China in transition; selected articles 1952-56 by writers for China Reconstructs. Peking, Foreign Languages Press, 1957. 434 p. illus. maps.

CHINA wins economic battles. Peking, Foreign Languages Press, 1950. iii, 58 p.

COMMUNIST PARTY. CHINA. National Congress, 1956. Full text of a report by Chou En-lai on proposals for a Second five-year plan, delivered on the opening day of the Congress in Peking on September 15, 1956. Peking, 1956. 24 p.

——. Proposals of the Eighth National Congress of the Communist Party of China for the Second five-year plan for development of the national economy, 1958-62. Report on the proposals for the Second five-year plan for development of the national economy [by] Chou En-lai. [Peking, 1956] 104 p. "Supplement to Hsinhua News Agency release."

———. Full text of a resolution on proposals for China's second five-year plan passed by the Congress at the final session in Peking on September 28, 1956. Peking, Foreign Languages Press, 1956. 13 p.

ECKSTEIN, ALEXANDER, 1915-   Summary of Conditions and prospects for economic growth in Communist China. Cambridge, Center for International Studies, Massachusetts Institute of Technology, 1954. 25 p.

ECONOMIC reconstructions in north China border regions. [n. p. ] 1943-     ? v.

L'ÉCONOMIE chinoise sur la voie du socialisme. Pékin, Éditions en langues étrangères, 1954. 132 p. illus.

GANGULI, BIRENDRANATH. Economic development in new China. Indian Council of World Affairs. Bombay, Oxford University Press [1955] 92 p.

GLUCKSTEIN, YGAEL. Mao's China: economic and political survey. London, Allen and Unwin, 1957. 438 p. tables. Boston, Boston Press, 1957.

GT. BRIT. Foreign Office. Correspondence between the Government of the United Kingdom of Great Britain and Northern Ireland and the Central People's Government of China on British trade in China. Peking, 12th April-5th July, 1952; with statement by the Secretary of State for Foreign Affairs in the House of Commons on 20th May, 1952. London, H. M. Stationery Off. , 1952. 7 p. (Its China, 1952, no. 1 ).

HSIA, RONALD, 夏修永, [Hsia Hsiu-yung] 1918-   Price control in Communist China. With an introd. by Douglas S. Paauw. New York, International Secretariat, Institute of Pacific Relations, 1953. iii, 81 p., 83-96 1.

———. Economic planning in Communist China. With a foreword by A. Doak Barnett. New York, International Secretariat, Institute of Pacific Relations, 1955. vi, 89 p.

HSIAO, CHI-JUNG, 蕭濟容, 1892-   Revenue and disbursement of Communist China. Kowloon, H. K., Union Research Institute [1954] 118 p. (Communist China problem research series [EC8] ).

HSIN, YING, 辛膺, 1915-   The price problems of Communist China. Kowloon, H. K., Union Research Institute [1954] 125 p. diagr. (Communist China problem research series [EC3] ).

———. The foreign trade of Communist China. Kowloon, H. K., Union Research Institute [1954] 161 p. diagr. (Communist China problem research series [EC4] ).

KIRBY, EDWARD STUART, 1909-   ed. Contemporary China; economic and social studies, documents, bibliography, chronology. [ Hong Kong] Hong Kong University Press, 1956-     v. illus.

LAVALLÉE, LEON. Économie de la Chine socialiste, par L. Lavallée [et autres] Genève, Librairie Rousseau, 1957. 512 p. maps, tables.

LI, FU-CHÜN, 李富春 1901-   Report on the first five-year plan for development of the national economy of the People's Republic of China in 1953-57; deliviered on July 5 and 6, 1955 at the Second Session of the First National People's Congress. Peking, Foreign Languages Press, 1955. 134 p.

———. Bericht über den ersten Fünfjahrplan zur Entwicklung der Volkswirtschaft in der Volksrepublik China von 1953 bis 1957, gehalten auf der zweiten Tagung des 1. Nationalen Volkskongresses vom 5. bis 6. Juli 1955, von Li Fu-dshun. [Übers. von Rose Gromulat] Berlin, Dietz, 1956. 116 p.

LIEU, D. K., 劉大鈞, 1890-   Industrial development in Communist China. [New York,, Sino-American Amity] c1955. 33 1.

NAN, HAN-CH'ÊN, 南漢宸, 1892-   Prospects for the development of economic relations between China and other countries; speech delivered at the International Economic Conference, Moscow, April 4, 1952. Peking, China Committee for the Promotion of International Trade, Chinese Chamber of Foreign Trade [1952] 15 p.

REMER, CHARLES FREDERICK, 1889-   Coal production in Communist China;

a paper on the economics of Communist China, prepared under a research grant from the Rackham School of Graduate Studies. Ann Arbor, University of Michigan, 1956. iii, 34 p. illus.

REVIEW on the economic situation of the Chinese mainland provinces during the year 1954. Taipei, Economic Stabilization Board, 1955. 92 p.

RIGGS, FRED WARREN, 1917-  The economics of Red China. New York, Foreign Policy Association, 1951. [62]-72 p. (Foreign policy reports, 27:6 ).

TA KUNG PAO, Hongkong. Trade with China, a practical guide. Hong Kong, Ta kung pao, 1957. 147 p. (p. 125-147 advertisements ).

UNION OF DEMOCRATIC CONTROL. 600 million customers in China; a report on Britain-China trade. Foreword by Harold Wilson. [London, 1954] 26 p. (A UDC publication).

U.S. Congress. Senate. Committee on Foreign Relations. Subcommittee on Technical Assistance Programs. Economic development in India and Communist China. Washington, Govt. Print. Off., 1956. 51 p. maps, tables.

———. Library of Congress. Legislative Reference Service. Economic development in India and Communist China [prepared by J. Clement Lapp of the Legislative Reference Service] Washington, U.S. Govt. Print. Off., 1956. v, 51 p. maps (part fold.) tables. (Staff study no. 6, Subcommittee on Technical Assistance Programs ).

———. Office of Strategic Services, Research and Analysis Branch. Economy of Communist North China, 1937-45: 1. Areas of economic control; 2. Summary of economic policies. Washington, 1945. 2 v. fold. maps. (Its R and A No. 3024.1 and 3024.2 ). Mimeographed.

VLADIMIROVA, I. Erfolge des wirtschaftlichen Aufbaus in der Volksrepublik China, von I. Vladimirova und V. Zamin. Berlin, Dietz, 1955. 111 p.

Die VOLKSREPUBLIK China auf der Leipziger Messe, 1953. Leipzig, Messeamt, 1953. 6 p. illus.

WENTZEL, ALBERT K. Die weltwirtschaftliche Position des neuen China. Ludwigsburg, Hans A. Waichel, 1954. ii, 39 p.

WHAT China exports. [1st ed.] Peking, Foreign Languages Press, 1954. 53 p. illus.

WAS China ausführt. Peking, Verlag für fremdsprachige Literatur, 1954. 51 p. illus. plates.

WU, YUAN-LI, 吳元黎, 1920-  An economic survey of Communist China. New York, Bookman Associates; London, Constable, 1956. x, 566 p. illus., maps.

Bibliographies and Dictionaries

U.S. Army Language School, Monterey, Calif. Civil affair terms. [Monterey] Army Language School, Far Eastern Language Division, Chinese-Cantonese Language Dept. [1951] 41 p.

ZEN, I-TU,孫任以都 1921-   Bibliography on Chinese social history; a selected and critical list of Chinese periodical sources, by E-tu Zen Sun and John De Francis.   New Haven, Institute of Far Eastern Languages, Yale University, 1952.  xii, 150 p.

General Works
Social Life as seen by Westerners

ARNOLD, GEORGE. Chopsticks. Illus. by the author.  Melbourne, National Press Pty., 1946.  154 p. illus.

AYSCOUGH, FLORENCE (WHEELOCK) 1878-1942. A Chinese mirror, being reflections of the reality behind appearance.  London, Cape; Boston, Houghton, Mifflin [1926] 464 p. illus., fold. map.

————. Un mirror chinois; traduit de l'anglais par Maurice Thiéry.  Paris, P. Roger [1926] 295 p. map, plates.

BARNES, GEORGE G. Enter China! A study in race contacts.  London, Edinburgh House Press, 1929.  168 p. "First published, April 1928. Third impression, May 1929."

BARTLETT, MYRTH. By the Bridge of a thousand ages; the adventures of Lingsan.  Los Angeles, Willing Pub. Co. [c1940] 9-232 p. illus.

BATISTE-MAYBORN, PIERRE. Essai sur les associations en Chine.  Paris, Plon-Nourrit et Cie, 1925.  208 p.

BRINES, CELIA R. Dragon tales.  Mountain View, Calif., Portland, Ore.  Pacific Press Pub. Association [1942] 5-125 p. incl. illus., plates, ports.

CABLE, MILDRED, 1880-1952. China, her life and her people, by Mildred Cable and Francesca French.  London, University of London Press [1946] 160 p. front., illus.(incl. map) plates, ports., diagrs.

CARTIER-BRESSON, HENRI, 1908-   D'un Chine à l'autre. Photographies de H. Cartier-Bresson.  Préface de Jean-Paul Sartre.  Paris, R. Delpire, 1954. 1 v. (chiefly illus.) (Collection Neuf, 14 ).

————. China gestern und heute.  Düssendorf, K. Rauch, 1955. 1 v. (unpaged, chiefly illus.).

————. From one China to the other. Photos. by Henri Cartier-Bresson. Text by Han Suyin [pseud. ] Edited by Robert Delpire.  New York, Universe Books; Toronto, Burns and MacEachern, 1956. 1 v. (chiefly illus., map).

————. China in transition; a moment in history. With an introd. and 144 photos. [Translated by Edward Hyams] London, Thames and Hudson [1956]  1 v. (chiefly illus.).

CHADOURNE, MARC, 1895-   Chine. Paris, Plon [1931] 293 p. illus.

————. China; translated from the French by Harry Block.  New York, Covici-Friede [c1932] 308 p. incl. plates.

CHILDERS, JAMES SAXON, 1899-   Through Oriental gates; the adventures of an unwise man in the East.  New York, London, D. Appleton, 1930. 333,[2] p. front., plates, ports.

COPLAND, DOUGLAS BERRY, 1894-   The Chinese social structure.  Sydney, Australasian Medical Pub. Co., 1948. 20 p. (George Ernest Morrison lectures

CORNABY, WILLIAM ARTHUR, 1860-1921. A necklace of peach-stones, "A string of Chinese peach-stones" rewritten, with appendix of Chinese lighter literature, illustrations and index. Shanghai, North-China Daily News and Herald, 1925. 401 p. col. front., illus.

CRANE, LOUISE. China in sign and symbol; a panorama of Chinese life, past and present. London, B.H. Batsford; Shanghai, Kelly and Walsh, 1927. xx, 227 p. plates (part col., part fold.).

CRESSY, EARL HERBERT. Understanding China; a handbook of background information on changing China. New York, Nelson [1957] 278 p. illus.

CROW, CARL, 1883-1945. Four hundred million customers, the experiences - some happy, some sad, of an American in China, and what they taught him. New York, Harper, 1937; London, H. Hamilton, 1937. 11-316, [1] p. illus.

————. 400 millions de clients: la Chine, vue par un commerçant; traduction de Claudine Decourcelle. Paris, Les Editions de France, c1938. iii, 257 p. illus.

————. Vierhundert millionen kunden. Autorisierte übersetzung aus dem Englischen von Richard Hoffmann. Berlin, P. Zsolnay, 1937. 311 p. illus.

————. My friends, the Chinese. London, H. Hamilton [1938] 277, [1] p. illus.

————. The Chinese are like that. New York [etc.] Harper, 1939. viii, 328 p.

————. Mes amis les chinois. La vie quotidienne en Chine. Traduit de l'anglais par Charles Mourey. Paris, Payot, 1939. 228 p. illus.

————. Foreign devils in the Flowery kingdom. New York, Harper, 1940. London, H. Hamilton [1941] xi, 340 p. illus.

DANBY, HOPE. My boy Chang. London, Gollancz, 1955. 222 p. illus.

DARUVALA, J.C. The Chinese exodus. Bombay, Hind Kitabs [1944] viii, 119 p. front. (group port.) plates, double maps.

DENBY, JAY. Letters of a Shanghai griffin. Shanghai, Kelly and Walsh, 1923. 438 p. illus.

EBERHARD, WOLFRAM, 1909-   Conquerors and rulers; social forces in medieval China. Leiden, Brill, 1952. xi, 129 p.

DUBOSCQ, ANDRÉ, 1876-   L'élite chinoise; ses origines, sa transformation après l'empire. Paris, Nouvelles éditions latines [1945] [9]-135 p.

ELIASSEN, SIGURD, 1884-   Dragon Wang's river. Translated by Katherine John from the Norwegian. New York, J.Day; London, Methuen [1957] 256 p. illus. Translation of Gamle Drage Wangs elv.

FARQUHARSON, RONALD. Confessions of a China-hand. London, Hodder and Stoughton [1950] New York, Morrow, 1951. 224 p. map (on lining papers ).

FAWCETT, RAYMOND, ed. China. London, P.R. Gawthorn [1951] 47 p. illus. (His How did they live?).

FISHER, MRS. WELTHY (HONSINGER) 1880-   Beyond the moon gate, being a diary of ten years in the interior of the Middle Kingdom. New York, Cincinnati, The Abingdon Press [c1924] 176 p. front., plates.

FÖLLMER, WILHELM. Schrei des Ostens, ein chinesisches Mosaik. Leipzig, Koehler und Voigtländer [1942] 300 p. plates.

FONTENOY, JEAN. Shanghaï secret, récit. Paris, B. Grasset [1938] 232 p.

————. Schanghai, Hölle des Ostens. Aus dem Französischen. Bern und Stuttgart, Hallwag, 1938. iv, 216 p.

————. The secret Shanghai. New York, Grey-hill Press [1939] 188 (i. e. 190) p.

[FRANKING, MAE M.]. My Chinese marriage, by M.T.F. New York, Duffield, 1921. 169 p.

GALBRAITH, WINIFRED. The dragon sheds his skin. London, J. Cape [1928] 221 p. front., plates.

————. In China now. New York, W. Morrow, 1941. 11-285 p.

GALE, ESSON McDOWELL, 1884-   Salt for the dragon; a personal history of China, 1908-45. [East Lansing] Michigan State College Press, 1953. 225 p. illus.

GREGG, EVA A. Hints from squints in China. Cincinnati, O., Printed by the

Caxton Press [c1923]  216 p. front., 1 illus., ports.

GROFF, GEORGE WEIDMAN, 1884-1955. Glimpses of China, 1939. Canton,
Lingnan University, 1939. [28] p. illus.

HAHN, EMILY, 1905-   The picture story of China. New York, Reynal and
Hitchcock [1946] [51] p. incl. front.(map) col. illus.

HAYES, ESTHER FRAYNE. At home in China. New York, W.Neale, 1931. x,
13-165 p. front., plates, ports.

HINZELMANN, HANS HEINZ, 1889-   O China, Land auf alten Wegen; wahr-
haftige Entdeckungen auf einer west-östlichen Lebensfahrt.    中國本地老道
Braunschweig, Schlösser Verlag [1948]  195 p.

HOBART, ALICE TISDALE (NOURSE) 1882-   By the City of the long sand; a
tale of new China. New York, Macmillan, 1926. xii, 329 p. illus., plates.

HODOUS, LEWIS, 1872-1949. Folkways in China. London, A. Probsthain, 1929.
viii, 248 p. plates. (Probsthain's oriental series. vol. 18 ).

HOSIE, DOROTHEA (SOOTHILL) lady, 1885-   Two gentlemen of China; an intimate description of the private life of two patrician Chinese families, their
homes, loves, religion, mirth, sorrow, and many other aspects of their family life, with an introduction by Professor Soothill. 2d ed. London, Seeley,
Service, 1924. 9-316 p. front., plates, ports.

——. Menschen in China; die politische und soziale Umwälzung in China von
dem täglichen Leben zweier chinesischer Patrizierfamilien aus gesehen, mit
einer Einführung von professor Soothill. Stuttgart, Berlin [etc.] Deutsche
Verlags-Anstalt, 1926. xii, 393, [1] p. plates, port. "Berechtigte übersetzung aus dem Englischen von Rudolf Nutt.''

——. The pool of Ch'ien Lung, a tale of modern Peking. London, Hodder and
Stoughton [1944]  175, [1] p. col. front.

HUTCHINSON, PAUL, 1890-1956. China's real revolution. New York, Missionary Education Movement of the United States and Canada [c1924]  x, 182 p.
front., plates, ports.

HUTCHINSON, JAMES LAFAYETTE. China hand. Boston, Lothrop, Lee and
Shepard, 1936. x, 418 p. incl. front., illus.

HUTSON, JAMES. Chinese life in the Tibetan foothills. Shanghai, Far Eastern
Geographical Establishment, 1921. 210 p. diagrs.

JACKSON, INNES. China only yesterday,    華土歸來 . [London] Faber and
Faber [1938] 288 p. front., illus.(map) plates, ports.

JENKINS, LAWRENCE WATERS, 1872-   Bryant Parrott Tilden of Salem, at a
Chinese dinner party, Canton: 1819. A Newcomen address. [Princeton, Printed at Princeton University Press] 1944. 28 p. illus.

KISCH, EGON ERWIN, 1885-1948. China geheim. Berlin, E. Reiss, 1933; 4.
Aufl. Berlin, Aufbau Verlag, 1949. 295 p.

——. La Chine secrète; traduit de l'allemand par Jeanne Stern. Paris, Gallimard [1935] 251 p. map. (Problèmes et documents ).

——. Secret China; translated by Michael Davidson. London, John Lane [1935]
vi, 279 p.

KUHN, MAY COLE. Lantern light. Mountain View, Calif., Portland,Ore., Pacific Press Pub. Association, 1939. 159 p. incl. front. illus.

KULP, DANIEL HARRISON, 1888-   Country life in South China; the sociology
of familism. Volume I. Phenix village, Kwangtung. New York, Bureau of
Publications, Teachers College, Columbia University, 1925. xxx, 367 p.col.
front., illus.(incl. maps) plates.

LEE, ESTHER (HAGGARD). The other side of the world; pages from the journal
of a young missionary in pre-Communist China. New York, Vantage Press
[c1956] 79 p. illus.

LEWIS, MRS. ELIZABETH (FOREMAN) 1892-   Portraits from a Chinese scroll;
illustrations by Virginia Hollinger Stout, calligraphy by Chen Chao-ming, 陳
兆銘 . Chicago, Philadelphia, John C. Winston [c1938]; London, Harrap,
1939. 267 p., plates.

McCORMICK, ELSIE. Audacious angles on China. Shanghai, Chinese-American Pub. Co., 1922. New York, Appleton, 1923. xi, [1], 3-305, [1] p. front. plates.

MÅNCHEN-HELFEN, OTTO, 1894-   China. Dresden, Kaden [1931] 232 p. illus.(map) (Die Weltpolitik, 3 ).

MAIER-HUGENDUBEL, MARTIN. Hinter der chinesischen Mauer. Stuttgart und Basel, Evang. Missionsverlag, 1929. 174 p. front., plates, port.

MOORE, NELLE E. On the other side of the world; stories of China. New York, C. Scribner [c1938] vi, [2], 216 p. illus.

MORRILL, SAMUEL. Lanterns, junks and jade. New York, Frederick A.Stokes, 1926. viii, 287 p. 1 illus., plan.

OBER, GEORGE. Mission to China. Los Angeles, Wetzel Pub. Co. [1943] 79 p. illus. (incl. ports.).

PAKENHAM-WALSH, WILLIAM SANDFORD, 1868-   Twenty years in China. Cambridge [Eng.] W. Heffer [1935] x, 127 p. front., plates, ports.

PERCHERON, MAURICE, 1891-   Intermède chinois. Paris, Denoël [1944] 222 p.

[PETERSON, HENRY WILLIAM CHRISTIAN] 1896-   Honourable and peculiar ways, by Pêh Der Chen [pseud. ]; with a foreword by Ernest Bramah. London, H.Hamilton [1932] 224 p. incl. front., illus.

POLITICAL AND ECONOMIC PLANNING. Poverty and progress in China. London, P.E.P., 1943. 15 p. (Planning, 209).

POWELL, CHARLES AUSTIN, 1887-   Bound feet. Boston, Warren Press [c1938] 3-339 p. plates, ports.

RASMUSSEN, ALBERT HENRY. China trader. New York, Crowell; London, Constable [1954] 274 p. illus.

————. Als die Zöpfe fielen. Zehn Jahre Zöllner und Kaufmann im alten China. Übers. von Willi Gustav Rickmer Rickmers. Wiesbaden, E. Brockhaus, 1956. 159 p. (Reisen und Abenteuer).

ROY, CLAUDE, 1915-   La Chine dans un miroir. Illustrations photographiques de W. Bischof [et al.] Illustrations littéraires traduites du chinois par Hsou Lien-tuan et l'auteur. Lausanne, Guilde du livre [1953] 152 p. illus. (part col.).

SEGERS, ARTHUR. La Chine; le peuple, sa vie quotidienne et ses cérémonies, avec une préface par jhr. mr. F. Beelaerts van Blokland. Anvers, Éditions "De Sikkel"; Paris, 1932. 242, 160 p. incl. plates.

SETON, GRACE (GALLATIN) "MRS. ERNEST THOMPSON SETON," 1872- Chinese lanterns. New York, Dodd, Mead, 1924. xv, 373 p. front., 1 illus., plates, ports., facsims.

SMITH, ARTHUR HENDERSON, 1845-1932. Moeurs curieuses des chinois. Traduit par B. Mayra et le Lt.-Cl. de Fonlonge. Paris, Payot, 1935. 311 p. plates. (Collection d'études, de documents et de témoignages pour servir à l'histoire de notre temps). 1er éd. 1927.

SOOTHILL, MRS. LUCY (FARRAR) d. 1931. A passport to China; being the tale of her long and friendly sojourning amongst a strangely interesting people, with a foreword by her daughter, Lady Hosie. London, Hodder and Stoughton, 1931. xi, [1], 339 p. front., illus.(plan) plates, ports.

STARRETT, VINCENT, 1886-   Oriental encounters; two essays in bad taste. Chicago, Normandie House, 1938. 11-45, [1] p.

STEEP, THOMAS. Chinese fantastics, 華國奇談. New York and London, The Century [c1925] viii, 222, [1] p. front.

TANDLER, JULIUS, 1869-1936. Volk in China; Erlebnisse und Erfahrung. Wien, Druck und Verlag "Thalia," 1935. 47 p.

THAN, WALTER. China ohne Zopf. Photos: Brüder Basch. Wien, Danubia-Verlag [c1949] 171 p. plates.

THORBECKE, ELLEN (KOLBAN). People in China; thirty-two photographic studies from life, with an introduction by Dr. W.J.R.Thorbecke. London [etc.]

G.G. Harrap [1935]  141 p. ,  1 l. incl. mounted plates. col. plates.

TOWNSEND, RALPH, 1900-    Ways that are dark; the truth about China.  New
York, G. P. Putnam, 1933.  vii-xiv, 336 p.

U. S. Office of Strategic Services. Research and Analysis Branch. Morale and
social conditions in Japan and occupied areas as reported by American repa-
triates.  [Washington] 1944.  ix l., 63 p. (Its R and A no. 1717).

La VIE moderne chinoise.  Pékin, Impr. de la "Politique de Pékin," 1932-34.
3 v. (Collection de la "Politique de Pékin").

WALN, NORA, 1895-    The House of exile.  Boston, Little, Brown, 1933. [3]-
337 p. col. front., illus.

————.  La maison d'exil. Moeurs et vie intime en Chine moderne. Traduction de
l'anglais de Michel Epuy.  Paris et Genève, J.H. Jeheber, 1934.  iv, 299 p.

————.  Süsse frucht, bittre frucht, China, übers. von Josephine Ewers-Bumiller und L. Günther.  Berlin, W. Krüger [c1935] 326 p.

WARR, WINIFRED. China; a handbook for leaders.  London, Edinburgh House
Press, 1941. 80 p. illus. (incl map, plan) (Practical books - 2 ).

WELLS, LAURA PRESTON. Stories from a Chinese hospital.  Shanghai, American Church Mission, 1930.  56 p. front., plates.

WIMSATT, GENEVIEVE BLANCHE. A griffin in China; fact and legend in the
everyday life of the great republic.  New York and London, Funk and Wagnalls Co., 1927.  xx, 252 p. col. front., plates.

## Social Life as seen by Chinese

BRIGGS, MARGARET (YANG) 1917-    Daughter of the khans, by Liang Yen [ 粱
琰 ] [pseud. ] New York, W. W. Norton [c1955]  285 p. illus.

CHANG, CHUNG-LI, 張仲禮, 1919-    The gentry in nineteenth century China:
their economic position as evidenced by their share of the national product.
Ann Arbor, University Microfilms [1953] ( [University Microfilms, Ann Arbor, Mich.] Publication no. 6408 ). Collation of the original: xi, 514 l. tables.  Thesis-University of Washington.

————.  The Chinese gentry; studies on their role in nineteenth century Chinese
society. Introd. by Franz Michael.  Seattle, University of Washington Press,
1955.  xxi, 250 p. diagrs. (University of Washington publications on Asia ).

CHAO, CHENG-HSIN, 趙承信 . An ecological study of China from segmentation
to integration.  Ann Arbor, Mich., 1933. iii, 207 l. incl. maps, tables. (U-
niversity microfilm. Pub. No. 320 ). Thesis-University of Michigan.

CHÊNG, CH'ÊNG-K'UN, 鄭成坤, 1906-    The dragon sheds its scales. New
York, New Voices Pub. Co., 1952. 192 p. illus.

CHENG, TCHENG, 盛成, [Shêng Ch'êng] 1899-    Ma mère. Préface de Paul
Valéry.  Paris-Neuchâtel, V. Attinger, 1928.  191 p. incl. front. (port.)
(His Vers l'unité. I ).

————.  Meine mutter. Mit einem Vorwort von Paul Valéry.  Berlin, G. Kiepenheuer, 1929.  xxiv, 151 p.

————.  A son of China; translated from the French by Marvin McCord Lowes;
preface by Paul Valéry.  New York, W. W. Norton [c1930] viii, 9-286 p.
Translation of Vers l'unité, I (Ma mère) and II (Ma mère et moi).

————.  Ma mère et moi à travers la révolution chinoise.  Paris, V. Attinger,
1929. 239 p. port. (His Vers l'unité, 2 ).

CHIANG, YEE, 蔣彝, 1903-    A Chinese childhood. 3d ed.  London, Methuen
[1946] xii, 304, [2] p. illus., 8 col. plates (incl. front., ports.). 1st ed.
1940.

————.  The same. [1st American ed. ] New York, John Day [1952] 303 p. illus.
(An Asia book ).

CHINA to-day through Chinese eyes, by Dr. T. T. Lew, 劉廷芳, Prof. Hu Shih,
胡適, Prof. Y. Y. Tsu, 朱友漁, Dr. Cheng Ching Yi, 誠靜怡. London, Student Christian Movement, 1922. 144 p.

————. Second series. By T. C. Chao, 趙紫宸, P. C. Hsu, 徐寶謙, T. Z. Koo, 顧子仁, T. T. Lew, 劉廷芳, M. T. Tchou, 朱懋澄, F. C. M. Wei, 韋卓民, D. Z. T. Yui, 余日章. London, Student Christian Movement, 1927. viii, 151 p.

FEI, HSIAO-T'UNG, 費孝通, 1911-   Peasant life in China; a field study of country life in the Yangtze valley. With a preface by Professor Bronislaw Malinowski. London, G. Routledge [1939] New York, Dutton, 1939, Oxford University Press, 1946. xxvi, 300 p. front., illus. (maps) plates, diagrs.

————. China's gentry; essays in rural-urban relations. Revised and edited by Margaret Park Redfield, with six life-histories of Chinese gentry families collected by Yung-teh Chow, 周榮德, and an introd. by Robert Redfield. Chicago, University of Chicago Press [1953] v, 289 p. illus.

HSU, FRANCIS L. K., 許烺光, 1909-   Under the ancestor's shadow; Chinese culture and personality. New York, Columbia Univ. Press, 1948. London, Routledge, 1949. xiv, 317 p. illus.

————. Religion, science, and human crises; a study of China in transition and its implications for the West. London, Routledge and K. Paul [1952] x, 142 p. illus. (International library of sociology and social reconstruction).

————. Americans and Chinese: two ways of life. New York, H. Schuman, 1953; London, Cresset Press, 1955. 457 p.

HU, CHIEN-MIN, 胡鑑民. Les transformations morales et sociales de la Chine depuis la révolution de 1911, avec une présentation de m. Wang King Ky, 王景岐, et une préface de m. Paul Otlet. [Bruxelles] 1927. 134 p. (Union des associations internationales. Publication n° 123, 1927).

HWANG, TSU-YÜ, 黃祖瑜. Der blühende Granatapfelbaum; eine einfache Geschichte einer chinesischen Familie. [Aus dem Englishcen übertragen und bearb. von Hanna Hindbeck] München, Winkler-Verlag [c1948] 259 p.

KUO, HELENA, 郭鏡秋, [Kuo Ching-ch'iu]. Peach path. London, Methuen [1940] xv, 239, [1] p.

LEE, BEATRICE D., 李哲民, [Li Chê-min] 1898-   Chih Ming's Chinese sketch book, as told by Beatrice Lee (Chih Ming) to Ida M. McCausland. Portland, Me., Falmouth Pub. House, 1948. 250 p.

LIN, YU-T'ANG, 林語堂, 1895-   My country and my people. New York, Reynal and Hitchcock [c1935] xviii, 382 p. illus., plates, facsim., diagrs.

————. The same. Rev. illustrated ed. New York, John Day [1939]; London, Heinemann, 1939. xxvi, 440 p. front., illus., plates, port., facsim.

————. La Chine et les chinois; traduit par S. et P. Bourgeois. Paris, Payot, 1937. 396 p. (Étude de documents et de témoignages pour servir à histoire de notre temps).

————. Mein Land und mein Volk. [Aus dem Englischen übertragen von W. E. Süskind] Stuttgart, Deutsche Verlags-Anstalt [1946] [c1935] 437 p. diagrs.

LO, MÊNG-TS'Ê, 羅夢冊, 1907-   Declaration on human welfare. [Hongkong] Chu Lieu (Main Current) Society [1951] 156 p.

LO, REN YEN, 羅隆炎, 1890-   China's revolution from the inside. New York, Cincinnati [etc.] Abingdon Press [c1930] 307 p.

LONG, KIA-SIANG, 龍家驤. Le mouvement social en Chine; ses causes et ses tendances. Lyon, Bosc frères et Riou, 1930. 157 p. Thèse-Univ. de Lyon.

LOWE, H. Y., 盧興源. The adventures of Wu; the life cycle of a Peking man. Peking, Peking Chronicle Press [c1941] 2 v. illus.

LYNN, JERMYN CHI-HUNG, 凌啓鴻, [Ling Ch'i-hung]. Social life of the Chinese (in Peking). Peking-Tientsin, China Booksellers, 1928. 182 p. plates.

MA, ROBERTA, 馬心儀, 1902-   China calls. Richmond, Va., William Byrd Press, 1938. 83 p. plates (1 double).

REMINISCENCES of a Chinese official. Revelations of official life under the Manchus. Tientsin, Tientsin Press, 1922. 518 p. front. "Reprinted from the Peking Gazette and the China Illustrated Review." French ed.: Moeurs des mandarins sous la dynastie mandchoue. Traduit par Eva Meyerovitch. Paris, Payot, 1935. 230 p.

SHEN, NELSON NAI-CHENG, 沈乃正. The changing Chinese social mind from
    1911 to 1922. Peking, Peking Express Press, 1924. 42 p.
T'ANG, LIANG-LI, 湯良禮, 1901-    The new social order in China. Shanghai,
    China United Press, 1936. xi, 282 p. diagr. ("China to-day" series. [6] ).
T'AO, L.K., 陶孟和, 1887-    Social changes. Shanghai, China Institute of Pa-
    cific Relations [1931] 15 p. Preliminary paper prepared for the 4th biennial
    conference of the Institute of Pacific Relations, Hangchow, 1931.
TING, CHOI-YUAN, 丁垂遠, 1922-    Floating clouds. [Berlin, 1948] 86 p.
    illus.
TSCHANG, YEN-YÜ, 張彥如. Soziale Frage u. ständische Sozialpolitik im
    Westen und in China. Weidlingau-Wien, O. Andreas, 1935. 76 p.
WU, KANG, 吳康, 1896-    Recent social changes and economic problems in
    China. [Taipei] Chinese Association for the United Nations, 1952. 43 p.
    (Unachina publications, Ser. I, 8 ).
YUAN, L.Z. Through a moon gate. Rev. ed. Shanghai, Mercury Press, 1948.
    162 p. illus. 1st ed. 1938.
ZEN, E-TU孫任以都, 1921-    ed. and tr. Chinese social history; translations
    of selected studies, by E-tu Zen Sun and John De Francis. Washington, A-
    merican Council of Learned Societies, 1956. xix, 400 p. maps. (American
    Council of Learned Societies. Studies in Chinese and related civilizations, 7).

## Social Customs and Folkways

ADAM, MAURICE, 1889-1932. tr. Us et coutumes de la région de Pékin, d'a-
    près le Je sia kieou wen k'ao,    日下舊聞考. Ch. 146-147-148. Pékin, A.
    Nachbaur, 1930. viii, 48 p. plates.
BREDON, JULIET. The moon year, a record of Chinese customs and festivals
    [by] Juliet Bredon and Igor Mitrophanow. With chart of the Chinese year.
    Shanghai, Kelly and Walsh, 1927. xi, 514, [xiii]-xx p. front., plates (2 col.)
    fold. diagr.
------. Das Mondjahr; chinesische Sitten, Bräuche und Feste; Darstellung und
    Kulturbericht. Berlin, P. Zsolnay [c1937] 527 p. front., plates, diagr.
------. Chinese New Year festivals; a picturesque monograph of the rites, cere-
    monies and observances in relation thereto. Shanghai, Kelly and Walsh, 1930.
    29 p. illus. (part mounted col.).
BURKHARDT, VALENTINE RODOLPHE, 1884-    Chinese creeds and customs.
    Hong Kong, South China Morning Post [1954] 2 v. illus.
CONSTANT, SAMUEL VICTOR, 1894-    Calls, sounds and merchandise of the
    Peking street peddlers. Peking The Camel Bell [1936?] xiv, 185 (i.e. 187)p.
    illus.(part col.; part mounted) plates, diagr.
CORMACK, ANNIE, "MRS. J.G. CORMACK." Chinese births, weddings and
    deaths. Peking, Printed at the North China Standard, 1923. 35 p. plates.
------. Chinese birthday, wedding, funeral, and other customs. 3d ed. Peking,
    China Booksellers [1927] 3-220 p. front., plates. 1st ed. 1922.
------. Everyday customs in China. Edinburgh and London, The Moray Press
    [1935] 264 p. front., plates.
CORTI, EGON CAESAR, conte, 1886-    Chinesisches Bilderbuch. Leipzig, Bib-
    liographisches Institut [c1935] 11-55, [1] p. col. illus. [Meyers bunte bänd-
    chen].
DER LING, princess, 德齡公主, d. 1944. Two years in the Forbidden city.
    New York, Dodd, Mead, 1924. ix, 383 p. front., plates, ports.
------. Kowtow. New York, Dodd, Mead [c1929] x, 322 p. front., plates.
------. Lotos petals. New York, Dodd, Mead [c1930] 267 p. front., illus.,
    plates.
EBERHARD, WOLFRAM, 1909-    Chinese festivals. New York, H. Schuman
    [1952] 152 p. illus. [Great religious festivals series].
GRAHAM, DOROTHY, 1893-    Through the moon door; the experiences of an

American resident in Peking. New York, J.H.Sears, 1926. x, 341 p. front., plates, port.

HUMMEL, MARGARET GIBSON. Fun and festival from China. New York, Friendship Press, 1948. 48 p. illus.

IMBERT, HENRI. Poésies chinoises sur les fêtes annuelles. Pékin, "La Politique de Pékin," 1924. 34 p. illus. (Collection de la "Politique de Pékin").

JAMESON, RAYMOND DE LOY, 1896-   Three lectures on Chinese folklore, delivered before the convocation of the North China Union Language School, March and April, 1932. Peiping, North China Union Language  School, cooperating with California College in China [1932] ix, 13-164 p.

KALFF, L. Der Totenkult in Südschantung, ein Beitrag zur Volkskunde des Landes. Yenchowfu, Verlag der katholischen Mission, 1932. viii, 109 p. illus., plates, diagr.

MORGAN, HARRY TITTERTON, 1872-   Chinese festivals. [Los Angeles, Broadway Press] 1941. 16 p. illus. [Chinese classics in miniature].

SWALLOW, ROBERT WILLIAM, 1878-   Sidelights on Peking life; introduction by Hardy Jowett. Peking, China Booksellers, 1927. xviii, 135 p. plates (incl. ports.) plan.

TIEFENSEE, FRANZ WILHELM. Wegweiser durch die chinesische Höflichkeits-Formen. 3.Aufl. Tokyo, Verlag der deutschen Gesellschaft für Natur-und Völkerkunde Ostasiens, 1924. 7-224 p. illus. diagrs. (Tokyo. Deutsche Gesellschaft für Natur-und Völkerkunde Ostasiens. Mitteil., 18).

TUN, LI-CH'ÊN, 敦禮臣, 1855-1911. Annual customs and festivals in Peking as recorded in the Yen-ching Sui-shih-chi, 燕京歲時記; translated and annotated by Derk Bodde. Peiping, H. Vetch, 1936. [vii]-xxii, 147 p. illus., plates (part col., 1 fold., 2 mounted) diagr.

## Magic and Superstitions

ADAM, MAURICE, 1889-1932. Chen Mou Tch'ang, 神木廠, le hangar du bois-genie. Pékin, La Politique de Pékin, 1927. 35 p. (Collection de la "Politique de Pékin").

ALEKSEEV, VASILIĬ MIKHAĬLOVICH, 1881-1951. The Chinese gods of wealth; a lecture delivered at the School of Oriental Studies, University of London, on 26th March, 1926. [London] Pub. by the School of Oriental Studies in conjunction with the China Society, 1928. 36 p. 24 plates (part col.).

BOUILLARD, GEORGES, 1862-1930. Notes diverses sur les cultes en Chine; les attitudes des Buddhas. 3e éd. Pékin, A. Nachbaur, 1933. 33 p. plates, illus.

CHOCHOD, LOUIS SIMON FORTUNÉ FRÉDÉRIC, 1877-   Occultisme et magie en Extrême-Orient: Indie-Indochine-Chine. Paris, Payot, 1949 (c1945). [7]-404 p. illus., diagrs. (Bibliothèque scientifique).

COMBER, LEON. Chinese magic and superstitions in Malaya. Singapore, Donald Moore, 1955. 80 p. illus. (Malayan Heritage, 5).

DAY, CLARENCE BURTON, 1889-   Chinese peasant cults; being a study of Chinese paper gods. Foreword by Clifford H. Plopper. Shanghai, Kelly and Walsh, 1940. xx, 243 p. col. front., plates (part col.) [Nanking theological seminary. English publications, 1].

DORÉ, HENRI, 1859-1931. Recherches sur les superstitions en Chine. Changhai, Impr. de la Mission Catholique, 1911-38. 18 v. illus. plates (part col.), ports., facsims.(part col.) (Variétés sinologiques No. 32, 34, 36, 39, 41-42, 44-46, 48-49, 51, 57, 61-62, 66).

———. Manuel des superstitions chinoises; ou, Petit indicateur des superstitions les plus communes en Chine. Chang-hai, Impr. de la mission catholique, 1926. v, 219 p.

ELLIOTT, ALAN JOHN ANTHONY. Chinese spirit-medium cults in Singapore. [London] Published for Dept. of Anthropology, London School of Economics and

Political Science [by Royal Anthropological Institute] 1955. 179 p. illus.
(Monographs on social anthropology, 14 ).

FÊNG, HAN-YI, 馮漢驥, 1902-　　The black magic in China known as ku [by] H.
Y. Fêng and J.K. Shryock. Philadelphia, American Oriental Society, 1935.
cover-title, 30 p. (Publications of the American oriental society. Offprint
series, 5 ).

GULIK, ROBERT HANS VAN, 1910-　　The mango "trick" in China; an essay on
Taoist magic. (In Asiatic Society of Japan. Transactions. Tokyo, 3d ser.,
v. 3 (1954) p. 117-169. plates ).

HEARN, LAFCADIO, 1850-1904, comp. Some Chinese ghosts; introduction by
Manuel Komroff. New York, The Modern Library [c1927] ix, [13]-203 p.
(The modern library of the world's best books) 1st ed. 1906.

HENTZ, CARL, 1883-　　Objets rituels, croyances et dieux de la Chine antique
et de l'Amérique. Anvers, Éditions "De Sikkel," 1936. 119, [122] p. illus.,
XII plates.

HSU, FRANCIS L.K., 許烺光, 1909-　　Magic and science in western Yunnan,
the problem of introducing scientific medicine in a rustic community. In co-
operation with the Yenching-Yunnan station of sociological research, National Yunnan University. New York, International Secretariat, Institute of Pacific Relations, 1943. v, 53 p. (Social change in southwest China - case stud-
y 3 ).

KIANG, CHAO-YUAN, 江紹原, 1898-　　Le voyage dans la Chine ancienne, con-
sidéré principalement sous son aspect magique et religieux; traduit du chinois par Fan Jen, 范仁. Shanghai, Commission mixte des oeuvres franco-
chinoises, Office de publications, 1937-　　375 p.

KOEHN, ALFRED. Harbingers of happiness; the Door Gods of China. Peiping,
Lotus Court, 1948. 38 p. col. illus.

LI, SHUN-FÊNG, 李淳風, 602-70. The great prophecies of China, by Li Chun-
feng and Yuan Tienkang, 袁天綱; translated and annotated by Charles L. Lee
[pseud.][ 顏樸生 ] New York, Franklin Co. [1950]　64 p.

LUM, CHUNG PARK, 林松柏. Chinese fortune telling. New York, 1930. 15 p.
illus.

―――. Chinese astrology and interpretations of dreams. New York, Lop Quan
and Co., 1932. 8 l. illus.

[MORGAN, HARRY TITTERTON] 1872-　　Chinese astrology. Edited for and
copyrighted by Quon-Quon company. Los Angeles, Calif, c1945. 20 p. illus.
[His Chinese classics in miniature]. A revision by T.C. Taylor of the work
originally edited by H.T. Morgan.

SCMITT, ERICH, 1893-　　Die Chinesen. Tübingen, Mohr, 1927. 110 p.

SOULIÉ, CHARLES GEORGES, 1878-　　Sciences occultes en Chine. Le main.
Paris, Éditions Nilsson, 1932. 136 p. illus.

WATERBURY, FLORANCE, 1883-　　Bird-deities in China. Ascona, Artibus
Asiae, 1952. 191 p. plates. (Artibus Asiae. Supplementum 10 ).

WILLOUGHBY-MEADE, GERALD. Chinese ghouls and goblins. London, Constable, 1928. xv, 431 p. front., plates.

YANG, KUN, 楊堃, 1901-　　Recherches sur le culte des ancêtres comme principe ordonnateur de la famille chinoise; la succession au culte, la succession
au patrimoine. Lyon, Bosc frères, M. et L. Riou, 1934. 174 p. Thèse-
Univ. de Lyon.

## Myth and Legends

COUCHOUD, PAUL LOUIS, 1879-　　ed. Mythologie asiatique illustrée. Paris,
Librairie de France [1928] x, 431 p. front., illus., plates (part col.).

―――. ed. Asiatic mythology, a detailed description and explanation of the my-
thologies of all the great nations of Asia, by J. Hackin [and others] with an
introduction by Paul-Louis Couchoud. London, G. G. Harrap [1932] 459,[1] p.

front., illus. col. plates. Translated by F. M. Atkinson.

COYAJEE, SIR JEHANGIR COOVERJEE, 1875-   Cults and legends of ancient Iran and China. Fort, Bombay, J. B. Karani [1936] 308, [xii] p. front.

CRANE, LOUISE. The magic spear, and other stories of China's famous heroes; with a foreword by Lin Yutang. New York, Random House [c1938] vi, xi-xx, [21]-244, ix-x p. incl. illus., plates.

DYSON, VERNE, 1879-   Forgotten tales of ancient China. Shanghai, Commercial Press, 1927. xiii, 384 p. front., illus.(incl. ports., maps).

———. Land of the yellow spring, pen and ink drawings by Arthur G. Learned. New York, Chinese Studies Press, 1937. xi, 143, [1] p. incl. front., illus.

FERGUSON, JOHN CALVIN, 1866-1945. Chinese [mythology] by John C. Ferguson, Japanese [mythology] by Masaharu Aneski. Boston, Archaeological Institute of America, Marshall Jones Co., 1938. xii, 416 p. illus., XLIV plates (part col., incl. front.) on 32 l., map. (The mythology of all races. vol. 8 ).

FUCHS, WALTER, 1902-   Der Wille der Kwan-yin. Eine chinesische Legende. Zürich und Stuttgart, Aldus Manutius Verlag, 1955. 46 p. plates (Kleine kostbarkeiten der Aldus Manutius-Drucke, 6 ).

GATES, MARY JEAN, 1887-   The Chinese model emperor lore. [Washington, D.C., 1936] 88 numb. l.

GILES, LIONEL, 1875-   tr. A gallery of Chinese immortals; selected biographies tr. from Chinese sources by Lionel Giles. London, J. Murray [1948] 128 p. (The Wisdom of the East series).

GRANET, MARÇEL, 1884-1940. Danses et légendes de la Chine ancienne. Paris, F. Alcan, 1926. 2 v. fold. tables, diagrs. (Travaux de l'Année sociologique).

GRIFFIS, WILLIAM ELLIOT, 1843-1928. China's story in myth, legend, and annals. Rev. ed. With additional chapters by Arthur Walworth. Boston and New York, Houghton Mifflin, 1935. x, [3]-336 p. front., plates. 1st ed. 1922.

HAYES, L. NEWTON. The Chinese dragon, with an introduction by Fong F. Sec, 鄺富灼. Shanghai, Commercial Press, 1922. xvi, 66 p. illus. (incl.ports.).

HENTZ, CARL, 1883-   Mythes et symboles lunaires (Chine ancienne, civilisations anciennes de l'Asie, peuples limitrophes du Pacifique) Apendice en langue allemande par Herbert Kühn. Anvers, Éditions "De Sikkel," 1932. xiii, 2-251, [1] p. illus., XIV plates.

———. Tod, Auferstehung, Weltordnung; das mythische Bild im ältesten China, in den grossasiatischen und zirkumpazifischen Kulturen. Mit Beiträgen von Herman Lommel und Hilde Hoffmann. Zürich, Origo Verlag [c1955] 2 v. illus. plates.

KRIEG, CLAUS WERNER. Chinesische Mythen und Legenden. Nacherzählt von C. W. Krieg. Zürich, Fretz und Wasmuth, 1946. iv, 298 p. illus. plates.

KÜHN, ALFRED. Berichte über den Weltanfang bei den Indochinesen und ihren Nachbarvölkern; ein Beitrag zur Mythologie des Fernen Ostens. Leipzig, Kommissionsverlag O. Harrassowitz, 1935. 3-176 p.

LALOY, LOUIS, 1874-1944. Légende des immortels d'après les auteurs chinois. Paris, A. Messin, 1922. 108 p.

LEE, ANDRÉ. Légendes chinoises. Pékin, Impr. de la "Politique de Pékin," 1937. 124 p. illus. (Collection de la "Politique de Pékin").

MacKENZIE, DONALD ALEXANDER, 1873-1936. Myths of China and Japan. London, The Gresham Pub. Co.[1923] xvi, 404 p. col. front., plates.(Myth and legend in literature and art ).

MUNN, WILLIAM. Chinese heroes in legend and history. London, Church Missionary Society [1925] 94, [2] p. front., illus.(maps) plates, ports.

TAN, J.M. Légendes chinoises. Préface de l'Abbé A. Boland. Louvain, A. C. J.S., 1929. 126 p

VALLEREY, GISÈLE. Contes et légendes de Chine. Paris, F. Nathan, 1936;

nouv. éd. Neuchâtel, Delachaux et Niestle, 1946. 254 p. illus., col. plates. (Collection des contes et légendes de tous les pays ).

WANG, YATES, 王一之 Iconology of heart and mind.  心神表象  Leiden, A. W. Sijthoff, 1949. 94 p. illus.

WERNER, EDWARD THEODORE CHALMERS, 1864-   A dictionary of Chinese mythology. Shanghai, Kelly and Walsh, 1932. xvii, 627 p.

————. Myths and legends of China. With thirty-two illustrations in colors by Chinese artists. London, G. Harrap, 1922; New York, Farrar and Rinehart [1933]; New ed. 1956. 7-453, [1] p. col. front., col. plates. (The myths series ).

## Symbolism

KOEHN, ALFRED. Embroidered wishes.  Peking, Lotus Court, 1943.  46 p. illus.

————. Window flowers; symbolical silhouettes for the Chinese new year.  Peiping, Lotus Court, 1948.  [10], 50, [2] p. col. illus. port.

————. Chinese flower symbolism. Tokyo, 1955. 26 p. 21 prints.

LOEWENSTEIN, PRINCE JOHN. Swastika and Yin-Yang. London, China Society, 1942. 28 p. incl. front., illus. (China society Occasional papers. New ser., 1 ).

MORGAN, HARRY TITTERTON, 1872-   Chinese symbolism. Los Angeles, Calif., c1941. 16 p. illus. [His Chinese classics in miniature].

————. Chinese symbols and superstitions. 100 illustrations from the Chinese. South Pasadena, Calif., P. D. and Ione Perkins, 1942. 192 p. incl. front., illus. (incl. music).

[————.] Chinese symbolism and its associated beliefs. Los Angeles, Quon-Quon company, 1945. 20 p. illus. [His Chinese classics in miniature].

WILHELM II, German emperor, 1859-1941. Die chinesische Monade; ihre Geschichte und ihre Deutung. Leipzig, K. F. Koehler, 1934. 66 p. incl. illus. (incl. maps) plates. col. front., col. plates.

WILLIAMS, CHARLES ALFRED SPEED, 1884-   Outlines of Chinese symbolism and art motives; an alphabetical compendium of antique legends and beliefs, as reflected in the manners and customs of the Chinese. 2d rev. ed.  Shanghai, Kelly and Walsh, 1932. xxi, 468, [1] p. col. front., illus., col. plates.

## Social Institutions
## Family and Marriage

ADDISON, J. T. Chinese ancestor worship, a study of its meaning and its relations with Christianity. Shanghai, Church literature committee of the Chung Hua Sheng Kung Hui, 1925. [3], vi, 85 p.

CHANG, TING-CHANG, 張鼎昌. Le mariage et la situation de la femme mariée en Chine au premier quart du xxe siècle. Paris, Rousseau et cie, 1930. [7]-130 p. Thèse-Univ. de Paris.

CHUNG, WÊN-HUI, 陳鐘文會 1903-   The family revolution in Communist China. Lackland Air Force Base, Tex., Air Force Personnel and Training Research Center, Air Research and Development Command, 1955. xii, 65 p. ( [U.S.] Human Resources Research Institute. Research memorandum, no. 35 ).

COMBER, LEON. Chinese ancestor worship in Malaya. Singapore, Donald Moore 1954. 41 p. plates. (Malayan heritage books, 1 ).

FÊNG, HAN-YI, 馮漢驥, 1902-   The Chinese kinship system. Philadelphia, 1937. 141-275 p. diagrs. "Reprint from Harvard journal of Asiatic studies, 2:2.

FREEDMAN, MAURICE. Chinese family and marriage in Singapore. London, H. M. Stationery Off., 1957. 249 p. illus., tables. ( [Gt. Brit.] Colonial Office. Colonial research studies, 20 ).

FRIED, MORTON HERBERT, 1923-   Kin and non-kin in Chinese society; an analysis of extra-kin relationships in Chinese society, with special reference to a selected community - Ch'u Hsien. Ann Arbor, University Microfilms, 1951. ( [University Microfilms, Ann Arbor, Mich.] Publication no. 2813 ). Collation of the original: ii, 281 l. illus., diagrs. Thesis-Columbia University.

——. Fabric of Chinese society; a study of the social life of a Chinese county seat. New York, Praeger [1953]; London, Atlantic Press, 1956. 243 p. map, diagrs.

GRANET, MARCEL, 1884-1940. Catégories matrimoniales et relations de proximité dans la Chine ancienne. Paris, F. Alcan, 1939. 254 p. diagrs. (part col.) (Bibliothèque de philosophie contemporaine ).

HAENISCH, ERICH, 1880-   Die Heiligung des Vater-und Fürstennamens in China, ihre ethischre Begründung und ihre Bedeutung in Lieben und Schriftum. Leipzig, S. Hirzel, 1932. 20 p. plates. (Sächsische Akademie der Wissenschaften zu Leipzig. Bericht über die Verhandlungen. Phil-hist. Kl. Bd. 84, Hft. 4 ).

HIGHBAUGH, IRMA, 1891-   Family life in west China. New York, Agricultural Missions, 1948. xi, 240 p.

HSIAO CHING, 孝經. Book of Filial Piety, copied and illustrated by Chao Meng-fu, 趙孟頫. Kowloon, H.K., Chi Sheng Book Co., 1956. 27 1 facim. 42 l.

HU, HSIEN-CHIN, 胡先晉, 1910-   The common descent group in China and its functions. New York, 1948. 204 p. illus. (Viking Fund publications in anthropology, 10 ).

KOEHN, ALFRED. Piété filiale en Chine. Peking, Lotus Court, 1943. 24 p.

——. Filial devotion in China. 2nd ed. Peking, Lotus Court, 1944. 24 l. Translation of the Erh-shih-ssu-hsiao 二十四孝 [24 examples of Filial Devotion] by Kuo chü-ching, 郭居敬 .

LANG, OLGA. Chinese family and society. New Haven, Yale University Press; London, G. Cumberlege, Oxford University Press, 1946. xv, [1], [3]-395 p. incl. tables.

——. La vie en Chine. Traduction de Aline Chalufour. [Paris] Hachette [1950] 287 p. (La Vie quotidienne).

LEVY, MARION JOSEPH, 1918-   The family revolution in modern China. Issued in coöperation with the Institute of Pacific Relations. Cmabridge, Harvard Univ. Press, 1949. xvi, 390 p.

LIN, TSIU-SEN, 林秋生 . Familienleben in China. Erlenbach-Zürich, E. Rentsch [c1943] 33 p. (on double leaves) (Schriften des Chinesischen Kultur-Dienstes).

LIN, YAO-HUA, 林耀華, 1910-   The golden wing, a sociological study of Chinese familism. London, K. Paul [1948] xv, 234 p. geneal. table. (International library of sociology and social reconstruction).

PON, SIAN, 彭襄. Le mariage pendant la période Tch'ouen ts'ieou. Paris, Lipschutz, 1936. 176 p. Thèse-Univ. de Lyon.

ROHNER, JOANNES. Die Kinderverlobung in China. Eine ethischrechtliche Untersuchung. Rome, Pontificia universitas gregoriana, 1951. 79 p.

SCHMITT, ERICH, 1893-   Die Grundlagen der chinesischen Ehe. Eine historisch-ethnographische Studie auf Grund des Gesetzbuchs der T'ang-Dynastie und Mandschu-Dynastie sowie ausgewählter Klassischer und philosophischer Literatur. Leipzig, Deutsche morganländische Gesellschaft, 1927. 223 p.

SCHRAM, LOUIS, 1883-   Le mariage chez les t'ou-jen du Kan-sou (Chine). Changhai, Impr. de la mission catholique, 1932. x, 189 p. 12 plates. (Variétés sinologiques, 58 ).

SIÉ, TON-FA, 謝東發. L'évolution psychologique et sociale de la famille en Chine. Le passé et le present. Boulogne-sur-Seine, Impr. d'études sociales et politiques, 1926. 31 p.

SOOTHILL, WILLIAM EDWARD, 1861-1935. The hall of light; a study of early Chinese kingship, edited by Lady Hosie and G. F. Hudson. London, Lutterworth

Press [1951] xxii, 289 p. illus., ports. (Lutterworth library, v. 38. Missionary research series, 18 ).

SU, SING GING, 徐聲金, 1892- The Chinese family system. New York, Columbia University, 1922. 109 p. Thesis-Columbia University.

WANG, TSE-SIN, 王自新. Le divorce en Chine. Paris, Les Éditions Domat-Montchrestien, 1932. iii, 267 p. fold. plates. (Institut de droit comparé. Études de sociologie et d'ethnologie juridiques. XV ). Thèse-Univ. de Paris, under title: Le divorce en droit chinois.

WILKINSON, HIRAM PARKES, 1866-1935. The family in classical China. Shanghai, Kelly and Walsh; London, Macmillan, 1926. 239 p. fold. geneal tables.

WU, PAO-AN, 吳保安, 1913- Kinship and law in feudal China; an inquiry into the nature of kinship and law in feudal China in the light of a comparison with kinship and law in feudal Europe. Cambridge, 1946. 227 p. Thesis-Harvard University.

YANG, CHING-KUN, 楊慶堃 , 1910- The Chinese family in the Communist revolution. [Cambridge, Center for International Studies, Massachusetts Institute of Technology, 1954] 373 l.

## Women in Traditional China

DAN, MRS. PAO TCHAO, 唐寶潮夫人. Hsiang Fei, 香妃. A love story of the Emperor Ch'ien Lung, by Madame Dan Pao Tchao, née Princess Shou Shan. Peiping, printed by the You Lien Press, 1934. 51 p. ports.

GRANTHAM, ALEXANDRA ETHELDRED, 1867- The twilight hour of Yang Kuei-fei, 楊貴妃; a dramatic poem in one act. Shanghai, Kelly and Walsh, 1923. 56 p.

HIBBERT, MRS. ELOISE TALCOTT. Embroidered gauze; portraits of famous Chinese ladies. London, John Lane [1938]; New York, E. P. Dutton, 1941. 332 p. front., plates, ports.

[HSI YUEN], 息園. Galerie des femmes vertueuses de la Chine; traduit par S. T. Wang. Pékin, la "Politique de Pékin," 1924. 118 p. illus. (Collection de la "Politique de Pékin").

HU, PING-SA, 朱胡彬夏 1886-1931. The women of old China; a review of the position of women in ancient China. Peiping, The Peking Leader, 1929. 10 p. (Peking Leader reprints, 45 ).

HUANG, SHU-CH'IUNG, 伍黄淑瓊 "MRS. WU LIEN-TEH." The most famous beauty of China; the story of Yang Kuei-fei. New York, D. Appleton, 1924. xv, 116, [1] p. mounted col. front., plates (part mounted, col.).

——. Yang Kuei-fei, the most famous beauty of China. London, Brentano [1924] xv, 103, [1] p. col. front., plates (part col.).

——. Hsi Shih, 西施, (pronounced See-she) beauty of beauties ( a romance of ancient China about 495-472 B.C.) Shanghai, Kelly and Walsh, 1931. xvi, 116 p. incl. col. front., illus. plates (part col.).

——. Chao Chün, 昭君 , beauty in exile. Shanghai, Kelly and Walsh, 1934. xvi, 168 p. col. mounted front., illus., plates (part col. mounted).

——. Tchao Kiun [Chao Chün], héroïne chinoise à la cour tartare avant l'ère Chrétienne. Traduit de l'anglais par Magdeline Cluzel. Avec une préface de Li Yu-ying, 李煜瀛. Versions rythmiques de Guillot de Saix. Paris, Gustave Paul Maisonneuve, 1939. 222 p. plates.

IMBERT, HENRI. Si-cheu, 西施, la Vénus chinoise; chansons traduites par Henri Imbert. Pékin, La Politique de Pékin, 1921. [6], 15 p. illus.(Collection de la "Politique de Pékin").

——. Les concubines chinoises célèbres, Pan Tsié-yu, 班嫟妤 et Tchao-kiun, 昭君; chansons traduites par Henri Imbert. Pékin, La "Politique de Pékin," 1921. 16 p. illus. (Collection de la "Politique de Pékin").

LIN, J. B. tr. La merveilleuse histoire de Pao-Se, 褒姒. [Conte chinois] Paris, G. Servant [1925] 58 p. col. plates.

MAO, HSIANG, 冒襄, 1611-93. The reminiscences of Tung Hsiao-wan, 董小宛
[ (影梅庵憶語) ] by Mao P'i-chiang,冒辟疆 ; translated into English by Pan
Tze-yen, 潘子延(Z. Q. Parker). Shanghai, Commercial Press, 1931. xv,
159 p.

O'HARA, ALBERT RICHARD, 1907-   The position of woman in early China according to the Lieh nü chuan, 列女傳, "The biographies of eminent Chinese
women." Washington, D. C., The Catholic University of America Press,
1945. xii, 301 p. (The Catholic University of America. Studies in sociology,
v. 16 ). 1947. 341 p. Thesis-Catholic University of America.

OLSCHAK, BLANCHE CHRISTINE. Frauen um den Drachenthron; Verführung
und Macht im Schicksal Chinas. Olten, Walter-Verlag [1956] 258 p. illus.
plates, map.

PANKING. Hsiang Fei, 香妃, la "Concubine Parfumée." Pékin, Impr. de la
"Politique de Pékin," 1922. 44 p. illus. (Collection de la "Politique de Pékin").

———. Galerie des femmes célèbres de la Chine. Pékin, Impr. de la "Politique
de Pékin," 1924. 79 p. illus. (Collection de la "Politique de Pékin").

SOULIÉ, CHARLES GEORGES, 1878-   La passion of Yang Kwé-feï, favorite
impériale, d'après les anciens textes chinois, par George Soulié de Morant.
Paris, L'Édition d'art [c1924] ix, [1], 201, [1] p. plates. ["Épopées et légendes"].

———. The passion of Yang Kwei-fei; from ancient Chinese texts, by George
Soulié de Morant; rendered into English by H. Bedford-Jones. New York,
Covici, Friede, 1928. 200 p.

SWANN, NANCY LEE, 1881-   Pan Chao, 班超, foremost woman scholar of
China, first century A. D.; background, ancestry, life, and writings of the
most celebrated Chinese woman of letters. New York, London, The Century
[c1932] xix, 179 p. incl. maps, geneal. tables, front., plates. Thesis-Columbia University.

WIMSATT, GENEVIEVE BLANCHE. The bright concubine and lesser luminaries;
tales of fair and famous ladies of China. Boston, J. W. Luce [c1928] xxi,
204 p. front., plates.

———. Apricot cheeks and almond eyes. New York, Columbia University Press,
1939. xviii, 123 p. front., plates, ports., facsim.

———. A well of fragrant waters, 浣花溪, a sketch of the life and writings of
Hung Tu, 薛濤 (洪度). Boston, John W. Luce [1945] 7-102 p. front.(port.)
facsim.

## Women in Modern China

[ALL-CHINA DEMOCRATIC WOMEN'S FEDERATION]. Women in new China.
Peking, Foreign Languages Press, 1949. 55 p. illus.

———. Chinese women in 1950. Peking, 1950. 71 p. illus.

———. Women in China to-day. Peking, Foreign Languages Press, 1952. 10
pts. in 1 v. illus. ports.

———. From struggle to victory; sketches of the fighting women of New China.
[2d ed. Peking, 1952] 112 p. ports.

———. Women of China. Peking, 1954. cover-title, 40 p. illus.(part fold.).

[———.] Femmes chinoises d'aujourd'hui. Pékin, Éditions en langues étrangères,
1954. 95 p. illus.

AYSCOUGH, FLORENCE (WHEELOCK) 1878-1942. Chinese women, yesterday
and to-day. Boston, Houghton Mifflin company, 1937; London, J. Cape,
1938. xiv, 324 p. illus. (incl. plan) 2 ports., (incl. front.).

BULLE, MIL'DA OTTOVNA. Leben und Kampf der chinesischen Arbeiterinnen
und Bäuerinnen. Übers. von Tranbenberg. Moskau, Verlagsgenossenschaft
Ausländischer Arbeiter, 1932. 39 p.

———. Chinese toiling women; how they are helping the Chinese soviets. Moscow, Co-operative Publishing Society of Foreign Workers in the USSR, 1933. 31 p. "Originally published by Modern books, London."

CH'EN, SOPHIA H.,任陳衡哲. The Chinese woman, and four other essays. 2nd ed. Peiping, 1934. ii, 100, [1] p.

CHENG, HSIU, 程琇, 1904-    La situation en droit privé de la femme chinois envisagée dans son évolution historique. Nancy, Impr. Bailly et Wettstein, 1935. 198 p. Thèse-Univ. de Nancy.

CHENG, SHOU-LIN, 鄭壽麟. Chinesische Frauengestalten; mit einem Vorwort von Bruno Schindler; illustriert von R. Hadl. Laipzig, Verlag der Asia major, 1926. 9-133 p. plates.

COOPER, ELISABETH (BEAVER), 1877-1945. My lady of the Chinese courtyard. Being a sequel to The letters of a Chinese lady. London, P. Davies, 1926. 126 p. plates, col. port. 1st ed. New York, 1914; London, 1920.

———. Dames de Chine; lettres d'un grande dame chinoise, adaptées d'après la version anglaise par Jeanne Foltz. Lausanne, Éditions Spes, 1931. iv, 139 p. illus.

DOCUMENTS of the women's movement of China. Peking, New China Women's Press, 1950. 46 p.

ESKELUND, KARL, 1917 or 18-    My Chinese wife, illustrated by Hans Bendix. Garden City, N.Y., Garden City Pub. Co. [1946] 247 p. illus.

FISHER, MRS. WELTHY (HONSINGER) 1880-    A string of Chinese pearls; ten tales of Chinese girls ancient and modern. New York, N.Y., Womans Press [1924] 3-187 p. illus.

FRICK, JOHANN. Die sozial-religiöse Stellung der Frau in Tsinghai. Wien, 1955. vii, 200 p. plates, map. Diss.-Univ. Wien.

GRISAR, ELIZABETH. La femme en Chine. Paris, Corrêa, 1957. 256 p. plates.

HOSIE, DOROTHEA (SOOTHILL) lady, 1885-    Portrait of a Chinese lady and certain of her contemporaries. New York, W. Morrow, 1930; London, Hodder and Stoughton, 1931. 404 p. front., plates, ports.

HSIEH, PING-YING, 謝冰瑩. Autobiography of a Chinese girl; a genuine autobiography. Translated into English with an introduction by Tsui Chi, 崔驥. With a preface by Gordon Bottomley. London, G. Allen and Unwin [1943] 216 p. front. (port.) illus. (facsims.).

———. Girl rebel, the autobiography of Hsieh Ping-ying, with extracts from her New war diaries; translated by Adet, 林如斯, and Anor Lin, 林無雙; with an introduction by Lin Yutang. New York, John Day [c1940] xviii, 270 p. incl. front.(facsim.) ports.

HSÜ, CHUNG-P'EI,朱徐鍾珮, 1917-    The position of women in Free China. Chinese women show their mettle in the arts. Taipei, China Culture Pub. Foundation, 1953. 18 p. (Pamphlets on Chinese affairs).

KOO, HUI-LAN (OEI), 顧黃蕙蘭. Hui-lan Koo [Madame Wellington Koo] an autobiography as told to Mary Van Rensselaer Thayer. New York, Dial Press [1943] vi, 421 p.

LOO, YU, 羅玉. La morale féminine en Chine à l'époque des Ming (1368-1644) Paris, Jouve et Cie, 1932. 153 p. Thèse-Univ. de Paris.

MARQUART, JAKOB. Die Frau in Schantung. Bilder aus Vergangenheit und Gegenwart. Ein Beitrag zur Volkskunde Chinas. Tsingtau, Missionsdruckerei Tsingtau, 1932. ix, [1], 93 p. illus.

MILLER, I.L. The Chinese girl, translated from the original manuscript in Russian by E. de Laberbis. Tientsin, 1932. ˙108 p. front., ports.

OEHLER-HEIMERDINGER, ELISABETH, 1884-    Der Weg der Ho moi; Lebensschicksale chinesischer Frauen. Stuttgart und Basel, Evang. Missionsverlag [1932] 46 p. illus.

SPICER, EVA DYKES. Chinese women and the war. Chungking, The China Information Committee [1940)] cover-title, 27, [1] p.

TCHENG, SOUMAY, 甤鄭毓秀, 1891-    Souvenirs d'enfance et de révolution.

Transcrits par B. Van Vorst. Paris, Payot, 1921. 255 p.

────. My revolutionary years, the autobiography of Madame Wei Tao-ming. New York, C. Scribner's, 1943. vi, 238 p.

TÊNG, YING-CH'AO, 周鄧潁超, 1902-  The women's movement in New China. [Peking] All China Democratic Women's Federation, 1952. 25 p. illus.

────. Women of China build for peace; report made at the reception in honor of the women delegates to the Peace Conference of the Asian and Pacific regions. [Peking] All-China Democratic Women's Federation, 1952. 26 p. illus.

VAN VORST, BESSIE (McGINNIS), 1875-  A girl from China (Soumay Tcheng). New York, Frederick A. Stokes, 1926. xi, 249 p.

WALN, NORA, 1895-  The street of precious pearls. New York, Womans Press, 1921. 96 p.

WANG, CH'ANG-PAO, 王長寶. La femme dans la société chinoise, sa situation sociale, civile et politique. Lettre-préf. de Mme. C. Brunschvicg, préf. de Georgette Ciselet. Paris, A. Pedone, 1933. xi, 252 p.

WOMEN and the way; Christ and the world's womanhood, a symposium by Madame Chiang Kai-shek, Mrs. Z. K. Matthews, Tsêng Pao-swen, 曾寶蓀, [and others]. New York, Friendship Press [c1938] xvii 198 p.

WOMEN of China. London, British United Aid to China, 1946. 16 p. illus.

WONG, SU-LING, 王淑玲. Daughter of Confucius, a personal history by Wong Su-ling and Earl Herbert Cressy. New York, Farrar, Straus and Young [1952] 381 p.

────. Töchter des Konfuzius. Geschichte eines Patrizier-Familie im China zwischen Gestern und Morgen, von Wong Su-ling und Earl Herbert Cressy. Ubers. von Susanna Rademacher. Hamburg, Kruger, 1954. 384 p.

YANG, BUWEI, 趙楊步偉, 1889-  Autobiography of a Chinese woman. English by Yuenren Chao. New York, John Day, 1947. xvi, 327 p. illus.(incl. music), plates, ports., maps.

## Secret Societies

FAVRE, BENOÎT, 1874-  Les sociétés secrètes en Chine; origine-rôle historique-situation actuelle, par le lieutenant-colonel B. Favre. Paris, G. P. Maisonneuve, 1933. [7]-222 p.

GLICK, CARL, 1890-  Swords of silence; Chinese secret societies, past and present, 洪門歷史, by Carl Glick and Hong Sheng-hwa, 洪聲華. New York, Whittlesey House [1947] xi, 292 p. front.

SCHLEGEL, GUSTAAF, 1840-1903. Thian ti hwui, 天地會. The Hung-league or Heaven-earth-league. A secret society with the Chinese in China and India. With an introduction and numerous cuts and illustrations. Batavia, Lange and Co., 1866; Reprint ed. 1957. [v]-xl, 253 p. illus., plates.

U.S. Office of Strategic Services. Research and Analysis Branch. Political implications of Chinese secret societies. Washington, 1945. 55 p. (Its R and A No. 2254).

WARD, JOHN SEBASTIAN MARLOW, 1885-  The Hung society, or, the Society of Heaven and Earth, by J. S. M. Ward and W. G. Stirling. London, Baskerville Press, 1925-26. 3 v. col. fronts., illus., plates (part col.) facsims. (part col.) diagrs.

## Slavery

BAUDRIT, ANDRÉ, 1896-  Bétail humain; rapt, vente, infanticide dans l'Indochine française et dans la Chine du Sud. 2. éd. Saigon [Société des imprimeries et librairies indochinoises] 1942 [i.e. 1943] 211 p. plates.

ERKES, EDUARD, 1891-  Das Problem der Sklaverei in China. Unveränderter Nachdruck. Berlin, Akademie-Verlag, 1954. 30 p. (Berichte über die Verhandlungen der Sächsischen Akademie der Wissenschaften zu Leipzig. Phil-

Hist. Kl. Bd. 100, Heft 1 ).
PIPPON, ANTON, 1909-   Beitrag zum chinesischen Sklavensystem, nebst einer Übersetzung des "Chung kuo nu pei chih tu" (Das Sklavensystem Chinas) von Wang Shih Chieh, 王世杰　中國女婢制度. Eine juristisch-soziologische Darstellung, von Toni Pippon.  Tokyo, Deutsche Gesellschaft für Natur-und Völkerkunde Ostasiens, 1936. iii-iv, 140 (i.e. 139) p. ("Mitteilungen" der Deutschen gesellschaft für natur- und völkerkunde Ostasiens. bd. XXIX, t. B).

## Social Surveys
## General Works

BATES, MINER SEARLE. The Nanking population: employment, earnings and expenditures; a survey conducted on behalf of the Nanking International Relief Committee, winter-spring, 1939. [Shanghai, Printed by the Mercury Press, 1939] cover-title, 32 p.

BURGESS, JOHN STEWART, 1883-1949. The guilds of Peking. New York, Columbia University Press; London, P.S. King, 1928. 270 p. (Studies in history, economics, and public law, no. 308 ).

BURNS, CECIL DELISLE, 1879-1942. Standard of living in China and Japan. An essay on policy. Prepared for the 4th bi-annual conference of the Institute of Pacific Relations to be held at Hangchow, 1931. London, Royal Institute of International Affairs, 1931. 22 numb. l.

DICKINSON, JEAN. Observations on the social life of a North China village (Chien Ying, Wu Ch'ing Hsien) Oct. -Dec. 1924. Peiping, 1928. 45 p. (Yenching University, Dept. of Sociology and Social Work, Publ. ser. C, 4 ).

GAMBLE, SIDNEY DAVID, 1890-   Peking, a social survey conducted under the auspices of the Princeton University center in China and the Peking Young men's Christian association. Foreword by G. Sherwood Eddy and Robert A. Woods.  New York, George H. Doran [c1921] xxiii, 25-538 p. front., illus. (plans) plates, diagrs.

————. The household accounts of two Chinese families.  New York, China Institute in America [c1931] cover-title, 23 p. tables.

————. How Chinese families live in Peiping; a study of the income and expenditure of 283 Chinese families receiving from $8 to $550 silver per month. Field work in charge of Wang Ho-ch'en, 王賀宸, and Liang Jen-ho, 粱人和. New York and London, Funk and Wagnalls, 1933. xvii, 348 p. front., illus. (incl. plan) plates, diagrs.

————. Ting Hsien, a North China rural community. Foreword by Y.C. James Yen, 宴陽初. Field work directed by Franklin Ching-han Lee, 李景漢. New York, International Secretariat, Institute of Pacific Relations, 1954. xxv, 472 p. illus., map.

LEE, FRANKLIN CHING-HAN, 李景漢, 1895-   Village families in the vicinity of Peiping, by F.C.H. Lee and T. Chin, 秦瓚. Peiping, Social Research Department, China Foundation, 1929. 65 p. (Its Bull., 2 ).

MENG, TIEN-PEI, 孟天培. Prices, wages and the standard of living in Peking, 1900-24 by Tien-pei Meng and Sidney D. Gamble. Peking, Peking Express Press [1926] 113 p. incl. tables, illus. (charts).

MILAM, AVA BERTHA, 1884-   A study of the student homes of China, with a foreword by Timothy Tingfang Lew, 劉廷芳. New York, Teachers College, Columbia University, 1930. viii, 98 p. (Studies of the International institute of Teachers College, Columbia University, 10 ).

SMYTHE, LEWIS STRONG CASEY, 1901-   War damage in the Nanking area, December, 1937 to March, 1938. Urban and rural surveys on behalf of the Nanking International Relief Committee, completed June, 1938. [Shanghai, Printed by the Mercury Press, 1938] v, 31, [33] l. incl. tables, fold. maps.

T'AO, L.K., 陶孟和, 1887-   Livelihood in Peking; an analysis of the budgets of sixty families. Peking, Social Research Department, China Foundation,

1928.   158, xxii p. incl. tables, forms. (Social research publications).

------.  The standard of living among Chinese workers. Preliminary paper prepared for the 4th biennial conference of the Institute of Pacific Relations to
be held in Hangchow, from October 21 to November 4, 1931. Shanghai, China
Institute of Pacific Relations, 1931.  37 p. incl. tables.

WOO, TOH, 吳鐸. An analysis of 2,330 case work records of the Social Service
department of the Peking Union Medical College.  Peiping, Institute of Social
Research, 1931.   20 p. (Its Bull., 5 ).

YANG, CHING-KUN, 楊慶堃, 1910-   A Chinese village and its early change
under communism.  Cambridge, Center for International Studies, Massachusetts Institute of Technology, 1954.  cover-title, 375 l.

YANG, MARTIN C., 楊懋春, [Yang Mou Ch'un] 1904-   A Chinese village: Tai-
tou, Shantung province.  New York, Columbia University Press, 1945; London, K. Paul, 1948.  xvii, 275 p. illus.(incl. maps, plans) diagr.

YENCHING UNIVERSITY, Peiping. Dept. of Sociology and Social Work. Study of
a typical Chinese town. What survey revealed in Ching Ho, North China, which
was taken as example, undertaken under the auspices of the Department of Sociology, Yenching University and reported by Leonard S. Hsü. Peiping, The
Leader Press, 1929.  16 p.

------.  Ching Ho, a sociological analysis: the report of a preliminary survey of
the town of Ching Ho, North China.  Peiping, Department of Sociology and
Social Work, Yenching University, 1930.  iii, ii, 146 p. incl. forms, tables,
illus.(charts) (Social Research ser., 1 ).

## New Life Movement

CHIANG, KAI-SHEK, 1886-   Outline of the New life movement. Translated by
Madame Chiang Kai-shek.  Nanch'ang, The Association for the Promotion
of the New Life Movement, 1930.  14 p.

------.  Chapters on national fecundity, social welfare, education, and health and
happiness. Written as supplements to Dr. Sun Yat-sen's lectures on The principle of people's livelihood. Rendered into English by Durham S. F. Chen, 陳
石孚.  Taipei, China Cultural Service [1952?] 107 p.

CHIU, CHENG-HO, 丘正歐. Le Mouvement de la vie nouvelle en Chine.  Paris,
Impr. R. Foulon, 1941.  [7]-142 p. Thèse-Univ. de Paris.

SOONG, MAYLING, 1897-   The new life movement in China, tr. by Madame
Chiang Kai-shek. [Calcutta] Calcutta Office, Chinese Ministry of Information, 1942.  cover-title, 19 p. port. (Pamphlet no. 1 ).

------.  La vie nouvelle.  Chungking, La Correspondant chinois, 1941. cover-title, 16 p.

## Crimes

[BARUCH, HUGO] 1907-   Chicago-Schanghai; Gangster in besonderer Verwendung, von Jack Bilbo ]pseud. ].  Berlin, Universitas [c1932] 221, [1] p.

BERTRAM, HANS, 1906-   Ruf der weiten Welt.  Berlin, Drei Masken Verlag
[c1937] 230, [1] p. plates, ports.

CHINA. Commission on Extraterritoriality. Chinese prisons (with plans and illustrations) Pub. by the Commission on Extraterritoriality.  Peking, 1925.
130 p. plates, 7 fold. plans, tables, form.

GEE, NATHANIEL GIST, 1876-1937. A class of social outcasts; notes on the
beggars in China.  Peking, Peking Leader Press, 1925.  30 p. (Peking leader reprints, 1 ).

GLASSPOOLE, RICHARD, 1788-1846. Mr. Glasspoole and the Chinese pirates;
being the narrative of Mr. Richard Glasspoole of the ship Marquis of Ely:
describing his captivity of eleven weeks and three days whilst held for ransom by the villainous ladrones of the China sea in the year 1809: together

with extracts from the China records and the log of the Marquis of Ely: and some remarks on Chinese pirates, ancient and modern, by Owen Rutter: and four engravings on wood by Robert Gibbings. [London] Golden Cockerel Press, 1935.  57, [1] p. front.

HOWARD, HARVEY JAMES, 1880-1956. Ten weeks with Chinese bandits, with illustrations from sketches and photographs by the author. New York, Dodd, Mead, 1926; Sydney, Cornstalk Pub. Co., 1927. xiv, 272 p. front., illus., plates, ports., facsim.

————. Zehn wochen bei chinesischen Banditen. Aus dem Englischen von Lothar Tobias. Leipzig, Brockhaus, 1930. 159 p.

LAMSON, HERBERT DAY, 1899-   Social pathology in China; a source book for the study of problems of livelihood, health, and the family. Shanghai, Commercial Press, 1934. xviii, 607 p.

LILIUS, ALEKO E. I sailed with Chinese pirates. London, Arrowsmith [1930] 245 p. front., plates, ports.

MATIGNON, JEAN JACQUES, 1866-   La Chine hermétique; superstitions, crime et misère (souvenirs de biologie sociale). Nouv. éd. Paris, Paul Geuthner, 1936. xx, 397 p. 42 plates (incl. facsims.) on 21 l.

PAWLEY, MRS. EDITH MURIEL (PHILLIPS) 1913-   My bandit hosts, by Tinko Pawley as told to Joy Packer. London, S. Paul [1935] 288 p. front., plates, facsim.

YEN, CHING-YUEH, 嚴景耀, 1905-   Crime in relation to social change in China. [Chicago, 1934] [1], 298-308 p. ''Reprinted from American journal of sociology, 11:3, November 1934.''

Labor Problems
General Works

ANDERSON, ADELAIDE MARY, 1863-1936. Humanity and labour in China; an industrial visit and its sequel (1923 to 1926). London, Student Christian Movement, 1928. xv, 285 p. front., plates, 7 ports. on 1 plate.

ARNOLD, JULEAN HERBERT, 1875-1946. Labor and industrial conditions in China, by Julean Arnold and William H. Gale. Washington, Govt. Print. Off., 1922. ii, 17 p. ( [U.S.] Bureau of foreign and domestic commerce. Trade information bull., 75 ).

CH'EN, TA, 陳達, 1896-   The labor movement in China. Peking, Peking Leader Press, 1927. cover-title, 30 p. (Peking leader reprints, 30 ).

CHINA. Ministry of Social Affairs. The social policies of China: population policy, labor policy, agrarian policy, social security policy. Nanking, 1947. 15 p.

CHINA FORUM. Five years of Kuomintang reaction; ed. by Harold R. Isaacs. Shanghai [China Forum Pub. Co.] 1932. 136 p. front., plates, map. ''Reprinted from the special May edition of the China Forum.''

EPSTEIN, ISRAEL, 1915-   Notes on labor problems in Nationalist China, with a supplement by Julian R. Friedman. New York, International Secretariat, Institute of Pacific Relations, 1949. viii, 159 p.

FANG, FU-AN, 房福安. Chinese labour; an economic and statistical survey of the labour conditions and labour movements in China. With the recent labour laws promulgated by the National government, introduction by Chen Ta. Shanghai, Kelly and Walsh, 1931. 185 p. plates, fold. tables.

FRIEDLANDER, LILIAN M. Child workers in China. Honolulu, 1927. 20 p. (Institute of Pacific Relations preliminary paper for 2nd general session, 1927 ).

GT. BRIT. Foreign Office. Papers respecting labour conditions in China. London, H. M. Stationery Off., 1925. 130 p. (China no. 1 (1925) ).

————. Memorandum on labour conditions in China. February 25, 1927. London, H. M. Stationery Off., 1927. 25 p. (China, no. 2 (1927) ).

HINDER, ELEANOR M. Life and labour in Shanghai, a decade of labour and social administration in the International settlement. New York, International

Secretariat, Institute of Pacific Relations, 1944. viii, 143 p.

INDUSTRIAL health in Shanghai, China. Shanghai, Chinese Medical Association [1935-37] 4 v. plates, tables (part fold.) diagrs. (Chinese medical association. Special report series no. 4, 6, 7, 9 ).

LATTIMORE, ELEANOR (HOLGATE) 1895-   Labor unions in the Far East. New York, American Council, Institute of Pacific Relations, 1945. 56 p.

LIANG, YUNG-CHANG, 梁永章, 1912-   The Kuomintang and the Chinese work-·er. Taipei, China Cultural Service [1954] 42 p. (Pamphlets on Kuomintang affairs ).

LIM, HY-SOON, 林熙春. La question ouvrière en Chine. Nancy, Poncelet, 1931. 160 p. Thèse-Univ. de Nancy.

LOWE, CHUAN-HUA, 駱傳華, 1902-   Facing labor issues in China. With introductions by Chen Kung-po, 陳公博, and Julean Arnold. London, G. Allen and Unwin [1934] v-xv, 211 p.

MA, CH'AO-CHÜN, 馬超俊, 1886-   History of the labor movement in China. Translated by Peter Min Chi Liang, 梁明致. Taipei, China Cultural Service, 1955.   169 p.

PU, SHOU-CH'ANG, 庸壽昌, 1921-   Labor policy in China. Cambridge, 1944. 191 p. Thesis-Harvard University.

[SNOW, HELEN (FOSTER) ] 1907-   The Chinese labor movement [by] Nym Wales [pseud.] New York, John Day [1945] xi, 235 p. illus.(map).

SOH, CHUAN-PAO, 束金保 , [Shu Chuan-pao]. La situation de l'ouvrier industriel en Chine. Gembloux, Impr. J. Duculot, 1937. 207, [1] p. (Université de Louvain. École des sciences politiques et sociales. [Collection] ).

TSING CHIN-CHUN, 曾錦春, [Tsêng Chin-chun]. Le mouvement ouvrier en Chine. Paris, P. Geuthner, 1929. 176 p. (Université de Lyon. Bibliotheca franco-sinica lugdunensis. Etudes et documents publiés par l'Institut franco-chinois de Lyon, t. VII ).

TSO, SHIH KAN SHELDON, 祝世康. The labor movement in China. Shanghai, Commercial Press, 1928. iv, 230 p.

U.S. Bureau of Foreign and Domestic Commerce (Dept. of Commerce). Industrial conditions in China. Washington, Govt. Print. Off., 1922. ii, 7 p. incl. tables. (Trade information bull., 61).

WANG, SIMINE, 王錫民 , [Wang Hsi-min]. Le travail industriel des femmes et des enfants en Chine,   中國婦女童工. Préface de m. Émile Vandervelde. Paris, A. Pedone, 1933. vi, 298 p. incl. tables.

WOU, MON-PENG, 吳孟班. L'évolution des corporations ouvrières et commerciales dans la Chine contemporaine; préface de Kao Lou. Paris, Paul Geuthner, 1931. [7]-299 p.

WOU, P., 吳本中, 1904-   Les travailleurs chinois et la grande guerre, 華工與 歐戰之關係. Préface de m. Marius Moutet. Paris, A. Pedone, 1939. 36 p.

## Legislation

ALLMAN, NORWOOD FRANCIS, 1893-   tr. China's National factory law (English and Chinese texts) promulgated by the National government, December 30, 1929; translation by N.F. Allman and Lowe Chuan-hua. Shanghai, China Weekly Review [1930] cover-title, 11, [10] p.

CHANG, LÉON Y., 張隆延. La législation du travail en Chine. Nancy, Impr. G. Thomas, 1936. [7]-137 p. Thèse-Univ. de Nancy.

CH'EN, TA, 陳達, 1896-   A study of the applicability of the factory act of the Chinese government. A preliminary survey of the Shanghai area. Shanghai, China Institute of Scientific Mangaement, 1931. 91 p. incl. tables, forms.

KOO, PING YUEN, 顧炳元 , ed. China's labor laws, 1929-35, promulgated by the National government; Chinese text with English translation. Shanghai, Commercial Press, 1935. xiii, 156 p.; 144 p.

KOUNG SHIEN-MING, 鞏賢明. Comment remédier à la situation tragique des

travailleurs chinois, une assurance sociale appropriée à la Chine. [Louvain,
E. Desbarax] 1927. [7]-254, [5] p. (Université de Louvain. École des sciences politiques et sociales. Collection ).

LAMB, JEFFERSON D.H., 林東海, [Lin Tung-hai] 1895-   The origin and development of social legislation in China. Edited by Maxwell S. Stewart. [Pe-
king, 1930] 73 p. (Publication of the Department of sociology and social work,
Yenching university, ser. C, no. 24, March 1, 1930 ).

————. The labour movement and labour legislation in China. Shanghai, China
United Press, 1933. xii, 252 p. (China united press ser., [4] ).

THANG, LE-VAN. L'oeuvre de l'Organisation International du Travail en Asie.
Marseille, Université de Marseille, 1932. 176 p.

WAGNER, AUGUSTA BERTHA, 1895-   Labor legislation in China. Peking,
Yenching University, 1938. iii, 301 p.

## Wages and Working Conditions

ARNDT, PAUL, 1870-   Der Arbeitslohn in China, von Paul Arndt, Djini Shen,
沈覲宜, und Chü-fen Lo, 羅巨份. Leipzig, Hans Buske Verlag, 1937. xii,
352 p. incl. tables.

LIN, SUNG-HO, 林頌河. Factory workers in Tangku. Peping, Social Research
Department, China Foundation, 1928. x, 128 p. incl. tables. plates.(Social
research publications).

LIU, HSIN-CHUAN, 劉心銓. Labor conditions in Chunghsing coal mine, Shantung. Peiping, Institute of Social Research, 1933. 45 p. (Its Bull., 7 ).

LOU, YEE-WEN, 盧郁文. Les œuvres sociales dans les chemins de fer chinois.
Paris, Bossuet, 1937. [11]-135, [1] p. illus.(map). Thèse-Univ. de Paris.

SHANGHAI. Bureau of Social Affairs. The index numbers of earnings of the factory laborers in greater Shanghai, July-December, 1928. [Shanghai, 1929]
1 v. (various pagings).

————. Wages and hours of labor, Greater Shanghai, 1929. Shanghai, Commercial Press, 1931. 139, xv, 153 p. incl. tables.

————. The cost of living index numbers of laborers, Greater Shanghai, January
1926-December 1931. Shanghai, Chung Hwa Book Co., 1932. 56, xiii, 35 p.
tables, diagrs.

————. Standard of living of Shanghai laborers. [Shanghai, Chung Hwa Book Co.,
1934] xi, 186, [2] p. tables.

————. Wage rates in Shanghai. [Shanghai] 1935. xii, 178 p. illus. (Its Labor
statistics series ).

SHIH, KUO-HÊNG, 史國衡. Labor and labor relations in the new industries of
southwest China, by Kuo-hêng Shih and Ju-k'ang T'ien, 田汝康, edited by
Francis L.K. Hsu, 許烺光 . New York, International Secretariet, Institute
of Pacific Relations, 1943. 45 p. (Social change in southwest China-case
study 2 ).

————. The labour situation in war-time interior China, by Kuo-hêng Shih and
Ju-k'ang T'ien; edited by Francis L.K. Hsu. [Kunming] Yenching-Yunnan
Station of Sociological Research, 1943. 45 l. diagr.

————. China enters the machine age; a study of labor in Chinese war industry,
by Kuo-hêng Shih with a supplementary chapter by Ju-k'ang T'ien; edited and
translated by Hsiao-tung Fei and Francis L.K. Hsu. Cambridge, Mass.,
Harvard University Press, 1944. xxiv, 206 p. incl. tables, diagr.

T'AO, LING, 陶苳. Women in Tientsin industries; a study of the working conditions of women and girls; by T'ao Ling and Lydia Johnson. Peking, Peking
Leader Press, 1928. cover-title, 11 p. (Peking Leader reprints, 40 ).

WANG, SHU-HSÜN, 王樹勳. Wages and labor mobility in a flour mill in Tientsin, translated by T.H. Ch'en, 陳宗漢 . Peiping, Institute of Social Research, 1932. 30 p. (Its Bull., 6 ).

## Industrial Disputes

ANDREWS, R. F. War on the Chinese workers. London [Friends of the Soviet Union] 1932. 24 p.

CH'EN, TA, 1896-    Analysis of strikes in China from 1918 to 1926. Peking [1927] 55 p. (Bureau of Economic Information Booklet ser., 4 ).

LIN, PETER WEI, 林暐 , 1894-    Chinese labor disputes since 1919. Nanking, Mei Chi Press, 1932. iii-iv, 118 p. tables (1 fold.).

SHANGHAI. Bureau of Social Affairs. Industrial disputes ( not including strikes and lockouts), Greater Shanghai, 1929. Shanghai, 1931. 269, ii, ii, 164 p. incl. tables, charts.

————. The same, Greater Shanghai, 1930. Shanghai, 1932. 160, xi, 124 p.

————. Report on industrial disputes in Greater Shanghai, July-December 1928, 1930, 1930-32. Shanghai, Dah Tung Book Co., 1929-34. 4 v. tables (part fold.),fold. charts,(double plate).

————. Strikes and lockouts, Greater Shanghai, 1929. Shanghai, Commercial Press, 1930. 291 p. charts, maps, tables.

————. Strikes and lockouts in Shanghai since 1918. Shanghai, Chung Hwa Book Co., 1933. xi, [2], 180 p.

————. Industrial disputes in Shanghai since 1928. [Shanghai, Chung Hwa Book Co.] 1934. viii, [2], 78, 252 p. tables, diagrs.

WU, LEONARD T.K., 吳祖光. An analysis of labor disputes in Hopei province and the cities of Peiping and Tientsin, January 1927-June 1929. Peiping, Institute of Social Research, 1930. 21 p. (Its Bull., 4).

## Labor since 1949

ALL-CHINA FEDERATION OF LABOR. Constitution of the All-China Federation of Labor, agreed unanimously by the sixth All-China labor conference, Harbin, August, 1948. New York, Committee for a Democratic Far Eastern Policy, 1949. 3 l.

————. Trade union delegations in China. Peking, 1952. 60 p. illus.

ALL-CHINA CONGRESS OF TRADE UNIONS. 7th, Peking, 1953. The Seventh All-China Congress of Trade Unions. Peking, Foreign Languages Press, 1953. 141 p. illus., ports.

ALL-CHINA FEDERATION OF TRADE UNIONS. China's women workers. [Peking, 1956] 1 v. (chiefly illus.).

ASIAN PEOPLES' ANTI-COMMUNIST LEAGUE. Slave labor under the Chinese Communist regime. [Taipei] 1955. 19 p.

CHINA (People's Republic of China, 1949-  ) Laws, statutes, etc. Labour insurance regulations. Peking, Workers' Press, 1952. 28 p.

————. The same. First promulgated by the Government Administration Council on Feb. 26, 1951, promulgated as amended by the Government Administration Council on Jan. 2, 1953. [2d ed. ] Peking, Foreign Languages Press, 1953. 34 p. 1st ed. 1952, 42 p.

————. The Trade union law of the People's Republic of China, together with other relevant documents. [3d ed. ] Peking, Foreign Languages Press [1952] 38 p. 1st ed. 1950.

————. La loi sur les syndicats ouvriers; suivi de deux autres documents. Pékin, Éditions en langues étrangères, 1950. 41 p.

————. Labour laws and regulations of the People's Republic of China. Peking, Foreign Languages Press, 1956. 87 p.

The CHINESE people celebrates May Day, 1952. [Peking, Workers' Press] 1952. 40 p.

CHINESE workers march towards socialism. Peking, Foreign Languages Press, 1956. 93 p. illus.

DETER, ADOLF. Das neue China und die chinesischen Gewerkschaften. Berlin,

Tribüne, 1954. 65 p. illus., port.

DEVERALL, RICHARD LAWRENCE GRACE, 1911-    People's China: sweat-
shop arsenal! 2d ed., rev. and enl. Tokyo, Printed by Toyoh Print. and
Book-binding Co., 1954. 489 p. illus.

DRIDZO, SOLOMON ABRAMOVICH, 1878-    The Pan-Pacific Trade Union Conference, Hankow, May 20-26, 1927, by A. Lozovsky [pseud.] Moscow, R.I.
L.U., 1927. 62 p.

HSIA, RONALD, 夏修永, 1918-    The role of labor-intensive projects in China's capital formation. [Working draft] Cambridge, Center for International
Studies, Massachusetts Institute of Technology, 1954. 103 l. illus.

LABOUR insurance in new China. Peking, Foreign Languages Press, 1953.
32 p. illus.

LIU, SHAO-CHI, 1900-    Manifesto and opening speech at the Trade Union Conference of Asian and Australian countries. Peking, 1949. Bombay, People's
Pub. House, 1950. 18 p.

MAO, TSÊ-TUNG, 1893-    Mind the living conditions of the masses and attend
to the methods of work. Peking, Foreign Languages Press, 1953. 10 p.

ONG, SHAO-ER, 翁紹耳, [Wêng Shao-êrh] 1917-    Labor problems in Communist China, to February 1953. Lackland Air Force Base, Tex., Air Force
Personnel and Training Research Center, Air Research and Development
Command, 1955. xv, 83 p. map, diagrs. ([U.S.] Human Resources Research Institute. Research memorandum, 42).

SU, WEI-CH'UAN, 蘇偉樁. Reform through labor in China, by Su Wei-ch'uan
and P'ei Yu-ming, 裴有明. Hong Kong, Asia Press, 1955. 113 p.

The SYSTEM of forced labor on mainland labor. [Taipei, 1956] 68 p. facsims.
Appendix: Laws, regulations and facts relating to political persecution and
slave labor. (Text in Chinese with English explanation).

TRADE unions in People's China. Peking, Foreign Languages Press, 1956.
58 p.

UNITED NATIONS. Economic and Social Council. Forced labor in Communist
China; report by the Secretary-General of United Nations and Director General of the International Labor Office before the 21st session. 221 p. (Document E/2815).

WORLD FEDERATION OF TRADE UNIONS. Working class in the struggle for
national liberation; reports and resolutions of trade union conference of A-
sian and Australian countries called by WFTU, Peking, Nov.-Dec. 1950.
Peking, 1951. 143 p.

WU, YUN-TO, 吳雲鐸. Son of the working class; the autobiography of Wu Yun-
to. [Translated by Huang Pin-chang and Tang Sheng] Peking, Foreign Languages Press, 1956. 224 p. illus.

Population
General Works

BALFOUR, MARSHALL C., 1896-    Public health and demography in the Far
East; report of a survey trip, September 13-December 13, 1948, by Marshall
C. Balfour [and others. New York] Rockefeller Foundation, 1950. ii, 132 p.
illus., maps.

CH'EN, CH'ANG-HENG, 陳長蘅, 1891-    Some phases of China's population
problem. Shanghai, 1930. 43 p. (XIXe session de l'institut international de
statistique, Tokio, 1930 ).

CH'EN, CHUNGSHEN S., 陳鍾聲, 1895-    The Chinese census of population
since 1912. Shanghai, 1930. 14 p. (XIXe session de l'institut international
de statistique, Tokio, 1930).

CH'ÊN, TA, 陳達, 1896-    Population in modern China. Chicago, University
of Chicago Press [1946] ix, 126 p. incl. tables.

——. Les problèmes démographiques en Chine. Paris, Dunod, 1950. 39, [1] p.

(Les Hommes et leur nourriture ).

CH'EN, WARREN H., 陳華寅. Population and other aspects of the workingmen's families. [Nanking, 1929] 57 p. incl. tables, diagrs.

———. An estimate of the population of China in 1929. Shanghai, 1930. 35 p. (XIXe session de l'institut international de statistique, Tokio, 1930).

CH'IAO, CH'I-MING, 喬啓明, 1898-   A study of the Chinese population. With a foreword by Edgar Sydenstricker. [New York, 1934] iii-iv, 56 p. illus. (map) diagrs. ''Reprinted from the Milbank memorial fund Quarterly bulletin, October, 1933, January, April, and July, 1934.''

———. An experiment in the registration of vital statistics in China by C. M. Ch'iao, Warren S. Thompson and D. T. Chen. Oxford, O., Scripps Foundation for Research in Population Problems, 1938.  115 p.

CHINESE ASSOCIATION FOR THE UNITED NATIONS. The balance between population and production. Taipei, Chinese Association for the United Nations, 1951.  21 p. (Unachina publications, ser. 1, 4 ).

HO, PING-TI, 何炳棣. The growth of the total population of China, 1750-1830, by Ping-ti Ho and Irene B. Tauber. Cambridge, Chinese Economic and Political Studies, Harvard University, 1956.  55 l. illus. (1956 Conference on the Chinese economy. Conference paper, 7 ).

LIEU, D.K., 劉大鈞, 1890-   The 1912 census of China. Shanghai, 1931. 27 p. diagrs. tables.

LIU, NANMING, 劉南溟. Contributions à l'étude de la population chinoise. Genève [Impr. et éditions Union, 1935] 252 p. tables. Thèse-Univ. de Paris.

## Internal Migration

CH'EN, HAN-SHÊNG, 陳翰笙, 1897-   Notes on migration of nan min to the Northeast. Shanghai, China Council, Institute of Pacific Relations, 1931. 31 p. incl. tables.

CHINESE colonization in Northern Manchuria, 1929-40. [n. p., 1945] 34 l.(Studies of migration and settlement. Translation ser. T-122 ).

HO, FRANKLIN LIEN, 何廉, 1895-   Population movement to the northeastern frontier in China. Preliminary paper prepared for the fourth biennial conference of the Institute of Pacific Relations to be held in Hangchow from October 21st to November 4th, 1931. Shanghai, China Institute of Pacific Relations [1931] 51 p. 4 fold. maps.

[PAN, QUENTIN] 潘光旦, 1899-   Chinese colonization in Manchuria. [n. p., 1929?] 24 numb. l.

TSAO, LIEN-EN, 曹勵恆. Chinese migration to the three eastern provinces. Shanghai, Bureau of Industrial and Commercial Information, Ministry of Industry, Commerce and Labor, 1930. 93 p. incl. tables. (Chinese Economic Journal booklet ser. 15 ).

YOUNG, CARL WALTER, 1902-39. Chinese colonization and the development of Manchuria. Honolulu, The Insitute of Pacific Relations, 1929.  5-53 p. 2 illus.(maps).

## Immigration and Emigration
## General Works

CH'ÊN, TA, 1896-   Chinese migrations, with special reference to labor conditions. July, 1923. Washington, Govt. Print. Off., 1923.  vi, 237 p. illus., plates, fold. maps. (U.S. Bureau of labor statistics. Bulletin, 340. Miscellaneous series ).

———. Emigrant communities in south China; a study of overseas migration and its influence on standards of living and social change. English version edited by Bruno Lasker. New York, Secretariat, Institute of Pacific Relations,1940. xvi, 287 p.

CHEN, TA, 陳達, 1896-  Japanese emigration to China. [New York?] Chinese Patriotic Committee of New York City [1921]  42 p. incl. illus.(map) tables.

DENNERY, ÉTIENNE. Foules d'Asie; surpopulation japonaise, expansion chinoise, émigration indienne.  Paris, A. Colin, 1930.  247 p. illus.(maps).

——. Asia's teeming millions: and its problems for the West, translated from the French by John Peile, with a foreword by Harold Cox.  London, J.Cape [1931] 248 p. front., illus.(maps) plates.

DJU, PETER, 朱伯奇. L'émigration japonaise depuis 1918.  Paris, P.Bossuet, 1937.  [11]-155, [2] p. incl. tables. Thèse-Univ. de Paris.

HUANG, TSENG-MING, 黃正銘, 1904-  The legal status of the Chinese abroad. Taipei, China Cultural Service, 1954.  347 p.

LU, YU-SUN, 陸雨聲. Programs of Communist China for overseas Chinese. Kowloon, Hong Kong, Union Research Institute [1956]  82 p. (Communist China problem research series, EC12 ).

MacNAIR, HARLEY FARNSWORTH, 1891-1947. The Chinese abroad, their position and protection; a study in international law and relations, with an introduction by V.K. Wellington Koo and a foreword by Fong F. Sec.  Shanghai, Commercial Press, 1924.  xxii, 340 p.

PYE, LUCIAN WILMOT, 1921-  Some observations on the political behavior of overseas Chinese.  Cambridge, Center for International Studies, Massachusetts Institute of Technology, 1954.  24 p.

Asia

BONE, ROBERT C. The role of the Chinese in Indonesia; a paper submitted to Yale University and the Foreign Service Institute, Dept. of State, in conjunction with a detail for the study of Indonesian and the Southeast Asia ares, 1950-51. [New Haven?] 1951.  148, 2 1. ( [U.S.] Foreign Service Institute. Monograph).

CATOR, WRITSER JANS. The economic position of the Chinese in the Netherlands Indies.  Chicago, University of Chicago Press, 1936; London, Oxford University Press, 1936.  xi, 264 p. illus.(map).

CHEN, SU-CHING, 陳序經, 1903-  China and Southeastern Asia.  Chungking, China Institute of Pacific Relations, 1945.  iii, 54 p. (China council series, 5.).

CHIANG, FÊNG-CH'ÊN, 蔣逢辰. The anti-Chinese riot in Korea in 1931, by F.C. Chiang and K.K. Chang.  Shanghai, 1931.  50 p.; 9 p. illus.

CHIEU, NGUYEN HUY. Le statut des Chinois en Indo-Chine.  Paris, Les Presses modernes, 1939.  123 p. Thèse-Univ. de Paris.

FENN, WILLIAM PURVIANCE, 1902-  Chinese schools and the education of Chinese Malayans; the report of a mission invited by the Federation Government to study the problem of the education of Chinese in Malaya. [By William P. Fenn and Wu Teh-yao, 吳德耀] Kuala Lumpur, Printed at the Government Press by H.T. Ross, 1951. iii, 42 p.

The FOOKIEN TIMES. Year book, 1949-55. [Manila] 6 v. illus.(part col.)ports.

HO, KUO-LIANG, 何國樑, 1919-  Some contemporary interests of the Chinese in the Southwest Pacific.  Ann Arbor, University Microfilms [1952] ( [University Microfilms, Ann Arbor, Mich.] Publication no. 2972). Collation of the original: v, 329 1. tables. Thesis-Princeton University.

HORSLEY, MARGARET WYANT, 1918-  Sangley: the formation of anti-Chinese feeling in the Philippines - a cultural study of the stereotypes of prejudice. Ann Arbor, University Microfilms, 1950. ( [University Microfilms, Ann Arbor, Mich.] Publication no. 1746 ). Collation of the original: i, 239 1. Thesis-Columbia University.

[KER, WILLIAM POLLOCK] 1864-1945. Chinese under British rule in Malaya, Hongkong and Weihaiwei. [n.p., 1929?] 45 numb. 1. In vol. XXVII of ''Documents of the third conference, Institute of Pacific Relations, Kyoto, Japan,

1929.''

LANDON, KENNETH PERRY, 1903- The Chinese in Thailand. London and New York, Oxford University Press, 1941. xi (i.e. ix), 310 p.

LEVASSEUR, GEORGES. La situation juridique des chinois en Indochine depuis les accords de Nankin (problèmes de droit international privé). 2e éd. Hanoi, Impr. d'Extrême-Orient, 1939. 262 p.

MEIJER, MARINUS JOHAN. The Chinese in Indonesia. [n.p., 195-] 60 l.

MOSOLFF, HANS. Die chinesische Auswanderung (Ursachen, Wesen und Wirkungen) unter besonderer Berücksichtigung der Hauptauswanderungs gebiete und mit einem ausführlichen Bericht über die chinesische Arbeiterbeschaffung für Samoa unter der deutschen Verwaltung. Rostock, C. Hinstorff, 1932. vii, 518 p. incl. tables. (Hamburger Schriften zur Wirtschafts-und Sozialpolitik, 22-23 ).

NEILL, DESMOND. Elegant flower; first steps in China. London, Murray [1956] 202 p. illus.

PHAN-VAN-THINH. Les Chinois au Viet-Nam. Paris, 1955. 170 p. map. Thèse-Univ. de Paris.

PLANTERS' ASSOCIATION OF MALAYA. Special Committee on Chinese Labour. Report. Kuala Lumpur, 1922. 35 p.

PURCELL, VICTOR WILLIAM WILLIAMS SAUNDERS, 1896- The Chinese in Malaya. Issued under the joint auspices of the Royal Institute of International Affairs and the Institute of Pacific Relations. London, New York, Oxford University Press, 1948. xvi, 327 p. fold. maps.

——. The position of the Chinese in Southeast Asia. Submitted by the IPR International Secretariat as a preparatory paper for the Eleventh Conference of the Institute of Pacific Relations to be held at Lucknow, India, Oct. 1950. New York, International Secretariat, Institute of Pacific Relations, 1950. 78 p. (Secretariat paper no. 3 ).

——. The Chinese in Southeast Asia. London, New York, Oxford University Press, 1951. xxxvii, 801 p. fold. maps.

——. The Chinese in modern Malaya. Singapore, D. Moore, 1956. 63 p. (Background to Malaya series, 9 ).

SIM, VICTOR, 优渭澤, ed. Biographies of prominent Chinese in Singapore, compiled under the editorial supervision of Victor Sim. Ed. de luxe in English and Chinese. Singapore, Nan Kok Publication Co. [cover 1950] i, 111, i, 110 p. (on double leaves) ports.

SKINNER, GEORGE WILLIAM, 1925- Report on the Chinese in Southeast Asia, December 1950. [Ithaca, N.Y.] Southeast Asia Program, Dept. of Far Eastern Studies, Cornell University [1951] v, 91 l.

——. Chinese community leadership in Bangkok together with an historical survey of Chinese society in Thailand. Ithaca, 1954. xxiv, 814 l. illus., maps. Thesis-Cornell University.

——. Chinese society in Thailand: an analytical history. Ithaca, N.Y., Cornell University Press [1957] xvii, 459 p. maps (part fold.) diagrs., tables.

SONG, ONG SIANG, 宋旺相, 1871-1941. One hundred years' history of the Chinese in Singapore; being a chronological record of the contribution by the Chinese community to the development, progress and prosperity of Singapore; of events and incidents concerning the whole or sections of that community; and of the lives, pursuits and public service of individual members thereof from the foundation of Singapore on 6th February 1819 to its centenary on 6th February 1919. London, J. Murray, 1923. xxii, 602 p. front., plates, ports.

SUN, FANG-SI, 1898- Die Entwicklung der chinesischen Kolonisation in Sudasien (Nan Yang) nach chinesischen Quellen. Jena, 1931. 63 p. incl. tables. Diss.-Univ. Jena.

T'IEN, JU-K'ANG, 田汝康, 1916- The Chinese of Sarawak; a study of social structure. London, Dept. of Anthropology, London School of Economics and Political Science [1953] 88 p. fold. maps, tables. (Monographs on social

anthropology, 12 ).
U.S. Office of Coördinator of Information. Research and Analysis Branch. Far
    Eastern Section. Our Chinese allies in Southeast Asia. [Washington] 1942.
    12 p. (Its Report no. 52 ).
WANG, WÊN-YÜAN, 王文元. Les relations entre l'Indochine française et la
    Chine; étude de géographie économique. Paris, P. Bossuet, 1937. 199,[1] p.
    diagrs. Thèse-Univ. de Paris.
WENG, KWONG-HAN, 溫廣漢. Essai sur l'immigration chinoise en insulinde.
    Paris, P. Bossuet, 1937. 199 p. map. Thèse-Univ. de Paris.
WILLIAMS, LEA E., 1924-    The rise of overseas Chinese nationalism in Neth-
    erlands India, 1900-16. Cambridge, 1956. 253 l. Thesis-Harvard Univer-
    sity.

United States
Chinese Exclusion

CITIZENS COMMITTEE TO REPEAL CHINESE EXCLUSION AND PLACE IMMI-
    GRATION ON A QUOTA BASIS, New York. [Miscellaneous publications] New
    York, 1943. 1 v.
McKENZIE, RODERICK DUNCAN, 1885-1940. Oriental exclusion, the effect of
    American immigration laws, regulations, and judicial decisions upon the Chi-
    nese and Japanese on the American Pacific coast. Chicago, University of
    Chicago Press [1928] viii, 9-200 p. diagrs.
[MENKEN, S. STANWOOD] 1870-    Total Chinese exclusion must end. [New
    York, 1943] cover-title, 3 p.
RIGGS, FRED WARREN, 1917-    Pressures on Congress; a study of the repeal
    of Chinese exclusion. New York, King's Crown Press, 1950. xii, 260 p.
SAWYER, JOHN B. Procedure in "section 6" and other Chinese immigration
    matters for the use of consular officers. Washington, Govt. Print. Off.,
    1926. iii, 54 p. incl. forms.
SHEN, TSO-CHIEN, 沈作乾. What "Chinese exclusion" really means. New
    York, China Institute in America, 1942. 58 p. [Hsueh-shu chien-kuo ts'ung-
    shu. No. 2].
STIDGER, OLIVER PERRY, 1873-    Higher lights on Chinese exclusion and
    expulsion. The immigration law of 1924 as it effects persons of Chinese de-
    scent in the United States, their business interests, their rights and their
    privileges. San Francisco [1924] 28 p.
U.S. Congress. House. Committee on Immigration and Naturalization. Repeal
    of the Chinese exclusion acts. Hearings before the Committee on immigra-
    tion and naturalization, House of representatives, Seventy-eighth Congress,
    first session, on H.R. 1882 and H.R. 2309, bills to repeal the Chinese ex-
    clusion acts, to put the Chinese on a quota basis, and to permit their natur-
    alization. May 19, 20, 26, 27, and June 2, and 3, 1943. Washington, Govt.
    Print. Off., 1943. iv, 283 p.
———. Repealing the Chinese exclusion laws. Report. [To accompany H.R.3070]
    [Washington, Govt. Print. Off., 1943] 7 p. ( [U.S.] 78th Cong., 1st sess.
    House. Rept. 732 ).
———. Congress. Senate. Committee on Immigration. Admission as nonquota
    immigrants of certain alien wives and children of United States citizens.
    Hearing before a subcommittee of the Committee on immigration, United
    States Senate, Seventieth Congress, first session, on S.2271, a bill to per-
    mit the admission, as nonquota immigrants, of certain alien wives and chil-
    dren of United States citizens. February 6, 1928. Washington, Govt. Print.
    Off., 1928. ii, 29 p.
———. Repealing the Chinese exclusion laws and to establish quotas. Report.
    [To accompany H.R.3070] [Washington, Govt. Print. Off., 1943] 9 p.([U.
    S.] 78th Cong., 1st sess. Senate. Rept. 535 ).

——. Dept. of State. Admission of Chinese into the United States. Supplement B of the Consular regulations. Notes to section 368. Effective October 1, 1936. Washington, Govt. Print. Off., 1936. iv, 49 p. incl. forms. ([Publication no. 910] Immigration series no. 3 ).

——. The same. Visa supplement B of the Foreign service regulations, notes to section XXII-2: January 1941. Washington, Govt. Print. Off., 1941. v, 35 p. incl. forms. [Its Publication 1542: Immigration series 3].

——. Laws, statutes, etc. Treaty, laws, and rules governing the admission of Chinese. Rules of October, 1926. Washington, Govt. Print. Off., 1926. iii, 44 p.

——. The same. Rules of October 1, 1926. Washington, Govt. Print. Off., 1934. iii, 87 p.

WURTZ, PIERRE. La question de l'immigration aux États-Unis; son état actuel. Paris, L. Dreux et M. Schneider, 1925. 334 p. Thèse-Univ. de Paris.

## Hawaii

BURROWS, EDWIN GRANT. Chinese and Japanese in Hawaii during the Sino-Japanese conflict. Honolulu, Hawaii group, American Council, Institute of Pacific Relations, 1939. 79 p.

The CHINESE of Hawaii. 1929- Honolulu, Overseas Penman Club, 1929-35 + 207 p. illus. (incl. ports.).

COULTER, JOHN WESLEY, 1893- Chinese rice farmers in Hawaii, by John Wesley Coulter and Chee Kwon Chun, 陳致昆. [Honolulu] University of Hawaii, 1937. 70, [2] p. illus. (maps) 2 plates, diagrs. (University of Hawaii. Research publications, 16 ).

GLICK, CLARENCE ELMER, 1906- The Chinese migrant in Hawaii; a study in accommodation. [n. p., 1942] [1], 734-743, 667-679 p. ''Reprinted from the American journal of sociology, vol. 43, March, 1938; vol. 47, March, 1942.''

KINNEY, WILLIAM A. Hawaii's capacity for self-government all but destroyed. Salt Lake City, F. L. Jensen [1927] [13]-206, 60 p.

LAM, FREDERICK WING KWAI, 林榮貴, 1894- A survey of the Chinese people in Hawaii, historically, educationally, commercially, religiously and socially. [Honolulu?] Institute of Pacific Relations, 1929. 14 numb. l.

LORDEN, DORIS M., 1908- The Chinese-Hawaiian family. [Chicago, 1935] cover-title, p. 453-463. ''Reprinted from the American journal of sociology, vol. 40:4, January 1935.''

SHAPIRO, HARRY LIONEL, 1902- The Chinese population in Hawaii. New York, American Council, Institute of Pacific Relations, 1931. 29 p. incl. tables. (Prepared for the fourth bi-annual conference of the Institute of Pacific Relations, Hangchow, 1931 ).

SMITH, WILLIAM CARLSON, 1883- The second generation oriental in America. Honolulu, Hawaii [1927] 36 p.

——. Americans in process; a study of our citizens of oriental ancestry, introduction by Romanzo Adams. Ann Arbor, Edwards Brothers, 1937. xv, 359 p. diagrs.

U.S. Congress. House. Committee on Immigration and Naturalization. Labor problems in Hawaii. Report. [To accompany H. J. Res. 171. ] [Washington, Govt. Print. Off., 1923] 9, 14 p. (67th Cong., 4th sess. House. Rept. 1717 ).

## California

CALIFORNIA. State Board of Control. California and the Oriental: Japanese, Chinese and Hindus. Report of State Board of Control of California to Gov. Wm. D. Stephens. June 19, 1920. Rev. to January 1, 1922. Sacramento, California State Print. Off., 1922. 250 p. incl. tables, charts, diagrs.

CALIFORNIA Chinese chatter, 加省華人之趣談 . San Francisco, A. Dressler,

1927. ix, 62 p. col. front. , illus.

CHUNG, WEN-HUI陳鍾文會, 1903-    Changing social-cultural patterns of the Chinese community in Los Angeles. Los Angeles, University of Southern California, 1952. xvii, 444 l. illus. , map (fold.). Thesis-University of Southern California.

COLMAN, ELIZABETH. Chinatown, U.S.A.; text and photographs. New York, John Day [1946]  31, [88] p. illus.

DOBIE, CHARLES CALDWELL, 1881-1943. San Francisco's Chinatown, illustrated by E.H. Suydam. New York, London, D. Appleton-Century, 1936. xiv, 336 p. col. front. , illus. , plates.

EVANS, HENRY. Curious lore of San Francisco's Chinatown, with illustrations from old prints. San Francisco, The Porpoise Bookshop, 1956. 31 p.

GENTHE, ARNOLD, 1869-1942. Old Chinatown; a photographic calendar for the year 1946. Oakland, Mills College [1946] [53] p. incl. illus.(incl. port.) plates.

GRAHAM, VIRGINIA TAYLOR, 1897-    The intelligence of Chinese children in San Francisco. [Baltimore, 1926] p. 43-71. Reprint from the Journal of comparative psychology. 6:1, February, 1926.

HOY, WILLIAM,    謝開. The Chinese six companies; a short, general historical resumé of its origin, function, and importance in the life of the California Chinese. San Francisco, Chinese Consolidated Benevolent Association (Chinese six companies) [c1942]  33, [1] p. ports. (part fold.).

LOWE, PARDEE, 劉裔昌, 1904-    Father and Glorious Descendant. Boston, Little, Brown, 1943. 3-322 p.

LUI, GARDING, 呂家定 , 1895-    Inside Los Angeles Chinatown. [Los Angeles? 1948] 207 p. illus. , ports. , maps.

McLEOD, ALEXANDER, 1895-    Pigtails and gold dust. Caldwell, Id. , Caxton Printers, 1947. 326 p. front. , plates, facsims.

MEARS, ELIOT GRINNELL, 1889-    Resident Orientals on the American Pacific coast; their legal and economic status. Chicago, University of Chicago Press [1928] xvi, 545 p. incl. tables, diagrs.

SAN FRANCISCO. Dept. of Public Health. The health of the Chinese in an American city-San Francisco. [San Francisco] 1939. 29 p. illus.

——. School of Social Studies. Living conditions in Chinatown, prepared by a study group in the School of Social Studies. San Francisco, 1939. 1 v.

SANDMEYER, ELMER CLARENCE, 1888-    The anti-Chinese movement in California. Urbana, University of Illinois Press, 1939. 127 p. ([Illinois. University] Illinois studies in the social sciences, 24:3 ).

SCHRIEKE, BERTRAM JOHANNES OTTO, 1890-    Alien Americans; a study of race relations. New York, Viking Press, 1936. xi, 208 p.

SHEPHERD, CHARLES REGINALD, 1885-    The ways of Ah Sin; a composite narrative of things as they are. New York, Fleming H. Revell [c1923] 223 p. front.

——. The story of Chung Mei; being the authentic history of the Chung Mei home for Chinese boys up to its fifteenth anniversary, October, 1938. Philadelphia, The Judson Press [c1938] 3-264 p. front. , plates, ports.

SPARKS, THERESA A. China gold. Fresno, Academy Library Guild, 1954. 191 p. illus.

WILSON, CAROL (GREEN) 1892-    Chinatown quest; the life adventures of Donaldina Cameron. Rev. ed. Stanford, Stanford University Press [1950] xiii, 197 p. illus. , ports.


New York and other Cities


CHEN, T'IEN-EN, 陳天恩, ed. Official Chinatown guide book. New York, [Henin and Co. ] 1939. 96 p. illus.(incl. ports. , plan).

CHÊNG, TÊ-CH'AO, 鄭德超, 1905-    Acculturation of the Chinese in the United

States; a Philadelphia study. Philadelphia, 1948. x, 280 p. illus., maps, tables. Thesis-University of Pennsylvania.

ENG, YING-GONG, 伍英光. Tong war! The first complete history of the tongs in America; details of the tong wars and their causes; lives of famous hatchet men and gunmen; and inside information as to the workings of the tongs, their aims and achievements, by Eng Ying Gong and Bruce Grant; with illustrations by Pedro Llanuza. New York, N. L. Brown, 1930. viii, [2], 11-287 p. front., plates.

FISK UNIVERSITY, Nashville. Social Science Institute. Orientals and their cultural adjustment; interviews, life histories and social adjustment experiences of Chinese and Japanese of varying backgrounds and length of residence in the United States. Nashville, Social Science Institute, Fisk University, 1946. x, 138 numb. l. (Its Social science source documents, 4 ).

GLICK, CARL, 1890-  Shake hands with the dragon, illustrated by Donald McKay. New York, London, Whittlesey House, McGraw-Hill Book Co. [c1941]; London, Herbert Jenkins, 1942. vii, [1], 327 p. incl. front., illus.

HAWKS, JEAN ELIZABETH. A study of Chinese-American children. [Baltimore, 1932] p. 203-223, 375-384. diagrs. ''Reprinted from the Journal of the American dietetic association, vol. VII, no. 3, 1931 and vol. VII, no. 4, 1932.''

HEYER, VIRGINIA. Patterns of social organization in New York City's Chinatown. Ann Arbor, University Microfilms [1954] ([University Microfilms, Ann Arbor, Mich.] Publication no. 8686 ). Collation of the original: 191 l. Thesis-Columbia University.

HUIE, KIN, 許芹, 1854-1935. Reminiscences. Peiping, San Yu Press, 1932. 115 p. plates, ports.

LEONG, GOR YUN, 梁果仁. Chinatown inside out; illustrated with photographs by Creighton Peet and others, and with old wood-engravings. New York, B. Mussey [c1936] 256 p. incl. front., illus. plates.

MENEELY, ALEXANDER HOWARD. The anti-Chinese movement in the Northwest. Seattle, 1922. 121 l. Thesis-Univ. of Washington.

PALMER, ALBERT WENTWORTH, 1879-  Orientals in American life. New York, Friendship Press [c1934] xi, 212 p.

TOW, JULIUS SU, 屠汝練, 1895-  The real Chinese in America; being an attempt to give the general American public a fuller knowledge and a better understanding of the Chinese people in United States. N[ew] Y[ork], Academy Press [c1923] xviii, 19-168 p. incl. front. (port.) plates, facsim.

TRULL, FERN COBLE. The history of the Chinese in Idaho from 1864 to 1910. Eugene, Ore., 1946. 235 l. Thesis-University of Oregon.

WU, CHARLES LING, 吳澤霖, 1900-  Attitudes toward negroes, Jews, and Orientals in the United States. [Columbus, O., H. L. Hedrick] 1930. 442, [7] l. Thesis-Ohio State University.


## Directories

CHINESE PUBLICITY BUREAU, Seattle. Chinese business directory and residents, Seattle-Tacoma-Spokane and vicinity; edited by Mor Cheolin, 馬超林. Seattle, 1950. 70 p.

LUM (JIMMY) ADVERTISING SERVICE, San Francisco. San Francisco Chinese directory; including Oakland-East Bay section. 1949. [San Francisco, Jimmy Lum] 1949. 72 p.

——. Map of San Francisco's Chinatown and vicinity. San Francisco, c1950. col. map.

SINO- AMERICAN PUBLICITY BUREAU, New York. Chinese directory of the Eastern States, 1953-54. New York, 1954. 1 v. (various pagings).

UNITED CHINESE ASSOCIATION OF NEW ENGLAND, Boston. The Chinese directory of New England. Boston, 1931. 96 p. illus. ports., plates.

## Canada, Central and South America

BRITISH COLUMBIA. Bureau of Provincial Information. Report on oriental activities within the province. Prepared for the Legislative Assembly.    Victoria, B.C., Printed by C.F.Banfield, 1927. 24 p. tables (1 fold.).

CANADA. Laws, statutes, etc. Chinese immigration act, 1923, and regulations.
Issued by the Minister of immigration and colonization. Ottawa, Canada,
1926. [Ottawa, F.A. Acland, printer to the King, 1926] 27 p. incl. form.
————. Chinese immigration act and regulations. Ottawa, Can., Minister of
mines and resources, 1939. 25 p. incl. forms.
————. Special Committee on Orientals in British Columbia. Report and recommendations. December, 1940. Ottawa, E. Cloutier, printer to the King,
1941. 20 p. incl. tables.

CHANG, CHING-CHIEH, 張景哲. The Chinese in Latin America, a preliminary
geographical survey with special reference to Cuba and Jamaica. College
Park, Md., 1956. 194 1. Thesis-University of Maryland.

CH'ÊNG, T'IEN-FANG, 程天放, 1899-    Oriental immigration in Canada.
Shanghai, Commercial Press, 1931. x, 306 p. map, tables, diagrs.

LUBBOCK, ALFRED BASIL, 1876-1944. Coolie ships and oil sailers. Glasgow,
Brown and Ferguson [1935] x, 180 p. front., plates, ports.

McINNES, TOM, 1867-    Oriental occupation of British Columbia. Vancouver,
Sun Pub. Co., 1927. 170 p.

MacINNIS, GRACE (WOODSWORTH) 1905-    Oriental Canadians, outcasts or
citizens? By Grace and Angus MacInnis. [Vancouver, B.C., The Federation-
ist Pub. Co., 1945?] 20 p.

STEWART, WATT, 1892-    Chinese bondage in Peru; a history of the Chinese
coolie in Peru, 1849-74. Durham, Duke University Press, 1951. x, 247 p.
illus., port., map. (Duke University publications).

WOODSWORTH, CHARLES JAMES, 1909-    Canada and the Orient; a study in
international relations. Issued under the auspices of the Canadian Institute of
International Affairs. Toronto, Macmillan Co. of Canada, 1941. xii, 321 p.
diagrs.

## Australia, New Zealand and Africa

CAMPBELL, PERSIA CRAWFORD. Chinese coolie emigration to countries within the British Empire. With a preface by the Hon. W. Pember Reeves. London, P.S. King, 1923. xxiii, 240 p. (Studies in economics and political science, no. 72 in the series of monographs by writers connected with the London school of economics and political science).

McNEUR, GEORGE HUNTER. The church and the Chinese in New Zealand.
Christchurch, Presbyterian Bookroom, 1951. viii, 56 p. illus. map.

MIAO, TUNG, 繆通, 1916-    Legal status of Chinese in the Union of South Africa. Johannesburg, Chiao Sheng Pao, 1947. 47 p.

SLEEMAN, JOHN H. C. White China; an Austral-Asian sensation. Sydney, The
Author, 1933. viii, 344 p.

[YÜAN, CHUNG-MING] 袁中明, ed. A book to commemorate a common victory,
issued by the Chinese community in N.S.W. [Sydney, Printed by Boylan and
Co.] 1945. 64 p.; 19 p. 2 port.

## Europe

JEROME, J.A. Chinese White; a study of Chinatown. London, Hampton Court
Books [1948] 195 p.

WHITTINGHAM-JONES, BARBARA. China fights in Britain; a factual survey of
a fascinating colony in our midst. London, W.H. Allen [1944] 68 p.

## Anthropology and National Minorities
### General Works

[BROOKBANK, THOMAS W.] Are the Chinese Semites? [Salt Lake City] Salt Lake Efficiency Ptg. Co., 1930. 33 p.

BURCKHARDT, CARL JACOB, 1891-  Gespräch in Peking. Olten, Vereinigung Oltener Bücherfreunde, 1942. 47 p. (Veröffentlichung der Vereinigung Oltener Bücherfreunde, 13 ).

EBERHARD, WOLFRAM, 1909-  Kultur und Siedlung der randvölker Chinas. Leiden, E.J. Brill, 1942. vii, [1], 506 p. 2 fold. maps. (T'oung pao. Suppl. au vol. 36 ).

————. Lokalkulturen im alten China. 1. Die Lokalkulturen des Nordens und Westens. Leiden, E.J. Brill, 1942. 447 p. (T'oung Pao. Suppl. au vol. 37 ).

————. The same. 11. Die Lokalkulturen des Südens und Ostens. Peiping, Catholic University, 1942. xiv, 588 p. (Monumenta Serica. Monog. 3 ).

GRANET, MARCEL, 1884-1940. Études sociologiques sur la Chine. Préf. de Louis Gernet; introd. de R.-A. Stein. Paris, Presses universitaires de France, 1953. 301 p. (Bibliothèque de sociologie contemporaine).

KARUTZ, RICHARD, 1867-  Die Völker Nord- und Mittel-Asiens. Stuttgart, Franckh, 1925. 7-120 p. illus.(incl. map) (Atlas der völkerkunde, bd.I ).

LI, CHI, 李濟, 1896-  The formation of the Chinese people; an anthropological inquiry. Cambridge, Harvard University Press, 1928. [3]-283 p. maps, tables, geneal, tab., diagrs.

MICHALSKI, IRENEUSZ. Skladniki rasowe Chińczyków. Les éléments raciaux des Chinois. Warszawa, Towarzystwo naukowe warszawskie, 1938. 73 p. illus. (maps) tables, diagrs. plates. (Prace antropologiczne Instytutu nauk antropologicznych i etnologicznych Towarzystwa naukowego warszawskiego. 3 ).

NATIONAL minorities in new China. 新中國少數民族的生活 [Peking, Foreign Languages Press, 1954] [12] col. plates (in portfolio).

POLICY towards nationalities of the People's Republic of China. Peking, Foreign Languages Press, 1953. 70 p.

SHIROKOGOROV, SERGEĬ MIKHAĬLOVICH, 1887-1939. Anthropology of northern China. Shanghai, 1923. ii, ii, 127 p. incl. maps, diagrs. (part fold.) fold. map. (Royal Asiatic society. North China branch. [Publications] Extra vol.II ).

————. Anthropology of eastern China and Kwangtung province. Shanghai, Printed by the Commercial Press, 1925. [v]-vi, 162 p. diagrs. (part fold.) (Royal Asiatic society. North China branch. [Publications] Extra vol.IV ).

————. Process of physical growth among the Chinese. v.1. The Chinese of Chekiang and Kiangsu, measured by V. Appleton. Shanghai, Commercial Press, 1925. 137 p. tables, diagrs.

STEVENSON, PAUL HUSTON, 1890-  Detailed anthropometric measurements of the Chinese of the North China plain. [Ch'angsha] Commercial Press, 1938. 39 p. diagrs., maps, tables. (Academia sinica. The Institute of History and Philology. Anthropologia sinica. No. 2 ).

STÜBEL, HANS, 1885-  Die Hsia min vom Tse-mu-schan; Ein Beitrag zur Volkskunde Chekiangs, 浙江景寧敕木山畬民調查記 ,von Hans Stübel und Li Hua-min, 李化民. Nanking, Institute of Social Sciences, Akademia Sinica, 1932. 115 p. illus.

TIEN, KHANG-KIAT. Genesis and the Chinese. Hong Kong, 1950. 97 p.

WANG, SHU-TANG, 王樹棠. China, land of many nationalities; a sketch. Peking, Foreign Languages Press, 1955. 63 p. illus.

————. China-Land der vielen Nationalitaten. Peking, Verlag für fremdsprachige Literatur, 1955. 71 p.

## Minorities-Southwestern China

CHANG, CHI-JEN, 張其仁, 1914-   The minority groups of Yunnan and Chinese political expansion into Southeast Asia. Ann Arbor, 1956. 208 l. Thesis - University of Michigan.

CHÊNG, TE-K'UN, 鄭德坤, 1907-   The ''South-Western barbarians.'' Chengtu, 1945. 22 p. (West China Union University. Museum. Translation ser., 1).

———. An introduction to the South-western peoples of China by Chêng Te-k'un and Liang Chao T'ao, 粱釗韜. Chengtu, 1945. 16 p. fold. map. (West China Union University. Museum. Guidebook ser., 7).

CREDNER, WILHELM, 1892-   Kulturgeographische Beobachtungen in der Landschaft im Tali (Yünnan) mit besonderer Berücksichtigung des Nan Tsao problems. Bangkok, 1935. Reprinted from the Journal of the Siam Society, vol. 27, pt. 2, p. 135-151 (April, 1935).

———. Cultural and geographical observations made in the Tali (Yunnan) region with special regard to the Nan-Chao problem. Translated from German by Major Erik Seidenfaden. Bangkok, Pub. by the Siam Society, 1935. cover-title, 20 p. 6 plates (incl. maps, II fold. tables).

DAUDIN, PIERRE. Contribution aux études ethnographiques sur les tribus du Yunnan et du Seutch'oan. Saigon, 1936. cover-title, 10 p. 5 plates.

DODD, WILLIAM CLIFTON, 1857-1919. The Tai race, elder brother of the Chinese; results of experience, exploration and research of William Clifton Dodd Compiled and edited by his wife. Cedar Rapids, Iowa, Torch Press, 1923. xxi, [2], 353 p. front., plates, ports.

FITZGERALD, CHARLES PATRICK, 1902-   The tower of five glories; a study of the Min Chia of Ta Li, Yunnan. London, Cresset Press, 1941. 280 p. plates, maps (1 fold.).

HENRY LESTER INSTITUTE OF MEDICAL RESEARCH, Shanghai. The Nosu tribes of west Szechuan; notes on the country and its peoples and on the diseases of the region, by E. R. Cunningham, Leslie G. Kilborn, James L. Maxwell [and others] with a foreword by J. L. Maxwell. Shanghai, 1933. 56 p. plates, facsim. fold. diagr.

HSU, ITANG, 徐益棠. Les trois grandes races de la province du Yun-nan. Paris, L. Rodstein, 1932. [5]-184 p.

IMBERT, HENRI. Les négritos de la Chine. Hanoi, Impr. d'Extrême-Orient, 1923. 11 p. illus.

STÜBEL, HANS, 1885-   Ein Dorf der Ta-Hua Miao in Yunnan; mit einem Beitrag von Inez de Beauclair. Hamburg, Gesellschaft für Natur und Völkerkunde Ostasiens, 1954. 80 p. illus. plates. (Deutsche Gesellschaft für Natur und Völkerkunde Ostasiens, Tokyo. Mitteilungen, 37 ).

T'IEN, JU-K'ANG, 田汝康, 1916-   Religious cults and social structure of the Shan States of the Yunnan-Burma frontier. London, 1948. ii, 250 p. Thesis- London School of Economics.


Lolo


DESSIRIER, JEAN LOUIS, d. 1915. À travers les marches révoltées; Ouest-chinois: Yun Nan-Se-Tchouen-Marches thibétaines; avec 61 gravures hors texte. Paris, Plon-Nourrit [1923] vii, 316 p. plates, ports.

POLLARD, SAMUEL, 1864-1915. In unknown China; a record of the observations, adventures and experiences of a pioneer missionary during a prolonged sojourn amongst the wild and unknown Nosu tribe of western China. Philadelphia, J.B. Lippincott; London, Seeley, Service, 1921. [11]-324 p. front., plates, 3 maps (2 fold.).

YOUNG, CHING-CHI, 揚成志. L'écriture et les manuscrits lolos. Genève, 1935. cover-title, 70, [2] p. incl. facsims. plates. (Publications de la Bibliothèque sino-internationale, Genève, nº 4 ). Published also as Thèse-Univ. de Paris.

## Moso

GOULLART, PETER. Forgotten kingdom. London, J. Murray [1955] 218 p. illus.

[LV-MBER IV-ZAW SSAW]. The romance of K'a-mä-gyu-mi-gkyi; a Na-khi tribal love story translated from Na-khi pictographic manuscripts, transcribed and annotated, by J. F. Rock. [Hanoi? Indo-China, 1939] 155 p. illus., XXXII plates (part col.) "Extrait du Bulletin de l'École française d'Extrême-Orient, t. XXXIX, 1939, fasc. I."

ROCK, JOSEPH FRANCIS CHARLES, 1884-   Studies in Na-khi literature. [Hanoi, 1938] 119 p. illus., XLI plates (part fold.; incl. facsims.) diagrs. "Extrait du Bulletin de l'École française d'Extrême-Orient, t. XXXVII, fasc. 1, 1937."

———. The ancient Na-khi Kingdom of southwest China. Cambridge, Harvard University Press, 1947 [i. e. 1948] 2 v. (xx, 554 p.) illus., ports., 4 fold. col. maps (in pocket of v. 2) (Harvard-Yenching Institute. Monograph series, v. 8-9 ).

———. The Mùan bpö ceremony; or, The sacrifice to heaven as practiced by the Na-khi. Peiping, Catholic University [1948] 160 p. plates. "Monumenta Serica. Reprint from vol. 8, 1948."

———. The Na-khi Nāga cult and related ceremonies. Roma, Is. M. E. O., 1952. 2 v. illus., plates (part col.) (Serie orientale Roma, v. 4, pt. 1-2 ).

———. The $^1$D'a $^3$Nv funeral ceremony with special reference to the origin of $^1$Na-$^2$khi weapons. Fribourg, Impr. St-Paul, 1955. 31 p. illus. Offprint of Anthropos, international review of ethnology and linguistics, v. 50, 1955.

———. The $^2$Zhi $^3$mä funeral ceremony of the $^1$Na-$^2$khi of southwest China; described and translated from $^1$Na-$^2$khi manuscripts. Vienna, St. Gabriel's Mission Press, 1955. xv, 228 p. 10 plates. (Studia Instituti Anthropos, v. 9).

## Miao

CHIU, CH'ANG-K'ONG, 邱長康. Die Kultur der Miao-tse nach älteren chinesischen Quellen. Hamburg, Kommissionsverlag Friederichsen, De Gruyter und co. m. b. h., 1937. 31, [1] p. 41 plates. (Mitteilungen aus dem Museum für völkerkunde in Hamburg. XVIII ).

GRAHAM, DAVID CROCKETT, 1884-   Songs and stories of the Ch'uan Miao. Washington, Smithsonian Institution, 1954. xi, 336 p. 24 plates (incl. ports.) map. (Smithsonian miscellaneous collections, v. 123, no. 1 ).

MICKEY, MARGARET PORTIA, 1889-   The Cowrie Shell Miao of Kweichow. Cambridge, The Museum, 1947. ix, 83 p. illus., maps. (Papers of the Peabody Museum of American Archaeology and Ethnology, Harvard University, v. 32, no. 1 ).

SAVINA, FRANCIS MARINA, 1876-   Histoire des Miao. 2. éd. Hongkong, Impr. de la Société des missions-étrangères, 1930. 303 p. illus. 1er éd., 1924.

## Yao

LEUSCHNER, FRIEDRICH WILHELM. Von den Ureinwohnern Chinas, erste Nachrichten eines Sachkundigen über das Volk der Jautze in den Bergen der Provinz Kwangtung. Mit einem Geleitwort von Siegfried Knak. Berlin, Heimatdienst-Verlag [1926] 96 p. illus.

LING, ZENG SENG, 凌純聲, 1901-   Recherches ethnographiques sur les Yao dans la Chine du Sud. Paris, Les Presses universitaires de France, 1929. vi, 151 p. front. (map). Thèse-Univ. de Paris, 1929.

## Minorities - South China

KRADER, RUTH S., 1911-   Ch'ih-ya, 赤雅, an account of non-Chinese peo-

ples of southern China. New Haven, 1946. v, 170 l. Thesis-Yale University.
LIU, HANS, 劉咸. Hainan, the island and the people. [Shanghai, China Journal
　　Pub. Co., 193-] 30 p. illus.
LUNT, CARROLL PRESCOTT, 1889-　　China, star of Asia's drama. Los An-
　　geles, Walton and Wright [c1941] 200, [5] p. front. (map).
NAGEL, SHERMAN A. At home with the Hakkas in South China. Mountain View,
　　Cal., Kansas City, Mo. [etc.] Pacific Press Pub. Association, 1921. 64 p.
　　illus. (Wide world series, 4 ).
ODAKA, KUNIO, 1908-　　Economic organization of the Li tribes of Hainan Is-
　　land. [Translation by Mikiso Hane. New Haven, Yale University, Southeast
　　Asia Studies, 1950] 95 l. illus., maps. (Yale Southeast Asia Studies. Trans-
　　lation series ).
RHEINWALD, OTTO. Die nichtchinesischen Stämme Südchinas, ein Überblick.
　　Tôkyô, Deutsche Gesellschaft für Natur- und Völkerkunde Ostasiens; Kom-
　　missionsverlag von O. Harrassowitz, Leipzig, 1942. 87 p. plates, fold.map.
　　(Mitteilungen der Deutschen Gesellschaft für Natur- und Völkerkunde Osta-
　　siens, Bd. 33, T.A.).
STÜBEL, HANS, 1885-　　Die Li-Stämme der insel Hainan; ein Beitrag zur Volks-
　　kunde Südchinas, unter Mitwirkung von P. Meriggi. Berlin, Klinkhardt und
　　Biermann, 1937. viii, 338 p. illus., 132 plates (part col.) on 66 l., fold.
　　map, 12 tables on 10 fold. l.
WIENS, HEROLD JACOB, 1912-　　China's march toward the tropics; a discus-
　　sion of the southward penetration of China's culture, peoples, and political
　　control in relation to the non-Han-Chinese peoples of south China and in the
　　perspective of historical and cultural geography. Hamden, Conn., Shoe
　　String Press [1954] xv, 441 p. illus., maps.
WIST, HANS, 1904-　　Die Yao im Südchina, nach berichten neuer Chinesischer
　　Feldforschungen. Berlin, D. Reimer, 1938. p. [73]-135. illus., plates incl.
　　maps. (On cover: Bässler-Archiv 21, 3 ).

Jews

[GINSBOURG, ANNA]. Jewish refugees in Shanghai. Shanghai, China Weekly Re-
　　view [1941?] vi, 32 p. plates.
LÖWENTHAL, RUDOLF, 1904-　　The Jewish press in China. Peking, Synodal
　　Commission in China, 1940. cover-title, p. 251-265. fold. tables. "Re-
　　printed from The religious periodical press in China."
—————. The Jews in China, an annotated bibliography. [Peking? pref. 1940] iv,
　　[119]-261 p. 1 illus., facsim. The first edition appeared in the Yenching jour-
　　nal of social studies, Peking, v. 1, no. 2, January, 1939, p. 256-291. "Re-
　　printed from the Chinese social and political science review, Peking. [v. 24,
　　no. 2, July-September, 1940].
—————. The early Jews in China: a supplementary bibliography. [Peking] Cath-
　　olic Univ. of Peking [1946] 353-398 p. At head of title: Folklore studies, pub-
　　lished by the Museum of Oriental Ethnology, the Catholic University of Pe-
　　king. Reprint from vol. v, 1946.
TORRANCE, THOMAS. China's first missionaries, ancient Israelites. London,
　　Thynne, 1937. 125 p. front., plates.
WHITE, WILLIAM CHARLES, bp., 1873-　　comp. Chinese Jews, a compilation
　　of matters relating to the Jews of K'aifeng Fu. Toronto, University of Toron-
　　to Press, 1942. 3 v. fronts., illus.(incl. facsims.) maps. [Monograph se-
　　ries of Chinese studies, no. 1, pt. 1-3].
WOO, H. SING. What a cultural Chinese thinks of the Jew? Asheville, N.C., The
　　Pelley Publishers, 1939. 24 p.
YIDDISH SCIENTIFIC INSTITUTE. Catalogue of the exhibition, Jewish life in
　　Shanghai, September 1948-January 1949. [Tr. from Yiddish] New York
　　[1948] 29 p.

# XII. PHILOSOPHY

## General Works

BECK, LILY (MORESBY) ADAMS, d. 1931. The story of oriental philosophy, by L. Adams Beck (E. Barrington) New York, Cosmopolitan Book Corporation, 1928. viii, 429 p. front., plates (1 fold. col.).

BERNARD, HENRI, 1897-   Sagesse chinoise et philosophie chrétienne; essai sur leurs relations historiques. Tientsin, Hautes Études, en vente à la procure de la Mission de Sienshien, 1935. 277, vi p.

————. The same. Paris, Cathasia [1950] 277, v p. (Les Humanités d'Extrême-Orient).

BRIÈRE, O. Les courants philosophiques en Chine depuis 50 ans (1898-1950). Changhai, 1949. [89] p. Reprinted from Bulletin de l'Université l'Aurore, Octobre, 1949.

————. Fifty years of Chinese philosophy, 1898-1950. Translated from the French by Laurence G. Thompson. Pref. by E. R. Hughes. London, Allen and Unwin [1956] 159 p.

CHAN, WING-TSIT, 陳榮捷, 1901-   An outline and a bibliography of Chinese philosophy. Rev. Hanover, N. H., 1955. 65 l. 1st ed. 1953.

————. Historical charts of Chinese philosophy. [New Haven] Far Eastern Publications, Yale University, 1955. unpaged.

CH'ÊN, LI-FU, 陳立夫, 1900-   Philosophy of life. [Tr. by Jen Tai, 任泰 ] With an introd. by Roscoe Pound. New York, Philosophical Library [1948] 148 p. diagrs.

CHÊNG, LIN, 鄭麐, 1901-   comp. and tr. Chinese wisdom; thoughts for harmonious and victorious living, compiled and translated by Chêng Lin and Lin Susan, 林素珊. Shanghai, World Book Co., 1947. vii, 71, 35 p. illus.

CHINESE philosophy: sayings of Confucius, sayings of Mencius, sayings of Lao Tzu, sayings of Chuang Tzu and Lieh Tzu. Decorations by Paul McPharlin. Mount Vernon, N. Y., Peter Pauper Press [1952?] 109 p. illus.

CHINESE philosophy of life. Girard, Kan., Haldeman-Julius Company [c1922] 51 p. (Ten cent pocket series no. 153, ed. by E. Haldeman-Julius ).

CHOW, YIH-CHING, 周毅卿. La philosophie chinoise. Paris, Presses universitaires, 1956. 128 p. (Que sais-je? Le point des connaissances actuelles, 707 ).

CREEL, HERRLEE GLESSNER, 1905-   Sinism; a study of the evolution of the Chinese world-view. Chicago, Open Court Pub. Co., 1929. vii, 127 p. Published also as thesis-University of Chicago.

————. Chinese thought, from Confucius to Mao-Tsê-tung. [Chicago] University of Chicago Press [1953]; London, Eyre and Spottiswoode, 1954. ix, 292 p.

————. La pensée chinoise de Confucius à Mao Tse-t'ung. Traduction de Jean-François Leclerc. Paris, Payot, 1955. 288 p. (Bibliothèque historique).

EBERHARD, WOLFRAM, 1909-   Beiträge zur kosmologischen Spekulation der Chinesen der Han-Zeit. Berlin, 1933. 100 p. diagrs. Diss.-Univ. Berlin. "Aus Baessler-archiv, band XVI, heft 1-2."

FAIRBANK, JOHN KING, 1907-   ed. Chinese thought and institutions; exploring twenty-five centuries of Chinese ideas in action. Chicago, University of Chicago Press, 1957; London, Oxford University Press, 1957. xiii, 438 p.

FANG, THOMÉ H., 方東美 , [Fang Tung-mei]. The Chinese view of life; the philosophy of comprehensive harmony. Hong Kong, Union Press [c1957] [xiv], 274 p.

FUNG, YU-LAN, 馮友蘭, 1895-   A comparative study of life ideals; the way of decrease and increase with interpretations and illustrations from the philosophies of the East and the West. Shanghai, Commercial Press, 1924. xii, 264 p. Thesis-Columbia University.

——. A history of Chinese philosophy; the period of the philosophers (from the beginnings to circa 100 B.C.) Translated by Derk Bodde, with introd.,notes, bibliography and index. Peiping, H. Vetch, 1937. 455 p. fold. map.

——. The spirit of Chinese philosophy. Tr. by E.R. Hughes. London, Kegan Paul [1947] xiv, 224 p.

——. A short history of Chinese philosophy, ed. by Derk Bodde. New York, Macmillan, 1948. xx, 368 p.

——. Précis d'histoire de la philosophie chinoise, d'après le texte anglais édité par Derk Bodde. Traduction de Guillaume Dunsteimer. Paris, Payot, 1952. 373 p. (Bibliothèque Scientifique).

——. A history of Chinese philosophy. Translated by Derk Bodde, with introd., notes, bibliography and index. Princeton, Princeton University Press,1952-53. 2 v. fold. map, diagrs.

FORKE, ALFRED, 1867-1944. The world-conception of the Chinese; their astronomical, cosmological and physico-philosophical speculations. London, A. Probsthain, 1925. xiv, 300 p. (Probsthain's oriental series, vol. 14 ).

——. Die Gedankenwelt des chinesischen Kulturkreises. München und Berlin, R. Oldenbourg, 1927. cover-title, 215 p.

——. Geschichte der alten chinesischen Philosophie. Hamburg, Kommissionsverlag, L. Friederichsen, 1927. xvi, 594 p. (Hamburgische universität. Abhandlungen aus dem gebiet der auslandskunde. bd. 25. Reihe B. Völkerkunde, kulturgeschichte und sprachen. bd. 14 ).

——. Geschichte der mittelalterlichen chinesischen Philosophie. Hamburg, Friederichsen, 1934. xii, 410 p. (Hamburgische universität. Abhandlungen aus dem gebiet der auslandskunde. bd. 41. Reihe B. Völkerkunde, kulturgeschichte und sprachen. bd. 21 ).

——. Geschichte der neueren chinesischen Philosophie. Hamburg, Friederichsen, 1938. xviii, 693 p. (Hansische universität. Abhandlungen aus dem gebiet der auslandskunde. bd. 46. Reihe B. Völkerkunde, kulturgeschichte und sprachen. bd. 25 ).

GRANET, MARCEL, 1884-1940. La pensée chinoise. Paris, La Renaissance du livre, 1934. xxiii, 614 p. diagrs. (L'évolution de l'humanité synthèse collective, [1. section, 25 bis] ).

GROUSSET, RENÉ, 1885-1952. Histoire de la philosophie orientale-Indie, Chine, Japon. Paris, Nouvelle Librairie Nationale, 1923. 376 p. (Bibliothèque française de philosophie ).

HACKMANN, HEINRICH FRIEDRICH, 1864-1935. Chinesische Philosophie. Mit einem bildnis Bodhidharmas. München, E. Reinhardt, 1927. 407 p. front. (Geschichte der philosophie in einzeldarstellungen. abt. I: Das weltbild der primitiven und die philosophie des Morgenlandes, bd. 5 ).

HOANG, TSEN-YUE, 黃曾樾 , [Huang, Tseng-yüeh]. Étude comparative sur les philosophies de Lao Tseu, Khong Tseu, Mo Tseu. Lyon, A. Rey; Paris, E. Leroux, 1925. xx, 299 p. (Annales de l'Université de Lyon. nouv. sér. ii. Droit, lettres. fasc. 37 ).

HU, SHIH, 胡適 , 1891-  The development of the logical method in ancient China. Shanghai, Oriental Book Co., 1922. 2, 10, 187 p.

HUANG, SIU-CHI, 黃秀璣 , 1913-  Lu Hsiang-shan, 陸象山 , a twelfth century Chinese idealist philosopher. New Haven, American Oriental Society, 1944. 116 p. diagrs. (American Oriental series, v. 27 ) Issued also as thesis-University of Pennsylvania.

HUGHES, ERNEST RICHARD, 1883-1956. Oxford and the comparative study of Chinese philosophy and religion; an inaugural lecture delivered in the examination schools on 20 November 1934. Oxford, The Clarendon Press, 1935. 23 p.

––––––. ed. The individual in East and West, edited by E. R. Hughes. London, Oxford University Press, H. Milford, 1937. vi, 197, [1] p.

––––––. ed and tr. Chinese philosophy in classical times, edited and translated by E. R. Hughes. London, J. M. Dent; New York, E. P. Dutton [1942] xlii, [1], 336 p. (Everyman's library, ed. by Ernest Rhys. Philosophy, [973] ).

HUMMEL, SIEGBERT. Polarität in der chinesischen Philosophie, dargestellt an Hand chinesischer Texte mit deutscher Übersetzung. Leipzig, O. Harrassowitz, 1949. vi, 36 p. (Forschungen zur Völkerdynamik Zentral- und Ostasiens, Heft 1 ).

[K'ANG HSI, emperor of China] 1655-1723. The Sacred edict; with a translation of the colloquial rendering, by F. W. Baller; prepared for the China Inland Mission. 6th ed. Shanghai, London [etc. ] China Inland Mission, 1924. vi, 216 p.

LIANG, CH'I-CHAO, 梁啓超, 1873-1929. The great Chinese philosopher K'ang Yu-wei. Introduction by Dai-ming Lee, 李大明. San Francisco, Chinese World [1953] cover-title, 68, [64] p.

LIANG, SI-ING, 梁錫英. La rencontre et le conflit entre les idées des missionnaires chrétiens et les idées des Chinois en Chine depuis la fin de la dynastie des Ming. Paris, Domat-Montchrestien, 1940. 159 p. Thèse-Univ. de Paris.

LIN, YU-T'ANG, 林玉堂, 1895-   The importance of living. New York, Reynal and Hitchcock [c1937]; London, Heinemann, 1938. xvi, 459 p.

––––––. The same. New York, John Day [1940] xvi, 459 p.

––––––. L'importance de vivre. Paris, Corréa, 1948. 288 p.

––––––. Weisheit des lächelnden Lebens. Aus dem Amerikanischen übertragen von Wilhelm Emmanuel Süskind. Stuttgart, Deutsche Verlags Anstalt, 1955. (c1938) 515 p. 1. Aufl. 1938.

––––––. Looking beyond. New York, Prentice-Hall; London, Bailey and Swinfen [1955] 387 p.

LUNG, CHÊNG-FU, 龍程芙, 1906-   The evolution of Chinese social thought. Los Angeles, University of Southern California Press, 1941. 40 p. (The University of Southern California. Social science series, 23 ). Extract from thesis-University of Southern California.

LYON, DAVID WILLARD, 1870-1949. Changing thought currents in modern China. Claremont, Calif., 1940. 20 p. (Claremont Oriental Studies, 3 ).

MALEBRANCHE, NICOLAS, 1638-1715. Entretien d'un philosophe chrétien et d'un philosophe chinois, suivi de l'Avis au lecteur. Avec une introduction et des notes par A. Le Moine. Marseille, Impr. et lithographie A. Ged, 1936. [11]-119 p. Thèse complémentaire-Aix-Marseille.

MASSON-OURSEL, PAUL, 1882-   La pensée en Orient. Paris, Colin, 1949. 215 p. (Collection Armand Colin, 255. Section de philosophie ).

MOORE, RUSSELL FRANKLIN, 1920-   Oriental philosophies, by William D. Gould, George B. Arbaugh [and] R. F. Moore. [3d ed., rev. ] New York, R. F. Moore Co. [1951] xiii, 220 p. First ed., by R. F. Moore, published in 1946.

––––––. ed. Readings in Oriental philosophies. New York, R. F. Moore Co. [1951] 116 p.

PORTER, LUCIUS CHAPIN, 1880-   comp. and tr. Aids to the study of Chinese philosophy, compiled by Lucius Chapin Porter. Translation by Fung Yu-lan, 馮友蘭, and Lucius Chapin Porter. [Peiping? 1934] 79 p. incl. tables, diagrs.

RICHARDS, IVOR ARMSTRONG, 1893-   Mencius on the mind; experiments in multiple definition. New York, Harcourt, Brace; London, Kegan Paul, 1932. xv, [1], 131, 44 p. front. (port.) diagr. (International library of psychology, philosophy and scientific method ).

SCHNUSENBERG, A. Terminologia philosophica latino-sinica, 拉丁中華哲學 辭典 auctoribus A. Schnusenberg et Th. Mittler, Editio tertia. Yenchowfu, E. typis missionis catholicae, 1935. ix p. 678 columns.

SCHWARTZ, FRIEDEBURG. China und das englische Schrifttum des 18. Jahrhunderts. Köln, 1943. 180 l. Diss.-Univ. Köln.

SHU, SEYUAN, 許思園, [Hsü, Ssŭ-yüan]. Answers to the grand problems of philosophy. [Wusih, Kiangsu] 1929. cover-title, 24 p.

――――. Une conception du bien moral. Paris, M. Vigne, 1941. 128 p.

SMALLEY, FRANK ALBERT. Chinese philosophy and religion. London, Produced by the Press and Publications Board of the Church Assembly for the Churches' Committee for Work Among Men in H. M. Forces, Westminster, 1947. 42 p. illus. (Religions of the East series, 4 ).

SPALDING, KENNETH JAY, 1879-  Three Chinese thinkers. [Mo-ti, Chuang-tzŭ and Hsün-tzŭ] Nanking, National Central Library [1947] 207 p. (International series of Chinese studies ).

TAZEROUT, MOHAND. La métaphysique intellectuelle d'Extrême-Orient. Rodez, Éditions Subervie [1955] 216 p. (His Au congrès des civilisés, 1 ).

THOMPSON, LAURENCE G., 1920-  Ta T'ung shu: the one world philosophy of K'ang Yu-wei. Claremont, Calif.[1954] vii, 458 l. Thesis-Claremont College.

TOMKINSON, LEONARD. Mysticism, ethics and service in Chinese thought. London, Seekers Association, 1956. 24 p. (Seekers Association. Pamphlets).

TSUCHIDA, KYOSON. Contemporary thought of Japan and China. New York, A. A. Knopf, 1927. xi, 13-239, [1] p. (Library of contemporary thought ).

VITALIS, J.H. Uralte chinesische Weisheit als moderne Weltauschaung. Bern, P. Haupt, 1944. 134 p.

WALEY, ARTHUR, 1889-  Three ways of thought in ancient China. London, G. Allen and Unwin [1939] 275, [1] p.

――――. The same. Garden City, N.Y., Doubleday, 1956. 216 p. (Doubleday anchor books, A75 ).

――――. Trois courants de la pensée chinoise antique. Traduction de G. Deniker. Paris, Payot, 1949. 198 p. (Bibliothèque scientifique).

――――. Lebensweisheit in alten China. Berechtigte Übersetzung von Eva Franziska Meister-Weidner. Hamburg, von Schröder, 1947. 227 p.

WANG, GUNG-HSING, 王恭行, 1908-  The Chinese mind. New York, John Day [1946] viii, 192 p.

WEBER, HARALD, 1881-1942. Die Weltdeuter des Ostens. Braunschweig, G. Westermann [c1927] 172 p.

WIEGER, LÉON, 1856-1933. Textes philosophiques; Confucianisme, Taoisme, Buddhisme. 2e éd., rev. et augmenté. [Hien-hsien] Impr. de Hien-hsien, 1930. 418 p. illus. 1st ed. 1906.

WILHELM, RICHARD, 1873-1930. Chinesische Lebensweisheit. Darmstadt, O. Reichl, 1922. 107 p.

――――. Chinesische philosophie. Breslau, F. Hirt, 1929. 128 p. illus., plates. (Jedermanns bücherei. Abt.: Philosophie ).

――――. Der Mensch und das Sein. Jena, E. Diederichs [c1931] v-x,[1], 337,[1] p. front.(port.).

――――. Weisheit des Ostens. Düsseldorf, E. Diederich [1951] 58 p. (Deutsche Reihe, Bd. 155 ).

WRIGHT, ARTHUR F., 1913-  ed. Studies in Chinese thought. With contributions by Derk Bodde [and others. Chicago] University of Chicago Press[1953] xiv, 317 p. illus. (Comparative studies in cultures and civilizations ).

YUAN, CHAUCER, 袁擢英. La philosophie morale et politique de Mencius. Paris, P. Geuthner, 1927. 324 p. incl. diagrs. (Université de Lyon. Études et documents publiés par l'Institut franco-chinois de Lyon, 2 ).

ZACH, ERWIN VON, 1872-1942. 1) Weitere Verbesserungen zu Forke's Geschichte der chinesischen Philosophie III.bd. 2) Sung Yü's Chiu pien. 宋玉九辨 [Batavia, 1939] 25 p.

ZACHARIAS, HANS CONRAD ERNEST, 1874-  Human personality, its historical emergence in India, China, and Israel. St. Louis, Herder, 1950. viii, 360 p. illus., maps.

ZENKER, ERNST VICTOR, 1865-    Geschichte der chinesischen Philosophie.
Reichenberg, Gebrüder Stiepel, 1926-27.  2 v.
———. Histoire de la philosophie chinoise; traduction par G. Lepage et Yves Le
Lay.  Paris, Payot, 1932.  527 p. (Bibliothèque historique).
ZOLLINGER, GUSTAV. Das Yang-und Yin-Prinzip ausserhalb des Chinesischen.
—Tau, Tau-t-an=Serm-an (der Spätere Hermes Trismegistos) Auf sprachver-
gleichender Basis gewonnene Ergebnisse über alte kulturelle Zusammen-
hänge. Bern, A. Francke, 1949.  63 p. illus.

## Confucian Classics
## I ching 易經

I CHING. I Ging; das Buch der Wandlungen, aus dem Chinesischen verdeutscht und
erläutert von Richard Wilhelm. Jena, E. Diederichs, 1924.  3 v. in 2.
———. The text of Yi king (and its appendixes) Chinese original, with English
translation by Z.D. Sung, 沈仲濤. Shanghai, China Modern Education Co.,
1935. xvi, 369, ii p. incl. diagrs.
———. I Ging, das chinesische Orakelbuck. In der Bearbeitung von Bill Behm.
Klagenfurt, J. Leon Sen., 1940.  139 p.
———. I Ging; das Buch der Wandlungen. Aus dem Chinesischen, neu übertragen
[von Mario Schubert] Zürich, W. Classen [1949] 95 p. (Vom Dauernden in
der Zeit, 48 ).
———. The I ching; or, Book of changes. The Richard Wilhelm translation rendered into English by Cary F. Baynes. Foreword by C.G. Jung. [New York]
Pantheon Books [1950]; London, Kegan Paul, 1951.  2 v. (Bollingen series,
19 ).
———. Das chinesische Orakelbuch I Ging [von] Bill Behm.  München, Drei
Eichen Verlag; Berlin, Weltweite-Verlag [1955].  173 p. 1. Aufl. 1940.
LIOU, TSE-HOUA, 劉子華, [Liu, Tzŭ-hua]. La cosmologie des Pa Koua et l'astronomie moderne. Situation embryonnaire du soleil et de la lune. Prévision
d'une nouvelle planète; exposé du système scientifique universel concernant
la genèse et l'évolution des mondes.  Paris, Jouve, 1940.  [5]-163, [1] p.
front.(port.) tables (1 fold.) diagrs. Thèse-Université de Paris.
MEARS, I. Creative energy; being an introduction to the study of the Yih king,
or Book of changes, with translations from the original text, by I. Mears and
L.E. Mears.  London, J. Murray [1931] xxiii, 239, [1] p. diagrs.
SUNG, Z.D., 沈仲濤, [Shen, Chung-t'ao). The symbols of Yi king; or, The
symbols of the Chinese logic of changes.  Shanghai, China Modern Education
Co., 1934. iii, [2], viii, 159 p. incl. diagrs.
WILHELM, HELLMUT, 1905-    Die Wandlung, acht Vorträge zum I-Ging.  Pe-
king, H. Vetch [1944] 157 p.
WILHELM, RICHARD, 1873-1930. Wandlung und Dauer; die Weisheit des I-Ging.
Düsseldorf, E. Diederichs [1956] 170 p.
YUAN, KUANG, 圓光. I ging: Praxis chinesischer Weissagung. Übersetzung
besorgte Fritz Werle.  München, O.W. Barth, 1951.  310 p. diagrs.
———. Méthode pratique de divination chinoise par le "Yi-king," avec préface
et notes explicatives de Tchou-Houa et Charles Canone. Dessins de Marcel
Nicaud.  Paris, Les Éditions Vega, 1952.  282 p. illus. (Bibliothèque des
arts divinatoires et des sciences conjectureles). 1er éd. 1950.

## Shu ching 書經

SHU CHING. Chou King; texte chinois avec une double traduction en français et
en latin, des annotations et un vocabulaire, par Séraphin Couvreur, S. J.
Sien Hsien, Impr. de la Mission catholique, 1927; 4th ed. 1934. 464 p. 2 fold.
maps.
———. The same. Les annales de la Chine [traduit] par Séraphin Couvreur.

Paris, Cathasia [1950] 464 p. (Les Humanités d'Extrême-Orient).

————. The Book of Documents [by] Bernhard Karlgren. Stockhom, 1950. cover-title, 81 p. Reprinted from the Bulletin of the Museum of Far Eastern Antiquities, No. 22.

KARLGREN, BERNHARD, 1889-  Glosses on the Book of Documents, 1-11. Stockholm, 1948-49. [276, 143] p. Reprinted from the Bulletin of the Museum of Far Eastern Antiquities, No. 20 and No. 21.

## Shih ching 詩經

SHIH CHING. Schi-king. Das Liederbuch Chinas, Gesammelt von Kung-fu-tse; hundert Gedichte, dem deutschen Angeeignet, nach Friedrich Rückert, von Albert Ehrenstein. [Wien, Gesellschaft für graphische Industrie; Leipzig, E. P. Tal und Co., 1922. 141, [1] p.

————. Cheu king. Texte chinois avec une double traduction en français et en latin, une introduction et un vocabulaire, par Séraphin Couvreur, S. J. 2. éd. Sien Hien, Impr. de la Mission catholique, 1926. 3. éd. 1934. xxxii, 555 p. illus., 2 fold. maps.

————. The classics of Confucius. Book of odes (Shi-king) by L. Cranmer-Byng. London, J. Murray, 1927. 56 p.

————. The book of poetry; Chinese text with English translation by James Legge. Reprint ed. Shanghai, Chinese Book Co., 1931. iv, 487 p. 1st ed., London, 1876.

————. The book of songs, translated from the Chinese by Arthur Waley. London, G. Allen and Unwin; Boston and New York, Houghton Mifflin [1937] Reprint ed. 1954. 358 p.

————. "Shu ist jagen gegangen"; chinesische Gedichte aus dem Schi-King, übertragen von W. M. Treichlinger. Zürich, Die Arche [1948] 61 p.

————. The book of odes. Chinese text, transcription and translation by Bernhard Karlgren. Stockholm, Museum of Far Eastern Antiquities, 1950. 270 p.

————. The classic anthology defined by Confucius. [Translator] Ezra Pound. Cambridge, Harvard University Press; London, Faber and Faber, 1954. 223 p.

HAN, YING, 韓嬰, fl. 150 B.C. Han shih wai chuan, 韓詩外傳: Han Ying's Illustrations of the didactic application of the Classic of songs; an annotated translation by James Robert Hightower. Cambridge, Harvard University Press, 1952. vii, 368 p. (Harvard-Yenching Institute. Monograph series, 11 ).

KARLGREN, BERNHARD, 1889-  The rimes in the Sung section of the Shi king. Göteborg, Elanders boktryckeri aktiebolag, 1935. 8 p. (Göteborgs högskolas årsskrift, XLI, 1935: 5 ).

LOON, P. VAN DER. Index to the Shih ching. Register zum Shih ching. Leiden, E. J. Brill, 1943. viii, 20 p.

TCHANG, TCHENG-MING, 張正明, [Chang, Chêng-ming]. Le parallélisme dans les vers du Cheu king. Changhai, Impr. et librairie de T'ou-sè-wè, Zi-ka-wei; Paris, P. Geuthner [1937] 100 p.

## I li, 儀禮 , Li chi, 禮記 , and Chou li, 周禮

I LI. Cérémonial; texte chinois et traduction par Séraphin Couvreur, S. J. 2. éd. Sien Hsien, Impr. de la Mission catholique, 1928. 667 p. 1er éd. 1916.

————. The same. [Reprint ed.] Paris, Cathasia [1951] 667 p. (Les humanités d'Extrême-Orient) 1er éd. 1916; 2e éd., 1928.

LI CHI. Li gi, das Buch der Sitte des älteren und jüngeren Dai; Aufzeichnungen über Kultur und Religion des alten China; aus dem Chinesischen verdeutscht und erläutert von Richard Wilhelm. Jena, E. Diederichs, 1930. xviii, 48, [2] p. incl. front.

————. Mémoires sur les bienséances et les cérémonies, par Séraphin Couvreur. [Reprint ed.] Paris, Cathasia [1950] 2 v. (Les Humanités d'Extrême-Orient) 2e éd., 1913.

CHOU LI. Le Tcheou-li; ou, rites des Tcheou, traduit pour la première fois du chinois par feu Édouard Biot. Paris, Impr. Nationale, 1851. [Reprint ed.] Peking, Wen tien-k'o, 1939. 3 v. illus. plates, plans, fold. map.

## Ch'un ch'iu, 春秋, and Tso chuan, 左傳

CH'UN CH'IU. Tch'ouen ts'iou et Tso-tchouan. La chronique de la principauté de Lôu [texte chinois avec traduction française] par Séraphin Couvreur. [Reprint ed.] Paris, Cathasia, 1951. 3 v. (Les Humanités d'Extrême-Orient ) 1er. éd., 1914.

FRASER, SIR EVERARD DUNCAN HOME, 1859-1922. Index to the Tso chuan, compiled by Everard D. H. Fraser, revised and prepared for the press by James Haldane Stewart Lockhart. London, New York [etc.] Oxford University Press, 1930. x, 430 p.

KARLGREN, BERNHARD, 1889-   On the authenticity and nature of the Tso chuan. Göteborg, Elanders boktryckeri aktiebolag, 1926. 65 p. (Göteborgs högskolas årsskrift. XXXII, 1926: 3 ).

————. The early history of the Chou li and Tso chuan texts. Stockholm, 1931. cover-title, 59 p. Reprinted from the Bulletin of the Museum of Far Eastern Antiquities, No. 3.

## Ssŭ shu, 四書

SSŬ SHU. Les quatre livres, avec un commentaire abrégé en chinois, une double traduction en français et en latin, et un vocabulaire des lettres et des noms propres, par Séraphin Couvreur, S. J. 3. éd. Sien Hsien, Impr. de la Mission catholique, 1930. vii, 748 p. 2e éd. 1910.

————. The same; avec la préface et le vocabulaire par Séraphin Couvreur. [Reprint ed.] Paris, Cathasia, 1949. 4 v. in 3 (vii, 654 p.) (Les Humanités d'Extrême-Orient ).

[————.] The four books: Confucian analects, The great learning, The doctrine of the mean, and the works of Mencius, with English translation and notes by James Legge. [Reprint ed.] Shanghai, Chinese Book Co. [1933] 1014 p.

————. The same; Confucian classics. Translated from the Chinese texts, rectified and edited with an introd. by Cheng Lin, 鄭麐. [Shanghai, World Publishers, c1948] xxxvi, 487 p. (Ancient Chinese classics series).

————. The gospel of China, "love virtue, and then the people will be virtuous." Edited and newly translated from the French of Pauthier with explanatory notes and prolegomena by Duncan Greenlees. Adyar, Madras, Theosophical Pub. House, 1949. lxxi, 180 p. port. (The World gospel series, 2 ).

————. Confucian analects; Dr. Legge's version. Edited with notes by Y. Ogaeri. Tokyo, Bunki Shoten [1950] 186 p.

CHUNG YUNG. The Chung-yung; or, The centre, the common, translated by Leonard A. Lyall and King Chien-kün. London, New York, Longmans, Green, 1927. vii-xxvii, 24 p.

————. Confucius; the unwobbling pivot and the Great digest; translated by Ezra Pound, with notes and commentary on the text and the ideograms, together with Ciu Hsi's "Preface" to the Chung yung and Tseng's commentary on the Testament. [n. p.] 1947. 52 p. (Pharos [no. 4] ).

————. The same. Bombay, Pub. for Kavitabhavan by Orient Longmans [1949] 44 p.

————. L'invariable milieu, Tschoûng-Yoûng; traduit du chinois par Abel Rémusat et préface par A. Volguine. Nice, Éditions des Cahiers astrologiques, 1952. 62 p. plates. (Les Maîtres de l'occultisme, 12 ).

————. Le Tchong yong, examen critique. Conférence donnée à la Faculté des Lettres le 23 février 1935 par Yoshio Takeuchi. Paris, J. Dumoulin, 1935. 14, [2] p. (Paris. Université. Institut d'études japonaise. Travaux et conférences, Fasc. 1 ).

CONFUCIUS. Les livres de Confucius; traduits et commentés par Pierre Salet. Paris, Payot, 1923. 102 p.

————. The sayings of Confucius, translated by Leonard A. Lyall. 2d ed. London, New York, Longmans, Green, 1925. xii, 112 p.

————. The same; a new translation of the greater part of the Confucian analects, with introduction and notes by Lionel Giles. London, J. Murray [1927] 132 p. (Wisdom of the East) "First impression September, 1907. Sixth impression August, 1927."

————. The wisdom of Confucius; a collection of the ethical sayings of Confucius and of his disciples. Edited by Miles Menander Dawson. Boston, International Pocket Library [c1932] 63 p. (International pocket library).

————. The Analects of Confucius, translated from the Chinese, with an introduction and notes, by Lionel Giles. Shanghai, Printed for the members of the Limited Editions Club by the Commercial Press, 1933. 114 numb. 1. plates.

————. Digest of the Analects. [version of Ezra Pound] Milan [P. Vera, 1937] [20] p.

————. The Analects of Confucius; translated and annotated by Arthur Waley. London, G. Allen and Unwin [1938] New ed. 1956. [11]-268 p.

————. The wisdom of Confucius, edited and translated with notes by Lin Yutang, 林語堂 . New York, The Modern Library; London, H. Hamilton [1938] xvii, 290 p. illus.(map) (The modern library of the world's best books).

————. Confucian analects; a selection from the philosophy and reflective writings of Confucius on harmony and equilibrium in living. Printed for the entertainment of the friends of Dr. C. C. Burlingame. New York and Hartford, 1939. 20 l.

————. The living thoughts of Confucius, presented by Alfred Doeblin. New York, Toronto, Longmans, Green, 1940; London, Toronto [etc.] Cassel and Co., 1942. 182 p. front.(port.) (The living thoughts library, ed. by A. O. Mendel).

————. The Analects; or, The conversations of Confucius with his disciples and certain others, as translated into English by William Edward Soothill, edited by his daughter Lady Hosie. London, New York [etc.] H. Milford, Oxford University Press [1941] lx, 254 p. front. (The World's classics, CDXLII ).

————. The conduct of life; the basic thoughts of Confucius [by] Miles Menander Dawson. New York, Garden City Pub. Co.[1941] xxi, 323 p. First published, 1915, under title: The ethics of Confucius. Also published, 1939, under title: The basic thoughts of Confucius; the conduct of life.

————. The conduct of life; the basic teachings of Confucius arranged for easy reading by Miles Menander Dawson. New York, The New Home Library [1942] v-xxi, 323 p.

————. Worte des Konfuzius; aus dem Buch der Gespräche. Bearb. und eingeleitet von Rudolf Wrede [pseud.] München, P. Hugendubel [c1942] 157 p.

————. The wisdom of Confucius, edited and translated with notes by Lin Yutang; illustrated by Jeanyee Wong, 黃如珍. New York, Modern Library [1943] xvii, [1], 265, [1] p. illus.(incl. map) col. plates. (Illustrated modern library).

————. Selections from the Confucian texts [in Chinese and English] by Arthur Lindsay Sadler. Sydney, Australian Medical Pub. Co., 1944. 55, 23 p.

————. The sayings of Confucius, illustrated and decorated by E. A. Cox. Leighon-Sea, Eng., F. Lewis [1946] 9-16 p. col. illus.

————. Les pages immortelles de Confucius, choisies et expliquées par Alfred Doeblin. Paris, Corrêa [1947] 233 p. (Collection Les Pages immortelles).

————. Lun-yü. Gespräche des Konfuzius. Aus dem Chinesischen von Irmgard Grimm. Heidelberg, Mölich, 1948. 113 p.

————. Konfuzius; Leben, Aussprüche, Weltanschauung [von] Waldemar Oehlke. Hamburg, Deutscher Literatur-Verlag [1949, c1948] 104 p.

————. La sagesse de Confucius. Présentation, introd. et notes de Lin Yutang. Traduction de l'anglais par Th. Bridel-Wasem. Paris, V. Attinger, 1949. 252 p. map. (Orient, 18).

————. Die goldene Mitte; Besinnliches aus dem Lun Yü, eingeleitet und übersetzt von Friedrich Thiel. Stuttgart, Schuler-Verlag, 1950. 163 p.

————. The best of Confucius, translated from the Chinese by James R. Ware. Garden City, N.Y., Halcyon House [1950] 192 p. illus.

————. Confucian analects; translated by Ezra Pound. New York, Kasper and Horton, 1952. 98 p. (Square dollar ser.) Reprinted from the Hudson Review.

————. The philosophy of Confucius in the translation of James Legge. With illus. by Jeanyee Wong, 黃如珍. Mount Vernon, N.Y., Peter Pauper Press [1953?] 220 p. illus.

————. Pensées morales. Traduit du chinois par René Brémond. Paris, Plon, 1953. 136 p. (Collection Jacques Haumont).

————. Gedanken und Gespräche des Konfuzius: Lun-yü. Aus dem Chinesischen Urtext neu übertragen und eingeleitet von Hans O.H. Stange. München, R. Oldenbourg [1953] 187 p.

————. So spricht Konfuzius (Lun-yü). [Auszug, dt.] Bearb. von W. Plügge. München-Planegg, O.W. Barth, 1954. 125 p. (Lebendige Quellen zum Wissen um die Ganzheit der Menschen).

————. Kung-fu-tse. Worte der Weisheit. Luin-yü. Die Diskussionsreden Meister Kung's mit seinen Schülern. Aus dem Urtext übertragen und erläutert von Haymo Kremsmayer. Wien, Europäischer Verlag, 1954. 128 p.

————. Gespräche (Lun-yü); aus dem Chinesischen verdeutscht und erläutert von Richard Wilhelm. Jena, E. Diederiche, 1923; Düsseldorf und Köln, E. Diederichs, 1955. xxxii, 255 p. front. port. 1.Aufl. 1910.

————. The sayings of Confucius. A new translation by James R. Ware. [New York] New American Library [1955] 125 p. (N.A.L. mentor books, 151 ).

————. Confucian analects. Translated and introduced by Ezra Pound. London, P. Owen [1956] 135 p.

————. Confucius, by Shigeki Kaizuka; translated [from the Japanese] by Geoffrey Bownas. London, G. Allen and Unwin; New York, Macmillan [1956] 191 p. illus. (Ethical and religious classics of East and West, no. 17 ).

MENCIUS. Mong dsi (Mong ko) Aus dem Chinesischen verdeutscht und erläutert von Richard Wilhelm. Jena, E. Diederichs, 1921. xix, 206, [1] p. incl. front. (port.) [Die religion und philosophie Chinas, 4].

————. Mencius, translated by Leonard A. Lyall. London, New York [etc.]Longmans, Green, 1932. xxviii, 277 p. col. front.

————. The book of Mencius (abridged) Translated from the Chinese by Lionel Giles. London, J. Murray [1942] 128 p. (The wisdom of the East series).

TA-HSÜEH. Ta hio, the great learning, newly rendered into the American language, by Ezra Pound. Seattle, University of Washington Book Store, 1928. 35 p. (University of Washington chapbooks, ed. by G. Hughes, 14 ).

————. The same, newly rendered into the American language by Ezra Pound. Norfolk, Conn., New directions [1939] 30 p. (New directions pamphlets, 4 ).

————. The great learning and The mean-in-action; newly translated from the Chinese, with an introductory essay on the history of Chinese philosophy, by E.R.Hughes. London, J.M. Dent [1942]; New York, E.P. Dutton, 1943. xii, 176 p.

————. Confucius: the great digest and Unwobbling pivot. Stone text from rubbings supplied by William Hawley; a note on the stone editions, by Achilles Fang, 方志彤. Translation and commentary by Ezra Pound. [New York, 1951]; London, P. Owen, 1952. 187 p. illus.

Confucius and Confucianism

AH KET, WILLIAM. Eastern thought with more particular reference to Confucius. Canberra, Australian Institute of Anatomy, 1933. 13 p. (George Ernest
Morrison lectures).

ARLINGTON, LEWIS CHARLES, 1859-1942. Some remarks on the worship offered
Confucius in the Confucian temple. Peiping, Peiping Chronicle, 1935. 8,
[20] p. plates. (China Chronicle, 10 ).

BIALLAS, FRANZ XAVER, 1878-1936. Konfuzius und sein Kult. Ein Beitrag zur
Kulturgeschichte Chinas und ein Führer zur Heimatsstadt des Konfuzius. Peking, Pekinger Verlag [c1928] 130 p. illus., ports., plans.

BONSALL, BRAMWELL SEATON. Confucianism and Taoism. London, Epworth
Press [1934] 127 p. (Great religions of the East).

BROWN, BRIAN, 1881-   ed. The story of Confucius, his life and sayings, with
introduction by Ly Yu Sang. 黎曜生   Philadelphia, David McKay [c1927] 265 p.
front. (port.) plates.

CHAN, NAY-CHOW, 陳汝舟, [Ch'en Ju-chow]. La doctrine du droit international chez Confucius. Paris, A. Pedone, 1941. 159 p.

CHANG, CH'I-YUN, 張其昀 1901-   A life of Confucius. Translated by Shih
Chao-yin, 時昭瀛. Taipei, China Culture Pub. Foundation, 1954. 113 p.

CHANG, KUANG-TSU, 張光楚. L'étude critique de la doctrine pédagogique de
Confucius. Bruxelles, Éditions Caducée, 1937. 184 p. Thèse-Univ.de Lille.

CH'EN, JOSEPH CHING-PAN. Confucius as a teacher. Toronto, 1940. 626 l.
Thesis-Univ. of Toronto.

CHÊNG, LIN, 鄭麐, 1901-   The study of ancient Chinese classics, a new approach. Shanghai, World Book Co. [1947] ii, 83 p. (Ancient Chinese classics ser.).

———. The teaching of the Four Books. [Shanghai] World Book Co. [1948] 36 p.

CHÊNG, T'IEN-HSI, 鄭天錫 , 1884-   China moulded by Confucius; the Chinese
way in western light. Published under the auspices of the London Institute of
World Affairs. London, Stevens, 1946. 264 p. front.(port.) illus.(map)
plates. (The Library of world affairs, 2 ).

———. La Chine, oeuvre de Confucius; la vie chinoise vue de l'Occident. Traduit
de l'original anglais par Auguste-Raynald Werner. Neuchâtel, Editions de
la Baconnière [1947]; Bruxelles, Office de Publicité [1948] iv, 416 p. illus.
map.

———. China, das Werk des Konfuzius; chinesisches Wesen im Lichte des Westens. [Aus dem Englischen übertragen von Anita Wiegand] Zürich, Rascher,
1949. 436 p. illus., port., map.

COLLIS, MAURICE, 1889-   The First Holy One. London, Faber and Faber;
New York, A.A. Knopf, 1948. 235 p. illus., maps.

COUCHOUD, PAUL LOUIS, 1879-   Japanese impressions, with a note on Confucius, tr. from the French of Paul-Louis Couchoud by Frances Rumsey,
with a preface by Anatole France. London, John Lane; New York, John
Lane company, 1921. xxiii, 155 p.

CREEL, HERRLEE GLESSNER, 1905-   Confucius, the man and the myth.
New York, John Day [1949]; London, Routledge and Kegan Paul [1951] xi,
363 p. map.

CREEL, LORRAINE JOHNSON, 1915-   The concept of social order in early
Confucianism. Chicago, 1943. 140 l. Thesis-University of Chicago.

CROW, CARL, 1883-1945. Master Kung; the story of Confucius. New York
and London, Harper, 1938. 344, [3] p. incl. front., plates.

———. Konfuzius Staatsmann, Heiliger, Wanderer; mit 12 Bildern nach chinesischen Vorlagen. Übers. von Richard Hoffmann. Berlin [etc.] P. Zsolnay,
1939. 391, [1] p. incl. plates.

DARRÉ, RICHARD WALTHER, 1895-   Vom Lebensgesetz zweier Staatsgedank-
en (Konfuzius und Lykurgos) Goslar, Verlag Blut und Boden [1940] 90 p.
plates, port. (Die Goslarer Volksbücherei [n. F.] 7 ).

DELIUS, RUDOLF VON, 1878-   Kungfutse, seine Persönlichkeit und seine

Lehre. Leipzig, P. Reclam jun.[c1930] 66, [2] p. (On cover: Reclams universal bibliothek, 7065 ).

DEVARANNE, THEODOR, 1880-   Konfuzius in aller Welt; ein tragisches Kapitel aus der Geschichte des Menschengeistes. Leipzig, J.C. Hinriches, 1929. 127 p.

EDWARDS, EVANGELINE DORA, 1888-   Confucius. London and Glasgow, Blackie [1940] xii, 146 p. ( What did they teach?).

FINGER, CHARLES J. The essence of Confucianism. Girard, Kan., Haldeman-Julius Co. [c1923] 64 p. (Pocket series, no. 471 ).

FOL, JEAN CHARLES. L'art de gouverner selon Confucius. Paris, La Nouvelle Édition [1947] 181 p.

FORD, EDDY LUCIUS, 1879-   A comparison of Confucian and Christian ideals. Foochow, Bing Ung press [192-?] 54 p.

GRIPEKOVEN, JEANNE. Confucius et son temps. Bruxelles, Office de Publicité, 1955; Neuchâtel, La Baconnière, 1955. 116 p. (Collections Lebegue et Nationale, 115 ).

HSIEH, TEHYI, 謝德怡, 1884-   Confucius said it first. Boston, Chinese Service Bureau [c1936] 91 p. front.(port.).

————. Konfuzius; eine Einführung in das Leben und Werken des Weisen und eine Auswahl seiner Gespräche und Gedanken. Übertr. von Ilse Krämer. Zürich, W. Classen [1954] 78 p. (vom Dauernden in der Zeit, 66).

HSU, C.Y., 徐慶譽. The philosophy of Confucius. With a foreword by J. Percy Bruce. London, Student Christian Movement, 1926. xxii, 23-63 p.

HSU, LEONARD SHIH-LIEN, 許仕廉, 1901-   The political philosophy of Confucianism; an interpretation of the social and political ideas of Confucius, his forerunners, and his early disciples. With a frontispiece of Confucius. London, G. Routledge, 1932. xxii, 257, [1] p. front. (The Broadway oriental library).

JOHNSTON, SIR REGINALD FLEMING, 1874-1938. Confucianism and modern China; the Lewis Fry memorial lectures, 1933-34, delivered at Bristol University. London, V. Gollancz, 1934; New York, D. Appleton-Century Co., 1935. 272 p. front., 1 illus., plates, facsim.

KAO, JEAN BAPTISTE, père, 高思謙, 1906-   La philosophie sociale et politique du confucianisme. Paris, [Schaebeek, "Votre imprimeur" Frans van Muysewinkel] 1938. 190, [2] p. Thèse-Univ. de Lille.

KENNEY, EDWARD HERBERT, 1891-   A Confucian notebook, by Edward Herbert [pseud.] With a foreword by Arthur Waley. London, Murray [1950] xiii, 89 p. (The Wisdom of the East series).

KITAMURA, SAWAKICHI, 1874-   Grundriss der ju-lehre. [Translated from the Chinese by Ferdinand Lessing and John Hefter.] Tokyo, Maruzen Co., 1935. xix, 372, 16 p. port., diagrs.

KOEHN, ALFRED. Confucius, his life and work. 2nd ed. Peking, Lotus Court, 1945. 42 p. illus.

KRAMERS, ROBERT PAUL. tr. K'ung tzu chia yü, 孔子家語; The school sayings of Confucius. Introduction, translation of sections 1-10. Leiden, E. J. Brill, 1949. vii, 379 p. (Sinica leidensia, 7).

KU, HUNG-MING, 1857-1928. Le catéchisme de Confucius; contribution à l'étude de la sociologie chinoise. Paris, M. Rivière, 1927. [9]-100 p.

The LIFE of Confucius, reproduced from a book entitled Shêng chi t'u, 聖蹟圖, being rubbings from the stone "Tablets of the Holy shrine. Shanghai, Kwang Hsueh Pub. House, Oxford University Press, China agency [1934?] 1 illus., 108 plates on 54 l.

LING, YU-SING, ed. Sketches of Confucius with illustrations. Foochow, Privately printed, 1948. 12 f. 12 col. plates.

LIU, WU-CHI, 柳無忌, 1907-   A short history of Confucian philosophy. [Harmondsworth, Middlesex] Penguin Books [1955] 229 p. (Pelican books, A333).

————. Confucius, his life and time. New York, Philosophical Library [c1955]

189 p.

MAGRE, MAURICE, 1877-    Le roman de Confucius.  Paris, Charpentier et
    Fasquelle, 1927.  216 p.

————.  Confucius and his quest, translated by Eliot Fay.  London, T.Butterworth
    [1929]  186 p.  front.

————.  The kingdom of Lu, the virtuous reforms of Confucius therein, something
    about his rival sage Lâo-tsze and more about that deplorable vagabond and
    clown Mong Pi, translated by Eliot Fay and illustrated by Kate Rowland.  New
    York, Cosmopolitan Book Corporation, 1929.  x, 178 p. front., illus.

PEETERS, JAN.  Eine Stimme aus der Sung-Zeit über die Heterodoxie: Lun-Yü,
    II, 16.  Breslau, 1938.  83 p. Diss.-Univ. Berlin.

ROE, CHUNGIL YHAN.  The true function of education in social adjustment, a
    comparative estimate and criticism of the educational teachings of Confucius
    and the philosophy of John Dewey with a view to evolving a project for a sys-
    tem of national education which will meet the needs of Korea.  Lincoln, Neb.,
    1927.  60 p. Thesis-Univ. of Nebraska.

ROSENKRANZ, GERHARD, 1896-    Der Heilige in den chinesischen Klassikern;
    eine Untersuchung über die Erlöser-Erwartung im Konfuzianismus und Taois-
    mus.  Leipzig, J.C. Hinrichs, 1935.  vii, 188 p. (Missionswissenschaftliche
    forschungen, hrsg. von der Deutschen gesellschaft für missionwissenschaft
    durch M. Schlunk, 9).

RYGALOFF, ALEXIS, 1922-    Confucius.  Paris, Presses universitaires de
    France, 1946.  [vii]-xii, 125 p. (Mythes et religions, collection dirigée par
    P.-L. Couchoud. [18] ).

SCHMITT, ERICH, 1893-    Konfuzius; sein Leben und seine Lehre.  Berlin,
    Deutsche Bibliothek [c1926]  216 p. plates (Die unsterblichen; die geistigen
    heroen der menschheit in ihrem leben und wirken, 3 ).

SHERLEY-PRICE, LIONEL DIGBY.  Confucius and Christ; a Christian estimate
    of Confucius.  Westminster [Eng.] Dacre Press [1951]  248 p. illus.

SHRYOCK, JOHN KNIGHT, 1890-    The origin and development of the state cult
    of Confucius; an introductory study.  New York, London, The Century Co.
    [c1932]  xiii, 298 p. illus.(plan).

SOULIÉ, CHARLES GEORGES, 1878-    La vie de Confucius (Krong Tse) par G.
    Soulié de Morant.  Paris, H. Piazza [1929]  213, [3] p. front.(port.) ("La
    sagesse antique").

————.  Les préceptes de Confucius (Krong Tse) par G. Soulié de Morant.  Paris,
    H. Piazza [1929]  xiv, [1], 164, [1] p. ("La sagesse antique").

STARR, FREDERICK, 1858-1933. Confucianism; ethics, philosophy, religion.
    New York, Covici-Friede, 1930.  ix, 3-250 p. incl. plates, ports. front.
    (port.).

WILHELM, RICHARD, 1873-1930. Kung-tse, Leben und Werk.  Stuttgart, From-
    mann, 1925.  210 p. front.(port.) (Frommanns klassiker der philosophie, be-
    gründet von †R. Falckenberg, 25 ).

————.  K'ungtse und der Konfuzianismus.  Berlin und Leipzig, W.de Gruyter,
    1928.  104 p.(Sammlung Göschen. [979] ).

————.  Confucius and Confucianism, translated into English by George H. Danton
    and Annina Periam Danton.  New York, Harcourt, Brace; London, Kegan
    Paul, 1931.  x, 181 p.

YANG, KEY P., 梁基伯, 1920-    An outline of the history of Korean confucian-
    ism, by Key P. Yang and Gregory Henderson.  Washington, State Dept.,1956.
    34 p.

YEH, GEORGE K.C., 葉公超, [Yeh, Kung Ch'ao] 1904-    The Confucian con-
    ception of jên.  London, The China Society, 1943.  14 p. (China Society Oc-
    casional papers. n.s.,3 ).

YETTS, WALTER PERCEVAL, 1878-1957. The legend of Confucius.  London,
    The China Society, 1943.  41 p. illus. (China Society Occasional papers, n.s.
    5 ).

YOUN, LAURENT EULSU, 1907-   Confucius, sa vie, son œuvre, sa doctrine.
Paris, Adrien Maisonneuve, 1943. [7]-126 p.

ZIA, Z.K., 謝頌羔, [Hsieh, Sung-kao]. The Confucian civilization. An introduction by Bishop Birney. Rev. ed. Shanghai, Commercial Press, 1925. viii,
90 p.

## Followers of Confucius
(Hsuntzu, Cheng I, Chou Tung-I, Chu Hsi, etc.)

CHENG, ANDREW CHIH-YI, 誠質怡, 1898-   Hsüntzu's theory of human nature
and its influence on Chinese thought. [Peking, 1928] 84, iii p. Thesis-Columbia University, 1928.

DUBS, HOMER HASENPFLUG, 1892-   Hsüntze, the moulder of ancient Confucianism. London, A. Probsthain, 1927. [xi]-xxxi, 308 p. (Probsthain's oriental series; vol.XV ).

GRAHAM, ANGUS CHARLES, 1919-   The philosophy of Ch'eng Yi-ch'uan,程頤
伊川, and Ch'eng Min-tao,程顥 明道 London, 1953. 350 l. Thesis-School of
Oriental and African Studies, University of London.

HSÜN-TZE, 荀子. The works of Hsüntze, translated from the Chinese, with
notes by Homer H. Dubs. London, A. Probsthain, 1928. 336 p. (Probsthain's oriental series. [vol.XVI] ).

HWANG, KIEN-CHUNG, 黃建中, 1890-   Hsun Tzŭ's logical doctrine and the
theory of probability. Nanking, Sino-Polish Culture Society, 1934. 18 p.

GABAIN, ANNEMARIE VON, 1901-    tr. Ein Fürstenspiegel: Das Sin-yü,新語,
des Lu Kia, 陸賈. Berlin, 1930. 82 p. Diss.-Univ. Berlin.

CHANG, CARSUN, 張嘉森, 1886-   The development of neo-Confucian thought.
With a preface by Arthur W. Hummel. New York, Bookman Associates,1957.
376 p.

CHÊNG, I., 程頤, 1033-1107. The philosophy of Chêng I; a selection of texts
from the complete works, edited and translated with introduction and notes
[by] Yung-ch'un Ts'ai, 蔡詠春. Ann Arbor, University Microfilms, 1950.
xiii, 376 p. (University Microfilms Publication No. 1756 ).

CHOU, TUN-I, 周敦頤, 1017-73. Ein Beitrag zur Kenntnis der chinesischen
Philosophie. T'ung su des Čeu-Tsí,周子通書, mit Ču-Hi's commentar, nach
dem Síng lì tsíng í, 性理精義; chinesisch mit mandschuischer und deutscher
Übersetzung und Anmerkungen hrsg. von Wilhelm Grube, kap. 1-20, fortge-
führt und beendet von Werner Eichhorn, kap. 21-40. Leipzig, Verlag Asia
Major, 1932. xvi, 173, 2 p. (China-Bibliothek der "Asia Major." Bd. 3 ).
[Grube's translation published in Wien, 1880-81].

CHOW, YIH-CHING, 周毅卿. La philosophie morale dans le néo-confucianisme
[Tcheou Touen-yi, 周敦頤 ] Préf. de Paul Demiéville. Paris, Presses universitaires de France, 1954 [c1953] xv, 230 p. (Bibliothèque de philosophie
contemporaine. Morale et valeurs).

EICHHORN, WERNER. Chou Tun-i, 周敦頤, ein chinesisches Gelehrtenleben
aus dem 11. Jahrhundert. Leipzig, Deutsche morgenländische Gesellschaft,
in kommission bei F.A. Brockhaus, 1936. 66 p. (Abhandlungen für die kunde
des Morgenlandes, mit unterstützung der Deutschen forschungs-gemeinschaft
hrsg. von der Deutschen morgenländischen gesellschaft. XXI, 5 ).

——. Die Westinschrift des Chang Tsai, 張載, ein Beitrag zur Geistesgeschich-
te der nördlichen Sung. Leipzig, Kommissionsverlag F.A. Brockhaus, 1937.
93 p. (Abhandlungen für die kunde des Morgenlandes, mit unterstützung der
Deutschen forschungsgemeinschaft, hrsg. von der Deutschen morgenländischen gesellschaft. XXII, 7 ).

CHU HSI. 朱熹 1130-1200. The philosophy of human nature, by Chu Hsi, translated from the Chinese, with notes by J. Percy Bruce. London, Probsthain
1922. xvi, 444 p.(Probsthain's Oriental series, vol. X).

——. Djin-si lu, 近思錄, vor. Dschu Hsi. Die Sung-konfuzianische Summa mit
dem Kommentar des Yä Tsai, 葉采. Übersetzt und erläutert von Olaf Graf.

Tokyo, Sophia University Press, 1953. 3 v. in 4. (Monumenta Nipponica monog. 12 ).

BRUCE, JOSEPH PERCY, 1861-1934. Chu Hsi and his masters; an introduction to Chu Hsi and the Sung school of Chinese philosophy. London, Probsthain, 1923. xvi, 336 p. diagrs. (Probsthain's Oriental series. vol. XI ).

LE GALL, STANISLAS, 1856-1916. Le philosophie Tchou Hi, sa doctrine, son influence. 2. éd. Changhai, Impr. de la Mission Catholique, 1923. 132 p. diagrs. (Variétés sinologiques, 6 ).

GRAF, OLAF, 1900-   Kaibara Ekiken, ein Beitrag zur japanischen Geistesge-schichte des 17. Jahrhunderts und zur chinesischen Sung-philosophie. Lei-den, E. J. Brill, 1942. x, 545 p.

HSU, PAO-CHIEN, 徐寶謙, 1892-1944. Ethical realism in neo-Confucian thought. [Peiping, 1933] vi, [2], 165, xix, [4] p. diagrs. Thesis-Columbia University.

PANG, CHING-JEN, 龐景仁. L'idée de Dieu chez Malebranche et l'idée de li chez Tchou Hi; suivies de: Du li et du k'i, traduction annotée du livre XLIX des Œuvres complètes de Tchou Hi. Paris, J. Vrin, 1942. 130 p. plates. Thèse-Univ. d Paris.

SARGENT, GALEN EUGENE. Tchou Hi contre le bouddhisme. Paris, Impr. Nationale, 1955. 158 p. Thèse-Univ. de Paris.

## Wang Yang-ming, 王陽明

CADY, LYMAN VANLAW. Wang Yang Ming's "intuitive knowledge"; a study. [Tsinan? 1936?] iv, 44 p. "Two lectures delivered at the School of Chinese studies, Peiping. Jan. 15th and 17th. 1936."

WANG, TCH'ANG-TCHE, 王昌祉, [Wang, Ch'ang-chih]. La philosophie morale de Wang Yang-ming. [n. p.] 1936. 217, [1], 31*p. Thèse-Univ. de Paris.

## Lao-tzŭ

LAO-TSŬ. Der Anschluss an das Gesetz; order, Der grosse Anschluss. Ver-such einer Wiedergabe des Tao-te-king von Carl Dallago. Insbruck, Breuner, 1921. 111 p.

LAO-TZŬ. Tao te king; das Buch des Alten vom Sinn und Leben, aus dem Chi-nesischen verdeutscht und erläutert von Richard Wilhelm. Jena, E. Dieder-ichs, 1921; Düsseldorf, Köhn, E. Diederichs, 1950. xxx, 119 p. 1. Aufl. 1911. 1957 ed. 160 p.

――――. Theosophie in China; Betrachtungen über des Tao-teh-king (Der Weg, die Wahrheit und das Licht) übers. aus dem Chinesischen des Lao-tze. Bearbei-tet von Franz Hartmann. Leipzig, Theosophische Central-Buchhandlung, 1922. 135 p.

――――. Tao teh king; by Lao Tzu; a tentative translation from the Chinese, by Isabella Mears. [2d. ed. ] London, Theosophical Pub. House, 1922. 111 p.

――――. The simple way [by] Laotze (the "old boy"); a new translation of the Tao-teh-king, with introduction and commentary by Walter Gorn Old. 3d. ed. Lon-don, W. Rider, 1922. xi, 186 p. 1st ed. 1904; 3rd ed. 1913; reprinted 1922.

――――. Des Laotse Tao-te-king. Deutsch von F. Fiedler; hrsg. von Gustav Wyne-ken. Hannover, P. Steegemann [1922] 97 p.

――――. Mensch, werde wesentlich! - Laotse sprüche. Deutsch von Klabund [pseud., i. e. Alfred Henschke]. Berlin-Zehlendorff, F. Heyder, 1922. 32 p.

――――. Le livre de la voie et de la vertu, Tao te king de Lao Tseu. Traduit et commenté par Pierre Salet. Paris, Payot, 1923. 96 p.

――――. Die Bahn und der rechte Weg des Lao-Tse; der chinesischen Urschrift nachgedacht von Alexander Ular. Leipzig, Insel-Verlag, 1923. 106 p. 1. Aufl. 1903.

――――. The simple way of Lao Tsze; an analysis of the Tao tĕh canon with comments by the editors of the Shrine of Wisdom. London, Shrine of Wisdom, 1924. 55 p. (Shrine of Wisdom. Manual no. 8).

——. Lao-tse's Taò tĕ kīng; aus dem Chinesischen ins deutsche übersetzt, eingeleitet und commentirt von Victor con Strauss. Leipzig, Verlag "Asia Major," 1924. lxxx, 357 p. front. (port.).

——. Laotse Wollen ohne Wahl; die Grundweisheit des Tao-te-king in freier Umschöpfung vergegenwärtigt von Elisabeth Hahn. Rudolstadt, Greifenverlag, 1924. 63 p.

——. Tao, a rendering into English verse of the Tao teh ching of Lao Tsze (B.C. 604) Wheaton, Ill., Theosophical Press [c1926] 1945. [7]-79 p.

——. The sayings of Lao Tzŭ, translated from the Chinese, with an introduction, by Lionel Giles. London, J. Murray; New York, Dutton [1926] [7]-53, [1] p. (Wisdom of the East series). "First edition May 1905; reprinted January 1926."

——. Laotse Tao teh king; vom Geist und seiner Tugend, übertragung von H. Federmann. 4. Aufl. München, C.H. Beck, 1926. ix, 101, [1] p.

——. [The philosophy of Lao Tze, translated by Wu-wu-tze [pseud.] Chengtu, 1926] 59 numb. 1. "Wu-wu-tze is a pseudonym. The translators are Dryden Linsley Phelps and Mr. Shae."

——. Tao-te-king, hrsg. und erläutert von J.G. Weiss. Leipzig, P. Reclam [1927] 92, [1] p. (Reclams universal bibliothek, nr. 6798).

——. The canon of reason and virtue, being Lao-tze's Tao-teh-king; Chinese and English by Paul Carus. Chicago and London, Open Court, 1927. 209 p. 1st ed. 1903.

——. Laotse (Tao teh king) translated from the Chinese by Shuten Inouye, with critical and exegetical notes, comparing various renderings in Chinese, Japanese and English, including new English versions by the translator. Tokyo, Duitokaku, 1928. 745, [2] p.

——. Die Bahn des All und der Weg des Lebens. Deutsch von E. Schröder. München, F. Bruckmann [1934] v, 101 p.

——. The way and its power; a study of the Tao tĕ ching and its place in Chinese thought, by Arthur Waley. London, G. Allen and Unwin [1934]; Boston, H. Mifflin, 1935. 11-262 p.

——. The way and its power; a study of the Tao te-ching and its place in Chinese thought, by Arthur Waley. London, G. Allen and Unwin; New York, Macmillan, 1956. 262 p. New York, Grove Press, 1958. 262 p.

——. Laotzu's Tao and wu-wei. 2d ed. rev. and enl. A new translation by Bhikshu Wai-Tao and Dwight Goddard. Interpretive essays by Henry Borel. Outline of Taoist philosophy and religion, by Dr. Kiang Kang-Hu, 江元虎. Santa Barbara, Calif., D. Goddard, 1935. 7-149 p.

——. The same. Thetford, Vt., D. Goddard, 1939. 139 p. 1st ed. 1919.

——. Tao teh king (The way of peace) of Lao-Tzu, 600 B.C. As re-stated by A.L. Kitselman II. [Palo Alto, Calif., The School of Simplicity, c1936] vii, 55 p.

——. Tao teh ching, translated and annotated by Hu Tse Ling, 胡子霖. Chengtu, Canadian mission press [1936] iv, 128 p.

——. Lao-tze's Tao teh king, the Bible of Taoism; English version by Sum Nung Au-Young, 歐陽心農 With an introduction by Merton S. Yewdale. New York, March and Greenwood [1938] 15-123 p.

——. The simple way [by] Laotze: (the 'Old boy') A new translation of the Tao-teh-king, with introduction and commentary by Walter Gorn Old. 7th ed. Philadelphia, David McKay [1939] xi, 186 p. "First edition September 1904. 3rd edition 1913.

——. Lao-tzu's The Tao and its virtue; translated and annotated by John C.H. Wu, 吳經熊. Shanghai, 1939-40. Reprint from Tien Hsia, v.9, p. 401-23,

498-521 (1939); v. 10, p. 66-99 (1940).

————. Lau Dse. Dau do djing des alten Meisters Kanon vom Weltgesetz und seinem Wirken. Neuübertragung von Franz Esser. Peking, Verlag der Pekinger Pappelinsel [c1941] 81, 6 p.

|————.] Tao tê ching, a new translation by Ch'u Ta-kao, 初大告. London, The Buddhist lodge [1942] 94 p. ''First published October, 1937. Third edition (war-time), 1942.'' Fourth edition, 1945, reprinted 1948.

————. Lao tze: The Tao-teh-king; a new translation with introduction and commentary (formerly published under the title ''The book of the simple way.'') By Walter Gorn Old. 8th ed. London, New York [etc.] Rider [1943] xi, [1], [3]-186 p. ''First edition, September 1904.''

————. Le doctrinal de Lao-tseu. Tr. by Stanislas Julien. Paris, Impr. de J. Haumont, 1944. 92 p. (Collection des petites œuvres).

————. The way of life according to Laotzu; an American version by Witter Bynner. New York, John Day [1944] 76 p.

————. The canon of reason and virtue, being Lao-tze's Tao teh king; Chinese and English by Paul Carus. Chicago, Open Court Pub. Co., 1945. [3]-209 p. front. illus. ''This booklet is an extract from the author's larger work, Lao-Tze's Tao teh king.'' 1st ed. 1903.

————. Die Weisheit des Ostens. Tao-te-king von Lao-tse, übertr. von O. Sumitomo. Zürich, Scientia [1945] 95 p. illus. plate. (Vom Dauernden in der Zeit, 3).

————. The way of life according to Laotzu; translated by Witter Bynner. [London] Editions Poetry London [1946] 74 p.

————. The way of acceptance, a new version of Lao Tse's Tao tê ching, by Hermon Ould. London, A. Dakers [1946] 95 p.

————. Führung und Kraft aus der Ewigkeit [Dau-dŏ-ging] Aus dem Chinesischen Urtext übertragen von Erwin Rousselle. [Wiesbaden] Insel-Verlag, 1946. 70 p. (Insel-Bücherei, 253).

————. Tao Te King; das Buch des Alten vom Weltgrund und der Weltweise, aus dem Chinesischen Urtext, neu übertragen und gedeutet von Haymo Kremsmayer. Salzburg, Igonta-Verlag, 1947. 122 p. illus.

————. The Tao teh of Laotse. A new version of the Chinese classic with comments and annotations by Frederick B. Thomas. [Oakland? Calif.] c1948. 122 l.

————. The wisdom of Laotse, tr., ed. and with an introd. and notes by Lin Yutang. New York, Modern Library [1948] xx, 326 p. (The Modern library of the world's best books [262]).

————. Lau Dse: Das als Weltgesetz und Vorbild. Deutsch von Vincenz Hundhausen. Peking, Pekinger Verlag, 1948. 83 p.

————. Kleines Laotse-Brevier. Zur Stärkung und Erleuchtung des Herzens in der Bedrängnis des Tages zusammengestellt aus dem Tao-te-king. [Hrsg. von Ferdinand Holzmann] Heidelberg, F. Holzmann, 1948. 8 p.

————. Das verborgene Juwel. Laotses Verkündung. Ausdeutung und Nachdichtung von Sprüchen aus dem Tao-te-king des chinesischen Weisen und Mystikers Laotse, von Josef Tiefenbacher. Stuttgart, Schuler Verlag, 1948. 108 p. plate. (Bücher d. Lebensweisheit).

————. The great Sindersis; being a translation [by Orde Poynton] of Tao tê-ching, attributed by tradition to Li Erh, 李耳 (Lao-tse). Adelaide, Hassell Press, 1949. [4] 1, 85 p.

————. Lao Tse Tao-Te-king. Textgestaltung und Einführung: Rudolf Backofen. Herausgeber: Werner Zimmermann. Thielle/Neuchâtel, Verlag Fankhauser [1949] 223 p.

————. La voie et sa vertu; texte chinois présenté et traduit par Houang Kia Tcheng, 黃家誠, et Pierre Leyris. Paris, Édition du Seuil, 1949. 133 p.

(Collection poètique bilingue).

———. Truth and nature, popularly known as Dawder-jing; appended with Chinese texts and the oldest commentaries, edited and translated with an introduction by Cheng Lin, 鄭麐. [Shanghai] World Book Co. [1950] xii, 71, 118, 24 p. (Ancient Chinese classics series).

———. Ho-Shang-Kung's 河上公 commentary on Lao-Tse. Translated and annotated by Eduard Erkes. Ascona, Artibus Asiae, 1950. 136 p. Reprinted from Artibus Asiae, 8, 9, 12, (1940, 1946 and 1949).

———. Das Buch von der grossen Weisheit. Deutsch von André Eckardt. Frankfurt a. M., A. Lutzeyer [1950] 53 p. plate (Besitz der Erde, 2).

———. Tao Te King. Aus dem Chinesischen übers. und kommentiert von Victor von Strauss. Bearbeitung und Einleitung von W. Y. Tonn. Zürich, Manesse Verlag, 1950. 420 p. (Manesse Bibliothek der Weltliteratur).

———. Tao te king; le livre du Tao et de sa vertu; traduction nouvelle suivie d'Aperçus sur les enseignements de Lao Tseu. Lyon, P. Derain, 1951. 245 p. (Collection Taôisme).

———. Li Ör-Lao tse Tao-te-King; älteste und Lehrer als Führer zum Wege Gottes und zum echten Leben. Aus dem Chinesischen Urtext neu übersetzt und gedeutet von E. Müller. Mit einer Auslegung ''Der Tempel des Tao''hrsg. von Gottfried Ginter. Bühl-Baden, Verlag Konkordia [1952] 66 p. port.(Grosse Erzieher der Menschheit, 1 ).

———. So spricht Lao tse. [Tao te king; übertragen von Walter Jerven] München-Planegg, O. W. Barth, 1952. 124 p. (Lebendige Quellen zum Wissen um die Ganzheit des Menschen).

———. Tao tö king, le livre de la voie et de la vertu. Texte chinois établi et traduit avec des notes critiques et une introd. par J.-J.-L. Duyvendak. Paris, Librairie d'Amérique et d'Orient, 1953. xiii, 187 p.

———. Tao te ching, the Book of the way and its virtue. Translated from the Chinese and annotated by J. J. L. Duyvendak. London, J. Murray [1954] vi, 172 p. facsim. (Wisdom of the East series).

———. The way of life. A new translation of the Tao tè ching, by R. B. Blakney. [New York] New American Library [c1955]; London, Muller, 1955. 134 p. (A Mentor book, M129).

## Commentaries

BAUMANN, CAROL. Reflections prompted by Laotse, a psychological approach. Berne, A. Francke, 1946. cover-title, [49]-61 p. ''Reprint from Bulletin de la Société suisse des amis de l'Extrême-Orient, vol. VIII, 1946.''

BOREL, HENRI, 1869-1933. The rhythm of life, based on the philosophy of Lao-Tse; translated by M. E. Reynolds from the Dutch of Henri Borel. London, J. Murray, 1921. 9-89 p. (Wisdom of the East series). Revised edition of the translation published by Luzac in 1904 and 1909 under title: Wu-wei.

———. Wu Wei, 無爲, Fantaisie inspirée par la philosophie de Lao Tsź; traduit du hollandais par Félicia Barbier. Paris, Éditions du monde nouveau, 1931. 108 p.

———. The same. Eine Auslegung der Lehren Laotses. Übersetzung und Vorwort von Werner Zimmermann. Salzburg, Rorschach; München, Friedeus-Verlag, 1947. 107 p.

CHANG, AMOS IH TIAO, 張一調, 1916-  The existence of intangible content in architectonic form based upon the practicability of Laotzu's philosophy. Princeton [Princeton University Press ] 1956. 72 p. illus.

EWALD, OSCAR, 1881-  Laotse. München, G. Müller, 1928. 86, [1] p. (Religio, religiöse gestalten und strömungen).

GRIFFITH, GWILYM OSWALD, 1882-  Interpreters of reality; a comment on Heracleitus, Lao-tse and the Christian faith. London, Lutterworth Press [label: Chicago, A.R. Allenson, 1946] 106 p.

ÎAN, KHIN-SHUN, 楊興順. Der chinesische Philosoph Laudse und seine Lehre, von Jang Ching-schun. [Übersetzt von G. Kahlenbach] Berlin, Deutscher Verlag der Wissenschaften, 1955. 136 p.

KARLGREN, BERNHARD, 1889-    The poetical parts in Lao-tsï. Göteborg, Elanders boktryckeri aktiebolag, 1932. 45 p. (Göteborgs högskolas årsskrift. XXXVIII, 1932: 3 ).

LÜTH, PAUL E.H., 1919-    Der seidene Mond. Die Legenden von Lao-tse und Li T'ai Po. Wiesbaden, Limes-Verlag [1947] 64 p.

MacINNES, TOM. The teaching of the Old Boy. London, Toronto, etc., Dent, 1928. ix, 11-227 p.

MAURER, HERRYMON, 1914-    The Old Fellow. New York, John Day [1943] viii, 296 p.

SAITSCHICK, ROBERT. Schöpfer Lebenswerte von Lao-tse bis Jésus. Zürich, Rascher Verlag, 1945. iv, 456 p.

STADELMANN, HEINRICH, 1865-    Laotse und die Biologie. [Genf, 1935] 22 p. illus. (Schriftenreihe der Bibliothek Sino-international, Genf, nº 2 ).

————. Die biologie des Laotse. Leipzig, Niels Kampmann, 1936. 20, [1] p.

[TRÖLTSCH, CHARLOTTE, FREIFRAU VON] 1876-    Lao-tse; die bisher unbekannte Lebensgeschichte des chinesischen Weisen und sein Wirken; Aufgenommen durch besondere Begabung eines Dazu berufenen. München, Verlag "Der Ruf" [1935] 345, [1] p.

WELCH, HOLMES. The parting of the way; Lao Tzu and the Taoist movement. Boston, Beacon Press [1957] 204 p. illus.

WILHELM, RICHARD, 1873-1930. Lao-tse und der Taoismus. 2. Aufl. Stuttgart, F. Frommann, 1948 [c1925] 164 p. group port. (Frommanns Klassiker der Philosophie, 26 ).

WULFF, KURT, 1881-1939. Acht Kapitel des Tao-tê-king. Hrsg. von Victor Dantzer. København, E. Munksgaard, 1942. 98 p. (Det Kgl. danske videnskabernes selskab. Historiskfilologiske meddelelser. XXVIII, 4 ).

## Chuang tzŭ and Others

CHUANG-TZŬ, 莊子. Dschuang Dsi. Das wahre Buch vom südlichen Blütenland, Nan hua dschen ging, 南華真經; aus dem Chinesischen verdeutscht und erläutert von Richard Wilhelm. Jena, E. Diederichs, 1923; Reprinted, 1940. xxiv, 267, [1] p. incl. front. port. 1. Aufl. 1912.

————. Chuang Tzŭ, mystic, moralist, and social reformer, translated from the Chinese by Herbert A. Giles. 2d ed., rev. London, B. Quaritch; Shanghai, Kelly and Walsh, 1926. xxviii, 466 p.

————. Die Weisheit des Dschuang-dse in deutschen Lehrgedichten [von] Vincenz Hundhausen. [Peking, Leipzig, Pekinger Verlag, c1926] 2 v.

————. Musings of a Chinese mystic; selections from the philosophy of Chuang Tzŭ; with an introduction by Lionel Giles. London, J. Murray [1927] 112 p. (Wisdom of the East series) 1st ed. 1906.

————. Chuang Tzŭ; a new selected translation with an exposition of the philosophy of Kuo Hsiang, 郭象, by Yu-lan Fung, 馮友蘭. Shanghai, Commercial Press, 1933. vi, [3]-164 p. 1st ed. 1931.

————. Reden und Gleichnisse; deutsche Auswahl von Martin Buber. [Zürich] Manesse Verlag [1951] 243 p. port. (Manesse Bibliothek der Weltliteratur) 1st ed. Leipzig, 1918.

————. Dichtung und Weisheit [von] Tschuang-tse. Aus dem Chinesischen Urtext übersetzt von Hans O.H. Stange. [Wiesbaden] Insel-Verlag [1954] 77 p.(Insel-Bücherei, Nr. 499).

BUNGARTZ, LOTHAR. Der Gedanke des "Nicht-Handelns" bei Chuang'tse. Ein

Beitrag zu den Staatsphilosophischen Spekulationen des chinesischen Altertums. Köhn, 1956. v, 147 p. Diss.-Univ. Köhn.

CHAN, WING-TSIT, 陳榮捷, 1901-    Philosophy of Chuang Tze. Cambridge,
1929. 248 p. Thesis-Harvard University.

LIE-TSŬ, 列子, B.C.450-375. Liä Dsi. Das wahre Buch vom quellenden Ur-
grund, Tschung hū dschen ging, 沖虛眞經. Die Lehren der Philosophen Lia
Yū Kou, 列禦寇, und Yang Dschu, 楊朱. Aus dem Chinesischen verdeutscht
und erläutert von Richard Wilhelm. Jena, E. Diederichs, 1921. xxix, 175 p.
plates. (Die Religion und Philosophie Chinas, Bd.8, 1 ).

## Mo Ti and Others

MO TI, fl. 400 B.C. Mê Ti des Sozialethikers und seiner Schüler philosophische
Werke, zum ersten male vollständig übersetzt, mit ausführlicher Einleitung,
erläuternden und textkristischen erklärungen versehen von professor Alfred
Forke. Berlin, Kommissionsverlag der Vereinigung wissenschaftlicher Ver-
leger, 1922. xiv, 638 p. (Mitteilungen des Seminars für orientalische sprach-
en an der Friedrich-Wilhelms-universität zu Berlin, beiband zum jahrg.XXIII/
XXV).

————. The social teachings of Meh Tse [translated by L. Tomkinson] Tokyo,Asi-
atic Society of Japan [1927] 184 p. (The Transactions of the Asiatic society of
Japan, 2d ser., vol.IV ).

————. The ethical and political works of Motse, translated from the original Chinese text by Yi-Pao Mei. London, A. Probsthain, 1929. xiv, 275 p. (Probsthain's Oriental series, 19 ).

GEISSER, FRANZ, 1913-    Das Prinzip der allgemeinen Menschenliebe im Re-
formprogramm Mo Ti's und seiner Schule und seine Aufnahme in China und
Europa. Uznach, Gebr. Oberholzer, Buchdr., 1947. xi, 25-75, 173-175 p.
Part of thesis-Zürich.

————. Mo Ti, der Künder der allgemeinen Menschenliebe. Bern, A. Francke,
1947. 180 p.

HOLTH, SVERRE. Micius; a brief outline of his life and ideas; with an introduction by Frank Rawlinson. Shanghai, Commercial Press, 1935. viii, 79 p.

LONG, WILBUR HARRY. Motze, China's ancient philosopher of universal love.
Peiping, College of Chinese Studies, California College in China [193-] 38 p.

MEI, YI-PAO, 梅貽寶, 1900-    Motse, the neglected rival of Confucius. London, A. Probsthain, 1934. xi, 222 p. fold. map. (Probsthain's Oriental series, 20 ).

ROWLEY, HAROLD HENRY, 1890-    The Chinese philosopher Mo Ti. (In John
Rylands Library, Manchester. Bulletin. Manchester, 1948. v. 31, p. 241-
276 ).

WILLIAMSON, HENRY RAYMOND. Mo Ti, a Chinese heretic; a short sketch of
his life and works. [Tsinan, The University Press, 1927] 38 p. "Lecture
delivered before the Literary society of Tsinanfu in November 1926."-Pref.

HUAI-NAN TZŬ, 淮南子, d.B.C.122. Tao, the great luminant; essays from
Huai nan tzu, with introductory articles, notes, analyses, by Evan Morgan;
foreword by J.C. Ferguson. London, Kegan Paul [1935] xlv, 287, [4] p.
incl. diagrs.

KOU, PAO-KOH, 顧保鵠, [Ku, Pao-ku]. Deux sophistes chinois: Houei Che,惠
施, et Kong-souen Long, 公孫龍. Paris, Impr. Nationale, 1953. viii,163p.
(Bibliothèque de l'Institut des Hautes Études chinoises, 8 ).

KUNG-SUN, LUNG, 公孫龍, 3d cent. B.C. Works; with a translation from the
parallel Chinese original text, critical and exegetical notes, punctuation and
literal translation, the Chinese commentary, prolegomena, and index, by
Max Perleberg. Hongkong, 1952. xxiii, 160 p.

LIU, SHAO, 劉邵, 3d cent. The study of human abilities; the Jen wu chih,人物

志, of Liu Shao, with an introductory study of J.K. Shryock. New Haven, American Oriental Society, 1937. x, 168 p. (American Oriental series, v.11).

BUNGER, KARL, 1903-    Studien über Religion und Staat in China. Tübingen,
1949. vii, 179 l. Diss.-Univ. Tübingen.

CHAN, WING-TSIT, 陳榮捷, 1901-    Religious trends in modern China. New
York, Columbia University Press, 1953. xiii, 327 p. (Lectures on the his-
tory of religions sponsored by the American Council of Learned Societies.
New series, 3 ).

————. Religiöses Leben im heutigen China. Übers. von Marcella Roddewig und
Grüfin Gertrud von Helmstädt. München-Planegg, O.W. Barth, 1955. 279 p.

CHÊNG, TE-KUN, 鄭德坤, 1907-    The religious outlook of the Chinese. London, The China Society, 1956. 8 p. (China Society Occasional Papers, 9 ).

CLENNELL, WALTER JAMES, 1867-    The historical development of religion
in China. London, The Theosophical Pub. House [1926] xv, 11-262 p. 1st
ed. 1917.

DE KORNE, JOHN CORNELIUS, 1888-    Chinese altars to the unknown God; an
account of the religions of China and the reactions to them of Christian missions. [Grand Rapids, Mich., 1926] ix-xiii, 139, [3] p. illus.

————. The Fellowship of goodness (T'ung shan she, 同善社 -a study in contemporary Chinese religion. [Grand Rapids, Mich., J.C. De Korne, 1941] vi,
109 (i.e. 124) numb. l. Thesis-Hartford seminary foundation, Kennedy school
of missions.

DAVARANNE, THEODOR, 1880-    Chinas Volksreligion; dargestellt nach einer
Rundfrage und verglichen mit den Grundlehren des Laotze, Konfuzius und
Buddha. Tübingen, J.C.B. Mohr (Paul Siebeck), 1924. 48 p. (Sammlung
gemeinverständlicher Vorträge, 107 ).

————. Der gegenwärtige Geisteskampf um Ostasien; der religions-und missions-
kundliche Ertrag einer Ostasienreise. Gotha, L. Klotz, 1928. vi, [1], 96 p.
(Bücherei der christlichen welt, 21 ).

ENDRES, FRANZ CARL, 1878-    Ethik des alltags. Zürich und Leipzig, Rascher [c1939] 135 p. plates, ports.

FARRÈRE, CLAUDE, 1876-    Forces spirituelles de l'Orient: Inde-Chine-Japon-
Turquie. [Paris] E. Flammarion [1937] [5]-244 p.

GLASENAPP, HELMUTH VON, 1891-    Die fünf grossen Religionen. Düssendorf, E. Diederichs Verlag, 1951-52. 2 v.

————. Les cinq grandes religions du monde. Traduit par Pierre Jundt. Paris,
Payot, 1954. 558 p. (Bibliothèque scientifique).

GLICK, CARL, 1890-    The secret of serenity; decorations by Joe Karov. New
York, Crowell [1951] 237 p.

GRAHAM, DAVID CROCKETT, 1884-    Religion in Szechuan province, China
(with twenty-five plates). Washington, Smithsonian Institution, 1928. 83 p.
plates on 13 l., diagrs. (Smithsonian miscellaneous collections. 8:4 ).

GRANET, MARCEL, 1884-1940. La religion des Chinois. 2. éd. Paris, Presses
universitaires de France, 1951. xi, 175 p. (Bibliothèque de philosophie contemporaine) 1er éd. Paris, Gauthier-Villars, 1922.

GROOT, JAN JAKOB MARIE DE, 1854-1921. Sectarianism and religious persecution in China; a page in the history of religions. Reprint ed. Peking, 1940.
2 v. plates. 1st ed. 1903-04.

GRÜTZMACHER, RICHARD HEINRICH, 1876-    Konfuzius, Buddha, Zarathustra,
Muhammed. Leipzig, A. Deichert, 1921. 92 p. port. (Lebensideale der

Menschheit, 2 ).

――――. Primitive und fernöstliche Religionen: China und Japan; eine religionsgeschichtliche Charakterkunde allgemeinverständlich dargestellt von professor dr. Richard H. Grützmacher. Leipzig, A. Deichert [1937] 49, [1] p.
(His Religionsgeschichtliche charakterkunde. [hft. 1] ).

HALL, MANLY PALMER, 1901-   The way of Heaven; and other fantasies told
in the manner of the Chinese. Los Angeles, Philosophical Research Society
[c1946] 184 p.

HARDIE, ALEXANDER, 1841-   Illustrious gentile Asiatics: Zoroaster, Buddha,
Confucius. Los Angeles, The Times-mirror Press, 1931. xx, 218 p.

HENTZE, CARL, 1883-   Objets rituels, croyances et dieux de la Chine antique
et de l'Amérique. Anvers, Éditions "De Sikkel," 1936. 119, [122] p. illus.
plates.

HUGHES, ERNEST RICHARD, 1883-1956. Religion in China, by E. R. Hughes
and K. Hughes. London, New York, Hutchinson's University Library, 1950.
151 p. (Hutchinson's university library: world religions, 39 ).

KATO, JOKEN. Religion and thought in ancient China. Cambridge, 1953. 44 p.
(Harvard-Yenching Doshisha Eastern cultural lectures, 3 ).

KERN, MAXIMILIAN, 1877-   Das Licht des Ostens; die Weltanschauungen des
mitteleren und fernen Asiens, Indien-China-Japan, und ihr Einfluss auf das
religiöse und sittliche Leben, auf Kunst und Wissenschaft dieser Länder.
Unter Mitwirkung von Museumsdirektor dr. Otto Fischer. Stuttgart, Union
deutsche-Verlagsgesellschaft [1922] 597 p. front., illus., 3 col. plates.

KING, PAUL HENRY, 1853-   Weighed in China's balance; an attempt at explanation. London, Heath, Cranton, 1928. 238 p.

KRAUSE, FRIEDRICH ERNST AUGUST, 1879-   Ju-Tao-Fo, 儒道佛. Die religiösen und philosophischen Systeme Ostasiens. München, E. Reinhardt,
1924. 588 p.

――――. Terminologie und Namensverzeichnis zu Religion und Philosophie Ostasiens. Beiheft zu Ju-Tao-Fo. München, E. Reinhardt, 1924. 226 p.

LEMAÎTRE, SOLANGE. Le mystère de la mort dans les religions d'Asie. Préface de Jacques Bacot. Paris, Presses universitaires de France, 1943. xi,
151, [1] p. (Mythes et religions. Collection dirigée par P. -L. Couchoud. [12]).

LIN, YU-T'ANG, 林語堂, 1895-   Chinese ideals of life. London, Watts and
Co. [1944] 32 p. (The Thinker's forum, 31 ).

LY HOI-SANG, 黎海生, 1870-1944. Book of everlasting gifts from ancient sages,
by Ly Hoi Sang in collaboration with Richard Alexander. New York, Long
Sang Ti Chinese Curios Co., 1927. 47 p.

MACLAGAN, PATRICK JOHNSTON, 1865-   Chinese religious ideas; a Christian valuation. London, Student Christian Movement, 1926. 238, [1] p.

MASPERO, HENRI, 1883-1945. Mélanges posthumes sur les religions et l'histoire de la Chine. Paris, Civilisations du Sud, S.A.E.P., 1950. 3 v.(Publications du Musée Guimet. Bibliothèque de diffusion, t. 57-59 ).

――――. Le Ming-T'ang, 明堂, et la crise religieuse chinoise avant les Han.
Bruges, 1951. 72 p. (Mélanges chinois et Bouddhiques, t. 9 ).

[MORGAN, HARRY TITTERTON] 1872-   Chinese religious beliefs. The ancient
religions-new pages of history. The three religions of China: Taoism, Confucianism, Buddhism. The new tide, rev. ed. Los Angeles, Calif. , Quon Quon
Company, c1944. 20 p. illus.(ports.) [His Chinese classics in miniature] 1st
ed. 1941.

NIVISON, DAVID SHEPHERD, 1923-   Communist ethics and Chinese tradition.
Cambridge, Center for International Studies, Massachusetts Institute of Technology, 1954. 83 l.

O'NEILL, FREDERICK WILLIAM SCOTT, 1870-   The quest for God in China.
New York, George H. Doran; London, G. Allen and Unwin, 1925. 272 p.

PERNITZSCH, MAX GERHARD, 1882-   Die Religionen Chinas. Berlin, W. de
Gruyter, 1940. 111 p. (Lehrbücher der Ausland-Hochschule an der Univer-

sität Berlin, 40 ).

RAWLINSON, FRANK JOSEPH, 1871-1937. Chinese ideas of the Supreme Being. Shanghai, Presbyterian Mission Press, 1927. 57 p.

———. Revolution and religion in modern China; a brief study of the effects of modern revolutionary movements in China on its religious life. Shanghai, Presbyterian Mission Press, 1929. [1], 97 p.

———. Chinese ethical ideals; a brief study of the ethical values in China's literary, social and religious life. Shanghai, 1934. x, 128 p.

REICHELT, KARL LUDVIG, 1877-1952. Religion in Chinese garment. Translated by Joseph Tetlie. New York, Philosophical Library [1951]; London, Lutterworth Press, 1951. 180 p. (Lutterworth library, v. 36. Missionary research series, 16 ).

———. Meditation and piety in the Far East; a religious-psychological study. Translated from the Norwegian [by] Sverre Holth. New York, Harper [c1954]; London, Lutterworth Press, 1954. 171 p. (Lutterworth library, v. 42. Missionary research series, 19 ).

ROSENKRANZ, GERHARD, 1896-    Fernost-wohin? Begegnungen mit den Religionen Japans und Chinas in Umbruch der Gegenwart. Heilbronn, E. Salzer, 1940. 304 p. illus.

ROWLEY, HAROLD HENRY, 1890-    Prophecy and religion in ancient China and Israel. [London] University of London, 1956. 154 p. (Jordan lectures in comparative religion, 4 ).

RUDD, HERBERT FINLEY, 1877-    Chinese social origins. Chicago, University of Chicago Press [1928] ix, 221 p.

SAUNDERS, KENNETH JAMES, 1883-1937. The ideals of East and West. Cambridge [Eng. ] The University Press, 1934. xxiii, 246, [2] p.

SCHMITT, ERICH, 1893-    ed. Die Chinesen. Tübingen, Mohr, 1927. 110 p. (Religionsgeschichtliches lesebuch. 2. erweiterte aufl., 6 ).

SHRYOCK, JOHN KNIGHT, 1890-    The temples of Anking and their cults; a study of modern Chinese religion. Paris, 1931. [5]-206 p. plates. Thesis-University of Pennsylvania, 1927.

SOOTHILL, WILLIAM EDWARD, 1861-1935. The three religions of China; lectures delivered at Oxford. 2d ed. London, New York [etc. ] Oxford University Press, H. Milford, 1923. 271, [1] p. illus.

———. Les trois religions de la Chine, traduit par G. Lepage. Paris, Payot, 1946. 270 p.

STEWART, JAMES LIVINGSTONE. Chinese culture and Christianity; a review of China's religions and related systems from the Christian standpoint. New York and Chicago, Fleming H. Revell [c1926] 316 p. illus.

TAN, YUN-SHAN, 譚雲山, 1901-    What is Chinese religion? Santiniketan, Sino-Indian Cultural Society of India, 1937. 16 p.

TIEN, TCHEU-KANG ANTOINE. L'idée de Dieu dans les huit premiers classiques chinois. Ses noms, son existence et sa nature étudiée à la lumière des découvertes archéologiques. Fribourg, Éditions de l'Oeuvre St. Justin, 1942. 224 p. Thèse-Univ. de Fribourg.

[VAN DURME, J.]. La notion primitive de "Dieu" en Chine. Bruges, Ch. Beyaert [1927] 16 p.

WEBER, MAX, 1864-1920. Konfuzianismus und Taoisms. Tübingen, J. C. B. Mohr, 1922. [260] p. (His Gesammelte Aufsätze zur Religionssoziologie, 1).

———. The religion of China: Confucianism and Taoism, translated and edited by Hans H. Gerth. Glencoe, Ill., Free Press, 1951; London, G. Allen and Unwin, 1952. xi, 308 p.

WERNER, EDWARD THEODORE CHALMERS, 1864-    The Chinese idea of the second self. Shanghai, Shanghai Times, 1932. 49 p.

WIEGER, LÉON, 1856-1933. Histoire des croyances religieuses et des opinions philosophiques en Chine depuis l'origine, jusqu'à nos jours. 2. éd. augm. [Sienhsien (Hokienfu)] Impr. de [Sienhsien] 1922. 796 p. illus. (incl. ports., plans).

――――. A history of the religious beliefs and philosophical opinions in China from the beginning to the present time. Translated by Edward Chalmers Werner. [Hsien-hsien] Hsien-hsien Press, 1927. 774 p. illus. (incl. plans).

――――. Bouddhisme chinois. Paris, Cathasia [1951] 2 v. illus. (Les Humanités d'Extrême-Orient).

YANG, YUNG-CH'ING, 楊永清, 1892-1956. China's religious heritage. New York, Nashville, Abingdon-Cokesbury Press [1943] 196 p.

YU, SHIH-YU, 于式玉. Religions secrètes contemporaines dans le nord de la Chine. Chengtu, 1948. [1] 1. 2, viii, 175 p. illus. (Studia serica. Monog. ser., 4 ).

Buddhism
Bibliographies
(See also Tibet - Literature)

BIBLIOGRAPHIE bouddique, v. 1-      Paris, P. Geuthner et Adrien Maisonneuve, 1930-date.

――――. Index: v. 1-6, 1938; v. 7-23, 1955.

HAMILTON, CLARENCE HERBERT, 1886-   Buddhism in India, Ceylon, China and Japan; a reading guide. Chicago, University of Chicago Press [c1931] viii, 107 p.

MARCH, ARTHUR CHARLES, 1880-   comp. A Buddhist bibliography. London, Buddhist Lodge, 1935. xi, 257, [1] p.

NANJIO, BUNYIU, 1849-1927, comp. A catalogue of the Chinese translation of the Buddhist Tripiṭaka, the sacred canon of the Buddhists in China and Japan. Oxford, Clarendon Press, 1883; [Tokyo, Japan, 1929] [ix]-xxxvi p., 480 col.

REGAMEY, C. Buddhistische Philosophie. Bern, A. Francke, 1950. 86 p.
(Bibliographische Einführungen in das Studium der Philosophie, 20/21 ).

TOKIWA, DAIJO, ed. Japanese alphabetical index of Nanjiō's Catalogue of the Buddhist Tripiṭaka, with supplements and corrections; ed. by Daijō Tokiwa and Unrai Ogiwara, assisted by Kōjun Minō. Tōkyō, Nanjiō-hakushi kinen kankōkwai, 1930. ix, 142, [4] p. port.

Dictionaries and Indexes

BAGCHI, PROBODH CHANDRA, 1898-1956. Deux lexiques sanskrit-chinois: Fan yu tsa ming, 梵語雜名, de Li Yen, 禮言, et Fan yu ts'ien tseu wen,梵語千字文, de Yi-tsing, 義淨. Paris, P. Geuthner, 1929-37. 2 v. (Sino-Indica; publications de l'université de Calcutta, 2, 3 ).

FAN FAN YÜ, 翻梵語. Fan-Fan-Yü, chaps. 43-55, 60-61; being a Chinese dictionary of Indian geographical names compiled in 517 A.D. from literature and accounts of travellers. The Chinese text transcribed into Devanagari and rendered into Sanskrit for the first time by Raghu Vira, together with restoration of Indian forms of names both geographical and literary. [Lahore, International Academy of Indian Culture, 1943] 11, 114 p. (Sarasvati vihara series, 14 ).

HACKMANN, HEINRICH FRIEDRICH, 1864-1935. Alphabetisches Verzeichnis zum Kao-seng-chuan, 高僧傳. Leiden, E. J. Brill, 1923. v, [81]-112 p. Reprinted from Acta Orientalia, v. 2.

――――. Erklärendes Wörterbuch zum chinesischen Buddhismus. Chinesisch-San-skrit-Deutsch. Nach seinem handschriftlichen Nachlass überarbeitet von Johannes Nobel. Leiden, E. J. Brill, 1951-52. 5 pts.

HŌBŌGIRIN, 法寶義林; dictionnaire encyclopédique du bouddhisme d'après les sources chinoises et japonaises, publié sous le haut patronage de l'Académie impériale du Japon et sous la direction de Sylvain Lévi et J. Takakusu. Rédacteur en chef, Paul Demiéville. Tōkyō, Maison franco-japonaise, 1929-

v. plates (part col.) illus. (incl. music).

————. Fascicule annexe. Tables du Taishō Issaikyo, nouvelle édition du Canon bouddhique chinois, publié sous la direction de J. Takakusu et K. Watanabe. Tōkyō, Maison franco-japonaise, 1931. cover-title, ii, 202 p.

NYANATILOKA, bhikku. Buddhist dictionary; manual of Buddhist terms and doctrines. Colombo, Frewin, 1950. [iii]-v, [13-189] p. fold. table. (Island hermitage publication, 1 ).

————. Buddhistisches Wörterbuch, kurzgefasstes Handbuch der buddhistischen Lehren und Begriffe in alphabetischer Anordnung. Konstanz, Christiani [1954] 277 p. (Buddhistische Handbibliothek, 3 ).

SCHMIDT, KURT. Buddhistisches Wörterbuch. Konstanz, C. Weller [1949, c1948] 110 p.

SOOTHILL, WILLIAM EDWARD, 1861-1935. A dictionary of Chinese Buddhist terms, with Sanskrit and English equivalents and a Sanskrit-Pali index, compiled by William Edward Soothill and Lewis Hodous. London, Kegan Paul, Trench, Trubner, 1937. xix, 510 p.


## General Works


ĀRYABHADRAKALPIKĀSŪTRA. Tausend Buddhanamen des Bhadrakalpa, nach einer fünfsprachigen Polyglotte hrsg. von Friedrich Weller. Leipzig, Verlag der Asia Major, 1928. xxv, 268, [2] p. diagrs.

BAGCHI, PRABODH CHANDRA, 1898-1956. Le canon bouddhique en Chine; les traducteurs et les traductions. Paris, P. Geuthner, 1927-38. 2 v. (Sino-Indica; publications de l'Université de Calcutta. t.I, 4 ).

BARTHÉLEMY SAINT-HILAIRE, JULES, 1805-95. Hiouen-Thsang, 玄奘, in India, translated from the French by Laura Ensor. [Reprint ed.] Calcutta, Susil Gupta, 1952. 104 p. [An extract from the author's Bouddha et sa religion, 1895].

BLOFELD, JOHN EATON CALTHORPE, 1913-   The jewel in the lotus; an outline of present day Buddhism in China. [London] Published for the Buddhist Society, London, by Sidgwick and Jackson [1948] 193 p. illus.

BOSE, PHANINDRA NATH. The Indian teachers in China. Triplicane, Madras, S.E., S. Ganesan, 1923. 148 p.

BOUILLARD, GEORGES, 1862-1930. Notes divers sur les cultes en Chine: Les attitudes des Buddhas. Pékin, A. Nachbaur, 1924. 28 p. plates.

BUDDHA, his life and teachings; illustrations by Jeanyee Wong, 黃如珍. Mount Vernon, N.Y., P. Pauper Press, 1954. 269 p. illus.

CHAVANNES, ÉDOUARD, 1865-1918. Contes et légendes du buddhisme chinois. Traduits du chinois. Paris, Bossard, 1921. 220 p. illus. fold. table. (Les classiques de l'Orient, 4 ).

CH'EN, KENNETH K.S., 陳觀勝, 1907-   A study of the Svāgata story in the Divyāvadāna in its Sanskrit, Pāli, Tibetan and Chinese versions. Cambridge, 1946. 107 p. Thesis-Harvard University. Reprinted from HJAS 9:3-4 (1947).

CHINESE BUDDHIST ASSOCIATION. Buddhism in China. Peking, Nationalities Pub. House, 1955. [2] l., 24 col. plates (in portfolio).

————. Statues and pictures of Gautama Buddha. Peking, Nationalities Pub. House, 1956. [8] p. plates (part col.).

————. Buddhists in new China. 中國佛教畫集. Peking, Nationalities Pub. House, 1957. 189 p. (chiefly illus., part col.).

CHOU, HSIANG-KUANG, 周祥光. T'ai Hsu, 太盧; his life and teachings. Allahabad, Indo-Chinese Literature Publications, 1956. 76 p.

CHOU, TA-FU, 周達夫. Three Buddhist hymns restored into Snaskrit from Chinese transliterations of the tenth century A.D. Bombay, 1946. 62 p. Thesis-Univ. of Bombay.

CLEATHER, MRS. ALICE LEIGHTON. Buddhism, the science of life, two monographs by Alice Leighton Cleather; also Tibetan initiates on the Buddha with

explanations and comments by Basil Crump. Peking, China Booksellers,
1928. 19, [1], [25]-50, [52]-183 p. front., plates, ports., facsim.

COOMARSSWAMY, ANANDA KENTISH, 1877-1947. Le pensée du Bouddha;texte
chinois, présentés par Ananda K. Coomarsswamy. Paris, Édition Corréa,
1949. 301 p.

DEMIÉVILLE, PAUL, 1894-   Les versions chinoises du Milindapañha. Hanoi,
1924. 258 p. plates, tables. (Hanoi. École français d'Extrême-Orient, Bull.
t. 24 ).

————. Sur l'authenticité du Ta tch'eng k'i sin louen,   大乘起信論 [ascr. to Aś-
vaghoşa] Tokyo, 1929. 78 p. Reprinted from Bulletin, Maison franco-japonaise, Tokio. t. 2, no. 2 ).

————. Le concile de Lhasa; une controverse sur le quiétisme entre bouddhistes
de l'Inde et de la Chine au VIII. siècle de l'ère chrétienne. Paris, Impr. Nationale de France, 1952. viii, 398 p. facsims. (Bibliothèque de l'Institut des
hautes études chinoises, v. 7 ).

DUTT, NALINAKSHA. Aspects of Mahāyāna Buddhism and its relation to Hīna-
yāna with a foreword by Prof. Louis de la Vallée Poussin. London, Luzac,
1930. xiii, 358 p. (Calcutta oriental series, 23 ).

ELIOT, SIR CHARLES NORTON EDGECUMBE, 1862-1931. Hinduism and Buddhism; an historical sketch. London, E. Arnold, 1921. 3 v.

ENNIN, 793-864. Diary; the record of a pilgrimage to China in search of the law;
translated from the Chinese by Edwin O. Reischauer. New York, Ronald
Press [1955] xvi, 454 p. col. port., maps (on lining papers).

FELLMANN, FREDERICK MARIA. Der Bodhisattva. Werdewege fernöstliche
Weisheit. Mit 15 chinesische Messerschnitte. Bremen, Z. Z. Schildhorst,
Dünen Verlag, 1947. 62 p.

GERNET, JACQUES, 1921-   Les aspects économiques du bouddhisme dans la
société chinoise du vᵉ au xᵉ siècle. Saigon, École française d'Extrême-Orient, 1956. 331 p. illus. (Publications de l'École française d'Extrême-Orient,
39 ).

GETTY, ALICE. The gods of northern Buddhism, their history, iconography and
progressive evolution through the northern Buddhist countries, with a general
introduction on Buddhism translated from the French of J. Deniker; illustrations from the collection of Henry H. Getty. Oxford, Clarendon Press, 1928.
lii, 220 p. col. front., plates (part col.) diagr.

GORDON, ELIZABETH ANNA. Asian Cristology [!] and the Mahāyāna; a reprint
of the century-old "Indian church history" by Thomas Yeates, and the further
investigation of the religion of the Orient as influenced by the apostle of the
Hindus and Chinese by E. A. Gordon. Tokyo, Meruzen and Co., 1921. xiii,
334 p. col. front., 1 illus., plates (part col.).

GROUSSET, RENÉ, 1885-1952. Sur les traces du Bouddha. Paris, Plon [1929]
iv, 329 p. front., plates, fold. map. 1957 ed.   312 p.

————. In the footsteps of Buddha. Translated from the French by Mariette Leon.
London, G. Routledge, 1932. xi, 352 p. front., plates, fold. map.

GULIK, ROBERT HANS VAN, 1910-   Siddham: an essay on the history of Sanskrit studies in China and Japan. Nagpur, 1956. 2 v. plates. (Sarasvati-
Vihara ser., 36 ).

HÄRTEL, HERBERT. Karmavācanā. Formulare für Gebrauch im buddhistischen
Gemeindeleben aus osturkistanischen Sanskrit-Handschriften. Göttingen,
1953. 178 p. Diss.-Univ. Göttingen.

HODOUS, LEWIS, 1872-1949. Buddhism and Buddhists in China. New York,
Macmillan, 1924. xi, 84 p. (The World's living religions).

HSIEH, TEHYI, 謝德怡, 1884-   Selected pearls of wisdom, and Buddhism.
Boston, Chinese Service Bureau [c1937] 95, [1] p. front. (port.).

HSÜAN-TS'ANG, 玄奘 , 603-664. Briefe der uigurischen Hüen-tsang-Biographie

von Annemarie von Gabain. Berlin, Verlag der Akademie der Wissenschaft-
en, 1938. 47 p. (Sitzungsberichten der Preussischen Akademie der Wissenschaften, Phil.-Hist. Kl. 1938. XXIX.).

KARUTZ, RICHARD, 1867-   Maria im fernen Osten; das Problem der Kuan
Yin. Leipzig, O.W. Barth, 1925. 99 p. illus.

KIMURA, RYUKAN. A historical study of the terms Hinayāna and Mahāyāna and
the origin of Mahāyāna Buddhism. [Calcutta] University of Calcutta, 1927.
xx, 203 p.

KITAYAMA, JUNYU, 1902-   Metaphysik des Buddhismus; Versuch einer philosophischen Interpretation der lehre Vasubandhus und seiner Schule. Stuttgart-Berlin, W. Kohlhammer [1934] xv, 268 p. (Veröffentlichungen des Orientalischen seminars der Universität Tübingen. 7. hft.).

LEE, PI-CHENG, 呂碧城, 188?-1943. Kwan Yin's saving power; some remarkable examples of response to appeal for aid, made to Kwan Yin by his devo-
tees. Collected, translated and edited by Pi-cheng Lee and published in England. Oxford, Printed at Kemp Hall Press, 1932. 39 p. port.

———. ed. and tr. An outline of Karma, edited, translated, and published by Pi-
cheng Lee of China. [n.p., 1941?] 97 p.

LEE, SHAO-CHANG, 李紹昌, 1891-   Popular Buddhism in China, with translations of ten Buddhist poems, thirty-two Buddhist proverbs, Hsüan ts'ang's
"Essence of the wisdom sutra," and Kumarajiva's "Diamond sutra." Introduction by Dr. Johannes Rahder. [Shanghai] Commercial Press, 1939. 52,
22 p. plates.

LIANG, CH'I-CH'AO, 梁啓超, 1873-1929. China's debt to Buddhist India, with
a biographical note by Herbert A. Giles. New York, The Maha Bodhi Society
of America [1927?] 15 p.

LIEBENTHAL, WALTER, 1886-   Sanskrit inscriptions from Yunnan, and the
dates of foundation of the main pagodas in that province. Peiping, Catholic
University Press, 1947. 40 p.

———. Sanskrit inscriptions from Yunnan. II. (and more about the pagodas and
statutes of that province). Santiniketan, 1955. 28 p. plates (Sino-Indian studies, 1 ).

McGOVERN, WILLIAM MONTGOMERY, 1897-   An introduction to Mahāyāna
Buddhism, with especial reference to Chinese and Japanese phases. London,
Kegan Paul; New York, E.P. Dutton, 1922. iv, 233, [1] p. diagrs.

Die MEDITATIONS-SŪTRAS des Mahāyāna-Buddhismus. Vorwort von Lama Govinda. Übers. und eingeleitet von R. von Muralt. Zürich, Origo, 1956. 2 v.

MUSES, CHARLES ARTHUR, 1919-   East-West fire; Schopenhauer's optimism
and the Lankavatara sutra; an excursion toward the common ground between
oriental and Western religion. London, J.M. Watkins; Indian Hills, Colo.,
Falcon's Wing Press, 1955. 67 p.

ORIENTAL philosophies, with an introduction by W.Y. Evans-Wentz. New York,
Russell F. Moore [1946] xii, 32 p. (American philosopher series).

PETZOLD, BRUNO, 1873-1949. The Chinese Tendai teaching; a lecture delivered
at the German Embassy in Tokyo before the Asiatic Society under the presiden-
cy of the German Ambassador, Dr. Solf. Tokyo, 193? 49 p. Reprinted from
an unidentified work.

RAGHU VIRA. Chinese poems and pictures on Ahiṁsā. Nagpur, International
Academy of Indian Culture, 1954. 101 p. illus. (Saraswatī-vihāra ser., 34 ).

REICHELT, KARL LUDVIG, 1877-1952. Der chinesische Buddhismus; ein Bild
von religiösen Leben des Ostens. Aus dem Norwegischen, übers. von W.
Oehler. Basel, Basler Missionsbuchhandlung, 1926. 230 p. front. plates.

———. Truth and tradition in Chinese Buddhism; a study of Chinese Mahāyāna
Buddhism, translated from the Norwegian by Kathrina Van Wagenen Bugge.
[4th ed.] rev. and enl. Shanghai, Commercial Press, 1934. [1st ed. 1927]
xii, 415 p. front., plates (1 col.).

REISCHAUER, EDWIN OLDFATHER, 1910-    Ennin's travels in T'ang China.
New York, Ronald Press [1955]  xii, 341 p.

ROBINSON, RICHARD, tr. Chinese Buddhist verse.  London, J. Murray [1954]
xxiv, 85 p. (Wisdom of the East series).

ROSENBERG, OTTO OTTONOVICH, 1888-1919. Die Weltanschauung des modernen Buddhismus im fernen Osten. Aus dem Russischen übers. von Ph. Schaeffer, mit einer biographischen Skizze von Theodor Stcherbatsky. Heidelberg,
Institut für Buddhismuskunde, 1924.  47 p. (Materialien zur Kunde des Buddhismus, 6 ).

SASAKI, SHIGETSU, 1882-1945. The story of the giant disciples of Buddha; Ananda and Maha-Kasyapa. From the Chinese version of the Sutras of Buddhism.
Restated in English by Sokei-ann Sasaki. [New York, First Zen Buddhism Institute, c1931]  32 p. illus.

SAUNDERS, KENNETH JAMES, 1883-1937, comp. Lotuses of the Mahāyāna.
London, J. Murray [1924]  63 p. (Wisdom of the East series).

SCHLINGLOFF, DIETER. Buddhistische Stotras aus ostturkistanischen Sanskrit-
texten. Berlin, Akademie Verlag, 1955.  132 p. (Deutsche Akademie der
Wissenschaften zu Berlin, Institut für Orientforschung. Veröffentlichung, 22.=
Sanskrittexte aus den Turfanfunden. 1 ).

SCHOTT, MAGDALENE. Sein als Bewusstsein; ein Beitrag zur Mahāyāna-Phil-
osophie. Heidelberg, C. Winters Universitätsbuchhandlung, 1935.  50 p.
(Materialien zur kunde des buddhismus, 20 ). Issued also as thesis-Univ.
Heidelberg.

SUZUKI, BEATRICE (LANE), 1878-1939. Impressions of Mahāyāna Buddhism
by Beatrice Lane Suzuki, edited by Daisetz Teitaro Suzuki. Kyoto, Eastern
Buddhist Society; London, Luzac, 1940.  x, 249 p. ports. (Ataka Buddhist
Library, 10 ).

————.  Mahāyāna Buddhism. With an introd. by D. T. Suzuki and a foreword by
Christmas Humphreys. [2d ed. enl.] London, D. Marlowe, 1948.  xxxx, 146 p.
1st ed. 1938.

TAI HSÜ, 太虛, 1890-1947. Lectures in Buddhism.  Paris [Imp. Union] 1928.
92 p. plates, port.

TAN, YUN-SHAN, 譚雲山, 1901-    Buddhism in China to-day.  Santiniketan,
Sino-Indian Cultural Society of India, 1937.  18 p.

————.  Ways to peace. Santiniketan, Sino-Indian Cultural Society of India, 1950.
23 p.

TUCCI, GIUSEPPE, 1894-    On some aspects of the doctrines of Maitreya [natha]
and Asaṅga, being a course of five lectures delivered at the University of Calcutta. Calcutta, The University, 1930.  vi, 81 p. (Calcutta. University. Read-
ership lectures).

UTSUKI, NISHU. The Shin sect; a school of Mahāyāna Buddhism, its teaching,
brief history, and present-day conditions, with photographs. Kyoto, Publication Bureau of Buddhist Books, Hompa Honganji, 1937.  ii, 45, [1] p. plates.

VALENTINO, HENRI. Le voyage d'un pèlerin chinois dans l'Inde des Bouddhas,
précédé d'un exposé des doctrines de l'Inde antique sur la vie et la mort.
Paris, G. P. Maisonneuve [1932] [9]-243 p. fold. map.

VISSER, MARINUS WILLEM DE, 1876-1930. The arhats in China and Japan.
Berlin, Oesterheld, 1923.  215 p. plates.

————.  The Bodhisattva Ākāśagarbha (Kokūzō) in China and Japan. Amsterdam,
Koninklijke Akademie van Wetenschappen, 1931.  47 p. (Verhandelingen der
Koninklijke Akademie van Wetenschappen te Amsterdam. Afdeeling Letter-
kunde. Nieuwe reeks, deel 30, 1 ).

WALEY, ARTHUR, 1889-    The reál Tripitaka, and other piaces. London, Allen
and Unwin; New York, Macmillan, 1952.  291 p.

WATTERS, THOMAS, 1840-1901. The eighteen lohan of Chinese Buddhist temples.
Reprint ed. Shanghai, Kelly and Walsh, 1925.  45 p. illus. 1st ed., 1899.

WEI, SHOU, 魏收, 506-572. Wei Shou on Buddhism, translated by James R.

Ware. Leiden, E.J. Brill, 1930. [81] p. Thesis-Harvard University. Reprinted from T'oung Pao, v. 30, p. 100-181.

——. Treatise on Buddhism and Taoism; an English translation of the original Chinese text of Wei-Shu CXIV and the Japanese annotation of Tsukamoto Zenryû, by Leon Hurvitz. [Kyoto] Jimbunkagaku Kenkyusho, Kyoto University, 1956. 25-103 p.

WELLER, FRIEDRICH, 1889-  Die Fragmente der Jātakamālā in der Turfansammlung der Berliner Akademie. Berlin, 1955. 54 p. illus. (Berlin. Deutsche Akademie der Wissenschaften. Institut für Orientforschung. Veröffentlichung. Hft. 24 ).

——. Tibetisch-Sanskritischer Index zum Bodhicaryāvatāra. Berlin, Akademie Verlag, 1952-55. 2 v. (Sächsische Akademie der Wissenschaften zu Leipzig. Phil.-Hist. Kl. Abhandlungen. Bd. 46, Heft 3; Bd. 47, Heft 3 ).

WIEGER, LÉON, 1856-1933. Amidsme chinois et japonais. Hien-Hien, Impr. de Hien-Hien, 1928. 51 p. illus.

——. ed. and tr. Bouddhisme chinois. Extraits du Tripitaka, des commentaires, tracts, etc. par Léon Wieger. Peking, H. Vetch, 1940; Paris, Cathasia, 1951. 2 v. illus. ports. (Les humanités d'Extrême-Orient) "Edition originale: Tome 1, 1910, Tome 2, 1913."

WINTERNITZ, MORIZ, 1863-  ed. Der Mahāyāna-Buddhismus, nach Sanskrit- und Prakrittexten. Tübingen, Mohr, 1930. vi, 88 p. (Religionsgeschichtliches Lesebuch. 2. erweiterte Aufl. 15 ).

WRIGHT, ARTHUR FREDERICK, 1913-  Fo t'u-teng, 佛圖澄, a biography. Cambridge, 1947. 84 p. Thesis-Harvard University.

YANG, I-FAN, 揚一帆. Buddhism in China. Kowloon, Hong Kong, Union Press [1956] 98 p. illus.

## Zen Buddhism

BENOIT, HUBERT. La doctrine suprême. Réflexions sur le bouddhisme Zen. Paris, Cercle du Livre, 1951. 240 p. (Les Univers de la connaissance).

——. The supreme doctrine: psychological studies in Zen thought; [translated from the French by Terence Gray] London, Routledge and Kegan Paul, 1955. xv, 248 p. diagrs.

DUMOULIN, HEINRICH. Die Entwicklung des chinesischen Ch'an nach Hui-nĕng, 慧能, im Lichte des Wu-mĕn-kuan, 無門關. 32 p. Reprinted from Monumenta Serica, v.6, 1941.

——. The development of Chinese Zen after the Sixth Patriarch in the light of Mumonkan. Translated from the German with additional notes and appendices by Ruth Fuller Sasaki. New York, First Zen Institute of America, 1953. xxii, 146 p. col. front., tables.

GODDARD, DWIGHT, 1861-1939. The Buddha's golden path; a manual of practical Buddhism based on the teachings and practices of the Zen sect, but interpreted and adapted to meet modern conditions. Rev. 2d ed. London, Luzac, 1931. x, 214 p. front., diagrs.

——. A Buddhist Bible, the favorite scriptures of the Zen sect; history of early Zen Buddhism, self-realisation of noble wisdom, the Diamond sutra, the Prajna paramita sutra, the sutra of the sixth patriarch, edited, interpreted and published by Dwight Goddard. Thetford, Vt., 1932. 316 p.

HU, SHIH, 胡適, 1891-  Ch'an (Zen) Buddhism in China, its history and method. Is Ch'an (Zen) beyond our understanding? Honolulu, University of Hawaii Press, 1953. 24 p. Reprinted from Philosophy East and West, 3:1, Apr. 1953.

HUI, HAI, 慧海. The path to sudden attainment; a treatise of the Ch'an (Zen) school of Chinese Buddhism. Translated by John Blofeld. London, published for the Buddhist society by Sidgwick and Jackson, [1948] 51 p.

HUI-NĔNG, 慧能, 638-713. Sutra spoken by the sixth patriarch, Wei Lang, on the high seat of the gem of law (message from the East) Translated by Wong

Mou-lam, 黄茂林. [Shanghai, Yu Ching Press, pref. 1930] 76 p.

_____. The sutra of Wei Lang (or Hui Neng) translated from the Chinese by Wong Mou-lam. New ed. by Christmas Humphreys. London, Pub. for the Buddhist Society by Luzac and Co., 1944. Rev. ed. 1953. 128 p.

SENZAKI, NYOGEN, ed. and tr. Buddhism and Zen, compiled, edited, and translated by Nyogen Senzaki and Ruth Strout McCandless. New York, Philosophical Library [1953] 91 p.

SUZUKI, DAISETZ TEITARO, 1870-　Essays in Zen Buddhism. (first series) London, Luzac, 1927. x, 423 p. plates.

_____. The same. (second series) London, Luzac, 1933. xii, 326 p. front., plates (1 fold.).

_____. The same. (third series) London, Luzac, 1934. xiv, 392 p. fold. front., plates (part fold.).

_____. The same. (first series) London, New York, Published for the Buddhist Society by Rider [1949]; New York, Harper, 1949. 383 p. illus. (His Complete works).

_____. The same. (second series) With 25 collotype reproductions of old masters. [Edited by Christmas Humphreys] London, Rider, 1950; Boston, Beacon Press, 1952. 348 p. plates. (His Complete works).

_____. The same. (third series) London, New York, Published for the Buddhist Society by Rider [1953] 367 p. illus. (His Complete works).

_____. Essais sur le Bouddhisme Zen. Préf. de Jacques Bacot; traduction de Pierre Sauvageot. Paris, A. Maisonneuve, Neuchâtel, Delachaux et Niestlé, 1941-46. 4 v. (Bouddhisme et Jaïnisme).

_____. Essai sur la Buddhisme Zen. Traduction sous la direction de Jean Herbert. Préface de J. Bacot. Paris, Albin Michel, 1954. 512 p. (Collection ''Spiritualités vivantes'').

_____. The training of the Zen Buddhist monk, with illustrations by Zenchu Sato. Kyoto, Eastern Buddhist Society, 1934; London, Luzac, 1934. xiv, 111 p. illus. plates.

_____. An introduction to Zen Buddhism. Kyoto, Eastern Buddhist Society, 1934. [3]-152, 8 p. [Ataka Buddhist library, 7].

_____. The same. With a foreword by C. G. Jung. New York, Philosophical Library [1949]; London, Rider, 1949. 136 p. (His Complete works).

_____. Die grosse Befreiung. Einführung in den Zen-Buddhismus. Geleitwort von C. G. Jung. Bearb. nach dem Englischen Original-Text von Heinrich Zimmer. Leipzig, C. Weller [1939] 3. Aufl., Konstanz, C. Weller, 1947. 188 p.

_____. Manual of Zen Buddhism. Kyoto, Eastern Buddhist Society, 1935; London, Luzac, 1936. x, 232 p. front., illus., plates (1 fold.) (Ataka Buddhist library, 8 ).

_____. The same. 2nd ed. London, New York, Published for the Buddhist Society, by Rider [1950] 192 p. illus. (His Complete works).

_____. The Zen doctrine of no-mind; the significance of the Sutra of Hui-neng (Wei-lang), 慧能. London, New York, Published for the Buddhist Society, by Rider [1949] 155 p. diagrs. (His Complete works).

_____. Le non-mental selon la pensée Zen. [Traduction de Hubert Benoit] 2e éd. Paris, Le Cercle du livre [1952] 216 p. diagrs. (Les Univers de la connaissance, 6 ).

_____. Living by Zen. London, New York, Rider [1950] 187 p. (His Complete works).

_____. Ein Leben aus Zen. Übers. von Ursula von Mangoldt. München-Planegg, O. W. Barth, 1955. 212 p.

_____. Studies in Zen. Edited by Christmas Humphreys. New York, Philosophical Library [1955]; London, Rider, 1955. 212 p. illus.

_____. Zen Buddhism, selected writings. Edited by William Barrett. Garden City, N. Y., Doubleday, 1956. 294 p. (Doubleday anchor books, A90).

WALEY, ARTHUR, 1889-　Zen Buddhism and its relation to art. London, Luzac,

1922. 31 p.

WATTS, ALAN WILSON, 1915- The spirit of Zen: a way of life, work and art in the Far East. London, J. Murray [1936] 136 p. (Wisdom of the East series).

———. Vom Geist des Zen, einem Lebens-und Schaffensstil im Fernen Osten. Aus dem Englischen übertragen von Julius Schwabe. Basel, Stuttgart, Schwabe, 1956. 141 p. (Sammlung Klosterberg. Neue Folge).

———. Zen Buddhism, a new outline and introduction. London, Buddhist Society, 1947. 20 p.

———. Zen. Stanford, Calif., J.L. Delkin [c1948] 41 p. illus.

———. The way of Zen. London, Thomas and Hudson, New York, Pantheon Books, Toronto, McClelland, 1957. xvii, 236 p. plates.

## Sacred Books, including Translations from Chinese and Tibetan Texts
## Sacred Books - Translations and Commentaries

AMITĀYUḤ-SŪTRA. Buddhabhāsita-amitāyuḥ-sūtra (The smaller Sukhāvatī-vyūha). Translated from the Chinese version of Kumārajīva, by Nishu Utsuki. Kyoto, Educational Department of the West Hongwanji, 1924. iii, vii, [1]-43 p.

ARTHAPADA-SŪTRA. Arthapada sūtra, spoken by the Buddha; translated by the upāsaka Che-kien, 支謙, under the Wu dynasty (222-280 A.D.), by P.V. Bapat. Santiniketan, Visva-Bharati, 1951. Parts 1-2 in 1 v. (Visva-Bharati studies, 13 ).

ASAṄGA. La somme du Grand Véhicule d'Asaṅga (Mahāyānasaṃgraha) par Étienne Lamotte. Louvain, Bureaux du Muséon, 1938-39. 2 v. in 4. (Bibliothèque du Muséon. 7 ).

AŚOKĀVADĀNA. Chinese version. La légende de l'empereur Açoka (Açoka-avadāna),阿育王傳, dans les textes indiens et chinois, par Jean Przyluski. Paris, P. Geuthner, 1923. xv, 459 p. (Annales du Musée Guimet. Bibliothèque d'études, t. 31 [i.e. 32] ).

[AŚVAGHOṢA]. Bruchstücke der Kalpanāmaṇḍitikā des Kumāralāta, hrsg. von Heinrich Lüders. Leipzig, Deutsch morganländische Gesellschaft, 1926. 208, [4] p. plates. (Preussische Turfan-Expeditionen. Kleinere Sanskrit-Texte, 2 ).

———. Das Leben des Buddha von Aṣvaghoṣa. Tibetisch und deutsch, hrsg. von Friedrich Weller. Leipzig, E. Pfeiffer, 1926-28. 2 v. (Leipzig. Universität. Forschungs-institut für vergleichende Religionsgeschichte. Veröffentlichungen. II, hft. 3, 8 ).

———. The principle and practice of Mahayana Buddhism; an interpretation of Professor Suzuki's translation of Ashvaghosha's Awakening of faith, by Dwight Goddard. Thetford, Vt., 1933. xxiv, 100 p.

[———.] The Buddhacarita: or, Acts of the Buddha. Published for the University of the Panjab, Lahore. Calcutta, Baptist Mission Press, 1935-36. 2 v. [Panjab university Oriental publications, 31-32].

———. Zwei zentralasiatische Fragmente des Buddhacarita [von] Friedrich Weller. Berlin, Akademie-Verlag, 1953. 26 p. facsims. (Abhandlungen der Sächsischen Akademie der Wissenschaften zu Leipzig. Philologisch-historische Klasse, Bd. 46, Heft 4 ).

———. Buddhacarita. Sacred books of the East, with critical and biographical sketches by Epiphanius Wilson. Rev. ed. New York, Willey Book Co., 1945. v, 457 p. plates.

AVALOKITASIṀHA. Dharma-Samuccaya. Compendium de la loi; recueil de stances extraites du Saddharma-Smṛty-upasthāna-sūtra par Avalokitasiṁha, chap. 1-5. Texte sanskrit édité avec la version tibétaine et les versions chinoises et traduit en français par Lin Li-kouang, 林藜光. Paris, Adrien-Maisonneuve, 1946. 292 p. (Paris. Musée Guimet. [Annales] Bibliothèque d'études, t. 53 ).

_____. Introduction au compendium de la loi, Dharma-Samuccaya [by Avalokita-
simha] L'aide-mémoire de la vrai loi, Saddharma-Smṛtyupasthāna-sūtra,
par Lin Li-kouang. Paris, Adrien-Maisonneuve, 1949. xv, 385 p. (Paris.
Musée Guimet. [Annales] Bibliothèque d'études, t. 54 ).

AVATAMSAKA-SŪTRA. The two Buddhist books in Mahāyāna (parts of the Ava-
tamsaka and other sūtras) compiled, translated and published by P. C. Lee,
呂碧城. 3rd ed. London, Luzac, 1939. 149 p.

BHAISHAJYAGURU VAIDŪRYAPRABHĀ TATHĀGATA. The sūtra of the lord of
healing. Translated into English from the Chinese version of Hsüan Ts'ang
by Walter Liebenthal; edited by Chou Su-chia, 周叔迦. Peiping, Society of
Chinese Buddhists [1936] xii, 32 p. fold. plates. (Buddhist scriptures ser.,
1 ).

[BLAVATSKY, HELENE PETROVNA (HAHN) ] 1831-91. The voice of the silence;
being chosen fragments from the "Book of the golden precepts." For the daily
use of lanoos (disciples). Translated and annotated by "H. P. B." Reprinted
from the original edition with notes and comments by Alice Leighton Cleather
and Basil Crump. Peking, Published under the auspices of the Chinese Buddhist Research Society, 1927. xi, 130 p. front. (facsim.), port.

BU-STON RIN-CHEN-GRUB-PA, 1290-1364. History of Buddhism (Chos-ḥbyung)
by Bu-ston. Translated from Tibetan by E. Obermiller. Heidelberg, In kommission bei O. Harrassowitz, 1931-32. 2 v. (Materialien zur kunde des buddhismus. 18.-19.).

BYA CHOS RIN-CHEN 'PHREN-BA. The Buddha's law among the birds; translation and commentary by Edward Conze; with a preface by J. Bacot. Oxford,
Cassirer, 1955. 65 p. front., illus.

[CANDRAKĪRTI]. Cinq chapitres de la Prasannapada, traduit et édité par Jan
Willem de Jong. Leiden, E. J. Brill, 1949. 167 p.

CATUSPARISATSŪTRA. Das Catuṣpariṣatsūtra. Eine kanonische Lehrschrift
über die Begründung der buddhistischen Gemeinde. Text in Sanskrit und Tibetisch, verglichen mit dem Pali nebst einer Ubersetzung der chinesischen
Entsprechung im Vinaya der Mūlasarvāstivādin. Auf Grund von Turfan-Handschriften hrsg. und bearb. von Ernst Waldschmidt. Berlin, Akademie Verlag, 1952. 1 v. (Deutsche Akademie der Wissenschaften zu Berlin. Abhandlungen. Klasse für Sprachen, Literatur und Kunst, Jahrg. 1952, 2 ).

CHANG, K'UN, 張琨, 1917-   Kaṭhinavastu, a vinaya text - a comparative study
of Sanskrit, Pali, Tibetan and Chinese texts. New Haven, 1955. 300 1.
Thesis-Yale University.

CHAO LUN, 肇論. The Book of Chao. A translation from the original Chinese.
With introduction, notes and appendices by Walter Liebenthal. Peiping, Catholic University Press, 1948. xvi, 195 p. (Monumenta Serica. Monog. 13 ).

[CHIH-I], 智顗, 531-597. Buddhist practice of concentration; dhyana for beginners, translation from the Chinese by Bhikshu Wai-dau and Dwight Goddard.
Santa Barbara, Calif., D. Goddard, 1934. viii, 59 p.

_____. Dhyâna pour les débutants (Traité sur la méditation) Suite de conférences
données par le grand maître Chih-chi du Tien-tai au temple de Shiu-ch'an
(dynastie des Sui 581-618) Traduction française de G. Constant Lounsbery
d'après la transcription du chinois du Bhikshu Wai-dau et de Dwight Goddard.
Paris, Adrien Maisonneuve, 1951 (c1944). 104 p.

CONZE, EDWARD, 1904-   ed. Buddhist texts through the ages. Newly translated from the original Pali, Sanskrit, Chinese, Tibetan, Japanese and Apa-
bhramsa. Edited in collaboration with I. B. Horner, D. Snellgrove, A. Waley.
Oxford, B. Cassirer; New York, Philosophical Library, 1954. 322 p. diagr.

DAŚABHŪMĪŚVARA. Glossary of the Sanskrit, Tibetan, Mongolian and Chinese
versions of the Daśabhūmika-sūtra, compiled by Jahannes Rahder. Paris,
P. Geuthner, 1928. viii, 202 p. (Buddhica. Documents et travaux pour l'é-
tude du bouddhisme. 2. sér.: Documents, t. 1 ).

DHAMMAPADA. Chinese version (Fa chü pi yü, 法句譬喻 ) English. Texts from
the Buddhist canon, commonly known as Dhammapada, with accompanying
narratives. Translated from the Chinese by Samuel Beal. Reprint ed. Calcutta, Susil Gupta, 1953. viii, 104 p. 1st ed. 1878.

DHARMASAMGRAHA. Der chinesische Dharmasamgraha; mit einem Anhang
über das Lakkaṇasuttanta des Dīghanikāya, hrsg. von Friedrich Weller. Leipzig, H. Haessel Verlag, 1923. 198 p. diagr.

DĪGHA-NIKĀYA. Das Chung-tsi-king, 眾集經 , des chinesischen Dīrghāgama;
übersetzt und mit anmerkungen von Siegfried Behrsing. Leipzig, Asia Major,
1931. 149 l. Diss. -Univ. Leipzig.

————. Brahmajālasūtra; tibetischer und mongolischer Texte; hrsg. von Friedrich Weller. Leipzig, O. Harrassowitz, 1934. 84 p.

DIVYĀVADĀNA. Udrāyaṇa, König von Roruka; eine buddhistische Erzählung.
Die tibetische Übersetzung des Sanskrittextes, hrsg., ins Deutsche übertra-
gen und mit einem Wörterbuch versehen von Johannes Nobel. Wiesbaden, O.
Harrassowitz, 1955- 2 v.

EHRET, FRANCES H. , 1910- Gāthās of the Saddharmapundarīka: a comparative study of the Sanskrit and Tibetan texts. Cambridge, 1949. 246 l. Thesis-
Harvard University.

FĀ-HEEN, 法顯 , fl. 399-414. The travels of Fa-hsien (399-414 A.D.), or,
Record of the Buddhistic kingdoms, re-translated by H.A. Giles. Cambridge
[Eng.] The University Press, 1923; 2nd impression, London, Routledge and
Kegan Paul, 1956. xvi, 96 p. front.

GERNET, JACQUES, 1921- Entretiens du Maître de Dhyâna Chen-houei, 神
會 , du Ho-tsö, 荷澤, (668-760 A.D.). Hanoi, 1949. x, 126 p. (Publ. de
École francais d'Extrême-Orient, 31 ).

GOKHALE, VASUDEV. Pratītyasamutpādaśāstra des Ullàngha, kritisch behan-
delt und aus dem Chinesischen ins Deutsche übertragen. Bonn, Scheur, 1930.
31 p. illus. Diss. -Univ. Bonn.

HOFFMAN, HELMUT, 1912- ed and tr. Bruchstücke des Ātānātikasūtra aus
dem zentralasiatischen Sanskritkanon der Buddhisten. Hrsg. und im Zusammenhang mit den Parallelversionen bearbeitet von Helmut Hoffmann. Leipzig, Deutsche morgenländische Gesellschaft, Kommission-Verlag, F. A.
Brockhaus, 1939. 105 p. plates (Preussische Turfan-Expeditionen. Kleinere
Sanskrit-texte, 5 ).

HSI-YÜN, 希運 , 9th cent. The Huang Po doctrine of universal mind, 黃檗傳心
法要, being the teaching of Dhyana master Hsi Yün as recorded by P'ei
Hsiu, 裴休, a noted scholar of the T'ang dynasty. Translated by Chu Ch'an,
竹禪, [John Blofeld] London, Buddhist Society, 1947. 52 p.

————. Le mental cosmique selon le doctrine de Huang Po. Selon les Annales de
P'ei Hsiu erudit bien connu sous la dynastie T'ang. Traduit de l'anglais par
Y. Laurence. Préf. du Swami Siddheswarananda. Introd. du Hubert Benoit.
Paris, Adyar, 1951. 143 p.

HSUAN-TS'ANG, 玄奘, 603 (ca)-664. Chang-Chen lun, 掌珍論; Karatalaratna;
or, The Jewel in hand. A logico-philosophical treatise of the Madhyamaka
school, by Acarya Bhavaviveka, translated into Sanskrit from the Chinese
version by N. Aiyaswami Sastri. Santiniketan, Visva-Bharati, 1949. 124 p.
(Visva-Bharati studies, 9 ).

HUI-K'AI, 慧開, 1184-1260. The gateless gate; translated from the Chinese by
Nyogen Senzaki and Saladin Reps. Los Angeles, J. Murray, 1934. 5-70 p.

[K'UO-AN], 廓庵, fl. 12th cent. 10 bulls; a Chinese classic translated by Nyogen Senzaki and Saladin Reps. Los Angeles, Devorss, 1935. [29] p.

LAÑKĀVATĀRA-SŪTRA. The Laṅkāvatāra-sūtra, edited by Bunyiu Nanjio. Kyoto, Otani University Press, 1923. x, 376 p. tables. (Bibliotheca Otaniensis,
v. 1 ).

————. Studies in the Lankāvatāra sūtra, one of the most important texts of Ma-

hayana Buddhism, in which almost all its principal tenets are presented, including the teachings of Zen, by Daisetz Teitaro Suzuki. London, G. Routledge, 1930. xxxii, 464 p. front. (port.) fold. tables.

————. The Laṅkāvatāra sūtra; a Mahayana text, translated for the first time
from the original Sanskrit by Daisetz Teitaro Suzuki. London, G. Routledge,
1932. xlix, 300 p. front., fold. plates. (Eastern Buddhist library).

————. Self realisation of noble wisdom; a Buddhist scripture; based upon Professor Suzuki's translation of the Laṅkāvatāra sūtra, edited, interpreted and
published by Dwight Goddard. [Thetford, Vt., c1932] 152 p.

————. An index to the Laṅkāvatāra sūtra (Nanjio edition) Sanskrit-Chinese-Ti-
betan, Chinese-Sanskrit, and Tibetan-Sanskrit, with a tabulated list of par-
allel pages of the Nanjio Sanskrit text and the three Chinese translations (Sung,
Wei, and T'ang) in the Taisho edition of the Tripitaka, compiled by Daisetz
Teitaro Suzuki. 2d, rev., and enl. ed. Kyoto, The Sanskrit Buddhist Texts
Pub. Society, 1934. 3-[214], x, 215-499 p.

LEVI, SYLVAIN, 1863-1935. ed. Mahā-Karmavibhaṅga (la grande classification
des actes) et Karmavibhaṅgopadeśa (discussion sur le Mahā-Karmavibhaṅga).
Textes sanscrits rapportés du Népal, édités et traduits avec les textes pa-
rallèlles en sanskrit, en pāli, en tibétan, en chinois et en koutchéen. Ouvrage
illustré le 4 planches: le Karmavibhaṅga sur les bas-reliefs de Boro-Budor,
à Java. Paris, E. Leroux, 1932. 270 p.

MAHĀ-PARINIBBĀṆA-SUTTA. Das Mahāparinirvāṇasūtra; Text in Sanskrit und
Tibetisch, verglichen mit dem Pāli nebst einer Übersetzung der chinesischen
Entsprechung im Vinaya der Mūlasarvāstivādins auf Grund von Turfan-Handschriften hrsg. und bearb. von Ernst Waldschmidt. Berlin, Akademie-Verlag, 1950-51. 3 v. (Abhandlungen der Deutschen Akademie der Wissenschaften zu Berlin. Philosophisch-historische Klasse. Jahrg. 1949-50. Nr. 1-3 ).

MAHĀVADĀNASŪTRAS. Das Mahāvadānasūtra; ein kanonischer Text über die
sieben letzten Buddhas. Sanskrit, verglichen mit dem Pāli, nebst einer Analyse der in chinesischer Übersetzung überlieferten Parallelversionen. Auf
Grund von Turfan-Handschriften hrsg. von Ernst Waldschmidt. Berlin, Akademie Verlag, 1953. 1 v. (Deutsche Akademie der Wissenschaften zu Berlin.
Klasse für Sprachen, Literatur und Kunst. Abhandlungen. Jahrg. 1952, 8 ).

MAHĀYĀNASŪTRAS. The sutra of 42 sections, and two other scriptures of the
Mahāyāna school. Newly translated from the Chinese by Chu Ch'an [John Blo-
feld] London, Buddhist Society, 1937. 38 p.

————. The Perfection of Wisdom; the career of the predestined Buddhas. A selection of Mahāyāna Scriptures translated from the Sanskrit by E. J. Thomas.
London, J. Murray [1952] 90 p. front. (Wisdom of the East series).

MĀTṚICHETA. Satapañcāśatka of Mātṛceṭa. Sanskrit text, Tibetan translation
and commentary, with an introduction, English translation and notes, edited
by David Roy Shackleton Bailey. Cambridge [Eng.] Cambridge University
Press, 1951. xi, 238 p.

MUS, PAUL, 1902-    La lumière sur les six voies. Tableau de la transmigra-
tion bouddhique d'après des sources sanskrites, pāli, tibétaines et chinoises
en majeure partie inédités. Paris, Institut d'ethnologie, 1939-    1 v. illus.,
plates. (Université de Paris. Travaux et mémoires de l'Institut d'ethnologie.
XXXV ).

NĀGĀRJUNA. Ga-las ḥjigs-med, die tibetische Version von Nāgārjuna's Kommentar Akutobhayā zur Mādhyamaka-kārikā; nach der Pekinger Ausgabe des
Tanjur hrsg. von Max Walleser. Heidelberg, Institut für Buddhismuskunde,
1923. 34-114 p. incl. facsims. (Materialien zur Kunde des Buddhismus, 2 ).

————. Yukti-ṣaṣṭikā; die 60 Sätze des Negativismus, nach der chinesischen Version übersetzt von Phil. Schaeffer. Heidelberg, Institut für Buddhismuskunde, 1924. 21 p. facsims. (Materialien zur Kunde des Buddhismus, 3 ).

————. Mahāyānaviṁśaka; reconstructed Sanskrit text, the Tibetan and the Chinese versions with an English translation; edited by Vidhushekhara Bhatta-

charya. Calcutta, Visva-bharati Bookshop [1931] 4, 44 p. (Visva-bharati studies, 1 ).

————. Vigrahavyāvarttanī. By Āchārya Nāgārjuna. With the author's own commentary. Edited by K. P. Jayaswal and Rāhula Sāṅkṛityāyana. [Patna, Bihar and Orissa Research Society, 1937] [4], x, [2], 2, 31, [1], 9 p. (Issued as appendix to the Journal of the Bihar and Orissa Research Society, vol. 23, pt. 3 ) (Sanskrit texts from Tibet, No. 4 ).

————. Siddha. Le traité de la grande vertu de sagesse (Mahāprajñāpāramitāśāstra) [tr.] par Étienne Lamotte. Pub. avec le concours de la Fondation universitaire de Belgique. Louvain, Bureaux du Muséon, 1944- 1 v. (Bibliothèque du Muséon, v. 18 ).

OBERMILLER, E. comp. Indices verborum Sanscrit-Tibetan and Tibetan-Sanscrit to the Nyāyabindu of Dharmakīrti and the Nyāyabindutīkā of Dharmottara, compiled by E. Obermiller from the edition of the Sanscrit and Tibetan texts by Th. Stcherbatsky. Leningrad, Akademiia Nauk, 1927-28. 2 v. (Bibliotheca Buddhica, 24-25 ).

————. Analysis of the Abhisamayālaṃkāra. Fasc. 1-11. London, Luzac, 1933-36. 275 p. (Calcutta Oriental ser. 27 ).

PRAJÑĀPĀRAMITĀS. Fragment of a Prajñāpāramitā manuscript from Central Asia, by B. B. Bidyabinod. Calcutta, Central Publication Branch, 1927.[4], 11, [2] p. facsims. (India. Archarological Survey. Memoirs, v. 32 ).

————. The commentaries on the Prajñāpāramitās. Edited with introduction and indices by Giuseppe Tucci. Baroda, Oriental Institute, 1932. 1 v. (Gaekwad's Oriental series. no. LXII ).

————. Die Prajñāpāramitā-Literatur, nebst einem Specimen der Suvikrāntavikrāmi-Prajñāpāramitā, von Tokumyo Matsumoto. Stuttgart, W. Kohlhammer, 1932. v, [3], 54, [2], 29 p. (Bonner orientalistische studien, 1 ).

————. The Diamond-sūtra: a Buddhist scripture. A new translation from the Chinese text of Kumārajīva by Bhikshu Wai-tao and Dwight Goddard. Santa Barbara, Calif., D. Goddard, 1935. 32 p.

————. Prajñā-pāramitā-ratna-guṇa-saṃcaya-gāthā; Sanscrit and Tibetan text, edited by E. Obermiller. Moscow, Akademiia Nauk, 1937. 15, [8]-125 p. (Bibliotheca Buddhica, 29 ).

————. The Diamond sūtra, 金剛經 ; or the jewel of transcendental wisdom; translated from the Chinese by A. F. Price, with a foreword by W. Y. Evans-Wentz. 2d ed. London, Buddhist Society, 1955. 75 p. 1st ed. 1947.

————. Selected sayings from the ''Perfection of Wisdom,'' selected and translated by Eduard Conze, from the Prajñāpāramitā scriptures of Mahāyāna buddhism. London, The Buddhist Society, 1955. 133 p. front.

PRĀTIMOKṢA. A comparative study of the Prātimokṣa, on the basis of its Chinese, Tibetan, Sanskrit and Pali versions by W. Pachow, 巴宙. Santiniketan, Sino-Indian Cultural Society, 1955. 219, 34 p. (Sino-Indian Studies Publ).

RATNAKŪṬA. Kāśyapaparivarta. The Kāçyapaparivarta, 大寶積經, a Mahāyānasūtra of the Ratnakūta class, edited in the original Sanskrit, in Tibetan and in Chinese by Baron A. von Staël-Holstein. [Shanghai, Commercial Press, 1926] xxvi, 234, [2] p.

————. Index to the Tibetan translation of the Kāçyapaparivarta, by Friedrich Weller. Cambridge, Mass., Harvard-Yenching Institute, 1933. vi, 252 p. (Harvard Sino-Indian series, 1 ).

SADDHARMAPUṆḌARĪKA. The lotus of the wonderful law; or, The lotus gospel, Saddharma pundarīka sūtra, Miao-fa lien hua ching, 妙法蓮華經, by W. E. Soothill. Oxford, Clarendon Press, 1930. xi, 275, [1] p. col. front., 13 plates.

SAMDHINIRMOCANA. Saṃdhinirmocana sūtra, l'explication des mystères; texte tibétain édité et traduit par Étienne Lamotte. Louvain, Bureaux du recueil, Bibliothèque de l'Université, 1935. 278 p. (Université de Louvain. Recueil de travaux publiés par les membres des Conférences d'histoire et de philologie. 2e sér., 34e fasc.).

SANGHABHEDAKAVASTU. Śāriputra et les six maîtres d'erreur. Fac-similé du manuscrit chinois 4524 de la Bibliothèque Nationale, présenté par Nicole Vandier-Nicolas. Avec traduction et commentaire du texte. Paris, Impr. Nationale, 1954. v, 32 p. facsim. of ms. fold. into 28 l., with col. illus. on verso. (Mission Pelliot en Asie centrale, Série in-quarto, 5).

SASAKI, SOKEI-ANN. The story of the giant disciples of Buddha, Ānanda and Mahā-Kāśyapa, from the Chinese version of the Sūtras of Buddhism. Restated in English. New York, First Zen Buddhism Institute, c1931. 32 p.

SASTRI, SHANTI BHIKSHU. Abhidharmāmṛta of Ghoṣaka, translated from the Chinese with notes and introductory study. Santiniketan, Visva-Bharati, 1953. iv, 8, 151 p.

[STHĪRAMATI]. A commentary to the Kāçyapaparivarta, edited in Tibetan and in Chinese by Baron A. von Staël-Holstein. Peking, Pub. jointly by the National Library of Peking and the National Tsinghua University, 1933. xxiv, 340 p.

SUKHĀVĀTĪ-VYŪHA. Buddhābhasita-amitayuh-sūtra (the smaller Sukhāvātī-vyūha) translated from the Chinese version of Kumārajīva, by Nishu Utsuki. Kyoto, Educational Dept. of the West Hongwanji, 1929. 43 p.

———. Sukhāvatī-vyūha in Manchu. Fučihi-I-Nomulaha-Abida-Nomun. Buddha-bhāshita-Amitāyus-Sūtra, edited by Y.C. Min, 閔泳珪, with three appendices. 1. Kumārajīva's Chinese text, Fo-shuo-o-mi-t'o-ching, 佛說阿彌陀經. II. A Korean translation Bul-sul-a-mi-ta-gyung issued in the early Li dynasty, A.D. 1464. III. Max Müller's English translation from the Sanskrit text, Sukhāvātī-vyhūa [sic] Seoul, Dong-guk University, 1950. 1 v. (unpaged).

The SUTRA of the teachings left by the Buddha, 佛遺教經, translated into Chinese by Kumārajiva in the latter part of the Tsin dynasty, 948-971 B.E.) [Osaka] K. Yamamoto [1952] 24 p.

SUVARṆAPRABHĀSA. Altan gerel, die westmongolische Fassung des Goldglanz-sūtra, nach einer Handschrift der Kgl. Bibliothek in Kopenhagen, hrsg. von Erich Haenisch. Leipzig, Asia Major, 1929. viii, 122 p.

———. Suvarṇaprabhāsa (Das Goldglanz-sūtra). Aus dem Uigurischen ins Deutsche übersetzt von W. Radloff. Nach dem Tode des Ubersetzere mit Einleitung von S. Malov herausgegeben. Leningrad, Akademii Nauk, 1930. 256 p. (Bibliotheca Buddhica, 27).

———. The Suvarṇaprabhāsa sūtra; a Mahāyāna text called "The Golden splendour." First prepared for publication by the late Prof. Bunyin Nanjio, and after his death revised and edited by Hokei Idzumi, under the auspices of the Keimeikwai. Kyoto, Eastern Buddhist Society, 1931. xxviii, 222 p. incl. tables. Sanskrit text.

———. Suvarṇabhāsottamasūtra; das Goldglanz-sūtra. Ein Sanskrittext des Mahāyāna-buddhismus, nach den Handschriften und mit hilfe der tibetischen und chinesischen Übertragungen hrsg. von Johannes Nobel. Leipzig, Otto Harrassowitz, 1937. liii, 275, [1] p. facsim. fold. tables.

———. The same. Ein Sanskrit-Text des Mahāyāna-Buddhismus, die tibetischen Übersetzungen mit einem Wörterbuch hrsg. von Johannes Nobel. Leiden, E. J. Brill, 1944-50. 2 v. facsim.

TRIPIṬAKA. Chinese version (Ta-tsang ching) French. Selections. Cinq cents contes et apologues extraits du Tripiṭaka chinois et traduits en français par Édouard Chavannes. Publiés sous les auspices de la Société Asitaique. Paris, E. Leroux, 1910-34. 4 v.

———. Fables chinoises du IIIe au VIIIe siècle de notre ère (d'origine hindoue) traduites par Édouard Chavannes, versifées par mme Édouard Chavannes; ornées de 46 dessins par Andrée Karpelès. Paris, Bossard [1921] 92, [3] p. incl. illus., plates.

———. English. Selections. Early Buddhist scriptures; a selection, translated and edited by Edward J. Thomas. London, Kegan Paul, Trench, Trubner, 1935. xxv, 232 p.

————. French. Selections. Les écrits primitifs du bouddhisme; choix de textes, traduits et édités par Edward J. Thomas. Traduit de l'anglais par S. Glachant. Paris, Adyar, 1949. 224 p.

————. German. Selections. Der ältere Buddhismus, nach Texten des Tripiṭaka, von M. Winternitz. Tübingen, Mohr, 1929. vi, 162 p. (Religionsgeschicht-liches Lesebuch. 2. erweiterte Aufl., 11 ).

TUCCI, GIUSEPPE, 1894-   ed. and tr. Pre-Diṅnāga Buddhist texts on logic from Chinese sources, translated with an introduction, notes and indices. Baroda, Oriental Institute, 1929. [373] p. (Gaekwad's Oriental series, XLIX).

————. ed. Minor Buddhist texts. Roma, 1956. 2 v. (Istituto italiano per il Medio ed Estremo Oriente. Serie orientale Roma, 9 ).

UDĀNAVARGA. The Udānavarga, verses collected from the Buddhist canon. Being the northern version of the Dhammapada, compiled by Dharmatrāta. Translated from the Tibetan of the Bkakhgyur and into metrical verse by Ayu Subhadra. London, Universalist Press [1946?]. 22 p.

VASU-BANDHU. L'Abhidharmakośa de Vasu-bandhu; traduit et annoté par Louis de la Vallée Pousson. Paris, P. Geuthner, 1923-31. 6 v.

————. Vijñaptimātratāsiddhi: la siddhi de Hiuan-Tsang, traduite et annotée par Louis de La Vallée Pousson. Paris, P. Geuthner, 1928-48. 3 v. (Buddhica; documents et travaux pour l'étude du bouddhisme. 1. sér.: Mémoirs, tome I, v, viii ).

————. Un système de philosophie bouddhique. Matériaux pour l'étude du système Vijñaptimātra par Sylvain Lévi. Paris, H. Champion, 1932. 206 p. plates. (Bibliothèque de l'École des hautes études. Sciences historiques et philologiques. 260. fasc.).

————. Wei shih er shih lun,　唯識二十論, or, The treatise in twenty stanzas on representation-only, by Vasubandhu. Translated from the Chinese version of Hsüan Tsang, Tripiṭaka master of the T'ang dynasty, by Clarence H. Hamilton. New Haven, American Oriental Society, 1938. 82 p. (American oriental series, v. 13 ).

————. Sanskrit restoration of Yuan Chwang's Vijnapti-matratāsiddhi-śāstra, by Rāhula Sānkṛtyāyana, with the help of Wong Mow-lam,　黃茂林. [Patna, K. P. Jayaswal, 1953] [2], 72 p. (Appendix to Journal of the Bihar and Orissa research society, v. 19 ).

WALDSCHMIDT, ERNST, 1897-   Bruchstücke des Bhikṣuṇī-Prātimokṣa der Sarvāstivādins; mit einer Darstellung der Überlieferung des Bhikṣuṇī-Prātimokṣa in den verschiedenen Schulen, hrsg. von Ernst Waldschmidt. Leipzig, F. A. Brockhaus, 1926. vi, 187 p. incl. tables. (Preussische Turfan-Expeditionen. Kleinere Sanskrit-Texte, 3 ).

————. Die Legende vom Leben des Buddha, in Auszügen aus den heiligen Texten; aus dem Sanskrit, Pali und Chinesischen übersetzt und eingeführt von Ernst Waldschmidt. Mit vielen zum teil farbigen Illustrationen wiedergegeben nach tibetischen Tempelbildern aus dem Besitz des Berliner Museums für Völkerkunde. Berlin, Volksverband der Bücherfreunde, Wegweiserverlag g.m.b.h. [c1929] 248 p. col. front., plates (part col.).

————. Bruchstücke buddhistischer Sūtras aus dem zentralasiatischen Sanskritkanon 1. Hrsg. und im Zusammenhang mit ihren Parallelversionen bearbeitet von Ernst Waldschmidt. Leipzig, Deutsche morgenländische Gesellschaft, 1932. 249 p. (Preussische Turfan-Expeditionen. Kleinere Sanskrittexte, 4 ).

WANG, JIH-HSIU, 王日休, [ 龍舒 ]. Laien-Buddhisms in China. Das Lung shu Ching T'u wên, 龍舒淨土文, des Wang Jih-hsiu aus dem Chinesischen übersetzt, erläutert und beurteilt von H[einrich Friedrich] Hackmann. Gotha/Stuttgart, F. A. Pertheus, 1924. xvi, 347 p.

Lamaism (See Tibet-Lamaism)

Taoism

BRÉMOND, RENÉ, tr. La sagesse chinoise selon le Tao. Pensées choisies et traduites par René Brémond. Paris, Librairie Plon, 1955. 208 p. (Éditions d'histoire et d'art ).

CLASSIC on the conformity of Yin. Schrift von Konformität des Yin. Translated and explained by Franz Huebotter. Tsingtao, Druck de Missionsdruckerei, 1936. 12 p.

ERKES, EDUARD, 1891-   Über den heutigen Taoismus und seine Literatur. [Leipzig, O. Harrassowitz, 1933] 10 p.

HACKMANN, HEINRICH FRIEDRICH, 1864-1935. Die dreihundert Mönchsgebote des chinesischen Taoismus. Amsterdam, Koninklijke Akademie van Wetenschappen, 1931. 60, [1], 23 p. (Verhandelingen der Koninklijke akademie van wetenschappen te Amsterdam, Afdeeling letterkunde. Nieuwe reeks, deel XXXII, 1 ).

HUMMEL, SIEGBERT. Zum ontologischen Problem des Dauismus (Taoismus) Untersuchungen an Lau Dsï, Kapitel 1 und 42. Leipzig, O. Harrassowitz, 1948. 45 p.

KENNEY, EDWARD HERBERT, 1891-   A Taoist notebook, by Edward Herbert [pseud.] London, Murray [1955] 80 p. (Wisdom of the East series).

LI,CHIH-CH'ANG, 李志常, 1193-1278. The travels of an alchemist; the journey of the Taoist, Ch'ang-ch'un, 邱長春, from China to the Hindukush at the summons of Chingiz Khan, recorded by his disciple, Li Chih-ch'ang. Translated with an introduction, by Arthur Waley. London, G. Routledge [1931] xi, 166 p. double front. (map) (The Broadway travellers).

LIN, T'UNG-CHI, 林同濟, 1906-   The other China. Chungking, Chinese-American Institute of Cultural Relations, 1944. cover-title, 16 p.

LIU, HSIANG, 劉向, 79-8 B.C. Le Lie-sien Tchouan, 列仙傳, biographie légendaires des immortels taoistes de l'antiquité, traduit et annoté par Max Kaltenmark. Pékin, Centre d'études sinologiques de Pékin, 1953. 204 p.

[MORGAN, HARRY TITTERTON] 1872-   Kuan Yin; the legends of the eight immortals. Los Angeles, Quon Quon Co., c1944. 16 p. illus. [His Chinese classics in miniature].

[POUVOURVILLE, ALBERT DE]. La voie rationnelle, par Matgioi [pseud.] 2. éd., rev. et corr. Paris, Éditions traditionnelles, 1941. 269 p. illus.

PRÉAU, ANDRÉ. La fleur d'or et Le taoïsme sans Tao. Paris, Bibliothèque Chacornac, 1931. 62 p. ''Réunit deux articles parus en février et avril 1931 dans la revue Le Voile d'Isis.''

SHIU, MAURICE POY, 梅樹培, 1911-   The eight immortals of the religion of Taoism in Chinese mythology. Illustrations by Thomas Shiu. [Chicago, Overseas Art Shop, c1941] [23] p. illus.

STEININGER, HANS. Hauch-und Körperseele und der Dämon bei Kuan Yin-tze, 關尹子; Untersuchungen zur chinesischen Psychologie und Ontologie. Leipzig, O. Harrassowitz, 1953. 93 p. (Sammlung Orientalistischer Arbeiten, 20 ).

T'AI-I CHIN-HUA TSUNG-CHIH. 太乙金華宗旨. Das Geheimnis der goldenen Blüte, ein chinesisches Lebensbuch. Übersetzt und erläutert von Richard Wilhelm, mit einem europäischen Kommentar von C.G. Jung. München, Dorn-Verlag [c1929] 161 p. front., illus., plates, diagr.

———. The same. Zürich und Leipzig, Rascher Verlag, 1939. xviii, 150 p. illus., plates, diagrs. front. New enl. ed. 1957.

———. The secret of the golden flower, a Chinese book of life, translated and explained by Richard Wilhelm, with a European commentary by C.G. Jung; with eleven plates and four text illustrations. Translated into English by Cary F. Baynes. London, Kegan Paul, 1931. ix, 151 p. incl. plates, diagrs. front. plates.

———. The same. New York, Wehman Bros. [1955] ix, 151 p. illus., plates.

T'AI-SHANG KAN-YING P'IEN. 太上感應篇. T'ai-shang kan-ying p'ien; treatise of the Exalted one on response and retribution; translated from the Chinese by Teitaro Suzuki and Dr. Paul Carus; containing introduction, Chinese text, verbatim translation, translation, explanatory notes and moral tales, edited by Dr. Paul Carus. With sixteen plates by Chinese artists and a front-ispiece by Keichyu Yamada. Chicago, Open Court Pub. Co.; London, Kegan Paul, 1926. [3]-139 p. front., illus., plates.

————. Le livre des récompenses et des peines; ouvrage taoiste traduit du chinois avec des notes et des éclaircissements, par Abel Rémusat. Précédé d'une notice historique sur la vie et les ouvrages d'Abel Rémusat, par Silvestre de Sacy. Nouv. éd. Paris, P. Geuthner, 1939. 113 p. (Les joyaux de l'orient, 3 ).

TEN BROECK, JANET RINAKER. A Taoist inscription of the Yüan dynasty: the Tao-chiao Pei, 道教碑, by J.R. Ten Broeck and Yiu Tung, 尤桐. Leiden, E.J. Brill, 1950. [66] p. plates. Reprinted from T'oung Pao 40:1-3, 1950.

WANG, SIANG, 王湘. Das Buch der irdischen Mühe und das himmlischen Lohnes; übertragen von Klabund [pseud.] Hannover, Steegemann [1921] 21 p. (Die Silbergäule, 109-110 ).

WIEGER, LÉON, 1856-1933, ed. and tr. Les pères du système Taoiste. 1: Lao-tzeu, 11: Lie-tzeu, 111: Tchouang-tzeu. Paris, Société d'édition Les Belles lettres [1950] 521 p. illus. (Cathasia. Série culturelle des hautes études de Tientsin).

ZENKER, ERNST VICTOR, 1865-   Der Taoismus der Frühzeit, die alt- und gemeinchinesische Weltanschauung. Wien, Hölder-Pichler-Tempsky, 1943. 56 p. (Akademie der Wissenschaften in Wien. Philosophisch-historische Klasse. Sitzungsberichte, 222. Bd., 2. Abhandlung).

## Islam

ALI, AHMED, 1908-   Muslim China. Karachi, Pakistan Institute of International Affairs [1949] 63 p.

ANDREW, G. FINDLAY. The crescent in north-west China. London, Philadelphia, China Inland Mission [1921] xii, 113 p. front., illus., plates, ports.

CHINA ISLAMIC ASSOCIATION. Moslems in China. Peking, Foreign Languages Press, 1953. unpaged (chiefly illus.).

————. The religious life of Chinese moslems. Peking, Nationalities Pub. House, 1956. 59 p. (chiefly illus.).

CORDIER, GEORGES. Les Musulmans au Yunnan. Hanoi, Impr. tonkinoise, 1927. 328 p.

FILCHNER, WILHELM, 1877-1957. Hui-Hui; Asiens Islamkämpfe. Berlin-Schöneberg, P.J. Ostergaard, 1928. 423 p. front (port.) illus. maps.

HARTMANN, MARTIN, 1851-1918. Zur Geschichte des Islam in China. Leipzig, W. Heims, 1921. xxiv, 152 p. illus. (Quellen und forschungen zur erd-und kulturkunde. bd. X ).

LEW, CHE, 劉智, fl. 1724. The Arabian prophet; a life of Mohammed from Chinese and Arabic sources. A Chinese Moslem work, by Liu Chai-lien, 劉介廉, translated by Isaac Mason. With appendices on Chinese Mohammedanism. Foreword by Rev. Samuel M. Zwemer. Shanghai, Commercial Press, 1921. xvii, 313 p. front., illus., plates, fold. maps, fold. plan, facsims.

MU MING, 穆鳴. Chinese-Moslems, The three centuries, translated by Chang Wen-chuan. Peking, 1955. 17, 38 p.

PICKENS, CLAUDE L. Annotated bibliography of literature on Islam in China. Hankow, Society of Friends of the Moslems in China, 1950. 72 p.

U.S. Office of Strategic Services. Research and Analysis Branch. Japanese infiltration among Muslims in China. [Washington] 1944. iii l., 146 p. (Its R and A no. 890.1 ).

————. Peoples and politics of China's northwest. Washington, 1945. 60 p.(Its R and A no. 1921 ).

Christianity and Foreign Missions

CARY-ELWES, COLUMBA, 1903-   China and the cross; a survey of missionary history. New York, P.J. Kenedy [1957]; London, Longmans, Green,
1957. 323 p. illus.
LATOURETTE, KENNETH SCOTT, 1884-   A history of Christian missions in
China. New York, Macmillan, 1929. xii, 930 p. fold. map.

Nestorianism

BERNARD, HENRI, 1897-   La découverte de nestoriens Mongols aux Ordos et
l'histoire ancienne du christianisme en Extrême-Orient. Tientsin, Hautes
Études, 1935. 75 p. Reprinted from Dossiers de la Commission synodale
de Pékin, Juin-juillet 1935.
COULING, CHARLOTTE ELIZA, 1860-   The luminous religion, a study of
Nestorian Christianity in China, with a translation of the inscriptions upon
the Nestorian tablet. London, Carey Press, 1925. 63, [1] p. front. "Reprinted from the 'Chinese recorder,' April and May, 1924."
DUVIGNEAU, AYMARD BERNARD, 1879-   L'expansion nestorienne en Chine
d'après Marco Polo. Pei-ping, Impr. des Lazaristes, 1934. 90 p. illus.,
plates. "Extrait du Bulletin catholique de Pékin, avril-novembre 1934."
FOSTER, JOHN. The church of the T'ang dynasty. London, Society for promoting Christian Knowledge; New York, Macmillan [1939] xvi, 168 p. fold.
map, fold. tables.
The HISTORY of Yaballaha III, Nestorian patriarch, and of his vicar, Bar Sauma,
Mongol ambassador to the Frankish courts at the end of the thirteenth century,
translated from the Syriac and annotated by James A. Montgomery. New York,
Columbia University Press, 1927. 82 p. (Records of civilization: sources and
studies, ed. under the auspices of the Department of history, Columbia University).
HOLM, FRITS, 1881-   My Nestorian adventure in China; a popular account of
the Holm-Nestorian expedition to Sian-fu and its results, with an introduction
by the Rev. Prof. Abraham Yohannan, illustrated with a map and thirty-three
photographs by the author and a frontispiece. New York, Chicago, Fleming
H. Revell, 1923. London, Hutchinson, 1924. 335 p. plates, 2 port. ( incl.
front.).
KLETT, HEINZ. Aufstieg und Untergang einer christlichen Missionsarbeit. Eine
Untersuchung über die Gründe, die zum Zusammenbruch und Untergang der.
Missionskirche die Nestorianer in Chine im Zeitalter der Tang-Dynastie ge-
führt haben. Greifswald, 1942. 99 1. Diss.-Greifswald Theol Fakultie.
The MONKS of Ḳûblâi Khân, emperor of China; or, The history of the life and
travels of Rabban Ṣâwmâ, envoy and plenipotentiary of the Mongol khâns to
the kings of Europe, and Marḳôs who as Mâr Yahbh-Allâhâ III became patriarch of the Nestorian church in Asia; translated from the Syriac by Sir E.A.
Wallis Budge. London [etc.] The Religious Tract Society [1928] xvi,335 p.
illus., XVI plates (incl. front., ports., facsims.).
MOULE, ARTHUR CHRISTOPHER, 1873-1957. Christians in China before the
year 1550. London, Society for promoting Christian Knowledge; New York
and Toronto, Macmillan, 1930. xvi, 293, [1] p. front., illus., plates, plans
(part fold.) facsims. (part fold.).
———. Supplement; a list of the Chinese words which are found in the book.

Shanghai, 1931. 14 p.

——. Nestorians in China; some corrections and additions. London, The China Society, 1940. 43 p. front., illus., facsims. (Sinological ser., 1 ).

NESTORIAN TABLET OF SIAN-FU. The Nestorian tablet and hymn; translations of Chinese texts from the first period of the church in China, 635-c.900, by John Foster. London, Society for promoting Christian Knowledge [1939] 26 p. (Texts for students, 49 ). Reprinted from the translator's The church of the T'ang dynasty. cf. p. 4.

ROSENKRANZ, GERHARD, 1896-   Die älteste Christenheit in China, in den Quellenzeugnissen der Nestorianer-Texte der Tang-Dynastie, mit einem Vorwort von Dr. Merkel. Berlin-Steglitz, Verlag der Ostasien-Mission, 1938. vii, 76 p. (Schriftenreihe der Ostasien-mission, 3/4).

SAEKI, YOSHIRŌ, 1871-   The Nestorian documents and relics in China. [2d ed.] Tokyo, Toho Bunkwa Gakuin: Academy of Oriental Culture, Tokyo Institute, 1951; 3rd ed. 1955. 1 v. (various pagings) illus., maps, facsims. 1st ed. 1916; reprint ed. 1937.

——. Catalogue of the Nestorian literature and relics. Tokyo, Maruzen, 1950. 50 p.


## Catholicism
## General Works

AUFHAUSER, JOHANN BAPTIST, 1881-   Christentum und Buddhismus im Ringen um Fernasien. Bonn und Leipzig, K. Schroeder, 1922. xii, 400 p. (Bücherei der kultur und geschichte, 25 ).

BECKMANN, JOHANNES, 1901-   Die katholische Missionsmethode in China in neuester Zeit (1842-1912) geschichtliche Untersuchung über Arbeitsweisen, ihre Hindernisse und Erfolge. Immensee, Schweiz, Verlag des Missionshauses Bethlehem, 1931. xvi, 202 p.

[BERTREUX, HENRI]. Au pays du dragon; illstrations de Shin-lou-ti. Paris, Maisonneuve et fils, 1922. 381, [2] p. illus., fold. map.

BIERMANN, BENNO MARIA, father, 1884-   Die Anfänge der neueren Dominikanermission in China. Münster in Westfalen, Aschendorff, 1927. [vii]-xxii, 236 p. illus. (maps) (Missionswissenschaftliche abhandlungen und texte, 10 ).

BOUSTON, GABRIEL M. Das blaue Tal; ein Chinabuch. Aus dem Flämischen übertragen von Georg Hermanowski. Recklinghausen, Paulus Verlag, 1954. 294 p. maps.

CATHOLIC CHURCH. Codex juris canonici. Tentamen sensum Codicis iuris canonici, litteris sinicis reddendi privatim susceptum et peractum a Cyrillo Rudolpho Jarre et Li Ki Jen, 李啓人. Shantung, Typis Missionis Catholicae Tsinan, 1943. xxii, 622 p.

CHANG, CHRYSOSTOMUS, 張基所. Essai d'une adaptation des exercises spirituels à l'âme chinoise. Rome, 1952. 31 p. Thèse-Pont. Univ. Gregoriana.

CHINA INFORMATION COMMITTEE. Catholic church activities in war afflicted China. Hankow, The Committee [1938] cover-title, 33 p. illus. (incl. ports., facsim.).

COSTANTINI, CELSO, abp. 1876-   Contra spem in spem. Le drame actuel des missions en Chine. Bruges, Abbayé du Saint-André, 1931. 439 p. (Les questions missionaires, 9 ).

CUENOT, JOSEPH, 1888-   La mission du Kouangsi; au pays des Pavillonsnoirs. Hong Kong, Impr. de Nazareth, 1925. 173 p.

——. Kwangsi, land of the Black banners, translated by Reverend George F. Wiseman. St. Louis, Mo., and London, B. Herder, 1942. xvii, 279 p. front.(map) ports.

DEVINE, W. The four churches of Peking. London, Burns, Oates and Washbourne [1930] 7-225 p. plates (1 col.) 2 port.

DURIEUX, A. La grande pitié de l'Église de Chine. Quelques faits, les causes.

Louvain, Éditions de l'Aucam, 1928. 47 p. (Les brochures de l'Aucam, 7 ).

ELIA, PASQUALE M. D', 1890-    Catholic native episcopacy in China; being an outline of the formation and growth of the Chinese catholic clergy, 1300-1926. Shanghai, Tu-sè-wè Printing Press, 1927. v, 107 p. front., plates, tables, diagrs.

————. The Catholic missions in China; a short sketch of the history of the Catholic church in China from the earliest records to our own days. Shanghai, Commercial Press, 1934. xi, 122 p. fold. tables.

FISCHER, HERMANN. China, das grösste Missionsland. Steyl, Verlag der Missiondruckerei [192?] 32 p. illus. (His Missions-album, 3.).

GARNIER, J. B. HENRI. Le Christ en Chine; morituri te salutant! Paris, Picart [1928] 261 p.

————. Les missionnaires de Chine répondent à M. Levaux. Dijon, Impr. de Bernigaud et Privat, 1948. 43 p.

GERVAIS, EMILE. Un mois en Chine avec les soeurs missionnaires N. D. des Anges du diocèse de Sherbrooke. Sherbrooke, Canada, Messager St. Michel, 1937. 129 p. illus. plates, port. map.

HUGON, JOSEPH, 1893-1929. Mes paysans chinois. Paris, Dillen et cie [1930] 206 p. incl. plates, front. illus. (incl. maps, ports.).

HUONDER, ANTON, 1858-1926. Der chinesische Ritenstreit. Aachen, Aachener Missionsdruckerei, 1921. 47 p. (Abhandlungen aus Missionskunde und Missionsgeschichte, 22 ).

HUSEMANN, DIETRICH. Die rechtliche Stellung christlicher Missionen in China. (Ein Beitrag zum Studium des Ausländerschutzes.) Berlin, C. Heymann, 1934. 119 p.

JENSEN, HANS-WERNER, 1912-    Christliche und nichtchristliche Eheauffassung dargestellt am Konfuzianismus. Eine Missionswissenschaftliche Untersuchung. Gütersloh, C. Bertelsmann, 1940. 134 p. (Allgemeine Missionsstudien, 24 ).

JUNOD, ENMY. Sur les bords du Fleuve Bleu. Petites nacelles dans les grandes eaux. Récits d'expériences missionnaires en Chine. Orange [chez l'auteur] 1931. iv, 290 p.

KASBAUER, SIXTA, 1888-    Du hast für mich dein Herz verschwendet; katholisches Frauenheldentum in China. Kevelaer, Butzon und Bercker [1956] 280 p.

KEARNEY, JAMES F. The four horsemen ride again. Shanghai, Impr. de T'ousè-wè, 1940. 219 p. (Portraits of China ser., 2 ).

LEBBE, VINCENT, 1877-1940. Problèmes missionnaires; une lettre inédité. Louvain, Éditions SAM, 1942. 27 p.

LEGRAND, FRANCIS XAVIER. Apostolat intellectuel en Chine: quelques suggestions pour l'après-guerre. Louvain, Éditions de l'Aucam [1947] 98 p.

————. The intellectual apostolate in China; preface by Thomas Cardinal Tien, 田耕莘. Hong Kong, Catholic Truth Society, 1949. 210 p.

LEVAUX, LÉOPOLD. La Chine et les missions. Liege, Pensée catholique, 1926. 36 p. (Études religieuses).

McGRATH, WILLIAM CECIL, 1896-    The dragon at close range. Scarboro Bluffs, Ont., St. Francis Xavier Seminary; Printed by A. B. C. Press, S. A., Shanghai, 1937. 13-209, [2] p. front., illus. (incl. ports.).

MARY JUST, Sister. China-1925; a mission investigation. [Cincinnati] Catholic Students' Mission Crusade [c1925] 55 p. (Paladin series).

————. Our neighbors the Chinese, by F. D. David. New York, Field Afar Press [1944] 92 p. plates, ports., double map. (World horizons series).

MARY ROSALIA, sister. One inch of splendor. Designs by Joseph Notarpole. New York, Field Afar Press [c1941] 3-90 p. illus., plates.

MATHIS, MARCIAN JOSEPH, 1918-    The constitution and supreme administration of regional seminaries subject to the Sacred Congregation for the Propagation of the Faith in China; a historical synopsis and a commentary. Washington, Catholic University of America Press, 1952. x, 172 p. map. (Catholic University of America. Canon law studies, 331 ).

MENKE, WILLIBRORD. Der gefesselte Schinfu. Erlebnisse eines deutschen Missionars unter chinesischen Räubern. Paderhorn, F. Schöningh, 1934. 128 p.

MERTENS, PIERRE XAVIER. La légend dorée en Chine; scènes de la vie de mission au Tchely sud-est (Vicarist apostolique de Sienhsien). Paris, Desclée de Brouwer, 1920; Paris, Spès, 1926. 2 v. illus. plates, map, facsims.

——. Gerbes chinoises. Paris, Castermann, 1935. 178 p. plates, map.

——. Du sang chrétien sur le fleuve Jaune. Actes de martyrs dans la Chine contemporaine. Paris, Spès, 1937. 192 p. map.

MEYER, BERNARD F., 1891-  Mission methods in China: like to leaven. Hong Kong, Catholic Truth Society, 1950. viii, 280 p.

MILLOT, RENÉ PIERRE. La Chine découvre le Christ. Paris, Fayard [1957] 218 p. (Bibliothèque Ecclesia, 36 ).

MOIDREY, JOSEPH TARDIF DE, 1858-  Notes sur les vingt-quatre dernières années des cinq regions synodales de Chine. Zi-ka-wei, Impr. de T'ou-sè-wè, 1930. 23 p. illus. (incl. map, tables).

PÉLOQUIN, BONAVENTURE. Débuts d'un missionnaire. Montreal, 1921. 224 p.

RENAUD, ROSARIO. Süchow, diocèse de Chine. Montréal, Éditions Bellarmin, 1955. 504 p. plates (incl. port.) maps, tables ("Service de Dieu," 14 ).

RENAULT-ROULIER, GILBERT, 1904-  Pourpre des martyrs [par] Rémy [pseud.] Paris, A. Fayard [1953] 379 p. illus.

ROSSO, ANTONIO SISTO, 1904-  Apostolic legations to China of the eighteenth century. South Pasadena, P.D. and I. Perkins, 1948. 502 p. facsims. Issued also as thesis, Columbia University.

RYAN, THOMAS F., 1889-  China through Catholic eyes. Hong Kong, Catholic Truth Society of Hong Kong; distributed by the Catholic Students' Mission Crusade, Cincinnati, Ohio [1942] [13]-149 p. illus. (incl. ports.) 1st ed. Hong Kong, 1941.

THAUREN, JOHANNES, 1892-  Die Missionen in Schantung, mit allgemeiner Einführung über China und die chinesische Mission. [Steyl, Missionsdruckerei, 1931] 94 p. fold. maps. (His: Die Missionen der Gesellschaft des göttliches Wortes in den heidenländern, 1.1.).

——. Die Mission in Kansu, Ost-Turkestan und Honan. [Steyl, Missionsdruckerei, 1931] 55, [1] p. fold. maps. (His: Die Missionen der Gesellschaft des göttliches Wortes in den heidenländern, 1.2.).

THIRY, IGNACE. La passion des Frères Maristes en Chine. 2e éd. Genval, Éditions Marie-Médiatrice, 1956. 93 p. port. plates.

VANHEE, LOUIS. Retraites modernes en Chine. Paris, Lethielleux, 1921. 43 p. (Bibliothèque des exercices de Saint-Ignace).

[VIANI,      ] 1690 (ca.)-1739. Die Niederlage des Papstes vor dem Drachenthron. Ein erstmals veröffentlichtes Dokument aus der Geschichte der römischen Kirche, aus dem Italienischen übers. und hrsg. von Herbert Melzig. Leipzig, T. Fritsch (jun.) [c1935] 63 p.

The VOICE of the church in China, 1931-32, 1937-38, with a preface by Dom Pierre-Célestin Lou Tseng-tsiang. London, New York [etc.] Longmans, Green [1938] xxv, 120 p.

WATHÈ, HENRY. La Chine qui s'éveille; nouvelle édition des fleurs et épines du Kiangsi. Vichy, 1926. xxi, 271 p. front. illus., map.

——. La belle vie du missionnaire en Chine; récits et croquis. Vichy, Maison du Missionnaire [1931] 2 v. front., plates, ports.

WILLEKE, BERNWARD HENRY, 1913-  Imperial government and Catholic missions in China during the years 1784-85. St. Bonaventure, N.Y., Franciscan Institute, 1948. xiv, 227 p. (Franciscan Institute publications. Missiology series, 1 ). Issued also as thesis, Columbia University.

WILMET, LOUIS, 1881-  Les Frères Maristes en Chine. Genval, Secrétariat des Oeuvres et Missions des Frères Maristes de Belgique, 1942. 108 p.

Franciscans

AROUD, CYPRIEN. La vie en mission. Paris, Maison du missionnaire, 1936.
312 p. plates.
————. En mission. Extraits de lettres 1890-1928. Paris, Impr. franciscaine
missionnaire, 1938. 298 p. (Collection missionarius).
AUMASSON, THEOBALD. La croix sur la pagode: Père Theodoric Baleţ, martyr
franciscain. 2e éd. Brive, Éditions Echo des Grottes, 1946. 95 p. illus.
BATTON, ACHATIUS, 1886- Wilhelm von Rubruk, ein Weltreisender aus dem
Franziskanerorden, und seine Sendung in das Land der Tataren. Münster in
Westf., Aschendorff, 1921. xii, 78 p. (Franziskanische studien, 6 ).
DAWSON, CHRISTOPHER HENRY, 1889- ed. The Mongol mission; narratives
and letters of the Franciscan missionaries in Mongolia and China in the thir-
teenth and fourteenth centuries. Translated by a nun of Stanbrook Abbey. New
York and London, Sheed and Ward, 1955. xxxix, 246 p. illus., fold. map.
(The Makers of Christendom).
GHELLINCK, JOSEPH DE, 1872- Les franciscains en Chine aux XIIIe et XIVe
siècles. Louvain, Belgique [1927] 2 v. (Xaveriana. 4e sér., no 42, juin
1927; no 44, août 1927. [Série Chine: no 3-4] ).
GIOVANNI DI PLANO CARPINI, abp. of Antivari, 1245-47. Johann de Plano
Carpini, Geschichte der Mongolen und Reisebericht 1245-47, übersetzt und
erläutert von Friedrich Risch. Leipzig, Pfeiffer, 1930. xvi, 405 p. (Leip-
zig. Universität. Forschungs-instituts für vergleichende Religions-geschichte.
Veröffentlichungen, 11. Reihe, Hft. 11).
HABIG, MARION ALPHONSE, 1901- In journeyings often; Franciscan pioneers
in the Orient. New York, Franciscan Institute, St. Bonaventure University,
1953. 319 p.
————. Pioneering in China; the story of the Rev. Francis Xavier Engbring, O. F.
M., first native American priest in China, 1857-95, with sketches of his missionary comrades, with a foreword by the Most Rev. Francis J. Beckman.
Chicago, Franciscan Herald Press, 1930. xiv, 17-155 p. front., ports.
HSIANG, PAUL STANISLAUS, 向保祿, 1917- The Catholic missions in China
during the Middle Ages, 1294-1368. Washington, Catholic University of A-
merica Press, 1949. xiii, 43 p. (The Catholic University of America. Studies
in sacred theology, 2d ser., [37] ). Excerpt from thesis-Catholic University
of America.
KOMROFF, MANUEL, 1890- ed. Contemporaries of Marco Polo, consisting
of the travel records to the eastern parts of the world of William Rubruck
[1253-55]; the journey of John of Pian de Carpini [1245-47]; the journal of
Friar Odoric [1318-30] and the oriental travels of Rabbi Benjamin of Tudela
[1160-73]. Edited by Manuel Komroff. New York, Boni and Liveright[cl928]
xxiii, [1], 3-358 p. illus. [The black and gold library].
LANGE, P. VITALIS. Das apostolische Vikariat, Tsinanfu; franziskanische Missionsarbeit in China. Werl, Provinzial-Missionsverwaltung, 1929. [211] p.
front. illus. plates, ports., maps, tables.
LHOTTE, CÉLINE. Dame Pauvreté chez les Mongols; L'épopée franciscaine de
Jean de Pian Carpin et de Guillaume de Rebrouck au XIII siècle [par Céline
Lhotte et Elisabeth Dupeyrat] Paris, Édition franciscaines [1947] 190 p.
MASS, OTTO, 1884- Die Wiedereröffnung der Franziskanermission in China
in der Neuzeit. Münster i. W., Aschendorffsche Verlagsbuchhandlung, 1926.
xxix, 183 p. (Missionswissenschaftliche Abhandlungen und Texte. 9 ).
O'SULLIVAN, DANIEL FRANCIS. Life sketch of Mother Mary Lawrence, F. M. M.
Boston, Propagation of the Faith [1925] 54 p.
RICCI, JEAN. Avec les Boxers chinois, traduit et préface par R. P. Théobald
Aumasson. Bordeaux, Missions franciscaines, 1948. 92 p.
ROMB, ANSELM M. Mission to Cathay, the biography of Blessed Odoric of
Pordenone. Paterson, N. J., St. Anthony Guild Press, 1956. 153 p.

RUYSBROEK, WILLEM VAN, 13th cent. Der Bericht des Franziskaners Wilhelm van Rubruk über seine Reise in das Innere Asiens in den Jahren 1253-55; erste vollständige Übersetzung aus dem Lateinischen, hrsg. und bearbeitet von Hermann Herbst. Leipzig, Griffel-Verlag, 1925. xxvii, 200 p. facsim. front. fold. map.

————. Reise zu den Mongolen 1253-55, übersetzt und erläutert von dr. Friedrich Risch. Leipzig, A. Deichertsche Verlagsbuchhandlung D. Werner Scholl 1934. viii, 336 p. ( [Staatliche forschungsinstitute in Leipzig] Veröffentlichungen des Forschungsinstituts für vergleichende religionsgeschichte an der Universität Leipzig. II. reihe, 13 ).

————. The journey of William of Rubruck to the eastern parts of the world, 1253-55, as narrated by himself, with two accounts of the earlier journey of John of Pian de Carpine. Tr. from the Latin and ed., with an introductory notice, by William Woodville Rockhill. London, Printed for the Hakluyt Society, 1900. Reprint ed. Peking, 1941. lvi, 304 p. fold. map. (Works issued by the Hakluyt society. 2d ser. no. IV ).

SALOTTI, CARLO, cardinal, 1870-   Sister Mary Assunta, the seraphic flower of the Franciscan missionaries of Mary, translated by Rev. Thomas F. Cullen. North Providence, R.I., Franciscan Missionaries of Mary, 1931. 249 p. front., plates, ports.

WYNGAERT, ANASTAAS VAN DEN, 1884-   ed. Sinica franciscana, collegit, ad fidem codicum redegit et adnotavit p. Anastasius van den Wyngaert. Ad Claras Aquas (Quaracchi-Firenze) apud Collegium s. Bonaventurae, 1929-54. 5 v. fold. maps.

See also Mongolia-missions

Jesuits

ALLAN, CHARLES WILFRID, 1870-   Jesuits at the court of Peking. Shanghai, Kelly and Walsh [1935] 300 p. plate, ports., facsim.

BERNARD, HENRI, 1897-   Aux portes de la Chine; les missionnaires du seizième siècle, 1514-88. Tientsin, Hautes Études, 1933. xxvii, 283 p.

————. Aux origines du cimetière de Chala, le don princier de la Chine au P. Ricci (1610-11). Tientsin, Hautes Études, 1934. 52 p. illus. fold. plan. Extract du Bulletin Catholique de Pékin, 1934.

————. L'apport scientifique du Père Matthieu Ricci à la Chine. Tientsin, Hautes Études, en vente à la Procure de la Mission de Sienshien, 1935. [7], 88 p.

————. Matteo Ricci's scientific contribution to China. Translated by Edward Chalmers Werner. Peiping, H. Vetch, 1935. 108 p. front., facsims.

————. Les îles Philippines du grand archipel de la Chine; un essai de conquête spirituelle de l'Extrême-Orient, 1571-1641. Tientsin, Hautes Études, en vente à la procure de la Mission de Sienhsien, 1936. viii, 227 p.

————. Le père Matthieu Ricci et la société chinoise de son temps (1552-1610). Tientsin, Hautes Études, 1937. 2 v.

————. Le voyage du Père de Fontaney au Siam et à la Chine, 1685-87, d'après des lettres inédites. Tientsin, Éditions Cathasia, 1942. cover-title, 54 p. "Extrait du Bulletin de l'Université l'Aurore, série III, tome III, 2."

————. Un correspondant de Bernard de Jussieu en Chine. Le Père Le Chéron d'Incarville, missionnarie francais de Pékin, d'après de nombreux documents inédits. Paris, J. Peyronnet, 1949. 58 p. plates. (Cathasia; série culturelle des Hautes études de Tientsin.) Reprinted from "Archives internationales d'histoire des Sciences" Tome 2, 1949.

BROU, ALEXANDRE, 1862-   Jésuites missionnaires; une siècle, 1823-1923. Paris, "Éditions Spes," 1924. vii, 93 p. incl. tables.

————. Cent ans de missions, 1815-1934; les jésuites missionnaires au XIXe et au XXe siècle. Paris, Éditions Spes, 1935. 312 p. illus. (maps).

CHABRIÉ, ROBERT. Michel Boym, jésuite polonais et la fin des Ming en Chine (1646-62) Contribution à l'histoire des missions d'Extrême-Orient. Paris, Pierre Bossuet, 1933. A-Q, i, [1], 283 p. maps.

CHEN, STANISLAUS, 陳鳳同. Historia tentaminum mission ariorum Societatis Jesu pro liturgia Sinica in saeculo. Rome, 1951. xvii, 189 p. Thèse-Pont. Univ. Urbanianam.

CRONIN, VINCENT. The wise man from the West. London, R. Hart-Davis; New York, Dutton, 1955. 300 p. illus.

DUHR, JOSEPH. Une Jésuite en Chine: Adam Schall, astronome et conseiller impérial (1592-1666). Adaptation de l'ouvrage du Père A. Väth. Louvain, Lessianum; Bruxelles, L'Édition universelle, 1936. 184 p. front. ports. (Museum Lessianum, Section missiologique, 23 ).

DUNNE, GEORGE HAROLD, 1905-   The Jesuits in China in the last days of the Ming dynasty. Chicago, 1947. Film copy of type-written manuscript. Positive. Collation of the original: 76 l. Part of thesis-University of Chicago, 1944.

FRANCISCO XAVIER, Saint, 1506-52. Briefe, 1542-52, ausgewählt, übertragen und kommentiert von Elisabeth Gräfin Vitzthum. [3. verb. Aufl.] München, Kösel-Verlag [1950] 364 p. front., fold. map. (Hochland-Bücherei).

HAY, MALCOLM [VIVIAN]. Failure in the Far East: why and how the breach between the western world and China first began. London, Spearman, 1957. xi, 202 p.

HERMAND, LOUIS. Les étapes de la mission du Kiangnan, 1842-1922. Zi-ka-wei, Impr. de la mission, Orphelinat de T'ou-sè-wè, 1926. vi, 59 p. incl. illus., port., maps, tables, diagr. fold. tables.

———. Les étapes de la mission du Kiangnan, 1842-1922 et de la mission de Nanking, 1922-32. Zi-ka-wei, Impr. de la mission, Orphelinat de T'ou-sè-wè, 1933. vi, 90 p. illus. (incl. ports., maps, diagrs.).

HUGON, JOSEPH, 1893-1929. La mission de Nankin. Vanves (Seine) Impr. franciscaine missionnaire [1925] 20 p. illus. (incl. map) diagr.

LA SERVIÈRE, JOSEPH DE. Les anciennes missions de la Campagné de Jésus en Chine 1552-1914. Changhai, Impr. de la mission, Orphelinat de T'ou-sè-wè, 1924. iv, 82 p. incl. front., illus. maps (1 fold.).

———. La nouvelle mission du Kiang-nan (1840-1922). Changhai, Impr. de la mission, Orphelinat de T'ou-sè-wè, 1925. iv, 50 p. illus. plates (ports.), map.

LAWLOR, RICHARD V., 1914-   The basic strategy of Matthew Ricci, S.J., in the introduction of Christianity in China. Romae, 1951. 32, [1] p. Thèse-Pont. Univ. Gregoriana.

MISSION du Kiang-nan, 1867-1925. Aperçu sur les oeuvres des religieuses auxiliatrices des âmes du purgatoires. Changhai, Le Presse Oriental, 1926. 89 p.

PFISTER, ALOYS, 1833-91. Notices biographiques et bibliographiques sur les Jésuites de l'ancienne mission de Chine, 1552-1773. Chang-hai, Impr. de la Mission catholique, 1932-34. 2 v. plates, facsims. (Variétés sinologiques, 59-60).

PLATTNER, FELIX ALFRED, 1906-   Jesuiten zur See; der Weg nach Asien. Ein Beitrag zur Geschichte der Entdeckungen. Zürich, Atlantis [1946] 367 p. plates, ports.

———. Jesuits go East. Translated from the German by Lord Sudley and Oscar Blobel. Dublin, Clonmore and Reynolds [1950]; Westminster, Md., Newman Press, 1952. 283 p. map (on lining papers).

PORTRAITS of China by American Jesuits in Shanghai, Nanking and Hai-Chow. Shanghai, Gonzaga College, 1936. 104 p. illus.

RICCI, MATTEO, 利瑪竇, 1552-1610. China in the sixteenth century: the journals of Matthew Ricci, 1583-1610; translated from the Latin by Louis J. Gallagher. With a foreword by Richard J. Cushing, Archbishop of Boston. New York, Random House [1953] xxii, 616 p. ports.

ROWBOTHAM, ARNOLD HORREX, 1888- Missionary and mandarin, the Jesuits at the court of China. Berkeley and Los Angeles, University of California Press, 1942. xi, 374 p. front., plates, ports.

SCHALL VON BELL, JOHANN ADAM, 湯若莖, 1592?-1666. Relation historique
[des événements qui se produisirent à l'occasion de la correction du calen-
drier chinois] Lettres et mémoires, édités par Henri Bernard. Texte latin
avec traduction française du P. Paul Bornet. Tientsin, Hautes Études,1942.
xvi, 462 p. (Série culturelle des Hautes Études de Tientsin).

SCHICK, JULIUS M. Diplomatic correspondence concerning the Chinese missions of the American Vincentians, 1929-34. Washington, D.C., Catholic
University of America, 1951. vi, 98 numb. l. map. Thesis-Catholic University of America.

SOULIÉ, CHARLES GEORGES, 1878- L'épopée des jésuites français en Chine
(1534-1928) par George Soulié de Morant. Paris, B. Grasset, 1928. 295,
[1] p.

TARANZANO, CHARLES. Sur les traces du Père Mathieu Ricci; tables analy-
tiques des principaux ouvrages du Père Henri Bernard, S.J. concernant l'Extrême-Orient, avec une liste bibliographique et différentes cartes. Tientsin,
Hautes Études, 1939. vi, 102 p. maps, plan.

TRIGAULT, NICOLAS, 金尼閣, 1577-1628. The China that was; China as dis-
covered by the Jesuits at the close of the sixteenth century [by] L.J. Gallagher,
S.J., from the Latin of Nicholas Trigault,S.J. Milwaukee, The Bruce Pub.
Co. [1942] xx, 199 p. front., ports., fold. map.

VÄTH, ALFONS, 1874-1937. Johann Adam Schall von Bell, S.J., Missionar in
China, kaiserlicher Astronom und Ratgeber am Hofe von Peking, 1592-1666;
ein Lebens-und Zeitbild. Köln, J.P. Bachem, g.m.b.h., 1933. xx, 380 p.
incl. illus. (incl. facsims.) geneal. tables. front. (port.) (Veröffentlichungen
des Rheinischen museums in Köln. 2. bd.).

VERBIEST, FERDINAND, 南懷仁, 1623-88. Correspondance de Ferdinand Verbiest de la Compagnie de Jésus (1623-88) directeur de l'observatoire de Pékin, par H. Josson, S.I., et L. Willaert, S.I. Bruxelles, Palais des aca-
démies, 1938. xxiv, 591, [1] p. [Académie royale des sciences, des lettres
et des beaux-arts de Belgique, Brussels. Commission royale d'histoire. Publications in-octavo. 49].

ZI-KA-WEI. BUREAU SINOLOGIQUE. Clergé chinois au Kiang-nan sous les Ta-
tsing en excluant les jésuites et les élèves du séminaire de Nan-king. Bureau
sinologique de Zi-ka-wei. Shanghai, Impr. de T'ou-sè-wè, près Zi-ka-wei,
1933. 67 p.

## Lazarists

BOUCHOT, JEAN. Les plagiats du R.P. Evariste Huc, Lazariste, ou l'art d'ac-
commoder les "Lettres édifiantes et curieuses." Hanoi, Impr. d'Extrême-
Orient, 1925. 23 p.

BRANDT, JOSEPH VAN DEN, 1883- comp. Catalogue des principaux ouvrages
sortis des presses des Lazaristes à Pékin de 1864 à 1930. Pékin, Henri Vetch,
1933. x, 124 p. facsims.

———. Les lazaristes en Chine, 1697-1935; notes biographiques recueillies et
mises à jour par J. van den Brandt. Peiping, Impr. des Lazaristes, 1936.
viii, 321 p.

CHATELET, ARISTIDE. Jean-Gabriel Perboyre de la Congrégation de la mission (Lazaristes) martyr. Meudon, Librairie vincentienne [1943] 364 p.
illus., ports.

HENRY, LÉON. Le siège du Pé-t'ang dans Pékin en 1900, le commandant Paul
Henry et ses trente marins. [Pékin, Impr. des Lazaristes du Pé-t'ang,
1921] vi, 366 p. illus., ports., plans.

HUBRECHT, ALPHONSE. Une effroyable hécatombe; les martyrs de Tientsin

(21 Juin 1870), d'après les documents contemporains. Pékin, Impr. des Lazaristes [1928] xxvi, 225 p. illus. (plan), plates, ports.
———. La mission de Pékin et les Lazaristes. Pékin, Impr. des Lazaristes,
1939. xliv, 382 p. front.(map) illus.
MONTGESTY, G. DE. Two Vincentian martyrs, Blessed Francis Regis Clet,
C. M., Blessed John Gabriel Perboyre, C. M., adapted from the French of
G. de Montgesty by Florence Gilmore. Maryknoll, N. Y., Catholic foreign
mission society of America [c1925] v, 182 p. front., plates, ports. The orig-
inal French edition appeared in 2 vols.: Soldat du Christ, le Bienheureux
François-Regis Clet, par G. de Montgesty, Paris, 1906; and Temoin du
Christ, le Bienheureux Jean-Gabriel Perboyre, par G. de Montgesty, Paris,
1905.
PLANCHET, JEAN MARIE. Documents sur les martyrs de Pékin pendant la per-
sécution des Boxeurs. Pékin, Impr. des Lazaristes, 1922-23. 2 v. illus.
(incl. plans) plates (part fold.) ports., maps ( 1 fold.).
———. Les Lazaristes à Suanhoafou, 1783-1927. Pékin, Impr. des Lazaristes,
1927. 185 p. illus. ports., fold. map.
———. Le cimetière et les oeuvres catholique de Chala, 1610-1927. Pékin, Impr.
des Lazaristes, 1928. vii, 287, [1] p. illus., plates, ports., fold. plans.
THOMAS, A. Histoire de la mission de Pékin. Paris, L. Michaud, 1923-25.
2 v illus. (incl. ports., plans) facsim.

## American Catholics

[BYRNE, PATRICK JAMES, bp., ] 1888-1950, ed. Father Price of Maryknoll; a
short sketch of the life of Reverend Thomas Frederick Price, missioner in
North Carolina, co-founder of Maryknoll, missioner in China. Compiled
from the letters of his friends by a priest of Maryknoll. Maryknoll, N. Y.,
Catholic Foreign Mission Society of America [1923] xv, 93 p. front., plates,
ports.
CARY, WILLIAM WALTER, 1887-   Story of the National Holiness Missionary
Society. Chicago, National Holiness Missionary Society, 1940. xii, 353 p.
double front., plates, ports., map.
CATHOLIC FOREIGN MISSION SOCIETY OF AMERICA. Maryknoll mission let-
ters, China; extracts from the letters and diaries of the pioneer missioners
of the Catholic Foreign Mission Society of America. New York, Macmillan,
1923-27. 2 v. plates, ports., maps.
———. Maryknoll mission letters, China. (1942-46) New York, Field Afar Press,
1942-46. 10 v. (semi-annual).
COSGROVE, JOSEPH G. Accent on laughter; a life sketch of Father Lawrence A.
Conley, M. M., Maryknoll missioner in South China. New York, McMullen
Books [c1952] 102 p.
DEASE, ALICE. Bluegowns; a golden treasury of tales of the China missions.
Maryknoll, N. Y., Catholic Foreign Mission Society of America, 1927. viii,
224 p. illus.
FORD, FRANCIS XAVIER, Bp., 1892-1952. Stone in the King's highway; selec-
tions from the writings of Bishop Francis Xavier Ford (1892-1952) with intro-
ductory memoir by Raymond A. Lane. New York, McMullen Books, 1953.
297 p.
GOODRICH, LUTHER CARRINGTON, 1894-   American catholic missions in
China. Peking, Express Press [1927] 18 p.
HAGSPIEL, BRUNO MARTIN, 1885-   Along the mission trail. Vol. 4: China.
Techny, Mission Press, S. V. D., 1927. 392 p. plates, map.
KROCK, GEORGE L. Stop killing dragons; letters to a Roman knight from a
Maryknoll missioner; illus. by Weda Yap. [New York] D. X. McMullen Co.
[1947] ix, 137 p. illus.
McSHANE, JOHN FRANCIS. My brother, the Maryknoll missionary; a life of the

Rev. Daniel Leo McShane, M. M. St. Meinrad. Ind., Abbey Press, 1932. 7-116 p. front., plates, ports.

MAGUIRE, THEOPHANE, father, 1898-    Hunan harvest. Milwaukee, The Bruce Pub. Co. [1946] xii, 191, [1] p. illus.

MURRETT, JOHN C. The story of Father Price: Thomas Frederick Price, co-founder of Maryknoll. New York, McMullen Books [1953] 116 p.

REID, RICHARD, 1896-    Three days to eternity; being the story of Father Sandy Cairns, Maryknoll missioner and modern apostle, by Richard Reid and Edward J. Moffett. Westminster, Md., Newman Press, 1956. 179 p.

TENNIEN, MARK A., 1900-    Chungking listening post. New York, Creative Age Press, inc. [1945] xiv, 201 p. front., plates, ports.

WALSH, JAMES EDWARD, bp., 1891-    Father McShane of Maryknoll, missioner in South China. New York, L. MacVeagh, Dial Press, Inc., 1932. 227 p. front., plates, ports.

——. The man on Joss Stick Alley. New York, Longmans, Green [1947] [6] l., 3-146 p. illus.

## Lives of Catholic Missionaries

AULITZKY, JOSEF M. Fu-Shenfu; ein Sohn des "heiligen Land Tirols" im "heiligen Lande des Konfuzius." Kurzes Lebensbild des Père Josef Freinademetz, des ersten österreichischen Missionars der Gesellschaft des Göttlichen Wortes. Mödling bei Wien, Missionsdruckerei St. Gabriel [1932] 32 p.

BAUDRY, FERDINAND. The life of Henry Dorié, Martyr. Translated by Lady Herbert. New York, The Catholic Publication Society, n. d. xii, 116 p.

BAUR, JOHANNES. Der Diener Gottes, P. Joseph Freinademetz SVD, 1852-1908; das Leben eines heiligmässigen Chinamissionärs. 3., verb. und erweiterte Aufl. Varone (Trento) Missionshaus des Göttlichen Wortes, 1942. 84 p. illus., ports.

BAZIN, MARIE RENÉ, 1883-    Mère Saint-Dominique, auxiliatrice du Purgatoire. Missionnaire en Chine 1842-1927. Paris, Spès, 1935. 260 p.

BEAUFAYS, IGNACE. Le père Victorin, martyr en Chine (1870-98). Bruxelles, Éditions du Chant d'oiseaux [1944] 49, [2] p.

BECKMANN, JOHANNES, 1901-    Msgr. Theodor Josef, Prokurator der Propaganda in China und erster apostolischer Präfekt von Hongkong 1804-42. Freiburg, Buchdruckerei St. Paul, 1942. 39 p.

BLARER, M. TH. DE. Soeur Marie de Saint-Nathalie, une des sept victimes de Tai-yuan-fou, 1900. Vanves (Seine), Impr. franciscaine missionnaire, 1932. 30 p. plates, ports.

BOLAND, A. Le Père Lebbe, était-il jeune? 3e éd. Louvain, Éditions SAM, 1941. 32 p.

——. Le Père Lebbe donne des conseils. Louvain, Éditions SAM, 1942. 32 p.

——. Le Père Lebbe et ses bibelots de luxe. Louvain, Éditions SAM, 1942. 43 p.

BOWLBY, APOLLINE, Sister, 1877-1942. A Sister of Charity in China (Sister Apolline Bowlby) during the wars, 1926-42. London, To be bought at St. Vincent's [1946] 87 p. plates, ports.

DE JAEGHER, RAYMOND J., 1905-    Father Lebbe, a modern apostle. Louvain, Éditions SAM; New York, Paulist Press, 1950. 40 p. front., illus.

DRAGON, ANTONIO. Le père Bernard. Montréal, Le Messager Canadien, 1948. 237 p. illus.

FLACHÈRE, A[UGUST]. Monseigneur de Guébriant: Le missionnaire. Préf. du duc de Broglie; lettre liminaire du R. P. Robert. Paris, Plon, 1946. 587 p. illus.

FOUCAULT, ALPHONSE GABRIEL, bp. 1843-1929. Le vénérable Jean-Matin Moÿe, missionnaire apostolique, fondateur des Soeurs de la Providence en Lorraine et des Vierges enseignantes en Chine. Lille, Desclée de Brouwer,

1929. x, 95 p.

———. The Venerable Jean-Martin Moÿe, apostolic missionary: founder of the Sisters of providence in Lorraine: and the Christian virgins in China; translated from the French of the Most Reverend A. G. Foucault by the Sisters of divine providence of Kentucky; foreword to the English translation by Reverend Peter Guilday. Melbourne, Ky., Sisters of Divine Providence of Kentucky [c1932] xii, 103 p. incl. front. (mounted port.) plates.

GARNIER, HENRI. Introduction à la vie réelle de Père Lebbe. Dijon, Impr. de Bernigaud et Privat, 1949-51. 2 v.

GERARDY, G. Le Père Lebbe et nous. 2e éd. Louvain, Éditions SAM, 1942. 32 p.

GOSSET, E. Le Père Lebbe chez les curés. 2e éd. Louvain, Éditions SAM, 1942. 31 p.

GOYAU, GEORGES, 1869-1939. Jean-Martin Moÿe, missionnaire en Chine, 1772-83. Paris, Alsatia, 1937. 234 p.

HENNINGHAUS, AUGUSTIN. P. Josef Freinademetz, SVD. Sein Leben und Wirken, zugleich Beiträge zur Geschichte der Mission Sud-schantung. 2 Aufl. Yenchowfu, 1926. vi, 653 p. front., ports., map.

H., M. L. [HINTON, MARY LOW]. Sister Xavier Berkeley (1861-1944) Sister of Charity of St. Vincent de Paul; fifty-four years a missionary in China, by M. L. H. With a foreword by John C. H. Wu. London, Burns, Oates, 1949. xxii, 257 p. plates, ports., map (on lining papers).

KASBAUER, SIXTA, sister, 1888-    Gold, Weihrauch und Myrrhe, Lebensbild von schwester Laurentiana Kraemer, Chinamissionarin. Steyl, post Kaldenkirchen, Rheinland, Missionsdruckerei [1941] 167, [1] p. front., plates, ports.

KERVYN, JOSEPH. Réminiscences des beaux jours passés. Bruxelles, Impr. F. van Buggenhoudt, 1949. 15 p.

LEBBE, VINCENT, 1877-1940. En Chine, il y a du nouveau: le Père Lebbe nous écrit. Liège, La Pensée catholique, 1930. 236 p. incl. front. plates, ports. maps (1 fold.).

———. Les monastères du Père Lebbe. Deux lettres du Père Lebbe présentées par G. Renirkens. Louvain, Éditions SAM, 1942. 32 p.

———. Le Père Lebbe, apotre moderne de la Chine. Lille, Éd. Catholicité, 1944. 24 p. illus. maps.

———. Pensées et maximes du Père Lebbe, apôtre de la Chine moderne (1877-1940) Recueillies et présentées par Léopold Levaux. [Bruxelles, Éditions universitaires, 1951] 118 p. port.

LECLERCQ, CHANOINE JACQUES. Vie du Père Lebbe, le tonnerre qui chante au loin. Paris, Casterman, 1955. 353 p. plates, ports. map. (L'Église vivante).

LEVAUX, LÉOPOLD. Le Père Lebbe (1877-1940), apôtre de la Chine moderne. Bruxelles, Éditions universitaires [1948] 468 p. illus. map.

LOETSCHER, ANTON. Robert zieht gegen die Räuber. Eine Abenteuer-Geschichte von P. Anton Loetscher. Der. Flieger von Tschitembo. Eine Missions-Geschichte aus ''Unsere Fahne.'' Umschlag und Zeichnungen von Armin Bruggisser. Luzern, Rex-Verlag, 1945. iv, 128 p.

[MARY OF ST. AUSTIN, mother]. Fifty-six years a missionary in China; the life of Mother St. Dominic, Helper of the holy souls, with a preface by Archbishop Goodier, S. J., and a foreword by the Bishop of Nanking. London, Burns, Oates [1935] xix, 249 p. front., plates, port.

MAZEAU, HENRY. L'heroîne de Pé-tang; Hélène de Jaurias. Paris, Téqui, 1928. 308 p.

———. The heroine of Pe-T'ang; Hélène de Jaurias, Sister of Charity (1824-1900). Translated from the French by an Ursuline, grand-niece of Hélène de Jaurias. New York, Benziger Brothers, 1928; London, Burns, Oates, 1928. viii, 252 p. front. (port.).

NANTEUIL, JACQUES. L'épopée missionnaire de Théophane Vénard. Paris,
Bloud et Gay [1950] 119 p.

PÉLOQUIN, BONAVENTURE. Débuts d'un missionnaire. Montreal, 1921. 224 p.

PLUS, RAOUL, 1882-  Jean-Martin Moÿe, prêtre de la Société des missions
étrangères de Paris. Foundateur des soeurs de la Providence. Paris, Beau-
chesne et ses fils, 1947.  173 p. illus.

———. Shepherd of untended sheep; John Martin Moÿe, priest of the Society of
the Foreign Missions of Paris, founder of the Sisters of Divine Providence.
Translated from the French by Sister James Aloysius [and] Sister Mary Gen-
erosa. Westminster, Md., Newman Press, 1950. xv, 180 p. illus., ports.

STENZ, GEORGE MARTIN. Life of Father Richard Henle, S. V. D. 2d ed. Techny,
Ill., Mission Press, 1921. 1st ed. 1915.

———. comp. Twenty-five years in China, 1893-1918. Techny, Ill., Mission
Press, 1924.  134 p. incl. front., illus.

TROCHU, FRANCIS, 1877-  Un martyr français au XIXe siècle, la bienheureux
Théophane Vénard, prêtre de la Société des missions-étrangères de Paris
(1829-61) d'après sa correspondance, les témoignages de sa cause et du nombreux documents inédits. Lyon, Paris, E. Vitte, 1929. xvi, 537, [1] p.
front. (port.) illus. (incl. maps, plan) fold. facsim.

WEBER, ELIZABETH JOSEPHINE, 1896-  Celestial honeymoon; the life of
Sister Catherine Buschman of the Daughters of Charity of St. Vincent de Paul.
Foreword by Mother Mary Joseph. New York, Benziger, 1950. viii, 167 p.

## Lives of Chinese Catholics

BARBIER, JEAN. Monseigneur Tchou, colporteur de chaussettes. Paris, Le
Centurion, 1955.  114 p. plates (L'aventure missionnaire, 3 ).

CASTEL, EUGÈNE, 1885-  Rose de Chine, Marie-Thérèse Wang, 汪大闺, 1er
avril 1917, 24 février 1932. Pékin, Impr. des Lazaristes, 1933. viii, 91,
[2] p. front., plates, ports., facsim.

———. Rose of China, 1917-32; translated from the French of Rev. E. Castel,
C. M., by Rev. Basil Stegmann, O. S. B. New York, Benziger Brothers, 1934.
x, 13-131 p. incl. front., illus., ports., facsim.

COUTURIER, J. Un séminariste chinois, fidèle imitateur de St. Jean Berchmans,
Berthélemy Zin, 1er Septembre 1903-4 juillet 1925. Changhai-Zi-ka-wei,
1926.  v, 46 p. incl. illus. port., facsims.

DEJAIFFE, J. Mgr. Yupin, 于斌, vous parle. Introduction d'Yvonne Poncelet.
Bruxelles, Éditions auxilliaires laiques des missions, 1945.  53 p. port.

DUHAMELET, GENEVIÈVE. Dom Lou, 陸徵祥, (1871-1949), homme d'État,
homme de Dieu. Bruxelles, Foyer Notre-Dame, 1954.  16 p.

LO, PA-HONG, JOSEPH, 陸伯鴻, 1875-1937. China's apostle of charity, Joseph
Lo Pa Hong, his life and works for the cause of God's poor. Shanghai, Catholic Mission Press, 1938.  24 p. illus.

LOU, TSENG-TSIANG, 陸徵祥, [Lu Chêng-hsiang], 1871-1949. Souvenirs et
pensées. Bruges, Desclée, de Brouwer [1945]; Paris, Éditions du Cerf,
1948.  171 p. illus. ports.

———. Ways of Confucius and of Christ. Translated by Michael Derrick. London, Burns, Oates, 1948. x, 140 p. plates, ports.

———. Konfuzianer und Christ. Deutsche Übertragung von Kaspar Hürlimann.
Luzern, Josef Stocker, 1947. iv, 219 p. illus. ports.

———. La rencontre des humanités et la découverte de l'Evangile. Bruges, Desclée, de Brouwer [1949] 152 p. illus. ports.

LY, ANDRÉ, 1692-1775. Journal d'André Ly, prêtre chinois, missionnaire et
notaire apostolique, 1746-63. Texte Latin; introduction par Adrien Launay.
2e éd. Hong Kong, 1924. xxiv, 707 p. 1er éd. Paris, 1906.

MALOOF, LOUIS JOSEPH. Adveniat regnum tuum, the story of China's first
cardinal [Thomas Tien, 田耕莘 ]. Tsingtao, Mission Press, S. V. D., 1946.

[13]-52 p. incl. plates, ports. front.

MASSON, JOSEPH, 1908-  Un millionnaire chinois au service des gueux: Joseph Lo Pa Hong, 陸伯鴻, Shanghaï 1875-1937. Lettre-préf. de Monseigneur
Costantini. Tournai, Casterman, 1950. 164 p. port. (Le Christ dans ses
témoins).

MERTENS, PIERRE XAVIER. Une petite martyr chinoise: Anne Wang de Ma-kia-
Tchoang. Paris, P. Lethielleux, 1935. ix, 54 p. plates.

OLICHON, ARMAND. La prêtre André Ly; missionnaire au Se-Tchoan, 1692-
1775. Paris, Blond et Gay, 1933. 421 p. plates, map.

SAINT-ANDRÉ-LEX-BRUGES, Belgium (Benedictine abbey). La benediction ab-
batiale du Reverendissime Père Lou et sa reception officielle à Gand. Bruges,
Abbaye de Saint-André, 1947. 54 p. illus. ports.

————. Les solennités de l'ordination sacerdotale du r. p. dom Pierre-Célestin
Lou Tseng-tsiang, O. S. B. Abbaye de Saint-André, le 29 juin 1935. [Schaer-
beek, Impr. F. van Muysewinkel, 1935] 39 p. front. (port.) plates (part col.).

SÉDÈS, JEAN-MARIE, 1913-  Le prêtre chinois André Ly. Paris, Desclée,
de Brouwer, 1943. 176 p.

SIH, PAUL K. T., 薛光前, [Hsüeh Kuang-ch'ien] 1909-   From Confucius to
Christ. New York, Sheed and Ward, 1952. 231 p. illus.

WU, JOHN C. H., 吳經熊, [Wu Ching-hsiung] 1899-   Gedanken während des
Haarschneidens. Ein Chinese über Europa; übertragen von Lotte Leber. Wien,
Amandus-Edition, 1946. 35 p. (Schriftenreihe "Symposion," 9 ).

————. De confucianisme au catholicisme. Rome, Pont. Univ. Gregoriana,1948.
45 p.

————. Dom Lou; sa vie spirituelle. Bruges, Desclée, de Brouwer, 1949. 71 p.
illus. ports.

————. Beyond East and West. New York, Sheed and Ward, 1951; London, Sheed
and Ward, 1952. xi, 364 p. ports.

————. Par delà l'Est et l'Ouest. Traduit de l'anglais par Franz Weyergans. Paris, Casterman, 1954; 2e éd., 1955. 272 p.

————. Jenseits von Ost und West. Übertragen aus dem Englischen. Mainz, Mat-
thias-Grünewald-Verlag, 1955. 323 p. illus.

————. The interior Carmel: the threefold way of love. New York, Sheed and
Ward, 1953. 257 p.

————. Le Carmel intérieur, ou Les trois étapes de la Voie d'amour. Traduit
par Franz Weyergans. Paris, Castermann, 1956. 232 p. (Église vivante).

YU PIN, PAUL,于斌, bp., 1901-   Eyes east, selected pronouncements of the
Most Reverend Paul Yu-Pin. Paterson, N. J., St. Anthony Guild Press, 1945.
ix, [1], 181 p.


## Catholicism under Communism


BAUER, THOMAS J. The systematic destruction of the catholic church in China.
New York, World Horizons Reports, 1954. 42 p. illus.

DE JAEGHER, RAYMOND J., 1905-   Que penser du communisme chinoise?
Louvain, Éditions SAM, 1947. 49 p. ports., plates, map.

————. The enemy within; an eyewitness account of the communist conquest of
China, by Raymond J. de Jaegher and Irene Corbally Kuhn. Garden City,
N. Y., Doubleday, 1952. 314 p.

————. Tempête sur la Chine par Raymond de Jaegher er Irene Corbally Kuhn,
traduit par Denise Meunier. Paris, Plon, 1953. 301 p. illus. port.

DRAGON, ANTONIO. En mission parmi les rouges. Montréal, Le Messager
Canadien, 1946. 128 p.

DUFAY, FRANCIS, 1916-   En Chine: l'étoile contre la croix. Hong Kong, Nazareth Press, 1952. 198 p.

————. L'étoile contre la croix. 9th éd. rev. et. augm. Tournai-Paris, Casterman, 1954. 240 p.

————. The star versus the cross; translated by Br. Cassien-Bernard. Hongkong, Nazareth Press [1953] 219 p.

————. Red star versus the cross; the pattern of persecution [by] Francis Dufay
and Douglas Hyde. London, Paternoster Publications [1954] 144 p.

————. Gesetz und Taktik des kommunistischen Kirchenkampfes. China als Mo-
dell. Detusche Bearb. von Josef Stierli. Frankfurt a. M. , Knecht, 1956.
260 p.

DUPERRAY, EDOUARD. Ambassadeurs de Dieu à la Chine. Tournai-Paris,
Casterman, 1956. 280 p. (Église vivante).

GAVER, ALAIN VAN. J'ai été condamné à la liberté. Préf. de Rémy. [Paris]
Le Centurion [1953] 221 p. illus.

GREENE, ROBERT W. , 1911-    Mon calvaire en Chine, traduit par Marguerite
Dubois. Paris, Corréd. , 1954. 256 p. (L'Esprit vivant).

————. Calvary in China. New York, Putnam [1953] London, Burns, Oates,
1954. 244 p.

GUETTIER, JEAN. Terreur sur le monde. Paris, Nouvelles éditions latines,
1956. 256 p.

HOMBURG, WILHELM. Zwei Jahre unter den Kommunisten Rot-Chinas. Hil-
trup, Verlag Herz-Jesumissionhaus, 1952. 151 p.

KASBAUER, SIXTA. Du hast für mich dein Herz verschwendet. Katholischen
Frauen heidentum in China. Kevelaer, Butzon und Bercker, 1956. 280 p.

LEFEUVRE, JEAN. Les enfants dans la ville; chronique de la vie chrétienne à
Shanghaï, 1949-55. 3. éd. Paris, Témoignage chrétien, 1956. 366 p. illus.
(La Collection Église vivante).

LEFFE, JEAN DE. Chrétiens dans la Chine de Mao. [Bruges] Desclée, De
Brouwer [1955] 136 p. (Questions actuelles).

LEGRAND, FRANCIS XAVIER, 1883-    Le communisme arrive au village chinois. Peiping, Scheut Editions; Bruxelles, Missions de Scheut, 1947. 44 p.
(Scheut Éditions, Série IV, 2 ).

————. When communism infiltrates a Chinese village. Taipei, Govt. Information Office, 1957. 23 p.

McCORMICK, JAMES A. Blueprint for enslavement. St. Paul, Minn. , Cate-
chetical Guild Educational Society, 1952. 64 p.

MARY VICTORIA, Sister. Nun in Red China. New York, McGraw-Hill [1953]
208 p.

MELIS, FRANCESCO, 1898-    Mon école dans la Chine en feu. Préf. du R. P.
Borsi. Paris, Julliard [1954] 254 p.

————. Pater Francesco und die Kinder Chinas. Ein Bericht ungewöhnlich Erlebnisse. Übers. von Eberhard Gauhe. Bonn, Verlag Bonner Buchgemeinde,
1955; Zürich, Die Arche, 1955. 231 p.

MONSTERLEET, JEAN, 1912-    Les martyrs de Chine parlent; l'empire de
Mao Tsé-Toung, contre l'église du Christ. Préf de Jean de Fabrègues. Paris, Amiot-Dumont [1953] 224 p. plates, ports. , fold. map. (Bibliothèque
catholique).

————. Martyrs in China. Translated by Antonia Pakenham. With a foreword by
John C. H. Wu. Chicago, H. Regnery Co. [1956]; London, Longmans, Green,
1956. 288 p. illus.

————. Chinas Märtyrer sprechen. Aus dem Französ. von Elisabeth Juhász.
Wien und München, Verlag Herold, 1955. 399 p. plates. (Abenteuer Christentum).

PALMER, GRETTA. God's underground in Asia. New York, Appleton-Century-
Crofts [c1953] 376 p.

————. Le maquis de Dieu en Asie. Traduit par Denise Meunier. Monaco, Éditions du Rocher, 1956. 329 p.

————. Chinas grosse Prüfung. Tatsachenbericht über die rote Christenverfol-
gung. Übers. und bearb. von Anton Lötscher. Luzern, Räber, 1954. 416 p.
illus.

RENAULT-ROULIER, GILBERT, 1904-    Pourpre des martyrs [par] Rémy
    [pseud.] Paris, A. Fayard [1953] 379 p. illus.
RIGNEY, HAROLD WILLIAM, 1900-    Four years in a Red hell; the story of
    Father Rigney. Chicago, H. Regnery Co., 1956. 222 p.
SAUVAGE, ÉDOUARD, 1901-    Dans les prisons chinoises. Provins, Seine-et-
    Marne [1957] 283 p. illus.
SCHÜTTE, JOHANNES. Die katholische Chinamission im Spiegel der rotchine-
    sischen Presse. Versuch einer Missionar. Münster, 1954. xxix, 608 l.
    Diss.-Münster. Katholische-Theol. Fakultät.
———. The same. Versuch e. Missionarischen Deutung. Münster i. W. Aschen-
    dorff, 1957. 394 p. map. (Missionswissenschaftl. Abhandlungen und Texte,
    21 ).
SCHYNS, JOSEPH, 1899-    Aveux spontanés. Anvers Omega [1954] 105 p.
SEFFER, JEAN. Fleur de pêcher; scènes vécues en Chine rouge. Toulouse,
    Apostolat de la prière [1954] 105 p. illus.
SPELLMAN, FRANCIS JOSEPH, 1889-    How red China tortures Protestant and
    Catholic missionaries. London, Friends of Free China Association, 1956.
    23 p. (Friends of Free China Association. Pamphlets, 1 ).
SWORD OF THE SPIRIT. Religious freedom in China. [Hinckley, Leics., S.
    Walker, 1954] 25 p.

Protestantism
Handbooks, Directories, etc.

The CHINA Christian year book. Shanghai, Kwang Hsüeh publishing house, 1910-
    19; Christian Literature Society, 1923-39. 21 v. Title varies: 1910-25, The
    China mission year book. 1926-39, The China Christian year book.
CHINA MISSION YEAR BOOK. See China Christian year book.
A CHINESE Bible encyclopedia (Sheng king peh k'o ch'uen shu) 聖經百科全書 ,
    based chiefly on the International standard Bible encyclopedia edited by Dr.
    James Orr, and containing many articles from other valuable works, with
    original articles written specially for the Chinese Bible encyclopedia. Shang-
    hai, Commercial Press, 1925. 4 v. fronts. (v. 2-3) illus., plates, double
    maps, facsim.
DIRECTORY of Protestant missions in China, edited for China Continuation Com-
    mittee by Charles Luther Boynton. Shanghai, Christian Literature Society,
    1916-50.    v. 1932-39 published by North China Daily News and Herald;
    1950-    published by National Christian Council of China.
DIRECTORY of Protestant missions [of China] 1943. [Chengtu] United Christian
    Publishers, 1943. 64 p.
LUTHERAN BOARD OF PUBLICATION, Hankow, Committee on Technical Theo-
    logical Terms. Dictionary of religious names and terms, 英漢宗教名彙 ,
    edited by the L. B. P. Committee on technical theological terms in consulta-
    tion with the Committee on theological literature. First and tentative edition.
    Hankow, Lutheran Board of Publication, 1935. 195 p.
NATIONAL CHRISTIAN COUNCIL OF CHINA. 1936 Handbook of the Christian
    movement in China under Protestant auspices, edited by Charles Luther Boyn-
    ton and Charles Dozier Boynton. Shanghai, Kwang Hsueh Pub. House, 1936.
    xvi, 352 p.
OSTASIEN-JAHRBUCH; Jahresbericht der Ostasien-Mission. 1921-41? Berlin,
    Ostasien-Mission. 21 v. ? illus.
OSTASIEN-MISSION, Berlin. 50 Jahre evangelischer Arbeit im Fernen Osten,
    1884-1934; Ostasien Jahrbuch 1934 im Auftrage des Zentralvorstandes, hrsg.
    von missionsdirektor Devaranne. Berlin, Ostasienmission, 1934. 152 p.
    illus. tables.

General Works

ALBAUGH, DANA M., 1897-    Between two centuries; a study of four Baptist
     mission fields, Assam, South India, Bengal-Orissa, and South China, edited
     by Baptist Board of Education, Department of Missionary Education. Phila-
     delphia, Judson Press [1935] 245 p. front. plates, ports.
ALEXANDER, MARY C., 1886-    Seedtime and harvest in the South China mis-
     sion of the Southern Baptist convention, 1845-1933. Richard, Va., Foreign
     Mission Board, Southern Baptist Convention, 1933. [11]-199 p. incl. tables.
     illus. plates, ports.
AMERICAN BAPTIST FOREIGN MISSION SOCIETY. Report of the intermission
     conference of delegates from associations and missions in China connected
     with the American Baptist Foreign Mission Society. Shanghai, 1922. 35 p.
ANDERSON, KENNETH, 1917-    This way to the harvest [by] Ken Anderson and
     Bob Pierce. Grand Rapids, Zondervan Pub. House [1949] 104 p. illus.,
     ports.
ANDERSON, PARK HARRIS. "He knoweth not how," a story of Chinese Baptist
     initiative for the information of Baptists and others. Nashville, Broadman
     Press [c1936] 7-174 p. illus. (incl. ports.).
ANTI-CHRISTIAN MOVEMENT, Shanghai. Anti-Christian movement: A collec-
     tion of papers originally issued by the Anti-Christian movement and transla-
     ted for the student Y.M.C.A. and Y.W.C.A. of China. 2nd ed. Shanghai,
     1925. 35 p.
AUGUSTANA EVANGELICAL LUTHERAN CHURCH. Board of Foreign Missions.
     Our second decade in China, 1915-25; sketches and reminiscences by mission-
     aries of the Augustana synod mission in the province of Honan. [Rock Island,
     Ill.] Board of Foreign Missions of the Augustana Synod [1926] 224 p. incl.
     front., illus., ports., maps.
———. Thirty years in China, 1905-35, the story of the Augustana synod mission
     in the province of Honan, as told by the missionaries; Gustav Carlberg, man-
     aging editor. [Rock Island, Ill.] The Board of Foreign Missions of the Augus-
     tana Synod [1937] 230 p. incl. front., illus., plates, ports., maps, diagrs.
BACON, MRS. BESSIE (BLANCHARD) 1887-1923. "With heaps o' love"; the
     story of four years in China, told in letters of Bessie Blanchard Bacon, edi-
     ted by her father, Charles Blanchard, "with the approval of the Foreign mis-
     sion department of the United Christian Missionary Society." Des Moines,
     Ia., Nichols Book and Travel Co. [c1925] 288 p. illus. (incl. ports.).
BACON, CHARLOTTE. Where East meets West in China. London and Edinburgh,
     Marshall, Morgan and Scott [1929] 96 p. illus.
BAKER, GILBERT. The changing scene in China. London, S.C.M. Press, 1946;
     New and rev. ed. New York, Friendship Press [1948] vii, 152 p.
BAKER, RICHARD TERRILL, 1913-    Methodism in China: the war years. [New
     York, Board of Missions and Church Extension, The Methodist Church] 1936.
     cover-title, [3]-46 p. illus. (incl. ports., double map).
———. Ten thousand years. The story of Methodism's first century in China.
     New York, Board of Missions and Church Extension, The Methodist Church,
     1947. 173 p.
BALLOU, EARLE HOIT, 1892-    Dangerous opportunity; the Christian mission
     in China today. New York, Friendship Press [c1940] xi, 211 p.
BALM, MRS. CATHERINE ATKINSON (MILLER) 1896-    Chinese ginger; recre-
     ation programs from China. New York, Missionary Education Movement of
     the United States and Canada [c1924] viii, 85 p. illus.
BALME, HAROLD, 1878-1953. The awakening of China in relation to the modern
     missionary program. London, Church Missionary Society [1921] 20 p.
———. What is happening in China? London, Edinburgh House Press, 1925.
     23 p.
BARBOUR, MRS. DOROTHY DICKINSON. Making the Bible desired. Garden
     City, N.Y., Doubleday, Doran, 1928. xii, 146 p.
BARCLAY, GWENDOLEN R. The way of partnership; with the C.M.S. in China.

London, Church Missionary Society, 1937.  3-97 p. plates (Partnership ser.).
BARHAM, MARIE. Blossom of the crag.  London, China Inland Mission, 1950.
   207 p.
BATES, MINER SEARLE, 1897-    Missions in Far Eastern cultural relations.
   New York, American Council, Institute of Pacific Relations [1942]  40 numb.
   l. (American council paper, 6 ).
BATTY, JANE AGNES STAUNTON. Our opportunity in China. 2d ed.  [London]
   Society for the Propagation of the Gospel in Foreign Parts, 19 13.  vi, [2],
   112, [112a]-112r p. front., plates, maps (1 fold.).
BEATON, KENNETH J. West of the gorges.  Toronto, United Church of Canada
   [c1948]  viii, 168 p. maps.
BEYER, GEORG. China als Missionsfeld.  Berlin, Buchhandlung der Berliner
   Evang. Missionsgesellschaft, 1923.  160 p. tables.
BITTON, NELSON. Pathfinders in China.  London, Livingston Press [1933] 80 p.
   front., plates, ports.
BOAZ, MAUD ELIZABETH. "And the villages thereof."  London, Marshall,
   Morgan and Scott [1925] vii, 173 p. front. plates.
————. The hundred-surname people.  London, Zenana Missionary Society, 1928.
   vii, 132 p. col. front., plates, ports.
BOSSHARDT, RUDOLF ALFRED. The restraining hand: captivity for Christ in
   China.  London, Hodder and Stoughton [1938]  288 p. front., ports., facsim.
BROCKMAN, FLETCHER SIMS, 1867-1944. I discover the Orient.  New York,
   London, Harper, 1935. xii, 211 p.
BROOMHALL, A.J., 1911-    Strong tower.  London, China Inland Mission
   [1947] 255 p. plates, maps.
————. Strong man's prey.  London, China Inland Mission, 1953.  256 p. illus.
BROOMHALL, MARSHALL, 1866-1937. Our seal; being the witness of the China
   Inland Mission to the faithfulness of God.  London, Philadelphia, China Inland
   Mission, 1933.  xiii, 173 p. front., plates, diagrs.
————. The Bible in China.  London, Philadelphia, China Inland Mission, 1934.
   xv, 190 p. front., illus., plates, facsims.
————. The answer of God; a doxology on the seventieth anniversary of the China
   Inland Mission, 1865-1935.  London, Philadelphia, China Inland Mission,
   1935.  x, 57 p.
————. By love compelled; the call of the China Inland Mission.  London, Hodder
   and Stoughton [1936]  x, 11-126 p.
BROWN, FREDERICK, 1860-    "Boxer" and other China memories.  London,
   A.H. Stockwell, 1936.  5-141 p. plates, port.
BROWN, T. COCKER. China's hour.  London, Livingstone Press, 1948.  79 p.
BRUCE, MICHAEL. Opportunity in China.  London, Society for Promoting Chris-
   tian Knowledge [1947] viii, 67 p.
BRYAN, ROBERT THOMAS, 1855-1946. Christianity's China creations.  Rich-
   mond, Va., Foreign Mission Board, Southern Baptist Convention [c1927]
   119 p. front., plates, ports.
BURGESS, ANDREW SEVERANCE, 1897-    In the lands of pagodas, temples
   and mosques. Ten studies in foreign missions.  Minneapolis, Augsburg Pub.
   House [1945]  160 p. illus. (incl. maps) diagrs. [The Teachers training
   course books].
BURT, ERNEST WHITBY, 1867-    Fifty years in China, the story of the Baptist mission in Shantung, Shansi and Shensi, 1875-1925.  London, Carey
   Press [1925]  127 p. incl. diagr. ports.
BUTLER, ROSA KATE (SMITH) "MRS. THOMAS BUTLER." Missions as I saw
   them; an account of a visit to the important centres of the United Methodist
   Missionary Society in China and Africa, with an interesting description of
   many of the places passed through and incidents of the journey, both grave
   and gay.  London, Seeley, Service, 1924.  9-284 p. front., plates, port.
   group.

CABLE, MILDRED, 1880-1952. Dispatches from northwest Kansu by Mildred
    Cable and Francesca French. London, China Inland Mission, 1925. 73,[1] p.
    illus. (map), plates.
CALDWELL, JOHN COPE, 1913-    China Coast family. Chicago, H. Regnery
    Co., 1953. 228 p. illus.
———. Our friends the tigers. London, Hutchinson [1954] 176 p. illus.
CARLBERG, GUSTAV. China in revival. Rock Island, Ill., Augustana Book Con-
    cern [c1936] 258 p. double map.
CARTWRIGHT, FRANK THOMAS, 1884-    From Foochow to the nation. A sou-
    venir of the Eastern Asia jubilee celebrating the seventy-fifth anniversary of
    Methodism's beginnings in Eastern Asia. Prepared for the Jubilee committee,
    Foochow, November 14-21, 1923. Shanghai, Union Print. and Service Agency,
    1923. 28 p. incl. table, front., illus., plates, ports.
CASSELMAN, ARTHUR VALE, 1874-    Red and black and gold. A record of the
    China mission, 1938 and 1939, Evangelical and reformed church. Philadel-
    phia, Board of Foreign Missions, Reformed Church in the United States,1940.
    128 p. illus. (front.).
CHAMBERLAIN, MARY ELEANOR (ANABLE) "MRS. W.I. CHAMBERLAIN."
    Fifty years in foreign fields, China, Japan, India, Arabia; a history of five
    decades of the Woman's board of foreign missions, Reformed Church in Amer-
    ica, 1875-1925, issued in its jubilee year by the Woman's Board of Foreign
    Missions, Reformed Church in America. New York [c1925] xv, 292 p. front.,
    plates, ports., fold. maps.
CHAO, TSU-CHEN, 趙紫宸, 1888-    The church in China and the church uni-
    versal; addresses at the annual meeting of the National Christian Council of
    China, May, 1923, by T.C. Chao and T.T. Lew, 劉廷芳. Shanghai, National
    Christian Council of China, 1923. 16 p.
CHAPMAN, BENJAMIN BURGOYNE. Flood-tide in China. London, Wesleyan
    Methodist Missionary Society, 1922. 79 p. front. plate (map).
CHENG, ANDREW CHIH-YI, 誠質怡, 1898-    Some problems confronting the
    Christian movement in China, as seen by a Chinese Christian, an address
    delivered in Martyr's Memorial Hall, Shanghai, April, 1927. Shanghai, Na-
    tional Christian Council, 1927. 16 p.
CH'ÊNG, MARCUS, 鄭仲桂, 1884-    Escape from Singapore; testimony of Mar-
    cus Cheng. Philadelphia, London, China Inland Mission [1944] 5-31 p.
———. Lamps aflame. The history of the Chungking theological seminary, with
    notes on some of the students. London, China Inland Mission, 1949. 120 p.
    ports.
CHIANG, KAI-SHEK, 蔣介石, 1886-    Selected speeches on religion, by Presi-
    dent and Madame Chiang Kai-shek. Compiled by Office of the Govt. Spokes-
    man. [Taipei?] 1952. 38 p.
———. Eastern messages by President and Madame Chiang Kai-shek. Taipei,
    Govt. Information Bureau, 1955. 12, 10 p.
CHINA BAPTIST CENTENARY CELEBRATION. A century of Christian conquest
    in Cathay, 1836-1936; records and addresses of the China Baptist centenary
    celebrations, held at Tung Shan, Canton, Oct. 13-18, 1936. [Canton] 1936.
    168 p. illus. plates.
CHINA CONTINUATION COMMITTEE. The Christian occupation of China; a gen-
    eral survey of the numerical strength and geographical distribution of the
    Christian forces in China, made by the Special committee on survey and oc-
    cupation, China Continuation Committee, 1918-21. Milton T. Stauffer, sec-
    retary and editor. Shanghai, China Continuation Committee, 1922. 13, 468,
    cxii p. illus. (incl. maps) tables, diagrs.
CHINA INLAND MISSION. "We wrestle." Being the short report of the China
    Inland Mission. London, China Inland Mission, 1930. 60 p.
———. Through fire; the story of 1938. London, Philadelphia, China Inland Mis-
    sion [1939] iv, 121 p. front.

———. Blossoms in the wilderness, edited by Anne Hazelton. London, China Inland Mission, 1941. 100 p. front. (port.), illus. (map), plates.

———. Attacking on all fronts; part of the story of the China Inland Mission in 1941, compiled by Bishop Frank Houghton. London, Philadelphia, China Inland Mission [1942?] 63 p.

———. The contested highway; part of the story of the China Inland Mission in 1942. Philadelphia, London, China Inland Mission [1943?] 78 p. front.(map).

———. According to plan, "I will build my church"; war time panorama of the China Inland Mission. London, Philadelphia, China Inland Mission [1944] 86 p. incl. front., illus.

———. God of the valleys: the story of the year 1949, containing the general director's survey of the China Inland Mission, edited by Anne Hazelton. London, China Inland Mission, 1950. 88 p.

———. Come wind, come weather; the story of the year 1950, edited by Anne Hazelton. London, Philadelphia, China Inland Mission, 1951. 77 p.

———. The hand that guided the story of the year 1951, edited by Anne Hazelton. London, China Inland Mission, 1952. 70 p. plates, table.

———. Ready sandals, the story of the year for 1952, edited by Anne Hazelton. London, China Inland Mission, 1953. 78 p.

———. Sound of abundance; the story of the year 1953, edited by Anne Hazelton. London, China Inland Mission, 1954. 77 p. illus. (Its annual report for 1953).

———. Lamp of grace, the story of the year for 1954, edited by Anne Hazelton. London, China Inland Mission, 1955. 78 p.

———. Swords drawn; the story of the year 1955, edited by Anne Hazelton. London, Philadelphia, China Inland Mission, 1956. 79 p.

———. Sounding chords; the story of the year 1956, edited by Eileen J. O'Rourke. London, Philadelphia, China Inland Mission, 1957. 69 p. (Its annual report for 1956).

CHIRGWIN, ARTHUR MITCHELL, 1885-   Conflict: China, Japan and Christ. London, Student Christian Movement Press [1939] 143, [1] p.

CHRISTIAN LITERATURE SOCIETY FOR CHINA, Shanghai. "No speedier way"; a volume commemorating the golden jubilee of the Christian Literature Society for China: 1887-1937. Shanghai, Christian Literature Society for China, 1938. vii, 143 p. plates, ports.

The CHRISTIAN movement in China in a period of national transition; three papers prepared at the request of the Department of social and industrial research for the Tambaram meeting of the International Missionary Council, by T.C. Chao, 趙紫宸, the Right Rev. the Bishop of Hong Kong and Dr. Roderick Scott. Mysore City, Wesley Press and Pub. House, 1938. 93 p.

CHRISTIANS in action; a record of work in war-time China, by seven missionaries. London, New York, Longmans, Green [1939] xii, 115 p.

CHURCH MISSIONARY SOCIETY, London. Manual on China. London, 1925. 96 p. illus.

———. China. London, Church Missionary Society, 1931. 70 p. plates. (Africa and the East ser.).

CHURCH OF CHRIST IN CHINA. An adventure in church union in China; origin, nature and task of the Church of Christ in China. New York, North American Advisory Committee, 1944. 31 p.

CLARK, SIDNEY J[AMES] W[ELLS] 1862-1930. The art of using the China missionary survey. [Shanghai, Printed by The Shanghai Mercury, 1922] 16 p.

———. The first stage in the Christian occupation of rural China. The "lifebringing" stage. London, World Dominion Press [1923?] cover-title, 8 p.

———. The indigenous church. London, World Dominion Press [1923?] cover-title, 24 p.

[———.] A paper on mission policy, organization and administration in China, by a business man. [Chester?, Eng. n.d.] 15 p.

COATES, CHARLES H. The Red theology in the Far East. London, C.J. Thynne and Jarvis, 1926. 202 p.

CODRINGTON, FLORENCE ISABEL, 1867-    Hot-hearted, 熱心 ; some women builders of the Chinese church. London, Church of England Zenana Missionary Society [1934] 111 p. col. front., plates, ports.

CONFERENCE OF MISSIONARY SOCIETIES IN GREAT BRITAIN AND IRELAND. Missionaries and the Chinese government. London, Edinburgh House Press, 1925. 7, [1] p.

COOKE, MRS. A. B. Honey Two of Lisu-land. Philadelphia, China Inland Mission [1932] 111 p. illus.

COUCHE, EDITH. Lighting Chinese lanterns. A cheerful missionary surveys the task. London, Chruch of England Zenana Missionary Society, 1941. 72 p. illus.

CRAWFORD, MARY K. The Shantung revival. Shanghai, China Baptist Publication Society [1933] 106 p. illus.

CRESSY, EARL HERBERT. Yellow rivers; adventures in a Chinese parish. New York and London, Harper, 1932. xiii, 153 p. incl. plates, front., illus.

——. China marches toward the cross. New York, Friendship Press, 1938. 79 p. double map.

CROUCH, ARCHIBALD ROY. Riksha rambles of Archie and Ellen; or, Adventures in Christian service. Cambria, Calif., Cambrian Press, 1937. 107 p.

——. Rising through the dust, the story of the Christian church in China. New York, Friendship Press [1948] viii, 179 p. fold. col. map.

CURTIS, CLAUDE HAMILTON, 1912-    A marine among the idols. Grand Rapids, Mich., Zondervan Pub. House [c1940] 79 p.

DECKER, JOHN WILLIAM, 1890-    Report on visit to South China; submitted to the Board of Managers of the American Baptist Foreign Mission Society. Nov.-Dec. 1933. [Hangchow?, 1934] 2-35 numb. l.

——. Report on visit to West China; submitted to the Board of Managers of the American Baptist Foreign Mission Society. [Hangchow?] 1934. 65 numb. l.

DEVARANNE, THEODOR, 1880-    Christus an Torii und Pagode, eine Handreichung für die Mission daheim. Gotha, L. Klotz, 1931. viii, 267 p.

DIFFENDORFER, RALPH EUGENE, 1879-    The situation in China; a report to the Board of foreign missions of the Methodist Episcopal Church of an official visit. New York, 1927. 70 p.

DINNEEN, A. M. D. Not of Gennesareth; romance and adventure in China. Wellington, N. Z., 1933. 143 p.

DIXON, STANLEY H. Chinese Christians face their war. London, Edinburgh House Press, 1939. 24 p. (War-time pamphlets, 2 ).

DRACH, GEORGE. ed. Our church abroad: the foreign missions of the Lutheran Church in America. Philadelphia, United Lutheran Pub. House, 1926. 277 p. front. plates, maps, tables.

EDDY, GEORGE SHERWOOD, 1871-    I have seen God work in China; personal impressions from three decades with the Chinese. New York, Association Press, 1944. ix, 137 p.

ELY, LOIS ANNA. Disciples of Christ in China. Indianapolis, United Christian Missionary Society, 1948. 62 p. illus.

FEDERATION OF WOMAN'S BOARDS OF FOREIGN MISSIONS. Toward friendship with China; outline for discussion course on China. Manchester-by-the-sea, Mass., North Shore Press, 1926. 112 p.

FISCHLE, ERNST, 1897-    Sechzehn Monate in chinesischer Gefangenschaft; mit einem Vorwort und 6 Zeichnungen von Ernst Walter. Stuttgart und Basel, Evang. Missionsverlag [1931] 190 p. front. (group port.) illus. (incl. map).

——. Seize mois de captivité chez les brigands chinois. Adapté de l'allemand par Gaston Victor Rosselet. Lausanne, Secrétariat romand de la Mission de Bâle, 1931. iv, 199 p. illus. plates.

——. Kidnapped in China; translated into English by Marie S. Christlieb, with six illustrations. Mangalore, Basel Mission Book and Tract Depository,

1932.  215 p. illus. plates.

———.  Ein Volk ohne Sünde und die Kirche Christi, von Ernst Fischle und Ernst Walter.  Stuttgart und Basel, Evang. Missionsverlag [1935] 30, [1] p.(Mission und Gemeinde 11/12 ).

FITCH MEMORIAL CHURCH, Shanghai. A virile, self-supporting church crippled by Japan's undeclared war.  Shanghai,. 1932.  26 p. plates.

FOREIGN MISSIONS CONFERENCE OF NORTH AMERICA. The present situation in China and its significance for Christian missions.  New York, Committee of Reference and Counsel, Foreign Missions Conference of N.A. [1925] 40 p.

———.  Addresses on China at the 34th annual session.  Atlantic City, N.J. Jan. 11-14 [1927]  New York, 1927.  45 p. diagr.

FOSTER, JOHN. The Chinese church in action.  London, Edinburgh House Press, 1933.  144 p. fold. map.

———.  Yarns on heroes of the church in China.  London, Edinburgh House Press, 1937.  71 p.

———.  The church and China.  [London, Edinburgh House Press, 1943]  18 p. (World issues, 17 ).

FRANKLIN, JAMES HENRY, 1872-   The Christian crisis in China.  New York, American Baptist Foreign Mission Society, 1931.  149 p. illus. incl. map.

FRITZ, K[ARL].  Christentum und nationale Strömungen in China.  Stuttgart, Evang. Missionsverlag;  Basel, Basler Missionsbuchhandlungen, 1927.  31 p.

FULTON, CHARLES DARBY, 1892-   Star in the east.  Richmond, Va., Presbyterian Committee of Publication [1938]  264 p. illus.

GALBRAITH, WINIFRED. Willow pattern, a picture of China to-day.  London, Edinburgh House Press, 1933.  63 p.

———.  New life in China; the growth of the church in war-time.  London, Edinburgh House Press, 1942.  24 p. (World issues, 2 ).

GALE, GODFREY LIVINGSTONE.  Interned in China.  London, Livingstone Press, 1946.  24 p.

GAMEWELL, MARY LOUISE (NINDE) 1858-1947.  Ming-Kwong, "city of the morning light."  West Medford, Mass., Central Committee of the United Study of Foreign Missions [c1924] 223 p. illus.

GARLICK, PHYLLIS L. Building the church: being the C.M.S. story of the year 1926-27.  London, Church Missionary Society [1927]  130 p. maps.

———.  Destiny at the door; China faces the future.  London, Church Missionary Society, 1945.  39 p.

GENG, GEORGE YUEN-HSIOH, 耿元學 , 1905-   The promotion of the economic welfare of the Chinese people through the Protestant church in China.  New York, 1951.  244 l. (Columbia University, Teachers College. Report Ed. D. Type B.).

GIH, ANDREW, 計志文 . The power of the gospel in war-torn China; a message reprinted from Winona echoes.  Grand Rapids, Mich., Zondervan Pub. House [1940]  5-15 p.

———.  His faithfulness: stories of miracles of a native mission, the "Evangelize China Fellowship."  Edited by Ruth J. Corbin.  London, Marshall, Morgan and Scott, 1955.  54 p. front. illus. 1st ed. 1937.

———.  Into God's family: a fascinating account of the lives and work of members of the famous Bethel evangelistic bands and some of their inspiring messages.  Rev. and enl. ed. London, Marshall, Morgan and Scott, 1955.  x, 11,233 p. port.

GLOVER, ARCHIBALD EDWARD, 1860?-   A thousand miles of miracle in China; a personal record of God's delivering pwer from the hands of the imperial Boxers of Shan-si. 17th ed.  London, Glasgow, Pickering and Inglis [1931] xvi, 372 p. front., plates, ports., facsims. 1st ed. 1904.

———.  The same. 22d ed. abridged by L.T. Lyall. Foreword by J.C. Pollock.  London, China Inland Mission; Lutterworth Press, 1957.  192 p. front.(port.) map. 1st ed. 1904.

GODDARD, FRANCIS WAYLAND, 1877-1958. A century of Baptist missions to the Chinese. [n.p.] 1935. 41 p. ports.

GOERTZ, PETER SIEBERT. A history of the development of the Chinese indigenous Christian church under the American Board in Fukien province. New Haven, 1933. v, 394, xii p. charts. Thesis-Yale University.

GOFORTH, JONATHAN, 1859-1936. "By my spirit." Foreword by Mrs. Rosalind Goforth. Grand Rapids, Mich., Zondervan Pub. House [1942] 138 p.

GRAY, W. PARKER. Report of a visit to China, 1929; by W. Parker Gray and C. E. Wilson. London, Baptist Missionary Society [1929] 58 p.

GREGG, EVA A. Hints from squints in China. Cincinnati, O., Printed by the Caxton Press [c1923] 216 p. front., 1 illus., ports.

GROSE, GEORGE RICHMOND, bp., 1869-  The new soul in China. New York, Cincinnati, Abingdon Press [c1927] 152 p.

HALL, RONALD OWEN, bp., 1895-  The art of the missionary; fellow-workers with the church in China. London, Student Christian Movement Press [1942] 77 p.

————. The missionary-artist looks at his job. New York, International Missionary Council, 1942. 64 p.

————. Chinese Christianity speaks to the West, by Ronald Owen Hall and T. Z. Koo, 顧子仁. London, Student Christian Movement, 1950. 30 p.

HARRIS, E. F. About China; compiled by E. F. Harris and A. M. Robinson. London, Church of England, Zenana Missionary Society, 1936. 62 p. front. illus. plates.

HARTENSTEIN, KARL. Die Kirche Chinas unter dem Kreuz, von Karl Hartenstein und Jakob Keck. Stuttgart, Evang. Missionsverlag, 1951. 36 p. (Weltmission heute, 1 ).

HARTWELL, GEORGE EVERSON, 1863-  "Granary of heaven." Toronto, Pub. by the Committee on missionary education, the Woman's Missionary Society, Literature dept. of the United Church of Canada [1939?] xii, 228 p. front., ports.

HAYES, EGBERT. Glimpses of a summer in Mongolia and a year's work in China; written for personal friends by Egbert and Eva M. Hayes. Shanghai, 1924. 68 p. illus.

HEEREN, JOHN J., 1875-1941. On the Shantung front; a history of the Shantung mission of the Presbyterian church in the U.S.A., 1861-1940 in its historical, economic, and political setting. New York, The Board of Foreign Missions of the Presbyterian Church in the United States of America, 1940. xiv, 264 p. front., maps.

HOBART, KENNETH GRAY. Early American Baptist missions to the Chinese. [Shanghai, Print. priv., 1939] cover-title, 68 p.

HODGKIN, HENRY THEODORE, 1877-1933. The missionary situation in China. An address delivered at the Foreign missions conference of North America in Atlantic City, N.J., Jan. 10-13, 1928. New York, 1928. 16 p.

HOLLISTER, MARY (BREWSTER), 1891-  Lady Fourth Daughter of China, sharer of life; cover design by I. Lai Cho, 卓宜來. Cambridge, Mass., The Central Committee on the United Study of Foreign Missions, 1932. 237 p. front., 1 illus., plates, double map.

HOPP, WALTER. Filmstreifen aus Ost-Kansu. Limburg a.d. Lahn, Druck der Limburger Vereinsdruckerei, 1930. 118 p.

HORNING, EMMA. Junior folks at mission study-China; a symposium written by missionaries in China, Emma Horning, Anna Seese, Grace Clapper, F. H. Crumpacker. Elgin, Ill., General mission board, Church of the Brethren [c1921] 64 p. col. front., illus. (maps) plates, ports.

HOUGHTON, FRANK, 1894-  The two hundred; why they were needed, how they responded, who they are, where they are. With foreword by the Rev. W. H. Aldis. London, China Inland Mission, 1932. 79 p. front., plates.

————. China calling. London, Philadelphia, China Inland Mission [1936] 187 p.

front., illus. (maps).

HOUGHTON, STANLEY, 1900-47. Chefoo, by Stanley Houghton, Edith B. Harman and Margaret Pyle, with foreword by F. McCarthy. London, Philadelphia, China Inland Mission, 1931. xi, 82 p. front., plates, ports., map.

HOWDEN, JOSEPH RUSSELL, 1872-    My mission to China. London, Marshall Bros., 1926. 126 p.

HUDSPETH, WILLIAM HARRISON. Stone gateway and the Flowery Miao, with special reference to Samuel Pollard's missionary work among the Miao. London, Cargate Press, 1937. 87 p. plates, port. map.

———. The Bible and China. London, British and Foreign Bible Society [1952] 47 p. map. (Third jubilee books, 1 ).

HUNG, WILLIAM, 洪業, 1893-    ed. As it looks to young China; chapters by a group of Christian Chinese. New York, Friendship Press; London, Student Christian Movement Press [1932] viii, 181 p.

HUNTINGTON, DANIEL TRUMBULL, bp., 1868-    The diocese of Anking. Hartford, Conn., Church Missions Pub. Co. [c1943] cover-title, 7-23,[2], 24-81 p. illus. (map) port.

HUNTINGTON, VIRGINIA ETHEL (HAIST) 1889-    Along the great river; illustrations by Lloyd Coe. New York, The National Council, Protestant Episcopal Church [c1940] 5-261, [1] p. illus.

HUSEMANN, DIETRICH. Die rechtliche Stellung christlicher Missionen in China. (Ein Beitrag zum Studium des Ausländerschutzes) Berlin, C. Heymann, 1934. v, 119 p.

INGLIS, THEODORA (MARSHALL). New lanterns in old China; with foreword by Isaac Taylor Headland. New York, Chicago, Fleming H. Revell [c1923] 175 p.

JANSEN, E.G. Jade engraved; New Zealand missionaries and their Chinese colleagues in Japan's "China incident." Christchurch, Presbyterian Bookroom [1947] xiii, 247 p. port., maps.

JENNESS, MARY. A wheelbarrowful of life; a dramatization of modern industry in China. New York, Missionary Education Movement of the United States and Canada [c1924] 23 p.

JOHNSON, CHRISTINE. For the women of China, and through Bible lands, translated from the Norwegian by Herman E. Jorgensen. Minneapolis, Norwegian Lutheran Church, 1927. 263 p. front. (port.) illus.

JOLLIFFE, R. ORLANDO. The Chinese church rides the storm. New York, Friendship Press [1946] 48 p.

JONES, CLARA J., 1900-    Above the tumult in China; illus. by Edward Sovik. Minneapolis, Augsburg Pub. House [1948] viii, 182 p. illus.

KÄSER, GUSTAV. Es ist kein Preis zu teuer. Eine Geschichte aus China. Basel, Basler Missionsbuchhandlung, 1940. iv, 31 p. illus.

KANE, J. HERBERT. Twofold growth. Philadelphia, Toronto, China Inland Mission [1947] xv, 181 p. front., plates, ports.

KELLY, MARY FRANCES E. Some Chinese friends of mine. Cincinnati, Powell and White, 1924. 196 p. front. (port.) illus.

KEMPGEN, WILHELM. Glaubenskampf am Tigertor, Not und Verheissung einer Hundertjährigen Missionsarbeit. Wuppertal-Barmen, Verlag der Rheinischen Missionsgeschichte, 1948. 171 p. front. (map).

KERSCHNER, MABEL GARDNER. Young China; a handbook for leaders of intermediate groups. New York, Missionary Education Movement of the United States and Canada, c1924. 94 p.

KEYTE, JOHN CHARLES, 1875-    In China now; China's need and the Christian contribution. London, United Council for Missionary Education; New York, George H. Doran, 1923. 160 p. front., illus.(map) plates, ports.

KILEN, JULIUS R. Forty years in China; a brief history of the Lutheran Brethren mission work in China, 1902-42. Fergus Falls, Minn. Borderbaandet Pub. Co., 1943. 156 p. map.

KILPPER, CHRISTIAN GOTTHILF, 1884-    Mein Räuberhauptmann; Erinnerung-

en eines Gefangenen. Stuttgart, Evang. Missionsverlag, 1934. 98 p.
——. My robber-captain; a true story; translated by W.J. Kilpper. Grand Rapids, Mich., Wm. B. Eerdmans Pub. Co. [c1936] [7]-166 p.
KNOTT, MARGARET C. The light approaching; China and the L.M.S., with epilogue by Cecil W. Knott. London, Livingstone Press [1928] 142 p. front. plates, ports., map.
——. Trek to the west; a story of modern China. London, London Missionary Society, 1946. 63 p. illus.
KUHN, ISOBEL. Precious things of the Lasting Hills. London, China Inland Mission, 1938. 79 p.
——. Nests above the abyss. Philadelphia, London, China Inland Mission [1947] x, 254 p. front., plates, ports.
——. Stones of fire. The story of a young Lisu tribe woman and the Lisu church since 1941. London, China Inland Mission, 1951. 152 p. plates.
LACY, WALTER NIND. A hundred years of China Methodism. Nashville, Abingdon-Cokesbury Press [1948] 336 p. map.
LAUTENSCHLAGER, STANTON. Far west in China. New York, Friendship Press [1941] 48 p. double map.
LAYMEN'S FOREIGN MISSIONS INQUIRY. Re-thinking missions; a laymen's inquiry after one hundred years, by the Commission of appraisal, William Ernest Hocking, chairman. New York and London, Harper, 1932. xv, 349 p. diagrs.
——. Supplementary series. v.2, v.5. Orville A. Petty, editor. New York and London, Harper, 1933. 2 v. illus. (maps) diagrs.
LEE, ESTHER (HAGGARD). The other side of the world; pages from the journal of a young missionary in pre-Communist China. New York, Vantage Press [c1956] 79 p. illus.
LEE, FREDERICK. Travel talks on China. Washington, D.C., South Bend, Ind. [etc.] Review and Herald Pub. Association [c1926] 7-254 p. incl. front., illus.
LEE, SHAU-YAN, 李守仁. How to win the Chinese. Norfolk, Va., 1946 (c1944) 151, [1] p.
LEGER, SAMUEL HOWARD, 1891- Education of Christian ministers in China, a historical and critical study. Shanghai, 1925. xi, 118 p. Thesis-Columbia University.
LEHMANN, ARNO. ed. Licht für Fernost. Dresden-A und Leipzig, C.L. Ungelenk, 1937. 64 p. (Die mission der kirche; missionsstunden aus dem gesamtgebiet der deutschen evangelischen weltmission).
LEHMANN, EMILY. Verborgene Brücken. Wuppertal, R. Brockhaus [1955] 126 p. illus.
LENNOX, WILLIAM GORDON, 1884- The health of missionary families in China, a statistical study. Denver, University of Denver, 1921. 121 p. incl. tables, front., plates.
——. A comparative study of the health of missionary families in Japan and China and a selected group in America. Denver, University of Denver, 1922. 44 p. incl. charts, tables.
LERRIGO, PETER HUGH JAMES, 1875- comp. Northern Baptists rethink missions; a study of the report of the Laymen's foreign missions inquiry. New York, Baptist Board of Education, Department of Missionary Education [1933] 128 p. illus.
LEWIS, IDA BELLE, 1887- Grains of rice from a Chinese bowl, with introduction by Prof. Isaac T. Headland. New York, Chicago, Fleming H. Revell [c1926] 5-123 p. front., plates.
LIBERTY, ERIC, 1902- Chinese students at the cross-roads. London, China Inland Mission [1948] 93 p. plates, group ports.
LIPPHARD, WILLIAM BENJAMIN, 1886- Out of the storm in China; a review of recent developments in Baptist mission field; issued by the Department of missionary education of the Board of Education of the Northern Baptist Con-

vention. Philadelphia and Boston, Judson Press [c1932]  201 p. front., illus. (maps).

LITTLE, LAURA NANCE. Darings in the dawn. Richmond, Va., Rice Press, 1938. 154 p. front. illus. plates, port.

LOBENSTINE, EDWIN CARLYLE, 1872-1958. The relation of church and mission in China; a statement prepared for the meeting of the International mission-ary council at Oxford, July 9th-16th, 1923. London, International Mission-ary Council [1923] 35 p.

LONDON MISSIONARY SOCIETY. Report of F. H. Hawkins of visit to China to at-tend the annual meeting of the China advisory council and the dedication of the new buildings of the Union Medical College, Peking, August-September, 1921. London, London Missionary Society, 1921. 75 p.

──────. Report by F. H. Hawkins on his visit to China, as special deputation from the directors, August 1927 to March 1928. London, London Missionary Soci-ety, 1928. 174 p.

LÜTTICHAU, ELLI. "In unsres Königs Namen": Reisetagebuchblätter der Mis-sionarinnen Gräfin Elli Lüttichau und Hildegard Spengler. Leipzig, Verlag und Bücherstube der Mädchen-Bibel-Kreise, 1927. 135 p. front. plates.

LUNDEEN, ANTON. In the grip of bandits and yet in the hands of God. [Rock Is-land, Ill., Augustana Book Concern, c1925] 143, [1] p. illus.

McMILLAN, ARCHIBALD MEMORY. For Christ in China. Nashville, Broad-man Press [1949, c1948] 141 p. illus.

MacNAIR, HARLEY FARNSWORTH, 1891-1947. Critical moments in the history of Christianity in China. A paper read before the Shanghai Missionary Associ-ation Nov. 3, 1925. Shanghai, 1925. 20 p.

McROBERTS, DUNCAN, 1912-  While China bleeds, introduction by H. A. Iron-side. Grand Rapids, Mich., Zondervan Pub. House [c1943]  162, [3] p.

──────. Pleading China. Grand Rapids, Mich., Zondervan Pub. House [1946] 141 p. plates, ports.

MADDOX, CATHERINE. The invincible company. London, Philadelphia, China Inland Mission [1951] 96 p. illus.

MANN, EBSENEZER JOHN, 1902-57. Testament of Grace. London, China In-land Mission, 1951. 70 p.

MANN, WALTER. Christianity in China: an exposure of foreign missions. Lon-don, Pioneer Press, 1927. 62 p.

MARBACH, OTTO, 1901-  Chinas not und Japans hoffnung; Reiseerinnerungen eines Ostasienfreundes. Bern und Leipzig, Verlag von Paul Haupt, 1929. 144 p. front. plates.

──────. 50 Jahre Ostasienmission; ihr Werden und Wachsen. Den Freunden der Ostasienmission zur Jubiläumsfeier im herbst 1934 freundlichst gewidmet. Berlin-Steglitz und St. Gallen, Verlag Ostasienmission [1934?] vii, 119 p. plates, ports.

MATHEWS, BASIL JOSEPH, 1879-1951. Torchbearers in China, by Basil Ma-thews and Arthur E. Southon. New York, Missionary Education Movement of the United States and Canada, c1924. 186 p. front., plates, ports.

MATHEWS, HAROLD SHEPARD. American Board of Commissioners for For-eign Missions; seventy-five years of the North China mission. Prepared in connection with the celebration of the seventy-fifth anniversary, Peking, 1935. Peking, 1942. 196 p.

METHODIST CHURCH (United States) Board of Missions. China, and what the Methodists are doing there. New York, Editorial department, Joint division of education and cultivation, Board of Missions and Church Extension [1941] 39 p. illus. (The World parish ser.).

MEYER, MINNA McEUEN. Chinese lanterns. Approved by the Committee on curriculum of the Board of Sunday Schools of the Methodist Episcopal Church. New York, Methodist Book Concern [1924] 142 p. front., plates.

MIAO, CHESTER S., 繆秋笙, [Miao Chiu-shêng] 1894-  ed. Christian voices in China. New York, Friendship Press [1948] viii, 216 p. illus., fold. col. map.

MITCHELL, FRED. Over to China; record of a visit. London, China Inland Mission, 1948. 115 p. front. illus.(map), plates.

MOENNICH, MARTHA L. On the China road. Introduction by H. A. Ironside. Grand Rapids, Mich., Zondervan Pub. House [1947] 150 p. plates.

MONCRIEFF, ASCOTT ROBERT HOPE, 1846-1927. Are ministerial missionaries needed? Shanghai, 1929. cover-title, 25 p.

MORTON, T. RALPH. Life in the Chinese church. London, Student Christian Movement Press [1931] 94 p.

NANKING THEOLOGICAL SEMINARY, Nanking. The great migration and the church in West China; report of a survey made under the auspices of the Nanking Theological Seminary and the National Christian Council of China. Shanghai, 1940. iv, 106 p.

NATIONAL CHRISTIAN CONFERENCE, Shanghai, 1922. The Chinese church as revealed in the National Christian conference held in Shanghai, Tuesday, May 2, to Thursday, May 11, 1922. Shanghai, Oriental Press [1922] viii, xi, 724 p. illus.

NATIONAL CHRISTIAN COUNCIL OF CHINA. The Christian occupation of Kiangsu, reprinted from the Survey prepared for the National Christian Conference 1922. Shanghai, National Christian Council, 1922? 31 p. incl. tables, illus. (maps).

——. The Christian occupation of Chekiang, reprinted from the Survey prepared by the National Christian conference 1922. Shanghai, National Christian Council, 1922? 22 p. incl. tables. illus. (maps).

——. Report of conference on the church in China to-day; the report of a conference of Christian workers with Dr. John R. Mott January 5-7, 1921. Shanghai, National Christian Council, 1926. [1], 166 p.

——. Report of the conference on Christianizing economic relations held under the auspices of the National Christian Council of China August 18-28, 1927. Shanghai, National Christian Council, 1927. 128 p.

——. The National Christian council; a five years' review, 1922-27. [Shanghai, National Christian Council, 1927] cover-title, 44 p.

——. The church in China and its relation to the churches of Europe and America. Prepared by the members of the China delegation to the meeting of the International missionary council, Jerusalem, April 1928. Shanghai, National Christian Council of China, 1928. 20 p.

——. The church literacy movement, 1930. Shanghai, National Christian Council of China, 1931. 44 p.

——. Christian cooperation in China as illustrated by the biennial meeting, Shanghai, May 5-11, 1937. Impressions, addresses, recommendations approved. Shanghai, National Christian Council of China, 1937. 49 p.

——. National Committee for Christian Religious Education in China. Religious education in the Chinese church: the report of a deputation, 1931. Shanghai, 1931. 296 p.

——. Education for service in the Christian church in China. The report of a survey commission, 1935. Shanghai, The Christian Literature Society, 1935. 120, 99-157 p.

NELSON, DANIEL, 1902-48. A compendium of basic characters in Chinese Christian thought. Hartford, 1943. 369 p. Thesis-Hartford Theological Seminary.

NICHOLS, NETTIE D. comp. God's faithfulness in Ningpo, compiled by Nettie D. Nichols and Joshua Bang. Springfield, Mo., General Council of the Assemblies of God, 1938. 48 p. illus.

NORDMO, JACOB M., 1882-   Demons despoiled. London, China Inland Missions, 1950. 95 p.

NOWACK, WILLIAM H. My Ebenezer, a personal testimony to the faithfulness of a prayer-hearing God. Green Bay, Wis., Reliance Pub. Co. [1946] [11]-

170 p.

[NOYES, HARRIET NEWELL]. History of the South China mission of the American Presbyterian church, 1845-1920. Shanghai, Printed at the Presbyterian Mission Press, 1927. 155 p. front., plates, ports.

ÖBERG, ELISABET. Light in the land of the shadow of death, sketches from the San-Miao orphanage at Saratsi, translated by Lizzie Lieden. Chicago, Emil Forslund Print. Co., 1926. 143 p. front., illus.

OEHLER, WILHELM, 1877- China und die christliche Mission in Geschichte und Gegenwart. Stuttgart, Evang. Missionsverlag, 1925. viii, 282 p. fold. map. (Handbücher für Missionsstudienkreise, 4 ).

―――. Chinas Erwachen auf dem nationalen, wirtschaftlichen und religiösen Gebiet; Erlebtes und Erforschtes. Wernigerode, "Die Aue" [1925] 137 p.

―――. Wege Gottes in China; das Hakkavolk und die Basler Mission. Stuttgart und Basel, Evang. Missionsverlag, 1931. 148 p. front., plates, ports., double map.

―――. China nach dem Kriege. Bad Salzuffen, MBK-Verlag, 1947. 24 p.(Wenn Gottes Winde wehen, 4).

OEHLER-HEIMERDINGER, ELISABETH, 1884- Über den gelben Storm. Geschichten von Chinesen. Stuttgart, Evang. Missionsverlag, 1922. 95 p. (Stuttgarter Missionsbücher, 1 ).

―――. Weihrauch und Gebet. Bilder aus dem chinesische Missionsarbeit. Stuttgart, Evang. Missionsverlag, 1924. 30 p. illus.

―――. Scènes de la vie missionnaire en Chine. Traduction de l'allemand par Ernest Morel. Bâle, Librairie des Missions, Neuchâtel, Delachaux et Niestlé, 1925. iv, 96 p. plates.

―――. Wie mir die chinesen Freunde wurden. Aus dem Tagebuch einer jungen Frau. Mit 8 original Aufnahmen von der Verfasserin. Stuttgart, Evang. Missionsverlag, 1925. 130 p.

OLDFIELD, WALTER HERBERT, 1879- Pioneering in Kwangsi; the story of Alliance missions in South China. Harrisburg, Pa., Christian Publications [c1936] 208 p. front., plates, ports.

ORCHARD, RONALD KENNETH. The situation of the China mission. London, Livingstone Press, 1951. 8 p.

ORR, JAMES EDWIN, 1912- Through blood and fire in China. London, Marshall, Morgan and Scott [1939] v, [1], 7-160 p. illus.(map) plates (incl. front., ports.).

OSS, JOHN. Mission advance in China. Nashville, Southern Pub. Association [1950, c1949] 284 p. illus., ports., map (on lining paper).

OSS, OLGA BERTINE (OSNES), 1897- Triumphs of faith; personal experience in service for the King by Mrs. John Oss. Takoma Park, Washington, D.C., South Bend, Ind., Review and Herald Pub. Association, c1935. 159 p. front. (port.).

OUR China mission. Part one: Hankow. St. Louis, Concordia Pub. House, 1926. 48 p. illus. (Men and Missions, 4).

PARKER, ALVIN P., 1850-1924. Southern Methodism in China. Nashville, Pub. House M.E. Church, South, 1924. 56 p. (Southern Methodist mission fields).

PASSIONISTS. Eyes East, interesting facts about China, presented by the Passionist missionaries. [Union City, N.J., The Sign, 193?] 72 p. illus.

PAYNE, JESSIE. The very heart of China. London, Carey Press [1930] viii, [100] p.

PEILL, SIDNEY GEORGE. Church planting [by] S.G. Peill and W.F. Rowlands. London, World Dominion Press [1924] cover-title, 12 p. [The indigenous church series] "Reprinted from World Dominion."

PENROSE, CECIL. The romance of China. London, Bible Churchmen's Missionary Society, 1927. 119, [1] p. plates.

PINSON, WILLIAM WASHINGTON, 1854- China in action; an elective course for adult and young people's classes, Sunday school teachers, and missionary committees. Nashville, Cokesbury Press, 1930. 176 p.

PORTER, LUCIUS CHAPIN, 1880-    China's challenge to Christianity. New York, Missionary Education Movement of the United States and Canada [c1924] vii, [1], 248 p. front.(port.) illus.(map) plates.

POTEAT, GORDON. Home letters from China; the story of how a missionary found and began his life work in the heart of China. New York, George H. Doran [c1924] vi, 9-159 p.

———. Stand by for China. New York, Friendship Press [c1940] x, 181 p.

POUSMA, RICHARD H. An eventful year in the Orient. Grand Rapids, Mich., Eerdmans, 1927. 233 p.

PRESBYTERIAN CHURCH IN CANADA. Together. Information on the cooperative effort of the Canadian Presbyterians with the Chinese Christians. [Toronto] Presbyterian Church in Canada, 1947. vii, 51 p.

PRESBYTERIAN CHURCH IN THE U.S.A. Tentative findings of the evaluation conference of the Presbyterian church in the U.S.A. held at Shanghai, Nov. 18-Dec. 3, 1926. [Shanghai, Presbyterian Mission Press, 1926] 105, viii p. incl. tables.

PRICE, FRANK WILSON, 1895-    We went to West China. [Nashville, Presbyterian Church in the United States, Executive Committee of Foreign Missions, 1943] 30 p.

———. China, twilight or dawn? New York, Friendship Press [1948] vi, 184 p. fold. col. map.

———. The rural church in China, a survey. [2d ed.] New York, Agricultural Missions, 1948. xi, 274 p. maps. (Studies in the world mission of Christianity, 9 ).

PRICE, PHILIP FRANCIS, 1864-1954. Our Chinese investment: sixty-years of the Southern Presbyterian church in China with biographies, autobiographies, and sketches of all missionaries since the opening of the work in 1867. Nashville, 1927? 187 p.

PROCTOR, JOHN THOMAS. [Mission administration in China] A paper read before the Shanghai missionary association, Oct. 3, 1922. Shanghai, 1922? cover-title, 18 p.

[PROTESTANT EPISCOPAL CHURCH IN THE U.S.A.]. Beyond the eight horizons. [New York, 1943?] cover-title, 56 p. plates, double map. (Building the church around the world).

QUENTIN, A.P. A Taoist pearl. London, Society for promoting Christian Knowledge; New York [etc.] Macmillan [1928] xv, [1], 143, [1] p. front., illus.

RATTENBURY, HAROLD BURGOYNE. The seven churches of China. Being a picture of the seven China districts of the Methodist Church. London, Cargate Press [1934] 111 p. map.

RAWLINSON, FRANK JOSEPH, 1871-1937, ed. Progressive ideals of Christian work in China, by resident workers. Shanghai, E. Evans [192-?] iii, 86 p.

———. Naturalization of Christianity in China (a study of the relation of Christian and Chinese idealism and life) Shanghai, Presbyterian Mission Press, 1927. viii, 216 p.

———. Western money and the Chinese church; an attempt to find a modern approach to an old practice. Shanghai, Presbyterian Mission Press, 1929. cover-title, ii, 71 p.

REES, RONALD DAVIS, 1888-    China faces the storm; the Christian church in China today, with a prologue and epilogue by George Osborn. London, Edinburgh House Press, 1937. 158 p.

———. China can take it. London, Edinburgh House Press, 1942. 64 p.

———. News from China. London, Livingstone Press, 1947. 48 p. map.

REICHELT, KARL LUDVIG, 1897-1952. The transformed abbot. Translated by G.M. Reichelt and A.P. Rose. London, Lutterworth Press [1954] 157 p. illus.

REYNOLDS, ARTHUR, 1909-    Change and challenge in China. London, China

Inland Mission, 1947. 99 p. plates, map.
———. Das neue China ruft. Übers. aus dem Englischen von Ursula von Reis-
witz. Bad Salzuflen, MBK Verlag, 1948. 48 p.
RICHARDSON, DONALD WILLIAM, 1879-   The church in China. Richmond,
Va., Presbyterian Committee of Publication [c1929] 224 p. plates, maps.
RICHTER, JULIUS, 1862-   Das Werden der christlichen Kirche in China. Gü-
tersloh, Bertelsmann, 1928. xvi, 584 p. fold. front. (Allgemeine Evangeli-
sche Missionsgeschichte, 4 ).
ROBINS, HENRY BURKE, 1874-   Christian progress in the Far East; a report
of a visit to Baptist mission fields in Japan, China and the Philippine Islands,
1920-21. New York, American Baptist Foreign Mission Society [1921] 51 p.
ROSE, JOHN RICHARD. A church born to suffer; being an account of the first
hundred years of the Methodist church in South China, 1851-1951. London,
Cargate Press, 1951. 172 p. illus. plates, tables.
ROSENKRANZ, GERHARD, 1896-   Der Nomos Chinas und das Evangelium;
eine Untersuchung über die Bedeutung von Rasse und Volkstum für die mis-
sionarische Verkündigung in China. Leipzig, J.C. Hinrichs, 1936. xii, 196 p.
(Missionswissenschaftliche forschungen, hrsg. von der Deutschen gesellschaft
für missionswissenschaft durch M. Schlunk, 10 ).
———. Fernost - wohin? Begegungen mit den Religionen Japans und Chinas im
Umbruch der Gegenwart. Heilbroun, E. Salzer, 1940. 304 p. illus.
———. Buddha und Christus im Ringen um die Seele Chinas. Ein Kapitel chine-
sischer Religionsgeschichte und seine Bedeutung für die christliche Mission.
Gütersloh, 1941. 58 p. (Allgemeine Missions-Studien, 25 ).
ROUTH, EUGENE COKE, 1874-   Evening and morning in China. Nashville,
Broadman Press [1950] ix, 125 p. illus.
ROWLANDS, E. End of an era; stories from Central China during the war years,
1938-45. London, Livingstone Press, 1947. 101 p. maps.
[ROWLANDS, WILLIAM FRANCIS]. Indigenous ideals in practice; a survey of
the evangelistic and church work in the district of Siaochang, with some ref-
erence to developments during the decade 1914-24. Siaochang, North China,
London Mission, 1925. 23 p. [Indigenous church series].
———. The same; evangelistic policy and work in the Siaochang field in North
China. London and New York, World Dominion Press [1932] 43 p. [Indige-
nous church series].
———. The plain and the people; life changing and church planting on the North
China plain. London, Livingstone Press, 1937? 110 p. front. plates.
———. Christ came to Bitter Market [Hopei]. London, Livingstone Press, 1951.
70 p. (Broadway Books, 1).
SADLER, J. True celestials: or, leaves from a Chinese sketch-book, by J.Sad-
ler assisted by W.H. Muncaster. London, S.W. Partridge and Co., n.d. 144 p.
SAUNDERS, J. ROSCOE, 1873-   The Chinese as they are. New York, Chicago,
Fleming H. Revell [c1921] 176 p. front., plates, ports., fold. map.
SCHÄPPI, GERTRUD. Heimgefunden. Vom Leiden und Reisen einer jungen Chi-
nesin. Stuttgart und Basel, Evang. Missionsverlag, 1929. iv, 30 p. illus.
———. Auf Bergpfaden in China. Aus dem Tagebuch einer Missionarin. Basel,
Basler Missionsbuchhandlung, 1943. iv, 96 p. illus.
SCHEURER, HANS. Die Letzten werden die Ersten sein. Aus dem Leben einer
chinesischen Frau. Stuttgart und Basel, Evang. Missionsverlag, 1937. iv,
19 p. illus.
SCHMAUSS, GEORG. Auf Missionspfaden in China; Reiseindrücke von Georg
Schmauss. Marburg, Spenerverlag und Druckerei, 1937. 87 p. plates.
SCHÖNLEBER, ANNA. Zwischen Lotosblüten und Gobistaub; Erlebnisse deut-
scher Schwestern in China. Stuttgart, J.F. Steinkopf [1955] 232 p. illus.
SCHULTZE, OTTO, 1872-   Wunderbare Führung eines Chinesenknaben. Stutt-
gart, Evang. Missionsverlag, 1921. 16 p. illus.
———. Der Fluch des Opiums und seine Bekämpfung in China. Basel, Basler

Missionsgesellschaft; Stuttgart, Evang. Missionsverlag, 1921. iv, 16 p. illus.

──. Lebensbilder aus der chinesischen Mission. 2. Aufl. Stuttgart, Evang. Missionsverlag, 1922. 90 p. (Stuttgarter Missionsbücherei, 4) 1st ed., Basel, 1905.

SCHWAGER, FRIEDRICH W. Kongregationale missionsarbeit in China. Redfield, S.D., 1927. 208 p. incl. illus.

SCOTT, CHARLES ERNEST, 1876- Answered prayer in China; some prayer-experiences of present-day Chinese Christians. Philadelphia, The Sunday School Times Co. [c1923] xv, 219 p.

──. Chinese twice-born: kingdom trophies in the Orient, introduction by Charles G. Trumbull. New York, Chicago, Fleming H. Revell [c1931] 159 p.

SCOTT, GEORGE A., 1904- In whose hands? A story of internment in China. London, China Inland Mission, 1947. 80 p.

SCOTT, PERCY MELVILLE. Is it worth while? (The present position of missions in China). London, Society for the Propagation of the Gospel in Foreign Parts, 1931. 24 p. (Problems of the mission field).

[SEAMAN, ROY] 1894- Ship that did not sink [a single outline history of the China Inland Mission], illustrated by Ellen Lister. London, China Inland Mission, 1952. 47 p.

SEWELL, WILLIAM GAWAN. China unbroken. London, Friends Service Council, 1940. 12 p. illus.

SHEBBEARE, U.K. China. London, Society for the Propagation of the Gospel in Foreign Parts, 1933. 105 p. map, plates (S.P.G. handbooks, n.s.).

SIMPSON, BARBARA. China post; letters in peace and war, with foreword by Pao-swen Tseng, 曾寶蓀. London, Edinburgh House Press, 1939. 103 p.

SKINSNES, CASPER C., 1886- Scalpel and cross in Honan. Minneapolis, Augsburg Pub. House [1952] 254 p. illus.

SKUES, ERIC. Shensi; China's mission to the Chinese. London, Society for the Propagation of the Gospel, 1935. 22 p. plates, ports.

SMITH, C. STANLEY. The development of Protestant theological education in China in the light of the history of the education of the clergy in Europe and America. Shanghai, Kelly and Walsh, 1941. xii, 171 p. (Nanking Theological Seminary. English publications, 2).

SMITH, DANIEL, 1907- Nosu nuggets from the Yunnan quarry. London, China Inland Mission [1940] 46 p. front., map.

SMYTHE, LEWIS STRONG CASEY, 1901- Changes in the Christian message for China by protestant missionaries. Chicago, 1928. v, 298, 8 l. Thesis-Univ. of Chicago.

SOONG, MAYLING, 蔣宋美齡, 1897- Christianity in China's national crisis. An address delivered at the Wuhan Monthly Missionary Prayer Meeting on April 6, 1938. Hankow, Printed by Chinese League of Nations Union [1938] 5 p. (Special publication ser., 14).

──. A propos du Resurgam de madame Chiang Kai-shek. Chungking, Le Correspondant chinois, 1940. cover-title, 20 p.

──. I confess my faith. New York, Board of Missions and Church Extension, the Methodist Church, 1943. 11 p.

──. The sure victory. [Westwood, N.J.] Revell [1955] 45 p.

SOUTHERN BAPTIST CONVENTION. A century for Christ in China. Richmond, Va., Foreign Mission Board, Southern Baptist Convention, 1936. 72 p. illus. map.

──. Southern Baptists in China. Richmond, Va., Foreign Mission Board, Southern Baptist Convention, 1939. 39 p.

SOUTHON, ARTHUR E. More yarns on China. London, Church Missionary Society, 1924. 79 p.

SPAICH, WILHELM. Erlebnisse einer Missionsschwester in China. Stuttgart und Basel, Evang. Missionsverlag [1928] iv, 16 p. illus.

SPEER, ROBERT ELLIOTT, 1867-1947. Report on Japan and China of the depu-
tation sent by the Board of foreign missions of the Presbyterian church in the
U.S.A. to visit these fields and to attend a series of evaluation conferences
in China in 1926; presented by Mr. Robert E. Speer and Dr. Hugh T. Kerr.
New York, Board of Foreign Missions of the Presbyterian Church in the U.S.
A., 1927. viii, 528 p. diagrs.
――――. ''Re-thinking missions'' examined; an attempt at a just review of the re-
port of the Appraisal commission of the Laymen's foreign mission inquiry.
New York, Fleming H. Revell [c1933] 7-64 p.
STAUFFER, MILTON THEOBALD, 1885-    Looking towards a Christian China;
a discussion course. New York, Missionary Education Movement of the Uni-
ted States and Canada [c1924] v, 7-128 p.
――――. China her own interpreter; chapters by a group of nationals interpreting
the Christian movement, assembled and edited by Milton Stauffer. New York,
Pub. for the Student volunteer movement for foreign missions by the Mission-
ary Education Movement of the United States and Canada [c1927] xv, 170 p.
(Christian voives around the world).
STEPHANY, MARIE. The power of the gospel in Shansi province. Springfield,
Mo., General Council of the Assemblies of God [1934] 45 p. illus.
STEWART, EMILY LILY, 1893-    Forward in western China; foreword by the
Archbishop of Sydney. London, Church Missionary Society, 1934. ix, [1],
77 p. col. front., illus.(map).
[STOCKWELL, FRANCIS OLIN] 1900-    Contacts in China; a book with a devo-
tional purpose, by a first termer. Foochow [Printed by the Bing Ung Press]
1932. 91 p. illus.
STOOKER, WILHELMINA. Friendship Center in China, a junior missionary pro-
ject, supervised by Wilhelmina Stooker, guided and recorded by Janet Hill.
New York, Missionary Education Movement of the United States and Canada
[c1924] viii, 84 p. plates.
STURTON, STEPHEN DOUGLAS, 1896-    From mission hospital to concentra-
tion camp. With a foreword by Will H. Hudspeth. London, Marshall, Morgan
and Scott [1948] 128 p. plates.
TAYLOR, JOSEPH, 1869-    West of the Yangtze gorges. Los Angeles, 1936.
[New York, 1944] 152 p.
TAYLOR, JOSEPH JUDSON, 1855-    Chinese missions, with an introduction by
Robert E. Chambers. New York, W. Neale [c1928] xiii, 15-103 p. front.
(port.).
TAYLOR, MARY GERALDINE (GUINNESS), 1862-1949. With P'u and his bri-
gands. London, China Inland Mission, 1922. xiii, 76 p. incl. front.
――――. The call of China's great north-west; or, Kansu and beyond. London,
Philadelphia, China Inland Mission [1923] viii, 215 p. front., plates, ports.,
fold. map.
THOMPSON, DOUGLAS W. Rise and build; Chinese pattern for village life. Lon-
don, Edinburgh House Press, 1949. 135 p.
THOMPSON, MAY BEL. Chinese teen-agers - and God! New York, Vantage
Press [1956] 206 p.
THOMPSON, PHYLLIS. There came a day. London, China Inland Mission, 1945.
94 p.
――――. King of the Lisu; illustrated by Carolyn Cranfield. London, China Inland
Mission, Lutterworth Press, 1956. 63 p. illus. map.
――――. Proving God: financial experiences of the China Inland Mission. London,
China Inland Mission, 1956. 143 p.
THROUGH toil and tribulation; missionary experiences in China during the war
of 1937-45 told by the missionaries. London, Carey Press [1947] 208 p.
plates, map (on lining-papers).
TINLING, CHRISTINE ISABEL, 1869-    Memories of the mission field. Foreword
by the Rev. F.B. Meyer. London, Morgan and Scott [1927] 158 p.

TOWNSEND, RALPH, 1900-   Ways that are dark; the truth about China. New York, G. P. Putnam, 1933. vii-xiv, 336 p.

TSU, YU YUE, 朱友漁, bp., 1886-   The Chinese church: partner in a world mission. New York, Friendship Press, 1944. 24 p.

TSUCHIYAMA, TETSUJI. Victory of the cross, or, an account of my trip in China. Winona Lake, Ind., Light and Life Press [1939] 39 p. front. (port.).

TVEDT, KRISTOFER N., 1884-   In captivity. Translated from Norwegian by Mrs. Mina Hellestad. Minneapolis, The Lund Press, 1937. 206 p. incl. front.

TYLER, ERNEST DELBERT. China at the crossroads; fifteenth award, essay winning first prize in competition of 1928, University of Kansas. [Lawrence, University of Kansas, 1929] [9]-44, [1] p. (Hattie Elizabeth Lewis memorial [essays in applied Christianity], XI ).

VASEL, MATHILDE. Licht im Dunkel; Gottes wunderbares Tun und Wirken in der Blindenschule der Liebenzeller Mission Changsha. Bad Liebenzell (Württ) Buchhandlung der Liebenzeller Mission [1937] 62, [1] p. illus. (incl. ports.).

WALLACE, EDWARD WILSON, 1880-1941. Christian missions in China. Shanghai. [n. p., 1929?] 24 numb. l.

WALTER, ERNST, 1886-   Chinesische Kirche im Wellenschlag der Zeit; zum hundertjährigen Jubiläum der Basler Mission im China. Basel, Basler Missionsbuchhandlung, 1946. iv, 107 p. front., plates, ports.

———. Sechzehn Monate Banditen-leben in China. Zeichnungen Fritz Krumenacher. Zürich, Schweizer. Jugendschriftenwerk, 1954. 32 p. illus.

WARD, RALPH ANSEL, 1882-   A memorandum of a few recent observations in China (from Peking). Peking, 1925. 21 p.

WARNSHUIS, ABBE LIVINGSTON, 1877-   comp. Data regarding the present legal position of American missionaries and missionary property in China. n. p., 1925. 6, [1] numb. l.

WATTS, ALICE. Silver; the story of a Chinese girl whose life has been touched and set aflame by the Spirit of God. By Miss Alice Watts and Miss Bessie B. Cordell. Chicago, National Holiness Association, Missionary Society [c1934] 24 p. illus. (ports.).

WELLER, PAUL. Aus Lenpin's Bergen; Bilder von chinesischem Leben und chinesischer Not. Mit Bildschmuck von Martha Welsch und 8 Bildtafeln. Stuttgart und Basel, Evang. Missionsverlag, 1929. 106 p. illus. plates. (Stuttgarter Missionsbücher, 16 ).

———. Chinesische Berglandsgestalten. Stuttgart und Basel, Evang. Missionsverlag, 1934. iv, 95 p. (Stuttgarter Missionsbücher, 20 ).

———. In Trübsal bewährt. Ein Frauenschicksal in China. Stuttgart und Basel, Evang. Missionsverlag, 1934. iv, 31 p. illus.

WHEELER, WILLIAM REGINALD, 1889-   Flight to Cathay; an aerial journey to Yale-in-China. With a foreword by Henry Sloane Coffin. New Haven, 1949. 81 p. fold. col. map.

WHITE, MARY CULLER, 1875-   comp. Stylus photographus; pictures of the Bible women and scholarship girls of the China mission. Nashville, Pub. House of the M. E. Church, South, 1922. 112 p. front. (port.).

WIETER, FRITZ. Das Ringen des Evangeliums um die Seele Chinas. Christus oder Konfuzius? Gütersloh, C. Bertelsmann, 1933. xi, 184 p. (Allgemeine Missions-Studien, 14 ).

WILEY, ELIZABETH ELLYSON, 1896-   Three pairs of hands. Nashville, Broadman Press [1948] 128 p. illus., ports. (Foreign mission study series).

WILLIAMS, BASCOM WINTON, 1860-   The joke of Christianizing China. New York, Peter Eckler Pub. Co., 1927. [3]-60 p. (Eckler large type series).

WILLIAMS, WALTER ROLLIN, 1909-   Ohio Friends in the land of Sinim; being a record of the missionary work in China under the direction of the Ohio yearly meeting of Friends' Church. Mt. Gilead, O. [1925] 229 p. illus. ports.

———. These fifty years with Ohio Friends in China; an intimate story of mis-

sionary work in China, under the direction of Ohio yearly meeting of the
Friends Church, 1890-1940. Damascus, O., Friends Foreign Missionary
Society of Ohio Yearly meeting [c1940] 315 p. illus. (incl. ports., maps).

WILSON, SADIE MAI. Chinese gateways; a course for juniors based on the
source book of materials, "What do you know about China?" Nashville,
Cokesbury Press, 1929. 64 p.

———. What do you know about China? A source book of materials. Nashville,
Cokesbury Press, 1929. 266 p. illus. (incl. music) plates, diagr.

WINSLOW, CAROLYN V. Tomorrow. Winona Lake, Ind., Young People's Missionary Society, 1945. 123 p. illus. (incl. map) ports.

WORKMAN, GEORGE BELL. The development of the motive of Protestant missions to China, 1807-1928. [New Haven] 1928. 3, 215 p. incl. charts.

WORLEY, HARRY WESCOTT. The central conference of the Methodist Episcopal Church; a study in ecclesiastical adaptation, or a contribution of the mission field to the development of church organization. Foochow, Printed by
the Christian Herald Mission Press, 1940. 397 p. [English publications of
the Nanking theological seminary, 4]. Thesis-Yale University.

WU, CHAO-KWANG, 伍朝光, 1904-    The international aspect of the missionary movement in China. Baltimore, Johns Hopkins Press; London, H. Milford, Oxford University Press, 1930. ix, 285 p. (Johns Hopkins University
studies in history and political science. Extra volumes. new ser., 11 ).

WU, YI-FANG, 吴贻芳, 1893-    ed. China rediscovers her West; a symposium
edited by Yi-fang Wu and Frank W. Price. London, G. Allen and Unwin [1942]
xiii, [1], 210 p. illus.

WUNDERLI, MARIE. Er kann trösten. Zwei Geschichten aus China. Stuttgart
und Basel, Evang. Missionverlag, 1931. iv, 30 p. illus.

YALE-IN-CHINA ASSOCIATION, INC., New Haven. The story of Yale in China.
New Haven, 1945. 11 p. illus. maps.

YANG, CHANG-TUNG, 楊昌棟. A program for the church of Ping-tan hsien,
Fukien, based on a study of twenty-seven successful rural churches and other
rural service organizations in the United States of America. Shanghai, Pub.
for the author by Kwang Hsueh Pub. House, 1935. v, 125 p. Thesis-Drew
University.

YOUNG, FLORENCE S. H. Pearls from the Pacific. London, Marshall Bros.
[1925] 256 p. front. (port.) map, plates.

ZIMMERMANN, KURT. ed. Fünfzig Jahre Allianz-China-mission. Grundsätz-
liches über Wesen und Arbeitsweise einer Allianz-mission in Mittel-China.
Wuppertal-Barmen, 1939. 96 p. illus.

## Medical Missions

ABBAS, KHWAJA AHMAD. And one did not come back! The story of the Congress medical mission to China; with a foreword by Lin Yutang. Bombay,
Sound Magazine (Publication dept.) [1944] 129 p.

ADOLPH, PAUL ERNEST, 1901-    Surgery speaks to China; the experiences of
a medical missionary to China in peace and war. Philadelphia, Toronto, China Inland Mission [1945] 195, [1] p. front. (port.) illus. (map) plates.

ALLAN, TED. The scalpel, the sword; the story of Dr. Norman Bethune, by
Sydney Gordon and Ted Allan. London, Hale [1954] 271 p. illus.

AYERS, THOMAS W. Healing and missions. Richmond, Va., Educational department, Foreign Mission Board, 1930. 123 p. front., plates, ports.

FEARN, ANNE (WALTER) 1867-    My days of strength; an American woman
doctor's forty years in China. 3rd ed. New York and London, Harper [c1939]
xiii, [1], 297 p. front., plates, ports.

HOLMAN, NELLIE (PEDERSON). My most unforgettable patients. New York,
Pageant Press [1953] 119 p.

HOUGHTON, FRANK, 1894-    George King, medical evangelist. London, China

Inland Mission, 1930. vii, 97 p. front. (port.) plates.

KEYTE, JOHN CHARLES, 1875-    Andrew Young of Shensi; adventure in medical missions. London, Carey Press [1924] 313, [1] p. front.

LEAVELL, GEORGE W. Some fruits of the Gospel; experiences of a medical missionary. Nashville, Tenn. Sunday School Board, Southern Baptist Convention [1928] 9-120 p. illus., port.

LIPPA, ERNEST M. Captive surgeon; adventures and misadventures of a doctor in Red China. New York, Morrow, 1953. 280 p.

——. I was a surgeon for the Chinese Reds. London, Harrap [1953] 240 p. illus.

——. J'étais médicin en Chine rouge. Traduit par René Jouan. Paris, Éditions France-Empire, 1955. 318 p. plates.

——. Chirurg hinter dem Bambusvorhang. Ins deutsche Übertr. von Helga Treichl. Wien, Ullstein, 1955. 300 p. map.

MORSE, WILLIAM REGINALD, 1874-    The three crosses in the purple mists, an adventure in medical education under the eaves of the roof of the world. Shanghai, Mission Book Co., 1928. ix, 306 p. plates (part col.) fold. plan.

OSGOOD, ELLIOTT IRVING, 1871-1940. China's crossroads. Cincinnati, O., Powell and White [1922] 229 p. front., plates, port.

PALMBORG, ROSS W. China letters, Seventh Day baptist medical missionary to China 1894-1940. Plainfield, N.J., The Recorder Press, 1942. 278 p. front.

POTEAT, GORDON. A Greatheart of the South, John T. Anderson, medical missionary. New York, George H. Doran [c1921] ix, 11-123 p. front., plates, ports.

"ROBIN, DOCTOR," pseud. What it feels like; letters from a doctor out East to a colleague at home. London, Student Christian Movement, 1926. 78 p.

SELMON, BERTHA EUGENIA (LOVELAND) 1877-    They do meet; cross-trails of American physicians and Chinese people. New York, Froben Press, 1942. xvii, 254 p. col. front., plates, ports., facsims.

SMITH, WILLIAM EDWARD. A Canadian doctor in West China; forty years under three flags. Toronto, Ryerson Press, 1939. xvi, 278 p. illus., front.

SPEER, ROBERT ELLIOTT, 1867-1947. "Lu Taifu," Charles Lewis, M.D., a pioneer surgeon in China. New York, Board of Foreign Missions, Presbyterian Church in the U.S.A., 193? 216 p. illus. ports.

## Lives of Protestant Missionaries

ADAMS, ARCHIBALD GUINNESS. Joseph Samuel Adams of China, an original contribution to the history of Protestant world missions in the form of a biographical record of the missionary career of his father. [New York, 1939] 2 v. Thesis-Union Theological Seminary.

ALBUS, HARRY JAMES, 1920-    Twentieth-century Onesiphorus, the story of Leslit M. Anglin and the Home of Onesiphorus. Grand Rapids, Eerdmans, 1951. 160 p. illus., ports.

ALEXANDER, MARY CHARLOTTE, 1874-    Charles Arthur Hayes of China: as Jesus served. Nashville, Broadman Press [1954] 24 p. illus. (More than conquerors, intermediate, 5).

ALLEN, YOUNG JOHN, 1836-1907. The diary of a voyage to China, 1859-60, edited by Arva Colbert Floyd. Atlanta, Ga., The Library, Emory University, 1943. 39 p. (Half-title: Emory University publications. Sources and reprints, ser.I).

AYLWARD, GLADYS. Gladys Aylward, one of the undefeated; the story of Gladys Aylward as told by her to R.O. Latham. London, Edinburgh House Press [1950] 48 p.

BARTHOLOMEW, ALLEN R. The martyr of Huping: the life story of William Anson Reimert, missionary in China. Philadelphia, Board of Foreign Missions,

Reformed Church in the United States, 1925. 157 p. illus., ports.

BEATON, KENNETH J. Serving with the sons of Shuh. Fifty fateful years in West China, 1891-1941. Toronto, United Church of Canada [1941] x, 238 p.

BOTHAM, OLIVE (TRENCH). Two pioneers; life sketches of Thomas and Mark Botham by Mrs. Mark Botham. London, China Inland Mission, 1924. viii, 9-140 p. incl. plan, front. ports.

BRODBECK, EMMA, 1892- Chicago missionary on the Burma road; letters of Emma Brodbeck, Ipin, Szechuan, West China, edited and published by Louise Hayes. [Chicago, c1941] cover-title, 3-35 p. illus. (incl. ports., maps).

BROOMHALL, MARSHALL, 1866-1937. F. W. Baller, a master of the pencil. London, China Inland Mission, 1923. iv, [56] p.

——. W.W. Cassels, first bishop in Western China. London, Philadelphia, China Inland Mission, 1926. xxiii, 378 p. front., illus.(plan, facsim.) plates, ports., fold. map.

BROWN, FRANK AUGUSTUS, 1876- Charlotte Brown, a mother in China; the story of the work of Charlotte Thompson Brown in China from 1909-49. [Carville? La., 1953] 100 p. illus.

BRYAN, FERREBEE CATHARINE, 1886- His golden cycle; the life story of Robert Thomas Bryan, by his daughter, F. Catharine Bryan. Richmond, Va., Rice Press, 1938. xvii, 297, [1] p. front., plates, ports., facsims.

——. At the gates; life story of Mathew Tyson and Eliza Moring Yates of China. Nashville, Broadman Press [1949] xxii, 374 p. illus. ports., facsims.

BUCK, PEARL (SYDENSTRICKER) 1892- The exile. New York, Reynal and Hitchcock [c1936] London, Methuen, 1936. [9]-315 p.

——. L'exilée. Traduit par Germaine Delamain. Paris, Stock, 1937. 251 p.

——. Die Frau des Missionars; roman. Deutsch von Richard Hoffmann. Berlin [etc.] P. Zsolnay, 1936. 326, [1] p.

——. Fighting angel; portrait of a soul. New York, Reynal and Hitchcock [c1936] London, Methuen, 1937. [9]-302 p.

——. The spirit and the flesh. New York, John Day [1944] 378 p.

BURGESS, ANDREW SEVERANCE, 1897- Lan Ta-tê, Landahl of China; illustrations by Ed. Sovik, jr. Minneapolis, Augsburg Pub. House [c1941] vii, [3], 116 p. incl. front., illus.(incl. map).

BURKE, JAMES COBB, 1915- My father in China, [William B. Burke] New York, Toronto, Farrar and Rinehart [1942] xiv, 431 p.

——. The same. London, M. Joseph [1945] 288 p.

BUSSEMER, KONRAD. Karl Engler: Lehrer und Missions-Inspektor, 1874-1923, zur Erinnerung an einen Begnadigten. Barmen, Allianz-China-Mission, 1925. 111 p. plates.

CANDLER, WARREN AKIN, bp., 1857- Young J. Allen, ''the man who seeded China." Nashville, Cokesbury Press, 1931. 245 p. front., ports.

CHAMBERS, CHRISTINE (COFFEE) 1885- Builder of dreams; the life of Robert Edward Chambers, by Ruth Carver Gardner and Christine Coffee Chambers. Nashville, Broadman Press [c1939] 200 p. plates, ports.

CHAPLIN, MAXWELL, 1890-1926. The letters of Maxwell Chaplin, edited by George Stewart, with a foreword by Robert E. Speer. New York, Association Press, 1928. ix, 3-239 p. front., plates, ports.

CRAIGHEAD, JAMES R.E. Hunter Corbett, fifty-six years a missionary in China. New York, Revell, c1921. 224 p. front., port.

CULLEN, ANDREW PATRICK. Lavington Hart of Tientsin. London, Livingstone Press [1947] 48 p. plates, port. (The Man and the work).

DE GRUCHÉ, KINGSTON. Dr. D. Duncan Main of Hangchow, who is known in China as Dr. Apricot of heaven below. London and Edinburgh, Marshall, Morgan and Scott [1930] 9-243 p. front., plates, ports.

DE MONTMORENCY, JAMES EDWARD GEOFFREY, 1866- Francis William Fox; a biography, with a prefatory note by G. P. Gooch. London, H. Milford, 1923. 141 p. front.(port.).

DUNAWAY, THOMAS SANFORD, 1872-1932. Pioneering for Jesus; the story of
Henrietta Hall Shuck. Nashville, Sunday School Board of the Southern Baptist
Convention [1930] 160 p. incl. front., illus.(incl. ports.).

DYSON, VERNE, 1879-    A Hong Kong governor [Sir John Bowring] and his famous hymns (and other essays). Macao, The Macao Review [1930] 20 p.
front.(port.).

EBERLE, EDITH. Macklin of Nanking; sketches by Rose Wright. St. Louis, Mo.,
Bethany Press [c1936] 173 p. illus.

ENGLISH, EUGENE SCHUYLER, 1899-    By life and by death; excerpts and lessons from the diary of John C. Stam. Grand Rapids, Mich., Zondervan Pub.
House [c1938] v-xii, [13]-62 p. illus.(facsim.) ports.

FOSTER, ARNOLD, 1846-1919. Arnold Foster. Memoir, selected writings, etc.
by various authors. London, London Missionary Society, 1921. 188 p. front.
(port.).

GAMMIE, ALEXANDER. Duncan Main of Hangchow. London, Pickering and Inglis [1935] 159 p. front., plates, ports.

GARSIDE, BETTIS ALSTON, 1894-    One increasing purpose; the life of Henry
Winters Luce. With an introd. by Henry P. Van Dusen. New York, F. H. Revell [1948] 271 p. illus., ports., map (on lining-papers).

GODDARD, FRANCIS WAYLAND, 1877-    Called to Cathay. New York, Distributed by the Baptist Literature Bureau [1948] 159 p. illus., ports., map,
geneal. table.

GOFORTH, ROSALIND (BELLSMITH) 1864-    Miracle lives of China, by Rosalind and Jonathan Goforth. New York and London, Harper, 1931. x, 157 p.

———. Goforth of China, [Jonathan Goforth] Grand Rapids, Mich., Zondervan
Pub. House [c1937]; London, Marshall, Morgan and Scott, Toronto, McClelland and Stewart, 1938. 364 p. front., plates (incl. music) ports.

———. Climbing; memories of a missionary's wife. Grand Rapids, Mich., Zondervan Pub. House [c1940] 216 p. front., ports.

GRAVES, FREDERICK R. Recollections, 1881-93. [Shanghai, 1928] 50 p.

GROSE, GEORGE RICHMOND, bp., 1869-    James W. Bashford, pastor, edu-
cator, bishop. New York, Cincinnati, Methodist Book Concern [c1922] 252 p.
front., plates, ports.

GUINNESS, JOY. Mrs. Howard Taylor, her web of time. Foreword by Amy Car-
michael. 2nd ed. London, China Inland Mission, 1950. vii, 369 p. plates,
ports.

HAMILTON, HORACE ERNST. China two generations ago; a family sketch of
Guy and Pauline Ernst Hamilton, Presbyterian medical missionaries in the
interior of North China. Denver, Big Mountain Press [1957] 102 p. illus.

HOLLOWAY, SADIE (LAWTON). Ida Deaver Lawton of China: happily ever after.
Nashville, Broadman Press [1954] 23 p. illus. (More than conquerors, intermediate no. 6 ).

HOUGHTON, FRANK, 1894-    Mason of Kwangchow. London, China Inland Mission, 1929. vii, 52 p.

HUIZENGA, LEE SJOERDS, 1881-1945. John and Betty Stam, martyrs. A short
story of the life and death of Mr. and Mrs. John C. Stam. Grand Rapids,
Mich., Zondervan Pub. House, c1935. 11-64 p. front., illus.(incl.ports.,
map).

———. The same. 2nd ed. Grand Rapids, Mich., Zondervan Pub. House,1935.
101 p. incl. front. illus.

———. Pressing on; an autobiographical sketch. Grand Rapids, Mich., Wm. B.
Eerdmans Pub. Co., 1946. 83 p. front.(port.) (Home devotional library).

HUPPENBAUER, HANS. Ein Wegbereiter Gottes in China, das Leben von Ernst
Ruff (1877-1944). Basel, Basler Missionsbuchhandlung [c1946] 64 p. port.

KAMIIZUMI, HIDENOBU. A Japanese pastor in Peking; a story of the Reverend
Yasuzo Shimidzu and his mission school for Chinese girls; translated from
Ai-no-kensetsusha (One who builds with love) by Hidenobu Kamiizumi. Tokyo,

Hokuseido Press, 1940. xii, 223 p. front., plates, ports.

KENDALL, R. ELLIOTT. Beyond the clouds. The story of Samuel Pollard of South-west China. London, Cargate Press, 1948. ix, 150 p. plates, map.

KERNAHAN, COULSON, 1858-  Cornaby of Hanyang, a great-souled missionary; an appreciation, with biographical chapters by Mrs. W.A. Cornaby, B.A. Introduction by the Rev. W.T.A. Barber and personal tributes by the Rev. Marshall Hartley and others. London, Epworth Press [1923] 156 p. front.(port.).

LAMBERTS, LAMBERTUS J. The life story of Dr. Lee S. Huizenga; an adventure in faith. Grand Rapids, Eerdmans, 1950. 194 p. ports.

LAWRENCE, UNA (ROBERTS) 1893-  Lottie Moon. Nashville, Sunday School Board of the Southern Baptist Convention [c1927] 317 p. illus.(incl. ports., map).

LYON, DAVID NELSON, 1842-1927. Youth and the China journey in 1869. [Pebble Beach, Calif., c1937] 31, [1] p. [White cloud papers. 1].

MacBEATH, ANDREW. W[illiam] H[enry] Aldis. Foreword by Frank Houghton. London, Marshall, Morgan and Scott [1949] 100 p. ports.

McCARTEE, DIVIE BETHUNE, 1820-1900. A missionary pioneer in the Far East; a memorial of Divie Bethune McCartee, ed. by Robert E. Speer. New York, Chicago, Fleming H. Revell [c1922] 224 p. front.

McINTYRE, EMMA H., 1879-  High privilege. Brisbane, W.R. Smith and Paterson, 1954. 97 p. illus.

MELROSE, PAUL C. On being a missionary. New York, Pageant Press [1957] 73 p.

MONTGOMERY, HENRY HUTCHINSON, 1847-  Charles Percy Scott, first bishop in North China, for fifty-three years a missionary in China. London, Society for the Propagation of the Gospel in Foreign Parts, 1928. x, 144 p. front. (port.), plates.

MOULE, ARTHUR EVANS, 1836-1918. Arthur Evans Moule, missionary to the Chinese; a memoir, by his six sons. London, The Religious Tract Society, 1921. 112 p. plates, ports.

MUELLER, JOHN THEODORE, 1885-  Great missionaries to China. Grand Rapids, Zondervan Pub. House [1947] 9-135 p.

MULLER, JAMES ARTHUR, 1884-  Apostle of China, Samuel Isaac Joseph Schereschewsky, 1831-1906. New York, Milwaukee, Morehouse Pub. Co., 1937. 279 p. front., plates, ports.

NICHOLS, BUFORD L. It happened in China; random glimpses of life in China as seen through the eyes of Buford L. Nichols. Nashville, Broadman Press [1948] 100 p. illus., ports.

PAKENHAM-WALSH, WILLIAM SANDFORD. Twenty years in China. Cambridge [Eng.] W. Heffer, 1935. x, 127 p. front. plates, ports.

PATTERSON, L.D. If two agree. Nashville, Publishing House of the M.E. Church, South, 1921. 102 p.

PAYNE, ERNEST ALEXANDER, 1902-  Harry Wyatt of Shanghai, 1895-1938. London, Carey Press, 1946. 83 p. front., plates, ports., map.

POLLARD, SAMUEL, 1864-1915. Eyes of the earth; the diary of Samuel Pollard, edited by R. Elliott Kendall. London, Cargate Press, 1954. 180 p. illus.

POLLARD, WALTER. The life of Sam Pollard of China; an account of the intrepid life of adventure, danger, toil and travel of a missionary in the far and little known interior of the vast Chinese empire, by his son, Walter Pollard. London, Seeley, Service, 1928. 13-188 p. incl. plates. front.(ports.)plates.

RATTENBURY, HAROLD BURGOYNE. David Hill, friend of China; a modern portrait. London, Epworth Press [1949] 214 p. port.

───. Greatheart; the tale of a country missionary, [Joseph Kimber Hill] London, Cargate Press [1953] 111 p.

REASON, JOYCE, 1894-  The witch of Ningpo. London, Edinburgh House Press, 1940. 31 p. (Eagle Books, 30).

SALLEE, ANNIE (JENKINS). W. Eugene Sallee, Christ's ambassador. Nashville,

Sunday School Board, Southern Baptist Convention [c1933] viii, 256 p. front., plates, ports., facsim.

———. Torchbearers in Honan. Nashville, Broadman Press [1948] 192 p. ports.

SCHLYTER, HERMAN. Karl Gützlaff, als missionar in China, with a summary in English. Lund, C. W. K. Gleerup; Copenhagen, E. Munksgaard, 1946. viii, 318 p. Diss.-Univ. Lund.

SMITH, JAMES FRAZER, 1858-   Life's waking part, being the autobiography of Reverend James Frazer Smith, pioneer medical missionary to Honan and missionary to Central India. Toronto, T. Nelson [c1937] 11, [1], 345 p. front.(port.).

SNOWDEN, RITA FRANCES. Never a dull moment; life and letters of Annie James. Christchurch [N. Z.] Presbyterian Bookroom [1948] 204 p. ports., map.

TAYLOR, FREDERICK HOWARD, 1862-1946. "By faith"; Henry W. Frost and the China Inland Mission, by Dr. and Mrs. Howard Taylor. Philadelphia, London, China Inland Mission, 1938. vii-xvii, 364 p. front., plates, ports., diagr.

TAYLOR, MARY GERALDINE (GUINNESS), 1862-1949. Guinness of Honan, by his sister Mrs. Howard Taylor. London, China Inland Mission, 1930. xi, 322 p. front., plates, ports.

———. Borden of Yale '09; "the life that counts," by Mrs. Howard Taylor. Philadelphia, China Inland Mission, 1930. rev. ed. 1952. xv, 285 p. plates, ports., map.

———. Margaret King's vision, by Mrs. Howard Taylor. Philadelphia, London [etc.] China Inland Mission, 1934. xiii, [1], 165 p. front., plates, ports.

———. Behind the ranges; Fraser of Lisuland, S. W. China, by Mrs. Howard Taylor. London and Redhill, Lutterworth Press and the China Inland Mission [1944] 255, [1] p. front., plates, ports.

———. The triumph of John and Betty Stam. Philadelphia, China Inland Mission, 1949. 129 p. ports. 1st ed. 1935.

THOMPSON, PHYLLIS. D. E. Hoste: "a prince with God," Hudson Taylor's successor as general director of the China Inland Mission, 1900-35. London, China Inland Mission, 1950. 222 p. illus. ports.

TOZER, AIDEN WILSON, 1897-   Let my people go! The life of Robert A. Jaffray. Harrisburg, Pa., Christian Publications [c1947] 127 p. port.

TROXEL, ELLEN (ARMOUR) 1875-   Cecil Troxel, the man and the work, by Mrs. Cecil Troxel and Mrs. John J. Trachsel. Chicago, National Holiness Missionary Society, 1948. 261 p. illus., ports., map (on lining-paper).

TURNER, WILLIAM H. Pioneering in China; introduction by Rev. J.H. King. Franklin Springs, Ga., Printed by the Publishing House of the P. H. Church [c1928] 17-312 p. front. (2 port.) illus., plates.

WALTER, ERNST, 1886-   Mein Leben und Die Mission. Stuttgart und Basel, Evang. Missionsverlag, 1932. iv, 48 p. incl. front. (port.), illus.

WALTERS, THOMAS B. Charles T. Studd, cricketer and missionary. London, Epworth Press, 1930. 126 p. front.(port.).

WHEELER, WILLIAM REGINALD, 1889-   John E. Williams of Nanking. New York, Fleming H. Revell [c1937] 222 p. front., plates, ports.

WHITE, MARY CULLER, 1875-   The days of June; the life story of June Nicholson. Kingstree, S.C., Kingstree Lithographic Co. [1952] 128 p.

———. Just Jennie; the life story of Virginia M. Atkinson. Atlanta, Tupper and Love [1955] 103 p. illus.

WILLIAMS, WALTER ROLLIN. Me and my house, by Walter R. and Myrtle M. Williams. Grand Rapids, Eerdmans [1957] 187 p. illus.

WOOD, H. G. Henry T. Hodgkin; a memoir. London, Student Christian Movement Press [1937] 281 p. front. plates.

Robert Morrison

BLOCHER, JACQUES A. Robert Morrison, l'apôtre de la Chine (1782-1834).Il-
lustrations de l'auteur. Paris, Les Bons semeurs, 1938. 86 p. incl. port.,
illus. map.
BROOMHALL, MARSHALL, 1866-1937. Robert Morrison, a master-builder.
London, Student Christian Movement, 1924. xvi, 238 p. front.(port.) 1 illus.
(plan) [The modern series of missionary biographies].
HAYES, ERNEST HENRY. Robert Morrison: China's pioneer. London, Living-
stone Press [1925] 128 p. front.(port.) illus. (map) (The Pioneer series, 4 ).
MEARS, JOHN. The King's men in China: Robert Morrison, Griffith John, Chiang
Kai-shek. Wellington, A.H. and A.W. Reed [1948] 109 p. illus. (His The
King's men series).
MORRISON, ROBERT,1782-1834. Robert Morrison: a souvenir of the centenary
celebrations. Hong Kong, Morrison Centenary Celebrations Committee,1934.
[4], 16 p. plates.
RIDE, LINDSAY. Robert Morrison, the scholar and the man, an illustrated cata-
logue of the exhibition held at the University of Hong Kong, September 4 to 18,
1957 to commemorate the 150th anniversary of Robert Morrison's arrival in
China. 54 p. illus.


## Hudson Taylor


BENOIT, JEAN PAUL. Puissance du Seigneur; vie d'Hudson Taylor. Strasbourg,
Éditions Oberlin, 1952 [c1946] 205 p. plates, ports., maps.
――――. Wind aus der Feuerwolke. Das Leben Hudson Taylors, übers. aus dem
Französischen. Konstanz, Christl.-Verlag, 195? 295 p.
BROOMHALL, MARSHALL, 1866-1937. Hudson Taylor, the man who believed
God. London, Philadelphia, China Inland Mission, 1929. xii, 244 p. front.
(port.) illus. (facsim.).
――――. Ein Mann der es mit Gott wagte. Aus dem Leben des grossen China-Mis-
sionars Hudson Taylor. 4. Aufl. Basel, Brunnen-Verlag, 1948. 62 p. illus.
(Brunnen-Bücherei, 7 ).
ELLIS, JAMES JOSEPH, 1853- J. Hudson Taylor, founder of China Inland Mis-
sion. London, Pickering and Inglis, 1929. 64 p. (Memoirs of Mighty Men).
――――. James Hudson Taylor; a little man who did great things for God. London,
Pickering and Inglis [1937] [9]-96 p. front.(port.), plates.
HELLER, MATHILDE. Die Geschichte einer Jugend, Hudson Taylor. Erzählt
von Mathilde Heller. Mit einer Einführung von Elisabeth Brnadt. Bad Salzu-
flen, MBK-Verlag [1938] 79 p. 2 port.
HUNNEX, MRS. GLORIA G. James Hudson Taylor, pioneer missionary of in-
land China. Anderson, Ind., Gospel Trumpet Co. [c1925] 154 p. front.(port.)
illus.
MILLER, BASIL WILLIAM, 1897- J.Hudson Taylor, for God and China. Grand
Rapids, Zondervan Pub. House [1948] 136 p.
OEHLER, ANNA. Das Wagnis des Glaubens; Leben und Werk Hudson Taylors.
Basel, Basler Missionsbuchhandlung [1948] 430 p. port. map.
RUDERSDORF, FRIEDHELM. Hudson Taylor, sein Werk und seine Missions-
methoden. Basel, Brunnen-Verlag [1942] 80 p. front.(port.) [Menschen, die
den ruf vernommen, 13.].
SCHULTZE, OTTO. James Hudson Taylor. Ein Glaubensheld im Dienste der
Evangelisation Chinas. 2.Aufl. Stuttgart, Evang. Missionsverlag; Basel,
Basler Missionsbuchhandlung, 1924. 236 p. plates, ports. map, tables.
1.Aufl. 1906.
TAYLOR, [FREDERICK] HOWARD, 1862-1946. Hudson Taylor. Foundateur de
la Mission dans l'intérieur de la Chine, 1832-1905, par le docteur et Madame
Howard Taylor: v. 1. adapté de l'anglais et abrégé par Jean Rouffiac. v. 2-3.
Traduit et adapté de l'anglais par MM Eugène Barnaud et Jean Barnaud.
Lausanne, Librairie des Semailles, 1922-23. 3 v. port. map.

------. Hudson Taylor in early years; the growth of a soul, by Dr. and Mrs. Howard Taylor, with introduction by Mr. D.E. Hoste. 6th impression. London, Philadelphia, China Inland Mission [1923] xxi, 511 p. front.,illus.(plan) plates, ports., fold. map. 1st ed. 1911.

------. Hudson Taylor's spiritual secret, by Dr. and Mrs. Howard Taylor. London, Philadelphia, China Inland Mission, 1932. 178 p. front.(port.).

------. Hudson Taylor and the China Inland Mission. The growth of a work of God, by Mr. and Mrs. Howard Taylor. London, China Inland Mission, 1934. xi, [1], 640 p. front. ports., fold. map. 1st ed., 1918.

------. J. Hudson Taylor: ein Lebensbild, von Howard Taylor und Geraldine Taylor. Neue Aufl. Merligen und Thoune, China Inland Mission, 1948-49. 2 v. illus. plates.

TAYLOR, JAMES HUDSON, 1832-1905. A retrospect. [17th ed.] London, China Inland Mission; agents: Lutterworth Press [1951] 126 p. illus.

THOMPSON, PHYLLIS. God's venturer, Hudson Taylor. London and Philadelphia, China Inland Mission, 1954. 110 p. port.

WÜRZ, FRIEDRICH. Hudson Taylor. Ein Missionsleben. Stuttgart und Basel, Evang. Missionverlag, 1929. 1v, 32 p. ports.

## Timothy Richard

EVANS, EDWARD WILLIAM PRICE. Timothy Richard [1945-1919], a narrative of Christian enterprise and statesmanship in China. London, Carey Press [1945] 160 p. front., plates, port.

GARNIER, ALBERT J. A maker of modern China, [Timothy Richard]. London, Carey Press [1945] 120 p. plates, 2 port. (incl.front.) facsim.

The MAN who could not be denied, [Timothy Richard]. [London, Carey Press, 1945] cover-title, 16 p.

SOOTHILL, WILLIAM EDWARD, 1861-1935. Timothy Richard of China, seer, statesman, missionary and the most disinterested adviser the Chinese ever had, with a foreword by Sir John N. Jordan, bart. London, Seeley, Service, 1924. 17-330 p. front., plates, ports.

WARR, WINIFRED. Far into China; the story of Timothy Richard, pioneer. London, Carey Press [1945] 32 p. plates.

## Lives of Chinese Protestants

BROOMHALL, MARSHALL, 1866-1937. In quest of God; the life story of pastors Chang and Ch'ü, Buddhist priest and Chinese scholar. London, Philadelphia, China Inland Mission [1921] xiii, 190 p. front., plates, ports., map, plan.

------. Marshall Feng, 'a good soldier of Christ Jesus.' Foreword by Major-General Sir George K. Scott Moncrieff. 5th ed. London, Philadelphia, China Inland Mission, 1924. x, 85 p. front.(port.group) plates.

------. General Feng, ein guter Streiter Jesu Christi. Berechtige deutsche Übersetzung nach dem 3. Auflage der 1924 englischer Original. Liebenzell, Buchhandlung der Liebenzeller Mission, 1924. iv, 97 p.

BROWN, MARGARET H. Mrs. Wang's diary, illustrated by Chang Hui-yuen. Shanghai, Christian Literature Society, 1936. ix, 161 p. illus.

BURGESS, ANDREW SEVERANCE, 1897-   Peng Fu, 彭福; a biography. Minneapolis, Augsburg Pub. House [c1939] 128 p. incl. plates, ports., map, facsim.

CAMPBELL-BROWN, C. Bruder Mao; ein chinesischer Strassenprediger. Zürich, Kanaresische Mission, 1926. 115 p.

CARTWRIGHT, FRANK THOMAS, 1884-   Life has no ceiling; a romance of changing China. New and rev. ed. New York, Friendship Press [1947] viii, 164 p. "Stories of James Cheng and Dorothy Lee, who were known in their earlier years not as James and Dorothy, but as Joo-mook and Daw-say."

CH'ENG, MARCUS, 鄭仲桂, 1884-    Marshal Feng - the man and his work. Shanghai, Kelly and Walsh [1926] 107 p. front., plates, ports.

————. After forty years, autobiography. London and Melbourne, China Inland Mission, 1948. 18 p. port.

CHIU, Y. T., 趙恩賜, [Chao Ên-tz'ŭ] 1890-    Meditations of a Christian Chinese. New York, Pageant Press [1956] 101 p.

CHURCH, M. M. tr. The seeker. The autobiography of a Chinese Christian. London, Church of England Zenana Missionary Society, 1931. 47 p.

EINE Chinesenfrau erzählt aus ihrem Leben. Übers. von Käthe Huber. Basel, Basler Missionsbuchhandlung, 1947. 32 p.

FORSYTHE, IRENE. Cheng's mother; decorated by Jim Lee. New York, Friendship Press [1948] 80 p. illus.

GIH, ANDREW, 計志文. Twice born - and then? The life story and message of Andrew Gih, autobiography, edited by J. Edwin Orr. London, Marshall, Morgan and Scott [1937] vii, 11-128 p.

HOLKEBOER, TENA. God's bridge; or, The story of Jin-gi. Grand Rapids, Mich., Wm. B. Eerdmans Pub. Co., 1944. 87 p. incl. front., illus., port.

HUNTER, EDWARD. The story of Mary Liu [ 劉永英]. London, Hodder and Stoughton, 1956; New York, Farrar, Straus and Cudahy, 1956. 248 p.

JÊN, CH'ÊNG-YÜAN, 任樫蓮. A tamarisk garden blessed with rain; or, The autobiography of Pastor Ren, translated and edited by Herbert Hudson Taylor and Marshall Broomhall. London, Philadelphia, China Inland Mission, 1930. xvii, 228 p. front. (port.) facsim.

LIU, LING-PI, 劉令璧. Chinaman's chance; the story of Harry Liu of the Pocket Testament League, by Harry Liu and Ellen Drummond. Chicago, Moody Press [1956] 143 p. illus.

McNEUR, GEORGE HUNTER. China's first preacher, Liang A-fa, 梁阿發, 1789-1855. Shanghai, Kwang Hsueh Pub. House, Oxford University Press, China agency [1934?] 123, [4] p. plates, ports, ports., map, facsim.

MAIR, ALEXANDER. Pastor Hsieh, a wayfarer for Christ. London, China Inland Mission, 1933. 24 p.

MOYER, ELGIN SYLVESTER, 1890-    Moy Gwong of South China; the story of Moy Gwong Han, 梅光顯, who burned out for the Lord. Elgin, Ill., Brethren Pub. House [1951] 77 p. illus., ports.

OSGOOD, ELLIOTT IRVING, 1871-1940. Shi, the story-teller; the life and work of Shi Kweipiao, Chinese story-teller and pastor. Cincinnati, O., Powell and White [1926] 228 p. front., plates, ports.

[SING, SAMUEL]. Captured by pirates: the adventure of a Chinese doctor [Samuel Sing] London, Church Missionary Society, 1930. 15 p.

TAYLOR, MARY GERALDINE (GUINNESS), 1862-1949. Pastor Hsi, 席勝魔, Confucian scholar and Christian. 20th ed. London, China Inland Mission, 1949. xvi, 293 p. maps. 1st ed. 1900.

TSAI, CHRISTIANA, 蔡蘇娟. Queen of the dark chamber; the story of Christiana Tsai as told to Ellen L. Drummond. Drawings by Ellen L. Drummond. Chicago, Moody Press [1953] 160 p. illus.

WELLER, PAUL. Ein chinesischer Volksmissionar Pan Nyen Sam. Stuttgart und Basel, Evang. Missionsverlag, 1929. iv, 27 p. illus.

WHITE, MARY CULLER, 1875-    Meet Mrs. Yu. [The true story of an outstanding Chinese Christian] New York, Abingdon-Cokesbury Press [1948] 212 p.

WOO, ESTHER, 伍蘇畫. Paradise in war, translated by Eleanor J. Woo. New York, Island Press Cooperative [1947] viii, 117 p. front., plates, ports. -

YÜ, DORA. God's dealings with Dora Yü, a Chinese messenger of the Cross. London, Morgan and Scott, 1927. 71 p.


Protestantism under Communism


ANDERSON, PALMER I., 1892-    Young China in the valley of decision. Minneapolis, Augsburg Pub. House [1953] 123 p.

BARNABAS, pseud. Christian witness in communist China. New York, More-
house-Gorham [1951]; London, S.C.M. Press, 1951; 2nd ed. 1952. 79 p.

———. Christliche Verkündigung im kommunistischen China, übers. und bearb.
Ökumenische Centrale in Frankfurt/M. München, Kaiser, 1951. 91 p. map.

BOYLE, SAMUEL E. The church in red China "Leans to one side." A documen-
ted study of the influence of communism on the Protestant churches in China.
Hong Kong, [The author] 1950. vi, 152 p.

BROWN, HOMER G. New China as we saw it, by Homer G. Brown and Muriel J.
Brown. St. Marys, Ontario, the author, 1956. 27 p.

BURGESS, ALEXANDER. Passport from China; tells the story of an empty Scottish pew. Glasgow, Maclellan, 1956. 307 p.

CHAU, PIK-KUM, 周伯琴, [Chou, Po-chin] 1891-    Commonism, a plan for im-
plementing the Christian answer to communism. With forewords by Hollington
K. Tong and John W. Bailey, and a biographical sketch of the author by
Charles R. Shepherd. New York, Exposition Press [1957] 256 p. illus.

CHILDE, DONALD B. China now; an account of the church in China today. London, Cargate Press [1955] 34 p.

CHINA: an object lesson, by an observer. London, Edinburgh House Press, 1951.
23 p.

CHINESE communists and mission properties; Preface by A.G.M. [n.p.,1926]
60 p.

FERRIS, HELEN. The Christian church in Communist China, by Helen Ferris
under the direction of Theodore H.E. Chen. Advance ed. [n.p.] 1952. 144 l.
(Studies in Chinese communism, ser. 2, 5).

———. The Christian church in Communist China, to 1952. Produced under Contract no. AF 33(038)-25075. Research accomplished under contract with Human Resources Research Institute, Maxwell Air Force Base, Alabama. Lackland Air Force Base, Texas, Air Force Personnel and Training Research
Center, Air Research and Development Command, 1956. xi, 76 p. map. ([U.
S.] Human Resources Research Institute. Research Memorandum, 45).

HARTENSTEIN, KARL. Dir Kirche Chinas unter dem Kreuz von Karl Hartenstein und Jakob Keck. 3. Aufl. Stuttgart, Evang. Missionverlag, 1952. 26 p.

HAYWARD, VICTOR E.W. "Ears to Hear," lessons from the China mission.
London, Edinburgh House Press, 1955. 64 p. (Tracts for the Times, 1).

HOYT, CHARLES. How Christianity fares in Chinese red areas. Nanking, Government Information Office, 1947? 30 p.

HUANG, K'UEI-YÜAN, 黃魁元, Bp., 1902-    Now I can tell; the story of a
Christian bishop under Communist persecution. New York, Morehouse-Gor-
ham Co., 1954. 222 p.

HUTLEY, K.H. Ordeal in Tingchow. London, Livingstone Press., 1939. 30 p.
map.

JAMES, ALFRED FRANCIS. Reports on deputation of Australian Churchmen to
mainland China. New York, Division of Foreign Missions, National Council
of the Churches of Christ in the U.S.A., 1957. 23 p. "Reprinted by the China
Committee of the Division of Foreign Missions."

JAMES, ANNIE. I was in prison; being a first-hand account of the experience of
one of the staff of the Presbyterian Mission in China at the hands of the Communists. Christ Church, N.Z., Presbyterian Book Room, 1952. 44 p. illus.

KIESOW, E. MARGARET. China: the challenge. London, Presbyterian Church
of England, 1954. 40 p. illus.

KOETHER, LUELLA G. Two hundred days as prisoners of the Chinese Communists, by Luella G. Koether and T. Janet Surdam. [Mason City? Iowa, 1956]
248 p.

KUHN, ISOBEL. Green leaf in drought-time; the story of the escape of the last
C.I.M. missionaries from Communist China. Chicago, Moody Press [1957].
160 p.

LACY, CREIGHTON, 1919-   Protestant missions in communist China.  New
    Haven, 1953.  xxxiii, 670 p. Thesis-Yale University.
LAPWOOD, RALPH. Through the Chinese revolution, by Ralph and Nancy Lap-
    wood.  London, Spalding and Levy [1954]  216 p.
LAUTENSCHLAGER, STANTON. With Chinese communists.  London, Edinburgh
    House Press, 1941.  24 p. illus.(map)  (World issues, 4).
McCAMMON, DOROTHY SNAPP, 1923-   We tried to stay. Scottdale, Pa., Her-
    ald Press [1953]  208 p. illus.
NELSON, DANIEL, 1902-48. The apostle to the Chinese communists.  Minneap-
    olis, Board of Foreign Missions of the Norwegian Lutheran Church of Ameri-
    ca [c1935]  xi, 139 p. incl. front.(port.) facsims.
ORCHARD, RONALD KENNETH. The situation of the China mission.  London,
    Livingstone Press, 1951.  8 p.
OUTERBRIDGE, LEONARD M. The lost churches of China.  Philadelphia, West-
    minster Press [1952]  237 p.
RUST, AMBROS, 1910-   Die rote Nacht; Schweizermissionare erleben den Kom-
    munismus in China.  Luzern, Schweizer Volksbuchgemeinde [1956];  München,
    Rex-Verlag, 1956.  264 p. illus.
STOCKWELL, FRANCIS OLIN, 1900-   With God in Red China; the story of two
    years in Chinese Communist prisons.  New York, Harper [1953]  256 p.
——.  Meditations from a prison cell; devotional talks from a Chinese commu-
    nist prison.  Nashville, Upper Room, 1954.  112 p.
THOMPSON, DOUGLAS WEDDELL. Into red starlight, line drawings by Paul
    Jefferies.  London, Edinburgh House Press, 1951.  104 p.
WEST, CHARLES C. [Materials gathered in the last months of missionary ser-
    vice in China, which ended in June 1950, for use in giving an insight into the
    place of the Christian forces in China under communist rule, and the response
    of Christian thinking and action to communist challenges] n. p. n. d.  various
    paging.
WITTENBACH, H. A. Eastern horizons.  London, Highway Press, 1954.  98 p.
    illus.


### Missionary Stories
(For foreign missions in Manchuria, Mongolia, Tibet, Sinkiang, etc., see
entries under respective areas )


DREYER, EDITH G. Light and shadow in China.  London, Philadelphia, China
    Inland Mission [194-?]  [9]-132 p. front. (port.) illus.(incl. map) plates.
DUNN, MARY NOREEN. Let's see China; a world friendship unit for junior girls
    and boys.  Nashville, Cokesbury Press [c1937]  78 p. illus.
EVANS, ALICE (PICKFORD) 1868-   Lee Chung; a son of Cathay.  Philadelphia,
    Boston [etc.] Judson Press [c1936]  3-174 p. incl. front., plates.
FISHER, LENA LEONARD. The River dragon's bride; being some story beads
    gathered in South China and strung on a thread of memory.  New York, Cin-
    cinnati, Abingdon Press [c1922]  142 p. front., illus., plates.
GRAHAM, JAMES ROBERT, 1863-   Incense-bearers of Han; stories of twice-
    born Chinese, foreword by E. Schuyler English.  Grand Rapids, Mich., Zon-
    dervan Pub. House [1941]  13-107 p.
HALL-LINDQUIST, ARTHUR. The tale of two steamer rugs.  Moline, Ill., Chris-
    tian Service Foundation [c1956]  202 p. illus.
HAYES, EVA FATIMA (MORRIS) comp. Tales from China.  New York, Friend-
    ship Press [c1940]  78, [1] p. illus.
HOLLISTER, MARY (BREWSTER), 1891-   South China folk.  New York [etc.]
    Fleming H. Revell [c1935]  141 p.
HUSTON, ROSE A. How Yung Fu saved a Bible, and other stories.  New York,
    London and Edinburgh, F. H. Revell [c1941]  64 p. front., plates.
LEWIS, ALICE HUDSON. Tales from China.  New York, Friendship Press [1948]

79 p. illus., map.

MENAGH, LOUISE. Young Canada in China, continuing the travels of Dick and
Mary Louise; for junior and internediate study. [Toronto] Women's Missionary Society of the Presbyterian Church in Canada, 1924. 213 p. plates.

MENKE, WILLIBRORD. Ki and Fu. Eine Erzählung aus der chinesischen Mission. Steinfeld-Eifel, Salvator-Verlag m. Tannerbauer, 1949. 223 p.

MILLER, BASIL WILLIAM, 1897-   Twenty-four missionary stories from China.
Kansas City, Mo., Beacon Hill Press [1948] 109 p.

NAIRNE, W. P. Yarns on heroes of China; a book for workers among boys. London, United Council for Missionary Education, n. d.   111 p.

OEHLER-HEIMERDINGER, ELISABETH, 1884-   Die Söhne aus dem Hause
Tsochhin; Erzählung aus China. Basel, Basler Missionsbuchhandlung [c1949]
159 p.

————. Niemand kann zwei Herren dienen. Eine Erzählung aus China. Stuttgart,
Evang. Missionsverlag; Basel, Basler Missionsbuchhandlung, 1955. 16 p.
(Von fernen ufern, 37).

PANTIN, MABEL. Flashlights on Chinese life, yellow dragon street and other
stories. London, Church of England Zenana Missionary Society, 1926. 55 p.
illus.

PATON, W. BERNARD. "The stanger people," a story and a challenge. London, Religious Tract Society, 1925. 151 p. plates.

SCHEURER, HANS. Im Banne des Drachenkönigs. Stuttgart und Basel, Evang.
Missionsverlag, 1938. iv, 31 p. illus. (Aus fernen Ländern, 5).

————. Ein Brand aus dem Feuer. Eine Erzählung aus China. Basel, Basler
Missionsbuchhandlung, 1942. iv, 16 p. illus. (Auf den Strassen der Welt, 18).

————. Im Schatten der Stammesburg. Erzählung aus China. Basel, Basler Missionsbuchhandlung, 1942. iv, 24 p. illus. (Von fernen Ufern, 7 ).

SPILLMANN, JOSEPH, 1842-1905. Die Brüder Yang und die Boxer. Eine Erzählung aus dem jüngsten Wirren in China. Freiburg, Herder und Co., 1923.
vii, 99 p. (Aus fernen Landen, 19).

————. The Yang brothers and the boxers; a story from the Chinese missions,
translated by H. A. Frommelt. Techny, Ill., Mission Press, 1930. [7]-132 p.
(Tales of foreign lands. vol. XIII ).

————. The Yang brothers; an unforgettable story of the Boxer uprising, adapted
by James Rogan. Techny, Ill., Mission Press [1951] 120 p. illus. (Tales of
valor series).

WELLER, PAUL. Eine von Vielen. Ein chinesisches Frauenlos. (Umschlag: Eine
Erzählung aus China) Stuttgart und Basel, Evang. Missionsverlag, 1933. iv,
32 p. illus.

WIGET, JOSEPH MARIA. Jungchristliches Heldentum in China. Das Leben des
Knaben Zyrill Sen und des Mädchens Maria Theresia Wang zwischen 1911 und
1932. Freiburg, Herder und Co., 1936. viii, 100 p. illus.

## Dictionaries

CHUANG, CHAI-HSUAN, 莊澤宣, 1895-    An Anglo-Chinese dictionary of educational terms.. Shanghai, Intelligence Press, 1930. 165 p.

T'AN, JÊN-MEI, 檀仁梅, 1908-    Dictionary of educational and psychological terms, by Jên-mei Tan and Hsi-chu Chen, 陳懿祝. Shaowu, Fukien, Dept. of Agricultural Education, Fukien Christian University, 1945. 346 p.

## General Works

ARNDT, CHRISTIAN OTTOMAR, 1899-    Education in China to-day, by Christian O. Arndt, K. Turosienski and Tung-yuan Fang, 方同源. Washington, D.C., Office of Education, 1944. 12 p. diagr. (Its leaflet, 69 ).

BECKER, CARL HEINRICH, 1876-1933. Educational problems in the Far and Near East; three lectures delivered in the institute. London, Pub. for the Institute of Education by Oxford University Press, H. Milford, 1933. 44 p. front.(port.) (University of London Institute of education. Studies and reports, I ).

BUCK, PEARL (SYDENSTRICKER) 1892-    Tell the people, talks with James Yen about the mass education movement. New York, John Day [1945] iii, 84 p.

————. The same. New York, American Council, Institute of Pacific Relations [c1945] 72 p. (I.P.R. pamphlets, 16).

BUSCH, HEINRICH, 1912-    The Tung-lin Academy and its political and philosophical significance. Ann Arbor, University Microfilms [1954] ([University Microfilms, Ann Arbor, Mich.] Publication 6587) Collation of the original: xvii, 246, 2 l. Thesis-Columbia University.

CHAI, YU HENG, 柴有恆. Étude sur l'obligation scolaire et l'enseignement primaire en France et en Chine (historique, comparaison et avenir). Paris, Domat-Montchrestien, 1935. 296 p. Thèse-Univ. de Paris.

CHANG, CH'I-YÜN, 張其昀, 1901-    Education in Free China. Taipei, China Culture Pub. Foundation, 1954. 20 p. illus. (Pamphlets on Chinese affairs).

CHANG, PE CHIN, 張伯謹, 1899-    The administrative reorganization of the educational system of a county in China based on the analysis of Cheng ting hsien. Ithaca, 1935. Abstract of thesis-Cornell University. 10 p.

CHANG, PENG CHUN, 張彭春, 1892-1957. Education for modernization in China; a search for criteria of curriculum construction in view of the transition in national life, with special reference to secondary education. New York, Teachers College, Columbia University, 1923. 92 p. (Teachers college, Columbia University. Contributions to education, 137 ). Issued also as thesis-Columbia University.

CH'ÊN, LI-FU, 陳立夫, 1900-    Chinese education during the war (1937-42). [Chungking?] Ministry of education, 1943. cover-title, ii, 41 p.

CH'EN, WEI-PING, 陳維屏. The new cultural movement in China. Canberra, Australian Institute of Anatomy, 1935. 15 p. (George Ernest Morrison lectures).

CHEN, WILLIAM JUNTUNG, 陳震東, 1915. Some controversies on Chinese culture and education. Ann Arbor, University Microfilms, 1951. ([University Microfilms, Ann Arbor, Mich.] Publication no. 2526). Collation of the original: 345 l. Thesis-Columbia University.

CHENG, HAWTHORNE,    鄭鈞. Education and research in China. Chungking, Chinese Ministry of Information, 1943. 63 p. (China Handbook ser., 10 ).

CHENG, RONALD YU-SOONG, 陳友松, [Ch'en Yu-sung] 1903-   The financing
   of public education in China; a factual analysis of its major problems of reconstruction. [Shanghai, Commercial Press, 1935] xvi, 300 p. fold. map,
   fold. tables, diagrs. (part fold.) Thesis-Columbia University.
——. The Nien-erh movement [ 念二社 ] in China, its working program and future plans, being a new method for tackling the problems of China, a plea for
   help from world-minded foreign friends. Shanghai, 1935. 30 p. illus.
CH'ÊNG, T'IEN-FANG, 程天放, 1899-   Educational developments and reforms
   in Free China. Taipei, Ministry of Education, 1953. 14 p.
——. Selected speeches and writings. Taipei, Ministry of Education, 1954.
   209 p.
CHINA. Ministry of Education. Education in Free China. Taipei [1952?] 47 p.
——. Preparatory Committee of the Regional Study Conference on Fundamental
   Education. Fundamental education in China, a report. Nanking, 1947. 96 p.
   illus.
——. Education statistics of the Republic of China. Taipei, 1957. 54 p. tables.
CHINESE NATIONAL ASSOCIATION OF THE MASS EDUCATION MOVEMENT,
   Peking. The Ting Hsien experiment in 1934. Peiping, Chinese National As-
   sociation of the Mass Education Movement [1934] 46 p. diagrs.
CHINNERY, JOHN DERRY, 1924-   Problems of literary reform in modern Chi-
   na. 345 l. Thesis-School of Oriental and African Studies, University of Lon-
   don, 195-.
CHU, DON-CHEAU, 朱宏潛, 1910-   Tao Hsing-chih, 陶行知, and Chinese ed-
   ucation. New York, 1953. 254 l. Thesis-Teachers College, Columbia Uni-
   versity.
CHU, PING-CHIEN, 朱炳乾, 1915-   A proposed administrative pattern of the
   Hsien (county) school system in China. New York, 1947. 231 l. illus.
CHU, YOU-KUANG, 朱有光, 1902-   Some problems of a national system of
   education in China; a study in the light of comparative education. Shanghai,
   Commercial Press [1933] xiii, [3]-394 p. diagrs. Thesis-Columbia Univer-
   sity.
CHÜ, SHIH-YING, 瞿世英, 1899-   Towards rural educational reconstruction.
   Ting-Hsien, Chinese National Association of the Mass Education Movement,
   1936. 30 p. tables, charts.
CHUANG, CHAI-HSUAN, 莊澤宣, 1895-   Tendencies toward a democratic sys-
   tem of education in China. Shanghai, Commercial Press, 1922. xvi, 176 p.
   Thesis-Columbia University.
DJUNG, LU-DZAI, 鍾魯齋, [Chung Lu-chai]. A history of democratic education
   in modern China. Shanghai, Commercial Press, 1934. xxxiii, 258 p. diagrs.
DUGGAN, STEPHEN PIERCE HAYDEN, 1870-1950. A critique of the report of
   the League of nations' mission of educational experts to China. [New York,
   1933] 40 p. (Institute of international education. 14th series. Bulletin no. 1,
   Jan. 9, 1933).
FAN, CHUNG-TEH, 范崇德, 1913-   Curriculum reorganization in rural China.
   [New York] 1948. 230 l. tables.
FANG, TUNG-YUAN, 方同源, 1900-   An improved program of secondary edu-
   cation in post-war China. Philadelphia, 1945. 201 l. incl. tables, diagr.
   Thesis-Univ. of Pennsylvania.
FENN, WILLIAM PURVIANCE, 1902-   The effect of the Japanese invasion on
   higher education in China. Kowloon, Hongkong, China Institute of Pacific
   Relations, 1940. 48 p. incl. tables. 3 fold. maps.
FORSTER, LANCELOT, 1882-   English ideals in education for Chinese students.
   Shanghai, Commercial Press, 1936. vi, 177 p.
FREYN, HUBERT. Chinese education in the war, prepared under the auspices of
   the Council of International Affairs, Chungking. Shanghai, Kelly and Walsh,
   1940. 137 p. map. ([Council of international affairs] Political and economic
   studies, 9 ).

FUGH, PAUL CHEN, 傅葆琛, 1895-    Reconstruction of the Chinese rural elementary school curriculum to meet rural needs in China. [Ithaca, 1924?] viii, 346 l. tables, diagrs. Thesis-Cornell University.

GALT, HOWARD SPILMAN, 1872-1951. A history of Chinese educational institutions. v. 1. To the end of the Five Dynasties (A. D. 960). London, A. Probsthain, 1951 [i. e. 1952]-    400 p. (Probsthain's oriental series, v. 28 ).

HART, S. LAVINGTON, 1858-    Education in China, a paper read before the China Society April 24, 1923. London, China Society, 1923. 22 p.

HSIAO, THEODORE E., 蕭恩承, [Hsiao En-ch'êng]. The history of modern education in China. Peiping, Peking University Press, 1932. xiv, [3]-164 p. illus.(map) plates, facsim., diagrs.

HUANG, CHING-SZE, 黃敬思, 1897-    Elementary supervision on a county basis by specialized agents in selected states; professionalized supervision of instruction in selected states on a county basis with application to China. [Peiping, Printed by Peiping Cultural Association] 1927. 4, iii, 177, 5 p. Thesis-Columbia University.

INTERNATIONAL INSTITUTE OF INTELLECTUAL CO-OPERATION. The reorganisation of education in China, by the League of nations' mission of educational experts: C. H. Becker, M. Falski, P. Langevin, R. H. Tawney. Paris, International Institute of Intellectual Co-operation, 1932. [7]-200 p. plates, III maps.

——. La réorganisation de l'enseignement public en Chine. Par la mission d'experts éducateurs de la Société des Nations: C. H. Becker, M. Falski, P. Langevin, R. H. Tawney. Paris, Institut internationale de cooperation intellectuelle, 1932. 245 p.

KAO, CHUNG-JU, 高仲儒. Le mouvement intellectuel en Chine et son rôle dans la révolution chinoise entre 1898 et 1937. Paris, 1952. 250, iii p. Thèse-Univ. de Paris. Also Pub. by the author at Aix-en-Provence, 1957.

KIANG, YING-CHENG, 江應澄. The geography of higher education in China. New York, 1955. xl, 282 l. maps, diagrs. tables. Thesis-Teachers College, Columbia University.

LEAGUE OF NATIONS. Delegation from China. Comments by the Chinese Delegation on the report of the League of Nations mission of educational experts to China. Geneva, 1932. 16 l.

LI CHOW, CHUNG-CHENG, 李周仲鏵 L'examen provincial en Chine (hiang che) sous la dynastie des Ts'ing (de 1644 à 1905 [i. e. 1911] ). Paris, Jouve et cie, 1935. 137 p. Thèse-Univ. de Paris.

LIN, PAOTCHIN, 林寶權, [Lin Pao-ch'üan]. L'instruction féminine en Chine (après la révolution de 1911). Paris, Geuthner, 1926. 188 p. tables (4 fold.) diagrs.

LUND, RENVILLE CLIFTON, 1923-    The Imperial University of Peking. Seattle, 1956. 358 l. Thesis-University of Washington.

MA, CHEN-LUAN, 馬承鑾. A proposed curriculum for the preparation of physical education teachers in middle schools of the Republic of China. New York, 1955. 227 l. Thesis-New York University.

MOHR, FRIEDRICH WILHELM, 1881-1936. Fremde und deutsche Kulturbetätigung in China; mit einem Anhang: Die Tung-chi Universität in Schanghai-Woosung von Max Linde. Münster i. W., Aschendorff, 1928. viii, 104 p. illus. plates.

MONROE, PAUL, 1869-1947. A report on education in China (for American educational authorities). New York, 1922. 41, [2] p. incl. tables. (The Institute of international education. Bulletin. 3d ser., 4 ).

NEW text-books of China. Tokyo, The Sokokusha [1932] iv, 109 p. On cover: Anti-foreign teachings in new text-books of China. Preface signed: The Sokokusha.

PAO, CHŪN-JIEN, 保君健, 1897-    China to-day, with special reference to higher education. Canberra, Australian Institute of Anatomy, 1937. 15 p.

(George Ernest Morrison lectures).

PEAKE, CYRUS HENDERSON, 1900-    Nationalism and education in modern
China. New York, Columbia University Press, 1932. xiv, 240 p. Issued also as thesis-Columbia University.

PURCELL, VICTOR WILLIAM WILLIAMS SAUNDERS, 1896-    Problems of Chinese education. London, Kegan Paul, 1936. viii, 261 p.

REGIONAL STUDY CONFERENCE ON FUNDAMENTAL EDUCATION, Nanking,
1947. Proceedings. Nanking, Ministry of Education, 1947. 100 p.

RUGH, ARTHUR DOUGLAS, 1907-    American influence in China's changing
education. [Seattle] University of Washington, 1940. iv, 207 l. incl. mounted illus. (group port.) tables. Thesis-University of Washington.

SAKAI, ROBERT K., 1919-    Politics and education in modern China. Cambridge, 1953. 318 l. Thesis-Harvard University.

SARDI, ALESSANDRO, barone, 1889-    Chine et cinema. Rome, Institut international du Cinématographie éducatif, 1932. 30 p.

SHEN, WEI-CHIH, 慎微之, 1896-    The role of education in postwar China.
Philadelphia, 1945. 199 l. Thesis-Univ. of Pennsylvania.

SHÜ, PEN-CHEN, 許本震, 1896-    Die chinesische Erziehungslage im Hinblick
auf die europäischen Reformen. Weimer, H. Böhlaus Nachfolger, 1928. iv,
105 p. diagrs. (Forschungen und Werke zur Erziehungswissenschaft, 2).

SMITH, HAROLD FRED, 1885-    Elementary education in Shantung; a study of
the reorganization of the curriculum in the elementary schools of rural Shantung, and plans for the preparation of teachers for these schools. Nashville,
Amessu, 1931. vi, 159, [1] p. Thesis-Columbia University.

TAI, CHEN-HUA, 臺鎮華, 1914-    A critical study of the resolutions of the
Chinese Federation of Educational Associations, 1915-26. New York, 1954.
206 l. Thesis-Teachers College, Columbia University.

TAI, CHIN-HSIEO, 尤戴清旭 1906-    The life and work of Ts'ai Yuan-p'ei, 蔡
元培. Cambridge, 1952. 208 l. Thesis-Harvard University.

TAO, W. TCHISHIN, 陶行知, 1893-1946. Education in China, 1924, by W. Tchishin Tao and C. P. Cheng, 程其保. Shanghai, Commercial Press, 1925.
39 p. plates.

TCHANG, EDOUARD HUAI, 張懷. L'organisation d'un institut des sciences
de l'éducation en Chine. Bruxelles, A. Dewit, 1929. viii, 231 p.

TCHANG, LAM, 陳廩. Étude sur l'organisation et le fonctionnement du service
de l'instruction publique dans la Chine moderne. Lyon, Bosc frères, M. et L.
Riou, 1939. 148 p. Thèse-Univ. de Lyon.

TENG, TSUI YANG, 鄧翠英, 1885-    Education in China; papers contributed by
the members of committees of the Society for the study of international education, ed. by T. Y. Teng and T. T. Lew, 劉廷芳. Peking, The Society for
the Study of International Education, 1923. [227] p. tables, diagrs.

TSAI, YUAN-P'EI, 蔡元培, 1868-1940. The development of Chinese education;
a paper read before the China Society on April 10, 1924. London, East and
West, Ltd., 1924. 11 p.

TSANG, CHIU-SAM, 曾昭森, [Tseng Ch'ao-shen] 1901-    Nationalism in school
education in China since the opening of the twentieth century. Hong Kong,
Printed by the South China Morning Post, 1933. [3]-241 p. Thesis-Columbia
University.

TSO, CHENG-EN, 左承恩. La mesure scientifique dans l'éducation en Chine.
Montpellier, Impr. Causse, Graillet et Castelnau, 1932. 190 p. illus. Thèse-
Univ. de Montpellier.

VEY, DÉ TCHAO, 魏德昭, [Wei Tê-ch'ao]. Le pouvoir d'examen en Chine.
Nancy, Impr. G. Thomas, 1935. [5]-140 p. Thèse-Univ. de Nancy.

WALMSLEY, LOUIS CALVIN. Western influences on Chinese national education.
Toronto, 1945. 213 l. Thesis-Univ. of Toronto.

WANG, SHIH-CHIEH, 王世杰, 1891-    Education in China. Shanghai, China
United Press, 1935. cover-title, 45 p. (China reconstruction series, 3).

WEI, WILSON SHIH-SHENG, 衞士生. The history of educational philosophy in
China. New York, 1934. 240 l. Thesis-New York University.

WONG, FENG-GANG, 黃方剛. Japanese influence on educational reform in China from 1895-1911. Peiping, Author's Bookstore, 1933. viii, 204 p.

WONG, YIN-KON. L'instruction publique de la Chine moderne. Paris, s.n.d'é-
dit, 1937. 171 p. Thèse-Univ. de Paris.

YEN, JAMES Y.C., 宴陽初, 1894-    The mass education movement in China.
[Shanghai, Commercial Press, 1925. ii, 25 p. illus.(incl. port., facsims.)
diagr.

YIN, CHILING, 殷芝齡, 1897-    Reconstruction of modern educational organizations in China. Shanghai, Commercial Press, 1924. xviii, 5-171 p.diagrs.

## Christian Colleges

ANDERSON, MARY RALEIGH, 1878-    Protestant mission schools for girls in
South China (1827 to the Japanese invasion). Mobile, Ala, Heiter-Starke
Print. Co., 1943. xxvii, 365, [8] p. illus., plates, ports. Thesis-Columbia
University.

BOONE UNIVERSITY, Wuchang. China's first library school. The Boone library
and its forward movements. [Wuchang? 1928] cover-title, [20] p. incl.illus.

CHINA CHRISTIAN EDUCATIONAL ASSOCIATION. Christian higher education in
China. A study for the year 1925-26, by Earl Herbert Cressy. Shanghai, China Christian Educational Association [1928] xii, 306, [5] p. maps, charts,
tables. (Bulletin, 20 ).

————. The correlated program in 1930 as adopted by the Council of Higher Education. Shanghai, China Christian Educational Association, 1930. 32 p. tables.

CHINA EDUCATIONAL COMMISSION. Christian education in China; the report
of the China educational commission of 1921-22. Shanghai, Commercial
Press, 1922. iii, iii, 390 p. incl. tables, fold. charts.

————. The same; a study made by an educational commission representing the
mission boards and societies conducting work in China. New York, Committee of reference and counsel of the Foreign Missions Conference of North A-
merica [c1922] xv, 430 p.

CHU, YOU-KUANG, 朱有光, 1902-    An educational experiment at Lingnan.
[Canton] Lingnan University, 1935. cover-title, 30 p. plates.(Lingnan University research lectures, 3 ).

[CONFERENCE ON CHRISTIAN EDUCATION IN CHINA, New York, 1925]. Chinese Christian education; a report of a conference held in New York City,
April 6th, 1925, under the joint auspices of the International Missionary
Council and the Foreign Missions Conference of North America. New York,
1925. 103 p.

CORBETT, CHARLES HODGE, 1881-    Shantung Christian University (Cheeloo).
New York, United Board for Christian Colleges in China, 1955. 281 p. illus.

DAY, CLARENCE BURTON, 1889-    Hangchow University, a brief history.
New York, United Board for Christian Colleges in China, 1955 [i.e. 1956]
183 p. illus.

[DUGGAN, STEPHEN PIERCE HAYDEN] 1870-1950. comp. Record of the testimonial dinner to Dr. Charles K. Edmunds, New York, March second, nineteen hundred twenty-two. [New York, 1922] 22 p. plates.

FOOCHOW, FUKIEN CHRISTIAN UNIVERSITY. What my education in Fukien
Christian University means to me. Foochow, 1938. 16 p. ports.

FORD, EDDY LUCIUS, 1879-    The history of the educational work of the Methodist Episcopal church in China; a study of its development and present trends.
Foochow, Christian Herald Mission Press, 1938. 294 p. fold. map.

GREGG, ALICE HENRIETTA, 1893-    China and educational autonomy; the
changing role of the Protestant educational missionary in China, 1807-1937.

Syracuse, N.Y., Syracuse University Press, 1946. xvi, 285 p. Thesis-Columbia University, 1945.

LAMBERTON, MARY, 1883-   St. John's University, Shanghai, 1879-1951. New York, United Board for Christian Colleges in China, 1955. 261 p. illus.

LEWIS, IDA BELLE, 1887-   A report of girls' schools in North China supported by the Women's foreign missionary society of the Methodist Episcopal church. Shanghai, Commercial Press [1921] 98 p. map, charts.

LI, ANTHONY C., 李景文 , 1920-   The history of privately controlled higher education in the Republic of China. Washington, D.C., Catholic University of America Press, 1954. 157 p.

LUTZ, JESSIE (GREGORY), 1925-   The role of the Christian colleges in modern China before 1928. Ithaca, 1955. vi, 375 l. Thesis-Cornell University.

MIAO, CHESTER S., 繆秋笙 , 1894-   Religion and character in Christian middle schools; a study of religious education in Christian private middle schools of China, by Chester S. Miao and Frank W. Price. Shanghai, China Christian Educational Association, 1929. iii-x, 240 p. incl. tables. plates, 2 plans.

[―――, ] ed. Education for service in the Christian church in China; the report of a survey commission, 1935. Shanghai, Pub. for The National Committee for Christian Religious Education in China, by the Christian Literature Society [1937?] 120, 99-157 p. 2 fold. tables.

MING SUM SCHOOL FOR THE BLIND, Canton. Ming Sum; the school of the understanding heart; the fiftieth anniversary 1889-1939. Hong Kong, Standard Press, 1939. 117 p. ports., illus.

NANCE, W.B., 1868-   Soochow University. New York, United Board for Christian Colleges in China, 1956. 163 p. illus.

NATIONAL COMMITTEE FOR CHRISTIAN RELIGIOUS EDUCATION IN CHINA. Education for service in the Christian church in China: the report of a survey commission, 1935; with a supplementary chapter by C. Stanley Smith. New York, Nanking Theological Seminary, Board of Founders [1945] 165 p. charts.

PRICE, FRANK WILSON, 1895-   ed. Religious life in Christian universities and colleges of China 1927-28. Shanghai, China Christian Educational Association, 1928. 47 p. (China Christian Educational Association. Bull. 24 ).

RELIGIOUS education in the Chinese church: the report of a deputation, 1931. Shanghai, National Committee for Christian Religious Education in China (National Christian Council of China) [1931] 296 p.

ST. JOHN'S UNIVERSITY, Shanghai. St. John's University, 1879-1929. [Shanghai, Printed by Kelly and Walsh, 1929?] 92, 58 p. front., plates, ports., fold. map.

SCOTT, RODERICK, 1885-   Fukien Christian University, a historical sketch. New York, United Board for Christian Colleges in China, 1954. 138 p. illus.

STUART, WARREN HORTON. The use of material from China's spiritual inheritance in the Christian education of Chinese youth; a guide and sourcebook for Christian teachers in China. Shanghai, Kwang Hsueh Pub. House, Oxford University Press, China agency, 1932. iii-ix, 93, 95-202, vii p. diagr. Thesis-Yale University.

TAYLOR, JOSEPH, 1869-   History of the West China Union University, 1910-35. Chengtu, Printed at the Canadian Mission Press [1936] 94 p. plates.

THURSTON, MATILDA S. (CALDER), 1875-1958. Ginling College. Part I [by] Mrs. Lawrence Thurston. Part II [by] Ruth M. Chester. New York, United Board for Christian Colleges in China, 1955 [i.e. 1956] 171 p. illus.

[UNITED BOARD FOR CHRISTIAN COLLEGES IN CHINA]. An impressive service; the story of the Christian colleges of China. [New York? 1940?] cover-title, 16 p. illus., map.

VAN PUTTEN, J. DYKE, 1899-   Christian higher education in China; contributions of the colleges of arts and sciences to Chinese life. [Chicago] 1937. ii numb. l., 64 p. Part of thesis-University of Chicago.

WALLACE, EDWARD WILSON, 1880-1941. The place of private schools in a national system of education. Shanghai, China Christian Educational Association, 1925. 26 p. (CCEA Bull. 5 ).

WALLACE, LYDIA ETHEL, 1880-    The history of Hwa Nan College, the woman's college of South China. New York, United Board for Christian Higher Education in Asia. 1956. 164 p.

WEBSTER, JAMES BENJAMIN, 1879-    Christian education and the national consciousness in China. New York, E. P. Dutton [c1923]  xi, 323 p.

## Survey of Educational Institutions

CHYNE, W. Y., 莊文亞 , [Chuang Wên-ya] ed. Handbook of cultural institutions in China. Shanghai, Chinese National Committee on Intellectual Co-operation, 1936. 282, xxiii p.

The EDUCATIONAL directory of China, a reference book for all interested in western education in China. 1914-21. Shanghai, The Educational Directory of China Pub. Co., 1914-22.    v. plates.

LIN, MOUSHÊNG, 林侔聖, 1906-    A guide to Chinese learned societies and research institutes. New York, China Institute in America [c1936] 3, [8], 5-48 p.

ACADEMIA SINICA. The Academia sinica and its national research institutes. (1931) Nanking, The Academia Sinica [1931]  3-173 p.  1st ed. 1929.

――――. Institute of Social Sciences, Nanking. The summary report of the Institute of social sciences, Academia Sinica. Kunming, Yunnan [etc.] 1938-    v.

AMOY. UNIVERSITY. The University of Amoy. Special publication in commemoration of its tenth anniversary. 1921-31. [Amoy, 1931] cover-title, 35, [13], 1, 187 p. illus., plates (part fold.) ports., diagrs.(part fold.).

CANTON. SUN YAT-SEN UNIVERSITY. The National Sunyatsen University, a short history. [Canton] Printed by Wai Hing Print. Co., 1935. viii, 160 p. plates (1 fold.) ports., diagrs. (1 fold.)  1st ed. 1931.  194 p.

――――. College of Engineering: a short history. Canton, National Sun Yatsen University, 1935. 54 p. plates.

――――. Institute of educational research. The Institute of educational research, Sun Yatsen University, Canton, China. 1928-32. [Canton, 1932] 26 p.  1st ed. 1930.

CHINA. Geological Survey. The National geological survey of China, 1916-22. A retrospect on the occasion of the opening of the Museum and library of the Survey in July, 1922. [Peking, 1922] 8 p.

――――. The same, 1916-31; a summary of its work during the first fifteen years of its establishment. Peiping, 1931. cover-title, 13, [32] p. plates.

CHINA INSTITUTE IN AMERICA. China institute in America, incorporated. New York, China Institute in America [1930] 15 p.  1st ed. 1928.

INSTITUTE OF SOCIAL RESEARCH, Peking. Institute of social research; a summary of its work, 1926-32, prepared for a Century of progress exposition at Chicago, 1933. Peiping, Institute of Social Research, 1933. 20, 36, [2] p.

NATIONAL ACADEMY OF PEIPING. The National Academy of Peiping. Kunking [etc.] 19-    v. plates.

NANKAI UNIVERSITY. Nankai Institute of Economics. Nankai institute of economics: its history and work, 1927-41. Shapingpa, Chungking, Nankai Institute of Economics, Nankai University, 1941. cover-title, 14 p. 1st ed. Tientsin, 1936. 26 p.

PEKING. PALACE MUSEUM. The Palace museum of Peiping. Peiping, The Palace Museum of Peiping, 1931. cover-title, 12 p. plates.

TSING HUA COLLEGE, Peking. Tsing Hua, 1911-21. A review. Published on the tenth anniversary of the founding of Tsing Hua College. Peking, 1921. 47, [3] p. incl. illus., ports., tables, diagr.

VERBAND FÜR DEN FERNEN OSTEN, Berlin. Denkschrift aus Anlass der feier-

lichen Einweihung der Tungchi technischen Hochschule in Schanghai-Woosung.
[Berlin-Schöneberg, Meisenbach Riffarth und Co.] 1924.   60, [6] p. illus.(incl.
ports.) plans (1 fold.).

## Chinese Students

ALL-INDIA STUDENTS' FEDERATION, Bombay. Lessons of China's student
movement.  Bombay, Printed by J. Bhatt at New Age Print. Press, 1950.
31 p. illus. port.

BONNINGUE, A. Étudients chinois; silhouettes et tendances.  Paris, Éditions
Alsatia, 1948.  130 p.

CHIANG, WÊN-HAN, 江文漢, 1908-   The ideological background of the Chinese
student movement.  New York, King's Crown Press, 1948.  x, 176 p. map
(on lining-papers) Thesis-Columbia University.

CHOU, HENRY HSÜEH CHANG, 周學章, 1894-1945. The measurement of composition ability.  [New York? 1923] 107 p. fold. tables, diagrs. Thesis-Columbia University.

CHOU, TS'Ê-TSUNG, 周策縦, 1916-   The May fourth movement and its influence upon China's socio-political development.  Ann Arbor, University Microfilms [1955] ([University Microfilms, Ann Arbor, Mich.] Publication no.
12,553) Collation of the original: 3, viii, 849 l. illus., tables. Thesis-University of Michigan.

FRANKE, WOLFGANG. Chinas kulturelle Revolution. Die Bewegung vom 4. Mai
1919.  München, Oldenbourg, 1957.  89 p. map. (Janus-Bücher, 1).

FREYN, HUBERT. Prelude to war; the Chinese student rebellion of 1935-36.
Shanghai, The China Journal Pub. Co., 1939.  122 p. plates.

HU, I, 胡毅, 1904-   An experimental study of the reading habits of adult Chinese.  Chicago, 1928.  x, 141 l. diagrs., mounted photos., tables. Thesis-
University of Chicago.

LIU, HERMAN CHAN-EN, 劉湛恩, 1896-1941. Non-verbal intelligence tests
for use in China.  New York, Teachers College, Columbia University, 1922.
viii, [2], 84 p. incl. illus., tables, diagrs. (Teachers College, Columbia
University. Contributiona to education, 126 ).

SEWELL, WILLIAM GAWAN. China through a college window.  New York, Friendship Press [1938] 183 p.

WANG, TSI CHANG, 王芷章 . The youth movement in China.  New York, New Republic, 1927.  xv, 245 p.

WEBSTER, JAMES BENJAMIN, 1879-1929. Interests of Chinese students.  Shanghai, Bureau of Publications, University of Shanghai, 1932.  cover-title, xxi,
166 p. (Studies in education and psychology, 1 ).

## Chinese Students Abroad

CHAO, THOMAS MING-HENG, 趙敏恆, 1904-   Shadow shapes; memoirs of a
Chinese student in America, by T. M. C.  Peking, Peking Leader Press, 1928.
215 p.

CHINA INSTITUTE IN AMERICA. Theses and dissertations by Chinese students
in America.  New York, China Institute in America [1927] cover-title, [2],
42 p. (Bulletin 4 ).

————. The same (supplementary list).  New York, China Institute in America
[1928?] cover-title, 12 p. (Bulletin 7 ).

————. The same, 1931-36, compiled by M. Hsitien Lin, 林俦聖.  New York,
China Institute in America [1936] 31 p.

————. Directory of Chinese university graduates and students in America. 1943,
1944, 1945, 1946-47.  New York, 1943-47.  4 v.

————. Directory of Chinese students in colleges and universities in the United

States of America. New York, 1951-date. 6 v.
————. Directory of Chinese members of American college and university facul-
ties. New York, 1951-date. 6 v.
————. A survey of Chinese students in American universities and colleges in the
past one hundred years. In commemoration of the one hundredth anniversary
of the graduation of the first Chinese from an American university, Yung
Wing, B.A., Yale 1854. A prelim. report. New York, 1954. 68 p. forms,
tables.
CHINESE STUDENTS' CHRISTIAN ASSOCIATION IN NORTH AMERICA. Direc-
tory of Chinese students in America. New York, Chinese Students' Christian
Association in North America, c1934/35-1943/44. 9 v.
CHINESE STUDENTS' ALLIANCE IN THE UNITED STATES OF AMERICA. The
handbook of the Chinese students in the U.S.A. [Chicago?] Chinese Students'
Alliance, U.S.A. [1922-34]    v.
CHU, JENNINGS PINKWEI, 朱斌魁, 1895-    Chinese students in America: qual-
ities associated with their success. New York, Teachers College, Columbia
University, 1922. 55 p. incl. tables, diagrs. (Teachers College, Columbia
University. Contributions to education, 127 ). Published also as thesis, Columbia University.
COMMITTEE ON EDUCATIONAL INTERCHANGE POLICY. Chinese students in
the United States, 1948-55; a study in government policy. New York, 1956.
14 p.
HUANG, LUCY, 黃仁華 1920-    Dating and courtship innovations of Chinese students in America. Chicago, 1954. 480 l. Thesis-Univ. of Chicago.
KAO, LIN-YING, 高麟英, 1918-    Academic and professional attainments of
native Chinese students graduating from Teachers College, Columbia Univer-
sity, 1909-50. New York, Teachers College, Columbia University, 1951.
153 l. map, tables.
KUNG, SAMUEL S., 龔希信, 1915-    Personal and professional problems of
Chinese students and former students in the New York metropolitan area.
New York, 1955. 186 p. Thesis-Teachers College, Columbia University.
LA FARGUE, THOMAS EDWARD, 1900-    China's first hundred. Pullman,
State College of Washington, 1942. xiv, 176 p. ports.
LIU, YUNG-SZI, 劉蓉士, [Liu Jung-shih] 1902-    The academic achievement
of Chinese graduate students at the University of Michigan, 1907-50. Ann
Arbor, University Microfilms [1956] Collation of the original: ix, 169 l. ta-
bles. Thesis-University of Michigan.
PARK, NO-YONG, 鮑訥榮, 1899-    Chinaman's chance. 2d ed.-rev. Boston,
Meador publishing company [1943] 198 p.
SZE, SZEMING, 施思明, 1908-    Chinese students in Great Britain. London,
China Society, 1931. 14 p.
U.S. International Educational Exchange Service. The program of emergency
aid to Chinese students, 1949-55. [Washington, 1956] v, 29 p. illus. (U.S.
Dept. of State. Publication 6343. International information and cultural se-
ries, 47 ).
WHO'S who of American returned students. Peking, Tsing Hua College, 1917.
viii, vi, 215, iv, iv p. 4 fold. tables.
WHO'S who of the Chinese students in America. Berkeley, Calif., Lederer,
Street and Zeus Co. [c1921-    v. front.(ports.)
YIEH, TSUNG-KAO, 葉崇高, 1906-    The adjustment problems of Chinese graduate students in American universities. Chicago, 1934. 127 p. Thesis-Uni-
versity of Chicago.

## Chinese Students and English Teaching

CHAO, SANKEY C., 趙世澤, 1921-    The teaching of English to Cantonese students: a critical study of some cultural and linguistic problems. New York,

1953. 153 1. Thesis-Teachers College, Columbia University.

LUM, CHUNG P., 林松柏 , [Lin Sung-po]. Anglo-Chinese commercial conversation and classified phrases. [New York, Walters and Mahon, inc., c1926] xxxvii, [1], 507, [1] p.

————. Anglo-Chinese practical conversation. 2d ed. [New York, Walters and Mahon, 1928, (c1926) ]. [194] p.

LIU, HSIAO-CHUAN, 劉笑娟, 1919-   Introducing English poetry to Chinese college students. New York, 1954.   172 1. Thesis-Teachers College, Columbia University.

LOH, D.Y., 陸殿揚. Practical English readers for junior middle schools. [Chungking] China Book Co. [1944?]-   6 v. illus.

MENG, TSE-HOU, 孟子厚. Select English short essays on current events. Shanghai, K'ai-Ming Book Store, 1936. vii, 180 p.

MICHIGAN. UNIVERSITY. English language Institute. An intensive course in English for Chinese students, by Charles C. Fries and Yao Shen, 优垚 . [Ann Arbor] English Language Institute, University of Michigan, 1946-   4 v. diagrs.

MOK, P.K., 莫泮芹, 1906-   The history and development of the teaching of English in China. Ann Arbor, University Microfilms, 1951. ([University Microfilms, Ann Arbor, Mich.] Publication no. 2546) Collation of the original: vii, 286 1. tables. Thesis-Columbia University.

RICHARDS, IVOR ARMSTRONG, 1893-   Basic in teaching: East and West. London, Kegan Paul, 1935.   112 p. front.(fold. tab.) (Psyche miniatures. General series, 72 ).

————. A first book of English for Chinese learners. Under the authority of the Orthological Institute of China. [Peiping, Yu Lien Press ], 1938.   426 p. illus.

SHUI, TIEN-TUNG, 水天同. Everyman's basic. Selections made under the authority of the Orthological Institute of China. [Peiping, 1937] v, 199 p. table.

T'ANG, CH'ING-I, 唐慶詒, comp. Selected modern English essays for college students. 2d ed. [Shanghai] Chung Hwa Book Co., 1947. 218 p.

YAO, MILTON T., 姚慕譚, comp. Specimens of English composition [for Chinese students]; selected and annotated by Milton T. Yao. [Shanghai] Commercial Press, 1946. x, 251 p.

YEN, ISABELLA YIYUN, 嚴倚雲 . English for speakers of Mandarin Chinese. Washington, American Council of Learned Societies, 1955. 356 p. illus.(American Council of Learned Societies. Program in English as a Foreign Language. Spoken English textbooks ).

## Youth Movement

BOY SCOUTS OF CHINA. Boy Scouts of China; general regulations, policy, organization and rules. [Shanghai? 1933?] 10 p.

CHINA. Ministry of Social Affairs. Child welfare work in China: a report. Nanking, 1947. 20, 17 p.

HSIAO, YUNLAY, 蕭雲來 , 1913-   Die Bedeutung der Formationserziehung für die Vorbereitung der Landesverteidigung in den Jugendorganisationen Deutschlands und Chinas. Weida, Thür. [194-] 101 p. diagrs. Diss.-Univ. Berlin.

HU, NAN, 胡蘭, 1902-   Étude comparée des programmes et des méthodes d'enseignement pour les enfants de 6 à 12 ans en Chine et en France. Paris, A. Pedone, 1935.   vi, 186 p. Thèse-Univ. de Paris.

HWANG, YUNTZE. Chinesische Kinderfreuden in Bild, Wort und Musik. Gedichte. Einleitung von Chiang Yee. Deutsche Texte von Herm. Scherchen. Zürich, Büchergilde Gutenberg, 1946.   46 p.

KOEHN, ALFRED. Kindesehrfurcht in China. Peiping, Lotus Court, 1943. [4], 24 p.

LEE, FRANK W., 李錦綸 , [Li Chin-lun] 1884-1956. Child welfare in China. New

York, Child Welfare Committee of America [1928] 11 p. ([Child welfare committee of America, inc.] Publication no. 56. Series 1928).

LI, HUAN, 李煥, 1916-    Features and missions. China Youth Corps for anti-communism and national salvation. Taipei, Youth Publishers, 1955. 14 p.

ROHNER, JOANNES. Die Kinderverlobung in China. Eine ethischrechtliche Untersuchung. Romae, Pontificia Universitas Gregoriana, 1951. 79 p.

RUDY, STELLA M. Children of China. Chicago, Rand, McNally, c1937. [64] p. illus.

SAUNDERS, J. ROSCOE, 1873-    China's children, a close-up view of China's boys and girls, prepared for the boys and girls of the West. New York, Chicago, Fleming H. Revell [c1929] 93 p. front., plates, ports.

TZEN, SHIAN-YUNG, 曾憲鎔, [Tseng Hsien-jung]. China youth warriors march. [Taipei] Youth Publishers [1953?] 20 p. illus.

UNITED SERVICE TO CHINA. One-fifth of the world's children. New York, United China Relief, 1944. 15 p. illus.

WEISS-SONNENBURG, HEDWIG. Li; das Buch vom kleinen Chinesen; Jugendbuch, von Hedwig Weiss-Sonnenburg. Leipzig, Payne Verlag [1938] 116, [1] p. incl. plates.

YUI, SHUFANG, 余蕭淑芳 Chinese children at play written and illustrated by Yui Shufang. London, Methuen, 1939. 21 p. illus.

## Education and Youth Movement in Communist China

ALL-CHINA DEMOCRATIC WOMEN'S FEDERATION. Children in new China. [Peking, 1952] 42 p.

ALL-CHINA FEDERATION OF DEMOCRATIC YOUTH. We build a new country, stories of young Chinese workers. Peking, Foreign Languages Press, 1950.

———. China's youth marches forward. Peking, Foreign Languages Press, 1950. 70 p. plates, illus.

———. Die Chinesische Jugend marschiert vorwärts. Peking, Verlag für Fremdsprachige Literatur, 1951. 70 p.

———. Chinese youth enjoys a happy life. [Peking?] 1953. 78 p. illus.

———. Jeunesse de la Chine nouvelle, par la Fédération nationale de la jeunesse democratique de Chine. Pékin, 1954. 38 l. (in portfolio) 1. éd. 1951, 80 p. illus.

———. The best sons and daughters of the Chinese people; stories of the heroic young fighters in the Chinese people's volunteers. [Peking, Foreign Languages Press ] 1954. 60 p.

———. Söhne und Töchter Chinas; Erlebnisse heroischer junger Kämpfer aus den Reihen der chinesischen Volksfreiwilligen-Armee. [Ins Deutsche übertragen von Johannes Schellenberger. 1. Aufl. Berlin] Verlag Neues Leben, 1955. 68 p. illus.

ALL-CHINA STUDENTS' FEDERATION. Students of New China. [Peking? 1952?] unpaged (chiefly illus.).

———. Chinese students. Peking, Foreign Languages Press, 1955. 36 p. illus.

ALL-CHINA YOUTH CONGRESS, 2d, Peking, 1953. The second All-China Youth Congress. Peking, All-China Federation of Democratic Youth, 1953. 34 p. illus.

ARENS, RICHARD, 1912-    The impact of communism on education in China, 1949-50. Chicago [Library, Dept. of Photographic Reproduction, University of Chicago] 1952. Microfilm copy (positive) of typescript. Collation of original: iv, 255 l. Thesis-University of Chicago.

CHAO, CHUNG, 趙聰. Students in mainland China, by Chao Chung [and] Yang I-fan, 楊一帆. Kowloon, Hong Kong, Union Research Institute [1956] v, 139 p. (Communist China problem research series, EC 13 ).

CH'EN, PO-TA, 陳伯達, 1905-    Speech before the study group of research members of Academia Sinica. Peking, Foreign Languages Press, 1953. 33 p.

CHI, TUNG-WEI, 齊東煒. Education for the proletariat in Communist China.
Kowloon, H.K., Union Research Institute [1954] cover-title, 73 p. (Communist China problem research series, EC6).

CHINA WELFARE INSTITUTE. Children's tears. Shanghai, China Welfare Institute, 1952. 76 p. plates.

CHINESE PEOPLE'S NATIONAL COMMITTEE IN DEFENCE OF CHILDREN.
New China through her children's eyes. Peking, Foreign Language Press,
1953. 73 p. illus.

————. Children in new China. Peking, Foreign Languages Press, 1953. unpaged
(chiefly illus.) 1954 ed. 40 p. illus.

————. Les enfants de la Chine nouvelle. 1954. [Pékin, Éditions en langues étran-
gères] 1954. 40 p. illus.

————. Our life [by children of New China] Peking, 1955. 71 p.

————. Children of China, 1956. Peking, Foreign Languages Press, 1956. cover-title, 39 p. (chiefly illus.).

————. Children of China. 1957. Peking, Foreign Languages Press, 1957. 48 p.

CHOU, EN-LAI, 1898-   Report on the question of intellectuals, delivered on
January 14, 1956 at a meeting held under the auspices of the Central Committee of the Communist Party of China. Peking, Foreign Languages Press,
1956. 44 p.

————. Bericht über die Frage der Intellektuellen. Gegeben am 14. Januar,
1956, auf einer vom Zentralkomitee der Kommunistischen Partei Chinas ein-
berufenen Sitzung zur Diskussion der Frage der Intellektuellen von Tschou
En-lai. Peking, Verlag für Fremdsprachige Literatur, 1956. 52 p.

CHUNG, SHIH, 鍾石. Higher education in Communist China. Kowloon, H.K.,
Union Research Institute [1953] cover-title, 97 p. (Communist China problem research series, EC2).

CULTURE and education in new China. Peking, Foreign Languages Press[1951?]
82 p. illus.

CULTURE, education and health in New China. Peking, Foreign Languages
Press, 1952. 40 p.

HAPPY youth of China. L'heureuse jeunesse chinoise. [Peking, Chinese Youth
Pub. House, 1955] 1 v. (unpaged).

HU, YAO-PANG, 胡耀邦. Unite all youth to march forward courageously in the
great ranks of the construction of our motherland; work report to the second
national congress of the New Democratic Youth League of China, June 24,
1953. [n.p., 1953] 25 p.

HUNTER, EDWARD, journalist. Brain-washing in Red China; the calculated
destruction of men's minds. New and enl. ed. New York, Vanguard Press
[c1953] 341 p. 1st ed. 1951.

KUO, MO-JO, 郭沫若, 1892-   L'instruction et la culture dans la Chine nouvelle. Pékin, Éditions en langues étrangères, 1950. 35 p.

LIAO, CH'ÊNG-CHIH, 廖承志, 1908-   Strive for the defence and construction
of our motherland; report to the second All-China Youth Congress. [n.p.,
1953?] 21 l.

LIN, EN-CHIN, 林恩卿. Educational changes in China since the establishment
of the People's Republic and some steps leading to them: a report. Philadelphia, 1953. 131 numb. l. (Pennsylvania. University. Studies in education,
57 ).

LINDSAY, MICHAEL, 1909-   Notes on educational problems in communist China, 1941-47, with supplements on developments in 1948 and 1949 by Marion
Menzies, William Paget, and S.B. Thomas. New York, International Secretariat, Institute of Pacific Relations, 1950. iii, 194 p.

NEW DEMOCRATIC YOUTH LEAGUE OF CHINA. Young builders of China.[Edi-
ted by the Central Committee of the New Democratic Youth League of China.]
Peking, Foreign Languages Press [1953] 75 p. illus., ports., map.

————. The second National Congress of the New Democratic Youth League of

China. Peking, Central Committee of the New Democratic Youth League of China, 1953. 78 p. port. illus.

PEOPLE'S CHINA. Nos progrès dans la culture et l'éducation. Pékin, Éditions en langues étrangères, 1954. 116 p. illus.

TS'UI, SHU-CH'IN, 崔書琴, 1906-57. From academic freedom to brainwashing; the tragic ordeal of professors on the Chinese mainland. Taipei, China Culture Pub. Foundation, 1953. 44 p. (Pamphlets on Chinese affairs).

WANG, CHARLES KILORD ATHEN, 王徵葵 1904- The control of teachers in Communist China; a socio-political study. Lackland Air Force Base, Tex., Air Force Personnel and Training Research Center, Air Research and Development Command, 1955. x, 61 p. ([U.S.] Human Resources Research Institute. Technical research report, 36 ).

WORLD FEDERATION OF DEMOCRATIC YOUTH. Young builders of new China; the report of the WFDY delegation which visited the Chinese People's Republic in September-October 1950, on new China and its youth. Bombay, People's Pub. House [1951] 61 p.

YANG, I-FAN, 楊一帆. The case of Hu Feng, 胡風. Hong Kong, Union Research Institute [1956] v, 169 p. (Communist China problem research series EC 16 ).

YEN, MARIA, 燕歸來, 1928- pseud. The umbrella garden; a picture of student life in Red China. Adapted from the Chinese by Maria Yen with Richard M. McCarthy. New York and London, Macmillan, 1954. 268 p.

———. China kratzt den Reisnapf aus. Übers. von Alexander Voill. Wien, Stuttgart, Wancura, 1956. 397 p.

# XV. LANGUAGE

## General Works

BODMAN, NICHOLAS CLEAVELAND, 1913-    A linguistic study of the Shih ming, 釋名 : initials and consonant clusters. Cambridge, Harvard University Press, 1954. xi, 146 p. (Harvard-Yenching Institute studies, 11 ). "The original version was presented as a doctoral dissertation to Yale University in June, 1950."

BOUSACK, CHRISTIAN. Chinesische Wortkunde. Neue Methode, die chinesische Sprache durch die Wortquell-Rechtschreibung tonrein sprechen zu lernen. Spezialausg. für Schantung. Münster i.W., Aschendorff, 1957. x, 106 p. (Veröffentlichungen des Instituts für Missionswissenschaft des Westfälschen Wilhelms-Universität Münster/Westfalen. Hft. 5 ).

DE FRANCIS, JOHN FRANCIS, 1911-    Nationalism and language reform in China. Princeton, Princeton University Press, 1950. xi, 306 p. Thesis-Columbia University.

DEMIÉVILLE, PAUL, 1894-    Matériaux pour l'enseignement élémentaire du chinois; écriture, transcription, langue parlée nationale. Paris, Adrien-Maisonneuve, 1953. 86 p.; 73 p.; 16 p.

FORREST, ROBERT ANDREW DERMOD, 1893-    The Chinese language. London, Faber and Faber [1948] 352 p. maps. (The Great languages).

HILLIER, SIR WALTER CAINE, 1849-1927. The Chinese language and how to learn it; a manual for beginners. 10th ed. London, Kegan Paul, 1942. viii, 297 p. incl. front.(facsim.).

HSIA, TAO-T'AI, 夏道泰, 1915-    China's language reforms. New Haven, Institute of Far Eastern Languages, Yale University, 1956. 200 p. (Mirror series A, 21).

KARLGREN, BERNHARD, 1889-    Philology and ancient China. Oslo, H. Aschehoug; Cambridge, Harvard University Press, 1926. 167 p. (Instituttet for sammenlignende kulturforskning. [Publikationer] ser. A: Forelesninger, VIII ).

———. Sound and symbol in Chinese. London, Oxford University Press, H. Milford, 1946 (c1923). 112 p. ([The world's manuals] Language and literature series).

———. The Chinese language, an essay on its nature and history. New York, Ronald Press Co. [1949] vi, 122 p.

LIN, FÊNG, 林峰 1909-    Memorandum; China's writing and language problem is solved at last. Shanghai, Liem Fueng Book House [1931] 5 p. tables.

LIU, FU, 劉復, 1891-1934. Les mouvements de la langue nationale en Chine. Paris, "Les Belles Lettres," Pékin, presse de l'université nationale, 1925. 56 p.

MARGOULIÈS, GEORGES, 1907-    La lanuge et l'écriture chinoises. Paris, Payot, 1943. [7]-272 p. (Bibliothèque scientifique).

MILLER, ROY ANDREW, 1924-    Problems in the study of Shuo-wen chieh-tzu, 説文解字. New York, 1953. xvi, 351 l. Thesis-Columbia University.

SCHINDLER, BRUNO, 1882-    ed. Hirth anniversary volume. London, Probsthain [1923] lxxxiii, 705 p. illus., port., col. maps (1 fold. in pocket).

SERRUYS, PAUL L., 1912-    Prolegomena to the study of the Chinese dialects of Han time according to Fang Yen, 方言. Berkeley, 1956. 605 l. Thesis-University of California.

TAN, YUN-SHAN, 譚雲山, 1901-    History of the Chinese language and literature. Santiniketan, Sino-Indian Cultural Society of India, 1952. 18 p.

TSCHARNER, EDUARD HORST VON, 1901-    Vom Wesen der chinesischen Spra-
    che. St. Gallen, H. Tschudy und Co., 1942. 30 p. Reprinted from Mittei-
    lungen der Schweizerischen Gesellschaft der Freunde ostasiatischer Kultur,
    III, 1941.
TUNG, T'UNG-HO, 董同龢, 1912-    Languages of China. Taipei, China Cul-
    ture Pub. Foundation, 1953. 14 p. (Pamphlet on Chinese Affairs).
WIEGER, LÉON, 1856-1933. Caractères chinois; etymologie, graphies, lexiques.
    5e éd. Hien-Hien, Impr. de Mission catholique, 1932. 943 p. illus.
──────. Chinese characters, their origin, etymology, history, classification and
    signification. A thorough study from Chinese documents. Translated into Eng-
    lish by L. Davrout, S.J. 2d ed., enl.and rev. according to the 4th French ed.
    Hsien-hsien, Catholic Mission Press, 1927. Re-issue. Peking. H. Vetch
    [1940] 820 p. illus.
WULFF, KURT, 1881-1939. Chinesisch und Tai; sprachvergleichende Untersu-
    chungen. København, Levin und Munksgaard, Ejnar Munksgaard, 1934. 260 p.
    (K.Danske videnskabernes selskab. Historisk-filologiske meddelelser.xx, 3).
──────. "Musik" und "Freude" im chinesischen. København, Levin und Munks-
    gaard, Ejnar Munksgaard, 1935. 39 p. (K. Danske videnskabernes selskab.
    Historisk-filologiske meddelelser. XXI, 2).

## Writing

ALLEN, WILLIAM DANGAIX, 1904-    100 Chinese picture-words; compiled by
    William D. Allen. Ideographs done by L.C.Lui. New York, Universal Pub.
    Co. [1936] cover-title, [16] p.
──────. Let's try Chinese, by William D. Allen and S.T. Shen, 沈守澤. Pre-
    pared by the Institute of Pacific Relations. [New York, 1936] 8 p.
BALLER, FREDERICK WILLIAM, 1852-1922. Mandarin primer, character an-
    alysis. Shanghai, China Inland Mission, 1926. 26 p.
BARRETT, DAVID DEAN, 1892-    A primer in the writing of Chinese charac-
    ters. 2d ed.,rev. Shanghai, Kelly and Walsh, 1936. [v]-xi, 98 p. 1st ed.
    1934.
BLAKNEY, RAYMOND BERNARD. A course in the analysis of Chinese charac-
    ters. Shanghai, Commercial Press, 1935 (c1926). vi, 384 p. front.
──────. The same. Peiping, College of Chinese Studies, 1948. 131 p.
CHANG, CHUNG-YUAN, 張鍾元, 1907-    A study of the relative merits of the
    vertical and horizontal lines in reading Chinese print. New York, 1942. 64 p.
    incl. tables, diagrs. (Archives of psychology. No.276 ). Thesis-Columbia
    University.
CHIANG, YEE, 蔣彝, 1903-    Some Chinese words to be learnt without a teach-
    er. [London, British United Aid to China, 1945] [36] p.
CHIANG, KER CHIU, 蔣克秋. How to write the Chinese characters listed in
    Mandarin made easy (the first ten lessons) [Singapore? 194-?] cover-title,
    28 p. illus.
CLEFS ou racines des caractères chinois. Cholon, Impr. My-khouan, 1943.
    28 p.
CREEL, HERRLEE GLESSNER, 1905-    Chinese writing. Washington, D. C.,
    American Council on Education, 1943. iv, 16 p. ([American council on edu-
    cation. Committee on Asiatic studies in American education] Asiatic studies
    in American education, 2 ).
DUN, FWU TARNG, 敦福堂. Aktualgenetische Untersuchung des Auffassungs-
    vorganges chinesischer Schriftzeichen. Leipzig, Akademie Verlagsgesell-
    schaft, 1939. [43] p. plate. Diss.-Univ. Jena.
FORKE, ALFRED, 1867-1944. Der Ursprung der Chinesen auf Grund ihrer alten
    Bilderschrift. Hamburg, L. Friederichsen, 1925. 31 p.
GILBERT, FRIEDRICH ROBERT. Die Bilderschrift von China und Japan als in-
    ternationale Weltschrift und ihre schnelle Erlernung nach der mebiwegal-

Methode. Berlin, New York, O. G. Zehrfeld, 1924. 47, [1] p.
——. Das ABC der Chinaschrift. [Ausgabe mit Begründung der Methode auf Seite 18a bis 18n] Berlin, Verlag von O. G. Zehrfeld, A-G, 1926. [106] p. tables.

GILLIS, IRVIN VAN GORDER, 1875-1948. The characters ch'ao and hsi. Peiping [Standard Press] 1931. 44 numb. l.

HACKMANN, HEINRICH FRIEDRICH, 1864-1935. Der Zusammenhang zwischen Schrift und Kultur in China. München, E. Reinhardt, 1928. 88 p. illus.

HATTORI, UNOKICHI, 1867- On the convenience and inconvenience of Chinese characters. Tokyo, Japan Council of the Institute of Pacific Relation, 1931. 18 p.

HOANG, KYUAN-CHENG, 黃涓生. Origine et évolution de l'écriture hiéroglyphique et de l'écriture chinoise. Nouv. éd. Paris, P. Geuthner, 1939. 95 p. (Université de Lyon. Étude et documents publiés par l'Institut franco-chinois de Lyon, 1). 1er éd., Lyon, 1926.

HUBRECHT, ALPHONSE. Étymologie des caractères chinois. Pékin, Impr. des Lazaristes, 1932. viii, 406 p.

JOBEZ, ROBERT. L'expertise en écriture des documents chinois. Tientsin, Hautes études; Paris, Recueil Sirey; [etc., etc.] 1940. 86 p. illus. (incl. facsims.) diagrs. (Le Droit chinois moderne, 6) 1er éd. 1930. 42 p.

JONES, J. IRA. 6000 Chinese characters with Japanese pronunciation and Japanese and English renderings, by J. Ira Jones and H. V. S. Peeke. [3d ed.] Tōkyō, Kyōbun kwan [1925] xix, 223 p.

KALFF, LAMBERT. Einführung in die chinesischen Schriftzeichen. Kaldenkirchen, Rhld., Steyler, 1954. 80 p.

KUNZE, RICHARD, 1873- Bau und Anordnung der chinesischen Zeichen; oder: Wie lernen wir leichter Zeichen lesen? Tôkyô, Deutsche Gesellschaft für Natur- und Völkerkunde Ostasiens, 1937. 47 p. ("Mitteilungen" der Deutschen gesellschaft für natur- und völkerkunde Ostasiens. bd. XXX, t. A [i. e. B] ).

LUC, KYNH, 盧謹, [Lu Chin]. An easy modern script for Chinese of all dialects taught in forty-five lessons. The teacher's book. Hong Kong, Nazareth Press, 1946. xii, 36 p.

MESTRE, ED. Quelques résultats d'une comparaison entre les caractères chinois modernes et les siao tchouan, 小篆. Paris, E. Leroux, 1925. 75 p. (Bibliothèque de l'École des hautes études. Sciences religieuses. 40. v.).

PURCELL, VICTOR WILLIAM WILLIAMS SAUNDERS, 1896- An index to the Chinese written language on a new non-radical system, with references to the dictionaries of Kanghi and Giles. Singapore, Printed at the Government Print. Off. by W. T. Cherry, government printer, 1929. xxiii, 419 p.

QUONG, ROSE, 鄺如絲, [Kuang Ju-ssŭ]. Chinese wit, wisdom and written characters. [New York] Pantheon Books [1944] [72] p.

SIMON, WALTER, 1893- The new official Chinese Latin script, gwoyeu romatzyh; tables, rules, illustrative examples. London, A. Probsthain, 1942. 63 p.

——. How to study and write Chinese characters; Chinese radicals and phonetics, with an analysis of the 1200 Chinese basic characters. London, Lund, Humphries, 1944. xliv, 405 p.

——. 1200 Chinese basic characters; an elementary text book adapted from the 'Thousand character lessons.' With a foreword by Wang Yun-wu. 2d rev. ed. London, Lund, Humphries, 1947; 3d rev. ed. 1957. xvi, 334 p. 1st ed. 1944.

TAI, T'UNG, 戴侗, 13th cent. The six scripts, 六書故; or, The principles of Chinese writing. A translation by L. C. Hopkins. With a memoir of the translator by W. Perceval Yetts. Cambridge, [Eng.] University Press, 1954. xxvii, 84 p. port., facsim.

TCHANG, TCHENG-MING, 張正明, [Chang Chêng-ming]. L'écriture chinoise et le geste humain, essai sur la formation de l'écriture chinoise. Changhai, Impr. et librairie de T'ou-sè-wè, Zi-ka-wei; Paris, P. Geuthner [1937]

205, [1] p. (Variétés sinologiques, 64 ). Thèse-Univ. de Paris.

TIPSON, ERNEST. Complete Chinese character course (graded) Kowloon, Hong Kong, Chinese Christian Literature Movement [pref. 1948] 158 p.

TU, HORACE TSOU CHOW, 杜佐周. The effects of different arrangements of the Chinese language upon speed and comprehension of silent reading; from the Psychological laboratories of the University of Iowa. [Worcester, Mass., 1930] p. 321-337. illus. Thesis-University of Iowa. Reprinted from Pedagogical Seminary and Journal of Genetic Psychology, 1930, 38.

U.S. Army. Forces in the Far East. List of the 1400 most frequently used Chinese characters. [n.p., 1st Radio Broadcasting and Leaflet Group, United States Army Forces, Far East, 195-] 48 p.

U. S. Army Language School, Monterey, Calif. Index of character in Chinese conversation. Presidio of Monterey, 1951. 12 p.

――――. Index to Chinese-Japanese character cards. Presidio of Monterey [195-?] [16] p.

――――. Practical exercise (character text) [Monterey] Army Language School, Far Eastern Division, Chinese-Cantonese Language Dept. [1952] 51 l.

VACCARI, ORESTE. Pictorial Chinese-Japanese characters, a new and fascinating method to learn ideographs, by Oreste Vaccari and Enko Elisa Vaccari. Tokyo, O. Vaccari; sold by the publisher and Brentano's New York [1950] xxxi, 264 p.

WAN, GRACE, 萬榮芳, [Wan Jung-fang]. Most commonly used Chinese characters and how to find them in dictionaries without using radicals [by] Grace Wan [and] Tao-tai Hsia, 夏道泰. New Haven, Institute of Far Eastern Languages, Yale University, 1957. 73 p. (Mirror series A, 22 ).

WHITAKER, KATHERINE POE KAN, 1912- 1200 Chinese basic characters; an adaptation for students of Cantonese of W. Simon's National Language version. With an introd. by W. Simon. London, Lund Humphries, 1953. xlii, 316 p.

WIESE, KURT, 1887- You can write Chinese. New York, Viking Press, 1945. [64] p. illus.(part col.).

WILDER, GEORGE DURAND, 1869-1946. Analysis of Chinese characters [by] G.D. Wilder and J.H. Ingram. [Peking] North China Union Language School, 1922. 2nd ed. 1934. xi, 364 p.

YEN, SUNG-PU, 閻松圃. The missionary's manual of Chinese penmanship, prepared by Yen Sung-pu and Harold A. Weller. Shanghai, China Inland Mission, 1937. 89, xvi p.

YEN, Y.C. JAMES, 晏陽初, 1894- 1000 Chinese foundation characters, by Y. C. James Yen and Daniel C. Fu, 傅智. [Toronto] School of Chinese Studies, University of Toronto, 1943-44. 4 v. illus.


## Conversation

ALDRICH, HARRY STARKEY, 1895- Hua yü hsü chih, 華語須知. Practical Chinese, including a topical dictionary of 5000 everyday terms, with a foreword by Nelson Trusler Johnson. Peiping, H. Vetch, 1931. 2 v.

――――. The same. American ed. New Haven, Dept. of Oriental Studies, Yale University, 1942. 2 v.

ANNAND, A.S. Every-day commercial Chinese as spoken in North China [Chinese text by Fan Chih-hsüeh, 樊志學] [Tientsin, 1926?] [1], 80 p.

BRANDT, ÎAKOV, 1869-1944. Introduction to spoken Chinese, 華言拾級 . Peking, Henri Vetch, 1940. xvii, [1], 240, 130 p.

――――. The same. New Haven, Pub. for the Dept. of Oriental Studies by Yale University Press; London, H.Milford, Oxford University Press, 1944. [v]-xvii, 240, 130 p.

――――. The same. Reprint ed. 1954. iv, 504 p.

CHAN, SHAU WING, 陳受榮, [Ch'en Shou-jung] 1906- Elementary Chinese, with romanization and exercises in speaking and writing. Stanford, Stanford

University Press [1951] xxxi, 468 p.

CHAO, TÊ-CHIEH, 趙德潔. Chinese conversation in the national language. London, Lund, Humphries, 1947. vii, 121 p.

CHIANG, KER-CHIU, 蔣克秋, [Chiang K'o-ch'iu]. Mandarin made easy, with pronunciation in Hokkien and Cantonese. 國語易解附閩粤譯音. 7th ed. Syonan, Chin Fen book store [1940] 2 v.

————. An advanced course in Mandarin, specially preared for students in the Cambridge classes. Singapore, The Chin Fen Book-store [1940?]-46. 2 v.

DARROCH, JOHN, 1865-  Chinese self-taught by the natural method. With phonetic pronunciation. Thimm's system. Philadelphia, David McKay [1944] vi, 154 p. (Marlborough's self-taught series [of European and Oriental languages]).

DAVID-BEY, MELIK S. La langue chinoise en 30 leçons suivie d'un manuel de conversation. Paris, Albin Michel, s.d. 115 p.

EASTLAKE, F. WARRINGTON. An Anglo-Chinese conversational dictionary, 華英會話文件辭典, rev. ed. for study and reference by F. Warrington Eastlake, ed. and tr. by P.S. Yie, 奚若. 12th ed. Shanghai, Commercial Press, 1921. 510 p.

DE FRANCIS, JOHN FRANCIS, 1911-  Beginning Chinese, by John De Francis, edited by Henry C. Fenn [and] George A. Kennedy. New Haven, Yale University Press, 1946. [vii]-ix, [1], 197 p. illus. (diagr.) (Yale linguistic series).

GILES, HERBERT ALLEN, 1845-1935. Chinese without a teacher, being a collection of easy and useful sentences in the Mandarin dialect, with a vocabulary. 10th ed. Shanghai, Kelly and Walsh, 1939. ii, 89, [1] p. 1st ed. 1872.

HARTWELL, GERALDINE L. English-Chinese conversation book for nurses, with list of terms and chart forms. [Shanghai] Kwang Hsueh Pub. House, 1948. 173 p.

[HOCKETT, CHARLES FRANCIS] 1916-  Spoken Chinese, basic course. [Madison, Wis.] Pub. for the United States Armed Forces Institute by the Linguistic Society of America and the Intensive language program, American Council of Learned Societies [1944-45] 2 v. ([U.S.] War dept. Education manual EM 506-507).

————. The same; by Charles F. Hockett and Chaoying Fang, 房兆楹. [Baltimore, Waverly Press, 1944-45] 2 v.

————. Guide's manual for Spoken Chinese, by Charles F. Hockett and Chaoying Fang. [New York] H. Holt [1945] 231 p. "Photo-lithoprint reproduction."

HUANG, LI-CH'ING. English and Chinese dialogues. 29th ed. Hong Kong, Empire Printing Co., 1938. 349 p.

KING, HARRY WILLIAM, 1893-  King's English-Chinese dictionary and phrase book (self pronouncing) Dallas, The Story Book Press [1944] 154 p.

————. "Chinese made easy" [Mandarin] A correspondence course. [Dallas] c1945. 100 l.

————. King's Way to say it in conversational Chinese (Mandarin) Dallas, King Publications [1944] 100 p.

LEE, WILLIAM POY, 李培, 1896-  A primer in Mandarin Chinese. [New York? 1948] c1949. 108 l.

LEI, WAI-HING, 李蕙馨. Chop suey; a mixture of the Chinese language, customs and culture, by Lei Wai-hing, Lei Wai-tsuen, 李蕙荃, Lin Shih-nge, 林士尊, [and] Gladys L. Smith. Boston, Mass. [Printed by John Worley company, c1940] [1], 5-158 (i.e. 159), [2] p. illus.

McHUGH, JAMES MARSHALL, 1899-  Introductory Mandarin lessons; or, Hua yü hsin chieh ching, 華語新捷徑. Shanghai, Kelly and Walsh, 1931. iii-xix, 251 p.

MATEER, CALVIN WILSON, 1836-1908. A course of mandarin lessons, based on idiom. 2d revised ed. 1906. Shanghai, Presbyterian Mission Press, 1922. iv, 3, 786 p. col. front.(fold. chart) 1st ed. 1892.

MICHIGAN. UNIVERSITY. English Language Institute. Mandarin Chinese for

English speakers; an oral approach, by Charles C. Fries and Yao Shen,优逹.
[Ann Arbor] 1950-        4 v. diagrs.

NUYTS, JOSEPH, 1898-   Le savoir-vivre en Chine. Peiping, 1946. vi, 138 p.
illus. (Scheut editions. Ser. 2: Practical mission life, v. 1 ).

PEKING. CALIFORNIA COLLEGE IN CHINA. Hua-wen-ch'u-chieh, 華文初階.
Chinese language lessons; Wade-Giles romanized translation for use with Chinese language records. Berkeley, California College in China [1948] 47 p.
1st ed. 1943, 312 p.

PHILIPPINE ISLANDS. Bureau of Internal Revenue. Manual of Chinese lessons.
Given to students of the Bureau of internal revenue at Manila by Juan Menca-
rini, instructor in Chinese. Manila, Bureau of Printing, 1928. 29 p.

RATAY, JOHN P., 1893-   Current Chinese; or, Shih yung hsin chung hua yü,
適用新中華語. Shanghai, Kelly and Walsh, 1927; London, K. Paul [1928]
2 v.

READ, BERNARD EMMS, 1887-1949. Hospital dialogue; English-Chinese sentences in dialogue for use by foreign practitioners in North China, with an
outline of Chinese medical history and English bibliography. 2d ed. Peking,
French Bookstore [1930] [1], 79 p.

SIMON, WALTER, 1893-   Chinese sentence series, first fifty lessons (with two
bibliographical appendices) by W. Simon and C.H. Lu, 陸建助. London, A.
Probsthain, 1942-44. 3 v.

————. Structure drill in Chinese. First fifty patterns by W. Simon and T.C.
Chao, 趙德潔. London, L. Humphries, 1945. x, 101 p. (Structure drill
through speech patterns, edited by B. Schindler and W. Simon. 1 ).

SUNG, YU-FENG, 宋育風. Chinese in 30 lessons, by Yu Feng Sung and Robert
Black. [Hollywood, Calif.] The Marcel Rodd Co., 1944. 126 p. incl. front.,
illus.(facsims.) Reproduced from type-written and manuscript copy.

SWADESH, MORRIS, 1909-   Chinese in your pocket. New York, H. Holt [1948]
xvi, 158 p. illus., maps.

TCHEN, YON-SUN, 陳榮生, [Ch'en Jung-shêng]. Je parle chinois. Paris, Adrien-Maisonneuve, 1945. 203 p.

TÊNG, SSŬ-YÜ, 鄧嗣禹 1906-   Conversational Chinese, with grammatical
notes; prepared by Têng Ssŭ-yü, assisted by Chao Ching-hui, 趙景暉, [and
others] Chicago, Univ. of Chicago Press [1947] ix, 441 p.

TEWKSBURY, MALCOLM GARDNER. Speak Chinese. New Haven, Pub. for the
Institute of Far Eastern Languages by Yale Univ. Press, 1948. xvi, 189 p.
(Mirror series A, 1 ).

U.S. Army Language School, Monterey, Calif. Practical exercises. Prepared
by Chinese-Mandarin Language Dept. Presidio of Monterey, 1951-   122 p.

USOV, SERGEĬ NĬKOLAEVĬCH, 1891-   A course of colloquial Chinese, 華語入
門. English edition, adapted from the sixth Russian edition of Kitaiskii raz-
gavornii yazik, in collaboration with C. Tyrwhitt. (Provisional issue) Peking,
H. Vetch, 1937-   2 v.

WANG, FANG-YÜ, 王方宇, 1913-   Chinese dialogues; edited by Henry C. Fenn
and Pao-ch'en Lee, 李抱辰. New Haven, Institute of Far Eastern Languages,
Yale University, 1953. vi, 385 p. (Mirror series A, 5 ).

WOOCHEFEE UNIVERSITY. Institute of Chinese Education. Everyday spoken
Chinese, compiled and published by the Institute of Chinese Education, Woochefee University. New York, 1945. 87 p.

## Readers

BALLER, FREDERICK WILLIAM, 1852-1922. An idiom a lesson; a short course
in elementary Chinese. 8th impression. Prepared for the China Inland Mission. London, Philadelphia, Morgan and Scott; Shanghai, China Inland Mission, 1934. ii, 106 p.

BRANDT, ĬAKOV, 1869-1944. Modern newspaper Chinese; progressive readings with vocabularies, notes and translations. 2d ed. Peking, H. Vetch, 1939. xii, 321 p. 1st ed. 1935.

BRUCE, JOSEPH PERCY, 1861-1934. Chinese, by J. Percy Bruce, E. Dora Edwards, [and] C.C. Shu, 舒慶春. Spoken by C.C. Shu. With phonetic transcription in the alphabet of the International Phonetic Association. 3d ed. London, Linguaphone Institute [193-?] 2 v. (Linguaphone oriental language courses).

BULLOCK, THOMAS LOWNDES, 1845-1915. Progressive exercises in the Chinese written language. 3d ed., rev. by H.A. Giles. Shanghai, Kelly and Walsh, 1923; London, Crosby Lockwood, 1923. 295, [1] p.

CHAN, SHAU-WING, 陳受榮, [Ch'en Shou-jung] 1906- Chinese reader for beginners, with exercises in writing and speaking, 中國國語入門. Stanford University, Calif., Stanford University Press; London, H. Milford, Oxford University Press [1942] v-xxvi, 348 p.

CHANG, TSÊ-CHIH, 張則之, comp. and tr. Practical Chinese with English translation, compiled and translated by Kinchen Johnson [pseud.] Peiping, Science Association, 1936. 1 v. (various pagings).

CHIANG, KER CHIU, 蔣克秋. Progressive Mandarin readers for internediate students, with vocabulary, 國語進階. Rev. ed. Singapore, Chung Hwa Mandarin Institution, 1940- 33 p.

CHIH, YÜ-JU, 郅玉汝, 1917- Selections from Chinese newspaper. New Haven, Institute of Far Eastern Languages, Yale University, 1953. 113 p. (Mirror series A, 12).

————. A primer of newspaper Chinese. New Haven, Institute of Far Eastern Languages, Yale University, 1956. 219 p. (Mirror series A., 12).

CREEL, HERRLEE GLESSNER, 1905- ed. Literary Chinese by the inductive method, prepared by Herrlee Glessner Creel, editor, Chang Tsung-Ch'ien, 張宗騫, [and] Richard C. Rudolph. Chicago, University of Chicago Press [1938-52] 3 v.

————. ed. Newspaper Chinese by the inductive method, edited by Herrlee Glessner Creel, Têng Ssŭ-yü, assisted by Josiah Whitney Bennett [and others] Chicago, University of Chicago Press [1943] viii, 265 p.

————. The same. Translations of text selections and exercises in Newspaper Chinese by the inductive method, prepared by Herrlee Glessner Creel and Têng Ssŭ-yü, assisted by Chou Nien-tz'ŭ, 周念慈. Chicago, University of Chicago Press [1943] vi, 56 p.

HAENISCH, ERICH, 1880- ed. Lehrgang der klassischen chinesischen Schriftsprache. 4. Aufl. Leipzig, O. Harrassowitz, 1953-56. 4 v. 1. Aufl. 1929.

HUANG, TZŬ-TAN. One hundred reading and conversational lessons in Mandarin, with English notes. Singapore, 1946-48. 4 pts.

[KENNEDY, GEORGE ALEXANDER] 1901- Chinese reading for beginners. [New Haven] Dept. of Oriental Studies, Yale University, 1939. [1], 24, 34 p.

————. The same. Key to Chinese reading for beginners. [New Haven] Dept. of Oriental Studies, Yale University, 1939. 44 p.

————. The same. [New Haven] Dept of Oriental Studies, Yale University, 1939 [i.e. 1942] 32, [1], 23 p. ([Yale University. Dept. of Oriental Studies] Mirror ser. A, 5).

————. Simple Chinese stories. [New Haven] Dept. of Oriental Studies, Yale University [1942] 40, 36 p. ([Yale University. Dept. of Oriental Studies] Mirror ser. A, 6).

————. ed. Stories from ancient China, ed. by Mary Rouse and George A. Kennedy. New Haven, Pub. for the Institute of Far Eastern Languages by Yale Univ. Press, 1949. x, 44 p.; 56 p. ([Yale University. Dept. of Oriental Studies] Mirror series A, 7).

LAMASSE, H. Sin kouo wen, 新國文; ou, nouveau manuel de langue chinois écrite, traduit et expliqué en français et romanisé selon les principaux dialectes, avec un appendice. 2e éd. Hong Kong, Impr. de la Société des missions-étrangères, 1922. 2 v.

LEE, PAO-CH'ÊN, 李抱辰, 1907-   Read about China. New Haven, Institute of Far Eastern Languages, Yale University, 1953. iv, 77 p.; 125 p. (Mirror series A, 16 ).

LEUNG, LOUIS LUEN, 梁鑾, 1887-   Introduction to Chinese language and culture. Book I. [Los Angeles] Mimeographed by the Los Angeles City College Mimeographing Dept., c1950-   93 p.

LEVY, HOWARD S. ed. Selections of modern Chinese literature. [Denver, 1954] unpaged.

LI, CHEN-CH'ING T.H., 李振青. Practical Chinese lessons; first book. Rev. ed. n.p., 1928. 101 p.

MENDELSON, MRS. ANNE. An improved method of learning Chinese, by Anne Mendelson and Chin Tzu-chi, 金子齊. [Tientsin, Printed by the Chihli Press, 1937] [iii]-vii, 180 p.

MORGAN, EVAN, 1860-   The new Chinese speaker; readings in modern Mandarin, 新官話彙編. 2d ed. Shanghai, Kelly and Walsh, 1933. 305 p.

ROESSLEIN, CHARLES GEORGE, 1910-   Fu Jen reader. Peking, Catholic University [1940] 394, iv p.

SAN TZŬ CHING, 三字經. The three character classic (composed by Wang Po Hou, 王伯厚, during the Sung dynasty, A.D. 960) English translation with notes, romanized into Mandarin, Cantonese and Hokkien by Chiang Ker Chiu, 蔣克秋. [Singapore, Chung Hwa Mandarin Institution, 1941] cover-title, 36 p.

SHA, CHIH-P'EI, 沙志培, 1903-   A Chinese first reader. Berkeley, University of California Press, 1938. xii, 36, iii, [1], 186 p. [University of California syllabus series, 262]. 1st ed. 1937.

SIMON, WALTER, 1893-   Chinese national language (Gwoyeu) reader and guide to conversation, by W. Simon and C.H. Lu, 陸建勳. 2d rev.ed. London, Lund, Humphries, 1954. 195 p. illus. 1st ed. 1943.

SOMMER, FRANCIS ERICH, 1890-   Reading Chinese, step by step. New York, Frederick Ungar Pub. Co. [1943] 28 p.

―――. The same. Synopsis of written Japanese in seven lessons, with exercises. A supplement. New York, Frederick Ungar Pub. Co. [1944] 23, [1] p.

TRITTEL, WALTER, 1880-   ed. Auswahl moderner chinesischer Prosastücke, von W. Trittel und M. G. Pernitzsch. Berlin und Leipzig, W. de Gruyter, 1936. 1, 404, iii p. (Lehrbuch der Ausland-Hochschule an der Universität Berlin, Bd. 38 ).

―――. Wörterbuch zur Auswahl moderner chinesischer Prosastücke, von W. Trittel und M.G. Pernitzsch. Leipzig, O. Harrassowitz, 1942. 245 p. (Sprachenkundliche Lehr- und Wörterbücher, Bd. 41 ).

U.S. Army Language School, Monterey, Calif. Newspaper Chinese. Prepared by Chinese-Mandarin Language Dept. Presidio of Monterey, 1954. 2 v.

―――. Màn tán jūng gwó. Read about China. Text. Presidio of Monterey, Chinese-Mandarin Language Dept., Army Language School, 1955. 78 p.

―――. All in the same boat (Túng jōu gùng jì). Rev. Presidio of Monterey, Calif., Chinese Mandarin Language Dept., Army Language School, 1956. 2 v.

VISSIÈRE, ARNOLD JACQUES ANTOINE, 1858-1930. Recueil de textes chinois à l'usage des élèves de l'École Nationale des Langues Orientales vivantes, Supplement No. 1. Glückstadt et Hambourg, J.J.Augustin, 1922. 16 p.

WANG, CHI-CHEN, 王際真, 1899-   ed. Readings in modern Chinese. New York, Columbia University Press, 1944. viii, [1], 219 p.

―――. ed. Readings in traditional Chinese. New York, Columbia University Press [1944] xiv, [1], 243 p.

―――. ed. Current Chinese readings. New York, Bookman Associates, 1950. 230 p.

WANG, FANG-YÜ, 王方宇, 1913-   Read Chinese, a beginning text in the Chinese character. New Haven, Institute of Far Eastern Languages, Yale University, 1952. 203 p. (Mirror series A, 4 ).

YANG, LIEN-SHÊNG, 楊聯陞, 1914-   Selected Chinese texts in the classical and colloquial styles. Cambridge, Mass., Published for the Harvard-Yenching Institute, Harvard University Press, 1953. xviii, 192 p.

## Phonetics and Romanization

BOUILLARD, GEORGES, 1862-1930. Essai sur une romanisation unique des sons de la langue chinoise. Pékin, n.d. [50] p.

CHAO, YUEN-REN, 趙元任, 1892-   An equivalent table between the national romanization and the Wade system. Peiping, Society for the Unification of the National Language, 1930. 35 p.

DREHER, JOHN JAMES, 1920-   A comparison of native and acquired language intonation. Ann Arbor, University Microfilms, 1950 [i.e. 1951] ([University Microfilms, Ann Arbor, Mich.] Publication no. 2396). Collation of the original: vii, 220 l. diagrs., tables. Thesis-University of Michigan.

HOCKETT, CHARLES FRANCIS, 1916-   Progressive exercises in Chinese pronunciation. New Haven, Institute of Far Eastern Languages, Yale University, 1951. 57 p. (Mirror series A, 2 ).

HOPE, EARL R. Linguistic psychology and the Romanization of Chinese. Pt.1: General survey of the problem. Ottawa, 1951-   121 p.

———. Karlgren's glottal stop initial in ancient Chinese, with particular reference to the hPhags-pa alphabet and to certain points of linguistic psychology. Ottawa, 1953. xii, 88 p.

JASMIN, ERNEST. The Chinese national language, taught in fifty lessons by means of a new alphabetical script. Hong Kong, Nazareth Press, 1946. 32 p.

JOU, BIENMING, 周辨明, [Chou Pien-ming] 1891-   Phonetic structure and tone behavior in Hagu (commonly known as the Amoy dialect) and their relation to certain questions in Chinese linguistics. Hamburg, 1930. 40 p.

———. A Quoyu pronouncing dictionary and cipher code. Amoy, Department of Linguistics, University of Amoy, 1937. 204 p.

———. Internationalizing the Chinese script: progress in quoyu romanization 1937-45. Amoy, College of Arts, National University of Amoy, 1945. 32, 11, 44, 11, 4 p.

KARLGREN, BERNHARD, 1889-   Études sur la phonologie chinoise. [Upsala, K.W. Appelberg]; Leyde, E.-J. Brill, 1915-26. Reprint ed. Peking, 1941. 898 p. illus., diagr. (Archives d'études orientales, pub. par J.-A. Lundell. v. 15).

———. The romanization of Chinese, a paper read before the China Society on Jan. 19, 1928. London, China Society, 1928. 24 p.

———. Grammata serica; script and phonetics in Chinese and Sino-Japanese. Stockholm [Gothenburg, Printed by Elanders boktryckeri a.-b.] 1940. 471 p. "Reprinted from: The Bulletin of the Museum of Far Eastern antiquities. No. 12."

———. Compendium of phonetics in ancient and archaic Chinese. London, Kegan Paul, 1954. 156 p.

———. Grammata serica recensa. Stockholm, 1957. 332 p. (BMFEA, 29, pt. 1).

LI CHIN-SHI, 黎錦西, 1890-   Chinese phonetic system and language (English translation) Tr. into English by Alex R. Mackenzie. 2d ed. Shanghai, Commercial Press, 1922. ii, 56, ii, ii, ii p. illus.

LIU, FU, 劉復, 1891-1934. Étude expérimentale sur les tons du chinois. Paris, Société d'édition "Les Belles lettres," 1925. viii, 121 p. illus., fold. tab., fold. diagrs. and atlas of XXVIII fold. plates on 14 l. (Collection de l'Institut de phonétique et des Archives de la parole, fasc. I ).

MARTIN, SAMUEL ELMO, 1924-   The phonemes of ancient Chinese. New Haven, American Oriental Society, 1953. 46 p. (Supplement to the Journal of the American Oriental Society, 16 ).

MERGENTHALER LINOTYPE COMPANY. China's national phonetic syllabary;
    or, Chu yin tzǔ-mu, 注音字母 . How it has been adapted to the linotype by
    the Mergenthaler linotype company. Brooklyn, N.Y. [1921] folder (7 numb.
    l. ).

MULLIE, JOSEPH, 1886-   Notions élémentaires de phonétique [chinoises] et
    alphabet général. Changhai, La presse orientale, 1922. vii, 119, 2 p. illus.
    tables.

PEOPLE'S CHINA. Draft scheme for a Chinese phonetic alphabet simplifying
    Chinese characters. Peking, 1956. 16 p.

ROSTHORN, ARTHUR VON, 1862-1945. Indischer Einfluss in der Lautlehre Chi-
    nas. Wien, Hölder-Pichler-Tempsky, 1941. 22 p. (Akademie der Wissen-
    schaften in Wien. Phil.-Hist. Kl. Sitzungsberichte, 219. Bd., 4. Abhandlung).

――――. Studien zur chinesischen Lautgeschichte. Wien, Hölder-Pichler-Temp-
    sky, 1942. 62 p. (Akademie der Wissenschaften in Wien. Phil.-Hist. Kl. Sitz-
    ungsberichte, 220. Bd., 1. Abhandlung).

RUSSELL, C. F. Rime store, 韻府 , (You Fer). Los Angeles, Reed Litho., 1954.
    48 p.

U.S. Army Language School, Monterey, Calif. Progressive exercises in Chinese
    pronunciation. Presidio of Monterey, Chinese-Mandarin Language Dept.[1952]
    66 p.

――――. Romanization list. [Presidio of Monterey] Army Language School, Chi-
    nese-Mandarin Dept., 1953. 16 p. 1st ed. 1951.

U.S. Army Map Service. Key to Wade-Giles romanization of Chinese characters,
    November 1944. Washington, D.C., War dept., Army Map Service, Corps
    of Engineers, U.S. Army [1944] 48 numb. l., 90, 8 p.

――――. Geographic Names Branch. Guide to special readings of Chinese charac-
    ters, for the use of place-name romanizers, prepared by the Orientalia Sec-
    tion, Geographic Names Branch, Army Map Service. [Washington, 194-?]
    cover-title, [21] l.

WANG, LI, 王力, 1901-   Une prononciation chinois de Po-Pei, 博白 , (pro-
    vince de Kouangsi) étudiée à l'aide de la phonétique expérimentale. Paris,
    E. Leroux, 1932. xii, 158 p. illus. map.

## Grammar

BALLER, FREDERICK WILLIAM, 1852-1922. A Mandarin primer. 14th ed.,
    rev. and enl. with supplement. Prepared for the China Inland Mission. Shang-
    hai, China Inland Mission; London, Philadelphia [etc.] Morgan and Scott, 1926.
    iv, [2], v-xxxviii, 462 (i.e. 522) p.

BRANDT, ĨAKOV, 1869-1944. Introduction to literary Chinese. Peking, North
    China Union Language School, 1927. 503, [1] p.

――――. The same. New York, Frederick Ungar Pub. Co. [1944?] 503, [1] p.

――――. Wenli particles, with a foreword by Hardy Jowett. Peiping, North China
    Union Language School, 1929. vii, 172 p.

BROUNER, WALTER BROOKS, 1869-   Chinese made easy, by Walter Brooks
    Brouner and Fung Yuet Mow, 馮悅茂 . With an introduction by Herbert A.
    Giles. Leiden, E.J. Brill, 1935. xiv, [2], 351 p. 1st ed. 1904.

CH'ÊN, THEODORE HSI-EN, 陳錫恩, 1902-   Elementary Chinese reader and
    grammar, by Theodore Hsi-En Chen and Wen-Hui Chung Chen, 陳鍾文會 ·
    South Pasadena, P.D. and Ione Perkins, 1945. ix, 209 p.

DARROCH, JOHN. Chinese grammar self-taught. London, E. Marlborough
    [1936] 156 p. (Marlborough's self-taught series [of European and Oriental
    languages]).

GABELENTZ, GEORG VON DER, 1840-93. Chinesische Grammatik, mit Aus-
    schluss des niederen Stiles und der heutigen Umgangssprache. [2. unveränder-
    te Aufl.] Berlin, Deutscher Verlag der Wissenschaften, 1953. xxvii, 549 p.

1st ed., 1881; Reprint ed., 1944.

———. The same. Nachtrag. [Bearb. von] Eduard Erkes. Berlin, Deutsche Verlag der Wissenschaften, 1956. 101 p.

———. Anfangsgründe der chinesischen Grammatik, mit Übungsstücken. New York, F. Ungar [1954] 150 p.

GILES, HERBERT ALLEN, 1845-1935. How to begin Chinese. The hundred best characters. Shanghai, Kelly and Walsh, 1925. vi, 72 p.

———. The same. The second hundred best characters. 2d ed. Shanghai, Kelly and Walsh, 1925. [v]-vi, 35, [1] p.

———. Short cuts to Chinese, including the two hundred best characters. New York, Padell Book Co., 1943. [144] p.

HAAG, KARL. Der Ausdruck der Denkordnung im Chinesischen. Heidelberg, C. Winter, 1940. 25 p.

KAO, MING-K'AI, 高名凱. Essai sur la valeur réelle des particules prépositionnelles en chinois. Paris, L. Rodstein, 1940. [7]-240 p. Thèse-Univ. de Paris.

LESSING, FERDINAND, 1882-   Vergleich der wichtigsten Formwörter der chinesischen Umgangssprache und der Schriftsprache. Ein Versuch. [Berlin, Reichsdruckerei, 1925] 58-138 p. (Mitteilungen des Seminars für orientalische sprachen zu Berlin, jahrg. XXVIII, abt. I: Ostasiatische studien. Sonderabdruck.).

MARGOULIÈS, GEORGES, 1907-   Petit précis de grammaire chinoise écrite. Paris, A. Maisonneuve, 1934. 64 p.

MATHEWS, ROBERT HENRY. Kuoyü primer; progressive studies in the Chinese national language. Shanghai, China Inland Mission, 1938. xlvi, 790 p.

MISCH, JOHANNES, 1909-   Der Konditionalsatz im klassischen Chinesisch. Berlin, 1935. 31 p. Diss.-Univ. Berlin.

MULLIE, JOSEPH, 1886-   The structural principles of the Chinese language, an introduction to the spoken language (Northern Pekingese dialect) Translated from the Flemish by A. Omer Versichel. Peiping, Bureau of Engraving and Printing, 1932-   3 v. (Anthropos; linguistische bibliothek. V-VII bd.).

———. Le mot-particule 之 tche. Leiden, E. J. Brill, 1942. vii, 237 p. Reprinted from T'oung Pao, v. 36, livr. 3-5.

SCHMITT, ERICH, 1893-   Einführung in das moderne Hochchinesisch, ein Lehrbuch für den Unterrichtsgebrauch und das Selbststudium nebst chinesischem Zeichenheft, von dr. Erich Schmitt und Lou Y†, 陸懿. Shanghai, M. Nössler, 1939. x, 117 p.

———. Chinesisches Zeichenheft zur Einführung in das moderne Hochchinesisch von dr. Erich Schmitt und dr. Lou Y†. Shanghai, M. Nössler und co., g. m. b. h., 1939. cover-title, 36 p.

SHADICK, HAROLD ERNEST, 1902-   Structural analysis of literary Chinese, by Harold E. Shadick and Hsin-min Wu, 吳新珉. Preliminary ed. Ithaca, Department of Far Eastern Languages and Division of Modern Languages, Cornell University, 1950. 129 p.

SIMON, WALTER, 1893-   Zur Rekonstruktion der altchinesischen Endkonsonanten. Partsl-II. Berlin, W. de Gruyter, 1927-28. [21], [30] p. (Berlin. Universität. Seminar für orientalische Sprachen. Mitteil. Bd. 30-31, Abt. 1).

TCHEN, TING-MING, 陳定民. Étude phonétique des particules de la langue chinoise. Préface de m. H. Maspero. Paris, Éditions Héraklès [1938] vi, 152 p. diagrs.

U.S. Army Language School, Monterey, Calif. Sentence drill, English for the Chinese-Mandarin language course. Presidio of Monterey [Chinese Language Dept.] 1951. 47 p.

———. Sentence patterns, English. [Monterey] Army Language School, Chinese-Mandarin Dept., 1953. 111 p.

WHYMANT, A. NEVILLE JOHN, 1894-   Colloquial Chinese (northern) London, Kegan Paul; New York, E. P. Dutton, 1922. v, [1], 106 p.

WIEGER, LÉON, 1856-1933. Chinois écrit. Précis. Grammaire. Phraséologie. 4e éd. [Sienhsien] 1929. 102 p.

YEN, ISABELLA YIYUN, 嚴倚雲, 1912- A grammatical analysis of Syàu Jīng. Ithaca, 1956. xi, 218 l. illus. Thesis-Cornell University.

ZACH, ERWIN VON, 1872-1942. Zum Ausbau der gabelentzschen Grammatik. Nebst v.d. Gabelentz' eigenen "Additions." Peking, Deutschland-Institut, 1944. 101 p.

## Dialects
### Peking and Northern

BRÖRING, THEODOR, 1883- Laut und Ton in Süd-Schantung. Mit Anhang: Die Töne in Nordostschantung, Peking, Sötshuän, Shanghai, Amoy und Canton. Hamburg, L. Friederichsen, 1927. 63 p. fold. map, diagrs. (Veröffentlichungen des Seminars für sprache und kultur Chinas an der hamburgischen Universität. nr. 2 ). 1. Aufl. 1924.

CHAO, YUEN-REN, 趙元任, 1892- A phonograph course in the Chinese national language. Shanghai, Commercial Press, 1925. xxii, 288 p.

―――. Mandarin primer, an intensive course in spoken Chinese. Cambridge, Harvard Univ. Press, 1948. viii, 336 p.

―――. The same. Character text for Mandarin primer. Cambridge, Harvard Univ. Press, 1948. 142 p.

DENIKER, GEORGE. Le mécanisme phonologique du parler de Pékin; précédé de deux notes sur les alphabets et sur les méthodes phonologiques. Pékin, A. Nachbaur, 1925. 75 p. plates, tables.

GASPERMENT, A. Étude de chinois, langue mandarin. 3e éd. Sienhsien, Impr. de la Mission catholique, 1925-26. 5 v. illus. fold. map, fold. table.

GERMAIN, ROBERT. Essai de description phonétique du dialecte de Pékin. Pékin, A. Nachbaur, 1923. 30 p.

GIET, FRANZ. Zur Tonität nordchinesischer Mundarten. Wien-Mödling, Verlag der Missionsdruckerei St. Gabriel, 1950. xx, 184 p. illus., maps (part col., 12 in pocket) (Studia Instituti Anthropos, v. 2 ).

JASMIN, ERNEST. L'étude du chinois par la romanisation interdialectique. Tours de phrases et grammaire selon le mandarin du nord, spécialement de Mandchourie. [Texte en caractères Chinois] Tientsin, Procure de la mission de Sienhsien, 1938. 2 v.

KERVYN, LOUIS MARIE. Clichés usuels de la langue mandarine. Tientsin, Scheut Mission, 1935. 387, 88, x p.

LAMASSE, H. Nouveau répertoire de la romanisation interdialectique. Hong Kong, Nazareth Press, 1951. 126 p.

LESSING, FERDINAND, 1882- Han yu t'ung shih. Lehrgang der nordchinesischen Umgangssprache. Bd. 1-11. Umschrift und Übersetzung von F. Lessing und W. Othmer. 2. Aufl. Schanghai, 1933. 160 p.

MITTLER, THEODOR, 1887- Chinesische Grammatik; Einführung in die Umgangssprache, mit besonderer Berücksichtigung der Shantungsprache, hrsg. von Theodor Mittler. Yenchowfu, Verlag der Katholischen Mission, 1927. xxxvii, 515 p.

OKAMOTO, M. A Chinese pronunciation dictionary in Peking dialect. 12th ed. Tokyo, Bunkyudo-Shoten, 1940. 244 p. 1st ed. 1902.

SYA, SYIN-KE, 夏心客 , [Hsia Hsin-k'o]. Mandarin in four weeks. 國語一月通 Taipei, Chi Ming Book Co. [1956] 3, xiv, 184, 43 p. fold. maps.

U. S. Army Language School, Monterey, Calif. Program of instruction for the Chinese-Mandarin language course; officer MOS 9330 and 9332; enlisted MOS 1267 and 1320; 30-OE-14. Presidio of Monterey, Chinese-Mandarin Language Dept., Army Language School, 1954. 24 p.

WANG, LIEN-TSENG, 王聯曾 . Recherches expérimentales sur les tons du pékinois. Amsterdam, 1937-38. 40, 48 p. (Archives néerlandaises de phonétique expérimentale, tome, 13 and 14 ).

WIEGER, LÉON, 1856-1933. Chinois parlé, manuel. Koan-hoa du nord, non-pé-
kinois. 4e éd. refondue. [Sienhsien, N. Vagner, S. J., 1936. [i. e. 1938] 1171 p.
1er ed., 1912.

YÜAN, YING-TS'AI, 袁英才. A guide to Mandarin, by Y. C. Yuen. Rev. ed.
Hong Kong, The author, printed by Caslon Printers, 1952. 50 (i. e. 100) p.

## Shanghai

HO, CHARLES. Shanghai dialect in 4 weeks, with map of Shanghai, by Charles
Ho [and] George Foe. Shanghai, Chi Ming Book Co., 1940. 102, 5, 9, 9 p.
illus., maps (part fold. col.).

McINTOSH, GILBERT. Conversations usuelles. Zi-ka-wei, Lithographie de
T'ou-sè-wè, 1921. 97 p.

———. Useful phrases in the Shanghai dialect, with index-vocabulary and other
helps. 5th ed. Shanghai, Presbyterian Mission Press, 1922. 121 p.

PARKER, R. A. Lessons in the Shanghai dialect. In romanized and character;
with key to pronunciation. [Shanghai? 1923?] iii, 221, 44 p. incl. fold. plates,
fold. forms.

POTT, F. L. HAWKS, 1864-1947. Leçons sur la dialecte de Changhai. Traduction et romanisation français par A. M. Bourgeois. Changhai, Impr. de la
mission catholique, 1939. 399 p. 1er éd., 1922.

U. S. Office of Strategic Services. Research and Analysis Branch. Notes on main
dialects of southeast China. [Washington] 1944. 4 l. fold. map. (Its R and A
no. 2478).

## Cantonese

BALL, JAMES DYER, 1847-1919. The Cantonese made easy: a book of simple
sentences in the Cantonese dialect, with free and literal translations, and
directions for the rendering of English grammatical forms in Chinese. 4th
ed. rev. and enl. Hong Kong, Kelly and Walsh, 1924. 1st ed. 1883.

———. Kelly and Walsh's English-Cantonese handbook. Containing common words
and phrases, printed without the Chinese characters, or tonic marks, the
sounds of the Chinese words being represented by an English spelling as far
as practicable. 6th ed. Shanghai, Kelly and Walsh, 1935. xi, 32 p. ''First
ed. 1886.''

CAYSAC, GEORGES. Introduction à l'étude du dialecte Cantonais. 2e éd. Hong
Kong, Catholic Truth Society, 1952 (c1926) iv, 348 p.

CHAN, YEUNG-KWONG, 陳陽光. Cantonese for beginners. Hong Kong, Man
Sang Printers, 1946. 71 p.

———. Everybody's Cantonese; combined progressive and beginner's course.
Hong Kong, Man Sang Printers, 1947. vii, 265 p.

CHAO, YUEN-REN, 趙元任, 1892- Cantonese primer. Cambridge, Pub. for
the Harvard-Yenching Institute, Harvard University Press; London, Oxford
University Press, 1947. vii, 242 p.

———. The same. Character text. Cambridge, Pub. for the Harvard-Yenching
Institute, Harvard University Press, 1947. 112 p.

CHIANG, KER-CHIU, 蔣克秋. Cantonese for beginners, 粵語易解, with a vocabulary. Singapore, Chin Fen Book-store, 1946 (c1941) 2 v.

COWLES, ROY T. A pocket dictionary of Cantonese. Cantonese-English with
English-Cantonese index. 2d ed. rev. and enl. Hong Kong, South China Peniel
Press, 1949. 1 v. (various pagings).

KOK, GERARD P., 1912- Speak Cantonese, by Gerard P. Kok and Po-fei
Huang, 黃伯飛. New Haven, Far Eastern Publications, Yale University,
1956. 432 p.

LEE, S. K., 李錫鈞, [Li Hsi-chün]. Cantonese simplified. Hong Kong, K. Weiss,

1954. 311 p. (Far East economic ser.) 1st ed. 1950.

MEYER, BERNARD F., 1891-   The student's Cantonese-English dictionary, by Bernard F. Meyer and Theodore F. Wemple. 3d ed., 1947. New York, Field Afar Press [1947] 843, [3], 136 p. 1st ed. 1935.

OAKELEY, R. H. Rules for speaking Cantonese. Kuala Lumpa, Printed by the authority of the Malayan Govt., 1953. ii, 192 p.

O'MELIA, THOMAS A., 1898-   First year Cantonese. 3d ed. Pref. by James E. Walsh. Hong Kong, Catholic Truth Society, 1954. 1 v. 2nd ed. 1941.

SERVUS, M. E. P. Locutions modernes. Dialecte cantonais. 粵法新詞句. Hong Kong, Impr. de la société des missions-étrangères, 1934. ii, 6, 827, 20 p.

SUNG, HOK-P'ANG, 宋學鵬, [Sung Hsueh-peng]. Cantonese conversation (with English notes). With preface by His Excellency Sir Cecil Clementi, the Rt. Rev. R. O. Hall and A. Morris. Hong Kong, 1934. 10, 10, 260 p.

TAM, WING KWONG, 譚榮光, [T'an Jung-kuang]. A new phonetic alphabet for the Cantonese dialect of the Chinese language. Hong Kong, Printed by the Yau Sang Print. Press, 1953. 28 p.

TIPSON, ERNEST. A Cantonese syllabary-index to Soothill's Pocket dictionary; incorporating all Cantonese colloquial characters and their meanings. London, Routledge and Kegan Paul, 1951. 79 p.

U. S. Army Language School, Monterey, Calif. Conversational Cantonese, Book II. [Presidio of Monterey] Army Language School, Far Eastern Language Division, Chinese-Cantonese Language Dept. [1951] 2 v.

———. Chinese-Cantonese. Presidio of Monterey, Chinese-Cantonese Language Dept., 1952. 4 v. in 5.

———. Chinese-Cantonese: basic course. v. 1. Presidio of Monterey, 1956-97 p. illus.

WELLS, HERBERT RICHMOND. Cantonese for every one; a simple introduction to Cantonese by H. R. Wells and Cheung Tün-chi, 張端始. Hong Kong, Wing Fat and Co., 1929. [60] p.

———. Commercial conversations in Cantonese and English. Hong Kong, Printed by Kae Shean Print. Co., 1931. 82, 52 p.

———. comp. An English Cantonese dictionary. Hong Kong, Kelly and Walsh, 1931. 227 p.

WHITAKER, KATHERINE PO KAN, 1912-   Characterization of the Cantonese dialect, with special reference to its modified tones. London, 1952. 2 v. Thesis-University of London, School of Oriental and African Studies.

———. Cantonese sentence series; an adaptation for students of Cantonese of W. Simon and C. H. Lu's "Chinese Sentence Series." London, A. Probsthain, 1954. xii, 150 p.

———. Structure drill in Cantonese, first fifty patterns. London, Lund Humphries, 1954. xxlx, 101 p. (Structure drill through speech patterns, 4).

YIU, T'UNG, 尤桐, 1896-   The T'ai-shan dialect. Ann Arbor, University Microfilms [1952] ([University Microfilms, Ann Arbor, Mich.] Publication no. 3073). Collation of the original: vi, 121 l. Thesis-Princeton University.

YUAN, YING-TS'AI, 袁英才. A guide to Cantonese (self-taught) by Y. C. Yuen. 5th ed. Hong Kong, The author, 1954. 50 p. 3rd ed. 1951.

## Other

BODMAN, NICHOLAS CLEAVELAND, 1913-   Spoken Amoy Hokkien, by N. C. Bodman, assisted by the staff of the Government Officers' language school, Federation of Malaya, and many others. Kuala Lumpur, Published by the authority of the Government, Federation of Malaya, 1955. 2 v.

CORBATÓ, HERMENEGILDO, 1894-   Chinese language; manual of the Foochow dialect. Revised for the California College in China by Paul P. Wiant. [Berkeley, Calif.] 1945. xviii, 206 (i. e. 207), 13, 5 numb. l. illus.

CORDIER, GEORGES,    -1936. Méthode pratique de langue chinoise.(dialecte yunnanais). Hanoi, Impr. tonkinoise, 1928. 159 p.

DROUGHT, JAMES MATTHEW. Introduction to Hakka. Hong Kong, Nazareth Press, 1926. 298 p.

EGEROD, SØREN. The Lungtu dialect: a descriptive and historical study of a south Chinese idiom. Copenhagen, Einar Munksgaard, 1956. xviii, 284 p.

FU, MAO-CHI, 傅懋勣. A study on the Lolo proverbs in and near the Taliang mountains. Hsichow, 1945. 15 p.

———. A descriptive grammar of Lolo. Cambridge, Eng., 1950. 382 p. plates. Thesis-Univ. Cambridge.

GROSVENOR, M. DONALD. A colloquial English-Chinese pocket dictionary in the Hankow dialect. Shanghai, Printed at the Presbyterian Mission Press, 1925. iii, [1], 269 p.

TIPSON, ERNEST. A pocket dictionary of the Amoy vernacular; English-Chinese. Singapore, Lithographers, 1934. 215 p.

WANG, SCHU-YÜN 王淑雲. Die Frage im Dialect von Tschang dschou. Eine experimental phonet. Untersuchung. Charlottenburg, Hoffmann, 1935. 83 p. Diss.-Univ. Berlin.

## Dictionaries
### English-Chinese; Chinese-English

CHAN, SHAU-WING, 陳受榮, [Chen Shou-jung] 1906- A concise English-Chinese dictionary, with romanized standard pronunciation. 2d ed. Stanford, Stanford University Press [1955] xvii, 416 p. 1st ed. 1946.

CHANG, S. M., 張湘玟, 1904- A concise English-Chinese dictionary, by S. M. Chang and Shirley Maxwell. [Hollywood, Calif.] Marcel Rodd, 1944. 7-191 p. Title also in Chinese on cover.

CHAO, YUEN-REN, 趙元任, 1892- Concise dictionary of spoken Chinese, by Yuen Ren Chao and Lien Sheng Yang, 楊聯陞. Cambridge, Pub.for the Harvard-Yenching Institute by Harvard Univ. Press, 1947. xxxix, 291 p.

CHENG, I-LI, 鄭易禮. A new English-Chinese dictionary with index in Chinese, by Cheng Yi-li and Tsao Cheng-shiu, 曹成修. [Peking] Sheng Huo, Tu Shu, Hsin Chih, San lien shu tien [1953] 2143 p.

CHIANG, KER-CHIU, 蔣克秋, [Chiang K'o-ch'iu]. A new English-Mandarin romanized dictionary, specially prepared for Mandarin students. [Syonan, Chin Fen book store, 194-?] 192, 6 p.

———. Chinese idioms in romanized Mandarin with literal and free translations in English. Syonan, Pub. by Chin Fen book store, 2604 [i.e. 1944] cover-title, 114 p.

CHINESE-ENGLISH dictionary; comprising over 3,800 characters with translations, explanations, pronunciations, etc., etc. Shanghai, Commercial Press, 1933. 282, 10 p.

CHÜ, CHUNG-FU, 瞿重福. T.F. Chu's Chinese-English dictionary. Shanghai, Little Book Co. [1932] 109, 42 p. (Little book special).

COMMERCIAL Press English and Chinese pronouncing condensed dictionary, revised by T.K. Yoh, 郁德基. Shanghai, Commercial Press, 1929. ii, [2], 693, 16, 21, 2 p.

A COMPREHENSIVE English-Chinese dictionary. Edited by Shih-fu Huang, 黃士復, and T'ieh Chiang, 江鐵. Shanghai, Commercial Press, 1937. xvi, 1502, 172 p. illus. 1st ed. 1928.

FENN, COURTENAY HUGHES, 1866-1953. The five thousand dictionary; a pocket dictionary and index to the character cards of the Yenching School of Chinese Studies (Peking language school) Compiled by Courtenay H. Fenn, with the assistance of Chin Hsien Tseng, 金憲曾. Shanghai, Mission Book Co., 1926. 2, 578, 49, 5, [2] p.

———. The five thousand dictionary, a pocket dictionary and index to the character cards of the North China Union Language School; compiled by Courtenay

H. Fenn, with the assistance of Chin Hsien Tseng. Peiping, North China Union Language School, cooperating with California College in China, 1932. 2, 2, 578 (i.e. 610), 50, 7, [2] p.

————. The five thousand dictionary, a Chinese-English pocket dictionary and index to the character cards of the College of Chinese Studies, California College in China, originally compiled by Courtenay H. Fenn, with the assistance of Chin Hsien Tseng. 5th ed., with additions and revisions by George D. Wilder and Chin Hsien Tseng. Peking [Printed at Union Press] 1940. xxxviii, 697 p. 1 illus.

————. Chinese-English pocket-dictionary. Rev. American ed. Cambridge, Harvard University Press, 1944 [c1942]. xxxvii, 694 p.

GILBERT, FRIEDRICH ROBERT. Mnemotechnisches Taschenlexikon der China-schrift. Tokyo, Taiheiyosha, 1934. xiii, 362 p.

————. A pocket-dictionary of Chinese characters on mnemonic principles. Tokyo, Sold at Maruzen Co., printed by Taiheiyosha [1936?] 42, 308, 47 p.

GOODRICH, CHAUNCEY, 1836-1925. A pocket dictionary (Chinese-English) and Pekingese syllabary. 15th thousand. Shanghai, Kwang Hsueh Pub. House, 1933. vii, 237, 70 p. 13th thousand published 1923, 14th thousand, 1927, both by Presbyterian Mission Press, Shanghai.

————. The same. New York, Columbia University Press, 1944. 237, 70 p.

GT. BRIT. War Office. General Staff. Geographical Section. Short glossary of Chinese. London [1943] cover-title, 30 p.

HARVARD-YENCHING INSTITUTE. Chinese-English dictionary project. Fascicle 39.0.1: preliminary print. Cambridge, Harvard University Press, 1953. 68, 27 p.

————. The same. Fascicle 39.0.1-3: preliminary print. Cambridge, Harvard University Press, 1953-54. 3 pts. in 2.

HILLIER, SIR WALTER CAINE, 1849-1927. An English-Chinese dictionary of Peking colloquial. New ed., enlarged by Sir Trelawny Backhouse and Sidney Barton. Shanghai, Printed at the Kwang Hsüeh Publishing House; London, Kegan Paul, 1933 (c1924). viii, 1030 p. Reprint ed. 1953.

HUNG, MING-HAN, 供明漢, comp. Chiu Yih's gem, new concise English-Chinese dictionary. Shanghai, Chiu Yih Book Co. [1950] ix, 1006, 38 p.

KARLGREN, BERNHARD, 1889-   Analytic dictionary of Chinese and Sino-Japanese. Paris, P. Geuthner, 1923. 436 p.

LEE, S.T., 李仕德, comp. A new complete Chinese-English dictionary. Kowloon, H.K., China Publishers Co., 1956. 1511, 68 p.

[LEE, YÜ-WÊN] 李玉汶. A new Chinese-English dictionary. Shanghai, Commercial Press [1937] 832, 73 p. 1st ed. 1918; 7th ed. 1925.

————. The same. American ed. Cambridge, Murray Printing Co., 1945; San Francisco, Service Supply Co., 1947. 832, 73 p.

LI, CHIH-YÜN, 厲志曇. The standard dictionary of English phrases, with bilingual explanations. Shanghai, Commercial Press, 1927. 897 p.

LI, RUMY, 李儒勉,   -1956. A practical English-Chinese, Chinese-English pocket dictionary. Shanghai, Chung Hua Book Co. [1931] [962] p.

MacGILLIVRAY, DONALD, 1862-1931. A Mandarin-romanized dictionary of Chinese, including new terms and phrases, with new supplement. 9th ed. Shanghai, 1930; London, Kegan Paul, 1930. x, 1145, 43 p.

MATHEWS, ROBERT HENRY. A Chinese-English dictionary, compiled for the China Inland Mission. Shanghai, China Inland Mission [etc.] 1931. 1232 p.

————. The same. English index. Shanghai, China Inland Mission, 1931. 184, [2] p.

————. Mathews' Chinese-English dictionary. Rev. American ed. Published for the Harvard-Yenching Institute. Cambridge, Harvard University Press, 1943; 7th printing, 1956. xxiv, 1226 p.

————. The same. A Chinese-English dictionary. Revised English index. Published for the Harvard-Yenching Institute. Cambridge, Harvard University

Press, 1944. 186 p.

MODEL English-Chinese dictionary with illustrative examples, edited by Chang Shih-lu, 張世鎏, and others. Shanghai, Commercial Press, 1934. iii-xvi, 1431 p. Rev. ed. 1935. xxiv, 1687 p.

MODEL English-Chinese dictionary, with illustrative examples, compiled by H. Bain, 平海瀾. Rev. ed. Shanghai, Commercial Press, 1949. 1711 p.

A MODERN English-Chinese dictionary, giving pronunciations, definitions and translations of a large vocabulary of words in common use, and thousands of phrases of frequent occurrence, with an appendix containing various useful tables. Shanghai, Commercial Press, 1931. iii, ii, lviii, 1555, [1] p.

MORGAN, EVAN, 1860-   Chinese new terms; revised and enlarged, with English translations, classifications, introduction and index. Shanghai, Kelly and Walsh, 1932. xiv, 614 p. 1st ed. 1903.

NASH, VERNON, comp. Trindex; an index to three dictionaries: Giles' Chinese-English dictionary, K'ang Hsi tzu tien, P'ei wen yun fu; in which are listed the 13,848 characters of Giles' dictionary, arranged in numerical sequence according to the Kuei hsieh system of converting characters into numerals devised by the editors of the Harvard-Yenching Institute Sinological index series. Peiping, Printed by Index Press, Yenching University [1936] lxx, 584, [2] p.

NELSON, DANIEL, 1902-48. An English-Chinese romanized dictionary. Minneapolis, Augsburg Pub. House [1944] xvi, 344 p. map (on lining-paper) [Series of Augsburg Publishing House lectureships, 1].

A NEW complete Chinese-English dictionary. Hong Kong, Chung Chien Pub. Co., 1956. 1224 p.

NIEH, N.Y., 倪灝森, [Ni Hao-sên]. An Anglo-Chinese dictionary of abbreviations and contractions with explanatory notes. Shanghai, Commercial Press, 1923. 224 p.

ONG, Y.F., 翁良, [Wêng Liang]. A complete dictionary of English phrases with bilingual explanations, by Y.F. Ong and Y.L. Yang, 楊士熙. [Shanghai] Commercial Press, 1939. 2, [vii]-xxvii, 1133 p. 1st ed. 1933.

A PRACTICAL English-Chinese dictionary; editors T.H. Lee, 李登輝, P.W. Kuo, 郭秉文, B.E. Lee, 李培恩 [and others] [Shanghai] Commercial Press [1935] iii-xiv, 1674 p.

QUO, JAMES C., 郭鋅. Concise English-Chinese dictionary, romanized; containing over 10,000 English words and expressions with equivalent Chinese characters and their romanized readings. Tokyo, Rutland, Vt., C.E. Tuttle Co. [1956] xi, 323 p.

SIMON, WALTER, 1893-   A beginners' Chinese-English dictionary of the national language (Gwoyeu) London, Lund, Humphries, 1947. cxxxiv, 880, 184 p. map (on lining-paper).

SOOTHILL, WILLIAM EDWARD, 1861-1935. The student's four thousand [characters] and general pocket dictionary. 17th ed. London, Kegan Paul, 1943. [iii]-xxxv, 428 p. 20th ed. 1952. 463 p.

TSANG, O.Z., 張鵬雲, [Chang P'êng-yün]. A complete Chinese-English dictionary, by O.Z. Tsang. Rev. ed. Shanghai, The Republican Press, 1932. iii, 756, 28, [6] p. 7th ed. 1923; Rev. ed. 1926.

——. The same. [New rev. ed. Hong Kong, Hop Kee Book Store, 1956] iii, 964, xxxvii, 30 p.

U.S. Army. 500th Military Intelligence Group. A Chinese-English dictionary of terms. [n.p., 1954] viii, 709 p.

U.S. Army Language School, Monterey, Calif. Consolidated vocabulary and notes index, Chinese-English. Presidio of Monterey, Chinese-Mandarin Language Dept., Army Language School, 1955. 2 v. (ii, 327 p.).

——. Chinese-Mandarin; consolidated vocabulary and index notes [introduced in the 12-month course] Presidio of Monterey, 1956. 2 v.

——. Chinese-Mandarin; eighteen months' course: advanced vocabulary. Presidio of Monterey, 1956-    2 v.

U.S. War Dept. Dictionary of spoken Chinese. Chinese-English, English-Chinese. Prepared by Charles F. Hockett and Fang Chao-ying. Washington, D.C., 1945. iii, 874 p. (War Dept. Technical Manual TM30-933).

WANG, I-T'ING, 王翼廷. A new Anglo-Chinese dictionary, by Wang I-Ting, Chao-Hsu Kwei, 桂紹旰 [and] Zung-Peh Chang, 張慎伯. Shanghai, Chung Hwa Book Co. [1948] ii, ii, 1075 p.

WEBSTER, NOAH, 1758-1843. Webster's collegiate dictionary with Chinese translation. Editors: P.W. Kuo, 郭秉文, S.L. Chang, 張世鎏. Shanghai, Commercial Press, 1933. xliii, 1768 p. front., illus., port.

YALE UNIVERSITY. Institute of Far Eastern Languages. IFEL vocabulary of spoken Chinese; edited by Po-fei Huang, 黃伯飛. New Haven, 1954. xvi, 347 p.

YEN, W.W., 顏惠慶, [Yen Hui-ch'ing] 1877-1950. ed. English and Chinese standard dictionary. Small type ed. Comprising 120,000 words and phrases with translations, pronunciations, definitions, illustrations, etc., etc., with a copious appendix. 3d ed. Shanghai, Commercial Press, 1921. [1307] p. illus.

———. ed. An abridged English and Chinese dictionary, comprising 65,000 words and phrases, with pronunciations, Chinese definitions, illustrations, etc., also a copious appendix. 4th ed. Shanghai, Commercial Press, 1922. 1441, 8,9,2 p. illus.

## French-Chinese; Chinese-French

AUBAZAC, LOUIS. Dictionnaire français-cantonnais. Nouv. éd. rev. et augm. Hongkong, Catholic Truth Society, 1955. 1106, 10, 139 p. 1st ed. 1909.

COUVREUR, SÉRAPHIN, 1835-1919. Petit dictionnaire chinois-français. Ho Kien-fou, Impr. de la mission catholique, 1923; reprint ed., Sien-hsien, 1930. xiv, 736 p. 1st ed. 1903.

———. Dictionnaire classique de la langue chinoise. Sien-hsien, Impr. de la Mission catholique, 1930. xii, 1080 p. 1st ed. 1904.

———. The same. Peiping, Henri Vetch, 1947. xii, 1080 p. Reprinted from 3rd ed. 1911.

DEBESSE, A. Petit dictionnaire chinois-français. 3. éd. refondue et augm. Chang-hai, Impr. de la Mission catholique, 1924; Paris, Adrien-Maisonneuve [1945] iii, [1], 559 p.

GAZTELU, J. Petit dictionnaire français-chinois, par J. Gaztelu. Hongkong, Impr. de Nazareth, 1928. xxi, 677, [6] p. [1st ed. 1900].

———. Lexique chinois français. Hong Kong, Impr. de la Société des missions étrangères, 1934. 119 p. 1st ed. 1906.

HSIAO, TZŬ-CH'IN, 蕭子琴. Nouveau dictionnaire français-chinois, par Hsiao Tzŭ-ch'in [et al] 8e éd.    Shanghai, Commercial Press, 1939 (c1923) 846 p.

LAPPARENT, J. DE. Petit dictionnaire chinois-français. Mandarin et dialecte de Changhai. 2e éd. Changhai, Impr. de la mission catholique à l'orphelinat de t'ou-sè-wè, 1929. vii, 474 p.

LAURE, CHARLES. Vocabulaire de la langue chinoise lai (franco-lai) précédé d'un essai grammatical. Hanoi, Impr. d'Extrême-Orient, 1924. 120 p.

LUC, KYNH, 盧謹, [Lu Chin]. Chinese-English-French dictionary, featuring a modern practical Chinese script. [n.p.] 1945. xxii, 702 p.

MÉDARD, JULES HENRI, 1883-    Vocabulaire français-chinois des sciences morales et politiques. Tientsin, Société française de librairie et d'édition [1927] ii, 1380, 16 p.

SAVINA, FRANÇOIS MARIE, 1876-    Dictionnaire étymologique français-nùng-chinois. Hong Kong, Société des missions étrangères, 1924. 528 p.

## German-Chinese; Chinese-German

DEUTSCH-chinesisches Standard-Handwörterbuch. Chefred: Huang Po-ch'iao, 黃伯樵. 3. Ausg. Shanghai, Chung-kuo k'o-hsüe t'u schu i-ch'i kung-sze, 1953. Leipzig, 1953. 1364 p.

KOLLECKER, C.A. Anhang zum chinesisch-deutschen Wörterbuch von Werner Rüdenberg, enthaltend die 6400 Schriftzeichen mit ihren Aussprache-und Ton-bezeichnungen in der Kantoner und Hakka-Mundart, bearbeitet von C.A.Kol-lecker. Hamburg, L. Friederichsen, 1925. 75 p.

KUNZE, RICHARD, 1873- Praktisches Zeichenlexikon, chinesisch-deutsch-japanisch, 6000 Zeichen etymologisch erklärt mit neuen praktischem Schlüs-sel. Nagoya, 1938. [720] p.

RÜDENBERG, WERNER. Chinesisch-deutsches Wörterbuch; 6400 Schriftzeichen mit ihren Einzelbedeutungen und den gebräuchlichsten Zusammensetzungen. 2. verb. Aufl. Hamburg, Friederichsen, 1936. ix, 686, [2] p. 1. Aufl. 1924.

STENZ, GEORG MARIA, 1869- Deutsch-chinesisches Wörterbuch. 2. verm. Aufl. [Shanghai, Sole agent: Van Chong Book Co.] 1947. vi, 773 p.

SUN, YUNG-CH'EN, 孫用震. Kleines deutsch-chinesisches Wörterbuch für den Anfang. 2 verm. Aufl. Bearb. von Sun Yung-chen und Wolfgang Franke unter Mitwirkung von Ku Hua, 顧華, und Ilse Martin. Peking, Deutschland Insti-tute, 1945. vii, 103 p. (Hilfsmittel für den deutschen Sprachunterricht in China, 1).

WILHELM, HELLMUT, 1905- Deutsch-chinesisches Wörterbuch, in Gemein-schaft mit chinesischen Fachgelehrten ausgearbeitet von Hellmut Wilhelm. Schanghai, M. Nössler, 1945. x, 1236 p.

## Other Dictionaries

CHINESISCH-Maleisch-Hollandsch-Engelsch Classificeerend-Woordenboek met Chineesche Uitspraak; a classified dictionary of Chinese-Malay-Dutch-Eng-lish with Chinese pronunciation, compiled by Li Joek Koey, 李毓慳. Bata-via, Kuo Min Book Co., 1931. xlix, 293, 2 p.

ESQUIROL, JOSEPH. Dictionnaire 'kaı nao-français et français-'kaı nao. Hong Kong, Impr. de la Société des Missions-étrangères, 1931. xliii, 519 p.

## Vocabularies

BRANDT, ÎAKOV, 1869-1944. Brandt's English-Chinese vocabulary. [New Ha-ven] Dept. of Oriental Studies, Yale Univ. [1944] 130 p. (Mirror series A, 13).

A CHINESE-English dictionary of terms. Compiled by 500th Military Intelligence [sic] Group, APO 613. [1954] viii, 709 p.

DAUDIN, PIERRE. L'écrin des gemmes en quatre caractères. 四字瓊林 Sai-gon, S.I.L.I., 1944. xvii, 557, 55, 50 p.

FENN, HENRY COURTENAY, 1894- ed. Chinese characters easily confused. New Haven, Institute of Far Eastern Languages, Yale University, 1953. ii p., 69 l., 71-84 p. (Mirror series A, 18).

HALL, RONALD ACOTT, 1892- The 3000 commonest Chinese terms, by Ron-ald Hall and Neville Whymant. London, Luzac, 1948. viii, 213 p.

INGRAM, JAMES HENRY, 187?-1936. Glossary of phrases found in "The three principles of the people" (San min chu i). Peking, 1930. 163 p.

KENNEDY, GEORGE ALEXANDER, 1901- A beginner's English-Chinese vo-cabulary. [New Haven] Dept. of Oriental Studies, Yale Univ., 1944. vii, 40 p. (Mirror series A, 10).

LI, CHI, 李祁. General trends of Chinese linguistic changes under communist rule. Berkeley, East Asia Studies, Institute of International Studies, Uni-versity of California, 1956. 42 p. (Studies in Chinese communist terminolo-

gy, 1 ).
————. Literary and colloquial terms in new usage. Terms topped by numerals. Berkeley, East Asia Studies, Institute of International Studies, University of California, 1957. 51 p. (Studies in Chinese communist terminology, 3 ).

NANKING. UNIVERSITY. An introductory analytical vocabulary for the study of Chinese, consisting of one thousand of the more frequently used characters. Prepared by the University of Nanking, Department of Missionary Training. [Nanking, 19-] 240 numb. l., 20 p.

SIMON, WALTER, 1893-  Gwoyeu romatzyh Chinese-English vocabulary, being a glossary to the Chinese sentence series. London, A. Probsthain, 1944. 54, [1] p.

SOSNOSKI, WALTER JOHN. Fun with Chinese. Waverly, N.Y., Mei Foo, 1940. 104 p.

STUART, J. LEIGHTON, 1876-  Chinese four-character phrases compiled with explanations. Peiping, Yenching University [1946] 24 p.

U.S. Army Language School, Monterey, Calif. Chinese-Cantonese civil affair terms. [Monterey] Army Language School, Far Eastern Language Division, Chinese-Cantonese Language Dept., 1951. 41 p.

————. Chinese Mandarin, eighteen months' course: a sketch of Chinese geography, vocabulary. Presidio of Monterey, 1956. 36 p.

WARE, JAMES ROLAND, 1901-  Vocabularies to the elementary Chinese texts used at Harvard University. Cambridge, Harvard-Yenching Institute, 1936. vi, 132 p.

————. Vocabularies to the intermediate Chinese texts used at Harvard University. Cambridge, Harvard-Yenching Institute, 1937. 160 p.

WONG, SING POO, 黃星甫, 1903-  Methodical guide to Chinese. [San Francisco?] c1953. [8] p.

## Lexicography and Indexing

[KENNEDY, GEORGE ALEXANDER] 1901-  Serial arrangement of Chinese characters. [New Haven] Dept. of Oriental Studies, Yale University, 1941. cover-title, 16 p. ([Yale University. Dept. of Oriental Studies] Mirror ser. A, no. 8).

————. ZH guide, an introduction to sinology. New Haven, Sinological Seminar, Yale University, 1953. 171 p. map.

KUEI, CHUNG-SHU, 桂中樞, 1897-  Kwei's system for the romanization of Chinese. New Haven, 1954. [10] l.

————. The three-positional system. New Haven, 1954. 8 p.

U.S. Army Language School, Monterey, Calif. Serial arrangements of Chinese characters. [Monterey] Army Language School, Chinese-Cantonese Dept., 1953. 18 p.

WANG, CHING-CH'UN, 王景春, 1883-  Gueeyin system of indexing. Claremont, Calif., College Press [1955] 23 l.

WONG, Y.W., 王雲五, [Wang, Yün-wu] 1888-  Wong's system for arranging Chinese characters, the revised four-corner numeral system by Y.W. Wong. Shanghai, Commercial Press, 1928. 143 p. First published, 1926, under title: Wong's system of Chinese lexicography, the four-corner numeral system.

## Miscellaneous

BOODBERG, PETER ALEXIS, 1903-  Exercises in Chinese parallelism. Berkeley and Los Angeles, University of California Press, 1943. 60 numb. l. (University of California syllabus series, 284 ).

————. UCI : an interim system of transcription for Chinese. Berkeley, University of California Press, 1947. 16 p. (University of California publications in East Asiatic philology, 1: 1).

CHAN, YING, 詹鎂, 1916-　The development of parallel reading comprehension examinations in English and Chinese at the graduate level. New York, 1953. 25 p. Thesis-Teachers College, Columbia University.

HEWES, MINNA, comp. Korean-Japanese readings of selected Chinese characters, compiled by Minna and Gordon Hewes. Washington, D.C., 1944. cover-title, 15, 15 numb. l.

HOLMES, GEORGE FOX, comp. A numerical index of Chinese names. Calcutta, Printed by the Calcutta General Print. Co., 1944. 89 p.

LEW, TIMOTHY TING-FANG, 劉廷芳 , [Liu T'ing-fang] 1891-1947. The psychology of learning Chinese; a preliminary analysis by means of experimental psychology of some of the factors involved in the process of learning Chinese characters. [Peking, 1924?] 377, ii p. illus., diagrs., facsim., tables. Thesis-Columbia University.

MANUEL, E. ARSENIO, 1909-　Chinese elements in the Tagalog language, with some indication of Chinese influence on other Philippine languages and cultures, and an excursion into Austronesian linguistics. With a historical introd. by H. Otley Beyer. Manila, Filipiniana Publications, 1948. xxv, 139 p.

OTTE, FRIEDRICH W.K. Translations from modern Chinese. 3d ed. Shanghai, Commercial Press, 1923. 2 v.

PEKING. COLLEGE OF CHINESE STUDIES. Language study courses of the College of Chinese Studies cooperating with California College in China, 1937. [Peking? 1937?] 12 p.

PERNITZSCH, MAX GERHARD. Chinesische Buchhaltung, von dr. M.G. Pernitzsch und H. Tittel. Tokyo, Verlag der Deutschen Gesellschaft für Natur- und Völkerkunde Ostasiens; [etc., etc.] 1927. 2, 84 p. plates, facsims. (Supplement der Mitteilungen der Duetschen gesellschaft für natur- und völkerkunde Ostasiens. [Supplementband, 10]).

WANG, FUNG-CHIAI, 王鳳階 , 1906-　An experimental study of eye-movements in the silent reading of Chinese. Chicago, 1934. v, 33 p. Part of thesis-University of Chicago.

# XVI. LITERATURE

## General Works

ALEKSEEV, VASILII MIKHAILOVICH, 1881-1951. La littérature chinoise; six conférences au Collège de France et au Musée Guimet (novembre 1926) Paris, P. Geuthner, 1937. 232 p. (Annales du Musee Guimet. Bibliothèque de vulgarisation, t. 52).

AYSCOUGH, FLORENCE (WHEELOCK), 1878-1942. Der Yangtse Kiang; Chinas grosser Strom, seine Legende und seine Poesie. Tokyo, Deutsche Gesellschaft für Natur- und Völkerkunde Ostasiens, 1937. 18 p. plates, map. (Mitteilungen der Deutsche Gesellschaft für Natur- und Völkerkunde Ostasiens, bd. 29, t. E ).

BÖTTGER, WALTER. Die ursprünglichen Jagdmethoden der Chinesen nach ihrer alten Literatur und der Paläographie. Leipzig, 1956. v, 105 l. Diss. - Univ. Leipzig.

BOVEN, HENRI VAN, 1911- Histoire de la littérature chinoise moderne. Peiping, Catholic University Press, 1946. 187 p. (Scheut editions. Sér. 1. Critical and literary studies, v. 2)

CHINESISCHE Liebesgeschichten. [Nach alten Quellen neu erzählt. Übertragungen von O. Sumitomo] Zürich, W. Classen [1947] 96 p. (Vom Dauernden in der Zeit, Kostbarkeiten alter und neuer Dichtung, 32).

CHOU, LING. 周麟 , 1915- ed. and tr. La sagesse chinoise; textes choisis et traduits du chinois par Chou Ling. Paris, La Jeune Parque [1947] (c1944) 45, iii p.

DAVIDSON, MARTHA. ed. A list of published translations from Chinese into English, French, and German. (Tentative ed.) Pt. 1: Literature. Ann Arbor, Pub. for ACLS by J. W. Edwards, 1952. Pt. 2: Poetry. New Haven, Pub. for ACLS by Far Eastern Publications, Yale University, 1957. 2 v.

DOBBINS, NATALIA. Feng ching, 中國風景 Chinese sketches. Los Angeles and San Francisco, Suttonhouse, 1933. 134 p. illus, (incl. music, plan) plates, ports.

EDWARDS, EVANGELINE DORA. Chinese prose literature of the T'ang period, A.D. 618-906. London, A. Probsthain, 1937-38. 2v. (Probsthain's oriental series, vol 23).

——. ed. The dragon book. London [etc.] W. Hodge, 1946 (c1938) 367 p. illus.

ERKES, EDUARD; 1891- Chinesische Literatur. Breslau, F. Hirt, 1922. 104 p. incl. plates. (Jedermanns bücherei... abt.: Literaturgeschichte).

GILES, HERBERT ALLEN, 1845-1935, ed. and tr. Gems of Chinese literature: prose. 2d ed., rev. and greatly enl. London, B. Quaritch, ltd., 1923. Shanghai, Kelly and Walsh, 1923.

——. A history of Chinese literature. New York and London, D. Appleton, 1927. v-viii, 448 p.

GILLIS, IRVIN VAN GORDER, 1875-1948, comp. The square, compass, line and plumb in Chinese literature. Peiping, 1937. [47] l.

GOODRICH, LUTHER CARRINGTON, 1894- The literary inquisition of Ch'ien-Lung. Baltimore, Waverly Press, 1935. xii, 275 p. [American council of learned societies [devoted to humanistic studies] Studies in Chinese and related civilizations, 1].

HIGHTOWER, JAMES ROBERT, 1915- Topics in Chinese literature; outlines and bibliographies. Rev. ed. Cambridge, Harvard University Press, 1953. ix. 141 p. (Harvard-Yenching Institute studies, 3) 1st ed. 1950.

HSIAO, CH'IEN, 蕭乾 , 1911- Etching of a tormented age; a glimpse of contemporary Chinese literature. London, G. Allen and Unwin. [1942] 48 p. (P.E.N. books).

————. Die chinesische Literatur der Gegenwart; ein Überblick. Einzig autorisierte Übersetzung von Joseph Kalmer. Herrliberg-Zürich, Bühl-Verlag [1947] 67p. (Bühl-Verlag-Blätter, 20).

HSU, SUNG-NIEN, 徐仲年, 1904- comp. and tr. Anthologie de la littérature chinoise des origines à nos jours, La Poésie. --Le roman. --Le théâtre. -- La philosophie. --L'histoire. Paris, Librairie Delagrave, 1933. 445 p. (Collection Pallas).

KALTENMARK-GHÉQUIER, ODILE. La littérature chinoise. Paris, Presses universitaires de France, 1948. 128 p. (Que sais-je? Le point des connaissances actuelles, 296).

KING, PEI-YUAN, 景培元, Étude comparative des divers éditions du Chouo fou, 說郛, Peiping, 1946. 22p. (Scripta sinica, 1)

LIN, YU-T'ANG, 林語堂 1895- Letters of a Chinese amazon; and, War-time essays. Shanghai, Commercial Press, 1934. xiv, 211 p. illus. (map).

————. ed. The wisdom of China and India, edited by Lin Yutang. New York, Random House [1942] xiii, 1104 p.

————. the same. [1st Modern Library giant ed.] New York, Modern Library [1955, c1942] 1104 p. (The Modern library of the world's best books. [A modern library giant, G59]).

————. The wisdom of China. London, M. Joseph [1944] new ed. 1954, 516 p.

LIU, WU-CHI, 柳無忌, 1907- ed. Readings in contemporary Chinese literature, edited by Wu-chi Liu and Tien-yi Li, 李田意. New Haven, Institute of Far Eastern Languages, Yale University, 1953- 3 v. (Mirror series C, 7).

LOCKE, M. A. The early life of Ou-yang Hsiu, 歐陽修, and his relation to the rise of the Ku-wen movement of the Sung dynasty. London, 1951. 2 v. Thesis-University of London, School of Oriental and African Studies.

LU, CHI, 陸機, 261-303. The art of letters; Lu Chi's "Wen fu, 文賦," A.D. 302, a translation and comparative study, by E.R. Hughes. With a fore-note by I.A. Richards. [New York] Pantheon Books [1951] xviii, 261 p. illus. (1 fold. col.) facsim. (Bollingen series, 29).

————. Rhymeprose on literature: The Wen-fu of Lu Chi (A.D. 261-303); translated and annotated by Archilles Fang, 方志彤. Cambridge, 1951. [39] p. Reprinted from HJAS, 14:3-4, December, 1951.

————. Essay on Literature; written by the third century Chinese poet Lu Chi, 陸機 translated by Shih-hsiang Chen, 陳世驤. Revised ed. Portland, Me., The Anthoensen Press, 1953. 35p. Previously published under title: Literature as light against darkness; being a study of Lu Chi's Essay on Literature in relation to his life, his period in medieval Chinese history, and some modern critical ideas; with a translation of the text in verse. Peiping, Peking University Press, 1948. 71 p. (Peking University semi-centennial papers, 2).

MARGOULIÈS, GEORGES, 1907- Le "fou" dans le Wen-siuan, 文選, étude et textes. Paris, P. Geuthner, 1926. 138 p.

————. Le kou-wen chinois, recueil de textes avec introduction et notes. Paris, P. Geuthner, 1926. cxxvii, 464p.

————. Évolution de la prose artistique chinoise. München, Encyclopädie-Verlag 1929. ix, 334 p. (China-encyclopaedia...section iv, v. 6a).

————. ed. and tr. Anthologie raisonnée de la littérature chinoise. Paris, Payot, 1948. 458 p. (Bibliothèque scientifique).

————. Histoire de la littérature chinois-Prose. Paris, Payot, 1949. viii, 336 p. (Bibliothèque historique).

MONSTERLEET, JEAN, 1912- Sommets de la littérature chinoise contemporaine. Paris, Domat [1953] 167 p. (Connaissance de l'Est).

MOTE, FREDERICK W. 1922- T'ao Tsung-i, 陶宗儀, and his Cho-keng-lu,輟耕錄. Seattle, 1954. 244 l. Thesis-Univ. of Washington.

NAGASAWA, KIKUYA, 1902- Geschichte der chinesischen Literatur und ihrer gedanklichen Grundlage nach Nagasawa Kikuya Shina gakujutsu bungeishi, übers. von Eugen Feifel. Peking, Catholic Univ., 1945. xii, 444 p.(Monumenta serica. Monograph series, 7).

PRŮŠEK, JAROSLAV. Die Literatur des befreiten China und ihre Volkstraditionen. [Übers. von Pavel Eisner und Wilhelm Gampert] Prag, Artia 1955. 736 p. illus.

REYNOLDS, PHILIP KEEP. The banana in Chinese literature, by Philip K. Reynolds, in collaboration with Mrs. C. Y. Fang, 杜聯喆. [Cambridge] Harvard-Yenching Institute [1940] cover-title, 165-181 p. incl. 3 plates. Reprinted from H. J. A. S. 5:2.

ROTTAUSCHER, ANNA, tr. Altchinesische Tiergeschichten. Aus dem chinesische Texten, übertragen von Anna Rottauscher. Wien, Neff, 1955. 264 p. plates (colored).

SCHÜLER, WILHELM, 1869-1935. ed. Proben chinesischer Literatur-und Umgangssprache-Selections from Chinese literature and everyday talk... unter Leitung von Wilhelm Schüler. Stuttgart, Otto Sperling, 1929. 1v. (various pagings).

SIÉ, KANG, 謝康, [HSIEH K'ANG] L'amour maternel dans la littérature féminine en Chine. Paris, A. Pedone, 1937. viii, 187, [1] p. Thèse-Univ. de Paris.

TSEN, TSONMING, 曾仲鳴, 1896-1939. Le Chine pacifique d'après ses écrivains anciens et modernes, morceaux choisis et traduits. Préface de M. Herriot. Lyon, J. Desvigne; Paris, E. Leroux, 1924. 101 p.

――――. Une goutte d'eau. Paris, E. Leroux; Lyon, J. Desvigne, 1925. 166 p. incl. tables, col. mounted front.

TSENG, KUNG, 曾鞏, 1018-1083. Tseng Kung: Ein Beitrag aus der Litteratur der Sung-Zeit von F. E. A. Krause. Heidelberg, C. Winter, 1922. 47, 17 p. map, (Von Portheim Stiftung. Heidelberger Akten, 1).

TSO, PING-NAN, 左炳南. Selections from Chinese classics with English translation. Batavia, Nan-Yang yin-shu-chü, 1948. 112 p.

WILHELM, RICHARD, 1873-1930. Die chinesische Literatur. Wildpark-Potsdam, Akademische Verlagsgesellschaft Athenaion, [1925-28] 199, [1] p. illus., v mounted pl. (4 col. )(Handbuch der Literaturwissenschaft, [lfg. 51, 59, 64, 70, 74, 93]).

WYLIE, ALEXANDER, 1815-1887. Notes on Chinese literature: with introductory remarks on the progressive advancement of the art; and a list of translations from the Chinese into various European languages. Reprinted. Shanghai, Presbyterian Mission Press, 1922. xl, 307 p. 1st ed. 1867.

YU, PING-YAO. 于炳耀. Title index to the Ssu k'u ch'üan shu, compiled by P. Y. Yu. under the supervision of I. V. Gillis. Peiping [Printed by the Standard Press] 1934. [422] p.

## Poetry: General Studies

BAXTER, GLEN WILLIAM, 1914- An index to the Ch'in ting tx'u p'u, 欽定詞譜, Cambridge, Harvard-Yenching Institute, 1951. viii, 71 l.

――――. Hua-chien chi, 花間集, Songs of tenth century China: a study of the first tz'u anthology. Cambridge, 1952. 317 p. Thesis-Harvard University.

――――. Index to the imperial register of tz'u prosody, Ch'in-ting tz'u-p'u. Prepared with a bibliographical note. Cambridge, Harvard University Press, 1956. xiii, 61 p. (Harvard-Yenching Institute studies, 15) First published in 1951 under title: An index to the Ch'in ting tz'u p'u.

BYNNER, WITTER, 1881- The persistence of poetry. San Fransisco, Book Club of California, 1929. 29, [1] p.

FENOLLOSA, ERNEST FRANCISCO, 1853-1908. The Chinese written character as a medium for poetry, by Ernest Fenollosa. An ars poetica. With a foreword and notes by Ezra Pound. New York, Arrow editions, London, S. Nott, 1936. 52 p. [Ideogramic series, ed. by Ezra Pound. I].

――――, the same. With offset of the Calcutta edition of Pivot. New York, J. Kasper, 1951. cover-title. 96 p. (Square dollar ser.).

FENG, SHU-LAN, 馮淑蘭, 1902- La technique et l'histoire du ts'eu. Paris, L. Rodstein, 1935. 254 (i.e. 258) p. Thèse-Univ. de Paris.

HO, AGNÈS,何陳學昭. Le "tse". Toulouse,Impr. toulousaine Lion et fils, 1934. 58, [2] p. Thèse-Clermont-Ferrand.

HOLZMAN, DONALD ALBERT, 1926- Yuan Chi, 阮籍, and his poetry. New Haven, 1953. iii, 266 l. Thesis-Yale University.

——. La vie et la pensée de Hi K'ang, 嵇康, 223-262 ap. J.-C.) Leiden, Published for Harvard-Yenching Institute [by] E.J. Brill, 1957. vii, 186 p. Thèse-Univ. de Paris.

HSU, RUTH RUBY (SCHMID), 許仕廉夫人 , comp.and tr. Chinese children's rhymes; with illustrations by Teng Kuei, 滕圭. Shanghai, Commercial Press, 1935. xxiv, 98 p. illus.

JABLONSKI, WITOLD. Les "siao-ha (i-eu) l-yu," 小孩兒語 , de Pékin; un essai sur la poésie populaire de Chine. Kraków, Nakładem Polskiej Akademja u Umiejetności, 1935. 193 p. fold. plates. (Polska akademja umiejetności, Prace Komisji orjentalistycznez, 19 ).

JUBY, PHYLLIS, ed. Chinese poetry, with an essay. Pretoria, J.L. Van Schaik, 1943. [5]-46 p. (Chinese culture series, 1).

LEPLAE,CHARLES. Chant sur la rivière; essai sur la poésie chinoise. Avec la collaboration de G. van den Bos. Précédé d'une étude sur la poésie T'ang par Luc Haesaerts. [Bruxelles] Éditions des artisted [1945] 185, [1] p., 2 l. incl. front. (port.).

LUH, CHIH WEI,陸志韋 , 1894- On Chinese poetry, five lectures. Peiping, 1935. 2-118 p.

MARGOULIÈS, GEORGES, 1907- Histoire de la littérature chinoise: poésie. Paris, Payot, 1951. 417 p. (Bibliothèque historique)

PURCELL, VICTOR WILLIAM WILLIAMS SAUNDERS, 1896- The spirit of Chinese poetry, an original essay; with illustrations from ancient Chinese drawings. Singapore, Kelly and Walsh, 1929. 43, [5] p. front., illus., plates.

TEELE, ROY EARL, 1915- Through a glass darkly; a study of English translations of Chinese poetry. Ann Arbor, 1949. xi, 173 p. Thesis-Columbia University.

TSEN, TSONMING, 曾仲鳴, 1896-1939. Essai historique sur la poésie chinoise. Lyon, J. Deprelle, 1922. 159 p. Thèse-Univ. de Lyon.

——. Histoire de la poésie chinoise. Shanghai, China United Press, 1936. 156 p.

## Translations

ACTON, HAROLD MARIO MITCHELL, 1904- tr. Modern Chinese poetry, translated by Harold Acton and Ch'en Shih-hsiang, 陳世驤. London, Duckworth [1936] 176 p.

ALLEY, REWI, 1897- comp. and tr. Peace through the ages; translations from the poets of China. Peking, 1954. 205 p. illus.

——.The people speak out; translations of poems and songs of the people of China. Peking, 1954. 107 p. illus.

ANTHOLOGIE D'ÉCRIVAINS CHINOIS de l'époque des T'ang. Traduit et présentée par Bruno Belpaire. Paris, Éditions universitaires, 1957. 416 p. (Encyclopédie universitaire).

AYSCOUGH, FLORENCE (WHEELOCK),1878-1942, tr. Fir-flower tablets;poems translated from the Chinese by Florence Ayscough. English version by Amy Lowell. Boston and New York, Houghton Mifflin, 1921. London, Constable, 1922. xcv, 227 p. front. (double map) plan, facsim.

——. Tablettes de fleur de sapin. L'adaptation anglaise de Amy Lowell; traduction française de Maurice Thiéry. Paris, E. Roger, 1928. 166 p. plates.

BETHE, HANS, 1876- Pfirsichblüten aus China. Mit 6 original-Lithographien von George A. Mathéy. Berlin, Rowohlt, 1922. 121 numb. l. illus.

——. Die chinesische Flöte. Nachdichtungen chinesischer Lyrik. Wiesbaden, Ingel-Verlag, 1955. 83 p. (Insel Bücherei, 465) 1st ed. 1929. 119 p.

BLACK, SHIRLEY MAXWELL, 1906- Rainbow skirts and feather jackets. Hollywood, Calif. W. M. Hawley, 1956. 44 p.

BÖHN, HANS. Lieder aus China, Nachdichtungen chinesischer Lyrik, mit seibzehn Zeichungen von Rudolf Grossmann. München, Callway, 1929. 62 p. incl. illus. plates.

CHAPIN, HELEN BURWELL, 1894-1950, tr. The round of the year; poems from the Chinese; prologue, epilogue and calligraphy by the translator, preface by Laurence Binyon. Mills College, Calif., Eucalyptus Press, 1936. 48 l.

Les CHANTS DE TSEU-YE, 子夜, et autres poèms d'amour. Traduits et annotés par Hsu Sungnien, 徐仲年. Pékin, Imrp. de la "Politique de Pékin," 1932. 25 p. (Collection de la "Politique de Pékin").

CHINESISCHE GEDICHTE IN VIERZEILERN AUS DER T'ANG ZEIT. Übers. und erweitert von Max Geilinger. Mit 6 Reproduktionen alter Gemälde aus dem kaiserlichen Palast zu Peking auf Tafeln und 20 Wiedergaben von Original-Pinselzeichnungen von Richard Hadl. Zürich, Rascher Verlag, 1944. iv, iv, 143 p.

CHRISTY, ARTHUR, tr. Images in jade; translations from classical and modern Chinese poetry. New York, E. P. Dutton, 1929. 191 p.

CH'U, TA-KAO, 初大告, tr. Chinese lyrics, translated by Ch'u Ta-kao, with a preface by Sir Arthur Quiller-Couch. Cambridge [Eng.] The University Press, 1937. xvii, 55, [1] p.

CLACK, ROBERT WOOD, tr. From bamboo glade and lotus pool. Emory University, Atlanta, Banner Press [c1937] 71 p. plates. [Verse craft series].

COLVIN, IAN DUNCAN, 1877-1938, comp. and ed. After the Chinese. London, P. Davis, 1927. lx, 75 p.

CRANMER-BYNG, LAUNCELOT ALFRED, 1872-1945, comp. A lute of jade; being selections from the classical poets of China, rendered with an introduction. New York, E. P. Dutton. London, J. Murray, 1934. 116 p. (The Wisdom of the East series) 1st ed. 1909, 2nd ed. 1911.

———. A feast of lanterns, rendered with an introduction. London, J. Murray, 1945. 95 p.(The Wisdom of the East series). 1st ed. 1916.

CURTISS, FLORENCE RISING, tr. Translations from the Chinese T'ang dynasty poets, 618-906 A. D. New York, 1952? 52 l.

DAUDIN, PIERRE, tr. Nocturnes chinois; poésies des T'ang et des Song. Saigon, France-Asie, 1950. 11 p.

DUTTON, HELEN (WILEY) tr. Secrets told in the bamboo grove. Peking, French Bookstore, 1940. 52, [2] p.

EHRENSTEIN, ALBERT, tr. China Klagt, Nachdichtungen revolutionärer chinesischer Lyrik aus drei Jahrtausenden. [Berlin, Malik-Verlag, c1924] 48 p. (Malik-Bücherei 8)

ESTEB, ADLAI ALBERT. Driftwood, and other poems; including translations of Chinese poetry. Mountain View, Calif. Pacific Press Pub. Assn. [1947] 127 p.

FLEISCHER, MAX, tr. Der Porzellanpavillon; Nachdichtungen chinesischer Lyrik. Berlin P. Zsolnay, 1927. 117, [1] p.

FLETCHER, WILLIAM JOHN BAINBRIGGE, 1879- Gems of Chinese verse; translated into English verse. Shanghai, Commercial Press, 1932. xxiii, 246 p.

———. More gems of Chinese poetry; translated into English verse. With comparative passages from English literature. Shanghai, Commercial Press, 1933. xv, 209 p.

The FLOWER LOVER AND THE FAIRIES, anonymous (circa fourteenth century) from the translation of Chi-chen Wang, 王際真, handwritten and illustrated by Jeanyee Wong, 黃如珍. New York, Archway Press [1946]. 36 p. illus. (The Scribe).

FORKE, ALFRED, 1867-1944. Dichtungen der T'ang-und Sung-Zeit. Aus dem chinesische Metrisch übertragen von Alfred Forke. Hamburg, Verlag Friedrichsen, de Gruyter and Co., 1929-1930, 2 v. (Hamburg. Universität.

Seminar für Sprache und Kultur Chinas. Veröffentlichungen, 3-4).

FRENCH, JOSEPH LEWIS, 1858-1936, ed. Lotus and chrysanthemum; an anthology of Chinese and Japanese poetry, selected and edited by Joseph Lewis
French. New York, Boni and Liveright, 1934. xxi, 237 p. 1st ed. 1927.

GILES, HERBERT ALLEN, 1845-1935, ed. and tr. Gems of Chinese literature:
verse. 2d ed., rev. and greatly enl. London, B. Quaritch, 1923. 6, 279, [1]
p.

——— . Select Chinese verses, translated by Herbert A. Giles and Arthur Waley,
Shanghai, Commercial Press, 1934. [v]-xi, 96 p.

HART, HENRY HERSCH, 1886- comp. and tr. A Chinese market: lyrics from
the Chinese in English verse. Foreword by E. T. C. Werner. Peking, French
Bookstore; San Francisco, J. J. Newbegin [c1931] xvii, [1]. 101 p.

———. tr. A garden of peonies,牡丹園, translations of Chinese poems into English verse. Stanford, Stanford University Press; London, H. Milford, Oxford University Press [c1938] xiii, 159 p.

———. comp. and tr. The hundred names, a short introduction to the study of
Chinese poetry, with illustrative translations. Berkeley, University of California Press, 1933. 2nd ed. 1935. 231 p.

———, comp. and tr. Poems of the hundred names; a short introduction to Chinese poetry, together with 208 original translations. [3d ed.] Stanford, Stanford University Press, 1954. 263 p. 1st ed. 1933 under title The hundred
names.

HAUSER, OTTO, 1876-1932. Die chinesische Dichtung. Mit vielen Kunstbeila-
gen. Berlin, Brandus, [1921] 2 p. 1. 67 p. front. plates, (incl. ports) (Die
Literatur Sammlung Brandus, 34).

HAUSMANN, MANFRED, 1898- ed. Hinter dem Perlenvorhang; Gedichte nach
dem Chinesischen. [Frankfurt am Main] S. Fischer, 1954. 79 p.

HEADLAND, ISAAC TAYLOR, 1859- ed. and tr. Chinese rhymes for children,
with a few from India, Japan and Korea. illustrated by Sui Wesley Chan.
New York, London [etc.] Fleming H. Revell company [c1933] 156 p. illus.

[HENSCHKE, ALFRED] 1891-1928. Das Blumenschiff; Nachdichtungen chinesischer Lyrik, von Klabund [pseud]. Berlin, E. Reiss, [1921] [56] p. illus.

[———]. Gesammelte Nachdichtungen: China. Japan. Persien. Wien, Phaidon
Verlag, 1930. 329, [1] p. Gesammelte werke in einzelausgaben).

[———]. Chinesische Gedichte; Nachdichtungen von Klabund [pseud]. Gesamt-
Ausgabe. Wien, Phaidon Verlag, [1933]. 130 p. col. plates.

[———]. Dichtungen aus dem Osten, von Klabund [pseud]. Wien, Phaidon-Ver-
lag, 1954 (c1929) 3 v.

HOFFMAN, ALFRED, 1911- Frühlingsblüten und Herbstmond春花秋月,ein Hol-
zschnittband mit Liedern aus der Sung-Zeit, 960-1279. Aus dem Chinesischen,
übertragen und erläutert von A. Hoffmann. Köhn, Greven Verlag, [1951].
108 p. illus.

HUNDHAUSEN, VINCENZ, 1878-1955, tr. Chinesische Dichter in deutscher
Sprache. Mit 2 Bildern nach Originalen des Wang Ting-dsche. Peking, Leipzig, Pekinger Verlag, 1926. 13-149 p. 2 mounted illus.

———. Chinesische Dichter des dritten bis elften Jahrhunderts. In deutscher
Nachdichtung. Mit 2 Bildern von Wang Ting-Dsche. Eisenach, E. Röth,
[1926) 149 p.

IVES, MABEL (LORENZ) tr. Chinese love songs, famous poems covering 26
centuries from the time of Confucius to the present; English verse renderings. Upper Montclair, N.J., B. L. Hutchinson [1949] 91 p. front.

LALOY, LOUIS, 1874-1944, comp. and tr. Poésies chinoises, tr. en français,
avec une introd, et des notes. [Fribourg] Egloff [1944] 102 p.

LEE, ALAN SIMMS, tr. Flower shadows, translations from the Chinese. London, E. Mathews, 1925. 47 p.

LEPEL, FELIX VON, 1899- comp. Die Jadeschale; ausgewählte Gedichte aus
dem alten China. Berlin-Reinickendorf, Chronos-Verlag [1944?] 16 p. (on

double leaves) illus. (Die Drei-Ringe-Reihe, Bd. 4)

LO, TA-KANG, 羅大綱, tr. Cent quatrains des T'ang; traduits du chinois. Préface de Stanislas Fumet, avec dix reproductions de peinture ancienne du Palais impériale de Pékin et en fac-similé une lettre de Louis Laloy. 2. éd.
Paris, Oreste Zeluck; Neuchâtel, La Baconnière, [1947]. 236 p. incl. facsim.

————. Homme d'abord, poète ensuite; présentation de sept poètes chinois. Avec
sept portraits anciens. Neuchâtel, La Baconnière [1948] 283 p. incl. mounted plates

LYON, DAVID WILLARD, 1870-1949, tr. Inside the moon gate; poems translated from the Chinese. Foreword by Ch'en Shou Yi, 陳受頤. Claremont, Calif., 63 p.

MCCLELLAND, HARDIN T. comp. and tr. Various Chinese poets, their biographies and selected poems, translated by Ma-k'uei-lun...[i.e.]Hardin T.
McClelland... Seattle, Wash. 1935. 520 numb. 1.

————. Art-themes in Chinese poetry, selected and translated by Ma K'uei-lun..
[i.e.] Hardin T. McClelland. Seattle, Wash., 1936. xi, 420 l. plates (part
fold), facsims.

MARTIN, RICHARD ARTHUR ORMSBY. Shan-Shui; translations of Chinese landscape poems. Melbourne, Meanjin Press, 1946. 6 p.

OEHLER-HEIMERDINGER, ELISABETH, 1884- tr. Das Frauenherz; chinesische
Lieder aus drei Jahrtausenden; ausgewählt und aus dem Chinesischen, übersetzt von Elisabeth Oehler-Heimerdinger. Stuttgart und Berlin, Union deutsche Verlags-gesellschaft, [1925] 173 p.

PAYNE, PIERRE STEPHEN ROBERT, 1911- ed. The white pony; an anthology
of Chinese poetry from the earliest times to the present day, newly translated. New York, John Day [1947]; London, G. Allen and Unwin, 1949. xxviii,
414 p.

PETER PAUPER PRESS, Mount Vernon, N. Y. Chinese love poems, collected
and published by the Peter Pauper Press. Mount Vernon, N. Y. [1942] 73 p.

LA POÉSIE CHINOISE. Anthologie des origines à nos jours. Préface, choix et
notices par Patricia Guillermaz. Paris, Seghers, 1957. 294 p. illus. map
(Collection Mélior).

REXROTH, KENNETH, 1905- One hundred poems from the Chinese. [New York]
New Directions [1956] 159 p.

ROUSSEL, ALBERT, 1869- Deux poèms chinois. Paroles de H.-P. Roché (d'après la traduction anglais de Giles). Favorite abandonnée (Li-I). Vois, de
belles filles (Huang Fu-Ian). [Op 47, No. 1-22]... Paris, Durand et Cie,
[1934] 3 p.

SHIH, MIN, ed. 石民, English translations of Chinese classics; an anthology of
Chinese poetry (from the Chou to T'ang dynasties) selected with notes by Shih
Min. Shanghai, Pei Sin Book Co., 1933. 4, vi, 231 p. (English translations
of Chinese classics).

SOULIÉ, CHARLES GEORGES, 1978- Florilège des poèms Song, 960-1277 après
J. C.; traduit du chinois par George Soulié de Morant. 3. éd. Paris, Plon-
Nourrit, 1923. ix, 233 p. (Collection d'auteurs étrangèrs).

————. tr. Anthologie de l'amour chinois; poèmes de lasciveté parfumée, traduits du chinois par George Soulié de Morant. Troisième édition. Paris,
Mercure de France, 1932. [iii]-xx, 247 p.

STOLZENBURG, WILHELM. Östlicher Divan; umdichtungen chinesischer Lyrik.
Baden, Ferdinand Acker, 1925. [41] p. (Els-druck, 7).

STRASSER, CHARLOT, 1884- Das Drachenpferd; chinesische Dichtungen, Betrachtungen darüber, nebst einer Einleitung von Hoo Chi-tsai, 胡世澤. Zürich, New York, Oprecht [c1942] 62 p. plate, ports.

T'ANG-SHIH SAN-PAI SHOU, 唐詩三百首. The jade mountain; a Chinese anthology, being three hundred poems of the T'ang dynasty, 618-906, translated by Witter Bynner from the texts of Kiang Kang-hu, 江元虎. New York,

————. Selections from the Three hundred poems of the T'ang dynasty, translated by Soame Jenyns. London, J. Murray, 1943. 116 p. (The wisdom of the East series, ed. by L. Cranmer-Byng [and] A.W. Watts) 1st ed. 1940.

————. A further selection from the Three hundred poems of the T'ang dynasty, translated by Soame Jenyns. London, J. Murray [1944] 95 p. (The Wisdom of the East series, ed. by L. Cranmer-Byng).

TCHANG, FONG, 張鳳. The paon; ancien poème chinois, traduit par Tchang Fong, suivi d'une étude de l'évolution poétique en Chine. Paris, Jouve et ' Cie, 1924. 43 p.

TCHOU, KIA-KIEN, 朱家健. Anthologie de la poèsie chinoise, par Tchou Kia-kien et Armand Gandon. Pékin, Impr. de la "Politique de Pékin," 1927. 64 p. illus.

TREVELYAN, ROBERT CALVERLEY, 1872- ed. From the Chinese. Oxford, The Clarendon Press, 1945. xvi, 92 p.

TS'AI T'ING-KAN, 蔡廷幹, 1861-1934? Chinese poems in English rhyme. Chicago, University of Chicago Press [c1932] xxi, 145, [1] p.

[TS'AO, SHANG-LING]. Le flûte de jade, 失笛記. Poésies chinoises, traduit par Franz Toussaint. Paris, L'édition d'art H. Piazza [1926] 138 p., 21. incl. col. plate, ("Ex oriente lux").

————]. The lost flute, and other Chinese lyrics; being a translation from the French, by Gertrude Laughlin Joerissen of the book of Franz Toussaint entitled "La flute de jade: poésies chinoise[s]." London, T.F. Unwin ltd. [1923] New York, Brentano, 1924. 177 p.

————]. The same. New York, The Elf, 1929. ix-xiv, 185 p.

TSEN, TSON-MING, 曾仲鳴, 1896-1939. tr. Ancient poèmes chinois d'auteurs inconnues. 中國無名氏古詩選譯. nouv. éd. rev. et augm. Lyon, J. Desvigne; Paris, E. Leroux, 1927. 118 p. illus. ler éd., 1923.

————. Rêve d'une nuit d'hiver (cent quatrains des Thang). Lyon, J. Desvigne; Paris, E. Leroux, 1927. 113 p. illus.,

UNDERWOOD, EDNA (WORTHLEY) 1873- tr. Three Chinese masterpieces, translated into English by Edna Worthley Underwood and Chi-Hwang Chu, 朱其璜. Portland, Me., Mosher press, 1927. [13] p.

WADDELL, HELEN JANE, 1889- comp. and tr. Lyrics from the Chinese. New York, H. Holt, [1935] xiv, 41 p.

WALEY, ARTHUR, 1889- tr. The temple, and other poems. With an introductory essay on early Chinese poetry, and an appendix on the development of different metrical forms. London, G. Allan and Unwin, [1923] 150, [1] p.

————. The same. New York, A.A. Knopf, 1923. 150 p.

————. [Poems from the Chinese] London, E. Benn, 1927. 31 p. (The Augustan books of English poetry, 2nd ser., 7).

————. One hundred and seventy Chinese poems. London, Constable, New York, Knopf, 1939. xii, 168 p. 1st ed. 1918.

————. Translations from the Chinese, illustrated by Cyrus LeRoy Baldridge. New York, A.A. Knopf, 1941; Toronto, Ryerson Press, 1941. 3-325 p. illus., col. plates.

————. Chinese poems, selected from 170 Chinese poems, More translations from the Chinese, The temple and The book of songs. London, G. Allen and Unwin ltd [1946]; 3rd impression, 1956. 213, [1] p.

WILHELM; RICHARD, 1873-1930, tr. Chinesisch-deutsche Jahres- und Tageszeiten; Lieder und Gesänge, verdeutscht von Richard Wilhelm, mit 16 Nachbildungen chinesischer Holzschnitte. Jena, E. Diederichs, 1922. 129 numb. 1., 21.

WONG, MAN, 黃斐 [Huang Wên] tr. Poems from China, 詩詞譯選, translated by Wong Man. Hongkong, Creation Books [1950] xvii, 241 p.

YOUNG, CLARA MARGARET (CANDLIN) 1883- The herald wind, transaltions of Sung dynasty poems, lyrics and songs with an introduction by L. Cranmer-Byng, foreword by Dr. Hu Shih. London, J. Murray [1933] 113 p. (The Wisdom of the East).

## Leading Poets: Chü Yuan 屈原

CHINESE PEOPLE'S COMMITTEE FOR WORLD PEACE. Commemoration of
Chü Yuan, Nicolaus Copernicus, François Rabelais, Jose Marti. Peking,
1953. 41 p. illus.

CH'Ü, YÜAN, 屈原, ca. 343-ca. 277 B.C. The Li sao, 離騷, an elegy on en-
countering sorrows, by Ch'ü Yüan, of the state of Ch'u (circa 388-288 B.C.)
Translated into English verse with introduction, notes, commentaries, and
vocabulary by Lim Boon Keng, 林文慶. With an introductory note by Sir Hugh
Clifford, and prefaces by H. A. Giles, Rabindranath Tagore, Chen Huan-
Chang, 陳煥章. Shanghai, Commercial Press, 1929. xxxviii, 200 p. illus.,
col. plate, maps (1 fold.) facsim.

———. Küh Yuan's "Fahrt in die Ferne" (Yüan yu, 遠遊) von Franz Biallas.
Leipzig, Verlag der Asia Major, 1928-31. Reprinted from Asia Major, v. 4.

———. Das älteste Dokument zur chinesischen Kunstgeschichte, T'ien-wen, 天
問... die "Himmelsfragen" des K'üh Yüan, übersetzt und erklärt von August Conrady, abgeschlossen und hrsg. von Eduard Erkes. Leipzig, Verlag
Asia Major, 1931. vii, 266 p. (China-Bibliothek der "Asia Major," Bd. 2).

———. The great summons, 招魂. From the translation of Arthur Waley.
Honolulu, The White Knight Press, 1949. 12 p.

———. Li sao, and other poems. Translated by Yang Hsien-yi and Gladys Yang.
Peking, Foriegn Languages Press, 1953. xvii, 84 p. plates.

———. The nine songs, 九歌; a study of shamanism in ancient China [by] Arthur
Waley. London, G. Allen and Unwin [1955] New York, Grove Press, 1956,
64 p.

## LI PO 李白

LI, PO, 李白, 705?-762. Quarante poésies de Li Tai-pé; texte, traduction et
commentaire par Bruno Belpaire. Paris, Impr. Nationale, 1921. 63 p.

———. Li-Tai-po: Gedichte. Aus dem Chinesischen übers. von Otto Hauser. 4.
Aufl. Berlin und Weimar, Duncker, 1922. x, 30 p. (Aus fremden Gärten. 1.)
1. Aufl. 1906.

———. Songs of Li-Tai-pe [and other Chinese poets] from the "Cancionerio chi -
nes" of Antonio Castro Feijo; an interpretation from the Portuguese by Jordan Herbert Stabler. New York, E. H. Wells, 1922. 43 p.

———. The works of Li Po, the Chinese poet, done into English verse by Shige-
yoshi Obata; with an introduction and biographical and critical matter translated from the Chinese. New York, E. P. Dutton, 1922; London, Dent, 1923;
New York, E. P. Dutton, 1928. xviii, 236 p. front. (port.).

———. La cigale éperdue; une transcription de Li Tai-peh d'après les caractères traduits et commentés par Yau Chang-foo, 姚昌復 [by] Jean Marie Guis-
lain. Paris, Albert Messein, 1925. 160 p. (Collection la phalange).

———. Poems of Li Po, the Chinese poet; done into vignettes by Frank Anken-
brand, jr.; foreword by Beaumont Bruestle. Haddon Heights, N. J., W. L.
Washburn, 1941. 53 l. incl. front. illus.

———. Der Pavillon aus Porzellan; Li-Tai-Pe's Spiegelgedicht in zwölffacher Ab-
wandlung, von Carl Albert Lange. Wedel (Holstein), Alster Verlag, 1946.
[27] p. illus.

———. Gedichte. Nach den unsterblichen des Li-Tai-Po von Hans Schiebelhuth.
Darmstadt, Darmstädter Verlag, 1948. 23 l.

BECKERATH, ERICH VON, 1891- Balladen um Li Tai-Pe. Lorch/Württ., Bur-
ger-Verlag, 1947. 55 p. illus.

HSU, SUNG-NIEN, 徐仲年, 1904- Essai sur Li Po, avec une préface de M. Maurice Courant. Pékin, Impr. de la "Politique de Pékin," 1934. v, 14 (i. e.

140) l. fold map. (Collection de la "Politique de Pékin").
——. Li Thai-po, son temps, sa vie et son oeuvre. Lyon, Boscfrères, M. et L. Riou, 1935. 193, [2] p. Thèse-Univ. de Lyon.
WALEY, ARTHUR, 1889-   The poetry and career of Li Po, 701-762 A.D. London, G. Allen and Unwin;  New York, Macmillan [1950] x, 123 p. (Ethical and religious classics of East and West, 3 ).

## Pai, Chü-i  白居易

PAI, CHÜ-I, 白居易, 772-846. Lieder eines chinesischen Dichters und Trinkers (Po Chü-i) übertragen von L. Woitsch. Mit Illustrationen von Richard Hadl. Leipzig, Verlag der Asia Major, 1925. iii, 110, [2] p. illus.
——. Aus dem Gedichten Po Chü-i's. Übers. von Erwin von Zach. Batavia, 1935. [12] p. "Overdruck uit het "Sin Po" gedenkboek 1910-1935, Batavia."
——. The everlasting woe. Ch'ang heng kuo, 長恨歌, by Po Chü-i (A.D. 772-846). Translated by Jen Tai, 任泰. Shanghai, Chung Hua Book Co., 1939. 27 p.

——. Po Chü-i as a censor; his memorials presented to Hsien-tsung during the years 808-810 [translated and explained by] Eugene Feifel. Ann Arbor, University Microfilms [ 1952] ([University Microfilms, Ann Arbor, Mich.] Publication no. 3885) Collation of the original: vii, 398 l. Feifel's thesis-Columbia University.
HOANG-XUAN-NHI. Plaintes d'une chinh-phou, femme dont le mari part pour la guerre, et autres poèmes. Paris, Stock (Delamain et Boutelleau) 1943. [9]-194 p., 2 l. "Plaintes d'une chinh-phou" was written in Chinese characters by Dang-trân-Côn in the 18th century. It was translated into Annamese by Doàn-thi-Diêm. cf. p. [21] "Le poète et la musicienne" was written by the Chinese poet, Po Chü-i. cf. p. [83].
LO, TA-KANG, 羅大綱. La double inspiration du poète Po Kiu-yi (772-846). Paris, P. Bossuet, 1939. [7]-156, [4] p. Thèse-Univ. de Paris.
WALEY, ARTHUR, 1889-  The life and times of Po Chü-i, 772-846 A.D. London, G. Allen and Unwin [1949] 238 p. port., fold. map, geneal. table.

## Su Shih, 蘇軾

SU, SHIH, 蘇軾, 1036-1101. Selections from the works of Su Tung-p'o, A.D. 1036-1101, translated into English, with introduction, notes and commentaries by Cyril Drummond Le Gros Clark and wood engravings by Averil Salmond Le Gros Clark; the foreword by Edward Chalmers Werner. London, J. Cape, 1931. 9-180 p. incl. plates. front. (port.).
——. The red cliff by Su Shih (1036-1101), popularly known as Su Tung-po; translated by Honcan Bough... with biographical notes of the author and of Ts'ao Ts'ao, 曹操, and Chou Yu, 周瑜. New York, H. Bough, 1934. 8 p.
——. The prose-poetry of Su Tung-p'o; being translations into English of the... [fu] with introductory essays, notes and commentaries by Cyril Drummond Le Gros Clark; the foreword by Ch'ien Chung-shu, 錢鍾書. Shanghai, Kelly and Walsh, 1935; London, K. Paul, 1935. vii-xxii, 280 p. plates, fold. facsim.
LIN, YU-T'ANG, 1895- The gay genius; the life and times of Su Tungpo. New York, J. Day Co. [1947] [3] l., v-xi, 427 p. illus., ports., map.
——. The same. London and Melbourne, Heinemann [1948] xii, 370 p. illus., map.

## T'ao Ch'ien, 陶潛

T'AO, CH'IEN, 陶潛, 372?-427? Tau Yüan-ming, ausgewählte Gedichte in deutscher Nachdichtung...von Vincenz Hundhausen. Peiping, Pekinger Verlag,

1928. 13-54 p. illus, (port. )

――――. Les poèmes de T'ao Ts'ien, traduit du chinois par Liang Tsong tai, 梁宗岱 ; préface de Paul Valéry; avec trois eaux-fortes originales de Sanyu et un portrait du poète d'après Hwang Shen. Paris, Lemarget, 1930. 79, [1] p., front., plates.

[――――]. T'ao Yuan-ming, par Wong Wen-po, 黃文博. Paris, Vigot Frères, 1934. viii, 128 p. Thèse-Univ. de Paris.

――――. T'ao the hermit; sixty poems by T'ao Ch'ien (365-427) Translated, introduced and annotated by William Acker. London, New York, Thames and Huddon [1952] 157 p.

――――. Poems; translated by Lily Pao-hu Chang, 張鄭寶瀌, [and] Marjorie Sinclair. Brush drawings by Tseng Yu-ho, 曾幼荷. Honolulu, University of Hawaii Press [1953] ix, 133 p. illus.

## Tu Fu, 杜甫

TU, FU, 杜甫, 712-770. The book of seven songs by Tu Fu, translated into English by Edna Worthley Underwood and Chi-Hwang Chu, 朱其璜. Portland, Me., Mosher Press, 1928. [13] p.

――――. Tu Fu, wanderer and minstrel under moons of Cathay, translated by Edna Worthley Underwood and Chi Hwang Chu, 朱其璜. Portland, Me., Mosher Press, 1929. v-liv, 246, [3] p. plates.

――――. Tu Fu, the autobiography of a Chinese poet, A. D. 712-770, including an historical year record, a biogrpahical index, and a topographical note, as well as maps, plans, and illustrations, arranged from his poems and translated by Florence Ayscough. London, J. Cape; Boston and New York, Houghton Mifflin [1929-34] 2 v. fronts, (ports. ) illus. (incl. plans) plates, fold. map.

――――. Tu-fu, China's great poet, the bard of T'sao t'ang ssu, 草堂寺. A translation of some of Tu Fu's poems written in Szechuan. By A. J. Brace. Translated with the hope of interesting Chinese students of English in studying English from Chinese sources. Chengtu, Rih hsin Press [1934?] cover-title, [ix]-xvii, 72 p. plates, port.

――――. Tufu's Gedichte (nach der Ausgabe des Chang Chin, 張縉 ) Buch xi-xx, übersetzt von Erwin von Zach. Batavia, 1936. 171 p. ([Zach, Erwin von] Sinologische beiträge, iii).

――――. Gedichte; übers. von Erwin von Zach. Edited with an introd. by James Robert Hightower. Cambridge, Harvard University Press, 1952. 2 v. (x, 864 p.) (Harvard-Yenching Institute studies, 8).

――――. Die grossen Klagen des Tu Fu. Nachdichtungen von Werner Helwig. Bremen, Schünemann, 1956. 91 p. plates.

HUNG, WILLIAM, 洪業, 1893- Tu Fu, China's greatest poet. Cambridge, Harvard University Press, 1952. x, 300 p. map (on lining papers).

――――. A supplementary volume of notes. Cambridge, Harvard University Press, 1952. 113 p.

### Other Poets

FAN, CH'ÊNG-TA, 范成大, 1125-1193. The golden year of Fan Cheng-ta, a Chinese rural sequence rendered into English verse by Gerald Bullett; with notes and calligraphic decorations by Tsui Chi, 崔驥. Cambridge [Eng.] University Press, 1946. 43, [1] p.

HAN, YÜ, 韓愈, 768-824. Poetische Werke, übers. von Erwin von Zach. Edited with an introd. by James Robert Hightower. Cambridge, Harvard University Press, 1952. xi, 393 p. (Harvard-Yenching Institute studies, 7).

LI, YÜ, 李煜, 937-978. Poems of Lee Hou-chu; rendered into English from the Chinese by Liu Yih-ling, 劉翼凌 , and Shahid Suhrawardy. With Chinese text.

Bombay, Orient Longmans [1948] xv, 79 p.

——. Die Lieder des Li Yü, 937-978, Herrschers der südlichen T'ang-Dynastie. Als Einführung in die Kunst der chinesischen Lieddichtung aus dem Urtext vollständig übertragen und erläutert von Alfred Hoffmann. Köln, Greven
Verlag [1950] xii, 274 p. illus.

LIN, PU, 林逋, 967-1028. Lin Ho-ching, 林和靖. Translated and annotated by
Max Perleberg. Hong Kong, K. Weiss, 1952. 150, [2] p. plates, port (Sino-
British publication, 1)

LU, YU, 陸游, 1125-1210. The rapier of Lu, patriot poet of China, translations
and biography by Clara M. Candlin (Mrs. W.A. Young) London, J. Murray
[1946] 68 p. (The Wisdom of the East series).

MENG CHIANG NÜ, 孟姜女(Chinese drum song) The lady of the long wall, a ku
shih, or drum song of China; translated from the Chinese by Genevieve Wimsatt and Geoffrey Chen (Chen Sun-han) New York, Columbia University Press,
1934. 13-84 p. incl. mounted front., mounted illus.

MÊNG, HAO-JAN, 孟浩然, 689-740. Biographies of Meng Hao-jan, translated
by Hans Hermann Frankel. Berkeley, University of California Press, 1952.
25 p. (California, University, Institute of East Asiatic Studies. Chinese dynastic histories translations. 1).

NA-LAN, HSING-TÊ, 納蘭性德, 1655-1685. Na-lan Sing-tö, par Wang Soo-ying,
王淑瑛, Paris, Vigot frères, 1937. 99, [12] p. incl. port., facsims. Thèse-
Univ. de Paris.

[SUNG, PO-JEN], 宋伯仁. The flowering plum, 梅花喜神譜 [poems; edited by]
Alfred Koehn. Peiping, Lotus Court, 1947. 62 p. (on double leaves) illus.

TSAO CHIH, 曹植, 192-232. Six poems of the Tsao Tzu-chien, 曹子建, translated by K'uai Shu-p'ing, 蒯淑平. Peiping, Peking National University, 1948.
31 p. (Peking University semicentennial papers, 14).

WANG, WEI, 王維, 699-759. Wang Wei, le poète... par Liou Kin-ling. Paris,
Jouve et Cie, 1941. 165, [1] p. plates.

WEN, TING-YÜN, 溫庭筠, -880. Wen Fei-ch'ing, 溫飛卿 und seine literarische
Unwelt von Lu I, 陸易. Wurzburg, Aumühle, 1939. 65 p.

YEN, YÜ, 嚴羽, 12th cent. Tsang-lang Discourse on poetry, 滄浪詩話, by Yen
Yü, translated from the Chinese by Peng Chun Chang, 張彭春, with a foreword by J.E. Spingarn. Pittsburgh, Laboratory Press, 1929. 10 p.

YÜ, HSÜAN-CHI, 魚玄機, 844-871. Selling wilted peonies; biography and songs
of Yü Hsüan-chi, T'ang poetess [by] Genevieve Wimsatt. New York, Columbia University Press, 1936. 119 p. ports.

YUAN, MEI, 袁枚, 1716-1798. Yuan Mei, eighteenth century Chinese poet by
Athur Waley. London, G.Allen and Unwin [1956] 227 p. port., map.


## Modern Poetry

AIKEN, CONRAD POTTER, 1889- A letter from Li Po, and other poems. New
York, Oxford University Press, 1955. 93 p.

ALLAN, PATRICIA. Shanghai picture-verse. Shanghai,Kelly and Walsh, [1939]
61 p. col. illus.

ALLEY, REWI, 1897- Gung ho; poems. Chosen and ed. by H. Winston Rhodes.
Christchurch, Caxton Press, 1948. 67 p. illus., ports.

——. Leaves from a Sandan notebook. [Prose and verse] Chosen and edited by
H. Winston Rhodes. Christchurch,Caxton Press, 1950. 64 p. illus., port.

——. This is China today, poems, chosen and edited by H. Winston Rhodes.
[Christchurch?] Rewi Alley Aid Group, 1951. 30 p.

BALL, EVELYN HANNA. Pictures of old Cathay. Kansas City, Kan., Printed
by the Johnston Typesetting and Printing Co., c1937. 3-42 numb. 1.

BREDON, JULIET. Chinese shadows, child songs, songs of the people. Temple
sketches. Peking, Printed by the Pei Ku'an Press, 1922. 91 p.

BURGESS, STELLA FISHER, 1881- A Peking caravan. [2d ed. Peking 1924]

Shanghai, Shanghai Times, 1924. 32 1.

CHAPIN, HELEN BURWELL, 1892-1950. Echoes. Berkeley, Printed at the Gillick Press, 1938. [62] p. mounted illus.

CHÊNG, CH'I-YÜ, 鄭啓愚 . New China in verse. Berkeley, Gillick Press, 1944. xxiv, 120 p.

CRARY, RUTH. Legends from ancient China. Mill Valley, Calif., Wings Press, 1952. 63 p.

FICKE, ARTHUR DAVISON, 1883- Christ in China; a poem, [Moline, Ill.] 1927. 40 p.

FROST, LOWELL CHESTER, 1882- Poems of Hua Lo. Los Angeles [Beverly Hills, McAndrew Press] 1946. ii-v, 3-78 p.

GARRETT, ERWIN CLARKSON, 1879- Jenghiz Khan, and other verses. Philadelphia, John C. Winston Co., 1924. 251 p.

GRAHAM, DOROTHY, 1893- Brush strokes on the fan of a courtesan; verse fragments in the manner of the Chinese, by Dorothy Graham and James W. Bennett. New York, H. Vinal, ltd., 1927. 46 p.

HANIGHEN, BERNARD DAVID, 1908- Pan Ku. [Poem. Winston-Salem, N.C.] c1953. 15 double 1.

HAUSHOFER, ALBRECHT, 1903-1945. Chinesische Legende, eine dramatische Dichtung. [Berlin, L. Blanvalet, 1949] 126 p. 1947 ed., 81 p.

HAUSMANN, MANFRED. Hinter dem Perlenvorhang. Gedichte nach dem Chinesischen. 2 neubearb. Aufl. Frankfurt a M., S. Fischer, 1956. 79 p.

HEAD, FRANCES NOWLIN. Chin Chin, Chinese man, pictures by Janet Laura Scott. New York, E. P. Dutton [c1931] 64 p.

HOROSE, S. La symphonie des ombres chinoises, idylle. Paris, Éditions de la Madeleine [c1932] xix, 267 p.

HSIEH, TEHYI謝德怡, 1884- Chinese epigrams inside out, and proverbs. New York, Exposition Press [1948] 75 p.

[HSIEH, WAN-YING, 謝婉瑩, 1902- Spring water, by Hsieh Ping Hsin, 謝冰心, [pseud.] translated by Grace M. Boynton. [Peking? 1929?] cover-title, 80 p.

KAIKINI, P. R. Shanghai: poems. Bombay, New Book Co., [1939] 63 p.

KASACK, HERMANN. Aus dem chinesischen Bilderbuch. [Gedichte]. Zeichnungen von Gaspar Neher. Frankfurt a.M., Suhrkamp, 1955. 49 p.

KEENEY, LOUELLA, 1882- Sky lanterns; vignettes of China, by Conly Keeney [pseud.] Los Angeles, Academy Publishers] 72 p.

KOMAI, GONNOSKE. Fuji-Yama and other poems, transcribed from the Chinese and Japanese originals. London, Eastern Press, [1934] 215 p.

KWAN, MOON,關文清[Kwan Wên-Ching] A Chinese mirror; poems and plays. Los Angeles, Phoenix Press, 1932. 68 p.

LEE, FRANK W., 李錦綸[Li Chin-lun], 1884-1956. Leaves from Chinese history in verse. [New York?] 1952-1955. 2 v.

LESTER, EMMA SERVICE. Poems to Wu; illustrations by C. Bockisch. Shanghai, Commercial Press, 1925. 3-70 p. front., illus.

LI, CHI, 李季, 1921- Wang Kuei and Li Hsiang-hsiang, 王貴與李香香. Translated by Yang Hsien-yi and Gladys Yang]. Peking, Foreign Languages Press, 1954. 33 p. illus.

———. Wang Gue und Li Hsiang-hsiang, von Li Dji. Peking, Verlag für Fremdsprachige Literatur, 1954. 34 p.

———. Songs from the Yumen oilfields,玉門詩抄. [Translated by Yuan Ko-chia] Peking, Foreign Languages Press, 1957. 48 p.

LOOMIS, FREDERIC, 1877-1949. In a Chinese garden,及時行樂. [Piedmont, Calif., Loomis Book Co., c1946]ii, 15 p. illus.

LUM, CHUNG PARK, 林松柏, [Lin Sung-po]. Chinese verse [by] Chung Park Lum, translation [by] Sui Peng糸一期; decoration [by] Edna Francess Edell. [New York, L. Quan and Co., c1927]. 169 p. front. (port.) illus.

MEISSNER, PATRICIA (JONES) 1923- Ilha Formosa; poems of Formosa. [Taipei, Chinese Petroleum Corp., 1954] 32 1.

NORTH, WILLIAM ROBERT, 1890- Chinese themes in American verse. Philadelphia, 1937. [11]-175 p. Thesis-University of Pennsylvania.

PAYNE, PIERRE STEPHEN ROBERT, 1911- ed. Contemporary Chinese poetry [an anthology] London, Routledge [1947] 168 p.

[RABBITT, JAMES A.] Ballads of the East, by Shamus A'Rabbitt [pseud.] illustrations by "Sapajou." Shanghai [A.R. Hager, 1937] 52 p. illus.

┣━━━━━┫. China coast ballads, by Shamus A'Rabbitt [pseud.] illustrations by "Sapajou." Shanghai [A.R. Hager, 1938] 3-125, [1] p. illus.

ROSSER; FLAVIA. Oriental lyrics. New York, Vantage Press [1955] 68 p.

SHEPHARD, ESTHER: The cowherd and the sky maiden, 牛郎織女, a retelling, in verse (decorated with rhyme and assonance) of an ancient Chinese legend, with an after-piece, explaining the background of the legend. San Jose, Calif., Pacific Rim Publishers [1950] 80 p. illus., facsims.

SWEENEY, THOMAS BELL, 1874- Makers of war. New York, Vantage Press [1951] 169 p.

TENNEY, HELEN. River of Golden Sands; verse impressions of China: 1915-20. New York, Exposition Press [1955] 95 p.

TSIANG, HSI-TSENG, 蔣希曾. Poems of the Chinese revolution, 中國革命詩 English ed. [New York, Printed by Liberal Press, c1929] cover-title, [3]-26 p.

WANG, CHAO-MING, 汪兆銘, 1884-1944. Poèmes et "tseu" choisis de Wang Ching-wei. Traduits et annotés par Hsu Sung-nien, 徐仲年. Pékin, Impr. de la "Politique de Pékin," 1932. 75 p. (Collection de la "Politique de Pékin")

━━━━━━. Poems of Wang Ch'ing-wei, translated into English with a preface and notes by Seyuan Shu, 許思園; foreword by T. Sturge Moore. London. G. Allen and Unwin. [1938] 96 p. front. (port)

WEISKOPF, FRANZ CARL, 1900- Des Tien Tschien Lied vom Karren. 田間趕 車傳. Nachdictung aus dem Chinesischen. Berlin, Dietz, 1954. 252 p.

WU MING FU. [pseud.] The wisdom of Wu Ming Fu, edited by Stanwood Cobb. New York, H. Holt [c1931] xii, 50 p.

━━━━━━. Patterns in jade of Wu Ming Fu, edited by Stanwood Cobb. Washington, Avalon Press [c1935] xi, [2] 52 p.

━━━━━━. The way of life of Wu Ming Fu, edited by Stanwood Cobb. Washington, Avalon Press [c1942] xi. [2] 58 p.

YEOU, TA, 尤達, [Yu, Ta] Nuits de Chine, 華夜集 [par] Yeou Ta. Introd. et adaptation de Joséphine. Paris, P. Seghers [1954] 39 p. (Collection P.S., no. 389).

## Plays: General Studies

ARLINGTON, LEWIS CHARLES, 1859-1942. The Chinese drama from the earliest times until to-day; a panoramic study of the art in China, tracing its origin and describing its actors (in both male and female rôles) : their costumes and make-up, superstitions and stage slang: the accompanying music and musical instruments: concluding with synopses of thirty Chinese plays, with a pien... by Mei Lan-fang and a foreword by H.A. Giles. Shanghai, Kelly and Walsh, 1930. xxxi, 177 p., 1 l., xxxv-xli, [1] p. incl. illus., plates, col. front.

━━━━━━. Le théâtre chinois depuis les origines jusqu'à nos jours; sources-rôles-costumes-grimages-superstitions-statuts-argot de scène-légendes- musique orchestrale-instruments de musique- programmes: une étude d'ensemble de l'art théâtral de la Chine suivie de trente résumés de pièces et enrichie de cent-quinze planches lithographiques en couleurs. Traduit de l'anglais par G. Uhlmann. Pékin, H. Vetch, 1935. xxi, 184, [25] p. incl. illus., plates, col. front.

BISHOP, JOHN LYMAN, 1913- A Chinese drama in eighteenth century Europe by

Marco Polo [pseud.] Cambridge, 1952. 24 p. (Susan Antholony Potter prize).

BUSS, KATE. Studies in the Chinese drama. Boston, The Four Seas Co. 1922,
New York, J. Cape and H. Smith [1930]. 97 p. incl. plates, facsim. front.
plates, port.

JOHNSTON, REGINALD FLEMING, 1874-1938. The Chinese drama, with six illustrations reproduced from the original paintings, by C. F. Winzer. Shan-
hai, Kelly and Walsh, 1921. 36 p. incl. 6 col. mounted pl.

LIU, CHÜN-JO, 劉君若 , 1925- A study of the Tsa-chü, 雜劇 of the 13th century
in China. Madison, 1952. 111, 185 1. Thesis-Univ. of Wisconsin.

LIU, JAMES, 劉若愚. Elizabethan and Yuan; a brief comparison of some conventions in poetic drama. London, the China Society, 1955. 12 p. front.
(China Society occasional papers, 8).

LOWE, H.    Y., 盧興源? Stories from Chinese drama; with illustrations by
the author. Peking, Peking Chronicle Press, 1942. xxli, 413, xxxviii, p. illus.

MILLER, ROBERT PICKENS, 1909- The particles in the dialogue of Yuan drama; a descriptive analysis. [New Haven] 1952. 88 1. Thesis-Yale University.

YANG, RICHARD FU-SEN, 揚富森 , 1918- Lü Tung-pin, 呂洞賓, in the Yüan
drama. Seattle, Wash. 1956. 212, 10, 7 1. Thesis-University of Washington.

ZUNG, CECILIA S. L.程修齡, 1903- Secrets of the Chinese drama; a complete
explanatory guide to actions and symbols as seen in the performance of Chinese dramas. With synopses of fifty popular Chinese plays and 240 illustrations, including 54 colour plates. Shanghai, Kelly and Walsh, 1937. xxv,
3-299 p. incl. front., illus. (part col.; incl. ports., plans, facsim.).

## Translations

ARLINGTON, LEWIS CHARLES, 1859-1942, ed. and tr. Famous Chinese plays,
translated and edited by L. C. Arlington and Harold Acton. Peiping, H. Vetch,
1937. xxx, 443, [1] p. front., plates.

CH'ING TING CHU, 慶頂珠 [ 打魚殺家] The fisherman's revenge, a Peking o-
pera. [Translated by Yang Hsien-yi and Gladys Yang] Peking, Foreign Languages Press, 1956. 53 p. illus.

[HSI HSIANG CHI], 西廂記. Das West-zimmer [hrsg. von] Vincenz Hundhausen;
ein chinesisches Singspiel in deutscher Sprache. Mit 21 Bildern nach chinesischen Holzschnitten. Peking, Leipzig, Pekinger Verlag, 1926. 355, [1] p.
front., plates.

[————]. L'amoureuse Oriole, jeune fille; roman d'amour chinois du xiii me
siècle, par Soulié de Morant. Avec dix illustrations chinoises. Paris, E.
Flammarion [c1928] [5]-246 p., incl. plates

[————]. Si syang ki, par Chen Pao-ki, 优寶基. Lyon, Bosc frères, M. and L.
Riou, 1934. 170 p. Chen's thèse-Univ. de Lyon.

[————]. The romance of the western chamber (Hsi hsiang chi); a Chinese play
written in the thirteenth century, translated by S. I. Hsiung,熊式一, with a preface by Gordon Bottomley. London, Methuen [1935] xxiii, 280, [2] p. incl.
front., illus.

[————]. The west chamber, a medieval drama, translated from the original Chi-
nese with notes by Henry H. Hart. Foreword by Edward Thomas Williams.
Stanford, Stanford University Press; London, H. Milford, Oxford University
Press [c1936] xxxix, 192 p.

[————]. Das Westzimmer. [hrsg. von] Vincenz Hundhausen. Ein chinesisches
Singspiel des 13. Jahrhunderts. In deutscher Nachdichtung nach den chinesischen Urtexten des Wang Sche-fu,王實甫 und des Guan Han-Tsching,關漢鄉
Mit 21 Holzschnitten eines unbekannten Meisters. Eisenach, Erich Röth,
1954. 355 p.

HUNG, SHENG, 供昇, 1645-1704. The palace of eternal youth, 長生殿. [Trans-
lated by Yang Hsien-yi and Gladys Yang. 1st ed.] Peking, Foreign Languages

Press [1955] 322 p., music ([16] p.) plates, port.

KAO MING, 高明, fl. 1345. Die Flaute,琵琶記 von Gau Ming. Ein chinesisches
Singspiel in deutscher Sprache von Vincenz Hundhausen. Mit zwanzig wiedergaben chinesischer Holzschnitte. Peking, Pekinger Verlag [c1930] 469 p.,
incl. plates.

——. The two wives (Die beiden Gattinnen); eight scenes of Kao Ming's classical drama, The Lute (Die Laute) in German language by Vincenz Hundhausen.
English text-book translated from the German. [n.p.n.d.] 75 p. plates.

LALOY, LOUIS, 1874-1944, tr. Trois drames de l'Asie; (Le songe de la vie,
drame en 4 actes et 1 prologue-Vikrâma et Ourvâsi, ou le Roi et l'apsára,
drame in 5 actes-Le chagrin au palais de Hán, drame en 5 actes). Neuchâtel,
Éditions de la Baconnière, 1943. 7-140 p., (Collection des cashiers du Rhone,
sér. blanche, 21).

LI, HSING-TAO, 李行道. HUI LAN CHI, 灰闌記. Hui lan ki. Der Kreidekreis;
Schauspiel in vier Aufzügen und einen Vorspiel, von Li Hsing-tao aus dem
Chinesischen übersetzt von Alfred Forke. Leipzig, Philipp Reclam jun. 1927.
91 p. (Reclams Universal Bibliothek, 768).

——. Der Kreidekreis; Spiel in fünf Akten nach dem Chinesischen von Klabund
[pseud] Wien, Phaidon Verlag [1929] 103 numb. 1. illus.[1. aufl. Berlin,
I.M. Spaeth, 1925].

——. The circle of chalk; a play in five acts, adapted from the Chinese by Klabund [pseud]. English version by James Laver. London, W. Heinemann,
1929. xii, 107 p.

——. Der Kreiderkreis, ein Spiel in sechs Bildern nach dem Chinesischen von
Johannes von Guenther. Potsdam, Rütten and Loening, 1942. 184 p.

——. The same. ein Spiel in sechs Bildern nach dem Altchinesischen (Li Hsing-
tao) von Johannes von Guenther; mit einer Einleitung des Verfassers. Stuttgart, Reclam [1953] 97 p. (Reclams Universal-Bibliothek, Nr. 7777).

——. The story of the circle of chalk; a drama from the old Chinese, translated
by Frances Hume [from the French of Stanislas Julien] with illus. by John
Buckland-Wright. London, Rodale Press [1954] 124 p. col. plates.

LIU YIN CHI, 柳蔭記. Love under the willows; a Szechuan opera. Liang Shanpo
and Chu Ying-tai, 梁山伯與祝英台. [Translated by Yang Hsien-yi and Gladys
Yang] Peking, Foreign Languages Press, 1956. 85 p. illus.

MA, CHIH-YUAN, 馬致遠, fl. 1251. Le rêve du millet jaune; Houang liang mong,
黃粱夢, drame taoiste du XIIIe siècle. Traduit du chinois par Louis Laloy.
Paris, Desclée de Brouwer [1935] 134, [5] p. illus. (Courrier des iles, 5).

RUDELSBERGER, HANS, 1868- ed. Altchinesische Liebes-Komödien, aus dem
chinesischen Urtexte ausgewählt und übertragen von Hans Rudelsberger.
Wein, A. Schroll and co. ges. m.b.h. [c1923] 116 p.incl. col. mounted front.,
illus., col. mounted plates.

TANG, HSIEN-TSU, 湯顯祖, 1550-1617. Der Blumengarten, 牡丹亭 von Tang
Hsian-Dsu. Ein chinesisches Singspiel in deutscher Sprache von Vincenz Hund-
hausen. Mit vier Wiedergaben chinesischer Holzschnitte. Peking, Pekinger
Verlag, [1933] 138 p. front. illus.

——. Die Rückkehr der Seele, 還魂記. Ein romantisches Drama. In deutscher
Sprache von Vincenz Hundhausen. Zürich, Leipzig, Rascher, 1937. 3 v.

——. Das Urteil in der zehnten Hölle. In deutcher Sprache von Vincenz Hundhausen. Peking, Pekinger Verlag, 1937. 32 p.

WANG, PAO-CH'UAN, 王寶釧. Lady Precious Stream; an old Chinese play done
into English according to its traditional style by S.I. Hsiung,熊式一. with a preface by Lascelles Abercrombie. London, Methuen, 1934. Acting ed. 1936.
xx, 168, [1] p. incl. front., plates.

——. The same. New York, Liveright Pub. Corp.; xx, 168. [1] p. incl. front.,
plates.

——. The same. New York, Los Angeles, S. French; London, S. French, c1937.
126 p. diagr.

Theatre

ALLEN, B     S. Chinese theatres handbook. Tientsin, La Librairie française [192-] 56 p. incl plates. front. (port.).

ALLEY, REWI, 1897- Peking opera; an introduction through pictures by Eva
Siao. Illus. and back cover by Kuan Liang. Peking, New World Press, 1957.
99 p.

CHEN, JACK, 陳伊範 The Chinese theatre. Illustrated by the author. London,
Dobson [1949] 63 p. illus. (part col.) (International theatre and cinema).

CHEN, LIN-JUI, 陳嶺端 . The Peking opera. Shanghai, 1956. 22 p. plates (part.
col.).

CHI, JU-SHAN, 齊如山, 1877- Répertoire des maquillages de théâtre; avec une
traduction françiase par André d'Hormon. [Shanghai, Shang-tien, 1934] 10 f.
69 col. figs. on 6 l.

CHIAO, CH'ÊNG-CHIH, 焦承志, 1902- Le théâtre chinois d'aujourd'hui. Paris,
E. Droz, 1938. 180 p. plates, (Bibliothèque de la société des historiens du
théâtre, 9).

CHINA MAGAZINE. Chinese opera. [New York? 1947?] [8] p. of illus., ports.
''Reprinted from the China magazine, February 1947.''

2e FESTIVAL INTERNATIONAL D'ART DRAMATIQUE. Le théâtre classique de
Chine. Paris, Agence littéraire et artistique parisienne pour les échanges
culturels, 1955. 71 p. illus. plates.

KALVODOVÁ. Chinese theatre [by] Kalvodová, Sís, [and] Vaniš. [Translated by
Iris Urwin. London, Spring House, 1957] 39 p. 47 plates (part col., 3 fold.
in pocket) (Spring books).

K'UN CH'U NIGHT, 崑曲晚會; two Chinese dramatic plays presented in the Great
Hall, University of Hong Kong, January 23, 1954 under the auspices of the
Institute of Oriental Studies and the Chinese Society of the University of Hong
Kong. Hong Kong, 1954. [4], 9 2 p. English text; 1 16 p. Chinese text,
plates.

LEUNG, GEORGE KIN, 梁社乾, [LIANG SHÈ-CH'IEN], 1899- Mei Lan-fang,
foremost actor of China. Shanghai, Printed at the Commercial Press, 1929.
xii, 132 p. front., col. plates, ports. (1 col.; part fold.).

———. Special plays and scenes to be presented by Mei Lan-fang on his American tour. Peking, 1929. 116 p. ports.

———. Three short addresses and articles, with a bibliography of the articles
and lectures on the Chinese theatre. [Shanghai] 1931. Cover-title, 21 p.

MEI, LAN-FANG, 梅蘭芳, 1894- Selections from the répertoire of operatic
songs and terpsichorean melodies of Mei Lan-fang recorded in both Chinese
and European notation by Professor Liu Tien-hua, 劉天華, assisted by Professor Ch'i ju-shan, 齊如山, and others. Peiping, 1929. 2 v. ports. in portfolio.

[MOY, ERNEST K., 梅其駒, 1895-1958] Mei Lan-fang: Chinese drama. [New
York, China Institute, 1929] cover-title, [40] p.

———. The Pacific coast tour of Mei Lan-fang, under the management of the Pacific Chinese dramatic club. San Francisco, 1930. 20 l. illus. incl. ports.

———. Mei Lan-fang; what New York thinks of him; compiled by Ernest K. Moy.
New York, 1930. 39 p. illus.

———. The first American tour of Mei Lan-fang. New York, China Institute in
America, 1930. 40 p.

POUPEYE, CAMILLE, 1874- Le théâtre chinois; 41 planches hor texte. Paris-
Bruxelles, Éditions ''Labor'' [1933] 194, [2] incl. front. plates.

ROY, CLAUDE. L'opéra de Pékin. Illustrés de photos de Pic, commentaires de
R. Ruhlmann. Paris, Cercle d'Art, 1955. 104 p. plates, illus. map.

SCOTT, ADOLPHE CLARENCE, 1909- The classical theatre of China. London,
Allen and Unwin [1957] 250 p. illus. (part col.)

SOULIÉ, CHARLES GEORGES, 1878- Théâtre et musique modernes en Chine, par George Soulié de Morant. Avec une étude technique de la musique chinoise et transcriptions pour piano par André Gailhard. Paris, P. Geuthner, 1926. vii-xvi, 195 p. illus., plates (incl. ports.).

TCHENG, MIEN, 陳綿, [CH'ÊN MIEN], 1901- Le théâtre chinois moderne. Paris, Les Presses modernes, 1929. 195 p. Thèse-Univ. de Paris.

———. Répertoire analytique du théâtre chinois moderne, 中國近代戲目分類注解. Paris, Jouve, 1929. 182 p.

TCHOU, KIA-KIEN, 朱家健, [CHU CHIA-CHIEN] Le théâtre chinois. Texte de Tchou Kia-kien. Peintures, sanguines et croquis d'Alexandre Jacovleff. Paris, M. de Brunoff, 1922. 30 p. illus.

———. The Chinese theatre. Translated from the French by James A. Graham. With illustrations from painting, sketches and crayon drawings by Alexandre Jacovleff. London, John Lane, 1922. 35 p. plates.

TSIANG, UN-KAI, 蔣恩凱. K'ouen k'iu, le théâtre chinois ancien. Paris, Ernest Leroux, 1932. 130 p. 1 illus. (music).

WANG, KUANG-CHI, 王光祈, 1898-1936. Über die chinesische klassische Oper. Genf, 1934. cover-title, 46, [2] p. illus. (music) Diss.-Univ. Bonn.

YOU, YA-OUI, 李尤亞偉 Le théâtre classique en Chine et en France d'aprés l'Orphelin de la Chine [by Voltaire] et l'Orphelin de la famille Tchao [by Chi Chünhsiang, 紀君祥 趙氏孤兒] Paris, Les Presses Modernes, 1937. vii, 187 p. Thèse-Univ. de Paris.

ZUCKER, ADOLF EDUARD, 1890- The Chinese theater, Boston, Little, Brown, 1925. xvi, 234 p. col. mounted front., plates (3 col. mounted).

## Shadow Theatres

BENTON, PAULINE. The Red gate players introduce the actors and plays of the Chinese shadow theatre. Text by Pauline Benton. Peking, Lotus Court, 1940. 18 l. col. front.

JACOB, GEORG, 1862-1937. Schattenschnitte aus Nordchina. hrsg. und mit einer Einleitung versehen von George Jacob. Hannover, H. Lafaire, 1923. 32 p. 31 col. plates.

———. Das chinesische Schattentheater, bearbeitet von Georg Jacob und Hans Jensen. Stuttgart, W. Kohlhammer, 1933. xv, 130 p. illus. (incl. facsim.) (Das orientalische Schattentheater, 3).

———. Einführung in die altchinesische Schattenspiele. Stuttgart, W. Kohlkammer, 1935. 39 p. illus.

LAUFER, BERTHOLD, 1874-1934. Oriental theatricals. Chicago, Field Museum of Natural History, 1923. 59 p. illus. plates (part fold), (Field Museum. Dept. of Anthropology, Guide. pt. 1.).

MARCH, BENJAMIN, 1899-1934. Chinese shadow-figure plays and their making. With 3 pieces from the Chinese: Visiting Li Er Ssu, Fox bewitchment, The exorcism. Edited with notes by Paul McPharlin. Detroit, 1938. 57 p. illus. (Puppetry imprints, handbooks xi).

MELCHERS, BERND, 1886- Chinesische Schattenschnitte, ein Bilderbuck, gesammelt und herausgegeben von Bernd Melchers. München, H. Bruckmann, 1921; 3. Aufl. Kassel, Lometsch, 1954. 64 numb. l. incl. illus. (part col.) plates (part col.) (Druck d. Arche 5).

———. The same. 4. erw. Aufl. Kassel, Lometsch, 1956. 4 ungez. bl. illus. (Druck d. Arche 5).

RAABE, JOSEF. Die Donnergipfel-Pagode. Ein Beitrag zur Geschichte des chinesische Schattenspiels. Bonn, 1940. 66 p. plates. Diss.-Univ. Bonn.

WIMSATT, GENEVIEVE BLANCHE. Chinese shadow shows. Cambridge, Harvard University Press, 1936. xvii, 68 p. col. front. illus.

## Modern Plays

[AITKEN, ANDREW] 1868-  Mr. Ling, an incarnate deity and the moon, by Wilcox Arnold [pseud.] London, Wilkinson bros., ltd. (1933?) 132 p. pl.

BUCK, PEARL (Sydenstricker) 1892-  Sun Yat-sen; a play. Preceded by a lecture by Hu Shih. [London, China Campaign Committee, 1944?] Cover-title, 32 p. illus. ports.

CARTER, IDA C    MESSER. "The new tide in China"; a pageant in two acts. [New York] c1925. 15 p.

CHANG, TAO-FAN, 張道藩, 1897-  Par sa propre faute; drame en cinq actes, Version française de Hsu Sung-nien, 徐仲年. Pékin, Impr. de la "Politique de Pékin," 1936. 85 p. illus. (Collection de la "Politique de Pékin").

CHEN, CHI-TUNG, 陳其通, 1916-  The long march. Peking, Foreign Languages Press, 1956. 168 p. plates. port. double map. music.

COLLIS, MAURICE, 1889-  The motherly and auspicious, being the life of the Empress Dowager Tzu Hsi in the form of a drama, with an introduction and notes. London, Faber and Faber, [1943]; New York, G. P. Putnam, 1944. 179 p. incl. geneal. tables, ports.

COLTON, JOHN, 1889-  The Shanghai gesture: a play; with an introduction by John D. Williams. New York, Boni and Liveright, 1926. 256 p.

DAKIN, LAURENCE. Marco Polo, a drama in four acts. Portland [Me.] Falmouth Pub. House, 1946. 3-53, [1] p.

FARRÈRE, CLAUDE, 1876-  Les tribulations d'un Chinois en Chine; comédie en 3 actes, tirée du roman de Jules Verne, par Claude Farrère et C. Méré. Paris, Hatchette, 1931. 46 p.

FIELD, ELLIOT, 1875-  Chinese gold; a play in a prologue and two acts. Boston, Walter H. Baker [c1935] 48 p.

FRISCH, MAX, 1911-  Die chinesische Mauer; eine Farce. Berlin, Suhrkamp, 1955. 154 p. 1. Aufl. Basel, B. Schwabe, 1947.

GAUTIER, JUDITH, 1846-1917. La fille du ciel; drame chinois. [15] éd. conforme à la représentation. Paris, Calmann-Lévy [1925] v. [3]-239 p.

GHÉON, HENRI, 1875-1944. Les trois sagesses du vieux Wang; drame chinois en quatre tableaux, d'après des documents authentiques. Paris, A. Blot, 1927. [9]-105, [1] p. (Les cahiers du théâtre chrétien. 13)

――――. Die drei Weisheiten des alten Wang. Ein chinesisches Missionsspiel in vier Bildern. Übers. von Karl Fry. 2. Aufl. Luzern, Rex-Verlag, 1944. lv, 76 p.

GRANTHAM, ALEXANDRA ETHELRED (von Herder) 1867-  The twight-house of Yang Kuei-fei; a dramatic poem in one act. Shanghai, Kelly and Walsh, 1923. 56 p.

GROVER, HARRY GREENWOOD, 1881-  As the petals fall; a pantomime with words, by Ho Go Go; translated from the original ancient manuscript by Harry Greenwood Grover. New York, Los Angeles, S. French; London, S. French, c1935. 14 p. diagrs.

HAYDEN, GEORGE. Bandit's return; a two-act play about China. London, Edinburgh House Press, 1951. 48 p. (Everyland plays).

HENSEL, PAUL, 1893-   Die Pagode Tien-ti; Schauspiel in vier Akten, von Paul Hensel-Haerdrich. Uraufgeführt am 12. februar 1942 im Braunschweigischen Staatstheater. Als unverkäufliches Manuskript vervielfältigt. Berlin-Charlottenburg, G. Kiepenheuer Bühnenvertriebs [c1942] xii (i.e. xiv), 115 p. plan.

HO, CHING-CHIH, 賀敬之, 1924-  The white-haired girl; an opera in five acts, by Ho Ching-chih and Ting Yi, 丁毅. [Translated by Yang Hsien-yi and Gladys Yang] Peking, Foreign Languages Press, 1954. 97, [8] p. illus.

――――. La fille aux cheveux blancs. Opéra chinoise en 5 actes par Ho Ching-chi et Ting-yi. Traduction de Jacques Dubois. Paris, Éditeurs français réunis, 1955. 224 p.

HOPKINS, MAY DE WITT. The oar song of the Emperor Wu-ti; a play in 4 acts and prologue. [ Philadelphia, 1946] 161 p.

HSIUNG, FU-HSI, 熊佛西, 1901- Chinesisches Bauernleben; drei Stücke aus
dem Chinesischen Landleben, von Hsiung Fu-hsi, übersetzt von W. Eichhorn.
Tôkyô, Deutsche Gesellschaft für Natur- und Völkerkunde Ostasiens, kommissionsverlag von O. Harrassowitz, Leipzig, 1938. 161 p.

HSIUNG, SHIH-I, 熊式一, 1902-   Mencius was a bad boy. London, Privately
printed [1934] 23 p.

————. The professor from Peking; a play in three acts with a preface by Lord
Dunsany. London,, Methuen [1939] xii, 198 p.

HU, K'O, 胡可, 1920- Steeled in battles; translated by Tang Sheng, 唐笙. Peking, Foreign Languages Press, 1955. 130 p. illus. port.

KU, TSONG-NEE, 顧宗沂. Modern Chinese plays; translated into English. With
a preface by Koo Chung I, 顧仲彝. Shanghai, The Commercial Press, 1941.
vi, 137 p.

KUO, MO-JO, 郭沫若, 1892- Chü Yuan, a play in five acts. Translated by Yang
Hsien-yi and Gladys Yang. Peking, Foreign Languages Press, 1953. 126 p.
illus.

————. K'iu Yuan. Traduction, préface et notes de Liang Pai-tchin. 6 éd. Paris, Gallimard, 1957. 206 p. (Collection Unesco d'oeuvres représentatives
connaissance de l'Orient. Série chinoises, 5).

LI, CHIH-HUA, 李之華. Struggle against counter-struggle, a one-act play. Peking, China, Cultural Press, 1950. 74 p.

LOO, DING, 魯汀. Hirse für die Achte; ein chinesisches Volkstück von Loo Ding,
Chang Fan [ und] Chu Shin-nan. Deutsche Fassung für das Berliner Ensemble
von Elisabeth Hauptmann und Manfred Wekwerth nach der Übersetzung aus
dem Chinesischen von Yuan Miao-tze. Leipzig, Hofmeister c1956. 82 1. illus.

MARTENS, ANNE COULTER. James Hilton's Lost horizon, dramatized by Anne
Coulter Martens and Christopher Sergel. Chicago, Dramatic Pub. Co.,[1942]
133 p. front. (port.) diagrs.

O'NEILL, EUGENE GLADSTONE, 1888-1953. A play, Marco Millions. New York,
Boni and Liveright, 1927. ix, 180 p.

OSTASIEN ALMANACH. Sonder-Ausgabe des ''Bühnenspiegel im Fernen Osten''
hrsg. aus Anlass der 25. Aufführung vom Deutschen Theater-Verein, Shanghai. Shanghai, M. Nössler, 1930. 213 p. illus.

PATON, MARGARET HAMILTON NOËL. More than conquerors. London, Edinburgh House Press, 1943. 16 p.

PEKING PEOPLE'S ART THEATRE. Between husband and wife; a play in one act
written collectively by the Peking People's Art Theatre; translated by Sidney
Shapiro. [ Peking, 1953] 22 p. illus. (Supplement to China Reconstructs No. 6).

REACH, JAMES. China boy, a comedy in three acts, by James Reach and Tom
Taggart. New York, Los Angeles, S. French; London, S. French, c1937.
112 p. diagr.

REASON, JOYCE, 1894- The wall between; a true tale from China. London,
Livingstone Press, 1946. 24 p. (Everyland Plays, 8).

SATURDAY AFTERNOON AT THE MILL and other one-act plays. Peking, Foreign Languages Press, 1957. 134 p.

SHEN, TUAN-HSIEN, 沈端先, 1901- The Test; a play in five acts, by Hsia Yen,
夏衍. Peking, Foreign Languages Press, 1956. 107 p.

SHU, CH'ING-CHUN, 舒慶春, 1898- Dragon beard ditch,    龍鬚溝, a play in
three acts by Lao Sheh [ pseud] Translated by Liao Hung-ying, 廖鴻英. Peking, Foreign Languages Press, 1956. 97 p. plates, ports.

SIÉ, S.  K.,謝壽康, 1894- Le jade brisé,李碎玉. Pièce en six tableaux, jouée
pour la première fois en Europe, le 17 mars 1927, au Théâtre Royal du Parc
de Bruxelles. Peiping, Impr. de la ''Politique de Pékin,'' 1928. 54 p.

————. Tse Kiou, 自救; Les Perles s'égrènent. Pièce en six tableaux, d'après
l'oeuvre originale de Chang Tao-fan, 張道藩. Bruxelles, Éditions ''Labor,''

1941. 157 p.

————. Tse Kiu (Save yourself). English adaptation of a play in six scenes by Chang Tao-fan. Rome, "Trumminelli," 1944. 148 p.

————. Marèse. Pièce en six tableaux et un prologue, d'après le roman de Julia Frezin. Berne, Chekiai, 1942. 171 p. (Collection "Chekiai").

SIKS, GERALDINE BRAIN. Marco Polo. Charleston, W. Va., Children's Theatre Press, c1941. 41 p. illus.

TAYLOR, GEORGE EDWARD, 1905- The phoenix and the dwarfs, a play in three acts, by George E. Taylor and George Savage. New York, Macmillan, 1944. xxxiv, 119 p.

TING, SY-LING, 丁西林, 1893- Théâtre chinois moderne; trois pièces de Ting Sy-ling: La Guepe, Dans l'ivresse, Mon cher mari. Traduit par Tchang Tien-ya. Pékin, Impr. de la "Politique de Pékin," 1932. 46 p. (Collection de la "Politique de Pékin").

VERÈ, DANIELE. Princess in Tartary: a play for marionettes. London, J. Murray, 1940. 60 p.

WAN, CHIA-PAO, 萬家寶, 1905- The sunrise, 日出; a play in four acts, by Tsao Yu, 曹禺, [pseud.] Done into English by Ho Yong 何永佶 with an introd. on modern Chinese drama. Shanghai, Commercial Press, 1940. 189 p.

THE WOMEN'S REPRESENTATIVE-three one-act plays. Peking, Foreign Language Press, 1956. 124 p.

WOLF, FREDERICK. Tai Yang erwacht. Ein Schauspiel unverkäuflich. [Bühnen] MS. Berlin, Aufbau-Bühnen Verlag, 1947. 97 p.

ZUNG, CECILIA SIEU-LING, 程修齡, 1903- Two too many; a Chinese comedy in fifteen scenes. New York, Los Angeles, S. French; London, S. French, c1939. 106, [5] p. plates, diagrs.

## Novels: General Studies

BIRCH, CYRIL, 1925- Ku chin hsiao shuo, 古今小説 : a critical examination. London, 1955. 499 l. Thesis-School of Oriental and African Studies, University of London.

BISHOP, JOHN LYMAN, 1913- The San-yen 三言 collections: a study of the colloquial short story in seventeenth century China. Cambridge, 1953. 252 p. Thesis- Harvard University.

————. The colloquial short story in China; a study of the San-yen collections. Cambridge, Harvard University Press, 1956. xi, 144 p. (Harvard-Yenching Institute studies, 14)

BUCK, PEARL (Sydenstricker), 1892- East and West and the novel. Sources of the early Chinese novel. Addresses before the convocation of the North China Union Language School, February 1932. Peiping, North China Union Language School cooperating with California College in China [1932] 40 p.

————. The Chinese novel; Nobel lecture delivered before the Swedish academy at Stockholm, December 12, 1938. New York, John Day [c1939] London, Macmillan, 1939. 59 p. front. (port).

CHINESISCHE NOVELLEN. Deutsche Fassung nach der französischen Übertragung durch Lo Ta-Kang, 羅大綱, von Richard B. Matzig. Umschlag von Peter Birkhäuser. Basel, Gute Schriften, 1946. iv, 80 p. (Gute Schriften Basel, 227).

EBERHARD, WOLFRAM, 1909- Die chinesische Novelle des 17.-19. Jahrhunderts; eine soziologische Untersuchung. Hrsg. mit Unterstützung des China-Instituts, Bern. Ascona (Schweiz) Artibus Asiae, 1948. xii, 239 p. (Artibus Asiae Supplementum 9).

EICHHORN, WERNER. Chinesische Liebes-Novellen. Bonn, E.A. Eriksen, 1948. 132 p. illus.

OU ITAÏ 吳益泰 [ WU I-T'AI] Essai critique et bibliographique sur le roman chinois. Paris, Les Éditions Vega, 1933. 192 p. illus.

PRŮŠEK, JAROSLAV. Die Literatur des befreiten China und ihre Volkstraditionen. [ Übers. von Pavel Eisner und Wilhelm Gampert] Prag, Artia 1955. 736 p. illus.

SCHYNS, JOSEPH, 1899- Romans à lire et romans à proscrire, 說部甄評. Tientsin, Chihli Press, 1946. 297, 23 p. (Scheut editions, Ser. 1. Critical and literary studies, 1).

————. 1500 modern Chinese novels and plays by Jos. Schyns and others. Present day fiction and drama in China by Su Hsueh-lin, 蘇雪林. Short biographies of authors by Chao Yen-sheng, 趙燕聲. Peiping, Catholic Univ. Press, 1948. iv, lviii, 484 p. (Scheut editions. Ser. 1, Critical and literary studies, v. 3).

[SHU, CH'ING-CH'UN], 舒慶春. T'ang love stories. An address by S. Y. Shu before the convocation of the North China Union Language School, February 1932. Peiping, North China Union Language School, 1932. 22 p.

WILLIS, DONALD S., 1917- The Nieh-hai-hua, 孽海花, and its place in the late Ch'ing social novel of protest. Seattle, 1951 100 l. Thesis-University of Washington.

Translations of Classical Novels: Chin ku ch'i kuan, 今古奇觀

[CHIN KU CH'I KUAN]. Die treulose Witwe, eine chinesische Novelle. Übertragung und nachwort von Eduard Grisebach. München, Hyperion-Verlag [1921] 98, [1] p.

————. A jolie fille, joli garçon; Le procès des épingles d'or; Miroir de beauté; Les amours de madame Fleur; adapté des Kin-Kou-Ki-Koan par Lucie Paul Margueritte. Paris, E. Flammarion [c1922]. vi, 269 p.

————. Die gelben Orangen der Prinzessin Dschau: aus dem chinesischen Urtext, von Walter Strzoda. München, Hyperion-Verlag, [1922]. 292 p. (Der chines. Novellensammlung Djin-gu-tji-guan, folge 1, Dichtungen des Ostens).

————. Chinesische Novellen, deutsch von Paul Kühnel. München, Georg Müller, 1924. xxix, 367, [3] p. (Meisterwerke orientalischer literaturen, 2). 1st ed. 1914.

————. The inconstancy of Madam Chuang, and other stories from the Chinese; translated by E. Butts Howell. With twelve illustrations by a native artist. Shanghai [etc.] Kelly and Walsh limited [19--]; London, T. W. Laurie, 1924. vii, 259 p. front., plates.

————. The restitution of the bride and other stories from the Chinese, translated by E. Butts Howell. With illustrations by a native artist. London, T. W. Laurie, [1926]; N. Y. Brentano, 1926. vii, 247 p. plates.

————. Die seltsame Hochzeitsfahrt; zwei chinesischen Novellen aus alter Zeit. Mit drei chinesischen Miniaturen. Aus den Urtexten übertragen von Anna von Rottauscher. Wien, W. Frick [1944] 77 p. plates (Wiener Bücherei, 14).

————. Chinesisches Novellenbuch. Deutsch von Eduard Grisebach. [Hrsg. und durchgesehen von Jan Tschichold] Basel, Birkhäuser [1945]. 228 p. [Sammlung Birkhäuser, Bd. 5].

————. Kin ku ki-kuan; chinesische Novellen, Ins Deutsche übersetzt von Eduard Grisebach. 3. durchges Aufl. Bremen-Horn, Dorn, [1947] 127 p. 1st ed. 1887.

————. Kin ku ki kwan: wundersame Geschichten aus alter und neuer Zeit; aus dem Chinesischen übers. von Franz Kuhn. [Zürich] Manesse Verlag [1952] 471 p. illus. (Manesse Bibliothek der Weltliteratur).

————. Blumenzauber; eine chinesische Novelle [entstammt dem Kin ku ki kuan] Die Übersetzung leisteten Tsou Ping-shou und Leo Greiner, eine letzte Redaktion Felix M. Wiesner. Zürich, Verlag die Waage [1953] 78 p. illus.

————. Chao-hsien-chün-chiao-sung-huang-kan-tzu, 趙縣君喬送黃柑子. Goldamsel flötet am Westsee. Erstmalig aus dem Chinesischen übers. von Franz Kuhn. Freiburg i Br., Klemm, 1953. 95 p. (Die Seemännchen, 4).

————. Chiang hsing k'o ch'ung hui chen chu shan. 蔣興哥重會珍珠衫. Das Perlenhemd; eine chinesische Liebesgeschichte. Aus dem chinesischen Urtext übertr. von Franz Kuhn. Leipzig, Insel-Verlag, 1928. 61 p. illus. (Insel-Bücherei, 216) 1948, 1956, 1957 ed., 51 p.

————. Chuang tzŭ hsiu ku p'ên ch'êng ta tao, 莊子休鼓盆成大道. Die treulose Witwe, eine chinesische Novelle. [Übertragung und Nachwort von Eduard Grisebach] München, Hyperionverlag [1921] 98 p.

————. Li yen k'ung chiung tu yu hsia k'o, 李研公窮途遇俠客. Li, Duke of Ch'ien and the poor scholar who met a chivalrous man. A Chinese novel, translated into English with full Chinese text in Peking colloquial by J. A. Jackson. Shanghai, Printed at the Methodist Publishing House, 1922. [4] p. 99 l.

————. [Mai yu lang tu chan hua k'uei], 賣油郎獨占花魁. Der ölhändler und das freudenmädchen; eine chinesische Geschichte in fünf Gesängen. Über. von Vincenz Hundhausen. [Peking, Leipzig, Pekinger Verlag, c1928]. 3 v.

————. [Mai yu lang tu chan hua k'uei] The oil vendor and the sing-song girl; a Chinese tale in five cantos, by Vincenz Hundhausen. Translated from the German by Fritz Ruesch. [New York, F. Ruesch, 1938] 3 v.

### Chin p'ing mei, 金瓶梅

CHIN P'ING MEI. The Adventures of Hsi Men Ching, translated from the Chinese, illustrated in black and white. [New York] Priv. print. for the Library of facetious lore [c1927] 215 p., incl. front., plates.

————. Djin ping meh, unter weitgehender Mitwirkung von Artur Kibat aus dem ungekürzten chinesischen Urtext übersetzt, und mit Erläuterungen versehen von Otto Kibat. Gotha, Engelhard-Reyher [1928-1932] 2 v.

————. Kin Ping Meh; oder, Die abenteuerliche Geschichte von Hsi Men und seinen sechs Frauen. Aus dem Chinesischen übertragen von Franz Kuhn. Leipzig, Insel-verlag [1930] 920 p.

————. Chin p'ing mei; the adventurous history of Hsi Men and his six wives, with an introduction by Arthur Waley. [English translation by Bernard Miall from the abridged version by Franz Kuhn (Insel-verlag, Leipzig)] London, John Lane [1939]; New York, G. P. Putnam, [c1940] vii-xxii, 852 p.

————. The Golden Lotus; a translation, from the Chinese original, of the novel Chin p'ing mei, by Clement Egerton. London, G. Routledge [1939]; New York, Grove Press, 1954. 4 v.

————. Episoden aus dem Leben Hsi Mens und seiner sechs Frauen. Aus dem Chinesischen übertr. und in neuer Fassung hrsg. von Mario Schubert. Zürich, W. Classen, 1950. 336 p.

————. Kin Ping Mei, ou la fin de la merveilleuse histoire de Hsi Men avec ses six femmes. Version française de J.-P. Porret. Paris, Le Prat [1953] 342 p.

————. Kin Ping Meh; order, Die abenteuerliche Geschichte von Hsi Men und seinen sechs Frauen. Aus dem Chinesischen übertragen von Franz Kuhn. Wiesbaden, Insel-verlag, 1955. 926 p. 1954 ed. 921 p.

### Ch'un meng so yen, 春夢瑣言

CH'UN MENG SO YEN, Ch'ung meng so yen. Trifling tale of a spring dream. A Ming erotic story, published on the basis of a manuscript preserved in Japan and introduced by R. H. van Gulick. Tokyo, 1950. 6, 19 p.

### Er nü ying hsiung chuan, 兒女英雄傳

[ER NÜ YING HSIUNG CHUAN] Wen K'ang, 文康: Die schwarze Reiterin; Roman aus der Tsing Zeit aus dem Chinesischen verdeutscht von Franz Kuhn. Zürich, Manesse Verlag, 1954. 954 p. illus. (Manesse Bibliothek der Weltliteratur).

├────]. La cavalière noire [par] Ouenn Kang; roman adapté de la version allemande de Franz Kuhn par Eugène Bestaux. Paris, Calmann-Lévy [1956] 299
p. (Collection "Traduit de").

## Erh tu mei, 二度梅

ERH TU MEI. Die Rache des jungen Meh oder Das Wunder der zweiten Pflaumen-
blüte. Roman. Aus dem Chinesischen übertr. von Franz Kuhn. Leipzig, Insel-Verlag, 1927. 331 p.

├────]. The same. Zürich, Verlag der Arche, 1949. 304 p.

## Fou shêng liu chi, 浮生六記

FOU SHÊNG LIU CHI. Shen Fu's, 沈復, Six chapters of a floating life, rendered into English by Lin Yu-tang. Shanghai, West Wind Monthly, 1935. xv, 326
p. illus.

## Hao ch'iu chuan, 好逑傳

[HAO CH'IU CHUAN]. La brise au clair de lune, "Le deuxième livre de génie,"
roman chinois traduit par George Soulié de Morant. Paris, B. Grasset, 1925.
364 p., incl. plates ("Les Cahiers verts" 57).

├────]. The breeze in the moonlight, "The second book of genius," translated
from the Chinese by George Soulié de Morant, and done into English by H. Bedford-Jones. New York and London, G. P. Putnam, 1926. xviii, 371 p. incl.
front., plates.

├────]. Die Geschichte einer vollkommenen Liebe, der klassische Liebesroman
der Chinesen. "Deutsche Übertragung von H. Brüggmann." Basel, Rhein
Verlag, 1926; Luzern, J. Stocker [1944]. viii, 286 p.

────. Eisherz und Edeljaspis; oder, Die Geschichte einer glücklichen Gatten-
wahl, ein Roman aus der Ming-Zeit. Übers. von Franz Kuhn. [Wiesbaden]
Insel-Verlag, 1947. 381 p. illus. 1st ed. Leipzig, 1926.

## Hsi yu chi, 西遊記

HSI YU CHI. Le singe et le pourceau; adventures magiques chinoises du Xllle.
siècle, adaptées par George Soulié de Morant; illustrations de André Wilder.
Paris, À la Sirène, 1924. 151 p. illus. col. plates.

────. The Buddhist Pilgrim's progress, by Helen M. Hayes, from the Shi yeu
ki, "The records of the journey to the Western paradise," by Wu Ch'eng-en,
吳承恩. New York, E. P. Dutton; London, J. Murray, 1930. 105 p. (The
Wisdom of the East series).

────. A mission to heaven, a great Chinese epic and allegory, by Ch'iu Ch'ang
Ch'un, 邱長春. Translated by Timothy Richard. [n. p.] 1940. xxxix, 362, vi p.
plates.

────. Monkey [by] Wu Ch'eng-en. Translated from the Chinese by Authur Waley. London, Allen and Unwin, 1942, 6th impression 1953; New York, John
Day [1943] 306 p.

────. The magic monkey, adapted from an old Chinese legend by Plato and Chris-
tina Chan, 陳智誠 智龍. [New York] Whittlesey House, McGraw-Hill
[1944] 50 p., illus. (part col.).

────. The adventures of Monkey, adapted from the translation made from the
Chinese of Wu Ch'eng-en by Arthur Waley. Illustrated by Kurt Wiese. New
York, John Day [1944] 143 p. illus.

────. Monkeys Pilgerfahrt, eine chinesische Legende. "Nach der englischen
Ausgabe von Arthur Waley: Wu Ch'êng-ên: 'Monkey.' Übersetzung aus dem

Englischen von Georgette Boner und Maria Nils." Zürich, Artemis-verlag [1946] 4 p. l., 464 p., illus.

## Hsing shih hêng yen, 醒世恆言

[HSING SHIH HÊNG YEN]. Glue and lacquer; four cautionary tales translated from the Chinese by Harold Acton and Lee Yi-hsieh, 李義協. Preface by Arthur Waley. With illustrations from drawings by Eric Gill interpreted on copper by Denis Tegetmeier. [London] The Golden cockerel press [1941] 139 p. incl. front., illus.

——. Four cautionary tales [from a collection, ed. and pub. in 1627 by Fêng Mêng-lung, 馮夢龍] Tr. from the Chinese by Harold Acton and Lee Yi-hsieh, 李義協: with a pref. by Arthur Waley. [London] J. Lehmann, 1947. 159 p.

——. Tse hiong hiong ti,      劉小官雌雄兄弟. The two brothers of different sex; a story from the Chinese. Translated from the French of Stanislans Julien by Frances Hume. Illustrated by Edy Legrand. London, Rodale Press, 1955. 51 p. col. illus.

SOULIÉ, CHARLES GEORGES, 1878- comp. and tr. Les contes galants de la Chine, par George Soulié de Morant. Paris, E. Fasquelle, 1921. 181 p.

[——]. The Chinese Decameron, now first rendered into English by Carlo de Fornaro. New York [The Lotus society] 1929. 205 p. incl. plates. front.

——. Der chinesische Dekameron, Berechtigte Übersetzung von Schiller Marmorek. Wien-Leipzig, Rhombus verlag [c1926] iv, 9-244 p., col. front., col. plates.

## Hung lou mêng, 紅樓夢

HUNG LOU MÊNG. Dream of the red chamber, by Tsao Hsueh-chin, 曹雪芹, and Kao Ngoh, 高鶚. Translated and adapted from the Chinese by Chi-chen Wang, 王際真, with a preface by Arthur Waley. Garden City, N. Y., Doubleday, Doran, 1929; London, Routledge, 1929. xxvii, 371 p. illus.

——. Der Traum der roten Kammer (Ein Roman aus dem frühen Tsing-zeit) von Tsao Hsueh-chin. Aus dem Chinesischen, übertragen von Franz Kuhn. Leipzig, Insel-Verlag, 1932. 788 p. fold. geneal. table, 1948 ed., 796 p.; 1956 ed. 859 p.

KOU, LIN-KE, 郭麟閣. [KUO LIN-KÔ]. Essai sur le Hong leou mong (Le rêve dans le pavillon rouge) célèbre roman chinois du xviiie siècle. Lyon, Bosc frères, M. and L. Riou, 1935. 17? p. Thèse-Univ. de Lyon.

LEE, CHEN-TONG, 李辰冬, 1907- Étude sur le Songe du Pavillon Rouge, [by Tsao Hsueh-chin and Kao Ngoh]. Paris, L. Rodstein, 1934. 146, [2] p. Thèse-Univ. de Paris.

LU, YUEH HWA, 盧月化, 1907- La jeune fille chinoise d'après Hong-leou-mong, Paris, Domat-Montchrestien, 1936. 113 p. Thèse-Univ. de Paris.

## I shan tsa tsuan, 義山雜纂

LI, SHANG-YIN, 李商隱, 813-858. The Miscellanea of I-shan: a little-known work of Li Shang-yin, ed. and tr. by E. D. Edwards. [London, 1930] [757]-785 p. "Reprinted from the Bulletin of the School of Oriental Studies, London Institution, vol. v, part iv, 1930."

——. Les notes de Li Yi-chan (Yi-chan tsa-ts'ouan). Traduit du chinois par Georges Bonmarchand. Tokyo, 1955. 84 p. (Bull. de la Maison Franco-japonaise, n. s. t. iv, 3).

## Ju lin wai shih, 儒林外史

[JU LIN WAI SHIH]. Jou lin wai che, par Wu Ching-tzǔ, 吳敬梓: le roman des

lettres; étude sur un roman satirique chinois par Ho Shih-chün, 賀師俊. Paris, L. Rodstein, 1933. 207 p.

——. The scholars by Wu Ching-tzŭ. [Translated by Yang Hsien-yi and Gladys
Yang] Peking, Foreign Languages Press, 1957. 721, [1] p. illus.

## Ko lien hua ying, 隔簾花影

[KO-LIEN HUA-YING]. Blumenschatten hinter dem Vorhang. Aus dem Chinesischen verdeutscht von Franz Kuhn. Freiburg in Br., H. Klemm, 1956. 784
p. fold col. map.

## Ku ching chi, 古鏡記

[KU CHING CHI]. Le mirror antique. Contes et nouvelles chinois des hautes é-
poques, traduit par Lo Ta-kang, 羅大綱. Neuchâtel, Baconnière [1943] iv,
281 p. illus. plates.

[——]. Der magische Spiegel; chinesische Märchen und Novellen aus den Zeiten der Blüte. Deutsche Fassung nach der französischen Übertragung durch
Lo Ta-kang von Richard B. Matzig. Bern, A. Francke [1944] 254 p. illus.

## Lao ts'an yu chi, 老殘遊記

[LIU, É] 1857-1909. Tramp doctor's travelogue, English version by Lin Yi-chin,
林疑今, and Ko Te-shun, 葛德順, with a foreword by G. N. Ling, 林玉霖.
[Shanghai] Commercial Press, 1939. vi, 263 p.

——. Mr. Decadent by Liu Ngo; translated by Yang Hsien-yi, 楊憲益, and G.
M. Taylor [Gladys Yang] Nanking, Tu Li Pub. Co., 1947. 319 p.

——. Mr. Derelict by Liu Ngo; translated by Yang Hsien-yi and G. M. Taylor
Gladys Yang. London, G. Allen and Unwin, 1948. 168 p.

——. The travels of Lao Ts'an, by Liu T'ieh-yün (Liu E); translated from the
Chinese and annotated by Harold Shadick. Ithaca, Cornell University Press
[1952] xxiii, 277 p. illus.

## Liao chai chih i, 聊齋誌異

P'U SUNG-LING, 1640-1715. Seltsame Geschichten aus dem Liao-chai. Übertragen aus dem Urtext von Erich Schmitt. Berlin, A. Häger, [c1924] 216 p.
plates, (Ex Oriente lux, 1. Abt.: China).

[——]. Strange stories from a Chinese studio, translated and annotated by Herbert A. Giles. New York, Boni and Liveright, 1925. xxiii, 488 p. 1st ed.
1880.

[——.] Contes magiques, d'après l'ancien texte chinois de P'ou Soung-lin
(L'Immortel en exil) Traduit par Louis Laloy. Paris, l'Édition d'art [1925]
xi, 213 p. (Épopées et légendes).

——. Der Pantoffel der kleinen Yen Dschi, 胭脂, zwei chinesische Novellen
aus alter Zeit mit drei chinesischen Miniaturen, aus den Urtexten übertragen
von Anna von Rottauscher. Wien, W. Frick, 1940. 72 p. col. plates, (Wiener Bücherei, 9).

——. Contes chinois, extraits du Liao-tchai-tche-yi traduits intégralement en
français par Pierre Daudin. Saigon, Impr. de l'Union, Ng.-v-Cua, 1940.
xii, 368, iv p. illus.

[——]. Chinese ghost and love stories. "A selection from the Liao-chai stories by P'u Sung-ling, translated by Rose Quong鄺如絲." [New York] Pantheon [1946] 9-329 p. illus.

——. Die Füchsin und die tote Geliebte. Eine chinesische Liebes-und Geister-
geschichte aus dem Liao Tschai (Liao Tschai Tsch-I). Berlin, Steuben-Ver-
lag, 1947. 20 p. (Steuben-Blätter, 21).

————. Gankler, Füchse und Dämonen. Aus dem Chinesischen. Übertr. von Erich
Peter Schrock und Liu Guan-ying, 劉冠英. Basel, B. Schwabe, 1955. 232 p.
plates (Sammlung Klosterberg, N. F.).

————. The painted skin, 畫皮; a tale from Strange stories from a Chinese studio. Adapted and illustrated by Cheng Shih-fa. Translated by Yu Fan-chin.
Peking, Foreign Languages Press, 1957. 40 p.

## P'ing kuei chuan, 平鬼傳

P'ING KUEI CHUAN. Dschung-Kuei, 鍾九傳. Bezwinger der Teufel (altes chinesisches Volksbuch, zum erstenmal unmittelbar aus der Ursprache übers und
mit Nachbildungen echter chinesischer Zeichungen veranschaulicht von Claude
du Bois-Reymond. Postdam, G. Kiepenheuer, 1923. 2 p. l. 7-279 p illus.

————. Dschung Kue; oder, Der Bezwinger der Teufel. Berlin, S. Fischer [1936]
[9]-325, [3] p. incl. plates.

## San kuo yen i, 三國演義

[LO KUAN-CHUNG], 羅貫中, 13th cent., supposed author. San kuo, or Romance
of the three kingdoms, by C. H. Brewitt-Taylor. An English version. Shanghai, Kelly and Walsh, 1925. 2 v. front. (fold, map).

————. Die drei Reiche (San kwo tschi) Roman aus dem alten China. Übertragen
und mit einem Nachwort versehen von Franz Kuhn. Berlin, G. Kiepenheuer
Verlag [c1940] 546 p. illus.

————. Die Schwurbrüder vom Pfirsichgarten. Roman aus dem alten China. Übertragen und mit ein Nachwort versehen von Franz Kuhn. 2. Aufl. Köhn and
Berlin, Kiepenheuer and Witsch, 1953. 462 p.

## Shih san ts'êng t'a, 十三層塔

SHIH SAN TS'ÊNG T'A. Die dreizehnstöckige Pagode; altchinesische Liebesgeschichten. Deutsch von Franz Kuhn. Berlin, Steiniger Verlage im Dom-Ver-
lag, [c1940] 488 p. Neu Aufl. 1956.

## Shiu hu chuan, 水滸傳

[SHUI HU CHUAN]. Les chevalièrs chinois, roman de moeurs et d'aventures,
traduit par Panking. Fékin, Impr. de la "Politique de Pékin," 1922. 8, 220
p. illus. (Collection de la "Politique de Pékin").

[————]. Räuber und Soldaten, Roman frei nach dem Chinesischen von Albert Ehrenstein. Berlin, Ullstein, [1927] 5-291, 2 p.

————. Robbers and soldiers, by Albert Ehrenstein, translated from the German
by Geoffrey Dunlop. New York, A. A. Knopf, 1929; London, G. Howe, 1929
3-268 p.

————. Die Rauber vom Liang schan moor. Mit sechzig Holzschnitten einer alten
chinesischen Ausgabe. Aus dem Chinesischen übertragen von Franz Kuhn.
Leipzig, Insel-verlag [1934] 839, [1] p. incl. plates.

————. All men are brothers[Shui hu chuan] translated from the Chinese by Pearl
S. Buck. 5th printing. New York, John Day [c1937] xiv, 1279 p. front.,
illus. 1st ed. 1933.

————. The same. With an introd. by Lin Yutang and illus. by Miguel Covarru-
bias. New York, For the members of the Limited Editions Club, 1948. 2 v.
col. illus.

————. The same. New York, Grove Press [1957, c1937]; London, Methuen,
1957. 2 v. illus. (xiv, 1279 p.).

————. Water margin, written by Shih Nai-an, 施耐菴, translated by J. H. Jackson, edited by Fang Lo-tien,方樂天. Shanghai, Commercial Press, 1937. 2 v

——. Selections; ed. by J. I. Crump, Jr. New Haven, Pub. for the Institute of Far Eastern Languages by Yale University Press, 1947. viii, 20 p.; 34 p. ([Yale University. Dept. of Oriental Studies] Mirror series C, no. 4).

[——]. Die Raüber vom Liang schan moor. Aus dem Chinesischen von Franz Kuhn. Wien, Heidelberg, Überreuter, 1955. 313 p.

IRWIN, RICHARD GREGG, 1909- The evolution of a Chinese novel: Shui-hu-chuan. Cambridge, Harvard University Press, 1953. ix, 231 p. (Harvard-Yenching Institute studies, 10).

## T'i kung an, 狄公案

T'I KUNG AN. Dee Goong An. Three murder cases solved by Judge Dee; an old Chinese detective novel translated from the original Chinese with an introduction and notes by Robert Hans van Gulick. Illustrated with three reproductions of original Chinese pictures, and six plates drawn by the author after ancient Chinese novels. Tokyo, Printed by Toppan Print. Co., 1949. xxiii, 237 p. plates.

## Yen tan tzŭ, 燕丹子

YEN TAN TZŬ. Prince Dan of Yann, short story written about B.C. 226; original text appended. With illus.; translated with an introd. by Cheng Lin, 鄭麐. [Shanghai, World Book Co., 1946] ii, 13 p.; 4, 6 p. illus. (Ancient Chinese classics series).

## Yü ching t'ing, 玉蜻蜓

SHEN, SHIH-SHING, 申時行, 1535-1614. Die Jadelibelle, Roman. 玉蜻蜓, aus dem Chinesischen von Franz Kuhn. Berlin, Schützen Verlag, 1936. 294 p.

——. The same. [Zürich] Manesse Verlag [1952] 279 p. (Manesse Bibliothek der Weltliteratur).

## Yü chiao li, 玉嬌梨

YÜ CHIAO LI. Ein chinesischer familien Roman. In deutsch Bearb. von Emma Wuttke-Biller. Leipzig, Ph. Reclam jun. [1922] 87 p.

——. Rotjade und Blütentraum. Ein chinesischer Liebesroman. Aus dem Urtexten übertragen von Anna von Rottauscher. Wien, Frick, 1941. 319 p.

——. Das Dreigespann; oder, Yü-kiao-li. [Roman. Übersetzung aus dem Chinesischen von Mario Schubert.] Bern, A. Scherz [1949] 451 p.

## Translation of Selections

BUBER, MARTIN, 1878- ed. Chinesische Geister-und Liebesgeschichten. Übers. von Martin Buber. Zürich, Manesse Verlag, Conzett and Ruber, 1948. 339 p. illus. (Manesse-Bibliothek der Weltliteratur) 1. ed. Frankfurt/M, 1920.

HSU, SUNG-NIEN, 徐仲年, 1904- Un enfant terrible: Siu Wen-tch'ang, 徐文長

——. Traduit des récits populaires de Mme Lin Lan, 林蘭. Peiping, lmpr. de la "Politique de Pékin," 1931. 19 p. (Collection de la "Politique de Pékin").

——. Contes choisis des T'ang. Pékin, Impr. de la "Politique de Pekin," 1935. 26, 128 p. (Collection de la "Politique de Pékin").

KUHN, FRANZ, 1889- tr. Chinesische Meisternovellen. Aus dem chinesischen Urtext übertragen von Franz Kuhn. Leipzig, Insel Verlag, 1941 [cl926] 95 p. (Insel-Bücherei, 387).

——. Das Tor der östlichen Blüte; Novellen aus dem alten China. Deutsch von Franz Kuhn. Düsseldorf, A. Bagel [1949] 336 p.

——. Und Buddha lacht, 彌勒佛 ; Geschichten aus dem alten China. Baden-

Baden, Kairos Verlag [1950]. 80 p. (Der Weltkreis, 11 ).
——. tr. Der Turm der fegenden Wolken, altchinesische Novellen, 李漁 十二樓 Aus dem Chinesischen übertragen von Franz Kuhn. Freiburg I. Br., H. Klemm [1951] 557 p.

LIN, YU-T'ANG, 林語堂, 1895- tr. A nun of Taishan (a novelette) and other translations. Shanghai, Commercial Press, 1936. x, 272 p.

ROTTAUSCHER, ANNA tr. Irrlicht und Morgen röte, fünf chinesische Erzählungen [ins Deutsche übertragen] Zürich, Verlag Die Waage [1955] 132 p. illus.
——. Altchinesische Tiergeschichten; aus dem chinesischen Texten. Wien, P. Neff, 1955. (c1947) 264 p. illus.

RUDELSBERGER, HANS, 1868- tr. Chinesische Novellen; aus dem Urtext übertragen von Hans Rudelsberger. Wien, A. Schroll, c1924. xx, 296 p. plates.

SOULIÉ, CHARLES GEORGES, 1878- comp. and tr. Trois contes chinois du XVlle siècle, traduites par G. Soulié de Morant. Paris, H. Piazza, [1926] 140 p. front. plates.

[——.] Love stories and gallent tales from the Chinese. English version by E. Powys Mathers. London, John Radker, 1928. 170 p. (Eastern love, 6).

——. Eastern shame girl. [Stories] Tr. from the French of George Soulié De Morant. Illus. by Marcel Avond. New York, Priv. print., 1929. 183 p. illus.

——. Chinese love tales; translated from the original of George Soulié de Morant, with illustrations by Valenti Angelo. New York, Three Sirens Press, 1935; Cleveland, World Pub. Co., 1935. 4 p. l., 11-161 p. incl. front., illus.

——. The same. Garden City, N.Y., Halcyon House [1950?] 161 p. illus. (Illustrated library).

YUAN, CHIA-HUA, 袁家驊, ed. Romance of the three kingdoms and A mission to heaven (selections) selected and annotated by Yuan and Shih, [石民]. Shanghai, The Peisin Book Co., 1931. 265 p. (English translations of Chinese classics. [vol. I]).

## Novels: Chinese Authors

CHANG, DIANA C.,張粲芳. The frontiers of love. New York, Random House [1956] 246 p.

CHANG, EILEEN,張愛玲. The rice-sprout song. New York, Scribner, 1955. 182 p.

——. Das Reispflanzerlied. Ein Roman aus dem heutigen China, übers. von Gabriele Eckehard. Düsseldorf, Köhn, Diederichs, 1956. 225 p.

——. Naked earth. Hong Kong, Union Press, 1956. 365 p.

CHANG, FA-SHUN, 張法舜. The Sky River. Illustrated by Jeanyee Wong黃如珍
——. New York, Lothrop, Lee and Shepard [1950] 156 p. illus.

——. Until the phoenix, a novel. New York, J. Day [1952] 310 p.

CHANG, HSIN-HAI, 張欣海, 1898- The fabulous concubine, a novel. New York, Simon and Schuster, 1956; London, J. Cape, 1957. 491 p.

CHANG, TIEN-YI, 張天翼, 1907- Stories of Chinese young pioneers. Peking, Foreign Languages Press, 1954. 49 p. illus.

——. Jeunes pionniers chinois-Récits. Pékin, Éditions en langues étrangères, 1954. 49 p.

——. Geschichten von Jungpionieren Chinas. Aus dem Chinesischen übers. von Tschen Yüan. Illus. von Dschang Wen-sin. Peking, Verlag für Fremdsprachige Literatur, 1954. 56 p.

CHANG, TSÊ-CHIH, 張則之, comp. and tr. Some famous Chinese stories, compiled and translated by Kinchen Johnson [pseud] for senior middle schools. Peiping, Chung Yuan Book Co., 1934. 395 p.

CHAO, CHING-SHÊN, 趙景深, 1902- comp. Contemporary Chinese short stories, compiled by Jörgensen. Shanghai, Pei hsin shu chü, 1946] 2 v.

in 1.

CHAO, SHU-LI, 趙樹理, 1905- Rhymes of Li Yu-tsai and other stories. With an introductory article by Chou Yang. Peking, Cultural Press, 1950. 195 p. illus.

———. Die Spruchlieder des Li Yu-T'sai von Dschau Schu-li. Peking, Kulturelle Presse, 1951. 109 p.

———. Die Lieder des Li Yü-ts'ai; eine Erzählung aus dem heutigen China. Übers von Jos. Kalmer. Berlin, Verlag Volk und Welt, 1950. 126 p.

———. Changes in Li Village. [1st ed. Translated by Gladys Yang] Peking, Foreign Languages Press, 1953. 224 p.

———. Die Wandlung des Dorfes Lidjiadschuang, von Dschao Schu-li. Deutsch von Tjen Nou. Berlin, Volk und Welt, 1952. 254 p.

CH'EN, T'ENG-KE, 陳登科, 1918- Living hell, translated [from Chinese] by Sidney Shapiro. Peking, Foreign Languages Press, 1955. 147 p.

CHIANG, HSIU-FÊNG, 蔣秀峯. Popular Chinese tales. 2d ed. Peiping, Printed by the Yu Lien Press, 1935. 62 p. illus. (map) plates.

CHIANG, PING-CHIH, 蔣冰之, 1907- When I was in Sha Chuan and other stories, by Ting Ling, 丁玲. Translated from the original Chinese by Kung Pu-sheng, 龔普生. Bombay, Kutub, 1945. 118 p.

———. The sun shines over the Sangkan River [by] Ting Ling [pseud.] Translated by Yang Hsien-yi, 楊憲益, and Gladys Yang] Peking, Foreign Languages Press, 1954. 348 p. illus.

———. Sonne über dem Sanggan von Ding Ling [pseud]. Berlin, Dietz Verlag, 1953. 468 p.

———. Sonne über dem Sangganfluss von Ding Ling, [pseud]. Übers. aus dem Russischen von Arthur Nestmann. Neubearbeitung. Berlin, Aufbau Verlag, 1954. 416 p.

CHIN, CHAO-YANG, 秦兆陽. Village sketches. Peking, Foreign Languages Press, 1957. 198 p.

CHOU, LI-PO, 周立波, 1908- The hurricane. [Translated from the Chinese by Hsu Meng-hsiung, 許孟雄. Illus. by Ku Yuan, 古元] Peking, Foreign Languages Press, 1955. viii, 409 p. illus., port.

———. Orkan, von Dschou Li-bo. Übers. aus dem Chinesischen von Yang En-lin, 楊恩林, und Wolfgang Müncke. Berlin, Tribune, 1953. 576 p.

———. The same. Wien, Stern-Verlag, 1954. 576 p. (Bücher der Zeit).

CHOU, SHU-JÊN, 周樹人, 1881-1936. Selected stories of Lu Hsun, 魯迅, [pseud]. Peking, Foreign Languages Press, 1954. 251 p. port.

———. Selected works of Lu Hsun [pseud.] Peking, Foreign Languages Press, 1956- v. illus.

———. Nouvelles de Lou Shun par Tchang Tien-ya. Pékin, Impr. de la "Politique de Pekin." 1932. 75 p. (Collection de la "Politique de Pekin").

[———]. The true story of Ah Q, by Lu-hsün [pseud.] Translated into English by George Kin Leung, 梁社乾. Shanghai, Commercial Press, 1927. vii, 100 p.

[———]. Ah Q and others, selected stories of Lusin [pseud.] Translated by Chi-chen Wang. New York, Columbia University Press, 1941. xxvi, 3-219 p.

———. The true story of Ah Q [by] Lu Hsun [pseud.] Peking, Foreign Langauges Press, 1953. 111 p. port.

———. La véritable histoire de Ah Q par Lou Sin [suivi de "Sur la véritable histoire de Ah Q." par Feng Soueh-feng, 馮雪峯] roman, traduit par Paul Jamati. Préface de Claude Roy. Paris, Éditeurs français réunis, 1953. 120 p.

———. Die wahre Geschichte des Ah Queh von Lu Hsin. Übers. aus dem Chinesischen von Herta Nan und Richard Jung. Mit einer Vorbemerkung und mit Anmerkungen von Richard Jung und mit einem Nachwort über das Werk und seinen Verfasser von Feng Hsüä-feng. Leipzig, List, 1954. 145 p.

———. Hesitation, by Lu Shun [pseud.] Compiled and annotated by Jörgensen, 趙景深. [Shanghai, Pei hsin shu chü, 1946] 271 p.

[———]. Segen, von Lu Hsün [pseud.] Aus dem Chinesischen übertragen von Joseph Kalmer. Herrliberg-Zürich, Bühl-Verlag [1947] 47 p. (Bühl-Verlag-Blätter, 21).

———. Erzählungen aus China, von Lu Hsün. Aus dem Russischen von Josi von Koskull. Berlin, Rütten und Löning, 1952. 100 p. (Kleine R und L-Bücherei).

———. Die Reise ist lang, gesammelte Erzählungen [von] Lu Hsün [pseud. Aus dem Chinesischen übers. von Joseph Kalmer] Düsseldorf, Progress-Verlag [1955] 524 p.

CHOW, YIH-ZAN, 周越然, 1885- Some Chinese tales. Shanghai, Commercial Press, 1928. vi, 107 p.

DER LING, princess 德齡公主 1944. Jades and dragons. New York, Mohawk Press [c1932] v, [2], 9-287 p. front. illus.. col. plates.

———. Golden phoenix, illustrated by Bertha Lum. New York, Dodd, Mead 1932. ix, 258 p. front., illus., plates.

HAI SCHANG SCHUO MONG JEN [pseud.], 海上說夢人. Fräulein Tschang, ein chinesisches Mädchen von heute, Roman; aus dem Chinesischen original übertragen von Franz Kuhn. Berlin [etc.] P. Zsolnay, 1931. 325, [1] p.

HAN, SUYIN, 韓素瑛, [pseud.] [唐珊瑚] Destination Chungking. Boston, Little, Brown, 1942; London, Cape, 1943. 3-367 p.

———. The same. New ed. London, Cape; New York, Clarke, Irwin, 1953. 291 p.

———. Manches Jahr bin ich gewandert; übers. von Dorothea Naumann-Preiswerk. 2. Aufl. Darmstadt, Baden-Baden, Genf, Holle Verlag, 1955. 359 p.

———. A many-splendored thing. Boston, Little, Brown [1952] 366 p.

———. The same. London, J. Cape [1952] 384 p.

———. Multiple splendeur. Traduction de Daria Olivier. Introduction de Malcom MacDonald. Paris, Stock, 1957. 445 p. illus.

———. Alle Harrlichkeit auf Erden, übers. von Isabella Nadolny. [Darmstadt] Genf, Holle Verlag, 1953. Stuttgart, Zürich, Salzburg, Europäischer Buchklub, 1955. 438 p.

———. ...and the rain my drink. Boston, Little, Brown [1956] 306 p. (An Atlantic Monthly Press book).

———. The same. London, J. Cape [1956] 319 p.

HO, RO-SE, 何若茜 Love and duty: the love story of a Chinese girl. Shanghai, Commercial Press, 1932 (c1926) 3 p. l. 169 p.

HSIAO, CH'IEN, 蕭乾, 1911- The spinners of silk. London, G. Allen and Unwin, [1944] 7-104 p.

———. Die Seidenraupen. [Einzig autorisierte Übertragung von Joseph Kalmer] Herrliberg-Zürich, Bühl-Verlag (1947) 172 p.

[HSIAO, CHÜN], 蕭軍, 1908- Village in August [by] T'ien Chün, 田軍,[pseud.] Introd. by Edgar Snow. [Tower books ed.] Clevelang, World Pub. Co. [1944, c1942] xix, 313 p.

[———]. The same. New York, Smith and Durrell [1942] xix, 313 p.

[———]. Das erwachende Dorf; Roman. Übers. aus dem Amerikanischen von Hartmut Rebitzki. Berlin, Kantorowicz, 1950. 229 p.

HSIUNG, SHIH-I, 熊式一, 1902- The bridge of heaven, a novel with a prefatory poem by John Masefield. London, P. Davies [1943]; N.Y. Putnam, 1943 [305 p.]. 394 p.

———. Le pont du ciel, roman, traduit de l'anglais par J. Giraud. Paris, R. Laffont, 1948. 432 p.

———. The story of Lady Precious Stream, a novel; with a pref. by J.B. Priestley. Illustrated by A.C. Chang, 張安治. London, Hutchinson, 1950. 176 p. illus. (part col.).

HSIUNG, TAI-MEI, 熊蔡岱梅 Flowering exile; an autobiographical excursion. London, P. Davies [1952] 287 p.

HSÜ, KUANG-YAO, 徐光耀, 1925- The plains are ablaze. [Translated by Sidney Shapiro. 1. ed.] Peking, Foreign Languages Press, 1955. 277 p. illus.

HUA, SHAN, 華山. The shepherd's message. Drawings by Liu Chi-yu, 劉繼卣.
Peking, Foreign Languages Press, 1954. 149 p. of illus.
———. Der Brief mit den Hahnenfedern. Übers. aus dem Russischen von Käthe
Heinz. Berlin, Verlag Kultur und Fortschritt, 1953. 51 p. (Kleine Jugend-
reihe).

KAO, YU-PAO, 高玉寶, 1927- Child labour. Adapted by Hsu Kuang-yu, 徐光
玉. Drawings by Chou Li, 周立, and others. Peking, Foreign Languages
Press, 1954. 95 p. illus.

KUO, HELENA, 郭鏡秋. I've come a long way. New York, London, D. Appleton-
Century, 1942. 369 p. front. (port.).
———. Westward to Chungking. New York and London, D. Appleton-Century,
[1944] 297, [1] p.

KYN, YN-YU J. B., 敬隱漁. Anthologie des conteurs chinois modernes; établié et traduite, avec une introduction. Paris, Les éditions Rieder, 1929.
190 p. (Les prosateurs étrangèrs modernes).
[———].comp. The tragedy of Ah Qui, and other modern Chinese stories. London, G. Routledge, 1930. xi, 146 p. (The golden dragon library) "Translated from the Chinese by J. B. Kyn Yn Yu and from the French by E. H. F. Mills."

LI, CHIN-YANG, 黎錦揚, 1917- The flower drum song, by C. Y. Lee. New
York, Farrar, Straus and Cudahy [1957] 244 p.

LI, FEI-KAN, 李芾甘, 1905- Living amongst heroes [by] Pa Chin, 巴金 [pseud.]
Peking, Foreign Languages Press, 1954. 132 p. illus.
———. Garten der Ruhe, von Pa Chin [pseud.] [autorisierte Übertragung aus
dem Chinesischen von Joseph Kalmer] München, Carl Hauser, [1954] 219 p.

LI KAO, 立高. Racing towards victory by Li Kao and others. Peking, Foreign
Languages Press, 1956. 184 p.

LI, TCHANG-CHIAN. Les écrivains contemporaine chinois, traduit des essais
critiques de Tchien Hsing-tsoun, 錢杏邨. Peiping, Impr. de la "Politique de
Pékin," 1933. 113 p. (Collection de la "Politique de Pékin").

LIANG, HSING, 梁星. Liu Hu-lan, 劉胡蘭, story of a girl revolutionary. Peking, Foreign Languages Press, 1953. 87 p.

LIM, BOON-KENG, 林文慶, 1869- Tragedies of Eastern life, an introduction to
the problems of social psychology. Shanghai, Commercial Press, 1927. 264
p.

[LIN, ADET]林如斯 1923- Flame from the rock, by Tan Yun [pseud.] New
York, John Day, 1943; London, Toronto, W. Heinemann [1944] 220 p.
———. Our family, by Adet and Anor Lin, 林無雙, with a foreword and comments
by Mei mei. New York, John Day [c1939] xiv, 256 p. front. (port. group)
illus.
———. Le roc ardent, roman [par] Tan Yun [pseud.] Tr. par Danièle Audiane.
Paris, Éditions du Pavois [1946] 323 p. (Bibliothèque internationale).
———. Das Mädchen und der Soldat, Roman von Tan Yün, [pseud.] Ins Deutche
Übertragen von Eva Maria Röder. Zürich, Fretz und Wasmuth, 1947. iv,
340 p.

[LIN, ANOR]林無雙 1926- War tide, a novel by Lin Taiyi. New York, John
Day [1943] 281 p.
———. Marée montante. Traduit de l'anglais par Marcelle Sibon. Paris, Stock,
1947. 367 p.
[———]. Das Leben ist stärker, Roman. Übertragen ins Deutsch von Lino Rossi.
Zürich, Büchergilde Gutenberg, 1945. iv, 352 p.
[———]. The golden ccin. New York, John Day, [1946] 5-306 p.

LIN, HAZEL AI CHUN, 林愛羣, 1913- The physicians, a novel. New York,
John Day, [1951] 250 p.

LIN, YU-T'ANG,林語堂,1895- Moment in Peking; a novel of contemporary Chi-
nese life. New York, John Day [1939]; Berne, A. Scherz, 1943; Garden City,
N. Y., Sun dial, 1942, 3-815 p.
———. Enfances chinoises, roman, traduit de l'anglais par François Fosca.

Genève, Éditions du Milieu du Monde, 1944. iv, 404 p.

————. Peking: Augenblick und Ewigkeit. Roman. Übers. von Lino Rossi. Zürich, Büchergilde Gutenberg, 1943. 2 v.

————. The same. Frankfurt a M., S. Fischer, 1951. 2 v.

————. With love and irony; illustrated by Kurt Wiese. New York, John Day [c1940]; Garden City, N. Y.; Blue Ribbon Books, 1945. xi, 291 p. illus.

————. Ein wenig Liebe...ein wenig Spott. Aus dem Amerikanischen übertragen von Ines Loos. Zürich, Rascher, 1943. iv, 309 p. illus.

————. A leaf in the storm, a novel of war-swept China. New York, John Day [c1941] 3-368 p. illus. (map).

————. The same. Berne, Phoenix Publishing Co., Scherz and Hallwag, 1947. 2 v. (The Scherz Phoenix Books, 83-84).

————. Feuille dans la tourmente, un roman de la guerre en Chine. Traduit par Charly Guyot, 1944. Neuchâtel-Paris, Delachaux et Niestlé, 1944. iv, 374 p.

————. Blatt in sturm. Roman aus dem kriegverheerten China. Übertragen ins Deutsch von Lino Rossi. Zürich, Büchergilde Gutenberg, 1944. iv, 454 p.

————. The same. Frankfurt a M. und Hamburg, G. B. Fischer, 1953. 543 p. (Die grossen Romane der Zeit).

————. Chinatown family, a novel. New York, John Day [1948] London, Heinemann; Toronto, Longmans, 1949. 307 p.

————. Chinesenstadt; Roman aus dem Englischen von Leonore Schlaich. Stuttgart, Deutsche Verlags-Anstalt, 1952. 365 p.

————. The same. Frankfurt a. M., Büchergilde Gutenberg, 1955. 390 p.

————. Miss Tu. London, W. Heinemann [1950] 124 p.

————. Die Kurtisane. [Erzählung] Übertr. aus dem Englischen von Leonore Schlaich. Stuttgart, Deutsche Verlags-Anstalt, 1951. 113 p. (Die Stern-Ausgaben).

————. tr. Widow, nun and courtesan; three novelettes from the Chinese, translated and adapted by Lin Yutang. New York, John Day [1951]; Toronto, Longmans, [1951] vi, 266 p.

————. Widow Chuan retold by Lin Yutang, based on Chuan chia chun by Lao Hsiang, 老向. London and Melbourne, W. Heinemann, 1952. viii, 158 p.

————. Famous Chinese short stories, retold by Lin Yutang. New York, John Day [1952] 299 p.

————. Die Botschaft des fremden chinesische Geschichten. Ins deutsche Übertragen von Ursula Löffler. Stuttgart, Deutsche Verlags- Anstalt, 1954. 340 p.

————. The vermilion gate, a novel of a far land. New York, John Day [1953] 438 p.

————. Leb wohl Sunganor. Roman aus einem fernen Land. Übers. von Maria Wolff. Berlin und Frankfurt a M., G. B. Fischer, 1954. 497 p. (Die grossen Roman der Zeit).

————. Lady Wu; a true story. London, Heinemann, 1957. 245 p. tables, diagrms.

LIU, BEATRICE, 劉艾碧珠. Little Wu and the watermelons. Illus. by Graham Peck. Chicago, Follett Pub. Co. [1954] 96 p. illus.

LIU, CHING, 柳青, 1916- Wall of bronze. [Translated by Sidney Shapiro] Peking, Foreign Languages Press, 1954. 283 p. illus.

LIU, PAI-YU, 劉白羽, 1915- Six A. M. and other stories. Peking, Foreign Languages Press, 1953. 149 p.

————. Six heures du matin. Pékin, Éditions de langues étrangères, 1953. 166 p.

————. Flames ahead. Peking, Foreign Languages Press, 1954. 166 p. map.

————. Flammen am Jangtse, Übers. von Walter Ecklelen. Berlin, Dietz, 1957. 212 p.

LO, KENNETH H. C., 羅孝建. Forgotten wave; stories and sketches from the Chinese seamen during the second World War, including the epic of Poo Lim, 彭廉, who sat alone on a raft and survived 133 days of the open Atlantic. Padiham [Eng.] Padiham Advertiser Ltd., 1947. 116 p. illus.

LOWE, H.  Y.,  盧興源? Stories from Chinese drama, with illustrations by the author. Peking, Peking Chronicle Press, 1942. xxii, 413, xxxxviii p. illus.

LU, A.K. L'histoire de Fou Sang-siang. Pékin, Impr. de la "Politique de Pékin." 1928. [2] 43 p. (Collection de la "Politique de Pékin").

LU, CHU-KUO, 陸柱國. Der Mensch ist stärker als Eisen, von Lu Tschu-kou. [Ins Deutsche übertragen von Yuan Miautse] Berlin, Verlag der Kasernierten Volkspolizei, 1956. 145 p. illus.

A NEW HOME and other stories, by contemporary Chinese writers. Peking, Foreign Languages Press, 1955. 165 p.

PAI, WEI, 白危, 1911- The Chus reach haven. [Translated by Yang Hsien-yi and Gladys Yang] Peking, Foreign Languages Press, 1954. 108 p.

REGISTRATION, and other stories, by contemporary Chinese writers. Peking, Foreign Languages Press, 1954. 226 p.

SHEN, TS'UNG-WÊN, 沈從文, 1902-   Nouvelles de Chen Tsong-wen par Tchang Tien-ya. Pékin, Impr. de la "Politique de Pékin," 1932. 40 p. (Collection de la "Politique de Pékin").

——. The Chinese earth; stories. Translated by Ching Ti and Robert Payne. London, G. Allen and Unwin [1947] 289 p.

SHEN, YEN-P'ING, 沈雁冰, 1896-   Schanghai im Zwielicht, Roman. Aus dem Chinesischen übertragen von Franz Kuhn. Dresden, W. Heyne, 1938. 477 p.

[——.] Chinesische Novellen von Mao Tun. Die Übers. aus dem Chinesischen von Wolfgang Schmalh. Hrsg. von Walter Donat. Berlin, Hermann Hübener, 1946. 64 p. illus. (Kleine drei Birken Bücherei, 9).

——. Der Laden der Familie Lin. Aus dem Chinesischen übersetzt von Joseph Kalmer. Berlin, Volk und Welt, 1953. 186 p.

[——]. Spring silkworms and other stories, by Mao Tun [pseud] Translated by Sidney Shapiro. Peking, Foreign Languages Press, 1956. 278 p. port.

[——]. Seidenraupen im Frühling. 2 Erzählungen von Mao Tun. Aus dem Chinesischen. Übertragen von Joseph Kalmer. Leipzig, Insel-Verlag, 1955. 78 p. (Insel-Bücherei, 589).

SHÊNG, CH'ÊNG, 盛成, 1899- Ma mère. Préface de Paul Valéry. Paris-Neuchâtel, V. Attinger, 1928. 191 p. incl. front. (port.) (His Vers l'unité. I).

——. Ma mère et moi. À travers la révolution chinoise. Paris et Neuchâtel, Éditions V. Attinger, 1929. iv, 240 p. (His Vers l'unité, 2).

——. A son of China; translated from the French by Marvin McCord Lowes; preface by Paul Valéry. New York, W.W. Norton [c1930] viii, 9-286 p.

——. Meine mutter. "Übersetzt von Paul Cohen-Portheim." Mit einem Vorwort von Paul Valéry. Berlin, G. Kiepenheuer, 1929. xxiv, 151 p.

SHIH, YEN, 石言. It happened at Willow Castle. Peking, Cultural Press, 1951. 71 p.

——. Das Gelöbnis des Li Yin. Eine Liebeserzählung aus dem neuen China. Leipzig, Paul List Verlag, 1953.   p.

SHU, CH'ING-CH'UN, 舒慶春, 1898-  Auprès du temple de la grande désolation (Ta-pei-sseu) par Lao Che, [pseud]. Traduit du chinois par Madame le docteur Chow Chung-cheng, 周仲錚. Amsterdam, 1940. [20] p. (China; een driemaandelyksch tydschrift, Jahr. 14, No. 1-2).

——. Rickshaw boy, by Lau Shaw [pseud.] Tr. from the Chinese by Evan King [pseud.] New York, Reynal and Hitchcock [1945] 315 p.

——. The same. Sketches by Cyrus Le Roy Baldridge. New York, Reynal and Hitchcock, 1945. 383 p. illus.

——. The same. Garden City, N.Y., Sun Dial Press [1946] 315 p.

——. The Same. London, M. Joseph [1946] 254 p.

——. Coeur-Joyeux, coolie de Pékin (Rickshaw boy) [par] Lao Sheh [pseud.] Roman chinois tr. par Jean Poumarat d'après la version anglaise d'Evan King [pseud.] Grenoble, B. Arthaud [1948, c1947] 438 p. (Collection "De par le monde").

——. Rikscha Kuli. Roman, von Lao Sheh. Deutsche Übertragung von Lena Frender. Zürich, Diana Verlag, 1947. iv, 446 p.

——. The quest for love of Lao Lee, by Lau Shaw (Lao Sheh) Tr. from the Chinese by Helena Kuo, 郭鏡秋  New York, Reynal and Hitchcock [1948] 306 p.

[——]. Divorce, tr. and adapted from the Pekinese of Venerable Lodge [pseud.] by Evan King [pseud.] [St. Petersburg] King Publications [1948] vii, 444 p.

——. Heavensent, by Shu She-yu, 舒舍予. London, J. M. Dent, 1951. 284 p.

——. The yellow storm [by] Lau Shaw [pseud. of] S. Y. Shu; translated from the Chinese by Ida Pruitt. New York, Harcourt, Brace [c1951] 533 p.

——. The drum singers, by Lau Shaw (S. Y. Shu) Translated from the Chinese by Helena Kuo. New York, Harcourt, Brace [1952] 283 p.

[SU, HSÜAN-YING], 蘇玄瑛, 1884-1918. The lone swan, 斷鴻零雁記 , by the Reverend Mandju, 曼殊, [pseud.] translated into English by George Kin Leung. Shanghai, Commercial Press, 1929. (c1924) xii, 147 p. incl. front. (port.) 1st ed. 1924.

——. Der wunde Schwan; die Aufzeichnungen des Möndes Man Ju. Roman. Aus dem Chinesischen übertragen von Anna von Rottanscher. Wien, Amandus-Edition, 1947. 152 p.

SU HUA, 凌叔華. Ancient melodies. With an introduction by V. Sackville West. London, Hogarth Press, 1953. 255 p. illus.

——. Nie verklungne Melodie (Erinnerungen). Mit einem Geleitwort von V. Sackville West. Übertragen aus dem Englischen von Sonja Mariasch. Zürich, Verlag der Arche, 1954. 240 p. illus.

SZE, MAI-MAI, 施蘊珍. Echo of a cry, a story which began in China. Illustrated by the author. New York, Harcourt, Brace, [1945]; London, J. Cape [1947] 3-203 p. illus.

——. Silent children, a novel. New York, Harcourt, Brace [1948] 189 p.

TCHENG, MIEN, 陳綿, 1901- Les contes merveilleux de la Chine. Paris, Éditions Nilsson, 1929? 125 p.

TCHOU, KIA-KIEN; 朱家健, tr. La septième petit Madame Tch'en, 陳七奶奶, adapté du chinois par Tchou Lan [陸] 腹郎. Traduit par Tchou Kia-kien. Pékin, A. Nachbaur, 1926. 232 p. plates. (scènes de la vie des maisons de thé).

TING, CZE-MING, 丁則民, comp. and tr. Short stories from China, translated from the Chinese by Cze Ming Ting; with an introduction by Agnes Smedley. Moscow, Co-operative Pub. Society of Foreign Workers in the U. S. S. R., 1935. 89, [1] p.

TS'AO MING, 草明, pseud., 1913- The moving force. Peking, Cultural Press, 1950. 214 p.

——. Die treibende Kraft. Übers. von Gerhard Mehnert. Berlin, Dietz Verlag, 1953. 207 p.

TSIANG, H.T., 蔣希曾 [CHIANG HSI-TSÊNG] China red (a novel) New York, The author [c1931] [11]-155, [1] p., 1 illus.

——. The hanging on Union Square with a foreword by Waldo Frank. N[ew] Y[ork], The author [1935] 222 p.

——. And China has hands. New York, R. Speller [1937] 164 p.

WANG, CHI-CHÊN, 王際真, 1899- tr. Traditional Chinese tales. New York, Columbia University Press, 1944. 225 p.

——. Contemporary Chinese stories. New York, Columbia University Press, 1944. ix, 242 p.

——. ed. Stories of China at war. New York, Columbia University Press, 1947; London, Oxford University Press, 1947. xi, 158 p.

WANG, HSI-DJIAN, 王希堅. Der gnädige Herr Wu. Roman. Berlin, Verlag Volk und Welt, 1954. 340 p.

WONG, JADE SNOW, 黃玉雪. Fifth Chinese daughter. [Autobiography] With illus. by Kathryn Uhl. New York, Harper [1950]; London, Hurst and Blackett, 1952 vii, 246 p. illus.

——. Ein chinesenmädchin in Frisco. Übers. von Doris Mühringer und Helmut Degner. Salzburg, Pallas-Verlag, 1954. 349 p. illus.

WONG, WILFRED SIEN-BING. The black hole of Shanghai (an inside story of kidnapping). Shanghai, China Critic Pub. Co., 194? 62 p. illus.

————. The mental autobiography of Bill Lee. Shanghai, China Critic Pub. Co., 1945. 55 p.

YANG, I, 揚儀, 1907-　Uncle Kao, a novel about the mistakes and difficulties encountered during the formation of agricultural cooperatives in their early days. Peking, Foreign Languages Press, 1957. 297 p.

YANG, SHUO, 揚朔, 1913-　A thousand miles of lovely land. [Translated by Yuan Ko-chia] Peking, Foreign Languages Press, 1957. 236 p. illus.

YEH, CHUN-CHAN, 葉君健, 1916-　The ignorant and the forgotten, nine stories. Eight original lithographs by Betty Dougherty. London, Sylvan Press, 1946. 159, [1] p. incl front., plates.

————. Mountain village; a novel. New York, G. P. Putnam; London, Sylvan Press, 1947. 3-248 p.

————. tr. Three seasons and other stories. London, Staples Press, 1947. 136 p.

————. They fly south. London, Sylvan Press, 1948. 208 p.

YU, TA-FU, 郁達夫, 1897-1945. Choix de nouvelles de Yu Ta-fou par Tchang Tien-ya. Pékin, Impr. de la "Politique de Pékin," 1933. 103 p. (Collection de la "Politique de Pékin").

YUAN, CHING, 袁靜. Daughters and sons, by Kung Chueh, 孔厥, and Yuan Ching; translated from the Chinese by Sha Po-li. New York, Liberty Press, 1952. 300 p.

————. Schüsse am Bayangsee; Roman [von] Kung Djüe und Yüan Djing. [Nach einer in "Chinese literature," Peking, erschienenen englischen Übersetzung ins Deutsche übertragen von Eduard Klein] Berlin, Verlag Volk und Welt, 1954. 362 p.

## Novels: Western Authors

ABBOTT, PAUL RICHARD. Within the four seas; a Shantung idyll. Shanghai, Commercial Press, 1930. [5]-279 p. front. plates.

ACTON, HAROLD MARIO MITCHELL, 1904-　Peonies and ponies, a novel. London, Chatto and Windus, 1941. vii, 310 p.

[AITKEN, ANDREW] 1868-　The great to be, by Wilcox Arnold [pseud.] London, Wilkinson Bros. [1930] 48 p.

[————]. Chinese folk-lore and Sequel to "The great to be" by Wilcox Arnold [pseud.] London, Wilkinson Bros., [1931] 48 p.

[————]. Mr. Ling, an incarnate deity and the moon, by Wilcox Arnold [pseud.] London, Wilkinson Bros [1933?] 132 p. plate.

ANDERSON, PAUL S., Pan Chao; a girl of old China. New York, Comet Press Books, [1954, c1953] 34 p. illus.

ANDERSON, WILLIAM ASHLEY. Yellow flood. New York, R. M. Mc Bride, 1932. 9-275 p.

ANDREWS, ROY CHAPMAN, 1884-　Quest in the desert; illustrated by Kurt Wiese. New York, Viking Press, 1950. 192 p. illus.

————. Quest of the snow leopard. Illustrated by Kurt Wiese. New York, Viking Press, 1955. 190 p. illus.

APPELL, GEORGE C., 1914-　The tin trumpet of China. New York, Duell, Sloan and Pearce [1950] 238 p.

APPLEGARTH, MARGARET TYSON 1886-　A china shepherdess. Philadelphia, Judson Press [1924] 3-323 p. illus.

ARCHER, CHARLES STANLEY, 1902-　Hankow return. Boston, Houghton Mifflin, 1941; London, Collins, 1941. 378 p.

————. China servant. London, Collins, 1946. 320 p. map.

ARNHOLD, VIRGINIA, 1909-　Celestial escapade, by Stella Kirby [pseud.] New York, Viking Press, 1951. 214 p.

AYSCOUGH, FLORENCE (WHEELOCK) 1878-1942. The autobiography of a Chinese dog, edited by his missus (Florence Ayscough) with writing-brush

sketches by Lucille Douglass. Boston and New York, Houghton Mifflin 1926.
London, Cape, 1926. xiv, 105 p. front., illus. plates.

BABSON, NAOMI LANE. All the tomorrows; a novel. New York, Reynal and
Hitchcock [c1939] 3-390 p.

BACHMANN, ROBERT. The hand of a thousand rings, and other Chinese stories.
New York, Cosmopolis Press, 1924. 252 p.

BAGLEY, WILLIAM CHANDLER, 1909- To far Cathay, tales of Marco Polo, illustrated by Nils Hogner. New York, T. Nelson, 1935. vi, 7-72 p. incl.
front., illus. (Our changing world).

BALL, DORIS BELL (COLLIER), 1897- China roundabout by Josephine Bell,
[pseud.] London, Hodder and Stoughton, 1956. 224 p.

BARING, MAURICE, 1874-1945. Tinker's leave. Garden City, N. Y. Doubleday,
1928; London, Heinemann, 1930. vii, 368 p.

BARRETT, WILLIAM EDMUND, 1900- The left hand of God. Garden City, N. Y.
Doubleday, 1951. 275 p.

BAUM, VICKI, 1888- Hotel Schanghai. Amsterdam, Querido-Verlag, 1939;
Wein, Bermann-Fischer, 1939. 689 p.

————. Shanghai '37; translated by Basil Creighton. New York, Doubleday, 1939;
Book League of America, 1940. viii, 619 p.

BEAUVOIR, SIMONE de, 1908- Les Mandarins. Roman. Paris, Gallimard,
1954. 579 p.

————. The mandarins, a novel. [Translated by Leonard M. Friedman] Cleveland, World Pub. Co., [1956]; London, Collins, 1957. 610 p.

BECHTEL, JOHN. The Shanghai mystery. Grand Rapids, Mich. Wm. B. Eerdmans Pub. Co., 1945. 88 p. illus.

BECK, LILY (MORESBY) ADAMS. The treasure of Ho; a romance. New York,
Dodd, Mead, 1924. 303 p.

BECKER, STEPHEN D    , 1927- The season of the stranger. New York,
Harper [1951] 278 p.

————. Shanghai incident, by Steve Dodge [pseud.] Cover painting by Lu Kimmel.
New York, Fawcett Publications [1955] 158 p. (Gold medal books, 456).

BENNETT, JAMES W. Plum blossoms and blue incense; and other stories of the
East, by James W. Bennett and Soong Kwen-ling. Shanghai, Commercial
Press, 1926; London, Kegan Paul, 1927. [3] -330 p. front. plates.

————. The Manchu cloud. New York, Duffield; London, J. Hamilton, 1927. 3-
329, [1] p.

————. The yellow corsair. New York, Duffield, 1927; London, J. Hamilton,
1928. 3-317, [1] p.

————. Dragon shadows. New York, Duffield, 1928. 286 p.

————. Son of the typhoon, a novel. New York, Duffield, 1928; London, Skeffington, 1929. 3-292 p.

————. Chinese blake. London, Skeffington, 1930. 288 p.

BENSON, STELLA, 1892-1933. Tobit transplanted. London and Toronto, Macmillan; New York, Harper, 1931. xii, 361, [1] p.

BISHOP, CHAIRE (HUCHET). The five Chinese brothers, by Clair Huchet Bishop
and Kurt Wiese. [New York] Coward McCann, [c1938] [50] p. illus.

BLAND, JOHN OTWAY PERCY, 1863-1945. Something lighter; with illustrations
by Mary MacLeod. Boston, Houghton, Mifflin, 1924. 256 p. col. front., col.
plates.

BLOOD, ADELE. The jade rabbit, by Adele Blood and Tam Marriott, illustrated
by Charles Fouqueray (Paris) London, The Diamond Press,[1926]; New York,
The Dial Press, 1927. 404 p.

BOYNTON, GRACE MORRISON, 1890- The River Garden of Pure Repose. New
York, McGraw-Hill [1952] 274 p. illus.

BREDON, JULIET. Le roman d'une ville interdite. Pékin, Impr. de la ''Politique de Pékin,'' 1930. 60 p. (Collection de la ''Politique de Pékin'').

----. Hundred Altars. New York, Dodd, Mead, 1934. viii, 336 p.

----. Hundert altäre, roman. "Deutsch von Richard Hoffmann." Berlin [etc.] P. Zsolnay, 1936. 462, [1] p.

BROWN, KAREN. The Shanghai lady, novelized by Karen Brown, adapted from John Colton's Drifting, illustrated with scenes from the photoplay, "a Universal picture," starring Mary Nolan. New York, Efrus and Bennett, [c1929] 238 p. front., plates.

BROWN, MARGARET H. "Heaven knows." London, Edinburgh House Press, 1939. 167, [1] p. front. plates.

BRULLER, JEAN, 1902- Les pas dans le sable: l'Amérique, la Chine et la France [par] Vercors [pseud.] Paris, A. Michel [1954] 288 p.

BRUNNGRABER, RUDOLF, 1901- Opiumkrieg; roman. Stuttgart-Berlin, Rowohlt [c1939] 326, [1] p.

----. The same. Leipzig, B. Tauchnitz, 1943. 308,[4]p. (Der Deutsche Tauchnitz, bd. 113).

BUCK, PEARL (Sydenstricker) 1892- East wind: west wind. New York, Grosset, 1930; John Day [c1930]; London, Methuen, 1931, cheap ed. 1934. 3-277, [1] p.

----. The same. [New York] American Mercury, [c1939] 126 p. [A Mercury book, 19].

----. The same. Cleveland, World Book Co.; Toronto, McClelland and Stewart, 1948. 277 p.

----. Vent d'Est, Vent d'Ouest. Traduit de l'anglais par Germaine Delamain. Paris, Édition du Dauphin, 1947; Genève, Édition de l'Echo illustré, 1949. xvi, 205 p.

----. Ostwind-Westwind; roman. "Deutsch von Richard Hoffmann." Berlin [etc.] P. Zsolnay, 1934; Zürich, Artemis Verlag, 1947. 274, [1] p.

----. The good earth. New York, John Day [c1931]; London, Methuen, 1931, cheap ed. 1934. 3-375, [1] p.

----. The same. Leipzig, B. Tauchnitz, 1932. 350 p. (Tauchnitz ed.).

----. The same, with an introduction by the author. New York, Modern Library [1934] v-xiii, 374, [1] p. (The modern library of the world's best books).

----. The same. New York, Triangle Books, 1939. 318 p.

----. The same. New York, Grosset and Dunlap. 1940. 374 p. (Madison square books).

----. The same. New York, Pocket Books, 1940. 348 p.

----. The same. Cleveland, World Pub. Co., 1944 318 p. (Tower Books).

----. The same, with illustrations by Howard Willard, introduction by Carl Van Doren. Cleveland and New York, The World Pub. Co. [1947] 292 p. 1 illus., plates. (The Living library).

----. The same. A school ed. by Jay E. Greene. New York, Globe Book Co. [1949] x, 325 p. illus.

----. The same. Standard ed., with an introd. by the author. New York, John Day [1949] xvi, 323 p.

----. La terre chinoise. Traduction de Théo Varlet. Préf. de G. Lepage. Paris, Payot, 1940. Lausanne, Payot, 1943. 375 p.

----. Die gute Erde, Roman des chinesischen Menschen. [Übertragung aus dem Englischen von Ernst Simon] München und Basel, Zimen-Verlag [1947?, c1933]; München, K. Desch, 1933. 405 p.

----. Sons. New York, John Day; London, Methuen, 1932. 3-467, [1] p.

----. The same. New York, Grosset and Dunlap, 1932. 467 p.

----. Les fils de Wang Lung. Traduit par Théo Varlet. Paris, Payot, 1933. 399 p.

----. Söhne, roman. "Deutsch von Richard Hoffmann." Berlin [etc.] P. Zsolnay, 1933; Zürich, Büchergilde Gutenberg, 1939; Artemis Verlag, 1948. 586, [1] p.

----. The young revolutionist. New York, Friendship Press [c1932]; London,

Methuen, 1932. 3-182 p.

――. Der junge Revolutionär. Aus dem Englischen übertragen von Ernst Simon. Basel, etc., Zinnen Verlag, 1934. iv, 244 p.

――. The same. München, K. Desch, 1947. 149 p.

――. The first wife and other stories. New York, John Day company; London, Methuen, 1933. 312 p.

――. La première femme de Yuan. Traduction de Germaine Delamain. Paris, Stock, 1945. 273 p.

――. Die erste Frau und andere Novellen. Berlin [etc.] P. Zsolnay, 1935. 313, [1] p.

――. The mother. New York, John Day; London, Methuen, 1934; Penguin Books, 1934; Cheap ed. 1936. 9-302 p.

――. The same. Cleveland and New York, The World Pub. Co., 1945. 302 p. (Tower Books).

――. La mère. Traduit par Germaine Delamain. Paris, Stock, 1935; Hazen, 1947; A. Brachet, 1948. 254 p. (Le cabinet cosmopolite).

――. Die Mutter, Roman. "Deutsch von Richard Hoffmann." Berlin [etc.] P. Zsolnay, 1934. 312, [1] p.

――. A house divided. New York, Reynal and Hitchcock [c1935] ; London, Methuen, 1935. cheap ed. 1937. 353 p.

――. The same. New York, Grosset, 1939. 353 p. (Novels of distinction).

――. The same. Cleveland and New York, The World Pub. Co. [1948] 287 p. (Forum Books).

――. La famille dispersée. Traduit par S. Campaux. Paris, Payot, 1935. 442 p.

――. Das geteilte Haus; roman. "Deutsch von Richard Hoffmann." Berlin [etc.] P. Zsolnay, 1935; Zürich, Artemis Verlag, 1948.

――. House of earth: The good earth; Sons; A house divided. New York, Reynal and Hitchcock [1935]; London, Methuen, 1936. 3-318, 467, 353 p.

――. Das Haus der Erde; Roman-Trilogie. [Die beruchtigte übersetzung besorgten Ernst Simon (Die gute Erde), Richard Hoffman (Sohne, und Das geteilte Haus)] Wien, P. Zsolnay, 1950. 1084 p.

――. This proud heart. New York, Reynal and Hitchcock [c1938] London, Methuen, 1938; cheap ed. 1940. 371 p.

――. The same. New York, Grosset, 1940. 371 p. (Novels of distinction).

――. Un coeur fier. Traduit par Germaine Delamain. Paris, Stock, 1939; Monaco, Édition du Rocher, 1945. 350 p.

――. Stolzes Herz, roman. "Deutsch von Richard Hoffmann." Berlin [etc.] P. Zsolnay, 1938. 490, [1] p.

――. The patriot. New York, John Day [c1939]; Toronto, Longmans; London, Methuen, 1939. 372 p.

――. The same. New York, Grosset, 1940. vii, 372 p. (Novels of distinction).

――. The same. Cleveland, The World Pub. Co., 1945. 302 p. (Tower Books).

――. The same. London, Methuen, 1950. 376 p. (Uniform ed.).

――. Le patriote. Traduit par Germaine Delamain. Paris, Stock, 1940. 324 p. (Le cabinet cosmopolite).

――. Land der Hoffnung, Land der Trauer! Roman. [Übertragen von Walter Gerull-Kardas] Zürich, Scientia AG. [c1940]; Neue Schweizer Bibliothek, 1951. 391 p.

――. Today and forever, stories of China. New York, John Day [c1941]; London, Macmillan, Toronto, Longman, 1941. Uniform ed. Methuen, 1950. 3-324 p.

――. Maintenant et à jamais. Traduit par H. De Beaune. Bruxelles, Édition de la Paix, 1947. 319 p.

――. Für Heut und alle Zeit. Übers. von F. Fiedler. Zürich, Scientia A.G., 1943; Neue Schweizer Bibliothek, 1951. iv, 383 p.

――. China sky. New York, Triangle Books [1942] 272 p. 1st ed. 1941.

――. Dragon seed, New York, John Day [c1942] London, Macmillan, 1942,

(London, Macmillan, 1942) 2nd ed. ; London, Methuen, 1949. 3-378 p.
———. The same. Garden City, N. Y., Sun Dial Press [1943] 3-378 p.
———. The same. Philadelphia, Triangle Books, the Blakiston Co.; Toronto,
Blue Ribbon Books, 1943. 378 p.
———. Fils de dragon; roman traduit de l'anglais par Jane Fillion. Genève, J.
H. Jeheber [1943] [9]-412 p.
———. Drachensaat, roman. "Einzig autorisierte Übertragung aus dem Ameri-
kanischen von Ernst Reinhard." [Bern] A. Scherz [c1942] 406 p.
———. The story of Dragon seed. New York, The John Day company [1944] 15 p.
———. Twenty-seven stories. Garden City, N. Y., Sun Dial Press [1943] 5-
312, 327 p.
———. The promise. New York, John Day [1943] London, Methuen, 1944. Uni-
form ed., Methuen, 1949. 248 p.
———. Promesse. Traduction de l'anglais par Jane Fillion. Genève, J. H. Je-
heber, 1945. iv, 285 p.
———. Das Gelöbnis. Übertragung von Ursula von Wiese. Bern, A. Scherz,
1945. iv, 318 p.
———. China flight. Philadelphia, Triangle books, the Blakiston company; To-
ronto, Blue Ribbon Books, 1945. 251 p.
———. Pavilion of women. New York, John Day [1946] London, Methuen, 1947.
316 p.
———. Die Frauen des Hauses Wu. Ins Deutsche Übertragen von Justinian Frisch.
Stockholm, Bermann-Fischer Verlag, 1948; Zürich, Buch-Gemeinschaft Ex
Libris, 1951. 474 p.
———. Far and near; stories of Japan, China, and America. New York, John
Day [1947]; Toronto, Longmans, 1947; London, Methuen, 1949. 250 p.
———. Zurück in den Himmel; Erzählungen aus China, Japon und Amerika. Ins
Deutsche Übertragen von Charlotte Kühner. Stuttgart, Victoria Verlag, 1954.
388 p.
———. Peony. New York, John Day [1948] 312 p.
———. Pivoine. Traduction de Germaine Delamain. Paris, Stock, 1949. 400 p.
———. Peony. Übertragen von Irene Mühlon. Bern. A. Scherz, 1949. 308 p.
———. Kinfolk. New York, John Day [1949]; London, Methuen, 1950. 406 p.
———. Liens de sang. Traduit par Lola Trance. Paris, Stock, 1950. 456 p.
———. Kinfolk. Übertragen aus dem Amerikanischen von Renate Hertenstein.
Bern, A. Scherz, 1950. 335 p.
———. The bondmaid. London, Methuen, 1949. 320 p.
———. The child who never grew. New York, John Day [1950], London, Methuen,
1951. 62 p. "Appeared as an article in the Ladies' home journal, May, 1950."
———. L'enfant qui ne devait jamais grandir. Traduction de Lola Trance. Pa-
ris, Stock, 1950. 128 p.
———. Geliebtes unglückliches Kind. [Berechtigte Übersetzung von F. Paster-
nak] Wien, P. Zsolnay, 1952. 84 p.
———. My several worlds, a personal record. New York, John Day [1954] 407 p.
———. Mein Leben-Miene Welten. Eine Autobiographie. Ins Deutsche Übertragung von Hans B. Wagenseil. Wien, München, Basel, K. Desch, 1955. 514 p.
port. illus.
———. Imperial woman; a novel. New York, John Day [c1956] 376 p.

## Works about Pearl Buck

PARDOEN, LÉON. Pearl Buck et la Chine. Lille, Société des auxiliaires des
missions, 1944. 36 p. ilus.
[WALSH, RICHARD JOHN] 1886- A biographical sketch of Pearl S. Buck. New
York, John Day, Reynal and Hitchcock [c1936] 28 p.
[YAUKEY, GRACE (Sydenstricker)] 1899- The exile's daughter, a biography of
Pearl S. Buck, by Cornelia Spencer [psued.] New York, Coward-McCann,
inc. [1944] 3-228 p. front., plates, ports.

BURGESS, STELLA FISHER. A Peking caravan. Shanghai, Printed by the Shanghai Times, 192? 32 numb. l. illus.

BURTON, MILES, 1903- Chinese puzzle. London, Collins, 1957. 254 p.

BYRNE, DONN, 1889-1928. Messer Marco Polo; illustrated by C. B. Falls. New York, Century; London, S. Low, Marston, 1921. 3-147 p., front., plates.

————. The same. New York, Modern Library [1942] 3-147 p. (The Modern Library of the world's best books. [43]).

CAHILL, HOLGER, 1893- Look south to the polar star. New York, Harcourt, Brace [1947] [3]-554 p.

CALDWELL, TAYLOR, pseud. The earth is the Lord's; a tale of the rise of Genghis Khan. New York, Scribner, 1941. 550 p.

CAMPBELL, THOMAS BOWYER. Far trouble. London W. Collins, [1931]; Philadelphis, Macrae Smith Co. [1932] 286 p.

CARDYFF, pseud. Twelve tales and one other. Shanghai, China Digest, 1937. 251 p.

CARNSON, MAXWELL. Monkeys of Hai Tu. London, Hutchinson, 1927. 288 p.

CAUSSE, FRÉDÉRIC, 1892- La gloire sous les voiles [par] Jean d'Agraives [pseud.] Paris, Berger-Levrault, 1933. vi, 206 p.

————. The same. Illus. de Henry Fournier. [Paris] Hachette [1938] 191 p. illus. (Bibliothèque de la jeunesse).

CLAIR, RENÉ, 1898- La princesse de Chine, suivi de De fil en aiguille. Paris, B. Grasset [1951] 237 p.

————. Die Prinzessin von China. Roman. Übertr. aus dem Französischen von N. O. Scarpi. Zürich, Diogenes Verlag, 1954; München, List, 1956. 132 p. (List-Bücher, 73).

CLEMOW, VALENTINE. Shanghai lullaby. London, Hurst and Blackett, [1937] ix, 13-288 p.

CLIFT, CHARMIAN. The big chariot, by Charmian Clift and George Johnston. Indianapolis, Bobbs-Merrill [1953] 342 p.

————. The same. Sydney, Angus and Robertson [1953] 320 p. illus.

CLIFT, WINIFRED LECHMERE. Seng Chang sees red, and other stories. London, Marshall Bros., 1928. 9-212 p.

COLERUS, EGMONT, 1888- Zwei Welten; ein Marco Polo Roman. Berlin [etc.] Paul Zsolnay Verlag [c1926] 707, [1] p.

CONQUEST, JOAN. Crumbling walls, frontispiece by Victor Beals. New York, Macaulay Co. [c1927] 382 p. front.

CONSTEN, HERMANN, 1878- Der Kampf um Buddhas Thron, mit 17 Bildtafeln und einem farbigen Einbandbilde. Berlin, Vossiche Buchhandlung [c1925] 233, [1] p. plates (part col.) (Pan-bücherei eines freien lesebundes, bd. IV).

CORLIEU, ROBERT. Lénine chez Confucius, roman de la Chine contemporaine. Paris, J. Tallandier [1930] 222 p. plates. (Collection du temps présent).

CRONIN, ARCHIBALD JOSEPH, 1896- The keys of the kingdom. Boston, Little, Brown, 1941. [3]-344 p.

————. The same. London, V. Gollancz, 1942. 254, [1] p.

————. The same. Berne, A. Scherz, 1942. iv, 376 p. (The Scherz-Phoenix Books, 1).

————. Les clés du royaume (The keys of the kingdom) roman. Traduit de l'anglais par G. de Tonnac-Villeneuve. Genève, Éditions du Milieu du Monde, 1942. iv, 383 p.

————. The same. Bruxelles, Éditions de la Paix [1946] 380 p.

————. Die Schlüssel zum Königreich, roman. "Einzig autorisierte Übertragung aus dem Englischen von Wilhelm du Fresne." [Bern] A. Scherz [c1942] 448 p.

CROIDYS, PIERRE, 1885- Mon ami le Fils du Ciel, roman. Paris, Fasquelle [1934] [7]-198 p.

CUTHRELL, MRS FAITH (Baldwin) 1893- American family. New York, Farrar and Rinehart, [c1935] xi, 388 p.

DAMIEN, C. L'orage dans de steppe, roman de moeurs subériennes. Pékin,

Impr. de la "Politique de Pekin," 1926. 144 p.

DANBY, HOPE. The illustrious emperor. Chicago, New York, Ziff-Davis Pub.
Co. [1946] 281 p. illus.

DEKOBRA, MAURICE, 1885- Shanghai honeymoon. New York, Philosophical
Library [1946] 316 p.

DÖBLIN, ALFRED. Die drei Sprünge des Wang-lun. Chinesische Roman. Baden-Baden, Keppler, 1946. 512 p.

DRAKE, BURGESS. Chinese white. London, Falcon Press, 1950. 317 p.

DRURY, WILLIAM PRICE, 1861- The flag lieutenant in China. London, Chapman and Hall, 1929. vii, 280 p.

DUFFIELD, ANNE. Miss Mayhew and Ming Yun; a story of east and west. New
York, Frederick A. Stokes, 1928. 3-311 p.

EDWARD, GEORG, 1869- Die chinesische Sklavin, Roman. Berlin, Globus Verlag [1940] 159, [1] p.

[EDWARDS, FREDERICK ANTHONY] 1896- Chinese dust, by J. van Dyke [pseud.]
London, Jarrolds [1933] 288 p.

———. Chinese lovesong. Garden City, N. Y., Doubleday, 1933. 3-325 p.

———. Chinese chapter, by J. Van Dyke [pseud.] London, Jarrolds [1934] vii,
11-288 p.

———. Peking madness [by] J. Van Dyke [pseud.] Garden City, N. Y., Doubleday, 1934. 300 p.

———. Passenger to Peking [by] J. Van Dyke. Garden City, N. Y., Doubleday,
1935. 300 p.

———. Chinese river. Boston, Lothrop, Lee and Shepard; London, R. Hale,
1937. 9-314 p.

———. And China lay sleeping, by J. Van Dyke, [pseud.] London, R. Hale, 1938;
New York, Ryerson Press, 1939. 285 p.

———. No coffins in China, by Charman Edwards, [pseud.] London, R. Hale,
1939. vii, 11-287 p.

———. Street of the many rickshaws, by J. Van Dyke, [pseud.] London, R. Hale,
New York, Ryerson Press, 1940. 288 p.

———. Chinese city [by] J. van Dyke [psued.] London, New York, T. V. Boardman [1946] 207 p.

EGGERS, KURT, 1905- Herz im Osten, der Roman Li Taipes des Dichters.
Stuttgart, Deutsche Verlags-Anstalt [c1935] 307, [1] p.

EKVALL, ROBERT BRAINERD, 1898- Tents against the sky; a novel of Tibet.
London, Gollancz, 1954; New York, Farrar, Straus and Yound[1955?]264 p.

ESPEY, JOHN JENKINS, 1913- Minor heresies. New York, A. A. Knopf, 1945.
3-202 p.

———. Tales out of school. New York, A. A. Knopt, 1947. x, 204 p.

———. The other city. New York, A. A. Knopf, 1950 [c1949] 211 p.

EWES, FRITZ. Ting, der "Nur flüsternd Genannte." Roman eines chinesischen
Napoleon der keinen Chronisten fand. Leipzig, Wehnert, 1938. 262 p.

FABER, JOHANNES GEORG, 1891- Die letzte Liebe des Kaisers Hüan Dsung,
Roman. Dresden und Leipzig, H. Minden [c1926] 100 p. incl. col. mounted
front.

FANE, LENOX. Legation street. London, T. Butterworth, [1925] 9-320 p.

FEDOROVA, NINA, 1895- The family. Boston, Little, Brown, 1940; London,
Collins, 1941. 3-346 p.

———. La famille (The family) Roman traduit de l'anglais par G. de Tonnac-
Villeneuve. Genève, Éditions du Rhône [1944] 7-302, [2] p.

———. The same. Paris, Édition de la Paix, 1948. 384 p.

———. Die Familie. Übertragung aus dem Amerikanischen von Lola Humm.
Bern, Hallwag, 1945. lv, 312 p. illus.

———. The children. Boston, Little, Brown, 1942; London, Collins, 1942. 386 p.

———. Kie Kinder. Übertragung aus dem Amerikanischen von Lola Humm. Bern
Hallwag, 1947. 347 p.

FITCH, ABIGAIL HETZEL. When the white camel rides. New York, Henkle-
Yewdale House, [c1936] 305 p.

FLEISCHMAN, ALBERT S. Shanghai Flame. New York, Fawcett Publications
[1955] 160 p. (Gold medal books, 514).

FLETCHER, JOSEPH SMITH, 1863- The Kuang-he vase. New York, Grosset
and Dunlap [1928?] 310 p.

FORD, JULIA ELLSWORTH, 1859- Consequences, introduction by John Haynes
Holmes, jacket illustration by Ellsworth Ford. New York, E. P. Dutton[1929]
xv, 342 p.

FRANK, JOSEF MARIA. Kleines Fräulein aus China. Roman. Frankfurt, Wien,
Forum-Verlag, 1953. 233 p. (Forum-Taschenbücher, 6).

FRASER, RONALD, 1888- Landscape with figures. London, T. F. Unwin[1925];
New York, Boni and Liveright, 1926. 285, [1] p. New York ed. 320 p.

———. Lord of the East. London, J. Cape [1956] 249 p.

FRONDAIE, PIERRE, 1884- Port-Arthur. Paris, Plon [1936] 270 p.

———. The same, a novel; authorized translation by Elisabeth Abbott. Philadelphia and New York J. B. Lippincott [c1938] 283, [1] p.

GAIDAR ARKADIĬ PETROVICH, 1904-1941. Timur and his gang [by] Arkady
Gaidar, translated by Zina Voynow, illustrated by Zhenya Gay. New York,
C. Scribner, 1943. vii, [2], 125 p. illus.

———. Timur and his squad; stories. [Translated from the Russian by Lucy
Flaxman; edited by Leonard Stoklitsky] Moscow, Foreign Languages Pub.
House, 1948. 542 p. illus.

———. Timur und sein Trupp, übers. aus dem Russischen von L. Klementinow
skaja. Bearb. von Ruth Gerull-Kardas. 5 Aufl. Berlin, Kinderbuchverlag,
1955. 108 p.

GALBRAITH, WINIFRED. Men against the sky. London, J. Cape [1940] 7-285 p.

[GALLOWAY, ALFRED DOUGLAS] 1881- Sampan Smith, a tale of the China
coast, by Shore Leith [pseud.] London, T. Butterworth [1938] 320 p.

GANN, ERNEST KELLOGG, 1910- Soldier of fortune. New York, W. Sloane
Associates [1954] 314 p.

GARSTIN, CROSBIE, 1887-1930. China seas, a novel of the East. London,
Chatto and Windus, 1930; New York, Frederick A. Stokes, 1931. 3-300 p.

GAUTIER, JUDITH, 1846-1917. The imperial dragon, translated by M.H. Bour-
chier. [New York] and London, Brentano's, 1928. 319 p. Translation of Le
dragon impérial, Paris, 1893.

GEER, ANDREW CLARE. Canton barrier. New York, Harper [1956] 282 p.

GELFAN, LEWIS DAVID. The embroidered city. Boston, Little, Brown, 1950.
368 p.

[GERAHTY, DIGBY GEORGE] The small general, a novel by Robert Standish
[pseud.] New York, Macmillan, 1945. v, 233 p.

———. The same. London, P. Davies [1945] vii, 241 p.

———. Mr. On Loong, a novel by Robert Standish [pseud.] London, P. Davies
[1946] 295 p.

———. The same. New York, Macmillan, 1947. 3-326 p.

———. Gentleman of China, a novel by Robert Standish [pseud.] London, P.
Davies [1949] 268 p.

———. The same. New York, Macmillan, 1953. 283 p.

———. A worthy man [by] Robert Standish [pseud.] New York, Macmillan; London, P. Davis, 1952. 278 p.

GERVAIS, ALBERT, 1892- Une fille de H'an. Paris, B. Grasset, 1928. [7]-
211 p.

———. Malven auf weisser Seide. Aus dem Französischen übertragen von Albert
freiherr von Bodman. Leipzig [etc.] W. Goldmann [1936]; München, Goldmann, 1954. 9-214, [1] p.

———. L'ombre du ma-koui. Paris, Gallimard [1936] [7]-274 p.

———. Im Schatten des Ma-kue; als Arzt im braune chinesischer Geisterwelt.

Deutsche Übertragen von Albert Freiherer von Bodman. Leipzig, W. Goldmann [ 1937]; München, W. Goldmann, 1952. 259 p. plates.

GILBERT, RODNEY YONKERS, 1889- The indiscretions of Lin Mang. London,
J. Murray [ 1929] 335 p.

GILMAN, LA SELLE, 1909- Shanghai deadline. New York, Dodge [c1936] 273 p.
——. The golden horde. New York, Smith and Durrell, [ 1942] 3-466 p.
——. The red gate. New York, Ballantine Books, 1953 [c1952] 212 p.
——. The dragon's mouth. New York, W. Sloane Associates, 1954. 310 p.

GILSON. CHARLES JAMES LOUIS, 1878- Held by Chinese brigands. New York,
Dodd, Mead, 1921; London, Oxford University Press, 1933. 302 p. col. front.

GIRAULT, YVONNE, 1896- La horde. Illustrations de Pierre Joubert. Paris,
Éditions Fleurus, 1953. 126 p. illus. (Collection Jean-François).

GLAUSER, FRIEDRICH. Der Chinese. [Kriminalroman] Zürich, Büchergilde
Gutenberg, 1957. 171 p.

GLICK, CARL, 1890- Three times I bow, with illustrations by Soriano. New
York, London, Whittlesey House, McGraw-Hill, [ 1943] vii, 259 p. illus.

GMELIN, OTTO, 1886-1940. Dschinghis Khan, der Herr der Erde, roman. Jena,
E. Diederichs [ 1930] 318 p.
——. The same. Jena, E. Diederichs [ 1943] 7-323, [ 1] p.

GODDEN, RUMER. Chinese puzzle. London, P. Davies, [ 1936] vii-viii, 149 p.

GOWEN, VINCENT HERBERT, 1893- Sun and moon. London, Duckworth
[ 1927] 319 p.
——. The same. Boston, Little, Brown, 1927. [3]-340 p.

GRAHAM, DOROTHY, 1893- Lotus of the dusk; a romance of China. New York,
Frederick A. Stokes, 1927. 3-310 p.
——. The China venture, a novel. New York, Frederick A. Stokes 1929. 3-328 p.
——. Wind across the world. New York, G. P. Putnam [ 1947] 3-278 p.

[GRANVILLE BAKER, LOLA MARIE THÉRÈSE] 1906- Yellow river, by Elena
Bochkovsky [ pseud. ] London, T. Butterworth, [ 1934] 315, [ 1] p.

GULIK, ROBERT HANS VAN, 1910- The Chinese maze murders; a Chinese detective story suggested by three original ancient Chinese plots. With 19 plates
drawn by the author in Chinese style. The Hague, W. Van Hoeve, 1956. 322 p.
illus. (A Judge Dee mystery).

HAHN, EMILY, 1905- Steps of the sun. New York, Dial Press, 1940. 313 p.
——. Mr. Pan. Garden City, N. Y., Doubleday, 1942. viii, 294 p.
——. The picture story of China, with pictures by Kurt Wiese. New York, Rey-
nal and Hitchcock [ 1946] [ 51] p. incl. front. (map) col. illus.
——. Miss Jill, a novel. Garden City, N. Y., Doubleday, 1947. 273 p.

[HALL, JOSEF WASHINGTON] Moonlady, by Upton Close [ pseud. ] New York,
London, G. P. Putnam 1927. viii, 375 p.

HANNA, WILLARD A. 1911- Destiny has eight eyes. New York and London,
Harper [ c1941] 305, [ 1] p.

HANSON, RITA MOHLER. The desert road to Shani Lun; a romance of Mongolia.
Portland, Or., Binfords and Mort [ c1939] 288 p. illus.

HANSTEIN, OTFRIED von. Der Schmuggler von Hankau. Wilhelmshaven, Hera-
Verlag, 1953. 169 p. illus.

HARRIMAN, MIRIAN. Ah-Ling of Peking; a romance of old China. New York,
George H. Doran [ c1923] 87 p.

HARVEY, MARION. The dragon of Lung Wang. New York, E. J. Clode, [ c1928]
vi, 9-310 p.

HEDLIN SVEN ANDERS, 1865- Tsangpo Lamas wallfahrt, die Pilger. Leipzig, F. A. Brockhaus, 1922. 346 p. illus.

HENEY, HELEN, 1907- The Chinese camellia, a novel. London, Collins [ 1950]
256 p.

HERSEY, JOHN RICHARD; 1914- A single pebble. New York, Knopf, 1956. 181 p.

HILTON, JAMES, 1900- 1954. Lost horizon. New York, M. Morrow, 1933,
Author's ed. 1936. London, Macmillan, 1937. 3-277 p.

———. The same. New York, Pocket Books [1944] 182 p. 1st ed. 1939.

———. The same; illus. by Kurt Wiese. Cleveland, World Pub. Co. [1948] 277 p. illus. (The Living library).

———. Les horizons perdus; roman traduit de l'anglais par Hélène Godard. Genève, J. H. Jeheber [1943] 296 p.

———. Irgendwo in Tibet. Übertragen von Herberth Egon Herlitschka. Berlin, Darmstadt, Deutsche Buch-Gemeinschaft; Zürich, Die Arche, 1954. 302 p.

HOBART, ALICE TISDALE (NOURSE) 1882- Within the walls of Nanking; poem by Florence Ayscough. New York, Macmillan, 1927; London, J. Cape [1928] 243 p. front., illus. (maps) plates.

———. Oil for the lamps of China. Indianapolis, Bobbs- Merrill [c1933] 403 p.

———. Lampes de Chine. Traduit de l'anglais par Gisèle d'Assailly. [Paris] Plon et Nourrit, 1937. 395 p. (Collection La Fayette)

———. The same. Paris, Intercontinentale- costard, 194? (Marabout, 3).

———. Petroleum für die Lampen Chinas; Roman "Aus dem Amerikanischen übertragen von Wilh. Ritter." [Zürich, Büchergilde Gutenberg, 1940]. 459 p.

———. The same. [Deutsche Übersetzung von Helene Schidrowitz] München, Zinnen-Verlag [1940] 462 p.

———. The same; Neue Ausg. München, Desch, 1949. 501 p.

———. Pidgin cargo. New York and London, Century [c1929] 5-315 p.

———. River supreme. Indianapolis, Bobbs-Merrill [c1934] 5-315 p. London, Cassell, 1936.

———. The same. New York, Triangle Books [1943] 5-315 p.

———. Les eaux tumultueuses. Traduit par Jacqueline Chassang. Liége-Paris, Maréchal, 1947. 283 p. (Couleur du monde).

———. Strom, du Schicksal; Roman um den Jangtsekiang. "Deutsche Übersetzung von Martha von Wagner." München, K. Desch [1946] 371 p.

———. Yang and yin; a novel of an American doctor in China. Indianapolis, Bobbs-Merrill [c1936]; London, Cassell, 1937. 366 p.

———. Das Haus der heilenden Hände. Übers. von Georg Anton Kern. München, Zinnen-Verlag, 1946; Neu Aufl. München, Desch, 1949. 454 p.

———. Venture into darkness. New York, London, Longmans, Green [1955] 367 p.

HOLLISTER, MARY (BREWSTER), 1891- Mai-Dee of the mountains, a story of present-day China. New York, Fleming H. Revell [c1933] 153 p.

———. Back of the mountain; a tale of young China and the People's party. New York, Fleming H. Revell [c1934] 155 p.

———. Mulberry village; a story of country life in China; illustrated by Kurt Wiese. New York, Dodd, Mead, 1936. vii, 287 p. incl. front., illus.

———. Beggars of dreams, pictures by Kurt Wiese, decorations from woodblocks cut especially for the book by Chinese artists in Shanghai. New York, Dodd, Mead, 1937. 234, [1] p. incl front., illus., plates.

———. Kee-kee and company; a story of American children in China; illustrated by Kurt Wiese. New York, Dodd, Mead, 1938. 3-192 p. incl. illus., plates.

———. Pagoda anchorage; a story of tea clipper days in China; illustrated by Margaret Ayer. New York, Dodd, Mead, 1939. vii, 268 p. incl. illus. plates.

———. Bright sky tomorrow; illustrated by Esther Wood. New York, Friendship Press [c1940] 122 p. illus.

HOROSE, S. La symphonie des ombres chinoises, idylle. Paris, Éditions de la Madeleine [c1932] xix, 267, [1] p.

HUELSENBECK, RICHARD, 1892- China frisst Menschen. Zürich und Leipzig, Orell Füssli [1930] 347 p.

HUGGINS, ALICE MARGARET, 1891- The red chair waits, by Alice Margaret Huggins [in collaboration with Earl Hoit Ballou and Hugh Laughlin Robinson] With decorations by Jeanyee Wong,黃如珍. Philadelphia, Westminster Press [1948] 256 p.

———. Day of the false dragon. Decorations by Jeanyee Wong. Philadelphia,

Westminster Press [ 1953] 160 p.

HUGHES, PAUL, 1916- Challenge at Changsha. New York, Macmillan 1945. 311 p.

HUNTER, BLUEBELL MATILDA, 1887- The Manchu empress. New York, Dial Press, 1945. iv, 355 p.

HURST, JOHN SHIRLEY. Then gilded dust. Indianapolis, Bobbs-Merrill [ 1943] 279 p.

HYDE, ROBERT, 1900- Winds of Gobi. New York, Brewer and Warren, Payson and Clarke 1930. 164 p.

JACQUES, NORBERT, 1880- Der Kaufherr von Shanghai; Roman. Berlin, Ullstein [ c1925] 289, [ 1] p.

JEFFRIES, GRAHAM MONTAGUE, 1900- Twilight of the dragon [ by] Peter Bourne [ pseud. ] New York, Putnam [ 1954] 371 p. illus.

JENSSEN, FRIEDRICH. Der chinesische Silberdollar, Kriminalroman. Berlin, Scherl [ 1943] 182 p.

JERNIGAN, MURIEL MOLLAND. Forbidden City. New York, Crown Publishers [ 1954] 346 p.

JONES, IDWAL. China Boy. Los Angeles, Primavera Press [ c1936] 132 p.

JUNKERMAN, HELEN BARRETT. Leng Fei, the Firefly; a lyrical fragment of ancient China. Illustrated by Wang Chi-yuan, 王濟遠 . New York, Exposition Press [ 1956] 30 p. illus.

KECK, MAUD. Mrs. Blair, a comedy of indiscretions. New York and London, Harper, 1938. 3-394 p.

KENT, LOUISE (ANDREWS) 1886- He went with Marco Polo; a story of Venice and Cathay; illustrated by C. Leroy Baldridge and Paul Quinn. Boston and New York, Houghton Mifflin, 1935. [ 3]-223 p. col. front., illus. (incl. maps).

KEON, MICHAEL, 1918- The tiger in summer. New York, Harper [1953] 314 p.

KEYTE, JOHN CHARLES, 1875- A daughter of Cathay; a novel. London, A. Rivers, [ 1926] 320 p.

————. Minsan, a novel. London, A. Rivers, 1927. 284 p.

KING, VERONICA. Anglo-Chinese sketches [ by] Veronica and Paul King. 3rd ed. Shanghai, Kelly and Walsh, 1927. [ 5]-132 p. 1st ed., 1903, under the pseudonym of William A. Rivers.

————. The chartered junk; a tale of the Yangtsze valley, [ by] Veronica and Paul King...2nd ed. Shanghai, Kelly and Walsh, 1927. 244 p. 1st ed., 1910, under the pseudonym of William A. Rivers.

————. The commissioner's dilemma: an international tale of the China of yesterday, by Veronica and Paul King. London, Heath, Cranton, 1929. 288 p.

————. Eurasia; a tale of Shanghai life, [ by] Veronica and Paul King...3rd ed. Shanghai, Kelly and Walsh, 1927. 265 p. 1st ed., 1907 under the pseudonym of William A. Rivers.

KOHLHÖFER, PAUL, 1895- Die Träne des Dschingis Chan, Kriminalroman. Berlin, Aufwärts-Verlag [ c1942] 247 p. (Der Aufwärts-Kriminal-Roman, 21).

KOMROFF, MANUEL, 1890- Jade Star. New York, Sloane [ c1951] 294 p.

KRAUTHOFF, BERNDT, 1907- Ich befehle; Kampf und Tragödie des Barons Ungern-Sternberg. Leipzig, B. Tauchnitz, 1944. 9-320 p. (Der Deutsche Tauchnitz, Bd. 131).

LAMBURN, JOHN BATTERSBY CROMPTON, 1893- Squeeze, a tale of China. London, J. Murray [1937] 318 p.

LANCING, GEORGE. Peking glass. London, S. Paul ltd. [ 1939] 11-256 p.

————. Lotus Blossom. New York, L. Furman, [ c1939] xi, 362 p.

————. Imperial motherhood. London, R. Hale [ 1945] 192 p.

————. The mating of the dragon, by George Lancing. London, R. Hale [ 1946] ix, 11-207 p.

————. Dragon in chains. London, R. Hale, [ 1947] 368 p.

————. Phonix triumphant. London, R. Hale, 1950. 365 p.

[ LANE, KENNETH WESTMACOTT] 1893- Hanging waters, a novel, by Keith

West [pseud.] New York, G. P. Putman [c1933] 256 p.
_____. The same; illustrated by Noel Syers. London, L. Dickson, 1933. 256 p. front., plates.
_____. Ma Wei slope, a novel of the T'ang dynasty. London, Cresset Press, 1944. 184 p.
_____. Winter Cherry, a novel of the T'ang dynasty. New York, Macmillan, 1944. 217 p.
_____. Peony. London, Cresset Press, 1945. 189 p.
_____. The same. New York, Macmillan, 1946. 213 p.
_____. The three blossoms of Chang-an [by] Keith West [pseud.] London, Cresset Press, 1942; New York, Macmillan, 1946. ix, 268 p.
_____. The widows of the magistrate; a novel by Keith West [pseud] London, R. Hale, 1949. 258 p.
LANGLEY, NOEL, 1911- The rift in the lute. London, A. Barker [1952]; New York, Coward-McCann, 1953. 192 p.
LAPIERE, RICHARD TRACY, 1899- Son of Han. New York, London, Harper, 1937. 314 p.
LAUBER, CÉCILE, 1887- Chinesische Nippes, Erzählungen und Gedichte. Zürich-Leipzig, Grethlein [1931] 126 p., [Seldwyla-bücherei, 23/24].
LEARNER, FRANK DOGGETT,            -1947. Tibetan journey. London, H. E. Walter [1949] xi, 71 p. illus., group ports.
LEAVELLE, ELIZABETH. Lustrous heroine. London, Hurst and Blackett, [1934] 7-285 p.
LEE, ANDRÉ. Le tireur de pousse-pousse (trois nouvelles). Pékin, Impr. de la "Politique de Pékin." 1933. 35 p. (Collection de la "Politique de Pékin").
LEWIS, ELIZABETH (FOREMAN) 1892- Young Fu of the upper Yangtze; illustrated by Kurt Wiese. Philadelphia, Chicago [etc.] John C. Winston [c1932] v, [1] 265 p. col. front., illus., col. plates
_____. Jung Fu wird Kupferschmied. Leben und Abenteurer eines wackeren Chinesenjungen. Nach dem Amerikanischen. Ausg. ins Deutsche Übertragung von Karl H. Coudenhove. Zeichnungen und Buchschmuck von Kurt Wiese. 6 Aufl. Graz, Salzburg, Wien, Pustet, 1950. 237 p.
_____. Ho-Ming, girl of new China; illustrated by Kurt Wiese. Philadelphia, Chicago, John C. Winston [c1934]; London, G. G. Harrap, 1935 v, [1] 266 p. col. front., illus., col. plates.
_____. Ho-Ming. Eine kleine Chinesin studiert. Nach dem Amerikanischen. Ausg. ins Deutsche Übertragung von Karl H. Coudenhove. Zeichnungen und Buchschmuck von Kurt Wiese. 4. Aufl. Graz, Salzburg, Wien, Pustet, 1950. 263 p.
_____. China quest, illustrations by Kurt Wiese. Toronto, Philadelphia John C. Winston [c1937]; London, G. G. Harrap, 1938. ix, 301 p. col. front., illus. col. plates.
_____. When the typhocn blows, illustrated by Kurt Wiese. Philadelphia, Toronto John C. Winston [1942] xi, 273 p. incl. col. front., illus.
LÖHNDORFF, ERNST FRIEDRICH. 1899- Yangtsekiang; ein Chinaroman. Bremen, C. Schünemann [c1940] 351 p.
MCCARTNEY, JAMES LINCOLN, 1898- Frustrated martyr, a novel of a medical missionary in West China. New York, Exposition Press [1953] 349 p.
MACKAY, MARGARET (MACKPRANG) 1907- Like water flowing. New York, Reynal and Hitchcock [c1938] 3-346 p.
_____. Lady with jade. New York, John Day [c1939] 3-510 p.
_____. Valiant dust. New York. John Day [c1941] 3-561 p.
_____. Great lady. New York. John Day [1946] 410 p.
MACLURE, JAN. Escape to Chungking. London, H. Milford, Oxford University Press, 1942. 192 p. illus.
MACWHIRTER, EDITH. Tibetan trumpet. London, Frederick Muller, 1953; Toronto, S. J. Reginald Saunders; Sydney, Shakespeare Head Press, 1953. 224 p.

MALRAUX, ANDRÉ, 1901- La condition humaine. Paris, Gallimard [1933],
402 p.

———. The same. Éd. rev. et corr. Généve, A. Skira, 1945; [Paris]Gallimard
1951(c1946). 404 p.

———. Man's fate (La condition humaine) translated by Haakon M. Chevalier.
New York, H. Smith and R. Haas, 1934; Random House, 1934. vi, 360 p.

———. The same. New York, Modern Library [1936] 360 p. (The Modern Library of the world's best books).

———. Storm in Shanghai (La condition humaine); translated from the French by
Alastair MacDonald. 2d ed. London, Methuen, [1935] 348 p.

———. Les conquérants. Paris, B. Grasset, [c1928]; Genève, A. Skira, 1945;
Lausanne, Guild du Livre, 1948. 9-269 p.

———. The conquerors, translated by Winifred Stephens Whale. New York, Harcourt, Brace [1929] 3-270 p.

———. The same. With a new postface translated by Jacques Le Clercq. Boston, Beacon Press [1956] 193 p. (Beacon paperback, BP30).

MARGUERITTE, LUCIE PAUL, 1886- La lanterne chinoise. Paris, Éditions
Bandinière, [c1930] 221 p.

———, tr. Le piège d'amour. Roman chinois moderne traduit d'un ouvrage de M.
Tchao Tcheng kieng. Paris, La nouvelle revue critique, [1925] 159 p. (Les
Maitres du roman, 14).

MARQUAND, JOHN PHILLIPS, 1893- Ming yellow. Boston, Little, Brown,
1935. 3-312 p.

MARSHALL, EDISON, 1894- The splendid quest. New York, H.C. Kinsey,
1934. 3-275 p.

———. Sam Campbell, gentleman. New York, H.C. Kinsey, 1935. 273 p.

———. Caravan to Xanadu, a novel of Marco Polo. New York, Farrar, Straus
and Young [1953] 371 p.

MARTIN, ARCHIBALD EDWARD, 1885- Chinese red mysteries. London, Reinhardt, 1955. 206 p.

MASON, RICHARD, 1919- The world of Suzie Wong. New York, World Pub. Co.
London, Collins, 1957. 344 p.

MASON, VAN WYCK, 1897- The Shanghai bund murders. Garden City, N.Y.
Pub. for the Crime Club, by Doubleday, 1933. xiii, 298 p.

———. The Hongkong airbase murders. Garden City, N.Y. Pub. for the Crime
Club, by Doubleday, 1937. 339 p.

———. The same. New York, Sun Dial Press, [1938?] 339 p.

MAUGHAM, WILLIAM SOMERSET, 1874- On a Chinese screen. London, W.
Heinemann, 1922. viii, 11-237 p.

———. The same. New York, George H. Doran [c1922] viii, 11-237 p.

———. The same. New York, George H. Doran [1926?] viii, 11-237 p. [Mur-
ray Hill library].

———. Le paravent chinois, texte français de madame E.R. Blanchet. Paris,
Les Éditions de France, c1933. 240 p.

———. The painted veil. London, Heinemann; New York, George H. Doran company [c1925] 9-289 p.

———. La passe dangereuse; texte français de Madame E.R. Blanchet. Paris,
Les Éditions de France, c1926. 279 p.

MECKAUER, WALTER 1889- Die Bücher des Kaisers Wutai, Roman; Geleitwort von Oskar Loerke. Berlin, Deutsche Buch-Gemeinschaft [c1928] 282,
[1] p.

———. The books of the Emperor Wu Ti, translated from the German by J.J.
Saville Garner. New York, Minton, Balch and Co.; London, M. Secker, 1931.
v, 215 p.

MERWIN, SAMUEL, 1874- In red and gold; illustrated by Cyrus Leroy Baldridge. Indianapolis, Bobbs-Merrill, [c1921] 352 p. front. plates.

———. Silk; a legend as narrated in the journals and correspondence of Jan Po;

illustrated by N. C. Wyeth. Boston and New York, Houghton Mifflin; London, Constable, 1923. 266, [1] p. col. front.

MILN, LOUISE (JORDAN) 1864-1933. Mr. and Mrs. Sên. New York, Frederick A. Stokes, 1923. 325 p.

――――. In a Shantung garden. New York, Frederick A. Stokes, 1924. 351 p.

――――. The soul of China, glimpsed in tales of today and yesterday. New York, Frederick A. Stokes, 1925. 311 p.

――――. Ruben and Ivy Sên. New York, Frederick A. Stokes, 1925. 360 p.

――――. It happened in Peking. New York, Frederick A. Stokes, 1926. 368 p.

――――. In a Yün-nan courtyard. New York, Frederick A. Stokes, 1927. 371 p.

――――. The flutes of Shanghai. New York, Frederick A. Stokes, 1928. 356 p.

――――. Red lily and Chinese jade; three chapters in the Chinatown life of Donald Martin, M. D. New York, Frederick A. Stokes. London, Hodder and Stoughton, 1928. viii, 326 p.

――――. By Soochow waters. New York, Frederick A. Stokes, 1929. New York, Frederick A. Stokes, 1929. 317 p.

――――. Mr. Wu. Based on the play "Mr. Wu" by H. M. Vernon and Harold Owen [16th printing] New York, Frederick A. Stokes, 1929. 314 p. 1st ed. 1920.

――――. Rice. New York, Frederick A. Stokes, 1930. 333 p.

――――. The vintage of Yon Yee. New York, Frederick A. Stokes, 1931. 360 p.

――――. Ann Zu-Zan, a Chinese love story. New York, Frederick A. Stokes, 1932. 341 p.

――――. Peng Wee's harvest. New York, Frederick A. Stokes, 1933. 346 p.

――――. A Chinese triangle. [London] Hodder and Stoughton [1933] 319 p.

MISSELWITZ, HENRY FRANCIS, 1900- Shanghai romance. New York, Harbinger House [1943] 127 p.

MITCHELL, DAVE. Red earth. New York, Vantage Press [1956] 295 p.

MORRIS, DONALD R. China station. [New York] Farrar, Straus, and Young [1951]; New American Library 1952; London, Hammond, Hammond, Co. 1952. 276 p. Cheaper ed. 1957, 224 p.

MORTON, JOHN BINGHAM, 1893- The Tibetan Venus; with illus. by Jean Charlot. London, New York, Sheed and Ward [1951] 230 p. illus.

MOSHER, JOHN S. Liar dice. New York, Simon and Schuster, 1939. 3-302 p.

NAGEL, SHERMAN A. Ah Sin, a factual novel of the Hakka Chinese. Grand Rapids, Mich., Wm B. Eerdmans, 1940. 272 p.

NEVILL, E. MILDRED, 1889- Ah Fu, a Chinese river boy, pictures by Elsie Anna Wood. New York, Friendship Press, c1932. 60, [1] p. col. illus. (Nursery series).

NOHARA, WILHELM KOMAKICHI, 1899- Erwin in Schanghai. Geschichte aus Chinas unruhtagen. Leipzig, Fritz Schneider, 1934. 112 p. illus.

OHTA, TAKASHI. The golden wind [by] Takashi Ohta and Margaret Sperry. New York, C. Boni, 1929. 9-269 p. (Paper books).

[O'MALLEY, MARY DOLLING (SANDERS)] Lady, 1889- Peking picnic, by Ann Bridge [pseud.] Boston, Little, Brown; London, Chatto and Windus, 1932. 3-354 [1] p.

――――. Peking picnic, by Ann Bridge [pseud.] Toronto, McClelland, 1932; New York, Grosset 1935. 3-354, [1] p.

――――. Pique-nique à Pékin (Peking picnic); roman. Texte français d'Henriette de Sarbois. Paris, Gallimard [c1940] 287, [1] p.

――――. The Ginger griffin, by Ann Bridge [pseud.] Boston, Little Brown; London, Chatto and Windus, 1934. 3-409 p.

――――. Der Gelbe Grief, Roman. "Übersetzt von Herbert E. Herlitschka." Zürich-Leipzig, Rascher [194-?] 382, [1] p.

――――. Four-part setting, by Ann Bridge [pseud.] Boston, Little, Brown 1939; London, Chatto and Windus 1939. 3-447 p.

――――. Gesang in Peking, Roman [von] Ann Bridge [pseud. Übertragung von

H. E. Herlitschka] Zürich, Humanitas Verlag [1941, c1942] 501 p.

O'NEAL COTHBURN. Master of the world. New York, Crown Publishers [1952] 405 p.

OSSENDOWSKI, FERDYNAND ANTONI, 1876-1945. Derriére la muraille chinoise. Roman contemporain. Traduction de Robert Bernard. Paris, Impr. De Lagny, 1927. 249 p.

OWEN, FRANK, 1893- The wind that tramps the world; splashes of Chinese color. New York, Lantern Press, 1929. 3-118 p.

——. The purple sea, more splashes of Chinese color. New York, Lantern Press, 1930. 153 p.

——. Della-Wu, Chinese courtezan, and other oriental love tales. New York, Lantern Press, 1931. 3-313 p.

[——]. Lovers of Lo-Foh, by Roswell Williams [pseud.] docorations by Steele Savage. [New York, C. Kendall, c1936] 287 p. illus.

——. The Scarlet hill. New York, Carlyle House, 1941. 367, [1] p.

——. The porcelain magician; a collection of oriental fantasies. Illustrated by Frances E. Dunn. New York, Gnome Press [1949, c1948] 256 p. illus.

——. Soochow the marine, by Reginald Owen and Paul Lees. London, Putnam [1951] vi, 218 p.

PACKARD, FRANK LUCIUS, 1877- Shanghai Jim. Garden City, N.Y., Pub. for the Crime Club by Doubleday, 1928. vi, 374 p.

PAGE, ISAAC MARSHALL, 1885- When the donkey jumped, and other stories. Philadelphia, London, China Inland Mission [1945] 94 p. illus., plates, 2 port. (incl. front.).

[PALAMOUNTAIN, ALAN]. Shanghai nights, by Tasman Ile [pseud.] [Shanghai?] The author [1929] 278 p.

PALEN, LEWIS STANTON. The red dragon; a China story of to-day. Boston and New York, Houghton Mifflin. 1927. vi, 290 p.

PATERSON, NEIL. The China run; being the biography of a great grandmother. London, Hodder and Stoughton, 1949. 95 p. incl. front.

PAYNE, PIERRE STEPHEN ROBERT, 1911- The Chinese soldier, and other stories. London, Toronto, W. Heinemann [1945] 165 p.

——. Love and peace. London, Toronto, W. Heinemann, 1945. viii, 207 p.

——. Liebe und Frieden, Roman. Berechtigt Übersetzung von Theresse Neumann. Wien, P. Zsolnay, 1946. 352 p.

——. Torrents of spring. New York, Dodd, Mead [1946] viii, 218 p.

——. The bear coughs at the North Pole. New York, Dodd, Mead [1947] 226 p.

——. A house in Peking. Garden City, N.Y., Doubleday, 1956. 320 p.

PETER, WILLIAM WESLEY, 1882- The great east gate. New York, Cleanliness Institute, 1929, 47 p.

——. The same. Shanghai, The Commercial Press, 1933. 56 p. illus.

——. Shanghai policeman; edited by Hugh Barnes. London, Rich and Cowan [1937] vii, 222 p. front. (port.), plates.

PETTIT, CHARLES, 1875- L'homme qui mangeait ses poux, roman chinois. Paris, E. Flammarion [c1922] 283 p.

——. Les amours d'une impératrice et d'un délicieux jeune homme; roman. Paris, E. Flammarion [c1922] 287 p.

——. L'impuissance d'un puissant général, roman chinois. Paris, E. Flammarion [c1926] 249 p.

——. The impotent general; translated by Una, lady Troubridge. New York, H. Liveright [c1931] 202 p.

——. The son of the grand eunuch. New York, Boni and Liveright, 1927; Avon Book Co. 1949. vi, 9-254 p.

——. Le fils du grand eunuque, roman de la vieille Chine. [Paris] P. Dupont [1947] 283 p. 1 éd., 1920.

——. La Chinoise qui s'émancipe. Paris, Les Éditions de France, c1927. 256 p.

————. La femme qui commanda à cinq cents millions d'hommes; Tseu-hi, impératrice de Chine (1835-1908). Paris, Éditions du Laurièr [1928] 316 p. (Collection "Les grandes figures").

————. The woman who commanded 500,000,000 men, translated from the French by Una, lady Troubridge. New York, H. Liveright [c1929] 319 p.

————. Elegant infidelities of Madame Li Pei Fou. New York, H. Liveright [c1928] 192 p.

————. Petal of-the-Rose, translated by Una, lady Troubridge. New York, H. Liveright [c1930] 249, [1] p. Translation of Petale de Rose et quelques Conzes. Paris, 1909.

————. The unfaithful lady. New York, Avon Book Co. [1948] 123 p. (New Avon library, 155) "Originally titled The elegant infidelities of Madame Li Pei Fou."

PITMAN, NORMAN HINSDALE, 1876-1925. Dragon lure: a romance of Peking in the days of Yuan Shih-kai). Shanghai, Commercial Press, 1925. 318 p. front. plates.

PONCINS, GONTRAN DE MONTAIGNE, vicomte de, 1900- From a Chinese city. Translated from the French by Bernard Frechtman. Garden City, N.Y. Doubleday, 1957. 256 p. illus. French ed. in press.

POSTON, MARTHA LEE. Ching-li, pictures i v Weda Yap. New York, T. Nelson [c1941] 40 p. col. illus.

————. The girl without a country, illustrated by Margaret Ayer. New York, Edinburgh T. Nelson [1944] 226 p. illus. (incl. map).

POZNER, VLADIMIR. Bloody Baron, the story of Ungern-Sternberg; translated from the French by Warre Bradley Wells. New York, Random House [c1938] 3-383 p.

PRITCHARD, WILLIAM THOMAS, 1909- The riddle of Chung Ling Soo. London, Arco, 1955. 300 p.

RIDEOUT, HENRY MILNER, 1877-1927. Tao tales. New York, Duffield, 1927. 3-382 p.

RITCHIE, ALICE, d. 1941. The treasure of Li-Po. With illus. by T. Ritchie. London, Hogarth Press [1948]; New York, Harcourt, Brace 1949. 127 p. illus.

RIVERAIN, JEAN, 1907- Marco Polo à travers l'Asie inconnue. 4 planches hors texte en couleurs et 55 compositions en noir par Néjad. Paris, Larousse [1954] 206 p. illus. (Contes et gestes historiques).

ROBERTS, C.  E. Not-a-care garage; a story of China. London, Edinburgh House Press, 1947. 96 p. illus. (Faraway tales, 8).

ROGERS, LETTIE (HAMLETT) 1917- South of heaven. New York, Random House [1946] 278 p.

————. The storm cloud. New York, Random House [1951] 309 p.

ROMANIELLO, JOHN. Bird of Sorrow. New York, P. J. Kenedy [1956]; London, W. H. Allen, 1957. 221 p. illus.

RUDINGER DE RODYENKO, STEPHEN PIERO SERGIUS, 1888- Small Me; a story of Shanghai life, by S. P. R. de Rodyenko. New York, The James A. McCann, [c1922] 217 p.

SAGENDORPH, KENT. Sin-Kiang castle. New York, Cupples and Leon [c1938] vi, 208 p. front. (His Dan Perry adventure stories).

SALZMANN, ERICH VON, 1876-1941. Das Geheimnis des Nashornbechers, Roman aus dem heutigen China. München, G. Müller [c1929] 274, [2] p.

SCHEURER-FLÜCKIGER, ROSA. Unsichtbare Mauern. Auf rauhen Wesen in Chinas Bergen. (Tatsachenbericht aus den Jahren 1921 bis 1928). Basel, Basler Missionsbuchhandlung, 1941. iv, 136 p. illus.

[SCHMIDT, JAMES NORMAN] 1912- An inch in time, by James Norman, [pseud.] New York, Books Inc., W. Morrow, 1944. 249 p.

SCHNEDITZ, GILBERT. Göttin Tschang; Untergang einer Dynastie. Wien, J. Günther, [c1940] 347 p. illus.

SCHOYER, PRESTON. The foreigners. New York, Dodd, Mead, 1942. viii, 617 p.

————. The indefinite river. New York, Dodd, Mead, 1947. vii, 325 p.

————. The ringing of the glass. New York, Dodd, Mead, 1950. 343 p.

SCHREIBER, HERMANN, 1892- Opfergang in Peking; ein Buch um das Sterben des Gesandten von Ketteler. Berlin, Scherl [c1936] 266, [1] p. front., plates, ports.

[SCHULKERS, ROBERT FRANC] 1890- The Chinese coin, by Seckatary Hawkins [pseud.] illustrations by Carll B. Williams. Cincinnati, R. F. Schulkers [c1926] 3-288 p. incl. front., illus.

SHEPHERD, CHARLES R. Lim Yik Choy, the story of a Chinese orphan. New York, London [etc.] Fleming H. Revell [c1932] 252 p.

SHERIDAN, JUANITA. The Chinese chop. Garden City, N. Y., Published for the Crime Club by Doubleday, 1949. 221 p.

SHORT STORY CLUB, SHANGHAI. Shanghai stories, by members of the Short Story Club, Shanghai. Shanghai, Kelly and Walsh, 1927. 310 p.

[SIMPSON, BERTRAM LENOX] 1877-1930. Her closed hands, by Putnam Weale [pseud.] New York, Macmillan, 1927. vi, 335 p.

————]. China's crucifixion, by Putnam Weal [pseud.] New York, Macmillan, 1928. 3-401 p.

————]. The port of fragrance, by Putnam Weale [pseud.] New York, Dodd, Mead, 1930. 3-314 p.

SMITH, BRADFORD, 1909- The arms are fair. Indianapolis, New York, The Bobbs-Merrill, [1943] 237 p.

SMITH, DON, 1909- China coaster; a novel of suspense. New York, Holt [1953] 211 p.

[SMITH, ERNEST BRAMAH]. Kai Lung's golden hours, by Ernest Bramah [pseud.]; with a preface by Hilaire Belloc. New York, George H. Doran, [c1923]; London, Richards Press, 1936. xiii, 17-333 p.

————]. The wallet of Kai Lung, by Ernest Bramah [pseud]; with an introduction by Grant Richards. London, G. Richards, 1923; New York, Doubleday, 1923; London, J. Cape (Traveller's library), 1926; Methuen, 1927. xi, 299 p.

————]. The story of Wan and the remarkable shrub, and The story of Ching-Kwei and the destinies, by Ernest Bramah [pseud.] Garden City, N. Y. Doubleday, [c1927] 98 p.

————]. Kai Lung unrolls his mat, by Ernest Bramah [pseud.] Garden City, N. Y., Doubleday, 1928. London, Richards Press, 1928. v, [1], 320 p.

————]. The mirror of Kong Ho, by Ernest Bramah [pseud.] London, Cayme Press, 1929. New York, Doubleday, 1930. x, 252 p.

————]. The moon of much gladness, related by Kai Lung, by Ernest Bramah [pseud.] London, Cassell, [1932] 316 p.

————. Kai Lung omnibus; containing The Wallet of Kai Lung, Kai Lung unrolls his mat, [and] Kai Lung's golden hours. London, P. Allen, Toronto, S. J. R. Saunders, 1936; Quality Press, 1938. 625 p.

————]. The return of Kai Lung, by Ernest Bramah [pseud.] New York, Sheridan House [1937]; Toronto, George J. McLoed, 1937. 319 p.

————]. Kai Lung beneath the mulberry-tree, by Ernest Bramah [pseud.] London, Richards Press [1940] Reprint, 1948. vi, 7-320 p.

[SOULIÉ, CHARLES GEORGES] 1878- In the claws of the dragon, by George Soulié de Morant. New York, A. A. Knopf, 1921. 7-297 p.

————. Le palais des cent fleurs, roman. Paris, E. Fasquelle, 1922. 271, [1] p.

————. Bijou-de-ceinture; ou, Le jeune homme qui porte robe, se poudre et se farde, roman. Paris, E. Flammarion [c1925] xv, [17]-249 p.

————. Ce qui ne s'avoue pas, même à Shanghaï, ville de plaisirs, roman. Paris, E. Flammarion [1927] 248 p.

————. Les lignes de la main d'après les chinois, par Soulié de Morant. Paris, Bernardin-Béchet, 1933. 1 v.

SOUPIRON, PAUL. La fille aux yeux de jade. Roman. Genève, Éditions du Rhône, 1946. iv, 239 p. (Collection Lugdunum, 5).

SOWERS, PHYLLIS (AYER). Some of the dragon. Illustrated by Margaret Ayer.

Chicago, A. Whitman 1942. 285 p. col. front., illus., col. plates.

SPERLING, ROBERT HELGI, 1912-  Piratin Fu.  München, W. Goldman [1952] 234 p. illus.

SPRINGER, THOMAS GRANT, 1873-  The red cord; a romance of China; with an introduction by John Luther Long, illustrations by S. Y. Pang.  New York, Brentano's [c1925]  xvi, 302 p. illus.

STEPANOV, ALEKSANDR NIKOLAEVICH, 1890-  Port Arthur, a historical narrative [tr. from the Russian by J. Fineberg]  Moscow, Foreign Languages Pub. House, 1947. 784 p.

STICKELBERGER, EMANUEL, 1884-  Der Reiter auf dem fahlen Pferd; ein Buch vom Mongolen Dschinggis-Khan und seinem abendländischen Gegenspieler.  Stuttgart, Verlag von J. F. Steinkopf [1938] 446, [1] p. fold. map, fold. geneal. tab.

STONE, GRACE (ZARING), 1896-  The bitter tea of General Yen, illustrated by Barbara Macfarlane.  Indianapolis, Bobbs-Merrill, [c1930]; London, Cobden-Sanderson, 1930; New York, Grosset and Dunlap, 1932. 9-322 p.

STUART FRANK STANLEY, 1904-  Caravan for China.  London, S. Paul and Co., ltd. [1939]; New York, Doubleday, 1941. 11-287 p.

TEILHET, HILDEGARDE (TOLMAN).  The assassins.  Garden City, N. Y. Doubleday 1946. 272 p.

TOMNOVEC, IDA ALLEN.  The building of the Wall of China, a novel.  New York, Exposition Press [1953] 160 p.

TREICHLINGER, WILHELM MICHAEL.  China bittet zu Tisch.  110 Spazierwege zu einer fremden Küche.  Zürich, Sanssouci, 1956. 72 p. illus.

UHSE, BODO.  Tagebuch aus China.  Mit Bildern von Werner Klemke.  Berlin, Aufbau-Verlag, 1956. 174 p. plates.

ULLMAN, JAMES RAMSEY, 1907-  The sands of Karakorum.  Philadelphia, Lippincott [1953] 254 p.

VARÈ, DANIELE, 1880-1956.  The maker of heavenly trousers.  Garden City, N. Y., Doubleday, 1936. vii-xii, 301 p.

———.  Der Schneider himmlischer Hosen, Roman.  "Deutsch von Annie Polzer."  Berlin [etc.] P. Zsolnay, 1936; Wien, Erasmus-Verlag, 1951. 318, [2] p.

———.  The same.  Zeichnungen von Josef Hegenbarth.  [Berlin-Lichterfelde, Wiking Verlag, 1944?] 128 p. illus. (Die Neue bücherei. [18/19]).

———.  The gate of happy sparrows.  Garden City, N. Y., Doubleday, 1937. xi-xix, 283 p.

———.  Das Tor der glücklichen Sperlinge, Roman in China.  "Deutsch von Viktor Polzer."  Berlin [etc.] P. Zsolnay, 1938; Berlin und Darmstadt, Deutche Buch-Gemeinschaft, 1953. 345, [1] p.

———.  Temple of costly experience.  London, Methuen, 1939, Toronto, S. J. R. Saunders, 1941. 250 p.

———.  Der Tempel der kostbaren Weisheit; Roman.  "Übers. von Lotte Leber."  Berlin, Wien [etc.] P. Zsolnay, 1940; Wien, Erasmus-Verlag, 1951. 345, [3] p. illus.

———.  Le maison des cinq vertus, Roman.  Traduit de l'anglais par Jean Muray.  Paris, Plon, 1947. ii, iii, 243 p. (Collection Feux croisés, 91).

———.  Novels of Yen-Ching.  London, Methuen, 1954. 656 p.

VOLK, GORDON.  Gold out of China.  London, S. Paul, [1946] 167 p.

WALLACE, FREDERICK WILLIAM.  Tea from China, and other yarns of the sea.  London, Hodder and Stoughton, [1927] 311 p.

WALLACE, KATHLEEN.  I walk alone.  London, W. Heinemann [1930] 3-337 p.

———.  The same.  Garden City, N. Y., Doubleday, 1931. 3-310 p.

———.  Without a stair.  London, W. Heinemann, [1933] 3-350 p.

———.  The same.  Garden City, N. Y., Doubleday, 1933. 3-303 p.

———.  Pity my simplicity.  London, Toronto, W. Heinemann, [1936] 3-323 p.

———.  Ancestral tablet.  London, Toronto, W. Heinemann [1938] 3-506 p.

———.  Rice in the wind.  New York, G. P. Putman, [1943] 3-294 p.

[WARD, ARTHUR SARSFIELD] 1853- Fu Manchu's bride. Garden City, N.Y., Pub. for the Crime Club, by Doubleday, 1933. v-vii, 319 p.

WARD, ROBERT SPENCER, 1906- Children of the black-haired people, by Evan King [pseud.] New York, Rinehart [1955] 435 p. illus.

WARNER, WILLIAM HENRY. The dragon's brood. New York, H.C. Kinsey, 1934. 296 p.

WATERBOER, HEINZ, 1907- Im Banne Dschingis-khans; auf den Spuren einer Forschungsreise zum Grabmal des grossen Reiters, Roman. Berlin, Volksverband der Bücherfreunde, Wegweiser-Verlag [1939] 382, [1] p.

———, Das mongolische Abenteuer, Roman. München, R. Piper [1941] 390, [1] p.

———. Hsiang Fei; eine Erzählung von Liebe und Treue. Tatsachennovelle aus der chinesischen Geschichte. Berlin-Friedenau, Spiegel Verlag [c1943] 91 p. ports.

WEBB, MARY GLADYS (MEREDITH) 1881-1927. The Chinese lion. London, B. Rota, 1937. 13 p.

WEBER, HARALD, 1881-1942. Enid, Roman einer Deutschen in China. Minden (Westf.) W. Köhler, 1943. 437 p.

WENDT, META. Tai-Sham. Eine chinesische Mutter. Breklum, Jensen, 1955. 15 p. plates.

[WESTLAKE, WILFRED]. All the tea in China, a Chinese misprint, by Wilfred Harvey [pseud.] London, S. French [1947] 28 p. illus. (French's acting edition, 969).

WIESE, KURT, 1887- The Chinese ink stick; text and drawings by Kurt Wiese. Garden City, N.Y., Doubleday, 1929. vi, 3-199 p. incl. illus., plates (part col.) col. front.

WILEY, HUGH, 1884- Manchu blood. New York, London, A.A. Knopf, 1927. [3]-306, [1] p.

WILSON, CHESLEY. Swing full circle. New York, Harcourt, Brace [1954] 312 p.

WILSON, DAVID CALDER. Chinese white; 3d. ed. London, Hutchinson [1927] 287 p.

WILSON, LOUISA. Broken journey. New York and London, Harper, 1935. 3-343 p.

WIMSATT, GENEVIEVE BLANCHE. A lady like the moon. New York, B. Ackerman, [1945] 304 p.

WINGATE, LITITIA BERYL (TUCKER). A servant of the mightiest, by Mrs. Alfred Wingate. London, C. Lockwood; New York, Brentano, 1927. 351,[1] p. front., plates.

———. Jen. London, C. Lockwood [1928] 284, [1] p. incl. illus. fold. map. geneal. tables.

———. The talisman of Kubla Khan, 1229-1298, by Mrs. Alfred Wingate. New York, R.M. McBride 1929. 284, [1] p. incl. 1 illus. geneal. tables. double front. (map).

WITTE, VIKTOR. Die Marionetten des Chang Loo. Kriminalroman. Wien, Rota-Verlag, 1954. 192 p. (Bären Reihe, 81).

WOODROOFFE, THOMAS. River of Golden Sand. London, Faber and Faber, [1936] 9-325 p.

———. Yangtze skipper. New York, Sheridan House [c1937] 306 p.

WOOLF, BELLA SIDNEY. Chips of China by Bela S. Woolf (Mrs. W.T. Southorn). Hong Kong, Kelly and Walsh, 1930. vii-ix, 82 p. illus.

WRIGHT, CONSTANCE. Their ships were broken. New York, E.P. Dutton, [c1938] 348 p.

WURM, ERNST, 1906- Yüan Schi-kai Tragödie eines Usurpators. Berlin, Zsolnay Verlag, K.H. Bischoff, 1942. 309, [1] p.

YARDLEY, HERBERT OSBORN, 1889- Crows are black everywhere, by Herbert O. Yardley and Carl Grabo. New York, G.P. Putnam [1945] 3-247 p.

[YAUKEY, GRACE (SYDENSTRICKER)] 1899- China trader. New York, John Day [1940] 3-362 p.

———. The missionary [by] Cornelia Spencer [pseud.] New York, John Day, 1947. 276 p.

ZUCKMANTL, PETER. Mongolisches Intermezzo. Darmstadt, Leske, 1953.
174 p.

## Tales and Short Stories

BAYLIN, J.R., tr. Contes chinois. Pékin, La Politique de Pékin, 1922. [6] p.
66 numb. 1. (Collection de la "Politique de Pékin").

BROWN, BRIAN, 1881- ed. Chinese nights entertainment; stories of old China,
selected and ed. by Brian Brown; foreword by Sao-Ke Alfred Sze, 施肇基.
New York, Brentano's [c1922] 222 p. front., plates

CHAN, CHIH-YI, 陳執毅. The good-luck horse, adapted from an old Chinese
legend by Chih-yi and Plato Chan, 陳智誠 New York, London, Whittlesey
House, McGraw-Hill [1943] [47] p. illus. (part col.).

CHI, YÜN, 紀昀, 1724-1805. Le lama rouge et autres contes, traduits par
Tcheng-Loh, 陳籙, et Mme. Lucie Paul-Margueritte, illustrés par C. Hauche-
corne. Paris, Éditions de l'Abeille d'or [1923?] [7]-131 p., illus.

CH'IEN, GOCHUEN, 錢歌川 Chinese fairy tales, with illustrations by the author.
London, Country Life, [1939] 73 p. illus., col. plates.

CHINESE FAIRY TALES, newly gathered from many sources, with illustrations
by Sonia Roetter. [Mt. Vernon, N.Y.] Peter Pauper Press [1946]; latest
ed. 1953. 76 p., incl. col. illus., col. plates.

CHINESISCHE ERZÄHLUNGEN. Auswahl. Mit einem Vorwort von N. Pachomow.
Berlin, Dietz-Verlag, 1953. 277 p.

CHINESISCHE VOLKAMÄRCHEN. Aus dem Russischen übers. von Manfred von
Busch. Illustriert von N. Kozergin. Berlin, Holz, 1954. 37 p.

CH'U, TA-KAO, 初大告. Stories from China, put into Basic English. London,
Kegan Paul, 1937. 84 p. front. (fold. tab.) (Psyche miniatures. General series, 89).

DAWN ON THE RIVER and other stories by contemporary Chinese writers. Peking, Foreign Languages Press, 1957. 170 p.

THE DRAGON KING'S DAUGHTER, ten Tang Dynasty stories. Peking, Foreign
Languages Press, 1954. 100 p. illus.

DIE TOCHTER DES DRACHKÖNIGS. Zehn Geschichten aus der Zeit der Tang
Dynastie. Peking, Verlag für Fremdsprachige Literatur, 1954. 100 p.

EBERHARD, WOLFRAM, 1909- ed. and tr. Chinesische Volksmärchen; ausgewählt und übertragen von W. Eberhard. Leipzig, Insel-Verlag, 1936, Neu
Aufl. 1953. 89 p. (Insel-Bücherei, 484).

_____. Chinese fairy tales and folk tales, collected and translated by W. Eberhard.
London, Kegan Paul, N.Y. Dutton, 1937. xiv, 304 p. "Translated from the
German by Desmond Parsons."

_____. Typen chinesischer Volksmärchen, bearbeitet von W. Eberhard. Hel-
sinki, Suomalainen Tiedeakatemia, Academia Scientiarum Fennica, 1937.
437 p. ([Folklore fellows] FF communications n:o 120).

_____. Volksmärchen aus Südost-China (Sammlung mr. Ts'ao Sung-Yeh, 曹松
葉) bearbeitet von W. Eberhard. Helsinki, Suomalainen Tiedeakatemia, Academia Scientiarum Fennica, 1941. 349 p. illus. (map) ([Folklore fellows] FF
communications n:o 128).

ERDBERG, OSKAR. Tales of modern China. Moscow, Co-operative Pub. Society of Foreign Workers in the U.S.S.R., 1932. 198 p.

ERZÄHLUNGEN AUS DEM NEUEN CHINA. Peking, Verlag für fremdsprachige
Literatur, 1955. 167 p.

EVERYDAY TALES OF CHINA AND JAPAN [with illustrations] London, Church
Missionary Society, 1938. 57 p.

FÊNG, HSÜEH-FENG, 馮雪峯, 1903- Fables. [Translated by Gladys Yang] Peking, Foreign Languages Press, 1953. 70 p. illus.

_____. Febeln. Peking, Verlag für Fremdsprachige Literatur, 1953. 56 p.

FORSTER-STREFFLEUR, SIDONIE. Was Li-Pao-ting erzählt. Chinesische

Sagen und Märchen, deutsch erzählt von S. Förster-Streffeur. Wien, A.
Schroll [ 1924] 140 p. , incl. front. , plates.

HALPHEN, J. Contes chinois; traduit du chinois. Paris, Champion, 1923. 196 p.

HSIEH, TEHYI. 謝德怡, 1884- ed. and tr. Chinese village folk tales. Boston,
B. Humphries [ 1949, c1948] 74 p. illus.

KE, HERTZ C.K., 葛傳槼. Chinese stories translated. Shanghai, Chung Hua
Book Co. , 1937. ii, 60 p. (Students' English library, 1).

KINGOME, RUBY FABRIS. Tales of a Chinese amah. Illustrated by Fei Cheng-
wu, 費成武. London, J. Nisbat [ 1952] viii, 178 p. col. illus.

LIM, SIAN-TEK, 林善德, 1904- Folk tales from China with illustrations by
William Arthur Smith. New York, John Day [ 1944] 160 p. incl. front. illus.

———. More folk tales from China; with illus. by William Arthur Smith. New
York, John Day [ 1948] 160 p. illus.

METZGER, BERTA. Picture tales from the Chinese, with drawings by Eleanor
Frances Lattimore. New York, Frederick A. Stokes, 1934. xii, 106, [3] p.
incl. illus. , plates.

MOLE, G.        E. Twenty-five Chinese stories told in simple English. Shanghai, Commercial Press, 1940. 25 p.

OLCOTT, FRANCES JENKINS. Wonder tales from China seas, illustrations
(except frontispiece) by Dugald Stewart Walker. New York, Longmans, Green,
1925. xviii, 238 p. col. front. , illus.

PANIKKAR, KAVALAM MADHAVA, 1896- comp. Modern Chinese stories.
Translated by Huang K'un. Delhi, Ranjit Printers and Publishers [ 1953]
429 p. illus.

PANKING. Contes chinois, traduit par Panking et Kou Hong-ming, 辜鴻銘. Pékin, La "Politique de Pékin," 1924. [6], 41, [3], 23 p. front. illus.

PITMAN, NORMAN HINSDALE, 1876-1925. Chinese fairy tales. New York,
Thomas Y. Crowell [ c1924] London, G.G. Harrap, 1923, 230 p. col. front.,
col. plates. 1st ed. 1910.

———. The same. Illustrated by Weda Yap. New York, Thomas Y. Crowell
[ 1945] 230 p. front. , col. plates.

ROSE, FRANCIS. The white cow, and other Chinese fairy tales as told by Lao
Tzu, written and illustrated by Francis Rose. London and Redhill, Lutterworth Press [ 1945]. 62 p. illus. (part. col. ).

SNOW, EDGAR, 1905- ed. Living China, modern Chinese short stories, compiled and edited by Edgar Snow; with an introduction by the editor and an essay on modern Chinese literature by Nym Wales. New York, Reynal and
Hitchcock [ 1937] 360 p. front. (port. ).

SOONG MAYLING, 1897- Little sister Su, a Chinese folk tale. [ New York,
John Day Co. , 1942] Cover-title, 19 l. illus.

TALES AND PARABLES of old China, translated by Lin Yutang. San Francisco,
The Book Club of California, 1943. [ 16] p. (Book club of California. Guar-
dians of the Pacific, 2).

TING, SIMON, 丁星. Selected short stories from Chinese classical literature.
with an introduction by Roxby Lefforge. Manila, New American Press, 1946.
95 p.

WANG, I-TING, 王翼廷. Fifty famous Chinese tales. Shanghai, Commercial
Press, 1934; Kwang Hsueh Pub. House, 1935. vi, 150 p., illus.

WELLS, HERBERT RICHMOND. tr. Gods, ghosts and devils; stories of Chinese
life and beliefs. Translated by H.R. Wells. Hong Kong, Wing Fat and Co.,
1935. 161 p

WILHELM, RICHARD, 1873-1930. ed. and tr. Chinesische Volksmärchen; übersetzt und eingeleitet von Richard Wilhelm; Jena, E. Diederichs, 1921. 409,
[ 1] p. front., plates. (Die Märchen der Weltliteratur, II. ser. Märchen des
Orients). 1. Aufl. 1911.

———. ed. The Chinese fairy book, ed. by Dr. R. Wilhelm, tr. after original
sources by Frederick H. Martens, with six illustrations in collor by George

W. Hood. New York, Frederick A. Stokes [c1921] vi, 329 p. col. front.,
col. plates.

————. tr. Chinesische Märchen. Aus dem Chinesischen übertragen von Richard
Wilhelm. Düsseldorf, Diederichs, 1955. 393 p. (Die Märchen der Weltliteratur).

————, Die Geister des gelben Flusses. Chinesische Märchen. Rudolstadt, Greifen Verlag, 1955. 362 p. illus.

WU, HO-MING,伍鶴鳴, tr. One hundred Chinese stories retold, with grammatical notes and equivalent Chinese. Shanghai. Sin Nien Book Co., 1948. 263 p.

YANG, HSIEN-I, 楊憲益, tr. The courtesan's jewel box; Chinese stories of the xth-xviith centuries. [Translated by Yang Hsien-yi and Gladys Yang] Peking, Foreign Languages Press, 1957. 553 p. illus.

YÜAN, CHIA-HUA, 袁家驊, ed. and tr. Contemporary Chinese short stories, ed. and tr. by Yuan Chia-hua and Robert Payne. London, New York, N. Carrington, 1946. 169 p. (Modern CHinese literature, 1).


## Wit and Humor

GILES, HERBERT ALLEN, 1845-1935, tr. Quips from a Chinese jest-book, translated by Herbert A. Giles. Shanghai, Kelly and Walsh, 1925. 146, iii p.

LIANG, SHIH-CH'IU, 梁實秋, 1901- The fine art of reviling, a translation from the Chinese by William B. Pettus. New York, The Typophiles, 1942. 28 p. (Typophile chap books, 6).

LIN, YU-T'ANG,林語堂 1895- The Little critic; essays, satires and sketches on China (First series: 1930-1932) Shanghai, Commercian Press, 1936. x, 299 p.

————. The same. (Second series: 1933-35) Shanghai, Commercial Press, 1935. x, 258 p.

————. L'humour chinois, ou Recueil d'essais, satires et esquisses, traduit de l'anglais. Pékin, Impr. de la "Politique de Pékin," 1936. 134 p. (Collection de la "Politique de Pékin").

————. Confucius saw Nancy, and essays about nothing. Shanghai, Commercial Press, 1937. viii, [2], 301 p., illus.

KAO, GEORGE,高克毅 1912- ed. Chinese wit and humor; introduction by Lin Yutang. New York, Coward-McCann [1946] xxxv, 347 p.

MCCORMICK, ELSIE. The unexpected diary of a Shanghai baby. 3rd ed. Shanghai, Chinese-American Pub. Co., 1923? ii, 96 p.

LA SATIRE CHINOISE, politique et sociale. Pékin, Impr. de la "Politique de Pékin," 1927-1935. 9 v. illus. (Collection de la "Politique de Pékin").

TONG, HOLLINGTON K., 董顯光, 1887- Gems of Chinese humor. Washington, 1957. 94 p.


## Proverbs

[BEILENSON, PETER] 1905- tr. Chinese proverbs from olden times. Mount Vernon, N.Y., Peter Pauper Press [1956] [62] p. illus.

BROWN, BRIAN, 1881- ed. The wisdom of the Chinese: their philosophy in sayings and proverbs, edited with an introduction by Brian Brown, and a preface by Ly Hoi Sang. Garden City, N.Y., Garden City Pub. Co. [1938] 208 p. front., plates. 1st ed. 1920.

————. The wisdom of the Orient; edited, with an introduction, by Brian Brown. Two volumes in one: The wisdom of the Chinese and The wisdom of the Hindus. Garden City, N.Y., Garden City Pub. Co. [1941] 7-208 p. vii-xxvi, 293 p.

FABRE, ALFRED. Film de la vie chinoise; proverbes et locutions. Hong Kong Impr. de la Société des missions étrangères de Paris, 1937. xviii, 694 p.

HART, HENRY HERSCH, 1886- comp. and tr. Seven hundred Chinese proverbs; translated by Henry H. Hart; foreword by Patrick Pichi Sun. Stanford, Stanford University Press; London, H. Milford, Oxford University Press [c1937].

xxviii, 83 p. illus.

——. Siebenhundert chinesische Sprichwörter. Unter Benützung der englischen Übersetzung von Henry H. Hart ins Deutsche übertragen von Margrit von Wyss-Vögtlin. Zürich, Rascher, 1945. iv, 112 p. 1. ed., 1942.

LUM, CHUNG PARK, 林松柏. Words of wisdom from Chinese sages. [New York, Walters and Mahon, c1933] 58 p.

[MORGAN, HARRY TITTERTON] 1872- Chinese proverbs. Edited for and copyrighted by Quon-Quon company. Los Angeles, Calif., c1944. 20 p. illus. [His Chinese classics in miniature].

PLOPPER, CLIFFORD HENRY, 1885- Chinese religion seen through the proverb. Shanghai, China Press, 1926. ix (i. e. xi), 381 p. front., illus., plates.

——. Chinese proverbs: the relationship of friends as brought out by the proverbs; economics as seen through the proverbs. Peiping, North China Union Language School cooperating with California College in China [1932] 47 p.

SCARBOROUGH, WILLIAM. A collection of Chinese proberbs. Revised and enlarged by the addition of some six hundred proverbs, by the Rev. C. Wilfrid Allan. Shanghai, Presbyterian Mission Press; London, Probsthain 1926. vi, 381, [2], xiv p.

SEN, YÜ-HSIU, 孫毓修, ed. Ancient Chinese parables, selected and edited by Yu Hsiu Sen. Translated by Kwei-ting Sen, 孫貴定. With a preface by H.J.C. Grierson. Shanghai, Commercial Press, 1927. xvi, 86 p.

[TREICHLINGER, WILHELM MICHAEL] Chinesische Spruchweisheit. 330 Chinesische Sprichworter. Ausgew. und aus dem Chinesischen. übers. von Wilhelm Michael Treichlinger. Zürich, Die Arche, 1956. 48 p. illus. (Die kleinen Bücher der Arche, 216).

YANG, HSIEN-YI, 楊憲益, tr. Ancient Chinese fables. [Translated by Yang Hsien-yi and Gladys Yang] Peking, Foreign Languages Press, 1957. 60 p.

New Literature

ALL-CHINA CONFERENCE of WRITERS and ARTISTS. 1st. Peking, 1949. The people's new literature; four reports. Peking, Cultural Press, 1950 [i. e. 1951] 136 p. 1st ed. 1950. 108 p.

——. Neue Volksliteratur in China. Vier Referate, die auf der ''Allchinesischen Konferenz der Schriftsteller und Künstler'' 1949, gehalten wurden. Berlin, Dietz, 1953. 88 p.

ANDERSON. COLENA MICHAEL, 1891- A study of two modern Chinese women authors: P'ing Hsin, 冰心, and Ting Ling, 丁玲. Claremont, Calif., 1954. ix, 252 l. Thesis-Claremont College.

BECKER, JOAN. Über die neue chinesische Literatur. Leipzig und Jena, Urania Verlag, 1955. 36 p. (Vorträge zur Verbreitg wissenschaftl. Kenntnisse, 77).

BOROWITZ, ALBERT, 1930- Fiction in communist China. Cambridge, Center for International Studies, Massachusetts Institute of Technology, 1954. 124 l.

CHAO, CHUNG, 趙聰. The Communist program for literature and art in China. Kowloon, H. K., Union Research Institute [1955] Cover title. 157 p. (Communist China problem research series, EC11).

CHOU, YANG, 周揚, 1908- China's new literature and art; essays and addresses. Peking, Foreign Languages Press, 1954. 156 p. port.

——. Die neue Volksliteratur, von Dschou Yang. Peking, Kulturelle Presse, 1950. 54 p.

DEUTSCHER SCHRIFTSTELLER KONGRESSES, Berlin. Aus der Literaturdiskussion in der Volksrepublik China. Gegen die bürgerliche Ideologie in der Literatur und Literaturkritik. Diskussionsmaterial zur Vorbereitung des 4. Deutschen Schriftstellerkongresses. Berlin, Deutscher Schriftstellerverband, 1955. 59 p. (Beiträge zur deutschen Gegenwartsliteratur, Heft 8).

GÖRSCH, HORST. China erzählungen. Ein Einblick in die chinesische Literatur.

Ausgewählt und zusammengestellt von Horst Görsch. Berlin, Volk und Wissen, 1953. 208 p. illus. (Literatur der Volksdemokratien, 2).

HSIA, PEARL,陳夏路韻 1919- The social thought of Lusin, 1881-1936. Chicago, 1953. 381 l. Thesis-Univ. of Chicago

KONG, KUG-LON, 康克倫. La littérature féminine dans la Chine d'aujourd'hui. Paris, Librairie sociale et économique, 1940. 118, [2] p. Thèse-Univ. de Paris.

KREBSOVA, BERTA. Lu Sün, sa vie et son oeuvre. Prag, 1953. 111 p. (Archiv Orientálni, Supplementa, 1).

LI, T'IEN-I, 李田意, 1915- ed. Selected readings in Chinese communist literature. New Haven, Institute of Far Eastern Languages, Yale University, 1954. 39 p.; 119 p. (Mirror series C, no. 6).

MAO, TSÊ-TUNG, 毛澤東, 1893- On literature and art. Translated by Ch'en Chia-k'ang, 陳家康, and Betty Graham. Chefoo, Chefoo News, [1942] iii, 42 p.

_____. Artistes et écrivains dans la Chine nouvelle; traduit du chinois par Ouang Che-liou. Paris, Pierre Seghers, [1949]. 50 p. (Poésie 49, brochure 19).

_____. Problems of art and literature. New York, International Publishers [1950] 2nd ed. 1951; Bombay, People's Pub. House, 1951. 48 p.

_____. Reden auf der Beratung über Literatur und Kunst zu Yenan. Peking, Kulturelle Presse, 1950. 69 p. illus.

_____. Reden an die Schriftsteller und Künstler im neuen China auf der Beratung in Yenan. Mit einem Nachwort von Anna Seghers. Hrsg. von der Deutschen Akademie der Künste. Berlin, Henschelverlag, 1953. 86 p. port.

_____. Talks at the Yenan forum on art and literature. Peking, Foreign Languages Press, 1956. 51 p. front. (port.).

SCHULTZ, WILLIAM RUDOLPH, 1923- Lu Hsun: the creative years. Seattle, 1955. xiii, 412 p. Thesis-Univ. of Washington.

SUNG, AI-LI,陳沈愛麗 Interdependence of roles in transitional China: a structural analysis of attitudes in contemporary Chinese literature. Cambridge, 1953. 310 l. Thesis, Radcliffe College.

WANG, CHÊNG-JU, 王燈如. Lu Hsün. Sein Leben und Werk. Ein Beitrag zur chinesischen Revolution. Berlin, 1939. 67 p. (Mitteilungen der Ausland-Hochschule, Bd. 42).


Juvenile Literature


ANDREWS, ROY CHAPMAN, 1884- All about dinosaurs; illustrated by Thomas W. Voter. New York, Random House [1953] 146 p. illus. (Allabout books).

ARMSTRONG, JOHN P. Chinese dilemma. Experimental ed. [Chicago, Sceince Research Associates, 1956] 64 p. illus. (Foreign relations series).

AYSCOUGH, FLORENCE (WHEELOCK), 1878-1942. Firecracker land; pictures of the Chinese world for younger readers. Boston and New York, Houghton Mifflin 1932. xiii, 351 p. front., illus.

BEAVER, ROBERT PIERCE, 1906- Below the Great Wall, Chinese folk tales for children; illus. by Harold Minton. Philadelphia, Christian Education Press [1947] 63 p. illus.

BEDIER, JULIE. The long road to Lo T'ing. New York, Longmans, Green, 1941. 25 p. illus.

BOWEN, VERNON. The wonderful adventures of Ting Ling; illustrated by Kurt Wiese. New York, D. McKay, c1952. unpaged. illus.

BUCK, PEARL (SYDENSTRICKER) 1892- The Chinese children next door. Drawings by William Arthur Smith. New York, John Day [1942] London, Methuen 1943. 62, [2] p. col. illus.

_____. Unsere kleinen chinesischen Freunde, übersetzung von Marianne Schön. Wien, P. Zsolnay, 1949. 57 p. illus.

——. The water-buffalo children, with drawings by William Arthur Smith. New York, John Day [1943]; London, Methuen, 1945. 59, [1] p., illus.

——. Die Kinder mit dem Wasserbüffel. [Übertragung: Inge Bauer] Linz, Pitts-burgh, Ibis-Verlag [c1948] 59 p. illus.

——. The dragon fish, illustrated by Esther Brock Bird. New York, John Day [1944]; Toronto, Longmans; London, Mathuen, 1946. 63 p. illus.

——. Der Drachenfisch. Übertragen von Bettina Hausmann. Zürich, Rascher, 1953. 110 p.

——. Yu Lan, flying boy of China, drawings by Georg T. Hartmann. New York, John Day, [1945] London, Mathuen, 1947. 60 p., incl. front., illus., plates.

BUDICH, CARL. Fernes China. 2 Aufl. Frankfurt a. M., Hirschgraben Verlag, 1956. 61 p. (Hirschgraben Lesereihe. Reihe 2, Bdch. 5).

BULLA, CLYDE ROBERT. White sails to China. Illustrated by Robert G. Henne-berger. New York, Crowell [1955] 84 p. illus.

——. Johnny Hong of Chinatown; illustrated by Dong Kingman, 曾景文. New York, Crowell [1952] 69 p. illus.

CARPENTER, FRANCES, 1890- Our little friends of China, Ah Hu and Ying Hwa. Illustrated by Curtiss Sprague. New York, Cincinnati, American Book Co. [c1937] 232 p. incl. col. front., illus. (part col.).

——. Tales of a Chinese grandmother; illustrated by Malthe Hasselriis. Gar-den City, N. Y., Doubleday, 1937; London, G. G. Harrap, 1938. xii, 261 p. col. front., illus., col. plates.

CHANDLER, ANNA CURTIS. Dragons on guard; an imaginative interpretation of old China in stories of art and history, with a foreward look by Anna Curtis Chandler; drawings by Margaret Ayer, foreword by Y.C. Yang, 楊永清. New York and Philadelphia, J. B. Lippincott, [1944] xv, 191 p. col. front., illus.

CHIANG, YEE, 蔣彝, 1903- Birds and beasts; a portfolio of drawings. London, Country Life, 1939. 12 plates.

——. Chin-pao and the giant pandas. London, Country Life [1942] 82, [2] p. col. front., illus., 3 col. plates.

——. Chinpao at the zoo. London, Methuen, 1941, New York, Transatlantic Arts, 1942. 96 p.

——. Lo Cheng: the boy who wouldn't keep still. Middlesex, Eng., Penguin Books, 1942. 32 p. illus. (Puffin picture books).

——. The men of the Burma road [illustrated by the author]. 3d ed. London, Methuen [1942]; New York, Transatlantic Arts and Studio, 1943, vii, 88 p. col. front., illus. plates.

——. Dabbitse; a story of a Chinese peasant boy and his water-buffalo. Lon-don, Transatlantic Arts, 1944. 66 p. London, J. Murray, 1955.

——. Dabbitse. Aus dem Englischen von Anita Wiegand. Zürich, Rascher, 1949. 64 p. illus. plates.

——. Yebbin, a guest from the wild. London, Methuen, 1947. 143 p.

——. Yebbin, le singe farceur; traduit par Jacqueline Des Gouttes. Neuchâtel et Paris,, Delachaux et Niestlé, 1948. 160 p. illus.

CHIN, STANLEY HONG, 陳連富. Two lands for Ming [by] Stanley Hong Chin [and] Virginie Fowler; illustrated by Stanley Chin. New York, C. Scribner, 1945. vi, [2], 248 p. illus.

CHINA WELFARE INSTITUTE. Under the sunshine of peace. Shanghai, People's Art Pub. House, 1956. 1 v. (unpaged).

CHRISMAN, ARTHUR BOWIE, 1889- The wind that wouldn't blow; stories of the merry Middle Kingdom for children, and myself, with silhouette decora-tions cut by Else Hasselriis. New York, E. P. Dutton, [c1927] xii, 355 p. illus.

——. Treasures long hidden; old tales and new tales of the East, illustrated by Weda Yap. New York, E. P. Dutton, 1941. 302, [1] p. illus.

CODRINGTON, FLORENCE ISABEL, 1867- Chopsticks, with 60 illustrations by

Helen Jacobs, extra illustrations by a Chinese artist and others. New York, Macmillan, 1929. 154 p. front., illus.

CONFUCIUS. Konfuzius: 50 Sprüche aus dem Chinesischen von Erika Spann-Rheinsch. Wien, Deutsche Verlag für Jugend und Volk, 1922. 16 p. (Sesam-Bücher, 38).

EASTON, FREDERICK HERBERT. Tales of a Chinese carrying pole; told by a pole. London, Religious Tract Society, 1929. 32 p.

EDWARDS, EVA D. Ling Ling, child of China, by Eva D. Edwards and Sung Sze-ai. San Francisco, Harr Wagner, 1939. vi, 217 p. illus. (incl. ports.).

ELDRIDGE, ETHEL J. Ling, grandson of Yen-foh; adapted from the Chinese by Ethel J. Eldridge; illustrated by Kurt Wiese. Chicago, A. Whitman, 1936. 29, [3] p. incl. col. front., col. illus.

————. Yen-foh, a Chinese boy, adapted from the Chinese; illustrated by Kurt Wiese. Chicago, A. Whitman, 1935. 29, [3] p. incl. col. front., col. illus.

FÊNG, TZU-K'AI. 豐子愷, 1898-  From Feng Tse-kai's drawings of children; selections made by Wang Chao-wen, 王朝聞. Peking, Foreign Languages Press, 1956. 95 p. illus.

FLACK MARJORIE, 1897-  The story about Ping, by Marjorie Flack and Kurt Wiese. [New York] Viking Press, c1933. [32] p. col. illus.

FÖRSTER-STREFFLEUR, SIDONIE. Die Lotosblume vom Hoangho. Eine Erzählung aus dem alten China. Illus. von Valerian Gillar. Wien, Verlag für Jugend und Volk, 1947. 87 p.

GAST, GUSTAV. Sven von Hedins abenteuerliche Reise durch Tibet: auf Sven von Hedins Werk "Abenteuer in Tibet" der Jugend und dem Volke. 28 Aufl. Stuttgart, Union, 1930. 202 p. illus. (Stuttgarter Jugendbücher, 9).

HANDFORTH, THOMAS, 1897-  Mei Li. New York, Doubleday, 1938. [52] p. illus.

HEINEN, JOSEF MARIA. Die Prinzessin von Chinesen. Ein lustiges Mädchenspiel. 6 Aufl. München, Höfling, 1953. 47 p. (Spiele des bunten Wagens, 81).

HEINTZ, KARL. Zauberflug nach China. Mit Zeichn. von Julius Himpel. Ravensburg, O. Maier, 1956. 32 p.

HEKKING, JOHANNA M. Pigtails; illustrations by Molly Castle. New York, Frederick A. Stokes, 1937. xiv, 112 p. incl. illus., col. plates.

HELMER, FREDERIC FLAGLER, 1870-  China chats; talks with children about things of China, compiled and arranged in story form. Philadelphia, Sunday School Times [c1925] 7-123 p. front., illus.

HERDMAN, THOMAS. Great plain of China. London, Longmans, Green, 1957. 40 p. illus. col. maps. col. diagrs. (Color geographies-unit 9).

HOLLISTER, MARY (BREWSTER), 1891-  River children; a story of boat life in China; illustrated by Kurt Wiese. New York, Dodd, Mead, 1935. 246 p. incl. front. illus. plates.

HOLTON, PRISCILLA. The spirit of the street, drawings by Gertrude Herrick, Boston, Chicago, Pilgrim Press [c1927] ix, [3]-157 p. illus.

————. Chinese children of Woodcutters' lane; illustrations by Gertrude Herrick Howe. New York, Friendship Press [c1932] [3]-68 p. illus.

HSIEH, TEHYI, 謝德怡, 1884-  Our little Manchurian cousin, with a foreword by Honorable Koliang Yih, 葉可樑, illustrated by Owl. Boston, L.C. Page, [c1933] x, 106 p. col. front., illus. (map) plates. [The little cousin series].

————. Chinese picked tales for children. Boston, Chinese Service Bureau [1948] 57 p. illus.

————. ed. and tr. Chinese village folk tales. Boston, B. Humphries [1949, c1948] 74 p. illus.

HSIUNG, SAI-SHENG, 熊塞聲. Mistress Clever. Adapted by Hsiung Seh-sheng and Yu Chin, 余金, drawings by Chen Yuan-tu, 陳綠圖, translated by Sidney Shapiro. Peking, Foreign Languages Press, 1955. 46 p. (chiefly illus.).

HUGGINS, ALICE MARGARET, 1891-  Fragrant Jade; illus. by Marybelle Kimball. Nashville, Broadman Press [c1948] 86 p. col. illus.

JANKE, BARBARA. Der dich liebet, der dich kennt. Erlebtes aus einem Kindergarten in China. Bad Salzuflen, MBK Verlag, 1947. 88 p. illus.

JEAN, SALLY LUCAS, 1878- Spending the day in China, Japan and the Philippines, by Sally Lucas Jean and Grace T. Hallock; illustrated by Jessie Gillespie. New York and London, Harper, 1932. xvii, 210 p. incl. illus., map. col. front.

KEEN, GRACE GRAHAM. Ah-Ming, a boy in China. Harrisburg, Stackpole, [c1938] 5-178 p. incl. front. (map) illus.

KENT, JUANITA RAY. Boys and girls in China; a world friendship unit for primary children. Nashville, Tenn., Board of Christian Education and Board of Missions, Methodist Episcopal Church, South, c1937. 80 p.

KETO, EMMA, 1907- Ting-Ling and Mee-Too. New York, Grosset and Dunlap, inc., c1937. [37] p. col. illus.

KINER, GRACE. Children of China; drawings by Ruth Kellogg. Chicago, Thomas S. Rockwell, 1931. 64 p. incl. front., illus.

KNIGHT, FRANK. Clippers to China, a junior novel; illustrated by Patrick Jobson. London, Macmillan; New York, St. Martin's Press, 1955. 268 p. illus.

KNOWLES CECILIA. Hua ma. The flower pony. With drawings by Leslie Atkinson. London, Falcon Press, 1947. 178 p. plates.

LATTIMORE, ELEANOR FRANCES, 1904- Little Pear, the story of a little Chinese boy, written and illustrated by Eleanor Frances Lattimore. New York, Harcourt, Brace, [c1931] 3-144 p. incl. illus., plates. front.

———. Jerry and the Pusa, written and illustrated by Eleanor Frances Lattimore. New York, Harcourt, Brace [c1932] 3-197, [1] p. incl. illus., plates. front.

———. Little Pear and his friends, written and illustrated by Eleanor Frances Lattimore. New York, Harcourt, Brace, [c1934] 3-178, [1] p. incl. illus. plates. front.

———. The story of Lee Ling, written and illustrated by Eleanor Frances Lattimore. New York, Harcourt, Brace, [c1940] 3-114 p. incl. front., illus, plates.

———. The questions of Lifu, a story of China, written and illustrated by Eleanor Frances Lattimore. New York, Harcourt, Brace, [1942] v. 104 p. incl. col. front., col. illus., col. plates.

———. Peachblossom, written and illustrated by Eleanor Frances Lattimore. New York, Harcourt, Brace [1943] 3-96 p. incl. front., illus., plates.

———. Three little Chinese girls. New York, W. Morrow, 1948. 128 p. illus.

———. Bells for a Chinese donkey; written and illustrated by Eleanor Frances Lattimore. New York, W. Morrow, 1951. 126 p. illus. [Morrow junior books].

———. Wu, the gatekeeper's son, written and illustrated by Eleanor Frances Lattimore. New York, W. Morrow, 1953. 128 p. illus. [Morrow junior books].

———. Willow Tree Village, written and illustrated by Eleanor Frances Lattimore. New York, W. Morrow, 1955. 128 p. illus. [Morrow junior books].

LEDERER, JOE, 1907- Fafan in China, ein Roman für dei Jugend, mit Bildern von Ingrid Wasa, Hrsg. und mit Notizen versehen von I. Carvalho. Amsterdam, J. M. Meulenhoff [1940] 133 p. illus. (Meulenhoffs Sammlung deutscher schriftsteller. [No. 84]) 1. Aufl. Wien and Leipzig, W. Frick, 1938. 190 p.

———. The same. Translated by Margaret Rounds. Illustrated by William Sanderson. [New York] Holiday House [c1939] 137 p. illus.

LEE, MELICENT HUMASON. Chang Chee, by Melicent Humason Lee and Jung Ho; pictures by Laura Bannon. New York, London, Harper, 1939. 137 p. incl. front., illus., plates.

LIANG, YEN, 梁衍, 1912- Dee Dee's birthday. New York, Oxford University Press, 1942. unpaged. illus. [Oxford books for boys and girls].

———. Tommy and Dee-Dee. New York, Oxford University Press, 1953. unpaged. illus. [Oxford books for boys and girls].

———. The pot bank. Philadelphia, Lippincott [1956] unpaged. illus.

LUX, HANNS MARIA, 1900- Felix und die Gesellschaft der Roten Laternen; eine
Jungengeschichte aus den Tagen des Boxeraufstandes 1900. [Zeichnungen von
Kurt Tetzmann] Reutlingen, Ensslin and Laiblin [1941] 203 p. illus. maps.

[MCCRADY, ELIZABETH F.   ] Ching Ling and Ting Ling. [New York] Platt
and Munk [1937?] [11] p. illus. (part col).

MATSON, MRS. EDLA C. Lee Ming and his sisters. Chicago, Covenant Book
Concern [c1929] 85 p. illus.

MEAD, MABEL CONVERSE. Children's books on China; reading for fun, with a
list for adults. New York [The New York Children's Bookshop] 1935. 31.
[1] p. illus.

MEADOWCROFT, ENID (LA MONTE) 1898- China's story, illustrated by Dong
Kingman, Weda Yap and Georgi Helms. New York, Thomas Y. Crowell
[1946] 92 p. incl. front., illus.

MEINCK, WILLI. Die seltsamen Abenteuer des Marco Polo. Textill. von Hans
Mau. 2. Aufl. Berlin, Kinderbuchverlag, 1956. 305 p.

MELCHERS, URSULA. Bim in China. Textzeichnungen von Walter Rieck. Köhn,
Schaffstein, 1954. 150 p.

MÜHLENWEG, FRITZ, 1898- Tausendjähriger Bambus. Nachdichtungen aus
dem Schi-King. Hamburg, Dulk, 1946. 53 p.

------. In geheimer Mission durch die Wüste Gobi; mit Geleitwort von Sven Hedin. Freiburg, Herder [1950]; 8. Aufl. 1956. xii, 359, 386 p.

------. Big Tiger and Christian; illustrated by Rafaello Busoni. [Translated by
Isabel and Florence McHugh] New York, Pantheon Books [c1952] 592 p. illus.

------. Grosser-Tiger und Kompass-Berg. Mit Geleitwort von Sven Hedin. 7.
Aufl. Freiburg, Herder, 1954. (c1950) xii, 359 p.

NEW JOY, a course on China for junior boys and girls. Part one: The story
with background notes, by Carolyn Titcomb Sewall; part two: The course, by
Charlotte Chambers Jones and others. New York, Friendship Press [c1932]
vi, 154 p.

PEASE, HOWARD, 1894- Shanghai passage; being a tale of mystery and adventure on the high seas in which Stuart Ormsby is shanghaied aboard the tramp
steamer "Nanking" bound for ports on the China coast, illustrated by Paul
Q. Forster. Garden City, N.Y., Doubleday, 1946. viii, 301 p. front., illus.
(Young moderns). 1st ed. 1929.

PERKINS, LUCY (FITCH) 1865-1937. The Chinese twins; illustrated by the author. Boston and New York, Houghton Mifflin, 1935. xvii, [3], 165, [1] p.
col. front., illus.

PRICE, OLIVE M. The Valley of the Dragon; a story of the times of Kublai
Khan. Illustrated by John Moment. Indianapolis, Bobbs-Merrill [1951] 250 p.
illus. [Stories of children in great times].

------. The story of Marco Polo; illustrated by Federico Castellon. Enid La
Monte Meadowcroft, supervising editor. New York, Grosset and Dunlap
[1953] 179 p. illus. (Signature books, 22).

PRICE, OLIVIA. The Middle country; a Chinese lad's adventures in his own land
illustrated by C. Le Roy Baldridge. Yonkers-on-Hudson, N.Y., Chicago World
Book Co., 1926. 176 p. incl. front., illus. (Children of the world).

REIN, ELIZABETH MARIA, 1897- Käfi, eine Dackel-und Kindergeschichte aus
dem fernen China. Ravensburg, O. Maier Verlag, [1951] 126 p.

REISS, MALCOLM. China boat boy; illustrated by Jeanyee Wong, 黃如珍. Philadelphia, Lippincott [1954] 157 p. ilius.

ROBERTS, CONSTANCE EVELYN. The loyalty of Rin Kong [a tale]. London,
Edinburgh House Press, 1935. 30 p.

------. Vagabond Wong, illustrated by Mabel R. Peacock. London, Edinburgh
House Press, 1936. 102 p.

------. Schoolboy refugee; a story of China. Illustrated by Neuville. London,
Lutterworth Press, 1940. 127 p.

------. Bandy Loo, a story of China. Illustrated by Mabel R. Peacock. London

Edinburgh House Press, 1942. 112 p.
——. Bell boy at the "Ocean"; a story of China. London, Highway Press, 1946. 63 p.
——. Not-a-care garage; a story of China. Illustrated by R. Kenneth McAll. London, Edinburgh House Press, 1947. 96 p.
——. Marriage of Min Lee; illustrated by Mabel R. Peacock. London, Edinburgh House Press, 1949. 78 p.
——. The young traveller in China. London, Phoenix House, 1951. 157 p. plates, map.
ROWE, DOROTHY, 1898- The rabbit lantern, and other stories of Chinese children; with introduction by Lucius Chapin Porter, illustrations by Ling Jui Tang. New York, Macmillan, 1925. xiii, 98 p. col. front., illus., col. plates.
——. The moon's birthday, and other stories of Chinese children, with illustrations by K'o Shuang-Shou and Ma Tzu-Yu. New York, Macmillan, 1927. 124 p. col. front., illus., col. plates.
——. Traveling shops, stories of Chinese children, pictures by Lynd Ward. New York, Macmillan 1929. 109 p. incl. illus., plates. col. front., col. plates.
SCHMIDT HEINRICH. Die Tina aus China. Illus. Wilhelm M. Busch. Heidelberg, Kemper, 1952. 190 p.
SHEELER HARRIET. An analysis of the cultural content of a selected list of children's books on China. Washington, D.C., 1952. 131 1. Thesis-Catholic University of America.
SHEN, MAO-CHÜN, 沈默君. Reconnaissance across the Yangtse, 渡江偵察記 Translated by Yu Fan-chin. Peking, Foreign Languages Press, 1956. 152 p. (chiefly illus.).
SOONG MAYLING, 1897- A letter from Madame Chiang Kai-shek to boys and girls across the ocean. Chungking, China Information Pub. Co., 1940. 26, 8 p. illus. (part col.).
SOWERS, PHYLLIS (AYER). Lin Foo and Lin Ching, a boy and girl of Chian; illustrated by Margaret Ayer. New York, Thomas Y. Crowell, [c1932] 3-121 p. incl. front., illus.
SPRIGGS, ELSIE HELENA. Wee Wong and Mary Jane Ann. London, Livingstone Press, 1932. 43 p. front. illus. (The Playmate Books, 1).
STILWELL, ALISON. Chin Ling, the Chinese cricket. New York, Macmillan 1947. [48] p. illus. (part col.).
THOMAS, LESLIE. The story on the Willow plate; adapted from the Chinese legend by Leslie Thomas, with illustrations by the author. New York, W. Morrow, 1940. 47, [1] p. incl. front., illus.
THOMPSON, PHYLLIS. They seek a city. London, Chian Inland Mission, 1940. 79 p.
——. Beaten gold: Mrs. Yen of the north suberb. London, Lutterworth Press, 1950. 176 p.
TIPPET, CHARLOTTE F. The clock man's mother and other stories. London, China Inland Mission, 1930. vii, 9-46 p. front.
——. The tin traveller. London, China Inland Mission, 1932. 47, [1] p. front. plates.
TREFFINGER, CAROLYN. Li Lun, lad of courage, illus. by Kurt Wiese. Nashville, Abingdon-Cokesbury Press [1947] 93 p. illus.
TROWBRIDGE, LYDIA JONES. Betty of the consulate; a little American girl's adventures in old China; illustrated by Louise Clasper Rumely. Garden City, N.Y., Doubleday, 1929. x, 205 p. incl. illus., plates. col. front.
TUNG, CHÜ-HSIEN, 董聚賢, comp. School-master Tungkuo,東郭先生. Adapted by Tung Chü-hsien and Yu Chin, 余金; drawings by Liu Chi-yu, 劉繼卣. Peking, Foreign Languages Press, 1954. 82 p. (chiefly illus).
TUNG, TSE-WEI, 董子畏. Chü Yuan, 屈原: Story of Tung Tse-wei, drawings by Liu Tan-tse, 劉旦宅. Translated by Chang Su-chu. Peking, Foreign Lan-

guages Press, 1957. 103 p.

WAGNER, MRS. MABEL GARRETT. Off to China; a course for primary children; with stories by Helen Firman Sweet. New York, Friendship Press [c1932] viii, 146 p.

WALTER, ERNST. 16 Monate Banditenleben in China. Zeichnungen: Fritz Krumenacher. Zürich, Jugendschriftenwerk, 1954. 32 p. illus.(Schweizer Jugendschriftenwerk, 509).

WANG, LIU-CHIN. The little white hen, drawn and written by Wang Liu-chin. Peking, Foreign Languages Press, 1956. 57 p. illus.

WEHRLI, KLARA. Fritz reist nach China. [Erzählung] Umschlag und Innenbilder von Willy Schnabel. Zürich, Schweizer. Jugendschriftenwerk, 1947. 32 p. illus.

WHITE, MARGARET POLLY (ROSSITER), 1901-    E Ming and E Ru; a story of child life in old Peking. New York, London [etc.] Fleming H. Revell [c1936] 3-91 p. incl. front.

WIESE, KURT, 1887- Liang and Lo. Garden City, N.Y., Doubleday, Doran, 1930. [56] p. col. illus.

WEISS-SONNENBURG, HEDWIG. Li, das Buch vom kleinen Chinesen, Jugendbuch. Berlin, Aufbau-Verlag, 1946. 103 p. illus.

WOOD, ESTHER, 1905- Silk and Satin lane, by Esther Wood; illustrated by Kurt Wiese. New York, Toronto, Longmans, Green, 1939. xii, 225 p. incl. front. illus.

————. Pepper Moon; pictures by Laura Bannon. New York-Toronto, Longmans, Green [c1940] 32 p. col. illus.

YANG, CHAO-LIN, 楊兆麟. Old Sun rejoins the co-op; story. Peking, Foreign Languages Press, 1955. 54 p. (chiefly illus.).

YOUNG, EVELYN, 1911- Wu and Lu and Li. New York, Oxford University Press [c1939] [31] p. col. illus.

————. The tale of Tai. London, New York, Oxford University Press [c1940] [31] p. col. illus.

# XVII. ARCHAEOLOGY AND FINE ARTS

## Bibliography

FREER GALLERY OF ART, Washington, D. C. Annotated outlines of the history of Chinese arts [by] Grace Dunham Guest, research associate, and Archibald G. Wenley, director. Washington, 1949. 1 v. (various pagings) illus. map. 1st ed. 1943.

ROWLAND, BENJAMIN, 1904- The Harvard outline and reading lists for Oriental art. Cambridge, Harvard University Press, 1952. 64 p.

## Archaeology

ACADEMIA SINICA. Institute of History and Philology. Chêng-tzŭ-yai: a report of excavations of the proto-historic site at Chêng-tzŭ-yai, Li-chêng Hsien, Shantung, by Fu Ssŭ-nien, 傅斯年, Liang Ssŭ-yung, 梁思永, Wu Gin-ding, 吳金鼎, Li Chi, 李濟, Tung Tso-ping, 董作賓, Kuo Pao-chün, 郭寶鈞, and Liu Yu-hsia, 劉嶼霞. Summary in English by Liang Ssu-yung. Nanking, Institute of History and Philology, Academia Sinica, 1934. xxvii, 105, xi, 30 p. col. front., plates, plans. (Archaeologia sinica, 1).

―――. Ch'êng-tzŭ-yai: the black pottery culture site at Lung-shan-chên in Li-ch'êng-hsien, Shantung Province [by] Li Chi, editor-in-chief [and others] Translated by Kenneth Starr. New Haven, Published for the Dept. of Anthropology, Yale University by the Yale University Press, 1956. 232 p. illus., plates, maps, diagrs. (Yale University publications in anthropology, no. 52).

ALLEN, WILLIAM DANGAIX, 1904- ed. Horses of Han; China's ancient life and legend seen in the rock carvings of the 2nd century. Ser. 1. Reproductions original size. New York, Universal Pub. Co., 1944. cover-title, [1] [14] plates.

ANDERSSON, JOHAN GUNNAR, 1874- An early Chinese culture. Peking, Geological Survey of China, 1923. 68, 46 p. illus., plates, maps. diagrs. Reprinted from the Bulletin, Geological Survey of China, No. 5.

―――. Essays on the Cenozoic of northern China. Peking, Geological Survey of China, 1923. 152 p; 4, 12 p. illus., ix plates (part fold. ) 3 fold. maps, 2 fold. tab. (China. Geological survey. Memoirs, ser. A, 3).

―――. Preliminary report on archäological research in Kansu. With a note on the physical characters of the prehistoric Kansu race, by Davidson Black. Peking, Geological Survey of China, 1925. 56, [22] p., 2, 50, [1] p. illus., plates (incl. fold. profile) (China. Geological survey. Memoirs, ser. A, 5).

―――. Children of the yellow earth; studies in prehistoric China, translated from the Swedish by E. Classen. London, Kegan Paul; New York, Macmillan, 1934. xxi, 345 p. illus. plates, double map, diagr.

―――. Researches into the prehistory of the Chinese. [Stockholm] 1943. 304 p. illus. (part col.) 200 plates, maps. Reprinted from Ostasiatiska samlingarna Bulletin, 1943. No. 15.

―――. The site of Chu chia chai. Stockholm, 1945. 63 p. illus., incl. maps, plans, diagrs, plates. Reprinted from Ostasiatiska samlingarna Bulletin, 1945. No. 17.

―――. Prehistoric sites in Honan. Stockholm, 1947. 124 p. illus., plates, fold. maps, diagrs. Reprinted from Ostasiatiska samlingarna Bull. 1947. No. 19.

ARNE, TURE ALGOT JOHNSSON, 1879- Painted stone age pottery from the province of Honan. Peking, Pub. for the Geological Survey of China, 1925. 40,

[32] p. illus., xiii plates (part col.) (China. Geological survey. Palaeontologia sinica. Ser. D, 1, fasc. 2).

BISHOP, CARL WHITING, 1881-1942. The beginnings of civilization in eastern Asia. (In Smithsonian institution. Annual report, 1940. Washington, 1941. p. 431-445. illus. (maps) 10 plates on 5 l.).

———. Origin of the Far Eastern civilizations: a brief handbook. Washington, Smithsonian Institution, 1942. 53 p. illus. (incl. maps, plans) plates, (Smithsonian institution. War background studies, 1).

BRITTON, ROSWELL SESSOMS, 1897-1951. Yin bone photographs. New York [Printed by the Commercial Press, for the Chalfant Publication Fund] 1935. 21, [1] p. illus.

———. Yin bone rubbings. New York [Printed by Acme photo-offset corp. for the Chalfant Publication Fund] 1937. 12, [2] p. illus.

———. Fifty Shang inscriptions. Princeton, N.J., Princeton University, the Library, 1940. 77, [1] p. illus., diagrs.

CHALFANT, FRANK HERRING, 1862-1914. The Couling-Chalfant collection of inscribed oracle bone, drawn by Frank H. Chalfant, edited by Roswell S. Britton. Shanghai, Commercial Press, 1935. 132 plates., 1 l.

———. Seven collections of inscribed oracle bone, drawn by Frank H. Chalfant, edited by Roswell S. Britton. New York [Printed by General Offset Co., for the Chalfant Publication Fund] 1938. 5, [1] p. 32 plates on 16 l.

CHÊNG, TE-K'UN, 鄭德坤, 1907- Prehistoric archaeology of Szechuan. Cambridge, 1941. 294 l. plates, tables, maps. Thesis-Harvard University.

———. Archaeological studies in Szechuan. London, Cambridge University Press, 1956. 344 p. plates, maps.

CREEL, HERRLEE GLESSNER, 1905- The birth of China; a survey of the formative period of Chinese civilization. London, J. Cape [1936]; New York, Reynal and Hitchcock, 1937. 3-395, [1] p. front., illus. (plan) xv plates. fold map, diagr.

———. The birth of China; a study of the formative period of Chinese civilization. New York, F. Ungar Pub. Co. [1954, c1937] 402 p. illus., map (on lining papers).

———. La naissance de la Chine: la périod formative de la civilisation chinoise environ 1400-600 av. J-C. Traduit de l'anglais par Clerc Salles, préface de Carl Whiting Bishop. Paris, Payot, 1937. 368 p. illus. map. (Bibliothèque historique).

———. Studies in early Chinese culture, first series, by Herrlee Glessner Creel Baltimore, Waverly Press, 1937. iii-xxii, 266 p. plates. [American council of learned societies. Studies in Chinese and related civilizations, 3].

EBERHARD, WOLFRAM, 1909- Early Chinese cultures and their development: a new working-hypothesis. (In Smithsonian institution. Annual report, 1937. Washington, 1938. p. 513-530. illus. (map)).

FREER GALLERY OF ART, Washington, D.C. Excavation of a West Han dynasty site at Yen-tzŭ Ko-ta, Wan Ch'üan Hsien, 萬全縣閻子坨墓 southwestern Shansi, conducted jointly in the autumn of 1930 by the Freer gallery of art of Washington, D.C., and the Shansi provincial library of T'aiyüan, Shansi. Shanghai [Printed at the press of Kelly and Walsh, 1932]. 44 p. [36] p. illus., xxi plates on 11 l., maps (1 fold.) fold. plan.

GRAHAM, DAVID CROCKETT, 1884- The ancient caves of Szechwan province. (In U.S. National museum. Proceedings. Washington, 1932. v. 80, art. 16. 13 p. illus., plates).

HANSFORD, S. Howard, 1899- A visit to An Yang. London, China Society, 1951. 14 p. plates.

HOPKINS, LIONEL CHARLES, 1854-1952. The Hopkins collection of inscribed oracle bone, drawn by Frank H. Chalfant, edited by Roswell S. Britton. New York [Printed by General Offset Company, 1939. [8] p. front. (port.) 66 pl. on 33 l.

LI, CHI, 李濟, 1896- The beginnings of Chinese civilization; three lectures illustrated with finds at Anyang. Seattle, University of Washington Press [1957] xvii, 123 p. illus., plates, map.

LIANG, SSU YUNG, 梁思永, 1903-1954. New Stone age pottery from the prehistoric site at Hsi-yin Tsun, Shansi, China. Menasha, Wis., American Anthropological Association [1930] cover-title, 76, [3] p. illus. (incl. plan) 18 plates on 9 l., diagrs. (Memoirs of the American anthropological association, 37).

MASPERO, HENRI, 1883-1943. The origins of the Chinese civilizations. (In Smithsonian institution. Annual report, 1927. Washington, 1928. p. 433-452).

MENZIES, JAMES MELLON, 1885-1957. The culture of the Shang dynasty, by James M. Menzies. (In Smithsonian institution. Annual report, 1931. Washington, 1932. p. 549-558).

NOTT, STANLEY CHARLES, 1902- Voices from the Flowery Kingdom; being an illustrated descriptive record of the beginnings of Chinese cultural existence, incorporating a complete survey of the numerous emblematic forces selected from nature by the ritualistic leaders of the Chinese throughout the ages, with an introd. by Byron E. Eldred. Illus. by twenty-four full page natural color plates, one hundred and three half-tone plates, reproduced from original photographs, seventy-nine line engravings made especially for the work by Mrs. Stanley Charles Nott. New York, Chinese Culture Study Group of America, 1947. xxv, 278 p. illus., plates.

SELIGMAN, CHARLES GABRIEL, 1873-1940. The Roman Orient and the Far East. (In Smithsonian institution. Annual report, 1938. Washington, 1939. p. 547-568. illus., 4 plates on 2 l. fold. map).

TCHANG, FONG, 張鳳 [CHANG FÊNG] Recherches sur les "os du Hônan." Quelques caractères de l'écriture ancienne. 甲骨刻字考異補釋 . Paris, P. Geuthner, 1925. 84 p. tables, Thèse-Univ. de Paris.

WHITE, WILLIAM CHARLES, 1873- Tombs of old Lo-yang; a record of the construction and contents of a group of royal tombs at Chin-ts'un, Honan, probably dating 550 B.C. Foreword by John C. Ferguson. Shanghai, Kelly and Walsh, 1934. xvi, 177 p. 10 l. xix-xxii p. col. front., illus., plates, maps, plans.

————. Bone culture of ancient China; an archaeological study of bone material from northern Honan, dating about the twelfth century, B.C. Toronto, University of Toronto Press, 1945. x, 233 p. incl. illus., plates. front., maps. ([Royal Ontario museum of archaeology] Museum studies, 4).

YETTS, WALTER PERCEVAL, 1878-1957. An-yang: a retrospect. London, China Society, 1942. 39 p. illus., maps. (China Society occasional papers. New series, 2).

SEE ALSO. Manchuria-Archaeology, Mongolia-Archaeology, Sinkiang-Archaeology, etc.

## Oriental Art

ARTS musulmans. Extrême-Orient: Inde, Indochine, Insulinde, Chine, Japon, Asie centrale, Tibet; par S. Élisséev, R. Grousset, J. Hackin, [e.a.] Paris, A. Colin, 1939. ix, [1] 496 p. illus. (incl. maps. plans) (Histoire universelle des arts, des temps primitifs jusqu'à nos jours, pub. sous la direction de Louis Réau. 4).

BALL, KATHERINE M. Decorative motives of oriental art. London, John Lane; New York, Dodd, Mead [1927] xxvi, 286 p. illus.

BERNOULLI, RUDOLF, 1880- Ausgewählte Meisterwerke ostasiatischer Graphik in der Bibliothek für Kunst und Kunstgewerbe in Berlin. Plauen im Vogtland, C. F. Schulz and Co., 1923. 110 p. illus. 40 plates, (Ostasiatische Graphik, 4).

BINYON, LAURENCE, 1869-1943. Asiatic art in the British museum (sculpture and painting). Paris and Brussels, G. van Oest, 1925. 74, [2] p. i, xiv

plates.

——. L'art asiatique au British Museum (sculpture et peinture). Paris, G. Van
Oest, 1925. 75 p. plates. (Ars Asiatica, 6).

——. The spirit of man in Asian art, being the Charles Eliot Norton lectures
delivered in Harvard university, 1933-34. Cambridge, Harvard University
Press, 1935. xv, 217 p. 70 plates.

——. Art of the Far East; landscapes, flowers, animals; 16 plates in colour
from the work of old Chinese and Japanese masters. London, New York,
Batsford [1950] 8 p. col. plates. (Iris colour books).

COHN-WIENER, ERNST, 1882- 1941. Das Kunstgewerbe des Ostens, Geschichte,
Stile, Technik. Berlin, Verlag für Kunstwissenschaft [1923] 256 p. col.
front., illus., col. plates.

——. Asia, Einführung in die Kunstwelt des Ostens; Indien, China, Japan, Islam. Berlin, R. Mosse [1929] 159, [1] p. illus.

FENOLLOSA, ERNEST FRANCISCO, 1853-1908. Epochs of Chinese and Japanese
art, an outline history of East Asiatic design. New and rev. ed., with copious
notes by Professor Petrucci. New York, Frederick A. Stokes; London, W.
Heinemann [1921] 2 v. col. fronts., illus. (incl. map) plates (part col., 2
double) diagr. 1st ed. 1912.

FISCHER, OTTO, 1886- 1948. Die Kunst Indiens, Chinas und Japans. 2 Aufl.
Berlin, Propyläen-Verlag [c1928] 643 p. illus., plates (part col.) maps.
(Propyläen-Kunstgeschichte, 4).

GROUSSET, RENÉ, 1885-1952. De la Grèce à la Chine. Monaco, Documents
d'art, 1948. xxxv, 104 p. (p. 1-88 plates) 9 plates (8 col.) 3 maps (part fold.).
(Orient et Extrême-Orient, 1).

HORVÁTH, TIBOR ANTAL. The art of Asia in the Francis Hopp Museum of eastern asiatic arts in Budapest. Budapest, Fine Arts Foundation, 1954. 25 p.

JAHRBUCH der asiatischen kunst. ed. by Georg Biermann. 1.-2. bd.; 1924-25.
Leipzig, Klinkhardt and Biermann [1924-25] 2 v. col. front., illus., plates.

KOECHLIN, RAYMOND, 1860-1931. Oriental art; ceramics, fabrics, carpets;
one hundred plates in colour, with introduction and descriptions by R. Koechlin and G. Migeon, translated by Florence Heywood. New York, Macmillan,
[1928] 7-20 p. c col. pl.

KÜMMEL, OTTO, 1874-1952. Die Kunst Ostasiens. Berlin, B. Cassirer, 1921.
48 p., 168 p. illus. (Die kunst des Ostens iv).

——. L'art de l'Extrême-Orient; traduction de Charlott Marchand. Paris, G.
Crès, 1923. 51, 166 p. incl. illus. plates (part double), facsims. (L'art de
l'Orient).

——. Ostasiatisches Gerät, ausgewählt und geschrieben von Otto Kümmel, mit
einer Einführung von Ernst Grosse. Berlin, B. Cassirer, 1925. 62 p., illus.
plates.

——. Die kunst Chinas, Japans und Koreas. Wildpark–Potsdam, Akademische
Verlagsgesellschaft Athenaion [c1929] 198 p. illus. (incl. maps) plates (part
col.) (Handbuch der kunstwissenschaft).

MARCH, BENJAMIN, 1899-1934. China and Japan in our museums, with an introduction by Frederick P. Keppel. A preliminary report prepared for the
third general session of the Institute of Pacific Relations to be held at Kyoto,
October 28th to November 9th, 1929. New York, American Council, Institute
of Pacific Relations [c1929].    xi, 122 p. plates.

MARTIN, HENRY MARIE RADEGONDE, 1852-1927. L'art indien, l'art chinois,
l'art indochinois. 2e éd. Paris, R. Ducher, [c1926] 36 p. illus. (His: La
grammaire des styles, pt. 12).

MÉLY, FERNAND de, 1851-1935. Périgueux au Fleuve jaune. Paris, Paul
Geuthner, 1927. 61 p. plates, map.

NEW ORIENT SOCIETY OF AMERICA. Oriental art in America; recent accessions
in American museums. Chicago, New Orient Society of America [c1937] [8]
p., plates.

PARIS. MUSÉE GUIMET. Bulletin archéologique du Musée Guimet. fasc. 1-2.
Paris et Bruxelles, G. van Oest et cie, 1921. 2 v. plates, port., map.
———. Études d'orientalisme, publiées par le Musée Guimet à la mémoire de
Raymonde Linossier. Paris, E. Leroux, 1932. 2 v. front. (port.) illus.
lxx pl. (part fold.)
———. Arts asiatiques. [Paris, Éditions des musées nationaux, 1950- v.
ROSS, sir EDWARD DENISON, 1871-1940. Eastern art and literature, with spe-
cial reference to China, India, Arabia and Persia. London, E. Benn [1928]
80 p. (Benn's sixpenny library, 3]).
ROWLAND, BENJAMIN, 1904- Art in East and West; an introduction through
comparisons. Cambridge, Harvard University Press, 1954. xiii, 144 p.
62 illus.
SCHUSTER, CARL, 1904- Joint-marks, a possible index of cultural contact between
America, Oceania and the Far East. Amsterdam, 1951. 51 p. illus., map.
(Koninklijk Instituut voor de Tropen. Mededeling no. 94. Afdeling Culturele
en Physische Anthropologie. no 39.).
SELIGMAN, CHARLES GABRIEL, 1873-1940. The Seligman collection of oriental art. London, Lund Humphries, 1957- v. illus. plates, maps. v 1:
Chinese, Central Asian and Luristan bronzes and Chinese jades and sculp-
tures. Introduction by S. Howard Hansford, xiii, 135 p.
SHANGHAI. Musée Heude. The Sowerby collection of Far Eastern art by Edmund Toeg. Shanghai, 1947. 16 p. illus. (Musée Heude. Notes d'archéolo-
gie et d'ethnologie chinoise. 1 juin 1947. v. 1. fasc. 2).
SPEISER, WERNER, 1908- Kultur Ostasiens, zwei Essays. Köln, Staufenver-
lag [1943] 7-77 p. (Staufen-bücherei, 36).
———. Die Kunst Ostasiens. Berlin, Safari-Verlag [c1946]; 2 Aufl. 1956. 355 p.
illus., plates (part col).
STUDIEN zur Kunst des Ostens. Josef Strzygowski zum sechzigsten Geburtstage
von seinen Freunden und Schülern; mit 260 Seiten und 126 Abbildungen. Wien
und Hellerau, Avalun-Verlag [1923] 7-257, [1] p., illus. (incl. plans) xxx
plates on 15 l.
VISSER, HERMAN FLORIS EDUARD, 1890- Asiatic art in private collections of
Holland and Belgium. Amsterdam, "De Spieghel" Pub. Co. [1948] 511 p.
223 plates (part col.).
WEBER, VICTOR FRÉDÉRIC, 1871- "Ko-ji hô-ten, 古事寶典 "; dictionnaire
à l'usage des amateurs et collectionneurs d'objets d'art japonais et chinois;
on y trouvera: l'explication des noms usuels et des noms propres qui se re-
contrent dans les ouvrages traitant de l'art et des religions de l'Extrême-
Orient; des renseignements sur les lieux célèbres de la Chine et du Japon,
ainsi que sur les nombreux personnages et héros historiques et légendaires;
la description des jeux, des moeurs et coutumes, des fêtes et des pratiques
religieuses ou laïques; les biographies, les signatures et autres signes particuliers des peintres, sculpteurs, ciseleurs, céramistes et autres artistes
et artisans; et enfin le résumé des contes et légendes de la Chine et du Japon
qui ont inspiré les artistes de ces deux pays dans l'illustration des ouvrages
et l'ornementation de leurs meubles et objets usuels. Le dictionnaire est illustré de plus de 2100 gravures et dessins intercalés dans le texte et sur 75
planches dont 5 en couleurs. Paris, L'auteur, 1923. 2v. col. fronts., illus.
plates (part col.).
WIENER BEITRÄGE ZUR KUNST- und Kulturgeschichte Asiens; Jahrbuch des
Vereines der freunde asiatischer Kunst und Kultur. Wien, 1926-1936. 10 v.
plates.

## Buddhist Art (See also Sculpture)

CHÊNG, TE-K'UN, 1907- Jun-huang studies in China. Chengtu, 1947. 14 p.
(West China Union University. Museum. Offprint ser., 10).

COHN, WILLIAM, 1880-  Buddha in der Kunst des Ostens; mit seiben Textabbildungen und hundertdreiundzwanzig Tafeln. Leipzig, Klinkhardt und Biermann, 1925. 5 p. iii-lxiv, 253 p. illus.

DAVIDSON, J      LEROY. The Lotus Sutra in Chinese art; a study in Buddhist
art to the year 1000. New Haven, Yale University Press, 1954. xvi, 105 p.
41 plates. (Yale studies in the history of art [ 8]).

DETROIT. INSTITUTE OF ARTS. Buddhist art. Detroit Institute of Arts, twen-
ty-fourth loan exhibition, October, 1942. [ Detroit, 1942] 62 p. incl. plates.
front. (map)

ECKE, GUSTAV, 1896-  The twin pagodas of Zayton; a study of later Buddhist
sculpture in China. Photographs and introduction by G. Ecke. Iconography
and history, by P. Demiéville. Cambridge, Mass., Harvard University
Press, 1935. viii, 95 p. front., 1 illus., plates (part fold.) fold, maps, fold.
plan. (Harvard-Yenching institute. Monograph series, II).

ROWLAND, BENJAMIN. 1904-  The wall-paintings of India, Central Asia and
Ceylon; a comparative study by Benjamin Rowland, jr., with an introductory
essay on the nature of Buddhist art by Ananda K. Coomaraswamy, with a
foreword by A. Townshend Johnson and colour plates by F. Bailey Vander-
hoef, jr. Boston, Printed at the Merrymount Press, 1938. ix-xiii, [ 1], 94
p. 36 plates (30 col.).

SECKEL, DIETRICH, 1910-  Buddhistische Kunst Ostasiens. [ Stuttgart] W.
Kohlhammer, 1957. 383 p. illus., plates, maps.

WARNER, LANGDON, 1881-1955. Buddhist wall-paintings, a study of a ninth-
century grotto at Wan Fo hsia. Cambridge, Harvard University Press, 1938.
xv, 33 p., plates, map. (Harvard-Radcliffe fine arts series).

YAMANAKA AND CO. Exhibition of Buddhist art of Asia dating from 2nd to 16th
century A.D. [ April 1st to 26th 1941] New York, Yamanaka and co., 1941.
8 p. illus.

## Chinese Art
## General Works

ARDENNE DE TIZAC, JEAN HENRI D'  , 1877-1932. Les animaux dans l'art
chinois. Cinquante planches en héliogravure et en couleurs. Introduction et
notices par H. d'Ardenne de Tizac. Paris, Librarie centrale des beauxarts,
1922. 7, [ 4] p. plates, (Les arts de l'Asie).

———. Animals in Chinese art; a collection of examples selected and described
by H. d'Ardenne de Tizac. With a preface by Roger Fry. London, Benn,
1923. [ 6] p., plates (part col.).

———. L'art chinois classique, ouvrage illustré de 30 gravures dans le texte et
162 gravures hors texte. Paris, H. Laurens, 1926. 364 p. illus., 104 plates.

———. Les hautes époques de l'art chinois d'après les collections du Musée Cernuschi. Paris, Éditions Nilsson [ 1930] [ 11] p. 24 mount. plates.

———. L'art décoratif chinois d'après les collections du Musée Cernuschi. Paris, Éditions Nilsson [ 1930] [ 14] p. 24 mounted plates.

ART AND ART CRAFTS OF ANCIENT CHINA. Essays on Chinese art written by
members of the literary department of the American Women's Club, Shanghai. Shanghai, 1921. 202 p. illus.

ASHTON, LEIGH, 1897 -  Chinese art, by Leigh Ashton and Basil Gray. London,
Faber and Faber [ 1935]; Boston, New York, Hale, Cushman and Flint, 1937.
397 p. incl. front., illus. (incl. map) plates.

———. The same. London, Faber and Faber, 1952; New York, Beechhurst
Press [ 1953] 366 p. illus. (part col.) map.

BACHHOFER, LUDWIG, 1894-  Chinesische Kunst. Breslau, F. Hirt, 1923. 80
p. incl. plates (Jedermanns bücherei, abt. : Bildende kunst).

———. A short history of Chinese art. [ New York] Pantheon [ 1946], London,
B. T. Batsford, 1947. 139 p., incl. col. front., illus. plates.

BINYON, LAURENCE, 1869-1943. The flight of the dragon; an essay on the theory and practice of art in China and Japan, based on original sources. London, J. Murray, 1944. 112 p. (Wisdom of the East) 1st ed. 1911.

BOODE, PETER. Notes for collectors of Chinese antiques (remote antiquity-end of Ming period) London, Commodore Press, 1943. 63 p. diagr.

BUHOT, JEAN, 1885-1952. Arts de la Chine. Photos. par Jacqueline Hyde. Paris, Éditions du Chène [1951] 172 p. illus.. (Arts du monde).

BURLING, JUDITH. Chinese art [by] Judith and Arthur Hart Burling. New York, Studio Publications, in association with Crowell [1953] 384 p. illus. (part col.).

CARTER, DAGNY (OLSEN). China magnificent; five thousand years of Chinese art. New York, Reynal and Hitchcock [c1935] xi, 225 p. incl. illus., plates.
──────. Four thousand years of China's art. New York, Ronald Press Co. [1948]; Rev. print. 1951. xix, 358 p. illus. maps.

CHATER, SIR CATCHICK PAUL, 1846-1926. The Chater collection, pictures relating to China, Hongkong, Macao, 1655-1860; with historical and descriptive letterpress, by James Orange. London, T. Butterworth, [1924] 528 p. incl. front., plates (part col) ports., maps (part fold.).

CHAVANNES, ÉDUARD, 1865-1918. De l'expression des voeux dans l'art populaire chinois. Paris, Éditions Bossard, 1922. 43, [1] p. illus. plates.

CHÊNG, T'IEN-HSI, 鄭天錫, 1884- Civilization and art of China; lectures by F. T. Cheng with note by Arthur Machen. London, W. Clowes, [1936] 39, [1] p. plates.

CHINESE ART: Introduction [by] Laurence Binyon; Painting and calligraphy [by] Laurence Binyon; Sculpture and lacquer [by] Leigh Ashton; The potter's art [by] R. L. Hobson; Bronzes [by] A. J. Koop; Jades [by] Una Pope-Hennessy; Textiles [by] Leigh Ashton. London, Kegan Paul, 1935. xvi, 111 p. xxiv plates (incl. front.).

COHN, WILLIAM, 1880- Chinese art. London, Studio, 1930. xvi, 75 p. col. front., plates.

CRANMER-BYNG, LAUNCELOT ALFRED; 1872-1945. The vision of Asia; an interpretation of Chinese art and culture. London, J. Murray [1932]; New York, Farrar and Rinehart, 1933. xi, 306 p. col. front.

DÉCORATION CHINOISE ET LE GOÛT CHINOIS. (paravents, laques, porcelaines, kakémonos, gravures) Paris, Guérinet, 1921. 1 v.

EDMUNDS, WILLIAM, 1852- Pointers and clues to the subjects of Chinese and Japanese art, as shewn in drawings, prints, carvings and the decoration of porcelain and lacquer. With brief notices of the related subjects. London, S. Low, Marston [1934] xiii, 706 p.

THE ENCYCLOPAEDIA BRITANNICA. Chinese art; a selection of articles from the new 14th edition of the Encyclopaedia Britannica, by the following authorities: R. L. Hobson, Laurence Binyon, A. F. Kendrick [and others] with many full page plates in colour and half-tone. A brief survey of the various arts and their periods in China. New York, Encyclopaedia Britannica; London, Encyclopaedia Britannica, [c1932] cover-title, [67] p. illus., plates (part col.) diagr. (Britannica booklet 1).

──────. The romance of Chinese art, by the following authorities: R. L. Hobson, Laurence Binyon, Oswald Sirén [and others] Garden City, N. Y., Garden City Publishing Co., [c1936] xv, 192 p. incl. col. front., illus., tables, diagr. plates (part col.).

FEDDERSEN, MARTIN, 1888- Chinesisches Kunstgewerbe. Berlin, Klinkhardt and Biermann [1939] 247 p. illus., fold. plates, map. fold. tab. (Bücherei des kunstsammlers, 1).

──────. The same; ein Handbuch für Sammler und Liebhaber. 2. neubearbeit. Aufl. Braunschweig, Klinkhardt and Beirmann [1955] xii. 302 p. illus., map. (Bibliothek für Kunst- u. Antiquitätenfreunde, 35).

FERGUSON JOHN CALVIN, 1866-1945. Survey of Chinese art. Shanghai, Commercial Press, 1939. 153 p. illus., plates. map, plans, facsims.

FRISCH, TERESA GRACE. Scythian art and some Chinese parallels. London, Oriental Art Magazine [ 1949] 22 p. illus. Part of thesis-Yale University.

FRY, ROGER ELIOT, 1866-1934. Chinese art; an introductory review of painting, ceramics, textiles, bronzes, sculpture, jade, etc., by Roger Fry, Laurence Binyon, A. F. Kendrick, Bernard Rachham, W. Perceval Yetts, Osvald Sirén, W. W. Winkworth. London, For the Burlington magazine by B. T. Batsford, [ 1925] vii, 62, ix-xviii p., col. front., illus. (incl. maps) plates (part col). (Burlington magazine monographs).

————. The same; with an introduction by Madame Quo Tai-chi, 郭泰祺, being a new and rev. ed., largely reillustrated, of the "Burlington magazine monograph, I": with 23 plates in colour and 62 from photographs. London, B. T. Batsford, [ 1935] xvi, 86 p. col. front., illus. (incl. maps) plates (part col. ).

————. The same. Being a new and rev. ed., largely re-illustrated, of the "Burlington magazine monograph, I. " New York, E. Weyhe [ 1946-47] xvi, 86 p. illus., plates (part col. ) maps.

GRANTHAM, ALEXANDRA ETHELDRED ( VON HERDER) 1867- Porcelain pagodas and palaces of jade, musings of an old collector. New York, E. P. Dutton; London, Methuen, 1929. xii, 210 p., front., plates.

————. The same; with twenty-eight illustrations. New York, E. P. Dutton; London, Methuen, 1939. xii, 210 p., front., plates.

GROUSSET, RENÉ, 1885- 1952. De la Chine au Japon. Monaco, Documents d' art [ 1951] xxvii, 93, [2] p. (p. 1-80 illus. ) 8 col. plates. (Orient et Extrême-Orient, 3).

————, La Chine et son art. Paris, Plon [ 1951] ix, 252 p. illus., plates, map. (Collection Ars et historia).

GUSTAF ADOLF, Crown Prince of Sweden, 1882- Selected Chinese antiquities from the collection of Gustaf Adolf, Crown Prince of Sweden. Ed. by Nils Palmgren. Stockholm, Generalstabens litografiska anstalts förlag, 1948. xv, 146 p. illus. (part col. ) map.

HÁJEK, LUBOR. Chinesische Kunst in tschechoslowakischen Museen. [ Deutsche Übersetzung, A. Kučerová] Fotografien von Werner Forman. Prag, Artia, 1954. 73 p., 241 plates (part col. ).

————. Chinese art [ in Czechoslovak museums] Photos. by Werner Forman. London, Spring Books [ 1955?] 84 p., 239 plates (part col. ).

HALLADE, MADELEINE. Arts de l'Asie ancienne. Thèmes et motifs. Tome 3: Chine. Paris, Presses universitaires, 1956. 96 p. (Paris, Musée Guimet [Publ.] ).

HANSFORD, S. Howard, 1899- A glossary of Chinese art and archaeology. London, China Society, 1954. xi, 104 p. illus. (China Society Sinological series, 4).

————. The study of Chinese antiquities: an inaugural lecture. London, 1955. 18 p.

HOBSON, ROBERT LOCKHART, 1872-1941. Chinese art; one hundred plates in colour reproducing pottery and porcelain of all periods, jades, lacquer, paintings, bronzes, furniture, etc., etc. Introduced by an outline sketch of Chinese art. London, E. Benn; New York, Macmillan, 1927. Rev. ed. 1954 14 p., 100 col. plates.

————. Cent planches en couleurs d'art chinois, reproduisant des pièces caracteristiques de toutes les époques: poteries et porcelains, jades, laques, bronzes, meubles, etc. et précédés d'un apercu historique sur l'art chinois. Traduction de J. V. Garnet. Paris, Levy [ 1927] 15 p. 100 col. plates.

HSIN, KWAN-CHUE, 邢光祖. An introductory note on Chinese art. [ Taipei? Ministry of Education, Republic of Chian, 1953] 30 p. illus.

HU, SHIH, 胡適, 1891- Inaugural address, November 17, 1944. [New York, The Chinese Art Society of America, 1944] [ 12] p.

JOURDAIN, MARGARET. [ EMILY] 188?-1951. Chinese export art in the eighteenth century, by Margaret Jourdain and R. Soame Jenyns. London, Country

Life; New York, Scribner, 1950. 152 p. (p. 73-144 illus.) col. front.

KARLBECK, ORVAR, 1879- Treasure seeker in China. Translated from the Swedish by Naome Walford. London, Cresset; New York and Toronto, Ambassador Books, 1957. 216 p. plates.

KELLY, CHARLES FABENS, 1885- The Chinese exhibition in London. La Salle, Ill., Published for the New Orient Society of America by the Open Court Pub. Co. [ 1936] 27 p. front. illus.

LION, DAISY (GOLDSCHMIDT) L'art chinois. Paris, Garnier frères, 1931. 209 p., illus. (Collection artistique Garnier).

————. Les arts de la Chine. Paris, Plon [ 1937] 60, [4] p. incl. front., illus. (Éditions d'histoire et d'art).

LOO, C. T. and CO., NEW YORK. An index to the history of Chinese art: an aide-mémoire for beginners. Reprint ed. New York, 1942 Cover-title, 8 p.

MCCLELLAND, ROBERT CRAWFORD. Some aspects of the arts and sciences in early China, from prehistoric times through the T'ang dynasty, ?-906 A.D. [ Norfolk] 1957. 21 l. (College of William and Mary [ -V.P.I. ] general publications series).

MACDONALD, JAMES STUART, 1878- The history and development of Chinese art. Canberra, Australian Institute of Anatomy, 1934. 16 p. (George Ernest Morrison lectures).

MARCUS, AAGE, 1888- Der blaue Drache. Lebenskunst und Bildkunst im alten China. Übers. von Hanna Kobylinski unter Mitwirkung von Walter Bauer. Zürich, Atlantis Verlag, 1949. 206 p. illus.

MENTEN, J   F   H   Sammlung J. F. H. Menten, chinesische Grabfunde und Bronzen. Hrsg. vom Kunstgewerbemuseum der Stadt Zürich. [ Zürich, 1948] 101 p. (p. 19-101 plates (part col.)).

MIGEON, GASTON, 1861-1930. L'art chinois. [ Paris] A. Morancé [ c1925] 36, [1] p., 57 (i.e. 58) plates (part col.) ([ Documents d'art] Musée du Louvre).

MORGAN, HARRY TITTERTON, 1872- ed. The romance of Chinese rietal art: Copper, bronze, cloisonné, brass, pewter. [Los Angeles, Distributor: Quon-Quon company] 1941. 16 p. illus. [His Chinese classics in miniature].

MUELLER, HERBERT, 1885- The Sunglin collection of Chinese art and archaeology, Peking. Catalog of exhibition, New York, May, nineteen thirty; with an introductory chapter on "Archaeology in China" and further contributions by Dr. Herbert Mueller (Peking) and 157 illustrations on 51 plates besides fifteen in the text. New York, N.Y., Herbert J. Devine Galleries [ c1930] 7-107, [1] p. incl. illus., plates.

MÜNSTERBERG, OSKAR, 1865- Chinesische Kunstgeschichte. 2 unveränd. Aufl. Esslingen a.N., P. Neff, 1924. 2 v. col. fronts., illus. col. plates.

————. A short history of Chinese art. New York, Philosophical Library [ 1949] London, Peter Owen, 1954. xiv, 227 p. 50 plates.

NEZU ART MUSEUM, TOKYO. Seizano seisho. Illustrated catalogue of the Nezu collection. Tokyo, Kaichiro Nezu, 1939-43. 10 v. in portfolio. plates.

NOTT, STANLEY CHARLES, 1902- comp. Chinese culture in the arts, being an illustrated descriptive record of the meaning of the emblematic and symbolic designs personified in the arts of China throughout the ages, with an introduction by H. Phelps Clawson. Illustrated by sixty-six halftone plates reproduced from original photographs; a fully descriptive map of China; together with one hundred eighty-seven line engravings made especially for the work from selected world-famous specimens of Chinese art by Mrs. Stanley Charles-Nott. New York, Chinese Culture Study Group of America, 1946. xx, 134 p. incl. col. front., illus. (incl. map) plates, ports.

PARIS. MUSÉE CERNUSCHI. Les hautes époques de l'art chinois, d'après les collections du Musée Cernuschi. Paris, Nilsson, [ 1932] [11] p. plates.

[ PARKES, KINETON ] 1865- Mystery of Chinese art. A Manchester collection reviewed [ Manchester] Printed by order of the Council of the Manchester

Chinese and Japanese Art Society, 1929. 44 p. incl. front., illus. (incl. port.).

PAUL-DAVID, MADELEINE, 1908- Arts et styles de la Chine. Paris, Larousse [1953] 199 p. illus., maps. (Arts, styles et techniques).

PELLIOT, PAUL, 1878-1945. Les influences européennes sur l'art chinois au XVIIe et au XVIIIe siècle. Conférence faite au Musée Guimet le 20 février, 1927. Paris, Impr. Nationale, 1948. Cover-title, 28 p. plates.

POMMERANZ-LIEDTKE, GERHARD. Chinesisches Kunstschaffen; Gegenwart und Tradition. Berlin, Henschelverlag, 1954. 159 p. illus.

PORTEUS, HUGH GORDON. Background to Chinese art. London, Faber and Faber [1935] 9-67 p. (Criterion miscellany, 42).

ROSE, SIR FRANCIS CYRIL, bart., 1909- Art seen through Chinese and western eyes; report of an address. London, China Society [1946] cover-title, 4 p.

ROSTOVTSEV, MÏKHAÏL ÏVANOVÏCH, 1870-1952- The animal style in South Russia and China; being the material of a course of lectures delivered in August 1925 at Princeton University under the auspices of the Harvard-Princeton fine arts club. Princeton, Princeton University Press; London, H. Milford, Oxford University Press; 1929. xvi, 112 p., xxxiii plates (Princeton monographs in art and archaeology, xiv).

SALMONY, ALFRED, 1890-1958. Sino-Siberian art in the collection of C. T. Loo. Paris, C. T. Loo, 1933. 119 p. plates, fold. map.

————. Antler and tongue; an essay on ancient Chinese symbolism and its implications. Ascona, Artibus Asiae, 1954. 57 p. illus. (part mounted) plates. (Artubus Asiae. Supplementum 13).

SEITZ, GUSTAV. Studienblätter aus China. Mit einem Geleitwort von Anna Seghers. Berlin, Aufbau Verlag, 1953. 10 illus.

SILCOCK, ARNOLD, 1889- Introduction to Chinese art. London, Oxford University Press, H. Milford, 1935. xvii, 268 p. front., illus., plates.

————. Introduction to Chinese art and history. London, Faber and Faber, 1947; New York, Oxford Univ. Press, 1948. xvi, 256 p. illus. (part col.) map (on lining-papers).

SIRÉN, OSVALD, 1879- Documents d'art chinois de la Collection Osvald Sirén publiés avec une préface de m. Raymond Koechlin, sous la direction de m. Henri Rivière, avec la collaboration de Serge Elisséèv, Gustaf Munthe, Osvald Sirén. Paris et Burxelles, G. van Oest, 1925. xiii, 88, [2] p. col. front., lx plates (Ars asiatica; études et documents pub. par Victor Goloubew vii].

————. A history of early Chinese art. London, E. Benn, 1929-1930. 4 v. illus. (incl. plans) plates.

————. Histoire des arts anciens de la Chine. Paris et Bruxelles, G. Van Oest, 1929-1930. 4 v. illus., plates. (Annales du Musée Guimet. Bibliothèque d' art. n. s. iii-iv).

SOULIÉ, CHARLES GEORGES, 1879- Histoire de l'art chinois de l'antiquité jusqu'à nos jours, par George Soulié de Morant, avec 77 illustrations dans le texte et 149 en phototypie hors texte. Paris, Payot, 1928. [7]-300, [1] p. illus., 80 plates on 40 l. (Collection l'art et le gout).

————. A history of Chinese art from ancient times to the present day, by George Soulié de Morant; translated by G. C. Wheeler. New York, J. Cape and H. Smith [1931] 295, [1] p. illus., 80 plates on 40 l.

SOWERBY, ARTHUR DE CARLE, 1885-1954. Nature in Chinese art, with two appendices on the Shang pictographs by Harry E. Gibson. New York, John Day [c1940] 203 p. incl. illus., plates. col. front., col. plates.

STRONG, HILDA ARTHURS. A sketch of Chinese arts and crafts. 2nd rev. ed. Peiping, H. Vetch, 1933. 3-329 p. front., illus., plates.

STUDIES IN CHINESE ART and some Indian influences (lectures delivered in connection with the International exhibition of Chinese art at the Royal Aca-

demy of Arts) by J. Hackin, Osvald Sirén, Langdon Warner [and] Paul Pelliot; with a foreword by Sir William Llewellyn. London, India Society [1938]
vii, 63, [1] p. plates.

TENG, KU, 滕固, 1901-1941. Chinesische Malkunsttheorie in der T'ang-und-
Sungzeit, Versuch einer geschichtlichen Betrachtung. Berlin, W. de Gruyter, 1935. 65 p. Diss.-Univ. Berlin.

TUPPER, EMILY HARTWELL. Birthplace: China; the life stories of some of
the Chinese animals and birds in the Seattle Art Museum, gathered together
by Emily Hartwell Tupper. Photos. by Earl Fields; one by C. F. Todd.
[Seattle? 1950] unpaged. illus.

WARNER, WORCESTER REED, 1846-1929. Selections from Oriental objects of
art collected by Worcester Reed Warner, most of which have been presented
to the Cleveland museum of art. Tarrytown, N. Y., 1921. 17-135 p. incl.
plates (part col.) col. front.

WEISS, RUTH. China's war art front. Chungking, China Information Committee,
1940. cover-title, 9 p.

WINGATE, LITITIA BERYL (TUCKER) The golden phoenix; essays on Chinese
art and culture. London, H. Jenkins, [1930] 252 p. front., 1 illus., plates.

WITH, KARL, 1891- Chinese art. [Pasadena, Calif., Esto Pub. Co.,c1940] cover-
title, [16] p. (Enjoy your museum, iiig).


## Exhibition Catalogues


ARDEN GALLERY, New York. Exhibition of imperial art treasures from Pe-
king's Forbidden city for the benefit of Mme. Chiang Kai-shek's fund for
Chinese war orphans, May 16th through October 28th. New York, Arden
Gallery [c1939] 24 p., front., illus.

BAHR, A. W. Rare stucco heads and figures from Honan province, important
carved wood and stone, archaic jades, early pottery, bronze and iron. The
collection of A. W. Bahr, sold by his order. Public sale by auction, April 28
and 29. New York, American Art Association, Anderson galleries, 1939.
38 p. illus.

BERN. KUNSTHALLE. Asiatische Kunst aus Schweizer Sammlungen; Ausstellung
veranstaltet von der Kunsthalle, Bern, in Verbindung mit der Schweizerischen
Gesellschaft der freunde ostasiatischer Kultur, 1. februar bis 30. märz 1941.
[Bern, Druck Büchler, 1941] 123 p. incl. col. front., 40 plates on 20 l.

BOSTON. MUSEUM OF FINE ARTS. The Charles B. Hoyt collection; memorial
exhibition, February 13-March 30, 1952. Boston, Museum of Fine Arts
[1952] 204 p. illus. (part mounted col.).

BREUER, A. Die Sammlung A. Breuer, Berlin; Ostasiatische Kunst, eingeleitet
von Otto Kümmel. Auktionsleitung: Paul Cassirer und Hugo Helbing. Berlin,
1929. 82 p. plates.

BRISTOL MUSEUM AND ART GALLERY, Bristol, Eng. The Schiller collection
of Chinese ceramics, jades and bronzes. Illustrated catalogue. [Bristol] The
Corporation [1948] 38 p. 14 plates. (Its Publication no. 1a).

BURCHARD, OTTO. Die Bestände der Firma Otto Burchard and Co., Berlin,in
liquidation. Chinesische Kunst. 1 Teil. Beschrieben von L. Reidemeister.
Versteigerung am 22 und 23 Marz 1935. Berlin, Paul Graupe, 1935. 78 p.

BURNET, H.K. Catalogue of the fine collection of important early Chinese bronzes,
rare archaic jades, paintings, lacquer, textiles, rugs, sculpture, Chinese
ceramics and various works of art, the property of H. K. Burnet, which will
be sold by auction by Messrs Sotheby and Co... the 2nd of April 1941 and two
following days [London, 1941] 101 p. front. illus. plates.

CATALOGUE OF AN EXHIBITION of Chinese art held in 1937 in the Dominion of
New Zealand. Aukland, 1937. iv, 49 p. illus.

CHENGTU. West China Union University. Museum. Guide book series, No. 1-9.
 Chengtu, 1945-46. 9 v. illus.
CHICAGO. ART INSTITUTE. Handbook of the department of oriental art.    Chi-
 cago, Lakeside Press, 1933. 62 p. illus.
CHINA. Organizing committee, International Exhibition of Chinese Art, London,
 1935-1936. The London International Exhibition of Chinese Art. Catalogue of
 exhibits at the preliminary exhibition in Shanghai, April 8th-May 1st, 1935.
 Nanking, Chinese Organizing Committee [ 1935] 160 (i. e. 172) p.
————. Illustrated catologue of Chinese government exhibits for the International
 Exhibition of Chinese Art in London [Shanghai, Commercial Press, 1936] 4 v.
 illus., plates, ports.
CHINESE WOMEN'S RELIEF ASSOCIATION OF NEW YORK. A loan exhibition of
 early Chinese art treasures, for the benefit of Chinese civilian war victims;
 this exhibition has been assembled from private collections including those of
 Mrs. William H. Moore, Mrs. Christian R. Holmes, Mrs. C. Suydam Cutting [ and others] none of the paintings, bronzes and and jades has ever been
 shown publicly. Arden Gallery   February 2nd to February 26th [ 1938] 38 p.
 illus. (incl. ports. ).
COX, JOHN HADLEY, 1913-  An exhibition of Chinese antiquities from Ch'ang-
 sha, lent by John Hadley Cox, March 26 to May 7, 1939. The Associates in
 fine arts at Yale University, Gallery of fine arts, Yale University, New Haven,
 Conn. [ Meriden, Conn., Printed by the Meriden Gravure Company, c1939]
 15 p. incl 5 plates on 3 l.
DETROIT. INSTITUTE OF ARTS. Art of India, China and Japan; picture book.
 [ Detroit] 1946 [ i. e. 1947] 28 p. illus.
————. The arts of the Ming dynasty. [ Detroit] 1952. 48 p. illus.
EUMORFOPOULOS, GEORGE, 1863-1939. Catalogue of the collection of Chi-
 nese ceramics, bronzes, gold ornaments, lacquer, jade, glass and works of
 art, formed by the late George Eumorfopoulos, esq. (Sold by order of Mrs.
 Eumorfopoulos and of the executors) which will be sold by auction by Messrs.
 Sotheby and co.  at their galleries 28th May, 1940, and three following days
 Illustrated catalogue (53 plates) [London, Printed by Kitchen and Barratt,
 ltd., 1940] [ 5]-152 p. colfl front., plates (part col. ).
FRIENDS OF THE FAR EASTERN ART. Exhibition of Chinese art, the Art gal-
 lery, Oct. 12 to Nov. 25, 1934. Mills College, Calif. [1934]  ix, 13-72 p.,
 48 plates on 24 l.
GENÈVE. GALERIE MOTTE. Chine, objets de haute curiosité. Exposition, Juil-
 let-Septembre, 1954. Genève, 1954? 12 p. fig.
GENÈVE. MUSÉE D'ETHNOGRAPHIE. Exposition des arts appliqués de la Chine
 et du Japon avec la collaboration de la Société suisse des amis de l'Extrême-
 Orient, 20 juin-15 septembre, 1942. [ Catalogue] Genève, 1942. iv, 72 p.
GESELLSCHAFT FÜR OSTASIATISCHE KUNST, Berlin. Ausstellung chinesischer Kunst, veranstaltet von der Gesellschaft für ostasiatische Kunst und
 der Preussischen Akademie der Kunste, Berlin, 12 Januar bis 2. April 1929.
 2. Aufl. Berlin, Würfel Verlag, 1929. 458 p. illus. (incl. plan).
————. Chinesische Kunst; Zweihundert Hauptwerke der Ausstellung der Gesellschaft für ostasiatische Kunst in der Preussischen Akademie der Künste, Berlin, 1929, hrsg. von Otto Kümmel. Berlin, B. Cassirer, 1930. 81 p., c]
 plates (part col. and mounted).
HUO, MING-CHIH PAUL, 霍明志. Preuves des antiquités. Pékin, 1930. 676 p.
 35, [ 2] p. incl. illus., plates, facsims. plates, ports.
KLEIJKAMP, JAN.    -1952. Early Chinese art: exhibited at the galleries of
 Henri Reinhardt and Sons, Inc. 1922. Catalogue with introduction by A. J.
 Kleijkamp [ of Royal art galleries, The Hague] New York, 1922. 46 p. col.
 front., plates.
————. Catalogue; finest examples from the famous collections of Petrucci, Ba-
 ron von der Heydt und Goloubew. Jan Kleijkamp galleries, early Chinese art,

jades, bronzes, sculptures, paintings, early potteries. New York, 1925. 21 l. mounted plates (part col. ).

————. The Santa Barbara Museum of Art presents an exhibition of masterpieces of Ancient China collected in China collected in China by Jan Kleijkamp during 1940-1941. October 19-November 23, 1941. New York, Kleijkamp, [ c1941] 39 p. illus.

————. The Detroit Institute of Arts presents an exhibition of masterpieces of ancient China, collected in China by Jan Kleijkamp during 1940-1941. May 19th-June 28th, 1942. New York, The Hague, Kleijkamp, [ 1942] 45, [ 2] p. incl. illus., xv pl. (incl. front. )

LETH, ANDRÉ. Chinese art; a selection of the exhibits shown at the Museum of Decorative Arts, Copenhagen, 1950. Copenhagen, Nyt nordisk forlag, 1953. [ 129] p. illus.

LONDON. INTERNATIONAL EXHIBITION OF CHINESE ART, 1935-1936. Catalogue of the International exhibition of Chinese art, 1935-36; patrons: His Majesty the King, Her Majesty Queen Mary, the President of the Chinese republic. 4th ed. London, Royal Academy of Arts [ 1935?] 2 pt. in 1 v. illus. (plan) 288 plates (incl. facsims. ) on 144 l., fold map.

————. The Chinese exhibition; a commemorative catalogue of the International exhibition of Chinese art, Royal Academy of Arts, November 1935-March 1936. London, Faber and Faber, [ 1936] xxviii, 160, [ 161] p. col. front., 160 plates (incl. facsims. ) on 80 l.

LONDON, ROYAL ACADEMY OF ARTS. Catalogue of the International exhibition of Chinese art, 1935-36 1st ed. London, Royal Academy of Arts, [ 1935] xxiv, 264, xxv-xxxiii p. fold map.

LOO, C. T. and CO., NEW YORK. Exhibition of Chinese, Indian and Cambodian art formed by C. T. Loo 9th to 21st Nov. 1931. New York, Wildenstein Gallery 1931 34 p. plates.

————. Exhibition of Chinese arts. New York. Special sale, November 1, 1941 to April 30, 1942. [ New York, Printed by the William Bradford Press, c1941] [ 163] p. illus.

————. An exhibition of figures in Chinese art in April of 1946. New York, [1946] 16 p. illus.

NEUCHÂTEL. MUSÉE D'ETHNOGRAPHIE. L'art artisanal de la Chine. [ Exposition] du 13 mai au 2 septembre, 1956. Organisée par l'Association du peu peuple chinois pour les relations culturelles avec l'étranger avec la collaboration du Musée d'ethnographie. Neuchêtel, 1956. 39 p. illus. 38 p.

NEW JERSEY. STATE MUSEUM, Trenton. Chinese art, from the neolithic age through the Sung dynasty; exhibition at the New Jersey State Museum, Trenton, from December 14, 1941 to January 26, 1942. [ Trenton, 1941] 24 p. front.

NOTT, STANLEY CHARLES, 1902- Chinese art of world renown, being a commemorative survey of the priceless Chinese art displayed at "Jadeholm, " compiled by Stanley Charles Nott, F.C.C.S.G. Illustrated by forty-six full page half-tone plates reproduced from original photographs made during the exhibition under the auspices of the Chinese culture study group of America, covering the Chinese art exhibition of Palm Beach, Florida, 1944. [ St. Augustine, The Record Press, 1944] xxi, 58 p. incl. front. (port. ) plates.

PARIS. MUSÉE CERNUSCHI. La découverte de l'Asie. Hommage à René Grousset. Paris, Musée Cernuschi, 1954. 157 p. plates.

————. L'art de la Chine des Song. Paris, Musée Cernuschi, 1956. 80 p. plates.

PARIS. MUSÉE DE L'ORANGERIE. Arts de la Chine ancienne; introduction de Georges Salles. [ Paris] Musêe de l'Orangerie, 1937. 237, [ 1] p. xxxii plates on 16 l. , fold. map.

PARIS. MUSÉE GUIMET. Guide-catalogue du Musée Guimet avec introductions concernant l'histoire, les religions et les arts des différents pays, par Odette Monod-Bruhl. Paris, Musée Guimet, 1939. 217 p. plates, fold. map.

PARISH-WATSON AND CO. Exhibition of decorative arts by Parish-Watson and
    Co., Inc., New York City. Rare old Chinese porcelains, potteries, bronzes
    and sculptures, early Persian faience, carpets and miniatures, French fur-
    niture and tapestries, English portraits. Vandyck galleries, Washington,
    D. C. [New York, G. T. Washburn and Co., 1924] Cover title, [10] p. illus.

PENNSYLVANIA. UNIVERSITY. University museum. The Chinese collections of
    the University Museum; a handbook of the principal objects, by Horace H. F.
    Jayne. Philadelphia, The University Museum, University of Pennsylvania
    [c1941] 62 p. incl. front., illus. (1 col.).

PORT ARTHUR. Kwantung Government Museum. Some exhibits in the govern-
    ment museum, New Town, Port Arthur. Port Authur, The Government Mu-
    seum of the Kwantung Government, 1932. 54 figures, with accompanying des-
    cription.

ST. PAUL. Gallery and School of Art. Loan exhibition; 3,000 years of Chinese
    art. November third through December first, 1940. St. Paul, Minn. [c1940]
    [44] p. illus.

SALMONY, ALFRED, 1890-1958. Asiatische Kunst; Ausstellung Köhn, 1926. Bear-
    beitet von Alfred Salmony mit Anmerkungen von Paul Pelliot. München, F.
    Bruckmann [1929] 80 p. 100 plates.

SELIGSOHN, RICHARD. Die Sammlung Richard Seligsohn, ostasiatische Kunst.
    Versteigerung den 27. oktober 1926 Auktionsleitung; Paul Cassirer und Hugo
    Helbing. [Berlin, Gedruckt bei H. Klokow, 1926] 39 p. x plates.

SIMON, THEODOR E. Sammlung Theodor E. Simon, Berlin; chinesische Kunst-
    gegenstände verzeichnet von L. Reidemeister; Gemälde, Möbel und euro-
    paische Porzellane de 18 Jahrhunderts verzeichnet von C. F. Foerster. Aus-
    stellung 2-4 Nov. Auktionsleitung Paul Cassirer und Hugo Helbing. Berlin,
    [1929] 44 p. plates.

STANFORD UNIVERSITY. Committee for Art. The magnificent Manchus; court
    art of the Ch'ing dynasty. [Exhibition] sponsored by the Committee for Art at
    Stanford in co-operation with the Stanford Museum at Stanford University,
    California, November 27, 1954 to February 5, 1955. [Stanford University,
    1955] 32 p. illus.

TOLEDO. Museum of Art. The art of Korea (Chosen) Manchuria (Manchukuo)
    Mongolia and Tibet; a selection of different phases of art from the interrelated
    countries of northeastern Asia. January, ninteen hundred forty-two, the To-
    ledo Museum of Art. [Toledo? 1941] [64] p. illus.

TONG-YING AND CO. Ancient Chinese art; the rare collection assembled by
    C. F. Yau, 姚昌復, president of Tong-ying and Co. including family treasures
    of the imperial princes. American art association, Inc., Managers. [New
    York, Lent and Graff Co., 1926] [13]-129, [2] p. col. mounted front. illus.

TORONTO. Royal Ontario museum of archaeology. Outline guide to the East
    Asiatic section. [Toronto, University of Toronto press, 1935] cover-title,
    22 p. illus.

VENICE. Mostra d'arte cinese. Exhibition of Chinese art. Catalogue. Venezia,
    Alfieri [1954] xxxviii, 273 p. illus. (part col.) 2 maps.

VEREENIGING VAN VRIEDEN DER AZIATISCHE KUNST, THE HAGUE. Tentoon-
    stelling van chinesische Kunst; Exhibition of Chinese art. Amsterdam, 1925,
    Stedelijk museum; Municipal museum, 13 September-18 October. Catalogus/
    Catalogue. [Amsterdam 1925] 5-99 p. plates.

————. The exhibition of Chinese Art of the Society of friends of Asiatic art, Am-
    sterdam, 1925, edited by H. F.E. Visser. The Hague, M. Nijhoff, 1926.
    viii, 39 p. lxvi plates. (part col., 1 mounted).

VICTORIA AND ALBERT MUSEUM, SOUTH KENSINGTON. Chinese art, the
    Eumorfopoulos collection. [London] Published under the authority of the
    Board of Education, 1936. 23, [1] p. front. plates.

WINKWORTH, STEPHEN D. Catalogue of the well-known and extensive collec-
    tions of Chinese pottery, porcelain, glass, Canton enamel, snuff bottles,
    cloisonne, bronzes, soapstone and fine old English furniture, the property of

Stephen D. Winkworth which will be sold by auction by Messrs. Sotheby and Co. on Tuesday, 26th of April 1938 and three following days. London, Kitchen and Barratt, 1938. [3]-129 p. front. plates, photos.

WORCH, EDGAR. Exhibition of the Edgar Worth collection of antique Chinese art at the Fifty-sixth Street galleries, Inc. New York City. New York, Flamingo Advertising Co., 1931. Cover-title, [10] p. illus.

YAMANAKA AND CO. Exhibition of Chinese art at the Fine Arts exposition, the Forum, Rockefeller center, New York City, November 1934. New York, Yamanaka and co., 1934. 52 p. illus. fold plates.

———. Collection of Chinese and other Far Eastern art, assembled by Yamanaka and co. New in process of liquidation under the supervision of the Alien property custodian of the United States of America. New York, Chicago [Printed by John B. Watkins, New York] 1943. [232] p. incl. col. front., illus. (1 col.).

## Architecture and Landscape Gardening

ADAM, MAURICE, 1889-1932. Yuen ming yuen. L'oeuvre architecturale des anciens jésuites au xviiie siècle. Peip'ing, Impr. des Lazaristes, 1936. xii, 44 p., front., illus., plates, ports., plans.

BOERSCHMANN, ERNST, 1873-1949. Baukunst und Landschaft in China; eine Reise durch zwölf Provinzen. Berlin, E. Wasmuth 1923. xxv p. plates. illus. (map) (Orbis terrarum).

———. Picturesque China, architecture and landscape; a journey through twelve provinces, translated by Louis Hamilton. New York, Brentano's [1923] xxvi, 288 p., illus., map.

———. China, architecture and landscape; a journey through twelve provinces, translated by Louis Hamilton. London "The Studio" [c1925] xxii p. plates. illus. (map) (Orbis terrarum).

———. La Chine pittoresque. Texte et vues originales. Paris, A. Calavas, 1923. xxv, 16 p. plates.

———. Chinesische Architektur. Berlin, E. Wasmuth, 1925. 2v. illus. plates.

BULLING, ANNELIESE, 1900- Die chinesische Architektur von der Han-Zeit bis zum Ende der T'ang-Zeit. Lyon, Impr. Franco-Suisse, 1935. 58 p. plates, Diss.–Univ. Berlin.

CH'ÊN, HUNG-SHUN, 陳鴻舜, 1905- Prince Kung's palace and its adjoining garden in Peking [by] H.-S. Ch'ên and G.N. Kates. Peking, H. Vetch [1941?] cover-title, 80 p. incl. plates. plan, fold. geneal. tab. Reprinted from Monumenta serica v. 5. (1940).

DEXEL, THOMAS. Chinesisches Steinzeug. Darmstadt, Schneekluth, 1957. 34 p. illus., map. (Wohnkunst und Hausrat, einst und jetzt, bd. 30).

DYE, DANIEL SHEETS, 1884- A grammar of Chinese lattice. Cambridge, Harvard University Press, 1937. 2v. illus., plates. (Harvard-Yenching institute. Monograph series. vol. v-vi).

———. The yin-yang dance of life and basic patterns, as seen in west China between December 1908 and April 1949. Penfield Downs, Pa., R.L. Balderston, 1950. 26 l. illus.

ELÉMENTS DE DÉCORATION CHINOISE; motifs décoratifs relevés dans les temples et yamens. Pékin, A. Nachbaur, 1931. 60 col. plates.

FABRE, MAURICE. Pékin, ses palais, ses temples et ses environs; guide historique et descriptif, illustré par Y. Darcy. Compositions originales de J. Malval. Tien-Tsin, Librairie française [c1937] xv, [1], 347, [1] p. front. illus., plates (part col.), 1 fold.) ports., fold. map, plans (part fold.).

FUGL-MEYER, H., 1894- Chinese bridges. Shanghai, Kelly and Walsh, 1937. ix, 138 p., front., illus., fold. map.

GRAHAM, DOROTHY, 1893- Chinese gardens: gardens of the contemporary scene; an account of their design and symbolism, illustrated from photographs taken by the author. New York, Dodd, Mead, 1938. xi, 3-255 p. col. front., plates.

GRANTHAM, ALEXANDRA ETHELDRED, 1867- The Ming tombs. Peking, Wu Lai-hsi, 1926. Cover-title, 21 p. illus.

HOWARD, EDWIN LACLEDE. Chinese garden architecture; a collection of photographs of minor Chinese buildings. Foreword by Everett V. Meeks. New York, Macmillan 1931. x p., col. front., plates.

HUBBARD, GILBERT ERNEST, 1885- The temples of the Western hills. Peking and Tientsin, La Librairie française, 1923. [3]-76 p. plates, photos., port., fold. map.

INN, HENRY, 1899- Chinese houses and gardens; edited by Shao Chang Lee. [李紹昌] New York, Hastings House [1950] xii, 148 p. illus. 1st ed. 1940.

ITŌ, CHŪTA, 1867-1954. Architectural decoration in China. Translated by Jiro Harada. Tokyo, Toho Bunka Gakuin, Academy of Oriental Culture, 1941- 5 v. illus., plates (part fold., part col.) col. maps (part fold.).

KELLING, RUDOLF. Das chinesische Wohnhaus. Mit einem ii. Teil über das frühchinesische Haus, unter Verwendung von Ergebnissen aus übungen von Conrady im Ostasiatischen Seminar der Universität Leipzig, von Rudolf Kelling und Bruno Schindler. Tokyo, Deutsche Gesellschaft für Natur- u. Völkerkunde Ostasiens, 1935. [1], ix, 128 p. illus., plates (1 col., 1 fold.) plans. Supplement der "Mitteilungen" der Deutschen gesellschaft für natur- und völkerkunde Ostasiens. supplementbd. xiii).

[LAUFER, BERTHOLD] 1874-1934. The Chinese gateway. Chicago, Field Museum of Natural History, 1922. cover-title, 7 p. plates. (Field museum of natural history. [Anthropology leaflet, no. 1]).

MELCHERS, BERND, 1886- China. Der tempelbau. Die Lochan von Ling-yänsï; ein hauptwerk buddhistischer plastik. Hagen i. W., Folkwang-Verlag g.m.b.h., 1922. 11-46, [159] p. incl. [121] p. of illus., xviii plans. (Schriften-reihe Kulturen der erde; material zu kultur- und kunstgeschichte aller völker. [Bilderwerke] bd. iv u. v. China ii. bd.).

MIRAMS, DENNIS GEORGE. A brief history of Chinese architecture. Introduction by H. E. Sir Archibald Clark Kerr and forword by A. E. Richardson. Shanghai, Kelly and Walsh, 1940. xxiv, 132 p. front., plates, 2 maps (1 fold.) fold. plan, diagrs.

NAWRATH, ALFRED, 1890- Indien und China, Meisterwerke der Baukunst und Plastik; mit 208 Abbildungen und einer Karte. Wien, A. Schroll [c1938] 64 p. plates, fold, map.

———. India and China; a photographic study. London, Cresset Press [1939] 39 p. plates.

POWELL, FLORENCE LEE. In the Chinese garden, a photographic tour of the complete Chinese garden, with text explaining its symbolism, as seen in the Liu yuan (the Liu garden) and the Shih tzu lin (the Forest of lions), two famous Chinese gardens in the city of Soochow, Kiangsu province, China. Text and photographs by Florence Lee Powell. New York, John Day [1943] 112 p. illus.

PRIP-MØLLER, JOHANNES, 1889- About Buddhist temples. Peiping, North China Union Language School cooperating with California College in China [1931] 33 p. illus.

———. Chinese Buddhist monasteries, their plan and its function as a setting for Buddhist monastic life. Copenhagen, G.E.C. Gad; London, Oxford University Press, 1937. 396 p. incl. illus. (incl. ports., map, plans (part col.) facsims.) plates (part fold., 1 col.).

SEKINO, TADASHI, 1868-1935. Summer palace and lama temples in Jehol. Tokyo, Kokusai Bunka Shinkokai (The Society for international cultural relations) 1935. 16, 2 p., mounted col. front., illus. (plan) plates. [Kokusai bunka shinkokai. Publications, series-B, no. 9].

SICKMAN, LAURENCE CHALFONT STEVENS. 1907- The art and architecture of China [by] Laurence Sickman [and] Alexander Soper. [Baltimore] Penguin Books [1956] xxvi, 334 p. illus., 190 plates, maps. (The Pelican history of art, Z10).

SIRÉN, OSVALD, 1879- The walls and gates of Peking, researches and impressions, illustrated with 109 photogravures after photographs by the author and fifty architectural drawings made by Chinese artists. London, John Lane [1924] xvii, 239 p. front., illus. (incl. plans) plates (2 col.) fold. map.

———. The imperial palaces of Peking; two hundred and seventy four plates in collotype after photographs by the author, twelve architectural drawings and two maps, with a short historical account by Osvald Sirén. Paris et Brussles, G. Van Oest, 1926. 3 v. plates, plans (part fold.).

———. Les palais impériaux de Pékin. Deux cent soixante-quatorze planches en héliotypie d'aprés les photographies de l'auteur, douze dessins architecturaux et deux plans evec une notice historique sommaire. Paris et Bruxelles, G. van Oest, 1926. 3 v. plates, plans (part fold.).

———. Gardens of China. New York, Ronald Press Co. [1949] xiv, 141 p. illus. [219] plates (part col.).

———. China and gardens of Europe of the eighteenth century. New York, Ronald Press Co. [1950] xiv, 223, 192 p. illus. (part col.).

SOPER, ALEXANDER COBURN, 1904- Four columns from a Chinese temple. Honolulu, Academy of Arts, 1947. 35 p. front., plates (Honolulu academy of arts. Special studies, 1).

VON ERDBERG, ELEANOR. Chinese influence on European garden structures, edited by Bremer Whidden Pond. Cambridge, Harvard University Press, 1936. [3]-221 p. front., illus., plates (Harvard landscape architecture monographs. i).

WÊN CHÊNG-MING, 文徵明, 1470-1559. An old Chinese garden; a three-fold masterpiece of peotry, calligraphy and painting, by Wen Chên Ming. studies written by Kate Kerby; translations by Mo Zung Chung. Shanghai, Chung Hwa Book Co. [1923?] 179 l. illus. (incl. facsims.).

WILSON, ERNEST HENRY, 1876-1930. China, mother of gardens, with map and sixty-one illustrations from photographs taken by the author. Boston, The Stratford [c1929] iii-x, 408 p. front., lx plates., fold. map, diagr.

WILSON, HARDY. Grecian and Chinese architecture. Melbourne, The author, 1937. 14 p., L mounted plates.

WOO, SHAO-LING, 吳紹璘. Der chinesische Hallenbau und seine Konstruktionen in der Tsing-Dynastie. Ein Vorbild für praktiksch Holzbau. Berlin, 1941. 103 l. illus. fig. Diss.-Berlin Tech. Hochs.

## Bronzes: General Works

ACKERMAN, PHYLLIS, 1893- Ritual bronzes of ancient China. New York, Dryden Press, 1945. vi, 114 p. incl. front., plates.

BERLIN. Staatliche Museen. Abteilung für Ostasiatische Kunst. Chinesische Bronzen aus der Abteilung für Ostasiatische Kunst an den Staatlichen Museen, Berlin. Berlin, A. Frisch [1928] 16 p. plates (3 Jahresgabe der Gesellschaft für ostasiatische kunst, Berlin).

BISHOP, CARL WHITING, 1881-1942. The bronzes of Hsin-chêng Hsien. (In Smithsonian institution. Annual report, 1926. Washington, 1927. p. 457-468. plates. ''Reprinted from the Chinese social and political science review, 8:2 April, 1924.''

BOUGH, HON-CAN. The Tsung Chow bell of the Emperor Ch'eng Wang, 1109 B. C. The history of the early Chow dynasty as given by the Emperor Ch'eng Wang (1115-1079 B. C.) in the inscriptions of the Tsung Chow bell. New York, London, G. P. Putnam, 1931. 133 numb. l., col. front., illus. (incl. ports., maps, facsims.).

BURCHARD, OTTO. Chinesische Bronzegefässe. Leipzig, E. A. Seemann, 1923.

12, 20 p. plates. (Bibliothek der Kunstgeschichte, 54).

CHICAGO. ART INSTITUTE. Chinese bronzes, in the collections of the Art Institute of Chicago. [Chicago] 1940. [1], 15 p. illus. (Its A Picture book).

——. Chinese bronzes from the Buckingham collection, by Charles Fabens Kelley and Ch'en Meng-chia, 陳夢家. [Chicago] 1946. 164 p. illus., 85 plates.

CULL, A    E    K. The Cull Chinese bronzes, by W. Perceval Yetts. [London] University of London, Courtauld Institute of Art, 1939. x, 197 p. illus., xxxv pl.

EUMORFOPOULOS, GEORGE, 1863-1939. The George Eumorfopoulos collection; catalogue of the Chinese and Corean bronzes, sculpture, jades; jewellery and miscellaneous objects, by W. Perceval Yetts. London, E. Benn, [1929- 2 v. illus. (incl. facsims.) plates (part col., part mounted).

FERGUSON, JOHN CALVIN, 1866-1945. A bronze table, with accompanying vessels. 陶齋舊藏古酒器考 . Peking, 1924. 19, 16 p.

——. The four bronze vessels of the Marquis of Ch'i, 陶齋舊藏四器考釋 Peking, 1928. cover-title, 10, [9] p. 1 illus., plates.

——. Two bronze drums. Peiping, 1932. Cover-title, 7 p., plates.

FOSTER, KENNETH E. The Viola Minor Westergaard Foundation presents a handbook of ancient Chinese bronzes. Rev. [limited] ed. [Claremont? Calif.] 1949. 96 p. illus.

FREER GALLERY OF ART, Washington, D.C. A descriptive and illustrative catalogue of Chinese bronzes, acquired during the administration of John Ellerton Lodge. (With 50 plates) Compiled by the staff of the Freer Gallery of Art. Washington, 1946. v, 108 p. illus. (incl. maps) plates. (Smithsonian institution. Freer gallery of art. Oriental studies, 3).

HACKENBROCH, YVONNE. The Lee collection. Toronto, University of Toronto Press, 1949. [19] p. plates.

HENTZE, CARL, 1883-    Frühchinesische Bronzen und Kultdarstellungen. Antwerpen, De Sikkel, 1937. 167, [1] p. and portfolio of plates (part mounted).

——. Die Sakralbronzen und ihre Bedeuting in den frühchinesischen Kulturen. Antwerpen, De Sikkel, 1941. 2 v. plates. (Studien zur frühchinesischen Kulturgeschichte, 1.).

——. Ko-und Ch'i-Waffen in China und in Amerika. Göttergestalten in der ältesten chinesischen Schrift von C. Hentze und Ch. Kim. Antwerpen, De Sikkel, 1943. 59 p. plates. (Studien zur frühchinesischen Kulturgeschichte, 2).

——. Bronzegerät, Kultbauten, Religion im ältesten China der Shang-Zeit. Antwerpen, De Sikkel, 1951. xix, 273 p. illus. and atlas (103 plates).

HEYDT, EDUARD freiherr VON DER, 1882-    Sammlung Baron Eduard von der Heydt. [Katalog] Berlin, B. Cassirer, 1932. 2 v. illus. (map) plates.

——. Sammlung Baron Eduard von der Heydt, Wien; Ordosbronzen, Bronzen aus Luristan und dem Kaukasus, Werke chinesischer Kleinkunst aus verschiedenen Perioden, bearbeitet von Viktor Griessmaier. Wien, Krystall-Verlag, 1936. 110, [2] p. illus. (Wiener beiträge zur kunst- und kultur-geschichte Asiens; jahrbuch des Vereines der freunde asiatischer kunst und kultur in Wien. Sonderpublikation anläszlich des zehnjährigen bestandes des Vereins).

KARLGREN, BERNHARD, 1889-    Yin and Chou in Chinese bronzes. Stockholm, 1935. cover-title, 9-156 p. plates. "Reprinted from: The Bulletin of the Museum of Far Eastern Antiquities, 8."

——. New studies on Chinese bronzes. Stockholm, 1937. Cover-title, 117 p. plates. "Reprinted from: The Bulletin of the Museum of Far Eastern Antiquities, 9."

KOOP, ALBERT JAMES, 1877-    Early Chinese bronzes. London, E. Benn; New York, Scribner, 1924. viii, 84, [1] p. plates, (part col.).

——. Le bronze chinois antique; traduit de l'anglais par Alix Guillain. Paris, Éditions A. Levy, [1924] vii, 94 p. plates (part col.) (Les arts de l'Asie).

——. Frühchinesische Bronzen; übers. von Anna Simons und Maria von Faber du Faur. Berlin, E. Wasmuth, 1924. 1, 46 p. plates.

KÜMMEL, OTTO, 1874-1952, ed. Jörg Trübner zum Gedächtnis. Ergebnisse seiner letzten chinesischen Reisen, bearbeitet und herausgegeben von Otto Kümmel. Berlin, Klinkhardt und Biermann, 1930. 148 p. front. (port. ) 4 mounted illus., 84 (i.e. 82) pl. ( 1 fold. ).

LAMAITRE, SOLANGE. Les agrafes chinoises jusqu'à la fin de l'époque Han. Paris, Les Éditions d'art et d'histoire, 1939. 57 p. incl. illus. plates, maps.

LAUFER, BERTHOLD, 1874-1934. ed. Archaic Chinese bronzes of the Shang, Chou and Han periods in the collection of Parish-Watson, accompanied by notes of B. Laufer. New York, Parish Watson, 1922. vi, 22 p. plates.

LEROI-GOURHAN, ANDRÉ, 1911-     Bestiaire du bronze chinois de style Tcheou, Paris, Les Éditions d'art et d'histoire, 1936. cover-title, 45 p. incl. illus. tab.

LOCHOW, HANS JUERGEN VON. Sammlung Lochow: Chinesischen Bronzen. Peking, [ Fu Jen Press], 1943-44. 2 v. illus., plates, (v. 1. edited by Gustav Ecke; v. 2, edited by the collector himself).

LOEHR, MAX. Beiträge zur Chronologie der älteren Chinesischen Bronzen. Berlin und Leipzig, W. de Gruyter, 1936. 41 p. Diss.-Univ. München.

LOO, C. T., et CIE. Bronzes antiques de la Chine appartenant à C. T. Loo, 盧 芹齋, et cie, par H. Tch'ou Tö-yi, 褚德彝 ; avec une préface et des notes de M. Paul Pelliot. Paris et Bruxelles, G. van Oest, 1924. 68 p. xi. pl.

————. Inlaid bronzes of the Han dynasty in the collection of C. T. Loo by Mikhail Rostovtzeff. Paris and Brussels, G. van Oest, 1927. 76 p. mounted ills. plates.

MA, CHANG-KEE, 馬長記 . The Ma Chang Kee collection, ancient Chinese bronzes, exhibited at the galleries of Ralph M. Chait, New York. [New York? 1932?] cover-title, 16 p.

MENZIES, JAMES MELLON, 1885-1957. Shang Ko; a study of the characteristic weapon of the bronze age in China in the period 1311-1039 B.C. Toronto, 1942. 2 v. plates. Thesis-Univ. of Toronto.

MINNEAPOLIS. INSTITUTE OF ARTS. A catalogue of the Chinese bronzes in the Alfred F. Pillsbury collection, by Bernhard Karlgren. Minneapolis, Published for the Minneapolis Institute of Arts by the University of Minnesota Press [ 1952] [ 16], 228 p. illus., 114 plates, port.

MÜNSTERBERG, HUGO, 1916-     Buddha's bronzes of the six dynasties period. Cambridge, 1941. 183 p. Thesis-Harvard University.

PASADENA, ART INSTITUTE. Far eastern culture: small Chinese bronzes and bronze mirrors. Pasadena, Calif., Pasadena Art Institute, 1947. [ 16] p. illus.

PEKING. NATIONAL PALACE MUSEUM. Chinese bronze age weapons; the Werner Jannings Collection in the Chinese National Palace Museum, Peking, by Max Loehr. Ann Arbor, University of Michigan Press; London, Oxford University Press, 1956. xiii, 233 p. illus., plates.

SALMONY, ALFRED, 1890-1958. The problem of Pre-Anyang bronzes. New York, [ n.p., 1952] 7 l. plates.

STOCKHOLM. HALLWYLSKA PALATSET. Catalogue of the collection of Chinese and Korean bronzes at Hallwye house, Stockholm. Stockholm, Centraltryckeriet, 1938. 96 p. illus., xxix pl. on 15 l., diagr.

————. ÖSTASIATISKA SAMLINGARNA. Yin and Chou researches; dedicated to the Royal academy of arts and the executive committee of the International exhibition of Chinese art, London, 1935-1936. Stockholm [ Printed by A. -b. H. W. Tullbergs boktryckeri] 1936. 9-154, 69 p. illus., plates (part col. ).

SWALLOW, ROBERT WILLIAM, 1878-     Ancient Chinese bronze mirrors. Peiping, H. Vetch, 1937. xii, [ 2], 78 p., front., plates.

TODD, OLIVER JULIAN, 1880-     Chinese bronze mirrors; a study based on the Todd collection of 1, 000 bronze mirrors found in the five northern provinces of Suiyuan, Shensi, Shansi, Honan and Hopei by Milan Rupert and O. J. Todd;

with 109 illustration.  Peiping, Printed by San Yu Press, 1935. iii, [2], 259 p. plates.

TRAUTMANN, OSKAR, 1877-1950. Frühe chinesische Bronzen aus der Sammlung Oskar Trautmann, hrsg. von Gustav Ecke. Peking, [Fu-jen Press] 1939. 23 l. 49 plates (in portfolio. ).

TRÜBNER, JÖRG, 1901-1930. Yu und Kuang zur Typologie der chinesischen Bronzen. Leipzig, Klinkardt und Biermann, 1929. 32 p. plates.

UMEHARA, SUEJI, 1893-    On the shapes of the bronze vessels of ancient China: an archaeological study. Kyoto, Institute of Oriental Culture, 1940. 13, 53 p. plates.

VAN HEUSDEN, WILLEM. Ancient Chinese bronzes of the Shang and Chou dynasties; an illustrated catalogue of the Van Heusden collection with a historical introduction by Willem Van Heusden. Tokyo, privately published, 1952. xi, 193 p. front. (col), illus. plates, map, tables.

VORETZSCH, ERNST ARTHUR, 1868-    Altchinesische Bronzen; mit 169 Abbildungen und einer Landkarte. Berlin, J. Springer, 1924. xxiv, 335, [1] p. illus., fold. map.

WATERBURY, FLORENCE, 1883-    Early Chinese symbols and literature: vestiges and speculations, with particular reference to the ritual bronzes of the Shang dynasty. New York, E. Weyhe, 1942. 164 p., front., plates.

WHITE, WILLIAM CHARLES, Bp., 1873-    Bronze culture of ancient China; an archaeological study of bronze objects from northern Honan, dating from about 1400 B.C.-771 B.C. [Toronto] University of Toronto Press, 1956. xviii, 219 p. illus. plates (part col.) maps. (Royal Ontario Museum, Division of Archaeology. Museum studies, 5).

## Exhibition Catalogues

CULL, A.   E.   K. Catalogue of the exhibition of ancient Chinese bronzes from the collection of A.E.K. Cull [by] W. Perceval Yetts. Durham, Durham University, School of Oriental Studies, 1953. Cover-title, 10 p. tables.

CHINESE ART SOCIETY OF AMERICA. Art of late eastern Chou; a loan exhibition [March 18 through May 7, 1952] New York, [The Society] 1952. 14 p. illus.

KARLGREN, BERNHARD, 1889-    Exhibition of early Chinese bronzes.   September, 1933. Stockholm, Museum of Far Eastern Antiquities, 1935. 64 p. plates.

LOO, C.T., and CO., New York. An exhibition of Chinese bronzes. Catalogue compiled by J. Leroy Davidson.    New York, C.T. Loo and Co., 1939. [16] p., plates.

———. An exhibition of ancient Chinese ritual bronzes, loaned by C.T. Loo and Co. The Detroit Institute of Arts, Detroit, Michigan, October 18 to November 10, 1940. [New York, Printed by the William Bradford Press, c1940] [78]p. incl. illus., plates.

———. Ancient Chinese bronzes and Chinese jewelry. An exposition of Chinese craftsmanship in the field of metal-work, which is comparable to the best of its kind in the world. Selected from the collection of C.T. Loo of New York City and shown in the special exhibition galleries of the Museum from Feb. 9 to March 2, 1941. [Toledo, The Toledo Museum of Art, 1941]. 48 p. illus.

MICHIGAN. UNIVERSITY. Museum of Art. Chinese buddhist bronzes; a loan exhibition under the joint auspices of Department of Fine Arts, Freer Fund [and] Museum of Art. April 13-May 7, 1950. [Ann Arbor, 1950] [15] p. 23 plates.

NEW YORK. METROPOLITAN MUSEUM OF ART. Chinese bronzes of the Shang (1766-1122 B.C.) through the T'ang dynasty (A.D. 618-906); an exhibition lent by American collectors and museums and shown in gallery D6 from October 19 through November 27. New York, 1938. xxxii, 29, [1] p., illus.,

plates.

ORIENTAL CERAMIC SOCIETY, London. Early Chinese bronzes from earliest times to the end of the Chou dynasty in B. C. 249; catalogue of an exhibition held from Nov. 7th to Dec. 15th 1951. London, [ 1951] 10 p. plates.

PARIS. MUSÉE CERNUSCHI. L'évolution des bronzes chinois archaïques d'après l'exposition franco-suédoise du Musée Cernuschi, mai-juin 1937; avec une préface de m. René Grousset. Paris, Les Éditions d'art et d'histoire, 1937. ix, [ 1], 64 p., front., illus., plates.

————. MUSÉE DE L'ORANGERIE. Bronzes chinois des dynasties Tcheou, Ts'in et Han. Préface et historique par Georges Salles. Musée de l'Orangerie, mai-juin 1934. Paris, 1934. 235 p. plates.

STUTTGART. STUTTGARTER KUNSTKABINETT. Chinesische Bronzen-Versteigerung, Freitag, 27 mai, 1955. Stuttgart, Roman Norbert Ketterer, [ 1955]. 20 p. illus.

YAMANAKA AND CO. Exhibition of ancient Chinese bronzes and buddhist art dating from Shang dynasty, 1766 B. C., to Yuan dynasty, A. D. 1367, Oct. 1938. New York, Yamanaka and Co., 1938. 58 p. incl. plates.

## Numismatics

CHANG, NAI-CHI, 張乃驊 . An inscribed Chinese ingot of the xii century A. D. New York, American Numismatic Society, 1944. 9, [ 1] p. front. plates. (Numismatic notes and monographs, 103).

COOLE, ARTHUR BRADDAN, 1900-  Coins in China's history. Tientsin, Student Work Department of the Tientsin Hui-wen academy, 1936. vi, 138 p. illus. (part col.).

————. A bibliography on far eastern numismatics and an union index of the currency, charms and amulets of the Far East. Peking, California College in China, College of Chinese Studies, 1940. ii-v, 421, [ 1] p.

CRAIG, ALAN DAVID, 1930-  The coins of Korea, and an outline of early Chinese coinages. Berkeley, Calif., c1955. 96 p. illus.

DAUDIN, PIERRE. Sigillographie sino-annamite. Saigon [ Impr. de l'Union, 1937] [v]-x, 321, [1] p. illus., plates, fold. tab.

GIBBS, HOWARD D. Chinese imperial names, a finding list of era and personal names on Chinese imperial coins, published under the direction of Numismatic Review. New York, J. B. Stack, M. Stack, c1944. [ 56] p.

GLATHE, HARRY. The origin and development of Chinese money. Shanghai, The China Journal Pub. Co., 1939. v-vi, 48 p. illus., plates.

IMBERT, HENRI. Les grands singes connus des anciens chinois. Pékin, Impr. de la "Politique de Pékin," 1922. 15 p. (Collection de la "Politique de Pékin")

JÖRGENSEN, HOLGER. Old coins of China; a guide to their identification. Arranged chronologically on twenty plates. n. p. 192? 6 p. illus.

KANN, EDUARD, 1880-  Illustrated catalogue of Chinese coins (gold, silver, nickel, and aluminum) [ Los Angeles] 1954 [ c1953] 476 p. 224 plates (incl. port., map).

SCHJØTH, FREDRIK, 1846-  The currency of the Far East, the Schjöth collection at the Numismatic cabinet of the University of Oslo, Norway; "What the Chinese say about their coins," by Fr. Schjöth. London, Luzac; Oslo, H. Aschehoug, 1929. 88 p. 132 plates on 66 l. (Publications of the Numismatic cabinet of the University of Oslo. no. 1).

SCHLÖSSER, RICHARD. Chinas Münzen, erläutert an der Sammlung im Missionsmuseum des Franziskanerklosters zu Dorsten in Westfalen. Werl in Westfalen, Franziskus-druckerei, 1935. 114 p. front., illus., plates (incl. ports.).

SIGLER, PHARES O. Sycee silver. New York, American Numismatic Society, 1943. 37 p. plates. (Numismatic notes and monographs, 99).

TSIANG, C. C., 蔣仲川 [ CHIANG CHUNG- CH'UAN] Illustrations of Chinese gold silver and nickel coins, 中國金銀鎳幣圖説 · Shanghai, Universal Stamp and Coin co. [1939] 4, 12, 3, 257 p. illus.

[WANG, SHOU-CH'IEN], 王守謙. Rare Chinese coins. [Shanghai, Universal
Coins and Stamps Co., 1935] cover-title, 104; cover-title, 7 p.1., 24 p.

WANG, YÜ-CH'UAN, 王毓銓, 1911-   Early Chinese coinage. New York, American Numismatic Society, 1951. viii, 254 p. plates, maps. (Numismatic
notes and monographs, 122).

## Jade: General Works

[ARNOLD, JULEAN HERBERT] 1875-1946. The alter of the green jade pagoda.
[Shanghai Printed by the  Mercury Press, 1933?] cover-title, [16] p.
illus.

BRITISH MUSEUM. Dept. of Oriental Antiquites and of Ethnography.  Chinese
archaic jades in the British Museum, by Soame Jenyns, deputy keeper.
[London] The Trustees of the British Museum, 1951. xxxviii p. 40 plates.

CHICAGO. ART INSTITUTE. Archaic Chinese jades, from the Edward and
Louise B. Sonnenschein collection. [Catalogue] by Alfred Salmony.  [Chica-
go] 1952. xiii, 279 p. 108 plates (1 col.).

DAVIS, FRANK, 1892-    Chinese jade, 2d. ed.  London, Commodore Press,
1944. 5-68 p. front., illus., plates. 1st ed. 1935. Pub. priv. by the author.

GOETTE, JOHN ANDREW, 1896-    Jade lore.  New York, Reynal and Hitchcock.
321 p. incl. col. front., illus., plates.

HANSFORD, S    HOWARD, 1899-   Chinese jade carving.  [London] Humphries, 1950. xi, 145 p. illus., maps.

LAUFER, BERTHOLD, 1874-1934. Jade; a study in Chinese archaeology and religion. [2d ed.] South Pasadena, P.D. and I. Perkins, 1946. xiv, 370 p. illus., col. plates. 1st ed. Chicago, 1912.

LIANG, WEI-MEI, 梁慧梅. An illustrated study of ancient jades, 古玉圖說
Hsin Huei, Len Hseung Yun, 1939. 1 v. plates (part col.).

LIU, T'I-CH'ING, 劉梯青. Ancient Chinese jade; explanatory notes on Mr. T.C.
Liu's unique collection of examples of Chinese art. U.S.A. representative:
Mr. Henry H. Wu, 吳協壎. Shanghai, H.H. Wu [1933] 85, [1] p. incl. illus.
(incl. ports.) plates.

LONG-SANG-TI CHINESE CURIOS CO., New York. Chinese jade, why called
"lucky stone." New York, Long sang ti 隆盛泰 Chinese Curios Co.,
[c1926] 47, [1] p. illus.

LOO, C.T., ET CIE. Jades archaïques de Chine appartenant à M.C.T. Loo,
publiés par M. Paul Pelliot. Paris et Bruxelles, G. van Oest, 1925. 120,
[8] p. xlvi plates.

MORGAN, HARRY TITTERTON, 1872-    The story of jade. Edited and copyrighted by H.T. Morgan. [Los Angeles, Broadway Press] 1941. 16 p. illus.
[Chinese classics in miniature].

NOTT, STANLEY CHARLES, 1902-    Chinese jade throughout the ages; a review
of its characteristics, decoration, folklore and symbolism, with an introduction by Sir Cecil Harcourt-Smith illustrated by 39 plates in colour and 109
from photographs together with 73 line engravings in the text.  London, B.T.
Batsford, [1936] xviii, 193 p. col. front., illus., plates (part col.) diagrs.

———. A catalogue of rare Chinese jade carvings, with an introduction by Lieut.-
General Sir Sydney Lawford, illustrated by forty-four plates from original
photographs. [St. Augustine, Printed by the Record Co.] 1940. xxii, 185 p.
incl. front., plates.

———. An analytical lecture surveying the geographical locations of Chinese jade,
[St. Augustine, Fla., Printed by the Record Co. c1941] 20 p. incl. double
map.

———. An expository historical résumé identifying one hundred and one famous
Chinese jades, illustrated with 103 reproductions from original photographs
and 21 line drawings. [St. Augustine, Fla., Printed by the Record Co. c1941]

26 p. front., plates, facsim.

――――. An illustrated annotation on the working and dating of Chinese jades, illustrated with fourteen reproductions from original photographs. Recording a lecture presented at the University of Florida, the fall session, October 20th, 1941. [St. Augustine, Fla., Printed by the Record Co., c1941] xii, 50 p. incl. col. front., 13 plates.

――――. An introductory lecture on the symbolic importance of Chinese jade. [St. Augustine, Fla., Printed by The Record Co., c1941] vi, 7-20 p.

――――. Chinese jades in the Stanley Charles Nott collection, being an illustrated descriptive record: exhaustively reviewing the symbolic ritualistic appurtenances of Chinese jades and their various sacrificial usages. Describing fully the involved formulas underlying Chinese religious services; the altar equipment and numerous superstitious practises, as they are perpetuated in Chinese jades produced throughout the ages. With an introduction by Dr. Lin Yutang and a foreword by Dr. Chih Meng; illustrated by one hundred and eighteen full page halftone plates reproduced from original photographs: together with one hundred and twenty-three line engravings, made specially for the work by Mrs. Stanley Charles Nott from selected world famous Chinese jades. Prepared as a handbook for visitors to the Jade room of the Norton gallery and school of art, West Palm Beach, Florida. [St. Augustine, Fla., Printed by the Record Co. 1942. xvi, 536 p. incl. col. front. (port.) illus., cxviii plates.

POPE-HENNESSY, Dame UNA (BIRCH),1876-1949. Early Chinese jades. London, E. Benn. 1923. [vii]-xx, 148, [1] p. illus., plates (part col.).

――――. A jade miscellany. London, Nicholson and Watson [1946] 60 p. illus., plates.

SALMONY, ALFRED, 1890-1958. Carved jade of ancient China. Berkeley, Printed at the Gillick Press, 1938. 85, [85] p. plates.

TANNER, P      de. Chinese jade, ancient and modern; descriptive catalogue, illustrating the most prominent pieces of a collection of jade articles, with special reference to sepulchral jades. Berlin, D. Reimer [etc.] 1925. 2 v. fronts., 1 illus., plates (part col., part fold.).

VASSAR COLLEGE. Art Gallery. Far eastern jades, Charles M. Pratt collection. [Poughkeepsie, N.Y. 1941] 7-62 p. front., plates.

VETLESEN, MAUDE (MONELL). Chinese jade carvings of the xvith to the xixth century, in the collection of Mrs. Georg Vetlesen; an illustrated descriptive record compiled by Stanley Charles Nott. Produced for private circulation only. [London, Printed by B.T. Batsford, 1939-40] 3 v. col. fronts., illus., plates (part col.).

WHITLOCK, HERBERT PERCY, 1868-1948. The story of jade, by Herbert P. Whitlock and Martin L. Ehrmann. New York, Sheridan House [1949] 222 p. illus., col. plates, map (on lining-papers).


Exhibition Catalogues


ARDEN GALLERY, New York. ''3000 years of Chinese jade.'' Arden Gallery, January 10th through February 11th, 1939. New York [c1939] 5-110 p. incl. plates.

CHÊNG TÊ-K'UN, 鄭德坤, 1907-   Chinese jade: an exhibition at Chengtu. Chengtu, 1945. 6 p. (West China Union University. Museum. Guidebook ser., 1).

CHINA INSTITUTE IN AMERICA. Exhibition of Chinese jade objects. Apr. 18-May 25 1946. New York, China Institute in America, 1946. [15] p. incl. illus.

――――. Exhibition of Chinese jade carvings, Sung to Ch'ien Lung loaned by a private American collector. May 3 through 23, 1954. New York, 1954. 10 p. plates.

LOO, C. T. and CO., New York. An exhibition of Chinese archaic jades. Arranged for Norton gallery of art, West Palm Beach, Florida, Jan, 20 to March 1, 1950. [New York, 1950.] 4 p. 60 plates.

MANCHESTER, ENG. Art Gallery. Catalogue of the John Yates collection of Chinese jade and other hard stones. Manchester, 1931. 26 p.

MICHIGAN. UNIVERSITY. Museum of Art. Early Chinese jades. A loan exhibition presented by the Museum of Art, University of Michigan, Alumni Memorial Hall, Ann Arbor, March 22 through April 22, 1953. [Ann Arbor, 1953] [26] p. plates.

ORIENTAL CERAMIC SOCIETY, London. Exhibition of Chinese jades from April 14th to June 9th [1948. London, 1948?] 17 p. 12 plates.

PENNSYLVANIA. UNIVERSITY. University Museum. Archaic Chinese jades; special exhibition, February, 1940. Philadelphia, University Museum [1940] 58 p. incl. front., illus.

SHANGHAI. City Museum of Greater Shanghai. Guide [to] Chinese early jade and porcelain exposition. Shanghai, 1937. 29 p.

WONG, K.    C. 王克秋? The Wong collection of ancient Chinese jades. London, Bluett and Sons, [1930] ix, 35 p. col. front., plates.

## Pottery and Procelain: General Works

ANDERSON, MALCOLM. The story of Chinese porcelain. Bexhill-on-sea, Eng., The author, 1952. Cover-title 52 p. plates, map.

BLUETT, EDGAR ERNEST. Ming and Ch'ing porcelains, a short treatise concerning some dated specimens together with some account of their distinguishing features; with a foreword by George Eumorfopoulos. London, Chiswick Press, 1933. 103, [1] p. plates, diagr.

BOERSCHMANN, ERNST, 1873-1949. Chinesische Baukeramik. Berlin, A. Lüdtke, 1927. 110 p. illus. (part mounted, incl. map) plates (part col.).

BONDY, WALTER, 1880-    Kang-hsi, eine Blüte-Epoche der chinesischen Porzellankunst, mit 16 Abbildungen im Text, 109 Tafelbildern in Wetzätzung und 6 Tafeln im Vierfarbdruck. München, Buchenau und Reichert [1923] 214, [2] p. incl. illus., plates. col. plates.

BOODE, PETER. Old Chinese pottery and porcelain recently collected in China by Peter Boode of the Hague. London, Bluett and Sons, 1934. 36, [1] p. incl. front., plates.

BRANKSTON, ARCHIBALD DOOLEY, 1902-1941. Early Ming wares of Ching-techen. Peking, H. Vetch, 1938. xvi, 102, [2] p. col. front., illus. (incl. maps) plates.

BRITISH MUSEUM. Dept. of Oriental Antiquities and of Ethnography. A guide to the pottery and porcelain of the Far East, in the Department of ceramics and ethnography; with 14 plates and 230 illustrations. [London] Printed by order of the Trustees, 1924. xvi, 168 p. front., illus. xiii plates.

———. Handbook of the pottery and porcelain of the Far East in the Department of oriental antiquities and of ethnography, by R. L. Hobson, with 20 plates and 260 illustrations. 2d ed. [London] Printed by order of the Trustees, 1937. xvi, 180 p. illus., xx plates (incl. front.).

BULLING, A    . The meaning of China's most ancient art; an interpretation of pottery patterns from Kansu (Ma Ch'ang and Panshan) and their development in the Shang, Chou, and Han periods. Leiden, E. J. Brill, 1952. xii, 150 p. illus.

BURCHARD, OTTO. Chinesische Grab-Keramik. Leipzig, E. A. Seemann [1922] 12 p. plates (Bibliothek der Kunstgeschichte, 30 ).

———. Chinesische Kleinplastik. Berlin, E. Wasmuth [1922] 10 p. plates. (Orbis pictus; Weltkunst-Bucherei, 12).

CARLYLE, RICHARD FREDRIC, 1905-    High lights on Chinese porcelain. New Orleans, B. Manheim Galleries, 1939. 72 p. plates.

CÉRAMIQUE orientale. Paris, E. Henri [1922] 3 p. 40 col. mounted plates.

CHÊNG, TÊ-K'UN, 鄭德坤, 1907- An introduction to Szechwan pottery. Chengtu, 1945. 21 p. (West China Union University. Museum. Guidebook ser., 2).

DAVID, SIR PERCIVAL VICTOR, bart., 1892- A catalogue of Chinese pottery and porcelain in the collection of Sir Percival David, by R. L. Hobson. London, Stourton Press, 1934. xl, 189, [1] p. plates (part col.).

DEXEL, THOMAS. Die Formen chinesischer Keramik; die Entwicklung der keramischen Hauptformen vom Neolithikum bis ins 18. Jahrhundert. Tübingen, E. Wasmuth [1955] 95 p. illus.

DUNCAN, ELSE SUENSON. The collecotr's first handbook on antique Chinese ceramics. [Washington] 1942. cover-title, 54 p. plates.

EUMORFOPOULOS, GEORGE, 1863-1939. The George Eumorfopoulos collection; catalogue of the Chinese, Corean and Persian pottery and porcelain, by R. L. Hobson. London, E. Benn, [1925-28] 6 v. plates (part mounted).

FARLEY, MALCOLM F., 1896-1940. Chinese porcelain; paper read before the Anti-cobweb society on May 20th, 1932, Foochow. [Foochow, Christian Herald Industrial Mission Press, 1933] 82 p.

FEDDERSEN, MARTIN, 1888- Chinesisches Porzellan, ein Brevier. Braunschweig, Kleinkhardt und Biermann [1956] 46 p. illus. (part col.).

———. Chinese porcelain. Braunschweig, Klinkhardt and Biermann, 1956. 46 p. illus. (part. col.).

———. La porcelaine chinoise. Paris, Les Presses universitaires, 1957. 20 plates (part. col.) (Mémentos illustrés).

FERNALD, HELEN ELIZABETH, 1891- Chinese pottery figurines. Toronto, Royal Ontario Museum of Archaeology, 1950. 4 p. plates.

FREER GALLERY OF ART, Washington, D. C. Ming porcelains in the Freer Gallery of Art. [Washington] Smithsonian Institution [1953] 38 p. (chiefly illus.).

FUCHS, EDUARD, 1870- Tang-plastik; chinesische Grabkeramik des vii. bis x. Jahrhunderts. Mit 6 Farbigen und 53 Schwarzen Tafeln. München, A. Langen [1924] 62 p., plates (6 col., incl. front.) (Kultur-und Kunstdokumente, i).

———. Dachreiter und verwandte chinesische Keramik des xv. bis xviii. Jahrhunderts. Mit 6 Farbigen und 52 schwarzen Tafeln. München, A. Langen [1924] 62 p. plates (6 col., incl. front.) (Kultur-und Kunstdokumente, ii).

GARNER, SIR HARRY MASON, 1891- Oriental blue and white. London, Faber and Faber [1954] xiii, 86 p. illus. (part col.) (The Faber monographs on pottery and porcelain).

GOIDSENHOVEN, JULES PIERRE VAN, 1889- La céramique chinoise sous les Ts'ing, 1644-1851. Bruxelles, R. Simonson; 1936. [9]-312 p., illus., plates (part col.).

———. La céramique chinoise; commentaires sur son évolution. Préf. par Daisy Lion-Goldschmidt. Bruxelles, Éditions de la Connaissance [1953, c1954] 213 p. 132 plates (28 col.).

GOW, LEONARD, 1859- Catalogue of the Leonard Gow collection of Chinese porcelain, by R. L. Hobson, [London, 1931] [xiii]-xxxix, 107, [1] p. plates (part col., 1 fold.; incl. front.).

GRAY, BASIL, 1904- Early Chinese pottery and porcelain. London, Faber and Faber [1953] xvi, 48 p. plates (part col.) (The Faber monographs on pottery and porcelain).

HARVARD UNIVERSITY. William Hayes Fogg Art Museum. The use of blue on Chinese porcelain of the Ming dynasty, 1368-1644. [Boston, 1947] [11] p. front.

HENTZE, CARL, 1883- Les figurines de la céramique funéraire; matériaux pour l'étude des croyances et du folklore de la Chine ancienne. Hellerau bei Dresden, Avalun-Verlag [1928] 2 v. plates.

———. Chinese tomb figures, a study in the beliefs and folklore of ancient China. With a foreword by W. Perceval Yetts. London, E. Goldston, 1928. xii, 105,

[1] p. plates.

HETHERINGTON, ARTHUR LONSDALE, 1881-   The pottery and porcelain factories of China; their geographical distribution and periods of activity. With a folding map of China. London, K. Paul; New York, E. P. Dutton, 1921. 15 p. fold. map.

——. The early ceramic wares of China, with one hundred illustrations of which twelve are in colour. New York, C. Scribner, 1922; London, E. Benn, 1922. Abridged ed., London, E. Benn, 1924. xvii, [1], 159, [1] p. col. front., plates (part col.).

——. Chinese ceramic glazes. [2d rev. ed.] South Pasadena [Calif.] P. D. and I. Perkins [1948] 114 p. illus. (part col.). 1st ed. Cambridge University Press, 1939.

HOBSON, ROBERT LOCKHART, 1872-1941. The art of the Chinese potter from the Han dynasty to the end of the Ming, illustrated in a series of 192 examples selected, described and with an introduction by R. L. Hobson and A. L. Hetherington. London, E. Benn; New York, A. Knopf, 1923. xx, 20 p., col. front., plates (part col.).

——. The wares of the Ming dynasty. With one hundred and twenty-eight illustrations of which eleven are in colour. London, Benn; New York, C. Scribner's 1923. xvi, 240 p. illus., plates (part col,; incl. front.).

——. Chinese pottery statute of a Lohan. London, British Museum, 1925. Cover-title, 7 p. col. plate.

——. The later ceramic wares of China, being the blue and white, famille verte, famille rose, monochromes, etc., of the K'ang Hsi, Yung Chêng, Ch'ien Lung and other periods of the Ch'ing dynasty. London, E. Benn, 1925. xxix, 155, [1] p. illus., plates (part col., part fold.; incl. col. front.)

——. Chinese porcelain and Wedgwood pottery, with other works of ceramic art. London, B. T. Batsford [1928] xii, 227 p. illus. plates, (Port Sunlight. Lady Lever art gallery, A record of the collections, 2 ).

——. Chinese ceramics in private collections, by R. L. Hobson, Bernard Rackham and William King. London, Halton and T. Smith, 1931. vii-xvi, 201, xvii-xxii p. illus., 32 col. mounted plates.

HONEY, WILLIAM BOWYER, 1889-   The ceramic art of China, and other countries of the Far East. London, Faber and Faber and the Hyperion Press [1945] vii, [1], 238 p. illus. (incl. map) 192 (i. e. 195) plates (3 mounted col.)

HSIANG, YUAN-P'IEN, 項元汴, 1525-1590. Noted porcelains of successive dynasties with comments and illustrations. Revised and annotated by Kuo Pao-ch'ang, 郭葆昌 , and John C. Ferguson. Peiping, Chih Chai Publ. Co., 1931. 200 l. incl. 85 col. plates, port.

HYDE, JOHN ALDEN LLOYD. Oriental Lowestoft, Chinese export porcelain. (Porcelaine de la Cie des Indes) With special reference to the trade with China and the porcelain decorated for the American market. [2d ed.] Newport, Monmouthshire, Ceramic Book Co. [1954] viii, 166 p. 36 plates (part col.) 1st ed. New York, C. Scribner, 1936.

JENYNS, SOAME, 1904-   Later Chinese porcelain; the Ch'ing Dynasty, 1644-1912. London, Faber and Faber [1951] xi, 104 p. 124 plates (part col.)(The Faber monographs on pottery and porcelain).

——. Ming pottery and porcelain. London, Faber and Faber [1953] xi, 160 p. 124 plates (part col.) (The Faber monographs on pottery and porcelain).

KOYAMA. FUJIO. The story of old Chinese ceramics; translated by Jiro Harada. Tokyo, Mayuyama, 1949. 30 p. plates, map.

LAN, P'U, 藍浦, d. 1795. Ching-tê-chên t'ao-lu, 景德鎮陶錄 ; or, The potteries of China, being a translation with notes and an introd. by Geoffrey R. Sayer. [London] Routledge and Kegan Paul [1951] xxiv, 139 p.

LIANG, SSU YUNG, 梁思永, 1903-1954. New stone age pottery from the prehistoric site at Hsi-yin Tsun, Shansi, China. Menasha, Wis., American Anthropological Association [1930] cover-title, 76, [3] p. illus. (incl. plan) plates, diagrs. (Memoirs of the American anthropological association, 37).

LION, DAISY (GOLDSCHMIDT) Les poteries et porcelaines chinoises. Paris, Presses universitaires, 1957. viii, 196 p. plates, (part. col.).

LOO, C. T., et Cie. Briques et objets céramiques funéraires de l'époque des Han, appartenant à C. T. Loo et cie, publiés par Olov Jansé. Paris, Les Éditions d'art et d'histoire, 1936. 39, [1] p., illus., plates.

MARCH, BENJAMIN, 1899-1934. Standards of pottery description. With an introductory essay by Carl E. Guthe. Ann Arbor, University of Michigan Press, 1934. 55 p. illus., plates (Michigan. University. Museum of anthropology. Occasional contributions, 3).

MARQUET DE VASSELOT, JEAN JOSEPH, 1871- La céramique chinoise, par J. J. Marquet de Vasselot et Mlle. M. -J. Ballot. [Paris] A. Morancé [c1922] 2 v. plates (part col.) (Documents d'arf. Musée du Louvre).

——. Chinese ceramics by J. J. Marquet de Vasselot and Mlle. M. -J. Ballot, translated by G. Brosseau and P. J. Angoulvent. Paris, A. Morancé [1922] 2 v. plates, (Documents d'art. The Louvre museum).

MEDCALF, C. J. B. Introduction to Chinese pottery and porcelain. With a foreword by Alan Barlow. Published for the Oriental Ceramic Society. London, Cresset Press, 1955. 64 p. illus.

MORGAN, HARRY TITTERTON, 1872- ed. Chinese porcelain and pottery. [Los Angeles, Broadway Press] 1941. 16 p. illus. [Chinese classics in miniature].

OSGOOD, CORNELIUS, 1905- Blue-and-white Chinese porcelain; a study of form. New York, Ronald Press, [1956] xvii, 166 p. illus., 64 plates.

PALMGREN, NILS, 1890- Kansu mortuary urns of the Pan Shan and Ma Chang groups. Plates I-XLI and 228 text figures. Peiping, Geological Survey of China, 1934. ix, 204, [82] p., illus., plates (part col.) (China. Geological survey. Palaeontologia sinica, ser. D, vol. iii, fasc. 1).

PELKA, OTTO, 1875- Chinesisches Porzellan. Leipzig, Schmidt und Günther, 1921. 148 p. col. front. plates (part col.) 1st ed. 1914.

PHILLIPS, JOHN GOLDSMITH. China-trade porcelain; an account of its historical background, manufacture, and decoration, and a study of the Helena Woolworth McCann collection. Cambridge, Published for the Winfield Foundation and the Metropolitan Museum of Art [by] Harvard University Press; London, Phaidon Press, 1956. xxi, 234 p. illus. (part col.) maps.

POPE, JOHN ALEXANDER, 1906- Fourteenth-century blue-and-white; a group of Chinese porcelains in the Topkapu Sarayi Müzesi, Istanbul. Washington, 1952. iii, 85 p. 44 plates (Freer Gallery of Art occasional papers, 2:1).

——. Chinese porcelains from the Ardebil shrine. Washington, Smithsonian Insitution, Freer Gallery of Art, 1956. xv, 194 p. illus., 142 plates (incl. map, facsim., plan).

REIDEMEISTER, LEOPOLD. Ming-porzellane in schwedischen Sammlungen; mit einem Geleitwort von J. Hellner. Berlin und Leipzig, W. de Gruyter, 1935. 34 p. plates.

RIVIÈRE, HENRI, 1864- La céramique dans l'art d'Extrême-Orient; recueil de cent soixante-deux pièces reproduites en couleurs d'après les originaux choisis dans les musées et dans les collections françaises et étrangères. Préface de Charles Vignier. Paris, A. Lévy, 1923. 2 v. mounted col. illus., 100 mounted col. plates.

RÜCKER-EMBDEN, OSCAR, 1865- Chinesische Frühkeramik, eine Einführung. Leipzig, K. W. Hiersemann, 1922. xii, 174 p. illus. plates, (part col.) map.

SCHMIDT, ROBERT, 1878-1952. Chinesische Keramik von der Han-zeit bis zum xix. Jahrhundert, hrsg. unter Mitarbeit von Alfred Oppenheim und Karl Bacher. Frankfurt a. M., Frankfurter Verlags-Anstalt, 1924. 117, [1] p., plates (part col. mounted).

THIEL, ALBERT WILLEM RUDOLF. Chinese pottery and stoneware. Los Angeles, Borden Pub. Co., 1953. xiv, 204 p. illus., plates (part col.).

VICTORIA AND ALBERT MUSEUM, South Kensington. Guide to the later Chinese porcelain, periods of K'ang Hsi, Yung Chêng and Ch'ien Lung, by W. B. Honey. London, Pub. under the authority of the Board of Education, 1927. xxi, 123 p. illus., plates [ Victoria and Albert museum, South Kensington. Publication, 183c].

———. Handbook to the W. G. Gulland bequest of Chinese porcelain, including some notes on the subjects of the decoration. London, H. M. Stationery Off., 1950. 57 p. 48 plates.

VOLKER, T    . Porcelain and the Dutch East India Company, as recorded in the Dagh-registers of Batavia Castle, those of Hirado and Deshima, and other contemporary papers, 1602-1682. [ Leiden, E. J. Brill, 1954] 243 p. plates, fold. maps, facsim. (Mededelingen van het Rijksmuseum voor Volkenkunde, Leiden, 11).

WHITE, WILLIAM CHARLES, 1873-   Tomb tile pictures of ancient China; an archaeological study of pottery tiles from tombs of western Honan, dating about the third century B. C. Toronto, University of Toronto Press, 1939. xx, 69 p. front., illus., plates (1 col.) 2 maps on 1 l. (Royal Ontario museum of archaeology. Museum studies, 1).

WILLIAMSON, GEORGE CHARLES, 1858-   The book of famille rose; with 19 plates in colour and 43 plates in collotype. London, Methuen, [ 1927] xxii, 231, [ 1] p. plates (part. col; incl. front. ).

WU, G. D., 吳金鼎[ WU CHIN-TING]. Prehistoric pottery in China. London, Pub. on behalf of the Courtauld Institute of Art, University of London, by Kegan Paul [ 1938] xi, [ 1], 180 p. illus. (map) plates.

ZIMMERMANN, ERNST, 1866-1940. Chinesisches Porzellan und die übrigen keramischen Erzeugnisse Chinas. 2. Aufl. Leipzig, Klinkhardt und Bier - mann, 1923. 2 v. plates (part col. ) map.

———. Altchinesische Porzellane im Alten Serai. Berlin und Leipzig, W. de Gruyter, 1930. 51 p. plates (part col. ) (Meisterwerke der türkischen museen zu Konstantinopel, hrsg. von Halil Edhem. bd. ii).

## Exhibition Catalogues

ALLARD, F. Collection F. Allard; catalogue de céramique de la Chine, Ming, Kanchi, Yung-ching et Kienlung. Paris, Galeries G. Petit, 1925. 35 p. plates.

ARNIM-MUSKAU, HERMANN GRAF VON. Sammlung Hermann Graf von Arnim-Muskau chinesische Keramik beschrieben von Leopold Reidemeister. Köln, Math. Lempertz Kunstauktionshaus [ 1951] 26 p. plates.

ART ASSOCIATION OF INDIANAPOLIS, INDIANA. John Herron Art Institute. Chinese ceramics of the Sung dynasty [ by Wilbur D. Peat] Indianapolis, John Herron Art Museum [ 194 ?] 15 p. illus. (part col. ) map.

BOSTON, MUSEUM OF FINE ARTS. Exhibition of Chinese ceramics lent by Mr. and Mrs. Eugene Bernat on Sept. 9 through Oct. 19, 1947. [ Boston, 1947] 37 p. plates.

———. Exhibition of Chinese ceramics and of European drawings. March 12-April 26, 1953. [ Portland, Me., Anthoensen Press, 1953] xii, 34 p. plates.

BROOKLYN INSTITUTE OF ARTS AND SCIENCES. Museum. Chinese ceramics, a catalogue of an anonymous loan collection. Exhibition, December 14, 1944 through February 4, 1945, the Brooklyn Museum, Brooklyn, N. Y. [ Brooklyn, 1944] 34 p. front., illus.

[ BUFFALO. MUSEUM OF SCIENCE] The art of the Chinese potter from prehistoric times to Kubla Khan. [ Buffalo, 1943] 6, [ 26] p. illus.

CHINA INSTITUTE IN AMERICA. Exhibition of three-color porcelain figures of the K'ang Hsi period. May 18-June 14, 1945. New York, 1945. 15 p. 21 numb. figs.

CHINESE ART SOCIETY OF AMERICA. Art of late eastern Chou; a loan exhibition [ March 18 through May 7, 1952] New York, 1952. 14 p. illus.

DAVID, SIR PERCIVAL VICTOR, bart. 1892-   Illustrated catalogue of tung, ju,
kuan, chün, kuang-tung and glazed I-hsing wares in the Percival David Foundation of Chinese Art, by S. Yorke Hardy. London, 1953. xiv, 44 p. illus.
———. Illustrated guide to the collection by Lady David. London, Percival David Foundation of Chinese art, 1956. ii, 28 p. plates.

DE FOREST, MRS. S.   K. Rare Sung and Ming porcelains and pottery, Ch'ing
decorated porcelains including ku-yüeh hsüan and other imperial wares, collection of Mrs. S.K. De Forest; sold by her order; with additions; public
sale January 11 [1936] [New York] American Art Association, Anderson
Galleries, inc., 1936. [48] p. illus.

ECKE, GUSTAV, 1896-   Hui Hsien ware in the collection of the Honolulu academy of arts. Honolulu, Academy of Arts, 1954. [11] p. front., plates,
(Special studies, 2).

EDINBURGH. ROYAL SCOTTISH MUSEUM. Chinese pottery and porcelain.
Edinburgh, H.M. Stationery Off., 1955. [4] p. 24 plates.

FRANKFURT A MAIN. Kunstgewerbe-Museum. Ausstellung chinesischer Keramik. Aus Frankfurter und auswärtigem Privat-und Museumbesitz vom juni
bis September 1923. Franfurt a. M., Englert und Schlosser, 1923. 151 p.
plates (part col.).

FRIENDS OF FAR EASTERN ART. Exhibition of Chinese tomb statuettes, San
Francisco Museum of Art, July 2 to August 30, 1937. San Francisco, [c1937]
ix, 13-43 p. plates.

GLASGOW. Art Gallery. The Chinese stonewares and porcelains in the Burrell
collection. Glasgow, 195?   36 p. plates.

GOLDSCHMIDT, JAKOB. Catalogue of the important collection of fine Chinese
enamelled porcelain of the 17th and 18th centuries, the property of Jakob
Goldschmidt, Esq., which will be sold at auction by Messrs. Christie, Manson and Woods on Wednesday, June 29, 1938 and following day. London,
Christie, Manson and Woods, 1938. 72 p.

HOLMES FOUNDATION, INC., New York.  Chinese ceramics and jades, Persian
pottery, Egyptian antiquities, Gothic and renaissance art, French furniture
of the xviii century and the empire and other art property; from the collection
of the late Mrs. Christian R. Holmes, now the property of Holmes Foundation,
inc, sold by order of the directors. Public auction sale April 15 to 18 inclusive. New York, Parke-Bernet Galleries, 1942. 234 p. incl. front., illus.,
plates.

HONGKONG. UNIVERSITY. Institute of Oriental Studies. Chinese tomb pottery
figures; catalogue of exhibition, 26th-28th September, 1953. [Hong Kong]
Hong Kong University Press, 1953. 15, [23] p. illus. (Its Catalogue series,1).

HUTTON, BARBARA, 1912-   The Barbara Hutton Collection of Chinese porcelain; [exhibition] Honolulu Academy of Arts, November 1956-January 1957.
[Honolulu, Honolulu Academy of Arts, 1957] 36 p. illus.

INSTITUTE OF ORIENTAL CERAMICS, Tokyo. Catalogue of the T'ang polychrome, compiled by the Institute of Oriental Ceramics. Tokyo, Iwanami,
1928. 36 1. 50 plates in portfolio.
———. Oriental ceramics, 1934-35. [Tokyo?] The Institute of Oriental Ceramics,
1936. 34 p. plates.

JOHNSON, A        BURLINGAME. Hand book of a collection of Chinese porcelains loaned by A. Burlingame Johnson. On exhibition in the Los Angeles museum of history, science and art. [Los Angeles] 1923. 149 p. incl. plates
mounted col. front. (Los Angeles museum of history, science and art. Miscellaneous publication, 3).

LOO, C. T. and CO., New York. An exhibition of figures in Chinese art in April
of 1946. New York, C.T. Loo and Co. 1946. [15] p. illus.
———. An exhibition of the wares of the Sung dynasty from March 29 to April 30,
1947. New York, C.T. Loo and Co., 1947. [10] p.

LOS ANGELES COUNTY MUSEUM. Chinese ceramics, from the prehistoric
    period through Ch'ien Lung; a loan exhibition from collections in America
    and Japan. Mar. 14 to Apr. 27, 1952. [Los Angeles, 1952] 119 p. illus.,
    map.
MANCHESTER, ENG. ART GALLERY. Catalogue of Chinese porcelain. [Man-
    chester] 1931. 22 p. plates.
MILLS COLLEGE, Oakland, Calif. Art Gallery. Early Chinese pottery; Mills
    college art gallery, Portland art museum; April, May, June 1941. [Berke-
    ley, Gillick Press, 1941] viii, [9]-45 p. 1 mounted illus., plates.
————. The potter's art in China (prehistoric through Sung), March 13-May 6,
    1955, Oakland, 1955. 24 p. illus.
NEW YORK, METROPOLITAN MUSEUM OF ART. Chinese porcelains in the Alt-
    man collection. New York, 1953. 111 p. 29 col. plates. (part col.).
ORIENTAL CERAMIC SOCIETY, London. Ming blue-and-white porcelain; cata-
    logue of an exhibition held from October 24th to December 21st, 1946. Lon-
    don [1948] 14 p. 4 plates.
————. Chinese ceramic figures; catalogue of an exhibition held from April 8th
    to June 21st, 1947. London [1948] 15 p. 5 plates.
————. Celadon wares; catalogue of an exhibition held from October 20th to Dec-
    ember 20th, 1947. London [1948] 19 p. 8 plates.
————. Monochrome porcelain of the Ming and Manchu dynasties; catalogue of an
    exhibition held from October 27th to December 18th, 1948. London [1948]
    22 p. plates.
————. Wares of the T'ang dynasty; catalogue of an exhibition held from April
    27th to June 8th, 1949. London [1949] 15 p. 4 plates.
————. Sung dynasty wares: Ting, ying ch'ing and Tz'u Chou; catologue of an ex-
    hibition held from November 9th to December 17th, 1949. London [1949] 15
    p. 4 plates.
————. Enamelled polychrome porcelain of the Manchu dynasty (1644-1912); cata-
    logue of an exhibition from May 23 to July 21, 1951. London, 1951. 19 p.
    plates.
————. Sung dynasty wares: Chün and brown glazes. Catalogue of an exhibition
    from May 1st to 31st, 1952. London, [1952] 16 p. plates.
————. Ju and Kuan wares; imperial wares of the Sung dynasty, related wares
    and derivatives of later date. Catalogue of an exhibition held from Nov. 12 to
    Dec. 13. 1952. London, 1952. 16 p. plates.
————. Pre-T'ang wares; catalogue of an exhibition held from April 29 to June 10,
    1953. London, 1953. 16 p. plates.
————. Catalogue of an exhibition of Chinese blue and white porcelain 14th to 19th
    centuries held from Dec. 16, 1953 to Jan. 23, 1954 at the Arts Council Gal-
    lery. London, 1953. [32] p. plates.
————. Catalogue of an exhibition of the arts of the T'ang dynasty, held from Feb.
    25 to March 30, 1955 at the Arts Council Gallery. [London, 1955]. 40 p.
    plates.
PASADENA, CALIF. ART INSTITUTE. An exhibition of old Chinese ceramics
    from the Late Chou dynasty through the Sung dynasty lent by Robert Hilton
    Simmons, Los Angeles. Pasadena, the Institute, 1953. 15 p. illus.
STOCKHOLM. HALLWYLSKA PALATSET. Catalogue of the collection of ceram-
    ic art of China and other countries of the Far East at the Hallwyl Museum,
    group XLVIII. Drawn up by Orvar Karlbeck. Stockholm, 1949. 212 p. illus.
    plates, map.
U.S. National Gallery of Art. Works of art from the Widener collection. Wash-
    ington, D.C., National Gallery of Art, 1942. 24 p.
VASSAR COLLEGE. Art Gallery. Far eastern ceramics, Charles M. Pratt col-
    lection. [Menasha, Wis., George Banta Pub. Co. 1940] 79, [1] p. incl.
    front., xii plates on 6 l.
WHITRIDGE, WILLIAM HALL; 1849-    Orientalia collected by Mr. and Mrs.

William H. Whitridge. Baltimore, Md., mcmxii. Baltimore museum of art loan exhibition, June 1 to October 15, 1930. [Baltimore, c1930] 131 p. plates.

YAMANAKA AND CO. Exhibition of Chinese pottery horses and camels, dating from the Han dynasty to the 20th century, September, 1934. New York, Yamanaka [1934] cover-title, [28] p. illus.

Paintings: General Works

ACKER, WILLIAM REYNOLDS BEAL, 1907- ed. and tr. Some T'ang and pre-T'ang texts on Chinese painting, translated and annotated. Leiden, E. J. Brill, 1954. lxii, 414 p. (Sinica Leidensia, 8).

BAHR, A W. Early Chinese paintings from A. W. Bahr collection, by Osvald Sirén. London, Chiswick Press, 1938. 116 p. incl. xxv (i.e. 27) mounted plates. (part col.).

BALL, KATHERINE M. 1859- Bamboo, its cult and culture, paintings by Wang Tseng-tsu, 王曾祖, imperial prince painter. Interpretative text and art analysis by Katherine M. Ball. Berkeley, Gillick Press, 1945. 7-109 p. incl. plates, double facsim.

BINYON, LAURENCE, 1869-1943. Chinese paintings in English collections. Paris and Brussels, G. Van Oest, 1927. 68 p. illus. plates.

———. Les peintures chinoises dans les collections d'Angleterre. Pairs et Bruxelles, G. Van Oest, 1927. 68 p. illus., lxiv plates. (Ars Asiatica; études et documents ix).

———. Painting in the Far East; an introduction to the history of pictorial art in Asia, especially China and Japan. 4th ed., rev. throughout. London, E. Arnold, 1934. xvi, 302 p. col. front., xli plates. 1st ed. 1908.

———. Art of the Far East, paintings from China and Japan; 15 plates in colour; with an introduction by Laurence Binyon. London, B. T. Batsford, [1936] 6 p. xv col. plates (Batsford's ''Art and nature in colour'' series).

———. Art of the Far East; landscapes, flowers, animals; 16 plates in colour from the work of old Chinese and Japanese masters. London, New York, Batsford [1950] 8 p. col. plates (Iris colour books).

BOSTON. MUSEUM OF FINE ARTS. Portfolio of Chinese paintings in the Museum (Han to Sung periods). A descriptive text by Kojiro Tomita. Cambridge, Pub. for the Museum of Fine Arts, Boston, by the Harvard University Press, 1933, 2nd ed. 1938. ix, [1], 20, [1] p. 144 plates.

BRITISH MUSEUM. Dept. of Prints and Drawings. Six Chinese paintings, reproduced in colour. [London and Banbury, Printed by H. Stone, 19--] 6 col. plates.

———. An index of Chinese artists represented in the Sub-department of Oriental prints and drawings in the British Museum, by Arthur Waley. [London] Printed by order of the Trustees, 1922. xii, 112 p.

BRODRICK, ALAN HOUGHTON. An outline of Chinese painting. New York, Transatlantic Arts [1949] London, Avalon Press, 1949. 40 p. 50 plates (part col.).

CH'EN, ALICE T. 陳蔡佩珠. How to paint landscapes in ancient Chinese technique; assisted with English text by her pupil, Ruth Stevens. Honkong [1955?] 93 p. illus.

CH'EN, JEN-DAO, 陳仁濤. The three patriarches of the Southern school in Chinese paintings. [A lecture given in the Sino-British Club of Hong Kong, Feb. 18, 1955] Hong Kong, 1955. 8 l.

CH'ÊNG, HSI, 程曦. The original spirit and cultural background of Chinese painting. English version translated by H. P. Wu, 吳鴻碧. Hong Kong, Sun Wah Print. Co. [1957] 55 p.; 43 p.

CHIANG, YEE, 蔣彝, 1903- The Chinese eye, an interpretation of Chinese painting; with a preface by S. I. Hsiung. 2d ed. London, Methuen, [1936] xvi,

240 p. illus., xxiv plates (incl. front.).

———. The same; 4th rev. ed. London, Faber and Faber, 1956.

———. Chinese painting, with an introduction and notes. [London] Faber and Faber [1953] 24 p. mounted col. illus. (The Faber gallery of oriental art).

CHINESE ART SOCIETY OF AMERICA. Kung Hsien, 龔賢 , and the Nanking school: some Chinese paintings of the 17th century. A loan exhibition. Introduction by Aschwin Lippe. New York, China House, 1955. 10 p. plates.

COHN, WILLIAM, 1880-  Chinese painting. [2d rev. ed.] London, Phaidon Press [1951]; New York, Oxford Univ. Press, 1951. 112 p. 275 illus. (part mounted col.) 1st ed. 1948.

———. Peinture chinoise. London, Phaidon Press, 1948. 29 p. illus. plates.

———. Chineesche Schilderkunst. London, Phaidon Press, 1948. 29 p. illus., 177 plates.

CONTAG, VICTORIA, comp. Maler- und Sammler-stempel aus der Ming- und Ch'ing-zeit, gesammelt und bearbeitet von Victoria Contag und Wang Chi-ch'üan, 王季銓. [Shanghai] Commercial Press, 1940. lxxv, 631 p. illus.

———. Die Beiden Steine; Beitrag zum Verständnis des Wesens Chinesischer Landschaftsmalerei. Braunschweig, H. Klemm [1950] 101 p. 32 plates.

———. Zwei Meister chinesischer Landschaftsmalerei, Shih-T'ao, 石濤, und Shih-ch'i 石谿: Ein Beitrag zum Verständnis des Wesens chinesischer Landschaftsmalerei. Baden-Baden, W. Klein [1956] 101 p. plates.

DESIGNS from the Tunhuang caves. With an introd. by Wang Hsun, 王遜. Designs copied by Chou Shao-Miao and Wu Mi-Feng. Peking, Foreign Languages Press, 1956. 20 l. (in portfolio).

DIEZ, ERNST, 1878-  Shan shui, dei chinesische Landschaftsmalerei. Wien, W. Andermann, 1943. 7-87 p. illus. 60 plates.

DUBOSC, JEAN PIERRE. Paintings by Chinese masters, Pao hui chi, 寶繪集. Twelve paintings reproduced in collotype from the collection of J. P. Dubosc. Peking, 1937. [5] p. plates.

DUTHUIT, GEORGES, 1891-  Mystique chinoise et peinture moderne. Paris, Chroniques du jour, 1936. 172 p. illus.

———. Chinese mysticism and modern painting. Paris, Chroniques du jour; London, A. Zwemmer [c1936] 155, [16] p. incl. 60 plates.

EUMORFOPOULOS, GEORGE, 1863-1939. The George Eumorfopoulos collection; catalogue of the Chinese frescoes, by Laurence Binyon. London, E. Benn, [1927] vii, 22 p. l.col. mounted plates.

———. The same; catalogue of the Chinese, Corean and Siamese paintings, by Laurence Binyon. London, E. Benn, [1928] vii, 39 p. plates (part col. mounted).

FEI, CH'ENG-WU, 費成武. Brush drawing in the Chinese manner. London, Studio Publications, 1957. 95 p. front. illus. (How to do it ser. 73).

FERGUSON, JOHN CALVIN, 1866-1945. Stories in Chinese paintings. [Shanghai, 1925] cover-title, p. [110]-133. Reprinted from the Journal of the North China branch of the Royal Asiatic society, vol. lvi. 1925.

———. Chinese painting. Chicago, University of Chicago Press [c1927] ix, 199 p. plates (part col.) port.

FINSTERBUSCH, KÄTE. Das Verhältnis des Schan-hai-djing zur bildenden Kunst. Berlin, Akademie-Verlag, 1952. 136 p. illus. (Abhandlungen der Sächsischen Akademie der Wissenschaften zu Leipzig. Phil-Hist. Kl. Bd. 46, 1).

FISCHER, OTTO, 1886-1948. Die chinesische Malerei der Han-dynastie, mit 80 Lichtdrucktafeln und einer Farbtafel. Berlin, P. Neff, 1931. xi, 150 p. plates (part fold., 1 col.).

———. Kunst des Fernen Ostens; Landschaften, Blumen, Tiere; 15 Farbtafeln nach Bildern alter chinesischer und japanischer Meister; Einführung von Otto Fischer. Bern, Iris Verlag [c1935] 10 p. xv col. plates (Iris bücher, hrsg. von H. Zbinden).

——. Chinesische Landschaftsmalerei 3., new bearb. und bereicherte Aufl. Mit 135 Bildwiedergaben. Berlin/Wien, P. Neff, 1943. 222 p. illus., 106 plates (part fold.).

FLEURS et papillons chinois. Introduction de P. W. Meister. Traduction de Eugène Bestaux. Paris, Arts et métiers graphiques, 1956. 8 p. col. plates (Le Verger, 3).

GRANTHAM, ALEXANDRA ETHELDRED, (von Herder), 1867- Wang Wei paysagiste. Pékin, Impr. de la "Politique de Pékin," 1922. 24 p. (Collection de la "Politique de Pékin").

GROSSE, ERNST, 1862-1927. Die ostasiatische Tuschmalerei. Mit 160 Tafeln. Berlin, B. Cassirer, 1923. 5-51 p. 160 plates (Die Kunst des Ostens, vi).

GROUSSET, RENÉ, 1885-1952. L'art de l'Extrême Orient; paysages, fleurs, animaux. 15 planches en couleurs d'après les tableaux des vieux maîtres chinois et japonais. Text de René Grousset. Paris, Plon [c1936] 10 p. 15 col. plates. (Collection "Iris").

——. Art of the Far East: landscapes, flowers, animals. 16 plates in color from the work of old Chinese and Japanese masters. Introduction by René Grousset. New York, Toronto, Oxford University Press [1945] 10 p. col. front., xv col. plates (Iris books) 1st ed. 1939.

HACKNEY, LOUISE WALLACE. Guide-posts to Chinese painting, edited by Paul Pelliot. Boston and New York, Houghton Mifflin, 1927. xii, 221 p. front., plates.

[HARADA, KINJIRO] The pageant of Chinese painting. Tokyo, The Otsuka-kogeisha, 1936. 8, [41] p. 1000 plates.

JENYNS, SOAME, 1904- A background to Chinese painting, with a preface for collectors by W. W. Winkworth. London, Sidgwick and Jackson, 1935. xxviii, 208, [1] p. plates (incl. front.).

KUO, HSI, 郭熙, b. ca. 1020. An essay on landscape painting, by Kuo Hsi; translated by Shio Sakanishi; a foreword by L. Cranmer-Byng. London, J. Murray [1935] 64 p. (The wisdom of the East series).

KUO, JO-HSU, 郭若盧, fl. 1074. Experiences in painting (T'u-hua chien-wên chih, 圖畫見聞志 ) An eleventh century history of Chinese painting, together with the Chinese text in facsimile; translated and annotated by Alexander Coburn Soper. Washington, American Council of Learned Societies, 1951. xiii, 216 p. facsim.: [68] p. (American Council of Learned Societies. Studies in Chinese and related civilizations, 6).

LAUFER, BERTHOLD, 1874-1934. T'ang, Sung and Yüan paintings belonging to various Chinese collectors, described by Berthold Laufer. Paris and Brussels, G. van Oest, 1924. 17 p. xxx plates.

LEE, SHERMAN E. 1918- Chinese landscape painting. Cleveland, Cleveland Museum of Art [1954] 169 p. illus.

——. Streams and mountains without end; a Northern Sung handscroll and its significance in the history of early Chinese painting, by Sherman E. Lee and Wen Fong, 方聞. Ascona, Switzerland, Artibus Asiae, 1955. 57 p. ·llus., 25 plates. (Artibus Asiae. Supplementum 14).

LEYDEN, JO VAN. Chinesische Landschaften. [With a commentary in German, English and French] Zürich, Verlag der Arche [1948] 13 p. 15 plates. (Die Kleinen Bücher der Arche, 57, 58).

LIN, TSIU-SEN, 林秋生 [LIN, CHIU-SHÊNG] Chinesische Legenden aus dem Chinesischen mit vier Farbenlichtdrucken nach chinesischen Gemälden aus dem 17. Jahrhundert. Berlin, A. Metzner [1938] [20] p. 4 col. mounted plates.

——. Meisterwerke chinesischer Malerei 12. bis 18. Jahrhundert, eingeleitet von Lin Tsiu-sen, mit acht Faksimile-reproduktionen in 13-farbigem Photochrom. Zürich, Amstutz, Herdeg, 1943. 12 p. 8 col. plates.

——. Masterpieces of Chinese painting; 12th to 18th centuries. With an introd. with 8 facsim. reproductions in 13-colour photochrome. [2d ed.] Zürich,

Amstutz, Herdeg, 1947. 12 p. 8 col. plates (in portfolio).

——. Meisterwerke chinesischer Tuschezeichnungen, 7. bis 13. Jahrhundert. 22 Reproduktionen. 2. Aufl. Zürich, Amstutz, Herdeg [c1948] [8] p. illus. 1 ed. 1946.

MA, YUAN, 馬遠, 1190-1224. Pécheurs chinois; un chef-d'oeuvre de la peinture Song. Pékin, Impr. de l'Ile de peupliers, c1938. 1 p. plates.

——. Chinese fishermen; a masterpiece of the Sung dynasty. Peking, The Poplar Island Press, c1938. [2] p. plates.

MARCH, BENJAMIN, 1899-1934. Some technical terms of Chinese painting. Baltimore, Waverly Press, 1935. xiii, 55, [1] p. 1 illus., plates. [American council of learned societies. Studies in Chinese and related civilization, 2].

MEYER, AGNES ELIZABETH (ERNST) 1887-   Chinese painting as reflected in the thought and art of Li Lung-mien李龍眠1070-1106, by Agnes E. Meyer. [2d ed.] New York, Duffield, 1923. ix-xii, [2], 251, [1] p. plates.

MOORE, ADA (SMALL) 1858-1954. A study of Chinese paintings in the collection of Ada Small Moore, by Louise Wallace Hackney and Yau Chang-foo, 姚昌復. London, New York, Oxford University Press, 1940. xvi, 279 p. plates (part col., part fold.) ports., facsims.

——. ——Supplement.   [Distinguished scholars feast before parting, by Shēn Chou, 沈周. London, New York, Oxford University Press, c1941] 10 p.

MÜNSTERBERG, HUGO, 1916-   The landscape painting of China and Japan. Rutland, Vt., C.E. Tuttle Co. [1955] xv, 144 p. col. front., 101 plates.

NEW YORK. METROPOLITAN MUSEUM OF ART. Chinese paintings; a picture book. New York [The Museum Press] 1940. 20 plates, [Its Picture books].

——. Portraits of the court of China, by Alan Priest. [New York] Metropolitan Museum of Art, 1942. 5 p. 22 plates.

——. Ch'ing Ming Shang Ho,清明上河圖, spring festival on the river. A scroll painting (ex. coll. A. W. Bahr) of the Ming Dynasty after a Sung Dynasty subject, reproduced in its entirety and in its original size in a portfolio of 23 collotype plates and 12 enl. details, with an introd. and notes by Alan Priest, curator of Far Eastern art. New York, 1948. [15] p. [30] plates (in portfolio).

ODIN, ULRICH. Peintures chinoises et japonaises de la collection Ulrich Odin, avec une introduction et des notices de m. Ulrich Odin, et un avant-propos de m. Sylvain Lévi. Paris et Bruxelles, Les Éditions G. van Oest, 1929. vii, 62, [2] p. plates. (Ars asiatica; études et documents xiv).

P'ANG, YUAN-CHI, 龐元濟. Masterpieces of Chinese painting by famous painters from T'ang dynasty to Ch'ing dynasty, 7th to 19th centuries A.D. Collection of P'ang Shu-chai, 龐虛齋, esq. Edited by Fan Pai-yen, 樊伯炎, Wu Yen-chen, 吳彥臣, P'and Ping-li, 龐冰履, and others. Shanghai, Mo-yuan publishers, c1940. 3 v. illus.

PAYER VON THURN, RUDOLF, ritter, 1867-1932. Chinesische Miniaturen. Leipzig-Wien, Thyrsos-Verlag, 1924-   2 p. 12 col. plates. (Erste veröffentlichung aus den schätzen der Familien-fideikommiss-bibliothek des ehem. kaisers von österreich).

PELLIOT, PAUL, 1878-1945. Notes sur quelques artistes des six dynasties et des T'ang. Leide, E. J. Brill, 1923. cover-title, 77 p. "Extrait du T'oung pao. 2e série, vol. 22, 1923."

POUZYNA, I    V. La Chine, l'Italie et les débuts de la renaissance (xiiie-xive siècles) Paris, Les Éditions d'art et d'histoire, 1935. 102 p. plates.

PRIEST, ALAN, 1898-   Aspects of Chinese painting. New York, Macmillan, 1954. 134 p. illus. (part col.).

ROSTHORN, ARTHUR VON, 1862-1945. Malerei und Kunstkritik in China. Wien 1930. 18 p. plates. (Wiener Beitrag zur Kunst- und Kulturgeschichte Asiens, 4)

ROWLEY, GEORGE, 1892-   Principles of Chinese painting, with illustrations from the Du Bois Schanck Morris collection. Princeton, Princeton University Press, 1947. ix-x, [2], 111 p. illus., 48 (e.e. 50) plates (part fold., part col.) on 35 l. [Princeton monographs in art and archaeology. xxiv].

SAKANISHI, SHIO, 1899-   tr. The spirit of the Brush, being the outlook of
Chinese painters on nature, from eastern Chin to five dynasties, A. D. 317-
960, translated by Shio Sakanishi. London, J. Murray [1939] 108 p. (The
wisdom of the East series).

SCHMIED, WIELAND, 1929-   Von den Chinesen zu den Kindern; Notizen zur Malerei. Mit einer Lithographie von H. Matisse. Wien, Bergland, 1957. 115 p.
front. (Neue Dichtung aus Österreich, 27/28).

SHIH, T'AO, 石濤.Chinesische Landschaften. 12 Tuschbilder, eingeleitet von Victoria Contag. Baden-Baden, Klein, 1955. 11 p. plates, (Der silberne Quell.
27).

SHIMADA, S. Painting of Sung and Yuan dynasties by S. Shimada and Y. Yonezawa. Tokyo, Mayuyama, 1952. vii, 47 p. cover-illus., plates.

SIRÉN, OSVALD, 1879-   Chinese paintings in American collections. Paris
and Brussels, G. van Oest, 1928. 109, [2] p. 200 plates. (Annales du Musée
Guimet. Bibliothèque d'art. n. s. ii).

———. Les peintres chinoises dans les collections Americaines. Paris et Bruxelles, G. van Oest, 1928. 112 p. plates. (Annales du Musée Guimet. Bibliothèque d'art. n. s. ii).

———. A history of early Chinese painting. London, Medici Society [1933] 2 v.
226 plates.

———. The Chinese on the art of painting; translations and comments. Peiping,
H. Vetch, 1936. 261 p. plates (incl. front.).

———. A history of later Chinese painting. London, The Medici Society, 1938.
2 v. 242 plates.

———. Chinese painting: leading masters and principles. pt. 1: The first millen
nium. New York, Ronald Press, London, P. Lund Humphries, 1956. 3 v.
plates.

SPEISER, WERNER, 1908-   T'ang Yin, 唐寅. Berlin, Walter de Gruyter,
1935. 43 p.

———. Meisterwerke chinesischer Malerei aus der Sammlung der japanischen
Reichsmarschälle Yoshimitsu und Yoshimasa. Berlin, Safari-Verlag [c1947]
50 p. 61 plates (1 col.).

———. Chinesische Gemälde der Ming- und Ch'ing-Zeit. Köln, Greven Verlag,
1950. [8] p. 12 plates (in portfolio).

SZE, MAI-MAI, 施蘊珍, tr. The Tao of painting. see Wang, Kai.

TSE, TSAN-TAI, 謝纘泰, 1872-   Ancient Chinese art (illustrated); a treatise
on Chinese painting. Hong Kong, South China Morning Post, 1928. 18 p. front.

VORETZSCH, ERNST ARTHUR, 1868-   comp. Chinesische Gemälde. Chinese
pictures. Tokio, Verlag Otsuka kogeisha, 1932. iv numb. l., v-vi p. 57
plates.

WALEY, ARTHUR, 1889-   An introduction to the study of Chinese painting.
London, E. Benn, 1923, N. Y. Scribner, 1923. xii, 261, [1] p. xlix plates
(incl. front.; part col.).

WANAMAKER, JOHN, firm, Philadelphia. A great carved and painted twelve-
fold Chinese screen of the late 17th and early 18th centuries, from the Imperial palace in Pekin. New York, Philadelphia, J. Wanamaker, 1928. 70 p.
illus. (1 col.).

WANG, CHUNG-YU, 王寵佑,1879-1958.The Chinese pictorial art: an essay on its
interpretation, with illustrations from Wang's private collection. Hankow,
1924. 6 p. illus.

WANG, FANG-CH'ÜAN, 王芳荃. Chinese free-hand flower painting. [Peiping,
1937] iii, 131 p. front., plates.

WANG, KAI, 王槩, fl. 1677. The tao of painting, a study of the ritual disposition of Chinese painting; with a translation of the Chieh tzŭ yüan hua chuan,
芥子園畫傳 ; or, Mustard Seed Garden manual of painting, 1679-1701, by
Mai-mai Sze, 施蘊珍. [New York] Pantheon Books; Toronto, McClelland and
Stewart, 1956. 2 v. illus., plates (part col.) (Bollingen series, 49).

WELLS, WILFRID H. Perspective in early Chinese painting. London, E. Goldston, 1935. 63, [1] p. plates.

WHITE, WILLIAM CHARLES, bp., 1873- An album of Chinese bamboos, a study of a set of ink-bamboo drawings A. D. 1785. [Toronto] University of Toronto Press, 1939. xv, 200 p. incl. col. front., illus., plates [Royal Ontario museum of archaeology. Museum studies, 2].

———. Chinese temple frescoes; a study of three wall-paintings of the thirteenth century. [Toronto] University of Toronto Press, 1940. xvii, 230 p. incl. col. front., illus., plates (part col.) map. [Royal Ontario museum of archaeology. Museum studies, 3].

WOU, TI-FEN, 何棣芬. [HO TI-FÊN]. La peinture de paysage en Chine à de l'époque Yuan. Paris, Jouve et Cie, 1932. 204 p.

YONEZAWA, YOSHIHO. Painting in the Ming dynasty. Tokyo, Mayuyama, 1956. 118 p. plates.

Exhibition Catalogues

BIGNOU GALLERY, New York. Ancient Chinese and modern Eupopean paintings May-June, 1943, Bignou Gallery. Text by A. C. Barnes and Violette De Mazia. [New York, 1943] [35] p. illus.

BUFFALO. FINE ARTS ACADEMY. Catalogue of an exhibition of Chinese paintings owned by Mr. and Mrs. G. Del Drago and exhibited at the Albright art gallery by special invitation March 15-Apr. 15, 1931. [Buffalo, 1931] 46 p. incl. front., illus.

BURCHARD, OTTO UND CO., Berlin. Altchinesische Malerei, Verzeichnis bearbeitet und mit einem Vorwort versehen von Otto Kümmel. 111. Sonderausstellung veranstaltet von Otto Burchard und Co., Berlin. Berlin, 1928. 23, [1] p. plates.

CAMBRIDGE, ENG. Fitzwilliam Museum. Illustrated catalogue of an exhibition of Chinese paintings from the Mu-Fei collection, with an introduction by Chêng Tê-k'un, 鄭德坤. Cambridge, Eng., 1954. 19 p.

DUBOSC, JEAN PIERRE. Catalogue de l'exposition des peintures chinoises de la collection J. P. Dubosc. Bibliothèque Nationale, Paris. Octobre, 1937. [Paris, 1937] xv, 21 p.

DÜSSELDORF. KUNSTSAMMLUNGEN DER STADT DÜSSELDORF. Ausstellung Chinesische Malerei, 15-20. Jahrhundert. Herausgeber: Werner Speiser. Einführung: Victoria Contag. Düsseldorf, 1950. 64 p. plates.

GENÈVE, MUSÉE RATH. Exposition d'art pictural chinois ancien et moderne organisée par la Bibliothèque sino-internationale, 5-27 juillet, 1947. Genève, 1947. 16 p. illus.

HAMBURG. MUSEUM FÜR KUNST UND GEWERBE. Chinesische Malerei der letzten vier Jahrhunderte; Ausstellung, 1. Oktober 1949 bis 9. Januar 1950. [Hamburg, 1950?] 56 p. 16 plates.

HARVARD UNIVERSITY. WILLIAM HAYES FOGG ART MUSEUM. Sixty Chinese and Japanese paintings, Fogg Museum of Art, Spring, 1945. [Cambridge, 1945] [8] p. front.

———. Masterpieces of Chinese bird and flower painting; a loan exhibition, October 30-December 14 1951. [Catalogue. Cambridge 1951] 29 p. illus.

KANSAS CITY, MO. WILLIAM ROCKHILL NELSON GALLERY OF ART and Mary Atkins Museum of Fine Arts. Exhibition of Chinese paintings 1948-1949. Kansas City, Mo. [1948] 37 l. Mimeographed.

LOO, C. T. and CO., New York. An exhibition of Chinese eighteenth century paintings, January 15 to Feb. 5, 1938. New York, C. T. Loo and Co. [c1938] [16] p. illus.

———. An exhibition of authorized Chinese paintings, April 1948, from the collection of Chang Ts'ung-yu, 張葱玉. New York, C. T. Loo and Co. [1948] 31 p.

————. Chinese frescos of northern Sung. New York, 1949. [30] p. illus. plates.

[OTTO, J. ] Chinesische Malerei und Kalligraphie. Ausstellung vom 14. 2. -
25. 4. 1954. Flensburg, Städtisches Museum, 1954. 8 p. illus.

PEKING. PALACE MUSEUM. Descriptive catalogue of an exhibition of calli-
graphies and paintings. National Palace Museum, December 1943-January
1944. Peking, 1944. 52 p.

PENNSYLVANIA. UNIVERSITY. UNIVERSITY MUSEUM. Handbook of Chinese
paintings in the collection of the museum, by Helen E. Fernald. Philadelphia, 1922. 64 p. incl. plates.

PETERSON, FREDERICK, 1859-    Catalogue of a collection of Chinese paintings
in the possession of Dr. Frederick Peterson, by Berthold Laufer. New York,
Priv. print, 1930. 51, [1] p.

PORTLAND, OR. ART MUSEUM. An exhibition of Chinese art held on the opening of the Solomon and Josephine Hirsch memorial wing. Portland, Portland
Art Association [1939] 14 p. incl. plates.

THE RENAISSANCE SOCIETY, CHICAGO. A catalogue of ancient Chinese paintings from the collection of Mr. G. Del Drago. New York; the Renaissance
society galleries, Goodspeed Hall, the University of Chicago, Sept. 28 to Oct.
25, 1941. [Chicago, 1941] 8 p. plates.

STOCKHOLM. NATIONAL MUSEUM. Catalogue of an exhibition of Chinese and
Japanese sculptures and paintings in the National Museum in Stockholm.
Stockholm, 1933. 35 p. (Nationalmusei utställningskataloger, 42).

————. An exhibition of Chinese paintings in the National museum, Stockholm.
Catalogue, by Osvald Sirén. [Stockholm] Nordisk rotogravyr [1936] 72 p.
32 plates.

————. Catalogue of an exhibition of Chinese paintings from the collection of the
National Museum, Stockholm, by Osvald Siren. [Stockholm] Nordisk roto-.
gravyr [1939] 38 p. plates.

VASSAR COLLEGE. ART GALLERY. Chinese painting, seventy-fifth anniversary
exhibition, May 22 to June 10, 1940. Poughkeepsie, [1940] [13] p. plates.

VIENNA. ÖSTERREICHISCHE MUSEUM FÜR KUNST UND INDUSTRIE. Ausstellung ostasiatische Malerei aus dem Museum von der Heydt, Eysden, Holland, Chinesisches Lackgerät aus verschiedenem Besitz, frühjar 1937. Wien,
Krystall-Verlag, 1937. 25 p. plates.

WILDENSTEIN AND COMPANY, INC. New York. Great Chinese painters of the
Ming and Ch'ing Dynasties, xv to xviii centuries. A loan exhibition for the
benefit of the Asia Institute, March 11 to April 2, 1949. New York, [1949]
71 p. illus.

YAMANAKA AND CO. Catalogue of Chinese portrait paintings of Ming dynasty
(1368-1643 A. D. ) New York, Yamanaka and Co. [1936?] Cover-title, 9 p.
plates.

ZÜRICH. HELMHAUS. Wegleitung für die Ausstellung [4 juin au 2 juillet à Zü-
rich]: Grosse chinesische Maler der Ming-und Tsing-Dynastien 1400-1750 und
chinesische Volkskunst, Gouaches und Farbendrucke von E. H. von Tsharner
und J. P. Dubosc. Zürich, 1950. 30 p. plates.

## Contemporary Paintings

BERN. KUNSTHALLE. Ausstellung chinesische Malerei der Gegenwart, 26 Aug-
ust-23 September 1934. Katalog mit Einleitung von Liu Hai-su, 劉海粟 .
Bern, 1934. iv, 40 p.

CHEN, SHU-JEN, 陳樹人 , 1883-1955. Les oeuvres récentes de Chen Shu-jen.
Changhai, Commercial Press, [c1937]. xl p. 24 plates (part. col. ) (Collection Chine-France; les maitres chinois contemporaine).

CH'I, PAI-SHIH, 齊白石 , 1861-1957. Farbige Pinselzeichnungen. Leipzig, Insel Verlag [1956] 34 p. (Insel-Bücherei, 583).

CHINESE ART CLUB, New York. National Chinese children art exhibition, June

18-July 8, 1939. New York, Chinese Art Club [1939] 74 p. illus.

CHOU, LING, 周麟, 1915-    La peinture chinois contemporaine de style tradi-
tionnel. Paris, Éditions Europe, 1949. 11 p. col. plates.

CONTEMPORARY CHINESE PAINTINGS. Peking, Foreign Languages Press,
1955. Cover-title, [2] p. 24 col. plates. German ed.: Chinesische Malerei
von heute. [2] p. 24 col. plates.

GESELLSCHAFT FÜR OSTASIATISCHE KUNST, Berlin. Ausstellung chinesische
Malerei der Gegenwart, veranstaltet unter förderung durch die regierung der
Chinesischen Republik von der Gesellschaft für Ostasiatische Kunst und der
Prussischen Akademie der Künste, Berlin, 20 januar bis 4 marz, 1934. Ber-
lin, Würfel Verlag, 1934. 67, [1] p. plates.

KAO, CH'I-FENG, 高奇峯. Painting series. Vol. 1. By the late "artistic sage"
Ko Kei-fung. Shanghai, Overseas-Chinese Pub. Co., 1935. 1 v. plates.

KINDERMALEREI aus dem neuen China. Peking, Verlag für fremdsprachige
Literatur, 1955. 33 p.

KWOK, DAVID 郭大維, [KUO TA-WEI], 1919-    Modern Chinese paintings by
David Kwok. [Chicago] Art Institute of Chicago, 1955. [7] p. 20 plates.

NEW YORK. METROPOLITAN MUSEUM OF ART. An exhibition of modern Chinese paintings; introductions by Hu Shih, Kinn-wei Shaw, 壽景偉, Lin Yutang [and] Alan Priest. January 15-March 14, 1943. New York, 1943. [16] p.
of illus.

――――. An exhibition of paintings by Kao Wêng, 高嵡翁, and Chang K'un-i, 張坤
儀; introductions by Hu Shih, Kao Wêng [and] Alan Priest. March 21-April
23, Metropolitan Museum of Art. New York, 1944. [18] p. of illus.

――――. Contemporary Chinese paintings; a catalogue of an exhibition sponsored
by the Chinese Art Research Society and the China Council for International
Cultural Co-operation. With forewords by V. K. Wellington Koo and Lin Yutang and an introd. by Alan Priest. New York, 1948. [12] p. 20 plates.

PARIS. MUSÉE CERNUSCHI. Thèmes traditionnels dans l'oeuvre de Ling Su-hua,
凌淑華. Paris, 1954. 15 p.

――――. Relevés de Touen-Houang et peintures anciennes de la collection Tchang
Ta-ts'ien, 張大千. Paris, 1956. 25 p. plates.

PARIS. MUSÉE D'ART MODERNE. Tchang Ta-ts'ien: peintre chinois. Paris,
1956. 17 p. plates, (part. col.).

PARIS. MUSÉE NATIONAL DU JEU DE PAUME. L'oeuvre de Tchang Shan Tse,
張善子, Mars 1939. Paris, 1939. cover-title, 15, [1] p. plates.

PREZZI, WILLIAM. Exhibition of paintings of Chinese objects by William Prezzi. Knoedler Galleries. May 21-June 8, 1945. [New York, 1945] [12] p.
front. plates.

TONG-YING AND CO., New York. A collection of Chinese paintings by Miss
Ching-chih Yee, 余靜芝, on exhibition from Nov. 14 to Dec. 24 at the galleries of Ton-ying and Co. New York [1938] 4 p. illus.

TSENG, YU-HO, 曾幼荷, 1923-    [Paintings] by Tseng Yu-ho. M. H. De Young
Memorial Museum, San Francisco, Nov. 7-Dec. 27, 1947. San Francisco,
1947. Cover-title, [6] p.

――――. Thèmes traditionnels dans l'oeuvre de Tseng Yu-ho. Paris, Musée Cernuschi, 1953. 8 p. illus.

――――. Tseng Yu-ho; peintures récentes, 2-18 mai 1957. Paris, Éditions Euros,
1957. 16 p. illus.

WANG, CHI-YUAN, 王濟遠, 1895-    Paintings by Wang Chi-yuan. New York,
Gallery of Modern Art, 1943. 8 p. illus.

――――. Chinese painting of the bamboo. New York, 1945. 12 p. illus. (part col.)

――――. Water-ink painting. New York, School of Chinese Brushwork, 1957.
[8] p. plates, facsims.

YEH, CH'IEN-YÜ, 葉淺予, 1907-    illus. China today, in art drawings. Foreword by Dr. C. J. Pao, 保君健. Introduction and commentary by Dr. Amiya

Chakravarty. [Calcutta] The Book Emporium[1944] vi, [7]-51 p. illus. (part mounted).

## Calligraphy

ALLEN, WILLIAM DANGAIX, 1904-  "Good luck". An easy introduction to the basis of Oriental arts, the art of calligraphy or "beautiful writing." A manual by William D. Allen and S.T. Shen, 优守犀 . New York, Universal Pub. Co., 1944. 15 l. illus.

CHIANG, YEE, 蔣彝 , 1903-  Chinese calligraphy; an introduction to its aesthetic and technique. With a foreword by Sir Herbert Read. [2d ed.] London, Methuen, Cambridge, Harvard University Press, 1954. xvi, 230 p. illus., facsims. 1st ed. 1938.

DRISCOLL, LUCY. Chinese calligraphy [by] Lucy Driscoll and Kenji Toda. Chicago, University of Chicago Press [1935] vii, 70, [1] p. incl. illus., facsims. front. (A monograph of the New Orient society of America).

SIRÉN OSVALD, 1879-  Huang T'ing-chien, 黃庭堅 , [1045-1105] on the art of calligraphy. Stockholm, 1952. 7 p.

YANG, YU-HSUN,揚毓珣 . La calligraphie chinoise depuis les Han. 2e. éd. Avec 32 planches et un index chinois. Paris, P. Geuthner, 1937. [5]-6, [7]-180, xiv p. xxxii plates (incl. facsims) on 19 l. double tab. 1er éd. 1933.

## Sculpture: General Works

[ARDENNE DE TIZAC, JEAN-HENRI D'] 1877-1932. Chinesische Tierplastik und Tierbilder. Eine Sammlung von Beispielen, ausgewählt und beschrieben von J.H. d'Ardenne de Tizac. Berlin, E. Wasmuth [1924] 11 p. plates.

———. La sculpture chinoise. Paris, G. van Oest, 1931. 49, [2] p. plates (1 double) (Bibliothèque d'histoire de l'art).

ASHTON, LEIGH, 1897-  An introduction to the study of Chinese sculpture. London, E. Benn; New York, C. Scribner, 1924. xviii, 113, [1] p. front, plates. map.

CENTRE D'ÉTUDES SINOLOGIQUES DE PÉKIN. Corpus des pierres scultées Han (estampages), edité par Fou Si-houa, 傅惜華 . Pékin, 1950-51. 2 v. plates. map.

CHICAGO. ART INSTITUTE. A Chinese Buddhist stele of the Wei dynasty in the collection of the Art Institute of Chicago. Chicago, 1927. 5 p. plates. (Oriental publications, 1).

COX, LEONARD BELL. The Buddhist cave temples of Yün-Kang and Lung-Mên. Canberra, Australian National University, 1957. 14 p. (George Ernest Morrison lecture in ethnology, 18).

FISCHER, OTTO, 1886-1948. Chinesische Plastik, München, R. Piper [1948] 200 p. 136 plates.

GLASER, CURT, 1879-  Ostasiatische Plastik. Berlin, B. Cassirer, 1925. 97 p. illus., plates (Die kunst des Ostens, hrsg. von W. Cohn, xi).

Les GROTTES de Yün-kang. L'art des Wei. Pékin, A. Nachbaur, 192-  6 p. plates.

GROUSSET, RENÉ, 1885-1952. La sculpture des Indes et de la Chine. Paris, Librairie des arts décoratifs [1939] 8 p. plates.

KING, GORDON, 1900-  The Buddhist cave temples at Yünkang. Peiping, Peiping Chronicle, 1935. 12, [24] p. illus. fold. maps.

LOO, C. T. and CO., New York. An exhibition of Chinese stone sculptures. New York, C.T. Loo and Co., 1940. [48] p. incl. xxxv plates.

MAHLER, JANE (GASTON). The Westerners among the figurines of the T'ang dynasty. Ann Arbor, University Microfilms, 1950. ([University Microfilms, Ann Arbor, Mich.] Publication no. 1878 ). 121 l. illus. maps, plan.

MIZUNO, SEIICHI, 1905-    Chinese stone sculpture. Tokyo, Mayuyama, 1950.
33 p. plates (part col.) map.
———. Yün-kang, the Buddhist cave-temples of the fifth century A.D. in North
China; detailed report of the archaeological survey carried out by the mission of the Tohobunka Kenkyusho 1938-45 [by] Seiichi Mizuno and Toshio Na-
gahiro. [Kyoto] Jimbunkagaku Kenkyusho, Kyoto University, 1951-    13 v.
illus., plates, maps.
[MORGAN, HARRY TITTERTON] 1872-    Chinese carvings. Edited for and copyrighted by Quon-Quon Co.    Los Angeles, Calif., c1944. 16 p. illus. [His
Chinese classics in miniature].
MULLIKIN, MARY AUGUSTA, 1874-    Buddhist sculptures at the Yun kang
caves, text and illustrations by Mary Augusta Mullikin, with additional illustrations by Anna H. Hotchkis. Peiping, H. Vetch, 1935. 66 p. incl. front.,
illus. (part col., mounted) plates (part col., mounted).
NEW YORK. METROPOLITAN MUSEUM OF ART. Chinese sculpture in the Metropolitan museum of art, by Alan Priest, curator of Far Eastern art. Photographs by Tet Borsig. New York, 1944. 81 p. plates.
PARIS. MUSÉE CERNUSCHI.  Yun-Kang and Nara; cocuments photographiques
sur l'art bouddique. Paris, Musée Cernuschi, 1952. 34 p. illus.
RUDOLPH, RICHARD C., 1909-    Han tomb art of West China; a collection of
first-and second-century reliefs [by] Richard C. Rudolph in collaboration
with Wen Yu, 聞宥. Berkeley, University of California Press, 1951. vii,
67, [81] p. plates, map, plans.
SALMONY, ALFRED,1890-1958. Chinesische Plastik, ein Handbuch für Sammler,
mit 129 Textabbildungen. Berlin, R.C. Schmidt, 1925. xi, 172 p. illus.
Bibliothek für kunst- und antiquitäten-sammler, xxvi).
SÉGALEN, VICTOR, 1878-1919. Mission archéologique en Chine (1914), par
Victor Ségalen, Gilbert de Voisins et Jean Lartigue. Paris, P. Geuthner,
1923-1935. 3 v. illus. (incl. maps, plans) Atlas of plates.
SHINKAI, TAKETARŌ,1868-1927. Rock-carvings from the Yun-kang Caves, se-
lected by Shinkai Taketaro [and] Nakagawa Tadayori; photographs by Yamamoto Akira and Kishi Masakatsu. Tokyo, Bunkyudo, 1921. 16 p. 200 plates.
(1 fold.) fold. plan.
SIRÉN, OSVALD, 1879-    Chinese sculpture from the fifth to the fourteenth cen-
tury; over 900 specimens in stone, bronze, lacquer and wood, principally
from northern China. With descriptions and an introductory essay. London,
E. Benn, 1925. 4 v. front., illus. (incl. plans) 623 pl.
———. La sculpture chinois du Ve au XIVe siècle; neuf cents spécimens en
pierre, bronze, laque, et en bois. Paris, G. van Oest, 1925. 4 v. illus.
(Annales du Musée Guimet. Bibliothèque d'art, n.s. l.).
———. Chinese and Japanese sculptures and paintings in the National Museum,
Stockholm. London, E. Goldston, [1931] 7-48 p. plates.
TORII, RYUZO, 1870-    Sculptured stone tombs of the Liao dynasty. [Peking]
Harvard-Yenching Institute, 1942. xiv, 134 p. illus., plates, map.
WITH, KARL, 1891-    Asiatische Monumentalplastik, mit einem Vorwort. [2.
Aufl.] Berlin, E. Wasmuth a.g. [1921] 16 p. 48 plates. (Orbis pictus; welt-
kunst-bücherei, 5).
———. Bildwerke Ost-und Südasiens aus der Sammlung Yi Yuan, mit begleiten-
dem Text von Karl With. Basel, B. Schwabe und Co. 1924. 9-74 p. plates.
———. Chinesische Kleinbildnerei in Steatit.  Oldenburg i. O., G. Stalling
[c1926] 142, [1] p. illus., plates (part col. mounted). (Sacramentum artis).

## Exhibition Catalogues

BERKELEY GALLERIES, London. Exhibition of Chinese sculpture at the Berkeley galleries. March-April, 1946. [London, 1946] [16] p. illus.
CHINESE ART SOCIETY OF AMERICA, INC. Small sculpture, Shang through

Sung dynasties (a (a loan exhibition). Feb. 19-Apr. 17, 1954. New York 1954. 20 p. illus.

KLEIJKAMP, JAN. -1952. The M. H. De Young memorial museum. San Francisco, presents an exhibition of Chinese sculpture, Han (206 B. C. -A. D. 220) to Sung (A. D. 960-1279) July 16 to August 15, 1944. Collection of Jan Kleijkamp and Ellis Monroe. [Fulton, N. Y., Morrill Press, 1944] 3-57 p. front., xxviii plates.

ORIENTAL FINE ARTS INC., New York. An exhibition of Chinese terra cotta sculpture from Han through T'ang dynasty. April 22-May 15, 1948. New York 1948. [14] p. illus.

PORTLAND, OR. ART MUSEUM. Exhibition of Chinese sculpture, July 15 through September 15, 1940. Portland, Or., Portland Art Museum [1940] [18] p. illus.

TOLEDO. MUSEUM OF ART. Sculptural forms in terra cotta from Chinese tombs; January, nineteen hundred thirty-nine, the Toledo Museum of Art. Toledo, Ohio. [Toledo? 1938?] [43] p. 15 plates.

## Woodcuts and Color Prints

CENTRE FRANCO-CHINOIS D'ÉTUDES SINOLOGIQUES, Peking. Exposition d'iconographie populaire; images rituelles du nouvel an. Pékin, Centre fran-do-chinois d'études sinologiques, 1942. xi, 239, [1] p. front.

————. Exposition d'ouvrages illustrés de la dynastie Ming. Pékin, Centre franco-chinois d'études sinologiques, 1944. xvi, 167, [1] xvi plates.

CHICAGO. ART INSTITUTE. Descriptive catalogue of Japanese and Chinese illustrated books in the Ryerson library of the Art Institute of Chicago, by Kenji Toda. Chicago [Printed at the Lakeside Press, R. R. Donnelley, 1931. xxxii, 466 p. illus., plates.

CHINA in black and white, a portfolio of wartime woodcuts. [New York, 1944] [15] p. illus.

————; an album of woodcuts by contemporary Chinese artists, with commentary by Pearl S. Buck. New York, John Day, [1945] 95 p. incl. front., illus.

CHINA MONTHLY REVIEW. Chinese woodcuts [and] paper cut-outs. Shanghai, 1953. [62] p. (on double leaves, chiefly illus.).

THE CHINESE WOODCUT, a new art for the 400 million. 11 prints of life and manners in present day China, with an introd. by Agnes Smedley. New York, Touchstone Press with the cooperation of the Tribune Subway Gallery [1948] [4] p. 11 plates (in portfolio) (Touchstone portfolios: Artists of the people, no. 5).

CHINESE WOODCUTTERS' ASSOCIATION. Woodcuts of war-time China, 1937-1945. Shanghai, Kaiming Book Co., [1946] 36 p.

CHINESISCHE Holzschnitte, Bildwahl und Geleitwort von Emil Preetorius. Leipzig and Wiesbaden, Insel-Verlag, 1954. 40 p. (Insel-Bücherei, 164).

CONTEMPORARY Chinese woodcuts. With forewords by Joseph Needham, Hetta Empson and Zdenek Hrdlicka. London, Fore Publications, 1950. xiv, 101 p. plates.

FISCHER, OTTO, 1886-1948. Chinesische Farbendrucke aus den beiden Lehrbüchern Chieh-Tse-Yuan Hua Chuan, 芥子園畫傳. Shih-Chu-Chai Shu Hua Tsih, 十竹齋書畫冊, Einleitung vom Emil Orlik. München, 1921. 15, iv p. plates. (Marées Gesellschaft. Drucke, 32).

————. Chinese woodcuts of seventeenth century; facsimile-reproductions, published by the Marees-society. Munich, R. Piper [192-?] 15 mounted col. plates.

GULIK, ROBERT HANS VAN, 1910- ed. Erotic colour prints of the Ming period, with an essay on Chinese sex life from the Han to the Ch'ing dynasty, B. C. 206- A. D. 1644. Tokyo, Priv. published, 1951. 3 v. in portfolio. illus. (part col.).

FOREIGN LANGUAGES PRESS. Woodcuts of new China. Peking, 1956. 40
   plates (in portfolio).
[HU, CHENG-YEN], 胡正言, 1582-1672. Chinesisches Gedichtpapier vom Meis-
   ter der Zehnbambushalle. 24 Faksimiles in der Originalgrösse, hrsg. von
   Jan Tschichold. Basel, Holbein-Verlag [1947] 22 p. col. plates.
———. Chinese poetry paper by the master of the Ten bamboo hall, with an intro-
   duction by J. Tschichold. Authorized translation by E. C. Mason. Baṣle,
   Holbein-Verlag, 1948. 22 p. col. plates.
KURTH, JULIUS, 1870-1947. Der chinesische Farbendruck. Mit 6 Farbigen,
   30 schwarzen Tafeln und 12 Abbildungen im Text. Plauen im Vogtland, C. F.
   Schulz, 1922. 87 p. illus., 36 plates (part col. and mounted) (Ostasiatische
   graphik 1).
LONDON. THE ARTS COUNCIL. Catalogue of an exhibition of printed Chinese
   letter papers; (loaned by Jan Tschichold). London, The Arts Council, 1950.
   36 p.
LOS ANGELES. COUNTY MUSEUM. Japanese and Chinese prints, lent by the
   collectors of southern California, selected, arranged and catalogued by Jud-
   don D. Metzgar. Los Angeles County Museum, Feb. 5 to March 2, 1941.
   [Los Angeles, 1941] [16] p.
MELCHERS, BERND, 1886-    ed. Blumen aus dem alten China; ausgewählt und
   engeleitet von Bernd Melchers. Kassel, F. Lometsch [1956] [31] p. (on
   double leaves) illus. (part col.).
METZGAR, JUDSON D. Chinese color prints, from the collection of the owner,
   Judson D. Metzgar. Los Angeles, Los Angeles County Museum, 1943. 18 p.
   illus.
MORI, S     H. Ukiyo-é paintings, Japanese and Chinese color-prints, the S.
   H. Mori collection; text by Frederick W. Gookin, with an appreciation by
   Gardner Teall, illustrated with one hundred and three halftone reproductions.
   New York, American Art Association inc. [1926] [163] p. front., illus.
NACHBAUR, ALBERT. Les images populaires chinoises. Pékin, A. Nachbaur,
   1931. 45 l. incl. mounted plates. 1er éd., 1926.
NEW YORK. METROPOLITAN MUSEUM OF ART. Chinese flower and fruit
   prints, from the Mustard seed garden and the Ten bamboo studios. Metropo-
   litan Museum of Art. New York and London, American Studio Books [1946]
   [4] p. xii mounted plates (10 col.).
SCHEER, MAXIMILIAN, 1896-    Der Holzschnitt im neuen China; mit einem
   Geleitwort von Maximilian Scheer. Dresden, Sachsenverlag, 1951. 138 p.
   illus. (Kunst und Welt).
TSCHICHOLD, JAN., 1902-    Der frühe chinesische Farbendruck. München,
   Prestel Verlag; Basel, Holbein Verlag, 1940. 13 l. 31. 16 col. plates.
   1953 ed. has title: Chinesische Farbendruck aus der Zehnbambus-halle.
———. L'estampe chinoise ancienne en couleurs. Traduit par Paul Roches.
   Bâle, Les Éditions Holbein, 1940. 3-13 numb. l., 16 col. pl.
———. Early Chinese color prints. [Authorized translation by Eudo C. Mason.
   New York, Beechhurst Press, 1953. 15, [2] p. (on double leaves) 16 col.
   plates.
———. Chinesische Farbendrucke aus dem Lehrbuch der Malerei des Senfkorn-
   gartens. Sechzehn Faksimiles in der Originalgrösse ausgewählt und eingeleit-
   et von Jan Tschichold. Basel, Holbein-Verlag [1941]; München, Prestel Verlag, 1942. 2 aufl. 1951. 5-11, [1] p. 16 pl. (part col.).
———. Chinese color-prints from the Painting manual of the Mustard Seed Garden; with an introd., 16 facsims. in the size of the originals. [Authorized
   English translation by Eudo C. Mason] London, Allen and Unwin [1952,
   c1951] 17 p. (on double leaves) plates (part col.) (The Holbein art books).
———. Der Holzschneider und Bilddrucker, Hu Chêng-yen, von Jan Tschichold;
   mit sechzehn Faksimiles nach Blättern der Zehnbambushalle. Basel, Hol-

bein-verlag [1943] 5-16 p. 16 plates (part col.) 1 1.

———. Papiergötter aus Peking. Basel, Baseler Druck und Verlags-Anstalt, 1951. 15 p. plates.

———. Hu Chêng-yen, a Chinese wood engraver and picture printer [by] Jan Tschichold; with 16 facsims from sheets in the Ten Bamboo Hall. Authorized English translation by Eudo C. Mason. London, G. Allen and Unwin, 1953. 5-16 p. plates (part. col.) (The Holbein art books).

———. Die Bildersammlung der Zehnbambushalle. Der Holzschneider und Bilddrucker Hu Chêng-yen. [2 Aufl.] Basel, Holbein-Verlag, 1953. 18 p. facs. plates (part. col.).

———. Chinesische Farbendrucke der Gegenwart, 北平箋譜 . Sechzehn Faksimiles in der Originalgrösse ausgewählt und eingeleitet von Jan Tschichold. Basel, Holbein- Verlag 1953. 7-17, [1] p. 16 col. pl. 1. ed. 1945.

———. Chinese color prints of today. [Authorized translation by Eudo C. Mason. 1st American ed.] New York, Beechhurst Press, 1953. 17 p. 16 col. plates.

VIETH VON GOLSSENAU, ARNOLD FRIEDRICH, 1889-    ed. 12 [i.e. Zwölf] Holzschnitte aus Volkschina. [Hrsg. von Ludwig Renn, pseud.] Erfurt, Thüringer Volksverlag, 1951. [8] p. 12 plates.

## Textiles, Tapestries and Embroideries

ARDENNE DE TIZAC, JEAN HENRI D,' 1877-1932. Les étoffes de la Chine; tissues et broderies. Paris, A. Calavas, n. d. [4], 4 p. plates (part col.) in portfolio. 1er éd. 1914.

———. The stuffs of China, weavings and embroideries; fifty-two collotype plates reproducing 84 fine examples in French collections selected and described by H. d'Ardenne de Tizac. London, E. Benn, 1924. 14 p. 52 pl.

BRODERIES CHINOISES. Paris, H. Ernst [19--?] 36 col. plates (5 double) mounted on 32 1. (4 double) in portfolio.

CAMMANN, SCHUYLER, 1912-    China's dragon robes. New York, Ronald Press Co., [1952] vii, 230 p. illus.

CHAI, FEI. Indigo prints of China, 中國藍印花布圖, compiled by Chai Fei [and others] Peking, Foreign Languages Press, 1956. [4] l., 48 plates.

———. Chinesische Blaumusterstoffe; zusammengestellt von Tschai Fi [et al.] Peking, Verlag für Fremdsprachige Literatur, 1956. [4] l. 48 plates.

CHINESE COSTUMES; illustrations hand painted,中華服制考略.Foreword by Hardy Jowett. Peiping, Chinese Painting Association of Peiping, 1932. 3 1. 24 col. plates.

EBERHARD, ALIDE. Die Mode der Han- und Chin- Zeit [von] Alide und Wolfram Eberhard. Antwerpen, De Sikkel, 1946. 127 p. illus.

GEIJER, AGNES, 1898-    Oriental textiles in Sweden. Copenhagen, Rosenkilde and Bagger, 1951. 139 p. illus., 104 plates (part col.)

HARADA, YOSHITO. Chinese dress and personal ornaments in the Han and six synasties. Tokyo, Toyo Bunko, 1937. 29 p. 168 p. illus., plates (The Toyo bunko ronso, series A, vol. 23).

LEE, JAMES ZEE-MIN,    李時敏 [LI SHIH-MIN] Chinese potpourri, 中國集錦 2nd ed. Hong Kong, Oriental Publishers, 1951. 329 p.

LEGGETT, WILLIAM FERGUSON, 1875-    The story of silk. [New York] Lifetime Editions, 1949. xiv, 361 p.

MINNEAPOLIS. INSTITUTE OF ARTS. Catalogue of an exhibition of imperial robes and textiles of the Chinese court, with a foreword by Alan Priest. Minneapolis, Minn., the Minneapolis Institute of Arts, April 13 to June 15, 1943. [Minneapolis, 1943.] 20 p. incl. front. plates.

MOH, JAMIN, 馬則民 [MA TSÉ-MIN] Principles and stichings of Chinese embroidery. 中國刺繡術 . Shanghai, Commercial Press, 1937. xviii, 46 p. illus. plates.

MUKDEN. MANCHOUKUO NATIONAL MUSEUM. Tsuan-tsu-ying-hua, 纂組英華 tapestries and embroideries of the Sung, Yüan, Ming and Ch'ing dynasties, treasured by the Manchoukuo National Museum, Mukden. Tokyo, Zauho Press, 1934-35. 2 v. in 5. 139 plates (part col., part mounted; 2 fold.).

NATIONAL costumes of China. Peking, 1957. 1 v. (unpaged) col. illus.

NEW YORK. METROPOLITAN MUSEUM OF ART. Chinese textiles; an introduction to the study of their history, sources, technique, symbolism, and use, by Alan Priest and Pauline Simmons. A new and rev. ed. New York, 1934. x, 96 p. incl. illus., plates. 1st ed. 1931-

————. Costumes from the Forbidden city, by Alan Priest, curator of Far Eastern art. New York, Metropolitan Museum of Art, 1945. 16 p. 56 plates.

PAUL, WILLIAM C. Old Chinese embroideries, a brief explanation of their symbolism; illustrations by the author. [New York, Kwong Yuen, 1929?] 15 p. illus.

SIMMONS, PAULINE. Chinese patterned silks. New York, Metropolitan Museum of Art, 1948. 40 p. illus.

SYLWAN, VIVI, 1870-    Woollen textiles of the Lou Lan people; introduction by Folke Bergman. Appendix: Spinning Tools and Spinning Methods in Asia, by G. Montell. Stockholm, 1941. 127 p. illus. plates. diagrs. (Reports from the scientific expedition to the north-western provinces of China under the leadership of Dr. Sven Hedin. The Sino-Swedish expedition. Publication 15 vii: 2).

————. Investigation of silk from Edsen-gol and Lop-nor, and a survey of wool and vegetable materials. Introd. by Gösta Montell. Stockholm, 1949. x, 180 p. illus. (part col.) port., maps. (Reports from the scientific expedition to the north-western provinces of China under the leadership of Dr. Sven Hedin. The Sino-Swedish Expedition. Publication 32. vii. Archaeology, 6).

TORONTO. ROYAL ONTARIO MUSEUM OF ARCHAEOLOGY. Chinese court costumes, by Helen E. Fernald. Toronto, 1946. 51 p. illus., 37 (i.e. 41) plates (part col.).

VICTORIA AND ALBERT MUSEUM, South Kensington. Dept. of Textiles. Brief guide to the Chinese embroideries. London, Pub. under the authority of the Board of education, 1931. 12, [1] p. front., plates [Victoria and Albert museum, South Kensington. Publication, 144 T] 1st ed. 1921.

————. Brief guide to the Chinese woven fabrics. London, Pub. under the authority of the Board of Education, 1938. 34 p. front., plates, 1st ed. 1925.

VUILLEUMIER, BERNARD. The art of silk weaving in China; symbolism of Chinese imperial ritual robes; foreword by Laurence Binyon; fourteen plates. London [The China Institute] 1939. x, 11-34, xxxv-xxxvi p. plates (incl. front.)

Rugs

CHICAGO. ART INSTITUTE. An exhibition of antique oriental rugs. Feb. 6 through Mar. 16, 1947. [Chicago, 1947] [70] p. illus.

GOULD, GEORGE GLEN. Monograph on Chinese rugs. Illustrated by Corinne Duncan. 2d ed. Washington, D.C., Woodward and Lothrop [c1926] 20 p. illus. 1st ed. New York, 1921.

GROTE-HASENBALG, WERNER, 1888-    Der Orientteppich, seine Geschichte und seine Kultur. Berlin, Scarabacus-Verlag, 1922. 3 v. front., illus., plates (part col.) fold. map.

————. Meisterstücke orientalischer Knüpfkunst. Newbearb. nach R. v. Oettingen und erweitert von Werner Grote-Hasenbalg. [Berlin, Scarabaeus-Verlag, 1922, c1921] 120 col. plates (in 2 portfolios).

————. Masterpieces of Oriental rugs, translated by G. Barry Gilford. New York, Brentano's [1922?] xi (i.e. ix), 121 p. front., illus. and 2 portfolios of col. plates.

————. Teppiche aus dem Orient; ein kurzer Wegweiser. 2 Aufl. Leipzig, H.

Schmidt und C. Günther [1938] 22 p. illus., 48 col. plates.

————. Carpets of the Orient; a short guide; translated by Marianne Brooke. Leipzig, Schmidt und Guenther [1939?] 23 p. front., illus., 48 col. plates.

HACKMACK, ADOLF. Der chinesische Teppich 2. Aufl. Hamburg, L. Frie- derichsen, 1926 (c1921) xi, 52 p. illus., plates (1 col.) map.

————. Chinese carpets and rugs. Authorized translation by Miss L. Arnold. Tientsin, La librairie française, 1924. x, 48 p. col. front., illus. plates, maps.

HAMBURG. MUSEUM FÜR KUNST UND GEWERBE. Orientalische Teppiche aus der vier Jahrhunderten. Ausstellung im Museum für Kunst und Gewerbe, Hamburg, 22 August bis 22 October, 1950. [Hamburg, 1950] [120] p. map. diags, plates.

HOSAIN, ALI. Les tapis d'Orient. Paris, Les Presses universitaires, 1956. 50 p. illus. plates (Mémentos illustrés).

————. Oriental carpets; Turkish, Persian, Chinese, etc. Braunschweg, 1956. 48 p. plates.

INDIANA. ART ASSOCIATION OF INDIANAPOLIS. Catalogue of oriental rugs in the collection of James F. Ballard. Indianapolis, Hollenbeck Press, 1924. xii, 206 p. incl. front. (ports.) illus.

LEITCH, GORDON B. Chinese rugs; with illustrations collected by the author. New York, Dodd, Mead [c1928] xii, 171 p. col. front., illus., plates.

NEW YORK. METROPOLITAN MUSEUM OF ART. A guide to an exhibition of oriental rugs and textiles, by M.S. Dimand. New York, May 13 through September 15, 1935. [New York, Metropolitan Museum of Art, 1935] xiii, 36 p. 35 plates.

RIPLEY, MARY CHURCHILL. The Chinese rug book, with seventeen half-tone illustrations. New York, Frederick A. Stokes, 1927. xviii, 66 p. front. illus. plates.

RYLANDER, GUSTAVE WILLIAM. Oriental rug lexicon. Pittsburgh, Pa., 1938. 32 p. plates.

ST. LOUIS. CITY ART MUSEUM. Inaugural exhibition of a collection of oriental rugs presented to the museum by James F. Ballard, opening November 21, 1929. St. Louis, 1929. 26 p. incl. front.

————. The Ballard collection of oriental rugs in the City Art Museum of St. Louis, by Maurice S. Dimand. St. Louis, 1935. [216] p. incl. front. (port.) plates (part mounted col.).

TAPIS anciens de la Chine. Paris, E. Henri [1932] [4] p. illus., 20 col. moun- ted plates.

TOLEDO. MUSEUM OF ART. A loan exhibition of oriental rugs, January 1937. Toledo, Toledo Museum of Art [1937] Cover-title, [21] p. illus. incl. map.

## Furniture

CESCINSKY, HERBERT, 1875-   Chinese furniture, a series of examples from collections in France, with an introduction. London, E. Benn, 1922. 20 p. plates, illus.

DUPONT, MAURICE, 1873-   Les meubles de la Chine (deuxième série) Cin- quante-quatre planches accompagnées d'une préface et d'une table descriptive. Paris, A. Calavas [1926] 6 p. 54 plates [Documents d'art décoratif].

————. Chinesische Möbel. Reihe 2. Stutthart, Hoffmann, 1926. 1 v. 54 plates.

ECKE, GUSTAV, 1896-   Chinese domestic furniture, one hundred and sixty- one plates illustrating one hundred and twenty-two pieces of which twenty-one in measured drawings. Peking, H. Vetch, 1944. 2 v. in 1. illus., 161 plates.

KATES, GEORGE NORBERT, 1895-   Chinese household furniture, from ex- amples selected and measured by Caroline F. Bieber and Beatrice M. Kates. Text by George N. Kates; photos. by Hedda Hammer Morrison. New York, Harper [1948] xiii, 125 p. illus., plates.

KRIEG, KLAUS WERNER. Chinesische Möbel der späten Ming-Seit und der
    frühen Ch'ing-Zeit. Basel, 1951. iv, 135 Bl. photos. Diss.-Univ. Basel.
ROCHE, ODILON. Les meubles de la Chine; cinquante-quatre planches accom-
    pagnées d'une préface et d'une table descriptive. Paris, Librairie des arts
    décoratifs [1921?] 6 p. 54 plates.
————. Chinesische Möbel. Stuttgart, Julius Hoffmann, 1924. 7 p. 54 plates.
STONE, LOUISE HAWLEY. The chair in China. Toronto, University of Toronto
    Press, 1952. x, 49 p. illus.


Lacquer


BALLOT, MARIE JULIETTE. 1868-    Les laques d'Extrême-Orient, Chine et
    Japon. Paris et Bruxelles, G. van Oest, 1927. 38 p. 32 plates. (Architec-
    ture et arts décoratifs).
CHINA INSTITUTE IN AMERICA  Exhibition of Chinese lacquer objects [from
    the collections of Fritz Low-Beer and C.T. Loo] February 16th through
    March 10th, 1945. New York [1945] 20 p. illus.
COUTRAIT, J    P    Manuel de vernissage, de laquage et de mise en cou-
    leurs laques de Chine. [Nouv. éd. rev. et augm. de formules nombreuses et
    de procédés nouveaux] Paris, C. Moreau [1948?] 296 p. (Les Livres utiles).
MÄNCHEN-HELFEN, OTTO, 1894-    Ausstellung Ostasiatische Malerei Chine-
    sisches Lackgerat. Wien, Krystall-Verlag, 1937. 25 p. plates.
SÉGUY, E    A. Les laques du Coromandel; 50 planches publiées sous la direc-
    tion et avec une introduction de E.A. Séguy. Nouv. éd. Paris, A. Lévy [1924?]
    3 p. 50 plates (part col.).
STRANGE, EDWARD FAIRBROTHER, 1862-1929. Chinese lacquer. London, E.
    Benn, 1926. xii, 71, [1] p. col. front., illus., plates (part col.).
VICTORIA AND ALBERT MUSEUM, South Kensington. Dept. of Woodwork. Cata-
    logue of Chinese lacquer, by Edward F. Strange. London, Printed under the
    authority of H.M. Stationery Off., 1925. vii, 36 p. front., illus., plates.
    [Victoria and Albert museum Publication 16iw].
ZEE, ZAI-ZIANG, 徐善祥, 1882-    The influence of concentration, temperature,
    and humidity on the drying of Chinese lacquer-oil varnishes. [New York]
    1925. 78 p. illus., diagrs. Thesis-Columbia University.


Ivories


COX, WARREN EARLE, 1895-    Chinese ivory sculpture. New York, Crown
    Publishers [1946] xiii, 17-112, [6] p. illus.
EASTHAM, BARRY CAULFIELD. Chinese art ivory. Tientsin, J.E. Paradissis,
    1940. 86 p. 32 plates.
LAUFER, BERTHOLD, 1874-1934. Ivory in China. Chicago, Field Museum of
    Natural History, 1925. cover-title, 78 p. illus., plates. (Field museum of
    natural history. Anthropology leaflet 21).
LION, LUCIEN. Étude sur les statuettes d'ivoire de l'époque Ming. Shanghai,
    T'ou sé-wé Orphanage Printing Press, 1936. 13 p. plates.
————. Les ivoires religieux et médicaux chinois d'après la collection Lucien
    Lion. Texte de Henri Maspero, René Grousset, Lucien Lion. Summary trans-
    lated into English by Lionel Hart. Paris, Les Éditions d'art et d'histoire,
    1939. 96 p. front., plates.
SASSOON, SIR [ELLICE] VICTOR, 1881-    The catalogue of Sassoon Chinese
    ivories in three volumes by S.E. Lucas. London, Country Life; New York,
    C. Scribner, 1950. 3 v. col. front., plates, illus.
SOWERBY, ARTHUR DE CARLE, 1885-1954. China and ivory. [n.p., 1936] 32 p.
    illus. ''Reprinted from the China Journal, 25:3, September, 1936.''

## Gold, Silver and other Jewelries

CHINA INSTITUTE IN AMERICA. Exhibition of ancient Chinese silver on the occasion of the silver anniversary of China Institute in America, May 21
through June 21, 1951. New York, 1951. 8 p.

GYLLENSVÄRD, BO. T'ang gold and silver. Stockholm, 1957. 230 p. fig.
plates. (Bulletin, Museum of Far Eastern Antiquities, 29: 2.).

KEMPE, CARL. Chinese gold and silver in the Carl Kempe collection; a catalogue by Bo Gyllensvärd. [Stockholm? 1953] 255 p. illus., plates.

LEMAÎTRE, SOLANGE. Les agrafes chinoises jusqu'à la fin de l'époque Han.
Paris, Les Éditions d'art et d'histoire, 1939. 57, [1] p. illus. (incl. maps)
ix pl.

NEW YORK. METROPOLITAN MUSEUM OF ART. Chinese jewelry, a picture
book. New York, 1944. 2 p. 20 plates, [Its Picture books] 1st ed. 1940.

PARISH-WATSON AND CO. The gold treasure of the Emperor Chien Lung of
China, by Berthold Laufer; exhibited by Parish-Watson and Co., New York.
Chicago, A Century of Progress, 1934. 32 p. incl. col. front., illus.

PERZYINSKI, FRIEDRICH. Chinesische Goldgegenstände und Textilien aus dem
Besitze von Friedrich Perzyinski, Rissen-Holstein, mit einem Vorwort von
William Cohn. Auktionsleitung P. Cassirer-H. Helbing. 54 p. incl. illus.
plates.

## Folk Arts

CHINESE PAPER CUT-OUTS, compiles by the Art Service Dept., Union of Chinese Artists. Peking, Distributed by Guozi Shudian, 1956. 6, [3] p. 20
plates (col. and mount.) in portfolio. Text in Chinese, Russian, English,
French and German.

FOLK ARTS OF NEW CHINA. Peking, Foreign Languages Press, 1954. 64 p.
illus. (part col.).

HAWLEY, WILLIS MEEKER, 1896-   Chinese folk design, a collection of cut-
paper designs used for embroidery, together with 160 Chinese art symbols
and their meanings. Hollywood, Calif., 1949. [4] p., 300 plates (part col.)
[16] p. illus.

SELECTED CHINESE PAPER-CUTS, 中國民間剪紙,選集。. [Peking, Guozi Shudian,1957?] [1] l. 17 mounted illus.(part col.).

SOONG, MAYING, 宋奚美英. The art of Chinese paper folding for young and
old, written and illus. by Maying Soong. New York, Harcourt, Brace[1948];
London, Thames and Hudson, [1955] xii, 132 p. illus.

## Christian Art

BORNEMANN, FRITZ. Ars sacra pekinensis. Die chinesisch-christliche Malerei an der katholischen Universität (Fu Jen) in Peking. Mödling bei Wien,
Missionsdruckerei St. Gabriel [c1950] 239 p. plates (part. col.).

FLEMING, DANIEL JOHNSON, 1877-   Each with his own brush; contemporary
Christian art in Asia and Africa. New York, Friendship Press [c1938] 85 p.
incl. front., illus., plates.

LAUFER, BERTHOLD, 1874-1934. Christian art in China. Peking, Reprinted
by the Licoph service, 1939. 100-118, [18] p. illus., plates. "Extract from
'Mitteilungen des Seminars für orientalische sprachen. Jahrgang xiii. Erste
abteilung, Ostasiatische studien. 1910'."

## Miscellaneous

CHINA INSTITUTE IN AMERICA. Exhibition of Chinese snuff bottles of the 17th
and 18th centuries. December 1, 1952 through January 31, 1953. New York

1952. 30 p. illus.

L'ENCRE DE CHINE dans la calligraphie et l'art japonnais contemporains. Exposition circulaire pour l'Europe. Kyōto, Bokubi-shuppansha, 1955. 36 p. plates.

HARCOURT-SMITH, SIMON. A catalogue of various clocks, watches, automata, and other miscellaneous objects of European workmanship dating from the xviiith and the early xixth centuries, in the Palace Museum and the Wu-ying-tien, Peiping. Peiping. The Palace Museum, 1933. 32 p. plates.

HITT, HENRY C. Old Chinese snuff bottles; notes, with a catalogue of a modest collection [by] Henry C. Hitt. 2d ed. Bremerton, Wash., 1945. v, 110 p. incl. illus. 3 mounted phot., map. front. (mounted phot.).

[HSIANG, HUAI-SHU], 項懷述, 18th cent., comp. Recueil de cachets sur la Montagne jaune, traduits et annotés par Pierre Daudin. [Saigon, Imp. de l'Union NG-Yan-Cua, 1932?] 110 p. illus.

HUNG, WILLIAM, 洪業, 1893-    The inkslab in Chinese literary tradition. [Peking, 1940] ii, 21 p. (Occasional papers by the scholars, fellows and their advisers in Chinese studies at Yenching University, 3).

MA, HÊNG. 馬衡, 1880-1955. The fifteen different classes of measures as given in the Lü li chih, 律曆志, of the Sui dynasty history; translated by John C. Ferguson. Peping, 1932. cover-title, 16, 16 p. plates, facsims.

MI, FU, 米芾, 1051-1107. Mi Fu on ink-stones, translated by R. H. van Gulick, with an introduction and notes. Peiping, H. Vetch, 1938. viii, 4, 70, 2 p. incl. front., (port.) illus. (incl. map, facsim.).

TOLEDO. MUSEUM OF ART. Exhibition of East asiatic glass; an exhibition of glass from regions of Asia east of the Himalaya mountains representing twenty-five hundred years of East asiatic interest in glass making. [October 3-31, Toledo, 1948] 28 p. illus.

WERNER, EDWARD THEODORE CHALMERS, 1864-    Chinese weapons. Shanghai, Royal Asiatic Society North China Branch, 1932. 41 p. 59 plates. (Royal Asiatic society (North China branch) [Publications] Extra vol.).

## Music and Musical Instruments

BECKER, BABETTE M. 1901-   Music in the life of ancient China: from 1400 B.C. to 300 B.C.  Chicago [Library, Dept. of Photographic Reproduction, University of Chicago] 1957. Microfilm copy (positive) of typescript. Collation of the original: 98 l. Thesis-University of Chicago.

CHAO, MEI-PA, 趙梅伯, 1907-   The yellow bell, a brief sketch of the history of Chinese music. Baldwin, Md., 1934. ix-xi, 13-61 p. illus. (incl. music) 2 port. (incl. front.).

COHN, JAMES. The construction of Chinese music: a survey of origins and theory, a report for musicology seminar. New York, 1950. 18 p.

DANIÉLOU, ALAIN. The Cycle of Fifths: the musical theory of the Chinese. In: Introduction to the study of musical scales. London, India Society, 1943. pt. III.

ECKARDT, HANS. Chinesische Musik. In: Die Musik in Geschichte und Gegenwart. Kassel, Bärenreiter-Verlag, 1952. Bd. 2, p. 1195-1216.

EDELMAN LILY. Music in China and Japan; classroom material.  New York, Service Bureau for Intercultural Education [c1940] [11], 20 l. ([Bureau for Intercultural Education, New York, Publications] O-23).

EDER, MATTHIAS. Das Jahr im chinesischen Volkskied. Peiping, Catholic University of Peking, 1946. 160 p.

GULIK, ROBERT HANS VAN, 1910-   On three antique lutes. [Tokyo, 1938] [155]-189, xvi (i.e. 10) plates. Reprinted from the Transactions of the Asiatic society of Japan, second series, vol. xvii.

———. The lore of the Chinese lute; an essay in ch'in ideology. Tokyo, Sophia University, 1940. viii, xi-[xii], 224, 13 p. front., illus., plates, facsims., fold. tab. (Monumenta nipponica monographs).

———. Hsi K'ang, 稽康, and his poetical essay on the lute.  Tokyo, Sophia University, 1941. 90 p. col. front., (Monumenta nipponica monographs).

HOWARD, FLORENCE. Lecture recital on Chinese music, Monday evening, February 5, at the Washington Hotel. [Washington, 1934] 4 p.

JIRÁNEK, JAROSLAV. Volkschina in der Musik. [Hrsg. vom Ministerium für Kultur, Hauptabteilung künstlerische Lehranstalten. Dresden, Verlag der Kunst, 1955] 42 p. illus. (Studienmaterial für die künstlerischen Lehranstalten. Musik, Heft 1, 1955).

KAO, MING, 高明, fl. 1345. Lute song, by Kao-Tong-Kia. Adapted for Broadway presentation by Will Irwin and Sidney Howard. Misic by Raymond Scott. Lyrics by Bernard Hanighen.  Chicago, Dramatic Pub. Co. [1955] 92 p. 1st ed. 1954.

KISHIBE, SHIGEO.  The origin of the p'i p'a with particular reference to the five stringed p'i p'a preserved in the Shôsôin. (In Asiatic society of Japan. Transactions. Tokyo [etc.] 1940. 2d ser., v. 19, p. [259]-304. illus. (map) plates).

KORNFELD, FRITZ. Die tonale Struktur Chinesischer Musik. Mödling bei Wien, St. Gabriel Verlag, 1955. 143 p. plates, (St. Gabrieler Studien, 16).

LEPEL, FELIX VON. Die Musik im alten China. Eine Kulturgeschichtliche Studie. Berlin-Charlottenburg, Selbst-Verlag, 1954. 16 p.

LEVIS, JOHN HAZEDEL. Vocal and instrumental recitals with explanatory talks on the music of China.  New York, Recital arrangement Arthur Judson, 1932. 4 p. illus. (port.).

———. John Hazedel Levis in concert lectures on "The Chinese through their music." Vocal and instrumental recitals with explanatory talks. [New York,

1934] 4 p. illus. (port.).

————. Foundations of Chinese musical art; illustrated with musical compositions. Peiping, H. Vetch, 1936. [v]-xiii, 233, [1] p. incl. mounted front., illus. music) diagrs.

MA, HIAO-TS'IUN, 馬孝駿 . La musique chinoise de style européen. Paris, Jouve, 1941. 135 p. illus. (music) Thèse-Univ. de Paris.

MENG, CHIH, 孟治, 1900-    Remarks on Chinese music and musical instruments. New York, China Institute in America [c1932] 14 p. illus. (incl. music) diagrs.

[ MORGAN, HARRY TITTERTON] 1872-    Chinese music, ed. for and copyrighted by Quon-Quon Co. Los Angeles, c1944. 16 p. illus., music. (His Chinese classics in miniature).

PICKEN, Laurence. Chinese music. In: Grove's Dictionary of Music and Musicians. 5th ed. London, Macmillan, 1954. v. 2, p. 219-248.

PISCHNER, HANS. Musik in China. Berlin, Henschelverlag, 1955. 152 p. illus. ports., fold. map.

REINHARD, KURT. Chinesische Musik. Eisenach, E. Röth [1956] 246 p. illus. (part col.) facsims., music (Das Gesicht der Völker).

RICHARD, MARY (MARTIN) ''MRS: TIMOTHY RICHARD,'' 1843-1903. Paper on Chinese music, read before the China branch of the Royal Asiatic society, Shanghai, November, 1898. Repeated (by request) before the Shanghai literary and debating society, January 4th, 1899. [4th ed] Shanghai, Presbyterian Mission Press, 1923. 40 p. front., (port.) illus., plates.

ROGERS, MARY JAMES, sister. Music in the Maryknoll mission field; the problem and our efforts to meet it. [Maryknoll, N.Y., Sisters' Motherhouse] 1938. 75 numb. 1. illus. (music) (Maryknoll teacher training school, Maryknoll, New York. Bulletin, 4).

SCHNEERSON, G. Die Musikkultur Chinas. Übers. aus dem Russischen von Renate Schubert. Leipzig, Hofmeister, 1955. 212 p. illus.

SHIAO CHAO CHINESE MUSIC RESEARCH INSTITUTE, Shanghai. The Shiao Chao Chinese music research institute in commemoration of its tenth anniversary presents its orchestra in a concert of classical Chinese music. Lyceum Theatre, Shanghai. Nov. 1, 1935. Shanghai, Mercury Press, 1935. 16, [20] p. front. illus. plate.

U. S. Library of Congress. Orientalia Division. Books on East Asiatic music in the Library of Congress printed before 1800. [Washington, Govt. Print. Off., 1945] 121-133 p. ''Reprinted from the Supplement to the Catalog of early books on music, 1944.''

VAN AALST, J    A. Chinese music. Published by order of the Inspector General of Customs. Peiping, Re-issued by the French Bookstore, 1933. iv, 84 p. front., illus. (incl. music) plates, diagrs. (China. [Inspectorate general of customs] Imperial maritime customs. ii. - Special series, 6). 1st ed. 1884.

WERNER, EDWARD THEODORE CHALMERS, 1864-    Chinese ditties. Tientsin, Tientsin Press, 1922. 56 p.

WILHELM, RICHARD, 1873-1930, ed. Chinesische Musik. [Frankfurt a. M., China-Institut, 1927] 64 p. illus., 3 plates (1 mounted) diagrs.

WONG, FLORENCE FENG-YEE, 黃奉儀, [HUANG FENG-I] 1918-    Music education in modern Chinese schools. New York, 1952. 189 1. charts, music. Thesis-Teachers College. Columbia University.

## Musical Compositions

ALL-CHINA FEDERATION OF DEMOCRATIC YOUTH. Songs of new China. Peking, Foreign Languages Press, 1953. 47 p.

ANSON, GEORGE, 1904-    Chinese chatter; piano solo. New York, Edward B. Marks Music Corp., 1953.

BANTOCK, SIR GRANVILLE. 1868-1946. China national and patriotic songs; arranged for solo voice or chorus with pianoforte accompaniment. London, W. Paxton, 1946.

CHANSONS POPULAIRES CHINOISES. Traduites par Ting Oueng, 丁篁. Pékin, Impr. de la "Politique de Pékin," 1935. 40 p. (Collection de la "Politique de Pékin").

[CH'ÊNG, MAO-YÜN] 程懋筠. The Chinese national anthem, arranged as a song or piano solo by Granville Bantock. London, W. Paxton [1943] 3 p.

———. National anthem of the Republic of China; issued on the occasion of 40th anniversary of the founding of the Republic, October 10, 1911-1951. [Translated by Tu Ting Hsiu, 杜庭修; acc. by Chao Yüan-Jen, 趙元任] New York, Chinese News Service [1951] [4] p. col. illus., ports.

CHEREPNIN, ALEKSANDR NIKOLAEVICH, 1899-    [Songs on Chinese poems, Op. 71] Seven songs on Chinese poems; English version by the composer. Bonn, M. P. Belaieff, 1956. 28 p.

———. The lost flute; for narrator and orchestra. Version for narrator, piano and percussion. Texts from Chinese poems translated by Gertrude Joerissen. Score. New York, Alec Templeton, 1956. 36 p.

CHINA RECONSTRUCTS. Folk songs from China. Shanghai, 1955. 12 p. (Supplement to China Reconstructs, No. 9).

CHOU, WEN-CHUNG, 周文中, 1923-    Seven poems of the T'ang dynasty; translated by Louise Varèse. New York, New Music, 1952. Score (36 p.) (New Music 25:4).

EICHHEIM, HENRY, 1870-1942. [Oriental impressions. Chinese sketch] Oriental impressions, Chinese sketch. For flute, oboe, violin, viola, harp, and percussion instruments (bells of metal and wood) 1921. score ([8] l.).

GOULD, MORTON, 1913-    New China march; based on the Chinese song "Work as one" by Shu Mo. New York, Mills Music, [c1943] 7 p. and 28 pts.

GRAVES, STELLA MARIE. Min river boat songs, by Stella Marie Graves; tunes collected by Malcolm F. Farley. New York, John Day [1946] 48 p.

HO, LÜ-T'ING, 賀綠汀. Longing for the past; piano-solo. Edited by Alexandre Tcherepnine. Peping, Commercial Press; New York, G. Schirmer [c1936] [4] p. ([Collection] Alexandre Tcherepnine, no. 9).

———. Four songs. Tokyo, Ryuginsha, c1936. 12 p. (Collection Alexandre Tcherepine, 23).

———. Evening party and "Sangidema." Peking, Foreign Languages Press, 195? 22 p.

HSI, HSING-HAI, 冼星海, --1945. Yellow River cantata, 黃河大合唱. text by Kwang Wei-yuan, 光未然, adapted for American use by Wallingford Riegger. New York, Leeds Music Corp., 1946.

HSU, ROSABEL, 徐欣. Free China; Chinese march-polka. Tsi u Chung Kao [or] Dou yeu Chung Koa. Rev. ed. Words by Dick Rogers, music by Rosabel Hsu. New York, Shapiro, Bernstein and Co., 1952.

HUNKINS, EUSEBIA SIMPSON, 1902-    comp. Six old Chinese melodies; music [compiled and] transcribed by Eusebia Simpson Hunkins. [Illustrations by Ruth E. Taylor, edited for flute by Frederick Wilkins] Athens, O., Lawhead Press, 1949.

JACOBS, A    GERTRUDE, comp. The Chinese-American song and game book, compiled by A. Gertrude Jacobs; illustrations by Chao Shih Chen, 趙世珍, music by Virginia and Richard Mather, text romanization by Ching Yi Hsu, 徐敬儀, Chinese characters by Yun Hsia, 夏雲. New York, A. S. Barnes, [1944] 96 p. incl. front. (port.) illus. (part col.).

K'EH, CHENG-HO, 柯政和. Chinese folk songs selected by K'eh Cheng-ho. Peiping, China Music Co., 1934. 16 p.

KOO, TS ZUNG, 顧子仁, 1887-    comp. Songs of Cathay, an anthology of songs current in various parts of China among her people. 4th impression. Shanghai, The Association Press [1930] [59] p.

————. Folk songs from China. English text by Irene Gass and Arthur Waley; music arranged by Reginald Redman; edited by Maurice Jacobson. London, The Hon. Lady Cripps, J. Curwen: New York, G. Schirmer, c1943. 23 p. (Curwen edition, 906001).

KWOH, HUAN-SHOU孟郭煥綏. 1916-    Feng young flower drum song; Song: Chinese folk song. English version by Chih Meng, melody traditional, accompaniment by Kwoh Huan-shou. New York, 1952.

————. Purple bamboo; a lullaby, song: Chinese folk song, English version by Chih Meng, melody: traditional, accompaniment by Kwoh Huan-shou. New York, 1952.

————. Wong ching-long; Song: traditional, arrangement: Kwoh Huan-shou. On arrangement and piano accompaniment; Chih Meng. New York, 1952.

LEE, DAI-KEONG, 1915-    A bitter love; original poem by Li Po (705-762 A. D.) translated by Witter-Bynner. New York, Sprague-Coleman, 1946. (c1942).

————. A farewell to a friend; original poem by Li Po, translated by Witter-Bynner. New York, Sprague -Coleman, 1946 (c1942).

————. In spring. [Words by Li Po, translated by Witter Bynner] New York, Sprague-Coleman, 1946 (c1942).

————. East and West; text by Hermann Hagedorn, arranged for mixed voices, S. A. T. B. With baritone and soprano solo, with piano accompaniment. New York, Mills Music, 1946.

[LEE, PAO-CHÊN]; 李抱辰, 1907-    comp. China's patriots sing. [Enl. ed. Calcutta, Chinese Ministry of Information, 1944?] cover-title, 53 p. 1st ed. 1939.

[————] comp. Songs of fighting China. [New York, Chinese news service, 1944] cover-title, 53 p.

LIEBERMANN, ROLF, 1910-    Chinesische Liebeslieder nach Übersetzungen von Klabund. Chinese love songs after the translation by Klabund. English version by Eric Smith. Gesang und Klavier. Wien, Zürich, London, Universal Edition, 1956. vi, 48 p.

LINEBARGER, PAUL MYRON WENTWORTH, 1871-1939. Sun Yatsen anniversary songs. Words and music by Paul M. Linebarger. Washington,1935. 6 p.

————. Les chansons anniversaires pour Sun Yat Sen, foundateur de la République de Chine. Paroles et musique de Paul Myron Linebarger. 3e éd. [Paris, Impr. Chaffange et Cie, 1936] Cover-title, 3-42 p. [1er éd., Shanghai,1933].

LIU, LIANG-MO, 劉良模, comp. China sings; folk-songs and fighting songs of China arranged and translated by Evelyn Modoi. New York, C. Fischer, c1945. 28 p.

————. High is the blue sky (a Chinese children's song). Author and composer unknown, arranged by Liu Liang-mo and Donna Nichols. New York, United China Relief, 1945.

LUM, MARYETTE HAWLEY. Farmer's song. Chinese work song arranged for 4-part chorus. English words by Berta Metzger and Maryette Lum. Peiping, China Music Co., 1934. 8 p.

————. Fisherman's song: ancient Chinese poems by Cheng Pan-chiao, 鄭板橋, translated and harmonized by Maryette Lum. Peiping, China Music Co., c1934. 10 p.

————. Songs of Chinese children, a collection of Chinese folk songs and songs based on Chinese folk-rhymes and folk-tunes. Illustrations by Lin Yu Ts'ang, 林甫蒼. New York, Los Angeles [etc.] Suttonhouse Publishers, [c1939] 32 p. incl. front., illus. 1st ed. Tientsin, 1936. (c1937).

MA, KO, 馬可. North Shensi suite, 陝北組曲. Peking, Foreign Languages Press, 195? 32 p.

MA, SZE-CHUNG, 馬思聰. Longing for home, 思鄉曲. Peking, Foreign Languages Press, 1952. 16 p.

————. North frontier dance,塞外舞曲. Peking, Foreign Languages Press, 1952. 25 p.

SONGS and dances of the Chinese youth. Peking, Foreign Languages Press, 1957.

1 v. (unpaged) chiefly illus. (part col).

UNITED SERVICE TO CHINA. Cheer China. New York 194? 64 [i.e. 72] p. illus.

WANG, HSIN. 王莘. Song of the motherland, 歌唱祖國. Peking, Foreign Languages Press. 1952. 3 p.

WIANT, BLISS 1895- The pagoda; thirteen songs from China. Arranged for group singing and translated by Bliss Wiant. 3rd ed. Delaware, O., Cooperative Recreation Service, c1946. 31 p.

————. Chinese lyrics; a collection of twenty-seven compositions of ancient, classic, folk and modern songs, ed. by T. Tertius Noble. Arr. with piano accompaniment by Bliss Wiant. Text tr. by Bliss Wiant and others. New York, J. Fischer [1947] 55 p. illus.

WILSON, DON. Chinese morning song; S.S.A., lyric by Don Wilson. Arranged from a Chinese folk tune, with piano acc. New York, Bourne, 1948.

YANG, ERNEST Y. L., 楊蔭瀏, 1900- Chinese Christian hymns; by Chinese writers, with Chinese tunes, selected from the Chinese hymn book Hymns of Universal Praise. English translations by Frank W. Price. [Edited by Ernest Y. L. Yang and Bliss Wiant. Principally close score] New York, c Frank W. Price, 1953.

YAO, CHIN-HSIN, 陳姚錦新, 1914- The flower drum and other Chinese songs [by] Chin-hsin Yao Chen and Shih-hsiang Chen, 陳世驤; foreword by Pearl S. Buck, preface by Henry Cowell. New York, John Day [1943] 64 p. incl. front. illus.

## Sports

ALL-CHINA ATHLETIC FEDERATION. Five national sports meets, 1953. Peking, People's Sports Pub. House, 1953. 1 v. (chiefly illus.).

————. Sport flourishes in New China. Peking, Foreign Languages Press, 1955. 32 p. (chiefly illus.).

[————]. China's sports to-day. Peking, Foreign Languages Press, 1956. 24 p. plates.

————. Sports in China. Peking, 1956. 1 v (chiefly illus.).

ALL-CHINA FEDERATION OF TRADE UNIONS. Workers' sports in China. [Peking] Workers Press [1956] 42, [4] p. of illus. (part. col.).

CH'ÊN, YEARNING K., 陳炎林, [CH'ÊN YEN-LIN] T'ai-chi ch'üan, its effects and practical applications. Shanghai [1947] vi, 184 p. illus., diagrs.

HOH, GUNSUN, 郝更生 1899- Physical education in China. Shanghai, Commercial Press, 1926. xvii, 314 p. fold. front., illus., fold. plate.

KIANG, LIANG-KWE, 江良規. Die Leibesübungen in alten China. Wurzburg, Triltsch, 1939. 59 p. (Körperliche Erziehung und Sport. Beiträge zur Sportwissenschaft, 2).

WEE, KOK ANN, 黃國安, 1897- Physical education in Protestant Christian colleges and universities of China. New York, 1937. vii, 105 p. diagrs. Issued also as thesis, Columbia-university.

## Hunting

CALDWELL, HARRY R. Blue tiger; introduction by Roy Chapman Andrews. New York, Abingdon Press [c1924]; London, Duckworth, 1925. 3-261 p. front., plates.

WONG-QUINCEY, J., 王文顯, 1886- Chinese hunter; foreword by Lin Yutang. New York, The John Day; London, R. Hale, 1939. 383, [1] p. front., illus. (map) plates, ports., diagr.

————. Souvenirs d'un chasseur chinois. Avant-propos de Lin Yutang. Paris, Payot, 1941. 413 p. (Bibliothèque géographique).

## Games: Chess

GRUBER, KARL. Das chinesische Schachspiel; Einführung mit Aufgaben und
Partien. Peking [etc.] Siebenberg-Verlag, 1937; Wien, Krey im Komm.,
1938. [4], 117 p. front.
——. Chinese chess; translated by Maria G. Ruck. Peiping, Siebenberg Ver-
lag, [1937]. iv, 117 p. plate, front. diagr. in pocket.
PECORINI, DANIELE, conte, 1872-    The game of wei-chi. With a foreword by
Professor H. A. Giles. London, New York, Longmans, Green, 1929. vii,
128, [14] p. incl. diagrs.
WILKES, CHARLES FRED, 1926-    A manual of Chinese chess. San Francisco,
Yamato Press [1952] 33 p. illus.

## Majong

AMERICAN CODE OF LAWS FOR MAH-JONG; mixed-hand one-double cleared-
hand games, adapted and endorsed by Jean Bray and others. New York, J.
H. Smith, 1924. 40 p.
AUCTION bridge and mah jong magazine. v. 1-2; Feb.-Sept. 1924. [New York,
John H. Smith, 1924] 2 v. illus. monthly.
BABCOCK, JOSEPH PARK. Babcock's rules for mah-jongg; the red book of
rules. 2d ed., rev. and enl., including full code of official laws and examples
of illustrative hands. San Francisco, Mah-jongg Sales Company of America;
1923) ii-vii, 117 p. illus.
——. Babcock's Regeln für Mah Jongg. 2 Aufl. Durchgesehen und erweitert
mit offizielen Regeln und Beispielen und erlauternden Partien. Frankfurt a.
M., Mah-Jongg Co., 1924. vii, 118 p. illus.
——. The laws of mah-jongg, 1925 code, revised and standardized by Joseph
Park Babcock and an associated committee. Containing also the new game du-
lo, by Mr. Babcock. Salem, Mass., Parker Brothers, [c1925] 48 p. port.
BOULON, F    GEORGE. Standard rules and instructions for the Chinese game
of ma chiang (sparrow) with notes on the American and one suit games. [New
York, A. J. Brandt] c1924. 32 p. illus.
BRAY, JEAN. How to play mah jong, 2d ed., rev. and much enl., with an added
chapter on special bonus scores and "limit hands." New York and London,
G. P. Putnam, 1923. x, 162 p. illus.
BREWSTER EUGENE VALENTINE, 1869-    Mah-jong simplified and one hun-
dred winning points, all the fine points in mah-jong at a glance. New York,
Brewster, [c1924] 35 p.
CAMPBELL, WINIFRED W. Mah-jong scoring combinations and conventions.
[Forsyth, Mont., Times-Journal, 1924] [4] p.
CECIL, VIOLA L. New mah jongg, by Viola L. Cecil and Lenore Medinets. 2nd
ed. New York, The author, 1937. 41 p. illus.
——. Maajh, the American version of an ancient Chinese game. [New York,
Printed by Hallco, c1938] 53 p. illus.
——. Maajh. 5th rev. ed. New York, The author, 1943. v, 48 p. illus.
CHINESE SPARROW GAME, or, Mah jongg; the ancient game of China. Boston,
Chinese Mah Jongg Co. [1923] 12 p. illus.
CHUE, JOHN ALFRED. The mastering of mah jongg. Hongkong, Yew Kee,
c1925. iv, 58 p. illus.
DIRECTIONS of playing "Chinese game of four winds." Hong Kong, Man Shing
Press, 1956. 22 p.
DOUGLASS, SILAS J. Instruction, suggestion and rules for playing the Chinese
game. Pasadena, Calif., c1923. 16 p.
[DOYEN, CLAUDE FAY]. Rules for playing mah-jongg (the sparrow) and sugges-
tions for play, by "Hendersonia" [pseud.] [Washington, D. C., Beresford
Linotype Co., c1922] cover-title, 16 p. plates.

DWIGGINS, ELMER. White dragons wild, and how to win at ma jong; an advanced study of the world's most wonderful game as adapted to American playing. [Los Angeles, Phillips Printing Co., c1924] 61 p. illus. (port.).

FOSTER, ROBERT FREDERICK, 1853-    The laws of mah jong (pung chow, etc.) for 1924, as proposed for the American game. New York, Vanity Fair [c1923] cover-title, 45 p.

———. Foster on mah jong. New York, Dodd, Mead, 1924. ix, 262 p. illus.

———. Twenty-point mah jong, with the American standard code of laws for all forms of the game. New York, Dodd, Mead, 1924. xi, 157 p. illus.

GERSTLE, RALPH J   F.   The green book of rules and regulations for majong. 3d ed., rev. and enl., with illustrated cuts and examples, showing a comprehensive and detailed method of play. [Chicago] Ma-jong Club of Chicago [c1923] 55, [1] p. incl. illus., plates.

[HARR, LEW LYSLE] 1882-    Pung-chow, the game of a hundred intelligences. Worcester, Mass., Pung-Chow Co. [c1922] [17] p. col. illus.

[———]. Pung chow in ten minutes (without a teacher) New York, Shanghai, Pung Chow Co., c1923. [27] p. illus. (part col.).

———. How to play pung chow, the game of a hundred intelligences, also known as mah-diao, mah-jong, mah-cheuk, mah-juck, and pe-ling. Rev. and enl. ed. New York and London, Harper, [c1923] 128 p. illus. 1st ed. 1922.

HARTMAN, LEE FOSTER, 1879-    Standardized mah jong; a manual of tactics for mixed hands, cleared hands, one-double game, and the American code of laws for mah-jongg. New York and London, Harper, 1924. xvii, 311 p. illus. (part col.).

HIRSCHFELD, OSCAR D. Mah-jongg; eine Einführung in das altchinesische Spiel. Leipzig, Grethlein, 1924. 47 p. incl. tables. illus. plates.

HOE, SANG M., 何生文. Mah jongg, the ancient game of China. New York, Long San Ti Chinese Curio Co., 4th ed. c1923. 34 p. 1st ed. 1922.

HOW TO PLAY MAH-JONG. Shanghai, Chun Wah Trading Co., 192? 24 p.

INTERNATIONAL MA CHIANG PLAYERS' ASSOCIATION. The laws of ma chiang, as adopted by the International ma chiang players' association. New York, 1924. [54] p.

IRWIN, FLORENCE, 1869-    The complete mah jong player. New York, Brentano's [1924] xii, 206 p. illus., diagr.

[ISRAEL, ARTHUR JULIUS]. How to play mah-jong, rules which govern the play in the principal American, European and Chinese clubs in Shanghai, Hongkong and Peking, as well as in the American and British fleets in the Far East. [New York, Oriental Export Co., c1923] cover-title, 24 p. illus.

KAN, ANDREW. Mah jong; a complete description of the game with authoritative rules, -liberally illustrated. Detroit, Shanghai Trading Co. [c1924] 47 p. illus.

KANAI, SHOZO. Mah jong for beginners, based on the rules and regulations of the Mah jong Association of Japan, by Shozo Kanai and Margaret Farrell. Tokyo and Rutland, Vt., Tuttle, 1952. 62 p. illus.

KRICK, LEONARD B. The blue book of mah-jong, the royal game. Chicago, Beatty Brothers [c1924] [36] p. illus., diagr.

LANE, THOMAS. Modern mah jong. Rev. ed. Chicago, Rand McNally, 1938. 64 p. illus.

LE HAIN, G.   M. Mah jongg. Montreal, Renouf Pub. Co., 1924. x, 86 p.

LEE, CHIANG. Mah jong and how to play it. 3rd ed. London, T. de la Rue, 1923. 95 p.

LIM, YANG-CHOW. The original rules of the ancient Chinese game, maa-jok. Seattle, Y.C. Lim, c1923. 9-50 p. front., illus.

LY, YU-SANG, 黎曜生, 1889-    Sparrow: the Chinese game called ma-ch'iau; a descriptive and explanatory story. New York, Long Sang Ti; Chinese Curios Co. [c1923] xiii, 128 p. col. front., illus.

MAH-JONGG LEAGUE, London. The official standardised rules of the Mah-jongg league limited.  Mah-jongg; rules for playing in the Chinese manner, with a foreword by the Hon. President, Miss Sybil Thorndike, with some "don'ts" for players; written and illustrated by Olga Racster.  London, Heath, Cranton;  Philadelphia, David McKay, 1924. 52 p. incl. front., illus.

MEYERSON, DOROTHY SKLAREW. "That's it, " the authentic system of playing Chinese tiles. [ Forest Hills, N. Y., 1937. 48 p. illus.

MORGAN, CASEY BRUCE, 1867-   Ma jong scoring made easy, and notes on playing; the scoring table analysed and discussed, thereby permanently fixing it in the player's memory. New York, Brentano's [ c1924] 41 p.

MORRIS  WILLIAM C. The game of mahjuck; Chinese dominos - also called mah chang, moh tsiah, pung chow and mah jongg. "Old in China-new in America." Description of pieces, details of playing, manner of scoring, suggestions for discarding, percentages and penalties, comments and memoranda. [ Los Angeles, Morris and Lelevier, c1922] 40 p.

[NAFTALY, PHILIP]  How to play ma jong. [San Francisco, Bowles-Broad Printing Works] c1922. cover-title 8, [ 1] p. illus.

[———]. Rules and directions for the Chinese game of "ma cheuck" (sparrows), also known as "ma jong," "mah diao," "pung-chow," "le ping" and other translations of the different Chinese dialects. A simple and complete explanation of the original Chinese game, tr. and comp. from Chinese rule books, and aided by Chinese experts of the game. [San Francisco, Bowles-Broad Printing Works] c1923. cover-title, 23, [ 1] p. illus.

NANYANG BROTHERS, INC., New York. Rules for playing mah jong.  New York, Nanyang Brothers, [ c1923] [ 15] p. illus.

NEVIN, ROBERT W. Complete instructions for mah jong.  New York, Hollis Press, c1924. [ 11] p. illus.

[ RIXFORD, LORING P. ] The dragon rule book for sparrow, ma ch'iau. [ New York, c1924] cover-title, 16 p. illus.

[ ROBERTSON, MARIAN]. Mah jong score book, with rules and definitions. This book may be used as a permanent record if desired, by dating each score page. New York, Wilmerding and Wilmerding [ c1924] [ 124] p.

ROBERTSON, MAX. Game of mah jong. 6th ed. London, Whitcombe and Tombs, 1941. 48 p.

[ ROSENBLATT, MARTIN STERN]. Majong (the game of sparrow) San Francisco, S. and G. Gump, [ c1922] cover-title, 12 p. illus.

RULES and how to play mah-jongg. Lahore, India, Civil and Military Gazette, 1946. 17 p.

SCOTT, VERN E. Official rules for pe-ling as played with cards. [San Francisco, Greeley, c1923] 16 p. plates.

———. Official rules for pe-ling, the original Chinese game played by the mandarins for centuries. [San Francisco, Greeley, c1923] 15 p. illus.

SNYDER, HENRY M. The ma-jung manual, with introduction by Ezra H. Fitch. Rev. ed. Boston and New York, Houghton Mifflin, 1924. xiii, [ 1], 209, [ 1] p. front., illus., plates. 1st ed., 1923.

The STANDARD rules of Mah Jongg and how to play it.  Harborne, Eng., Chad Valley Co., 1954 (c1923) 23 p.

STERLING, HAROLD. Standard rules and instructions for the Chinese game of mah chang (sparrow). 3d ed. [Albany, N. Y., Oriental Arts Co., c1923] 21 p. illus.

TCHOU, KIA-KIEN, 朱家健, [CHU CHIA-CHIEN]. Le jeu de mah-jong tel qu'il est joué par les Chinois (Préface de Lucien Corpechot) Paris, Éditeurs associés, 1924. 142 p.

TOW, JULIUS SU, 屠汝煉, 1895-   The outline of mah jong; how to play and how to win, the real Chinese methods. [New York, Printed by The Pacific Printing Co., c1924] 64 p. illus.

WARREN, EMILY STANLEY, " MRS. PRESCOTT WARREN." The game of ma chiang.  New York, Thomas Y. Crowell [ c1924] x, 402 p. incl. front., illus.

WEI, WING LOCK, 韋榮胳, 1892-1935. The theory of mah jong, its principles, psychology, tactics, strategies, and fine points, including the complete Chinese rules of play. Boston, Small, Maynard [c1925] viii, 76 p. illus.

WILCOX, CONSTANCE GRENELLE. Mah-jongg; the play of one hundred intelligences, in a prologue and one act, with music in the Chinese manner by Harvey Worthington Loomis. Boston. C.C. Birchard, [c1923] 75, [1] p. plates.

WINTERS, EDGAR S. Ma cheuk (also called "mah jong," "pung chow" and "ma-jung") as played by the Chinese. New York, E. P. Dutton, [c1923] 161 p. incl. front., illus.

WORK, MILTON COOPER. Mah-jongg, up-to-date, including the American official laws of mah-jongg. Philadelphia, John C. Winston [c1924] 177 p. front. (5 port.) illus.

# XIX. NATURAL SCIENCE

## General Works

ACADEMIA SINICA. National Research Council. Science bibliography of China, 中國科學著作目錄 . Nanking, 1936. 9 pts. (various pagings).

BERNARD, HENRI. La science européenne au tribunal astronomique de Pékin (xviie-xixe siècles) Conférence faite au Palais de la découverte le 16 juin 1951. Paris [1952] 39 p. illus., port., map. facsims., diagr. (Conférences du Palais de la découverte. Sér. D, Histoire des sciences, no 9).

GLATHE, A. Die chinesischen Zahlen. Tokyo, Deutsche Gesellschaft für Natur- und Völkerkunde Ostasiens, 1932. 47 p. illus. (incl. facsims., ports.) (Tokyo. Deutsche Gesellschaft für Natur-und Völkerkunde Ostasiens. Mitteil. Bd. 26, Teil B).

HOANG, PIERRE,黃伯祿, [HUANG PÊ-LU], 1830-1909. Catalogue des éclipses de soleil et de lune relatées dans les documents chinois et collationnées avec le canon de Th. Ritter v. Oppolzer. Changhai, Impr. de T'ou-sè-wè, 1925. vi, 169 p. (Variétés Sinologiques, 56).

KWA, TAK-MING, 柯德明 , [K'O TÊ-MING]. The fundamental operations in bead arithmetic; how to use the Chinese abacus. Manila, P.I., 1922. 52 p. illus.

LANCHESTER, GEORGE. The Yellow Emperor's south-pointing chariot. [Lecture delivered to the China Society, Feb. 3, 1947] With a note by A. C. Moule. London, China Society [1947] cover-title, 6 p. illus.

LI, SHU-HUA, 李書華, 1890- Origine de la boussole. Cambridge, 1954. 2 pts. in 1. illus. plates. Reprinted from Isis, 45: 139.

MORGAN, LEONARD GEOFFREY. The teaching of science to the Chinese, with a foreword by A. H. Crook. Hong Kong, Kelly and Walsh, 1933. xxi, 150 p.

NEEDHAM, JOSEPH, 1900- Chinese science. London, Pilot Press [1945] 71, [9] p. illus.

————. Science and civilisation in China, by Joseph Needham with the reaearch assistance of Wang Ling, 王鈴. Cambridge [Eng.] University Press, 1954- v. illus., maps (2 fold.). Contents.-v. 1. Introductory orientations. - v2. History of scientific thought.

PEKING. NATIONAL UNIVERSITY. The fortieth anniversary papers of the National university of Peking. (Peiping? 1944] cover-title, 171 numb. 1. plates (2 mounted) maps (part fold.) diagrs. (part mounted).

SCESNEY, F C. The Chinese abacus. [Buffalo] c1944. 68 l. illus.

SCIENCE SOCIETY OF CHINA. The Science Society of China; its history. organization and activities. In commomoration of the formal opening of the Science Society of China Library in Shanghai and the new Biological Laboratory in Nanking. Shanghai Science Press, 1931. cover-title, 31, [38] p. plates. fold. diagr. 1st ed. 1929.

SHANGHAI SCIENCE INSTITUTE. Library. List of scientific periodicals in the library of the Shanghai Science Institute. [Shanghai] 1934. cover-title, 83 p.

SINO-BRITISH SCIENCE CO-OPERATION OFFICE. Science outpost; papers, 1942-1946. Ed. by Joseph Needham and Dorothy Needham. London, Pilot Press, 1948. 313 p. illus., ports., maps.

SIU, RALPH GUN HOY, 蕭根開 [HSIAO KEN-KAI], 1917- The Tao of science; an essay on Western knowledge and Eastern wisdom. Cambridge, Technology Press, Massachusetts Institute of Technology and New York, John Wiley, 1957. 180 p.

TARANZANO, CHARLES. Vocabulaire des sciences: mathematiques, physiques et naturelles. Sien Hsien, Impr. de la Mission catholique, 1923-36. 2 v.

Supplément au vocabulaire français-chinois des sciences; classifications, tableaux synoptiques. Sien Hsien, Impr. de la Mission catholique, 1923. 120 p. illus. Supplément: Radioélectricité par Marcel Lichtenberger. Sien Hsien, Impr. de la Mission catholique, 1938.

TOKUNAGA, SHIGEYASU, 1874-    Natural science research of the first Scientific Expedition to Manchoukuo. [Tokyo?] 1934. 76 p. illus. (incl. ports.) plates (1 fold.) fold. map. (Report of the first Scientific expedition to Manchoukuo, 1933. Section 1).

TWISS  GEORGE RANSOM, 1863-    Science and education in China; a survey of the present status and a program for progressive improvement, published under the auspices of the Chinese National Association for the Advancement of Education, Peking, China. Shanghai, Commercial Press, 1925. ix, 361 p.

U. S. Library of Congress. Science Division. Chinese scientific and technical serial publications in the collections of the Library of Congress. Washington, 1955. vii, 55 p.

WANG, LING, 王鈴. The Chiu-Chang Suan-Shu, 九章算術, and the history of Chinese mathematics during the Han dynasty. Cambridge, Eng., 1956. 300, 255 p. Thesis-University of Cambridge.  255 l.

WORLD FEDERATION OF SCIENTIFIC WORKERS. The social responsibility of scientists; report of meeting held in Peking, China, on Paril 3, 1956, to celebrate the tenth anniversary of the founding of the World Federation of Scientific Workers. Peking, All-China Federation of Scientific Societies, 1956. 67 p.

YAP, POW-MENG, 葉寶明 [YEH, PAO-MING]. The place of science in China. London, China Campaign Committee [1945?] 22, [2] p.

Astronomy

BURGAUD, MAURICE. Le pendule élastique inversé. Son spplication au nivellement des instruments astronomiques. Quelques essais. Changhai, Impr. de la Mission catholique à l'Orphelinat de T'ou-sè-wè, 1939, iv, 28 p. illus. plates, diagrs. (Annales de l'Observatoire astronomique de So-Se. T. 22, fasc. 1).

FANG, J    T., 方俊. Report on stronomical determination of latitude and longitude. Nanking, Geological Survey of China, 1936. cover-title, 45 p. illus., tables (2 fold.) 2 fold, diagr. (China. Geological survey. Geological memoirs, ser. B, no. 9).

KAO, KIUN,高平子. Conversion des dates chinoises en jours de la période julienne, 史日長編. Nanking, National Research Institute of Astronomy, 1932. 171 p. (Its monographs, 1).

KAO, LOU, 高魯, 1876-1947. The past and the future of the Peking central observatory. Peking, Central Observatory, 1925. 20, 21 p.

———. Le passé et l'avenir de l'Observatoire central de Pékin. Pékin, Publication de l'Observatoire central [1925] 21, [1] 20 p. 21, [1] p. illus. (incl. charts).

———. L'évolution des asterismes chinois,    星象統箋 . Nanking, National Research Institute of Astronomy, 1933. 159, vi p. (Its Monographs, 2).

LEJAY, PIERRE. Exploration gravimétrique de l'Extrême-Orient. [Paris, Soc. gén. d'impr. et d'éd.] 1936. [5]-75 p. incl. tables, diagrs. charts (part fold.) diagr.

LÜBKE, ANTON, 1890-    Der Himmel der Chinesen; mit Abbildungen im Text und 76 Abbildungen auf 39 Tafeln. Leipzig, R. Voigtländer [c1931] 141 p. illus. (incl. music) 39 plates. (incl. diagr.).

SAUSSURE, LÉOPOLD DE, 1866-1925. Les origines de l'astronomie chinoise. Paris, Librairie orientale et américaine Maisonneuve frères [1940] x, 594, [4] p. diagrs. ''Réproduction photomécanique posthume d'articles parus dans le Tóung pao.''

T'IEN WÊN T'U, 天文圖. The Soochow astronomical chart [by] W. Carl Rufus and Hsing-chih Tien 田興智. Ann Arbor, University of Michigan Press, 1945.    v, 24 p. maps, charts.

YU, CH'ING-SUNG, 余青松, 1898-    The total solar eclipse of September 21, 1941. Kunming, National Research Institute of Astronomy, 1940. 9 p. incl. tables, fold. map.

ZI-KA-WEI, Observatoire. Annales de l'Observatoire astronomique de Zô-sè (Chine) fondé et dirigé par les missionaries de la Compagnie de Jésus. Changhai, Impr. de la Mission catholique à l'orphelinat de T'ou-sè-wè, 1907-1943. 22 v. plates, diagrs.

————. Notes de sismologie. No. 1-11 (1920-1931). Zi-ka-wei, Impr. de T'ou-sè-wè, 1921-1931.    v.

————. Cooperation de l'Observatoire de Zi-ka-wei à la revision internationale des longitudes. Changhai, Impr. de la Mission catholique à l'Orphelinat de T'ou-sè-wè, 1927. 1 p. iii, 156 p. plates (incl. ports. diagrs. (part col., part fold.) (Annales de l'Observatoire astronomique de Zo-Se. T. 16).

————. Fifty years of scientific work. Paris, G. Roüan, 1928. [44] p. illus. plates.

————. Cinquante ans de travail scientifique. Paris, G. Roüen, 1928. unp. illus. plates.

————. Amas et champs d'étoiles d'après des plaques photographiques prises de 1900 à 1925 par le Père S. Chevalier. Étoiles de la nebuleuse d'Orion d'après six plaques prises de 1902 a 1923. Changhai, Impr. de la Mission catholique à l'Orphelinat de T'ou-sè-wè, 1930. 61 p. (Annales de l'Observatoire astronomique de Zô-Sè. T. 18, fascicule 1 ).

————. Catalogue de la zone -0° 50 à -0° 50′(equin. 1920) d'après les photographies du tour de l'equateur, par le Père S. Chevalier. Changhai, Impr. de la Mission catholique à l'Orphelinat de T'ou-sè-wè, 1930. 61 p. (Annales de l'Observatoire astronomique de Zô-Sè. T. 13).

————. Cooperation de l'Observatoire de Zi-ka-wei à la revision internationale des longitudes, Octobre-Novembre 1933, par Pierre Lejay, Maurice Burgaud E. de la Villemarque. Changhai, Impr. de la Mission catholique à l'Orphelinat de T'ou-sè-wè, 1934. 99 p. plates, tables, diagr. (Annales de l'Observatoire de Zô-Sè. T. 20).


Meteorology


ACADEMIA SINICA. Collected scientific papers, 1919-1949: meteorology. [European languages ed.] Peking, 1954-    1 v. maps, charts, diagrs., tables.

————. National Research Institute of Meteorology. The Institute of meteorology; its organization and work. Pei-chi-ko, Nanking, China, Printed at the Science Press, 1931. (c 1929) 12, 5, [2], 6-10 p. plates.

————. Bulletin of the upper air current observations, v. 1-6, 1930-1935. Nanking, 1930-1935. 6 v. illus. diagrs. tables.

————. Climatological data. Chungking, 1943-1945. 3 v. tables.

ALBRECHT, FRITZ, 1896-    Ergebnisse von dr. Haudes Beobachtungen der Strahlung und des Wärmehaushaltes der Erdoberfläche an den beiden Standlagern bei Ikengüng und am Edsen-Gol, 1931-32, unter Mitwirkung von Paul. Brosse. Stockholm [Leipzig, Druck von F. A. Brockhaus] 1941. 352 p. incl. illus., tables, diagrs. plates. (Reports from the Scientific expedition to the north-western provinces of China under the leadership of Dr. Sven Hedin. The Sino-Swedish expedition. Publication 14, ix. Meteorology, 2).

BERNING, WARREN W. A report on the military climatology of Chinese Turkestan and Tibet, by Warren W. Berning and John Van Vessem. Pasadena, 1942. 17 p. diagrs. (Military climatology, v. 1).

BRUZON, ÉTIENNE, 1894-    Le climat de l'Indochine et les typhons de la Mer de Chine, par E. Bruzon. [et] P. Carton. Hanoi, Impr. d'Extrême-orient,

1929. 141 p. illus., plates, maps (part fold.) charts (part fold., part col.) diagrs. (part fold., part col.).

CANTON. METEOROLOGICAL OBSERVATORY. Monthly meteorological bulletin. v. 1-4, 1935-1938. Canton, 1935-1938. 4 v.

CHANG, CH'I-YUN, 張其昀, 1901-　Climate and man in China. Taipei, China Culture Pub. Foundation, 1953. 23 p. illus., maps, (Pamphlet on Chinese affairs).

CH'EN, PARKER C., 陳宗器. Preliminary report on the results of geomagnetic survey in China, 1946-47; by Parker C. Chen and Liu Ching-ling, 劉慶齡. Nanking, 1948. 78-87 p. (Academia Sinica. Institute of Meteorology. Scientific Papers, Contribution No. 172).

CHÊNG, CHUEN-SHU, 程純樞. Central Weather Bureau of China: a brief survey (May 1948). Shanghai, 1948. 1 v. (various pagings), tables.

———. Chinese synoptic weather patterns. Shanghai, Shanghai Observatory, 1949. 116 p. maps, tables.

CHU, COCHING,竺可楨. 1890-　The climate of Nanking during the period 1905-1921. Nanking, National Southeastern University, 1922. 16 p. charts, (Annual report of meteorology station).

———. Climate provinces of China. Nanking, National Research Institute of Meteorology, 1929. 11 p. maps, plates, (Its Memoirs, 1).

———. Circulation of atmosphere over China. Nanking, National Research Institute of Meteorology, 1932. 15 p. plates (Its Memoirs, 4).

———. A brief survey on the climate of China. 中國氣候概論. Nanking, National Research Institute of Meteorology, 1936. 26 p. 35 p. fold. maps, tables, (Its Memoirs, 7) Reprint ed. 1944 (U.S. Army Air Forces. report, 805).

———. Circulation of atmosphere over China. Edited and reprinted by the Weather Division, Hdqrs., U.S. Army Air Forces. Washington, 1944. 27 p. illus. charts, tables. (U.S. Army Air Forces. [Translation and reports ser.]).

———. The temperature of China by Chu Coching, John Lee, 呂炯, and Chang Pao-kun, 張寶堃. Nanking, National Research Institute of Meteorology, 1947 (c1940) xxx, 934 p. tables. Appendix. 1947. (c1940) v. 16 p. 30 charts.

CONFERENCE OF DIRECTORS OF FAR EASTERN WEATHER SERVICES, Hongkong, 1930. Report of proceedings, with appendices and list of delegates. Hong Kong, Royal Observatory, 1930. 68 p. illus. tables.

DODINGTON, E A M. Weather in the China Seas and in the western part of the North Pacific Ocean. London, H. M. Stationery Off., 1945. 3 v. illus., maps (part fold. part col.) ([Gt. Brit.] Meteorological Office. [Publications, official] 404a-404c).

FROC, LOUIS 1859-　Typhoon of August 5 to 23. 1924. Shanghai, T'ou-sè-wè Press. 1925. 12 p. fold. map.

———. Code de Zi-ka-wei. Historique. Rapport présenté par R. Père L. Froc à la Conférence des directeurs des services météorologiques d'extrême-orient tenue à Hong Kong, fin avril 1930. Changhai, 1930. 4 p.

GAFFNEY, THOMAS. A report on the military climatology of central and southern China, by Thomas Gaffney, Herbert Plagge and George Weber. Pasadena, 1942. 42 p. maps, tables, diagrs, (Military climatology, v. 1).

GHERZI, ERNESTO, 1886-　Houie et microseismes sur la cote de Chine. Changhai, T'ou-sè-wè Orphanage Printing Press, 1927. 12 p. plates (part fold.) (Obs. de Zi-ka-wei. Notes de seis., 8).

———. Le tremblement de terre du 23 mai 1927 près de Liangchow, Kansu occidental. Shanghai, T'ou-sè-wè Orphanage Printing Press,1927. 9 p. charts (part fold.) (Observ. de Zi-ka-wei. Notes de seis., 9).

———. Typhoons in 1926-1937. Shanghai. T'ou-sè-wè Orphanage Printing Press, 1927-1938. 6 v.

———. Étude sur la pluie en Chine. (1873-1925) Chang-Hai, Impr. de la mission catholique, à l'Orphelinat de T'ou-Sè-Wè, 1928. 2 v. illus., fold. map, col.

charts, diagrs. (part fold., part col.).

——. Étude sur les microseismes cuases par le froid. Ondes de dilatation et ondes de compression. Changhai, T'ou-sè-wè Orphanage Printing Press, 1929. 23 p. plates (fold) (Obs. de Zi-ka-wei. Notes de seis., 10).

——. Recherches radiogoniométriques sur la marche des typhoons et relévements radiogoniométri à Changhai. Paris, 192? 18 p.

——. The winds and the upper air currents along the China coast and in the Yangtse valley. Shanghai, Catholic mission press Tou-sè-wè, 1931. 240, [7] p. plates, charts, diagrs. (part col.).

——. Typhoons in 1930. Shanghai, T'ou-sè-wè Orphanage Printing Press, 932. 20 p. charts.

——. Typhoons in 1931 (some data about typhoon centres) To the members of the Shangahi general chamber of commerce. T'ou-sè-wè Orphanage Printing Press, 1933. 38 p. 4 fold. maps 2 fold. diagr.

——. Atlas de l'humidité relative en Chine. Shanghai, Impr. de T'ou-sè-wè, 1934. [31], 13 p. (chiefly maps, diagrs.) (Obs. de Zi-ka-wei).

——. Atlas thermométrique de la Chine. Shanghai, Impr. de T'ou-sè-wè, 1934. [3] p. 16 maps, (Obs. de Zi-ka-wei).

——. Typhoons in 1934 (set caused by tropical cyclones.) To the members of the Shanghai general chamber of commerce. [Shanghai] T'ou-sè-wè Orphanage Printing Press, 1936. 43 p. 4 fold. charts, fold. tab.

——. Typhoons in 1938 (the steering of typhoons) Shangahi, T'ou-sè-wè Orphanage Printing Press, 1939. 30 p. charts.

——. Climatological atlas of East Asia. Shanghai, Tou-sè-wè Press, 1944. viii, 175 p col. maps.

——. The meteorology of China. [Macau, Imprensa Nacional, 1951]- 2 v. fold. col. maps, diagrs.

GT. BRIT. Hydrographic Office. China sea pilot. 1st ed., 1937. London, Pub. for the Hydrographic Dept., Admiralty, by H. M. Stationery Off., 1937-38. 3 v. illus., plates, maps, charts, tables, diagr.

——. The same. 2nd ed. London, 1950-1951. 2 v. illus., maps (part fold. col.) diagrs., tables.

——. Meteorological Office. Meteorological report on South China south of a line Shanghai-Tsinlingshan. London, Meteorological Office, 1945. 60 p. illus. incl. tables, front (map), charts, diagrs. (Its Aviation meteorological report, 29).

——. Quarterly surface current charts of the western North Pacific Ocean, westward of longitude 160° W., with monthly chartlets of the China Seas. 2d. ed. Prepared in the Marine Branch of the Meteorological Office. London, H. M. Stationery Off., 1949. 25 p. charts. (Its [Publications, official] 485).

HAUDE, WALDEMAR. Ergebnisse der allgemeinen meteorologischen Beobachtungen und der Drachenaufstiege an den beiden Stanlagern bei Ikengüng und am Edsen-gol 1931/32. Stockholm, Bokförlags aktiebolaget Thule, 1940. 328 p. incl. facsims., tables. plates (1 double) map, fold, diagrs. (Reports from the Scientific expedition to the northwestern provinces of China under the leadership of Dr. Sven Hedin. The Sino-Swedish expedition. Publication 8. ix. Meteorology. 1).

HUANG, HSIA-CHIEN, 黃廈千. Frontogenetic regions in the Far East, 1937. Washington, Govt. Print. Off., 1944. iv, 56 p. illus., charts. On cover: U.S. navy reprint, chief of naval operations, Aerology section, Washington, D. C.

——. Air masses of North China. Chungking, National Research Institute of Meteorology, 1940. 25 p. charts, tables, (Its Memoirs, 13(3)).

JAW, JEOU-JANG, 趙九章 [CHAO CHIU-CHANG]. A preliminary analysis of the air masses over eastern China. Nanking. National Research Institute of Meteorology, 1935. 12, 24 p. maps, tables, diagrs, (Its Memoirs, 6).

JONG, PIN-CHEN, 張丙辰 [CHANG P'ING-CH'ÊN]. Chinese air mass analysis.

Nanking, Institute of Meteorology, 1948. 17 p. illus. charts, tables, (Its Memoirs 15:3).

LEE, JOHN, 呂炯 [LÜ CHIUNG]. Preliminary study on the application of polar front theory to the winter cyclones along the lower Yangtze valley. Nanking, National Research Institute of Meteorology, 1930. 51 p. figs. (Its Memoirs, 2).

——. Dynamical effect of eastern Chinese coastal winds and its influence upon the temperature. Chungking, National Research Institute of Meteorology, 1938. 48 p. illus. tables, diagrs. (Its Memoirs 12:1).

LI, SJAN-ZSI, 李憲之 [LI HSIEN-CHIH]. Die Kälteeinbrüche in Ostasien. Ohlan i Schl., Eschenhagen, 1935. 79 p. Diss.-Univ. Berlin.

LINGNAN UNIVERSITY, Freeman Meteorological Observatory. Daily meteorological record, 1919-1937. [Canton] 1919-1937.

LOA, DAVID KAI-FOO, 羅開富 [LO K'AI-FU] 1913- Climatic atlas of China proper. [n.p.] 1944. [2] 1., 3, 92 maps. Scale of maps ca. 1:14,400,000. Issued also as thesis, Clark University.

LU, ALFRED, 盧鋈, [LU WU] 1911- The monthly pressure distribution and the surface winds in the Far East. Chungking, National Research Institute of Meteorology, 1939. 25 p. illus. tables, diagrs. (Its Memoirs 12:4) Reprinted by the U.S. Army Air Forces and issued as Its report, 803.

——. The cold wave of China; edited and reprinted by the Weather division, Hdqrs. U.S. Army Air Forces. Washington, 1944. v, 31 p. illus. charts, diagrs. tables, (U.S. Army Air Forces. [Translation and reprints ser.]).

——. Climatological atlas of China. Chungking, Central Weather Bureau, 1946. 94 maps.

NATIONAL TSING HUA UNIVERSITY. Quarterly meteorological bulletin, v. 1-5 1932-1936. Peiping, 1932-1936.

NELSON, ROY W. Climate and weather of the coast of China, by Roy W. Nelson and Roger F. Wilcox. Pasadena, 1942. 19 p. diagrs. (Calif. Inst. of Tech.).

NETHERLANDS. METEOROLOGISCH INSTITUUT. Oceanographic and meteorological observations in the China seas and in the western part of the North Pacific ocean. U.S. Navy reprint. Washington, Chief of Naval Operations, Aerology section, 1945. Cover-title, 80 p. of charts.(Its Navaer 50-IR-173).

NUTTONSON, M. Y. Ecological crop geography of China and its agro-climate: analogues in North America. Washington, American Institute of Crop Ecology, 1947. 28 p. illus. map, tables (part. fold) (Its International agro-climatological ser. Study No. 7).

ORTON, ROBERT B. The utilization of 500 millibar charts in forecasting for the Chinese area-spring season. Washington, Hdqrs. Air Weather Service, 1945. 6 p. illus. charts, (Its Technical report, 105-59A).

POND, ALONZO WILLIAM, 1894- Climate and weather in the Central Gobi of Mongolia. Rev. Maxwell Air Force Base, Ala., Arctic, Desert, Tropic Information Center, Air University, 1954. 1 v. (various pagings) map (on cover) tables. ([U.S.] Arctic, Desert and Tropic Information Center. ADTIC publication D–101).

SODERGREN, A. R. Mean air currents and fronts of China. An analysis of the work of Mr. Tu Ch'ang-wang on this subject. Pasadena, 1942. 9 p. diagrs. (Calif. Inst. of Tech.).

SUNG, SHIO-WANG, 沈孝鳳 [SHEN, HSIAO-HUANG]. Extratropical cyclones of eastern China and their characteristics. Nanking, National Research Institute of Meteorology, 1931. 60 p. figrs. (Its Memoirs, 3).

TAO, SHIH-YEN, 陶詩言. The mean surface air circulation over China. Nanking, Institute of Meteorology, 1948. 7 p. charts, (Its Memoirs 15:4).

TOKYO. CENTRAL METEOROLOGICAL OBSERVATORY OF JAPAN. Aerological data of Manchuria (radiosonde). Tokyo, 194-.

TSIANG, P. J., 蔣丙然, 1886- La température de Tsingtao. Tsingtao, 1929. viii, 69 p. plates.

TSINGTAO. OBSERVATORY. Results of the meteorological observations made at Tsingtao for the lustrum, 1916-1920. [Tsingtao] 1921. 40 p.
———. Code for meteorological wireless messages, issued by the Tsingtao Observatory. Tsingtao, 1924. 11 p.
———. Annular eclipse of the sun, May 9, 1948. Tsingtao, 1947. Cover-title, 20 p. fold. map. (Its Memoir, 11).
TU, CH'ANG-WANG,徐長望 . Some regional rainfall types of China. The tabulation by Li Liang-chi, 李良騏, and the discussion by Tu Chang-wang. Nanking, National Research Institute of Meteorology, 1935. 25 p. tables, diagrs. (Its Memoirs, 5).
———. Climate provinces of China. Nanking, National Research Institute of Meteorology, 1936. 22 p. maps, (part fold.) tables, diagrs. (Its Memoirs, 8).
———. A preliminary study on the mean air currents and fronts of China. Nanking, National Research Institute of Meteorology, 1937. 12 p. illus. diagrs. (Its Memoirs 11:3).
———. China weather and world oscillation with applications to long-range forecasting of floods and droughts of China during the summer. Nanking, National Research Institute of Meteorology, 1937. 54 p. illus. tables, diagrs. (Its Memoirs, 11:4).
———. The air masses of China. Chungking, National Research Institute of Meteorology, 1938. 50 p. illus. charts, tables, diagrs. (Its Memoirs 12:2).
———. A preliminary study on the climatological conditions of the free atmosphere of China. Chungking, National Research Institute of Meteorology, 1939. 14 p. illus. charts, diagrs. tables, (Its Memoirs 13:2).
———. The frontology of North China. Kunming, U.S. AAF Weather Central, 1945. ii, 95, iii p. illus. charts, diagrs, tables. (U.S. Dept. of the Air Force. Air weather service tech. rept. 105-67).
U. S. ARMY AIR FORCES. Forecasting and related problems in China. Washington, Hdqrs. U.S. Army Air Forces, 1944. iv, 25 p. illus. map, (Its Tech. rept. 105-32).
———, Weather and climate of China. Washington, Govt. Print. Off., 1945. 2 v. illus. charts, tables, diagrs., (Its Tech. rept. 105-34).
U.S. DEPT OF THE AIR FORCE. Maxwell Air Force Base, Ala. Climate and weather in the central Gobi of Mongolia, by Alonzo W. Pond. Maxwell Air Force Base, Arctic, Desert, Tropic Information Center, Air University, 1951. 1 v. tables, (ADTIC publication D-101).
U.S. Hydrographic Office. Currents in the South China, Java, Celebes and Sulu Seas. Washington, 1945. [2] l., col. charts (Its H.O. pub. no 236).
———. Ocean currents in the vicinity of the Japanese islands and China coast. Washington, 1945. 3 l. charts. (Its H.O. pub. no. 237).
———. Sailing directions for the western shores of the China Sea, from Singapore Strait to and including Hong Kong. 4th ed. Washington, Govt. Print. Off., 1951 [i.e. 1952- ] 1 v. (loose-leaf) charts (1 col. in pocket) (Its H.O. pub[lication] no. 125) First ed. published in 1915 as v. 4 of its Asiatic pilot.
———. Sailing directions for the coast of China; the Yalu River to the approach to Hong Kong, the Yangtze River, Taiwan (Formosa) and the Pescadores Islands. 5th ed. Washington, Govt. Print. Off., 1951- 1 v. (loose-leaf) charts (1 col. in pocket) (Its H.O. pub[lication] no. 124). First ed. published in 1910 as v. 3 of the Asiatic pilot.
U.S. Office of Coordinator of Information. Research and Analysis Branch. Far Eastern Section. Weather and war in the Far East. [Washington] 1941. 4 l. map (Its Memorandum no. 4).
U. S. Weather Bureau. Flying conditions between Irkutsk-Urga-Lanchow-Chungking, by C.E. Lamoureaux. Washington, 1942. 15 p. (Its Special rept. 81).
———. Flying conditions in Shantung, Tsingtao. by L.C. Miller. [Washington, 1943] 13 p. illus. (Its Special rept., 333).

――――. Hainan Island: a climate report, by L.C. Miller. Washington, 1943. 10 p. (Its Special rept., 312).

WANG, TEHCHIH.王德基. Die Dauer der ariden, humiden und nivalen Zeiten des Jahres in China. Tübingen, 1941. 33 p. fig. map. Diss.-Univ. Tübingen.

WARD, WILLIAM CURTIS. Weather conditions prevailing in the interior of China. Pasadena, 1942. 10 p. tables, diagrs. (Calif. Inst. of Tech.).

YAO, CHEN-SHENG, 幺枕生. The stationary cold fronts of central China and the wave disturbances developed over the lake basin. Chungking, National Research Institute of Meteorology, 1939. 17 p. diagrs. (Its Memoirs 13:1).

ZI-KA-WEI. Observatoire. Bulletin des observations. v. 1-27. (1873-1931) Zi-ka-wei, 1877-1933.

――――. Bulletin aérologique, sondages faits à Zi-ka-wei et à Hankow. Janvier 1931-juillet 1937. Shanghai, 1931-37. tables.

――――. Notes de météorologie physique. fasc. 1-9. Changhai, Impr. de T'ou-sè-wè près Zi-ka-wei, 1934-1939. v. plates, tables, diagrs. (part col.).

――――. Bulletin aérologique. Température, 1930. 1932-1934. Données thermométriques obtenues sur la ligne aérienne: Shanghai-Chungking. Shanghai, 1935. v. tables.

――――. Supplément pour 1932. Sondages exécutés à bord du U.S.S. Houston. Shanghai, 1936? 9 p. tables.

## Chemistry

CHEMICAL WORKERS' TRADE UNION OF CHINA. China's chemical workers. Peking, Foreign Languages Press, 1953. 17 p. illus.

CHIKASHIGE, MASUMI, 1870-    Alchemy and other chemical achievements of the ancient Orient; the civilization of Japan and China in early times as seen from the chemical point of view, tr. by Nobuji Sasaki. Tokyo, Rokakuho U-chida, 1936.    vii, 102 p. illus., plates (1 col.).

JOHNSON, OBED SIMON, 1881-    A study of Chinese alchemy. Shanghai, Commercial Press, 1928.    xi, 156 p. Published also as thesis: University of California.

LI, CH'IAO-P'ING, 李喬苹, 1897-    The chemical arts of old China; with a fore-word by Tenney L. Davis. Easton, Pa., Journal of Chemical Education [1948] viii, 215 p. illus.

RUSSIAN-Chinese-English chemical and technological dictionary,    俄中英化學化工術語 , compiled by T'ao Kun, 陶坤, and Wang Sung-shan, 王松山 . Peking, Chinese Academy of Sciences, Bureau of Publications, 1955. 768 p.

TSAO, HUI C., 曹惠羣. An English-Chinese vocabulary of chemical terms, compiled by Hui C. Tsao and William H. Adolph. Shanghai, Publication Committee, China Medical Missionary Association, 1922. 20 p.

WANG, CHENG-MING, 王承明 . Russian-Chinese-English chemical and technical dictionary,    化工術語彙編 . Shanghai, Chung-kuo-k'o-hsueh tu-shu-i-ch'i-kung ssu, 1954. iii, 279 p.

WANG, CHI CHE, 王季茝 , 1894-    The chemistry of Chinese preserved eggs and Chinese edible birds' nests. [Baltimore, 1921] p. 429-452. diagrs. Thesis-University of Chicago. ''Reprinted from the Journal of biological chemistry, December, 1921.''

ZEE, ZAI-ZIANG, 徐善祥, [HSÜ SHAN-HSIANG], 1882-    A modern English-Chinese chemical lexicon, compiled by Zee Zai-ziang and Chêng Lan-hua, 鄭蘭華 . Shanghai, Chung kuo k'o hsueh tu shu i ch'i kung ssu, 1951. xiv, 1625 p.

## Geology
### Bibliographies

CHI, YUNGSHEN SHIAOCHING, 計榮森 , 1907-    Bibliography of Chinese geology for the years 1934-35. Nanking, National Research Council, Academia

Sinica, 1936. 57 p.
——. Bibliography of Chinese geology for the years 1936-1940. Peipei, National Geological Survey of China, 1942. vi, 147 p.
CHINA. Geological Survey. Bibliography of Chinese geology. Bibliography of geology and allied sciences of Tibet and regions to the west of the Chinsha-chiang, by T. C. Tseng, 曾鼎乾. Nanking, National Geological Survey of China, 1946. viii, 114 p.
——. The same : bibliography of geology and geography of Sinkiang, by Hsiao-Fang Li, 李孝芳. Pub. by the National Geological Survey of China under the Ministry of Economic Affairs. Nanking, 1947. 213 p.
——. Library. List of papers in the Bulletin of the Geological Society of China 1922-1933. Peiping, The Library, National Geological Survey of China [1933] cover-title, 20 p.
WANG, CH'UNG-YU, 王寵佑, 1879-1958. Bibliography of tungsten from 1918 to 1922 and from 1922 to 1924. [Peking, 1924?] 26 p. Reprinted from the Journal of the Association of Chinese and American engineers, 5:2. 1924.
——. Bibliography of antimony from 1917 to 1924. [Peking?] 1925. 21 p. Reprinted from the "Journal of the Association of Chinese and American engineers." 6:3 1925.
——. Bibliography of the mineral wealth of China from 1918 to 1924. Peking, 1925. 17 p. Reprinted from the Journal of the Association of Chinese and American engineers. 6:5 1925. 1st ed.: Bibliography of the mineral wealth and geology of China published in London, 1912. 2d. ed: [covering the years 1912-17] published in Shanghai, 1917, followed by a supplement, 1918.
YOUNG T.I., 楊遵儀 [YANG TSUN-I]. Bibliography of Chinese geology up to 1934, with a preface by C. Y. Wang, 王寵佑. [Peiping] National Academy of Peiping, 1935. ix, 241 p.

## General Works

BARBOUR, GEORGE BROWN. 1890-    The loess of China. (In Smithsonian institution. Annual report, 1926. Washington, 1927. p. 279-296. illus., 6 plates) "Reprinted from the China journal of science and arts, 3:8, August, 1925 and 3:9, September, 1925."
——. The geology of the Kalgan area. Peking [Printed by the Drukkerij Holland, Amsterdam] 1929. xi, 148, 148a-f, [2] p.; 1 p. 2, 26 p. incl. illus., tables, fold. front., plates (1 fold.) 2 fold. maps. (China. Geological survey. Memoirs, ser. A, no. 6, October 1929).
BAUER, HEINRICH WILHELM, 1913-    Der Bergbau in China. Leipzig, Druck von E. Gärtner, 1936. 127 p. Inaug.-Diss.-Berlin.
——. Chinas Schätze? Eine Studie über den Chinesischen Bergbau. Berlin, Jung-Verlag [1938] 126 p. fold. map.
CARLSON, ELLSWORTH C. The Kaiping mines (1877-1912) Cambridge, Chinese Economic and Political Studies, Harvard University; distributed by Harvard University Press, 1957. 174 p. (Chinese Economic and Political Studies. Special series).
CHAO, YA-TS'ENG, 趙亞曾, 1898-1929. The geology of the Tsinlingshan and Szechuan. By Y. T. Chao and T. K. Huang, 黃汲清. Peiping, Geological Survey of China and the Section of Geology of the National Academy of Peiping, 1931. v, 228 p. 4, 48 p. illus., 19 plates (incl. fold. maps) and atlas of 20 plates (17 maps, 3 diagr.) (China. Geological survey. Memoirs, ser. A, no. 9).
CHINA. GEOLOGICAL SURVEY. General statement on the mining industry. Peking and Peipei, 1921-1945. 7 v. tables (part fold.) (Its special report Nos. 1-7).
——. NATIONAL CONSTRUCTION COMMISSION. A brief description of the mining and metallurgical industries undertaken by the National Construction Commission. Nanking, 1930. 8 p. incl. tables.

COLLINS, WILLIAM FREDERICK. Mineral enterprise in China. Rev. ed. With
  maps and sketches. Tientsin, Tientsin Press, 1922. iii-xv, 410 p. maps
  (part fold. ) 1st ed. London, 1918.

HEIM, ARNOLD ALBERT, 1882-   Tseliutsin in Szechuan, the oldest bore field
  of the world. Canton, The National Sun Yatsen University, 1930. iv, 7 p.

————. Geology of Canton with general geological map 1:50, 000. By Arnold Heim,
  K. Krejci-Graf and Lee Cheng-San, 李承三. Canton, 1930. cover-title, 29,
  [20] p. [20] p. illus., 10 plates, fold. col. amp. (Kwangtung. Geological
  survey. Special publication no. 7).

————. Tectonical study of Omei-Shan, Szechuan; with 1 plate of coloured sketch-
  maps, 2 plates of sections and map, 3 plates of photographs and 8 figures in
  the text. Canton, 1932. 53, [48] p. [2] p. illus., vi plates (incl. 2 fold.
  maps, fold. diagr. ) (Kwangtung. Geological survey. Special publication no.
  xiii).

————. Tectonical sketch of the Yangtse from Itshiang to the Red basin; with 6
  plates and 7 figures in the text. Canton, 1933. cover-title, 39, [41] p. illus.
  vi plates (incl. fold. map. fold. diagr. ) (Kwangtung. Geological survey. Special publication no. xiv).

HEINTZLEMAN, PERCIVAL STEWART, 1880-   Mining and metallurgical in-
  dustries in central China. Washington, Govt. Print. Off., 1922. ii, 9 p.
  ([ U. S. ] Bureau of foreign and domestic commerse (Dept. of commerce)
  Trade information bulletin, 26).

HO, PEI-YANG, 何丕揚 . The production of tungsten in China. Tientsin, Hautes
  études, 1941. 26 p. (Tientsin. Institut des hautes études industrieles et commerciales. Economic studies, 16).

HSIEH, CHIA-YUNG, 謝家榮, 1896-   Foreign interests in the mining industry
  in China, by C. Y. Hsieh and M. C. Chu, 朱懋澄 . Shanghai, China Institute
  of Pacific Relations, 1931. 54 p. tables.

————. Geology of the iron deposits in the lower Yangtze region by C. Y. Hsieh
  with collaboration of C. C. Sun, 孫健初 , Y. C. Cheng, 程裕祺 , and K. Chern,
  陳愷 . Peiping, Geological Survey of China, 1935. 191, xviii p. 2, 78 p.
  incl. illus., tables, profiles. plates, (incl. fold. maps) (China. Geological
  survey. Geological memoirs, ser. A, no. 13).

————. A review of the stratigraphy, structure, and geological history of the
  Szechuan red basin and the occurrence of natural gas, oil, brines and rock
  salt contained therein with special discussions of their origin and future prospects. Nanking, 1945. 23, 2 l. tables.

HSÜ, K'O-CH'IN, 徐克勤 . Geology and tungsten deposits of southern Kiangsi by
  K. C. Hsü and I. Ting, 丁毅 . Pehpei, Chungkung, Geological Survey of China,
  1943. 10, 360 p. 75 p. incl. illus., tables, diagrs. plates, fold. maps (1 in
  pocket) (China. Geological survey. Memoirs, ser. A, no. 17).

HUANG, T. K., 黃汲清 [ HUANG CHI-CH'ING], 1904-   On major tectonic forms
  of China. Chungking, Pub. by the National Geological Survey of China under
  the Ministry of Economic Affairs, 1945. iv, 165, 13 p. plates, fold. maps (in
  pocket) (China. Geological survey. Geological memoirs, ser. A, no. 20).

JUAN, VEI-CHOU, 阮維周 , 1912-   Mineral recources of China. [n. p., 1946]
  399-474 p. incl. illus. (maps) tables. "Reprinted from Economic geology,
  41:4 June-July, 1946."

KAO, P'ING, 高平 . Geology of western Kiangsi, with 10 text fugures and 14
  plates, by P. Kao and K. C. Hsü, 徐克勤 . Pehpei, National Geological Survey of China, 1940. 72 p. illus., fold. maps (1 in pocket) diagr. (China.
  Geological Survey. Memoirs, ser. A, no. 16).

KWEICHOW. GEOLOGICAL SURVEY. On the establishment of the heavy industrial centres of Kweichow in reference to the distribution of the chief mineral
  resources-the geology of Lung-Tou-Shan coal field, etc. [ Kweichow, 1945]
  [30] p. 2 fold. maps.

LEE, JONQUEI S., 李四光 [LI SSÙ-KUANG] 1889-   Fusulinidoe of north China.

Peking, Geological Survey of China, 1927. vii, 172 p. 10 p. incl. illus.,
tables. plates, fold. chart, diagrs. (China. Geological survey. Palaeontologia sinica, ser. B., vol. iv, fasc. 1).

――――. A geological guide to the Lungtan district, Nanking, by J.S. Lee and S.
Chu, 朱森. With a geological map under separate cover. Nanking, National
Research Institute of Geology, Academia Sinica, 1932. 25, [2] p. 13 p. 5
plates 1 fold. ).

――――. The geology of China. London, T. Murby, 1939. xv, 528 p incl. illus.,
plates, diagrs. maps (part double).

――――. Quaternary glaciations in the Lushan Area, Central China. Nanking, Institute of Geology, Academia Sinica, 1947. 70, 60 p. 16 plates, fold. map (in
pocket) (Academia Sinica. Monograph of the Institute of Geology, ser. B, v.
2).

LEINUNG, A. Das Pechwan-Kohlengebiet (Provinz Szechwan) Shanghai, 1937.
Microfilm copy. Negative. Collation of the original; iv, 25 l. illus. maps.

LI, CHING-YUAN, 李慶遠, 1913-   Potential sources of aluminum in southwestern China, by Chingyuan Y. Li and C. Y. Hsieh. (In Mining technology. v. 10,
no. 1 Jan. 1946. 6 p. maps, diagrs.)

LI, KUO-CH'IN, 李國欽, 1892-   Tungsten: its history, geology, ore-dressing,
metallurgy, chemistry, analysis, applications, and economics, by K.C. Li
and Chung-Yu Wang, 王寵佑. 3d. ed. New York, Reinhold [1955] xx, 506 p.
illus. (part col.) maps. (Am[erican] C[hemical] S[ociety] Monograph series,
no. 130). 1st ed. 1943.

LI YUEH-YEN, 李悅言. Salt deposits of Szechuan. Pehpei, National Geological
Survey of China, 1944. cover-title, 6, 202 p. incl. tables, plates. maps, plans,
diagrs. (China. Geological survey. Memoirs, ser. A, no. 18).

LIAO, Y   J., 廖友仁. Report on the Shanwupoa tin field, Kianghua, Hunan (summary) by Y. J. Liao and Y. T. Hsu, 許原道. (In Hunan. China. Geological
survey. Bulletin. Changsha, 1934. [no.] 17. Economic geology 11. p. 1-5,
1-30. plates. (incl. fold. col. map)).

――――. Report on the geology of Yangmeishan coal field, I-Chang, by Y. J. Liao
and T. Y. Liu, 劉祖彝. (In Hunan. Geological survey. Bulletin, Changsha,
Hunan, 1936. no. 18 (Econ. geol. 12) p. 17-21, 57-66 incl. tab., diagr. fold.
col. map).

LICENT, ÉMILE. Notes géologiques sur la région de Ki ning hien et sur les vol-
cans de Koan ts'ounnze et de Kong Keueh t'eou. Tientsin, Mission de Sien
Hsien, 1932. 11 p. (Publication du Musée Hoang ho Pei ho, 5).

――――. Les collections néolithiques du Musée Hoang ho Pei ho. Tientsin, Mission de Sien Hsien, 1932. 98 p. (Publications du Musée Hoang ho Pei ho, 14).

LIU. CHI-CH'ÊN, 劉季辰. Preliminary report on the geology and mineral resources of Kiangsu, by C.C. Liu and J.C. Chao, 趙汝鈞. Peking, Commercial Press, 1924. 34, [90] p. tables (1 fold.) [Memoirs of the Geological survey of China. Ser. A, no. 4].

――――. Report on the Shui Kou Shan lead and zinc mine, Hunan, by C.C. Liu, C.
C. Tien, 田奇瓗, and C. Y. Ou Yang, 歐陽超邁. Changsha, Hunan, 1927.
13 p. 2, 5, 59 p. incl. illus. tables, diagrs. plates. (incl. fold. map) 3 fold.
plans. (Hunan, China. Geological survey. Bulletin 1. Economic geology 1).

MATHIEU, FRANÇOIS FELIX, 1886-   La stratigraphie du bassin houiller de
Kaiping (Chine). La flore paléozofque du bassin houiller de Kaiping (Chine)
par F. Stockmans et F. F. Mathieu. Bruxelles, Musée royal d'histoire naturelle de Belgique, 1939. 164 p. illus.

MENG, HSIEN-MIN, 孟憲民, 1900-   Geology of the Tung-chuan district, northeastern Yunnan by H. M. Meng [and others]. Nanking, National Research
Institute of Geology, 1948. 68 p. maps (3 fold.) (Academia Sinica. National

Research Institute of Geology. Memoirs, 17).

OINOUYE, YOSHICHIKE. Geological survey report on the oil shales in Mao-Ming Hsien, Kao-Chou district, Kwangtung, South China. Translation prepared by Engineer Intelligence Division, Office of the Engineer, Headquarters United States Army Forces, Far East. Tokyo, 1955. 42 l. map, tables, (U.S. Army. Corps of engineers. Far East command. [Pacific surveys] report, 41).

PAN, CHUNG-HSIANG, 潘鍾祥, 1906-　The geology and metallogenetic provinces of eastern Asia. Minneapolis, 1946. ix, 288 l. illus., fold, plates, Thesis- Univ. of Minnesota.

SMITH, WILFRED. A geographical study of coal and iron in China, with an introduction by Percy M. Roxby. [Liverpool] University Press of Liverpool; London, Hodder and Stoughton, 1926. 83 p. maps (2 fold. in pocket).

SUN, CHIEN-CHU, 孫健初. Geology of Suiyuan and southwest Chahar by C.C. Sun. Peiping, National Geological Survey of China, 1934. v, 80, [72] p. incl. illus. tables. plates. and Atlas of 7 col. maps, diagrs. (China. Geological survey. Geological memoirs, Ser. A, no. 12).

SURVEY REPORT on the mines of North China (second party). By B (Otsu) party of non-official staff, headquarters of the Japanese garrison in China. Tokyo, 1954. v, 227 l. maps, diagrs. tables. (U.S. Army, Corps of engineers. Far East command. [Pacific surveys]-Reports, 14).

TEGENGREN, FELIX REINHOLD. The iron ores and iron industry of China, including a summary of the iron situation of the circum-Pacific region. Peking, Geological Survey of China, 1921-24. 2 v. incl. illus., plates (part fold.) tables (part fold.) and atlas of 39 plates (col. maps, diagrs) (Memoirs of the Geological survey of China, ser. A. no. 2, October, 1921, and December, 1923).

T'IEN, CH'I-CH'IUNG, 田奇瑪 , 1899-　Reports on the geology of Tzemenchiao, Fenghuanshan, and Huping Permian coal fields, Sianghsiang, Hunan, by C.C. Tien, H.C. Wang, 王曉青 , and S.Y. Kuo, 郭紹儀. Changsha, 1928. 7, [32] p. illus., 3 maps, fold. diagr. (Hunan, China. Geological survey. Bulletin 7; economic geology 4).

―――. Reports on the Pan-Hsi antimony mine, Yi-Yang, Hunan, by C.C. Tien, S.Y. Kuo and H.C. Wang. Changsha, 1928. 13, [40] p. incl. tables, diagrs. fold. map, fold. diagr. (Hunan, China. Geological survey. Bulletin 5; economic geology 3).

―――. Report on the Shang-Wu-Tu manganese deposit, Central Hunan, by C.C. Tien and H.C. Wang. Report on the Siangtan gypsum and salt deposit, Central Hunan, by C.C. Tien, S.Y. Kuo and H.C. Wang. Changsha, 1928. 15 p. 52 p. incl. illus., tables, 6 plates (incl. fold. map) (Human, China. Geological survey. Bulletin 4; economic geology 2).

―――. A study of the Devonian sections in Changsha and Sientang districts, Central Hunan. Changsha, 1928. 25, [14] p. illus., fold. diagr. (Hunan. Geological survey. Bulletin ii(Geology i)).

―――. Report on the geology and mineral resources of Hsinhu, Hunan. By C.C. Tien, H.C. Wang and S.Y. Kuo. Changsha, 1929. 12, [50] p. incl. tables, diagrs. fold. map. (Hunan. Geological survey. Bulletin 8; economic geology 5 ).

―――. Geological reconnaissance along the projected line between Changsha and Pingshih stations of the Canton-Hankow railway, by C.C. Tien, H.C. Wang and T.Y. Liu, 劉祖彝. Changsha, 1933. 9, [60] p., illus., iv plates (incl. front. (fold. map)) (Hunan. Geological survey. Bulletin 16, Geology 3).

―――. The geology of Changsha, Hsiangtan, Hengshan, Hengyang, Hsianghsiang, and Shaoyang districts, central Hunan, by C.C. Tien, H.C. Wang, and Y.T. Hsu, 許原道. Changsha, 1933. 47, [122] p., plates,fold. map. 2 fold. diagr. (Hunan. Geological survey. Bulletin 15, Geology 2).

———. The iron ores of Hunan (no. 1), by C.C. Tien, H.C. Wang and T.Y. Liu. Changsha, 1934. 8, [108] p. incl. illus., tables. plates, maps (part fold.) (Hunan. Geological survey. Memoir, ser. A, vol. i).

———. Report on the Wuhsi antimony deposit, Yuanling, Hunan (summary), by C.C. Tien and H.C. Wang. (In Hunan, China. Geological survey. Bulletin. Changsha, 1934. [no.] 17, Economic geology 11. p. 6-7, 31-46 p. vii plates, on 4 l. (incl. diagr.)).

———. The manganese ores of Hunan, by C.C. Tien, H.C. Wang, Y.T. Hsu and T.Y. Liu. Changsha, 1935. 8, 43, 5 p. illus., plates, maps (part fold.)(Hunan. Geological survey. Memoir, ser. A, vol. ii).

———. Geology and mineral resources of n.w. Tzŭli district. (In Hunan. Geological survey. Bulletin. Changsha, Hunan, 1936. no. 18 (Econ. geol. 12) p. 1-10, 1-38 incl. tables, diagrs. plates (incl. fold. map)).

———. Report on the coal field of Wulitun, Chenhsi, by C.C. Tien and H.C. Wang. (In Hunan. Geological survey. Bulletin. Changsha, Hunan, 1936. no. 18 (Econ. geol. 12) p. 22-24, 67-71. fold. map).

———. Report on the geology of Paohotang coal field, Shaoyang, by C.C. Tien and J.L. Hsu, 徐瑞麟. (In Hunan. Geological survey. Bulletin. Changsha, Hunan, 1936. no. 18 (Econ. geol. 12) p. 11-16, 39-56 incl. tab., diagrs. plates. (incl. fold. map) fold. profile).

TING, CHEN-WEI, 丁陳威. Extraction of alumina and potash from Chinese alunite by the kalunite process. Taipei, Taiwan Fertilizer Co., 1952. 38 p. (Research bull., 8).

TING, V. K., 丁文江. 1887-1936. The Permien of China and its bearing on Permian classification, by V.K. Ting and A.W. Grabau. Washington, D.C., 1934. 14 p. illus. plate. Reprinted from Report of XVI International geological congress, Washington, 1933.

———. The Carboniferous of China and its bearing on the classification of the Mississippian and Pennsylvanian, by V.K. Ting and A.W. Grabau. Washington, D.C., 1934. 17 p. illus. plate. Reprinted from Report of XVI International geological congress, Washington, 1933.

———. Report on the geology and tin mines of Kochiu district, Yunnan. Nanking, National Geological Survey of China, 1937. 2, 2, 51 p. illus., 2 maps (1 fold.) diagrs. (China. Geological survey. Memoirs and Chinese, ser. B, no. 10).

TSEN, PAK-LIANG, 曾伯良 [TSÊNG PO-LIANG], 1891- Recherches sur quelques minerais chinois de tungstène et de molybdène. Paris, P. Geuthner, 1928. 79 p. fold. map (Université de Lyon. Bibliotheca Franco-Sinica Lugdunensis. Études et documents pub. par l'Institut franco-chinois de Lyon, t. 6).

TUNG, C., 董常. Vocabulary of mineralogical, petrological and geological terms. Peking, Geological Survey of China, 1923. cover-title, [74] p.

VILLA, EDWARD MANSO DE, 1888- The study of mines in China, Indochina and Malaya. Hong Kong, Printed by the Hong Kong Daily Press, ltd., 1935. ciii, 226 p. incl. tables. plates (1 fold., incl. front.) fold. map, fold. form.

WANG, C. F., 王正黻, 1890-1951. A syllabus of mining conditions in the three eastern provinces. [Mukden, 1929] 11 p. In vol. xxi of "Documents of the Third conference, Institute of Pacific relations, Kyoto, Japan, 1929."

WANG, CHUNG YU, 王寵佑, 1879-1958. The mineral resources of China. [Tientsin, Tientsin Press, [n.d.] 54 p. incl. tables.

———. Antimony: its geology, metallurgy, industrial uses and economics. 3d ed. rev. London, C. Griffin [1952] 170 p. illus. 1st ed. 1909.

WANG, FELIX DJAHUNG, 王家鴻, 1900- Chinas Eisenproduktion und Eiseneinfuhr. Mauen-Berlin, Freyhoff, 1933. v, 69 p. Diss.-Univ. Berlin.

WANG, HSIAO-CHING, 王曉青. Report on the Matienhsu coal field, Yunghsin, Hunan (summary), by H.C. Wang and H.C. Hsiu, 粟顯伏. (In Hunan, China. Geological survey. Bulletin. Changsha, 1934. [no.] 17. Economic geology 11, p. 10, 55-58. plates).

————. Report of the Tungchungkou gold deposit, Yuanling, Hunan (summary). (In Hunan, China. Geological survey. Bulletin. Changsha, 1934. [no.] 17. Economic geology 11. p. 8-9. 47-54. iv plates on 2 l. (incl. map, plan)).

————. The geology of Changsha-Changteh district, Hunan, by H.C. Wang and T.Y. Liu. Changsha, 1936. 21, 106, 12 p. illus., xi plates on 6 l. 2 fold. maps (1 in pocket) diagrs. (Hunan. Geological survey. Memoir, ser. B, v. 1).

————. The antimony ores of Hunan, by H.C. W. ng, Y.T. Hsu and K.C. Liu, 劉國昌. Changsha, 1938. 12, 182 p. illus., plates, maps, profiles, tables, diagrs. (Hunan, China. Geological survey. Memoir, ser. A, vol. iv).

WANG, YIUCHANG TSENSHAN, 王臻善, 1889-   The Shuitung coal field, Hsienschen Hsien, Anhui. [Shanghai? 1926] 20 p. illus., 2 maps (1 fold.) diagrs. Reprinted from the Far Eastern review, v. 22 January 1926.

WONG, WILLIAM A. 黄著勳. Mineral wealth of China. Shanghai, Commercial Press, 1927. 129 p. front. (fold. map).

YEH, LIEN-TSUN, 葉連俊 . Geology of central and southern Kansu, by L.T. Yeh and S.C. Kwan, 關士聰 . Pehpei, National Geological Survey of China, 1944. cover-title, 7, 72, 12 p. xii fold, plates, (incl. maps, profiles, diagrs.) in pocket. (China. Geological survey. Memoirs, ser. A, no. 19).

YIH, LIANG-FU, 葉良輔 . The igneous geology of the Nanking hills, by Liang F. Yih and T.Y. Yü, 喻德淵 . [Shanghai] 1934. 83, 137 p. illus., plates, fold. maps (in pocket) tables (part fold.) (Academia sinica. National research institute of geology. Monograph, ser. B, v. 1).

## Paleontology

BIEN, M. N., 卡美年 [PIAN MEI-NIEN]. On the fossil Pisces, Amphibia and Reptilia from Chou-koutien localities 1 and 3. Peiping, Geological Survey of China, 1934. 32 p. 2 p. incl. illus., tables. plates ([China. Geological survey] Palaeontologia sinica, ser. C, vol. x, fasc. 1).

————. Preliminary observations on the Cenozoic geology of Yunnan [n. p., 194-] Microfilm copy made by Microfilms, inc. Positive. Collation of the original, as determined from the film: 180-204 p. maps, profiles. "Reprinted from the Bulletin of the Geological Society of China, vol. xx, no. 2, 1940."

————. Cave and rock-shelter deposits in Yunnan, by M.N. Bien and L.P. Chia, 買蘭坡 [n. p., n. d.] Microfilm copy made by Microfilms, inc. Positive. Collation of the original, as determined from the film: 326-347 p. illus. map. Reprinted from the Bulletin of the Geological Society of China, v. 18, nos 3-4, 1938.

————. "Red Beds" of Yunnan, [n. p., 194-] Microfilm copy made by Microfilms, inc. Positive. Collation of the original: 158-198 p. maps (2 fold.) profiles. "Reprinted from the Bulletin of the geological Society of China, vol. xxi, nos. 2-4, 1941."

BLACK DAVIDSON, 1884-1934. The human skeletal remains from the Sha Kuo T'un cave deposit in comparison with those from Yang Shao Tsun and with recent North China skeletal material. Peking, Published by the Geological Survey of China, 1925. 148, [18] p. plates, tables. (China. Geological survey. Palaeontologia sinica. ser. D, v. 1, fasc. 3).

————. On a lower molar hominid tooth from the Chou kou tien deposit. Peking, Geological Survey of China, 1927. 28, vi, [24] p. illus. plates (China. Geological survey. Palaeontologia sinica, ser. D, v. 7, fasc. 1).

————. A study of Kansu and Honan aeneolithic skulls and specimens from later Kansu prehistoric sites in comparison with north China and other recent crania. Peking, Geological Survey of China, 1928-   1 v. tables (part fold.) diagrs. (part fold.) (China. Geological survey. Palaeontologia sinica, ser. D, vol. vi, fasc. 1).

————. On an adolescent skull of Sinanthropus pekinensis in comparison with an adult skull of the same species and with other hominid skulls, recent and fossil. Peiping (Peking) Geological Survey of China, 1930. 144 p. incl. illus. tables. plates. (China. Geological survey. Palaeontologia sinica, ser. D. v. 7, fasc. 2).

———. Fossil man in China; the Choukoutien cave deposits with a synopsis of our present knowledge of the late Cenozoic in China, by Davidson Black, Teilhard de Chardin, C.C. Young and W.C. Pei; edited by Davidson Black, with a foreword by Wong Wen Hao. Peiping, The Geological Survey of China, and the Section of Geology of the National Academy of Peiping, 1933. x, 166 p. 4 p. incl. illus., tables. 9 fold. plates (incl. maps) (China. Geological survey. Memoirs, ser. A, no. 11).

BOHLIN, BIRGER, 1898-   Die familie Giraffidae mit besonderer Berücksichtigung der fossilen Formen aus China. Peking, Published by the Geological Survey of China, 1926. 178 p. 13 l. incl. illus., tables. ([China. Geological survey] Palaeontologia sinica; ser, c, vol. iv, fasc. 1).

———. Cavicornier der Hipparion-fauna nord-Chinas. Plates 1-xx and 142 figures of text. Peiping, Geological Survey of China, 1935. 166, 5 p. incl. illus. tables. xx plates (China. Geological survey. Palaeontologia sinica, ser. c. vol. ix, fasc. 4).

———. Eine tertiäre Säugetier-fauna aus Tsaidam. With plates i-ix and 215 figures of text. Peiping, Geological Survey of China, 1937. [5]-111 p. illus., ix plates (Reports from the Scientific expedition to the north-western provinces of China under leadership of Dr. Sven Hedin. The Sino-Swedish expedition. vi. Vertebrate palaeontology: 1) At head of title: Palaeontologia sinica. Ser. C, vol. xiv, fasc. 1.).

———. Oberoligozäne Säugetiere aus dem Shargaltein-tal (western Kansu). With 2 plates and 136 figures of text. Nanking, The Geological Survey of China, 1937. 66 p. illus., plates. (Reports from the Scientific expedition to the northwestern provinces of China under leadership of Dr. Sven Hedin. The Sino-Swedish expedition. Publication 5. vi. Vertebrate palaeontology:2). At head of title: Palaeontologia sinica. New ser. C, no. 3. Whole ser. no. 107.

———. Einige jungtertiäre und pleistozäne Cavicornier aus Nord-China. Uppsala, Almqvist und Wiksella boktryckeri-a-b., 1938. 54 p. illus. diagrs. (Nova acta Regiae societatis scientiarum Upsaliensis. ser. iv, v. 11, No. 2).

———. The fossil mammals from the Tertiary deposit of Tabenbuluk, western Kansu. Stockholm, 1942-   2 v. illus., plates,fold. map, diagrs. (Reports from the scientific expedition ot the north-western provinces of China under leadership of Dr. Sven Hedin. The Sino-Swedish expedition. Publication 20, and 28).

———. [Tertiary mammals of China] Stockholm, Thule, 1937-1946. 4 v. in 1. illus. plates, fold. col. map, tables. (Report from the scientific expedition to the northwestern provinces of China under leadership of Dr. Sven Hedin. The Sino-Swedish expedition. Publications 17, 5, 20, 28, vi: Vertibrate Palaeontology, 1-4).

———. Some mammalian remains from Shih-ehr-ma-ch'eng, Hui-hui-p'u area, western Kansu. Stockholm, 1951. 46, [1] p. illus. (Reports from the scientific expedition to the north-western provinces of China under leadership of Dr. Sven Hedin. The Sino-Swedish Expedition. Publication 35, vi. Vertebrate palaeontology, 5).

BOULE, MARCELLIN, 1861-1942. Le paléolithique de la Chine par M. Boule, H. Breuil, E. Licent et P. Teilhard. Paris, Masson et Cie, 1928. viii, 138, [1] p. illus. plates, maps, (Archives de l'institut du paléontogie humaine, Mémoire, 4).

BREUIL, HENRI, 1877-   Bone and antler industry of the Choukoutien sinanthropus site. English translation by Miss M. E. Boyle. Peiping, Geological Survey of China, 1939. iv, 92 p. plates. (China. Geological survey. Palaeontologia sinica. New ser. D, no. 6. Whole ser. no. 117).

BRUSSELS. INSTITUT ROYAL DES SCIENCES NATURELLES DE BELGIQUE.

Contribution à la connaissance de la stratigraphie et de la tectonique du Jurassique à couches de houille dans la Chine septentrionale, par F.-F. Mathieu. Contribution à l'étude de la flore jurassique de la Chine septentrionale, par F. Stockmans et F.-F. Mathieu. Bruxelles, 1941. 67 p. 7 plates.

CAMP, CHARLES LEWIS, 1893-   Dinosaur remains from the province of Szechhuan, China. Berkeley, Calif., University of California Press, 1935. covertitle, 467-471 incl. illus., plates (University of California publications. Bulletin of the Department of geological sciences. v. 23, no. 15).

CHANG, HSICHIH, 張席褆  On some fossil mammals from Kwangsi, South China; with 3 plates and 5 textfigures. Canton, 1934. cover-title, 14, [11] p. illus. plates. (Kwangtung. Geological survey. Special publication, no. xv).

CHANG, MING-SHAO, 張鳴韶 . Brachiopoda from the Orthis bed of the Neichia formation of central China. Peiping, Geological Survey of China, 1934. 28 p. 3 p. illus., plates. (China. Geological survey, Palaeontologia sinica, ser. B, vol. i, fasc. 3).

CHAO, YA-TS'ÊNG, 趙亞曾 , 1898-1929. Fauna of the Taiyuan formation of north China, -Pelecypoda. Peking, Geological Survey of China, 1927. 64 p. 4 p. incl. tables. plates (China. Geological survey. Palaeontologica sinica, ser. B, vol. ix, fasc, iii).

——. Productidoe of China. Peking, Geological Survey of China, 1927-28. 2 v. illus., plates, tables, diagrs. ([China. Geological survey. Palaeontologia sinica, ser. B, vol. v, fasc. ii-iii).

——. Carboniferous and Permian spiriferids of China. Peiping, Geological Survey of China, 1929. 133 p; 6 p. incl. illus., tables. plates. (China. Geological survey. Palaeontologia sinica, ser. B, vol. xi, fasc. 1).

CH'ÊN, HSÜ, 陳旭. Fusulinidoe of south China. Peiping, Geological Survey of China, 1934-   1 v. plates, tables, diagrs. (China. Geological survey. Palaeontologia sinica, ser. B, vol. iv, fasc. 2).

CHI, YUNGSHEN SHIAOCHING, 計榮森 , 1907-   Weiningian (Middle Carboniferous) corals of China. Peiping, Geological Survey of China, 1931. 70 p. 5 p. plates, fold. tables. (China. Geological survey. Palaeontologia sinica, ser. B, vol. xii, fasc. 5).

——. Lower Carboniferous syringoporas of China. Peiping, Geological Survey of China, 1933. 48 p; 5 p. plates. (China. Geological survey. Palaeontologia sinica, ser. B, vol. xii, fasc. 4).

——. Additional fossil corals from the Weiningian limestones of Hunan, Yunnan and Kwangsi provinces, in sw. China, Peiping, Geological Survey of China, 1935. 38 p; 8 p. illus., plates, fold. table. (China. Geological survey. Palaeontologia sinica, ser. B, vol. xii, fasc. 6 ).

CHU, S., 朱森 . Corals and Brachiopoda of the Kinling limestone, with v plates and 7 text-figures. Nanking, Published by the National Research Institute of geology, Academia sinica, 1933. 73, [4] p. illus. (Academia sinica. National research institute of geology. Monograph, ser. A. v. 2 ).

COLBERT, EDWIN HARRIS, 1905-   Pleistocene mammals from the limestone fissures of Szechwan, China [by] Edwin Harris Colbert [and] Dirk Albert Hooijer. New York, 1953. 134 p. illus., 40 plates, map. tables (Bulletin of the American Museum of Natural History, v. 102, article 1).

DEXEL, THOMAS. Zur Frage der spätneolithischen Kulturen Nordchinas. Göttingen, 1950. 206 l. Diss. –Univ. Göttingen.

FONTAINE, HENRI. Étude et revision des tabules et heliolitides du Devonien d'Indochine et du Yunnan. Saigon, Impr. Le Van Tan, 1954. 86 p. plates, diagrs. tables, (Vietnam. Centre national de recherches scientifiques et techniques. Archives géologiques du Vietnam, 2).

GRABAU, AMADEUS WILLIAM, 1870-1946. Ordovician fossils of north China, with plates i -ix and 20 text figures. Peking. Published by the Geological Survey of China, 1922. 127 p; [2] p. illus., 1x pl. (China. Geological survey. Palaeontologia sinica, ser. B, vol. 1, fasc. 1).

————. Palaeozoic corals of China. Peking, Geological Survey of China, 1922-1928. 2 v. illus., plates, diagrs. (China. Geological survey. Palaeontologia sinica, ser. B, v. 2, fasc. 1-2.

————. Stratigraphy of China. Peking, Published by the Geological Survey, Ministry of Agriculture and Commerce, 1923-28. 2 v. illus., plates (part fold.) maps (part fold.) profiles, tables (part fold.) diagrs.

————. Silurian faunas of eastern Yunan. Peking, Published by the Geological Survey of China, 1926. 100 p. illus., plates, tables. (China. Geological survey. Palaeontologia sinica. Ser. B., v. 3, fasc. 2).

————. Contributions to geological science by graduates of the National University; an address delivered at the celebration of the thirty-first anniversary of the founding of the university. Peiping, 1930. 16 p.

————. The Grabau anniversary volume. Peiping, 1931. xx, 352 p. illus. plates, maps (part fold.) (Bull. of Geological Soc. of China, vol. 10).

————. Devonian Brachiopoda of China. Peiping, Published by the Geological Survey of China, 1933- 1 v. illus., plates, tables (part fold.) (China. Geological survey. Palaeontologia sinica, ser. B., v. 3, fasc. 3.

————. Early Permian fossils of China. Peiping, Geological Survey of China, 1934-1936. 2 v. illus., plates, tables. (China. Geological survey. Palaeontologia sinica, ser. B, vol. viii, fasc. 3.).

————. Palaeozoic formations in the light of the pulsation theory. [Peiping] University Press, the National University of Peking, 1936- 4 v. illus., fold. maps, fold. profiles.

————. The Amadeus William Grabau memorial volume. Nanking, 1947. 408 p. front. (port.) illus. plates, maps (part fold.) (Bull. of Geological Society of China, vol. 27).

HALLE, THORE GUSTAF, 1884-    Fossil plants from south-western China by T.G. Halle. With stratigraphical note, by V.K. Ting, Peking, Geological Survey of China, 1927. 26 p. 4 p. plates. (China. Geological survey. Palaeontologia sinica, ser. A, vol. i, fasc. ii).

————. Palaeozoic plants from central Shansi. Peking, Geological Survey of China, 1927. 64 l., 316 p. incl. 2 maps, tables, diagr. plates, fold. diagr. (China. Geological survey. Palaeontologia sinica, ser. A, vol. ii, fasc. i).

————. Some seed-bearing pteridosperms from the Permian of China. With 6 plates and 3 figures in the text. Communicated November 28th by O. Juel and O. Rosenberg. Stockholm, Almqvist and Wiksells boktryckeri-a.-b., 1929. 24 p. illus., plates. (Kungl. svenska vetenskapsakademiens handlingar. 3. ser., bd. 6, n:o 8).

————. On Drepanophycis, Protolepidodendron and Protopteridium, with notes on the Palaeozoic flora of Yunnan. Plates v, and 2 figures of text. Nanking, Published by the Geological Survey of China, 1936. 38, 3 p. illus., plates (China. Geological survey. Palaeontologia sinica, ser. A, v 1, fasc. 4).

HOOIJER, DIRK ALBERT. A mastodont tooth from Szechwan, China [by] Dirk A. Hooijer and Edwin H. Colbert. [Chicago] Chicago Natural History Museum, 1951. 129-134 p. illus. ([Chicago. Natural History Museum. Publication] no. 683).

HOPWOOD, ARTHUR TINDELL, 1897-    Fossil Proboscidea from China. With plates I-VIII. Peiping, Geological Survey of China, 1935. 108 p; 3 p. incl. tables. viii plates. (China. Geological survey. Palaeontologia sinica, ser. C, vol. ix, fasc. 3).

HSÜ, SINGWU CHIEH,   許傑 , 1901-    The graptolites of the lower Yangtze valley with 7 plates and 37 text-figures. Nanking, 1934. 106, [23] p. incl. illus., tables, plates. (Academia sinica. National research institute of geology. Monograph. ser. A. vol. iv).

————. Fresh-water gastropods from Tertiary and Quaternary deposits of Kwangsi, S. China. Peiping, Geological Survey of China, 1935. 48 p.; 4 p. incl. illus., tables, diagrs. plates. (China. Geological survey. Palaeontologia sinica, ser. B, vol. vi, fasc. 2).

————. Gastropods from the Siashu formation. Nanking, Geological Survey of China, 1936. 50 p. 6 p. incl. tables, diagrs. plates, (China. Geological Survey . Palaeontologia sinica, ser. B, vol. vi, fasc. 3).

HU, HSEN-HSU, 胡先驌 , 1894-   A Miocene flora from Shantung province, China. Part I. Introduction and systematic considerations [by] Hsen Hsu Hu and Ralph W. Chaney. Part II. Physical conditions and correlation [by] Ralph W. Chaney and Hsen Hsu Hu. Washington, D.C., 1940. vi, 147 p. incl. illus. (map) tables. 57 plates on 53 l. ([Carnegie institution of Washington] Contributions to paleontology).

HUANG, T. K., 黃汲清 [HUANG CHI-CH'ING] 1904-   . Permian corals of southern China. Peiping,Geological Survey of China, 1932. 163 p; 5 p. illus. plates. (China. Geological survey. Palaeontologia sinica, ser. B, vol. viii, fasc. 2).

————. The Permian formations of southern China. Peiping, Geological Survey of China, 1932. iii, 140 p; 2, 18 p. incl. illus., tables. 6 plates (incl. fold. maps) (China. Geological survey. Memoirs, ser. A, no. 10).

————. Late Permian Brachiopoda of southwestern China. Peiping,Geological Survey of China, 1932-33. 2 v. illus., plates. (China. Geological survey. Palaeontologia sinica, ser. B, vol. ix, fasc. 1-2).

KOENIGSWALD, GUSTAV HEINRICH RALPH VON, 1902-   Gigantopitheous blacki von Koenigswald, a giant fossil hominoid from the Pleistocene of southern China. New York, 1952. 295-325 p. illus., tables. (Anthropological papers of the American Museum of Natural History, v. 43, pt. 4).

LÖNNBERG, EINAR, 1865-   On a new fossil porcupine from Honan with some remarks about the development of the Hystridae. Stockholm, Peking, Geological Survey of China, 1924. 15 p. plates. (China. Geological Survey. Palaeontologia sinica, ser. C, v. 1, fasc. 3).

LOUDERBACK, GEORGE DAVIS, 1874-   The stratigraphic relations of the Jung Hsien fossil dinosaur in the Szechuan red beds of China. Berkeley, Calif., University of California Press, 1935. cover-title, p. 459-466 incl. tables. (University of California publications. Bulletin of the Department of geological sciences. v, 23, no. 14).

LOWE, PERCY ROYCROFT, 1870-   Struthious remains from northern China and Mongolia; with descriptions of Struthio wimani, Struthio anderssoni and Struthio mongolicus, spp. nov. With a note on remains of carinate birds, by Dorothea M.A. Bate. Peiping, 1931. 47 p. illus., plates. (China. Geological survey. Palaeontologia sinica, ser. C, vol. vi, fasc. 4).

MA, T'ING-YING, H., 馬廷英 . On the seasonal growth in Palaeozoic tetracorals and the climate during the Devonian period. Nanking, Geological Survey of China, 1937. 96 p; 6 p. plates, fold. map, tables (1 fold. ) ([China. Geological survey] Palaeontologia sinica, ser. B, vol. ii, fasc. 3).

————. On the growth rate of reef corals and its relation to sea water temperature. Nanking, Geological Survey of China, 1937. 226 p; 7 p. incl. tables, diagrs. and [atlas] of 2 l. [227]-426 p.,plates ([China. Geological survey] Palaeontologia sinica, ser. B, vol. xvi, fasc. 1).

————. Research on the past climate and continental drift. Yungan and Taipei, The author, 1943-1953. 6 v. plates, maps (part fold. ).

————. Subaerial erosions and amounts of sliding of the rigid shell of the globe in the Pacific Basin since the end of the Cretaceous. Taipei, 1953. 6; 7 p. illus. tables, (Oceanographica Sinica, 1:1).

————. Deposition of geosynclinal formations and the origin of petroleum. Taipei, 1953. 48 p. diagr. tables (2 fold. ) (Oceanographica Sinica 1:2).

ODHNER, NILS HJALMAR, 1884-   Non-marine Mollusca from Pliocene deposits of Kwangsi, China. With III plates and an Appendix on recent Chinese shells in fossil occurrence. Peking, Published by the Geological Survey of China, 1930. 34 p. plates. (China. Geological survey. Palaeontologia sinica, ser. B, v. 6, fasc. 4 ).

——— . Shells from the San Men series. Peking, Published by the Geological
Survey of China [Stockholm, Cederquists grafiska aktiebolag] 1925. 18, [2]p;
vi, [6] p. illus., plates (China. Geological survey. Palaeontologia sinica,
ser. B, v. 6, fasc. 1).

P'AN, CHUNG-HSIANG, 潘鐘祥, 1906-    Older Mesozoic plants from north
Shensi. Nanking, Geological Survey of China, 1936. 76 p; 6 p. plates (incl.
map, diagr.) (China. Geological survey. Palaeontologia sinica. ser. A, vol.
iv, fasc. 2).

PATTE, ÉTIENNE, 1891-       Étude de quelques fossiles paléozoiques et meso-
zoiques recueillis en Indochine et au Yunnan. I. Fossiles recueilli au cours
de la mission Jacob et Dussault au Laos (1921-1922) II. Ammonites du Trias
supérieur du Tonkin. III. Fossile du Dévonien et du Trias recueillis au Yunnan par m. Fromaget. iv. Rhétien marin du Yunnan. Par Étienne Patte. Ha
Hanoi, Impr. d'Extrême-Orient, 1922. 71 p. plates. ([Indo-China, French]
Service géologique de l'Indo-Chine. Mémoires, v. 9: fasc. 1).

——— . Fossiles paléozoiques et mésozoiques du sud-ouest de la Chine. Avec 4
planches. Peiping, Geological Survey of China, 1935. 50, 14 p. plates (China.
Geological survey. Palaeontologia sinica, ser. B, vol xv, fasc. 2).

PEARSON, HELGA SHARPE, 1898-    Chinese fossil Suidae. Peking, Geological
Survey of China, 1928. 75 p. incl. illus., tables. plates. (China. Geological
survey. Palaeontologia sinica, ser. c, v. 5, fasc. 5).

P'EI, WÊN-CHUNG, 裴文中, 1903-    Mammalian remains from locality 5 at
Chouk'outien. Peiping, Geological Survey of China, 1931. 18 p; 2 p. incl.
illus., tables. plates. (China. Geological survey. Palaeontologia sinica, ser.
C, vol. vii, fasc. 2).

——— . Choukoutien excavations. Peiping, The National Geological Survey of
China and Institute of Geology of the National Academy of Peiping, 1934. 4,
2, 6, 68 p., illus., plates (2 fold.) fold. map. (China. Geological survey.
Memoirs, ser. B, no. 7).

——— . On the Carnivora from locality 1 of Choukoutien. Peiping, The Geological Survey of China, 1934. 216 p; 5 p. incl. illus., tables, diagrs. plates.
(China. Geological survey. Palaeontologia sinica, ser. C, vol. viii, fasc. 1).

——— . On the mammalian remains from locality 3 at Choukoutien. Peiping,
1936. 120 p; 3 p. incl. illus., tables, plates. ([China. Geological survey]
Palaeontologia sinica, ser. C, vol. vii, fasc. 5).

——— . Le rôle des phénomènes naturels dans d'éclatement et le façonnement des
roches dures utilisées par l'homme préhistorique. Paris, 1936. 78 p. illus.
plates, diagrs. Thèse-Univ. de Paris. "Extrait de la Revue de géographie
physique et de géologie dynamique. Volume ix, fascicule 4."

——— . Le rôle des animaux et des causes naturelles dans la cassure des os.
Peiping, Geological Survey of China, 1938. 60 p. illus., plates. (China. Geological survey. Palaeontologia sinica. New ser. D, no. 7. Whole ser. no.
118).

——— . The upper cave industry of Choukoutien. Peiping, Geological Survey of
China, 1939. 58 p. illus., plates, diagrs. (China. Geological survey. Palaeontologia sinica. New ser. D, no. 9. Whole ser. no. 120).

——— . An attempted correlation of Quaternary geology, paleontology and prehistory in Europe and China. London, Institute of Archaeology, 1939. 16 p̄. 2
fold. tab. (London. University. Institute of archaeology. Geochronological
table no. 1).

——— . The upper cave fauna of Choukoutien. Chungking, Geological Survey of
China, 1940. iv, 100 p. incl. illus., tables. plates, fold. diagr. (China, Geological survey. Palaeontologia sinica. New ser. c, no. 10. Whole ser. no.
125).

PING, CHI, 秉志, [PING CHIH], 1889-    Cretaceous fossil insects of China.
Peiping, Geological Survey of China, 1928. 56 p; 7 p. illus., plates, map.

(China. Geological survey. Palaeontologia sinica, ser. B, vol. xiii, fasc. 1).
——. Fossil terrestrial gastropods from north China. Peiping, Geological Survey of China, 1929. 30 p; 7 p. illus., plates (China. Geological survey. Palaeontologia sinica, ser. B, vol. vi, fasc. 5).
——. Tertiary and Quaternary non-marine gastropods of north China. Peiping, Published by the Geological Survey of China in cooperation with the Section of Geology, National Academy of Peiping, 1931. 39 p; 8 p. illus., plates. (China. Geological survey. Palaeontologia sinica; ser. B, vol. vi, fasc. 6).

REED, FREDERICK RICHARD COWPER, 1869-    Palaeozoic and Mesozoic fossils from Yun-nan. Calcutta, Government of India Central Publication Branch, 1927. 331, vi p. plates. (India. Geological survey. Memoirs. Palaeontologia indica. n. s., vol. x, no. 1).

RINGSTRÖM, TORSTEN JONAS, 1895-    Nashörner der hipparion-fauna Nord Chinas. Peking, Geological Survey of China, 1924. [3], 156, [30] p. illus., plates, tables. ([China. Geological survey] Palaeontologia sinica, ser. C, vol. I, fasc. 4).
——. Über Quartäre und Jungtertiäre rhinocerotiden aus China und der Mongolei. Peking, Geological Survey of China, 1927. 21, [1] p. incl. illus., tables. plates. (China. Geological survey. Palaeontologia sinica, ser. C, vol. iv, fasc. 3).

SCHAUB, SAMUEL, 1882-    Über einige fossile Simplicidentaten aus China und der Mongolei. Basel, Komm. E. Birkhäuser et Cie, 1934. iv, 40 p. plates, figs. (Abhandlungen der Schweizerischen palaeontologischen Gesellschaft, Bd. 54, 2).

SCHLOSSER, MAX. Fossil primates from China. Peking, Published by the Geological Survey of China, 1924. 14, [4] p. plates. (China. Geological survey. Palaeontologia sinica, ser. C, vol. I, fasc. 2).

SEFVE, IVAR, 1886-    Die Hipparionen Nord-Chinas. Peking, Published by the Geological Survey of CHina, 1927. 93 p. incl. illus., tables, diagrs. plates. (China. Geological survey. Palaeontologia sinica, ser C, vol. iv, fasc. 2).

SHÊNG, HSIN-FU, 盛莘夫 . Lower Ordovician trilobite fauna of Chekiang. Peiping, Geological Survey of China, 1934. 28 p; 3 p. plates. (China. Geological survey. Palaeontologia sinica, ser. B, vol. III, fasc, 1).

SMITH, GRAFTON ELLIOT, 1871-1937. The discovery of primitive man in China. (In Smithsonian institution. Annual report, 1931. Washington, 1932. p. 531-547. illus., plates.
——. The significance of the Peking man, lecture delivered at the University of Edinburgh, Friday, 30th January 1931. [Edinburgh, London, Oliver and Boyd, 1931] 20 p. illus., plates. (The Henderson trust lectures.-no. 11).

STENSIÖ, ERIK ANDERSSON, 1891-    Sinamia zdanskyi, a new amiid from the Lower Cretaceous of Shantung, China. With 17 plates and 20 figures in the text. Peiping, Published by the Geological Survey of China, 1935. 48 p; 2 p. illus., plates. ([China. Geological survey] Palaeontologia sinica, ser. C, vol. III, fasc. 1 ).

SUN, YÜN-CHU, 孫雲鑄, 1897-    Contributions to the Cambrian faunas of north China. Peking, Geological Survey of China, 1924. 109 p; 24 p. incl. map. plates. (China. Geological survey. Palaeontologia sinica, ser. B, vol. I, fasc. IV).
——. Ordovician trilobites of central and southern China. Peiping, Geological Survey of China, 1931. 47 p; 2 p. III plates. (China. Geological survey. Palaeontologia sinica, ser. B, vol. VII, fasc. 1).
——. Ordovician and Silurian graptolites from China. Peiping, Geological Survey of China, 1933. 69, [1] p; 5 p. plates (China. Geological survey, Palaeontologia sinica, ser. B, vol. xiv, fasc. 1).
——. Lower Ordovician graptolite-faunas of north China. Peiping, Geological Survey of China, 1935. 20 p; 2 p. plates. (China. Geological survey. Palaeontologia sinica, ser. B, vol. xiv, fasc. 2).

——. Bases of the chronological classification with special reference to the Paleozoic stratigraphy of China. Kunming, National University of Peking, 1941. Cover-title, 21 p. incl. tables.

——. Preliminary notes on the stratigraphy and structure of the Paoshan region, W. Yunnan. Peiping, Yu Lien Press, 1947. 26 p. illus. plates, (Peking. National Univ. of Peking. Geological institute. Contributions, 32).

SZE, H. C., 斯行健 [SSÜ HSING-CHIEN]. Beiträge zur mesozoischen Flora von China. Peiping, Geological Survey of China, 1933. 91, [1] p; 2 p. incl. tables, plates (China. Geological survey. Palaeontologia sinica, ser A, vol. IV, fasc. 1).

——. Fossile Pflanzen aus Shensi, Szechuan und Kueichow. Peiping, Geological Survey of China, 1933. 44 p; 7 p. plates. (China. Geological survey. Palaeontologia sinica, ser. A, vol. I, fasc. 3).

——. On the occurrence of Neuropteris gigantea Sternb. in Kiangsi, by H. C. Sze and Kouta Chan, 陳國達. [n. p., 194-] Collation of the original, as determined from the film; 196-200 p. plate, map. From the Bulletin of the Geological Society of China, v. 22, nos. 3-4, Dec. 1942.

——. Die mesozoische Flora aus der Hsiangchi Kohlen Serie in Westhupeh. Nanking, National Geological Survey of China, 1949. 71 p. plates. (China. Geological Survey. Palaeontologia sinica, new ser. A, no. 2, Whole ser. no. 133).

——. Older mesozoic plants from the Yenchang formation, northern Shensi. Peking, Institute of Paleontology and Laboratory of Vertebrate Palaeontology, 1956. p. 113-217. (Palaeontologia Sinica. n. s. A, 5, whole number 139).

TEILHARD DE CHARDIN, PIERRE. Preliminary observations on the Pre-Loessic and Post-Pontian formations in western Shansi and northern Shensi, by P. Teilhard de Chardin and C. C. Young. Peiping, Geological Survey of China and the Section of Geology of the National Academy of Peiping, 1930. 54 p; 20 p. incl. illus. plates (incl. fold. map) (China. Geological survey. Memoirs, ser. A, no. 8).

——. Fossil mammals from the late Cenozoic of northern China, by P. Teilhard de Chardin and C. C. Young. Peiping, Geological Survey of China, 1931. 88 p; 5 p. illus., plates, map. (China. Geological survey. Palaeontologia sinica, ser. C, vol. ix, fasc. 1).

——. Fossil mammals from locality 9 of Choukoutien. Nanking, Published by the Geological Survey of China, 1936. [5]-70, [2] p. illus., plates. (China. Geological survey. Palaeontologia sinica, ser. C, vol. vii, fasc. 4).

——. On the mammalian remains from the archaeological site of Anyang, by P. Teilhard de Chardin and C. C. Young. Nanking, Geological Survey of China, 1936. ii, [1], [5]-78 p; 8 p. illus. plates (1 fold.) ([China. Geological survey] Palaeontologia sinica, ser. C, vol. xii, fasc. 1).

——. The proboscidians of south-eastern Shansi, by P. Teilhard de Chardin and M. Trassaert Nanking, Geological Survey of China, 1937. 84, 4 p. incl. illus., map, tables. (China. Geological survey. Palaeontologia sinica, ser. C, v. 13, fasc. 1).

——. The pliocene Camelidae, Giraffidae, and Cervidae of south-eastern Shansi, by Teilhard de Chardin and M. Trassaert. Nanking, Geological Survey of China, 1937. 68, [8] p. illus. plates, (Palaeontologia sinica, n. s. C., no. 1).

——. The fossils from locality 12 of Choukoutien. Nanking, Published by the Geological Survey of China, 1938. 50 p. illus. (incl. map) plates, diagr. ([China. Geological survey] Palaeontologia sinica, n. s. C., no. 5, whole ser. no. 114).

——. Cavicornia of south-eastern Shansi, by P. Teilhard de Chardin and M. Trassaert. [Nanking] Published by the Geological Survey of China, 1938. 106 p. incl. illus., tables. plates. ([China. Geological survey] Palaeontologia sinica, n. s. C, no. 6, whole ser. no. 115).

——. The fossils from locality 18, near Peking. Chungking, Geological Survey of China, 1940. 100 p. illus., plates. (China. Geological survey. Palaeontologia sinica. n. s. C, no. 9. whole ser. no. 124).

——. The fossil mammals from locality 13 of Choukoutien by Teilhard de Chardin and Pei Wen-chung. Pehpei, Geological Survey of China, 1941. iii, 118 p. illus. (Palaeontologia sinica, n. s. C, no. 11).

——. Réflexions sur le progrès. Peking, 1941. 27 p.

——. Early man in China, Pékin, Institut de Géobiologie, 1941. xi, 99 p. illus. map (Institut de géobiologie. [Publ. ], 7).

——. Chinese fossil mammals; a complete bibliography analysed, tabulated, annotated and indexed. Pékin, Institut de Géobiologie, 1942. 142 p.

——. Fossil man, recent discoveries and present problems, a lecture given at the Catholic University of Peking. Peking, H. Vetch, 1943. 28 p. illus. diagrs.

——. Le néolithique de la Chine, par Pierre Teilhard de Chardin et Pei Wen-chung. Pékin, Institut de Géobiologie, 1944. xiv, 100 p. illus. 2 fold. maps. (Institut de géobiologie. [Publ. ] 10).

——. La question de l'homme fossile; découvertes récentes et problèmes actuels. Paris, Éditions Psyché [1948] 33 p. illus. (Collection Psyché. Petites études).

T'IEN, CH'I-CH'IUNG, 田奇瑂, 1899- Crinoids from the Taiyuan series of north China. Peking, Geological Survey of China, 1926. 58 p; 6 p. incl. illus. plates, (China. Geological survey. Palaeontologia sinica, ser. B, vol. v, fasc. 1).

——. Lower Triassic Cephalopoda of south China. Peiping, Geological Survey of China, 1933. 53 p; 2 p. incl. tables. plates, (China. Geological survey. Palaeontologia sinica, ser. B, vol. xv, fasc. 1).

——. Devonian Brachiopoda of Hunan. Changsha, Geological Survey of China, 1938. iv, 192, 7 p. incl. illus., tables, diagrs. plates. (China. Geological survey. Palaeontologia sinica, n. s. B, no. 4, whole ser. no. 113).

WEIDENREICH, FRANZ, 1873-1948. Observations on the form and proportions of the endocranial casts of Sinanthropus pekinensis, other hominids and the great apes: a comparative study of brain size. Peiping, 1936. 50 p. incl. illus. (incl. diagrs.) tables. (China. Geological survey. Palaeontologia sinica, ser. D, vol. vii, fasc. 4).

——. The dentition of Sinanthropus pekinensis; a comprative odontography of the hominids. With tables I-XXVII and an atlas containing plates I-XXXVI and 49 diagrams. Peiping, 1937. v, 180 p. incl. tables. and atlas of plates, 49 diagr. ([China. Geological survey] Palaeontologia sinica, new ser. D, no. 1. Whole ser. no. 101).

——. The mandibles of Sinanthropus pekinensis: a comparative study. With text figures 1 to 100, tables I to XVII and plates I to XV. Peiping, 1938. 162, 5 p. incl. illus., tables, diagrs. plates ([China. Geological survey] Palaeontologia sinica, ser. D, vol. 7, fasc. 3).

——. Six lectures on Sinanthropus pekinensis and related problems. Pehpei, 1939. Cover-title, 110 p. plates. Reprinted from the Bull. of the Geological Society of China, v. 19, No. 1.

——. The extremity bones of Sinanthropus pekinensis. With tables I to XX, and plates I to XXIV. Peking, Geological Survey of China, 1941. 150 p. incl. tables. plates. (China. Geological survey. Palaeontologia sinica. New ser. D, no. 5. Whole ser. no. 116).

——. The skull of Sinanthropus pekinensis; a comparative study on a primitive hominid skull. With tables I-XXXVIII and plates I-XCIII. Pehpei, Geological Survey of China, 1943. xxi, 484, [2] p. incl. plates, diagrs. (China. Geological survey. Palaeontologia sinica. New ser. D, no. 10. Whole ser. no. 127).

——. Giant early man from Java and south China. New York, 1945. 134 p. illus. (incl. map) plates, tables (1 fold. ) diagrs. (Anthropological papers of the American museum of natural history. v. 40: pt. 1).

------. The shorter anthropological papers of Franz Weidenreich published in
the period 1939-1948; a memorial volume compiled by S. L. Washburn and
David Wolffson. New York, Viking Fund, 1949. vii, 267 p. illus.

WIMAN, CARL JOHAN JOSEF ERNST, 1867-1944. Die Dreide-dinosaurier aus
Shantung. Peking, Geological Survey of China, 1929. 67 p; 3 p. incl. illus.,
tables, diagr. plates (part fold.) (China. Geological survey. Palaeontologia
sinica, ser. C, v. 6, fasc. 1).

------. Fossile Schildkröten aus China. Peiping, Geological Survey of China,
1930. 56 p; [2] p. incl. illus., tables. plates (3 fold.) (China. Geological
survey. Palaeontologia sinica, ser. C, v. 6, fasc. 3).

YIN, TSAN-HSÜN, 尹贊勳, 1902-    Gastropoda of the Penchi and Taiyuan series of north China. Peiping, Geological Survey of China, 1932. 53 p; 2 p.
incl. tables. plates, (China. Geological survey. Palaeontologia sinica, ser.
B, vol. xi, fasc. 2).

------. Upper Palaeozoic ammonoids of China. Peiping, Geological Survey of
China, 1935. 44 p; 5 p. illus., plates (China. Geological survey. Palaeontologia sinica, ser. B, vol. xi, fasc. 4).

YOH, SÊN-SHING,樂森璕 , 1899-    The coral fauna of the Chihsia limestone of
the lower Yangtze valley, by S.S. Yoh and T.K. Huang. Peiping, Geological
Survey of China, 1932. 72 p; 10 p. plates. (China. Geological survey. Palaeontologia sinica, ser. B, vol. viii, fasc. 1).

YOUNG, CHUNG-CHIEN, 楊鍾健,Fossile nagetiere aus Nord- China. Peking,
Geological Survey of China, 1927. 82, [6] p; 2 p. incl. tables. plates. (China. Geological survey. Palaeontologia sinica, ser. C, vol. v, fasc. 3).

------. On the mammalian remians from Chi Ku Shan near Chou Kou Tien. Peiping, Geological Survey of China, Section of Geology, National Academy of
Peiping, 1930. 24 p; 2 p. 1 illus., plates. (China. Geological survey. Palaeontologia sinica, ser. C, vol. vii, fasc. 1).

------. On the Artiodactyla from the Sinanthropus site at Chou-k'outien. Peiping, Geological Survey of China, 1932. 158 p. incl. illus., tables. plates.
(China. Geological survey. Palaeontologia sinica, ser. C, vol 8, fasc. 2).

------. On the fossil vertebrate remains from localitites 2, 7 and 8 at Choukoutien. Peiping, Geological Survey of China, 1932. 24, [4] p. illus., plates.
(China. Geological survey. Palaeontologia sinica, ser. C, v. 7, fasc. 3).

------. Fossil man and summary of Cenozoic geology in China. Peiping, Geological Survey of China, 1933. 4, 4, 2, 106 p. illus., plates, fold. maps, fold.
diagrs. (China. Geological survey. Geological memoirs, ser. B, no. 5).

------. On the Insectivora, Chiroptera, Rodentia and primates other than Sinanthropus from locality 1 at Choukoutien. Peiping, Geological Survey of China,
1934. 160 p; 4 p. incl. illus., tables. plates. ([China. Geological survey]
Palaeontologia sinica, ser. C, vol. viii, fasc. 3).

------. Fossil reptiles in China. Peiping, National Geological Survey of China
and the Institute of Geology of the National Academy of Peiping, 1935. 4, 4,
56, [3] p. illus., plates, fold. map, tables (2 fold.) (China. Geological survey. Geological memoirs ser. B, no. 8).

------. On a new nodosaurid from Ninghsia. Peiping, Geological Survey of China, 1935. 34 p; 2 p. illus., plates (China. Geological survey. Palaeontologia
sinica, ser. C, vol. xi, fasc. 1).

------. Miscellaneous mammalian fossils from Shansi and Honan. Peiping, Geological Survey of China, 1935. 56 p; 1 p. illus., plates. (China. Geological
survey. Palaeontologia sinica, ser. C, vol. ix, fasc. 2).

------. A complete osteology of Lufengosaurus huenei Young (gen. et sp. nov.)
from Lufeng, Yunnan, China. Pehpei, Geological Survey of China, 1941.
53 p. illus., plates (part fold.) (China. Geological survey. Palaeontologia sinica. New ser. C, no. 7. Whole ser. no. 121).

------. On Lufengosaurus magnus Young (sp. nov.) and additional finds of Lufengosaurus huenei Young. Nanking, Published by the Geological Survey of Chi-

na, 1947. 53, 2 p. illus. (China, Geological survey. Palaeontologia sinica, n. s. C, no. 12. Whole ser. no. 132).

YÜ, CHIEN-CHANG,俞建章 . The Ordovician Cephalopoda of central China. Peiping, Geological Survey of China and Section of Geology, National Academy of Peiping, 1930. 101 p; 18 p. illus., plates. (China. Geological survey. Palaeontologia sinica; ser. B, vol. I, fasc. 2 ).

————. Lower Carboniferous corals of China. Peiping, Geological Survey of China, 1933. 211 p; 11 p. plates. (China. Geological survey. Palaeontologia sinica, ser B, vol xii, fasc. 3).

ZDANSKY, OTTO. Jungtertiäre carnivoren Chinas. Peking, Geological Survey of China, 1924. 149 p; 2 p. illus., plates, map, tables. (China. Geological survey. Palaeontologia sinica, ser. C, v. 2, fasc. 1).

————. Quartäre carnivoren aus Nord-China. Peking, Published by the Geological Survey of China [Stockholm, Cederquists grafiska aktiebolag] 1925. 26, [3] p. incl. illus., tables. plates. (China. Geological survey. Palaeontologia sinica, ser. C, V. 2, fasc. 2).

————. Fossile hirsche Chinas. Peking, Geological Survey of China [Stockholm, Cederquists grafiska aktiebolag] 1925. 90, [4] p., incl. illus., tables. plates, (China. Geological survey. Palaeontologia sinica, ser. C, v. 2, fasc. 3).

————. Peracamelus gigas, Schlosser. Peking, Geological Survey of China [Stockholm, Cederquists grafiska aktiebolag] 1926. 44 p., illus., plates (China. Geological survey. Palaeontologia sinica, ser. C, v. 2, fasc. 4).

————. Weitere, Bemerkungen über fossile Cerviden aus China. Peking, Published by the Geological Survey of China, 1927. 19 p. incl. illus., tables. plates (China. Geological survey. Palaeontologia sinica. ser. C, vol. v, fasc. 1).

————. Die Säugetiere der Quartärfauna von Chou-k'ou-tien. Peking, Geological Survey of China, 1928. 146 p. incl. illus., tables, diagrs. plates. (China. Geological survey. Palaeontologia sinica, ser. C, vol. v, fasc. 4).

————. Die Alttertiären Säugetiere Chinas nebst stratigraphischen Bemerkungen. Peiping, Geological Survey of China, 1930. 87 p. incl. illus., tables, plates. (China. Geological survey. Palaeontologia sinica, ser. C, vol. vi, fasc. 2).

————. Equus und andere Perissodactyla. Peiping, Geological Survey of China, 1935. 54 p. 2 p. incl. tables. plates. (China. Geological survey. Palaeontologia sinica, ser. C, vol. vi, fasc. 5).

## Botany

### Bibliographies

LIOU, HO, 劉厚[LIU HOU]. Aperçu bibliographique sur les anciens traités chinois de botanique, d'agriculture, de séricuculture et de fungiculture, 中國植物學書目考. par Liou-Ho et Claudius Roux avec 2 planches hors texte. Lyon. Impr. Bosc frères et Riou, 1927. cover-title, 39 p. plates.

MERRILL, ELMER DREW, 1876-1956. A bibliography of eastern Asiatic botany, by Elmer D. Merrill and Egbert H. Walker. Sponsored by the Smithsonian Institution, Arnold Arboretum of Harvard University, New York Botanical Garden, Harvard-Yenching Institute. Jamaica Plain Mass., Arnold Aboretum of Harvard University, 1938. xiii 719 p.

### General Works

BELVAL, HENRI. Contribution à la flore du Kiang-sou, Changhai, 1931. 17 p. (Musée Heude. Notes de botanique chinoise, 1.).

BRETSHNEÏDER, ÉMILIÏ VASÏL'EVÏCH, 1833-1901. Botanicon Sinicum. Notes on Chinese botany from native and western sources. London, Trübner, 1882-1895 [Tokyo, Royal Asiatic Society, 1937] 3 v. Facsimile edition. Vols II and III have imprint: Shanghai [etc.] Kelly and Walsh, limited. Issued originally in the Journal of the North-China branch of the Royal Asiatic Society, new series, vols. XVI, XXV, XXIX, 1882-1895.

————. History of European botanical discoveries in China. Leipzig, Unveränderte Nachdruck von K. F. Koehlers Antiquarium, 1935. 2 v. Has also imprint of original edition: London, Sampson Low, Marston and company, limited, 1898.

CHEN, PAN-CHIEH, 陳邦傑, 1907- Studien über die ostasiatischen Arten der Pottiaceae. 1. Dresden, C. Hienrich, 1940. 76 p. illus. Diss.-Univ. Berlin.

CHEN, LUETTA,陳秀英, [CH' ÊN HSIU-YING] 1910- A revision of the genus Sabia Colebrooke. The Chinese and Indo-Chinese species of Ormosia, by E. D. Merrill and Luetta Chen. Jamaica Plain, Mass., Arnold Arboretum of Harvard University, 1943. 120 p. illus. (Sargentia; a continuation of the Contributions from the Arnold arboretum of Harvard university. III).

CHIAO, CH'I-YÜAN, 焦啓源. Kiangsu grasses. Contribution from the Herbarium, College of Agriculture and Forestry, University of Nanking. (Chengtu, Szechuan) 1943. iii, 115 p.

CHIU, SHIN FOON, 趙善寬. Toxicity studies of insecticidal plants in southwestern China. Canton, College of Agriculture, National Sun Yatsen University, 1944. 54 p.

CHOW, HANG-FAN, 周漢藩. The familiar trees of Hopei. Peiping, Peking Natural History Bulletin, 1934. xii, 374 p. illus. ([Peking society of natural history] Handbook, 4).

CHUN, WOON-YOUNG, 陳煥鏞, [CH'ÊN HUAN-YUNG], 1895- Chinese economic trees. Illustrated with 100 plates. [Shanghai] Printed by the Commercial Press [1921] xxvii, [1] 309, ix p. front., illus.

CHUNG, HSIN HSUAN, 鍾心煊, 1892- A catalogue of trees and shrubs of China. Shanghai, 1924. 4, ii, 271 p. (Memoirs of the Science society of China. 1:1).

COURTOIS, FRÉDÉRIC, 1860-1928. Flore de la région montagneuse du Ngan-Hoei. Enumération des plantes récoltées et déterminées par le P. Courtois au cours des années 1906-1922; editées par H. Belval. Changhai, 1933. viii, [1], 169, 14 p. fold. plate, fold. map, (Musée Heude. Notes de botanique chinoise, 2.).

COWAN, JOHN MACQUEEN, ed. The journeys and plant introductions of George Forrest, v. M.H. Edited by J. Macqueen Cowan with the assistance of members of the staff of the Royal Botanic Garden, Edinburgh, and E. H. M. Cox. London, Published for the Royal Horticultural Society by Oxford University Press, 1952. xi, 252 p. illus. (part col.) port., fold. col. map.

COX, EUAN HILLHOUSE METHVEN, 1893- ed. The plant introductions of Reginald Farrer. London, New Flora and Silva, 1930. xi, 113 p. incl. front. (port.) plates. col. plates.

————. Plant-hunting in China; a history of botanical exploration in China and the Tibetan marches. London, Collins, 1945. 3-230 p. col. front., illus. (maps) plates (incl. ports.) diagr.

DE VOL, CHARLES EDWARD, 1903- Ferns and fern allies of east central China. Changhai, 1945. 154 p. plates, (Musée Heude. Notes de botanique chinoise, 7).

FANG, WÊN-P'EI, 方文培. A monograph of Chinese Aceraceae. Nanking, Science Society of China, 1939 [i. e. 1940] cover-title, ix, 346 p. illus. (Contributions from the Biological laboratory of the Science society of China. Botanical series, xi).

————. Icones plantarum omeiensium. Chengtu, National Szechuan University, 1942-1945. 2 v. illus.

————. Commemoration volume in commemoration of Dr. Fang Wen-pei's ten years service in the National Szechuan University. Chengtu, National Szechuan University, 1947. 32 p.

[FORBES, FRANCIS BLACKWELL] 1839-1908. Enumeration of all the plants

known from China proper, Formosa, Hainan, the Corea, the Luchu archipe-
lago, and the island of Hongkong; together with their distribution and synonymy. [London, Linnean Society, 1886-1905. Peking, The Licoph Service,
1939?] 3 v. plates (1 fold.) fold. map.

GARDNER, NATHANIEL LYON, 1864-1937. A new species of Entophysalis from
China, and notes on other species of the genus. Berkeley, University of California Press, 1927. cover-title, p. [369]-372. 72 plates. (University of California publications in botany. 13:17).

―――. On a collection of Myxophyceae from Fukien province, China. Berkeley,
University of California Press, 1927. cover-title, 20 p. 5 plates. (University
of California publications in botany, 14:1).

GARVEN, HUGH SHAW DUNN. Wild flowers of north China and south Manchuria.
Peiping, Peking Natural History Bulletin, 1937. 117 p., [203] p. of illus.
([Peking society of natural history] Handbook, 5).

GEE, NATHANIEL GIST, 1876-1937. List of plants in Kiangsu province. Shanghai, Science Society of China, 1921. 178 p.

GROFF, GEORGE WEIDMAN, 1884-1955. The lychee and lungan with eleven appendices, including contributions by Frederick V. Coville, Walter T. Swingle,
Edward Goucher, and Michael J. Hagerty, all of the United States Department of Agriculture. New York, Orange Judd, 1921. iii, 188 p. front., plates
(1 col.).

―――. Plants of Kwangtung province and their Chinese names. Washington,
1921. 3 pts in 9 v.

―――, Plants of Lungt'aushan. Canton, Lingnan University, 1930. cover-title,
138 p. front. (map), (Lingnan University. Science Bull., 2 ).

HANDEL-MAZZETTI, HEINRICH RAPHAEL EDUARD, freiherr von. 1882-1940.
Plantae novae sinenses; diagnosibus brevibus descriptae a Dre. Heinr. Handel-Mazzetti. 20-39 fortsetzung. [Wien] 1920-1926. 7 v. (Wien. Akademie
der Wissenschaften. Math-Naturw. Kl. v. 57-63).

―――. Naturbilder aus Südwest-China; Erlebnisse und Eindrücke eines öster -
reichischen Forschers während des Weltkrieges, mit einer Karte und 148
Bildern nach Aufnahmen des Verfassers, darunter 24 Autochromen. Wien
und Leipzig, Österreichischer Bundesverlag für Unterricht, Wissenschaft
und Kunst, 1927. xiv, 380 p. illus., plates (part col.) fold. map (in pocket).

―――. Symbolae sinicae. Botanische Ergebnisse der Expedition der Akademie
der Wissenschaften in Wien nach Südwest-China 1914-1918. Unter Mitarbeit
von Viktor F. Brotherus, Heinrich Handel-Mazzetti, Theodor Herzog, [u. a. ]
Hrsg. von Heinrich Handel-Mazzetti. Wien, J. Springer, 1929-37. 7 v.
plates.

HAO, KIN-SHEN, 郝景盛. Synopsis of Chinese Salix. Dahlem bei Berlin [ Buchdruckerei H. Lotze, inh. E. Sandau] 1936. iv, 123 p. plates (Repertorium
specierum novarum regni vegetabilis. Hrsg. von Friedrich Fedde. Beihefte.
bd. 93).

HOFFMANN, WILLIAM EDWIN, 1896- Lingnan trees, a list of trees growing
on Lingnan university campus. Canton, 1942. 15 p. (Lingnan natural history
survey and museum, Special publ. 11).

HU, HSEN-HSU, 胡先驌, 1894- ed. Icones plantarum sinicarum, ed. by Hsen-
Hsu Hu and Woon-Young Chun, 陳煥鏞. Shanghai, Commercial Press, 1927-
1935. 4 v. plates.

―――. Icones filicum sinicarum, by Hsen Hsu Hu and Ren Chang Ching, 秦仁昌.
Nanking, 1930-37. 4 v. plates.

HU, SHIU-YING, 胡秀英, 1910- Flora of China, family 153: Malvaceae. [ Jamaica Plain, Mass.] The Arnold Arboretum of Harvard University, with the
support of the China International Foundation, 1955. 80 p. illus.

HWANG, LIANG, 黃亮. A preliminary study on bacterial soft rot of Brassica
pekinensis and other vegetables in China. Nanking, College of Agriculture
and Forestry, University of Nanking, 1935. 26 p. illus. tables, (Its. Bull.,
33).

IMBERT, HENRI. La Pivoine, reine des fleurs en Chine. Pékin, La "Politique de Pékin," 1922. 11 p. illus. (Collection de la "Politique de Pékin").

————. Le nélombo d'Orient (Lotus); fleur sacrée des bouddhistes. Pékin, La "Politique de Pékin," 1922. 13 p. illus. (Collection de la "Politique de Pékin").

JAO, CHIN-CHIH, 饒欽止, 1900-    Studies on the freshwater Algae of China. I. Zygnemataceae from Szechwan. Nanking, 1935. p. 551-645 incl. illus., plates. Thesis-University of Michigan. "Papers from the Department of botany and herbarium of the University of Michigan, no. 541. "

KINGDON-WARD, FRANCIS, 1885-1958. The romance of plant hunting. London, E. Arnold, 1924. xi, 275 p. front., plates.

KLAUTKE, PAUL. Nutzpflanzen und Nutztiere Chinas. Hannover, Hahnsche Buchhandlung, 1922. 159, [1] p. illus. (Weltwirtschaftliche abhandlungen, v. bd.).

KOEHN, ALFRED. Fragrance from a Chinese garden. Peking, Lotus Court, 1942.[7], 62 p. col. plates. "Poems and stories concerning 18 of China's most revered plants and trees from the enlarged edition of Wang Hsiang-chin's, 王象晉 Chün-fang p'u, 羣芳譜 . "

KOZLOV, I. Renonculacées. Traduit du manuscrit russe par E. de Laberbis. Tientsin, Mission de Hsien-Hsien, 1933. 43 p. (Publications du Musée Hoang-ho Pai-ho, 22).

KURTÉN, BJÖRN. The Chinese Hipparion fauna; a quantitative survey with comments on the ecology of the machairodonts and hyaenids and the taxonomy of the gazelles. Helsinfors, 1952. 82 p. (Societas Scientiarum Fennicae. Commentations biologioae, xiii, 4).

LAUFER, BERTHOLD, 1874-1934. The American plant migration pt. 1. The potato. Prepared for publication by C. Martin Wilbur. [Chicago, 1938-1 v. front. (port.) illus. (Field museum of natural history, Publication 418.

LEE. SHUN-CHING, 李順卿, 1892-    Forest botany of China. Shanghai, Commercial Press, 1935. [iii]-xlvii, 991 p. illus.

LI, HUI-LIN, 李惠林, 1911-    The Araliaceae of China, with fourteen text-figures. Jamaica Plain, Mass., Arnold Arboretum of Harvard University, 1942. 134 p. illus., diagr. (Sargentia; a continuation of the Contributions from the Arnold arboretum of Harvard university. II).

————. A revision of the genus Pedicularis in China. Philadelphia, Academy of Natural Sciences, 1948-1949. 2 pts. in 1 v. illus. plates, fold map. (Proceedings of the Academy of Natural Sciences of Philadelphis, v. 100-101).

————. Floristic relationships between eastern Asia and eastern North America. Philadelphia, American Philosophical Society, 1952. 371-429 p. maps. (Transactions of the American Philosophical Society, new ser., v. 42, pt. 2).

————. Chinese flower arrangement. Philadelphia, Hedera House, 1956. 122 p. illus.

LIMPRICHT, WOLFGANG. Botanische Reisen in den Hochgebirgen Chinas und Ost-Tibets. Dahlem bei Berlin, Verlag des Repertoriums, 1922. viii, 515 p. plates, fold. maps. (Repertorium specierum novarum regni vegetabilis. Beihefte. bd. xii).

LING, LEE, 凌立 1910-    A contribution to the knowledge of the Ustilaginales in China. Kew, Surrey, Imperial Mycological Institute, 1945. 12 p. illus. (Mycological papers, 11).

LINGNAN UNIVERSITY, Canton. A list of plants growing in the Lingnan University campus and vicinity. Canton, 1947. 3 p. 113 numb. l.

LIOU, HO, 劉厚. Lauracées de Chine et d'Indochine; contribution à l'étude systématique et phytogéographique. Paris, Hermann, 1934. xii, 226, [2] p. illus., plates, map. diagr.

LIU, JU-CH'IANG, 劉汝強, 1895-    Systematic botany of the flowering families in North China. 130 illustrations of common native plants, 170 figures on descriptive terms. (2d ed.) Peiping, H. Vetch, 1934. xvi, 218 p. illus. 1st ed. 1931.

MCCLURE, FLOYD ALONZO, 1897-    New genera and species of Bambusaceae from eastern Asia. Canton, Lingnan University, 1940. cover-title 67 p. (Lingnan university science bulletin, 9).

MASAMUNE, GENKEI. Flora Kainantensis sive enumeratio plantarum sponte crescentium hucusque rite cognitarum. [Taihoku, Taihoku University] 1943. xv, 443 p.

METCALF, FRANKLIN POST, 1892-1955. Trees, shrubs, vines and herbaceous plants in the Lingnan campus and vicinity. Canton, Lingnan University, 1937. 58 p.

————. Flora of Fukien and floristic notes on southeastern China. [Canton] Lingnan University, 1942-    1 v. illus. (maps) tables.

NATIONAL ACADEMY OF PEIPING. Laboratory of Botany. Flore illustrée du nord de la Chine: Hopei (Chihli) et ses provinces voisines. Publiée sous la direction de m. Liou Tchen-Ngo, 劉慎鍔, directeur du Laboratoire de botanique de l'Académie nationale de Peiping. Peiping, Académie nationale de Peiping, 1931-    2 v. plates.

P'EI, CHIEN, 裴鑑. The Verbenaceae of China. Shanghai, Science Society of China, 1932. 193 p. plates. (Memoirs of the Science society of China. 1:3).

PORTERFIELD, WILLARD MERRITT, 1893-    Bamboo and its use in China. Peking, Chinese Government Bureau of Economic Information, 1926. 77 p. incl. tables, illus. (Industrial and commercail information bureau. booklet ser. 2).

————. Wayside plants and weeds of Shanghai. Shanghai, Kelly and Walsh, 1933. v-xxx, 232 p. illus.

READ, BERNARD EMMS, 1887-1949. Flora Sinensis, Series A., v. 1. Peking, Department of Pharmacology, Union Medical College, 1927. 1 v.

[SCOTTISH ROCK GARDEN CLUB] George Forrest, v.M.H., explorer and botanist, who by his discoveries and plants successfully introduced has greatly enriched our gardens. 1873-1932. [Edinburgh, Printed by Stoddart and Malcolm, 1935] 89, [1] p. incl. plates, ports. front.

TENG, S. C., 鄧叔羣. A contribution to our knowledgeof the higher fungi of China. Chungking, National Research Institute of Zoology and Botany, 1939. ix 614 p.

————. Supplement to higher fungi of China. 1940. [25] p.

THOMAS, CECIL CALVERT, 1886-    The Chinese jujube. [Washington, Govt. Print. Off., 1936] 15 p. illus. (U.S. Dept. of agriculture. Department Bull. 1215).

WALKER, EGBERT HAMILTON. 1899-    Fifty-one common ornamental trees of the Lingnan university campus; a guide to the more important local trees, illustrated with fifty-five plates. Canton, Lingnan University, 1930. 166 p. illus. plates. (On cover: Science bulletin, no. 1) "Reprinted from Lingnan science journal, 6:1-2. January 24, 1930."

————. The plants of China and their usefulness to man. (In Smithsonian institution. Annual report, 1943. Washington, 1944. p. 325-361. plates. fold. map).

WICKES, DEAN ROCKWELL, 1883-    Flowers of Peitaiho. Peking, Peking, Leader Press, 1926. cover-title, 83, [4] p. illus. [Peking society of natural history. Handbook, 1].

YAMAMOTO, YOSHIMATSU. Contributiones ad floram Kainanensem. Hainan, Special affairs department of Headquarters, Japanese navy, 1942. 37 p. illus. plates, fold. col. map. (Special reports on the South Chinese and their environment, 1.).

YEH, HUI-LAN, 葉惠蘭, 1913-    Studies of the proteins of the tung nut (A. fordii). Ann Arbor, Mich., 1945. Film copy of type-written manuscript. Made in 1945 by University microfilms (Publication no. 704) Positive.    196 l. tables, diagrs.

YEN, WÊN-YÜ, 閻玫玉. Recherches systématiques, biologiques et cytologiques sur les ustilaginées de Chine. Paris, 1937. p. [157]-310, illus. plates. Thèse-Univ. de Paris. Reprinted from the Contributions of the Institute of botany of the National academy of Peiping.

## Zoology
### Mammals

ALLEN, GLOVER MORRILL, 1879-1942. The mammals of China and Mongolia. New York, American Museum of Natural History, 1938- 1 v. illus. (incl. maps) plates. (Central Asiatic expeditions. Natural history of Central Asia. Vol. xi).

ENGELMANN, CARL HEINRICH. Grossäuger Szetschwans, Sikongs und Osttibets, nach Ernst Schäfers Tagebüchern und Trophäen bearbeitet von Carlheinrich Engelmann mit Unterstützung der Deutschen Forschungsgemein- schaft. Berlin-Hermsdorf, In Kommission bei W. Stichel, 1938. 76 p. plates (Zeitschrift für Säugetierkunde. Sonderheft. Bd. 13).

HOWELL ALFRED BRAZIER, 1886- Mammals from China in the collections of the United States National museum. (In U.S. National museum. Proceedings. Washington, 1929. v. 75, art. 1. 82 p. 10 plates (incl. map).

JAKOVLEFF, B. Collection des mammifères du Musée Hoang ho Pai ho à Tientsin. Fam. Felidae, par B. Jakovleff. Traduit du manuscript russe par E. de Laberbis. Tientsin Mission de Sien Hsien. 1932. 19 p. (Publications du Musée Hoang ho Pai ho. 9).

MELL, RUDOLF, 1878- Beiträge zur Fauna Sinica. Berlin und Leipzig, W. de Gruyter, 1922. 4 v. illus. plates, (part col.).

ORR, ROBERT THOMAS, 1908- Mammals from Sikang, China. [San Fransisco] 1938. [307]-310 p. (Proceedings of the California academy of sciences. 4th ser., 23:22, September 1, 1938).

OSGOOD, WILFRED HUDSON, 1875- Mammals of the Kelley-Roosevelts and Delacour Asiatic expeditions. Chicago, 1932. p. 193-339. front. (map) 1 illus. plates. (Feild museum of natural history. Publication 312. Zoological series. 18:10).

POPE, CLIFFORD HILLHOUSE, 1899- China's animal frontier. New York, Viking Press, 1940. 192 p. illus.

[REEVES, CORA DAISY] 1873- Manual of the vertebrate animals of northeastern and central China, exclusive of birds. Shanghai, Chung Hwa Book Co., 1933. xxxi, [1], 806 p. illus.

SOWERBY, ARTHUR DE CARLE, 1885-1954. Mammals recorded from or known to occur in the Shanghai area. Chang-hai, Univ. L'Aurore, 1943. 15 p. illus. (Musée Heude. Notes de mammalogie, no. 2).

———. A new species of shrew from the Shanghai area. [Changhai, Univ. L' Aurore] 1945. [2] p. (Musée Heude. Notes de mammalogie, no. 3).

### Dogs and Horses

BECK, SALIM. The Mongolian horse, translated from the Russian. Tientsin, Société française de librairie et d'édition [c1926] xii, 163 p. incl. front., illus.

COLLIER, V W F. Dogs of China and Japan in nature and art. New York, Stokes, London, W. Heinemann, 1921. xix, 206 p. illus. (part col.).

DENLINGER, MILO GRANGE, 1890- The complete Pekingese. Silver Spring, Md. 1949. 112 p. illus., ports.

DIXEY, ANNIE COATH. The lion dog of Peking: being the astonishing history of the Pekingese dog. London, P. Davies [1931] 3-245, [1] p. front., plates.

HARMAN, IAN DENYS ANTHONY, 1911- Pekingese. London, Williams and Norgate [1949] 96 p. plates.

[JOHNS, ROWLAND] 1882- ed. Our friend the Pekingese. London, Methuen [1932]; New York, E.P. Dutton, 1933. vii, 86 p. front. (Our friend the dog series).

KOEHN, ALFRED. Royal favorites. Peiping, Lotus Court, 1948. 1 p. col. plates.

KRIEGER, GRACE A. Pet Pekingese by Grace A. Krieger. The health of your
pet, by P. R. Des Rosiers. Fond du Lac, Wis., All-Pets Books, 1954. 63 p.
illus.

LANSDOWNE, MRS. CHARMIAN. The imperial dog of China, the Pekingese.
Los Angeles, Wolfer Printing Co., c1934. 163 p. incl. front., illus., plates,
ports.

MORGAN, HARRY TITTERTON; 1872-   Chinese dogs. Written and edited by
H. T. Morgan. [Los Angeles] c1941. 16 p. illus. [His Chinese classics in
miniature].

NICHOLAS, ANNA KATHERINE. The Pekingese; a complete presentation with
illustrations of the origin, development, breeding, showing, training, kennel-
ing, care and feeding of this breed of dog. Chicago, Judy Pub. Co., 1952.
x, 11-141 p. illus. 1st ed., 1939.

THE PEKINGESE; a symposium by Lydia Hopkins and a chapter on the Pekingese
standard simplified, by Vinton P. Breese, together with a roster of the Pekingese clubs of America, and the directory of reliable Pekingese breeders
in America and England. New York, Field and Fancy Pub. Corp., 1924.
113 p. illus. incl. ports. (Popular dogs of the day, 6).

## Pandas

GOULD, ESTHER. I am a Panda. The story of the baby Giant Panda. Racine,
Wis., Whitman Pub. Co., 1938. 32 p.

GREGORY WILLIAM KING, 1876-   On the phylogenetic relationships of the
giant panda (Ailuropoda) to other arctoid Carnivora. New York, 1936. 29 p.
illus. (American Museum novitates, 878).

HARKNESS, RUTH. The lady and the panda, an adventure. New York, Carrick
and Evans, [c1938] 288 p. front., plates, ports.

———. The baby giant panda. New York, Carrick and Evans, [c1938] 126, [1]p.
incl. plates, ports.

RAVEN, HENRY CUSHIER, 1889-1944. Notes on the anatomy of the viscera of
the giant panda (Ailuropoda melanoleuca). New York, 1936. 23 p. illus.
(American Museum notvitates, 877).

ROOSEVELT, THEODORE, 1887-   Trailing the giant panda, by Theodore Roosevelt and Kermit Roosevelt; with a frontispiece from a painting by Carl Run-
gius and illustrations from photographs by Suydam Cutting and K. R. New
York, London, C. Scribner, 1929. x, 278 p. col. front., plates, ports.,
fold. map.

WARING, RUTH ANN. Su-lin, the real story of a baby giant panda, by Ruth Ann
Waring and Helen Wills. Chicago, Rand, McNally c1937. [34] p. illus.

## Birds

BANGS, OUTRAM, 1862-1932. Birds of western China obtained by the Kelley-
Roosevelts expedition. Chicago, 1932. p. 343-379. (Field museum of natural
history. Publication 314. Zoological series. 18:11).

CALDWELL, HARRY R. South China birds, by Harry R. Caldwell and John C.
Caldwell; a complete, popular and scientific account of nearly five hundred
and fifty forms of birds found in Fukien, Kwangtung, Kiangsi, Kiangsu and
Chekiang provinces. Illustrated by more than seventy-five original half tones
of birds in life, nests, eggs and haunts, from photographs by the authors, and
Morris Caldwell. Together with six colored plates by Prof. Andrew Allison.
Stories and legends by Muriel E. Caldwell. Shanghai, H. M. Vanderburgh
[1931] 447 p. col. front., 1 illus., plates (part col.).

GAYOT, CHARLES, 1882-1921. Les oiseaux de Chang-Hai. Observations ornitho-
logiques (1913-1920) Pub. par les P. P. Henry Dugout et Auguste Savio. Zi-
ka-wei, Chang-Hai, Impr. de l'Orphelinat de T'ou-sè-wè, 1922. iii, 59 p.
port.

GEE, NATHANIEL GIST, 1876-1937. A tentative list of Chinese birds; compiled by N. Gist Gee Lacy I. Moffett and G. D. Wilder. Peking. 1926-27. 370, 8 p. Reprinted from Peking Natural History Bull. 1:1-3.

GRESSITT, MARGARET K. A provisional bird calendar for Canton, China, by Margaret K. Gressitt and J. Linsley Gressitt. [Canton] 1942. Cover-title. 1C p. (Lingnan University, Canton, China. Natural History Survey and Museum. Special publication no. 10).

HEMMINGSEN, AXEL MARIUS, 1900-  Observations on birds in north eastern China, especially the migration at Pei-tai-ho Beach. Copenhagen [I kommission hos Munksgaard] 1951. 227 p. illus., map, diagrs. (Spolia zoologica Musei Hauniensis, 11.).

HOOSE, HARNED PETTUS. Peking pigeons and pigeon-flutes, a lecture delivered at the College of Chinese Studies, Peking. Peking, College of Chinese Studies, California College in China, 1938. 28 p. plates.

KOLTHOFF, KJELL. Studies on birds in the Chinese provinces of Kiangsu and Anhwei 1921-1922. Göteborg, Elanders boktr., 1932. 190 p. illus., map. (Göteborgs kungl. vetenskaps- och vitterhets-samhälles handlingar, 5. följden, ser. B, bd. 3, n:o 1) Meddelanden från Göteborgs musei Zoologiska avdelning, 59.

LA TOUCHE, JOHN DAVID DIGUES DE. A handbook of the birds of eastern China (Chihli, Shantung, Kiangsu, Anhwei, Kiangsi, Chekiang, Fohkien, and Kwangtung provinces). London, Taylor and Francis, 1925-1934. 2 v. illus. plates, fold. maps.

LAUFER, BERTHOLD, 1874-1934. The domestication of the cormorant in China and Japan. 4 plates in photogravure. Chicago, 1931. p. 201-262. plates. (Field museum of natural history. Publication 300. Anthropological series. 18:3).

RILEY, JOSEPH HARVEY, 1873-1941. A collection of birds from the provinces of Yunnan and Szechwan, China, made for the National Geographic Society by Dr. Joseph F. Rock. (In U.S. National museum. Proceedings. Washington, 1927. v. 70, art. 5. 70 p).

————. A second collection of birds from the provinces of Yunnan and Szechwan, China, made for the National Geographic Society by Dr. Joseph F. Rock. (In U.S. National museum. Proceedings. Washington, 1932. v. 80, art. 7. 91 p.).

————. Birds collected in Inner Mongolia, Kansu, and Chihli by the National Geographic Society's Central-China expedition under the direction of F.R. Wulsin. (In U.S. National museum. Proceedings. Washington, 1931. v. 77, art. 15. 39 p.).

SHAW, TSEN-HWANG, 壽振黃. The birds of Hopei province, with 506 illustrations in the text, 25 plates, and a map. Peiping, Fan Memorial Institute of Biology, 1936. 2 v. illus., plates, fold. map, diagr. (Zoologia sinica. Series B. The vertebrates of China. 15: 1).

SOWERBY ARTHUR DE CARLE, 1885-1954. Birds recorded from or known to occur in the Shanghai area. Chang-hai, Univ. L'Aurore, 1943. 212 p. illus. (Musée Heude. Notes d'ornithologie, 1).

WILDER, GEORGE DURAND, 1869-1946. Birds of northeastern China: a practical guide on studies made chiefly in Hopei province by George D. Wilder and Hugh W. Hubbard. Peking, Peking Natural History Society, 1938. v, 700 p. illus. maps, (Peking natural history bulletin. Handbook, 6).

WILKINSON, EDWARD SHELDON, 1883-  Shanghai birds; a study of bird life in Shanghai and the surrounding districts. Shanghai, North-China Daily News and Herald, 1929. xxi, 243 p. col. plates (incl. front.) plan.

————. The Shanghai bird year; a calendar of bird life in the country around Shanghai. Shanghai, North-China Daily News and Herald, 1935. 219 p. front., illus., plates.

## Reptiles and Amphibians

CHANG, MANGVEN L. Y., 張孟聞. Contribution à l'étude morphologique, biologique et systématique des amphibiens de la Chine. Paris, Picart, 1936. 145 p. incl. illus., tables. plates, Thèse-Univ. de Paris.

LIU, CH'ENG-CHAO, 劉承釗, 1902-  Secondary sex characters of Chinese Salientia. Ithaca, N.Y., 1934. 6 p. Abstract of thesis- Cornell university.

———. Secondary sex characters of Chinese frogs and toads. Chicago, 1936. p. 115-156. plates. (Zoological series. Field museum of natural history, 22:2 Publication 368).

———. Amphibians of western China. [Chicago] Chicago Natural History Museum, 1950. 400 p. illus. (part col.) maps. (Fieldiana: zoology memoirs, v, 2).

MASLIN, T PAUL. Snakes of the Kiukiang-Lushan area, Kiangsi, China. San Francisco, Tha Academy, 1950. 419-466 p. illus. (Proceedings of the California Academy of Sciences, 4th ser. 26:12).

MELL, RUDOLF, 1878-  Grundzüge einer Ökologie der chinesischen Reptilien und einer herpetologischen Tiergeographie Chinas. Berlin, W. de Gruyter, 1929. ix, 282 p. illus., col. plates, maps (part col.) (His Beiträge zur Fauna Sinica, 4).

POPE, CLIFFORD HILLHOUSE, 1899-  The reptiles of China: turtles, crocodilians, snakes, lizards, with 78 illustrations in the text, including a map, and 27 plates at end. New York, American Museum of Natural History, 1935. iii, 604 p. incl. illus., plates, fold. map, tables (1 fold.) (Central Asiatic expeditions. Natural history of Central Asia. vol.10).

SCHMIDT, KARL PATTERSON, 1890-  A new toad from western China, by Karl P. Schmidt and Ch'eng-chao Liu. [Chicago, 1940] 151-154 p. illus. (Field museum of natural history. Publication no. 471. Zoological series of Field museum of natural history, 24:13).

SOWERBY, ARTHUR DE CARLE, 1885-1954. Amphibians and reptiles recorded from or known to occur in the Shanghai area. Changahi, Université l'Aurore, 1943. Cover-title, 16 p. plates. (Musée Heude. Notes d'herpétologie, 1.).

STEJNEGER, LEONHARD HESS, 1851-1943. Chinese amphibians and reptiles in the United States National museum. (In U.S. National museum. Proceedings. Washington, 1926. v. 66, art. 25, 115 p. illus., diagrs.).

———. The green pit viper, Trimeresurus gramineus, in China. (In U.S. National museum. Proceedings. Washington, 1928. v. 72, art. 19. 10 p. illus.).

———. The Chinese lizards of the genus Gekko. (In U.S. National museum. Proceedings. Washington, 1934. v. 82, art. 3. 8 p.

## Fishes

CHINA. CENTRAL FISHERIES RESEARCH INSTITUTE. A general account of the fisheries industries of China-its present condition, and plans and requirements for development. Presented to the Chinese American Agricultural Collaboration Commission. Shanghai, the Institute, 1947. 22 l.

CHU, YÜAN-TING T. 朱元鼎, 1896-  Index piscium sinensium. [Shanghai, Dept. of Biology, St. John's University] 1931. iv, 290 p. (Biological bulletin of St. John's university, 1).

———. Fishes of the West Lake. [Hangchow, West Lake Museum] 1932. vi, 58 p. plates.

———. Comparative studies on the scales and on the pharyngeals and their teeth in Chinese cyprinids, with particular reference to taxonomy and evolution. [Shanghai, Department of Biology, St. John's University] 1935. x, 225, [2] p. plates (Biological bulletin of St.John's university, 2).

DREWS, ROBIN ARTHUR, 1913-  The cultivation of food fish in China and Japan; a study disclosing contrasting national patterns for rearing fish consistent with the differing cultural histories of China and Japan. Ann Arbor, University Microfilms [1952] (University Microfilms, Ann Arbor, Mich., Publication no. 3582) x, 263 l. illus. maps, tables.

EVERMANN, BARTON WARREN, 1853-1932. Fishes from eastern China, with descriptions of new species, by Barton Warren Evermann and Tsen-Hwang Shaw, 壽振黃. San Fransisco, The Academy, 1927. cover-title, p. [97]-122. (Proceedings of the California academy of sciences. 4th ser. 16:4 Jan. 31, 1927).

FOWLER, HENRY WEED, 1878- A small collection of fishes from Soochow, with descriptions of two new species. By Henry W. Fowler and Barton A. Bean. (In U.S. National museum. Proceedings. Washington, 1921. v. 58, p. 307-321. illus.).

————. A synopsis of the fishes of China. Hong Kong, 1931-34. 1 v. (various pagings) illus. Reprinted from Hong Kong Naturalist, vols 2-5.

FRY, FREDERICK ERNEST JOSEPH, 1908- Lethal temperature relations for a sample of young speckled trout, Salvelinus fontinalis, by F.E.J. Fry, J.S. Hart and K.F. Walker. On the artificial propagation of Tsing-fish. Matsya sinensis (Bleeker) from Yang-tsung Lake, Yunnan Province, China, by Tchang-Si, 張璽, and Yungpin Liu, 劉永斌. [Toronto] Univ. of Toronto Press, 1946. 47 p. diagrs. (University of Toronto studies. Biological series, 54).

HERVEY, GEORGE F. F.Z.S. The goldfish of China in the XVIII century. With a foreword by A.C. Moule. London, China Society, 1950. 66 p. illus. (China Society Sinological series, 3).

HOWELL, ALFRED BRAZIER, 1886- Contribution to the anatomy of the Chinese finless porpoise, Neomeris phocaenoides. (In U.S. National museum. Proceedings. Washington, 1927. v. 70, art. 13. 43 p. illus., plates.).

HSIAO, SIDNEY C., 蕭之的. Copepods from Lake Erh Hai, China. (In U.S. National Museum. Proceedings. Washington. v. 100 (1954) p. 161-200. illus.).

HUBBS, CARL LEAVITT, 1894- Asiatic fishes (Diploprion and Laeops) having a greatly elongated dorsal ray in very large postlarvae, by Carl L. Hubbs and Yuanting T. Chu. Ann Arbor, University of Michigan Press, 1934. 7 p. plates. (University of Michigan. Occasional papers of the Museum of zoology, 299).

KIMURA, SHIGERU. Description of the fishes collected from the Yangtze-kiang, by the late K. Kishinouye and his party in 1927-1929, Shanghai, 1934. Cover-title, [11]-247 p. plates (part fold.), fold. map, Reprinted from the Journal of the Shanghai Science Institute. Section iii, vol. 1.

KUHN, FRANZ, 1889- Der kleine Goldfischteich. Kolorierte Stiche nach chinesischen Aquarellen. Leipzig, Im Insel-Verlag, n.d. 42. [1] p. incl. col. plates.

MOULE, ARTHUR CHRISTOPHER, 1873-1957. A version of the Book of Vermilion Fish. 硃砂魚譜 Leiden, E.J. Brill, 1949. 82 p. Reprinted from T'oung Pao, 39: 1-3.

NICHOLS, JOHN TREADWELL, 1883- The fresh-water fishes of China. New York, American Museum of Natural History, 1943. xxxvi, 322 p. illus. (incl. map) 10 col. plates (Central Asiatic expeditions of the American museum of natural history. Natural history of central Asia, vol. 9).

PANNING, ALBERT, 1894- The Chinese mitten crab, (with nine plates) (In Smithsonian institution. Annual report, 1938. Washington, 1939. p. 361-375. 2 illus. (maps) plates, diagr.).

PETERS, NICOLÁUS, 1900- Die chinesische Wollhandkrabbe (Eriocheir sinensis H. Milne-Edwards) in Deutschland, von Nicolaus Peters und Albert Panning mit einem Beitrag von W. Schnakenbeck. Leipzig, Akademische Verlagsgesellschaft, 1935. viii, 180 p. illus. (incl. maps) (Zoologische anzeiger. Ergänzungsband zu bd. 104).

READ, BERNARD EMMS, 1887-1949. Common food fishes of Shanghai. Shanghai, North China Branch of the Royal Asiatic Society, 1939. 52 p. illus.

SHÊN, CHIA-JUI, 优嘉瑞. The brachyuran Crustacea of north China. Peiping, Fan Memorial Institute of Biology, 1932. x, 320 p. illus., plates, map. (Zoologica sinica, ser. A. Invertebrates of China, vol. ix, fasc. 1).

TCHANG, TCHUNG-LIN, 張春霖 [CHANG CHUN-LIN]. Cyprinidés du bassin du Yangtze. Contribution à l'étude morphologique, biologique et toxinomique. Paris, Hermann, 1931. [5]-171 p. illus., plates.

――――. The study of Chinese cyprinoid fishes. Peiping, Fan Memorial Institute of Biology, 1933- 2 v. illus., plates. (Zoologia sinica. Ser. B. Chordata of China. vol. ii, fasc. 1).

WU, HSIEN-WEN, 伍獻文. Contribution à l'étude morphologique, biologique et systématique des poissons hétérosomes (Pisces heterosomata) de la Chine. Paris, Jouve et Cie, 1932. 179 p. illus.

## Insects

CHAMBERLIN, RALPH VARY, 1879- Descriptions of new American and Chinese spiders, with notes on other Chinese species. (In U.S. National museum. Proceedings. Washington, 1924. v. 63, art. 13. 38 p. plates).

CH'EN, SICIEN H., 陳世驤. Recherches sur les Chrysomelinac de la Chine et du Tonkin. Paris, Société entomologique de France, 1934. 104 p. illus., maps. Thèse-Univ. de Paris.

CHÊNG, FUNG-YING, 鄭鳳瀛, 1915- Revision of the Chinese Mecoptera. Cambridge, The Museum, 1957. 118 p. illus., 23 plates. (Bulletin of the Museum of Comparative Zoology at Harvard College, v. 116, no. 1).

CHEKIANG. BUREAU OF ENTOMOLOGY. Miscellaneous publication. No. 1- Hangchow 1930- v. illus., plates, fold. maps. tables.

CHEO, MING-TSANG, 周明烊 , 1907- The Gyrinidae of China. [Peiping, 1934] p. [205]-237. plates. From the Peking natural history bulletin, 8:3.

FENG, HSIAO-TANG,馮斅棠 , 1899- Classification of Chinese Dytiscidae. [Peiping, 1933] p. [81]-146. plates. Thesis-Cornell university, From Peking natural history bulletin, 8:2. Dec. 1933.

GRESSITT, J  LINSLEY, 1914- The tortoise beetles of China (Chrysomelidae: Cassidinae) San Francisco, The Academy, 1952. 433-591 p. illus., maps. (Proceedings of the California Academy of Sciences, 4th ser. 27:17).

HOFFMANN WILLIAM EDWIN, 1896- An abridged catalogue of certain Scutelleroidea (Plataspidae, Scutelleridae, and Pentatomidae) of China, Chosen, Indo-China, and Taiwan. Canton, Lingnan University, 1935. iv, 294 p. illus. (maps) (Lingnan university science bulletin, 7).

――――. Notes on beetles of the genus Sagra (Coleoptera, Sagridae) [Canton, 1942] 8 p. (Lingnan University, Canton, China. Natural History Survey and Museum. Special publication, 6).

HUMMEL, DAVID, 1893- Zur Arthropodenwelt Nordwest-Chinas; Sammlungen David Hummels in den Jahren 1927-30; Insecta, Myriopoda, Arachnoidea. Sammlung von Aufsätzen, erschienen im Archiv für Zoologi, hrsg. von der Königl. Schwedischen Akademie der Wissenschaften. Stockholm Bokförlags aktiebolaget Thule 1937. 3 v. illus. plates. maps. (Reports from the scientific expedition to the north-western provinces of China under leadership of dr. Sven Hedin. The Sino-Swedish expedition Xa. Zoology. 1-3).

IMBERT, HENRI. Le grillon et la cigale en Chine. Pékin, Impr. de la "Politique de Pékin." 1923. 20 p. illus. (Collection de la "Politique de Pékin").

LAUFER, BERTHOLD, 1874-1934. Insect-musicians and cricket champions of China. Chicago, Field Museum of Natural History, 1927. cover-title, 27 p. plates (incl. front.) ([Field museum of natural history] Anthropology leaflet, 22).

MELL, RUDOLF, 1878- Biologie und Systematik der südchinesischen Sphingiden, zugleich ein Versuch einer Biologie tropischer Lepidopteren überhaupt von Rudolf Mell. Berlin, R. Friedländer, 1922. xxii, 177, 331 p. and atlas of 1 p. plates. (14 col.) map, 10 diagr. (His Beiträge zur fauna sinica (II) ).

--------. Zur Systematik und Ökologie der Sphingiden und Saturniiden von Chekiang (Samml. Höne). (Mit einer tafel. ) (In Mitteilungen aus dem Zoologischen museum in Berlin. Berlin, 1934. 20. bd., 2. hft., p. [ 337]-[ 366] plates).

--------. Inventur und ökologisches Material zu einer Biologie der südchinesischen Pieriden. Stuttgart, E. Schweizerbart, 1943. 132 p. plates (part col. )tables. (His Beiträge zur Fauna Sinica, 21) Zoologica. Original-Abhandlungen aus dem Gesamtgebiete der Zoologie, 36. Bd., 6. Lfg., Heft 100.

OUCHI, YOSHIO. Bibliographical introduction to the study of Chinese insects. Shanghai [ Kelly and Walsh, 1934-38. 4 pts. in 1 v. (The journal of the Shanghai science institute. Section III, vol. 2 (pp. 1-533) ); vol 3 (p. 17-88, 125-220, 233- 327).

SCHENKEL, E. Chinesische Arachnoidea aus dem Museum Hoangho-Peiho in Tientsin. Rio de Janeiro, 1953. 108 p. illus. (Rio de Janeiro. Museu Nacional. Boletim, n. s. Zoologia, 119).

TOUMANOFF, CONSTANTIN, 1903-  L'anophélisme en Extrême-Orient; contribution faunistique et biologique. Préface de E. Roubaud. Paris, Masson, 1936. viii. 434 p. illus., plans, tables (1 fold. ) diagrs. (Collection de la Société de pathologie exotique. Monographie 4).

WU, CHENFU F. , 胡經甫 [ HU CHING-FU], 1896-  Catalogus insectorum sinensium (Catalogue of Chinese insects) Peiping, Fan Memorial Institute of Biology, 1935-          3 v.

## Flies

ALDRICH, JOHN MERTON, 1866-1934. Five new parasitic flies reared from beetles in China and India. (In U. S. National museum. Proceedings. Washington, 1929. v. 74, art. 8. 7 p. ).

--------. New two-winged flies of the family Calliphoridae from China.  (In U. S. National museum. Proceedings. Washington, 1931. v. 78, art. 1. 5 p. illus. ).

KLOTS, ELSIE BROUGHTON. Chinese dragon-flies (Odonata) in the American Museum of Natural History.  New York, The Museum, 1947. 14 p. illus. (Amer. Museum Novitates, 1341, Apr. 7, 1947).

NEEDHAM, JAMES GEORGE, 1868-1957. A manual of the dragonflies of China; a monographic study of the Chinese Odonata. Peiping, Fan Memorial Institute of Biology, 1930. 344, 11 p. illus., plates (Zoologia sinica. Series A. Invertebrates of China. v. 11, fasc. 1).

WU, CHENFU F. , 胡經甫 [ HU CHING-FU], 1896-  Plecopterorum sinensium; a monograph of the stoneflies of China. (order Plecoptera). Peking, 1938. 225 p. illus. port.

## Mollusks and Worms

BARTSCH, PAUL, 1871-  Schistosomophora in China, with descriptions of two new species and a note on their Philippine relative. Washington, 1946. 7 p. illus. (Smithsonian miscellaneous collections. 104:20).

GATES, GORDON ENOCH, 1897-  New earthworms from China, with notes on the synonymy of some Chinese species of Drawida and Pheretima. City of Washington, Smithsonian Institution, 1935. 19 p. illus. (Smithsonian miscellaneous collections. 93:3).

--------. On some species of Chinese earthworms, with special reference to specimens collected in Szechwan by Dr. D. C. Graham. (In U. S. National museum. Proceedings. Washington, 1940. v. 85, p. 405-507, incl. tables.).

GRABAU, AMADEUS WILLIAM, 1870-1946. Shells of Peitaiho, by Amadeus W. Grabau and Sohtsu G. King, 金叔初 . 2d ed. rev. and enl. Peking, Peking Laboratory of Natural History, 1928. vi, 279 p. illus. (Peking Society of Natural History. Hand-book, 2).

--------. Studies of Gastropoda. Peiping, The National University of Peking, 1935.

viii, 159 p. illus. plates.

KIRK, EDWIN, 1884-     Tanaodon, a new molluscan genus from the middle Devonian of China. (In U.S. National museum. Proceedings. Washington, 1927. v. 70. art. 12, 4 p. plates).

SOWERBY, ARTHUR DE CARLE, 1885-1954. Three new land snails from Shansi, North China. Changhai, Université l'Aurore, 1945. [6] p. illus. (Musée Heude. Notes de malacologie, 6).

YEN, TENG-CHIEN. 閻敦健. Notes on the gastropod fauna of Szechwan province. (In Mitteilungen aus dem Zoologischen museum in Berlin. Berlin, 1938. 23. bd., 2. hft., p. [438]-[458] plates I).

———. Die chinesischen Land-und Süsswasser-Gastropoden des Natur-museums Senckenberg. Frankfurt a M., V. Klostermann, 1939. 234 p. plates, (Senckenbergische naturforschende gesellschaft. Abhandlungen 444).

———. Notes on some unfigured type-specimens of Chinese mollusks from the North Pacific expedition. [San Franscisco] 1944. [561]-586 p. plates. (Proceedings of the California academy of sciences, 4th ser., 23:38. August 22, 1944).

———. Notes on land and fresh-water mollusks of Chekiang Province, China. [San Francisco] 1948. 69-98 p. illus. (Proceedings of the California Academy of Sciences, 4th ser. 26:4).

# XX. AGRICULTURE AND FORESTRY

## General Works

ATTERBURY, MARGUERITE, 1896- A study of some phases of Chinese-American co-operation in promoting China's agricultural extension. Ann Arbor, University Microfilms [1954] ([University Microfilms, Ann Arbor, Mich.] Publication no. 8600). ix, 401 l. illus. Thesis-Columbia University.

CHANG, C.C., 張心一 , 1896- A proposed plan for taking China's first agricultural census. Shanghai, 1930. 9 p.

CHANG, HSIEN-CH'IU, 張憲秋 . Ecological crop geography atlas of China. Compiled under the auspices of National Agricultural Research Bureau, M.O.A.F. Nanking [by] Hsien-tsiu Chang, Shouchow Wu, 吳學周 [and] Cheng Yang, 楊 真 [Nanking] Ministry of Agriculture and Forestry, 1948. 2 v. (18, 18 maps).

CHEN, YAO-TUNG, 陳耀東 ? Le régime agraire en Chine. Lyon, Bosc et Riou, 1933. 222 p. Thèse- Univ. de Lyon.

CHINA. MINISTRY OF AGRICULTURE AND FORESTRY. Principles for enforcing the outlines of agricultural policy for China, by the Agricultural section of the Central Planning Board, represented by members of the Ministry of Agriculture and Forestry. Translated into English by Feng Shou-yu and by Conference of agricultural attaché and officials of the Ministry of Agriculture and Forestry. Chungking, 1945. 22 l. [mimeographed].

CHINA-UNITED STATES AGRICULTURAL MISSION. Report. Washington, 1947. xiv, 265 p. maps. (U.S. Office of Foreign Agricultural Relations. Report, 2).

COMMITTEE ON AGRICULTURAL ENGINEERING IN CHINA. A report on agriculture and agricultural engineering in China. J. Brownlee Davidson, Chairman. Chicago, [International Harvestor Co.] 1949. 259 p.

FARMERS' BANK OF CHINA. An agricultural survey of Szechwan province, China; a summary and interpretation by John Lossing Buck of a full report in Chinese by the Szechwan rural economics survey commettee of the Farmer's Bank of China in cooperation with the Department of agricultural economics, University of Nanking and directed by Chi-ming Chiao, 喬啓明 . Chungking, Farmer's Bank of China; New York, Distributed by International Secretariat, Institute of Pacific Relations, 1943. v, 63 numb. l. illus. (maps) diagrs.

FENG, RUI, 馮銳 , 1899-1936. A program of Chinese agriculture. Ithaca, 1924. ix, 373 p. illus. Thesis-Cornell University.

FUN, TSCHAUSCH, 豐傳詩 . Die Agarkrise in China. Wien, Eigen-Verlag, 1938. 32 p. Diss.-Univ. Wien.

KING, FRANKLIN HIRAM, 1848-1911. Farmers of forty centuries; or, Permanent agriculture in China, Korea and Japan. Edited by J. P. Bruce. London, J. Cape [1927] 379 p. illus. 1st ed. 1911.

LOVE, HARRY HOUSER, 1880- Application of statistical methods to agricultural research. Shanghai, Commercial Press, 1936. 501 p.

MENG, CHING-PENG, 孟慶彭 , 1919- Agricultural problems in China: a study of conditioning factors. Urbana, Ill., 1951. 179 l. Thesis-University of Illinois.

NANKING. UNIVERSITY. College of Agriculture and Forestry. Dept. of Agricultural Economics. Twenty-two years of agricultural economics; a review of the work of the Department of agricultural economics, College of Agriculture and Forestry, Universtiy of Nanking (1920-42) [Nanking] 1942. cover-title, 23 p.

SCOTT, JAMES CAMERON, 1905- Health and agriculture in China; a fundamental approach to some of the problems of world hunger. London, Faber and Faber [1952] 279 p. illus., map.

AGRICULTURE AND FORESTRY

SHAO, SUI-CHU, 邵雪初 . La question agraire en Chine. Nancy, Impr. Grandville, 1934. 172 p. Thèse-Univ. de Nancy.

SHÊN, TSUNG-HAN, 沈宗瀚 , 1895-  Agricultural resources of China. Ithaca,
Cornell University Press, 1951. xviii, 407 p. maps, tables.

TANG, CHI-YU,唐啓宇 1897-  An economic study of Chinese agriculture. [Itha-
ca, 1924?] viii, 514 p. illus. (maps) diagrs. Thesis-Cornell university.

TAWNEY, RICHARD HENRY, 1880-  A memorandum on agriculture and industry in China. Honolulu, Institute of Pacific Relations, 1929. 128 p. incl. tables.

————. Land and labour in China. London, G. Allen and Unwin; New York, Harcourt, 1932. [7]-207, [1] p.

————. The condition of China. Oxford, The Claredon Press, 1933. 24 p. (Earl
Grey memorial lectures).

TSOU, PIN-WEN, 鄒秉文 , 1892-  Proposed program of agricultural development in China. [Washington, D.C.] 1945. 26 numb. l.

UNITED NATIONS INTERIM COMMISSION OF FOOD AND AGRICULTURE.
Secretariat. Division of Area Studies. Area reference series: China. First
preliminary draft. Washington, 1944. 3 pts. in l v. [mimeographed].

UNITED NATIONS RELIEF AND REHABILITATION ADMINISTRATION. Report
of the regional agricultural rehabilitation officers' conference, Shanghai,
China, November 25 to 30, 1946. [Shanghai? 1946?] 119 l. illus.

VISSIÈRE, ARNOLD JACQUES ANTOINE, 1858-1930. Les chambres d'agriculture en Chine. Paris, Revue du Pacifique, 1923. 16 p.

WAGNER, WILHELM, 1886-  Die chinesische Landwirtschaft. Berlin, P. Parey, 1926. xv, 668 p. incl. illus., tables, diagrs. 2 fold. maps.

WANG, P'ING- HSUN, 王炳勳 . Agricultural resources of China and Japan with
a comparative survey. Tientsin, Hautes études, 1938. xii, 254 p. incl.
diagrs. illus. (charts), (Tientsin. Institut des hautes études industrieles et
commerciales. Economic studies, 12).

WILCOX, EARLEY VERNON, 1869-  Acres and people; the eternal problem of
China and India. New York, Orange Judd Pub. Co., 1947. 287 p. illus.

WITTFOGEL, KARL AUGUST, 1896-  Die ökonomische Bedeutung der agrikolen
und industriellen produktivkräfte Chinas. Stuttgart, W. Kohlhammer, 1930.
188 p. illus. Diss.-Univ. Frankfurt a. M.

————. Wirtschaft und Gesellschaft Chinas; Versuch der wissenschaftlichen Analyse einer grossen asiatischen Agrargesellschaft, 1. teil. Produktivkräfte,
Produktions- und Zirkulationsprozess. Leipzig, C.L. Hirschfeld, 1931.
xxiv, 767, [1] p. illus., fold. map, diagr. (Schriften des Instituts für sozial-
forschung an der Universität Frankfurt a. M.  3 bd.).

WU, YUAN-LI, 吳元黎 , 1920-  Agriculture. London, Chinese Ministry of information, 1945. 32 p. (China. Ministry of information (London). Pamphlets,
4).

YEH, HSIA-TI, 葉霞翟 , 1916-  A study of the farm security administration as
applicable to China's problems. Madison, 1944. ii, 171 l. Thesis-Univ. of
Wisconsin.

YUEN, MING-PAO, 袁民寶 , [YÜAN MIN-PAO]. Des systèmes agraires en
Chine. [Changhai, Impr. Jeanne d'Arc] 1922. cover-title, 63, [1], 2, 2, 80
p. Thèse-Univ. de Changhai (l'Aurore).


Agricultural Production

CHAO, TS'AI-PIAO, 趙才標 , 1903-  A statistical study of crop yields in 12 provinces in China. Ithaca, 1933. xvii, 215 p. incl. map, tables, diagrs. The-
ses-Cornell University.

CHINA. NATIONAL AGRICULTURAL RESEARCH BUREAU. China agricultural
estimates, 1931-1946. Nanking, Department of Agricultural Economics, National Agricultural Research Bureau, 1947. 93 l. [mimeographed].

NUTTONSON, MICHAEL Y      1904-  Ecological crop geography of China and its agro-climatic analogues in North America. Washington, American Institute of Crop Ecology, 1947. 28 p. map, tables. (Published also as Study no. 7 of the International agro-climatological series of the American Institute of Crop Ecology).

SCHMITZ-MANCY, GUIDO. Die landwirtschaftliche Produktion Chinas und ihre Bedeutung für den chinesischen Aussenhandel. Berlin, 1943. 215 p. map, Diss.-Univ. Berlin.

TWANMO, CHONG, 端木中 , [TUAN-MU CHUNG] Production of food crops in mainland China: prewar and postwar. Santa Monica, Calif., Rand Corp. [1956] 79 p. diagrs. tables. (Rand Corp. Research memorandum, RM-1659).

## Rice and Wheat

LE CLERC, JOSEPH ARTHUR, 1873-  Rice trade in the Far East. Washington, Govt. Print. Off., 1927. vi, 73 p. incl. tables, diagr. ([U.S.] Bureau of foreign and domestic commerce (Dept. of commerce) Trade promotion series, 46)

PAO, HUNG-HSIANG, 鮑鴻翔 . Wheat problems in China. Tientsin, Hautes études, 1937. vii, 98 p. (Tientsin. Institut des hautes études industrieles et commerciales. Economic studies, 8).

U.S. Dept. of State. Office of Intelligence Research. The world rice situation, 1945-46, with particular reference to the Far East. Washington, 1946. 23, [38] l. tables (Its [Report] no. 3499).

## Fruit and Vegetables

FABEL, L.B.A. The economic importance of fruit culture in China. Peiping, Catholic University and Chinese Catholic Agricultural Research Association, 1948. 113 p. (Agr. Extension Service Bull., 2).

HODGE, WALTER H          1912-  The Chinese waterchestnut [by W.H. Hodge and David A. Bisset. Washington, Govt. Print. Off.] 1955. 16 p. illus. (U.S. Dept. of Agriculture. Circular, 956).

KAO, HSUEH-CHUNG, 高學中 , 1907-  The availability of calcium from Chinese cabbage (Brassica pekinensis, Rupr.) New York, 1937 [i. e. 1938] 221-228 p. Reprinted from the Journal of biological chemistry, 123:1 (1938).

KRAUS, JAMES ELLSWORTH, 1909-  Chinese cabbage varieties, their classification, description, and culture in the central Great plains. [Washington, Govt. Print. Off., 1940] 20 p. illus. (U.S. Dept. of agriculture. Circular, 571).

LECTURES ON COMMODITIES VEGETABLE PRODUCTS. Tientsin, Hautes études, 1936. 172 p. (Tientsin. Institut des hautes études industrieles et commerciales. Economic studies, 3).

LIU, SU-YING, 劉素英 , 1916-  Studies of Litchi chinensis Sonn. Ann Arbor, University Microfilms [1954] ([University Microfilms, Ann Arbor, Mich.] Publication no. 8332). ix, 261 l. illus. maps, tables. Thesis-Univ. of Michigan.

READ, BERNARD EMMS, 1877-1949. Shanghai vegetables, by Bernard E. Read and W. Wagner. Shanghai, China Journal, 1940. 31 p. illus.

## Tea

CHINA. MINISTRY OF INDUSTRY. Shanghai tea exports, 1933. Shanghai, Shanghai Bureau of Inspection and Testing of Commercial Commodities, Ministry of Industry, 1933. 1 v. tables.

CHU, T          H. 朱祖晦 . Tea trade in central China. Shanghai, Published for China Institute of Pacific Relations by Kelly and Walsh, 1936. 259 p. incl. fold. tables.

HARRIMAN, WILLIAM KARL. The story of tea; illustrated by Ralph D. Dunkelberger. Philadelphia, The Penn Pub. Co. [c1938] 208 p. front., illus.

HUNG FU, 供絨 , 1906- La géographie du thé. 2e éd. Canton, 1934. cover-title, 181 p. incl. illus. (maps) tables, diagrs. plates. (Bibliothèque de l'Institut de géogrpahie de l' Université de Lyon et des "Études rhodaniennes").

TSAO, JUO-CHING, 曹若青 , 1903- Der chinesische Tee auf dem europäischen und Amerikanischen Markte. Engelsdorf-Leipzig, C. U. M. Vogel, 1929. 92 p. map, chart.

TORGASHEV, BORIS PAVLOVICH. China as a tea producer; areas of cultivation, methods of planting and manufacture, export trade, production and consumption, both in China and abroad, with fifty-nine statistical tables. Shanghai, Commercial Press, 1926. ix, 252 p. plates.

## Soybean Products

CHANG, YET-OY, 張月愛 , 1913- Soybean products as supplements to rice in Chinese diets, with special reference to their protein and calcium content. Ann Arbor, University Microfilms [ 1954] ([ University Microfilms, Ann Arbor, Mich.] Publication no. 8626) Collation of the original: 60 l. plates, tables. Thesis-Columbia University.

CHEN, PHILIP STANLEY, 陳學勤, 1903- Soybeans for health, longevity, and economy, by Philip S. Chen with the assistance of Helen D. Chen. 陳馮媛真 . South Lancaster, Mass., Chemical Elements [ 1956] 241 p. illus.

CHIU, YAN-TSZ, 趙恩賜 , [ CHAO EN-TZ'Ǔ] 1890- Studies of the physical and chemical properties of soy bean milk. [ Canton, The Shameen Printing Press, 1927] 38 p. incl. plates, diagrs. Thesis-Cornell university.

HORVATH, ARTHEMY A. The soybean as human food. Peking, Chinese Government Bureau of Economic Information, 1927. 86 p. (Booklet ser., 3).

## Tung Oil

CHANG, CHIA-CHU, 張嘉鑄 , 1902- China tung oil and its future. Hong Kong, China Vegetable Oil Corporation [ pref. 1940] 129 p. illus. (incl. map) diagrs. (1 fold. ) (Ch[ hina] v[ egetable] o[ il] c[ orporation] Leaflet, 8).

——. A general survey of China tung oil industry. Submitted to the Chinese-American Agricultural Collaboration Commission. Shanghai, 1946. 17 numb. l.

CHI, HENG, 紀蘅 . The trade in tung oil of China and its prospects. Tientsin, Hautes études, 1936. 119 p. (Tientsin, Institut des hautes études industrieles et commerciales. Economic studies, 5).

HO, K'AI, 賀闓 , 1902- Bibliography on tung tree and tung oil, 世界桐油文獻 compiled by K. Ho and H. Liu, 劉瑚 . With a foreword by Chung-Yu Wang, 王寵佑 . [ Hankow] The Government Testing Bureau of Hankow, 1937. vii, 175 p.

STEVENS, GEORGE H. Stevens' China wood oil formulary, a companion book to the four volume compilation entitled Patents, technology and bibliography of China wood oil. 2nd ed. Newark, N. J., 1926 (c1924) 1, x, 457 numb. l. 24 p. plates.

——. Information on Chinese wood oil. Newark, N. J., The author, 1925. 15 p. illus.

TAYLOR, WILLIAM MYERS, 1896- China wood oil. Washington, Govt. Print. Off., 1923. iv, 21 p. incl. tables, diagrs. fold. chart ([ U. S. ] Bureau of foreign and domestic commerce (Dept. of commerce) Miscellaneous series, 125).

THOMSON, JAMES CLAUDE, 1889- A study of Chinese wood oils; with special reference to the isolation and the characterization of isomeric eleostearic acids. New York, 1933. 35 p. diagrs. Thesis-Columbia University.

WELZ, CHRISTOPHER JOHN. Studies in the chemistry of Chinese wood oil. [ Easton, Pa., 1927] 15 p. 1 illus., diagrs. Thesis-Cornell University, 1926. "Reprinted from Industrial and engineering chemistry 19:1 January, 1927."

## Sericulture

BUCHANAN, RALPH E. The Shanghai raw silk market.  New York, Prepared for and published by the Silk Association of America [c1929] 3-76 p. illus.

HOWARD, CHARLES WALTER, 1882-1928. The sericulture industry of south China. [n. p.] 1923. 32 p. plates.

————. A survey of the silk industry of south China, by C. W. Howard and K. P. Buswell, Hong Kong, 1925. 208 p. plates, maps, (Lingnan agricultural bull., 12).

KEH, KINTSON, 葛敬孫. A preliminary plan for the improvement of sericulture in China.  Chinkiang, 192- .  24 p. (Chinkiang station of the International Committee for Improvement of Sericulture in China).

LIEU, D. K. 劉大鈞, [LIU TA-CHÜN], 1890-  The silk reeling industry in Shanghai.  Shanghai, 1938. cover-title, viii, 142 p. incl. tables (part fold.) diagrs. (The China institute of economic and statistical research. [Publications] 1:2).

————. The silk industry of China. Issued under the auspices of the China Institute of Pacific Relations and the China Institute of Economic and Statistical Research.  Shanghai, Kelly and Walsh, 1940. xviii, 266 p. incl. tables (part fold.) diagrs.

SHANGHAI INTERNATIONAL TESTING HOUSE. A survey of the silk industry of Central China, by the Shanghai international testing house of the United States Testing Co., Inc. Under the auspices of the Silk Association of America. Shanghai [Printed by the Shanghai Times] 1925. cover-title, 100 p. fold, map, plans, diagrs. (1 fold.).

SIAO, TSEN-TSAN, 蕭貞昌, 1900-  Die chinesische Seidenindustrie. Leipzig, L. A. Klepzig, 1929. 92 p., 1 l. Diss.-Leipzig.

SILK ASSOCIATION OF AMERICA. Sericultural development in China.  New York, Silk Association of America [c1928] 29 p.

TSING, TUNG-CHUN, 曾同春, [ TSENG T'UNG-CH'UN] De la production et du commerce de la soie en Chine.  Paris, P. Geuthner, 1928. 228 p. map. diagrs. (Université de Lyon. Bibliotheca Franco-Sinica Lugdunensis. Études et documents pub. par l'Institut franco-chinois de Lyon, t. 4).

## Other

FENG, CHE-FANG, 馮澤芳, 1899-  Genetical and cytological studies of species of Asiatic and American cottons.  [Chicago, 1935] 1 p. 485-504. illus. Thesis-Cornell university. From Botanical gazette, v. 96, March, 1935.

LEE, HSIEN-WEI 李顯威. The tobacco in China.  Tientsin, Hautes études, 1934. 59 p. (Tientsin. Institut des hautes études industrieles et commerciales. Economic studies, 1).

LIU, CHIN-T'AO, 劉錦濤. Egg industry in Tientsin.  Tientsin, Hautes études, 1941. 46 p. (Tientsin. Institut des hautes études industrieles et commerciales. Economic studies, 18).

READ, BERNARD EMMS, 1877-1949. Shanghai foods. 4th ed.  Shanghai, China Nutrition Aid Council, 1948. 117 p. (China Medical Association, Special report ser., 8).

U. S. Coordinating Committee on Foreign Food Facts. Food supply in the Ningpo-Wenchou area, Chekiang Province, China, prepared by the Ningpo-Wenchou Working Group of the Coordinating Committee on Foreign Food Facts.  Washington, 1945. 89 p. map.

WANG, CH'I-TUNG, 王祈棟. Eggs industry in China.  Tientsin, Hautes études, 1937. ii, 106 p. (Tientsin. Institut des hautes études industrielles et commerciales. Economic studies, 9).

YANG, CH'ÊNG-YÜ, 楊承裕. Groundnuts production and trade in China.  Tientsin, Hautes études, 1938. 187, [3] p. illus., plates, maps, (Tientsin, Institut des Hautes Études industrielles et commerciales. Economic studies,14).

## Land Tenure and Utilization: Land Ownership

ANDERSON, CHARLES ARNOLD. Chinese peasant, by Charles A. Anderson and
Mary Bowman. Lexington, University of Kentucky, 1950. 287 p.

BUCK, JOHN LOSSING, 1890- Farm ownership and tenancy in China. Shanghai,
National Christian Council [ 1927] 31 p.

CH'ÊN HAN-SENG,' 陳翰笙 , 1897- The present agrarian problem in China.
Shanghai, China Institute of Pacific Relations, 1933. 32 p. Preliminary paper
prepared for the 5th biennial conference of the Institute of Pacific Relations,
Banff, 1933.

――――. Agrarian problems in southernmost China. Shanghai, Published for Lingnan University, Canton by Kelly and Walsh, 1936. viii, 144 p.

――――. Landlord and peasant in China; a study of the agrarian crisis in south
China. With a preface by Frederick V. Field. New York, International Publishers, 1936. xvii, 144 p. incl. tables.

――――. Industrial capital and Chinese peasants; a study of the livelihood of Chinese tobacco cultivators, by Chen Han-seng, assisted by Wong Yin-seng.
Chang Hsi-chang and Huang Kuo-kao. With an introd. by Karl August Wittfogel. Shanghai, Kelly and Walsh, 1939 [ i. e. 1940]. xxiii, 97 p. map, diagr.
tables.

――――. The Chinese peasant. [ London, G. Cumberlege, Oxford University Press
[ 1945] 31 p. (Oxford pamphlets on Indian affairs, no. 33).

――――. Frontier land systems in southernmost China; a comparative study of agrarian problems and social organization among the Pai Yi people of Yunnan
and the Kamba people of Sikang. New York, International Secretariat, Institute of Pacific Relations, 1949. vi, 156 p.

LAMB, JEFFERSON P. H., 林東海 [ LIN, TUNG-HAI] 1894- The development of
the agrarian movement and agrarian legislation in China. Shanghai, Commercial Press, 1934. 228 p. 1st ed. 1931.

LEE, SHU-CHING, 李樹青 , 1908- Social implications of farm tenancy in China.
Chicago, 1950. 268 l. Thesis-Univ. of Chicago.

## Land Utilization

BUCK, JOHN LOSSING, 1890- An economic and social survey of 150 farms, Yen-
shan county, Chihli province, China. [ Nanking], 1926. Cover-title, 110 p.
(Nanking. University. College of Agriculture and Forestry. Bull. 13).

――――. Chinese farm economy; a study of 2866 farms in seventeen localities and
seven provinces in China. Chicago, Pub. for the University of Nanking and
the China Council of the Institute of Pacific Relations by the University of Chicago Press [ 1930] xii, 476 p. incl. illus. (map) tables, diagrs., forms, plates,
plans (1 fold.).

――――. Land utilization in China, a study of 16, 786 farms in 168 localities, and
32, 256 farm families in twenty-two provinces in China, 1929-1933. Shanghai,
Commercial Press, ltd. [ 1937] 3 v. illus. (maps) plates, diagrs. and atlas
of xii, 146 p. incl. maps, plates.

――――. The same; New York, Reproduced by the Council on Economic and Cultural Affairs, 1956. xxxii, 494 p. illus. maps.

――――. Some basic agricultural problems of China. Submitted by the International
Secretariat as a document for the Tenth Conference of the Institute of Pacific
Relations to be held at Stratford-on-Avon, England, Sept. 1947. New York,
International Secretariat, Institute of Pacific Relations [ 1947] 62 l. (Secreta-
riat paper no. 1).

CHAPMAN, BENJAMIN BURGOYNE. The climate regions of China; a preliminary report of the China land utilization study, prepared by the Department of

Agricultural Economics, College of Agriculture and Forestry, University of Nanking. Nanking, 1933. 62 p. incl. tables, illus. (charts), (Its. Bull. n.s., 3).

CHANG, P'EI-KANG, 張培剛, 1913- Agriculture and industrialization; the adjustments that take place as an agricultural country is industrialized. Cambridge, Harvard Univ. Press, 1949. xii, 270 p. illus. (Harvard economic studies, v. 85).

HENSON, EDWIN RAY, 1896- Report on the agricultural rehabilitation program in China. Distributed by the International Secretariat, IPR, as a supplementary document for the Tenth Conference of the Institute of Pacific Relations, Stratford-upon-Avon, Eng., Sept. 1947. New York, Institute of Pacific Relations, 1947. 19 l.

INSTITUTE OF PACIFIC RELATIONS. Agrarian China; selected source materials from Chinese authors, compiled and translated by the Research staff of the secretariat, Institute of Pacific Relations, with an introduction by R. H. Tawney. Shanghai, Kelly and Walsh, 1938; London, G. Allen and Unwin, 1939. xviii, 257 p. (Its International research series).

KEH, CHI-YANG, 葛啓揚, 1909- Land utilization in China and in the United States. [East Lansing, Mich., ] 1944. Film copy of type-written manuscript. Made in 1944 by University microfilms (Publications no. 638) Positive. Collation of the original: vii, 104 numb. l. incl. tables. fold. maps.

TASCHDJIAN, E. Agricultural economy and farm management with reference to China. Peiping, Catholic University of Peking, 1945. 66 p. (Agricultural extension service Bull., 1).

WANG, VINCENT YU-SAN, 王育三, L'économie agricole de la Chine. Louvain, Vlaamsche Boekenhalle, 1925. 188 p. illus. (maps, 1 double) [ Bibliothèque de l'École des sciences politiques et sociales de Louvain].

WILMANNS, WOLFGANG OTTO, 1893- Die Landwirtschaft Chinas. Berlin, P. Parey, 1938. 87 p. illus. (incl. map) [Gernamy] Reichs-und pr. ministerium für ernährung u. landwirtschaft. Berichte über landwirtschaft. n.f., 133. sonderheft). (At head of title: Aus dem Institut für landwirtschaftliche betriebslehre an der Universität Leipzig. Summaries in German, English, French and Spanish.

WONG, WEN-HAO, 翁文灝, 1889- The distribution of population and land utilization in China. Prepared for the 5th biennial conference of the Institute of Pacific Relations to be held at Banff, 1933. [Shanghai] China Institute of Pacific Relations, 1933. 11 p.

## Rural Economy

CHEN, YIN-KWONG, 陳延光. Die landwirtschaftlichen Genossenschaften in China, und die Anwendbarkeit der Systeme des deutschen landwirtschaftlichen Genossenschaftswesens auf ihre Fortbildung. Leipzig, H. Buske, 1937. 114 p. (Beiträge zur genossenschaftskunde; schriften des Seminars für genossenschaftswesen an der Universität Halle-Wittenberg hft. 5).

CHIANG, SHANG-YI, 姜尚義. Les coopératives de crédit agricole en Chine. Nancy, Impr. centrale de l'est, 1931. 131, [1] p. Thèse-Univ. de Nancy.

CHINA. National Economic Council. Rural reconstruction in Kiangsi. Nanchang, 1935. 18 numb. l. (Its. Special bull., 1).

CHINA INSTITUTE OF ECONOMIC AND STATISTICAL RESEARCH, Shanghai. A study of the rural economy of Wuhing, Chekiang. Shanghai, China Institute of Economic and Statistical Research, 1939. v, 121 p. incl. tables, diagrs.

FEI, HSIAO-T'UNG, 費孝通, 1911- Earthbound China; a study of rural economy in Yunnan, by Hsiao-tung Fei and Chih-i Chang, 張之毅. Rev. English ed. prepared in collaboration with Paul Cooper and Margaret Park Redfield. London, Routledge and K. Paul [1949] xv, 319 p. plates, maps, tables (International library of sociology and social reconstruction).

FOOD AND AGRICULTURE ORGANIZATION OF THE UNITED NATIONS. Training rural leaders; Shantan Bailie School, Kansu Province, China. Washington, 1949. vi, 136 p. illus., maps.

──────. L'École Bailie de Chantan; la formation de dirigeants de coopératives
rurales. Washington, 1949. vi, 144 p. illus., map.

HAN, WEN-TON, 韓聞洞. Le crédit agricole en Chine et les amendements pro-
posés. Nancy, Impr. G. Thomas, 1936. [5]-156 p. Thèse-Univ. de Nancy.

HO, FRANKLIN LIEN, 何廉, 1895- Rural economic reconstruction in China.
Preliminary paper prepared for the sixth conference of the Institute of Paci-
fic Relations held at Yosemite, California, August 15-29, 1936. [Shanghai]
China Institute of Pacific Relations, 1936. 59 p.

HSÜ, PAUL C., 徐寶謙, 1892-1944. Rural cooperatives in China. Honolulu,
Institute of Pacific Relations, 1929. 16 p. (Institute of Pacific Relations, 1st
conference, Kyoto, 1929).

LI, YU-I, 李有益. Three types of rural economy in Yunnan, by Yu-i Li, Hsiao-
tung Fei, 費孝通, and Tse-i Chang, 張之毅, edited by Hsiao-tung Fei. New
York, Institute of Pacific Relations, 1943. 35 p. (Social change in southwest
China-case study 1).

LO, WAN-SEN, 羅萬森, 1904- Probleme der Agrarkreditpolitik in China. Wür-
zburg-Aumühle, K. Triltsch, 1941. 142 p. incl. illus. (2 maps) tables. 2 diagr.

──────. Problems of agricultural credit policy in China (Probleme der agrarkreditpolitik in China) (Translated from German into English by Francis J.
Weiss) Wuerzburg-Aumuehe, K. Triltsch, 1941. 151 numb. l.

MALONE, CARROLL BROWN, 1886- The study of Chinese rural economy, by
C. B. Malone and J. B. Tayler. Peking, 1924. 14, 65 p. incl. tables, diagrs.
(China. International famine relief commission. Publ. ser. B., 10).

MARTIN, HARRY S. Recent development in agricultural work in Tunghsien by
Harry S. Martin and James A. Hunter, edited by Maxwell S. Stewart. Pei-
ping, 1930. 14 p. (Yenching University. Dept. of Sociology and Social Work,
Publ. ser. C. 24).

PEO, YU, 卜愈, [PU YU]. Associations de crédit mutuel rural et associations
similaires en Chine (Ts'ing-Houei) Ouvrage honoré d'une subvention de l'Institut des hautes études chinoises de l'Université de Paris. Paris, Domat-
Montchrestien, 1936. 157, [1] p. diagrs.

SCHOLZ, HARTMUT-DIETER. Die Formen der ländlichen Siedlung in China.
Bonn, 1949. 184 l., plate, map. Diss.- Univ. Bonn.

SHANTUNG. Institute of Rural Reconstruction. Rural reconstruction in Tsouping.
Tsinan, 1935. Cover-title, 16p. port. (Its Rural reconstruction ser., 1).

STRICKLAND, CLAUDE FRANCIS, 1881- Rural finance and cooperation. Shanghai, Chung Hwa Book Do., [1937?] ii, 459 p. fold. tables. (China. National
economic council. Cooperative commission. Publications. Series D, no. la).

SUN, HO-SHENG, 孫和生, 1923- Cooperative farming systems and their application in China. East Lansing, 1954. x, 215 p. Thesis-Michigan State University.

TSCHANG, WEN-HSI, 常文熙, 1904- Die chinesische Pacht. Würzburg, Triltsch, 1934. 81 p. Diss. -Univ. Berlin.

YANG, CHING-KUN, 楊慶堃. A North China local market economy, a summary
of a study of periodic markets in Tsouping hsien, Shantung. New York, Institute of Pacific Relations, 1944. 41 numb. l. mimeographed.

## Land Reform: Nationalist China

CHANG, HSUN-YANG, 張勛祥. Das chinesische Bodenrecht. Unter besonderer
Berücksichtigung des ᴄϪtsche Rechts. Göttingen, 1949. vii, 264 l. Diss-
Univ. Göttingen.

CH'EN, CH'ENG, 陳誠, 1896- An approach to China's land reform. Taipei,
Cheng Chung Book Co., 1951. 106 p. illus.

CH'EN, LI-FU, 陳立夫, 1900-  The function of the Commission on land research
    and planning.  Nanking, International Relations Committee [1935] 36 p.
———.  Report on land investigation.  Translated by Chao Hsi-lin, 趙錫麟.  Nan-
    king, International Relations Committee, 1935.  83 p. incl. tables.
CHINA.  Laws, statutes, etc.  The Chinese land law and the law governing the en-
    forcement of the Chinese land law.  [amended and promulgated on April 29
    1946 by the National government of the Republic of China] Translated by the
    Land division, Joint Commission on Rural Reconstruction, 1949.  Taipei,
    1949.  37, 9 p.
———.  Code Foncier; promulgué et mis en vigueur le 29 avril 1946.  Traduction
    française par André Bonnichon et André Song Kia-Hoai.  Teintsin, Hautes é-
    tudes, 1946.  94 p. (Collection ''Le droit chinois moderne'').
———.  The land-to-the-tiller act, passed by the Legislative Yuan on Jan. 20,
    1953 and promulgated by the President of the Republic of China on Jan. 26,
    1953.  Taipei, 1953.  1 v. (various pagings).
DRAGONI, CARLO.  Report on agricultural reform in China.  Nanking, National
    Economic Council, 1933.  60 p.
FREE CHINA REVIEW.  Land reform in Free China.  Taipei [1953] i, 65 p.
HSIAO, CHÊNG, 蕭錚, 1905-  The theory and practice of land reform in China.
    Taipei, Chinese Research Institute of Land Economics, 1953.  80 p.
JOINT COMMISSION ON RURAL RECONSTRUCTION IN CHINA (U.S. and China)
    Land-to-the-tiller program in Formosa.  Taipei, 1955.  12 p.
KLEIN, SIDNEY, 1923-  The pattern of land tenure reform in East Asia after
    world war II.  New York, 1956.  398 p. Thesis-Columbia University.
SHÊN, TSUNG-HAN, 沈宗翰, 1895-  Agricultural and land programs in Free
    China; increase production and farmer security.  Taipei, Govt. Information
    Bureau, 1954.  cover-title, 85 p. plates, diagrs., tables.
———.  Land to the tiller in Free China.  Taipei, China Culture Pub. Foundation,
    1954.  13 p. illus. (Pamphlets on Chinese affairs).
TANG, HUI-SUN, 湯惠蓀, 1900-  Land-to-the-tiller policy and its implementa-
    tion in Taiwan, by Tang Hui-sun and Chen Jen-lung, 陳人龍.  Taipei, 1954.
    16 p.
———.  Land reform in free China.  Taipei, Joint Commission on Rural Recon-
    struction, 1954.  336 p. illus., maps, diagrs., facsims.

### Land Reform: Communist China

AGRICULTURE in new China.  Peking, Foreign Languages Press [1953] 51 p.
    illus.
ASIAN PEOPLES' ANTI-COMMUNIST LEAGUE.  The food policy of the Chinese
    Communists.  [Taipei] 1955.  35 p.
———.  The Chinese Communist agricultural collectivization.  [Taipei] 1957. 40 p.
CHAO, KUO-CHÜN, 趙國鈞, 1918-  A historical survey of the land policy of the
    Chinese communists, 1921-1950.  Cambridge, Center for International Stu-
    dies, Massachusetts Institute of Technology, 1954.  vii, 108 l.
———.  Land policy of the Chinese communist party.  1921-1953.  Ithaca, N.Y.,
    1954.  vii, 4, 375 l.
———.  Agrarian policies of mainland China; a documentary study (1949-1956)
    Cambridge, Distributed by Harvard University Press, 1957.  xiii, 276 p.
    (Chinese Economic and Political Studies.  Special series).
CH'EN, PO-TA, 陳伯達, 1905-  Notes on Mao Tse-tung's ''Report of an inves-
    tigation into the peasant movement in Hunan.''  Peking, Foreign Languages
    Press, 1954.  62 p.
CHINA (People's Republic of China, 1949-    ) Laws, statutes, etc.  The Agrarian
    reform law of the People's Republic of China and other relevant documents.
    [4th ed.]  Peking, Foreign Languages Press [1952] 85 p.
———.  La loi sur la reforme agraire de la République populaire de Chine suivie

de deux autres documents. Pékin, Éditions en langues étrangères, 1950. 64 p.
——. Model regulations for an agricultural producer's co-operative; adopted by the Standing Committee of the National People's Congress of the People's Republic of China on March 17, 1956, at its 33rd meeting. Peking, Foreign Languages Press, 1956. 51 p.
——. Model regulations for advanced agricultural producers' co-operatives, adopted on June 30, 1956, by the First National People's Congress of the People's Republic of China at its third session. Peking, Foreign Languages Press, 1956. 33 p.
COMMITTEE FOR FREE ASIA, INC. Land reform: Communist China, Nationalist China, Taiwan, India and Pakistan. [San Francisco 1953] 68 p.
COMMUNIST PARTY. CHINA. Co-operative farming in China; decisions on the development of agricultural producers' co-operatives adopted by the Central Committee of the Communist Party of China. Peking, Foreign Languages Press, 1954. 34 p.
——. Decisions on agricultural co-operation, adopted at the sixth plenary session (enlarged) of the Seventh Central Committee of the Communist Party of China, October 11, 1955. Peking, Foreign Languages Press, 1956. 54 p.
——. The draft programme for agricultural development in the People's Republic of China, 1956-1967. Peking, Foreign Languages Press, 1956. 43 p.
——. Entwurf des Programms für die Entwicklung der Landwirtschaft in der Volksrepublik China 1956-67. Unterbreitet vom Politbüro d. ZK der Kommunist Partei Chinas am 23 Jan. 1956. Peking, Verlag für fremdsprachige Literatur, 1956. 26 p.
——. Socialist upsurge in China's countryside. Peking, Foreign Languages Press, 1957. 504 p.
DUMONT, RENÉ, 1904-  Révolution dans les campagnes chinoises. Paris, Éditions du Seuil [ 1957] 462 p. illus., maps. (Collections Esprit "Frontière ouverte").
GANGULI, BIRENDRANATH. Land reform in new China. Delhi, Ranjit Printers and Publishers, 1954. 74 p.
GOEL, SITA RAM. China is red with peasants' blood. Calcutta, Society for Defence of Freedom in Asia [ 1953] 92 p. (Inside Communist Slave-Empire series, 3).
HSIAO, CH'IEN, 蕭乾, 1911-  How the tillers win back their land. Peking, Foreign Languages Press, 1951. 148 p. illus.
——. Befreites Land. Wie die chinesischen Bauern ihr Land wiedergewannen. Berlin, Kongress-Verlag, 1953. 144 p. illus.
MAO, TSE-TUNG, 毛澤東, 1893-  Agrarian reforms in China by Mao Tse-tung and Liu Shao-chi. Hong Kong, 1948. 41 p. Reprinted from China Digest, June 1, 1948.
——. Significance of agrarian reforms in China, by Mao Tse-tung and Liu Shaochi. [Bombay, Published by J. Bhatt for People's Pub. House, 1950] 41 p.
——. Report of an investigation into the peasant movement in Hunan. Peking, Foreign Languages Press, 1953. 64 p. port.
——. The question of agricultural co-operation. Peking, Foreign Languages Press, 1956. 39 p.
——. Fragen des genossenschaftlichen Zusammenschlusses in der Landwirtschaft. Referat auf die Beratung des Sekretäre der Provinz, Stadt-und Gebietskomitees der Kommunistischen Partei Chinas am 31. Juli 1955. Berlin, Dietz, 1956. 35 p.
MUTUAL aid and co-operation in China's agricultural production. Peking, Foreign Languages Press, 1953. 38 p.
NOT winter but spring and other stories on mutual aid and co-operation in Chinese agriculture. Peking, Foreign Languages Press, 1956. 193 p.
ONG, SHAO-ER, 翁紹耳, [WÊNG SHAO-ÊRH] 1917-  Chinese farm economy after agrarian reform. Lackland Air Force Base, Tex., Air Force Personnel and Training Research Center, Air Research and Development Command,

1955. 32 p. (Human Resources Research Institute, Research Memorandum).
————. Agrarian reform in Communist China to 1952. Lackland Air Force Base, Tex., Air Force Personnel and Training Research Center, Air Research and Development Command, 1955. xviii, 61 p. illus., map. (Human Resources Research Institute. Research memorandum no. 41).

ORIENS, pseud. Land reform in China. With a foreword by David Mitrany. London, Batchworth Press [1952] 48 p. (Background books).

TÊNG, TZǓ-HUI, 鄧子恢, 1897- The outstanding success of the agrarian reform movement in China. Peking, Foreign Languages Press, 1954. 20 p.

WANG, TE-HUA, 王德華, 1922- Land reform in the People's Republic of China. Iowa City, 1952. 226 l. Thesis-State University of Iowa.

WITTFOGEL, KARL AUGUST, 1896- Mao Tse-tung, liberator or destroyer of the Chinese peasants? New York, Free Trade Union Committee, American Federation of Labor [1955] 22 p.

## Livestock

CH'ÊN, CHIH-CH'ANG, 陳之長. A report to His Excellency, Governor Ma Hung Kwei, 馬鴻逵, on a short animal production reconnaissance trip in Ninghsia Province, August 23rd to September 9th 1943, under auspices of the Republic of China, Ministry of Education, Province of Ninghsia [and] the United States of America, Department of State, Division of Cultural Relations. By C. C. Chen, Y. H. Tsou, 鄒樹文 [and] Ray G. Johnson. [Chungking? 1943?] 27, 10 l. plates, ports.

THE FOREIGN TRADE ASSOCIATION OF CHINA. Goatskin. [Shanghai, Commercial Press, 1936] cover-title, 31 p. tables, diagrs. (China export commodity series, 1).

JOHNSON, RAY GEORGE, 1902- An animal production reconnaissance trip through Sikong Province of the Republic of China, May 23, 1943 to July 14, 1943. [Washington 1943?] 1 v. (various pagings) illus., ports., map.

LEVINE, CARL OSCAR. Butchering and curing meats in China. Canton, 1921. iii, [1], 41, [1] p. plates, (Canton Christian College, Bull, 27).

PHILLIPS, RALPH WESLEY, 1909- Livestock improvement in China. Chungking, Ministry of Agriculture and Forestry, 1944. cover-title 160 p. maps.
————. The livestock of China, by Ralph W. Phillips, Ray G. Johnson and Raymond T. Moyer. Washington, Govt. Print. Off., 1945. vi, 174 p. incl. illus. (incl. maps) tables. [U.S. Dept. of state. Publication 2249. Far eastern series 9].

## Forestry

NATIONAL BUREAU OF INDUSTRIAL RESEARCH. Forest products laboratory, a brief account of its plan and works with abstracts of some publications (September 1939-December 1944). Kiating, Szechuan, 1946. 20, 64 p.

HSU, YUN-CHUN, 徐永椿. A preliminary study of the forest ecology of the area about Kunming. Stanford, Natural History Museum of Stanford University, 1950. 12 p. (Contributions from the Dudley Herbarium, 4:1).

HU, CHARLES Y, 虎犡如, [HU CHIAO-JU], 1910- The agricultural and forestry land-use of Szechuan basin. Chicago, 1946. ii-x, 157 (i.e. 170) p. incl. illus. (map) tables, diagrs. plates, 12 fold, maps. Thesis-Univ. of Chicago.

## Flood Control and Famine Relief

ALLEY, REWI, 1897- Man against flood; a story of the 1954 flood on the Yangtse and of the reconstruction that followed it. Peking, New World Press [1956] 109 p. illus.

CHINA. National Flood Relief Commission. Compendium showing dykes and other works constructed by National Flood Relief Commission [edited by T.C. Hsi,

席德炯 ] [Shanghai, Printed by the China Science Corporation] 1932. 10,
[28] p. plates (part fold.) maps (part fold.) tables.

———. The work of the National flood relief commission of the National Government of China, August 1931-June 1932. Shanghai, 1932. 30 p. plates, fold.
map.

———. Report of the National flood relief commission, 1931-1932. Shanghai
[Printed at the Comacrib Press] 1933. 304 p., 1 l., [12] p. fold. map (in
pocket) tables (part fold.) diagrs. (1 fold.).

CHINA (People's Republic of China, 1949-   ) Ministry of Water Conservancy.
Water conservancy in new China. Shanghai, People's Art Pub. House, 1956.
1v. (unpaged chiefly illus.).

CHINA INTERNATIONAL FAMINE RELIEF COMMISSION. Annual report. 1922-
1936. Peking, 1923-1937. 15 v. plates, tables (China international famine
relief commission. Publication[s] ser. A, no. 1-15).

———. History, organization and policy. Peking, 1923. cover-title, 10 p. (China international famine relief commission. [Publications] ser. B, no. 3).

———. The C.I.F.R.C. fifteenth anniversary book, 1921-1936. Peiping, 1936.
cover-title, 38 p. incl. illus., plates, ports., maps, diagrs. (China international famine relief commission publication. ser A, no. 47)

CHINESE FOREIGN FAMINE RELIEF COMMITTEE, Shanghai. Report on speci-
fic flood relief and prevention problems in Chekiang Province. Shanghai,
1925. iii, 40 p. maps (part fold.) diagrs.

FREEMAN, JOHN RIPLEY, 1855-1932. Flood problems in China. [New York,
1922] cover-title, p. 1113-1167. illus. (kncl. maps) fold. pl. xx. Reprinted
from Proceedings, Am. Soc. C.E. for May, 1922.

HUPEH FLOOD RELIEF COMMITTEE. Hankow's greatest flood catastrophe in
a century. Hankow, China, Hupeh Flood Relief Committee [1931] cover-
title, 8, 44 p. incl. illus., fold. plates.

KEH, CHI-YANG, 葛啓揚, 1909-  TVA program and the water control program
for China. Knoxville, Tenn., 1945. iii, 53 numb. l.

MACNAIR, HARLEY FARNSWORTH, 1891-1947. With the White cross in China;
the journal of a famine relief worker with a preliminary essay by way of introduction. Peking, H. Vetch, 1939.   viii, [3]-123 p., illus. (plans) fold.
map, tables.

MALLORY, WALTER HAMPTON, 1892-  China: land of famine, with a fore -
word by Dr. John H. Finley. New York, American Geographical Society,
1926. xvi, 190 p. incl. front., illus., maps (American geographical society.
Special publication, 6).

NANKING. UNIVERSITY. College of Agriculture and Forestry. The 1931 flood
in China: an economic survey by the Department of Agricultural Economics,
College of Agriculture and Forestry, the University of Nanking, in cooperation with the National Flood Relief Commission. Nanking, The University of
Nanking, College of Agriculture and Forestry, 1932. 74 p. incl. tables. fold.
map. ([Nanking. University. College of agriculture and forestry] Bulletin no.
1 (new series) April, 1932).

PEKING UNITED INTERNATIONAL FAMINE RELIEF COMMITTEE. The North
China Famine of 1920-1921, with special reference to the west Chihli area.
Being the report of the Peking united international famine relief committee.
Peking [Printed by the Commercial Press works] 1922. viii, 175 p. illus.,
fold. map.

RED CROSS. U.S. American National Red Cross. The report of the American
Red cross commission to China. Washington, D.C., The American National
Red Cross, 1929. 103 p. [Red cross. U.S. American national Red cross.
ARC circular 270].

———. American Red cross famine relief in China, 1920-1921, from the Report
of the China Famine Relief, American Red cross. [New York] Russell Sage

Foundation [1943] 25 p. ([Russell Sage foundation, New York] Administration of relief abroad, a series of occasional papers. [8]).

SHANSI. WATER CONSERVANCY COMMISSION. Regulation of the Fen Ho, for flood protection and conservancy of winter flow as an aid to irrigation. A report prepared from surveys made in 1933. Taiyuan, 1934. 27 p. plates, map.

TODD, OLIVER JULIAN, 1880- Two decades in China, comprising technical papers, magazine articles, newspaper stories and official reports connected with work under his own observation. Peking, the Association of Chinese and American Engineers, 1938. xviii, 604 p. front. plates, port., maps, fold. table.

U.S. Congress. House. Committee on Appropriations. Famine relief in China. Hearing before subcommittee of House Committee on appropriations in charge of deficiency appropriations. Sixty-sixth Congress, third session. Washington, Govt. Print. Off., 1921. 12 p.

## Bibliographies

HUEBOTTER, FRANZ, 1881- A guide through the labyrinth of Chinese medical writers and medical writings, a bibliographical sketch. Kumamoto, Japan, 1924. 2-74 numb. l.

PEKING. UNION MEDICAL COLLEGE. Bibliography of the publications from the laboratories and clinics of the Peiping union medical college and hospital. v. [1/2]- 1915/25-1926-1940. Peiping, 1926-1941. 5 v.

——. Selected contributions from the Peking union medical college. v. 1-6. Peking, China [1921-1926] 6 v. illus., plates, maps, tables, diagrs.

——. Dept. of Surgery. The gist of articles by the staff of the Department of Surgery, Peking Union Medical College. No. 1- Peiping, 1930/31-

## Directories and Dictionaries

CHANG, CHUNG-HSI. 張崇熙. Foreign Chinese medical terms — Medizinische Vokabulien. Hangchow, Hsin-i-shu-chü, 1953. 2, 402, 4 p.

CHEN, M. C., 陳文駐 [CH'EN WEN-CHU] 1898- A selected list of Chinese materia medica. New York, Chinese Chamber of Commerce of New York, 1948. 111 p.

The CHINESE medical directory [1st]- 1928- Shanghai, The Chinese medical association, 1928- v. plates, maps. Title varies: 1928...Medical guide, with classified list of medical suppliers (At head of title, National medical association of China) 1930...Medical directory (At head of title: National medical association of China) 1932- The Chinese medical directory [Published by the Chinese medical association].

COUSLAND, PHILIP BRUNELLESCHI, 1861- An English-Chinese lexicon of medical terms, by Philip B. Cousland. 5th ed. --with the assistance of Teh-Ching Leo, 魯德馨. Based on the new official terminology and reprinted with separate list of the latest additional terms. [Shanghai] Publication Committee, China Medical Association, 1926. 20, 254 p., 1st ed., 1908.

——. English-Chinese medical lexicon. 10th ed. rev. and enl. by Teh-ching Leo, and P. L. McAll. Shanghai, Chinese Medical Association, 1949. 449 p.

GENERAL COMMITTEE ON SCIENTIFIC TERMINOLOGY. Latin-English-German-Chinese madical terminology; edited by Teh-ching Leo and others. Shanghai, 192? 520 p.

HO, HUAI-TE, 何懷德. 俄英中醫學辭彙 Russian-English-Chinese medical dictionary by Ho Huai-te and Tien Li-chih, 田立志. Peking, Jen-min-wei-sheng-ch'u pan-she, 1954. 714 p.

JÊN, P'ING. 任平. [Latin-Chinese medical dictionary] 拉華醫學辭典 Shanghai, Hsi-nan-i-hsueh shu-shê, 1953. 2, 413, 35 p.

LIU, CH'ING. 柳青, comp. [Chinese-Latin-English-German handbook of drugs] Shanghai, Hsi-nan i-hsueh shu-shê, 1954. 15, 111 p.

SHANGHAI. Municipal Council. Register of medical practitioners, dentists, and veterinary surgeons. [Shanghai, 193- ] v. annual.

SONG, KOU-PING, 宋國賓. Song Kou-ping's French-English-Chinese medical etymology. Shanghai, 1937. 402 p.

TZ'U TIEN PIEN I-WEI-YUAN HUI. 辭典編譯委員會. English-Chinese modern medical dictionary. 英漢新醫辭典. 3rd ed. Shanghai, Hsin-i shu-chü, 1953 (c1949) 836 p.

WU, CHIEN-AN, 吳建庵. comp. A pocket medical dictionary for nurses and

medical students. 4th ed.  Shanghai, Kuang hsieh shu-chü, 1951. 272, 86,
14 p. 1st ed. 1949.
ZIA, DA-ZUNG, 謝大任 [HSIEH TA-JEN] The etymology of medical terms for
medical students.  Shanghai, Lungmen Books, Inc., 1951. vi, 175 p.

## Chinese Drugs

CHEN, SZE YEE, 陳思義. Illicium religiosum, Siebold, mang tsao; a phyto-
chemical study.  Philadelphia, Pa. [1929] 72 p. illus. Thesis-University of
Wisconsin.  Reprinted from the American journal of pharmacy, vol. 101,
August, September and October, 1929.
CHING, LI-PIN, 經利彬. Note pour servir à l'étude des matièrs médicales de
Chine. Peiping, Impr. des Lazaristes, 1936. 20 p. illus.
GRIEBLING, FRANK A. comp. Imported Chinese crude drugs. [n.p.] 1949. 551.
―――. Imported Chinese proprietary preparations. [n.p.] 1949. 59 l.
HAYDEN, ALICE HAZEL, 1909- A chemical study of ma huang by Alice H.
Hayden and C.B. Jordan.  [Washington, D.C., 1933] p. [616]-625, 1 l.
Abstract of thesis-Purdue university. ''Reprinted from the Journal of the A-
merican pharmaceutical association, 22:7. ''
HUANG, YAN-KAI. Über Krebstherapie der altchinesischen Medizin und deren
Verwertungsmöglichkeiten in der Nachbehandlung der heutigen Heilverfahren.
München, J.F. Lehmanns Verlag, 1937. 15 p. Diss. -Univ. Erlangen.
ISHIDOYA, TSUTOMU, 1891- Chinesische Drogen, Pt. 1. Keijo, Verlag von
dem Pharmakologischen Institut der Kaiserlichen Universität, 1933. 138, 7 p.
illus.
LEUNG, (T.) HERB CO.; LOS ANGELES. Chinese herbal science; its principles
and methods, comprising its treatment of various prevalent diseases, useful
information on matters of diet and testimonials; a guide to health. [Los An-
geles], Calif., 1928. 76 p. illus., ports.
LEUNG, TO-CHING, 1906- Contribution à l'étude de la radix ginseng, pana-
cée du peuple chinois. Lyon, 1932. 84 p. Thèse-Univ. de Paris.
LOU, TZE-CHING, 樓子岑. Studies on certain Chinese drugs. London, 1950.
vii, 140 p. plates, map.
MCCLURE, FLOYD ALONZO, 1897- The flora of a Canton herb shop, by F.A.
McClure and Hwang Ts'ui-mae.  Canton, Lingnan University, 1934. cover-
title, 32 p. plate. (Lingnan university science bulletin, 6).
MONOD, HENRI DUCIMETIÈRE. La république populaire de Chine et l'industrie
pharmaceutique.  Paris, Chambre syndicate des fabricants de produits phar-
maceutiques, 1957. 144 p. map.
MOSIG, ALFRED. Der Arzneipflanzen-und Drogenschatz Chinas und die Bedeutung des Pên-Ts'ao Kang-Mu   本草綱目  als Standardwerk des chinesischen Materia Medica, [von] Alfred Mosig [und] Gottfried Schramm.  Berlin,
Verlag Volk und Gesundheit, 1955. 71 p. illus. (''Pharmazie, '' Beih. 4).
OFFE, HANS-ALBERT, 1912- Über das krötengift Cinobufagin, einen herzwirk-
samen Bestandteil der chinesischen Droge Ch'an su.  Bottrop i.W., Postberg
1937. v, 27 p. Diss.-Univ. Göttingen.
PRISHVIN, MIKHAÏL MIKHAÏLOVICH, 1873- Jen sheng: the root of life; English
version by George Walton and Philip Gibbons; foreword by Julian S. Huxley.
New York, G.P. Putnam, 1936. vii, 177 p. incl. front., illus.
READ, BERNARD EMMS, 1887-1949. Botanical, chemical, and pharmacological reference list to Chinese materia medica. [Peking, Printed by Bureau
of Engraving and Printing] 1923.   v, 38 p.
―――. Plantae medicinalis Sinensis, 2d ed. Bibliography of Chinese medicinal
plants from the Pen Ts'ao Kang Mu 1596 A.D., by Bernard E. Read [and]
Liu Ju-ch'iang, 劉汝強. Peking, Dept. of pharmacology, Peking Union Medical College, in collaboration with the Peking Laboratory of Natural History,
1927. xi, 106 p. (Flora Sinensis, ser. A, v. 1).

——. Materia medica tables and notes. 10th ed. Published by Council on publication, the Chinese Medical Association. Shanghai, Kwang Hsueh Pub. House, 1934. 172 p.

——. Chinese materia medica. From the Pen ts'ao kang mu by Li Shih-chen, 李時珍, A.D. 1597. Peiping, Peking Natural History Bulletin, 1931-1941. 6 v. illus., plates.

——. A compendium of minerals and stones used in Chinese medicine from the Pên ts'ao kang mu, by Li Shih-chên, 1597 A.D. Compiled by B.E. Read and C. Pak. 2nd ed. Peiping, Peking Natural History Bulletin, 1936. viii, 98 p. 1st ed., 1928.

——. Chinese medicinal plants from Pen ts'ao kang mu. A.D. 1596. 3rd edition of a Botanical, chemical and pharmacological reference list. [Peiping, China] Peking Natural History Bulletin, 1936. xvi, 389 p. Second edition published under title: Plantae medicinalis Sinensis.

——. Famine foods listed in the Chiu-huang pen-ts'ao, 救荒本草, giving their identity, nutritional values and notes on their preparation. Shanghai, Henry Lester Institute of Medical Research, 1946. 90 p. illus.

ROI, JACQUES. Plantes médicinales chinoises d'après le traite célèbre de pharmacopée, le Pen ts'ao kang mu (1590). [Peking, 1942] 142 p. illus. Reprinted from Collectanea Commissionis Syndolis, 15 ).

——. Atlas de plantes médicinales chinoises. Changhai, Université l'Aurore, 1946. Cover-title, 125 plates. (Musée Heude. Notes de botanique chinoise, 8).

——. Traité des plantes médicinales chinoises. Paris, P. Lechevalier, 1955. 488 p. plates.

## Chinese Medicine

BARATOUX, JEAN E., 1902- Précis élémentaire d'acuponcture avec repérage anatomique des points et leurs applications thérapeutiques. Avec 26 planches. Paris, E. Le François, 1942. [7]-170 p., illus.

BUSSE, ERNST. Akupunktur-Fibel. Die Praxis der chinesischen Akupunkturlehre von Ernst und Paul Busse. München, Pflaum, 1954. 56 p. illus.

COLLE, HENRY. Outlines to a general and biographical history of pharmacy and medicine in Asia. [9 v] Vol. 4: Central Asia. Vol 6: China. San Francisco, The author, 1951. 2 v. illus. Typescrit.

FERREYROLLES, PAUL, 1881- L'acupuncture chinoise (thérapeutique énergétique) Lille, Éditions S.L.E.L. [1953] 200 p. illus.

HUANG-TI NEI-CHING SU-WEN. 黃帝內經素問. Huang Ti nei ching su wên, the Yellow Emperor's classic of internal medicine. Chapters 1-34 translated from the Chinese with an introductory study by Ilza Veith. Baltimore, Williams and Wilkins, 1949. xix, 253 p. illus., port. The translator's thesis-Johns Hopkins University.

HUEBOTTER, FRANZ, 1881- Zwei berühmte chinesische Ärzte des Altertums, Chouen-yü I, 淳于意, und Hoa T'ouo, 華陀. 2. Aufl. Tokyo, Deutsche Gesellschaft für Natur-und Völkerkunde Ostasiens, 1927. 48 p. (Mitteilungen der Deutschen gesellschaft für natur-und völkerkunde Ostasiens. bd. 21 t. A).

——. Die chinesische Medizin zu Beginn des xx. Jahrhunderts und ihr historischer Entwicklungsgang. Leipzig, Verlag der "Asia major," 1929. [5]-356 p. illus. (China-bibliothek der "Asia major," bd. I).

——. Chinesisch-Tibetische Pharmakologie und Rezeptur. Ulm/Donau, Hang, 1957. 180 p. ports. illus. (Panopticum medicum, 6).

HUME, EDWARD HICKS, 1876-1957. The Chinese way in medicine. Baltimore, Johns Hopkins Press, 1940. 189 p. front. (port.) illus., plates (1 fold.) fold tables. (Publications of the Institute of the history of medicine, the Johns Hopkins university. 3d ser.: The Hideyo Noguchi lectures, vol. 6).

KERVYN, JOSEPH. Médicine chinoise. Choses vues. Bruxelles, Impr. F. Van Buggenhoudt, 1947. 15 p.

LEPRINCE, ALBERT. L'acupuncture à la portée de tous. Manuel théorique et
    pratique de l'acupuncture chinoise et des méthodes qui en dérivent. Paris,
    Dangles [1945] 174, [2] p. illus.
LEUNG, TIT-SANG, 梁鐵生. Akupunktur und Räucherung mit Moxa. Übers.
    von Werner Zimmermann. München, Drei Eichen Verlag, 1954. 86 p.
LUI, GARDING,呂家定, 1895- Secrets of Chinese physicians. Los Angeles,
    B. N. Robertson [1943] 165 p., illus.
MORSE, WILLIAM REGINALD, 1874- Chinese medicine, with 16 illustrations.
    New York, P. B. Hoeber, 1934. xxiii, [1] 185 p. illus., plates (Clio medica:
    a series of primers on the history of medicine 11).
NAKAYAMA, T. Acupuncture et medicine chinoises vérifiées au Japon. Paris,
    Hippocrate, 1934. 90 p. illus.
NGUYEN-VAN-QUAN. Acupuncture chinoise pratique; sur quelques recherches
    touchant la médicine traditionelle sino-japonaise. Paris, Picart, 1936. 126
    p. illus.
NIBOYET, J.  E.  H. Essai sur l'acupuncture chinoise pratique. Paris, Édi-
    tions Dominique Wapler, 1951.  v, 358 p. illus. fold. tables.
OTTO, JOHANN H.      F. Das Dau, Tao, in der chinesischen Heilkunst.
    Hamburg, Anthropologisches Institut, 1954. 10 p. (Anthropologie, 62).
RIJCKEVORSEL, EDITH VAN. Le message de l'acupuncture. 2. éd. Paris,
    1950. 22 p.
RAKUSEN, CHARLESWORTH PERCIVAL, 1894- History of optics in China.
    [Shanghai] The Committee on Medical History of the National Medical Asso-
    ciation of China, 1937. cover-title, 1077-1107 p. "Published as a special
    number by the Committee on medical history of the National medical associa-
    tion of China."
SCHÖNEWALD, ANNELIESE. Die chinesische Medizin und ihre Berührungspunkt
    mit der frühen Abendländischen, vor allem der griechischhippokratischen Me-
    dizin. München, 1940. 28 l. Diss. -Univ. München.
SOULIÉ, CHARLES GEORGES, 1878- Précis de la vraie acuponcture chinoise.
    Doctrine, diagnostic, thérapeutique; par George Soulié de Morant. 6. éd.
    Paris, Mercure de France, 1936. 199 p. illus. plates. 1947 ed., 201 p.
————. L'acuponcture chinoise,  鍼灸法, par George Soulié de Morant. Paris,
    Mercure de France, 1939-41. 2 v. illus., plates, facsim.
————. The same. Préface du P. Mériel. Avant-propos du M. Martiny. Paris,
    Lafitte, 1957. 1000 p., plates (part col.) map.
VEITH, ILZA. Some philosophical concepts of early Chinese medicine. [Basa-
    vangudi, Bangalore] 1950. 15 p. (Indian Institute of Culture. Transaction, 4).
WONG, K. CHIMIN, 王吉民, [WANG, CHI-MIN] History of Chinese medicine;
    being a chronicle of medical happenings in China from ancient times to the
    present period, by K. Chimin Wong and Wu Lien-teh, 伍連德. 2d ed. Shang-
    hai, National Quarantine Service, 1936. xxviii, 906 p. illus., plates (incl.
    front., ports., plan, facsims.) diagrs. 1st ed. Tientsin Press, 1932.
ZIMMERMANN, WERNER, 1893- Chinesische Weisheit und Heilkunst [von]
    Werner Zimmermann [und] Leung Tit-sang, 梁鐵生. München, Drei Eichen
    Verlag [1954] 51 p. illus. ports.

Western Medicine in China

BALME, HAROLD, 1878- China and modern medicine; a study in medical mis-
    sionary development, with preface by Sir Donald MacAlister. London, United
    Council for Missionary Education, 1921. 224 p. front., plates, port.
BASIL, GEORGE CHESTER, 1902- Test tubes and dragon scales in collabora-
    tion with Elizabeth Foreman Lewis. Philadelphia, John C. Winston Co.
    [c1940] xi, [1], 316 p. illus.
BECKER, ROLF. Beitrag zur Frage der Verbreitung und Bekämpfung von Kala-
    Azar (Leichmaniose) in China. Halle/Saale, 1950. 35 l. tables. Diss. -Univ.

Halle.

CHANG, KWEI, 張奎, 1906-  Studies on hookworm disease in Szechwan Province, West China, by K. Chang and co-workers. Baltimore, Johns Hopkins Press, 1949. x, 152 p. illus., maps. (The American journal of hygiene; monographic series, 19).

CHINA DEFENCE LEAGUE. Aid for China must go on; medical work in the northwest border region. Hong Kong, Central Committee of the China Defence League, [1940] 20 p. illus.

———. In guerrilla China; report of China Defence League. New York, China Aid Council, 1943; Sydney, Current Book Distributors, 1945. 72 p. illus.

CHINESE SOCIETY OF PATHOLOGY AND MICROBIOLOGY. Pathology and microbiology, being mainly proceedings of the Chinese Society of Pathology and Microbiology held in Canton, November 5—8, 1935. Peiping, 1936. 518 p. illus. plates, (Chinese medical journal. Suppl. 1).

———. The same; issued by the Chinese Society of Pathology and Microbiology on the occasion of the visit to Chian of Dr. Hans Zinsser. Peiping, 1938. vi, 600 p. illus. plates, (Chinese medical journal. Suppl. 2).

CONFERENCE ON THE PRESENT MEDICAL SITUATION IN CHINA, College of Physicians and Surgeons, New York, 1946. New York, American Bureau of Medical Aid to China, 1946. ii, 67 l.

CORT, WILLIAM WALTER, 1887-1942. Researches on hookworm in China, embodying the results of the work of the China hookworm commission, June, 1923 to November, 1924, by W. W. Cort, J. B. Grant, N. R. Stoll and other collaborators. Baltimore, Md., 1926. v-ix, 398 p. incl. illus., maps, tables, diagrs. plates. (The American journal of hygiene;monographic series, 7).

FAR EASTERN ASSOCIATION OF TROPICAL MEDICINE. 9th congress. Nanking, 1934. Transactions of the ninth congress held in Nanking, China, October 2-8, 1934. Edited by Wu Lien-teh and C. Y. Wu, 伍長耀. Nanking, the National Health Administration, 1935. 2 v. front. (facsim.) illus., plates (1 col.) ports., maps, tables (part fold.) diagrs.

FAUST, ERNEST CARROLL, 1890-  Studies on Clonorchis sinensis (Cobbold) by Ernest Carroll Faust and Oo-Keh Khaw, 許甫階, assisted by Yao Ke-Fang, 姚克方. and Chao Yung-An, 趙永安; with a consideration of the molluscan hosts of Clonorchis sinensis (Cobbold) in Japan, China and southeastern Asia and other species of molluscs closely related to them, by Bryant Walker. Illustrated with 14 plates and 33 text figures. Baltimore, Md., 1927. vii-xi, 284 p. illus., plates (1 fold.) fold. maps, tables (1 fold.) diagrs. (1 fold.) (The American journal of hygiene; monographic series, 8).

FLOWERS, WILFRED STEPHEN. A surgeon in China; vivid personal experiences of Dr. W. S. Flowers with a British Red cross unit. London, Carey Press [1946] cover-title, 52 p. illus. (incl. ports., map) diagr.

FRAZIER, CHESTER NORTH, 1892-  Racial variations in immunity to syphilis; a study of the disease in the Chinese, white, and Negro races [by] Chester North Frazier and Li Hung-chiung, 李鴻週. Chicago, Univ. of Chicago Press [1948] xi, 122 p. diagrs.

GAJDOS, STEPHAN. Studies on typhus fever in China, by Stephan Gajdos, and Joseph Chang 張廣民. Peiping, Catholic University Press, 1933. 59, iii p. plates, diagrs. (The Catholic university of Peking science publications. Contributions from the Microbiology laboratory).

HUME, EDWARD HICKS, 1876-1957. Doctors east, doctors west; an American physician's life in China. New York, W. W. Norton [1946]; London, Allen and Unwin, 1949. 278 p. front., plates, port. French ed.: Docteur en Chine. Bruxelles et Paris, Éditions de la Paix, 1952. (Vies de medicine).

———. In ärztlicher Mission; das Leben eines Amerikanischen Arztes in China. Übers. von Suzan von Wittek. Lizenzausig, Linz, Demokratische Druck-und Verlagsgesellschaft, 1949. 302 p. illus.

―――. Doctors courageous. New York, Harper [1950] xiv, 297 p. illus. ports.

JEFFERYS, WILLIAM HAMILTON, 1871-  The diseases of China, including Formosa and Korea (Jefferys and Maxwell) 2d ed. by James L. Maxwell. With
  176 illustrations. Shanghai [Printed by A. B. C. Press] 1929. ix, 530 p.
  illus., plates (1 col.) 1st ed. Philadelphia, 1910.

JEN, HUEI-CHIA, 任會嘉, 1909-  Le choléra à Changhai dans ces dix dernières
  années (1926-1935) Paris, 1937. 48 p. Thèse-Univ. de Paris.

LI, HUAN-HSIN, 李煥新, 1901-  Die Wurminfektionen des Menschen in China.
  Hamburg, Christiaus, 1936. 62 p. Diss.-Univ. Hamburg.

LYMAN, RICHARD SHERMAN, ed. Social and psychological studies in neuropsychiatry in China, edited by R. S. Lyman, V. Maeker and P. Liang, 梁孟
  娟, Peking, Published for the Division of Neuropsychiatry, Peking Union Medical College, by H. Vetch, 1939. [3]-377, [3] p. incl. tables, diagrs., forms
  (part fold.) plates.

MCCARTNEY, JAMES LINCOLN, 1898-  Chinese military medicine. Reprinted
  from United States naval medical bulletin, volume 25, no. 4. Washington,
  Govt. Print. Off., 1927. 34 p. incl. illus., table plates.

MCCLURE, ROBERT BAIRD, 1900-  The Red cross at work in China (Dr. R. B.
  McClure) Compiled by F. M. Osborn. [Sheffield, Eng., Sheffield newspapers,
  1943?] 48 p. illus. ["China chronicle" series].

NORTH MANCHURIAN PLAGUE PREVENTION SERVICE. Reports edited by Wu
  Lien-teh, 伍連德. Tientsin, Teintsin Press, 1914-1922. 3 v. plates, ports.,
  fold maps, diagrs. Imprint varies.

―――. Manchurian plague prevention service memorial volume, 1912-1932. Edited by Wu-Lien-teh. Shanghai, National Quarantine Service, 1934. 469 p. col.
  front., illus. (incl. plan) plates, ports., diagrs.

POWELL, LYLE STEPHENSON, 1893-  A surgeon in wartime China. Lawrence,
  Kan., University of Kansas Press, 1946. 233 p. plates, group ports.

RASMUSSEN, OTTO DURHAM, 1888-  Chinese eyesight and spectacles. 4th rev.
  ed. Tonbridge, Tonbridge Free Press [1949] 64 p. illus.

SCHULZ, GERTRUD. Kurzer Überblick über die Krankheiten der Europäer in
  China. Gewonnen aus dem Krankenberichten des Tropengenesungsheims Tü-
  gingen. Tübingen, 1943. 32 l. tables. Diss.-Univ. Tübingen.

SMITH, ROBERT GILLEN, 1913-  History of the attempt of the United States
  Army Medical Department to improve the effectiveness of the Chinese Army
  Medical Service, 1941-1945. Ann Arbor, University Microfilms, 1950 [i.e.
  1951] ([University Microfilms, Ann Arbor, Mich.] Publication no. 2130) Mi-
  crofilm copy of typescript. Positive. Collation of the original: 238 l. tables.
  Thesis-Columbia University.

SNAPPER, ISIDORE, 1889-  Chinese lessons to western medicine. A contribution to geographical medicine from the clinics of Peiping Union Medical College, by I. Snapper. With a foreword by Geroge R. Minot. New York, Inter-
  science Publishers, 1941. x, 380 p. incl. illus., tables, diagrs.

STURTON, STEPHEN DOUGLAS, 1896-  Medical work in China. London, The
  China Society [1946] Cover-title, 5 p.

TS'AI, CHEOU-K'ANG, 蔡壽康. L'épidémiologie du choléra en Chine. Strassbourg, Éditions Argentoratum, 1934. 45 p. Thèse-Univ. de Strassbourg.

TSEN, EDGAR T.  H., 陳宗賢 [CH'EN TSUNG-HSIEN] Notes on biologic thera-
  peusis. Peking, Central Epidemic Prevention Bureau, 1923. 73 p. plates,
  (Its. Bull. 1).

UNITED SERVICE TO CHINA. Western medical assistance to China during 1943-
  44 in the field of medicine and health, prepared by Tania M. Cosman. [New
  York, 1944- 1 v.

U. S. Bureau of Medicine and Surgery. Epidemiology of kala azar in China, by
  Robert J. Dicke and Tsai-yu Hsiao, 蕭彩瑜. Washington, D.C., Bureau of
  Medicine and Surgery, Navy Dept., 1946. cover-title, ii, 83 p. illus., fold
  map.

————. Epidemiology of the diseases of naval importance in Manchuria, prepared by Tsai-yu Hsiao, entomologist, Division of preventive medicine. Washington, D.C., Bureau of Medicine and Surgery, Navy Dept., 1946. v, 54 p. incl. tables. Reproduced from type-written copy.

U.S. WAR DEPT. Medical and sanitary data on southeastern China. Washington, Govt. Print. Off., 1945. 94 p. tables, (War Dept. Technical Bull. TB Med. 171).

WU, LIEN-TÊ, 伍連德, 1879-  Plague in the Orient with special reference to the Manchurian outbreaks. Tientsin, Tientsin Press, 1921. Cover-title, 18 p. illus.

————. A treatise on pneumonic plague. [Nancy, Paris, Strasburg, Printed by Berger-Levrault, 1926] xiv, 466 p., plates, fold. map. plan.

————. A new survey of plague in wild rodents and pneumonic plague. Shanghai, National Quarantine Service, 1933. 118 p. Reprinted from National Quarantine Serve reports. ser. 3.

————. Cholera; a manual for the medical profession in China, by Wu Lien-teh. J. W. H. Chun, 陳永漢, R. Pollitzer, C. Y. Wu, 伍長耀, Illustrated with one colour and twenty-three half-tone plates. Shanghai, National Quarantine Service, 1934. xxii, 197 p. col. front., plates.

————. Plague, a manual for medical and public health workers, by Wu Lien-teh J. W. H. Chun, R. Pollitzer and C. Y. Wu. With one hundred and three illustrations, of which six are in colour. [Shanghai] Weishengshu National Quarantine Service, 1936. xxxiii, 547 p. illus. (incl. maps, plan) plates (incl. front., ports., facsims.; part col.) diagrs.

## Hospitals and Medical Schools

CADBURY, WILLIAM WARDER, 1877-  At the point of a lancet; one hundred years of the Canton hospital, 1835-1935, by William Warder Cadbury and Mary Hoxie Jones. Shanghai, Kelly and Walsh, 1935. xvii, 304 p. front., plates, ports., plan, facsim.

CANTON. CANTON HOSPITAL. Report, 1877-1941. Canton, 1878-1941. v. illus. annual (irregular).

FABER, KNUD HELGE, 1862-  Report on medical schools in China. [Geneva, 1931] 47 p. (Series of League of Nations publications. iii. Health. 1931. iii. 8).

————. Report sur les écoles de médecine en Chine. Genève, Service des Publications, Société des Nations, 1931. iv, 54 p.

PEKING. UNION MEDICAL COLLEGE. Addresses and papers, dedication ceremonies and Medical conference, Peking Union Medical College, September 15-22, 1921. Peking, [Concord, N.H., Rumford Press] 1922. xiv, 416 p. front., plates (incl. ports., plans) diagrs.

————. Laboratory manual of the Department of bacteriology and immunology, Peiping Union Medical College, prepared under the direction of C.E. Lim, 林宗揚. 2d ed. Peiping, [Kwang Yuan Press] 1935. 190 p. incl. tables, 2 diagr. 1st ed. 1929.

————. Committee on the Hospital. Formulary; a list of drugs and preparations selected as official for use in the Peking Union Medical College hospital. 4th ed. Peiping, P.U.M.C. Press, 1932. ix, 69 p.

————. Dept. of Anatomy. A catalogue of the first 400 specimens of the human embryological collection in the Department of Anatomy of the Peking Union Medical College, edited by A.B. Droogleever Fortuyn. Shanghai, Printed at the Presbyterian Mission Press, 1927. Cover-title, 94 p.

————, Manual for the medical services. 5th ed. Revised by the staff of the Department of Medicine and edited by F.R. Dieuaide. Peking, 1936. vi, 204 p. fold plates.

SNELL, JOHN A. An inquiry into the present efficiency of hospitals in China with special reference to recent grwoth. Presented at the general conference of the Chinese Medical Association, 1934. 93 p. (Chinese Medical Association.

Special report ser. 1.)

SPENCER, BARBARA. Desert hospital in China. London, Jarrolds [1954]; New York, Roy Publishers, 1955. 192 p. illus.

———. Mon hôpital dans le désert chinois. Traduit par Gabrielle Rivers. Paris, Julliard, Sequana, 1955. 225 p. illus. (photos), maps. (Collection Sciences et voyages).

TSINAN. CHEELOO UNIVERSITY. Shantung Christian University: twenty-five years in Tsinan. Tsinan, n. d. 31 p. plates.

## Public Health

ASSOCIATION FOR THE ADVANCEMENT OF PUBLIC HEALTH IN CHINA. Memorandum on the need of a public health organisation in China. Presented to the British Boxer Indemnity Commission by the Association for the Advancement of Public Health in China. Peking, 1926. 108 p. diagrs.

CH'EN, CHIH-CHIEN, 陳志潛. Public health in rural reconstruction at Ting Hsien. [Ting Hsien], 1934. 50 p.

———. Development of systematic training in rural public health. Annual report. Ting Hsien, 1935. 38 p.

CHINA. CENTRAL EPIDEMIC PREVENTION BUREAU. Annual report, 1st- 1922/23- Peking, 1923- . 1919-Apr. 1922 as Central Plague Prevention Bureau; Apr. 1922-Oct. 1925 as Central Epidemic Prevention Bureau; Oct. 1925-1937 as National Epidemic Prevention Bureau.

———. Report 1919-1934; being a review of its activities from its foundation in March 1919 to June 1934. Peiping, 1934. vi, 170 p. illus. plates, photos, tables.

CHINA. CENTRAL FIELD HEALTH STATION. Report of the Central field health station. 1st Apr. 1931/Dec. 1933- Shanghai, North-China Daily News and Herald, 1934- .

CHINA. NATIONAL HEALTH ADMINISTRATION. National public health activities, a pictorial survey. Nanking, 1934. 54 l.

CHINA. National Quarantine Service. Quarantine regulations of the republic of China. [n. p., 1931?]. 53 p. incl. fold. tab., forms.

———. Reports, Ser. 1-7 (1930-1937) Shanghai, 1931-1937. 7 v. illus. map.

———. National quarantine service; memorial volume, 1934. Edited by Wu Lien-teh and C. Y. Wu. Shanghai, 1934. xii, 326 p. illus. ports.

CHINA. Public Health Administration. Preparatory papers: Report of China [for the] Intergovernmental Conference of Far-Eastern Countries on Rural Hygiene. [Geneva, 1937] 109 p. maps (1 fold.) (Series of League of Nations publications. iii Health. 1937. iii. 11).

CHINESE MEDICAL ASSOCIATION. Minimum nutritional requrement for China; report of the Committee on Nutrition of the Council of Public Health of the Chinese Medical Association. Shanghai, 1938. iii, 32 p. tables (Its Special report series, 10).

FOLTZ, EUGEN. Die Ernährung in China. Hannover-Wülfel, Horman, 1941. 37 p. Diss. - Univ. Frankfurt.

HOU, HSIANG-CH'UAN, 侯祥川. Nutritional studies in Shanghai, by H. C. Hou, P. G. Mar, T. G. Ni, 倪章祺, and B. E. Read, the Division of physiological sciences, Henry Lester Institute of Medical Research, Shanghai. A report upon the nutritional status of certain Shanghai groups 1937-39, dietary surveys and a study of the value of various food supplements. [Shanghai, 1940?] 92 p. incl. illus., plates, tables, diagrs. (Chinese medical association. Special report series, 12).

JOINT COMMISSION ON RURAL RECONSTRUCTION IN CHINA (U. S. and China). Report on rural health work. 1948/50- [n. p.] v. annual.

KING, P. Z., 金寶善 [CHIN PAO-SHAN] 1893- Selected papers by the staff of the National health administration and Central field health station, 1934. Edited by P. Z. King. With a foreword by J. Heng Liu, 劉瑞恆. Nanking, 1935. viii, 330 p. incl. illus., tables (1 fold.) diagrs. plates.

LEAGUE OF NATIONS. Health organisation. Proposals of the National Government of the Republic of China for collaboration with the League of Nations on health matters. [Geneva, 1930] 51 p. (C. 118. M. 38. 1930. iii [C. H. 842]).

——. Health organisation. Collaboration with the Ministry of Health of the National Government of the Republic of China. Completion of the survey of Chinese ports and report on the reorganisation of the port health services, in conformity with the request of the National Government of China. [Geneva, 1930] 70 p. 2 diagr. (1 fold.) At head of title: Official no.: C. H. 906. Geneva, September 16th, 1930. League of nations.

PETER, WILLIAM WESLEY, 1882- Broadcasting health in China; the field and methods of public health work in the missionary enterprise. Shanghai, Presbyterian Mission Press, 1926. 89 p. illus. (incl. ports.).

SZE, SZEMING.施思明, 1908- China's health problems, [3rd ed.] Washington, D.C., Chinese Medical Association, 1944. 76 p. 1st ed. 1942.

UNITED NATIONS EDUCATIONAL, SCIENTIFIC AND CULTURAL ORGANIZATION. The healthy village; an experiment in visual education in West China. Paris [1951] 119 p. illus. (Its Monographs on fundamental education, 5).

——. La santé au village; une expérience d'éducation visuelle en Chine. Paris [1952] 129 p. illus. (part col.) (Its Monographies sur l'éducation de base, 5).

YUAN, I-CHIN, 袁貽瑾, 1899- The influence of heredity upon the duration of life in man based on a Chinese genealogy from 1365 to 1914. Baltimore, 1931. 81 p. Thesis-John Hopkins University.


## Chinese Food and Cookery

AU, MAN SING, 歐萬勝, 1906- ed. Chinese cookery. Honolulu, Creart Publications, 1932. 46, [2] p.

——. The Chinese cook book; covering the entire field of Chinese cookery in the Chinese order of serving, from nuts to soup, compiled and edited for the American cook by Mr. M. Sing Au; with decorations by Warren G. Troutman. Reading, Pa., Culinary Arts Press, c1936. 47 p. illus.

CH'EN, JOSEPH S., 陳尚球 [CH'EN SHANG-CHIU]. Composition of Chinese foods [by] Joseph S. Ch'en and Olivia L. Li, 李彩璘. Taipei, Dept. of Biochemistry, National Defence Medical Center [195-] 38 p. tables.

CHAN, SOU, 陳壽[CH'ÊN SHOU] The House of Chan cookbook. Drawings by Sui Lan Loh, 陸秀蘭. Garden City, N.Y., Doubleday, 1952. 190 p. illus.

CHEN, EDWARD WING-SHING, 陳華全, [CH'ÊN HUA-CHUAN]1921- A practical encyclopaedia of Chinese cookery. [Victoria? Australia, 1954. 112 1.

CHÊNG, S. K. 鄭紹經 [CHENG SHAO-CHING] Chinese cookery book. London, The proprietors of: The Shanghai Restaurant, 1936. 102 p.

CHÊNG, T'IEN-HSI, 鄭天錫, 1884- Musings of a Chinese gourmet; food has its place in culture [by] F. T. Cheng. London, Hutchinson [1955] 155 p.

CHINESE foodstuffs and how to use them; tested recipes for foreign dishes made from Chinese products. Preface by Bernard E. Read. Shanghai, Kelly and Walsh, 1940. iii-xvi, 146 p.

The EPICURE in China; eight complete Chinese epicurean dinners. San Francisco, Colt Press [1939] [13]-63, [1] p. col. illus.

FENG, DOREEN YEN HUNG, 馮彥鴻. The joy of Chinese cooking, written and illustrated by Doreen Yen Hung Feng. New York, Greenberg, 1951?; London, Faber and Faber [1952] 227 p. illus.

FIELD, MOIRA. Easy Chinese dishes for today, by Moira Field and Chung San Chao. London, John Lane [1943] vii, 55 p.

FRANCETTA, Sister. The art of Chinese cooking, by [Sister M. Francetta and Sister Regia] the Benedictine sisters of Peking. Illus. by M. Kuwata. Tokyo, C. E. Tuttle Co. [1956]; London, Arco, 1957. 94 p. illus.

HAWCOCK, EMORY. Practical and profitable Chinese recipes. [ New York, J.O. Dahl, c1933] cover-title, 32 p. (Little gold business books).

HONG, WALLACE YEE, 余鳳棠. The Chinese cook book. New York, Crown Publishers [ 1952] 261 p. [International cook book series].

JACKSON, LENLI. 100 simple Chinese recipes. London, New Europe Pub. Co., 1946. 35 p. [New Europe cookery series].

KAO, LOIS TERESA. Cookery book on local food. Singapore, Straits Printers [ 1946] xvi, 102 p.

KWON, GEORGE I. Oriental culinary art, by George I. Kwon and Pacifico Magpiong; an authentic book of recipes from China, Korea, Japan and the Philippines. Los Angeles, G. I. Kwon [ c1933] 11-115 p.

LAMB, CORRINNE. The Chinese festive board; line-drawings and paper-ends by John Kirk Sewall. Peiping, H. Vetch [ 1935] 153 p. front., illus., plates.

LECOURT, HENRI. La cuisine chinoise. Pékin, A. Nachbaur, 1925. 141 p.(on double leaves) illus.

LEE, M.    P.    李孟萍 . Chinese cookery; a hundred practical recipes; with decorations by Chiang Yee, 蔣彝.  London, Faber and Faber [ 1943]; New York, Transatlantic, [ 1945] 74 p. incl. front., illus.

LIAO, TSUI-FENG林廖翠鳳. Cooking with the Chinese flavor, by Tsuifeng Lin and Hsiangju Lin, 林相如. Englewood Cliffs, N. J., Prentice-Hall [ 1956] 196 p. illus. English ed.: London, Heinemann, 1957. xiv, 215 p.

LIU, DOLLY,劉周佩. "Chow"; secrets of Chinese cooking, with selected recipes, illustrated by Henry Liu. Shanghai, Kelly and Walsh, 1939. vi, viii, 183 p. front. (ports. ) illus. (1 col. ) plates (part col. ).

———. The same. Rutland, Vt., C. E. Tuttle, 1952. ix, 174 p. illus.

LOW, HENRY, 劉渠. Cook at home in Chinese. New York, Macmillan, 1938; rev. ed. 1951. 274 p.

LO, KENNETH, 羅孝建[ LO HSIAO-CHIEN] Cooking the Chinese way. New York, and London, Arco Pub. Co. [ 1955] 154 p. illus.

MANDARIN chop suey cook book, containing authentic translations of the best recipies of leading Chinese chefs and directions for preparing various popular and healthful Chinese dishes exactly as they are prepared in the Orient. Chicago, Pacific Trading Co., 1928. 96 p. illus.

MITCHELL, ALICE MILLER, comp. Oriental cookbook. [Chicago] Chicago Oriental Council, 1950. 110 p. illus.

MOORE, ALICE. Chinese recipes, letters from Alice Moore to Ethel Moore Rook; cover design by Royal Rook. Garden City, N. Y., Doubleday, Page, 1923.  xiii, 113 p. illus.

MORGAN, HARRY TITTERTON, 1872-  Chinese recipes. 2d ed. Edited and copyrighted by H. T. Morgan. Los Angeles, c1942. 16 p. [His Miniature books of information on China and things Chinese ].

OLIVER, FRANK. Chinese cooking. London, Deutsch, 1955. 232 p. illus. (Cookery books, ed. by Elizabeth David).

PANKING. Livre de cuisine d'un gourmet poéte. Pékin, Impr. de la ''Politique de Pékin'', 1924. 64 p. (Collection de la ''Politique de Pékin'').

SEARLE TOWNLEY. Strange newes from China: a first Chinese cookery book. with 101 rare and choice Chinese recipes and decorations by the author. London, A. Ouseley, 1932; N. Y. Dutton, 1933. 231 p. illus.

SHEN, MEI-LON, pseud. The ancestral recipes of Shen Mei Lon. [A scroll of favorite Chinese dishes adapted for American kitchens. New York, Richards Rosen Associates] c1954. 140 p. illus.

SIA, MARY (LI), 謝李靈生 . Chinese chopsticks; a manual of Chinese cookery and guide to Peking restaurants, by Mary Li Sia (Mrs. Richard H. P. Sia) 2d ed. Peking, Peking International Women's Club, 1938. xvii, 144 p. front., plates.

———, Chinese cookbook. Honolulu, University of Hawaii Press, 1956. 148 p. illus.

SOU SAN, WILLIAM, 林建安, [ LIN CHIEN-AN] Chinese culinary in plain English. 2nd ed.  Brisbane, Austrailia, The author, 1953. 104 p.

WING  FRED 傅恩永 [FU EN-JUNG] 1896-   New recipes.  [New York, Edelmuth Co. c1941] cover-title, [28] p.

————.  Old Chinese recipes, simplified and tested by Mabel Stegner.  [New York]
   United Service to China, [1946] cover-title, 50 p.  illus.

————.  New Chinese recipes, using only ingredients easily obtainable in neighbor-
   hood stores.  Tested by Mabel Stegner.  [9th print.  New York, Edelmuth Co.,
   1951] 111 p. illus. 1st ed. 1941.

WONG, CHIN-CHONG, 黄軫章 [HUANG CHÊN-CHANG] Chinese American, European cook book.  [San Francisco, Chong Sing Co., 1925] 5, 77, 553, [1], 52
   (i. e. 54) p., illus. (port.).

WONG, GAIL KUM TING, 黃金靜, [HUANG CHIN-CHING] 1901-   Authentic
   Chinese recipes. [Rev. 2d ed.  Honolulu? c1955] 151 p. illus. 1st ed. 1954.

WONG, RICHARD. Enjoy Chinese cooking at home,中國廚書.  New York, Dragon
   Inn, 195-  74 p. illus.

WU, WOOT-TSUEN梁伍恬泉, 1915-  Composition of foods used in Far Eastern
   countries, by Woot-tsuen Wu Leung, R. K. Pecot, and B. K. Watt.  Washington [Govt. Print. Off.] 1952. 62 p. tables. (U. S. Dept of Agriculture. Agriculture handbook, 34).

YANG, KUANG-TEH, 揚光德. Fifty Chinese recipes,中國食譜.  Peking, China
   Reconstructs, 1957. 40 p. illus. (Supplement to China Reconstructs).

YANG, PU-WEI,趙揚步偉, 1889-  How to cook and eat in Chinese. Rev., enl. ed.
   New York, J. Day [1949] xviii, 262 p. illus.

————.  The same.  London, Faber and Faber, 1956. 286 p. illus.

YEP, HUNG-HEE, 葉融羲, 1916-  Chinese recipes for home cooking: complete
   recipes and methods of preparation for the most popular, famous and traditional Chinese dishes. 5th ed.  Sydney, Horwitz Publications, 1955 (c1951)
   144 p. illus.

YOUNG WOMEN'S CHRISTIAN ASSOCIATIONS. Honolulu. Chinese home cooking;
   recipes of Cantonese dishes, by the Chinese committee, International institute, Y. W. C. A., Honolulu, Hawaii.  [Honolulu, T. H., Printed by Paradise
   of the Pacific, c1941] 86 (i. e. 88) p. col. front., illus.

# XXII.  NORTHEASTERN  PROVINCES  (MANCHURIA)

## Bibliographies

[AUSTRALIA. JOINT SERVICE STAFF, Washington, D.C.] Manchuria; handbook of selected reference material. [Washington, D.C.] 12 pts.

CHINESE EASTERN RAILWAY CO. Economic Bureau. What to read about Manchuria. Harbin, Economic Bureau, Chinese Eastern Railway, 1933. 11 p. illus.

FUCHS, WALTER, 1902- Beiträge zur mandjurischen Bibliographie und Literatur. Tôkyô, Deutsche Gesellschaft für Natur- und Völkerkunde Ostasiens, 1936. 146 p; 8 p. illus. (Supplement der "Mitteilungen" der Deutschen gesellschaft für natur- und völkerkunde Ostasiens. supplement bd. xiv).

INTER-ALLIED RAILWAY COMMITTEE. Short list of books on the Russian Far East and northern Manchurai. [Harbin] Secretariat, Inter-Allied Railway Committee, 1922. iv, 52 p.

NEW YORK. PUBLIC LIBRARY. The Manchus; a list of references in the New York Public Library, comp. by John L. Mish. [New York, 1947. 5 p.

TAGUCHI, MINORU. Histoire de l'étude de Mandchourie en France; annexe: Bibliographie de Mandchourie en langue française. Dairen, Dairen-Bibliothèque, 1933. cover-title, 24 p. (Recherches sur les bibliographies de Mandchourie et de Mongolie, 1).

U. S. Consulate. Mukden. List of Manchukuo publications issued between August and December, 1937, inclusive. [n.p., 1938] 9 l.

U. S. Library of Congress. Reference Dept. Manchuria; a selected list of bibliographies, compiled by Peter A. Berton, consultant in Manchurian bibliography, with the assistance of Helen Dudenbostel Jones, bibliographer, General Reference and Bibliography Division. Washington, 1951. iv, 15 p.

———. Manchuria; an annotated bibliography, compiled by Peter A. Berton, consultant in Manchurian bibliography, with the assistance of members of the Orientalia Division and the General Reference and Bibliography Division. Washington, 1951. xii, 187 p. maps.

## Description and Travel

AKIMOTO, SHUNKICHI. Manchuria scene. Tokyo, Taisho Eibun Sha [1933] 334 p. front. (port.).

AUGUSTIN, REINHARD. Durch Mandschukuo; abenteuerliche Erlebnisse im Lande des Opiums. Buchschmuck und Umschlagzeichnung von Friedrich Kasshofer-Kerner. Reichenberg, Sudentendeutscher Verlag Franz Kraus, 1936. 149, [1] p. illus. (incl. map).

BARBER, NOEL. Trans-Siberian. London G.G. Harrap [1942] 180 p. plates, 2 port. (incl. front.).

BERTRAND, GABRIELLE. Seule dans l'Asie troublée; Mandchoukuo-Mongolie, 1936-1937. Préface de Louis Audouin-Dubreuil. Paris, Plon [1937] 312 p. plates (1 double) port., fold. map.

CAMENZIND, JOSEF MARIA, 1904- Zwischen Amur und Sungari; Reiseerlebnisse eines Schweizers in der Mandschurei. Zürich, Verein Gute Schriften [1948] 64 p. (Gute Schriften, 8).

CHINESE EASTERN RAILWAY. Guide book and directory for the health resorts of the Chinese Eastern Railway. Harbin, 1923. 75 p.

CORDES, ERNST, 1908- Das jüngste Kaiserreich; schlafendes-wachendes Mandschukuo. Frankfurt a. M., Societäts-verlag [1936] 225 p., plates, ports.,

map.

FISCHER, EMIL SIGMUND, 1865-1945. Beobachtungen auf Reisen in Korea und der Mandschurei. Wien [1931] 20 p. (Cover1title: "Abdrücke aus den Mitteilungen der Geographischen Gesellschaft in Wien").

———. My 1932 journey around the world; particular notes on the Trans-Siberian Railway and Manchuria. Tientsin, Tientsin Press, 1932. 13 p.

———. The present outlook in Manchuria. Tientsin, Tientsin Press, 1935. 10 p.

LARROUY, MAURICE, 1882-   Eaux glacées; Mandchourie-Japon-Canada-États-Unis. Paris, A. Fayard [c1934] [7]-446 p.

LINDT, AUGUST RODOLPHE. Special correspondent; with bandit and general in Manchuria. London, Cobden-Sanderson [1933] 292 p. front., plates, map.

———. Im Sattel durch Mandschukuo; als Sonderberichterstatter bei Generälen und Räubern. Leipzig, F.A. Brockhaus, 1934. 272 p. incl. front. (port.) illus., maps.

LISSNER, IVAR, 1909-   Taiga. [Hamburg] Hoffmann und Campe [1951] 296 p.

MATHESON, R.   O. Modern Manchuria, a series of articles written for the Chicago Tribune. Dairen, Printed by the "Manshu Nichi-Nichi-Shimbum," 1926. Cover-title, 11 p.

MELZER, FRITHJOF. Malaria, Gold und Opium, mit Stötzners Hei lung kiang-Expedition in die unerforschte Mandschurei. Mit einem Geleitwort von Georg Cleinow. 2. Aufl. durchgesehen und eingeleitet von Walther Stötzner. Leipzig, M. Möhring [1932? c1929] 246 p. illus. ports., maps.

MONCHARVILLE, MAURICE  1864-   Pages africaines et asiatiques. Paris, A. Pedone, 1938. 302 p.

OSSENDOWSKI, FERDYNAND ANTONÏ, 1876-1944. From president to prison, in collaboration with Lewis Stanton Palen. New York, E. P. Dutton [c1925] viii, 360 p.

PLAETSCHKE, BRUNO. Das Bergland der nordwestlichen Mandschurei; Ergebnisse topographischer Erkundungen und landschaftskundlicher Untersuchungen. Gotha, J. Perthes, 1937. 101, [1] p. plates, maps (part fold.) (Ergänzungsheft nr. 232 zu "Petermanns mitteilungen").

SCHALEK, ALICE THERESE EMMA, 1874-   Japan, das Land des Nebeneinander; eine Winterreise durch Japan, Korea und die Mandschurei. Breslau, F. Hirt, 1925. 403, [1] p. illus. (incl. ports., maps).

SORGE, WOLFGANG, 1891-   Erlebtes Mandschukuo, die Jugend eines altneuen Kaiserreiches. Berlin, Kommodore Verlag [1938] 308 p. plates, ports., fold. map.

SOUTH MANCHURIA RAILWAY COMPANY. Illustrated guide book for travelling in Manchoukuo, with sketch map. Dairen, 1934. 83 p. illus., maps.

———. Port of Dairen. [Darien] S[outh] M[anchuria] R[ailway] 1923. cover-title, 48 p. illus., plates, maps, tables.

———. Dairen. 1939. [Tokyo] General-directorate of Railways, The South Manchurian Railway Co. [1939] 30 p. illus. fold. map.

———. Mukden. 1939. [Tokyo] General-directorate of Railways, The South Manchurian Railway Co. [1939] 28 p. illus. fold. map.

———. Ryojun. [Tokyo] General-directorate of Railways, The South Manchuria Railway Co. [1939] 19 p. illus. map.

TAMAKI, TERUNOBU. A brief guide to battle-fields in Port Arthur. [Rev. and enl. ed. Dairen] 1929. 26 p. illus.

## Manchu and Tungus Languages

BENZING, JOHANNES. Lamutische Grammatik, mit Bibliographie, Sprachproben und Glossar. Wiesbaden, F. Steiner, 1955. viii, 254 p. (Akademie der Wissenschaften und der Literatur. Veröffentlichungen der Orientalischen Kommission, 6).

———. Die tungusischen Sprachen; Versuch einer vergleichen- den Grammatik.

Mainz, Verlag der Akademie der Wissenschaften und der Literatur; in Kommission bei F. Steiner, Wiesbaden [1955, i.e. 1956] 151 p. (Akademie der Wissenschaften und der Literatur. Abhandlungen der Geistes- und Sozialwissenschaftlichen Klasse, Jahrg. 1955, Nr. 11).

GRUBE, WILHELM, 1855-1908. Die Sprache und Schrift der Jŭcen, 女眞. Reprint ed. [Tientsin, 1941. xi, 147 p. 1. ed., Leipzig, 1896.

HAUER, ERICH, 1878-1936. Handwörterbuch der Mandchusprache, 滿獨辭典 Tokyo, Deutsche Gesellschaft für Natur- und Völkerkunde Ostasiens. Wiesbaden, Kommissionsverlag O. Harrassowitz, 1952-55. x, 1052 p.

MÖLLENDORFF, PAUL GEORG VON, 1848-1901. A Manchu grammar, with analyzed texts. Shanghai, Printed at the American Presbyterian Mission Press, 1892. [Peking, Wên tien ko shu-chuang, 1938] 52 p., Photoprinted 1934; reprinted 1938.

SHIROKOGOROV, SERGEĬ MIKHAĬLOVICH, 1887-1939. A Tungus dictionary; Tungus-Russian and Russian-Tungus. Photogravured from the mss. Tokyo, Minzokugaku Kyōkai, 1944. 258 p.

TANGGU MEYEN. Tanggu meyen and other Manchu reading lessons. Romanised text and English translation side by side. By M. Forbes A. Fraser. London, Luzac, 1924. vii, 184 p.

## History

CHAN, YU LAI, 陳汝禮 [CH'EN JU-LI], 1915-    A history of the alien conquests of China through the Liao area. Washington, 1951. xiii, 419 l. maps (part fold.) Thesis-Georgetown University.

CLYDE, PAUL HIBBERT, 1896-    International rivalries in Manchuria, 1689-1922. (2d ed. rev.) Columbus, The Ohio State University Press, 1928. xv, 323 p. fold. front. (map).

GILBERT, LUCIEN. Dictionnaire historique et géographique de la Mandchourie; ouvrage illustré de nombreuses gravures et de plusieurs cartes. Hong Kong, Impr. de la Société des missions-étrangères, 1934. xx, 1040 p. incl. illus., tables, plates, ports., maps, facsims, geneal. tables.

LI, CHI, 李濟, 1896-    Manchuria in history, a summary. Peiping, Peking Union Bookstore, 1932. cover-title, 43 p. plates (incl. facsims.) fold. maps, fold. tables.

NING, E    C., 寧恩承. Historical account of the Laio-Ning province (South Manchuria) and the Manchus. Mukden, Printed by Northeastern University factory, Printing department [1929?] 27 p.

STAUFFER, ROBERT BURTON, 1920-    Manchuria as a political entity: government and politics of a major region of China, including its relations to China proper. Minneapolis, 1954. 624 l. Thesis-Univ. of Minnesota.

## Foreign Relations
See also Foreign Relations- China and Japan; China and Russia

AKAGI, ROY HIDEMICHI, 1892-    Understanding Manchuria; a handbook of facts, (3d ed., rev.) New York, 1932. viii, 79 p. illus. (map).

[AMANO, MOTONOSUKE], 1901-  comp. Brief history of Japan's rights and interests in Manchuria, compiled by M. Amano and Y. Koizumi. Dairen, Research Off., South Manchuria Railway Co., 1932.    v. 67 p. (South Manchuria Railway Co. "Chosaka" Pamphlet, 2).

BALET, JEAN CYPRIEN, 1867-    Le drame de l'Extrême-Orient; la Mandchourie; historique, politique, économique, son avenir; préface de François de Tessan. Paris, Payot, 1932. 222 p. illus. (map) (Bibliothèque politique et économique).

————. Das Drama des Fernen Ostens. Die Mandschurei, Geschichte, Politik, Volkswirtschaft, ihre Zukunft. Übers. von Nora Sinnreich. Wien, Österr.

Journal, 1932. 207 p. fold. map.

BATE, H. MACLEAR, 1908-  Manchuria and Korea; asiatic flashpoint. London, H.G. Morris [1948] 24 p.

[BISSON. THOMAS ARTHUR] 1900-  Basic treaty issues in Manchuria between Japan and China. New York, Foreign Policy Association [1931] [381]-394 p. illus. (map) (Foreign policy reports. 6:21, December 23, 1931).

BÖCHER, HERBERT. Der Vertraute des Marschalls Tschang-Hsüehliang erzählt. Ein Deutscher zwischen Chinesen, Japanern und Räubern. Erlebnisse des Sportlehrers Herbert Böcher von der chinesischen Universitat Mukden. (Ms.) Stuttgart, Dieck, 1932. 1 v. (unpaged).

————. Chinois, japonais et brigands. Récit d'un familiar du Maréchal Tchang Tsueliang. Traduction originale de l'allemand, par Maurice d'Aubigné. Paris, Éditions Montaigne, Fernand Aubier, 1932. 176 p. (Collection des documents).

BONNEAU, GEORGES, 1897-  Japon et Mandchourie. Ôsaka, Ôsaka taishi keizairemmei; Paris, Vanier, 1932. 45, [1] p. illus.

CATHOLIC ASSOCIATION FOR INTERNATIONAL PEACE. Manchuria: the problem in the Far East. Study presented to the Catholic Association for International Peace by the Asia committee. Washington, D.C., Catholic Association for International Peace [1934] 69 p. [Catholic association for international peace] Pamphlet, 12).

DAIREN. CHAMBER OF COMMERCE AND INDUSTRY. What Chinese fugitive soldiers and hunghudze are capable of; into what awful condition they threw South Manchuria; long list of shocking outrages charged against them. Dairen, Manchuria, Chamber of Commerce and Industry [1933] vi, 40 p. map.

DASHIN´SKII, S. Japan in Manchuria, edited by N. Fokin. New York, Workers Library Publishers [1932?] London, Modern Books, 1932. 47, [1] p. incl. 2 maps (1 double).

EDDY, GEORGE SHERWOOD, 1871-  The world's danger zone. New York, Farrar and Rinehart, [c1932] vi, 3-119 p.

ETHERTON. PERCY THOMAS, 1879-  Manchuria, the cockpit of Asia, by Colonel P.T. Etherton and H. Hessell Tiltman, with sixteen reproductions from photographs and a map. New York, Frederick A. Stokes, 1932. x, 327 p. front., plates, fold. map.

FANG, EDWIN LO-TIEN, 方樂天. Manchuria; a second Korea? An outline of Japan's Manchuria policy from its inception to its climax. Shanghai, Commercial Press, 1934. xi, 430 p. maps.

FOCHLER-HAUKE, GUSTAV, 1906-  Die Mandschurei; eine geographisch-geopolitische Landeskunde, auf Grund eigener Reisen und des Schrifttums. Heidelberg, K. Vowinckel, 1941. xv, 448 p. front., illus., plates, fold. maps. (Schriften zur wehrgeopolitik, 3).

HSIAO, SHUN-CHING, 蕭純錦, 1894-  Is Manchuria vital to Japan's existance? Shanghai, China Institute of International Relations, 1932. 26 p.

HSU, SHU-HSI, 徐淑希, 1892-  Japan's rights and position in Manchuria [a review of C. Walter Young's Japan's jurisdiction and international legal position in Manchuria] Peiping, 1932. 41 p. facsim.

ITO, TAKEO, 1895-  Chins's challenge in Manchuria; anti-Japanese activities in Manchuria prior to the Mukden incident. [Dairen] South Manchuria Railway Co. [1932] 117 p.

JAPAN. Consulate. Harbin. Sino-Japanese relations; improbity and corruption practiced by former military cliques in North Manchuria. Harbin, 1932. 57 p. illus., fold. map.

————. Ministry of Foreign Affairs. Relations of Japan with Manchuria and Mongolia [n.p.] 1932. x, 203, 47 p. fold. map (On cover: Document B).

————. The same. Les relations du Japon avec la Mandchourie et la Mongolie. [n.p., 1932] xii, 209 p., xi, 46 p. incl. tables. fold. map. (Document B).

JAPAN ECONOMIC FEDERATION. China's treaty violations in Manchuria. Tokyo, Japan Economic Federation, 1932. 23, 7 p. map.

THE JAPANESE expedition to Chientao. Why it was sent and what it did. Seoul, Seoul Press, 1921. 51 p.

JONES, FRANCIS CLIFFORD. Manchuria since 1931. London, Royal Institute of International Affairs [ 1949] vii, 256 p. fold. map.

——. Manchuria in 1945-1946. Constitutes part of a larger IPR research report which is being undertaken under the auspices of the Royal Institute of International Affairs on "Developments in Manchuria since 1931." Submitted by the Royal Institute of International Affairs as a document for the Tenth Conference of the Institute of Pacific Relations to be held at Stratford-upon-Avon, England, September 1947. London, Royal Institute of International Affairs, 1947. 11 l. (United Kingdom paper, 3).

LATTIMORE, OWEN, 1900-  Manchuria, cradle of conflict. New York, Macmillan, 1932. Rev. ed. 1935. xviii, 343 p. maps (part fold. ).

LEO; T. Y. Manchuria-hunger of the East Asiatic "Boches." New York, Chinese Patriotic Association, 1931. 16 p.

LIN, CHING-JÜN, 林景潤, 1898-1947. The Liaotung case. New York, Chinese Students Club, Columbia University, 1923. 8 p.

LONG, JOHNSON. La Mandchourie et la doctrine de la porte ouverte. Paris, A. Pedone, 1933. 208 p. Thèse-Univ. de Paris.

LUM, YING-WU, 林英武, ed. A brief study of the Manchurian question. Chicago, The mid-west branch of the Kuomintang, the Chinese Nationalist party in America, 1931. 31 p.

MANCHURIA YOUNG MEN'S FEDERATION. An appeal by Japanese people concerning the Manchurian problem. [Dairen?] Manchuria Young Men's Federation [1931] 34 p. plates, facsims.

MILLARD, THOMAS FRANKLIN FAIRFAX, 1868-1942. The A B C's of the Manchuria question. Shanghai, Weekly Review of the Far East, 1921. cover-title, 15 p.

MITSUO, KIMISUKE. How does an average Japanese feel about the situation in the Orient? Delivered at the Quota Club, Washington, D. C., Thursday, January 10th, 1935. [New York, 1935] cover-title, 22 p.

O'CONROY, TAID. The menace of Japan. London, Hurst and Blackett, [ 1933]; New York, H. C. Kinsey, 1934. 294 p. front., plates, ports., facsim.

PAN, STEPHEN C. Y., 潘朝英, 1908-  American diplomacy concerning Manchuria. Washington, Catholic University of America, 1938. xvi, 385 p. Thesis-Catholic University of America.

PARLETT, SIR HAROLD GEORGE, 1869-1945. A brief account of diplomatic events in Manchuria. Published under the auspices of the Royal Institute of International Affairs, 1929. London, Oxford University Press, H. Milford [ 1929] viii, 93, [1] p. fold. map.

PRICE, ERNEST BATSON, 1890-  The Russo-Japanese treaties of 1907-1916 concerning Manchuria and Mongolia. Baltimore, Johns Hopkins Press, 1933. xiv, 164 p. incl. map. facsims.

ROMANOV, BORIS ALEKSANDROVICH, 1889-  Russia in Manchuria, 1892-1906. Translated from the Russian by Susan Wilbur Jones. Ann Arbor, Mich., Published for American Council of Learned Societies by J. W. Edwards [ 1952] x, 549 p. (Russian Translation Project series of the American Council of Learned Societies, 15).

ROYAMA, MASAMICHI, 1895-  Japan's position in Manchuria. A paper prepared for the third biennial conference of the Institute of Pacific Relations, Kyoto, 1929. [Tokyo] The Japanese Council, Institute of Pacific Relations [ 1929] 1 p. l., iii (i. e. iv), ii, 103 p. fold. map.

SAKAMOTO, NAOMICHI. L'affaire de Mandchourie. Paris, Recueil Sirey, 1931. 33 p. fold. map.

SAKURAI, TADAYOSHI, 1879-  Niku-dan, Menschenopfer; Tagebuch eines japanischen Offiziers während der Belagerung und Erstürmung von Port Arthur.

Übers. von A. Schinzinger. 2. Aufl. Tokyo, Nippon Sekai-Koron-sha, 1940. 206 p. plates, ports., fold map, facsims. [1. Aufl., Freiberg, J. Beilefeld, 1911. English title: Human bullets, a soldier's story of Port Arthur. Boston, Houghton, Mifflin, 1907. 269 p.].

SOKOLSKY, GEORGE EPHRAIM, 1893-   The tinder box of Asia. Garden City, N.Y., Doubleday, Doran, 1933. xii, 453 p. illus. (maps).

SOUTH MANCHURIA RAILWAY COMPANY. "Present Manchuria and Mongolia." Dairen, South Manchuria Railway Co., 1924. iv, 116 p. illus., fold. map. 1st ed., 1921.

SPIELMANS, VICTOR. Russland und Japan im Fernen Osten. Berlin-Spandau, Obelisk-Verlag [c1935] 88 p. incl. tables. fold. map (in pocket).

STEWART, JOHN ROBERT, 1910-   Manchuria since 1931. Prepared for the sixth conference of the Institute of Pacific Relations, held at Yosemite park, California, from August 15th to 29th, 1936. New York, Secretariat, Institute of Pacific Relations, 1936. 53 p. ([Institute of Pacific relations] Secretariat papers. no. 2).

[TAKADA, RYUICHI] A brief sketch of the Kwantung government, illustrated with photographs, diagrams and maps. Dairen, Mammo Bunka Kyokai (Manchuria Enlightening Society) 1926. ii, 79, 2 p. plates, fold. map.

U.S. Army. Far East Command. Japanese preparations for operations in Manchuria, Jan. 43-Aug. 45. Prepared by Military History Section, Headquarters, Army Forces Far East. [Tokyo?] Distributed by Office of the Chief of Military History, Dept. of the Army [1953] 1 v. (various pagings) illus., maps. (Japanese monograph, 138).

U.S. Dept. of State. Conditions in Manchuria. Message from the President of the United States transmitting, in response to Senate resolution no. 87, a report by the Secretary of State relative to the existing conditions in Manchuria. Washington, Govt. Print. Off., 1932. iii, 56 p. (72d Cong., 1st sess. Senate. Doc. 55).

U.S. and BRITAIN'S attitude toward Manchurian situation; statement and release of the U.S. State department and British protest to Soviet government with Secretary Byrnes' speech of "Seven notes." Shanghai, International Publishers, 1946. 24 p.

VESPA, AMLETO, 1888-   Secret agent of Japan. Boston, Little, Brown, 1938. xiv, [3]-301 p. front., plates, ports., facsims.

YOUNG ARTHUR MORGAN, 1874-   Imperial Japan, 1926-1938. London, G. Allen and Unwin, [1938] [9]-328 p.

YOUNG, CARL WALTER, 1902-1939. The international relations of Manchuria; a digest and analysis of treaties, agreements, and negotiations concerning the three eastern provinces of China, prepared for the 1929 conference of the Institute of Pacific Relations in Kyoto, Japan. Chicago, Pub. for the American Council, Insititue of Pacific Relations, by the University of Chicago Press [c1929] xxx, 307 p. incl. front. (map).

———. Japan's special position in Manchuria; its assertion, legal interpretation and present meaning. Baltimore, Johns Hopkins Press; London, H. Milford, Oxford University Press, 1931. xxxiv, 412 p. incl. double map. (His Japan's jurisdiction and international legal position in Manchuria, 1).

———. The international legal status of the Kwantung leased territory. Baltimore, Johns Hopkins Press; London, H. Milford, Oxford University Press, 1931. xxx, 249 p. incl. map. (His Japan's jurisdiction and international legal position in Manchuria, 2).

———. Japanese jurisdiction in the South Manchuria railway areas. Baltimore, Johns Hopkins Press; London, H. Milford, Oxford University Press, 1931. xxxv, 332 p. incl. double map. (His Japan's jurisdiction and international legal position in Manchuria, 3).

Japanese Occupation
General Works

[BISSON, THOMAS ARTHUR] 1900-  Japan and Manchoukuo.  New York, Foreign
Policy Association, [1932] p. [87]-98. (Foreign policy reports. 7:8 June 22,
1932).

CHENG, HSIAO-HSÜ, 鄭孝胥, 1859-1938. Wang tao (the kingly way).  [Dairen,
Printed by the Manchuria daily news, 1934] 41 p. port.

CHINA. Ministry of Foreign Affairs. How ''Manchoukuo'' was created. Nanking,
Waichiaopu, The Intelligence and Publicity Department, 1933. 66 p. (China.
Ministry of foreign affairs. Information Bull. 7).

CHINA UNITED PRESS, Shanghai. The puppet state of ''Manchoukuo.''  Shanghai,
China United Press, 1935. viii, 278 p. fold. map (''China today'' series.[4]).

COLLIER, D.    M.    B. Manchoukuo, jewel of Asia, [by] D. M. B. Collier
and Lt. Col. C. L'E. Malone.·  London, G. Allen and Unwin [1936] [7]-267,
[1] p. illus. (map) plates. (incl. front.).

——. Le Mandchoukuo, joyau de l'Asie. Naissance d'un pays, population,
moeurs, etc. du Mandchoukuo, par D. M. B. Collier et Lt. Col. C. L'E. Malone. Traduit par Robert Waldteufel. Paris, Payot, 1938. 234 p. map, (Bib-
liotèque géographique).

[DORFMAN, BEN DAVID] 1902-  Two years of the Manchoukuo régime.  New
York, Foreign Policy Association [1934]  p. [169-180. illus. (map) (Foreign
policy reports. 10:14 September 12, 1934).

ENDO, R. Japan, China and Manchukuo; the kingly way. Tokyo, The Eastern
Asiatic Society Press, 1933. 157 p.

FISCHER, JACOB. Mandschukuos Kampf und Sieg.  Hamburg, O. Meissner,
1933. 3, 4, 342 p. front., plates, ports., maps (1 fold.) fold facsim., col.
diagr..

[GORMAN, GEORGE WILLIAM ALOYSIUS] 1888-  Manchoukuo, the world's
newest nation; facing facts in Manchuria, by P. Ohara [pseud.]  Moukdon
[Darien, Printed by the Manchuria Daily News] 1932. ii, 5, 168 p. ports.

——. Freedom: Manchuria's plea for independence.  Mukden, Manchu Hsieh-
ho hui, 1935. 32 p.

HISHIDA, SEIJI GEORGE, 1874-  The Manchoukuo question in its wider aspects,
with special reference to John Bassett Moore's discussion of international affairs.  Tokyo [Maruzen]1934. iii-ix, [2], 86 p., port.

HUSSEY, HARRY, 1882-  ''Manchoukuo'' in relation to world peace. Things not
told in the report of the Commission of Enquiry.  [Geneva, 1932] 113 p.

ISHII, KIKUJIRO, 1866-1945. Manchoukuo and the Manchu question.  Tokyo,
League of Nations Association of Japan, 1932. 18 p.

JAPANESE CHAMBER OF COMMERCE OF NEW YORK. Manchukuo; the founding
of the new state in Manchuria.  New York, Japanese Chamber of Commerce,
1933. 44 p. front. (fold. map).

KAWAKAMI, KIYOSHI KARL, 1875-  Manchoukuo, child of conflict.  New York,
Macmillan, 1933.  viii, 311 p. plates, ports., diagr.

KWANTUNG LEASED TERRITORY. General outline of the administration of the
Kwantung Government.  Port Arthur, South Manchuria, 1932. 29 p. 1st ed.
1926. 62 p.

——. The Kwantung government, its functions and works, 1934. The Kwantung
government, January, 1934.  [Dairen, The Manchuria Daily News, 1934] vii,
210 p. plates, maps (part fold.) tables (part fold.) 1st ed. 1929.

——. Ordinance no. 17, issued by the Government of the Leased Territory of
Kwangtung on April 25th, 1933, for the control of opium in the South Manchuria Railway Zone. Communicated by the representative of Japan. Geneva, 1934. 4 p. At head of title: League of Nations. Advisory Committee on
Traffic in Opium and Other Dangerous Drugs.

LEWISOHN, WILLIAM. Manchoukuo revisited; a study of the political and com -
mercial aspect of Manchoukuo made on an extensive tour of the country.

Shanghai, North China Daily News and Herald, 1935. 43 p. illus.

MANCHOUKUO, a pictorial record. Le Mandchoukouo, chronique illustrée.
[Tokyo and Osaka, Asahi Shimbun Pub. Co., 1934] 329 p., incl. plates.

MANCHOUKUO, a comprehensive pictorial presentation. Tokyo, Japan, Asahi
shimbun sha, 1940. [169] p. illus.(1 col.).

MANCHOUKUO. Bureau of Information. An outline of the Manchoukuo empire.
1939. Dairen, Manchuria Daily News [1939] 241 p.

MANCHURIA. Manciu-cuo vigoroso nei fotografi. Die junge Mandschurei in Bildern. Young Manchoukuo in pictures. [Hsinking? 1938] 119 plates on 50 l.
1 col. mounted illus.

MANCHURIA. Dept. of Civil Affairs. Historical significance of the establishment of Manchukuo. Compiled and published by the Department of civil affairs,
the Manchukuo government, March 10, 1932. [n.p., 1932] cover-title, 24 p.

MANCHURIA. Dept. of Foreign Affairs. A genera' outline of Manchoukuo. Hsinking, 1932. 71 p.

――――. Aperçu général sur le Mandchoukouo. Hsinking, 1932. 72 p.

――――. Manchoukuo and the League of Nations. Hsinking, 1933. Cover-title, 36 p.
(Department of foreign affairs. Publications. Series, 4).

――――. Manchoukuo: handbook of information. Published by Bureau of information and publicity, Department of Foreign Affairs, Manchoukuo government
Hsinking [Dairen, Printed by the "Manshu nippo-sha"] 1933. vi, 161, [1] p.
plates, ports., fold. map, fold, diagr.

――――. The voice of the people of Manchoukuo. Compiled by Bureau of information and publicity, Department of Foreign Affairs. Hsinking [1933?] cover-
title, iii, [2], 38, [178] p.

MANCHURIA. General Affairs Board. Manchoukuo, a pictorial sketch. [Hsin-
king? 1937] cover-title, [36] p. of illus. (incl. facsims.).

MANCHURIA. State Council. An outline of the Manchoukuo empire, 1939. Edited
by the Bureau of information, Manchoukuo State council, Hsinking. Dairen,
Manchuria Daily News [1939] 241 p.

THE MANCHURIA DAILY NEWS. Manchoukuo gives birth to new culture; questions and answers, 1940. Hsinking, Manchoukuo, The Manchuria Daily News
[1940] 80 p. plates, ports.

――――. Souvenir enthronement supplement, March 1st, 1934. Issued in celebration of the enthronement of His Majesty P'u Yi as first emperor of the Empire of Manchoukuo. [Hsinking] 1934. 102 p.

――――. Manchoukuo-Soviet border issues, compiled by Noboru Hidaka. Dairen,
Manchuria Daily News, 1938. 261 p. illus. (map) plates.

――――. Nomonhan incident; brief account of the recent clash between the invading
Soviet-Outer Mongol forces and Manchoukuo-Japanese troops along the Outer
Mongolia-Manchoukuo frontier; a vivid report of a foreign correspondent
from the scene of the incident. Dairen, Manchuria Daily News, 1939. 24 p.
illus., plates, map.

――――. The same. Manchoukuo-Outer Mongolia border clashes. 2d issue; June-
July, 1939. Dairen, Manchuria Daily News [1939] 47 p. plates, map.

――――. Progressing Manchoukuo. [Dairen?] The Manchuria Daily News, 1940.
61 p. illus.

MATSUI, IWANE, 1878- La question de la Mandchourie et de son indépendance;
quelques reflexions sur des points fondamentaux. The question of Manchuria
and its independence; some reflections on fundamental points. Genève, Kundig, 1932. [3]-63, [4] p.

REA, GEORGE BRONSON, 1869-1936. Manchukuo; back to first principles! Address delivered before an assembly in the hall of the Athénée at Geneva, on
October 14, 1932. Genève, Kundig, 1932. 5-43, [1] p.

――――. Le Mandchoukouo. Revenons aux principes. Conférence faite à Genève,
le 14 Octobre 1932. Genève, Kundig, 1932. 44 p.

――――. The independence of Manchoukuo. Paper read before the members of the legal fraternity of Gamma eta gamma, the George Washington law school, Washington, D.C., on November 23, 1933. [Washington? D.C., 1933] 5-71p.

———. The case for Manchoukuo. New York, London, D. Appleton-Century, 1935. xi, 3-425 p. front., plates, ports., fold. map.

SAITO, HIROSI, 1886-1939. Japan and Manchuria: speech at the Fabian summer school, Rowledge, Nr. Burnham, Surrey, [Eng.] 26th August, 1932. [London] 1932. 14 p.

———. Manchukuo, the new-born state: an address at Columbia University School of Journalism, October 11, 1932. [Washington] 1932. 15 p.

———. Future prospects of Manchukuo: an address at the University of Kentucky, December 9, 1932. [Washington] 1932. 11 p.

SCHERER, JAMES AUGUSTIN BROWN, 1870- Manchukuo: a bird's-eye view. Tokyo, Hokuseido Press, 1933. 145 p., front., plates, ports., 2 maps (1 fold.) 2 facsim. (1 fold.).

SOUTH MANCHURIA RAILWAY COMPANY. Answering questions on Manchuria. [Dairen] 1939. x, 81 p. illus., col. maps (1 fold) 1st ed. 1936.

———. A pictorial outline of Manchuria. Dairen, 1939. 1 v.

U.S. ARMY. Forces in the Far East. Small wars and border problems. Prepared by Military History Section. [n.p.] Distributed by Office of the Chief of Military History, Dept. of the Army [1956- 1 v. maps, tables. (Its Japanese studies on Manchuria, v. 11).

U.S. DEPT. OF STATE. "Manchukuo" precedents. Official documents covering the period 1932-1938 concerning the American policy toward Manchuria. Washington [1938] 1 v. (Various pagings).

U.S. OFFICE OF STRATEGIC SERVICES. Research and Analysis Branch. Programs of Japan in Manchukuo, with biographies. Assemblage #53. Honolulu, 1945. 2v. (Its R and A 3117).

VÈVRE, E de. La reconnaissance de jure de la régence de Mandchourie et le Traité des neuf puissances. Paris, Rousseau, 1932. [7]-137 p.

WONG, WILLIAM. Henry Pu Yi and the Japanese, 1924-1945; a study in puppetry. Berkeley, 1951. iv, 103 l. Thesis-Univ. of California

WOODHEAD, HENRY GEORGE WANDESFORDE, 1883- A visit to Manchukuo. Shanghai, Mercury Press [1932] 112 p. front., plates, ports., fold. map.

WOU, P. 吳本中, 1904- La vérité sur la Mandchourie. Préface de m. Ch. Rousseau. Paris, A. Pedone, 1936. x, [5]-291 p. fold. map.

YANAIHARA, TADAO. Manshu mondai. Problem of Manchuria. Tokyo, Iwanami, 1936. 2, 2, 278, [4] p.

## Treaties, Etc.

CARNEGIE ENDOWMENT FOR INTERNATIONAL PEACE. Division of International Law. Manchuria, treaties and agreements. Washington, The Endowment, 1921. xiv, 220 p. fold. map. (Pamphlet series of the Carnegie endowment for international peace. Division of international law, 44).

MANCHURIA. Treaties. Agreement for the cession to Manchoukuo of the rights of the Union of Soviet Socialist Republics concerning the North Manchuria Railway (Chinese Eastern Railyway). Tokyo, March 23, 1935. (In American journal of international law. Concord, N.H., 1936. v. 30. suppl., p. 85-104).

———. Freundschaftsvertrag zwisch Mandschukuo und Deutschen Reich. Tokyo, 1938. 12 p.

———. Friendship, commerce and navigation between Manchoukuo and Italy. Tokyo, 1938. 12 p.

———. Accord entre le gouvernement d'Italie, le gouvernement du Japon et le gouvernement du Mandchoukuo pour regler les exhanges commerciaux et les paiements y afferents entre l'Italie d'une part et le Japon et le Mandchoukuo d'autre part. Tokyo, 1938. 24 p.

———. Notes exchanged between Manchoukuo and Poland relating to the question of rendering normal, the legal status of respective consulates. Tokyo, 1938. 27 p.

———. Records of treaties, conventions, etc. between Manchoukuo and foreign states. v. 1. Hsinking, Foreign Office, 1941. 643 p. fold plates.

## Laws, Statutes, etc.

KUSABA AND COMPANY. Patents, utility models, designs and trade marks in Japan, Manchukuo and China, 1935. Tokyo, 1935. 31 p. (Circular no. J. 17).

MANCHURIA. LAWS, STATUTES, etc. Proclamations, statements and communications of the Manchoukuo government. Hsinking, 1932. Cover-title, 22 p. (Department of foreign affairs. Publications. Series, 1).

———. The Chief executive's proclamation, the Organic law of Manchoukuo and other laws governing various government offices. Hsinking, [1932] cover-title, 45 p. (Department of foreign affairs. Publications. Series, 2).

———. The Patent law and the Disign law of Manchoukuo. [Hsinking?] The Patent Invention Office [1936?] cover-title, 60 p.

NAKAMATSU PATENT AND LAW OFFICE, Tokyo. Manchukuo. Patent, design and trade mark laws with regulations for their enforcement. Tokyo, Nakamatsu International Patent and Law Office [pref. 1936] ii, 124 p.

VOGT, KARL, 1878-  ed. and tr. Das neue Mustergesetz fuer Manschukuo (Gebrauchsmuster- und Geschmacksmuster-gesetz) Übers. von Karl Vogt. Tokio, 1936. 14 p.

———. Das neue Patentgesetz fuer Manschukuo, übers. von Karl Vogt. Tokio, 1936. 44 p.

## Year-books and Directories

The DIRECTORY of Manchukuo.     満洲商工年鑑 .  Dairen, Orient Pub. Co., 1938-39. 1 v. illus.

JAPAN-MANCHOUKUO YEAR BOOK, 1934-1941. Tokyo, Japan-Manchoukuo Year Book Co., 1934-1941. 8 v. plates, maps, tables, diagrs.

ORIENT YEAR BOOK, 1942. Tokyo, Asia Statistic Co., 1942. 1364 p. plates, maps, tables, diagrs. [a continuation of Japan-Manchoukuo Year Book].

## Economic Conditions
### General Works

ADACHI, KINNOSUKÉ, 1871-1952. Manchuria; a survey. New York, R. M. Mc-Bride, 1925. xvii, 401 p. front. (port.) plates, maps (part fold.).

———. Tales of three cities in Manchuria. South Manchuria Railway Co., 1933. Tokyo, Herald Press, 1933. 27 p. illus.

BANK OF KOREA. Economic history of Manchuria, compiled in commemoration of the decennial of the Bank of Chosen. Seoul, 1921. x, 303 p. plates, ports., fold. map, tables.

BAYLIN, J.  R. L'est chinois; historique. Contrats divers et documentation economique succincts sur la Mandchourie. Pékin, Éditions A. Nachbaur, 1929. 54 p. plates, map, (Le droit chinois moderne, 3).

CENTRAL BANK OF MANCHOU. The Central bank of Manchou and appendix of laws pertaining thereto. 1935 (revised) Hsinking, The Central Bank of Manchou [1936?] iii, 91 p.; 22p. plates (part col.) diagr. 1st ed. 1932. 35 p.

———. Semiannual report on economic conditions in Manchoukuo. 1937-1939. Hsinkiang, 1938-40. 3 v.

———. Manchoukuo's business and finance, March 1937. Hsinking, The Central Bank of Manchou, [1937] 23 p.

CHEN, CHAO-SHUNG, 陳兆熊. La vie du paysan en Mandchourie (les trois provinces de l'est de la Chine). Paris, P. Bossuet, 1937. 160 p. diagr. Thèse-Univ. de Paris.

CHIH, PIAO, 際彪, 1885-    A general outline of Manchoukuo's construction programme. [Tokyo] The Foreign Affairs Association of Japan, 1933. 18 p. illus. (maps) pl.

CHINESE EASTERN RAILWAY. Economic Bureau. Statistical year book. Harbin, 1923-1935. 13 v. tables.

CHUGAI SHOGYO SHIMPO. Industrial expansion of Japan and Manchoukuo. 1936 edition. Tokyo, Chugai shogyo shimpo-sha [1935] 5-108 p. incl. illus., mounted col. plates.

DAIREN. CHAMBER OF COMMERCE AND INDUSTRY. Economic conditions in Manchuria. Dairen, Dairen Chamber of Commerce and Industry, 1934. cover-title, 60 p.

DALBANK. The Far Eastern bank "Dalbank" (Established in Harbin); a review of its activities during the first five-year period of its existence, 1923-1928. Harbin, 1928. Cover-title, 13, [1] p.

FEIS. HERBERT, 1893-    The international trade of Manchuria. New York, Carnegie Endowment for International Peace, Division of Intercourse and Education [1931] 68 p. illus. (map) diagrs. (Studies in world economy, 3).

The FOREIGN trade of Manchoukuo since its inception. [Dairen] The South Manchuria Railway Co. [1939] cover-title, 55 p. incl. tables.

HOU, SHU-T'UNG, 侯樹彤. Japanese bank-notes in Manchuria. Peiping, 1931. 28 p. (Yenching Political Science Ser., 13).

HSIAO, CHÜ, 蕭蘧, 1897-1947. Manchuria; a statistical survey of its resources, industires, trade, railways, and immigration. Preliminary paper prepared for the third biennial conference of the Institute of Pacific Relations, October 28 to November 9, 1929. Tientsin, 1929. 52, [2] p. incl. tables (part fold.) 2 fold. maps.

ÎASHNOV, EVGENÏÏ EVGEN'EVICH. Chinese agriculture in northern Manchuria, by E. E. Yashnov. Digest and translation by Lewis L. Lorwin. [Honolulu?] Institute of Pacific Relations, 1929. 16 numb. l.

JAPAN ECONOMIC FEDERATION. Economic and financial conditions in Japan, Manchoukuo and China; addresses by Kazuo Aoki. Toyotaro Yuki, Naoki Hoshino, Tetsusaburo Tanaka [and] Shih-ching Wang, 汪時璟. Tokyo, Japan Economic Federation, 1939 vii, 58 p. (East Asia economic intelligence series, 2).

————. The heavy industry of Manchoukuo; present conditions of the exploitation of natural resources in Manchoukuo. Tokyo, Japan Economic Federation, 1940. viii, 83 p., fold. map, tables (1 fold.) (East Asia economic intelligence series, 3.).

————. The currency and finance of Manchoukuo. Tokyo, Foreign Relations Council, Japan Economic Federation, 1940.    vi,    35, [1] p., incl. tables. (East Asia economic intelligence series, no. 7).

KANAI, KIYOSHI, 1884-    Economic development in Manchoukuo. Prepared for the sixth conference of the Institute of Pacific Relations to be held at Yosemite, California, August 15th to 29th, 1936. Tokyo, Japan Council, Institute of Pacific Relations, 1936.    v, 3-69 p. fold. tab. (Japan council papers, 15).

KINNEY, HENRY WALSWORTH, 1879-    Modern Manchuria. Rev. ed. Dairen, 1929. viii, 87 p. plates, fold, map.

————. Manchuria today. Dairen [Osaka, Printing by Hamada Printing Co., ] 1930. 100 p. plates, fold. map.

KRAMER, IRVING I. Japan in Manchuria. Tokyo, Foreign Affairs Association of Japan, 1954. 54 p.

MAIER, HANS, 1897-    Die Mandschurei in Weltpolitik und Weltwirtschaft. Leipzig, Deutsche wissenschaftliche Buchhandlung, 1930. 59 p. plates (Added t.-p.: Weltwirtschaftliche vorträge und abhandlungen, 9).

MANCHURIA. Economic construction program of Manchukuo. Issued on its first anniversary by the Manchukuo government, March 1, 1933. New York office of the South Manchuria Railway Co. [New York? 1933] cover-title, 3-15 p. fold. map.

————. Dept. of Finance. Annual returns of the foreign trade of Manchoukuo, 外國貿易統計年報. 1932-1937. [Hsinking? 1933-1938. 6 v. tables.

————. Monthly returns of the foreign trade of Manchoukuo, 外國貿易統計月報. 1933-Aug, 1940. Hsinking, 1933-1940. 8 v. map, tables.

————. General survey of conditions in Manchoukuo, with special emphasis on economic development. Hsinking [Printed by Kōlokutosho Printing Works] 1936. cover-title 59 p. incl. tables.

————. Foreign Office. Economic conditions in Manchoukuo. [Hsinking?] 1940. 111 p.

MANCHURIAN AFFAIRS INFORMATION BUREAU. Industry of Manchoukuo; a rough sketch. Hsinking, 1934. 40 p.

THE MANCHURIA DAILY NEWS. Manchoukuo's natural resources and their development; questions and answers. Appendix: The five-year industrial development plan of Manchoukuo. [Dairen] The Manchuria Daily News [1939] 64 p. plates.

————. Special companies in Manchoukuo; their mission and activities. [Dairen] The Manchuria Daily News, 1940. 108 p. plates.

THE MANCHURIAN STAPLE PRODUCE YEAR-BOOK, 重要物產統計年鑑 1st-2nd, 1909/1920, 1920/1923. Dairen, Manchurian Staple Produce Merchants Association, 1921-1924. 2 v. tables, diagrs.

MANSHU TOKUSAN CHUOOKAI, Hsinking. Agricultural products in Manchouko. Hsinking, The Manchurian Agricultural Products Institute [193- ] 32 p.

MATSUOKA, YOSUKE, 1880-1946. Economic co-operation of Japan and China in Manchuria and Mongolia, its motives and basic significance. [Dairen? Manchuria, 1929?] 19 p.

————. An address on Manchuria, its past and present, and Reply to Prof. Shuhsi-Hsu's, 徐㹠庶, criticisms and observations. Third biennial conference, Institute of Pacific Relations. Kyoto, Japan, 1929. 30 p.

————. La Mandchourie, hier et aujourd'hui; exposé de la politique japonaise, suivi de sa réponse aux critiques du professeur Shuhsi-Hsu. Traduction et préface de N. Sakamoto. [Paris, N.R. Money, imprimeur, 1931] cover-title, 5-47, [1] p.

————. Building up Manchuria. Tokyo, The Herald of Asia [1938?] 247 p. front., plates, ports.

[THE ORIENTAL ECONOMIST] Manchuria industrial development corporation. [Tokyo, The Oriental Economist of Japan, 1938] 50 p.

ROYAL INSTITUTE OF INTERNATIONAL AFFAIRS. Notes on the economic consequences of recent events in Manchuria, compiled in the Study groups department of Chatham House. Prepared for the fifth bi-annual conference of the Institute of Pacific Relations, to be held at Banff, Canada, August 14th to 28th, 1933. London, Royal Institute of International Affairs [1933] cover-title, 29 (i.e. 30) numb. l. incl. tables.

SAKATANI, YOSHIRO, baron, 1863-1941. Manchuria: a survey of its economic development based in part on material prepared under the supervision of Baron Y. Sakatani, revised by Grover Clark. Prepared for the Division of Economics and History of the Carnegie Endowment for International Peace. [New York, 1932] xv, 305 l. tables.

SCHUMPETER, ELIZABETH BOODY, ed. The industrialization of Japan and Manchuko, 1930-1940: population, raw materials and industry. Contributors: G.C. Allen, E.F. Penrose, M.S. Gordon [and] E.B. Schumpeter. New York, Macmillan, 1940. xxviii, 944 p. tables (5 on 3 fold. l. in pocket) diagr.

SIMON, PAUL. L'organisation économique et sociale du Manchoukuo. Louvain, Secrétariat de la Société scientifique, 1937. 208 p. fold. maps.

SOUTH MANCHURIA RAILWAY COMPANY. Manchuria, where east meets west. [New York] South Manchuria Railway [c1924] 20, [1] p. illus.

————. Manchuria, land of opportunities. Illustrated from photographs, with diagrams and maps. Rev. ed. New York, South Manchuria railway company,

1924. ix, 98 p. plates, fold. map. 1st ed. 1922.

———. [1st]-8th report on progress in Manchuria, 1907/28-1936. Dairen, The South Manchuria Railway Co., 1929-1937. 6 v. plates, ports., fold. maps, fold. plans, col. diagrs.

———. Agriculture of Manchuria and Mongolia. Dairen, Agriculture Office, South Manchuria Railway Co. [1928] iii, 82 p. incl. tables. plates.

———. Bean oil industry in Manchuria. Dairen, South Manchuria Railway Co., 1936. 38 numb. l. incl. tables.

———. Immigration of Japanese farmers into Manchuria. [Dairen] South Manchuria Railway Co. [1938?] cover-title, 42 p.

———. New York Office. Economic construction program of Manchukuo. New York, 1933. 15 p.

TACHI, SAKUTARŌ, 1874-    The principle of the open door in China and Manchoukuo. [Tokyo? Foreign Affairs Association of Japan, 1937] 33 p.

THIEL, ERICH. Mandschukuo; Führer durch die mandschurische Wirtschaft. Hrsg. von Hiyoshi Kato; bearb. von Erich Thiel. Königsberg (Pr) Ost-Europa-Verlag [1937] vi, 79 p. fold. map.

WOLFF, OTTO, firm, Cologne. [Manchurian projects; commercial papers. n. p., 193-?] Microfilm copy. Negative. Collation of the original. 1 v. (various pagings).

YAMANARI, KYOROKU. The monetary policy of Manchoukuo. Prepared for the sixth conference of the Institute of Pacific Relations to be held at Yosemite, California, August, 1936. Tokyo, Japan Council, Institute of Pacific Relations, 1936. 24 p. (Japanese council papers, 13).

YEH, KUNG-CH'O, 葉恭綽, 1880-    An industrial tour around Manchuria. Peking, Office of the High Industrial Commissioner, 1921. 126 p. illus.


1945-


CHAO, KUO-CHÜN, 趙國鈞, 1918-.  Northeast China (Manchuria) to-day.  Cambridge, Center for International Studies, Massachusetts Institute of Technology, 1953. 131 p.

CHENG, CHO-YUAN, 鄭竹園. Anshan Steel Factory in Communist China.  Kowloon, Union Research Institute [1955] 98 p. (Communist China problem research series, EC9).

CHINESE ASSOCIATION FOR THE UNITED NATIONS. A report on Russian destruction of our industries in the North-eastern Provinces. [Taipei] 1952. 27 p. (Unachina publications, series l, 7).

CLUBB, OLIVER EDMUND, 1901-    Chinese communist development programs in Manchuria, with a supplement on Inner Mongolia. New York, International Secretariat, Institute of Pacific Relations, 1954. 46 p. tables. (Secretariat paper, 3).

KAO KANG, 高崗, 1902-1955. La reconstruction économique du nord-est de la Chine; titre original: Mettons-nous à l'avant du front de la reconstruction économique du Nord-Est. [Un rapport fait le 13 mars 1950 au 1er Congrès des délégués du Parti communiste chinois du Nord-Est] Pékin, Éditions en langues étrangères, 1950. ii, 46 p.

PAULEY, EDWIN WENDELL, 1903-    Report on Japanese assets in Manchuria to the President of the United States, July 1946. [Washington, Govt. Print. Off., 1946] 1 v. (various pagings) illus., maps (part fold.).

U. S. DEPT. OF STATE. Division of Research for the Far East. Economic significance of the Nationalist defeat in Manchuria; a short-term appraisal. Washington, 1948. 14 p. (Its OIR report No. 4821) Mimeographed.

———. The economic importance of Manchuria to the United States. Washington, 1948. 55 p. (Its. OIR report No. 4160) Mimeographed.

WATROUS, GEORGE D. Kwantung leased territory, a brief summary of its economy. Prepared for the Foreign Economic Administration. [Washington]

1945. 9 p. incl. tables. (Japanese trade studies).

## South Manchuria Railway

BAYLIN, J.    R. Chemins de fer de Mandchouri. Lignes parallèles au Sud-
Mandchourien- le Kirin-Hoeining.  Pékin, Impr. de la "Politique de Pékin,"
1932. 36 p. map. (Collection de la "Politique de Pékin").

CHANG, PAO-YUAN, 張寶源, 1905-  Die Eisenbahnen in der Mandschurei.
Leipzig, 1930. 100 p. map. Diss.-Univ. Leipzig.

CHANG, PIN-YANG, 張炳揚. Étude sur la chemin de fer chinois de l'Est.   Nancy, Impr. Grandville, 1932. 222 p. Thése-Univ. de Nancy.

HOUANG, TCHANG-SIN, 黄昌愼. Le problème du chemin de fer chinois de l'Est.
Paris, Les écrivains réunis, 1927. 457 p. fold. maps. Thèse- Univ. de Paris.

KADONO, CHOKYURO, 1867-   Development of railways in Manchoukuo. Prepared for the sixth conference of the Institute of Pacific Relations to be held
at Yosemite, California, August 15th to 29th, 1936. Tokyo, Japan Council,
Institute of Pacific Relations, 1936. 27 p. front. (fold. map) (Japanese council papers, 12).

KANAI, KIYOSHI, 1884-  The South Manchuria Railway Company's part in the
economic development of Manchoukuo. Prepared for the sixth conference of
the Institute of Pacific Relations to be held at Yosemite, California, August
15 to 29, 1936.  Tokyo, Japan Council, Institute of Pacific Relations, 1936.
31 p. (Japanese council papers, 10).

KENNAN, GEORGE, 1845-1924.  Harriman's Far Eastern plans; the inside history of the American attempt to gain control of the South Manchuria Railway
as a link in the Harriman round-the-world transportation system. (Extracted
from "E. H. Harriman," a biography by George Kennan, published by Houghton Mifflin, Boston and New York) [n. p., n. d. ] Microfilm copy (positive) Collation of the original, as determined from the film: 225-229 p. port. Detached
from Far Eastern Review, April 1923.

KINGMAN, HARRY LEES, 1892-   Effects of Chinese nationalism upon Manchurian railway developments, 1925-1931.  Berkeley, University of California
Press, 1932. cover-title xi, 97 p., fold. map. (University of California publications in international relations. 3:1).

KINNEY, HENRY WALSWORTH, 1879-   Manchuria and the South Manchuria
Railway Company.  Dairen, The Manchuria Daily News, 1927. 57 p. plates,
fold. map.

———. Modern Manchuria and the South Manchuria Railway Company. [ Tokyo,
Printed by the Japan Advertiser Press] 1928. viii, 91, [1]p. plates, fold. map.

———. La Mandchourie moderne et la Campagnie du Chemin de Fer Sud-Mandchourien.  Paris, 1929? 89 p. plates, fold. col. map.

SOUTH  MANCHURIA RAILWAY COMPANY.  South Manchuria Railway.  Dairen,
The South Manchuria Railway Co.,  1923. Cover-title, vi, 185 p. illus. fold.
map. 1st ed. 1920.

———. A brief survey of the Manchoukuo state railways. 2d ed.  Mukden, 1936.
2, 51 p. 1st ed. 1934.

———. South Manchuria Railway, the pioneer on the Continent.  Tokyo, 193-  90 p.

———. The same; October, 1939.  Dairen, South Manchuria Railway Co [ 1939]
5-57 p. illus. (incl. map) 1935 ed. 54 p.

TCHENG, KUI-I, 鄭揆一. La Cie du chemin de fer Sud-Mandchourien et l'em-
prise japonaise en Mandchourie, préface de son excellence le dr. Wellington
Koo.  Paris, P. Bossuet, 1939. 4, [9]-316 p. map, diagr.

## Chinese Eastern Railway

CHANG, TAO-HSING,  張道行, 1908-   International controversies over the Chinese Eastern Railway.  Shanghai, Commercial Press, [ 1936] ix, 289 p. Thesis - University of Iowa, 1934.

CHINESE EASTERN RAILWAY. An abridged outline of the historical survey of the Chinese Eastern Railway. Introduction and Chapter 1, 1896-1923. Compiled by E. X. Nilus. [Harbin, 192-   ] 1 v. (various pagings).

———. Chinese Eastern Railway, 1920-1923. Harbin, 1924. 25 p. incl. tables, diagrs.

———. North Manchuria and the Chinese Eastern Railway. Harbin, C. E. R. Printing Office, 1924. xvii, 454 p. incl. illus., ports., diagrs. plates, maps (1 fold.) plan.

———. The Chinese Eastern Railway and its zone. Harbin, 1928. 32 l. incl. mpas, diagrs. (part col. ). 1st ed. 1923.

[———]. L'Est chinois, historique. Contrats divers et documentation économique succincte sur la Mandchourie.    Pékin, A. Nachbaur, 1929. 54 p. incl. tables. plates, map. (Encyclopédie des questions chinoises).

———. Germany-Lithuania-Latvia-Estonia-China-Japan. Freight through traffic in transit via U. S. S. R. (German-Far Eastern traffic). Harbin, 1932. 20 p. incl. tables, fold. map.

———. Land Dept. Transactions. Bulletin, nos. 1-2. 2 v.

FOREIGN POLICY ASSOCIATION, New York. The Chinese Eastern Railway. [New York, Foreign Policy Association, 1926] 10 numb. l. illus. (map) (Information service 2:1, February 27, 1926).

SOKOLSKY, GEORGE EPHRAIM, 1893-    The story of the Chinese Eastern Railway. Shanghai, North-China Daily News and Herald, 1929. 68 p.

TONG, HOLLINGTON K., 董顯光, 1887-    Facts about the Chinese Eastern Railway situation (with documents) Pub. under the auspices of the Committee for Public Enlightenment of the Northeastern Provinces. [n. p., 1929] [3]-183 p. plates, port.

TSAO, LIEN-EN, 曹勵恆. The Chinese Eastern Railway - an analytical study. Shanghai, The Bureau of Industrial and Commercial Information, Ministry of Industry, Commerce and Labor, [1930] cover-title, ii, 198 p. fold. map.

YAVDYNSKY, J    A The Chinese-Eastern Railway problem in contemplation of law. Shanghai, 1934. 35 p.

YU, Y. C. FISHER, 余英傑, 1899-    The Chinese Eastern Railway; its redemption by the Chinese government, and the financial involvements. Cambridge, Mass. 1925. Cover-title 19 p. illus. map.


## Social Conditions

KOBAYASHI, MASATOSHI. Manners and customs in Manchoukuo, compiled by M. Kobayashi and N. Hidaka. Dairen, Manchuria Daily News, 1942. 121 p. illus.

THE MANCHURIA DAILY NEWS. Manchoukuo's policy for the eradication of opium smoking. [Dairen] Printed and published by The Manchuria Daily News, 1939. 25 p. plates.

NAGASHIMA, T. Opium administration in Manchoukuo. Tokyo, South Manchuria Railway Co. 1938. Cover-title, 27 p. Reprinted from Contemporary Manchuria, 3:1.

SHIROKOGOROV, SERGEĬ MIKHAĬLOVICH, 1887-1939. Social organization of the Manchus. A study of the Manchu clan organization. Shanghai, 1924. vi, 194 p. illus. (Royal Asiatic society. North China branch. [Publications] Extra vol. III).

U. S. OFFICE OF STRATEGIC SERVICES. Research and Analysis Branch. Social conditions, attitudes, and propaganda in Manchuria, with suggestions for American orientation toward the Manchurians. [Washington] 1942. 33 p. (Its R. and A no. 295).


## Minorities

JOCHELSON, VLADIMIR IL' ICH, 1855-1937. The Yukaghir and the Yukaghiriz-
    ed Tungus. Leiden, E. J. Brill; New York, G. E. Stechert, 1926. xvi, 469 p.
    illus., xxviii pl., fold. map. (Memoir of the American museun of natural
    history. [vol. xiii, pt. i-iii]).
LATTIMORE, OWEN, 1900-    The Gold tribe, "Fishskin Tatars" of the lower
    Sungari. Menasha, Wis., American Anthropological Association [1933]
    cover-title, 77 p. illus. (incl. plans) (Memoirs of the American anthropolo-
    gical association, 40).
SHIROKOGOROV, SERGEĬ MIKHAĬLOVICH. 1887-1939.    Social organization of
    the northern Tungus, with introductory chapters concerning geographical dis-
    tribution and history of these groups. Shanghai, Commercial Press, 1929.
    xiv,    427 p. illus., col. plates, maps (part fold. ).
———. Psychomental complex of the Tungus. London, K. Paul, Trench, Trub-
    ner, 1935. xvi, 469 p. illus. (incl. music) diagrs.

## Foreign Missions

ANNUAIRES DES MISSIONS CATHOLIQUE DU MANCHOUKUO. Moukden, Impr.
    de la mission catholique, 1935-    2v?
BECKMANN, JOHANNES, 1901-    Heilungkiang; Land, Leute, Mission. Immen-
    see (Schweiz) Verlag des Missionshauses Bethlehem, 1932. 96 p. illus. (incl.
    ports., map).
CHRISTIE, IZA (INGLIS) "Mrs. Dugald Christie. " Jackson of Moukden. Lon-
    don, Hodder and Stoughton [1923] 155 p. front. (port. ) plates. [Master mis-
    sionary series]
———. The Chinese; a study of influences operating in China with special refer-
    ence to Manchuria. Edinburgh, United Free Church of Scotland, [1926] 103
    p. front. plates, maps, (The races beyond series).
———. Dugald Christie of Manchuria, pioneer and medical missionary; the story
    of a life with a purpose, by his wife, with foreword by Sao-ke Alfred Sze.
    London, J. Clarke [1932] 231, [1] p. front., plates, ports.
CONSIDINE, JOHN JOSEPH, 1897-    When the sorghum was high. A narrative
    biography of Father Gerard A. Donovan of Pittsburgh, Pennsylvania, a Mary-
    knoll missioner slain by bandits in Manchukuo. New York, Toronto, Long -
    mans, Green [1941] 177 p., plates, ports.
MACKENZIE, ALEXANDER R. Church and missions in Manchuria; a survey of
    a strategic field. London, World Dominion Press, 1928. viii, [11]-63 p.
    maps (1 fold. ) diagrs. [World dominion survey series].
MORTON, T    Ralph. To-day in Manchuria; the young church in crisis. Lon-
    don, Student Christian Movement Press; New York, Friendship Press, [1939]
    128 p. incl. front. (map).
WEIR, MARGARET (GRILLS). Andrew Weir of Manchuria. London, J. Clarke
    and Co., 1936. 255 p. front. plates, port.

## Art and Archaeology

ANDERSSON, JOHAN GUNNAR, 1874-    The cave-deposit at Sha Kuo T'un in
    Fengtien. Peking, Geological Survey of China, 1923. 58, [26] p. illus.,
    plates (1 col. ) (China. Geological survey. Palaeontologia sinica, ser. D., 1,
    fasc. 1).
[HAMADA, KOSAKU] P'i-tzu-wo; prehistoric sites by the river Pi-liu-ho, South
    Manchuria. Tokyo and Kyoto, The Toa-koko-gaku-kwai, or the Far-Eastern
    Archaeological Society, 1929. [164] p. illus., plates (part col., part fold. 1
    mounted) maps, 2 tables. (1 fold. ) (Archaeologia orientalis., i).
[———]. Hung-shan-hou, Ch'ih-fêng, prehistoric sites at Hung-shan-hou, Ch'ih-
    fêng, in the province of Johel. [Tokyo] The Tôa-kôkogaku-kwai, or the Far
    Eastern Archaeological Society, 1938. [174] p. col. mounted front., illus.,

plates (part col., part double) plan, maps. (Archaeologia orientalis, vi).

HARADA, YOSHITO. Lo-lang, a report on the excavation of Wang Hsü's tomb in the "Lo-lang" province, an ancient Chinese colony in Korea, with the collaboration of King Tazawa; with appendix, On human bones, teeth and hair found in Wang Hsü's tomb, by Dr. K. Kiyono, etc. By order of the Faculty of letters, Tokyo Imperial University. Tokyo, The Toko-shoin, 1930. xi, 53 p; 3, [ 19] p., [ 100] p. illus. (part mounted) plates (part fold., part col.) maps, diagrs.

[————]. Mu-yang-ch'êng; Han and pre-Han sites at the foot of mount Lao-t'ieh in south Manchuria. Tokyo and Kyoto, The Tôa-kôkogaku-kwai, or the Far-Eastern Archaeological Society, 1931. [202] p. illus. (part mounted) plates (part col., part fold.) maps, plans, fold. tab. (Archaeologia orientalis, ii).

[————]. Tung-ching-ch'êng; report on the excavation of the site of the capital of P'o-hai. [Tokyo] The Tôa-kôko-gakukwai, or the Far-Eastern Archaeological Society, 1939. [186] p. illus. (1 col. mounted) plates (part col., part fold.) fold. maps, plans (part fold.) (Archaeologia orientals, v).

KANAZEKI, T. Yang-t'eou-wa; fouille d'un site préhistorique dans la Baie de Hatowan près de Rioziun, en Mandchourie meridionale, par T. Kanazeki, S. Muzune and S. Miyake. Tokyo, La société archéologique de l'Asie orientale, 1942. ii, vii, 8, 4, 7, 162 p. illus., plates, (part. fold) (Archaeologia orientalis, B. Ser., 3).

[MORI, OSAMU] Ying-ch'êng-tzŭ, the Han brick-tomb with fresco-paintings, etc., near Chien-Mu-ch'êng-j, South Manchuria. Tokyo and Kyoto, The Tôakôkogaku-kwai or The Far Eastern Archaeological Society, 1934. [84] p. illus., plates (1 double) map, plans (1 double) (Archaeologia orientalis., iv).

[SHIMADA, SADAHIKO] Nan-shan-li, brick-tombs of the Han dynasty at the foot of Mt. Lao-t'ieh, South Manchuria. Tokyo and Kyoto, The Tôakôkogaku-kai, or the Far-Eastern Archaeological Society, 1933. [176] p. illus., plates (part col.) maps, plans (1 fold.) (Archaeologia orientalis, iii).

TOKUNAGA, SHIGEYASU, 1874- Report of diggings at Ho-chia-kou, Ku-hsiang-tung, Kirin, Manchoukuo. By Shigeyasu Tokunaga and Nobuo Naora. [Tokyo?] 1934. 119, 7 p., illus. (incl. plans) fold. table, plates, (Report of the first Scientific expedition to Manchoukuo 1933. Section ii. Part i).

————. Palaeolithic artifacts excavated at Ho-chia-kou in Ku-hsiang-tung, Manchoukuo, by Shigeyasu Tokunaga and Nobuo Naora. [Tokyo, University Press] 1936. 107 p., illus., plates. (Report of the first Scientific expedition to Manchoukuo 1933. Section vi. Part ii).

## Natural History, Geology and Paleontology

AHNERT, ÉDUARD ÉDUARDOVICH. Mineral resources of North Manchuria. Peiping, [Geological Survey of China] 1929. 262 p.; 2, 2, 108 p. incl. tables (part fold.) plates, maps (part fold.) (China. Geological survey. Memoirs, ser. A, no. 7).

EMOTO, YOSHIKADZU. Myxomycetes of Jehol. [Tokyo, University Press] 1936. 3, [1] p. plates. (Report of the first Scientific expedition to Manchoukuo. Section iv. Part iii [no. 1]).

ENDO, RIUJI. The Canadian and Ordovician formations and fossils of South Manchuria. Washington, Govt. Print. Off., 1932. iii, 152 p. plates, 5 fold. maps (4 in pocket) (Smithsonian institution. United States National museum. Bulletin 164).

————. The Sinian and Cambrian formations and fossils of southern Manchoukuo, by Riuji Endo and Charles Elmer Resser. Mukden, Educational Institute, South Manchuria Railway Co., 1937. ix, 474 p., plates (incl. fold. map) (Manchurian science museum. Bulletin i).

ENDÔ, SEIDÔ. Fossil Juglans from Ku-hsiang-tung, Kirin, Manchoukuo. Tokyo, 1936. 8 p. plates. (Report of the First Scientific expedition to Manchoukuo. Sect. 11, pt. 3).

FLORIN, RUDOLF, 1894- Zur alttertiären Flora der südlichen Mandschurei. Mit Tafel i-iii und 3 Textfiguren. Peking, Published by the Geological Survey of China, 1922. 52, [8] p. illus., plates (China. Geological survey. Palaeontologia sinica, ser. A., vol. i, fasc. 1).

HSINKING. Hsinking Gaiji Club. Hunting in Manchuria, 1940. [Hsinking] 1940. 114 p. plates.

IHARA, KEINOSUKE. Geology of the Hsing-lung-hsien area. [Tokyo?] 1935. 10 p. illus., fold. col. map. (Report of the first Scientific expedition to Manchoukuo. Section ii. Part ii [no. 2] ).

JAPAN. ARMY. General Staff, Kwantung. Geologic columnar sections of the fluviatile deposits in east Manchuria. Translation prepared by Engineer Intelligence Division, Office of the Engineer, edited by E. Paseur. Tokyo, 1956. 128 l. fold. maps (in pocket) diagr. (U.S. Army. Corps of Engineers, Far East. [Pacific Surveys, Reports] 149).

————. The same. Topographic and geologic descriptions of North Manchuria. (Topography and geology of Manchuria, Part II, Chapter 2). Translation prepared by Engineer Intelligence Division, Office of the Engineer, Hdgrs U.S. Army Forces, Far East, Tokyo. Tokyo, 1956. vi, 91 l. illus. fold map. (U.S. Army. Corps of Engineers, Far East. [Pacific Surveys, Reports] 136).

KITAGAWA, MASAO. Lineamenta florae manshuricae; or, an enumeration of all the indigeneous vascular plants hitherto known from Manchurian empire together with their synonymy, distribution and utility. Hsinking [The Institute of Scientific Research, Manchoukuo] 1939. 487 p. illus. plates, map, (Report of the Institute of scientific research, Manchoukuo. v. 3, app. 1).

MATSUSHITA, SUSUMU. On the geology along the southern half of the Antung-Mukden line of the South Manchurian Railway. Ryojun, 1930. 1 v. (Ryojun College of Engineering. Publication, 5).

MATSUZAWA, ISAO. The geology along the route between Ku-pei-kow and Luanping, Je-ho province in Manchuria. [Tokyo?] 1935. 8 p. 1 illus., fold. col. map. (Report of the first Scientific expedition to Manchoukuo. Section ii. Part ii [no. 3]).

MORI, TAMEZO, 1884- A handlist of the Manchurian and eastern Mongolian vertebrata. [Keijo, Korea] 1927. 10, 2, 186, 23 p.

————. The fresh water fishes of Jehol. [Tokyo] 1934. 28, 61 p., 1 illus., plates (1 col.) (Report of the first Scientific expedition to Manchoukuo 1933. Section v. Pt. i).

————. Mammalia of Jehol and the district north of it. Tokyo, 1939. 84, 3, [1] p. incl. illus, tables, plates (part col.) (Report of the first Scientific expedition to Manchoukuo, Section V, division 2, pt. 4).

MURAKAMI, HANZÔ. Geology of the An-shan iron mine district, South Manchuria. With 26 plates and 6 text figures. [Dairen] South Manchuria Railway Co. 1921. 53 p., illus., plates, maps (1 fold.).

NAKAI, TAKENOSHIN, 1882-1952. Plantae novae jeholenses i. By Takenoshin Nakai and Masao Kitagawa. [Tokyo, University Press] 1934. 71 p. plates (part double) (Report of the first Scientific expedition to Manchoukuo 1933. Section iv. Part i).

————. Contributio ad cognitionem florae manshuricae, by Takenoshin Nakai, Masaji Honda, and Masao Kitagawa. [Tokyo, University Press] 1935. 187 p. illus., plates (part double) (Report of the first Scientific expedition to Manchoukuo 1933. Section iv. Part ii).

————. Index florae jeholensis cum appendice: Plantae novae vel minus cognitae ex Manshuria, by Takenoshin Nakai, Masaji Honda, Yoshisuke Satake, and Masao Kitagawa. [Tokyo, University Press] 1936. 108 p., plates (2 double) (Report of the first Scientific expedition to Manchoukuo 1933. Section iv. Part iv).

NIINOMY, KUNITARO. The magnesite deposits of Manchuria. [Lancaster, Pa.

1925] Cover-title, p. 25-53,illus. (incl. map) Thesis-Cornell University.
Reprinted from Economic geology, 20:1, Jan.-Feb. 1925.

SAITO, RINKI. General review of the geology of Manchuria. (Explanatory text
to the geological map of Manchuria and adjacent areas, scale 1:3,000,000).
Translation prepared by Engineer Intelligence Division, Office of the Engineer. Hdgrs. U.S. Army Forces, Far East, Tokyo: Tokyo, 1956. 82 p.
diagrs (part. fold), tables, (U.S. Army. Corps of Engineers, Far East.
[Pacific Surveys, Reports] 124).

SHIMIZU, SABURÔ. The geology of the Cheng-teh area, Je-ho province, Manchuria, by Saburô Shimizu and Isao Matsuzawa. [Tokyo?] 1935. 32 p. incl.
illus., tab. profiles (1 fold.) fold. map. (Report of the first Scientific expedition to Manchoukuo. Section ii. Part ii [no. 1]).

SOUTH MANCHURIA RAILWAY COMPANY. List of plants in Manchuria and Mongolia. [Dairen, South Manchuria Railway Company, Agricultural Bureau,
Dept. of Industry, 1925] 2, 379, 379-381, xxxv p.

――――. Geological Institute. Explanatory text to the geological map of Manchuria.
Dairen, 1925. 1 v. fold. plates (incl. maps, tables, diagrs.).

――――. The geology and mineral resources of South Manchuria. Dairen, Geological Institute, South Manchuria Railway Co., 1926. 25 p. fold. map (in pocket) tables.

――――. Geology and geographical description of northwestern Manchuria. Reports
on studies and research. v. iii. Translation prepared by Engineer Intelligence
Division, Office of the Engineer. Hdgrs. U.S. Army Forces, Far East, Tokyo. Tokyo, 1955. 233 1,maps (part fold.) diagrs (part fold.) tables, (U.S.
Army. Corps of Engineers. Far East Command. [Pacific surveys. Reports]
35).

SOWERBY, ARTHUR DE CARLE, 1885-1954. On a new silurid fish from the Yalu
river, South Manchuria. (In U.S. National museum. Proceedings. Washington, 1922.    v. 60, art. 13. 2 p.).

――――. The naturalist in Manchuria. With photographs and sketches by the author.
Tientsin, Tientsin Press, 1922-23. 5 v. in 3,fronts. (v. 1, col. mounted) illus., plates (2 col. mounted, 1 fold.) fold. maps.

TEILHARD DE CHARDIN, PIERRE. Sur la découverte de couches mésozoiques.
à poissons dans la région de Hailar (Barga). Tientsin, Mission de Sien-
Hsien, 1934. 5 p. (Musée Huang-ho Peiho de Tientsin. Publications, 33).

TOHEIDA, BUNKICHI. Useful minerals and their distribution in South Manchuria.
Dairen, Geological Institute, South Manchuria Railway Co. 1921. 11 p.

VOEIKOV, A. D. [WOEIKOFF, A. D.] Climate conditions of horticulture in Manchuria. Harbin, Chinese Eastern Railway, Land Dept., 1928. 55, 23 p.
plates, map.

――――. What can the Manchurian flora as well as the flora of neighbouring countries give to gardens of Manchuria itself and other countries with cold cli-
mates. With 48 photographs in 16 tables. Harbin, 1941. 134, [5] p. plates.

Bibliographies

[AUSTRALIA. JOINT SERVICE STAFF, Washington, D.C.] The Mongolias; handbook of selected reference material. [n.p.] 1949- 8 pts.

CHANG, CHIH-YI, 張之毅, 1911-   A bibliography of books and articles on Mongolia. [London? 1951?] 49 p. Reprinted from the Journal of the Royal Central Asian Society, London, 37:2-3, 1950.

KNOEPFMACHER, HUGO, 1890-   Outer Monglia; a selection of references. New York, New York Public Library, 1944. 13 p. "Reprinted from the Bulletin of the New York public library, October 1944."

WASHINGTON (STATE) UNIVERSITY. Far Eastern and Russian Institute. Bibliography of the Monglian People's Republic. New Haven, Human Relation Area Files, 1956.   v, 101 p. (Behavior science bibliographies).

Description and Travel

ALIOSHIN, DMITRI. Asian odyssey. New York, H. Holt [c1940] 322 p. front. (port.) plates, facsim.

——. The same. London, Cassell [1941] 311 p. illus. (map)

BARZINI, LUIGI GIORGIO, 1908-   Mongolische Reise, aus dem italienischen übersetzt von Horst Wolf. Mit 48 Bildern. Leipzig, A.H. Payne [1940] 175, [1] p. incl. plates.

BOSSHARD, WALTER, 1892-   Kühles Grasland Mongolei, Zauber und Schönheit der Steppe. Mit 71 Aufnahmen des Verfassers. Zürich, Fretz und Wasmuth [1949] 217 p. plates, ports., maps. [1. Aufl. Berlin, 1938].

——. Sous la yourte mongole, à travers les steppes de l'Asie centrale. Traduit de l'allemand par Marie Laure Rouveyre. Paris, Amiot-Dumont, 1954. 220 p. illus., plates, ports., map. (Bibliothèque des voyages).

CABLE, MILDRED, 1880-1952. The Gobi desert [by] Mildred Cable with Francesca French. London, Hodder and Stoughton [1942]; New York, Macmillan, 1944. 303 p. col. front., plates (part col.) maps (1 fold.).

——. Wall of spears: the Gobi desert by Mildred Cable and Françesca French, illustrated by Joan Kiddell-Monroe. London, Lutterworth Press, [1951] 177 p. illus.

CAMMANN, SCHUYLER, 1912-   The land of the camel; tents and temples of Inner Mongolia. New York, Ronald Press Co. [1951] x, 200 p. illus., ports. mpa.

CRESSEY, GEORGE BABCOCK, 1896-   The Ordos desert of Inner Mongolia. [Granville, Ohio] 1933. Cover-title, [93] p. illus. maps, tables. (Denison University Bull. vol 33, Jour. of scientific laboratories, vol 28, Art. 4).

DETTMANN, HANS EDUARD, 1891-   Mit Sven Hedin durch die Wüste Gobi. Berlin, F. Schneider, 1943. 83 p. illus., ports., map.

DIGBY, GEORGE BASSETT, 1888-   Tigers, gold, and witch-doctors. New York, Harcourt, Brace [c1928] 341 p. front., plates.

HARTMANN, EDGAR VON. Auf tausendjähriger Karawanenstrasse durch die Mongolei; mit 48 Bildern in Tiefdruck. Berlin, Bong [c1933] 185, [1] p., incl. plates, ports., map.

HASLUND-CHRISTENSEN, HENNING, 1896-1948. Tents in Mongolia (Yabonah) adventures and experiences among the nomads of Central Asia; translated from the Swedish by Elizabeth Sprigge and Claude Napier; with 64 plates and a map. New York, E.P. Dutton [c1934] ix-xvi, 366 p. front., illus. (incl. music) plates, ports., maps (1 double).

——. Jabonah, Abenteuer in der Mongolei; mit einem Geleitwort von Sven Hedin; mit zwei Karten. Leipzig, Insel- Verlag, 1944. 302 p., illus. (plan, music) 2 maps on fold. 1.

——. Men and gods in Mongolia (Zayagan) with 57 illustrations and a map. "Translated from the Swedish by Elizabeth Sprigge and Claude Napier." London, K. Paul, 1935. xvi, 358 p. incl. front., illus. plates (1 double; incl. music) ports., fold. map.

——. More travels and adventures in Mongolia; a youth edition of Men and gods in Mongolia; prepared by Eleanor Graham. London, K. Paul, 1936. xi, 331 p. front., 1 illus., plates, ports.

——. Zajagan; Menschen und Götten in der Mongolei. Mit einem Vowort von Sven Hedin. Stuttgart, Union Deutsche Verlag-Gesellschaft [1936] 276 p. chart. front. illus (incl. music), plates, ports.

——. Mongolian journey. [Tr. from the Danish by F. H. Lyon] London, Routledge and K. Paul [1949] x, 232 p. illus., fold. map.

HEDIN, SVEN ANDERS, 1865-1952. Auf grosser Fahrt; meine Expedition mit Schweden, Deutschen und Chinesen durch die wüste Gobi, 1927-28. Mit 110 Bunten und einfarbigen Abbildungen und einer Routenkarte. Keipzig, F. A. Brockhaus, 1929. xii, 346, [1] p. front., illus. (map) plates (part col.)

——. Across the Gobi desert; with 114 illustrations and three maps. "Translated from the German by H. J. Cant." London, G. Routledge 1931; New York York, E. P. Dutton, 1935. xxi, [1],402 p. front., plates, ports., maps (2 fold.)

——. Rätsel der Gobi, die Fortsetzung der grossen Fahrt durch Innerasien in den jahren 1928-1930. Mit 74 Abbildungen nach Aufnahmen und Feichnungen des Verfassers und seiner Mitarbeiter, sowie zwei vierfarbigen Karten. Leipzig, F. A. Brockhaus, 1931. ix, 335 p. front., plates, ports.

——. Riddles of the Gobi desert; with 24 illustrations; translated from the Swedish by Elizabeth Sprigge and Claude Napier. London, Routledge, 1933; New York, E. P. Dutton. 1933. x, 382 p. front., plates, ports.

——. Durch Asiens Wüsten. [Reprint ed.] Wiesbaden, F. A. Brockhaus, 1956. 192 p. illus. plates, ports.

HUC, ÉVARISTE RÉGIS, 1813-1860. Souvenirs d'un voyage dans la Tartarie et le Thibet pendant les années 1844, 1845 et 1846, Nouv. éd. annotée et illustrée par J. M. Planchet. Pékin, Impr. des Lazaristes, 1924. 2 v. fronts. (ports.) fold maps.

——. L'empire chinois, faisant suite à l'ouvrage instítulé Souvenirs d'un voyage dans la Tartarie et le Thibet. Nouv. éd. annotée et illustrée par J. M. Planchet. Pékin, Impr. des Lazaristes, 1926. 2 v.

——. Souvenirs d'un voyage dans la Tartarie, le Thibet et la Chine. Nouv. éd. pub. et préfacée par H. d'Ardenne de Tizac. Paris, Plon-Nourrit et cie [c1925-28] 4 v. fronts. (ports.) fold. maps. [1st ed. Paris, 1850].

——. Travels in Tartary [by] Évariste-Régis Huc (Père Huc) edited by H. d'Ardenne de Tizac, translated from the French by W. Hazlitt. New York and London, A. A. Knopf, 1927. ix, 229, [1] p. front., illus. (incl. map) (Blue jade library).

——. Travels in Tartary. Thibet and China, 1844-1846, translated by William Hazlitt; now edited with an introduction by Professor Paul Pelliot. New-York and London, Harper [1928] 2 v. front. (fold. map) (The Broadway travellers).

——. High road in Tartary. An abridged revision of Abbé Huc's Travels in Tartary, Tibet and China during the years 1844-5-6. Ed. by Julie Bedier [pseud.] Illus. by Joseph Notarpole. New York, C. Scribner, 1948. viii, 219 p. illus. map (on lining-papers).

KOZLOV, PETR KUZ´MICH, 1863-1935. Mongolei, Amdo und die tote Stadt Chara-Choto. Die Expedition der Russischen geographischen Gesellschaft 1907-1909. Mit einem Anhang, 4 Karten und 129 Bildern. Autorisierte Übersetzung aus dem Russischen von dr. L. Breitfuss und Paul Gerhard Zeidler;

mit einem Geleitwort von Sven v. Hedin, hrsg. von Wilhelm Filchner. Berlin, Neufeld und Henius, 1925. xiii, [1] p. 304 p., [2] p. illus. (incl. ports.) maps.

———. Die Mongolei, Amdo und die tote Stadt Chara-choto. [ Übers. von Helmut Sträubig] Leipzig, F.A. Brockhaus, 1955. 424 p. illus., ports., map.

LATTIMORE, OWEN, 1900-  The desert road to Turkestan. Boston, Little, Brown, 1929. xv, 373 p. front., plates.

———. Mongol journeys. New York, Doubleday, Doran; Toronto, McClelland, 1941. x, 324 p. front. (port.) 1 illus., plates.

———. The same. London, J. Cape ; Toronto, Nelson [ 1941] 284 p. incl. front. (port.) 1 illus., plates.

LESSING, FERDINAND, 1882-  Mongolen; Hirten, Briester und Dämonen. Berlin, Klinkhardt und Biermann [ c1935] 211 p. illus.

LIEBERENZ, PAUL KARL, 1893-  Mit Sven Hedin durch Asiens Wüsten, nach dem Tagebuch des Filmoperateurs der Expedition, Paul Lieberenz, bearb. von dr. Arthur Berger; mit 16 Abbildungen. Berlin, Volksverband der Bücherfreunde, Wegweiser-Verlag [ c1932] 383, [1] p. plates, ports.

LIGETI, LAJOS, 1902-  . Rapport préliminaire d'un voyage d'exploration fait en Mongolie chinoise, 1928-1931. Publié par la Société Kőrősi-Csoma. Budapest, Envente chez Otto Harrassowitz, Leipzig, 1933. 64 p. plates (incl. facsims.) fold. map.

MONTELL, GÖSTA, 1899-  Durch die Steppen der Mongolei; mit einem Vorwort von Sven Hedin und zahlreichen Abbildungen nach Aufnahmen des Verfassers. Stuttgart, Union deutsche Verlagsgesellschaft [ 1938] 175, [1] p., front., plates, ports.

ÖBERG, TORGNY. Im Schatten der grossen Mauer. Erlebnisse und Abenteuer in Chinas Grenzland. Aus dem Schwed. übers. von Ilse Meyer-Lüne. Zürich, Orell Fussli, 1957. 222 p. illus.

OSSENDOWSKI, FERDYNAND ANTONI, 1876-1944. Beasts, men, and gods. 32d ed.] New York, Blue Ribbon Books [ 1931, c1922] xii, 325 p. [ 1st ed. New York, Dutton, 1922].

———. Bêtes, hommes et dieux. Traduit de l'anglais par Robert Renard. Paris, Plon-Nourrit [ 1924] [4], iii, 275 p. fold. map.

———. Tiere, Menschen und Götter. Beasts, men and gods. Einzig berichtigte deutsche Übersetzung der amerikanischen Originalausg., hrsg. von Wolf von Dewall. Frankfurt a. Main, Frankfurter Societäts-Druckerei [ c1924] 369 p. illus.

PENSEL, ERNST. Mit dem Mercedes durch Asiens Wüsten. Halb um den Äquator vom Okzident zum Orient. Stuttgart, Riegler, 1956. 194 p. illus. map.

PEVTSOV, MIKHAIL VASIL´EVICH, 1843-1902. Wo man mit Ziegeltee bezahlt; Bericht einer Reise durch die Mongolei und die nördlichen Provinzen des inneren China. [Aus dem Russischen übertragen von Heinz Müller] Leipzig, F.A. Brockhaus, 1953. 307 p. fold. map.

STEFFEN, ALBERT, 1884-  Irrfahrten des Lebens aus Erlebnissen und Tagebuchaufzeichnungen. Anhang: Bilder aus der Mogolei, Land und Leute, Sitten und Gebräuche. Langnau, Emmenthaler Blatt, 1934. 148 p. front., plates, ports., map. facsims.

STRASSER, ROLAND, 1886-  The mongolian horde; translated from the German by R.T.G. [Rachel Theodsia Gribble Knight] With an introduction by Sir Michael Sadler. London, Toronto, J. Cape; New York, J. Cape and H. Smith [ 1930] 346, [1] p. incl. illus., plates. front. [Academy books, 5].

———. Mongolen, Lamas und Dämonen; Reiseberichte aus Tibet und der Mongolei. Mit vielen Zeichnungen des Verfassers. Berlin, Deutsche Buch-Gemeinschaft, [ c1932] 333, [3] p. incl. 1 illus., plates. map.

WALN, NORA, 1895-  Sommer in der Mongolei. ''Aus dem englischen manuskript übersetzt von Josephine Ewers-Bumiller und L. Günther.'' Berlin, W. Krüger [ c1936] 278 p., front., plates.

Mongolian Language
Dictionaries

BLEICHSTEINER, ROBERT, 1891-1954. Wörterbuch der heutigen mongolischen Sprache mit kurzem Abriss der Grammatik und ausgewählten Sprachproben, unter Mitwirkung von W. A. Unkrig zusammengestellt von R. Bleichsteiner und W. Heissig. Wien-Peking, Siebenberg-Verlag, 1941. 135, [1] p.

BOBERG, FOLKE. Mongolian-English dictionary. Stockholm Förlaget Filadelfia; Copenhagen, Ejnar Munksgaard, 1954-55. 3 v.

HALTOD, MATTHEW. Mongol-English practical dictionary with English word reference list, [compiled by Matthew Haltod, and others, for the Evangelical Alliance Mission. Chicago, Evangelical Alliance Mission, 1953?] 3, xii, 679 p.

KOWALEWSKI, JÓZEF SZCZEPAN, 1800-1878. Dictionnaire mongol-russe-français par Joseph Étienne Kowalewski. Kasan, Impr. de l'Université, 1844-49. [Peiping, French bookstore, 1933] 3 v.

MOSTAERT, ANTOINE, 1881-  Dictionnaire ordos. Peking, Catholic Univ., 1941-44. 3 v. (Monumenta serica; journal of oriental studies of the Catholic University of Peking. Monograph 5).

RAMSTEDT, GUSTAV JOHN, 1873-1950. Kalmückisches Wörterbuch. Helsinki, Suomalais-Ugrilainen Seura, 1935. xxx, 560 p. (Lexica Societatis Fenno-Ugricae, 3).

SMEDT, A  de. Le dialecte monguor parlé par les Mongols du Kansou occidental, par A. de Smedt et A. Mostaert. Vienne et Pékin, 1929-1945. 3 v.

TREXEL, D. A. comp. Mongolian vocabulary (modern Khalkha language). Mongolian-English, English-Mongolian. Washington, Govt. Print. Off., 1953. 725 p. (On cover: U. S. Department of the Army).

Grammar and Readers

AUSTIN, WILLIAM M. 1914-  A Mongol reader [by] William M. Austin, Gombojob Hangin, 抗京 [and] Urgunge Onon, 伍如恭格 Washington, American Council of Learned Societies; London, Bailey and Swinfen, 1956. 248 p. (American Council of Learned Societies. Program in Oriental Languages. Publication. Series A: Texts, 3).

BUCK, FREDERICK HOLDEN. Comparative study of postpositions in Mongolian dialects and the written language. Cambridge, Harvard University Press, 1955. xvii, 158 p. illus., map, facsims., table. (Harvard-Yenching Institute studies, 12) Thesis-Harvard University.

CHINGGALTAI, comp. A grammar of the Mongol language. Translated from the original Mongol for the Evangelical Alliance Mission at Hong Kong, 1951; revised in 1952. Hong Kong, the Evangelical Alliance Mission, 1952. 173 p.

CROWLEY, WASHINGTON IRVING, 1897-  Introduction to literary Mongolian grammar; grammar and easy reading. Hollywood, Birmingham, Pangloss Publications, 1946. x, 53 p., (Pangloss Mongolian series, 1).

DÖRFER, GERHARD. Zur Syntax der geheimen Geschichte der Mongolen. Berlin, 1954. 218 l. Diss.-Univ. Berlin.

GRØNBECH, KAARE, 1901-  An introduction to classical (literary) Mongolian; introduction, grammar, reader, glossary, by K. Grønbech and John R. Krueger. Wiesbaden, O. Harrassowitz, 1955. 108 p. charts.

HAMBIS, LOUIS, 1906-  Grammaire de la langue mongole écrite. Paris, A. Maisonneuve, 1945 [i. e. 1946]- 108 p.

HAENISCH, ERICH, 1880-  Grammatische Besonderheiten in der Sprache des Manghol un Niuca Tobca'an. Helsinki, 1950. 24, [2] p. illus. (Studia orientalia edidit Societas Orientalis Fennica, 14:3).

―――. Zur japanischen Phototypie-Ausgabe des fünfsprachigen Wörterspiegels. Berlin, Akademie Verlag, 1953. 18 p. facsim. (Deutsche Akademie der Wissenschaften zu Berlin. Institut für Orientforschung. Veröfftlichung. 16).

LEWICKI, MARIAN. La langue mongole des transcriptions chinoises du XIVe siècle. Le Houa-yi-yi-yu, 華夷譯語 de 1389. Édition critique précédée des observations philologiques et accompagnée de la réproduction phototypique du texte. Wrocław, Nakł. Wrocławskiego Towarzystwa Nankowego, 1949. 228 p. (Travaux de la Société des Sciences et des Letters de Wrocław. Sér. A, nr. 29).

PELLIOT, PAUL, 1878-1945. Les systemes d'écriture en usage chez les anciens Mongols. [Lipsiae, 1925] 289 p.

POPPE, NIKOLAĬ NIKOLAEVICH, 1897-  The groups *uya and *üge in Mongol languages. Helsinki, 1950. 15 p. (Studia orientalia edidit Societas Orientalis Fennica, 14:8).

——. Khalkha-Mongolische Grammatik, mit Bibliographie, Sprachproben und Glossar. Wiesbaden, F. Steiner, 1951. xii, 188 p. (Akademie der Wissenschaften und der Literatur. Veröffentlichungen der Orientalischen Kommission, Bd. 1).

——. Grammar of written Mongolian. Wiesbaden, O. Harrassowitz, 1954. xii, 195 p. (Porta linguarum orientalism, neue ser., 1).

——. Introduction to Mongolian comparative studies. Helsinki, Suomalais-ugrilainen Seura, 1955. 300 p. (Suomalais-ugrilaisen Seuran toimituksia, 110).

RUDNEV, ANDREĬ DMĪTRIEVĪCH. Lectures on the grammar of the Mongolian written language; translated by A. I. Ward from the Russian original: Lektsii po grammatike mongolskago pismennago yazyka, chitannyya v 1903-1904 akademicheskom godu. 1st ed. St. Petersburg, 1905. [Tientsin, 1933] xiv, 155 numb. l.

SHMĪDT, ĪAKOV ĪVANOVĪCH, 1779-1847. Grammaire mongole de Schmidt, traduite de l'allemand en 1845. Peiping, Impr. des Lazaristes, 1935. 2 v.

STREET, JOHN CHARLES., 1930-  The language of the secret history of the Mongols. New Haven, 1955. 281 l. Thesis-Yale University.

WHYMANT, A. NEVILLE JOHN, 1894-  A Mongolian grammar, outlining the Khalkha Mongolian with notes on the Buriat, Kulmuck, and Ordoss Mongolian. London, K. Paul, 1926. viii, 74 p.

Mongolian Literature
incl. Folklore and Music

FARQUHAR, D. A description of the Mongolian manuscripts and xylographs in Washington, D. C. London, 1955. 70 p. Reprinted from Central Asiatic Journal 1:3.

GESAR (Romances, etc.) Gessar Khan, told by Ida Zeitlin, illustrated by Theodore Nadejen. New York, George H. Doran [c1927] viii p., 11-203 p. col. illus.

HAENISCH, ERICH, 1880-  Ein buddhistischer Druckfragment vom Jahre 1312. Berlin, Akademie Verlag, 1954. 22 p. facsims (Mongolica der Berliner Turfan-Sammlung 1: Deutsche Akademie der Wissenschaften zu Berlin. Klasse für Sprachen, Literatur und Kunst. Abhandlungen. Jahrg. 1953. nr. 3).

[HASLUND-CHRISTENSEN, HENNING] 1896-1948. comp. The music of the Mongols pt. 1. Stockholm [Tryckeri aktiebolaget Thule] 1943-  100 p. mounted col. front., illus. (incl. music) plates, port., fold. map. (Reports from the scientific expedition to the north-western provinces of China under the leadership of Dr. Sven Hedin. The Sino-Swedish expedition. Publication 21. viii. Ethnography. 4.

HECKEN, JOSEPH Van, 1905-  Études mongoles. 1. la littérature mongole chrétienne. 2. Les travaux linguistiques. Schöneck, Administration: Neue Zeitschrift für Missionswissenschaft, 1947. iv, 27 p. (Les Cahiers de la Nouvelle Revue de Science Missionnaire, 4).

HEISSIG, WALTHER, 1913-  Die Pekinger lamaistischen Blockdrucke in mongolischer Sprache; Materialien zur mongolischen Literaturgeschichte. Wiesbaden, O. Harrassowitz, 1954. xv, 220 p. facsims. (Göttinger asiatische

Forschungen 2).

LIGETI, LAJOS, 1902-    Catalogue du Kanjur mongol imprimé.  Budapest, Société Kőrősi Csoma, 1942. 2v (Bibliotheca Orientalis Hungarica, 3).

——.  Le Subhāsitaratnanidhi Mongol; un document du moyen Mongol.  Pt. 1: Le
manuscrit Tibéto-Mongol en reproduction phototypique avec une introduction.
Budapest, Société Kőrősi Csoma, 1948. xiii, 124 p. incl. plates. (Bibliotheca Orientalis Hungarica, 6).

MOSTAERT, ANTOINE, 1881-    ed. Textes oraux ordos, recueillis et publiés
avec introduction, notes morphologiques, commentaires et glossaire.  Pei-
p'ing, Cura Universitatis catholicae Pekini edita; en vente aux Éditions H.
Vetch, 1937.  lxx, 768 p. (Monumenta serica; monograph series, 1).

——.  Folklore ordos; traduction des Textes oraux ordos.  Peip'ing, Catholic
Univ., 1947. viii, 605 p. (Monumenta serica; Monograph series, 11).

NIRGIDMA, Torgot princess, comp. Dix-huit chants et poèmes mongols, recueillis par la princesse Nirgidma de Torhout et transcrits par madame Hum-
bert-Sauvageot. Avec notations musicales, texte mongol, commentaires et
traductions.  Paris, P. Geuthner, 1937. 31, 28 p. incl. map. (Bibliothèque
musicale du Musée Guimet, dirigée por P. Stern. [Musique orientale-mu-
sique des régions lointaines] 1. sér., t. iv).

POPPE, NICOLAI NIKOLAEVICH, 1897-    Mongolische Volksdichtung; Sprüche,
Lieder, Märchen und Heldensagen. Khalkhamongolische Texte mit deutscher
Übersetzung, einer Einleitung und Anmerkungen. Wiesbaden, Franz Steiner,
1955.  x, 287 p. (Akademie der Wissenschaften und der Literatur.  Mainz.
Orientalische Kommission. Veröffentlichungen, 7).

TAYLOR, ARCHER, 1890-    An annotated collection of Mongolian riddles.  Philadelphia, American Philosophical Society, 1954. 319-425 p. (Transactions of
the American Philosophical Society, new ser., 44:3).

WELLER, FRIEDRICH, 1889-    Zum Mongolischen Tanjur.  Berlin, Akademie
Verlag, 1949. 35 p. (Sächs. Akademie der Wissenschaften. Phil.-Hist. Kl.
Bericht über die Verhandlungen. Bd. 97, Heft 2).

——.  Über den Quellenbezug eines mongolischen Tanjurtextes.  Berlin, Akademie-Verlag, 1950. 51, 114 p. illus. (Abhandlungen der Sächsischen Akademie der Wissenschaften zu Leipzig. Phil-Hist. Kl. Bd. 45, Heft 2).

——.  Zum Blockdruckfragmente des mongolischen Bodhicaryāvatāra der Berliner Turfansammlung.  Berlin, Akademie Verlag, 1955. 29 p. (Mongolica
der Berliner Turfan-sammlung. 1a: Deutsche Akademie der Wissenschaften
zu Berlin. Klasse für Sprachen, Literatur und Kunst. Abhandlungen. Jahrg.
1954, nr. 2).

## History
### General Works

ALTAN TOBČI. Altan tobči; a brief history of the Mongols, by bLo-bzań bsTan-
'jin; with a critical introduction by Antoine Mostaert and an editor's foreword
by Francis Woodman Cleaves.  Cambridge, Harvard University Press, 1952.
xxvi, iv, 161, 193 p. (Harvard-Yenching Institute. Scripta mongolica, 1).

——.  The Mongol chronicle Altan tobči. Text, translation and critical notes by
Charles R. Bawden.  Wiesbaden, Harassowitz, 1955. x, 205 p. (Göttingen
Asiatische Forschungen, 5).

BOUVAT, LUCIEN. L'empire mongol (2ème phase).  Paris, E. de Boccard, 1927.
364 p. (Histoire du monde  t. viii³).

CLEAVES, FRANCIS WOODMAN, 1911-    The sino-mongolian inscription of 1362
in memory of Prince Hindu, 忻都公.  Cambridge, 1949. 133 p. plates. Reprinted from HJAS, 12: 1-2 June, 1949.

——.  The sino-mongolian inscription of 1335 in memory of Chang Ying-jui, 張應
瑞.  Cambridge, 1950. 131 p. plates. Reprinted from HJAS, 13: 1-2, June
1950.

——.  The sino-mongolian inscription of 1338 in memory of Jiguntei, 竹溫台.

Cambridge, 1951. 104 p. plates. Reprinted from HJAS, 14:1-2, June 1951.
———. The sino-mongolian inscription of 1346. Cambridge, 1952. 123 p. plates, Reprinted from HJAS, 15:1-2, June 1952.
———. The Mongolian documents in the Musée de Téhéran. Cambridge, 1953. 107 p. plates. Reprinted from HJAS, 16:1-2, June 1953).
———. The Bodistw-a čari-a Awatar-un Tayilbur of 1312, by Čosgi Odsir. Cambridge, 1954. 129 p. plates. Reprinted from HJAS, 17:1-2, June, 1954.
———. An early Mongolian loan contract from Qara Qoto. Cambridge, 1955. 49 p. Reprinted from HJAS 18:1-2, June 1955.
DE BECKER, JOSEPH ERNEST, 1863-1929. Notes on the Mongol invasion of Japan. Yokohama, Printed at the "Japan Gazette" Press, 192? 20 p. fold. plates.
DÖRRIE, HEINRICH, 1911-    Drei Texte zur Geschichte der Ungarn und Mongolen: Die Missionsreisen des Fr. Julianus O. P. ins Uralgebiet (1234/5) und nach Russland (1237) und der Bericht des Erzbischofs Peter über die Tartaren. Göttingen, Vandenhoeck and Ruprecht, [1957] 126-202 p. (Akademie der Wissenschaften in Göttingen. Nachrichten. 1 Jg. 1954, 6).
GRIGOR, of Akanc', 13th cent. History of the nation of the archers (the Mongols) by Grigor of Akanc' hitherto ascribed to Marak'ia the monk. The Armenian text, edited with an English translation and notes, by Robert P. Blake and Richard N. Frye. The Mongolian names and terms in the History of the nation of the archers by Grigor of Akanc' [by] Francis Woodman Cleaves. Cambridge, Published for Harvard-Yenching Institute by Harvard University Press, 1954. 180 p. First published in 1870 in Armenian, and also in English under title: Relics of Armenian literature: the history of the T'at'ars. "Reprinted from HJAS, 12:3-4 December 1949. pp. 269-443."
GROUSSET, RENÉ, 1885-1952. L'empire des steppes: Attila. Gengis-Khan. Tamerlan. Avec 30 cartes et 20 figures dans le texte. Paris, Payot, 1939. [7]-639 p. illus. (incl. maps) (Bibliothèque historique).
———. L'empire mongol (1re phase). Paris, E. de Boccard, 1941. xii, 583 p., fold. maps. (Histoire du monde. t. viii3).
HAENISCH, ERICH, 1880-    Steuergerechtsame der chinesischen Klöster unter der Mongolenherrschaft. Eine kulturgeschichtliche Untersuchung mit Beigabe dreier noch unveröffentlichter Phagspa-Inschriften. Leipzig, S. Hirzel, 1940. 74 p. (Bericht über die Verhandlungen der Sächs Akademie der Wissenschaften. Phil-hist. Kl., Bd. 92, Heft 2).
———. Die Kulturpolitik des mongolischen Weltreichs. Berlin, W. de Gruyter, 1943. 30 p. map. (Preussische Akademie der Wissenschaften. Vorträge und Schriften, Heft 17).
———. Die viersprachige Gründungsinschrift des Tempels An-yüan-miao in Jehol v. Jahre 1765, übersetzt und erläutert von Erich Haenisch. Wiesbaden, In Kommission bei F. Steiner [1951] 22 p. fold. facsim. (Akademie der Wissenschaften und der Literatur, Mainz. Abhandlungen der Geistes-und Sozialwissenschaftlichen Kl. Jahrg 1950, Nr. 15).
———. Sino-Mongolische dokumente vom Ende des 14 Jahrhunderts. Berlin, Akademie Verlag, 1952.    60, xxvi p. facsims. (Deutsche Akademie der Wissenschaften zu Berlin. Kl. für aprachen, literatur und kunst, Jahrg. 1950, 4).
HAMBIS, LOUIS, 1906-    Le chapitre cvii du Yuan che; les généalogies impériales mongoles dans l'histoire chinoise officielle de la dynastie mongole. Avec des notes supplémentaires par Paul Pelliot. Avec 71 tableaux dont 10 horstexte. Leiden, E. J. Brill, 1945. xii, 181 p. fold. geneal. tables. (T'oung pao; archives concernant l'histoire, les langues, la géographie, l'ethnographie et les arts de l'Asie orientale, revue dirigée par Paul Pelliot et J. J. L. Duyvendak...Suppl. au vol. xxxviii).
———. Le chapitre cviii du Yuan che; les fiefs attribués aux membres de la famille impériale et aux ministres de la cour mongole d'après l'histoire chinoise officielle de la dynastie mongole. Leiden, E. J. Brill, 1954. iv. geneal.

tables. (T'oung pao. Archives concernant l'histoire, les langues, la géographie, l'ethnographie et les arts de l'Asie orientale. Monographie 3.

HEISSIG, WALTHER, 1913-    Bolur erike, "eine Kette aus Bergkristallen"; eine mongolische Chronik der Kienlung-Zeit von Rasipungsuy (1774/75) literaturhistorisch untersucht. Peiping, Fu-Jen Univ., 1946. xi, 225 p 3 facsims. (Monumenta serica; journal of oriental studies of the Catholic University of Peking. Monograph series, 10).

HOWORTH, SIR HENRY HOYLE, 1842-1923. History of the Mongols, from the 9th to the 19th century. London, Longmans, Green. 1876-1927. 4 v. in 5. fold. maps.

HUNG, WILLIAM, 洪業, 1893-    The transmission of the book known as "The Secret History of the Mongols." Cambridge, 1951. 59 p. Reprinted from HJAS 14: 3-4, Dec., 1951.

KRAUSE, FRIEDRICH ERNST AUGUST, 1879-    Die Epoche der Mongolen; ein Kapitel aus der Geschichte und Kultur Asiens. Berlin, 1924. 60 p. (Berlin. Universität. Seminar für orientalische Sprachen, Mitteil. Bd. 26, Abt. 1).

MENG KU SHIH HSI PU, 蒙古世系譜. Mongyol horjigid oboy-un teüke von Lomi (1732). Hrsg. und mit Einleitungen versehen von Walther Heissig und Charles R. Bawden. Wiesbaden, O. Harrassowitz, 1957. 140 p. facsims. (Göttinger asiatische Forschungen, 9).

MOSTAERT, ANTOINE, 1881-    Trois passages de l'Histoire secrète des Mongols. Helsinki, 1950. 5, [2] p. illus. (Studia orientalia edidit Societas Orientalis Fennica, 14:9).

————. Sur quelques passages de l'Histoire secrète des Mongols. Cambridge, 1950-1952. [76] [164] [122] p. Reprinted from HJAS, 13:3-4, December 1950, 14:3-4, December 1951, 15:3-4, December 1952.

MUNIER, PAUL. Trois grands empires de nomades d'Asie. Conférence prononcée le 28 janvier 1937 à l'Université indochinoise sous les auspices de la Société de géographie de Hanoi. Hanoi, Impr. d'Extrême-Orient, 1937. 27 p. fold. maps. (Cahiers de la Société de géographie de Hanoi. 33. cahier, 1937).

OHSSON, CONSTANTIN MOURADGEA D'OHSSON, friherre d', 1779-1851. Histoire des Mongols, depuis Tchinguiz-Khan jusqu'à Timour Bey, ou Tamerlan; par m. le baron C. D'Ohsson. La Haye et Amsterdam, Les frères Van Cleef, 1834-35. Reprint ed. Tientsin, 1940. 4 v. fold. map. fold. geneal. tables.

OLBRICHT, PETER. Das Postwesen in China unter der Mongolenherrschaft im 13. und 14. Jahrhundert. Wiesbaden, O. Harrassowitz, 1954. 110 p. (Göttinger asiatische Forschungen, 1).

OLSCHKI, LEONARDO, 1885-    Guillaume Boucher; a French artist at the court of the Khans. With ten illustrations and a map of Asia. Baltimore, Johns Hopkins Press, 1946.    viii, 125 p. plates, fold. map.

POKOTILOV, DMITRIĬ DMITRIEVICH, 1865-1908. History of the Eastern Mongols during the Ming dynasty from 1368 to 1631. Chengtu, Chinese Cultural Studies Research Institute, West China Union University, 1947-[49] 2 v. (Studia serica. Monog. ser. A, 1) Translation of Istoriĭa vostochnykh mongolov v period dinastii Min, 1368-1634. Contents. -pt. 1. Translation of the Russian text, by Rudolf Löwenthal -pt. 2. Additions and corrigenda, by Wolfgang Franke.

POPPE, NIKOLAĬ NIKOLAEVICH, 1897-    The Mongolian monuments in ḥP'agspa Script. 2d. ed. Translated and edited by John R. Krueger. Wiesbaden, Harrassowitz, 1957. xii, 147 p. illus. charts, map. (Göttinger asiatische Forschungen, 8).

POUCHA, PAVAL. Die geheime Geschichte des Mongolen als Geschichtsquelle und Literaturdenkmal. Ein Beitrag zu über Erklarung. Prag, 1956. 247 p. illus. photos, fold. map. (Archiv Orientální, Supplement 4).

SERRUYS, HENRY, 1911-    The Mongols in China during the Hung-wu period (1368-1398) Ann Arbor, University Microfilms [1955] ([University Microfilms, Ann Arbor, Mich.] Publication no. 12, 321). viii, 403 l.

————. Sino-Jürčed relations during the Yung-Lo peroid, 1403-1424. Wiesbaden, O. Harrassowitz, 1955. viii, 118 p. (Göttinger asiatische Forschungen, 4).

SSANANG SSETSEN, Chungtaidschi. Geschichte der Ost-Mongolen und ihres Für-sten-hauses, verfasst von Ssanang Ssetsen Chungtaidschi der Ordus; aus dem Mongolischen übersetzt, und mit dem Originaltexte, nebst Anmerkungen, Er-läuterungen und Citaten aus andern unedirten Originalwerken hrsg. von Isaac Jacob Schmidt. St. Petersburg, Gedruckt bei N. Gretsch, 1829. Reprint, ed. Peking, 1940. xxiv, 509 p.

————. Eine Urga-Handschrift des mongolischen Geschicthswerks von Secen Sa-gang (alias Sanang Secen) [hrsg. von] Erich Haenisch. Berlin, Akademie-Verlag, 1955. [204] p. on 102 p. facsims. (Deutsche Akademie der Wissen-schaften. Institut für Orientforschung. Veröffentlichung, 25).

————. Erdeni-yin Tobči, Mongolian chronicle by Sayang Sečen. With a critical introduction by Antoine Mostaert, and an editor's foreword by Francis Wood-man Cleaves. Cambridge, Harvard University Press, 1956. 4v. plates. (Harvard-Yenching Institute. Scripta Mongolica, 2).

VICHNEVSKY, LUDMILA, 1903-    La Russie, l'Asie, l'Occident, dans le passé, le présent et l'avenir [par] Amir Ali [pseud.] Paris, Distributeur: Maison du Livre francais [1952] 197 p. illus.

YÜAN-CH'AO PI-SHIH, 元朝祕史. Untersuchungen über Yuan-ch'ao pi-shih. Die geheime Geschichte der Mongolen, von Erich Haenisch. Leipzig, Hirzel, 1931. 100 p. facsims. (Sächs. Akademie der Wissenschaften. Abhandlungen. Phil.-Hist. Kl. 41, 4).

————. Manghol un Niuca Tobca'an (Yüan-ch'ao pi-shi) Die geheime Geschichte der Mongolen, aus der chinesischen Transkription (ausgabe Ye Têh-hui, 葉德輝) im mongolischen Wortlaut wiederhergestellt von Erich Haenisch. Leip-zig, O. Harrassowitz, 1937-1939. 2 v.

————. Onyaku-Mobun-Gencho-hishi, 音譯蒙文元朝祕史; a romanized re-presentation of the Yuan-ch'ao pi-shih (a secret history of the Mongols) in its original mongolian sound, by Shiratori Kurakichi. Tokyo, Toyo Bunko, 1942. 13, 610, 5 p. (Toyo Bunko Publications, ser. c, 8).

————. Die geheime Geschichte der Mongolen. Aus einer mongolischen Nieder-schrift des Jahres 1240 von der Insel Kode'e im Keluren-Fluss. Erstmalig übers. und erläutert von Erich Haenisch. 2 verb. Aufl. Leipzig, O. Harras-sowitz, 1948. xviii, 196 p. illus., maps. ''Der Originaltext erschien 1937 unter dem Titel 'Manghol un niuca tobca' an.' '' 1. Aufl. 1941, xxxii, 209 p.

————. Histoire secrète des Mongols. Restitution du texte mongol et traduction française des chapitres i à vi. par Paul Pelliot. Paris, Librairie d'Amérique et d'Orient, 1949. ii, 196 p. (Oeuvres posthumes de Paul Pelliot, 1).

ŽAMCARANO, CYBEN ŽACARONOVIČ, 1880-    The Mongol chronicles of the seventeenth century, translated from the Russian by Rudolf Löwenthal. Wies-baden, O. Harrassowitz, 1955.    x, 95 p. (Göttinger asiatische Forschungen, 3).

## Genghis Khan

BARCKHAUSEN, JOACHIM, 1906-    Das gelbe Weltreich; Lebensgeschichte ein-er Macht. Berlin, Buch-und Tiefdruck Gesellschaft [c1935] 291 p. maps.

————. L'empire jaune de Genghis-Khan, préface et traduction du dr. George Montandon. Avec trois cartes. Paris, Payot, 1935. [7]-277, [2] p. incl. illus. (maps) geneal. tab. (Bibliothèque historique).

[CHAROL, MICHAEL] 1894-    Das Erbe Tschingis-Chans. Stuttgart, Deutsche Verlags-Anstalt [1935] 294, [1] p. front., illus., plates, ports., 2 double maps, fold. geneal. table. Author's pseud., Michael Prawdin, at head of title. Berlin ed. Rutenberg, 1935, 364 p.

[————]. Tschingis-Chan; der Sturm aus Asien. Stuttgart, Deutsche Verlags-An-stalt [1937] 236, [1] p. front., illus. (maps) plates, ports., facsim.

[_____]. Tschingis-Chan und sein Erbe . Ergänzte und bis auf die Gegenwart
fortgefürte ausg. Stuttgart, Deutsche Verlags-Anstalt [c1938] 532, [1] p.
front., illus. (incl. maps) plates, ports., facsim., fold. geneal. tab. 1957
ed. 377 p.

————. Genghis Khan [par] Michaël Prawdin [pseud.] Traduction par André Cog-
niet. Paris, Payot, 1951. 231 p. illus. (Bibliothèque historique).

————. The Mongol Empire, its rise and legacy, by Michael Prawdin [pseud.]
Translated by Eden and Cedar Paul. [2d impression] London, Allen and Unwin [1952] 581 p. port., maps, geneal. table. 1st ed. 1940.

FOX, RALPH WINSTON, 1900-   Genghis Khan; with 8 illustrations and 2 maps.
New York, Harcourt, Brace [c1936] xiii, 285 p. incl. front., 1 illus.
plates, maps (1 fold.).

GRENARD, FERNAND, 1866-   Gengis-Khan. Paris, A. Colin, 1935. 206, [2]
p. (Ames et visages).

GROUSSET, RENÉ, 1885- 1952. Le conquérant du monde (vie de Gengis-Khan)
Paris, A. Michel [1944] [7]-380 p., plates,fold. maps, fold, geneal. table.

KRAUSE, FRIEDRICH ERNST AUGUST, 1879-   Cingis Han; die Geschichte
seines Lebens nach den chinesischen Reichsannalen. Heidelberg, Carl Winter, 1922. 111 p. tables, (Von-Portheim-Stiftung. Heidelberger Akten, 2).

LAMB, HAROLD, 1892-   Genghis Khan, the emperor of all men. New York,
R. M. McBride, 1928.   viii, 13-279 p. incl. maps. plates (part double)ı
2 port. (incl. front.).

————. The same; Philadelphia, Blakiston [1944] viii, 270 p. incl.  maps. (The
New home library].

————. Dschingis Khan, Beherrscher der Erde; deutsch von Dagobert von Mikusch;
mit einem Titelbild und 2 Geländekarten. Leipzig, P. List [c1928] vii, 297,
[2] p. incl. maps. front. (port.).

————. Boy's Genghis Khan [by] Harold Lamb, edited and adapted by James Gilman, illustrated by William Siegel. New York, R. M. McBride, 1930. xiii,
245 p. incl. front., illus., plates.

————. Genghis Khan and the Mongol horde; illustrated by Elton Fax.  New York,
Random House [1954] 182 p. illus. (World landmark books, W-12).

LIDDELL HART, BASIL HENRY, 1895-   Great captains unveiled. Edinburgh
and London, W. Blackwood, 1927. [3]-274 p. illus. (maps, plans) Jenhis
Khan: p. 3-34.

MARTIN, HENRY DESMOND, 1908-   The rise of Chingis Khan and his conquest
of North China; introd. by Owen Lattimore. Edited by Eleanor Lattimore.
Baltimore, Johns Hopkins Press, 1950. xvii, 360 p. port., maps (3 fold. in
pocket).

PERCHERON, MAURICE, 1891-   Les conquérants d'Asie. Paris, Payot, 1951.
253 [3] p. maps. (Bibliothèque historique).

————. Sur les pas de Gengis Khan. Paris, Del Duca, 1956. 311 p. map.

ROBERTS, MICHAEL. Orion marches; poems by Michael Roberts. London, Faber and Faber limited [1939] 7-96 p.

SHÊNG WU CH'IN CHÊNG LU,　聖武親征錄． Histoire des compagnes de Gengis
Khan.  Cheng-wou ts'in-tcheng lou. Traduit et annoté par Paul Pelliot et
Louis Hambis. Leiden, E. J. Brill, 1951- v. 1,513 p.

STICKELBERGER, EMANUEL. Gesammelte Werke in 12 Einzelbänden. Bd. 2:
Der Reiter auf dem fahlen Pferd. Ein Buch vom Mongolen Dschinggis-Khan
und seinem abendländischen Gegenspieler. Frauenfeld, Huber und Co., 1947.
iv, 398 p. plate, map.

THE TARIKH-I JAHÁN--GUSHÁ OF ALÁ'U 'DIN ' ATÁ MALIK I-JUWAYNI
(composed in A. H.  658-A. D. 1260) Part 1: containing the history of Chingtz
Khán and his successors. Edited with an introduction, notes and indices from
several old MSS by Mírzá Muhammad Ibn ' Abdu'l Wahháb-i-Qazvíni. London
and Leyden, 1952. 94 p. (Gibb Memorial Ser. xvi, 1).

VLADÍMIRTSOV, BORÍS ÍAKOVLEVÍCH, 1884-1931. The life of Chingis-Kahn.

Translated from the Russian by Prince D. S. Mirsky. Boston and New York, Houghton Mifflin; London, Routledge, 1930. vii-xii, 172 p.
——. Genghis Khan. Introduction historique de René Grousset. Traduction par Michel Carsow. Paris, Adrien Maisonneuve, 1948. xxxii, 158 p. map.
WALKER, CYRIL CHARLES, 1892-  Jenghiz Khan. With seven maps in colour. London, Luzac, 1939 [i. e. 1940] 215 p. maps (part fold. ).

## Timur

AḤMAD IBN MUḤAMMAD, called IBN 'ARABSHĀH, d. 1450. Tamerlane, or Timur, the great amir, translated by J. H. Sanders from the Arabic life by Ahmed ibn Arabshah. London, Luzac, 1936. xviii, 341 p. front., double map.
CHAMPDOR, ALBERT. Tamerlan. Avec 6 cartes. Paris, Payot, 1942. [9]-246 p. illus. (maps) (Bibliothèque historique).
[CHAROL, MICHAEL] 1894-  L'Empire mongol et Tamerlan, par Michael Prawdin. Préface et traduction de George Montadon. Paris, Payot, 1937. 296 p. illus. ports, maps, general. table, (Bibliothèque historique).
GONZÁLEZ DE CLAVIJO, RUY, d. 1412. Embassy to Tamerlane, 1403-1406; translated from the Spanish by Guy Le Strange with an introduction. London, G. Routledge [1928] xv, 375 p. maps, plans. (The Broadway travellers, ed. by Sir E. Denison Ross and Eileen Power).
IBN KHALDŪN, 1332-1406. Ibn Khaldūn and Tamerlane, their historic meeting in Damascus, 1401 A. D. (803 A. H.) A study based on Arabic manuscripts of Ibn Khaldūn's "Autobiography," with a translation into English, and a commentary by Walter J. Fischel. Berkeley, University of California Press, 1952. x, 149 p. illus. facsims.
KAMAL, AHMAD, 1914-  The seven questions of Timur, translated by Ahmad Kamal from an original Turki manuscript by Ahmad, descended of Karu Yusuf ibn Kara Yakub. The month: Rabi'ul'awwal, the year: 1357. Santa Ana, Calif., Fine Arts Press, 1938. [22] p., incl. col. front. (port.) illus.
LAMB, HAROLD, 1892-  Tamerlane,the earth shaker. New York, R. M. Mc Bride 1928. ix p., 15-340 p. front. (port.) plates (part double) double maps.
——. The same. Garden City, N. Y. Garden City Pub. Co. [1932] ix, 340 p. front. (port.) plates, double maps. (A star book).
——. The march of the barbarians. New York, Doubleday, Doran, 1941. xv, 389 p., 1 illus., maps, geneal. table.
——. The earth shakers. [1st ed.] Garden City, N. Y., Doubleday, 1949. ix, 689 p. illus., maps. "Originally published as separate books entitled The march of the barbarians and Tamerlane."
MELZIG, HERBERT, 1909-  Timur; Verhängnis eines Erdteils. Zürich, Europa Verlag [1940] 204 p. plates.
NIZĀM AL-DĪN, Shāmī. Histoire des conquêtes de Tamerlan, intitulée Ẓafarnāma, Niẓāmuddīn Šāmī, avec des additions empruntées au Zubdatu-t-Tawārīh-i Bāysunġurī de Ḥāfiẓ-i Abrū. Édition critique par Felix Tauer. Praha, Orientální ústav-Oriental institute, 1937-  1 v. (Monografie Archivu orientálního; studies, texts and translations, issued by the Czechoslovak Oriental institute, Prague; vol. 5).
SCHILTBERGER, JOHANNES, b. 1380 or 81. Reise in die Heidenschaft; was ein bayerischer Edelmann von 1394 bis 1427 als Gefangener der Türken und Mongolen in Kleinasien, Ägypten, Turkestan, der Krim und dem Kaukasus erlebte. Der alten Chronik nacherzählt von Rose Grässel. Hamburg, Classen et Goverts [1947] 135 p. illus., fold. map.
TĀG AS-SALMĀNĪ. Sams al-Husn. Eine Chronik vom Tode Timurs bis zum Jahre 1409. Persischer Text in Faks (Hs Lālā İsma 'Īl Efendi 304) Ins deutsch übertr. und kommentiert von Hans Robert Roemer. Wiesbaden, Steiner, 1956. iv, 147 p. (German text), 177 p. (Arabian text) illus. (Akademie der Wissenschaften und der Literatur, Veröffentlichung der Oriental. Kommission, 8).

## Mongols in Russia and Iran

GREHOV, BORIS DMITRIEVICH, 1882-    La Horde d'Or; la domination tatare au xiiie et au xive siècle de la mer Jaune à la mer Noire [par] B. Grekov et A. Iakoubovski. Traduit du Russe par François Thuret. Paris, Payot, 1939. 251 p. plates, map, (Bibliothèque historique).

HANSTEIN, OTFRID VON, 1869-    Beim Grosskhan der goldenen Horde; die Reisen und Erlebnisse des Venetianers Marco Polo in Asien und am Hofe des Mongolen-Grosskhans Chubilai in Kambalu (Peking) im 13. Jahrhundert. Leipzig, Leipziger Graphische Werke A. G. [1928] 153 p. front. (port.) illus. maps, (Sammlung Interessanter Entdeckungsreisen, 3).

PELLIOT, PAUL, 1878-1945. Notes sur l'histoire de la Horde d'Or; suivies de Quelques noms turcs d'hommes et de peuples finissant en "ar." Paris, Adrien-Maisonneuve, 1949 [cover 1950] 292 p. (His Oeuvres posthumes, 2).

PHILLIPS, G.   D.   R. Dawn in Siberia; the Mongols of Lake Baikal. London, Frederich Muller, 1942. 196 p.

SPULER, BERTOLD, 1911-    Die Mongolen in Iran; Politik, Verwaltung und Kultur der Ilchanzeit 1220-1350. Leipzig, J.C. Hinrichs, 1939. xvi, 533 p. fold. map (in pocket) (Iranische Forschungen, Bd. 1).

——. Die goldene Horde; die Mongolen in Russland, 1223-1502. Leipzig, O. Harrassowitz, 1943. xvi, 556 p. 2 fold. maps (in pocket) 2 fold. geneal. tab. (Das Mongolische weltreich; quellen und forschungen, hrsg. v. Erich Haenisch u. H. H. Schaeder. ii).

——. Geschichte der islamischer Länder; ein Überblick. ii. Die Mongolenzeit. Berlin, Wissenschaftliche Editionsgesellschaft, 1948; Leiden, E. J. Brill, 1948. 76 p. fold. maps, fold. table, (Handbuch der Orientalistik [10]).

TAYLOR, OTIS ELLERY, 1893-    Architecture of northwest Persia under the Il-Khân Mongols. [Chicago, 1940] 122 p. incl. illus., plates, map, plans. Part of thesis-University of Chicago, 1939.

VERNADSKY, GEORGE, 1887-    The Mongols and Russia. New Haven, Yale University Press; and London, G. Cumberlege, Oxford University Press, 1953. xi, 462 p. maps. geneal. tables. (Half title: a history of Russia, by George Vernadsky and Michael Karpovich, v. 3).

## Inner Mongolia

CHANG, YIN-T'ANG, 張印堂, 1902-    The economic development and prospects of inner Mongolia (Chahar, Suiyuan, and Ningsia). Shanghai, Commercial Press, 1933. xiv, 243 p. front., plates, maps.

HEISSIG, WALTHER, 1913-    Der mongolische Kulturwandel in den Hsingan-Provinzen Mandschukuos. Wien, W. Exner, 1944. 97, [1] p. illus., plates, maps. (Asien-Schriftenreihe, 1).

——. Ostmongolische Reise. Darmstadt, C. W. Leske, 1955. 169 p. illus. map, (Reisen und Länder).

INNER MONGOLIA TODAY. [Peking] Nationalities Pub. House; distributed by Guozi Shudian, 1957. 175 p.

LARSON, FRANS AUGUST, 1870-1957. Larson, duke of Mongolia. Boston, Little, Brown, 1930. [3]-296 p. front., plates, ports.

——. Die Mongolei und mein Leben mit den Mongolen. [Aus dem Englischen übertragen von Ruth Andreas-Friedrich] Mit 14 Bildern. [Berlin] G. Kiepenheuer [193-] 232 p. plates, port.

LATTIMORE, OWEN, 1900-    The Mongols of Manchuria; their tribal divisions, geographical distribution, historical relations with Manchus and Chinese, and present political problems; with maps. New York, The John Day company [c1934] 311, [1] p. maps (2 fold.).

MA, HO-T'IEN, 馬鶴天. Chinese agent in Mongolia; translated by John De Francis. Baltimore, Johns Hopkins Press, 1949. xvi, 215 p. map (on lining papers).

MONGOLIA. Laws, statutes, etc. Constitutional laws promulgated at Alashan, July-August, 1949, by the anti-communist Government [under Prince Teh] Hong Kong? 1949? Microfilm copy made in 1950 by the Library of Congress. Negative.

MONTAGU, Hon. IVOR GOLDSMID SAMUEL, 1904-    Land of blue sky, a portrait of modern Mongolia. London, D. Dobson [1956] 191 p. illus.

OOST, JOSEPH VAN, 1877-    Notes sur le T'oemet. Changhai, Impr. de la Mission catholique, 1922. iii, 190 p. illus. (music), map. (Variétés sinologiques, 53).

————. Au pays des Ortos (Mongolie) Paris, Dillen [1932] 135 p. illus. (incl. facsim., music) plates, fold, maps.

THE PEKING CHRONICLE. Meng Chiang (autonomous government of Inner Mongolia) as seen by foreign correspondents. [Peking, The Peking Chronicle, 1939] 70 p. illus.

WASHINGTON (STATE) UNIVERSITY. Far Eastern and Russian Institute. A regional handbook on the Inner Mongolia autonomous region. Seattle, 1956. lv, 555 l. maps, tables. (HRAF-60, Wash.-7).

## Outer Mongolia (Mongolian People's Republic)

ALINGE, CURT. Mongolische Gesetze; Darstellung des geschriebenen mongolischen Rechts (Privatrecht, Strafrecht u. Prozess) Leipzig, T. Weicher, 1934. vii, 157 p. (Leipziger rechtswissenschaftliche studien, herausgegeben, von der Leipziger juristen-fakultät, 87).

BLAGOVESHCHENSKIĬ, M    N. Die Mongolische Volksrepublik. Stenogramm einer im Auditorium maximum der Unionsgesellschaft zur Verbreitung wissenschaftlicher und politischer Kenntnisse in Moskau gehaltenen Vorlesung. Übers. von G. Weinhold. Red., W. Fickenscher. Berlin, Verlag Kultur und Fortschrift, 1951. 53 p. illus. (Sowjetwissenschaft).

CARNEGIE ENDOWMENT FOR INTERNATIONAL PEACE. Division of international law. Outer Mongolia, treaties and agreements. Washington, The Endowment, 1921. vii, 39 p. (Pamphlet series of the Carnegie endowment for international peace. Division of international law, 41).

DUNN, EDWARD. The truth about Outer Mongolia. Shanghai, the author, 1935. 32 p., plates, ports., diagr.

FAR EASTERN REPUBLIC. Letters captured from Baron Ungern in Mongolia. Washington, 1921. 7 p.

FRITERS, GERARD MARTIN, 1911-    Outer Mongolia and its international position. Edited by Eleanor Lattimore, with an introd. by Owen Lattimore. Baltimore, Johns Hopkins Press, 1949. London, Allen and Unwin, 1951. xlvii, 358 p. maps.

GELETA, JÓZSEF. The new Mongolia, by Ladislaus Forbath, as related by Joseph Geleta; translated from the Hungarian by Lawrence Wolfe. London, Toronto, W. Heinemann [1936] 276 p. plates, ports.

HEISSIG, WALTHER, 1913-    Das gelbe Vorfeld, die Mobilisierung der chinesischen Aussenländer; mit 8 Kartenskizzen und mehreren Abbildungen. Heidelberg [etc.] K. Vowinckel, 1941. 163 p. illus. (incl. maps) (Schriften zur wehrgeopolitik, bd. 2).

KERVYN, LOUIS MARIE. Ourga, 1912-1930; la politique chinoise en Mongolie. Pékin, Impr. de la "Politique de Pékin", 1932. 258 p. plates, ports.

————. L'empire chinois et les barbares. Pékin, Impr. de la "Politique de Pékin," 1933. 5 p. 5-74 numb. l. (Collection de la "Politique de Pékin"). 1st ed. 1929.

KOROSTOVETS, ĬVAN ĬAKOVLEVĬCH. Von Cinggis Khan zur Sowjetrepublik; eine kurze Geschichte der Mongolei unter besonderer Berücksichtigung der neuesten Zeit, unter Mitwirkung von Erich Hauer mit 38 Abbildungen, einer Über-

sichtskarte der Mongolei und einem Geleitwort von Otto Franke. Berlin und
Leipzig, W. de Gruyter und co., 1926. x, 351 p. front., plates, ports.,
fold. map.

LATTIMORE, OWEN, 1900-     Nationalism and revolution in Mongolia. With a
translation from the Mongol of Sh. Nachukdorji's Life of Sukebatur, by Owen
Lattimore and Urungge Onon. New York, Oxford University Press, 1955.
x, 186 p.

———. The same. Leiden, E. J. Brill 1955. x, 186 p.

LEVIN, ISAAK OSIPOVICH, 1876-     La Mongolie historique, géographique, politique. Avec une carte. Paris, Payot, 1937. [7]-252 p. illus. (double map)
(Bibliothèque géographique).

MISSHIMA, YASUO. A Japanese view of Outer Mongolia; being a condensed translation of "The Outer Mongolian people's republic," by Yasuo Misshima and
Tomio Goto. Translated and summarized from the Japanese by Andrew J.
Grajdanzev. New York, International secretariat, Institute of Pacific
tions, 1942. 1 p. l., 1 numb. l., 1 l., 66 numb. l.

MONGOLIA (MONGOLIAN PEOPLE'S REPUBLIC) Constitution. Constitution
(Fundamental law of the Mongolian People's Republic) Ulan-Bator [19   ]97 p.

MONGOLIA, YESTERDAY AND TODAY. [Tientsin, Tientsin Press, c1924]69 p.

DIE MONGOLISCHE VOLKSREVOLUTION und das Lebenswerk des Marschalls
Tschoibalsan: Kurzer Abriss der Geschichte der mongolischen Volksrevolution [von] H. Tschoibalsan; Leben und Wirken des Marschalls Tschoibalsan
[von] J. Zedenbal. [1. Aufl.] Berlin, Dietz, 1954. 127 p.

MURPHY, GEORGE, 1924-     Economic development of the Outer Mongolian economy in recent times. Seattle, 1956. 385 l. Thesis-Univ. of Washington.

MURZAEV, ÉD     M. Die Mongolische Volksrepublic; physisch-geographische
Beschreibung. [Deutsch von F. Tutenberg. 1. Aufl.] Gotha, Geographisch-
Kartographische Anstalt, 1954. 523 p. illus., port., maps (part fold. col. in
pocket).

PHILLIPS, G     D     R. Russia, Japan and Mongolia. London, F. Muller ltd.
[1942] 104 p.

PRICE, ERNEST BATSON, 1890-     The Russo-Japanese treaties of 1907-1916
concerning Manchuria and Mongolia. Baltimore, the Johns Hopkins press,
1933. xiv, 164 p. incl. map, facsims.

RIAZANOVSKII, VALENTIN ALEKSANDROVICH, 1884-     Customary law of the
Mongol tribes (Mongols, Buriats, Kalmucks) part i-iii. Harbin, "Artistic
Printing-House," 1929. 306, [2] p. (Memoirs of the Faculty of law in Harbin,
vol. viii).

———. Fundamental principles of Mongol law. Tientsin, 1937. 338 p.

RUPEN, ROBERT ARTHUR, 1922-     Outer Mongolian nationalism, 1900-1919.
Ann Arbor, University Microfilms [1954] ([University Microfilms, Ann Arbor, Mich.] Publication no. 8363) 386 l. maps. Thesis-Univ. of Washington.

TAN, TENNYSON, 譚襐愼, 1898-     Political status of Mongolia. Shanghai,
Mercury Press, 1932. 144 p. map.

WASHINGTON (STATE) UNIVERSITY. Far Eastern and Russian Institute. Mongolian People's Republic (Outer Mongolia) New Haven, Printed by Human Relations Area Files [1956-     3 v. maps (1 fold. col. in pocket) diagrs. HRAF,
Subcontractor's monograph, HRAF-39).

WEI, YING-PANG, 魏英邦. L'independence de facto et de jure de la Mongolie
extérieure. Paris, A. Pedone, 1947. 14 p. Reprinted from Revue générale
de droit international public, 1947.

ZLATKIN, I     IA. Die mongolische Volksrepublik; geschichtlicher Abriss.
Berlin, Dietz, 1954. 315 p. illus.

Tannu Tuva (Uriankhai)

GRANÖ, JOHANNES GABRIEL, 1882-     Itinerarien und Landschaftsprofile J. G.

Granös aus Uranchai (Tannu-Tuwa) und der Nordmongolei, bearbeitet und gezeichnet von A. K. Merisuo; mit Vorwort und einleitendem Text von J. G. Granö sowie einem Verzeichnis der Gesteinsproben von Pentti Eskola. Helsinki [Druckerei-a. g. der Finnischen Literaturgesellschaft] 1938. 42 p. illus. (facsim.) fold. map, 12 fold. diagr. ([Geografiska sällskapet i Finland, Helsingfors] Acta geographica: 6, n:o 1).

————. Mongolische Landschaften und Örtlichkeiten; eine Geographie physiognomischer Typen und einheitlicher Räume nach Reisebeobachtungen und Wegeaufnahmen in Uranchai (Tuwa) und der Nordmongolei aus den jahren 1906, 1907 und 1909. Helsinki [Druckerei-a. g. der Finnischen Literaturgesellschaft] 1941-    291 p. illus. (incl. maps) Ɪᴀᴄ., diagrs. ([Geografiska sällskapet i Finland, Helsingfors] Acta geographica 7, n:o2-).

HAUSEN, HANS, 1884-    ed. The upper Yenissei drainage area (territory of Uriankhai). Helsingfors [A.-b. F. Tilgmanns tryckeri] 1925. 185, [1] p. illus., 3 fold. maps, diagrs. ([Geografiska sällskapet i Finland, Helsingfors] Acta geographica 1, n:o 1).

LEIMBACK, WERNER. Landeskunde von Tuva, das Gebiet des Jenissei-Oberlaufes. Gotha, J. Perthes, 1936. 124 p. plates, fold. maps. (Ergänzungsheft nr. 222 au Petermanns Mitteilungen).

MÄNCHEN-HELFEN, OTTO, 1894-    Reise ins asiatische Tuwa; mit 28 Photobildern. Berlin, Der Bücherkreis, 1931. 172 p. incl. plates.

PEHRMAN, GUNNAR, 1895-    Über ein Nickeleisen aus Tannuola (Mongolei). Åbo, Åbo akademi, 1923. 12 p. plates (Acta Academiae aboensis. Mathematica et physica. iii, 1).

PRINTZ, HENRIK, 1888-    The vegetation of the Siberian-Mongolian frontiers (the Sayansk region) by Henrik Printz. [Trondhjem] K. Norske videnskabers selskab [1921] 458 p. illus., plates, maps. (Contributiones ad floram Asiae interioris pertinentes... iii).

## Economic and Social Conditions

ABERLE, DAVID FRIEND, 1918-    The kinship system of the Kalmuk Mongols. Albuquerque, University of New Mexico Press, 1953. 48 p. diagrs. (University of New Mexico publications in anthropology, no. 8).

BOYER, MARTHA HAGENSEN, 1911-    Mongol jewellery; researches on the silver jewellery collected by the First and Second Danish Central Asian Expeditions under the leadership of Henning Haslund-Christensen, 1936-37 and 1938-39. København, I kommission hos Gyldendal, 1952. 223 p. illus. (part col.) port., fold. map. (Nationalmuseets skrifter. Etnografisk raekke, 5).

CONOLLY, VIOLET. Soviet economic policy in the East; Turkey, Persia, Af- ghanistan, Mongolia and Tanu Tuva, Sin Kiang. London, Oxford University Press, H. Milford, 1933. ix, 168 p. fold. map.

GEHRING-KIENE, MARTHA VERENA, 1899-    Grüne Steppen, weisse Jurten; Erlebnisse einer Schweizer Familie in der Mongolei [von] Verena Winter [pseud.] Aarau, H.R. Sauerländer [1951] 266 p. illus.

HANSEN, HENNY HARALD. Mongol costumes; researches on the garments collected by the First and Second Danish Central Asian Expeditions under the leadership of Henning Haslund-Christensen, 1936-37 and 1938-39. København, I kommission hos Gyldendal, 1950. xx, 199 p. illus., map. (Nationalmuseets skrifter. Etnografisk raekke, 3).

KARAMYSHEV, V. Mongolia and western China; social and economic study. Tientsin, La Librairie française, 1925. xxvii, 401 p. incl. front. plates., fold. maps.

KERVYN, LOUIS MARIE. Moeurs et coutumes mongoles; oeuvre posthume. Gembloux, J. Duculot [1949?] 251 p. illus. maps.

MILLER, ROBERT J., 1923-    The socio-political and economic aspects of the monastery in Inner Mongolia. Seattle, 1955. 338 l. Thesis-Univ. of Washington.

OTTO, JOSEPH ALBERT, 1901-    L'évasion du monastère lama.  Bruges, Oeuvre St. Charles, 1935. 111 p.

PERCHERON, MAURICE, 1891-    Dieux et démons, lamas et sorciers de Mongolie. Préf. de Paul Claudel.  Paris, Denoël [ 1953] 267 p. illus. (His Le tryptique mongol, 1).

SCHRAM, LOUIS, 1883-    The Monguors of the Kansu-Tibetan frontier: their origin, history, and social organization. With an introd. by Owen Lattimore. Philadelphia, American Philosophical Society, 1954. 138 p. illus., group port., maps. (Transactions of the American Philosophical Society, new ser., v. 44, pt. 1).

——. The Monguors of the Kansu-Tibetan frontier: their religious life.  Philadelphia, American Philosophical Society, 1957. 164 p. illus. (Transactions of the American Philosophical Society, new ser., v. 47, pt. 1.).

SMITH, MABEL WALN. Land of swift-running horses; a summer of adventures in Mongolia. Drawings by Imre Hofbauer. London, Harrap[ 1956]216 p. illus.

VLADIMIRTSOV, BORIS ÍAKOVLEVICH, 1884-1931. Le régime social des Mongols; le féodalisme nomade. Préf. par René Grousset. Traduction par Michel Carsow. Paris, A. Maisonneuve, 1948. xviii, 291 p. fold. col. map. (Publications du Musée Guimet. Bibliothèque d'études, t. 52).

VREELAND, HERBERT HAROLD, 1920-    Mongol community and kinship structure. 2d. ed.  New Haven, Human Relations Area Files, 1957. ix 359 p. illus. maps, plans. (Behavior science monographs). 1st ed. 1953.

## Foreign Missions

BROUGHTON, DOUGLAS G. Mongolian plains and Japanese prisons. London, Pickering and Inglis, 1947. 71 p. illus., ports., map (on lining-paper).

CONGREGATION OF THE IMMACULATE HEART OF MARY. Directorium seminariorum (in Sinis). Pekini, Missionariis congregationis immaculati cordis Mariae (Scheut), [ 1949] xxxix, 745 p.

CRISTIANI, LÉON. Les fils de Saint François et de Saint Dominique chez les Mongols. Liége, Pensée Catholique, 1932. 32 p. (Collection Études religieuses).

DIEU, LÉON. La mission belge en Chine. 2. éd.  Bruxelles, Office de publicité, 1944. 118, [ 2] p. front. (port. ) (Collection nationale 2. sér., nr. 15).

——. A l'ombre de la Grande Muraille.  Charleroi, J. Depuis, 1944. 169 p.

HECKEN, JOSEPH VAN, 1905-    Les missions chez les mongols aux temps modernes. Peiping, Imrp. des Lazaristes, 1949. 254 p.

——. Les réductions catholiques du pays des Ordos; une méthode d'apostolat des missionnaires de Scheut. Schoneck/Beckenried (Suisse), 1955-56. 102 p. Reprinted from Neue Zeitschrift für Missionswissenschaft. v. 11-12.

LEYSSEN, JACOBUS, 1889-    Formatio cleri in Mongolia. Pekini, Ex typ. Lazaristarum, 1940. 154 p. illus. ports.

——. The Cross over China's wall. Peking, Lazarist Press, 1941. 174 p. illus. (incl. ports., map) diagr.

——. Le triomphe de la charité; ou, le contennaire de l'oeuvre de la Saint-Enfance, avec une lettre-préface de S. E. le Délégué Apostolique et de plusieurs évêques de Chine. Pékin, Impr. des Lazaristes, 1943. xxi, 236 p. illus. plates, ports.

LA MISSION BELGE EN CHINE, par un missionnaire de Scheut.  Bruxelles, Office de Publicité, 1942. 123 p. ports. (Collection Nationale, 15).

NAIRNE, W    P. Gilmour of the Mongols. London, Hodder and Stoughton, [ 1924] xi (e.e. ix), 206 p. 2 port. (incl. front. ) 2 maps. [ Master missionary series].

PELLIOT, PAUL, 1878-1945. Les Mongols et la papauté.  Paris, A. Picard,

1923. 1 v. in 3 (222 p.) illus., facsim. "Extrait de la Revue de l'orient
chrétien. 3e série, t. iii (xxiii), nos 1 et 2 (1922-23), pp. 3-30."

REASON, JOYCE, 1894-  In Mongol tents. London, Livingstone Press, 1939.
16 p.

SINO-MONGOLICA. Bijdragen door de missionarissen van Oost-Mongolië; mémoires des missionnaires de la Mongolie orientale. jaarg. 1-3, aflevering 3;
1920/21-1925-26. [Louvain, W.A. Grootaers; 1939] 3 v. in 1. No nos.
issued 1922/23-1924/25.

TROIS MISSIONNAIRES AUX MAINS DES BRIGANDS: Les Pères Soenen, Van
Praet et De Clippele. Anvers, Impr. De Vièvre, 1926. 184 p. incl. illus.
ports, map.

See also Christianity and Foreign Missions-Franciscans.

## Art and Archaeology

EGAMI, NAMIO. Inner Mongolia and the region of the Great Wall, by Namio E-
gami and Seiichi Mizuno. Tokyo and Kyoto, Far Eastern Archaeological Society, 1935. viii, 16, [349] p. illus. plates, map. (Archaeologia orientalis.
Ser. B., 1.).

HARADA, YOSHITO. Shang-Tu; the summer capital of the Yuan dynasty in Dolon
Nor, Mongolia, by Yoshito Harada and Kazuchika Komai. English resumé of
the Japanese text by Jiro Harada. Tokyo, The Far Eastern Archaeological
Society [1941] 1 v. (various pagings) illus. plates, plans, facsim. (Archaeologia orientalis ser. B., 2).

MARINGER, JOHN. Contribution to the prehistory of Mongolia, a study of the
prehistoric collections from Inner Mongolia. Together with the catalogue prepared by Folke Bergman. Stockholm, 1950. xii, 216 p. illus., maps (1 fold.
col.) (Reports from the sceintific expedition to the north-western provinces
of China under the leadership of Dr. Sven Hedin. The Sino-Swedish Expedition. Publication 34. vii. Archaeology, 7).

THE MONGOLIAN PLATEAU, pt. 1., 蒙古高原論 . Tokyo, The East Asia Archaeological Society, 1942. 1 v. plates (part fold.) ports, fold. maps, (Archaeologia orientalis, ser. B, 4).

SOMMARSTRÖM, BO., 1923-  Archaeological researches in the Edsen-gol region, Inner Mongolia. Together with the catalogue prepared by Folke Bergman. Stockholm, Statens Etnografiska Museum, 1956 [i.e. 1957]- 1958. 2 v.
illus., fold. col. maps. (Reports from the scientific expedition to the north-
western provinces of China under the leadership of Dr. Sven Hedin. The Sino-
Swedish Expedition. Publication 39. vii. Archeology, 8-9) Translated from
Swedish ms. by Kathleen Pain.

TAMURA, JITSUZŌ, 1904-  Tombs and mural paintings of Ch'ing-ling, Liao
imperial mausoleums of eleventh century A.D. in Eastern Mongolia; detailed
report of archaeological survey carried out in 1935 and 1939, by Jitsuzo Tamura and Yukio Kobayashi. English summary by Shinobu Iwamura and Wilma
Fairbank. [Kyoto] Dept. of Literature, Kyoto University, 1952-53 [v. 1,
1953] 2 v. illus., plates (part col., part fold.) maps (part fold.).

TREVER, KAMILLA VASIL'EVNA. Excavations in Northern Mongolia, 1924-
1925. Leningrad, 1932. 73, [2] p. 33 plates. (Memoirs of the Academy of
History of Material Culture, 3).

## Natural History, Geology and Paleontology

ANDREWS, ROY CHAPMAN, 1884-  Across Mongolian plains: a naturalist's account of China's "great northwest," photographs by Yvette Borup Andrews.
New York, London, D. Appleton, 1921. N.Y. Blue Ribbon Books, 1931. xxiv,
276 p. front., plates, ports., map.

————. On the trail of ancient man; a narrative of the field work of the Central

Asiatic expeditions, with an introduction and a chapter by Henry Fairfield Osborn, illustrated with photographs by J. B. Shackelford. New York, Garden City Pub. Co. [1935] (c1926) vii-xviii, 375 p. front., illus. (incl. maps) plates, ports.

——. Auf der Fährte des Urmenschen; Abenteuer und Entdeckungen dreier Expeditionen in die mongolische Wünste. Leipzig, F.A. Brockhaus, 1927. 287 p. front. (port.), illus., map, plates.

——. The new conquest of central Asia; a narrative of the explorations of the Central Asiatic expeditions in Mongolia and China, 1921-1930, with chapters by Walter Granger, Clifford H. Pope [and] Nels C. Nelson, and summary Statements by G. M. Allen, R. C. ANdrews, C. P. Berkey [and others] With 128 plates and 12 illustrations in the text and three maps at end. New York, American Museum of Natural History, 1932. 1, 678 p. col. front., illus., plates, (incl. ports.) (part fold.) maps (part fold.) diagrs. (Central Asiatic expeditions, Natural history of central Asia, i).

——. This business of exploring. New York, London, G. P. Putnam, 1935. xix, 288 p. front., plates, ports., facsim.

——. Exploring with Andrews, a narrative of a life of exploration; selections for younger readers from the writings of Roy Chapman Andrews. New York, G. P. Putnam, 1938. vii, 226 p. front., plates, ports.

——. Heart of Asia; true tales of the Far East. New York, Duell, Sloan and Pearce [1951]; London, A. Barker, 1952. 224 p.

BERKEY, CHARLES PETER, 1867-1955. Geology and prehistoric archaeology of the Gobi desert, by Charles P. Berkey and N.C. Nelson. New York, 1926. 16 p. illus. (incl. map) (American Museum novitates, 222).

——. Geology of Mongolia; a reconnaissance report based on the investigations of the years 1922-1923, by Charles P. Berkey [and] Frederick K. Morris, with 44 plates and 161 illustrations in the text, six maps in pocket at end. New York, American Museum of Natural history, 1927. xxxi, 475 p. col. front., illus., plates (1 col.) maps (part fold.) diagrs. (Central Asiatic expeditions of the American museum of natural history. Natural history of Central Asia, ii).

BOHLIN, BIRGER, 1898-    A contribution to our knowledge of the distribution of vegetation in Inner Mongolia, Kansu and Ching-hai. Stockholm, 1949. 95 p. illus., maps (1 fold. col.) (Reports from the scientific expedition to the northwestern provinces of China under the leadership of Dr. Sven Hedin. The Sino-Swedish Expedition. Publication 33. xi. Botany, 3).

——. Fossil reptiles from Mongolia and Kansu. Appendix: Details of a new moulding and casting method, by Eric Stahl. Stockholm, Statens Etnografiska Museum, 1953. 113 p. illus., 9 plates, map. (Reports from the scientific expedition to the north-western provinces of China under leadership of Dr. Sven Hedin. The Sino-Swedish Expedition. Publication 37. vi. Vertebrate palaeontology, 6).

CLEMENTS, JULIUS MORGAN, 1869-    Gold placer area in Mongolia. Washington, Govt. Print. Off., 1922. 14 p. incl. tables. ([U.S.] Bureau of foreign and domestic commerce. Trade information bulletin, 4).

COLBERT, EDWIN HARRIS, 1905-    An upper Miocene suid from the Gobi desert. New York, 1934. 7 p. illus. (American Museum novitates, 690).

——. Palaeotragus in the Tung Gur formation of Mongolia. New York, 1936. 17 p. illus. (American Museum novitates, 874).

——. Tertiary deer discovered by the American Museum Asiatic expeditions. New York, 1936. 21 p. illus. (American Museum novitates, 854).

——. A new anchitheriine horse from the Tung Gur formation of Mongolia. New York, 1939. 9 p. illus. (American Museum novitates, 1019).

——. Some cervid teeth from the Tung Gur formation of Mongolia, and additional notes on the gnera Stephanocemas and Lagomeryx. New York, 1940. 6 p. illus. (American Museum novitates, 1062).

GILMORE, CHARLES WHITNEY, 1874-1945. Two new dinosaurian reptiles from Mongolia with notes on some fragmentary specimens. New York, 1933. 20 p. illus. (American Museum novitates, 679).

GRABAU, AMADEUS WILLIAM, 1870-1946. The Permian of Mongolia; a report on the Permian fauna of the Jisu Honguer limestone of Mongolia and its relations to the Permian of other parts of the world... with a chapter on the relations of the Jisu Honguer formation to the general geology of Mongolia, by Charles P. Berkey and Frederick K. Morris, with 72 illustrations in the text and 35 plates at end of volume. New York, American Museum of Natural history, 1931. xliii, 665 p. illus., plates, maps (1 fold.) tables (1 fold.) diagrs. (Central Asiatic expeditions of the American museum of natural history. Natural history of Central Asia, iv).

GRANGER, WALTER, 1872-1941. Discovery of Cretaceous and other Tertiary strata in Mongolia, by Walter Granger and Charles B. Berkey. New York, 1922. 7 p. illus. (map.) (American Museum novitates, 42).

————. Protoceratops andrewsi, a pre-ceratopsian dinosaur from Mongolia, by Walter Granger and William K. Gregory. New York, 1923. 9 p. illus. (American Museum novitates, 72).

————. An apparently new family of amblypod mammals from Mongolia, by Walter Granger and William K. Gregory. New York, 1934. 8 p. illus. (American Museum novitates, 720).

GREEN, FITZHUGH, 1888- Roy Chapman Andrews, dragon hunter, with 31 illustrations. New York, London, G. P. Putman 1930. ix, 173 p. front., plates, ports.

GREGORY, WILLIAM KING, 1876- On Protoceratops, a primitive ceratopsian dinosaur from the lower Cretaceous of Mongolia, by William K. Gregory and Charles C. Mook. New York, 1925. 9 p. illus. (American Museum novitates, 156).

HÖRNER, NILS, 1896- Some notes and data concerning dunes and sand drift in the Gobi desert. 40 p. plates, maps., fig. (Reports from the scientific expedition to the north-western provinces of China under the leadership of dr. Sven Hedin. The Sino-Swedish expedition. iii. Geology:5).

KOHMURA, TAIJI. Die Veredelung des mongolischen Schafes; Kreuzungsversuche am mongolischen Fettschwanzschaf mit dem Rambouilletmerino in besonderer Rücksicht auf die Vererbung der Wollcharaktere und des Wollertrags. Tokyo, Maruzen, 1938. iv, 75 p., xix plates., diagrs.

MATSUZAWA, ISAO. The geological history of the Mongolian plateau and the history of the physiographic development. Translation prepared by the Engineer Intelligence Division, Office of the Engineer, Hdqrs. U.S. Army Forces, Far East, Tokyo. Tokyo, 1955. 83 p. maps, diagrs. (U.S. Army. Corps of Engineers. Far East command. Pacific surveys, Report, 23).

MILLER, GERRIT SMITH, 1869- Revised determinations of some Tertiary mammals from Mongolia. Peking, Geological Survey of China, 1927. [3]-20 p. (China. Geological survey. Palaeontologia sinica, ser. c, v. 5, fasc. 2).

MURAKAMI, HANZŌ. Mica deposits of Inner Mongolia. Translation prepared by Military Geology Branch, U.S. Geological Survey, for Intelligence Division, Office of the Engineer, Hdqrs. U.S. Army Forces, Far East, Tokyo, 1953. 6 l. (U.S. Geological Survey. Pacific geological surveys, report, 161).

NORLINDH, TYCHO, 1906- Flora of the Mongolian steppe and desert areas. pt. 1. Stockholm, 1949. 139 p. illus., maps (1 fold.) (Reports from the scientific expedition to the north-western provinces of China under the leadership of Dr. Sven Hedin. The Sino-Swedish Expedition. Publication 31. xi. Botany, 4.

SCHLOSSER, MAX. Tertiary vertebrates from Mongolia. Peking, Published by the Geological Survey of China, 1924. 132, [4] p., illus., plates, (China. Geological survey. Palaeontologia sinica, ser. c, vol. i, fasc. 1).

SOUTH MANCHURIA RAILWAY COMPANY. Investigation of the eastern part of

Inner and Outer Mongolia, by Party No. II, pt. 1-3. Dairen, Investigation
Section, General Affairs Dept., South Manchurian Railway Co., 1927. 3 pts.
illus. maps, (part col., 2 fold.) diagrs. tables.

————. Excerpt from Investigation of the eastern part of Inner and Outer Mongolia (by Party No. 11): Part 11. Commerce, agriculture and geology. Published by Investigation Section, General Affairs Department, 1927. Translation prepared by Engineer Intelligence Division, Office of the Engineer.
Hdqrs. U. S. Army Forces, Far East, Tokyo. Tokyo, 1955. 28 l. maps.
fold. table, (U.S. Army. Corps of Engineers, Far East. [Pacific Surveys.
Reports] 33).

TEILHARD DE CHARDIN, PIERRE. Étude géologique sur la région du Dalai-
Noor. Paris, Société géologique de France, 1926. 56 p. incl. illus. plates,
2 fold. col. maps. (Mémoires de la Société géologique de France. nouv. sér.,
t. 3, fasc. 3).

WALKER, EGBERT HAMILTON, 1899-    Plants collected by R. C. Ching, 秦仁
昌, in southern Mongolia and Kansu province, China. Washington, Govt.
Print. Off., 1941.    v, 563-675, vii-xiii p. 1 illus., plates. (Smithsonian
institution. U.S. National museum. Contributions from the U. S. National
herbarium, v. 28, pt. 4).

# XXIV. TIBET

## Bibliographies

[AUSTRALIA, JOINT SERVICE STAFF, Washington, D. C.] Tibet-Sinkiang-Tannu Tuva; handbook of selected reference material. [n. p. ] 1949-  7 pts. mimeographed.

FAZY, ROBERT. Essai d'une bibliographie raisonnée de l'exploration tibétaine. St. Gallen, Buchdr. H. Tschudy und Co., 1940. iv, 20 p. Reprinted from the Bulletin de la Société suisse des amis de l'Extrême-Orient, décembre, 1940.

SHAFER, ROBERT, 1893-  Bibliography of Sino-Tibetan languages. Wiesbaden, O. Harrassowitz, 1957. xl, 211 p.

## Description and Travel

BACOT, JACQUES, 1877-  Le Tibet et les Tibétains. Monaco, Impr. de Monaco, 1925. 29 p. (Société de Conférences, Monaco. [Conférences No. 17].

BAILEY, FREDERICK MARSHMAN, 1882-  China-Tibet-Assam; a journey, 1911. London, J. Cape [1945] 175 p. front. (port. ) 1 illus. (music) plates, maps (1 fold. ).

———. No passport to Tibet. London, Hart-Davis, 1957. 294 p. illus.

BEHAGUE, JOHN C. I found Shangri-La. [Birmingham, Eng. ] Eagle Publications and Publicity [1947] 46 p. illus.

BHANJA, K. C. Mystic Tibet and the Himalaya. Darjeeling, Gilbert, 1948. 306 p. plates, photos.

BYRON, ROBERT, 1905-1941. First Russia, then Tibet. [London] Macmillan, 1933. xvi, 328 p. col. front., illus., plates, ports.

CHAPMAN, FREDERICK SPENCER, 1907-  Lhasa, the holy city; with an introduction by Sir Charles Bell. London, Chatto and Windus, 1938; New York, Harper, 1939. xiv, 342 p., col. front., plates (part col. ) ports., maps ( 1 fold. ).

———. Memoirs of a mountaineer: Helvellyn to Himalaya. Lhasa, the holy city. [Rev. ed.] London, Chatto and Windus, 1951. 446 p. illus.

CONNOLLY, LOUISE, 1862-1927. Tibet; the country, climate, people, customs, religion, resources. Newark, N. J., Newark Museum Association, 1921. xi, 37 p. incl. front. (map) illus.

DAVID-NEEL, ALEXANDRA, 1874-  À pied et en mendiant de la Chine à l'Inde à travers le Thibet: voyage d'une Parisienne à Lhassa. Paris, Plon, [1927]. xii, 332 p. front. fold. map, plates, ports.

———. My journey to Lhasa; the personal story of the only white woman who succeeded in entering the forbidden city, illustrated with many photographs taken by the author. New York and London, Harper, 1927. xviii, 310 p. front., plates, ports.

———. Arjopa; die erste Pilgerfahrt einer weissen Frau nach der verbotenen Stadt des Dalai Lama. 2. Aufl. [Aus dem Englischen von Ada Ditzen] Leipzig, F. A. Brockhaus, 1930. 322 p. plates, ports., map.

———. Mönche und Strauchritter; eine Tibetfahrt auf Schleichwegen [aus dem Französischen von Karl Pfannkuch]. Leipzig, F. A. Brockhaus, 1933. 290 p. front., illus. (incl. map).

———. Grand Tibet; au pays des brigands gentilshommes; avec 26 gravures et une carte. Paris, Plon [1933] ii, 356 p., plates, ports., fold. map.

———. Tibetan journey. London, John Lane, [1936] x, 275 [1] p. front., plates, ports., fold. map.

——. A l'ouest barbare de la vaste Chine. Paris, Plon [ 1947] ii, 301 p. illus. ports., fold. map.

——. Land der Is; in Chinas wildem Westen. [ Übertragen von Herbert Furreg. Wien] Ullstein [ 1952] 270 p. illus.

DOUGLAS, WILLIAM ORVILLE, 1898-    Beyond the high Himalayas. Garden City, N.Y., Doubleday, 1952. 352 p. illus. (part col. ) maps (on lining papers).

DUNCAN, MARION HERBERT, 1896-    The Yangtze and the yak; adventurous trails in and out of Tibet. Alexandria, Va., Privately printed, 1952. x, 353 p. illus., ports., maps (1 on linging papers, 4 fold. in pocket).

EASTON, JOHN. An unfrequented highway through Sikkim and Tibet to Chumolaori. London, Scholartis Press, 1928. xi, [1], 132, [2] p. front., plates.

EMMERICH, FERDINAND. Asiatenwache Erlebtes in Südost-Tibet. Leipzig, Fr. Seybold, 1922. 79 p. (Seynolds Volksbücher, 12).

——. Von Birma nach Tibet. Leipzig, Staneck, 1935-1936. 241 p. illus. (His Reisebericht).

——. Auf Schleichwegen nach Tibet. Leipzig, Staneck, 1936. 247 p. (His Reisebericht).

ENDERS, GORDON BANDY. Foreign devil; an American Kim in modern Asia. New York, Simon and Schuster, 1942; London, J. Gifford [ 1945] 3-307 p.

FORD, ROBERT, 1923-    Wind between the worlds. New York, D. McKay Co. [ 1957] 338 p.

——. Captured in Tibet. London, Harrap [ 1957] 256 p. illus. ports.

FORMAN, HARRISON, 1904-    Through forbidden Tibet; an adventure into the unknown. New York, Longmans, Green, 1935. xii, 275 p. front., plates, ports., facsims. London ed. Jarrods, 1936, xii, 288 p.

GLÜCK, JULIUS F. Tibet; Ausstellung im Linden-Museum [ Stuttgart, 1955] 20 p.

HAMSA, bhagwan, 1878-    The Holy mountain; being the story of a pilgrimage to lake Mānas and of initiation on mount Kailās in Tibet, by Bhagwān Shri Hamsa; translated from the Marāthi by Shri Purohit. swāmi; with an introduction by W. B. Yeats. London, Faber and Faber, [ 1934] 7-202, [ 1] p. front. (port. ) plates.

HANBURY-TRACY, JOHN. Black river of Tibet; foreword by Admiral Sir William Goodenough, G. C. B. With 24 illustrations and a map. London, F. Muller, [ 1938] xi, 305 p. front., plates, ports.

HANSTEIN, OTFRIED VON. Ins Verbotene Tibet; Abenteuer-Erzählung. Wien und Innsbruck, Hartleben, 1953. 215 p.

HARRER, HEINRICH, 1912-    Sieben Jahre in Tibet; mein Leben am Hofe des Dalai Lama. [ Wien] Ullstein [ 1952] 266 p. illus.

——. The same. [ Gekürzte Ausg. Wien] Ullstein [ 1954] 191 p. illus. (Bunte leuchtende Welt).

——. Seven years in Tibet; translated from the German by Richard Graves. With an introd. by Peter Fleming. London, R. Hart-Davis, 1953. 288 p. illus.

——. The same. New York, Dutton, 1954 [ c1953] 314 p. illus.

——. Sept ans d'aventures au Tibet; traduction de Henri Daussy. Ouvrage orné de 40 héliogravures. Paris, Arthaud [ 1953] 271 p. illus., ports., fold. map. (Collection "Les Clefs de l'aventure, " 4).

——. Meine Tibet-Bilder. Text: Heinz Woltereck. Seebruck am Chiemsee, Heering-Verlag, 1953. 232 p. illus. (part col. ) ports. (part col. ) map (on lining paper).

HAYDEN, SIR HENRY HUBERT, 1869-1923. Sport and travel in the highlands of Tibet, by Sir Henry Hayden and César Cosson, with an introduction by Sir Francis Younghusband. London, R. Cobden-Sanderson [ 1927] xvi, 262 p. front., plates, ports., fold. map (in pocket).

HEICHEN, WALTER, 1876-    Der Todesgang der Karawane; ein Tatsachenbericht über Sven Hedins reisen durch Tibet, von Walter Heichen. Mit bildern

von M. Wulff.  Berlin, A. Weichert [ 1936] 112 p. incl. front., plates., facsim.

HERRMANN, WILHELM KARL.  Ein Ritt für Deutschland.  Mit 1 Titelbild und
228 Abbildungen nach eigenen Aufnahmen des Verfassers, 14-Zeichnungen im
Text und 6 Karten.  Berlin-Leipzig, Nibelungen-verlag, 1940.  591 p. front.,
illus., plates (1 fold. ) ports., facsims., fold. map.

HUC, ÉVARISTE RÉGIS, 1813-1860.  Un français à Lhasa; voyage en Tartarie
et au Thibet.  Paris, Éditions Montsouris, 1942.  96 p.  map, (Collection
Dauphine).

―――. Découverte du Thibet (1845-46).  Paris, Flammarion, 1934.  96 p. illus.
(Collection Bonnes Lectures).

HUGUENIN, CYRANO.  Voyage au coeur du monde.  Lausanne, Éditions Les Gé-
meaux [ 1946] 357 p.

ILLION, THEODORE.  Rätselhaftes Tibet; in Verkleidung unter Lamas, Räubern
und wahrhaft Weisen.  Hamburg, Uranus-Verlag [ c1936] 143 p. plates, port.

―――. In secret Tibet; in disguise amongst lamas, robbers, and wise men.  A
key to the mysteries of Tibet.  London, Rider [ 1937] ix-xi, 13-190 p.

IUSOV, B        V. Tibet; kurzer geographischer Abriss.  Hrsg. von W. J. Awar-
in und E. M. Mursajew.  [ Übers. von Martin Brandt]  Leipzig, Bibliographisches Institut, 1953.  80 p. illus.

KAULBACK, RONALD .  Tibetan trek.  London, Hodder and Stoughton, 1934.
iii-ix, [ 11]-300 p. front., plates, ports, 2 maps.

―――. Salween.  London, Hodder and Stoughton [ 1938] xi, 331 p. front., illus.
plates, ports., maps.

―――. The same; New York, Harcourt, Brace [ c1939] 331 p. front., illus.,
plates, ports., maps (1 fold. ).

KIDD, WALTER J. What made Tibet mysterious? Notes on Tibet's topography,
history and religion.  Newark, N. J., Newark Museum Association, 1921-22.
16 p. illus.

KNIGHT, G.      E.       O. Intimate glimpses of mysterious Tibet and neighboring
countries. 4th ed.  London, The Golden Vista Press, 1930.  72 p. port.

KRUPARZ, HEINZ, 1929-    Shisha Pangma; Reisebilder aus Indien, Nepal und
Tibet. Geleitwort von Wilhelm Filchner.  95 Schwarzweissfotos, 8 Farbbilder
[ und] 2 Landkarten.  Wien, Kremayr und Scheriau [ 1954] 190 p. illus.

LAFUGIE.        Au Tibet.  Préf. de Alexandra David Neel.  Couverture, illus. et
photographies de l'auteur.  Paris, J. Susse [ 1949] 214 p. illus., ports. (Collection  Voyages et aventures ).

LANDOR, ARNOLD HENRY SAVAGE, 1865-1924.  Auf verbotenen Wegen.  Leipzig, F. A. Brockhaus, 1923.  159 p. front. (port. ) illus. (incl. map) plates.
[ Reisen und abenteuer, 22].  3 aufl. 1898.  511 p.

MA, SHAO-YUN, 馬少雲, [ MA YANG, 馬揚].  Tibet; a geographical, ethnological, and historical sketch, derived from Chinese sources.  With 6 maps and
plans. By W. Woodville Rockhill 1891.  Peking, Wên tien ko shu chuang, 1939.
Cover-title, 133, 185-291 p. fold. plates (part col. ) fold maps. A translation
of parts of the Wei Ts'ang t'u chih, 衛藏圖識 .

MACDONALD, DAVID.  Touring in Sikkim and Tibet.  Kalimpong, 1930; Calcutta,
Thacker, Spink, 1943.  2, 126 p. fold. map.

―――. Tibet.  [ London ] H. Milford, Oxford University Press [ 1945] 31, [ 1] p.
(Oxford pamphlets on Indian affairs, no. 30).

―――. Valley of a thousand knives.  London, Grey Walls Press, 1948.  198 p.
(Falcon Press Book).

MCGOVERN, WILLIAM MONTGOMERY, 1897-    To Lhasa in disguise; an account of a secret expedition through mysterious Tibet.  London, T. Butterworth, [ 1924]; New York and London, Century, c1924.  352 p. front., illus.
(maps) plates, ports.

―――, Als Kuli nach Lhasa, eine heimliche Reise nach Tibet.  Aus dem Englisch-
en übers. von Martin Proskauer.  Berlin, A. Scherl [ 192  ] 296 p. illus.,

ports., maps.

MARAINI, FOSCO. Secret Tibet; translated from the Italian by Eric Mosbacher. Foreword by Bernard Berenson. Illustrated with 70 photos. by the author. New York, Viking Press, 1952. xii, 306 p. illus., ports., maps (on lining paper).

———. The same; with an introductory letter by Bernard Berenson. Illustrated with 60 double colour plates from photos, by the author. Translated from the Italian by Eric Mosbacher. London, Hutchinson [ 1952] 251 p. illus.

———. Tibet secret (Segreto Tibet) Préf. de Bernard Berenson; traduit de l'italien par Juliette Bertrand. Ouvrage orné de 68 héliogravures d'après des photos. de l'auteur. Paris, B. Arthaud [ 1952] 311 p. illus. (Collection 'Exploration,'' 4).

———. The same. Paris, Club des libraires de France, 1957. 328 p. illus. (photos). map.

———. Geheimnis Tibet, übers. von Lotte Leber. München und Wien, Andermann, 1953. 286 p. plates.

MELE, PIETRO FRANCESCO. Tibet. Photographs and text by P. F. Mele. Introduction by G. Dainelli. London, G. Allen and Unwin, 1957. 100 p. plates, photos.

MERRICK, MRS. HENRIETTA (SANDS). Spoken in Tibet. New York, London, G. P. Putnam, 1933. v-xvi, 19-198 p. front., plates, ports., map.

MIGOT, ANDRÉ, 1892-  Caravane vers Bouddha; un Français à travers la Haute-Asie mystique. Préf. d'Alexandra David-Neel. Paris, Amiot-Dumont [ 1954] 228 p. illus. (Bibliothèque des voyages).

———. Tibetan marches; translated from the French by Peter Fleming. London, R. Hart-Davis; New York, Dutton, 1955. 288 p. illus.

———. The same; Harmondsworth, Penguin Books, 1957. 253 p. plates, map.

———. Vor den Toren Tibets. Deutsche Übertragen von Leonore Schlaich. Stuttgart, Scherz und Goverts, 1955. 288 p. plates.

O'CONNOR, SIR WILLIAM FREDERICK TRAVERS, 1870-  On the frontier and beyond; a record of thirty years' service, by Lieut.-Colonel Sir Frederick O'Connor. London, J. Murray [ 1931] xiv, 355 p. front., illus. (map) plates, ports.

PALLIS, MARCO, 1895-  Peaks and lamas, with one plate in colour, ninety-five photogravure illustrations, and three maps. London and Toronto, Cassell, 1946. ix-xx, 428 p. front., illus. (incl. maps) plates (1 col.) ports. ''First edition October 1939. Third (revised) edition June 1942.''

———. The same. [ Rev. and completely reset] New York, A.A. Knopf, 1949. xvii, 397, xiii p. illus., ports., maps.

PATTERSON, GEORGE NEILSON, 1920-  Tibetan journey. London, Faber and Faber [ 1954] 232 p. illus.

———. Journey with Loshay. New York, Norton [ 1954] 248 p. illus.

PELLIOT, PAUL, 1878-1945. Asie contrale et Tibet. Missions Pelliot et Bacot (Documents exposés au Musée Guimet). Paris et Bruxelles, G. van Oest, 1921. 38 p. plates, (Bull. archéologique du Musée Guimet, facs. 2).

———. Le voyage de mm. Gabet et Huc à Lhasa. [n. p., n. d. ] [ 133]-178 p. On cover: T'oung-pao. Tirage à part.

QUELING, HANS, 1903-  Im Land der schwarzen Gletscher; eine Forscherfahrt nach Tibet. Frankfurt a. M., Societäts-Verlag [ c1937] 291 p., plates, ports., map.

REIFENBERG, JAN GEORG. Siedlung im tibetischen Hochland. Grundlagen und Erscheinungsformen, geographisch betrachtet. Freiburg, 1949. 123 l. plate, map. Diss.-Univ. Freiburg.

RIENCOURT, AMAURY DE. Roof of the world, Tibet, key to Asia. New York, Rinehart [ 1950] x, 322 p. illus., ports., maps.

———. Lost world: Tibet, key to Asia. London, Gollancz, 1951. 317 p. illus., maps.

——. Le toit du monde. Tibet et Asie. Traduit par René Jouan. Paris. Éditions France-Empire. 1955. 316 p. illus. (photos).

——. Tibet im wandel Asiens. übers. aus dem Amerikanischen von Lothar Tobias. Wiesbaden. F. A. Brockhaus. 1951. 286 p. illus. maps.

RIJNHART, SUSI. Unter Lama und Lumpen in Tibet. Die Tibetreise von Susi und
Petrus Rijnhart. Nacherzählt von Friedemann Schaefer. Stuttgart, Evang.
Missionsverlag, 1956. 15 p. (Auf den Strassen der Welt. Missionshefte d.
Jungen Gemeinde, 34).

ROEDER, HEINRICH VON. Gold in Tibet. Bens Abenteuer auf dem Dach des
Erde; von Heinrich von Roeder und Friedrich von Stülpnagel. Textzeichnungen: Alfred Heller. Hamberg, Bayer Verlag-Anstalt, 1952. 175 p.

ROERĬCH, NĬKOLAĬ KINSTANTĬNOVĬCH, 1874-1947. La joie de l'art. L'âge de
pierre; traduit de l'anglais. A travers le Thibet. Notes de voyage; traduit du
russe. Précédé d'une introduction par M. de Vaux-Phalipau et Georges Chkla-
ver. Paris, Éditions de la Revue du vrai et du beau, 1928. xvii, 18-62 p.
illus.

——. Altai-Himalaya; a travel diary; with twenty reproductions from paintings.
New York, Frederick A. Stokes company, 1929. xix, 407 p. front. (port.)
plates.

——. Heart of Asia. New York, Roerich Museum Press, 1930. 3-170 p. (New
era library, ser. ii-"Lights of Asia," book i).

——. Shambhala, with a frontispiece in colors by Svetoslav Roerich. New
York, Frederick A. Stokes, 1930. viii, 316 p. col. front. (port.).

——. Roerich, compiled and edited by the publishers. New York, Corona Mun-
di, inc., International Art Center [c1924] v-ix, [66] p. illus., port.

——. Nicholaĭ Konstantĭnovĭch Roerĭch: his life and creations during the past
forty years, 1889-1929; with 122 plates, of which 36 are in four colors and
86 in two colors or tinted half tones. New York, Central Book Trading Co.
1931. 47 p. incl. front. (mounted col. port.) illus. (1 mounted col.) 119
plates (part col.).

SCHÄTZ, JOSEF JULIUS, 1887-    Heiliger Himalaya; Menschen und Berge,
Götter, Geister und Dämonen. München, F. Bruckmann [1952] 120 p. illus.

SCHARY EDWIN GILBERT, 1893-    In search of the mahatmas of Tibet; with
forewords by Canon C. E. Tyndale-Biscoe and David Macdonald. London,
Seeley, Service [1937] xiii,[2] p., 1 1.,19-312 p.front. 1 illus. (map) plates,
port., facsims.

SÍS, VLADIMÍR. Der Weg nach Lhasa; Bilder aus Tibet, [von] Vladimír Sis [und]
Josef Vaniš. [Deutsch von M. Vaničková] Prag, Artia, 1956. 54 p. 224
plates (part col.).

——. On the road through Tibet, vy Vladimír Sís and J. Vaniš. Translated by
Iris Urwin. London, Spring Books, 1956. 52 p. plates.

TAFEL, ALBERT, 1877-1935. Meine Tibetreise; eine Studienfahrt durch das
nordwestliche China und durch die innere Mongolei in das östliche Tibet. 2.
Ausg. Stuttgart, Union Deutsche Verlagsgesellschaft [1923? c1914] iv, 499 p.
illus., plates (part col.) port., fold. map.

TEICHMAN, SIR ERIC, 1884-1944. Travels of a consular officer in eastern Tibet, together with a history of the relations between China, Tibet and India,
by Eric Teichman, with original maps of eastern Tibet and photographs taken
by the author. Cambridge [Eng.] The University Press, 1922. xxiii, [1],
248 p. plates, maps (1 fold., in pocket).

THOMAS, LOWELL JACKSON, 1923-    Out of this world; across the Himalayas
to forbidden Tibet. New York, Greystone Press [1950] 320 p. illus. (part
col.) ports. (part col.) col. maps (on lining papers).

——. The same. London, Macdonald [1951] 238 p. illus.

TICHY, HERBERT, 1912-    Weisse Wolken über gelber Erde, eine asiatische
Reise. Wien, Ullstein, 1951 [1948] 376 p. illus., map (on lining-papers).

——. Zum heiligsten Berg der Welt; auf Landstrassen und Pilgerpfaden in Af-

ghanistan, Indien und Tibet. Geleitwort von Sven Hedin. [5., durchgesehene
Aufl.] Wien, Buchgemeinschaft Donauland [1953, c1937] 199 p. plates, fold.
maps (part col.).

——. Tibetan adventure; travels through Afghanistan, India and Tibet; with a
preface by Sven Hedin. London, Faber and Faber, [1938] 261 p. plates, 2
fold. maps. "Translated from the German by Ian F. D. Morrow and L. M.
Sieveking."

——. Drei Buben im Himalaya. Wien-Mödling, St. Gabriel-Verlag; Kaldenkirchen, Steyler Verlag Buchhandlung, 1954. 32 p. (Frische Saat. 34).

TRINKLER, EMIL, 1896-1931. Tibet: sein geographisches Bild und seine Stellung im asiatischen Kontinent. München, C. Wolf und Sohn, 1922. 146 p.
map, plates.

——. Das Land des Dalai Lama. Berlin, R. Hobbing, 1930. 96 p. illus. (Die
Welt im Bild).

WIEDEMANN, HEINZE, ed. Tibet, Indien, Ceylon. Frankfurt a. M., Hirsch-
graben-Verlag, 1957. 64 p. (Hirschgraben-Lesereihe. Reihe 2, Buch. 12).

WIGNALL, SYDNEY. Prisoner in red Tibet. London, Hutchinson, 1957. 264 p.
illus., plates.

WINNINGTON, ALAN. Tibet; record of a journey. London, Lawrence and Wishart, 1957. 235 p. illus.

YOUNGHUSBAND, SIR FRANCIS EDWARD, 1863-1942. Peking to Lhasa; the narrative of journeys in the Chinese empire made by the late Brigadier-General
George Pereira compiled by Sir Francis Younghusband from notes and diaries
supplied by Major-General Sir Cecil Pereira. London, Constable, 1925. x,
293 p. front., plates, ports., fold. maps.

——. The heart of a continent, commemorating the fiftieth anniversary of his
journey from Peking to India by way of the Gobi desert and Chinese Turkestan,
and across the Himalaya by the Mustagh pass. London, J. Murray [1937]
vii-xvi, 246 p. front., illus., plates, port., fold. map.

ZETLAND, LAWRENCE JOHN LUMLEY DUNDAS, 2d marquis of, 1876- Lands
of the thunderbolt, Sikhim, Chumbi and Bhutan, by the Earl of Ronaldshay.
London Constable, 1923. xvii, 267 p. front., plates., fold. map.

## Tibetan Language: Dictionaries

BHATTACHARYA, VIDHUSHEKHARA, mahamahopadhyaya. Bhota-prakāśa; a
Tibetan chrestomathy. With introduction, skeleton grammar, notes, texts
and vocabularies. [Calcutta] University of Calcutta, 1939. lix, 578 p. front.
(facsim.).

BLO-BSAÑ MIN-'GYUR RDO-RJE, lama. A Tibetan-English primer, by Lama
Lobzang mingyur dorje. Rev. ed. [Calcutta, University of Calcutta] 1938.
37 p.

——. Tibetan reader, 1-111. Tibetan-English vocabularies. Calcutta, University of Calcutta, 1951. 3 v.

CHE-RIÑ-DBAÑ-RGYAL. Dictionnaire tibétain-sanscrit, par Tse-ring-ouang-
gyal (Che riñ dbañ rgyal). Reproduction phototypique publiée par J. Bacot.
Paris, P. Geuthner, 1930. 3 p. facsim.: 101 p. (Buddhica. Documents et
travaux pour l'étude du bouddhisme. 2. sér.: Documents, t. 2).

EDGAR, JAMES HUSTON, 1871 or 72-1936. English-Giarung vocabulary.
[Chengtu,] Harvard-Yenching committee of the West China Union University
[1935?] 63 p. "Supplement to volume v, Journal of the West China border research society."

GIRAUDEAU, P. Dictionnaire français-tibétain, Tibet oriental [par] S. E. Mgr.
Giraudeau et Francis Goré. Paris, Adrien-Maisonneuve, 1956. 310, 24 p.

GÕ, MINORU, 1904- ed. An Eastern Tibetan dictionary (revised) and a study
of the Eastern Tibetan language, with special reference to the initial conso-
nants. Edited by Minoru Gõ [and others], Okayama, Minoru Gõ, 1954. 303 p.

map.

GOULD, SIR BASIL JOHN, 1883- 1956. Tibetan syllables, by Sir Basil Gould and Hugh Edward Richardson. [London, H. Milford, Oxford university press, 1943. x, 119, [ 1] p.

——. Tibetan word book, by Sir Basil Gould and Hugh Edward Richardson with a foreword by Sir Aurel Stein [London] H. Milford, Oxford University Press, 1943. xvi, 447 p.

HACKIN, JOSEPH, 1886-1941, ed. and tr. Formulaire sanscrit-tibétain du Xe siècle, édité et traduit par Joseph Hacken. Paris, P. Geuthner, 1924. ix, 27, 130 p. (Mission Pelliot en Asie Centrale, sér. petit in-octavo, 2).

JÄSCHKE, HEINRICH AUGUST, 1817-1883. A Tibetan-English dictionary, with special reference to the prevailing dialects. To which is added an English-Tibetan vocabulary. London, K. Paul, 1934. xxii, 671 p.

——. The same. [London] Routledge and Paul, 1949. xxii, 671 p.

NISHIO, KYŌO, 1901-  comp. A Tibetan index to the Mahavyutpatti, with its Sanskrit equivalents. Sakaki ed. Kyoto, Isseido Pub. Co. [1941] 305 p.

SIMON, WALTER, 1894-  Tibetisch-chinesische Wortgleichungen: Ein Versuch. Berlin, W. de Gruyter, 1930. 72 p. (Berlin. Universität. Seminar für orientalische Sprachen. Mitteil. Bd. 32, Abt. 1).

## Grammar and Readers

BACOT, JACQUES, 1877-  Grammaire du tibétain littéraire. Paris, Librairie d'Amérique et l'Orient, 1946-48. 2 v. Vol. 2 has subtitle: Index morphologique (langue littéraire et langue parlée).

BELL, SIR CHARLES ALFRED, 1870-1945. Grammar of colloquial Tibetan. 3d ed. Alipore, Bengal, Superintendent, Govt. Print. Bengal Govt. Press, 1939. x, [2], 184 p. fold. map (in pocket) fold. facsims.

BERNARD, THEOS, 1908-  A simplified grammar of the literary Tibetan language. Santa Barbara, Tibetan Text Society, 1946 [c1947] ix, 65 p. facsim.

BOUDA, KARL, 1901-  Die Beziehungen des sumerischen zum baskischen, westkaukasischen und tibetischen.  Leipzig, O. Harrassowitz, 1938. 23 p. (Mitteilungen der Altorientalischen gesellschaft, xii, bd., hft. 3).

DBYAŃS-CAN-GRUB-PA'I-RDO-RJE, lama. Tibetische Nationalgrammatik. i. teil: Das Sum-cu-pa und Rtags-kyi-'ajug-pa des lama Dbyańs-can-grub-pairdo-rje. Ein Kommentar zu den gleichnamigen Schriften Thon-mi Sam-bhota's. Übersetzt und erklärt, von Johannes Schubert. [Berlin, Reichsdruckerei, 1928] 59, [1] p. Inaug.-Diss. (Johannes Schubert)-Berlin.

DURR, JACQUES A. Morphologie du verbe tibétain. Heidelberg, C. Winter, 1950. 192 p. (Bibliothek der allgemeinen Sprachwissenschaft. 3. Reihe, Darstellungen und Untersuchungen aus einzelnen Sprachen).

——. ed. Deux traités grammaticaux tibétans. Commentaire développé des çlokas du Sum rTags, admirable collier de perles des savants, par Situ (çlokas 12, 13, 14, 15 et 25 du rTags'aJug) et Examen définitif ou commentaire élucidant les notions difficiles du rTags'aJug appelé Miroir de pur cristal, Dvangs Shel Me Long, par Don'aGrub. Heidelberg, C. Winter, 1950. 95 p. (Bibliothek der allgemeinen Sprachwissenschaft. 3. Reihe: Darstellungen und Untersuchungen aus Einzelnen Sprachen).

GOULD, SIR BASIL JOHN, 1883-1956. Tibetan sentences, by Sir Basil Gould and Hugh Edward Richardson. [London, H. Milford, Oxford university press, 1943. v, 137 p.

JÄSCHKE, HEINRICH AUGUST, 1817-1883. Tibetan grammar; addenda by A. H. Francke, assisted by W. Simon. 3. Aufl. Berlin, Walter de Gruyter, 1929. vi, 161 p.

——. Tibetan grammar. Supplement of readings with vocabulary, by John L. Mish. New York, F. Ungar Pub. Co. [1954] 126 p. First ed. published in 1865 under title: A short practical grammar of the Tibetan language.

KOERBER, HANS NORDEWIN VON. Morphology of the Tibetan language; a con-
tribrution to comparative Indosinology. Los Angeles, Suttonhouse [1935]
xii, 230 p.
LALOU, MARCELLE. Manuel élémentaire de tibétain classique; méthode empi-
rique. Paris, A. Maisonneuve, 1950. v, 111 p.
MILLER, ROY ANDREW, 1924-    The Tibetan system of writing. Washington,
American Council of Learned Societies; London, Bailey and Swinfen, 1956.
30 p. (American Council of Learned Societies. Program in Oriental Lan
guages. Publications. Series B: Aids, no. 6).
ROERICH, GEORGE NICHOLAS, 1902-    Dialects of Tibet; the Tibetan dialect
of Lahul. New York, Urusvati Himalayan Reaearch Institute of Roerich Museum [1933] 107 p. (Tibetica, v. 1). Issued also in Journal of Urusvati Hima-
layan Research Institute of Roerich Museum, v. 3 (1933) p. 83-189.
——. Text-book of colloquial Tibetan. Dialect of Central Tibet, by George N.
Roerich and Tse-Trung Lopsang Phuntshok. Bengal, 1957. iv, 238 p.
ROL-PA'I-RDO-RJE, grand lama of Peking, 1736-1795. Tibetische National-
grammatik; das Sum cu pa und Rtags kyi 'ajug pa des Grosslamas von Peking
Rol pai rdo rje. Ein Kommentar zu den gleichnamigen Schriften Thon-mi
Sambhoṭa's auf Grund der Erklärung des lamas Chos-skyoṅ-bzaṅ-po, lo-tsa-
ba von Johannes Schubert. Leipzig, Offizin R. Hadl, 1937. 104 p.(Artibus
Asiae, curat editionem Richard Hadl. Suppl. i).
THONMI SAMBHOṬA, fl 632. Une grammaire tibétaine du tibétain classique.
Les ślokas grammaticaux de Thonmi Sambhoṭa, avec leurs commentaires,
traduits du tibétain et annotés par Jacques Bacot. Paris, P. Geuthner, 1928.
iv, 231 p. fold. facsims. (Annales du Musée Guimet, Bibliothèque d'études-
t. 37).
U.S. Work projects administration. California. Sino-Tibetan linguistics. Produced on a Work projects administration project. Sponsored by University of
California through A.L. Kroeber, Dept. of anthropology. Supervised by Robert Shafer [and] Paul K. Benedict. Berkeley, Calif., 1937-41. 16 v. in 15.
tables.

Other Tibetan Dialects

READ, ALFRED FRANK CHARLES, 1907-    Balti grammar. London, Royal
Asiatic Society, 1934. iv, 108 p. (James G. Forlong fund, vol. xv).
THOMAS, FREDERICK WILLIAM, 1867-1956. Nam, an ancient language of the
Sino-Tibetan borderland; text, with introd., vocabulary and linguistic studies.
London, Oxford Univ. Press, 1948. x, 469 p. fold. map, facsims. (Publica-
tions of the Philological Society, 14).
WALSH, ERNEST HERBERT COOPER, 1865-    A vocabulary of the Tromowa
dialect of Tibetan spoken in the Chumbi valley (so far as it differs from standard Tibetan), together with a corresponding vocabulary of Sikhimese and of
Central (standard) Tibetan compiled by E.H.C. Walsh, I.c.s. (the corresponding Sikhimese words supplied by Sub-inspector S.W. Laden La, Bengal
police.). Calcutta, Bengal-Secretariat Book Depot, 1905. x, 34 p.
WOLFENDEN, STUART NORRIS, 1889-    Outlines of Tibeto-Burman linguistic
morphology, with special reference to the prefixes, infixes and suffixes of
classical Tibetan and the languages of the Kachin, Bodo, Nâgâ, Kuki-Chin
and Burma groups. London, Royal Asiatic-Society, 1929. xv, 216 p. fold.
tab. (Prize publication fund. vol. xii).

Tibetan Literature: Bibliographies

KAUJUR. A comparative analytical catalogue of the Kanjur division of the Tibetan Tripitaka; edited in Peking during the K'ang Hsi era, and at present kept
in the library of the Otani Daigaku, Kyoto, in which the contents of each sutra

are collated with their corresponding parts in the existing Sanskrit, Pali, and Chinese texts, and in which page references to the Narthang and the Derge edition of the Tripitaka are also entered. Kyoto, Otani Daigaku library, 1930-32. 14, 477 p.

LALOU, MARCELLE. Catalogue du fonds tibétains de la Bibliothèque Nationale par Marcelle Lalou. Paris, P. Geuthner, 1931-    1 v. (Buddhica. Documents et travaux pour l'étude du Bouddhisme. 2 sér. Documents, t. 4).

PARIS. BIBLIOTHÈQUE NATIONALE. Répertoire du Tanjur d' après le catalogue de Palmyr Cordier, par Marcelle Lalou avec une préface de Paul Pelliot. Paris, Durand, 1933. viii, 239 p.

————. État des manuscrits sanscrits, bengalis et tibétains de la collection Palmyr Cordier, par Jean Filliozat. Paris, Imprimerie Nationale, 1934. cover-title, 19 p. "Extrait du Journal asiatique (janvier-mars 1934)"

————. Inventaire des manuscrits tibétains de Touen-houng conservés à la Bibliothèque Nationale (Fonds Pelliot tibétain), par Marcelle Lalou. Paris, Adrien-Maisonneuve, 1939-1950. 2 v.

SENDAI, TOHOKU UNIVERSITY. A catalogue of the Tōhoku University collection of Tibetan works on Buddhism, by Yenshô Kanakura, Ryujo Yamada [and others] Sendai, Seminary of Indology, Tōhoku University [1953] 531 p.

UI, HAKUJU, 1882-    A complete catalogue of the Tibetan Buddhist canons (Bkaḥ-ḥgyur and Bstan-ḥgyur) edited by Hakuju Ui, Munetada Suzuki, Yenshô Kanakura [and] Tōkan Tada. Sendai, Published by Tōhoku Imperial University aided by Saitô Gratitude Foundation, 1934. 2, 2, 701, 3 p. with catalogue-index, 124 p.

## General Works

BACOT, JACQUES, 1877-    ed. and tr. Représentations théâtrales dans les monastères du Tibet; trois mystères tibétains. Tchrimekundan, Djroazanmo, Nansal, traduits avec introduction, notes et index. Bois gravés d'après les dessins de V. Goloubew. Paris, Éditions Bossard, 1921. 298 p. illus. (Les Classiques de l'Orient, 3).

————. ed. Three Tibetan mysteries: Tchrimekundan, Nasal, Djroazanmo, as performed in the Tibetan monasteries; translated from the French version of Jacques Bacot (with an introduction, notes, and index) by H. I. Woolf. Illustrated from native designs by V. Goloubew. London, G. Routledge; New York, E. P. Dutton [1924] 267, [1] p. incl. front., plates. (Broadway translations).

————. Le poète tibétain Milarépa, ses crimes, ses épreuves, son Nirvāna, traduit du tibétain avec une introd. et un index. 40 bois de Jean Buhot d'après une iconographie tibétaine de la vie de Milarépa. Paris, Éditions Bossard, 1925. 302 p. illus. (Classiques de l'Orient, 11).

————. La vie de Marpa, le "traducteur," suivi d'un chapitre de l'Avadāna de l'oiseau Nīlakaṇṭha. Extraits et résumés d'après l'édition xylographique tibétaine. Paris, P. Geuthner, 1937. 115, [1] p. front. (port.) (Buddhica. Documents et travaux pour l'étude du bouddhisme. 1. sér.: Mémoires, t. vii).

BKA'GYUR. Tibetan tales: stories from the "Dsange Blun" (The Wise and the Foolish), from an ancient collection of stories on the wise and foolish actions of men, attributed to the Buddha Gautama and compiled after his death by his disciple, Ananda. Translated from the Tibetan by Anointte K. Gordon. London, Luzac, 1953. 72 p. illus.

DAVID-NEEL, ALEXANDRA, 1874-    Mipam; ein Tibetischer Roman. Leipzig, F. A. Brockhaus, 1935. 335 p.

————. Textes tibétains inédits. Paris, La Colombe [1952] 199 p.

————. Unbekannte tibetische Texte. Übers. von Ursula von Mangoldt. München-Planegg, O. W. Barth, 1955. 171 p. (Weisheitsbücher der Menschheit).

DRI MED KUN IDAN. Ti-me-kun-dan, prince of Buddhist benevolence, a mystery play, translated from Tibetan text by Millicent H. Morrison. London, J. Murray, 1925. 128 p. (Wisdon of the East Series).

DUNCAN, MARION HERBERT, 1896- Harvest festival dramas of Tibet. Hong Kong, Orient Pub. Co. [1955] 275 p. illus.

EKVALL, ROBERT BRAINERD, 1898- Tibetan voices. Drawings by Jean Hammond. New York and London, Harper [1946] 63 p. illus.

FRANCKE, AUGUST HERMANN, 1870-1930. Tibetische Hochzeitslieder, übers. nach Handschriften von Tag-ma-cig. Mit einer Einleitung über die Mythologie der tibetischen Sagenwelt und Bildern, meist nach Aufnahmen des Verfassers, von A. H. Francke. Lieder in die ursprünglichen Versmasse übertragen von Anna Paalzow. Hagen i W. [etc.], 71 p. illus. plates. (Kulturen der Erde. Textwerke).

GESAR (Romances, etc). La vie surhumaine de Guésar de Ling, le héros thibétain, racontée par les bardes de son pays. Préface par Sylvain Lévi. Paris, Éditions Adyar, 1931. lxiv, 346 p., plates, ports. At head of titel: Alexandra David-Neel et le lama Yongden.

———. The superhuman life of Gesar of Ling, the legendary Tibetan hero, as sung by the bards of his country, by Alexandra David-Neel and the lama Yongden; preface by Sylvain Lévi, rendered into English with the collaboration of V. Sydney. London, Rider, 1933. 7-286 p.

———. The same. [New York, C. Kendall, c1934] vi, 390 p.

GOS LO-TSÃ-BA GŽON-NU-DPAL, 1392-1481. The Blue annals. Edited and translated by George N. Roerich. Calcutta, 1949-53. 2 v. (Asiatic Society of Bengal. Monog. 7).

JEWETT, ELEANORÉ MYERS. Wonder tales from Tibet, illustrations by Maurice Day. Boston, Little, Brown, 1922. ix, 183 p. col. front., col. plates.

JUNGBAUER. GUSTAV 1886- ed. Märchen aus Turkestan und Tibet. Jena, E. Diederichs 1923. 3-317, [2] p. incl. front., 1 illus. (Die märchen der weltliteratur [23]).

KANJUR. Tibetanische Märchen. Berlin, Junker, 1923. 224 p. Inhaltsverzeichnis.

———. Tibetan tales. derived from Indian sources, translated from the Tibetan of the Kahgyur by F. Anton von Schiefner, and from the German into English by W. R. S. Ralston, with an introduction. New ed. with a preface by C. A. F. Rhys Davids. London, G. Routledge; New York, E. P. Dutton [1926] v. [2], [vii]-ixv, 368 p. (Broadway translations).

MI-LA RAS-PA, 1038-1122. Milaraspa; tibetische Texte in Auswahl übertragen von Berthold Laufer. Hagen i. W., Folkwang-Verlag, 1922. 78 p. plates, (Kulturen der Erde. Textwerke.).

———. Chants from Shangri-la; original translation from the Tibetan by Flora Beal Shelton revised and edited by Dorris Shelton Still. Palm Springs, Calif., D.S. Still, [c1939] 93 p. illus. plates.

———. Sieben Legenden [übersetzung von sieben ausgewählten Kapitelnder "Hunderttausend Gesänge" von] Helmut Hoffmann. München, O. W. Barth, 1950. 127 p. illus.

———. Milarepa, magicien poète ermite tibétain (XIe siècle) Traduction de Jacques Bacot; eauxfortes de Georges Braque. Paris, Maeght, 1950. 1 v.

NO-RUB-CAN. Les contes de No-rub-can (contes thibétains) suivis de La légende de Na-ro-pa. Bruxelles, Les Éditions de Belgique, 1939. [7]-210, [2] p.

NOEL, SYBILLE (GRAHAM). The magic bird of Chomo-lung-ma; tales of mount Everest, the turquoise peak, by Sybille Noel, illustrated by A. Avinoff. Garden City, N. Y., Doubleday, Doran 1931. 310 p. front., illus., plates.

PELLIOT, MARIANNE. Le sorcier du Lac Vert. Paris, Adrien-Maisonneuve, 1950. 95 p.

SANGHARAKSHITA. Messengers from Tibet and other poems. Bombay, Hind Kitabs, 1954. 50 p.

SHAHIDULLAH, MUHAMMAD, ed. Les chants mystiques de Kānha et de Saraha; les Dohākoṣa (en apabhraṃśa, avec les versions tibétaines) et les Caryā (en vieux-bengaḷi) avec introduction, vocabulaires et notes, édités et traduits par

M. Shahidullah. Paris, Adrien-Maisonneuve, 1928. [ix]-xii, 234, [2] p. (Textes pour l'étude du bouddhisme tardif). Issued also as the author's thesis, Univ. de Paris.

SHELTON, ALBERT LEROY, 1875-1922. Tibetan folk tales, translated by A. L. Shelton. (Shelton of Tibet) edited with an introduction by Flora Beal Shelton, illustrated by Mildred Bryant. New York, George H. Doran [c1925] xiv p. 17-192, [1] p. incl. plates. col. front.

SHELTON, FLORA BEAL. Folk tales of Tibet; illustrated by Mary Forrester. Dallas, Story Book Press, 1951. 38 p. illus.

SIMONSSON, NILS. Indo-tibetische Studien; die Methoden der tibetischen Uber-setzer, untersucht im Hinblick auf die Bedeutung ihrer Übersetzung für die Sanskrit philologie. Uppsala, 1957. 1 v. (290 p. ) facsims. Diss.-Univ. Up-psala.

THOMAS, FREDERICK WILLIAM, 1867-1956. ed. and tr. Tibetan literary texts and documents concerning Chinese Turkestan, selected and translated by F. W. Thomas. London, Royal Asiatic Society, 1935-1955. 3 v. (Oriental translation fund. New series).

——. Ancient folk-literature from northeastern Tibet. Berlin, Akademie Verlag, 1956. x, 76, 204 p. plates, map, (Abhandlungen der deutsche Akademie des Wissenschaften zu Berlin. Kl. für Sprachen, Literatur und Kunst. Jg. 1956, H 3).

TOUSSAINT, GUSTAVE CHARLES: Le Dict de Padma (Padma thang Yig), Ms. de Lithang. Traduit du Thibétain. Paris, E. Leroux, 1933. 540 p. plates. (Bibliothèque de l'Institut des Hautes Études Chinoises, 111).

TUCCI, GIUSEPPE, 1894-   ed. and tr. Tibetan folksongs from the district of Gyantse, collected and translated by Giuseppe Tucci. Ascona, Switzerland, Artibus Asiae Publishers, 1949. 89 p. mounted illus. (Artibus Asiae. Supplementun 7).

YONGDEN, LAMA. La puissance du néant, roman tibétain, adaptation française de Alex. David-Neel. Paris, Plon, 1954. 256 p.

——. Die Macht des Nichts. Ein Tibetischer Roman, übers. aus dem Französischen von Curt Meyer-Clason. Wiesbaden, F. A. Brockhaus, 1956. 200 p.

## History and Foreign Relations

AOKI, BUNKYŌ, 1886-   Study on early Tibetan chronicles, regarding discrepancies of dates and their adjustments; a report of study for 1954-1955 by the subsidy from the Ministry of Education, Japan. Tokyo, Nippon Gakujutsu Shinkokai (Japan Society for the Promotion of Science) 1955. 10, vi, 161 p. tables. Photolithographed from ms. copy.

BACOT, JACQUES, 1877-   ed. and tr. Documents de Touen-houang relatifs à l'histoire du Tibet [par] J. Bacot, F. W. Thomas [et] Ch. Toussaint. Paris, P. Geuthner, 1940 [i. e. 1946] 204 p. facsims. (Annales du Musée Guimet. Bibliothèque d'études, t. 51).

BANERJEE, ANIL CHANDRA. The problem of Tibet. Calcutta, Uttarayan [1951] 16 p. (Uttarayan monograph on current affairs, no. 11).

BELL, SIR CHARLES ALFRED, 1870-1945. Tibet, past and present. Oxford, Clarendon Press, 1924. xiv, 326 p. col. front., plates (part col. ) ports., fold. maps.

——. Tibet einst und jezt. Deutsch von E. H. Bollog. Leipzig, F. A. Brockhaus 1925. xv, 335 p. illus. map.

CAMMANN, SCHUYLER, 1912-   Trade through the Himalayas; the early British attempts to open Tibet. Princeton, Princeton University Press, 1951. x, 186 p. illus., maps.

CLARK, GROVER, 1891-1938. Tibet, China and Great Britain; notes on the present status of the relation between these countries. Peking, Peking Leader Press, 1924. Cover-title, 57 p.

DAS, TARAKNATH. British expansion in Tibet. Calcutta, N. M. Raychowdhury [1927] 137 p.

DAVID-NEEL, ALEXANDRA, 1874-    Le vieux Tibet face à la Chine nouvelle. Paris, Plon [1953] 244 p. illus., ports., fold. col. map.

———. Altes Tibet, neues China. Übers. von Fritz Montfort, 1955. Wiesbaden, F. A. Brockhaus, 1955. 203 p. plates, map.

DOCUMENTS AND SPEECHES ON THE PEACEFUL LIBERATION OF TIBET. Peking, People's China, 1951. 15 p.

ENDERS, GORDON BANDY. Nowhere else in the world, by Gordon B. Enders with Edward Anthony; with sixty-four photographs. New York, Farrar and Rinehart [c1935] x, 434 p. incl. illus. (map) plates, ports.

———. The same; London, Hurst and Blackett, 1936. 304 p.

FILCHNER, WILHELM, 1877-1957. Sturm über Asien, Erlebnisse eines diplomatischen Geheimagenten, mit vielen Abbildungen, Karten und Vollbildern nach Skizzen des Verfassers. Berlin, Neufeld and Henius [c1924] vii, [1], 310 p. front., plates, ports., maps (part fold.)

———. Wetterleuchten im Osten, Erlebnisse eines diplomatischen Geheimagenten. Mit einem Porträt des Verfassers, 6 Federzeichnungen von Ottokar Luke, 10 ganzseitigen Bildtafeln mit 15 Abbildungen, 3 Karten, und 2 Plänen. Berlin, P. J. Oestergaard [pref. 1927] 300 p. illus., ports., fold. maps.

GT. BRITAIN. Central Office of Information. Tibet, background to the Chinese invasion. London, Reference Division, Central Office of Information, 1950. 5 p. (No. R. 2048).

HSIN HUA News Agency. Agreement on measures for peaceful liberation of Tibet. [Peking? 1951?] 11 p. illus.

LAI, TZE-SHENG, 雷子聲. Le problème thibétain. Paris, A. Pedone, 1941. [vii]-ix 186 p. Thèse-Univ. de Paris.

LEE, WEI KUO, 李惟果, 1905-    Tibet in modern world politics (1774-1922). New York, 1931. [7]-148 p. illus. (maps) Thesis-Columbia University.

LI, FANG-KUEI, 李方桂, 1902-    The inscription of the Sino-Tibetan treaty of 821-822. Leiden, E. J. Brill, 1956. 99 p. Reprinted from T'oung Pao, vol. XLIV, 1-3.

LI, TIEH-TSENG, 李鐵錚, 1906-    The historical status of Tibet. New York, King's Crown Press, Columbia University, 1956 [c1954] xi, 312 p. Issued also in microfilm form, as thesis, Columbia University, under title: A historical study of the status of Tibet.

———. The problem of Tibet in Sino-British relations. London, 1956. v, 460 l. Thesis-London School of Economics.

PETECH, LUCIANO. China and Tibet in the early 18th century; history of the establishment of Chinese protectorate in Tibet. Leiden, E. J. Brill, 1950. x, 286 p. 2 fold. maps. (T'oung pao: archives concernant l'histoire, les langues, la géographie, l'ethnographie et les arts de l'Asie orientale. Monographie 1).

RICHARDSON, H. E. ed. Ancient historical edicts at Lhasa and The Mu Tsung/ Khri Gtsug Lde Brtsan Treaty of A. D. 821-822 from the inscription at Lhasa. London, Royal Asiatic Society of Great Britain and Ireland, 1952. iii, 186 p. plates. (Its Prize publication fund, 19).

SHÊN, TSUNG-LIEN, 沈宗濂, 1899-    Tibet and the Tibetans, by Tsung-lien Shên and Shên-chi Liu, 劉匣祺. Foreword by George E. Taylor. Stanford, University Press; London, Oxford Univ. Press, [1953]. 199 p. illus.

TCHEOU, MEI-LI, 周美荔. Le Tibet et ses relations internationales depuis le VIIe siècle à nos jours. Paris, 1950. 171 l. Thèse-Univ. de Paris.

TUCCI, GIUSEPPE, 1894-    Le Thibet et la situation asiatique. Paris, 1950. 24 p. "Relation presentée le 5 juin 1950 au Centre d'études de politique étrangère à Paris."

WILLIAMS, EDWARD THOMAS, 1854-1944. Tibet and her neighbors. Berkeley, Calif., University of California Press, 1937. cover-title, 1 p. 99-139. (University of California publications. Bureau of international relations. 3 :2).

## Social Conditions: General Works

BELL, SIR CHARLES ALFRED, 1870-1945. The people of Tibet. Oxford, Clarendon press, 1928. xix, 319, [1] p. front., plates (1 col.) maps (part fold.).

DUNCAN, MARION HERBERT, 1896-    The Mountain of silver snow. Cincinnati, O., Powell and White [c1929] 240 p. front., plates, ports.

EKVALL, ROBERT BRAINERD, 1898-    Cultural relations on the Kansu-Tibetan border. Chicago, University of Chicago Press [c1939] xiii, [2], 87 p. illus. (map) (University of Chicago publications in anthropology. Occasional papers, 1).

————. Tibetan sky lines. New York, Farrar, Straus and Young; London, Gollancz, 1952. 240 p. illus.

HERMANNS, MATTHIAS, 1899-    Die A mdo pa-Grosstibeter; die sozial-wirtschaftlichen Grundlagen der Hirtenkulturen Innerasiens. [Freiburg, 1948?] xvi, 325 p. illus., 4 fold. maps.

————. The Indo-Tibetans. The Indo-Tibetan and Mongoloid problem in the Southern Himalaya and North-Northeast India. Bombay, K. L. Fernandes, 1954. xvi, 159 p. illus. map.

[ILLION, THEODORE]. Tibeter über das Abendland; Stimmen aus dem geheimnisvollen Tibet. [Von] Burang [pseud.] [3. Aufl.] Salzburg, Igonta-Verlag, 1947. 215 p.

LAUFER, BERTHOLD, 1874-1934. Use of human skulls and bones in Tibet. Chicago, Field Museum of Natural History, 1923. cover-title, 16 p. fold. pl. (Field museum of natural history. [Anthropology leaflet, 10]).

LEARNER, FRANK DOGGETT. Rusty hinges; a story of closed doors beginning to open in north-east Tibet. London and Philadelphia, The China Inland Mission, 1933. xi, 13-157 p. front., plates, ports.

MACDONALD, DAVID. The land of the lama; a description of a country of contrasts and of its cheerful, happy-go-lucky people of hardy nature and curious customs; their religion, ways of living, trade and social life, by David Macdonald. With a foreword by the Right Hon. the Earl of Ronaldshay. London, Seeley, Service, 1929. 283 p. front. (port.) illus. (incl. plan, facsims.) plates, fold. map.

————. Moeurs et coutumes des Thibétains. Traduction française par R. Bilot. Paris, Payot, 1930. 262 p. plates, (Collection d'études, documents et de temoignages pour servir à l'histoire de notre temps).

————. Twenty years in Tibet, intimate and personal experiences of the closed land among all classes of its people from the highest to the lowest [by] David Macdonald. With a foreword by the Earl of Lytton. Philadelphia, J. B. Lippincott, [1932] London, Seeley, 1932. 7-318 p. front., plates, ports., fold. map.

PEMBA, TSEWANG Y. Young days in Tibet. London, J. Cape [1957] 184 p.

RIBBACH, SAMUEL HEINRICH. Drogpa Namgyal, ein Tibeterleben.    München-Planegg O. W. Barth-Verlag gmbh. 1940. 7-263 p. front., plates.

SHERAP, PAUL, 1887-    A Tibetan on Tibet; being the travels and observations of Mr. Paul Sherap (Dorje Zödba) of Tachienlu; with an introductory chapter on Buddhism and a concluding chapter on the devil dance, by G. A. Combe. London, T. F. Unwin [1926] xx, 212 p. front. (ports.) fold. map.

VIERZIG, KATHARINA. Beiträge zur Kenntnis tibetischer Pharmakologie. Jena, 1949. 79, iv, 1. Diss. -Univ. Jena.

## Lamaism

ARYA MAHABALA-NAMA-MAHYANA-SUTRA. Tibétan (mss. de Touen-Houang) et chinois, by F. A. Bischoff, 1956. Paris, P. Geuthner, 1956. 126 p. plates.

(Buddhica. Documents et travaux pour l'étude du bouddhisme. 1 sér. Mémoirs, t. 10).

BARDO THÖDOL. The Tibetan Book of the dead; or, The after-death experiences on the Bardo plane, according to Lāma Kazi Dawa-Samdup's English rendering, by W. Y. Evans-Wentz. With foreword by Sir John Woodroffe. 2d ed. London, New York, Oxford Univ. Press, 1949. 1, 248 p. illus., plates, port., facsim. 1st ed. 1927.

――――. The same; with a psychological commentary by Dr. C.G. Jung, and introducting foreword by Lāma Anagarika Govinda, and a foreword by Sir John Woodroffe. 3rd ed. London, Oxford University Press, 1957. lxxxiv, 249 p. front., illus., plates.

――――. Le livre des morts tibétain, ou Les expériences d'après la mort dans le plan du Bardo. Suivant la version anglaise du Lāma Kazi Dawa Samdup, editée par W. Y. Evans-Wentz. Traduction française de Marguerite La Fuente, precédée d'une préface de Jacques Bacot. Paris, Adrien-Maisonneuve, 1933. viii, 226 p. illus.

――――. Das tibetanische Totenbuch; oder, Die nach-Tod-Erfahrungen auf der Bardo-Stufe. Nach der englischen Fassung des Lāma Kazi Dawa-Samdup hrsg. von W. Y. Evans-Wentz. Übers. und eingeleitet von Louis Göpfert-March; mit einer Einführung und einem psychologischen Kommentar von C.G. Jung und einem Vorwort von Sir John Woodroffe. 5., umgearb. und erweiterte Aufl. Zürich, Rascher Verlag, 1953. lxxiii, 265 p. illus.

BELL, SIR CHARLES ALFRED, 1870-1945. The religion of Tibet. Oxford, Clarendon Press, 1931. xv, [1] 235, [1] p. col. front., plates, ports., 3 maps (2 fold.) 2 facsim.

――――. Portrait of the Dalai lama. London, Collins, 1946. 414 p. plates. (part col., 1 double; incl. front., ports., facsims.).

BERNARD, THEOS, 1908- Heaven lies within us. New York, C. Scribner, 1939. xiv, 326 p. incl. front., illus.

――――. The same; London, Rider [1941] 256 p. incl. front., illus.

――――. Penthouse of the gods; a pilgrimage into the heart of Tibet and the sacred city of Lhasa. New York, and London, C. Scribner, 1939. xii, 344 p. front., plates, ports.

――――. Land of a thousand buddhas; a pilgrimage into the heart of Tibet and the sacred city of Lhasa. With 83 illustrations. London, Rider [1940]. 320 p. front., plates, ports.

BLEICHSTEINER, ROBERT, 1891-1954. Die gelbe Kirche; Mysterien der buddhistischen Klöster in Indien, Tibet, Mongolei und China. Wien, J. Belf [c1937] 272 p. plates, plans.

――――. L'église jaune. Traduction de Jacques Marty. Paris, Payot, 1950. 292 p. (Bibliothèque historique) 1st ed. 1937.

BOUCHOT, JEAN. Le Temple des Lamas. Pékin, Impr. de la "Politique de Pékin," 1923. 68 p. illus.

BOUILLARD, GEORGES, 1862-1930. Notes divers sur les cultes en Chine: Les ornements rituels des temples lamaïques et bouddhiques. Pékin, A. Nachbaur 1924. 10 p.

――――. Le temple des lamas; temple lamaiste de Yung Ho Kung à Pékin. Description, plans, photos, cérémonies. Pékin, A. Nachbaur, 1931. 127, [1] p. illus., plates, (part. fold.) fold. plan.

BROMAGE, BERNARD. Tibetan yoga. London, Aquarian Press; Toronto, Smithers and Bonellie, 1952. 244 p. front. plates.

CLARK, WALTER EUGENE, 1881- ed. Two Lamaistic pantheons, edited with introduction and indexes by Walter Eugene Clark from materials collected by the late Baron A. von Staël-Holstein. Cambridge, Harvard University Press, 1937. 2 v. plates, facsims. (Harvard-Yenching institute. Monograph series.

vol. iii-iv).

CONTRIBUTIONS to ethnography, linguistics, and history of religion. Stock-
holm, Statens Etnografiska Museum, 1954. 128 p. illus., map, facsims.
(Reports from the scientific expedition to the north-western provinces of
China under the leadership of Dr. Sven Hedin. The Sino-Swedish Expedition.
Publication 38. viii. Ethnography, 6).

DAVID-NEEL, ALEXANDRA, 1874-    Heilige und Hexer; Glaube und Aberglaube
im Lande des Lamaismus, nach eigenen Erlebnissen in Tibet dargestellt von
Alexandra David-Neel, [aus dem Französischen von Ada Ditzen] Leipzig,
F.A. Brockhaus, 1931. 295 p. front., map, plates, ports.

————. Mystiques et magiciens du Thibet. Préface de A. d'Arsonval. Avec 25
gravures hors texte. Paris, Plon [1929] vi, 306 p., plates, ports.

————. With mystics and magicians in Tibet. With an introduction by Dr. A. d'Arsonval, and 29 illustrations from the author's photographs. London, John
Lane [1931]; Harmondsworth, [Eng.] Penguin Books, 1938. xiv, 320 p.
front., plates, ports.

————. Magic and mystery in Tibet. With an introduction by Dr. A. d'Arsonval.
[New York, C. Kendall, 1932] xii, 320 p. plates, ports.

————. Initiations lamaïques; des théories-des pratiques-des hommes; avec 36
gravures hors-texte. Paris, Adyar, 1930. Nouv. éd. 1957. 284 p. plates,
ports.

————. Initiations and initiates in Tibet. Authorised translation by Fred Rothwell.
London, Rider [1931] 224 p. plates, ports.

————. Meister und Schüler; die Geheimnisse der lamaistischen Weihen; auf
grund eigener Erfahrungen dargestellt von Alexandra David-Neel. "Aus dem
französischen von Ada Ditzen." Mit 36 Abbildungen. Leipzig, F.A. Brockhaus, 1934.

————. Magie d'amour et magie noire, scènes du Tibet inconnu. Paris, Plon
[1938] iii, 246 p.

————. Liebeszauber und schwarze Magie. München-Planegg, O.W. Barth,
1952. 267 p.

ELLAM, JOHN E. Buddhism and lamaism; a study of the religion of Tibet. Calcutta, Thacker, Spink and Co., 1924. 45 p.

————. The religion of Tibet; a study of Lamaism. London, J. Murray [1927]
127 p. (Wisdom of the East).

FILCHNER, WILHELM, 1877-1957. Kumbum Dschamba Ling, das Kloster der
hunderttausend Bilder Maitreyas; ein Ausschnitt aus Leben und Lehre des
heutigen Lamaismus. Mit 208 Abbildungen auf Kunstdrucktafeln nach eigenen
Aufnahmen, 412 Skizzen des Verfassers im Text, einer Lichtdruck-und einer
Buntdrucktafel sowie einer Klosterkarte. Leipzig, In kommission bei F.A.
Brockhaus, 1933. xvi, 555, [1] p. front., illus., plates (1 col.) port., diagrs.

————. Kumbum; Lamaismus in Lehre und Leben. Mit Originallegenden (tibetisch, mongolisch, chinesisch) und 7 Bildtafeln nach Originalaufnahmen des
Verfassers. [1. Aufl. Zürich] Rascher 1954. 298 p. illus.

FRANCKE, AUGUST HERMANN, 1870-1930. Geistesleben in Tibet. Gütersloh,
C. Bertelsmann, 1925. 80 p. facsims, front. plates (Allgemeine Missions-
studien, 2).

GOVINDA, ANAGARIKA BRAHMACARI. Grundlagen tibetischer Mystik; nach den
esoterischen Lehren des Grossen Mantra Om Mani Padme Hûm, von Lâma
Anagarika Govinda (Anangavajra Khamsum-Wangchuk) Aufnahmen tibetischer
Plastik von Li Gotami. Zürich, Rascher Verlag, 1957. 357 p. illus.

HERMANNS, MATTHIAS, 1899-    Himmelsstier und Gletscherlöwe. Tibetische
Mythen, Sagen und Fabeln. Auf einer Völkerkundlichen Forschungsreise in
Tibet aufgenomen. Kassel, Erich Röth, 1956. 260 p. ("Das Gesicht der Völ-
ker").

——. Mythen und Mysterien; Magie und Religion der Tibeter. Köln, B. Pick [1956] 400 p. illus.

HOFFMANN, HELMUT, 1912-    Quellen zur Geschichte der tibetischen Bon-Religion. Mainz, Verlag der Akademie der Wissenschaften und der Literatur; in Kommission bei F. Steiner, Wiesbaden [1950] 319 p. illus., plates (part col.) fold. map. (Akademie der Wissenschaften und der Literatur. Abhandlungen der Geistes- und Sozialwissenschaftlichen Klasse, Jahrg. 1950, Nr. 4)

——. Die Religionen Tibets. Bon und Lamaismus in ihrer geschichtlichen Entwicklung. Freiburg, München, Alber, 1956. 214 p. illus. plates.

HUMMEL, SIEGBERT. Lamaistische Studien. Leipzig, O. Harrassowitz, 1950. 212 p. port. plates, facsims. maps, (Forschungen zur völkerdynamik zentral und ostasiens, 5).

KRASINSKI, CYRILL VON KORVIN. Die tibetische Medizinphilosophie; der Mensch als Mikrokosmos. Zürich, Origo Verlag [1953] xl, 363 p. tables. (Mainzer Studien zur Kultur- und Völkerkunde, Bd. 1).

LALOU, MARCELLE. Les religions du Tibet. Paris, Presses universitaires, 1957. 104 p. (Collection Mythes et religions).

LAUPPERT, NORBET, ed. Briefe tibetanischer Weiser. Graz, Adyar-Verlag, 1954. 164 p.

LESSING, FERDINAND, 1882-    Yung-ho-kung, an iconography of the Lamaist cathedral in Peking, with notes on Lamaist mythology and cult. v. 1. in collaboration with Gösta Montell. Stockholm [Göteborg, Elanders boktryckeri aktiebolag] 1942. 179 p. mounted col. front., illus., plates, fold. plan (in pocket) diagrs. (Reports from the scientific expedition to the north-western provinces of China under the leadership of Dr. Sven Hedin. The Sino-Swedish expedition. Publication 18. viii. Ethnography. 1).

LOBSANG RAMPA, T. The third eye; the autobiography of a Tibetan lama. Illustrated by Tessa Theobald. London, Secker and Warburg; New York, Doubleday, c1956. 256 p.

——. Das dritte Auge. Ein tibetanischer Lama erzählt sein Leben. Aus dem Englischen übertra. von Herbert und Waltraut Furreg. München, Piper, 1957. 315 p.

LUCAS, HEINZ. Lamaistische Masken. Das Masken-und Tanzfeste aus Tibet, Mongolei, Nepal, Bhutan und Sikkim. Kassel, Erich Töth, 1956. 160 p. plates.

MARQUÈS-RIVIÈRE, JEAN. Le bouddhisme au Thibet. Paris, Éditions Baudinière [1936] [7]-250 p., illus., plan.

——. Le yoga tantrique, hindou et thibétain. Paris, Véga, [c1938]. 126, [1]p. illus. (Collection "Asie").

——. Tantrik yoga, Hindu and Tibetan. Translated by H. E. Kennedy. London, Rider [1940] ix-xiv, 15-126 p. illus.

——. A l'ombre des monastères thibétains. Préface de Maurice Magre. [Nouv. éd.] Paris et Neuchâtel, V. Attinger, 1956. (c1930) xxiii, [25]-208 p. incl. front. (Orient, 5).

MIGOT, ANDRÉ, 1892-    Études tibétaines. 1. Réflexions sur l'histoire des relations sino-tibétaines. II. Le lamaïsme, petit essai d'explication et de compréhension. III. Les lamas-souvrains du Tibet (Dalai-Lama et Panchen-Lama). Saigon, France-Asie, 1955. 12, 38, 28 p.

NAGAO, GADJIN MASATO. A study of Tibetan Buddhism; being a translation into Japanese of the exposition of Vipaśyanā in Tsoñ-kha-pa's lam-rim chen-mo with annotation and prefatory remarks. Tokyo, Iwanami Shoten, 1954. lxi, 446 p.

NEBESKY-WOJKOWITZ, RENÉ DE. Der Kult und die Ikonographie der tibetischen Schutzgottheiten. Wien, 1955. 623 p. plates.

——. Oracles and demons of Tibet; the cult and iconography of the Tibetan protective deities. 's-Gravenhage, Mouton, 1956. xiv, 666 p. illus., plan.

——. Wo Berge Götter sind. Drei Jahre bei unerforschten Völkern des Himalaya. Stuttgart, Deutsche Verlags-Anstalt, 1955. 267 p. illus. plates, fold. map.

———. Where the gods are mountains: three years among the people of the Himalayas, translated from the German by Michael Bullock. London, Weidenfeld and Nicolson, 1956. 256 p. plates.

[RAS-CHŪN] The story of a reverend saint Milarepa, the greatest of hermits, showing the way of deliverance and omniscience, as translated from the French [of Jacques Bacot] by Anna R. Arocha. n.p. 194? [2] p. 43 numb. l. Typescript.

———. Tibet's great hogī, Milarepa. A biography from the Tibetan, being the Jetsün-kahbum, or biographical history of Jetsün-Milarepa, according to the late Lāma Kazi Dawa-Samdup's English rendering, edited with introd. and annotations by W.Y. Evans-Wentz. 2d ed. London, New York, Oxford University Press, 1951. xxviii, 315 p. illus. (1 col.) 1st ed. 1928.

———. Milarepa. Tibets grosser Yogi auf dem Weg zu Wissen und Erlosung. Pfullingen, Baum, 1956. xix, 204 p.

ROCK, JOSEPH FRANCIS CHARLES, 1884-    The Na-khi Nāga cult and related ceremonies. Roma, Is. M.E.O., 1952. 2 v. illus., plates (part col.)(Serie orientale Roma, v. 4, pt. 1-2).

SCHULEMANN, GUNTHER, 1889-    Geschichte der Dalai-Lamas. Leipzig, O. Harrassowitz, 1957. 519 p. plates, map.

SNELLGROVE, DAVID, 1909-    Buddhist Himalaya: travels and studies in quest of the origins and nature of Tibetan religion. Oxford, Bruno Cassirer, 1957. 364 p. illus.

STEIN, R.    A. L'épopée tibétaine des Gésar dans sa version lamaïque de Ling. Paris, Presses universitaire, 1956. 399 p. (Paris, Musée Guimet. Annales. Bibliothèque d'études, 61).

TUCCI, GIUSEPPE, 1894-    Travels of Tibetan pilgrims in the Swat valley. Calcutta, Greater India Society, 1940. 103 p. (Greater India Studies, 2).

UNTO thee I grant, rev. by Sri. Ramatherio [pseud.] A private, limited ed. San Jose, Calif., Supreme Grand Lodge of AMORC [1948] viii, 112 p. (Rosicrucian library, v.5).

TIBETISCH-MYSTISCHE LEBENSWEISHEIT, übers. aus dem Englischen. Munchen-Planegg. O.W. Barth, 1953. 198 p.

WADDELL, LAURENCE AUSTINE, 1854-    The Buddhism of Tibet; or, Lamaism, with its mystic cults, symbolism and mythology, and in its relation to Indian Buddhism. 2d ed. Cambridge [Eng.] W. Heffer, 1934. 598 p. incl. front., illus. fold. plates. 1st ed. 1895.

WENTZ, WALTER YEELING EVANS, ed. Tibetan yoga and secret doctrines; or, Seven books of wisdom of the great path, according to the late Lāma Kazi Dawa-Samdup's English rendering; arranged and edited with introductions and annotations to serve as a commentary by W.Y. Evans-Wentz, with a foreword by Dr. R.R. Marett. London, Oxford University Press, H. Milford, 1935. xxiv, 389, [1] p. front., plates (1 col.) facsims. 2d ed. 1958. 432 p.

———. Le yoga tibétain et les doctrines secrèts; ou, Les sept livres de la sagesse ou grand sentier, suivant la traduction du Lāma Kasi Dawa-Samdup; edité par W.Y. Evans-Wentz, avec introductions et commentaires. Traduction française du Marguerite La Fuente. Paris, A. Maisonneuvre, 1948. 365 p. front. illus.

———. Yoga und Geheimlehren Tibets. [Die deutsche Bearbeitung und Übersetzung erfolgte durch Alterego] München-Planegg, O.W. Barth, 1937. 286 p.

———. The Tibetan Book of the great liberation; or, The method of realizing nirvāṇa through knowing the mind, preceded by an epitome of Padma-Sambhava's biography and followed by Guru Phadampa Sangay's teachings. According to English renderings by Sardar Bahādur S.W. Laden La and by the Lāmas Karma Sumdhon Paul, Lobsang Mingyur Dorje, and Kazi Dawa-Samdup. Introduc-

tions, annotations, and editing by W. Y. Evans-Wenta. With psychological
commentary by C. G. Jung. London, New York, Oxford University Press,
1954. lxiv, 261 p. 9 plates.

———. Das tibetischei Buch der grossen Befreiung. Die autor. Übers. besorgte
Alterego. Psychologische Kommentar: C. G. Jung. München, O. W. Barth,
1955. 378 p. plates.

YOSHIMURA, SHYUKI, 1908-    ed. Tibetan Buddhistology. With the illustrations, an introductory note and the texts. Kyoto, Research Society for Eastern Sacred Books, Ryukoku University, 1953-54. 2 v.

## Foreign Missions

BULL, GEOFFREY T    1921-    When iron gates yield. London, Hodder and
Stoughton [ 1955] 254 p. illus.

CRISLER, CLARENCE CREAGER, 1877-1936. China's borderlands and beyond.
Takoma Park, Washington, D. C.; South Bend, Ind., Review and Herald Pub.
Co. [ c1937] 346 p. front., plates, ports.

CROIDYS, PIERRE, 1885-    Du Grand-Saint Bernard au Thibet ''Sur la terre
des esprits'', une équipe héroïque s'en va bâtir à 3, 000 mètres un nouveau
Saint-Bernard. Paris, Spès, [ 1949] 192 p. map.

———. Ins Land der Geister. Vom Grossen Sankt Bernard nach Tibet. Übers.
aus dem Französischen von Gerold Schmid. Luzern, Räber-Verlag, 1949.
192 p. maps.

DESIDERI, IPPOLITO, 1684-1733. An account of Tibet; the travels of Ippolito
Desideri of Pistoia, S. J., 1712-1727. Edited by Filippo de Filippi, with an
introduction by C. Wessels, S. J. Rev. ed. London, G. Routledge [ 1937]
xviii, 477, [ 1] p. plates (incl. mounted col. front. ) fold. map. 1st ed. 1932.

EKVALL, ROBERT BRAINERD, 1898-    Gateway to Tibet; the Kansu-Tibetan
border. Introduction [ by] Rev. William Christie. Harrisburg, Pa., Christian Publications, [ c1938] 198 p. front., plates, ports.

FAZY, ROBERT. La p. Ippolito Desideri à Lhasa, 1716-1721 et son exposé de
la religion tibétaine. St. Gall, H. Tschudy et Cie, 1945. iv, 45 p. Reprinted
from Bull. de la Société suisse des amis de l'Extrême-Orient, v. 6 (1944).

GORÉ, FRANCIS, 1883-1954. Trente ans aux portes du Thibet interdit, 1908-38.
Hong Kong, Maison de Nazareth, Impr. de la Société des Missions étrangères
de Paris, 1939. 388 p. illus. ports., maps (1 fold).

LEHMANN, ARNO, ed. Das Kreuz im Lande des Lotus. Dresden, C. L. Ungelenk, 1936. 64 p. (Die Mission der Kirche; Missionsstunden aus dem Gesamtgebiet der Deutschen Evangelischen Weltmission).

LOUP, ROBERT. Martyr au Thibet. Maurice Tornay, chanoine régulier du
Grand-St. -Bernard, 1910-1949. 2. éd. Fribourg. Éditions ''Grand-St. -Ber-
nard-Thibet'' [ 1953] 280 p. illus., ports., map. 1st ed. 1950.

———. Martyr in Tibet; the heroic life and death of Father Maurice Tornay, St.
Bernard missionary to Tibet. Translated from the French by Charles Daven-
port. New York, D. McKay Co. [ 1956] 238 p. illus.

MCINTOSH, AMY. The man in the skeepskin: a tale of Tibet. London, China Inland Mission, 1950. 51 p. illus. map.

———. The story of Drolma, daughter of Tibet, London, China Inland Mission,
1951. 56 p. illus. map.

MACLAGAN. SIR EDWARD DOUGLAS, 1864-    The Jesuits and the Great Mogul.
London, Burns, Oates and Washbourne, 1932. xxi. 433, [ 1] p. incl. illus.
(geneal. tables) map. front., plates, port., map.

MOULES, LEONARD C    J. Three miles high. London, Christian Literature
Crusade [ 1948] 115 p. illus., maps.

PATTERSON, GEORGE NEILSON, 1920-    God's fool. London, Faber and Faber
[ 1956] 251 p. illus.

———. The same. Garden City, N. Y., Doubleday, 1957. 251 p. illus.

SHELTON, ALBERT LEROY, 1875-1922. Pioneering in Tibet; a personal record of life and experience in mission fields. New York, Fleming H. Revell [c1921] 214 p. front. (part.) plates.

——. Shelton of Tibet; with an introduction by J. C. Ogden and The afterglow, by Edgar Dewitt Jones. New York, George H. Doran [c1923] xv, 21-319 p. front., plates, ports.

SIMONNET, CHRISTIAN. Thibet; voyage au bout de la chrétienté. Paris, Éditions du Monde nouveau [1949] 186 p. illus., maps. (Collection Hommes et cité).

VAN DYCK, HOWARD. William Christie, apostle to Tibet. Harrisburg, Pa., Christian Publications [1956] 176 p. illus.

WESSELS CORNELIUS. Early Jesuit travellers in Central Asia, 1603-1721. The Hague, M. Nijhoff, 1924. xvi, 344 p. front., plates., fold. map, facsims.

## Art - General Works

BACOT, JACQUES, 1877- Kunstgewerbe in Tibet. Berlin, E. Wasmuth, [1924] [12] p. plates (part. col.).

BRYNER, EDNA. Thirteen Tibetan tankas. [Indian Hills, Colo.] Falcon's Wing Press [1957, c1956]; London, Arthur F. Bird; Toronto, Burns and MacEachern, 1956. xxv, 153 p. illus.

CHÊNG TE-K'UN, 鄭德坤, 1907- An introduction to Tibetan culture by Chêng Te-K'un and D. Michael Sullivan. Chengtu, 1945. 40 p. (West China Union University. Museum. Guidebook ser., 6).

DECORATION tibétaine; préface de Jacques Bacot. Paris, A. Calavas [1924?] [12] p. plates (part col.) Issued in portfolio.

GORDON, ANTOINETTE K. The iconography of Tibetan Lamaism. New York, Columbia University Press, 1939. xxxi, 129 p. col. front., illus., plates (part col.).

——. Tibetan religious art. New York, Columbia University Press, 1952. xvi, 104 p. illus. (part col.) ports.

HOFFMANN HELMUT, 1912- Die Gräber der tibetischen Könige im Distrikt 'P'yonsrgyas. Göttingen, Vandenhoeck und R., 1950. 14 p. (Akademie der Wissenschaften in Göttingen. Nachrichten. Phil-Hist. kl. Jg. 1950).

HUMMEL, SIEGBERT. Geheimnisse tibetanischer Malereien. Leipzig, O. Harrassowitz, 1949. vii, 102 p. plates. (Forschungen zur Völkerdynamik Zentral-und Ostasiens, 2).

——. Elemente der tibetischen Kunst. Leipzig, O. Harrassowitz, 1949. 92 p. (Forschungen zur Völkerdynamik Zentral-und Ostasiens, 3).

——. Geschichte der tibetischen Kunst. Leipzig, O. Harrassowitz, 1953. 123 p. illus., plates (part col.) fold. map.

——. Tibetisches Kunsthandwerk in Metall. Mit 18 Bildtafeln nach Aufnamen von W. Gursky. Leipzig, O. Harrassowitz, 1954. 27 p. 18 plates.

——. Die lamaistiche Kunst in der Umwelt von Tibet. Leipzig, O. Harrassowitz, 1955. 149 p. illus. plates (part. col.) fold. map.

MAÑJUŚRĪ. Iconographie des étoffes peintes (paṭa) dans le Mañjuś-rīmūlakalpa, par Marcelle Lalou. Paris, P. Geuthner, 1930. 116 p. plates. (Buddhica. Documents et travaux pour l'étude du bouddhisme 1. sér.: Mémoires, t. 6).

MARCHAIS, JACQUES. Jacques Marchais. New York [1944- ] 16 p. illus. (incl. port.) [Concerning the author's Tibetan art collection.]

——. Objects from the Tibetan Lamaist collection of Jacques Marchais. [Brooklyn, Printed at the Comet Press, c1941] cover-title, [31] p. illus. (incl. port.).

MEURS, W J G van. Tibetan temple paintings. Tibetaansche tempelschilderingen. English translation by May Hollander. 2d ed. with an introd. by P. H. Pott. Leiden, Brill, 1953. 21 p. illus.

MONOD-BRUHL, ODETTE. Peintures tibétaines. pt. 1. [Paris] A. Guillot
    [1954] cover-title,48 p. col. plates. (Art et archéologie).
NEWARK MUSEUM ASSOCIATION, Newark, N. J. The religious art of Tibet-
    A bibliography. Newark, 1951. 26 p.
PANDER, EUGEN. Iconographie du Buddhisme d'après le Professeur Pander.
    Pékin, Albert Nachbaur, 1933. 44 col. plates on 23 l.
PARIS. MUSÉE GUIMET. La sculpture indienne et tibétaine au Musée Guimet.
    Paris, E. Leroux, 1931. 24 p. plates.
ROERICH, GEORGE, NICHOLAS, 1902-    Tibetan paintings. Paris, P. Geuth-
    ner, 1925. 95 p. col. mounted front., plates.
------. The animal style among the nomad tribes of northern Tibet.   Prague,
    Seminarium Kondakovianum, 1930. 41 p. illus., map, plates.
SCHMID, TONI, 1897-    The cotton-clad Mila, the Tibetan poet-saint's life in
    pictures. Stockholm, Statens etnografiska museum, 1952. 126 p. illus., 31
    plates (part col.) (Reports from the scientific expedition to the north-western
    provinces of China under the leadership of Dr. Sven Hedin. The Sino-Swedish
    Expedition. Publication 36. viii. Ethnography, 5).
TUCCI, GIUSEPPE, 1894-    Shrines of a thousand Buddhas; exploring for Tibet's
    hidden art, by Dr. Giuseppe Tucci in collaboration with Capt. E. Ghersi,
    translated by Mary A. Johnstone. New York, R. M. McBride, [1936] 272 p.
    illus. (plans) plates, ports., double map.
------. Indo-tibetica. Roma, Reale accademia d'Italia, 1932-1941. 4 v. col.
    fronts. illus., plates (part col.) facsims., fold. maps, diagrs. (Reale acca-
    demia d'Italia. Studi e documenti. 1).
------. Tibetan painted scrolls. Translated from the Italian by Virginia Vacca.
    Roma, Libreria dello Stato, 1949. 2 v. (xv, 798 p.) illus. and portfolio (256
    plates (part col.) ).
------. The tombs of the Tibetan kings. Roma, Is. M. E. O., 1950. viii, 117 p.
    illus. (Serie orientale Roma, 1).

### Exhibition Catalogues

BERKELEY GALLERIES, London. Exhibition of the art of Tibet and neighbouring
    countries at the Berkeley galleries, Dec. 1945-Jan. 1946. [London, 1945]
    [14] p. incl. map, illus.
BRITISH MUSEUM. Guide to an exhibition of Indian and Persian paintings and il-
    luminated mss.; with specimens of the art of eastern Turkestan, Tibet, Bur-
    ma and Siam. [London] Printed by order of the Trustees, 1922. 16 p.
CAMMANN, SCHUYLER, 1912-    Catalogue of Tibetan objects from the collec-
    tions of the Peabody Museum, Harvard University. Cambridge, 1939. 74 p.
    (Course report for Anthropology 20 d).
CHÊNG, TE-K'UN, 鄭德坤, 1907-    Tibetan painting: an exhibition at Chengtu.
    Chentu, 1945. 7 p. (West China Union University. Museum. Guidebook ser.,
    9).
CUTTING-VERNAY EXPEDITION FOR THE AMERICAN MUSEUM OF NATURAL
    HISTORY, 1935. The Cutting-Vernay Tibetan exhibition, showing the collec-
    tion of temple banners, embroideries, and the domestic material collected by
    the Cutting-Vernay expedition for the American Museum of Natural History.
    Lhasa and Shigatse, 1935. The collection will be placed on exhibition from
    Monday, May eleventh, until Saturday, May sixteenth. [New York? 1936?]
    [44] p. col. illus.
HANOI. MUSÉE LOUIS FINOT. La collection tibétaine par Claude Pascalis.
    Hanoi, École française d'Extrême-Orient, 1935. 155 p. plates.
LIVERPOOL. PUBLIC MUSEUMS. Tibetan exhibition: Catalogue of exhibits,
    March, 1953. Liverpool, 1953. ii, 105 p.
NEWARK MUSEUM ASSOCIATION, Newark, N. J. Tibetan objects shown by the
    Newark Museum Association in the Public library building, Dec. 6 to Jan. 31,

1921-1922. Catalog of objects. [Newark, 1921?] ii, [3]-24 p.
NEWARK MUSEUM ASSOCIATION, Newark, N.J. Catalogue of the Tibetan col-
lection and other lamaist articles. Newark, 1951. 2 v. illus.
PARIS. MUSÉE GUIMET  Guide-catalogue du Musée Guimet; les collections
bouddhiques (exposé historique et iconographique) Inde centrale et Gandhâra,
Turkestan, Chine septentrionale, Tibet, par J. Hackin, conservateur du Mu-
sée Guimet. Paris et Bruxelles, G. van Oest, 1923. 175 p. plates.
PARIS. MUSÉE CERNUSCHI. [Catalogue] Tibet, Bannières et miniatures, 22
fevr - 28 Avr. 1952. Paris, Impr. Municipal, 1952. 52 [1] p.
POTT, P.   H., 1918-   Introduction to the Tibetan collection of the National
Museum of Ethnology, Leiden. Leiden, E.J. Brill, 1951. 184 p. illus.,
plates, port., map. (Mededelingen van het Rijksmuseum voor Volkenkunde,
Leiden, no. 8 en 9).
ROERICH MUSEUM, New York. Exhibition of Tibetan paintings, sculpture and
art objects collected by the Roerich Central Asian Expedition. New York,
Roerich Museum, 1929. 14 p. incl. front. and plates.

## Geological and Geographical Explorations

BURDSALL, RICHARD LLOYD. Men against the clouds; the conquest of Minya
konka, by Richard L. Burdsall and Arthur B. Emmons, 3rd, with contributions by Terris Moore and Jack Theodore Young. New York, London, Harper, 1935. xiii, 292 p. incl. maps, diagrs. front., plates, ports.
BURRARD, GERALD, 1888-   Big game hunting in the Himalayas and Tibet,
with sections by Col. A. G. Arbuthnot, W. B. Cotton, Col. G. H. Evans, Sir
Otway Wheeler-Cuffe, bart., and F.C. Lowis. London, H. Jenkins, 1925.
320 p. front., illus., plates, maps (part fold.)
BURRARD, SIR SIDNEY GERALD, 1860-   A sketch of the geography and geology of
the Himalaya mountains and Tibet, by Colonel S. G. Burrard and H. H. Hayden.
Revised by Colonel Sir Sidney Burrard and A. M. Heron. Delhi, Manager of pub-
lications, 1933. x, 359, xxxii p. plates (part fold.) maps (part fold.) diagrs.
DAINELLI, GIOTTO, 1878-   Buddhists and glaciers of western Tibet. Trans-
lated from the Italian by Augus Davidson. With 32 plates and map. London,
K. Paul, 1933. xiii, 304 p. front., plates, double map.
DALLONI, MARIUS. Mission au Tibeati (1930-1931). Dirigée par M. Dalloni.
Paris, Gauthier-Villars, 1934-1935. 2 v. illus. plates, fold. maps, diagrs.
FILCHNER, WILHELM, 1877-1957. Quer durch Ost-Tibet. Mit 24 Bildern und
2 Karten. Berlin, E.S. Mittler 1925. x, 195 p. plates, ports., 2 fold. maps.
————. Om mani padme hum; meine China- und Tibetexpedition, 1925-28; mit
103 Abbildungen und Skizzen, sowie einer Übersichtskarte. Leipzig, F.A.
Brockhaus, 1929. ix, 352 p. front., illus. (incl. plans) plates, ports., maps
(1 fold.).
————. The same. Neue, gekürzte Ausg. mit 33 Zeichnungen von Heiner Roth-
fuchs. 4 Aufl. Wiesbaden, E. Brockhaus, 1953 [c1950] 186 p. illus.
————. In China, auf Asiens Hochsteppen, im ewigen Eis; Rückblick auf fünfund-
zwanzig Jahre der Arbeit und Forschung. Mit 39 Bildern und 19 Karten.
Freiburg im Breisgau, Herder, 1930. [ix]-x, 202 p. front., (port.) illus.
plates, maps.(Fremdland-fremdvolk, eigenartige landschaften, länder und
völker der erde).
————. Im Machtbereich des Dalai-Lama. Mit 7 Abbildungen.  Leipzig, F.A.
Brockhaus, 1944. 63, [1] p. plates. "Gekürzt aus: Om mani padme hum.
Meine China-und Tibetexpedition 1925/28."
GREGORY  JOHN WALTER, 1864-1932. To the Alps of Chinese Tibet; an ac-
count of a journey of exploration up to and among the snow-clad mountains of
the Tibetan frontier, by J. W. Gregory and C. J. Gregory. London, Seeley,
Service, 1923. 17-321 p. illus. plates (incl. front.) fold. map, diagrs.
GUIBAUT, ANDRÉ. Ngolo-Setas: deuxième expédition Guibaut-Liotard au Tibet.

1940. Paris, Susse, 1947. 231 p. illus. maps. (Voyages et Aventures).

——. Tibetan venture in the country of the Ngolo-Setas; second Guibaut-Liotard expedition. Translated by Lord Sudley. London, J. Murray [1947] 206 p.
plates, ports., maps.

HEDIN, SVEN ANDERS, 1865-1952. Southern Tibet; discoveries in former times
compared with my own researches in 1906-1908. Stockholm, Lithographic
Institute of the General Staff of the Swedish Army [1916]-22 [v. 1, '17] 11 v.
in 9. illus., plates (part col., part fold.) maps (part fold.) diagrs. and atlas.
3 v.

——. Im Herzen von Asien: Zehntausend Kilometer auf unbekannten Pfaden.
6th Aufl. Leipzig, F.A. Brockhaus, 1929. 2 v. plates, port. maps.

——. A conquest of Tibet. London, Macmillan; New York, E.P. Dutton, 1934;
Garden City, N.Y. Halcyon Press, 1941. viii, 11-400 p. incl. front. (port.)
illus.

——. Im verbotenen Land. Mit zahlreichen Zeichnungen vom Verfasser. Aus
dem Schwedischen.Übertragen von Theodor Flade. Leipzig, P. Reclam jun.
[1937] 147, [3] p. illus. (incl. map) [Reclams universal-bibliothek, nr.
7370, 7371].

——. Eroberungszüge in Tibet. 4. Aufl. Leipzig, F.A. Brockhaus, 1942.
329 p. incl. front. (port.) illus. fold. map.

——. Wildes heiliges Tibet. Mit zahlreichen Zeichnungen vom Verfasser. Aus
dem Schwedischen übertragen von Theodor Flade. Leipzig, P. Reclam jun.
[1944] 77 p. illus. (Reclams Universal-Bibliothek, 7334).

——. The same; Stuttgart, Reclam [1952] 77 p. illus. (Reclams Universal-Bibliothek, Nr. 7334).

——. Transhimalaja; Entdeckungen und Abenteuer in Tibet. Mit 34 Abbildungen
aud Tafeln nach Aufnahmen und Zeichnungen des Verfassers, 1 Karte im Text
und 1 vierfarbigen Übersichtskarte. Neue [gekürzte] Ausg. [bearb. von Suse
Brockhaus] Wiesbaden, E. Brockhaus] 1951. 441 p. illus. (Klassiker der
Entdeckung).

——. Abenteuer in Tibet. [Reprint ed.] Wiesbaden, F. A. Brockhaus, 1956.
166 p. [16. Aufl. 1920, 404 p.].

HEIM, ARNOLD ALBERT, 1882-    Minya Gongkar, Forschungsreise ins Hoch-
gebirge von Chinesisch Tibet; Erlebnisse und Entdeckungen. Mit 3 Tafeln
(karten, panoramen) 26 Zeichnungen im Text und 147 Photographien, darunter
6 farbige Tafeln. Bern-Berlin, H. Huber, 1933. 244 p. incl. maps. illus.
(incl. music) plates (1 fold.; part col. mounted) fold. maps. diagrs.

KASHYAP, S    R. Some geographical observations in Western Tibet. [n.p.]
1930. Cover-title [223-236 p. illus., plates. "From the Journal and proceedings, Asiatic Society of Bengal (new series) vol xxv, 1929, no. 1."

KINGDON-WARD, FRANCIS, 1885-1958. The mystery rivers of Tibet; a description of the little-known land where Asia's mightiest rivers gallop in harness
through the narrow gateway of Tibet, its peoples, fauna, and flora, with many
illustrations and 3 maps. London, Seeley, Service, 1923. 11-316 p. front.,
plates, maps (1 fold.).

——. The riddle of the Tsangpo gorges. With contributions by the Right Hon.
the Earl Cawdor. London, E. Arnold, 1926. xv, 328 p. front., plates., fold.
map.

——. A plant hunter in Tibet. London, J. Cape [1934] 317 p. front., plates,
2 fold. maps.

——. Assam adventure. London, J. Cape [1941] 7-304 p. front., plates, ports.,
maps (1 fold.).

MARGERIE, EMMANUEL DE, 1862-    L'oeuvre de Sven Hedin et l'orographie
du Tibet. Paris, Imprimerie Nationale, 1929. cover-tile, 139 p. illus.,
plates, port., maps (2 fold.). "Extrait du Bulletin de la Section de géographie
du Comité des travaux historiques et scientifiques, 1928."

NORIN, ERIK, 1895-    Geological explorations in western Tibet. Appendices by

F. Heritsch, K. Metz and H. Frebold. Stockholm, 1946. xi, 214 p. plates, maps (1 fold. col.) profiles. (Reports from the scientific expedition to the north-western provinces of China under the leadership of Dr. Sven Hedin. The Sino-Swedish Expedition. Publication 29. iii. Geology. 7).

PRANAVĀNANDA, Swami. Exploration in Tibet. With an introd. by Syamaprasad Mookerjee and foreword by S. P. Chatterjee. [2d ed. Calcutta] University of Calcutta, 1950. xxxii, 302 p. plates, ports. fold. maps (in pocket) [1st ed. 1939, xx, 160 p.].

REED, FREDERICK RICHARD COWPER, 1869-    Upper Carboniferous fossils from Tibet. Calcutta, Government of India Central Publication Branch, 1930. 37 p. plates (India. Geological survey. Memoirs, Palaeontologia indica, n. s. vol 16).

ROERICH, GEORGE NICHOLAS, 1902-    Trails to inmost Asia; five years of exploration with the Roerich central Asian expedition, with a preface by Louis Marin. New Haven, Yale University Press; London, H. Milford, Oxford University Press, 1931. xx, 504 p. front., 1 illus., plates, ports., fold. map.

――――. Sur les pistes de l'Asie Centrale; texte française de M. de Vaux-Phalipan, préface de Louis Marin. Paris, P. Geuthner, 1933. viii, 296 p. plates, ports., fold. map.

SCHÄFER, ERNST, 1910-    Berge, Buddhas und Bären; Forschung und Jagd in geheimnisvollem Tibet. Mit 32 Tafeln nach photographischen Aufnahmen des Verfassers und 2 Karten. Berlin, P. Parey [1933] x, 316 p. illus. (maps) plates, ports.

――――. Unbekanntes Tibet; durch die Wildnisse Osttibets zum Dach der Erde. Tibetexpedition 1934/36. Berlin, P. Parey [c1937] viii, 294 p. plates, ports., maps.

――――. Dach der Erde; durch das Wunderland Hochtibet. Tibetexpedition 1934/36. Mit 83 Abbildungen des Verfassers. Berlin, P. Parey [c1938] xii, 292 p. plates, ports., fold. map.

――――. Ornithologische Ergebnisse zweier Forschungsreisen nach Tibet. Bernburg, 1938. 349 p. illus. plates. Diss.- Univ. Berlin.

――――. Tibet ruft; Forschung und Jagd in den hochgebirgen Osttibets, Tibetexpedition 1931/32. Mit 49 Abbildungen und 2 Karten. Berlin, P. Parey [1942] 290 p. plates, maps. "Das vorliegende werk ist zugleich eine vollkommene neugestaltung von 'Berge, buddhas und bären'."

――――. Geheimnis Tibet, erster Bericht der Deutschen Tibet-Expedition, Ernst Schäfer, 1938/39. München, F. Bruckmann [c1943] 183 p. illus., col. plates, map.

――――. Über den Himalaja ins Land der Götter; auf Forscherfahrt von Indien nach Tibet. [Braunschweig] Vieweg-Verlag [c1950] 200 p. plates, port., map (on lining paper).

――――. Fest der weissen Schleier; eine Forscherfahrt durch Tibet nach Lhasa, der heiligen Stadt des Gottkönigtums. [3. Aufl. Braunschweig] Vieweg-Verlag [1952] 199 p. illus. [Forschung und Abenteuer] [1. Aufl. 1949; 2. Aufl. 1950].

――――. Unter Räubern in Tibet; Gefahren und Freuden eines Forscherlebens. [Braunschweig] Vieweg-Verlag [1952] München, Goldmann, 1954. 215 p. illus. (Goldmanns gelbe Taschenbücher, 321).

TUCCI, GIUSEPPE, 1894-    Secrets of Tibet; being the chronicle of the Tucci scientific expedition to western Tibet (1933) by Dr. Giuseppe Tucci and Captain E. Ghersi. Translated from the Italian edition by Mary A. Johnstone. London, Blackie, 1935. xiv, 210 p. front., illus. (plans) plates, ports., fold. maps, facsims.

――――. To Lhasa and beyond; diary of the expedition to Tibet in the year MCMXL-VIII. With an appendix on Tibetan medicine and hygiene, by R. Moise. [Translated by Mario Carelli. Roma] Instituto poligrafico dello Stato [1956] 195 p. illus. map.

## Bibliographies

HU, HUEN-YONG, 胡煥庸, 1901-   Books and articles on Sinkiang (in Western languages) compiled by Huen-yong Hu and Chen-kang Tung, 童承康. Chung-king, Institute for the Promotion of Dr. Sun Yat-sen's Industrial Plan, 1943. 47 p. (National Central University. Dept. of Geography, Bull. B: 2).

## Description and Travel

AMBOLT, NILS PETER, 1900-   Karavan; travels in Eastern Turkestan. Trans-lated from the Swedish by Joan Bulman. London and Glasgow, Blackie, [1939] xiii, 191 p. col. front., plates (part col.) ports., fold. map. Swedish ed.: Karavan. Stockholm, 1935.
———. Karawanen, im Auftrag Sven Hedins durch Innerasien; mit einem Geleit-wort von Sven Hedin, 100 Bunten und einfarbigen Abbildungen und einer Karte. 2. aufl. Leipzig, F.A. Brockhaus, 1941. 191 p. col. front., plates (part col.) parts., map.
BATESON, WILLIAM, 1861-1926. Letters from the Steppe, written in the years 1886-1887 by William Bateson; edited, with an introduction, by Beatrice Bate-son. London, Methuen [1928] xvi, 222 p. front. (port.) illus., map.
BOSSHARD, WALTER, 1892-   Durch Tibet und Turkestan. Reisen im unberühr-ten Asien. Stuttgart, Strecker and Schröder, 1930. xiv, [1], 245, [1] p. front., plates, ports. maps.
———. Hazards of Asia's highlands and deserts. London, Figurehead [1932] 138, [1] p. front., illus. (maps) plates. (Pioneer series).
CABLE, MILDRED, 1880-1952. Through Jade gate and central Asia; an account of journeys in Kansu, Turkestan and the Gobi desert, by Mildred Cable and Francesca French, with an introduction by Rev. John Stuart Holden. London, Constable [1927] xvi, 304 p. front., plates, fold. map.
———. Par la porte de jade; odysée de trois femmes missionairies dans le Kan-sou, le Turkestan, et le désert de Gobi, [par] Mildred Cable et Francesca French; introduction de John Stuart Holden; traduit du l'anglais par Margue-rite Faguer. Paris, Plon, [1935] 332 p. fold. map. port.
DAVIDSON, BASIL, 1914-   Turkestan alive; new travels in Chinese Central Asia. London, Cape [1957] 255 p. illus.
DETTMANN, HANS EDUARD, 1891-   Unter Chinesen, Türken und Bolschewik-en. Photos und Buchschmuck vom Verfasser. Berlin, F. Schneider [c1939] 91 p. illus., map.
ETHERTON, PERCY THOMAS, 1879-   In the heart of Asia. London, Constable, 1925; Boston and New York, Houghton Mifflin, 1926. xii, 305 p. fold. map.
———. The last strongholds. London, Jarrolds, 1934. 5-297 p. front., plates, ports.
———. Across the great deserts. London, Lutterworth Press [1948]; New York, McGraw-Hill, [1948] 183 p. plates, maps (on lining-papers).
FILCHNER, WILHELM, 1877-1957. Bismillah! Vom Huang-ho zum Indus. 8. Aufl. Leipzig, F.A. Brockhaus, 1942 [c1938] 347 p. illus., ports., fold. col. map. [1. Aufl. 1938].
———. The same; mit 32 Textzeichnungen von Heiner Rothfuchs. Wiesbaden, E. Brockhaus, 1951. 191 p. illus.
———. A scientist in Tartary; from the Hoang-ho to the Indus; translated by E.O. Lorimer. London, Faber and Faber [1939] 391 p. front., illus., plates,

ports., fold. map.

FLEMING, PETER, 1907-    News from Tartary; a journey from Peking to Kashmir, London, J. Cape [1936] Reprint ed., 1945. 384 p. front., plates, fold.
map.

──── . Au coeur de la Tartarie; traduit par S. et P. Bourgeois. Paris, Nouvelle revue française, 1938. 294 p. front (map).

──── . Travels in Tartary: One's company and News from Tartary. London,
J. Cape [1948] 603 p. fold. maps.

GOERGER, ANDRÉ. En marge de la croisière jaune; de Moscou en Chine, de
Beyrouth à Srinagar, le "tour du monde", trois mois en Chine. Avec 121
gravures et une carte hors-texte. Paris, Rieder, 1935. [vii]-viii, 310 p.
plates (incl. front.) fold. map.

HEDIN, SVEN ANDERS, 1865-1952. Drei Jahre im innersten Asien. Braunschweig, G. Westermann, 1921. 157 p. illus. (Wissenschaftliche Volksbücher für Schule und Haus, 21).

──── . General Prschewalskij in Innerasien. Leipzig, F.A. Brockhaus, 1922.
158, [1] p. front., illus. (incl. maps) plates, ports. (Reisen und abenteuer,
19).

──── . An der schwelle Innerasiens. Leipzig, F.A. Brockhaus, 1923. 159 p.
front. (port.) illus. (incl. map) plates. [Reisen und abenteuer. 23].

──── . Big Horse's flight; the trail of war in Central Asia, translated by F.H.
Lyon. London, Macmillan, 1936. xv, 247, [1] p. front., plates, ports.,
fold. map, facsims. (1 fold.).

──── . The flight of "Big Horse"; the trail of war in Central Asia, translated
by F.H. Lyon. New York, E.P. Dutton, 1936. v-xv, 247, [1] p. front.,
plates, ports., facsims. (1 double).

──── . Die Flucht des Grossen Pferdes. 11. Aufl. Leipzig, F.A. Brockhaus,
1943. 299 p. illus., ports., fold. col. map.

──── . The wandering lake; translated from the Swedish by F.H. Lyon; with 32
illustrations, 76 sketches and 10 maps. New York, E.P. Dutton, 1940. x p.
291 p. front., illus., plates, ports., maps (1 fold.).

──── . Der wandernde See. Mit 151 Abbildungen und 10 Karten. 9. Aufl. Leipzig, F.A. Brockhaus, 1942. 295 p. front., illus., plates, ports., maps (1
fold.).

──── . The Silk road, translated from the Swedish by F.H. Lyon; with 31 plates
and a map. New York, E.P. Dutton, [c1938] viii, 322 p. front., plates,
ports., maps (1 fold.).

──── . Die Seidenstrasse. Mit 91 Abbildungen und 2 Karten. 9. Aulf. Leipzig,
F.A. Brockhaus, 1942. 263, [1] p. front., illus., plates, ports., mpas (1
fold.).

KAMAL, AHMAD, 1914-    Land without laughter. New York, C. Scribner,
1940. 4, 3-346 p. front. (group port.) illus. (facsims.).

KUCZYNSKI, MAX HANS, 1890-    Steppe und Mensch, kirgisische Reiseeindrücke und Betrachtungen über Leben, Kultur und Krankheit in ihren Zusam-
menhängen. Leipzig, S. Hirzel, 1925. 187, [1] p.

LATTIMORE, ELEANOR (HOLGATE), 1895-    Turkestan reunion, decorations
by Eleanor Frances Lattimore. New York, John Day; Toronto, McLeod,
1934; London, Hurst and Blackett, 1935. xi, 308 p. illus.

LATTIMORE, OWEN, 1900-    High Tartary. Boston, Little, Brown, 1930. xiv,
370 p. front., plates, ports., fold. map.

LE COQ, ALBERT VON, 1860-1930. Von Land und Leuten in Ostturkistan; Berichte und Abenteuer der 4. deutschen Turfanexpedition. Leipzig, J.C. Hinrichs, 1928. vii, [1], 183, [1] p. illus. (incl. maps, plans) plates (incl.
ports.).

LIAS, GODFREY. Kazak exodus. London, Evans Bros. [1956] 230 p. illus.

MACARTNEY, CATHERINA THEODORA (BORLAND) lady. An English lady in
Chinese Turkestan. London, E. Benn, [1931] 236 p. front., illus. (map)

plates.

MAILLART, ELLA KATHERINE, 1903-   Des Monts Célestes aux Sables Rouges. Paris, B. Grasset [1934] [3]-300 p. illus. (maps) plates.

———. Turkestan solo; one woman's expedition from the Tien Shan to the Kizil Kum, translated by John Rodker. New York, G. P. Putnam [c1935] 3-307 p. front., plates, ports.

———. Turkestan Solo. Deutsch von Hans Reisiger. Stuttgart, Rowohlt, 1941. 312 p.

———. Oasis interdites de Pékin au Cachemire; illustré de 32 pages hors-texte en hélio et de cartes. Paris, B. Grasset [1937] [7]-281 p. plates, ports., maps (1 fold.).

———. Forbidden journey-from Peking to Kashmir, Translated by Thomas Mc-Greevy. London, W. Heinemann, [1937] xvi, 312 p. front., plates, ports., facsim., maps (1 fold.).

———. Verbotene Reise von Peking nach Kaschmir. Deutsch von Hans Reisiger. Berlin, Rowohlt [1938] 302 p. front., plates, ports., fold. map.

MANNERHEIM, CARL GUSTAF EMIL; friherre, 1867-1951.   Across Asia from west to east in 1906- 1908. Helsinki, 1940. 2 v. front. (port.) illus. plates, maps. (part fold.) facsims, diagrs.

NAZAROV, PAVEL STEPANOVICH. Hunted through central Asia, by P.S. Nazá-roff; rendered into English from the Russian of the author's manuscript by Malcolm Burr with frontispiece and map. Edinburgh and London, W. Black-wood, 1932. xi, 331, [1] p. front. (port.).

———. Moved on! From Kashgar to Kashmir, by P.S. Nazaroff, rendered into English from the Russian manuscript of the author by Malcolm Burr. London, G. Allen and Unwin, [1935] 317 p. front., plates, ports., fold. map.

OSSENDOWSKI, FERDYNAND ANTONI, 1876-1944. Man and mystery in Asia, by Ferdinand Ossendowski in collaboration with Lewis Stanton Palen. New York, E. P. Dutton [c1924] xvi, 343 p. front. (port.).

———. L'homme et le mystère en Asie; traduit de l'anglais par Robert Renard. Paris, Plon-Nourrit, [1925] 6, vii, 306, [1] p. fold. map.

———. In den Dschungeln der Wälder und Menschen. Einzig berechtigte deutsche Ausg., hrsg. von Wolf von Dewall. Frankfurt a M., Frankfurter Societäts-Druckerei [1924] 399 p. fold. map.

PHILIPE, ANNE. Caravanes d'Asie du Sinkiang su Cachemire. Paris, Julliard, Sequana, 1955. 253 p. illus. (photos), maps, (La croix du sud).

RAWICZ, SLAVOMIR. The long walk; a gamble for life as told to Ronald Down-ing. New York, Harper [1956] 239 p. illus.

SCHOMBERG, REGINALD CHARLES FRANCIS, 1880-   Peaks and plains of cen-tral Asia, with colour photographs by Captain George Sherriff. London, M. Hopkinson, 1933. 288 p. col front., col. plates, maps (1 fold.).

SCHULTZ, ARVED VON, 1883-   Kaschgar (chinesisch Turkestan), Stadt und Landschaft. Hamburg, O. Meissner, 1921. 51 p. plates, 2 maps (1 fold.) (Mitteilungen aus dem Seminar für geographie der hamburgischen Universi-tät).

SHIPTON, DIANA. The antique land. Decorations by Jill Davis. London, T. Brun [1950] 219 p. illus., ports., maps (on lining papers).

SHIPTON, ERIC EARLE, 1907-   Blank on the map; with a foreword by T. G. Longstaff. London, Hodder and Stoughton [1938] xv, 299, [1] p. front., illus. plates, ports., maps (1 fold.).

———. Mountains of Tartary. Photos. by the author. London, Hodder and Stough-ton [195-] 224 p. illus.

SKREDE, WILFRED, 1921-   Par-dessus le toit du monde. Traduit du norvé-gien par Marguerite Gay et Gerd de Mautrod. Paris, Nouvelles Éditions de Paris [1951] 249 p. illus. Norwegian ed., published in 1949, has title: Veien over verdens tak. Oslo, Gyldendal. 187 p.

———. Across the roof of the world; translated from the Norwegian by M. A. Michael. London, New York, Staples Press [1954]; New York, Norton, 1955; London, World Distributors, 1956. 255 p. illus.

SKRINE, CLARMONT PERCIVAL, 1888-   Chinese Central Asia, with an introduction by Sir Francis Younghusband. With a frontispiece in colour, 5 panoramas and 2 maps, 51 other illustrations. London, Methuen [1926] xvi, 306 p. col. front., 1 illus. (music) plates (2 fold.) port., fold. map.

STRONG, ANNA LOUISE, 1885-   The road to the grey Pamir. Boston, Little, Brown, 1931. 289 p. front. illus., (map) plates, ports.

TEICHMAN, SIR ERIC, 1884-1944. Journey to Turkistan. London, Hodder and Stoughton, [1937] xiv, 15-221 p. plates, ports., fold. map.

TILMAN, HAROLD WILLIAM, 1898-   China to Chitral. With 69 photos. taken by the author. Cambridge [Eng.] University Press, 1951. 123 p. illus.

TRINKLER, EMIL, 1896-1931. Im Land der Stürme, mit Yak- und Kamelkarawanen durch Innerasien; mit 124 Bunten und einfarbigen Abbildungen nach Aquarellen und Aufnahmen des Verfassers und einer Karte des Reisewegs der Deutschen Zentralasien-Expedition, 1927-28. Leipzig, F.A. Brockhaus, 1930. 242, [1] p. col. front., plates (part col.) ports., fold. map.

——. The stormswept roof of Asia; by yak, camel and sheep caravan in Tibet, Chinese Turkistan and over the Kara-Koram. London, Seeley, Service, 1931. 11-312 p. front., plates. fold. map.

VASEL, GEORG. Flammen in der Wüste; Erlebnisse eines deutschen Flugpioniers in Innerasien. Mit 21 Aufnahmen und einer Karte. Berlin, Ullstein [1936] 264, [1] p., illus. (double map) plates, ports.

——. My Russian jailers in China; translated from the German by Gerald Griffin. London, Hurst and Blackett [1937] 288 p. plates, ports.

[WADDINGTON, JEAN PENDRELL] 1893-   Lueurs d'Asie; de l'Himalaya aux mers de Chine. Préface du maréchal Franchet-d'Esperey. Paris, Picart, 1935. 3- [9]-191, [1] p. front. (port.) plates. fold. map.

WILSON, HELEN CALISTA. Vagabonding at fifty, from Siberia to Turkestan, by Helen Calista Wilson and Elsie Reed Mitchell. New York, Coward, McCann, 1929. v-viii p. 9-335 p. front. (map) plates.

## Turki and Other Languages

BANG-KAUP, WILLY, 1869-1934. ed. Türkische Turfan-Texte in Verbindung mit A. von Gabain und G.R. Rachmati, hrsg. von W. Bang-Kaup. Berlin, Verlag der Akademie der Wissenschaften, 1930-1954. 8 pts. 30, 22, 31, 20, 102, 124, 105 p. plates.

BASKAKOV, NIKOLAI ALEKSANDROVICH. The Turkic languages of Central Asia: problems of planned culture contact. [London] Central Asian Research Centre [1952?] 52 p.

BIDWELL, CHARLES EVERETT, 1923-   A structural analysis of Uzbek. [Washington, American Council of Learned Societies, 1955] 140 p. (American Council of Learned Societies [Devoted to Humanistic Studies] Program in Oriental Languages. Publications. Series B: Aids, no. 3).

FRANKLE, ELEANOR, 1913-   Word formation in the Turkic languages. [New York] Columbia Univ. Press, 1948. 109 p. Thesis-Columbia Univ.

JARRING, GUNNAR, 1907-   Studien zu einer osttürkischen Lautlehre. [Translated by] E.Blauert and H. Müller. Lund, Borelius; [etc., etc., 1933] xv p. 126, 53 p., illus. (map) fold. facsim., diagrs. Akademische abhandlung-Lund.

——. ed. Materials to the knowledge of Eastern Turki; tales, poetry, proverbs, riddles, ethnological and historical texts from the southern parts of Eastern Turkestan, with translation and notes. Lund, C.W. K. Gleerup [1946-51]. 4 v. (Lunds universitets ärsskrift, n.f., avd. 1, bd. 43, nr. 4, bd. 44, nr. 7.

KOERBER, HANS NORDEWIN VON. Comparative study of the Turkish, Mongol, and Japanese languages, a brief résumé. Los Angeles, the University of

Southern California Press, 1937. 19 p. (The University of Southern California. Language and literature series, 3).

LENTZ, WOLFGANG, 1900-    Pamir-dialekte. 1. Materialien zur Kenntnis der Schugni-Gruppe. Göttingen, Vandenhoeck und Ruprecht, 1933-  1 v. illus. (maps) facsims. (Ergänzungshefte zur Zeitschrift für vergleichende sprachforschung auf dem gebiete der indogermanischen sprachen, nr. 12).

————. Zeitrechnung in Nuristan und am Pamir. Berlin, Akademie der Wissenschaften, in kommission bei W. de Gruyter, 1939. 211, [1] p. illus. (incl. maps) fold. tables (Abhandlungen der Preussischen akademie der wissenschaften. Jahrg. 1938. Philosophisch-historische klasse, nr. 7).

LÖWENTHAL, RUDOLF, 1904-    The Turkic languages and literatures of central Asia, a bibliography. Washington [1956] xii, 173 p.

MENGES, KARL HEINRICH, 1908-    Glossar zu den volkskundlichen Texten aus Ost-Türkistan II. Mainz, Verlag der Akademie der Wissenschaften und der Literatur; in Kommission bei F. Steiner. Wiesbaden [1954] 139 p. (Akademie der Wissenschaften und der Literatur. Abhandlungen der Geistes- und Sozialwissenschaftlichen Klasse. Jahrg. 1954, Nr. 14).

RAQUETTE, GUSTAF RICHARD, 1871-1945. English-Turki dictionary, based on the dialects of Kashgar and Yarkand. Lund, C. W. K. Gleerup; [etc., etc., 1927] [2]. ii, 139 p. (Lunds universitets årsskrift. n. f., avd. 1, bd. 23, nr. 4).

————. ed. Eine kaschgarische Wakf-Urkunde aus der Khodscha-Zeit Ost-Turkestans. Lund, C. W. K. Gleerup; Leipzig, O. Harrassowitz [1930] 24 p. fold. facsim. (Lunds universitets årsskrift, n. f., avd. 1, bd. 26, nr. 2).

————. ed. Tāji bilä Zohra; eine osttürkische Variante der Sage von Tahir und Zohra. Lund, C. W. K. Gleerup [1930] 128 p. (Lunds universitets årsskrift. n. f., avd. 1, bd. 26, nr. 6).

ROSS, SIR EDWARD DENISON, 1871-1940, ed. Dialogues in the eastern Turki dialect on subjects of interest to travellers, collected and edited by Sir E. Denison Ross and Rachel O. Wingate. London, Royal Asiatic society, 1934. xii, 48 p. (James G. Forlong fund, vol. xi).

SAKIR, SA'ADAT, 1907-    ed. Qazaqisch, bearbeitet von dr. S. Šäkir und dr. K. Menges. Berlin, Institut für Lautforschung an der Universität Berlin, in Kommission bei O. Harrassowitz, Leipzig, 1935. 19 p. (Lautbibliothek; texte zu den sprachplatten des Instituts für lautforschung an der Universität Berlin, hrsg. von D. Westermann. Nr. 148).

SIMPSON, C.   G. Some features of the morphology of the Oirot (Gorno-Altai) language. iii, 68 p. (Central Asian Research Centre, Publ.).

WIENER, THOMAS GUSTAV, 1917-    Kazakh oral art and literature with special emphasis on the impact of the October revolution. Ann Arbor, University Microfilm, 1950 [i. e. 1951] ([University Microfilms, Ann Arbor, Mich.] Publication no. 2137). Collation of the original: ii, 548 l. map., diagr., tables. Thesis-Columbia University.

WURM, STEFAN. Der özbekische Dialekt von Andidschan. Phonetische und morphologische Studien, Texte. Brünn, In Kommission bei R. M. Rohrer, 1945. 1 v. (Akademie der Wissenschaften in Wien. Philosophisch-historische Klasse. Sitzungsberichte, 224. Bd., 3. Abhandlung).

## History

AHMAD, HAFIZ MANZOORUDDIN. Kampf um leere Räume, Turan, Turkestan, Tibet. Leipzig, W. Goldmann [1940] 153, [1] p. illus. (map) ("Weltgeschehen").

BAGCHI, PRABODH CHANDRA, 1898-1956. India and Central Asia. Calcutta, National Council of Education, Bengal, 1955. 184 p. illus.

BARTHOLD, VASILĬ VLADIMIROVICH, 1869-1930. Turkestan down to the Mongol invasion. 2d ed., translated from the original Russian and revised by the author with the assistance of H. A. R. Gibb. Printed by the Oxford University

Press for the Trustees of the "E. J. W. Gibb memorial." London, Luzac, 1928. 2nd ed. 1956. xix, [1], 513, [1] p. fold. map. ("E. J. W. Gibb memorial" series. New series, v).

————. 12 Vorlesungen über die Geschichte der Türken Mittelasiens, Deutsche Bearbeitung von Theodor Menzel. Berlin, Deutsche Gesellschaft für Islamkunde, 1935. 278 p. (Die Welt des Islams, bd. 14-17. Beiband).

————. Histoire des Turcs d'Asie Centrale. Adaptation française par mme. M. Donskis. Paris, Adrien-Maisonneuve, 1945. [3]-202 p. incl. geneal. table. 2 fold. maps (Initiation à l'Islam. Collection pub. sous le patronage de l'Institut d'études islamiques de l'Université de Paris. iii).

————. Four studies on the history of Central Asia. Translated from the Russian by V. and T. Minorsky. v. 1: A short history of Turkestan. A history of Semirechyé. Leiden, E. J. Brill, 1956. xvi, 184 p.

————. L'Asie ancienne centrale et sud-orientale d'après Ptolémée. Avec 23 cartes en noir et 1 en couleur. Paris, Payot, 1930. 426 p. maps (part fold.) diagrs. (Bibliothèque géographique).

BUGRA, MOHAMMED EMIN, 伊敏. Eastern Turkestan's struggle for freedom and Chinese policy. Istanbul, Osmanbey Mat. 1954. 32 p.

CHAVANNES, ÉDOUARD, 1865-1918. Documents sur les Tou-Kiue (Turcs) occidentaux. Recueillis et commentés, suivi de notes additionnelles. Avec une carte. (Présenté à l'Académie impériale des sciences de St-Pétersbourg le 23 août 1900). Paris, Adrien-Maisonneuve [1942] iv, 378, 110 p. front. (fold. map).

CH'EN, TSU-YUEN, 陳宗鎣. Histoire du défrichement de la Province du Sinkiang sous la dynastie Ts'ing. Paris, Jouve et Cie, 1932. 180 p. maps. Thèse-Univ. de Paris.

CHU, CHIA-HUA, 朱家驊, 1893- Taiwan and Sinkiang (Formosa and Chinese Turkistan) Taipei, Chinese Association for the United Nations, 1954. 55 p. (Unachina publications, ser. L 11).

CHU, WEN-DJANG, 朱文長, 1914- The policy of the Manchu government in the suppression of the Moslem rebellion in Shensi, Kansu and Sinkiang from 1862 to 1878. Seattle, 1955. 439 l. Thesis-Univ. of Washington.

FRANCKE, AUGUST HERMANN, 1870-1930. Königsnamen von Khotan (A-maca) auf tibetischen Dokumenten der Turkistan-Sammlungen von London und Berlin. Berlin, 1928. 8 p.

FUNINGGAN 富寗安, d. 1728. Zum Dsungarenkrieg im 18. Jahrhundert; Berichte des Generals Funingga, aus einer mandschurischen Handschrift übers. und an Hand der chinesischen Akten erläutert von Eva S. Kraft. Leipzig, O. Harrassowitz, 1953. viii, 191 p. map, facsim. (Das Mongolische Weltreich; Quellen und Forschungen, Bd. 4). Original ed., issued in 1949 as the editor's thesis, has title: Berichte des Generals Funinga aus dem Dsungarenkrieg i. xviii. Jrh.

HAMBIS, LOUIS, 1906- La Haute-Asie. Paris, Presses universitaires de France, 1953. 134 p. illus. ("Que sais-je?" Le point des connaissances actuelles, 573).

HAMILTON, JAMES RUSSELL, 1921- Les Ouïghours à l'époque des cinq dynasties d'après les documents chinois. Paris, Impr. nationale, 1955. 201 p. fold. map, facsims. (Bibliothèque de l'Institut des hautes études chinoises, 10).

HO, DAVID 何昌熾. L'oeuvre colonisatrice de la Chine dans le Turkestan chinois. Paris, Recueil Sirey, 1941. 128 p. Thèse-Univ. de Paris.

JACOBSON, HARALD, 1910- Rise of Turkish power in Central Asia; history of the Eastern Turks (522-745) Chicago, 1938. 56 l. Lithoprinted ed. 22 p. Thesis-University of Chicago.

LATTIMORE, OWEN, 1900- Pivot of Asia; Sinkiang and the inner Asian frontiers of China and Russia, by Owen Lattimore with the assistance of Chang Chih-yi, 張之毅 [and others.] Boston, Little, Brown, 1950. xii, 288 p.

maps.

MCGOVERN, WILLIAM MONTGOMERY, 1897-    The early empires of Central
    Asia; a study of the Scythians and the Huns and the part they played in world
    history, with special reference to the Chinese sources. Chapel Hill, Univer-
    sity of North C. roliana Press, 1939. xiii, 529 p. illus.(maps) plates.

NOBEL, JOHANNES, 1887-    Central Asia: the connecting link between East and
    West and other lectures. Nagpur, International Academy of Indian Culture,
    1952. 160 p. (Sarasvati Vihara ser. 26).

NORINS, MARTIN RICHARD. Gateway to Asia: Sinkinag, frontier of the Chinese
    far west; introduction by Owen Lattimore, illustrated with maps and photo-
    graphs; issued in co-operation with the International Secretariat, Institute of
    Pacific Relations. New York, John Day [ 1944] 200 p. illus. (maps) plates.

PELLIOT, PAUL, 1878-1945. La Haute Asie. Paris, L'Édition artistique, J.
    Goudard, [n.d.] 37 p. illus. plates. Cover-title: "Explorations et voyages
    dans la Haute-Asie."

WU, AITCHEN K., 吳靄辰, 1892-    Turkistan tumult, with 16 plates and 2 end-
    paper maps. London, Methuen, [ 1940] xiii, 278, [2] p. front., plates,
    ports.

## Economic and Social Conditions

CLARK, MILTON J., 1920-    Leadership and political allocation in Sinkiang
    Kazak society. Cambridge, 1955. 353 l. Thesis-Harvard University.

EGART, MARK. The ferry; sketches of the struggle for socialism in the Altai
    mountains. London, M. Lawrence, 1932. 151 p. plates (part double).

GOLAB, LUDWIG WAWRZYN. A study of irrigation in East Turkestan. [ Trans-
    lated from the German by James E. Mertz] Freiburg in der Schweiz, Druck
    und Kommissionsverlag: Paulusdruckerei [ 1951] Cover-title, 187-199 p. illus.
    Reprinted from Anthropos, v. 46, 1951.

HARVA, UNO, 1882-    Die religiösen Vorstellungen der altaischen Völker. Hel-
    sinki, Suomalainen tiedeakatemia; [ etc., etc., 1938] 634 p. illus. ([ Folklore
    fellows] FF communications, 125).

HUDSON, ALFRED EMMONS, 1904-    Kazak social structure. New Haven,
    Published for the Department of anthropology, Yale University, by the Yale
    University Press; London, H. Milford, Oxford University Press, 1938. 109 p.
    incl. map. (Yale university publications in anthropology, 20).

KAZAK, FUAD. Ostturkistan zwischen den Grossmächten; ein Beitrag zur wirt-
    schaftskunde Ostturkistans. Königsberg (Pr.), Berlin, Ost-Europa Verlag,
    1937. viii, 160 p. incl. tables. fold. map. (Osteuropäische forschungen.
    Neue folge, 23).

KRADER  LAWRENCE. Kinships systems of the Altaic speaking peoples of the
    Asiatic Steppe. Cambridge, 1953. 660 l. charts, diagrs. Thesis-Harvard
    University.

——. The Kazakhs; a background study for psychological warfare, by Lawrence
    Krader and Ivor Wayne. [ Washington] George Washington University, Human
    Resources Research Office, 1955. viii, 154 p. maps, diagrs., tables (George
    Washington University [ Washington, D. C. ] Human Resources Research Office.
    Technical report 23).

SAMOLIN, WILLIAM, 1911-    The Turkisation of the Tarim Basin up to the Çara-
    Çytay; a preliminary survey of the problems involved. Ann Arbor, University
    Microfilms [ 1954] ([ University Microfilms, Ann Arbor, Mich. ] Publication
    no. 6696) Microfilm copy of typescript. Positive. Collation of the original:
    iv, 362 l. map, facsim. Thesis-Columbia University.

## Foreign Missions

CABLE, MILDRED, 1880-1952. The challenge of Central Asia; a brief survey of

Tibet and its borderlands, Mongolia, north-west Kansu, Chinese Turkistan, and Russian Central Asia. By Mildred Cable, F. Houghton, R. Kilgour, A. McLeish, R. W. Sturt, and Olive Wyon. London, New York, World Domini-on Press, 1929. iv, [9]-136 p. fold. maps. [World dominion survey series].

——. Something happened, by Mildred Cable and Francesca French. London, Hodder and Stoughton, 1933; New York, Frederick A. Stokes, 1934. 320 p. front., plates, port., fold. map.

——. The making of a pioneer: Percy Mather of Central Asia, by Mildred Cable and Francesca French. New York, Frederick A. Stokes, 1936. 288 p. front., plates, ports., fold. map.

——. The perpetual challenge of Central Asia. London, Central Asian Mission 1937? 7 p. double map.

——. The story of Topsy, little lonely of Central Asia, by Mildred Cable and Francesca French. London, Hodder and Stoughton, [1937] viii 9-212 p. front. illus. plates, ports.

——. George, Hunter, apostle of Turkestan, by Mildred Cable and Francesca French. London, China Inland Mission [1948] 107 p. plates, ports., map (on lining-papers).

——. Grace, child of the Gobi, by Mildred Calbe and Francesca French. Re-print ed. London, China Inland Mission, 1949. 56 p. illus. 1st ed. 1933.

THE CHALLENGE OF CENTRAL ASIA. London, World Dominion Press [192-?] cover-title, 32 p. fold. map. (World dominion survey series).

EASTERN AND CENTRAL ASIA. [London, New Mildmay Press, 1935?] 33 p. (World to-day series).

FRENCH, EVANGELINE. A desert journal; letters from central Asia, by Evan-geline French, Mildred Cable [and] Francesca French. London, Constable, 1934; 2nd ed. London, Hodder and Stoughton, 1939. ix, 261 p. front., plates, ports., fold. map.

MINGANA ALPHONSE, 1881-1937. The early spread of Christianity in Central Asia and the Far East: a new document. Manchester, The University Press, 1925. 80 p. Reprinted from the Bulletin of the John Rylands Library, 9:2).

## Art and Archaeology

BERGMAN, FOLKE, 1902-1946. Archaeological researches in Sinkiang, espe-cially the Lopnor region; by Folke Bergman; descriptive lists of textiles by Vivi Sylwan, appendices by Sten Konow and Hjalmar Ljungh; with 20 half tone plates, 2 coloured plates, 36 collotype plates, and 52 illustrations and maps in the text. Stockholm, Bokförlags aktiebolaget Thule, 1939. 258 p. illus. (incl. maps) plates (2 col.) (Reports from the scientific expedition to the north-western provinces of China under the leadership of Dr. Sven Hedin. The Sino-Swedish expedition. Publication 7. vii, Archaeology. 1).

GRÜNWEDEL, ALBERT, 1856-1935. Die Teufel des Avesta und ihre Beziehun-gen zur Ikonographie des Buddhismus Zentral-Asiens. Berlin, O. Elsner, 1924. 448, 113 p. illus., double pl.

HACKIN, JOSEPH, 1886-1941. Recherches archéologiques en Asie Centrale (1931). Paris, Les Éditions d'art et d'histoire, 1936. 35 p. illus. map, plan. diags.

HERRMANN, ALBERT, 1886- Lou-lan; China, Indien und Rom im Lichte der Ausgrabungen am Lobnor; mit einem Vorwort von Sven Hedin. Leipzig, F. A. Brockhaus, 1931. 160 p. front., illus. (incl. maps, plans) plates (incl. fac-sims.).

HJORTSJÖ, CARL HERMAN, 1914- Das Schädel- und Skelettgut der archäolo-gischen Untersuchungen in Ost-Turkistan, von Carl-Herman Hjorstjö und An-ders Walander. Stockholm [Tryckeri aktiebolaget Thule] 1942. 89 p. illus. (incl. map) plates (Reports from the Scientific expedition to the north-western provinces of China under the leadership of Dr. Sven Hedin. The Sino-Swedish expedition. Publication 19. vii. Archaeology. 3).

LE COQ, ALBERT VON, 1860-1930. Die buddhistische Spätantike in Mittelasien. Berlin, D. Reimer [etc.] 1922-33. 7 v. illus. (part mounted; incl. maps, plans) plates (part col.).

———. Bilderatlas zur Kunst und Kulturgeschichte Mittel-Asiens. Mit 255 Abbildungen. Berlin, D. Reimer [etc.] 1925. [5]-107 p. illus.

———. Auf Hellas spuren in Ostturkistan; Berichte und Abenteuer der II. und III. deutschen Turfan-Expedition, mit 108 Abbildungen im Text und auf 52 Tafeln sowie 4 Karten. Leipzig, J. C. Hinrichs, 1926. xi, 166 p. illus. (incl. maps. plans) plates (incl. ports.).

———. Buried treasures of Chinese Turkestan; an account of the activities and adventures of the second and third German Turfan expeditions, translated by Anna Barwell. London, G. Allen and Unwin, [1928] [7]-180 p. illus. (incl. plans) plates (incl. ports.).

STEIN, SIR MARK AUREL, 1862-1943. Serindia; detailed report of explorations in Central Asia and westernmost China carried out and described under the orders of H. M. Indian Government by Aurel Stein. Oxford, Clarendon Press, 1921. 5 v. illus., plates (part fold., part col.) 94 (i. e. 96) fold. maps, 59 plans (part fold.) facsims. (part fold.).

———. Memoir on maps of Chinese Turkistan and Kansu from the surveys made during Sir Aurel Stein's explorations, 1900-01, 1906-08, 1913-15. With appendices by Major K. Mason and J. de Graaff Hunter, Dehra Dun, Trigonometrical Survey Office, 1923. xv, 208 p. front., plates. [India. Survey of India dept. Records of the survey of India, vol. xvii]

———. Innermost Asia; detailed report of explorations in Central Asia, Kan-su, and eastern Īrān, carried out and described under the orders of H. M. Indian Government by Sir Aurel Stein. Oxford; Clarendon Press, 1928. 4 v. plates (part col., 1 fold.) plans. facsims., fold. maps.

———. Ancient Khotan, detailed report of archaeological explorations in Chinese Turkestan, carried out and described under the orders of H. M. Indian Government by M. Aurel Stein. Reprint ed. Peking, 1940. 2 v. illus., 153 plates (part col.; incl. plans, facsims.) fold. map in pocket. [1st ed. Oxford, 1907].

———. On ancient Central-Asian tracks; brief narrative of three expeditions in innermost Asia and north-western China. With numerous illustrations, colour plates, panoramas and map from original surveys. [London, Macmillan, 1933] Reprinted ed. Peking, 1941. xxiv, 342 p. plates (part fold.) ports., fold. map.

WALDSCHMIDT, ERNST, 1897- Gandhara, Kutscha, Turfan; eine Einführung in die frühmittelalterliche Kunst Zentralasiens; mit 119 Abbildungen und Karte auf 66 Tafeln und im Text. Leipzig, Klinkhardt und Biermann [c1925] 115 p. illus. (incl. plans) plates, map.

## Tunhuang Finds: General Works

ANDREWS, FREDERICK HENRY. Wall paintings from ancient shrines in Central Asia; recovered by Sir Aurel Stein; described by Fred H. Andrews. Published under the orders of the Government of India. London, Oxford University Press, 1948. xxxiv, 128 p. illus., fold. map, and portfolio (32 plates (part col.)).

DELHI. CENTRAL ASIAN ANTIQUITIES MUSEUM. Catalogue of wall-paintings from ancient shrines in Central Asia and Sīstān, recovered by Sir Aurel Stein, described by Fred H. Andrews. Delhi, Manager of Publications, 1933. [v]-xiii, 201 p. plates (incl. plans; 1 fold.) fold. map.

———. Descriptive catalogue of antiquities recovered by Sir Aurel Stein during his explorations in Central Asia, Kansu and eastern Iran, by Fred H. Andrews Delhi, Manager of Publications, 1935. [v]-x, 36, 37-445 p. 1 illus., plates, fold. map.

GILES, LIONEL, 1875-1958. Descriptive catalogue of the Chinese manuscripts from
    Tunhuang in the British Museum. London, Trustees of the British Museum,
    1957. xxv, 334 p.
MASPERO, HENRI, 1883-1945, ed. Les documents chinois de la troisième ex-
    pédition de Sir Aurel Stein en Asie centrale. London, Trustees of the Brit-
    ish Museum, 1953. xii, 268 p. 40 plates (facsims.).
PARIS. Musée Guimet. Manuscrits et peintures de Touen-houang; Mission Pel-
    liot 1906-09. Collections de la Bibliothèque et du Musée Guimet. [Paris] Édi-
    tions des Musées nationaux, 1947. 41, [3] p. fold. map.
PELLIOT, PAUL, 1878-1945. Les grottes de Touen-houang; peintures et sculp-
    tures bouddhiques des époques des Wei, des T'ang et des Song. Paris, P.
    Geuthner, 1914-24. 6 v. in 3 plates (Mission Pelliot en Asie Centrale. Sé-
    rie in quarto. 1.).
STEIN, SIR MARK AUREL, 1862-1943. The thousand Buddhas; ancient Buddhist
    paintings from the cave-temples of Tun-huang of the western frontier of Chi-
    na, recovered and described by Aurel Stein, with an introductory essay by
    Laurence Binyon. Published under the orders of H. M. Secretary of State for
    India and with the co-operation of the Trustees of the British Museum. Lon-
    don, B. Quaritch, ltd., 1921. xii, 65 p. plates and portfolio of plates.
VINCENT, IRENE (VONGEHR). The sacred oasis; caves of the thousand Bud-
    dhas, Tun Huang. With a pref. by Pearl Buck. London, Faber and Faber
    [1953] 114 p. illus.
WALEY, ARTHUR, 1889-    A catalogue of paintings recovered from Tun-huang
    by Sir Aurel Stein, preserved in the Sub-department of Oriental prints and
    drawings in the British museum, and in the Museum of Central Asian antiqui-
    ties, Delhi. London, Printed by order of the Trustees of the British Museum
    and of the Government of India, 1931. lii, 328 p. diagrs.

### Khotanese Texts

BAILEY, HAROLD WALTER, 1899-    ed. Khotanese texts. Cambridge [Eng. ]
    The University Press, 1945-56. 3 v.
————. ed. Khotanese Buddhist texts. London, Taylor's Foreign Press, 1951.
    ix, 157 p. (Cambridge oriental series, 3).
BOYER, AUGUSTE M., ed. Kharoṣṭhi inscriptions discovered by Sir Aurel
    Stein in Chinese Turkestan, transcribed and edited by A. M. Boyer, E. J.
    Rapson and E. Senart. Published under the authority of His Majesty's Sec-
    retary of State for India in council. Oxford, The Clarendon Press, 1920-27.
    2 v. plates.
BURROW, THOMAS. The language of the Kharoṣṭhi documents from Chinese
    Turkestan. Cambridge [Eng.] The University Press, 1937. ix, 134 p.
————. tr. A translation of the Kharoṣṭhi documents from Chinese Turkestan.
    London, Royal Asiatic Society, 1940. vi, 151 p. (James G. Forlong fund,
    vol. 20 ).
CODICES khotanenses, India office library, Ch. ii 002, Ch. ii 003, Ch. 00274,
    reproduced in facsimile. With an introduction by H. W. Bailey. Copenhagen,
    Levin and Munksgaard, 1938. xiii p., facsims.: 183 p. (Monumenta lingua-
    rum Asiæ maioris, edidit K. Grønbech. II ).
JĀTAKASTAVA. The Jātakastava; or, "Praise of the Buddha's former births."
    Indo-Scythian (Khotanese) text, English translation, grammatical notes, and
    glossaries. [By] Mark J. Dresden. Philadelphia, American Philosophical
    Society [1955] 397-508 p. (Transactions of the American Philosophical Soci-
    ety, new ser., v. 45, pt. 5).
KONOW, STEN, 1867-1948. Saka studies. Oslo [Glückstadt and Hamburg, Prin-
    ted by J. J. Augustin] 1932. vi, 198 p. (Oslo. Etnografiske museum. Bulletin
    5).
————. Ein neuer Saka-Dialekt. Mit 8 Tafeln. Berlin, Verlag der Akademie der

Wissenschaften, in Kommission bei W. de Gruyter, 1935. 54 p. 1 illus.,
plates (facsims.; 1 fold.).
————. Khotansakische Grammatik, mit Bibliographie, Lesestücken und Wörter-
verzeichnis. Mit einer Schrifttafel. Leipzig, O. Harrassowitz, 1941. vi,
130 p. fold. facsim. (Porta linguarum orientalium; sammlung von lehrbüchern für das studium der orientalischen sprachen, hrsg. von Richard Hartmann, 22 ).
————. A medical text in Khotanese, Ch. ii 003 of the India Office Library. With
translation and vocabulary, ed. by Sten Konow. Oslo, I kommisjon hos J.
Dybwad, 1941. 104 p. (Avhandlinger utg. av det Norske videnskapsakademi
i Oslo. II. Hist.-filos.klasse, 1940, no. 4 ).

### Sogdian Texts

BENVENISTE, ÉMILE, 1902-    Textes sogdiens. Édités, traduits et commentés par É. Benveniste. Paris, P. Geuthner, 1940. ix, 284 p. (Mission Pelliot en Asie-centrale. Série in-quarto, 3 ).
————. Vessan Tara Jataka. Texte sogdien, édité, traduit et commenté par É.
Benveniste. Paris, P. Geuthner, 1947. x, 137 p.
BERLINER soghdische Texte. 1: Bruckstücke einer soghdischen Version der
Georgspassion (C 1). Hrsg. von Olaf Hansen. Berlin, Akademie der Wissenschaften in Kommission bei W. de Gruyter, 1941. 38 p. facsims. (Preussischen Akademie der Wissenschaften. Abhandlungen. Phil.-Hist. Kl. Jahrg.
1941, 10 ).
————. II. [hrsg. ] von Olaf Hanson. Wiesbaden, Franz Steiner Verlag, 1955.
100 p. plate, facsims. (Mainz. Akademie der Wissenschaften und der Litera-
tur. Abhandlungen der Geistes-und Sozialwissenschaftlichen Kl. Jahrg. 1954,
15 ).
CODICES sogdiani; manuscrits de la Bibliothèque nationale (Mission Pelliot) reproduits en fac-similé, avec une intoduction par E. Benveniste. Copenhague,
E. Munksgaard, 1940. [ix]-xiii p., facsims.: 215 p. (Monumenta linguarum
Asiæ maioris, edidit K. Grønbech. III ).
GAUTHIOT, ROBERT, 1876-1916. Essai de grammaire sogdienne avec préface
de A. Meillet. Paris, P. Geuthner, 1914-29. 2 v. maps, facsim. (Mission
Pelliot en Asie Centrale. Série petit in octavo, 1, 3 ). Pt. 1. published post-
humously; Pt. 2. Morphologie, syntaxe et glossaire par Émile Benveniste.
————. ed. and tr. Le sûtra des causes et des effets du bien et du mal; édité et
traduit d'après les textes sogdien, chinois et tibétan par Robert Gauthiot et
Paul Pelliot. Paris, P. Geuthner, 1920-28. 2 v. in 1. 52 facsims. (Mission
Pelliot en Asie Centrale. Série-in-quarto, 2).
GERSHEVITCH, ILYA. A grammar of Manichean Sogdian. Oxford, B. Black-
well, 1954. xiii, 307 p. (Publications of the Philological Society, 16). Thesis-
University of London.
HENNING, WALTER BRUNO HERMANN. Sogdica. London, Royal Asiatic Soci-
ety, 1940. 67 p. (James G. Forlong fund, vol. 21 ).
MUELLER, FRIEDRICH WILHELM KARL,, 1863-1930. ed. and tr. Soghdische
Texts. 11. Aus dem Nachlass hrsg. von W. Lentz. Berlin, Akademie der
Wissenschaften in Kommission bei W. de Gruyter, 1934. 106 p. (Preussi-
schen Akademie der Wissenschaften. Sitzungbericht. Phil.-Hist. Kl. 21 ).
[v. 1 appeared in 1912].
————. Reste einer soghdischen Übersetzung des Padmacintamanidharani-sûtra.
Berlin, W. de Gruyter, 1926. 8 p.
REICHELT, HANS, 1877-    ed. and tr. Die soghdischen Handschriftenreste des
Britischen Museums, in Umschrift und mit Übersetzung. Heidelberg, C.
Winter's Universitätsbuchhandlung, 1928-31. 2 v.
WELLER, FRIEDRICH, 1889-    Zum soghdischen Vimalakīrtinirdeśasūtra.
Leipzig, Deutsche morgenländische Gesellschaft, Kommissionsverlag F.A.

Brockhaus, 1937. 87 p. (Abhandlungen für die kunde des Morgenlandes, mit unterstützung der Deutschen forschungsgemeinschaft hrsg. von der Deutschen morgenländischen gesellschaft. 22:6 ).

## Tokharian Texts

FILLIOZAT, JEAN, ed. and tr. Fragments de textes koutchéens de médecine et de magie. Texte, parallèles sanskrits et tibétains, traduction et glossaire. Paris, A. Maisonneuve, 1948. 155 p. map, facsims.

KRAUSE, WOLFGANG, 1895-   Westtocharische Grammatik. Heidelberg, C. Winter, 1952-      v. (Indogermanische Bibliothek. 1. Reihe, Lehr- und Handbücher ).

LÉVI, SYLVAIN, 1863-1935. ed. and tr. Fragments de textes koutchéens, Udāna-varga, Udānastotra, Udānālamkāra et Karmavibhaṅga; publiés et traduits, avec un vocabulaire et une introduction sur le "tokharien," par m. Sylvain Lévi. Paris, Impr. nationale, 1933. 161 p. (Cahiers de la Société asiatique. 1. sér. II ).

POUCHA, PAVAL. Institutiones linguae Tocharicae. Praha, Státnf pedagogicke nakl, 1955. xiii, 466 p. (Archiv orientálnf. Monografie, v. 15 ).

SIEG, EMIL H., 1866-   Tocharische Sprachreste. Sprache A., hrsg. von E. Sieg und W. Siegling. Berlin, W. de Gruyter, 1921. 2 v. plates (Königlich Preussische-Turfan-Expeditionen).

————. The same. Sprache B. hrsg. von E. Sieg und W. Siegling. Göttingen, Vandenhoeck und Ruprecht, 1949. 1 v. plates (Berlin. Deutsche Akademie der Wissenschaften).

————. Tocharische Grammatik, im Auftrage der Preussischen Akademie der Wissenschaften, bearb. in Gemeinschaft mit Wilhelm Schulze von Emil Sieg und Wilhelm Siegling. Göttingen, Vandenhoeck und Ruprecht, 1931. 6, 518 p. (Göttlinger sammlung indogermanischer grammatiken und wörterbücher).

————. tr. Ubersetzungen aus dem Tocharischen. Berlin, Akademie der Wissenschaften, in Kommission bei W. de Gruyter, 1944-      1 v. (Abhandlungen der Preussischen Akademie der Wissenschaften. Philosophisch-historische Klasse. Jahrg. 1943, Nr. 16).

## Geological and Geographical explorations

ALAI-PAMIR EXPEDITION, 1928. Wissenschaftliche Ergebnisse der Alai-Pamir Expedition 1928, im Auftrage der Notgemeinschaft der deutschen Wissenschaft, hrsg. von H. von Ficker und W. R. Rickmers. Berlin, D. Reimer/E. Vohsen, 1932. 3 v. in 6. illus., plates (part fold.) fold. maps, diagrs. Contents. -t. 1. Geodätische, topographische und glaziologische Ergebnisse, von Richard Finsterwalder. - t. II. Geologische Untersuchungen im nordwestlichen Pamir-gebiet und mittleren Trans-Alai von Ludwig Nöth. - t. III. Beitrag zur faunistik des Pamir-gebietes, von W. F. Reinig.

AMBOLT, NILS PETER, 1900-   Latitude and longitude determinations in eastern Turkistan and northern Tibet derived from astronomical observations. With 74 illustrations, in the text, two maps and one table in pocket at end. Stockholm, Bokförlags aktiebolaget Thule, 1938. 143 p. illus., fold. map, fold. plan, fold. table, diagrs. (Reports from the Scientific expedition to the north-western provinces of China under the leadership of Dr. Sven Hedin. The Sino-Swedish expedition. Publication 6. II. Geodesy. 1).

————. Relative Schwerkraftsbestimmungen mit Pendeln in Zentralasien. Stockholm, 1948. 112 p. illus., maps (2 fold.) tables. (Reports from the scientific expedition to the northwestern provinces of China under the leadership of Dr. Sven Hedin. The Sino-Swedish Expedition. Publication 30. II. Geodesy, 2 ).

BLEEKER, WOUTER, 1904-   Meteorologischen zu den 3 holländischen Karakorum-Expeditionen. Amsterdam, 1936. 27 p. figs., tables (Kon. Akad. van Wetenschappen, Proceedings 39: 6-8, 1936 ).

BOHLIN, BIRGER, 1898-    Notes on some late Palaeozoic localities in the Nanshan se of Tun-huang. Stockholm, Bokförlags aktiebolaget Thule, 1937. 53 p. incl. front. (map) illus. plates. (Reports from the Scientific expedition to the north-western provinces of China under the leadership of Dr. Sven Hedin. The Sino-Swedish expedition. Publication 3. III. Geology. 2 ).

BORCHERS, PHILIPP. Berge und Gletscher im Pamir, mit Beiträgen von Eugen Allwein, Richard Finsterwalder, Wolfgang Lentz, Erwin Schneider und Karl Wien, hrsg. unter Mitwirkung des Deutschen und österreichischen Alpenvereins. Mit 8 Tafeln in Kupfertiefdruck, 103 Bildern auf Kunstdrucktafeln und 2 Karten. Stuttgart, Verlag von Strecker und Schröder [1931] xi, [1], 259, [1] p. front., plates, 2 maps.

BOSSHARD, WALTER, 1892-    Botanische Ergebnisse der deutschen Zentral-Asien-Expedition 1927-28, hrsg. vom Botanischen Museum der Universität Zürich. Bearb. von E. Schmid, V. Czurda, H. Skuja, J. Thériot, A. Zahlbruckner, Zürich 1932. 76 p. plates. (Repertorium specierum novarum, Bd. 31; Zürich. Universität. Mitteil. aus dem Botanische Museum, 143).

CHEREPOV, I. A. Die Rätsel des Tienschan. [Aus dem Russischen übertragen von Alexander Böltz] Dresden, Sachsenverlag, 1954 [cl953]. 173 p. illus.

DU RIETZ, TORSTEN. Igneous rocks of Nanshan; a study in Caledonian igneous rocks. Introduction by Gerhard Bexell. Stockholm [Tryckeri aktiebolaget Thule] 1940. 117 p. incl. illus., tables, diagrs., plates, maps. (Reports from the scientific expedition to the north-western provinces of China under the leadership of Dr. Dven Hedin. The Sino-Swedish expedition. Publication 12. III. Geology. 4).

FICKELER, PAUL. Der Altai; eine Physiogeographie, mit 7 Tabellen, 1 Kurventafel, 5 Karten und 14 Abbildungen. Gotha, G. Perthes, 1925. viii, 202 p. plates, fold. maps, fold. diagr. (Ergänzungsheft nr. 187 zu "Petermanns mitteilungen").

FILCHNER, WILHELM, 1877-1957. Kartenwerk der Erdmagnetischen Forschungsexpedition nach Zentral-Asien 1926-28. Gotha, J. Perthes, 1933. 255 p. illus., fold. maps. (Ergänzungsheft nr. 215- zu "Petermanns mitteilungen").

FILIPPI, FILIPPO DE, 1869-1938. The Italian expedition to the Himalaya, Karakoram and Eastern Turkestan (1913-14), with chapters by G. Dainelli and J. A. Spranger. Illustrated with two coloured plates by R. W. Spranger, 15 panoramas, four maps in colour and over 300 illustrations in the text from photographs by C. Antilli and other members of the expedition. London, E. Arnold, 1932. xvi, 528 p. col. front., illus. (incl. plans) plates (1 col., part fold.) maps (part fold.). "Translated by H. T. Lowe-Porter from the Italian edition as revised by the author, with an additional chapter on the scientific results."

FISCHER, EMIL SIGMUND, 1865-1945. Zum Gedächtnis Jörg Trübner's und Emil Trinkler's letzte Expedition. Tientsin, 1931. 44 p.

FREBOLD, HANS, 1899-    Untersuchungen über die Fauna und Stratigraphie des marinen Tertiärs von Ostturkistan. Stockholm [Aktiebolaget H. W. Tullberg] 1940. [7]-35 p. illus. (map) plates. (Reports from the scientific expedition to the north-western provinces of China under the leadership of Dr. Sven Hedin. The Sino-Swedish expedition. Publication 11. v. Invertebrate pälaeontology. 2).

HEDIN, SVEN ANDERS, 1865-1952. History of the expedition in Asia, 1927-35, by Sven Hedin, in collaboration with Folke Bergman. Stockholm [Göteborg, Elanders boktryckeri aktiebolag] 1943. 4 pts. mounted front., illus. (incl. plans) plates (1 fold) ports., maps (part fold.) (Reports from the scientific expedition to the north-western provinces of China under the leadership of Dr. Sven Hedin. The Sino-Swedish expedition. Publication 23-26).

HEIM, MAURICE. Sur les pentes du Pamir. Paris, R. Chiberre, 1922. [9]-
334 p., 1 l.

HUANG, T. K. 黃汲凊 [Huang Chi-ch'ing] 1904-    Report on geological investigation of some oil-fields in Sinkiang. By T. K. Huang, C. C. Young, 楊
鍾健 , Y. C. Cheng, 程裕淇 , T. C. Chow, 周宗俊 , M. N. Bien,
卞美 , and W. P. Weng, 翁文波 , Nanking, Geological Survey of China,
1947. vii, 118, 3 p. maps, profiles. (China. Geological Survey. Memoirs,
ser. A. No. 21).

HYLLNINGSSKRIFT tillägnad Sven Hedin på hans 70-årsdag den 19 febr. 1935.
Edited by Axel Wallén. Stockholm, I distribution: Generalstabens litografiska anstalt [1935]. xvi, 668 p. illus., plates (part col., part fold.) port.,
maps (part fold.) diagrs. (part fold.).

ÍAKOVLEV, ALEKSANDR EVGEN'EVICH), 1887-1938. Dessins et peintures
d'Asie, exécutés au cours de l'Expédition Citroën Centre-Asie; troisième
mission G. M. Haardt, L. Audouin-Dubreuil, édité sous la direction de
Lucien Vogel. Paris, J. Meynial [1934]. [30] p. illus., 50 col. plates
(incl. ports.).

LE FÈVRE, GEORGES, 1892-    Expédition Citroën Centre-Asie; la croisière
jaune; troisième mission Haardt-Audouin-Dubreuil; préface d'André Citroën;
introduction de L. Audouin-Dubreuil; avec 95 gravures, 3 cartes hors texte
et 3 cartes dans le text. Paris, Plon [1933]. xlvi, 368 p. front., plates,
ports., maps (part fold.).

———. An Eastern odyssey; the third expedition of Haardt and Audouin-Dubreuil;
preface by André Citroën; introduction by L. Audouin-Dubreuil; translated
and adapted by Major-General Sir E. D. Swinton. ⟨Ole Luk-Oie⟩ London, V.
Gollancz, 1935; Boston, Little, Brown, 1935. 368 p. front., plates, ports.,
fold. map.

LENTZ, WOLFGANG, 1900-    Auf dem Dach der Welt; mit Phonograph und
Kamera bei vergessenen Völkern des Pamir. Berlin, Deutsche Buchgemeinschaft. [c1931]. 353 p. illus. (maps) plates.

LÖWENECK, SIGMUND. Aus den wissenschaftlichen Ergebnissen der Merz-
bacher'schen Tianschan-Expeditionen; Beitrage zur Kenntnis des paläozoikums
im Tienschan. München, Verlag der Bayerischen Akademie der Wissenschaften in Kommission bei der C. H. Beck'schen Verlagsbuchhandlung, 1932.
141 p. plates. (Bayerische Akademie der Wissenschaften. Math. Natur.
Abteilung. Abhandlungen, n. f. 11).

MAGNUSSON, ADOLF HUGO, 1885-    Lichens from Central Asia. Stockholm,
1940-44. 2 pts. illus., maps (1 fold.). (Reports from the scientific expedition to the north-western provinces of China under the leadership of Dr.
Sven Hedin. The Sino-Swedish Expedition. Publication 13. xi. Botany, 1;
Publication 22. xi. Botany, 2).

NORIN, ERIK, 1895-    Geology of western Quruq tagh, eastern T'ien-Shan.
With 43 plates and 19 illustrations in the text, three plates of sections and
two maps in pocket at end. Stockholm, Bokförlags aktiebolaget Thule, 1937.
xv, 194 p., incl. illus., tables, diagrs. plates, maps (part fold., 2 in
pocket) 3 fold. profiles. (Report from the Scientific expedition to the north-
western provinces of China under leadership of Dr. Sven Hedin. The Sino-
Swedish expedition. iii. Geology. i). [Full name: Erik Stephan Norin]

———. Geologic reconnaissances in the Chinese T'ien-shan. Appendices by
F. Heritsch, F. Kahler, and B. Bohlin. With 33 illustrations in the text,
23 plates, 3 maps, and one plate of sections at end of volume. Stockholm
[Tryckeri aktiebolaget Thule] 1941. xii, 229 p. illus., plates, maps (part
fold. tables, diagrs., profiles (part fold.) (Reports from the scientific expedition to the north-western provinces of China under the leadership of Dr.
Sven Hedin. The Sino-Swedish expedition. Publication 16. iii. Geology.
6).

———. The Tarim basin and its border regions. Leipzig, Akademische

Verlagsgesellschaft, Becker und Erler kom.-ges., 1941. cover-title, 36,
[4] p. illus., maps (1 fold). (Regionale geologie der erde, hrsg, von K.
Andrée, H. A. Brouwer und W. H. Bucher. Bd. 2: Palaeozoische tafeln
und gebirge. Abschnitt ivb).

PFANN, HANS. Führerlose Gipfelfahrten in den Hochaplen, dem Kaukasus, dem
Tian-schan und den Anden. Einbandzeichnung von Otto Brandhuber. Berlin,
Röth, 1941. iv, 255 p. illus.

PRINZ, GYULA, 1882-      A magas Tiensán, irta Prinz Gyula. Der hohe-
Tienschan. Mit 156 Abbildungen und 11 Tafeln, alle von Verfasser gezeichnet. Hrsg. von der dem Kgl. ung. Ackerbauministerium unterstehenden
Königlich ungarischen geologischen Anstalt. Budapest [etc.] Dunántúl Pécsi
egyetemi könyvkiadó és nyomda r.-t., 1939. 352 p. illus., plates (part
fold., incl. maps, profiles) ([Hungary. Földtani intézet] Mitteilungen aus
dem jahrbuch der Kgl. ungar. geolog. anstalt, bd. 33).

PRZHEVAL'SHIĬ, NIKOLAĬ MIKHAĬLOVICH, 1839-88. Hanhai. Von Kuldscha
über den Tianschan und zum Lobnor. [Hrsg. von Herbert Butze. Übers.
von Alexander Böltz] Leipzig, Bibliographisches Institut, 1952. 248 p.
illus., maps. (Sammlung Volk und Buch).

———. In das Land der wilden Kamels. Von Kiachta zu den Quellen des Gelben
Flusses, die Erforschung des nördlichen Randgebietes von Tibet und der Weg
über den Lobnor durch das Tarimbecken; übers. von Helmut Sträubig.
Leipzig, F. A. Brockhaus, 1954. 339 p. illus. plates. (Sammlung Volk
und Buch).

REGNÉLL, GERHARD, 1915-      On the Siluro-Devonian fauna of Chöl-tagh,
eastern T'ien-shan. Pt. 1. Stockholm [Esselte ab. Stockholm, Aktiebolaget H. W. Tullberg] 1941. 64 p. illus., plates. (Reports from the scientific expedition to the north-western provinces of China under the leadership
of Dr. Sven Hedin. The Sino-Swedish expedition. Publication 17. v. Invertebrate palaeontology. 3).

REYMOND, ANDRÉ. Sur le peuplement entomologique de l'Asie centrale.
Paris, Revue de géographie physique et de géologie dynamique, 1937. 285,
[1] p. illus., xx pl., fold, maps. Thèse - Univ. de Paris.

RICKMERS, WILLY RICKMER, 1873-      Alai! Alai! Arbeiten und Erlebnisse der deutsch-russischen Alai-Pamir-Expedition, mit 90 Abbildungen,
25 Diagrammen, 2 Panoramen und 1 Karte des Arbeitsgebiéts der Expedition. Leipzig, F. A. Brockhaus, 1930. 299, [1] p. front., illus., plates
(1 fold.) ports., maps.

ROI, JACQUES. Phytogeography of Central Asia. Peking, 1941. 35 p. illus.
maps, (Peking. Institut de Géo-biologie. [Publ.] 5).

RUDENKO, SERGEĬ IVANOVICH, 1885-      Der zweite Kurgan von Pasyryk.
Arbeitsergebnisse der Expedition des Institutes für Geschichte der materi-
ellen Kultur der Akademie der Wissenschaften der UdSSR v. J. 1947; vor-
läufiger Bericht, ins Deutsche übertragen von Ida-Maria Görner. Berlin,
Verlag Kultur und Fortschritt. 1951. 96 p. illus., 29 plates. ("Sowjetwissenschaft," Beiheft 16).

SINO-SWEDISH EXPEDITION, 1927-35. Reports from the scientific expedition
to the north-western provinces of China under the leadership of Dr. Sven
Hedin. The Sino-Swedish expedition. Stockholm, Bokförlags aktiebolaget
Thule, 1939.      v. illus., plates. (works in this series are cited individu-
ally).

TRINKLER, EMIL, 1896-1931. Wissenschaftliche Ergebnisse der Trinkler-
schen Zentral-Asien Expedition, bearbeitet von E. Trinkler und H. de Terra.
Berlin, D. Reimer, E. Vohsen, 1932. 2 v. illus., plates, maps. (part
fold.) diagrs. Contents: I. Geographische Forschungen im Westlichen
Zentralasien und Karakorum-Himalaya von Emil Trinkler. II. Geologische
Forschungen im westlichen K'un-lun und Karakorum-Himalaya, von Hellmut
de Terra.

TROEDSSON, GUSTAF TIMOTEUS, 1891-    On the Cambro-Ordovician faunas
of western Quruq tagh, eastern T'ien-shan. With an appendix: Report on a
collection of graptolites from the Charchaq series of Chinese Turkistan, by
O. M. B. Bulman. With plates i-x and 8 figures of text. Nanking, Pub-
lished by the Geological Survey of China, 1937. [7]-74, 6 p. illus., plates.
(Reports from the Scientific expedition to the north-western provinces of
China under leadership of Dr. Sven Hedin. The Sino-Swedish expedition.
Publication 4. v. Invertebrate paleontology: 1).
VISSER, PHILIPS CHRISTIAN, 1882-    ed. Wissenschaftliche Ergebnisse
der niederländischen Expeditionen in den Karakorum und die angrenzenden
Gebiete in den Jahren 1922, 1925, und 1929-30. Hrsg. von Ph. C. Visser
und Jenny Visser-Hooft. Leipzig, in Kommission bei F. A. Brockhaus,
1935. xviii, 499 p. illus. plates, fold. map, diagrs.
YOUNG, CHUNG-CHIEN, 楊鍾健 , 1897-    A new dinosaurian from Sinkiang,
Nanking, Published by the Geological Survey of China, 1937. 28, 4 p. incl.
illus., tables. plates. (China. Geological survey. Palaeontologia sinica.
New series C, no. 2. Whole series, no. 105).
ZATULOVSKII, D. M. Auf den Gletschern und Gipfeln Mittelasiens. Übers.
von Hellmut Schöner. Leipzig, Bibliographisches Institut, 1953. 400 p.
illus. (Sammlung "Volk und Buch").

# XXVI.  TAIWAN (FORMOSA)

## Bibliographies

[AUSTRALIA.  JOINT SERVICE STAFF, WASHINGTON.] Formosa; handbook of selected reference material. [n. p., 12 pts., 1949?-].

STANFORD UNIVERSITY.  China Project.  Bibliography of Taiwan (Formosa). New Haven, Human Relation Area Files, 1956.  37 p. (Behavior science bibliographies).

## Description and Travel, 1921-45

BIGELOW, POULTNEY, 1855-     Japan and her colonies; being extracts from a diary whilst visiting Formosa, Manchuria, Shantung, Korea and Saghalin in the year 1921. New York, Longmans, Green, 1923.  xii, 276 p. front., plates, ports.

FOGHT, HAROLD WALDSTEIN, 1869-     Unfathomed Japan; a travel tale in the highways and byways of Japan and Formosa, by Harold and Alice Foght; with maps and numerous illustrations by the authors and others.  New York, Macmillan, 1928.  xvii, 438 p. incl. front., illus., plates, ports., facsims. fold. map.

FORMOSA.  (Government-General of Taiwan, 1895-1945).  Progressive Formosa.  Taihoku, 1926.  108 p.  map, plates.

FRANCK, HARRY ALVERSON, 1881-     Glimpses of Japan and Formosa. With some kodak snapshots by the author.  New York and London, Century, [c1924].  xi, 235 p. front., plates.

GOLDSCHMIDT, RICHARD BENEDICT, 1878-     Neu-Japan; Reisebilder aus Formosa, den Ryukyuinseln, Bonininseln, Korea and dem südmandschurischen Pachtgebiet.  Mit 215 Abbildungen und 6 Karten.  Berlin, J. Springer, 1927.  vi, 303 [1] p.  illus. (incl. maps).

LANDSBOROUGH, MARJORIE.  In beautiful Formosa; being a personally-conducted tour of boys and girls to view the people, the scenery, and the work of the missionaries in strange and lovely places. London, R. T. S., 1922.  141 p. front., plates.

———.  More stories from Formosa. London, Presbyterian Church of England, [1932].  142 p. front. (map), plates, ports.

PSALMANAZAR, GEORGE, 1679?-1763.  An historical and geographical description of Formosa.  Giving an account of the religion, customs, manners etc. of the inhabitants.  Together with a relation of what happen'd to the author in his travels; particularly his conferences with the Jesuits, and others, in several parts of Europe.  Also the history and reasons of his conversion to Christianity, with his objections against it (in defence of paganism) and their answers.  London, R. Holden, 1926.  xlviii, 288 p.  plates. [A fabrication. The author's real name is unknown.  "Psalmanazar...wrote in Latin, and the main portion of his manuscript was translated by Mr. Oswald...What was not due to his own imagination he borrowed from Verenius's 'Descriptio regni Japoniae et Siam' (Amsterdam, 1649) or Candidius's 'Voyages'." - Dict. nat. biog.].

RUTTER, OWEN, 1889-     Through Formosa; an account of Japan's island colony. London, T. F. Unwin, [1923].  288 p. front., illus. (map), plates.

TAIWAN.  A record of Taiwan's progress, 1936-37 ed.  Issued by Kokusai Nippon kyokai, Tokyo, Japan.  Edited, compiled and designed by Hideo Naito. Tokyo, 1937.  xii, 334 p.  plates, ports., facsims.

TAIWAN, A UNIQUE COLONIAL RECORD. 1937-8 ed. Issued by Kokusai Nippon kyokai, Tokyo, Japan. Edited, compiled and designed by Hideo Naito.
[Tokyo, 1938]. xii, 350, 6 [2] p. plates (part col.), ports., facsims.

TAKEUCHI, SADAYOSHI. Taiwan. Rev. ed. [Taihoku, Niitakado, 1927.] 40,
8, 1470, 51 [1] p. illus. (incl. ports., maps, diagrs.), plates, fold. map,
fold. table.

TERRY, THOMAS PHILIP, 1864-       Terry's guide to the Japanese empire, including Korea and Formosa, with chapters on Manchuria, the Trans-Siberian
railway, and the chief ocean routes to Japan; a handbook for travellers with
8 specially drawn maps and 23 plans. Rev. ed. Boston, Houghton Mifflin;
London, Constable, 1928. cclxxxiv (i. e. 272), 799 (i. e. 787) p. maps (part
fold., incl. front.) plans (part fold.)

TIETJENS, EUNICE (HAMMOND), 1884-       Japan, Korea and Formosa, edi-
ted by Burton Holmes; text by Eunice Tietjens, illustrations by Burton
Holmes. Chicago, Wheeler Pub. Co. [c1940]. xi, [1], 419 p. illus. (The
Burton Holmes travel stories.)

TRAUTZ, FRIEDRICH MAX, 1877-       Japan, Korea und Formosa, Landschaft,
Baukunst, Volksleben. Aufgenommen von A. von Graefe, G. von Estorff,
Gertrud Fellner, Herbert Ponting u. a. Mit einem Geleitwort von W. H. Solf.
Berlin, Atlantis-Verlag [1930]. liv p., plates. (Orbis terrarum [reihe 3, bd.
26]).

------. Japan, Korea and Formosa; the landscape, architecture, life of the people; photographs by A. von Graefe, G. von Estorff and others. London, "The
Studio," [1931?]. xxix p., plates. (Orbis terrarum).

UKERS, WILLIAM HARRISON, 1873-       Japan and Formosa. New York, Tea
and Coffee Trade Journal Co., c1925. 58 p. illus. (incl. ports., maps.)
(Little journey series.)

U. S. NAVY. Pacific Fleet and Pacific Ocean Areas. Information bulletin.
Formosa, Takao area and Koshun peninsula. [n. p.] 1944. cover-title, 73 p.
illus. (incl. maps, charts.) (Its Cincpac-Cincpoa bulletin no. 119-44.)

U. S. OFFICE OF NAVAL OPERATIONS. Taiwan (Formosa). [Washington]
Office of the Chief of Naval Operations, Navy Dept., 1944. xv, 198 p. incl.
illus. (incl. maps), tables, diagrs. (Its Civil affairs handbook.)

------. Economic supplement. Prepared by Far eastern unit, Bureau of foreign
and domestic commerce, Department of commerce for Occupied areas section, Chief of Naval Operations. [Washington] Office of the Chief of Naval
Operations, Navy Dept., 1944. xiv, 127 p. incl. illus (incl. maps), tables.
(Its Civil affairs handbook.)

WALTON, WILLIAM HEWARD MURRAY. Scrambles in Japan and Formosa.
London, E. Arnold, [1934]. 304 p. incl. map. front., plates, maps (2 fold.).

1945-

BRISTOL, HORACE. Formosa; a report in pictures. Tokyo, East-West [1954].
unpaged. illus.

CALDWELL, JOHN COPE, 1913-       Let's visit Formosa, island home of Free
China. New York, J. Day [1956]. 71 p. illus.

CANADA. Dept. of Mines and Technical Surveys. Geographical Branch. Taiwan (Formosa); a geographical appreciation. Ottawa, 1952. xi, 59 p. maps.
(Its Foreign geography information series, 5).

CH'EN, CHÊNG-SIANG, 陳正祥. Cities and rural towns of Taiwan. Taipei, Institute of Agricultural Geography, 1953. 8 p. 9-40 p. (Its Research report,
48).

------. Keelung. Keelung, Taiwan, Keelung Municipal Government, 1954. 44
p. illus.

------. The city of Taipei. Taipei, Fu Min Geographical Institute of Economic
Development, 1956. 19 p. fold. diagrs. (Its Research report, 71).

CHINA. Ministry of Communications. Aeronautical information publication, Taiwan flight information region. Taipei, Civil Aeronautics Administration, 1952. 1 v. maps.

CHINESE NEWS SERVICE, NEW YORK. Free China's island province of Taiwan (Formosa). New York, 1953. 4 p. illus.

DUNN, GORDON T. Formosa, the island beautiful. London, China Inland Mission, 1954. 31 p. map. (Fields for reaping ser., 5).

MACMILLAN, HUGH. Then till now in Formosa. Taipei, British and Canadian Presbyterian Missions, 1953. 102 p.

TAIWAN PICTORIAL, TAIPEI. Taiwan, land of progress. Taipei, 1956. 92 p. illus.

U. S. ARMY. Far East Command. General Staff. Military Intelligence Section. Information report on facilities in Formosa. Tokyo, 1946. 123 p. illus. maps.

## History, Politics and Government, 1921-1945

FORMOSA. (Government-General of Taiwan, 1895-1945.) Laws, statutes, etc. Opium ordinance of Formosa, revised in 1929 in accordance with the provisions of the International Convention concluded at Geneva in 1925. Communicated by the Japanese Government. Geneva, 1929. 20 l.

——. The Kodama report; translation of Japanese plan for aggression, 1902. New York, American Council, Institute of Pacific Relations, 1945. 32 l.

U. S. OFFICE OF NAVAL OPERATIONS. Japanese administrative organization in Taiwan (Formosa). [Washington], 1944. viii, 71 p. illus. (Its Civil affairs handbook.).

——. Taiwan (Formosa), the Pescadores Islands. [Washington], 1944. viii, 39 p. illus., maps. (Its Civil affairs handbook.).

——. Taiwan (Formosa) Taihoku province. [Washington], Office of the Chief of Naval Operations, Navy Dept., 1944. xii, 209 p. incl. illus. (incl. maps), tables. (Its Civil affairs handbook.).

——. Taiwan (Formosa) Takao Province. [Washington], Office of the Chief of Naval Operations, Navy Dept., 1944. x, 136 p. incl. illus. (incl. maps), tables. (Its Civil affairs handbook.).

——. Taiwan (Formosa) Tainan province. [Washington], Office of the Chief of Naval Operations, Navy Dept., 1944. x, 106 p. incl. illus. (incl. maps), tables. (Its Civil affairs handbook.).

——. Taiwan (Formosa) Taichu province. [Washington], Office of the Chief of Naval Operations, Navy Dept., 1944. xiii, 235 p. incl illus. (incl. maps), tables. (Its Civil affairs handbook.).

——. Taiwan (Formosa) Shinchiku province. Opnav 13-25. [Washington], Office of the Chief of Naval Operations, Navy Dept., 1944. xi, 110 p. illus., maps. (Its Civil affairs handbook.).

——. Taiwan (Formosa) Karenko and Taito provinces. Opnav 13-24. [Washington], Office of the Chief of Naval Operations, Navy Dept., 1944. x, 101 p. illus., maps. (Its Civil affairs handbook.).

## 1945-

BALLANTINE, JOSEPH WILLIAM, 1888-    Formosa, a problem for United States foreign policy. Washington, Brookings Institution, 1952. 218 p. illus.

BATE, H. MACLEAR, 1908-    Report from Formosa. New York, Dutton, 1952. 290 p. illus.

——. Report from Formosa. London, Eyre and Spottiswoode, [1952]. 210 p. illus.

CHANDRA, ROMESH. Hands off Taiwan! The "Formosa question" and its solution. Madras, All India peace council, 1955. 8 p.

CHANG, CH'I YÜN, 張其昀, 1901-   An outline of history of Taiwan. Taipei, China Culture Pub. Foundation, 1953. 32 p. port., maps. (Pamphlets on Chinese affairs.) Reprinted from Free China review, April and May, 1952.

———. The spirit of Taiwan. Taipei, China Culture Pub. Foundation, 1953. 11 p. (Pamphlets on Chinese affairs.)

CHINA. (People's Republic of China, 1949-   ). Embassy. New Delhi. China will liberate Taiwan. New Delhi, 1955. 90 p.

DURDIN, TILLMAN, 1907-   . China and the world, by Tillman Durdin. The rebirth of Formosa, by Robert Aura Smith. [New York, Foreign Policy Association] 1953. 63 p. illus., maps. (Headline series, 99.)

FITCH, GERALDINE. Formosa beachhead. Chicago, H. Regnery Co., 1953. 267 p.

GIGON, FERNAND, 1908-   . Formose; ou les tentations de la guerre. Paris, Documents du Monde [1955]. 187 p. plates, maps. (Collection Documents du Monde.)

GT. BRIT. Central Office of Information. The problem of Formosa. London, H. M. Stationary Off., 1950. 4 p. (No. R. 2063.)

HAN, LIH-WU, 杭立武, 1902-   Taiwan today. [Rev. ed.] Taipei, Hwa Kuo Pub. Co., 1952. 162 p. [1st ed. 1951].

HILLIS, DICK, 1913-   . Shall we forfeit Formosa? Grand Rapids, Mich., Zondervan Pub. House, 1956. 32 p.

HSIEH, JAMES CHIAO-MIN, 謝覺民 , 1918-   Successive occupance patterns in Taiwan. Syracuse, N.Y., 1953. 417 l. illus., maps, diagrs. Thesis-Syracuse University.

IMPORTANT documents concerning the question of Taiwan. Peking, Foreign Languages Press, 1955. 183 p.

KIERMAN, FRANK ALGERTON, 1914-   . The fluke that saved Formosa. Cambridge, Center for International Studies, Massachusetts Institute of Technology, 1954. 12 p. illus.

LIAO, JOSHUA, 廖文奎 [Liao Wên-kuei], 1905-1952. Formosa speaks [by] Joshua Liao. The memorandum submitted to the United Nations in Sept., 1950, in support of the petition for Formosan independence by the Formosan League for Re-emancipation. [Hongkong?] 1950; London, Bailey and Swinfen, 1954. 59 p.

RECTO, CLARO M., 1890-   . Senator Claro M. Recto on the Formosa question. Foreword and epilogue by Juan Collas. [n. p., 1955] 119 p. illus.

RIGGS, FRED WARREN, 1917-   . Formosa under Chinese Nationalist rule. New York, Macmillan, 1952. ix, 195 p. map.

SCHAFFER, GORDON, 1905-   . Formosa; secrets behind the crisis. [London, Britain-China Friendship Association, 1955.] 11 p.

SHIEH, MILTON J. T., 謝然之 [Hsieh Jan-chih], 1912-   Taiwan and democratic world. [Documents of foreign relations concerning Formosa] edited by Milton J. T. Shieh. Taipeh, Shin Sheng Pao Daily News, 1951 [i. e. 1952] 89 p.; 2, 81 p. illus., ports.

STANFORD UNIVERSITY. China Project. Taiwan (Formosa). New Haven, Printed by Human Relations Area Files [1956]. 2 v. (viii, 680 p.) maps, diagrs. (HRAF. Subcontractor's monograph, HRAF-31).

TAIWAN. Information Dept. The administrative achievements of Taiwan province in the past six years. [general report on Taiwan's provincial administration made by Governor K. C. Wu, 吳國楨 , at the first session of the Provisional Provincial Assembly on December 12, 1951]. Taipei, 1952. 17 p.

———. Taiwan's provincial administration during the first half of 1952; a general report made by Governor K. C. Wu before the Provisional Provincial Assembly on June 12, 1952. Taipei, 1952. 27 p.

———. The guiding principles of Taiwan provincial administration; an administrative report made by Governor K. C. Wu before the 3rd session of the Taiwan Provisional Provincial Assembly on December 15, 1952. Taipei, 1953. 21 p.

——. Taiwan provincial administration; a general report made by O. K. Yui, 俞鴻鈞, before the Taiwan Provisional Provincial Assembly on June 22, 1953. Taipei, 1953. 34 p.

——. Taiwan provincial administration, its point of emphasis and its progress; a general report made by Governor O. K. Yui before the fifth session of the Provisional Provincial Assembly of Taiwan on December 14, 1953. Taipei, Dept. of Information, Taiwan Provincial Govt., 1953. Cover-title, 39 p.

TAIWAN. Information Office. Taiwan; ten years of progress. Taipei, 1956. 104 p. illus.

TAIWAN NEWS SERVICE. An infamous riot; story of recent mob violence in Taiwan. Taipei, 1947. 72 p.

TAYLOR, GEORGE EDWARD, 1905- . Formosa. Cambridge, Center for International Studies, Massachusetts Institute of Technology, 1954. 42 p. (Communist bloc program. China project E/54-7.)

TSONG, Y. T. Memoranda on the Formosan independence movement. Tokyo, 1949. 156 p.

UNITED NATIONS ASSOCIATION OF GREAT BRITAIN AND NORTHERN IRE-LAND. Formosa. London, United Nations Association, 1955. 16 p. map.

U. S. PRESIDENT, 1953- (Eisenhower). Security of the United States of America; message from the President of the United States. [Washington, Govt. Print. Off., 1955.] 4 p. (84th Cong., 1st sess. House of Representatives. Document no. 76.)

WOODMAN, DOROTHY. Facing facts in Formosa; a challenge to peace. New ed. [London, Union of Democratic Control, 1951.] 11 p.

YUI, O. K., 俞鴻鈞, 1898- Report on action taken by the government regarding the incident on May 24, 1957, in Taipei. Taipei, Govt. Information Off., 1957. 41 p. tables, plates, plan.

## Economic Conditions

BANK OF TAIWAN. Economic Research Dept. Taiwan financial statistics monthly, 台灣金融統計月報. Taipei, 1952- .

CHEN, NAI-RUENN, 陳迺瀾, 1926- Formosa's national income; concepts, estimation, methods and distribution. Urbana, [1955]. 59 l. tables. Thesis-University of Illinois.

CHINA. Economic Stabilization Board. A review of the economic situation of the Republic of China, July 1954-June 1955. Taipei, 1955. 116 p.

——. Directorate General of Telecommunications. Telecommunications in Taiwan, China. Taipei, 1956. 15 p. illus.

——. Industrial Development Commission. Clay deposits in northwestern Taiwan. By Pei-yuan Chen, 陳培源. Taipei, 1955. 37 p. fold. map, tables. (Its I D C survey report, 1.).

——. Inspectorate General of Customs. The trade of China 1955, 1956, 1957. (Taiwan) 中國進出口貿易統計年刊. Taipei, 1956-58. 3 v. charts.

——. Ministry of Economic Affairs. Pamphlets. Taipei, 1955. 10 v. in 1. illus. maps, diagrs. tables. Contents: Four year economic development plan of Taiwan. 8 p.; Taiwan agriculture in progress. 24 p.; Taiwan electric power in expansion. 24 p.; Fertilizer Taiwan. 12 p.; Taiwan fisheries. 16 p.; Forestry Taiwan. 12 p.; Taiwan's handicrafts. 12 p.; Petroleum in Taiwan. 12 p.; Taiwan sugar. 16 p.; Taiwan textile industry. 12 p.

——. Ministry of Finance. Dept. of Statistics. Index numbers of the import and export trade of China (Taiwan), 台灣進出口貿易指數, 1955-date. Taipei, 1955-date.

——. National Resources Commission. Industrial enterprises of National Resources Commission in Taiwan; general information. [Taipei], 1951. 1 v. (various pagings) illus., maps (part fold.)

———. National Resources Commission. General information of Taiwan fertilizer company. Taipei, 1951. 19 p. illus.

———. National Resources Commission. General information of Chinese Petroleum Corporation. Taipei, 1951. 51 p. illus. maps, diagrs. tables.

———. National Resources Commission. N.R.C. and economy of Taiwan. Taipei, 1951. 8 l.

CHINESE ASSOCIATION FOR THE UNITED NATIONS. The Economic Cooperation Administration program in Taiwan. Taipei, Chinese Association for the United Nations, 1951. 34 p. (Unachina publications, ser. 1, 5.)

DIRECTORY OF TAIWAN. 1951-1957. [Taipeh, China News and Publication Service.] 7 v. illus.

FORMOSA (GOVERNMENT-GENERAL OF TAIWAN, 1895-1945). Annual return of the trade of Taiwan (Formosa), 1900-1938. [Taihoku], 1901-39. 39 v. col. diagrs., tables. Title varies: 1900-1917, Annual return of the foreign trade of Taiwan (Formosa).

———. Returns of the trade of Taiwan (Formosa) for the twenty five years from 1896 to 1920 inclusive. The Government of Taiwan. [Taihoku? 1921?] 51, 544 p. incl. tables.

———. Returns of the trade of Taiwan (Formosa) for the thirty years (1896-1925). The Customs, Government of Taiwan. Taihoku, 1926? 59, 641 p.

———. Returns of the trade of Taiwan for forty years, 1896-1935. [Taihoku, 1936?]. 703 p. of tables.

———. Delegation to Postal Union Congress. 9th, London, 1929. Taiwan (Formosa). Its system of communications and transportation, submitted by the Japanese delegate for Taiwan to the ninth conference of the International Postal Union, held at London, May 1929. The Government-General of Taiwan. [Taihoku? 1929.] 50 p. plates, fold. map.

GINSBURG, NORTON SYDNEY, 1921- . The economic resources and development of Formosa. New York, International Secretariat, Institute of Pacific Relations, 1953. 58 p. maps (on cover), diagrs. (on cover).

GRAD, ANDREW JONAH, 1899- . Formosa today; an analysis of the economic development and strategic importance of Japan's tropical colony. New York, International Secretariat, Institute of Pacific Relations, 1942. v, 193 p. map, tables. (I.P.R. International research series.)

HO, CH'UN-SUN, 何春蓀. Mineral resources of Taiwan. Prepared for Ministry of Economic Affairs. [Taipei?] 1953. vi, 313 p. maps (part col., part fold.) tables.

HSING, MO-HUAN, 邢慕寰. Capital formation in Taiwan 1951-1953, a preliminary finding. Taiwan, Industrial Development Commission, ESB, 1955. 22 p.

INTERNATIONAL TRADE MONTHLY, TAIPEI. Taiwan exports. Taipei, 1957. 1 v. (unpaged, chiefly illus.)

LI, LAMP, 李傑, [Li Chieh]. The structure and geographical distribution of Taiwan's industries. [Taipei?] 1954. 14 p. illus.

LI, MABEL KWAN-WAI, 李坤維, 1922- The tax system of Taiwan. New York, 1956. 2 v. (typescript) Thesis-New York University.

LING, HUNG-HSÜN, 淩鴻勛, 1894- Industrial development of Taiwan. Taipei, China Culture Pub. Foundation, 1953. 35 p. (Pamphlets on Chinese affairs).

PAO, KE YUNG, 包可永, 1908- . Report on Taiwan's industries. [Nanking], 1947. 14 numb. l. charts.

PROPERTY IN TAIWAN; a survey of references found in documents translated by Research Unit #2 prior to 1 October 1944. [n.p., 1945?] 168 l.

TEIKOKU GINKŌ KAISHA YŌROKU (Catalogue of banks and concerns in the empire) 1940, Taiwan, pp. 1-46. Translated by Military Government Translation Center, Naval School of Military Government and Administration, New York, N.Y., translator: Amino Ichirō. [New York, 1941?] 2 v.

TAIWAN. Bureau of Accounting and Statistics. Report on family living studies of wage earners and salaried employees in Taiwan, May 1954 to April 1955. v, 224, 17 p. charts, tables.

————. Custom House. Annual trade statistics, Taiwan, 1950- Keelung, 1951- v.

————. Dept. of Communications. Annual statistical data of Taiwan communications and transportations, 1946-date. 台灣交通統計彙報 . Taipei, 1947-date. 10 v.

————. Dept. of Communications. Monthly statistical report on Taiwan transportaion. 台灣交通統計月報 . Taipei, 1954-date.

————. Dept. of Communications. Taiwan communications. (1946-) Taipei, 1947. 1 v.

————. Provincial Government. Lists of import and export articles for Taiwan province (promulgated on 19th September 1949). Taipei, 1950. 70 p.

————. Provincial Government. Bureau of Accounting. Taiwan monthly of commodity price statistics, 台灣物價統計月報 , 1949- . Taipei, 1949-date. v.

————. Railway Administration. Railways in Taiwan. Taipei, 1952. 41 p.

————. Railway Administration. Taiwan Railway. Taipei, 1955. 70 p. illus. col. map.

TAIWAN FERTILIZER COMPANY, LTD. Taiwan Fertilizer Co., Ltd. 1957. Taipei, 1957. 1 v. (unpaged.)

TAIWAN POWER COMPANY. Sun-moon Lake hydro-electric power development. Taipei, 1948. [13] p. illus.

————. Tien-leng hydro-electric project. Taipei, 1952. 24 p.

————. Electric power in Taiwan today. Taipei, 1952. 33 p. illus., map.

————. Taiwan electric power in expansion. Taipei, 1955. 24 p.

TAIWAN PULP AND PAPER CORPORATION. Report. [n.p.] v. annual.

U.S. ECONOMIC COOPERATION ADMINISTRATION IN CHINA. U.S. economic assistance to Formosa, 1 January to 31 December 1950. 46 p. maps.

U.S. MUTUAL SECURITY MISSION TO CHINA. Economic progress on Formosa. [Washington? 1952.] 20 p. illus.

————. Urban and industrial Taiwan, crowded and resourceful, by Arthur F. Raper. Taipei, 1954. vii, 370 p. illus., maps, diagrs., tables.

————. Economic development on Taiwan, 1951-1955. Taipei, 1956. 87 p. illus. (part col.) maps, diagrs.

————. Area and resources survey: Taiwan, by Willert Rhynsburger, area and resources analyst. Taipei, 1956. viii, 198 p. maps, diagrs., tables.

U.S. TARIFF COMMISSION. Annotated tabular survey of the trade of Japan proper, including that with Korea and Formosa. Prepared for the Foreign Economic Administration. [Washington], 1945. 228 p. tables. (Japanese trade studies.)

WANG, SHI-FU, 王世富. The correlation of money and price in Taiwan, 1953-1955. Taipei, 1956. 68 p. illus.

WESTINGHOUSE ENGINEERING COMPANY OF ASIA, NEW YORK. Rehabilitation and development program of the Taiwan Power Company. Pre-project engineering report authorized by CUSA-ECA Joint Committee for Reconstruction and Replacement. New York, 1949. 1 v. (various pagings.) plates, maps (1 fold.), plans.

YIN, K. Y., 尹國墉 , 1903-     . My views on Taiwan's economy. Taipei, China Cultural Pub. Foundation, 1953. 14 p. (Pamphlet on Chinese affairs.)

## Population and Statistics

BARCLAY, GEORGE W., 1923-     . Colonial development and population in

Taiwan. Princeton, Princeton University Press; London, Oxford University Press, 1954. xviii, 274 p. maps, diagrs., tables.

——. A report on Taiwan's population to the Joint Commission on Rural Reconstruction. Princeton, Office of Population Research, Princeton University, 1954. xii, 120 p.; diagrs., tables.

TAIWAN. Bureau of Accounting and Statistics. Results of the 7th population census of Taiwan, 1940; including appendix with partial results of special household surveys of 1944-1945. Taipei, 1953. Cover-title, xi, 190 p. tables (1 fold.)

——. Dept. of Statistics. Life tables of Taiwan, 1936-1940. 2d issue. [n.p.] 1947. x, 176 p. diagrs.

## Social Conditions

CALDWELL, JOHN COPE, 1913-    . Still the rice grows green; Asia in the aftermath of Geneva and Panmunjom. Chicago, H. Regnery Co., 1955. 312 p. illus.

FREE CHINA RELIEF ASSOCIATION. FCRA relief work in Kinmen and Matsu. [Taipei, 195-] 1 v. (unpaged). illus.

——. Employment services and vocational assistance of Chinese refugees in Taiwan. [Taipei, 195-] 1 v. (unpaged). illus.

——. Our support of the anti-communist escapees fleeing to freedom. [Taipei, 1957.] 1 v. (unpaged). illus.

——. The evacuation of overseas Chinese from North Vietnam and the relief work. [Taipei, 1956.] 1 v. (unpaged). illus.

——. Resettlement of war disabled refugees; a significant project completed by FCRA in cooperation with FERP, U.S.E.P. Taipei, 1956. 40 p.

HSU, SHIH-CHÜ, 許世鉅 , 1905-  Public health program in Taiwan, by S. C. Hsu and James C.M. Wang, 王紀民 . Taipei, 1953. 42 p. charts (JCRR. Rural health ser., 1.).

MOODY, CAMPBELL N. The king's guests, a strange Formosan fellowship. London, H.R. Allenson, [1932]. 144 p. front., plates.

TAIWAN. Provincial Health Administration. Taiwan tuberculosis control program. Annual report. Taipei, 1953. v. illus.

——. Provincial Health Administration. Annual report on trochoma control program in Taiwan province. Taipei [1953?] v.

## Education

FORMOSA (GOVERNMENT-GENERAL OF TAIWAN, 1895-1945.) Annual report on education in Formosa. [Tokyo] 19  . v. plates, tables, diagrs.

FORMOSAN EDUCATION ASSOCIATION. Modern Formosa, with special reference to education. [Taihoku?] Formosan Education Association [1923?] cover-title, 32 p.

SASSANI, ABUL HASSAN K., 1911-    . Education in Taiwan (Formosa). [Washington] U.S. Dept. of Health, Education, and Welfare, Office of Education [1956]. v, 34 p. illus. (U.S. Office of Education. Bulletin, 1956, 3.)

TAIWAN PROVINCIAL FARMERS ASSOCIATION. The Taiwan new rural extension education movement with thirty good examples. Taipei, 1956. 28, 38 p. illus.

## Ethnology

JAPAN. Imperial Academy. Dictionnaire de termes de droit coutumier des aborigènes de Formose, 高砂族慣習法語彙 . Tokyo, L'Académie impériale, 1941. vi, 200 p. col. map.

KANO, TADAO. The illustrated ethnography of Formosan aborigines: the Ya-

mi tribe, by Tadao Kano and Kōkichi Segawa.  Contribution from The Shibu-
sawa Institute for Ethnographical Research (Nippon-Jōmin-Bunkwa-Kenkyū-
sho). Tokyo, Seikatsusha, 1945.  2, 2, 6 p.  419 plates.
McGOVERN, JANET B. (MONTGOMERY). Among the head-hunters of Formosa; with a preface by R. R. Marett. Boston, Small, Maynard; London, T.
F. Unwin, 1922.  220 p.  front., plates, map.
————.  Unter den Kopfjagern auf Formosa. [Die Übersetzung aus dem Englischen besorgte Frances Kulpe.] Stuttgart, Strecker und Schröder, 1923.  vii,
127 p.  illus., plates, port., map.
NORBECK, EDWARD, 1915-        .  Folklore of the Atayal of Formosa and the
mountain tribes of Luzon.  Ann Arbor, University of Michigan Press, 1950.
iv, 44 p.  fold. map.  (Anthropological papers, 5.)
RE, ARUNDELL DEL, 1892-         .  Creation myths of the Formosan natives.
[Tokyo], Hokuseido Press, [1951].  75 p.  illus.
WHITEHORN, JOHN.  He led them on;  the story of the Christian movement
among the Paiwan tribe of Formosa [by] John Whitehorn and Edward Band.
London, British and Foreign Bible Society, [1955].  32 p.  illus.

## Meteorology

T'AI-PEI (CITY) RAIN STIMULATION RESEARCH INSTITUTE.  A condensed report on experiments of rain making over Sun-moon Lake. [Taipei], 1952.
4 1.  fold. map, table.
TAIWAN. Weather Bureau. The list of treatises, 1946. Taipeh, [1946].  8 p.
Cover title.

## Natural History and Geology

CHINESE PETROLEUM CORPORATION.  Summaries of manuscripts presented
at the symposium on petroleum geology of Taiwan in the celebration of the
tenth anniversary, June 1, 1956.  Taipei, 1956.  2, 43, [2, 18] p.
JUAN, VEI-CHOW, 阮維周 , 1912-    Physiography and geology of Taiwan.  Taipei, China Culture Pub. Foundation, 1954.  45 p. illus. (Pamphlets on Chinese affairs).
KANEHIRA, RYŌZŌ. Anatomical characters and identification of Formosan
woods with critical remarks from the climatic point of view, with 300 micro-
graphs. Taihoku, Bureau of Productive Industries, Govt. of Formosa, 1921.
2, 317 p.  illus., plates.
————.  Identification of the important Japanese woods by anatomical characters.
Supplement to the Anatomical characters and identification of Formosa woods,
etc.  Taihoku, Bureau of Productive Industries, Govt. of Formosa, 1921.
104 p.  plates.
————.  Identification of Philippine woods by anatomical characters.  Supplement
to the Anatomical characters and identification of Formosan woods, etc.  Taihoku, Govt. Research Institute, 1924.  73 p.  plates.
————.  Formosan trees indigenous to the island.  Formosa, Department of Forestry, Govt. Research Institute, 1936.  [iii]-x, 574 [i.e. 754] p.  plates,
map.
MASAMUNE, GENKEI. ed. Short flora of Formosa, or, An enumeration of
higher cryptogamic and phanerogamic plants hitherto known from the island
of Formosa and its adjacent islands. Taihoku, The Editorial Department of
"Kudoa," 1936. 410 p.  front.
SASAKI, SHUN-ICHI, 1888-       . List of plants of Formosa. Taihoku, Natural
History Society of Formosa, 1928.  xxvi, 8, 562 p.
SAWADA, KANEYOSHI. List of fungi found in Formosa. [Taihoku, Government-
General of Formosa, 1931.] cover-title, 103 (i.e. 111) p.
SONAN, JINHAKU. Insect pests of the tea-plant in Formosa. Taihoku, Govt.

Research Institute, 1924. 1 v. illus., col plates, fold. map, diagrs. (part
fold.) (Formosa. Government Research Institute. Dept. of agriculture. Report no. 12.)

TAIHOKU. Government Research Institute. A catalogue of the government herbarium by Syun'iti Sasaki. Taihoku, Department of Forestry, Govt. Research
Institute, 1930. vii, 592 p. (Its Report, 9.).

——. Taihoku University. Faculty of Science and Agriculture. Memoirs. v.
1-31, no. 1; Jan. 1930- Oct. 1942. [Taihoku.] 31 v. in 25. illus. (part col.),
maps. irregular.

——. Taihoku University. Faculty of Science. Memoirs. 1943-45. Series
1: Mathematics, Physics, Chemistry. Series 2: Zoology, Botany. Series
3: Geology.

——. Geological Survey. Bibliography of geology of Taiwan, by T. P. Yen,
顏昌波 , C. S. Ho, 何春蓀 , and P. Y. Chen, 陳培源 . Taipei, Geological Survey of Taiwan, 1947. 58 p.

TAKAHASHI, RYOICHI. Observations on the Coccidae of Formosa. Taihoku,
Govt. Research Institute, 1929-   1 v. illus. (Formosa. Dept. of agriculture. Government Research Institute. Report 40.)

——. Aleyrodidae of Formosa. Taihoku, Govt. Research Institute, 1932-
2 v. illus. (Formosa. Dept. of agriculture. Government Research Institute.
Report 59, 60.)

TSOONG, P. C., 鍾補勤 , 191--54. A preliminary survey of the vegetation of
the south Cha-Tien mountains, 插天山之初步植生調查 . Taipei, 1954. 36 p.
(Taiwan Forestry Research Institute. Bull. 41.).

YAMAMOTO, YOSHIMATSU. Supplementa Iconum plantarum Formosanarum,
auctore Yoshimatsu Yamamoto. Taihoku, Department of Forestry, Govt. Research Institute, 1925-32. 5 v. illus. plates.

## Agriculture

ANDERSON, WALFRED ALBIN, 1892-   . Farmers' associations in Taiwan;
a report to the Joint Commission on Rural Reconstruction, Economic Cooperation Administration Mission to China. Taipeh, 1950. 70, 2 p. tables.

CHANG, JEN-HU, 張鏡湖 , [Chang Ching-hu], 1928-   Agricultural geography
of Taiwan. Taipei, China Cultural Service [c1953]. ii, 86 p. maps (part fold.,
part col.), diagrs.

CHANG, HSIEN-TSIU, 張憲秋 . Problems of tea production in Taiwan. Taipei,
1953 28 p. illus. (JCRR. Plant Industry ser., 2.).

——. Crop variety improvement and seed multiplication work in Taiwan; a
summary report by H. T. Chang, C. F. Cheng, 鄭仲孚 , and others. Taipei,
1956. 35 p. tables. (JCRR. Plant Industry ser., 7.).

——. Natural environment and crop distribution in Taiwan. Taipei, 1956. 42
p. illus. maps, tables. (JCRR. Plant industry ser., 13.)

CHANG, HSUIN-SHWEN, 張訓舜 . The rice and seed multiplication system in
Taiwan. Taipei, 1956. 22 p. illus. tables. (JCRR. Plant Industry ser., 12).

CH'ÊN, CHÊNG-SIANG, 陳正祥 . Sugar industry of Taiwan. Taipei, 1955.
45 p. (Fu Min Institute of Agricultural Geography. Research report, 58.)

——. The agricultural regions of Taiwan. Taipei, 1956. 49 p. map, diagrs.
(Fu Min Geographical Institute of Economic Development. Research report,
70.)

CHENG, CHUNG-FU, 鄭仲孚. Crop improvement and seed distribution of upland
food crops in Taiwan. Taipei, 1956. 54 p. tables. (JCRR. Plant Industry
ser., 11.).

CHINESE RESEARCH INSTITUTE OF LAND ECONOMICS. A brief description
of the Chinese Research Institute of Land Economics. Taipei, 1952. 11 p.

CHU, HAI-FAN, 朱海帆 . Green manure crops in Taiwan. Taipei, 1954. 32 p.
illus. (JCRR. Plant Industry ser., 3.).

FAR EAST AGRICULTURAL CREDIT WORKSHOP, Manila and Baguio, 1956.
Delegation of the Republic of China. Working papers on agricultural credit in
Free China. Taipei, 1956. [89] p.

FAR EAST SEED IMPROVEMENT CONFERENCE, Taiwan, 1956. Proceedings.
Taipei, 1956. 216 p.

GILL, TOM, 1891-      . Forest policy and program for Taiwan. Taipei, 1952.
15 p. (JCRR. Forestry ser., 2.)

HSIAO, CHENG, 蕭錚 , 1905-  Agricultural loans made by the Land Bank of
Taiwan in 1955, inspection report. Taipei, 1955. 83 p.

HSIEH, SAN-CHUNG, 謝森中 . Farm price reporting in Taiwan, compiled by S.C.
Hsieh and T.S. Kuo, 郭志嵩 . Taipei, 1952. 36 p. tables. (JCRR. Economic
digest ser., 1.).

———. Rice and sugarcane competition on paddy land in Central Taiwan. Minneapolis, 1957. 113 l. Thesis---University of Minnesota.

HUNTER, JAMES AUSTIN, 1898-      . The rinderpest epidemic of 1949-50,
Taiwan (Formosa). Taipei, 1951. 8 p. illus. (JCRR. Animal industry
ser., 1.)

JOINT COMMISSION ON RURAL RECONSTRUCTION IN CHINA (U.S. and China).
Summary report, the JCRR assistance program. 1951-date. Taipei, 1951-

———. General report. [1st]-7th. Taipeh, 1948-date. 7 v.

———. The program of the Joint Commission on Rural Reconstruction in China;
its organization, accomplishments and lessons for rural reconstruction elsewhere in Asia. [Washington], Economic Cooperation Administration, [1951?]
40 p. illus., map.

———. The Joint Commission on Rural Reconstruction in China; its policies,
procedures, and program [by William H. Fippin. n.p., 1953]. 58 p. illus.

———. General agricultural statistics of Taiwan with a summary of JCRR project status. Taipei, 1952-57. 6 v.

———. Rural Taiwan, problem and promise, by Arthur F. Raper. Taipei, 1953.
296 p. illus., maps.

———. A study on the export potentiality and elasticity of agricultural products
in Taiwan. Prepared by the Plant Industry and Rural Economics divisions,
JCRR, in cooperation with Committee D of the Economic Stabilization Board
of the Executive Yuan. Taipei, 1954. 22 p. tables. (JCRR. Economic digest ser., 5.)

——— . Tachen report, compiled by Hsu Woo-ping, 徐吳斌 . Taipei, 1954.
176 p. (JCRR. Food and Fertilizer ser.)

——— . Plant Industry Division. On the agricultural mechanization in Taiwan.
Taipei, 1956. 13 p. (Its PID-C-005.)

KUNG, PETER, 龔弼 . The distribution of rice varieties and their trend of
changes in the recent three decades in Taiwan. Taipei, 1956. 24 p. maps,
diagrs., tables. (JCRR. Plant Industry ser., 10.).

———. Rice culture in Taiwan. Taipei, 1956. 20 p. illus. tables. (JCRR.
Plant industry ser., 9.)

LEE, ROBERT C. T., 李崇道 . Hog cholera control program in Taiwan. Taipei, 1953. 74 p. tables, map. (JCRR. Animal industry ser., 2.)

———. A preliminary report on the lapinized hog cholera vaccine in Taiwan.
Taipei, 1954. 51 p. illus., tables. (JCRR. Animal industry ser., 5.)

LUH, CHI-LIN, 陸之琳. Citrus culture in Taiwan. Taipei, 1953. 29 p. illus.
(JCRR. Plant industry ser., 1.)

———. Recent improvement on pineapple and citrus fruit production in Taiwan.
Taipei, 1956. 28 p. illus. (JCRR. Plant industry ser., 8.)

———. Vegetable production in Taiwan and its problems. Prepared under the
direction of H. T. Chang 張憲秋 . Taipei, 1956. 32 p. illus. (JCRR. Plant
industry ser., 6.)

MA, FENGCHOW C., 馬逢周 . A Preliminary study of farm implements used
in Taiwan province, by Fengchow C. Ma, T. Takasaka and Ching-wen Yang

揚景文 . Taipei, 1955. 331 p. illus. diagrs. (JCRR. Plant industry ser., 4.)

MATSUMOTO, TAKASHI. Monograph of sugarcane diseases in Taiwan. Taipei, 1952. 61 p. col. plates. (JCRR. Monograph.)

MOYER, RAYMOND TYSON, 1899- . The JCRR program on Formosa: a summary and evaluation. Taipei, 1951. 171.

NEWSOM, ISAAC ERNEST, 1883- . Animal disease in Taiwan. Taipei, 1953. 23 p. (JCRR. Animal industry ser., 3.)

SHEN, TSUNG-HAN, 沈宗瀚 , 1895- . The agricultural four-year plan at work in Taiwan. Taipei, 1954. 22 p. Reprinted from Free China Review, April, 1954.

TAIPEI. National Taiwan University. College of Agriculture. Memoirs v. 1- Taipei, 1946.

——. Special Publications No. 1. Taipei, 1955.

——. National Taiwan University. Forest Experiment Station. Technical bulletin. No. 1- Taipei, 1952.

TAIWAN. Dept. of Agriculture and Forestry. Taiwan agricultural year book, 1920- date. Taipei, 1921-date.

——. Dept. of Agriculture and Forestry. Report of investigation on ownership and operation of arable land; agricultural basic survey. Issued under the auspices of the Joint Commission on Rural Reconstruction. Taipei, 1950. ix, 173 p.

——. Dept. of Agriculture and Forestry. Report of investigation of farm economy for rice and miscellaneous cropping farm family; agricultural basic survey. Issued under the auspices of the Joint Commission on Rural Reconstruction. Taipei, 1952. 610 p. tables.

——. Dept. of Agriculture and Forestry. Series of agricultural programs. No. 1- (February, 1954) Taipei, 1954.

——. Dept. of Agriculture and Forestry. A summary report on rural reconstruction in Taiwan. Taipei, 1956. 46 p.

——. Land Bureau. Statistics on landownership classification in Taiwan, China, 1952. Taipei, 1953. xvii, 184 p. (chiefly tables).

——. Land Bureau. Land reform in Taiwan. [Taipei] 1955. 158 p.

TAIWAN Pineapple Corporation. A five-year plan for the rehabilitation of pineapple plantation and its canning industry in Taiwan, 1951-1955. [n. p.] 1950. 30 p. illus.

——. Effect of irrigation on pineapple leaves by T. Eguchi and M. Ikeda. Taipei, 1952. 20 p.

TAIWAN Provincial Agricultural College. Department of Agricultural Economics. Rice and sugarcane competition in Taiwan; report on JCRR project TW-M-17. Intra-regional competition between rice and sugarcane in the use of paddy land in Taichung district. Taipei, 1953. 98 1.

TSUI, YOUNG-CHI, 崔永楫 , 1908- . Farm income of Taiwan in 1952. [compiled] by Y. C. Tsui and S. C. Hsieh, 謝森中 . Taipei, 1954. 181 p. charts, tables. (JCRR. Economic digest ser., 4.)

——. A study of peanuts in Taiwan. Taipei, 1955. 118 p. tables, map. (JCRR. Economic digest ser., 6.)

UNITED NATIONS. Economic and Social Council. Economic Commission for Asia and the Far East. Digues et protection de berges sur les rivières de Taiwan. Lake Success, 1950. 56 p.

U. S. Office of Naval Operations. Agriculture in Taiwan (Formosa). [Washington] Office of the Chief of Naval Operations, Navy Dept., 1945. vi, 130 p. incl. illus. (incl. maps) plates, tables, diagrs. (Its Civil affairs guide).

WANG, I-T'AO, 王益滔 , 1902- . The miracle of . 375, by Yi-tao Wang and Wen-chi Tung, 董文琦 . Hongkong, Newsdom Co. [c1952] 50 p. illus.

WANG, TSE-TING, 王子定 . Propagation of cryptomeria by the cutting method in relation to the age of branches. [Taipei, National Taiwan University, Forest Experiment Station, 1952. 14 p. (Technical Bull. 1).

————. Root development of the dominent, the intermediate, and the suppressed trees in a cryptomeria stand. [Taipei, National Taiwan University, Forest Experiment Station, 1952. 18 p. (Technical Bull., 3).

YANG, YUEH-HENG, 揚月恆 . Yeast-feeding demonstration in selected primary schools, Taipei area, Taiwan, 1953-54. Taipei, 1955. 16 p. tables. (JCRR. Food and fertilizer ser., 1.).

YEH, SHING-MIN, 葉新明 . Rural land taxation in Taiwan, compiled by S. M. Yeh, and T. S. Kuo, 郭志嵩 . Taipei, 1952. 54 p. tables. (JCRR. Economic digest ser., 2.).

————. Rice marketing in Taiwan. Taipei, 1955. 98 p. (JCRR. Economic digest ser., 7.).

ZEHNGRAFF, PAUL [JOHANNES], 1902- . Forest conditions in Taiwan. Taipei, 1951. 59 p. (JCRR. Forestry ser., 1.).

Fisheries

CH'EN, TUNG-PAI, 陳同白 , 1900- . Milkfish culture in Taiwan. Taipei, 1952. 17 p. (JCRR. Fisheries ser., 1.).

————. The culture of Tilapia in rice paddies in Taiwan. Taipei, 1954. 30 p. illus. (JCRR. Fisheries ser., 2.).

LIANG, YUN-SHANG, 梁雲生 . A check-list of the fish specimens in the Taiwan Fisheries Research Institute. Taipei, 1951. 35 p. (Its. Laboratory of Biology. Report, 3.).

RICH, WILLIS HORTON, 1885- . Fisheries statistics, research and education in Taiwan. [Washington?] Office of Industry and Natural Resources, FOA Mutual Security Mission to China, 1953. 14 p.

TANG, YUN-AN, 唐允安 . On the processes and ridges on the pectoral fin rays of the males of Hypophthalmichthys molitrix (C. and A.) and Aristichthys nobilis (Richard). [Taipei] Taiwan Fisheries Research Institute, 1954. 12 p. (Fish culture report 1 ).

————. Effect of soil-fertilization and water-fertilization on the production of plankton bottom organisms and goldfish in ponds. [Taipei] Taiwan Fisheries Research Institute, 1954. 10 p. tables (Fish culture report 2).

U. S. Foreign Economic Administration. The fishing industry in Taiwan (Formosa). Prepared by Supply and Resources Service, Office of Economic Programs, Foreign Economic Administration, for Military Government Section, Central Division, Chief of Naval Operations. [Washington] Office of the Chief of Naval Operations, Navy Dept., 1944. viii, 32 p. illus., fold. map. ([U. S. Office of Naval Operations] Civil affairs guide).

U. S. Office of Naval Operations. Civil affairs guide; the fishing industry in Taiwan (Formosa). Washington, D. C., 1944. 32 p. (Op. Nav. 13-29).

# XXVII. HONG KONG

## Description and Travel

C., S. Hong Kong, "Isle of Beauty": the new handbook and guide. Hong Kong, Commercial Press, 1928. 106 p.

CLIFT, WINIFRED LECHMERE. Looking on in Hong Kong. London, Oliphants, 1927. 65 p.

DAVIS, S. G., 1907- . Hong Kong in its geographical setting. London, Collins [1949] 226 p. illus., maps.

DE ROME, F. J. Notes on the harbour of Hong Kong, by F. J. De Rome and V. Evans. Hong Kong, Ye Olde Printers, 1932. 19 p.

———. Notes on the new territories of Hong Kong, by F. J. De Rome, V. Evans, and E. C. Thomas. Hong Kong, Ye Olde Printers, [n. d.] Cover-title, 32 p. maps.

EPPSTEIN, JOHN, 1895- . Hong Kong. London, British Society for International Understanding, 1951. 20 p. illus. maps. (British survey popular ser., 118).

FAR EAST ENTERPRISE. Faree's tourist guide to Hong Kong. 5th edition. Hong Kong, [1954] 116 p. illus.

FORSTER, LANCELOT, 1882- . Echoes of Hong Kong and beyond. Hong Kong, Ye Olde Printers, 1933. 114 p.

GOODWIN, RALPH BURTON, 1902- . Passport to eternity. London, Arthur Barker, 1956. 192 p. front. (port.) plate (map).

GT. BRIT. Central Office of Information. Free port of the East: Hong Kong. New York, British Information Services, 1953. 21 p. illus. map, diagrs.

———. Central Office of Information. Hong Kong: outpost of freedom. London, Central Office of Information, 1954. 20 p. illus. map.

HAHN, EMILY, 1905- . Hong Kong holiday. Garden City, N. Y., Doubleday, 1946. viii p., 1 l., 305 p.

HAVEN, VIOLET SWEET. Hong Kong for the week-end! Impressions of a 23,500-mile jaunt over the Pacific via the China Clipper; with a foreword by Lowell Thomas. Boston, Contemporary Features, 1939. 56 p. illus. (incl. ports.) (Around the globe with Violet Sweet Haven; a new series of travelettes, 1).

HEYWOOD, GRAHAM SCUDAMORE PERCIVAL, 1903- . Rambles in Hong Kong. Hong Kong, 1938. 59 p.

HONG KONG. Attorney General. Street index of the city of Victoria, etc., etc., Hong Kong, by John Whyatt, acting assistant attorney general. 25th issue. Hong Kong, Printed by Noronha, 1938. Microfilm copy. Collation of the original, as determined from the film: lxx, 363 p.

———. Public Relations Office. Hong Kong. 2nd ed. Hong Kong, Public Relations Office, 1955. 48 p. illus. plan.

———. A diplomatic press survey, special edition of the "Diplomatic Bulletin." London, Diplomatic Press and Pub. Co., 1953. 30 p. illus. maps.

———. A brief history and guide of Hong Kong and the new territories. Hong Kong, Kelly and Walsh, 1924. 144 p. plates, fold. maps.

HONG KONG TRAVEL ASSOCIATION. Handbook of Hong Kong, the Riviera of the Orient. [The standard guide to Hong Kong and the new territories] Hong Kong, [1936] xx, 147 p. illus., plates, ports., fold maps (part col.).

HURLEY, R. C. Picturesque Hong Kong--British crown colony--and dependencies. Hong Kong, 1925. 160 p.

INGRAMS, WILLIAM HAROLD, 1897- . Hong Kong. London, H. M. Stationery

Off., 1952. xii, 307 p. illus. (part col.) maps (The Corona Library).

JOUGLET, RENÉ, 1884-    . Le capitaine de Hong Kong, couverture en couleur de Gustave Alaux. Paris, Colbert, 1944. 297 p. (Mer et outre-mer).

KESSEL, JOSEPH, 1898-    . Hong Kong et Macao. 16. éd. Paris, Gallimard, 1957. 276 p. (L'Air du temps).

PEPLOW, S. H. Hong Kong, around and about, by S. H. Peplow and M. Barker. 2nd ed. Hong Kong, Ye Olde Printerie, 1931. 196 p.

RAND, CHRISTOPHER. Hong Kong, the island between. New York, Knopf, 1952. 244 p.

The SHORT cut to beauty: Hong Kong's Peak Tram. [Hong Kong? 1935]. Cover title. 16 p. illus., map.

SILENT guide to Hong Kong. Hong Kong, Tell-the-World Pub. Co., 1937. 44 p.

STERICKER, JOHN. Hong Kong in picture and story [by] John and Veronica Stericker. Hong Kong, 1953. 175 p. illus., col. maps (on lining papers).

——. Hong Kong in picture; 100 photographs and two maps from the book Hong Kong in picture and story, by John and Veronica Stericker. [Special forces ed.] Hong Kong, 1954. 118 p. (chiefly illus.).

——. The Hong Kong gift book, by John and Veronica Stericker. Hong Kong, 1954. 52 p. plates (part col., 4 in pocket) port., maps (1 fold. col.).

SWEET, S. A. A Hong Kong sketch book. Hong Kong, Ye Olde Printerie, 1931. ix, 21 p.

TRIANGULATION of Hong Kong and New Territories. Hong Kong, 1931? 35 p. fold. map, tables.

WEISS, K. Hong Kong guide, with comprehensive street index, 22 maps and 20 views of Hong Kong. Hong Kong, the author; London, Bailey and Swinfen, 1953. xiv, 304 p. plates, maps.

WEMBLEY. British Empire Exhibition. Hong Kong: a history and a description. Hong Kong, 1924. 41 p.

——. British Empire Exhibition. Hong Kong section, British Empire exhibition. The Chinese street. Hong Kong, 1924. 32 p.

——. British Empire Exhibition. Where to shop in Hong Kong. Hong Kong, British Empire Exhibition, 1924. 32 p.


## History and Archaeology

CLARK, RUSSELL S. An end to tears. Sydney, P. Huston [1946] 180 p.

DAVIS, S. G. 1907-    . The geology of Hong Kong from the basic work of R. W. Brock, S. G. Davis [and others. Hong Kong, Government Printer, 1952]. iv, 210 p. illus. fold. maps.

FABIAN SOCIETY, London. Strategic colonies and their future, papers prepared for the Fabian Colonial Bureau, with an introduction by A Creech Jones, and maps by J. F. Horrabin. London, Fabian Publications and V. Gollancz [1945] 36. p. illus. (map) ([Fabian society, London] Research series, 100).

HEANLEY, C. M. A contribution to the prehistory of Hong Kong and the New Territories, by C. M. Heanley and J. L. Shellshear. Hanoi, 1932. 14 p. plates.

HO, STANLEY DZU-FANG, 何祚犨 , 1913-    . A hundred years of Hong Kong. Ann Arbor, University Microfilms [1952] ([University Microfilms, Ann Arbor, Mich.] Publication no. 2973) Collation of the original: 1 v. (various pagings) diagrs., tables. Thesis--Princeton University.

HONG KONG, a short history of the colony and an outline of the present political situation in China. 3d ed., rev. Hong Kong, Publicity Bureau for South China [1928]. 86 p. fold. plates.

——. Historical and statistical abstract of the Colony of Hong Kong, 1841-1930. 3d ed. Hong Kong, Printed by Noronha and Co., Govt. Printers, 1932. v, 105 p. tables.

[KER, WILLIAM POLLOCK] 1864-    . Chinese under British rule in Malaya,

Hong Kong and Weihaiwei. [n. p., 1929?] 45 numb. 1.(typescript).

MILLS, LENNOX ALGERNON. British rule in eastern Asia; a study of contemporary government and economic development in British Malaya and Hong
Kong. Issued under the auspices of the Secretariat, Institute of Pacific Relations, International research series. London, Oxford university press, H.
Milford, 1942. viii, 581 p., 1 l. fold. maps.

SAYER, GEOFFREY ROBLEY, 1887-    . Hong Kong: birth, adolescence, and
coming of age. London, Oxford University Press, 1937. viii, 232 p. incl.
plates (2 maps) col. front., plates, diagrs.

TCHEOU, CHE-LONG, 周詩農 [Chou Shih-nung] Hong Kong. Paris 1952. 117 l.
Thèse--Univ. de Paris.

WOOD, WINIFRED A. A brief history of Hong Kong. Hong Kong, Printed by
South China Morning Post [1940] 278, iv p.


## Siege, 1941

BROWN, WENZELL. Hong Kong aftermath. New York, Smith and Durrell,
1943. 283 p.

CANADA. Commissioner on the Canadian Expeditionary Force to the Crown
Colony of Hong Kong. Report on the Canadian expeditionary force to the
crown colony of Hong Kong, by Right Hon. Sir Lyman P. Duff, royal commissioner, pursuant to Order in Council, P. C. 1160. Ottawa, E. Cloutier,
printer to the King, 1942. 61 p.

————: Commissioner on the Canadian Expeditionary Force to the Crown Colony
of Hong Kong. Rapport concernant le Corps expéditionnaire canadien envoyé
dans la colonie de la couronne de Hong Kong, soumis par le très honorable
Sir Lyman P. Duff... en conformité de l'arrêté en conseil C. P. 1160. Ottawa, E. Cloutier, Impr. du roi, 1942. 64 p.

DEW, GWEN, 1907-    . Prisoner of the Japs. New York, A. A. Knopf, 1943;
London, Hutchinson, 1944. v-viii, 309, [1] p. fold. front. (map).

DUDLEY, MARION, 1895-    . Hong Kong prison camp, [New York] c1942.
10 numb. 1. (Typescript).

GOODWIN, RALPH BURTON, 1902-    . Hong Kong escape. London, A. Barker
[1953] 223 p. illus.

HONG KONG. Royal Hong Kong Defence Force. A record of the actions of the
Hong Kong volunteer defence corps in the battle for Hong Kong, December
1941. Hong Kong, 1956. 61 p.

HARROP, PHYLLIS. Hong Kong incident. London, Eyre and Spottiswoode [1943]
[3]-192 p. plates (incl. front. (group port.)).

LAN, ALICE Y, 藍如溪, [Lan Ju-hsi] We flee from Hong Kong, by Alice Y.
Lan and Betty M. Hu, 胡美蓮 . Grand Rapids, Mich., Zondervan Publishing House, Toronto, Evangelical Publishers, 1944. 125 p. front., plates,
ports.

MARSMAN, JAN HENDRIK, 1892-    . I escaped from Hong Kong. New York,
Reynal and Hitchcock [1942] 3-249 p. front. (port.).

NORRIS, RONALD. The Passionists in China, a series of articles. [n. p.]
1942. 78, [2] p. illus. (incl. ports., maps).

PROULX, BENJAMIN A. Underground from Hong Kong. New York, E. P. Dutton,
1943. 214 p.

RYAN, THOMAS F, 1889-    . Jesuits under fire in the siege of Hong Kong, 1941,
a composite narrative. London and Dublin, Burns, Oates and Washbourne,
1944. 188 p. front., plates, group port.

SATO, YUKIJ. Hong Kong under the military administration of Japan. [Trans-
lation] Hong Kong, 1944. Microfilm copy (positive) of typescript. Collation
of the original: 26, 40 l.

U. S. Bureau of Foreign and Domestic Commerce. Hong Kong under Japanese
occupation; a case study in the enemy's techniques of control, prepared by

Robert S. Ward, American consul, detailed to the Far Eastern Unit, Bureau
of Foreign and Domestic Commerce, Dept. of Commerce. [Washington] 1943.
6, iii, 105, 148 p. illus., ports., fold. map.
————. Office of Coordinator of Information. Research and Analysis Branch.
Hong Kong. Dec. 31, 1941.[Washington, 1941]. 3, [1] 1. (Its. R and A no. 33).

## Administration

ABERCROMBIE, SIR PATRICK, 1879-    . Hong Kong; preliminary planning re-
port. London, Crown Agents for the Colonies, 1949. 24 p. fold. plans.
COLLINS, SIR CHARLES HENRY, 1887-    . Public administration in Hong Kong.
London, Royal Institute of International Affairs [1952] ix, 189 p.
GT. BRIT. Colonial Office. Annual report on Hong Kong. 1946-date. London,
H. M. Stationery Off., 1946-date. v. illus., fold. map. (Its. Colonial annual
reports.
HONG KONG. Administration reports. 1908-1915, 1917-1938. [Hong Kong] 1910-
1939. v. illus., fold. maps (part col.).
————. Hong Kong Blue Books, 1901-1940. Hong Kong, 1902-1941. 40 v.
————. Estimate of revenue and expenditure, 1929, 1931-33. Hong Kong, 1928-
32. 4 v. tables.
————. Letters patent and royal instructions to the Governor of Hong Kong, to-
gether with standing orders of the Legislative Council of Hong Kong, amend-
ed to June, 1953. Hong Kong, Govt. Printer, 1953. 51 p.
————. Report on Hong Kong. 1946-date. Hong Kong 1947-date. v. illus., maps.
————. Audit Dept. Report by the Director of Audit. 1951/52- Hong Kong, Govt.
Printer, 1952-  v.
————. Census Office. Report on the census of the colony for 1921. Hong Kong,
1921. 82 p. incl. tables.
————. Census Office. Report on the census of the colony of Hong Kong taken on
the night of March 7, 1931, by W. J. Carrie...Superintendent of the Census.
Hong Kong, Noronha and Co., 1931. 111 p. incl. forms, tables, charts, col.
plans.
————. Civil Aviation Dept. Annual departmental report by the Director of Civil
Aviation. 1949/50- Hong Kong, Govt. Printer, 1950- v.
————. Co-operative and Marketing Dept. Departmental report by the registrar
of co-operative societies and director of marketing. Hong Kong, Govt. Print-
er, 1951/52- v. annual. (Hong Kong. Annual departmental reports).
————. Custodian of Property and Custodian of Enemy Property. Departmental
report. Hong Kong, Govt. Printer, 1951/52- v. (Hong Kong annual depart-
mental reports).
————. Dept. of Statistics. Report of the Government Statistician. 1948/49-
[Victoria?] v. annual.
————. Fire Brigade. [Annual departmental report by the] chief officer, Fire
Brigade. Hong Kong, 1952/53. v.
————. Hong Kong Govt. Office in London. Departmental report by the Director,
1951/52- Hong Kong, Govt. Printer, 1952-  v. (Hong Kong annual department-
al reports).
————. Housing Authority. Report. 1954/55- Hong Kong, Govt. Printer, 1955-
date. v. illus.
————. Labour Dept. Annual departmental report by the Commissioner of Labour.
Hong Kong, Govt. Printer. v.
————. Land Office. Departmental report of the land officer and registrar of
marriages. 1947/48-  [Hong Kong] 1948-   v.
————. Legislative Council. Report of the meetings of the legislative council.
"Hong Kong Hansard." Session, 1892-1940. Hong Kong, 1893-1940. v.
————. Legislative Council. Sessional papers laid before the legislative council
of Hong Kong, 1894-1940. 1946-date. Hong Kong, 1894-1940, 1946-date. v.

———. Marine Dept. Annual departmental report by the Director of Marine. 1951/52- Hong Kong, Govt. Printer, 1952- v.

———. Medical dept. Medical and sanitary reports. 1913-1940. Victoria, 1932-1941. v. fold map, tables, diagrs.

———. Police Dept. Annual departmental report, 1949/50- [Hong Kong] 1950- v. annual.

———. Post Office Dept. Annual departmental report by the postmaster general. 1928-date. Hong Kong, Govt. Printer, 1928-date. v.

———. Post Office Dept. The Hong Kong postal guide. 1929- Hong Kong, 1930- v.

———. Public Relations Office. Report. 1951/52- Hong Kong, Govt. Printer, 1952- v. annual. (Hong Kong. Annual departmental reports).

———. Public Services Commission. Report. 1st- 1950-52-date. Hong Kong, Govt. Printer, 1952-date. v.

———. Public Works Dept. Annual departmental report by the Director of Public Works. 1952/53- Hong Kong, Govt. Printer, 1953- v. annual.

———. Rating and Valuation Dept. Departmental report by the commissioner of rating and valuation. 1951/52- Hong Kong, Govt. Printer, 1952- v. annual. (Hong Kong. Annual departmental reports).

———. Register General's Dept. Departmental report. Hong Kong, Govt. Printer, 1951/52- v. annual. (Hong Kong. Annual departmental reports).

———. Registry of Trade Unions. Annual departmental report by the Registrar of trade unions. 1955/56. Hong Kong, Govt. Printer, 1956. 1 v.

———. Rent Control Committee. Rent control; report of a committee appointed by the Governor in February 1952. Hong Kong, [Govt. Printer] 1953. 140 p.

———. Riot Compensation Advisory Board. Report. Hong Kong [1957] 11 p.

———. Salaries Commission. Report of the Hong Kong Salaries Commission, 1953-54. Hong Kong, Govt. Printer [1954] 121 p. tables.

———. Salaries Commission. Revised scheme for salaries and allowances, Hong Kong, 1955. Hong Kong, Govt. Printer [1955] 105 p.

———. Secretariat for Chinese affairs. Report of the Secretary for Chinese affairs. Stanley, 1928-1940; 1950-date. v. tables (part. fold.).

———. Stores Dept. Departmental report by the Government stores and sand monopoly. Hong Kong, Govt. Printer, 1950/51-date. v. annual. (Hong Kong annual departmental reports).

———. Supreme Court. Annual departmental report by the registrar, Supreme Court. 1950/51- Hong Kong, Govt. Printer, 1952-date. v. (Hong Kong. Annual departmental reports).

———. Treasury. Report by the accountant general. 1950/51- Hong Kong, Govt. Printer, 1951- v. annual.

———. Urban Council. Departmental report. 1950/51- Hong Kong, 1951-date. v. annual.

MACINTOSH, DUNCAN WILLIAM, 1904-    . Policing Hong Kong. [Hong Kong?] 1952. 8 p. illus.

## Laws, Statutes, etc.

HONG KONG. Laws, statutes, etc. The ordinances of Hong Kong, 1844-1923 (prepared under the authority of ordinance no. 18 of 1923) Edited by Arthur Dyer Ball. Hong Kong, printed by Noronha and Co., 1924-27. 6 v.

———. Laws, statutes, etc. The ordinances of Hong Kong [1844-1914 (1937 ed.) (Prepared under authority of Ordinance no. 51 of 1936) Edited by John Alexander Fraser. Hong Kong, Printed by Noronha and Co., government printers, 1938-41. 2 v.

———. Laws, statutes, etc. (Indexes) Index to the ordinances of Hong Kong, 1924-1933, still in force at the end of 1933. Compiled for the Government of Hong Kong by Mr. H. K. Holmes. Hong Kong, Printed by Noronha and Co. [1934] xxii, 102 p.

———. Laws, statutes, etc. Hong Kong Port regulations; being an abstract of portions of the Merchant shipping ordinance, 1899, Ordinance no. 10 of 1899, as amended up to 31st May, 1922. Required to be delivered to masters of vessels pursuant to Section 44 of the said Ordinance, with certain other information, extracts and notices affecting such masters. Hong Kong, Printed by Noronha and Co. [192-] 131 p.

———. Laws, statutes, etc. The regulations of Hong Kong [1844-1931](1937 ed.) (Prepared under authority of Ordinance no. 51 of 1936) Edited by John Alexander Fraser. Stanley, Printed at the Hong Kong prison, 1938-41. 3 v. illus.

———. Laws, statutes, etc. Hong Kong war emergency legislation; being a collection of regulations made under the Emergency powers (defence) acts, 1939 and 1940, as applied to this colony by order of His Majesty in Council, and of orders, directions, etc., made under these regulations, as amended up to and including 28th February, 1941, with a list of references to other emergency legislation. Prepared by John Alexander Fraser. Hong Kong, Printed by Noronha and Co., 1941. xv, 209 p.

———. Laws, statutes, etc. The laws of Hong Kong, containing the ordinances enacted until and including the 1st day of September, 1950, and subsidiary legislation made thereunder. Prepared under the authority of the Revised edition of the laws ordinance, 1948, by J. B. Griffin [and others. Rev. ed., 1950] Hong Kong [Noronha, 1951] 11v.

———. Laws, statutes, etc. The regulations of Hong Kong, including proclamations, orders in council, etc. Hong Kong, 1951-52. 2 v. annual.

———. Laws, statutes, etc. The business regulation ordinance, 1952, passed by the Legislative Council on 14th May, 1952. Hong Kong, O. K. Print. Press, 1952. 12, 4 p.

———. Laws, statutes, etc. Prisons; ordinance no. 17 of 1954. Hong Kong, Govt. Printer, 1954. 85 p.

MELLO, ALOŸSIUS DE. A manual of the law of extradition and fugitive offenders applicable to the eastern dependencies of the British empire (the Straits settlements, Hong Kong, India, Ceylon, and the protected states of Malaya and Borneo). 2d ed. Singapore, Printed at the Govt. Print. Off., 1933. 4, xix, 637 (i. e. 649) p.

### Economic Conditions

### General Works

CH'EN, FRANCIS J., 陳鵬 . The Jaycee movement in Hong Kong. Hong Kong, Tong Ham, 1954. 97 p.

COMMERCIAL and industrial Hong Kong; a record of 94 years progress of the colony in commerce, trade, industry and shipping (1841-1935). Hong Kong, The Bedikton Co., 1935. 200 p. illus, ports. tables.

GT. BRIT. Hong Kong Currency Commission. Hong Kong currency. Report of a commission appointed by the Secretary of State for the Colonies. May, 1931. London, H. M. Stationery Off., 1931. 67 p. incl. tables, diagr. ([Parliament. Papers by command] Cmd. 3932).

HONG KONG. Chinese Manufacturers' Union. Record of the 14th exhibition of Hong Kong products. Hong Kong, 1956. 128 p. illus.

———. Dept. of Commerce and Industry. Hong Kong trade statistics. 1930- Hong Kong. 1930-    v.    Quarterly, 1920 -Apr./May/June 1930; monthly, July 1930-Apr. 1953. No statistics collected June 1925-Mar. 1930. Title varies: -2d quarter 1925, Hong Kong trade and shipping returns. -2d quarter 1930-Dec. 1953, Hong Kong trade returns.

———. Dept. of Commerce and Industry. Annual departmental report by the Director of Commerce and Industry. 1949/50- Hong Kong, Govt. Printer, 1950- v. illus.

———. Dept. of Commerce and Industry. Hong Kong imports and exports classification list. [Rev. ed. Hong Kong, Govt. Printer, 1953] 113p.

——. Dept. of Commerce and Industry. Commercial guide to Hong Kong [3rd ed.] Hong Kong, Published by Beatrice Church, Advertising and Publicity Bureau for the Dept. of Commerce and Industry, 1953. 180 p. 1st. ed. 1949.

——. Dept of Commerce and Industry. Trade bulletin. September 1954-date. Hong Kong, 1954-date. 1v. illus.

——. Economic Commission. Report of the commission appointed by His Excellency the Governor of Hong Kong to inquire into the causes and effects of the present trade depression in Hong Kong and to make recommendations for the amelioration of the existing position and for the improvement of the trade of the colony, July 1934-February 1935. Hong Kong, Noronha and Co., 1935. 71 p. incl. tables.

——. General Chamber of Commerce. Report of the General Committee of the Hong Kong General Chamber of Commerce, 1920-1940, 1954-date. Hong Kong, 1921-1940, 1954-date.

——. Imports and Exports Dept. Report of the superintendent of imports and exports, 1919-1928. Hong Kong, 1920-1929. 10 v. annual.

——. Imports and Exports Dept. Annual report. Hong Kong, Govt. Printer, 1946/47-date.

——. Imports and Exports Dept. Hong Kong trade returns. [annual] [Hong Kong] v. tables.

——. Inland Revenue Dept. Annual departmental report by the Commissioner of Internal Revenue, 1950/51-date. Hong Kong, 1951-date.

——. Junior Chamber of Commerce. This is Hong Kong 1955, an economic report. [Hong Kong, 1955] 37 p.

——. Kowloon-Canton Railway. Annual departmental report by the general manager [Kowloon-Canton Railway, British Section] Hong Kong, Govt. Printer. 195- v. (Its Annual departmental reports).

——. Statistical Dept. A report on post war movements in the cost of living in Hong Kong. Hong Kong, 1950. iii, 69 p. illus.

——. Stock Exchange. Handbook of stocks and shares of the principal public companies of Hong Kong. Comparative figures 1949-1951. [Hong Kong, 1952] 44 l.

——. Wholesale Vegetable Marketing Organisation. Report. 1947/48- [Hong Kong] 1948- v. annual.

HONG KONG British Industries Fair Committee. Directory of Hong Kong Products. Hong Kong, 1954. 46 p. illus.

HONG KONG textiles annual, edited by Pong Ding Yuen, 龐鼎元 . 1st- 1955- Hong Kong Cotton Merchants' Association, 1955-

KING, FRANK H. H. The monetary system of Hong Kong, with a chapter on the monetary system of Macao. Hong Kong, Weiss; London, Bailey and Swinfen, 1953. viii, 151 p. illus.

MA, RONALD A. 馬榮立 , 1923-    . The national income of Hong Kong, 1947-1950, by Ronald A. Ma and Edward F. Szczepanik. Hong Kong, University Press, 1955. viii, 70 p. tables, graphs.

U. S. Consulate. Hong Kong. Hong Kong. Annual economic report. 1951- Hong Kong, 1951-

WEMBLEY. British Empire Exhibition. The British colony of Hong Kong. Handbook of export trade. Hong Kong, 1924. 60 p.

## Transportation

GT. BRIT. Air Ministry. Bangkok-Hong Kong civil air transport service. Note by the Secretary of State for Air on the principal provisions proposed to be embodied in an agreement with Imperial airways, ltd., for the operation by them of an improved air transport service connecting Hong Kong with the

main empire air route. London, H. M. Stationery Off., 1938. 3 p. ([Parl-
iament. Papers by command] Cmd. 5871).
HONG KONG. Report of an inter-departmental committee on a scheme for air-
port development at Hong Kong. Hong Kong, 1953. 1 v.
————. Colonial Secretary's Dept. Papers on the development of Kai Tak airport.
[Hong Kong, 1954] 1 v. (various pagings).

## Directories and Yearbooks

ANGLO-Chinese directory of Hong Kong. Rev. ed. Hong Kong, Publicity Bureau
for South China, 1923. xiv, 748 p. port.
BUILDERS, engineers and manufacturers classified directory, Hong Kong. 1952-
Hong Kong, International Trade Journal, 1952- 1 v.
BUSINESS directory of Hong Kong and Macao. 1953-date. [Hong Kong] Canton
Business Directory Co. 1953-date. v. annual.
CANTON, Hong Kong and Macau commercial directory. Hong Kong, South China
Advertising Co., 1931.
COMMERCE, industry, finance; the official guide and directory on commerce,
industry and finance in the British crown colony of Hong Kong. 1949- [Hong
Kong] Dept. of Commerce and Industry. v. illus. biennial.
HONG KONG. Dept. of Commerce. Directory of commerce, industry and finance,
an official guide and directory, 1957. Hong Kong, Marklin Advertising, 1957.
195 p. illus., tables.
————. General Chamber of Commerce. Classified directory of members, 1957.
Hong Kong, 1957. 1 v.
HONG KONG and Far East builder directory, 1956/57. Hong Kong, Hong Kong
Building Service, 1956.
HONG KONG and South China business directory, 1936. Hong Kong, The Pub-
licity and Commercial Bureau, 1936. v. illus. fold map, fold plans.
HONG KONG and South China Hong list, 1935. Hong Kong, The Publicity and
Commercial Bureau, 1935. 1 v.
HONG KONG builders, engineers, decorators classified directory. 1954- Hong
Kong, Terry Advertising Agency.
HONG KONG CHINESE MANUFACTURERS' UNION. Classified directory of mem-
bers. English ed. Hong Kong. 1956- 1 v. illus. annual.
HONG KONG CHINESE TEXTILE MILLS ASSOCIATION. Directory of registered
members. 1949. Hong Kong, 1949. 88, 134 p.
HONG KONG commercial year book, with a complete directory of firms and man-
ufactories. Hong Kong, Chinese General Chamber of Commerce. 1951- v.
illus.
HONG KONG $ (dollar) directory, 1935- Hong Kong, Local Print. Press, 1936-
The HONG KONG exporter and Far Eastern importer. 1947- Hong Kong, Standard Press, 1948-
HONG KONG trade index; Hong Kong, Manila, Japan and South Africa, compiled
by M. V. Vásquez, 1950, 1951. Hong Kong, M. V. Vásquez, 1950, 1951. 2 v.
illus.
LEB'S Trade and shopping guide of Hong Kong. Hong Kong, L. E. Basto, 1928.
xx, 464 p.
O. K. business directory. 1952- Hong Kong, [O. K. Print. Press] 1953. 2 v.
Cover title: Hong Kong, Japan business directory.
PHARMACEUTICAL, chemical and cosmetic classified directory of Hong Kong.
1952/53-date. [Hong Kong] Terry Advertising Agency, 1953-date.

## Social Conditions

CATHOLIC directory and year book, 1954- Hong Kong, Catholic Truth Society.

v. Superseded Catholic directory for the diocese of Hong Kong.

FREE CHINA RELIEF ASSOCIATION. FCRA relief work in Hong Kong and Macao. [Taipei, 1956?] 1 v. (unpaged) illus.

GT. BRIT. Colonial office. Hong Kong. Papers relative to the mui-tsai question. Presented by the Secretary of State for the Colonies to Parliament by command of His Majesty, November, 1929. London, H. M. Stationery Off., 1929. 77 p. incl. form. ([Parliament. Papers by command] Cmd. 3424).

──── . Mui-tsai Commission. Mui tsai in Hong Kong and Malaya. Report of commission. London, H. M. Stationery Off., 1937. viii, 314 p. incl. tables (1 fold.) (Colonial office. Colonial no. 125).

HALL, RONALD OWEN, bp., 1895-        Hong Kong: what of the church? London, Edinburgh House Publications, 1952. 24 p.

HASLEWOOD, HUGH LYTTLETON, 1886-        Child slavery in Hong Kong, the mui tsai system. London, Sheldon Press, 1930. ix, 130 p. front.

HONG KONG. Traffic in women and children. Annual report for 1925 from the Hong Kong government. Geneva, 1926. 2 numb. 1. At head of title: League of nations. Official no.: C. 416. M.152. 1926.iv. [C. T. F. E. 315]

──── . Report of the government of Hong Kong on the traffic in opium and dangerous drugs. Hong Kong, 1930-32. 3 v. tables (part. fold.).

──── . Commissioner of Prisons. Department report by the Commissioner of Prisons for the financial year 1954/55. Hong Kong, Govt. Printer, 1955. 1 v. tables (Annual departmental reports).

──── . Committee on Chinese Law and Custom. Chinese law and custom in Hong Kong; report of a Committee appointed by the Governor in October, 1948. [Hong Kong, Govt. Printer, 1953] vii, 315 p. diagrs., tables.

──── . Committee on Colony's Position with regrad to Obligations incurred under International Opium Convention, 1912. Report of the committee appointed by H. E. the governor to consider the colony's position with regard to the obligations incurred under the International opium convention, 1912. [Hong Kong, 1924] 6 p.

──── . Governor 1930-1935 (Sir William Peel) Report by the governor of Hong Kong on the mui-tsai question. London, H. M. Stationery Off., 1930. 4 p. ([Gt. Brit. Parliament. Papers by command] Cmd. 3735).

──── . Governor, 1937-1940 (Sir Geoffry Northcote) Report by the Governor of Hong Kong on the mui tsai in the colony for the half-year ended 30th November, 1938. Geneva, 1939. 80 p. (mimeographed).

──── . Governor, 1956. (A. Grantham) Report on the riots in Kowloon and Tsuen Wan, October 10th-12th, 1956, together with covering dispatch dated the 23rd December, 1956, from the Governor of Hong Kong to the Secretary of State for the colonies. Hong Kong, 1956. 55 p.

──── . Mui-tsai Committee. Mui-tsai in Hong Kong. Report of the committee appointed by His Excellency the Governor, Sir William Peel. London, H. M. Stationery Off., 1936. 83 p. ([Gt. Brit. Parliament. Papers by command] Cmd. 5121).

HONG KONG REFUGEES SURVEY MISSION. The problem of Chinese refugees in Hong Kong; report submitted to the United Nations High Commissioner for Refugees by Edvard Hambro, chief. Leyden, A. W. Sijthoff, 1955. x, 214 p. illus., fold. map.

LO, Sir Man Kam, 羅文錦 . Comments on the Report of the Committee on Chinese law and custom in Hong Kong. [Hong Kong, Govt. Printer, 1953] 18 p.

## Education

FISHER, N. G. A report on government expenditure on education in Hong Kong, 1950. Hong Kong, 1951. 59 p. (Sessional paper No. 33, 1951).

HONG KONG. Committee on Higher Education. Report of the Committee on Higher education in Hong Kong, tabled in the Legislative Council 17th September,

1952. Hong Kong, Govt. Printer, 1952. vii, 74 p. tables, diagrs.

———. Festival of the Arts. Souvenir program of the second festival of the arts, 3-25 March 1956. Hong Kong, 1956. 64, [36] p. illus.

———. Festival of the Arts. Souvenir programme, 28th September to 2nd November, 1957. Hong Kong, 1957. 73 p.

———. Technical Education Investigating Committee. A report on technical education and vocational training in Hong Kong, presented by the Technical Education Investigating Committee, 30th October, 1953. [Hong Kong] 1953. 170 p.

———. University. The University of Hong Kong; its origin and growth by W. W. Hornell. Hong Kong, 1926. 58 p. incl. tables.

———. University. Engineering Society. Hong Kong University engineering journal. v. 1- 1929- [Hong Kong] v. illus. annual. Publication suspended 1941-48.

———. University. Medical Society. The Elixir; Hong Kong University medical society magazine. No. 1- 1950- Hong Kong, 1950-

[HORNELL, SIR WILLIAM WOODWARD] 1878-    The University of Hong Kong, 1912-1933. A souvenir. Hong Kong, Newspaper Enterprise Ltd., 1933. 36 p. plates, ports.

JENNINGS, WILLIAM IVOR, 1903-    A report on the University of Hong Kong, September 1953, by William I. Jennings and Douglas William Logan. Hong Kong, University Press, 1954. [1] 117 p. tables.

PRIESTLEY, K. E. Mental health and education in Hong Kong, by K. E. Priestley and Peryl R. Wright. [Hong Kong] Hong Kong University Press, [1956] 97 p. (University of Hong Kong Extra-mural lecture series).

## Meteorology

HONG KONG. Royal Observatory. Magnetic results. 1884-1941; 1949-date. Hong Kong, 1885-date. v. illus.

———. Royal Observatory. Annual departmental report by the Director. 1900-date. Hong Kong, Govt. Printer. 1900-date.

———. Royal Observatory. Monthly meteorological bulletin; containing detailed results of observations made at the Royal Observatory, Hong Kong, and the daily weather reports from various stations in the Far East. Jan. 1913-32. Hong Kong, 1913-1932. v. Ceased publication Dec. 1932. Superseded by its Meteorological results.

———. Royal Observatory. Monthly seismological bulletin, 1913-1940. Hong Kong, 1914-1940. v. charts, tables.

———. Royal Observatory. The winds of Hong Kong, by T. F. Claxton. Hong Kong, Noronha and Co., 1921. 105 p. incl. diagrs., tables.

———. Royal Observatory. Meteorological results. 1933-1941; 1949-date. Hong Kong. 1934-1941; 1949-date. v. annual.

———. Royal Observatory. The upper winds of Hong Kong, from observations made with pilot balloons, 1921-1932, by G. S. P. Heywood, under the direction of C. W. Jeffries, director. Hong Kong, Printed by Noronha and Co., 1933. 13 p. plates, tables.

———. Royal Observatory. Typhoon tracks, January 1947-date. Hong Kong, 1947-date.

———. Royal Observatory. Monthly weather summary; Southeast Asia and the Western Pacific. Hong Kong, 1949. 1 v. (loose-leaf).

———. Royal Observatory. A brief general history of the Royal Observatory, containing extracts from contemporary records, annual reports and memoranda, by L. Starbuck, assistant director. Hong Kong, Govt. Printer, 1951 34 p. illus.

———. Royal Observatory. Hong Kong meteorological records and climatological notes, 60 years, 1884-1939, 1947-1950. Edited by J. E. Peacock, scientific officer. Hong Kong, Govt. Printer, 1952. ii, 45 p. illus., maps, tables, diagrs. (Its R. O. T. M., 5).

## Natural History and Agriculture

GIBBS, L. Common Hon Kong ferns; illustrations and descriptions of forty-two common Hong Kong ferns. Hong Kong, Kelly and Walsh, [1927]. x. 84 p. illus.

HERKLOTS, GEOFFREY ALTON CRAIG. Flowering shrubs and trees; first twenty. Hong Kong, The University, 1937. 34 p. illus. plates.

——. Orchilds, first twenty. Hong Kong, The University, 193?. 62 p. illus. plates. (Hong Kong nature ser.).

——. Common marine food-fishes of Hong Kong, by G. A. C. Herklots and S. Y. Lin. 2nd ed. Hong Kong, 1940. 4, 89 p. illus. diag.

——. Vegetable cultivation in Hong Kong. [2nd. ed.] Hong Kong, South China Morning Post, 1947. 208 p. illus. [1st ed., 1941].

——. Hong Kong birds. Hong Kong, South China Morning Post [1953] 233 p. plates.

HONG KONG. Agricultural Dept. Report. 1948/49-49/50 [Hong Kong] 1949-51. 2 v.

——. Botanical and Forestry Dept. Report, 1893-date. Hong Kong, 1894-date. annual.

——. Dept. of Agriculture, Fisheries and Forestry. Annual departmental report by the Director of Agriculture, Fisheries and Forestry. 1950/51- Hong Kong, Govt. Printer, 1951- v. illus.

——. Dept. of Agriculture, Fisheries and Forestry. A review of forestry in Hong Kong with policy recommendations, by A. F. Robertson, forestry officer. Hong Kong, Govt. Printer, 1953. 30 p.

——. Dept. of Agriculture, Fisheries and Forestry. Report on agriculture in Hong Kong, with policy recommendations, by W. J. Blackie, Director. Hong Kong, Govt. Printer [1956] 93 p.

——. Fisheries Dept. Report of the Director of Fisheries. 1948/49-49/50. [Hong Kong] 2 v.

——. Fisheries Dept. Report of the director of fisheries on the Fish Marketing Organization. 1948/49- [Victoria?] 1949- v. diagrs.

——. Gardens Dept. Report by the Superintendent of Gardens. 1948/49-49/50. [Hong Kong] 1949-

HONG KONG HORTICULTURAL SOCIETY. Occasional notes of the Hong Kong Horticultural Society. no. 1- Feb. 1931- Hong Kong [1931- v. plates.

The HONG KONG naturalist; a quarterly illustrated journal principally for Hong Kong and South China. v. 1- Jan. 1930- Hong Kong, Newspaper Enterprise Ltd., 1930- v. illus., plates (part col.).

HONG KONG UNIVERSITY fisheries journal. no. 1- Dec. 1954- Hong Kong University Press. v. illus., maps. Supersedes Journal of the Hong Kong fisheries research station.

JOURNAL of the Hong Kong fisheries research station. v. 1-2, no. 1; Feb. 1940-Mar. 1949. Hong Kong, Printed by the South China Morning Post. 2 v. illus. Publication suspended Oct. 1940-Feb. 1949.

POPE, CLIFFORD HILLHOUSE, 1899-   A new ranid frog (Staurois) from the colony of Hong Kong [by] Clifford H. Pope and J. D. Romer. [Chicago] Chicago Natural History Museum, 1951. 609-612 p. illus. ([Chicago. Natural History Museum. Publication] no. 675).

TRAGEAR, THOMAS REFOY, 1897-   Land Utilization in Hong Kong, with map in 8 colors of Hong Kong and the New Territories (Sept. 1954), scale 1:80,000. Hong Kong, University Press, 1955. 8 p. map.

# XXVIII. MACAO

## Bibliography

BOXER, CHARLES RALPH, 1904-    Algumas notas sôbre a bibliografia de Macau [por] C. R. Boxer e J. M. Braga. Macau, Escola tipográfica salesiana, 1939. 30 p.

BRAGA, JOSÉ MARIA. A biblioteca do capitão C. R. Boxer. Macau, Escola tipográfica do Orfanato, 1938. 14 p. front. (port.) illus. (facsims.) "Separata do 'Boletim eclesiástico da diocese de Macau'."

## Description and Travel

BRAGA, JOSÉ MARIA. Macao fairs and exhibitions and handbooks to the charity and commercial fair, 1928; edited by Henrique Nolasco da Silva. Macao, Macao Publicity and Information Bureau, 1928. 7-54 p. illus. plates.

CORREIA, AFONSO. Macau, terra nossa; solar de Portugal no oriente. Macau, Impr. Nacional, 1951. 265 p.

MACAO. A visitor's handbook to romantic Macao. [2nd ed.] Pub. by the Publicity Office, Port Works Department, Macao. [Macao] Printed by N. T. Fernandes e filhos, 1928. 40 p., 1 l. front. (map) plates.

———. Anuário de Macau. 1921-1931? Macau [1921-1931?]Superseded by Anuário de Macau (Macao. Repartição central dos serviços economicos)?.

———. Repartição Central dos Serviços Economicos. Anuário de Macau. 1-ano; 1932- [Macau, 1932- At head of title, 1932-35: Colônia de Macau. Inspecção dos serviços económicos; 1936-: Colônia de Macau. Repartição central dos serviços económicos. Title varies: 1932-37, Directório de Macau. 1938- Anuário de Macau.

MACHADO, JOSÉ SILVEIRA. Macau, sentinela do passado. Macau, Secção de Propaganda e Turismo, 1956. 113 p.

MONTALTO DE JESUS, CARLOS A. Historic Macao; international traits in China old and new. 2d ed., rev. and enl. Macao, Salesian Print. Press, 1926. 4, 515, 6 p. plates, ports., fold. plan.

POMBAL, MARQUÊS DE, 1875-    Macau. In: Grande Enciclopédia Portuguesa e Brasileira. Lisbon, Editorial Enciclopédia, 1935-45, v. 15, p. 706-716.

PORTUGAL. Ministerio do Ultramar. Anuário colonial. 1916- Lisboa, Impr. Nacional, 1916- Publication suspended 1919-25. Issued by the Ministry under its earlier name: Ministerio das Colonias.

REGO, FRANCISCO DE CARVALHO E. Macau. Macau, Impr. Nacional, 1950. 112 p. illus., ports.

TEIXEIRA, MANUEL. Camões em Macau, contribuições para o estudo do problema. Macau, Impr. Nacional, 1940. 68 p. incl. plates.

## History

BOXER, CHARLES RALPH, 1904-    ed. A aclamação del Rei D. João iv em Goa e em Macau; relações contemporâneas reeditadas e anotadas. Lisboa, Tip. de J. Fernandes júnior, 1932. 74 p. facsims.

———. A derrota dos Holanedses, em Macau no ano de 1622; subsidios inéditas, pontos controversos, informações novas. Macau, Escola tipografica de Orfanato, 1938. 43 p. plan.

———. Macau na época da restauração (Macau three hundred years ago) Macau,

Impr. Nacional, 1942. 5-231 p. front. (port.) illus., plates (part fold.) facsims.

——. Subsídios para a história dos capitáis gerais e governadores de Macau (1557-1770) Macau, 1944. 106 p. illus.

——. Expediçoes militares portuguêsas em auxílio dos Mings contra os Manchus, 1621-1647. Macau, Escola Tipográfica Salesiana [194-?] 23 p. plates.

——. The Portuguese padroado in East Asia and the problem of the Chinese rites, 1576-1773. Macau, Impr. Nacional, 1948. 30 p. "Separate do n. 1 do Boletim do Institvto Portvgves de Hong Kong."

——. Fidalgos in the Far East, 1550-1770; fact and fancy in the history of Macao. The Hague, M. Nijhoff, 1948. xii, 297 p. plates, ports., maps.

BRAGA, JOSÉ MARIA. O inicio da imprensa em Macau. Macau, Escola tipográfica do Orfanato, 1938. 26 p. incl front. (facsim.)'' Separata do 'Boletim eclesiástico de Macau'.''

——. O primeiro acordo Luso-chines. Realizado por Leonel de Sousa em 1554. [Annotated by J. M. Braga] Macau, 1939. 17 p.

——. Tamão dos pioneiros portugueses. Macau, Escola tipográfica salesniana, 1939. 27 p.

——. With the flowery banner; some comments on the Americans in Macao and South China. Macao, 1940. 56 p.

——. Macao in 1515; remarks on Dr. Armando Cortesão's edition of the "Suma oriental" of Tomé Pires. Macau, Impr. Nacionale, 1949. 10 p. (Instituto Português de Hong Kong).

——. The western pioneers and their discovery of Macao. Macau, Impr. Nacional, 1949. 248 p.

——. Les pionniers de l'Occident et la découverte de Macao. Traduit de l'anglais par Maurice Echinard. Saigon, France-Asie [1950] 59 p. Reprinted from France-Asie, Décembre, 1950.

BRAGA, JOSÉ PAULO DE OLIVEIRA, 1905-    Em luta com os corsários da China. Lisboa, A. M. Teixeira, 1946. 217 p. (Aventuras d'aquém e d'além-mar, 1).

BRAZÃO, EDUARDO, 1907-    A política europeia no extremo oriente no século xix e as nossas relações diplomáticas com a China. Porto, Livraria Civilização, 1938. 87 p.

——. Apontamentos para a história das relações diplomáticas de Portugal com a China, 1516-1753. Lisboa, Divisão de Publicações e Biblioteca, Agência Geral das Colónias, 1949. 210 p.

COLOMBAN, EUDORE DE, pseud. Resumo da história de Macau. Refundido e aumentado pelo editor Jacinto José do Nascimento Moura. Macau, Tip. do Orfanato da I. C., 1927. 148 p. [1] p. illus., ports., maps.

——. Histoire abrégée de Macau. Pékin, Impr. de la Politique de Pékin, 1928. 2 v. illus. plates, ports, map, facsims. (Collection de la "Politique de Pékin").

CORTESÃO, ARMANDO, 1891-    Primeira embaixada europeia à China, o boticário e embaixador Tomé Pires e a sua "Suma oriental" Lisboa "Gráfica lisbonense"] 1945. 88 p. incl. map. (Cadernos da "Seara nova." Secção de estudos históricos).

EMBAIXADA de Macau ao Japão em 1640; relação contemporânea publicada e anotada por C. R. Boxer. Lisboa, Impr. da Armada, 1933. 52 p. maps, facsims. "Separata dos 'Anais do Club Militar Naval' tomo lxii, nos. 9 e 10.''

FRAZÃO DE VASCONCELLOS, JOSÉ AUGUSTO DO AMARAL, 1889-    A aclamação del rei d. João IV em Macau (subsídios históricos e biográficos) Lisboa, Agência geral das Colónias, 1929. 55 p. illus. (incl. facsims) "Separata do no. 53 do 'Boletim du Agência geral das Colónias'.''

GOMES, ARTUR LEVY. Esboço da história de Macau, 1511 a 1859. [Macau] Repartição Provincial dos Serviços de Economia e Estatística Geral (Secção de Propaganda e Turismo) [cover 1957] 409 p. illus.

GOMES, LUIZ G., 高美士 . Curiosidades de Macau antiga. Macau, 1945.  150 p.
"Separata da 'Renascimento'."

INSTRUCÇÃO para o bispo de Pequim e outros documentos para a historia de
Macau. Prefácio de Manuel Múrias.  Lisboa, Agência geral das Colónias,
1943.  380 p.

MACAO. Arquivos de Maçau, publicação oficial. vol. 1-3, ser. 2, v. 1, junho
de 1929-41. [Macau?] 1929-1941.

PIRES DE LIMA, DURVAL RUI. A embaixada de Manuel de Saldanha ao Impera-
dor K'hang hi em 1667-1670. (Subsídios para a história de Macau) [ Lisboa,
Tipografia e Papelaria Carmona, 1930] 23 p. fold geneal. table.

PORTUGAL. Agencia Geral do Ultramar. Divisão de Publicações e Biblioteca.
Instrução para o bispo de Pequim e outros documentos para a historia de Ma-
cau; prefácio de Manuel Múrias. [Lisboa] Divisão de publicações e biblioteca,
Agência Geral das Colonias, 1943. xiv, 380 p.

———. Direcção dos Serviços Diplomaticos, Geograficos e de Marinha. Memorandum sobre a questão de Macau; documentos. Ed. reservada. Lisboa, Impr.
Nacional, 1921. 532 p.

———. Ministerio do Ultramar. Arquivo das colónias. v. 1- (no. 1-      ); Lisboa, 1917- Monthly, July 1917-June 1919; quarterly, Apr. /June 1922-
Publication suspended July 1919-Mar. 1922, July 1922-1928. Issued 1917-
by the Ministry under its earlier name: Ministerio das Colonias.

RODRIGUES, FRANCISCO, 1873-    A aclamação de D. João IV em Macau pat-
riotismo e traição. Lisboa, 1944. 14 p. Reprinted from Revista Brotéria,
38:6.

SERRANO, FRANCISCO. Elementos historicos e etnograficos de Mação. [Ma-
ção, Tipografia Ferreirense, 1935] 220 P.

SILVA REGO, ANTONIO DA. A presença de Portugal em Macau. Lisboa, Divisão de publicações e biblioteca, Agência Geral das Colónias, 1946. xiii, 111 p.

YIN, KUANG-JÊN, 印光任 fl. 1744. Ou- mun kei-leok 澳門記略 . Monografia
de Macau, por Tcheong-Ü-Lâm 張汝霖 , e Ian-Kuong-Iâm 印光任 . Tradução
de chinês por Luís G. Gomes 高美士 . Editada pela Repartição Central dos
Serviços Económicos, Secção de Publicidade e Turismo. Macau, Impr. Nacional, 1950. 250 p. plates.

## Biography

BOXER, CHARLES RALPH, 1904-    Antonio de Albuquerque Coelho, esbóço-
biográfico. [Macau, Tipografia da Imaculada Conceição, 1939] 57 p. illus.,
facsims.

———. Antonio Coelho Guerreiro, e as relações entre Macau e Timor, no com-
éço do século xviii. [Macau] Escola Tipográfica do Orfanato da Imaculada
Conceição de Macau, 1940. 49 p. illus., fold, map.

———. Breve relação da vida e feitos de Lopo e Inacio Sarmento de Carvalho,
grandes capitãis qve no secvlo xvii honraram Portvgal no Oriente. Macau,
Impr. Nacional, 1940. 9-72 p. incl. geneal. tab. plates, facsims.

———. "Adonde hay valor hay honor." Esboço biográfico do almirante Luis Vel-
ho (1624-1669) Lisboa, 1948. 40 p. facsim.

TEIXEIRA, MANUEL. Galeria de macaenses ilustres do século dezanove. Macau, Impr. Nacional, 1942. 17-659 p. plates, ports., facsim.

## Politics and Government

ESPARTEIRO, JOAQUIM MARQUES. Alguns problemas magnos de Macau; breve
memória descritiva e justificativa. Macau, Impr. Nacional, 1952. 37 p.

MACAO. Boletim oficial do govêrno da província de Macau [weekly] 1900-date.
[Macau, Impr. Nacional, 1900-date.

———. Obras e melhoramentos efectuados em Macau. 1947-50. Macau, 1950-
v. illus. triennial.

——. Comissão de Valorização das Ilhas da Taipa e Coloane. Resumo das actas da Comissão da Valorizaçãs das Ilhas da Taipa e Coloane e da Comissão do Plano de Fomento. Macau, Impr. Nacional, 1956. 30 p.

——. Concelho. Compilação dos acordãos do Conselho de província publicados no boletins oficiais da província de Macau. [Annual] Macau, 194?- .

——. Conselho de Administraçao das obras públicas. Projecto de orçamento para o ano econômico de 1... Macau, 192- v. tables (part fold.).

——. Conselho do Governo. Acta da sessão [em] 7 de novembro [do ano de] 1918-1941? [Macau, Impr. Nacional, 1918-4-?

——. Direcção dos Correios e Telegrafos. Relatorio e estatistica dos correios e telegrafos. 1927-- Macau, 1928- .

——. Direcção dos Correios e Telegrafos. Serviço radiotelegráfico internacional. Taxas radiotelegráficas por palavra (em francos ouro) e respectivas instruções em vigor desde 15 de março de 1932. [Macau] Impr. Nacional, 1932. 17 p. incl. tables.

——. Governador, 1951- (Esparteiro) No primeiro biénio de governo; discursos e alocuções, brindes e mesagens [1951-1953] Macau, Ediçaõ da Repartição central dos serviços econômicos (Secção de propaganda e turismo) 1953. 271 p.

——. Repartição Tecnica das Obras Publicas. Caderno geral de encargos das obras, aprovado pela p. p. no. 2:091, de 16-5-1936. [Macau, Impr. Nacional, 1936] 67 p.

——. Repartição Tecnica das Obras Publicas. Conta da gerência. [Annual] Macau. 1941-

## Laws and Statutes

(Materials dealing with Portuguese colonies frequently include discussion of Macao. These titles are generally excluded from the present bibliography; they should, however, be consulted especially for laws, statutes, etc.)

MACAO. Ordem à fôrca armada da guarnição da colónia de Macau. Macau, 19? v. forms.

——. Laws, statutes, etc. Reorganização da administração civil e financeira da colónia. Macau, Impr. Nacional, 1921. Cover-title, xvii, 86 p. incl. forms.

——. Laws, statutes, etc. Tabela dos emolumentos e taxas de varias licenças, aprovadas pelos diplomas legislativos provinciais de 19 de novembro de 1924. Macau, Impr. Nacional, 1924. 30 p.

——. Laws, statutes, etc. Regimento do Tribunal administrativo, fiscal e de contas de Macau, aprovado pelo diploma legislativo provincial no. 43, de 17 de agosto de 1927. Macau, Impr. Nacional, 1927. Cover-title, 39 p.

——. Laws, statutes, etc. Compilação de legislação e mais disposições de execucao permanente, publicadas em... 1926-27. no Boletin oficial da colónia de Macau. Macau, Impr. Nacional, 1927. 2 v. illus. tables, forms.

——. Laws, statutes, etc. Regulamento para a concessão de terrenos na colonia de Macau, aprovado pelo diploma legislativo no. 268, de 21 de novembro de 1932. (Publicado no Boletim oficial no. 48, de 26 de novembro de 1932) Macau, Impr. Nacional, 1932. 19 p.

——. Laws, statutes, etc. Código de trânsito, aprovado pelo diploma legislativo no. 285, de 29 de março de 1933. Macau, Impr. Nacional, 1933. 33 p. 4 fold. plates.

——. Laws, statutes, etc. Regulamento da lotaria da Santa casa da misericórdia de Macau, alterado por deliberação da assemblea geral da Irmandade de mesma Santa casa, realizada em 17 de março de 1933. Aprovado pela portaria provincial no. 1:135, de 15 de maio de 1933 (Boletim oficial no. 23, de 10 de junho de 1933) Macau, Impr. Nacional, 1933.

——. Laws, statutes, etc. Regulamento para o serviço de abastecimento de água na cidade de Macau, aprovado pela portaria provincial no. 1:132-A, de 10 de maio de 1933 (Boletim oficial no. 20, de 20 de maio de 1933) Macau, Impr. Nacional, 1933. 13 p.

——. Laws, statutes, etc. Regulamento da Caixa económica postal. Aprovado pela P.p.no. 1:946, de 9-11-1935 (B.o.no. 45, de 9-11-1935) Macau, Impr. Nacional, 1935. Cover-title, 116 p. incl. forms (part fold.).

——. Laws, statutes, etc. Regulamento de recrutamento privativo. Aprovado pela P.p. no. 1:905, de 7-9-1935 (B.o.no. 36, de 7-9-1935) Macau, Impr. Nacional, 1935. 138 p. incl. tables, forms (part fold.).

——. Laws, statutes, etc. Regulamento para o comércio de armas, munições e explosivos e industrias de panchões e fogos de artificios. Aprovado pelo Diploma legislativo no. 342, de 16-12-1933. Macau, Impr. Nacional, 1935. 112 p. incl. forms (1 fold.).

——. Laws, statutes, etc. Regulamento para o serviço do material de guerra aprovado pela Portaria provincial no. 2:192, de 26-9-1936 (Boletim oficial no. 39, de 26-9-1936) Macau, Impr. Nacional, 1936. 54 p. incl. forms.

——. Laws, statutes, etc. Regulamento das escolas regimentais da guarnição militar de Macau aprovado pela Portaria provincial no. 2:162, de 15 de agosto de 1936 (Boletim oficial no. 33, de 15-8-1936) Macau, Impr. Nacional, 1936. Cover-title, [3]-32 p. incl. forms (1 fold.).

——. Laws, statutes, etc. Regulamentos do Corpo da policia de segurança pública, dos Serviços das policias administrativa e de investigação criminal e da Policia maritima. Aprovados, respectivamente, pelas P.P. nos. 2:427, 2:428 e 2:429, de 31-12-1937 (Suplemento ao B.o.no. 52/1937) Macau, Impr. Nacional, 1938. Cover-title, 37, 14, 22 p.

——. Laws, statutes, etc. Regulamento para o comércio de armas, munições e explosivos e indústria de panchões e fogos de artifício, aprovado pelo Diploma legislativo no. 645 de 23 dezembro de 1939. (Publicado no Boletim oficial no. 51 de 1939) com as alterações introducidas pelo Diploma legislativo no. 688, de 26 de outubro de 1940 (publicado no Boletim oficial no. 43 de 1940) Macau, Impr. Nacional, 1939. 62 p., 58 p. incl, forms.

——. Laws, statutes, etc. Regulamento do Corpo de salvação pública, aprovado pelo P.p. no. 2:759, de 30 dezembro de 1939. Macau, Impr. Nacional, 1940. Cover-title, 23 p.

——. Laws, statutes, etc. Regulamento das instalações radioeléctricas, aprovado por Diploma legislativo no. 702, de 15 de março de 1941, publicado no Boletim oficial no. 11 de 1941. Macau, Impr. Nacional, 1941. 16 p.; 14 p.

——. Laws, statutes, etc. Regimento do Conselho do govêrno, aprovado por Diploma legislativo no. 703, de 22 de março de 1941. Publicado no Boletim oficial no. 12 de 1941. Macau, Impr. Nacional, 1941. Cover-title, 10 p.

——. Laws, statutes, etc. Remodelação dos vencimentos dos funcionários civis e militares da colónia de Macau. Autorizada pelo Decreto no. 31:344, de 26 de junho de 1941 e aprovada pelo Diploma legislativo no. 718, de julho de 1941. Macau, Impr. Nacional, 1941. Cover-title, 41 p.

——. Laws, statutes, etc. Código de trânsito, aprovado pela Portaria provincial no. 3:024, de 28 de dezembro de 1940. Macau, Impr. Nacional, 1941. Cover-title, 34 p.; 28 p. iv pl. on 2 fold. 1.

——. Laws, statutes, etc. Regulamento do imposto do sêlo, aprovado pelo Diploma legislativo no. 701, de 15 de março de 1941. Macau, Impr. Nacional, 1941. 95 p.

PORTUGAL. Laws, statutes, etc. Código de justiça militar. Aprovado pelo decreto no. 11:292, de 26 de novembro de 1925, com as alterações introduzidas pelo decreto no. 12:393, de 27 de setembro de 1926. Macau, Impr. Nacional, 1926. Cover-title, 141 p.

——. Laws, statutes, etc. Regulamento de disciplina militar colonial; aprovado por decreto no. 21:828, de 4 novembro de 1932. Macau, Impr. Nacional, 1933. 76 p. incl, fold tables, forms.

——. Laws, statutes, etc. Carta orgânica do império colonial português. Macau, Impr. Nacional, 1934. 71 p.

——. Laws, statutes, etc. Reforma administrativa ultramarina (publicada no. 2. suplemento ao no. 52 do "Boletim oficial" de 30 dezembro de 1933). Macau, Impr. Nacional, 1934. Cover-title, 325 p. incl. illus., forms.

——: Laws, statutes, etc. Leis orgânicas do império português. Luanda, Impr. Nacional, 1935. 421 p.

——. Laws, statutes, etc. Regulamento das concessões de licenças para o estabelecimento e exploração de instalações eléctricas nas colónias portuguesas aprovado por Decreto no. 24:455/1935 (Boletim oficial no. 9, de 2 de março de 1935) Macau, Impr. Nacional, 1935. 41 p.

——. Laws, statutes, etc. Regulamento de betão armado, aprovado por Decreto no. 25:948, de 16-10-1935. Publicado no B.o. da colonia de Macau, no. 52, de 28-12-1935. Macau, Impr. Nacional, 1936. Cover-title, 80 p. incl. illus., tables, diagrs.

——: Laws, statutes, etc. Carta orgânica do império colonial português (nova publicação ordenada pela portaria ministerial no. 8:699, com as rectificações constantes das leis nos.1:948 e 1:900, dos decretos nos. 26:180 e 27:067 e da portaria ministerial no. 8:730.) (Publicada no Boletim oficial no. 26 de 1937) Macau, Impr. Nacional, 1937. 70 p.

## Foreign Missions

BOXER, CHARLES RALPH, 1904-   A propósito dum livrinho xilográfico dos Jesuítas de Pequim  (século xviii); ensaio histórico. Macau, Impr. Nacional, 1947. 20 p. (on double leaves), facsim.: 14 double 1.

BRAGA, JOSÉ MARIA. A igreja de s. Domingos e os dominicanos em Macau. Macau, Orfanato de Imaculada Conceição, 1939. 46 p. front., plates.''Macau, centro das nossas missões,'' by Jesus Gaio (p. 33-46) reprinted from Albertina, October, 1938.

——. Tomb-stones in the English cemeteries at Macao. Macao, Printed by Tipografia mercantil de N. T. Fernandes e filhos, 1940. [3]-59 p. plates.

PIMENTEL, FRANCISCO, d. 1675.  Breve relação da jornada que fez à corte de Pekim o senhor Manoel de Saldanha, embaixador extraordinario del rey de Portugal ao emperador da China, e Tartaria (1667-1670), escrita pelo padre Francisco Pimentel, e documentos contemporaneos. Compilados e anotados por C. R. Boxer e J. M. Braga. Macau, Impr. Nacional, 1942. 74, xlii p.

RODRIGUES, FRANCISCO, 1873-   Jesuitas portugueses astronomos na China, 1583-1805. Porto, Tipografia Porto Medico, 1925. 125 p. plates.

TEIXEIRA, MANUEL. Macau e a sua diocese. Macau, Tipografia do Orfanato salesiano, 1940- 2 v. plates, maps (1 fold.).

——. A fachada de S. Paulo, texto do  padre Manuel Teixeira, ilustrações do barão de Reichenau. [Macau, Impr. Nacional, 1941] 9-57 p. illus., 4 pl. (1 fold.).

## Medicine and Public Health

[BRAGA, JOSÉ MARIA]. Early medical practice in Macao, by J. A. Kollard [pseud.] Macao, Inspecção dos serviços economicos [1935] 24 p.

CAEIRO DA MATTA, JOSÉ, 1883-   La colonie de Macao et la question du trafic de l'opium. Lisbonne, 1940. 95 p.

MACAO. Direcção dos Servi ços de Saude e Higiene. Boletim sanitario. Macau, 1931-38?

PEREGRINO DA COSTA, PEDRO JOAQUIM. Relatórios das epidemias de cólera de 1937 e 1938. Macau, Impr. Nacional, 1938. [3]-70 p. fold. map, fold. diagrs.

——. Medicina Portuguesa no Extremo-Oriente, Siao, Molucas, Japão, Cochin-

china, Pequim e Macau. Bastora, Tipografia Rangel, 1948. 237 p.
SOARES, JOSÉ CAETANO. Macau e a assistência (panorama médico-social)
Lisboa, Agência Geral das Colónias, Divisão de Publicações e Biblioteca,
1950. 543 p. illus. port.

## General and Other

GOMES, LUIS G., 高美士 . Lendas chinesas de Macau. Macau-Oriente, Noticias
de Macau, 1951. 340 p. (Colecção Noticias de Macau, 5).
MACAO. Comissão Central de Assistência Publica. Assistência em Macau.
[Macau, 1951] 88 p. illus.
———. Comissão Executiva da Participação de Macau na Exposição Portuguêsa
em Sevilha. Catálogo geral da representação de Macau na exposição portuguêsa em Sevilha, 1929. Macau, N. T. Fernandes e Filhos, 1929. 25 p. illus.
———. Comissão Executiva da Participação de Macau na Exposição Portuguêsa
em Sevilha. Monografias, atigos, mapas e gráficos estatisticos, coligidos para
a Representação da Colónia de Macau na Exposição Portuguesa em Sevilha,
1929. Macau, N. T. Fernandes e Filhos, 1929. 132 p. charts, statistics.
———. Conselho Inspector de Instrução Publica. Anuário do ensino de Macau.
1939-40. Macau, Impr. Nacional. v.
———. Repartição Central dos Serviços Economicos. Movimento industrial e
comercial. 1929/30-1937/38. [Macau, 1933-38].
———. Serviços económicos. Monografia da visita do Ministro do ultramar a
Macau, de 18 de junho a 1 de julho, 1952. Coordenação de David Barrote [Ma-
cau, 1952] 328 p. illus. ports.
———. Serviço meteorológico. Notas cientificas. No. 1-date. Macau, 1952-date.
———. Serviço meteorológico. Resultados das observações meteorológicas de
Macau. V. 1-date. Macau, Impr. Nacionale, 1952-date. v. tables. [Monthly].
———. Servico meteorológico. Resultados das observações meteorológicas de
Macau, v. 1-date. Macau, 1952-date. [Monthly].
The MACAO review. v. 1-2 (December 1929-December 1930) Macao, 1929-30.
2 v.
MOSAICO. [Monthly] v. 1- Macau, 1950-
REGO, FRANCISCO DE CARVALHO E. Dialecto macaense, apresentado ao Col-
loquium international de Estudos Luso-Brazileiros. Macau, Impr. Nacional,
1950. 33 p.
U. S. Treaties, etc., 1923- (Coolidge) Parcel-post convention between the United
States of America and the Portuguese colony of Macao. [Washington, Govt.
print. Off., 1927] 12 p.

# APPENDIX I: SERIAL PUBLICATIONS

## General

AGENCE CHEKIAI. Bulletin. [Weekly] Berne. 193?-42?
———. Information télégraphiques, 1933-35. Shanghai, 1933-35.
AMERASIA: a Review of America and the Far East, v. 1-11, March 1937-July 1947. New York, 1937-47//.
ANNALES franco-chinoises publiées trimestriellement par l'Institut franco-chinois de l'Université de Lyon. [1. ]- Mars 1927- Lyon, Institut franco-chinois [1927-1934].
ASIA; Asian Quarterly of Culture and Synthesis. v. 1- [Quarterly] (no. 1-  ); Mar. 1951- [Saigon] 1951- [Editor: R. de Berval].
ASIA and the Americas. v. 1- July 1898-1946. [New York, 1898-1946] Irregular, 1898-Feb. 1902; monthly, Apr. 1902- Title varies: 1898-Jan. 1917, Journal of the American Asiatic association. Mar. 1917-Oct. 1942, Asia. Nov. 1942-1946, Asia and the Americas.
ASIA Calling. v. 1- [Santa Monica, Calif., American-Oriental Friendship Association] 1947- .
ASIAN Horizons. v. 1- [London, Asian Publications], 1948-51//
ASIATICA. [Bollettino dell'Istituto italiano per il Medio ed Estremo Oriente] anno-1-9. [Roma, 1935-43? Monthly, 1935; bimonthly, 1936- Title varies: 1935, Bollettino dell'Istituto italiano per il Medio ed Estremo Oriente.
ASIEN Berichte. [1.]-5 Jahrg. (Heft 1-22); Feb. 1939- Wien, Siebenberg-Verlag, 1939-44. Title varies: 1939, Berichte des Asien Arbeitskreises. Issued 1939 by Reichsstudentenführung, Aussenamt.
ASSOCIATION amicale franco-chinoise. Bulletin, 1-11. Paris, 1907-1930.
ASSOCIATION amicale sino-française. Bulletin. v. 1- Shanghai, 1933-
AUSTRALIA-China Association, Sydney. Report. 1-3 Sydney [1944-46].
BULLETIN de l'Association française des amis de l'Orient. v. 1- Paris, 1921-38.
BULLETIN periodique de la presse chinoise. No. 1-41. Paris, 1917-1923.
CANTON. v. 1, no. 1-5; Apr.-Oct. 1939. [Monthly] [Canton, Oriental Cultural Association] 1939//?
CANTON Truth. v. 1- Aug. 19, 1933- Canton, National Publishers, 1933-1937? Supersedes China Truth.
CARAVAN; Magazine of the Far East. v. 1-4, no. 2, Jan. 1936-Apr. 1939// Peking, 1936-39.
CHINA [the official publication of the China Society of America, inc.] v. 1- Jan. 1924-33. New York, 1924-33.
CHINA. [Quarterly] Amsterdam, Nederlandsch-Chineesche Vereeniging. 1925-.
CHINA. v. 1, No. 1- Sept. 15, 1928- Shanghai, 1928- .
CHINA. Chinese New Service. China Information Bulletin v. 1-2 New York, Jan. 1948-Jan. 1949.
The CHINA Critic; the only Chinese owned and edited English weekly. v. 1- May 31, 1928-1940// Shanghai, The China Critic Pub. Co. [1928-40].
CHINA Digest. v. 1-  ; Nov. 7, 1925- Shanghai, 1925-?
The CHINA Express and Telegraph. London, 1858-1931// 1860 as China express. 1861-1921 as London and China express. 1925-1931 as China express and telegraph.
CHINA Journal. v. 1-35. Shanghai, China Society of Science and Arts and the Shanghai Chemical Society, 1923-1941//.
The CHINA Monthly. v. 1-11, no. 3. [New York] 1939-1950.

CHINA Monthly Review. v. 1- [Shanghai, Millard Pub. Co.] 1917-1950. Publication suspended Dec. 13, 1941-Oct. 13, 1945. Title varies: 1917-May 28, 1921: Millard's review of the Far East. (May 17-July 5, 1919: Millard's China national review)— June 4, 1921-July 1, 1922: The Weekly review of the Far East.— July 8, 1922-June 16, 1923: The Weekly review.— June 23, 1923-1950: The China weekly review.

The CHINA Outlook. [Monthly] v. 1- Dec. 1, 1927- [Peking, 1927-1928//.

CHINA Outlook. [Weekly] v. 1-7, Jy 26, 1935-July 15, 1937. n. s. v. 1, Jan. 15-Jy 30, 1938. Shanghai, 1935-38. Superseded by Voice of New China.

CHINA Press Weekly. v. 1-3 no. 29; Feb. 25, 1933-Jy 14, 1934; [n. s.] 1-3 no. 1-75) Aug 11, 1935-Dec. 1937. Shanghai, 1933-37.

The CHINA Quarterly. v. 1- Shanghai, 1935-1941//.

CHINA Review. v. 1-6; July 1921-Sept. 1924. New York, China Trade Bureau, 1921-24.

CHINA Review. [Bi-monthly] v. 1, nos. 1-4; Feb.-Aug. 1932. New York, 1932.

CHINA Review. v. 1-5, no. 13; Oct. 1931-May 1938// London, 1931-38.

CHINA Review; a Review devoted to Anglo-Chinese Affairs. [Monthly] v. 1-2// Dec. 1947-48. [London, British United Aid to China] Formed by the union of China tomorrow and B.U.A.C. review.

CHINA Society of America. Pamphlets. no. 1-3, 1922; s2 no. 1-3, 1923. New York, 1922-1923//.

CHINA Tomorrow. v. 1-2. Nov. 1928-Je/Jy 1930// Peiping, 1928-30.

CHINA Tomorrow. [Quarterly] v. 1, no. 1-5; Apr. 1946-June 1947// [London] 1946-47. Caption title, Apr.-Sept. 1946: China tomorrow and Orient review. In Dec. 1947 united with B.U.A.C. review to from China review.

CHINA Truth, devoted to the development of China and the world affairs. v. 1-5, no. 17. April 20, 1929-Aug. 12, 1933. Canton, 1929-1933// Superseded by Canton Truth.

CHINA Weekly Review, see China Monthly Review.

Le CHINE; revue bi-mensuelle illustrée, rédigée par un comité franco-chinois. Nos. 1-73. Pékin, A. Nachbaur, 1921-1925//.

CHINE. v. 1- 1935- Paris, 1935-

Le CHINE et le monde. t. 1-3. Paris, Les Presses universitaires de France, 1925-1929//

CHINE illustrée. China illustriert. China illustrated, No. 1- Août, 1935- Genève, Bibliothèque Sino-Internationale, 1935-

Le CHINE libre, Bulletin hebdomadaire d'information. v. 1- Paris, Ambassade de la République de Chine, 1952-

CHINESE Affairs. v. [1]-6, no. 13; June 10, 1928-Dec. 15, 1934// Nanking [etc.] International Relations Committee [1928-34] 6 v. in 5. illus. Weekly, 1928-May 31, 1933; semimonthly, June 15, 1933-Dec. 15, 1934. Issues for 1928-31 (nos. 1-154/155) do not bear volume numbering but they constitute v. 1-3. Publication suspended from De. 1931 to May 1932 both inclusive. 1928-May 31 have subtitle: A weekly survey of important events relating to China (varies slighty).

CHINESE Digest. v. 1-6. San Francisco, China Cultural Society of America, 1935-1940//

The CHINESE Nation. v. 1-3, no 15. June 18, 1930-June 1932. Shanghai, [1930-32//

CHINESE Opinions on Current Events (translated from Chinese Periodicals) [Weekly] June, 1936- Shanghai, 1936-

CHINESE Press. [Weekly] v. 1-6, no. 24; Nov. 22, 1941-Oct. 29, 1943. San Francisco, Calif. [C. Leong] 1941-43.

The CHINESE Republic. [Weekly] v. 1- May 7, 1932-36// [Shanghai, 1932-36].

COUNCIL of International Affairs, Nanking. Information Bulletin. v. 1-2. Nanking, 1936-1937.

EAST and West. [Quarterly] year 1- Apr. 1950- [Rome, Istituto italiano per il

Medio ed Estremo Orient].

EAST Wind (the only magazine designed for the Chinese in America). v. 1-3, no. 2. Cleveland, East wind Printers, 1945-47//

FAR EASTERN Affairs. no. 1- New York, St. Martin's Press, 1957- (St. Antony's papers, no. 2.).

FAR Eastern Information Bureau. Bulletin. v. 1- v. 2, no. 2. Nanking, 1929-1930.

FAR Eastern monthly, Hankow. See Pan-Pacific monthly.

The FAR EASTERN Quarterly; Review of Eastern Asia and the adjacent Pacific islands. v. 1- Nov. 1941-1956. Ithaca, N. Y. [etc.] Published for the Far Eastern Association by Cornell University Press [etc.]. Superseded by the Journal of Asian Studies, Nov. 1956.

FAR EASTERN Survey. v. [1]- [New York] 1932- Biweekly, 1932-49; biweekly (monthly in summer), 1950- Title varies: Mar. 3, 1932-Dec. 21, 1934, Memorandum.

FRANCE-ASIE; revue de culture et de synthèse franco-asiatique. [Monthly] [Saigon], 1946- .

MILLARD PUBLISHING COMPANY, Shanghai. Monthly report; a monthly newsletter. v. 1- Shanghai, 1946- Issued 1946 by the China weekly review (later China monthly review).

MILLARD'S Review. See China Monthly Review.

MODERN China Monthly. 1st- issue; Taipei, 1950- .

The NEW China. [Monthly] v. 1-2. Peiping, 1930-31// Published by the Journalism club of Yenching university, (in cooperation with the New China publishing association.

The ORIENT; occidental life in the Far East, published in the interest of the U. S. Military and Naval forces. [Monthly] v. 1- Shanghai, 1924.

ORIENT et Occident.. [Monthly] [1.]-2. année (t. 1-5); Jan. 1922-juin 1923. Paris, E. Leroux, 1922=23.//

ORIENT-NACHRICHTEN. 1-5. Jahrg; [Semimonthly] Berlin, Deutscher Orient-Verein, 1935-39. Superseded by Der Nahe Osten.

OSTASIATISCHE Rundschau; die Zeitschrift für den Fernen Osten. 1- 1 Feb. 1920-44. Berlin, Deutscher Überseedienst, 1920-22; Hamburg, Wirtschaftdienst, 1923-44.

OSTASIEN. Bd. 1-2. Berlin, Junker und Dünnhaupt, 1943-44. Issued by Deutsches Auslandswissenschaftliches Institut.

OST-West-Korrespondenz (Monthly); Hrsg. von Yunlay Hsiao. v. 1- 1947- Berlin-Charlottenburg, 1947-.

PACIFIC Affairs. -Dec. 1927; [new ser., v. 1]- Jan. 1928- Honolulu and New York, Institute of Pacific relations [1928]-

PACIFIC Data, from the Institute of Pacific relations, Honolulu, Hawaii. no. 1-30; Aug. 15, 1927-Dec. 20, 1928.// Honolulu, 1927-28. 30 1. semimonthly (Sept. -Dec. 1928, irregular) Continued in Pacific Affairs.

PACIFIC Digest. [Monthly] v. 1- Oct. 1937-38// [Kweilin, 1937-38.

PAN-Pacific Monthly. No. 1-38. Hankow, 1927-1930// 1927-Mar. 1928 as Pan-Pacific Worker; April 1928-Mar. 1929 as Far Eastern Monthly.

PEKING Magazine. v. 1- (no. 1-6); July-Dec. 1931. [Peking, Pacific Pub. Co., 1931]// 1 v. in 2. illus. monthly. Title of v. 1, no. 1-4, reads: Peking; news and views of China.

The PEOPLE'S Tribune; an organ of national revolutionary thought and opinion. v. 1-16, March, 1931-May 16, 1937. Shanghai, United China Press, 1931-37.

La POLITIQUE de Pékin; revue hebdomadaire illustrée. Pékin, 1919-194?

ROYAL Central Asian Society, London. Journal. v. 1- London, 1914-.

SINO-Indian Journal. v. 1- Santiniketan, Sino-Indian Cultural Society in India, 1947-.

The TIMES Week. v. 1-6, no. 9. Mar. 1, 1943-Aug. 1, 1945// [Shanghai] Shanghai Times, 1943-45. Weekly, Mar. 1-July 26, 1943; biweekly (irregular) Aug. 2, 1943-Aug. 1, 1945.

The SOUTH China Monthly Review. v. 1-2; Oct. 1928-May 1929. [Canton, Canton Tourist Bureau, etc., 1928-29]//.

VOICE of new China; a bi-lingual fortnightly. v. 1-7. Nanking [New China Pub. Co., 1938-41// Supersedes China outlook (Shanghai).

WEST and East Monthly. v. 1- Taipei, 1956-.

## China at War

ASIANA; the Monthly News-Magazine of East Asia. Shanghai, 1941- //.

CHINA. no. 1- Apr. 1945- [New Delhi] Published under the auspices of the Office of the Commissioner of the Republic of China in India.

CHINA. Chinese New Service. [Release. Series] SA. no. [1]- Sept. 1943- New York, 1943-.

——. American press opinion, 1948-50. New York, 1948-.

CHINA. Chinese News Service. News from China; weekly summary of China news based on press reports received from China. no.  -166;  -Mar. 30. 1949. New York, 194-.

CHINA Air Mail; fortnightly newsletter service on Far Eastern affairs. no. 1- Hong Kong, 1939- Editor: 1939- Guenther Stein.

CHINA at War. v. 1-15. Hankow, etc. China Information Committee, 1938-1945. Suspended Jan-Apr. 1946 and superseded by China Magazine.

CHINA Campaign Committee. China Bulletin. No. 1-7 London, 1937-38//.

——.Miscellaneous publications. No. 1- London, 1938-//.

——. China Newsletter. London, 1946-//.

CHINA Correspondent. Dec. 1943-Sept. 1944. [Calcutta, 1943-44]//.

CHINA Defence League. News Letter. n. s. No. 1-36, April 1, 1939-November, 1941. Hong Kong, 1939-41.

The CHINA Fortnightly. v. 1-3. [Chungking, Central news agency, 1939-41]//.

CHINA Forum; a weekly review. v. 1-6, no. 1; Feb. 19, 1938-July 20, 1940. Hankow and Chungking [etc., 1938-40]// 6 v. in 5. Published under the auspices of the Chinese League of nations union. Publication suspended from Oct. 1, 1938 to March 11, 1939.

CHINA Information Bulletin. [Weekly] no.  -170; Sept. 12, 1945. Calcutta, Chinese Ministry of Information.

CHINA Information Service, Washington, D. C. [Bulletin] no. 1-61// Washington, D. C., 1938-41//.

CHINA Magazine. [New York, etc., Chinese News Service, etc.] 1946-49. Supersedes China at War.

CHINA Today. La Chine d'aujourd'hui. Китай сегодня [no. 1]-July 1939-40. [Hong Kong, China Branch, International Peace Campaign, 1939-40.

——. champion of China's unity, democracy and independence. v. 1-8, no. 3; 1933-Mar. 1942. [New York, American friends of the Chinese people, etc., 1934-42] 8 v. in 7. illus. (incl. ports., maps) Monthly. No numbers were issued for Dec. 1940, June and Nov. 1941. Superseded by Amerasia.

CHINESE League of Nations Union. Sino-Japanese issue series. no. 1- Sept. 1937-38// Hankow [etc., 1937-38].

CHINESE Mind; an interpretation. [Monthly] v. 1, no. 1-11/12. Ja-N/D 1943// New York, People's Foreign Relations Assn. of China, 1943.

The CHINESE Mercury; quarterly journal for world's English-reading public. v. 1- Columbia, Mo., 1937-39//.

CHINESE People's Correspondence. v. 1- San Francisco, 1951-// Editor: China News Association.

CHINESE Press Views. no. 1-32. [London] China association [1940-41] Editor: E. M. Gull. Mimeographed.

CONTEMPORARY China; a reference digest. v. 1- [Biweekly] May 25, 1941-May 13, 1946// New York, Chinese news service, [etc.] 1941-46//.

FACTS and Opinions concerning the Far East; a reference digest. no. 1- Feb. 1940- New York, 1940-.

FAR EAST Bulletin, news and views from China. Kowloon, H. K., Kuosin News Agency, 1940-41.

FAR EASTERN Affairs Pamphlets. [v. 1, no. 1- [San Francisco, D. W. Ryder] 1938- Editor: D. W. Ryder. [1939 as the Far Eastern affairs monthly].

The FAR EASTERN Digest. [Hong Kong, Far Eastern digest, 1939-.

FAR Eastern Mirror. v. 1- Feb. 15-Sept. 10, 1938-// Hong Kong, 1938. Monthly, Feb.-Mar. 1938; semimonthly (irregular) Apr. 1938- vol. 1, no. 1 was published in Hankow.

FRANCE. Services d'information en Chine. Bulletin d'information. [Weekly] Chungking, 1944-.

FRIENDS, Society of. American Friends Service Committee. Bulletin on work in China. No. 1- Jan. 10, 1942-47. Philadelphia, 1942-47// irregular.

KUO-MIN NEWS AGENCY. [Press releases] [daily] [Nanking?].

"Das NEUE China," Sektion der Kuomintang in Deutschland. Schriftenreihe zur Ostasien-Frage. Nr. 1-4. Berlin, 1937-38.

NEW China. [Weekly, irregular] ser. [1]-3, no. 20; July 7, 1939-July 21, 1942. Washington, D. C., China Information Service, 1939-42// Publication suspended from Dec. 29, 1939 to July 5, 1940 and from May 1 to Sept. 8, 1941, inclusive.

The XXth Century (monthly) v. 1-5. Shanghai, the XXth Century Pub. Co., 1939-43. Editor: Klaus Mehnert.

UNITED CHINA RELIEF, INC. News of China. V. 1-8, no. 3. Sept. 1942-49. New York, 1942-49// Supersedes its Newsletter, Sept. 1942-Dec. 1943. Suspended June 1946-May 1947.

UNITED China Relief Series. no. 1- Chungking, China, The China publishing company, 1941-.


## Chinese Studies

ACADEMIA Sinica. Annals. No. 1- Taipei, 1954-.

ACTA Orientalia. v. 1- Lund, 1922-

——. t. 1- Budapest, Magyar Tudományos Akadémia, 1950-.

AMERICAN ORIENTAL SOCIETY. Journal of the American Oriental Society, v. 1- 1843/49- Boston, etc., 1849- Index v. 1-20 in v. 21; 21-40 in v. 44.

ARCHIV Orientálnf. v. 1- Praha, Orientálnf ústav, 1929-.

ASIA Major. v. 1-10, Jan. 1924-35; n. F., Bd. 1, Heft 1, 1944; New ser., v. 1- 1949- London, Taylor's Foreign Press [etc.] [Published in Leipzig, 1924-44].

ASIAN Review. v. 1-10 (no. 1-20) Jan. 1886-Oct. 1890; 2d ser., v. 1-10 (no. 1-20) Jan. 1891-Oct. 1895; 3d ser., v. 1-34 (no. 1-68) Jan. 1896-Oct. 1912; new ser., v. 1- no. 1- ) Jan 1913- [London, East and West, etc.] 1886- Quarterly (every 6 weeks, 1914-17) Title varies: 1886-90, 1913, The Asiatic quarterly review. — 1891-1912, The Imperial and Asiatic quarterly review and Oriental and colonial record (varies)— 1914-52, The Asiatic review.

ASIATISCHE Studien. Études asiatiques. [Quarterly] v. 1- 1947- Bern, A. Francke, 1947- Journal of the Schweizerische Gesellschaft für Asienkunde and supersedes its Mitteilungen.

BERLIN. UNIVERSITÄT. Seminar für Orientalische Sprachen. Mittheilungen des Seminars für Orientalische Sprachen an der Königlichen Friedrich Wilhelms Universität zu Berlin. jahrg. 1-41. Berlin und Stuttgart, W. Spemann, 1898-1938.

BULLETIN of Chinese Studies. Chengtu, 1941-1948//.

CHINA SOCIETY, LONDON. Paper. No. 1-13. London, 1915-1925//.

——. Sinological Series. No. 1- London, 1940-.

CHINA SOCIETY, Singapore. Annual. Singapore, 1952-.

CHINESE Culture: a Quarterly Review. v. 1, No. 1-  (July 1957-  ) Taipei,
    Chinese Cultural Research Institute, 1957-.
The CHINESE Repository. v. 1-20; May 1832-Dec. 1851. Canton [etc.] Printed
    for the proprietors. Reprint edition, Peking, 1940.
CLAREMONT Oriental Studies; an occasional publication of the Society for orient-
    al studies at Claremont colleges. no. 1-5. [Claremont, Calif., 1939-43.
DEUTSCHE Gesellschaft für Natur- und Völkerkunde Ostasiens, Tokyo. Mitteil-
    ungen. bd. 1- (1873/76+) Yokohama [etc., 1873-92]; Tôkyô [etc., 1893]-date.
    Supplement. bd. 1-  Yokohama [1889]; Tôkyô [etc., 1892]-date.
——. Nachrichten. no. 1- 20. Juli 1926-.
DEUTSCHE Morgenländische Gesellschaft. Zeitschrift. Bd. 1-  Leipzig, 1847-
ÉCOLE FRANCAISE D'EXTRÊME-ORIENT, Hanoi. Bulletin de l'École francaise
    d'Extrême-Orient. t. 1- Hanoi et Saigon, 1901- Quarterly, 1901-11; irreg-
    ular, 1912-.
HARVARD Journal of Asiatic Studies. v. 1-  Apr. 1936- Cambridge, Harvard-
    Yenching institute, 1936-.
INSTITUT belge des hautes études chinoises, Brussels. Mélanges chinois et
    bouddhiques. Tome 1-19. Louvain, M. Istas, 1933-51.
——. Rapports, No. 1-6, 1929-31, 1932-33, 1933-35, 1935-36, 1936-37, 1937-
    38. Bruxelles, 1931-39. 6 v.
JOURNAL asiatique. t. 1- Paris, Société asiatique, 1822-.
JOURNAL of East Asiatic Studies. v. 1- Oct. 1951-  Manila, University of Ma-
    nila, 1951-.
JOURNAL of Oriental Literature. v. 1- Honolulu, 1947-  Annual (irregular)
    1947-52; semiannual 1953-  Publication of the Oriental Literature Society,
    University of Hawaii.
JOURNAL of Oriental Studies. v. 1- [Semiannual] [Hong Kong] Hong Kong Uni-
    versity Press, 1954-.
LONDON. UNIVERSITY. School of Oriental and African Studies. Bulletin. v. 1-
    London, 1917-.
MONUMENTA Serica; journal of oriental studies of the Catholic university of
    Peking. v. 1- 1935/36-48; 1949/55-  Peiping, and Nagoya, [1936-date.
The NEW China Review. v. 1-4. Mar. 1919-Dec. 1922// Shanghai, New China
    Review Office [1919-22// Editor: Mar. 1919- Samuel Couling.
ORIENS. v. 1- [2 no. a year] Leiden, E. J. Brill, 1948- "Milletlerarasi Şark
    Tetkikleri Cemiyeti mecmuasi. Journal of the International Society for Orient-
    al Research.''
ORIENS Extremus; Zeitschrift für Sprache, Kunst and Kultur des Länder des
    Fernen Ostens. [Heft] 1-  Weisbaden, O. Harrassowitz, 1954-.
ORIENT et Occident. 1. -  année; août 1934-  Genève, Bibliothèque sino-inter-
    nationale [1934-36// Editor: Tienshe Hu].
PHI THETA annual; papers of the Oriental languages honor society, University
    of California. Berkeley, 1947-.
ROYAL ASIATIC SOCIETY OF GREAT BRITAIN AND IRELAND. London. Jour-
    nal. v. 1-  London, 1834-.
——. North China Branch, Shanghai. Journal. v. 1-2, 1858-60; n. s. v. 1-73,
    1864-1948. Shanghai, 1858-1948.
——. North China Branch, Shanghai. Extra volumes. v. 1-  1915-.
SCHWEIZERISCHE Gesellschaft für Asienkunde. Mitteilungen. v. 1-8. St. Gal-
    len, 1839-1946// Superseded by Asiatische Studien.
SINICA [Zeitschrift für Chinakunde und Chinaforschung] 1-17 jahrg.; 1925-42//
    Heidelberg, N. Kampmann, 1925-42. ''Veröffentlichung des China-instituts
    zu Frankfurt am Main.'' Title varies: v. 1 (1925-27) Chinesische Blätter für
    Wissenschaft und Kunst. v. 2-  (1927- ) Sinica. Editor: Richard Wilhelm,
    Erwin Rouselle.
SINOLOGICA; Zeitschrift für chinesische Kultur und Wissenschaft. Review of
    Chinese culture and science. [Quarterly] v. 1-  1948-  Basel, Verlag für

Recht und Gesellschaft, 1948-
SINOLOGISCHE Arbeiten. [Heft] 1-3. Peking, Deutschland-Institut, 1943-45.
STOCKHOLM. Östasiatiska samlingarna. Bulletin. no. 1-  Stockholm, 1929-.
STUDIA Orientalia. v. 1- Helsinki, Societas Orientalis Fennica, 1925-.
T'IEN Hsia Monthly. v. 1-  Aug. 1935-  [Shanghai, Kelly and Walsh, ltd., 1935-
    41//.
TOKYO. TŌYŌ BUNKO. Memoirs of the Research department of the Toyo bunko
    (the Oriental library) no. 1-  Tokyo, Toyo Bunko, 1926-
T'OUNG pao. Archives concernant l'histoire, les langues, la géographie, l'ethno-
    graphie et les arts de l'Asie orientale. v. 1-10, avril 1890-99; sér. 2. v. 1-
    Leiden, E. J. Brill, 1890-date. Index général, 1890-1944. Leiden, E. J. Brill,
    1953.
WENNTI Papers. v. 1-  New Haven, Sinological Seminar, Yale University, 1954-.

## Communist and Anti-Communist

ALL-CHINA DEMOCRATIC WOMEN'S FEDERATION. Women of China [Quarterly]
    1952-date. Peking, Foreign Languages Press, 1952-date.
ASIAN Peoples' Anti-Communist League. Bulletin. v. 1- Taipei, 1954- date.
CANADIAN Far Eastern Newsletter, 1948-  Toronto, 1948-  Editor: James C.
    Endicott.
CHINA (People's Republic of China, 1949-) Diplomatische Mission, Germany
    (Democratic Republic, 1949-) Presse-Bulletin, Berlin, 1952-54.
——. Embassy, Germany (Democratic Republic, 1949-) Bulletin, 1954-  Ber-
    lin, 1954-.
——. Legation. Switzerland. Bulletin d'information. Berne, 1952-.
CHINA Digest. [biweekly] v. 1-5. Hong Kong, 1946-50// Superseded by Peo-
    ple's China.
CHINA News Analysis: weekly study of Communist China, economic, political,
    cultural, social conditions and development. Kowloon, H. K. 1, Ag 25, 1953-.
CHINA Pictorial. [Monthly] Jan. 1951- [Peking].
CHINA Reconstructs. v. [1]-  Peking, 1952-.
FAR East Spotlight. v. 1-6, no. 3. New York, Committee for A Democratic
    Far Eastern Policy, 1945-50// v. 1, no. 1-13 as Committee's Information
    Bulletin; v. 2, no. 1-v. 3, no. 4 as Spotlight on the Far East.
FREE China and Asia; a monthly report on the free Chinese struggle against
    communism, vol. 1, no. 1, 1954-  Taipei, Asian People's Anti-communist
    League, 1954-.
FREE China Information. No. 1- London, 1952-.
FREE China Review. [Monthly] v. 1- [Taipeh] 1951-.
PEOPLE'S China. [Semi-monthly] v. 1-  Peking [Foreign Languages Press],
    1950-.
UNION Research Service. [Semiweekly] [v. 1]-  Kowloon, H. K., 1955-.
U. S. Consulate. Hong Kong. Current Background. Hong Kong, 1950-.
——. Survey of China Mainland Press. Hong Kong, 1950-.
——. Survey of Hong Kong Press. Hong Kong, 1950-.
——. Chinese Communist Propaganda Review. Hong Kong, 1951-.
——. Highlights of Chinese Communist Press. Hong Kong, 1952-.
U. S. Embassy. Thailand. Translations from the Chinese Press. Bangkok, 1955-.

## Economics and Foreign Trade

ANGLO-CHINESE CHAMBER OF COMMERCE. London. Journal of the Anglo-
    Chinese Chamber of Commerce. London, 1947-.
ASSOCIATION économique franco-chinoise. v. 1, Paris, 1921-.
AUSTRALIA-NEW ZEALAND and Far East Trade. [London, Millington Publica-
    tions, etc.] see Far East Trade

BANK OF CHINA. Financial and Commercial Monthly Bulletin. v. 1-6, No. 1,
     January 1930-January 1939// 1930-34 as its Financial Market Statistics.
——. Fortnightly letter on economic conditions in China. No. 1-? Chungking,
     1943-45//.
——. Monthly Economic Review. No. 1- Taipei, 1950-.
BRITISH Chamber of Commerce Journal. v. 1-7. Shanghai [1915-21//].
BULLETIN commercial d'Extrême-Orient. Shanghai, v. 1, 1916-39.
CENTRAL BANK OF CHINA. Bulletin. v. [1]-6. no. 3. Mar. 1935-Sept. 1940//
     Shanghai and Chungking, 1935-40. Quarterly. Pub. by the bank's Economic
     Research Dept.
——. Central Bank Monthly. n. s. v. 1-4, no. 2. Shanghai, 1946-49//.
CHINA. National Tariff Commission. Statistical Series, 1-6. Shanghai, 1930-37.
CHINA. News Service. Economic Weekly Bulletin. no. [1]- New York, 1946-48.
     Title varies: Oct. 7, 1946-Aug. 11, 1948, Economic bulletin.
CHINA-AMERICA COUNCIL OF COMMERCE AND INDUSTRY. Annual Report.
     1944/45- [New York, 1945].
——. China Trade News. v. 1-3. [New York] 1944-47//.
CHINA Corporation Digest. [New York?] 1944-45. Continuation of William Hunt's
     China Letter 1-9.
The CHINA Economic Annual. 1940- Tokyo, Japan Manchoukuo Year Book Co.,
     1940-.
CHINA Economist. [Weekly] v. 1-5, no. 6, Apr. 5, 1948-May, 1949// [Shang-
     hai, Millard Publishing Co.] "Economic supplement of the China weekly re-
     view" (later China monthly review).
The CHINA Exporter. [Quarterly] no. 1-3. [Shanghai, S. B. Bosack, 1939-40//.
CHINA News and Views Digest ("Economic digest") Shanghai, 1939-41//.
CHINA Trade and Economic Newsletter. v. 1- London, British Council for the
     Promotion of International Trade, 1955-.
CHINA Trade Monthly. v. 1- Shanghai, Foreign Trade Association of China,
     1947-49//.
The CHINESE Economic and Statistical Review. v. 1-8. Jan. 1934-41. Shang-
     hai, China Institute of Economic and Statistical Research [1934-41//].
CHINESE Economic Journal and Bulletin. v. 1-20; Jan. 1927-June 1937. [Shang-
     hai] Bureau of Foreign Trade, Ministry of Industry; [etc., etc., 1927-37].
The CHINESE Economic Monthly. v. 1-3; Oct. 1923-Dec. 1926, Peking, Chinese
     Government Bureau of Economic Information, 1923-26.
CHINESE INDUSTRIAL COOPERATIVES. Gung Ho News. June 1946-March 1949.
     Shanghai, 1946-49//.
COOPERATIVE LEAGUE OF CHINA. Taipei. Chinese Cooperator, No. 1- Tai-
     pei, 1953-.
DEUTSCHE Handelskammer Schanghai. Jahresbericht. 1929/30. Schanghai, 1930.
EAST Asia Economic Intelligence Series. no. 1- Tokyo, 1939-.
FAR EAST Trade. [London, Millington Publications] 1947-53. Title varies:
     —Dec. 1947, China trade and engineering.—Jan. 1948-May, Nov. 1951, May
     Nov. 1952, Far East trade and engineering.—Mar.-Oct. 1953, Australia-
     New Zealand and Far East trade.
FAR EASTERN Economic Review. v. 1. Oct. 16, 1946+ Hong Kong, [E. E. Hal-
     pern] 1946-.
FAR EASTERN Investor's Year-Book; a chronicle of companies and trade. [1st]-
     1925- Shanghai, "Capital and trade" [1925]-.
FINANCE and Commerce (Weekly), v. 1-38, No. 23, 1920-Dec. 1941. Shanghai,
     1920-41// Title varies: v. 1-12, China and Far East Finance and Commerce.
FOREIGN TRADE ASSOCIATION OF CHINA. South Seas Trade Series 1-V//
     Shanghai, 1926-36.
INDUSCO Bulletin. v. 1-12. [New York, American Committee in Aid of Chinese
     Industrial Cooperatives], 1941-52//. Monthly -Aug. 1948; quarterly (irregular)

autumn 1948-52.
INSPECTION and Commerce. v. 1-8. Shanghai, [1930-37].
NANKAI Social and Economic Quarterly. v. [1]-12. [Tientsin, etc., 1928-41.
  Publication suspended from Aug. 1937 to Dec. 1939, inclusive. Title varies:
  1928-33, Nankai weekly statistical service. 1934, Monthly bulletin on econo-
  mic China. 1935- Nankai social and economic quarterly.
NATIONAL Economic Bulletin, Nos. 1-2, Aug. -Sept. 1928. New York, China
  National Economic Bureau, 1928.
NATIONAL Reconstruction. v. 1- New York, Committee on Wartime Planning
  for Chinese Students in the United States, 1942-47.
OSTASIATISCHER Verein Hamburg-Bremen. Jahresbericht. Hamburg, 1929-.
THREE-MONTHLY economic review [of] China, Hong Kong, North Korea. Lon-
  don, Economist Intelligence Unit, 1955- Title varies: -Dec. 1955, Quarterly
  economic review of China and Hong Kong.
THREE-MONTHLY economic review of Japan, Formosa, S. Korea. London,
  Economist Intelligence Unit, 1955- Title varies: -Nov. 1955, Quarterly
  economic review of Japan.
U. S. Bureau of Foreign and Domestic Commerce. Far Eastern Financial Notes.
  [Washington, 1925-40.
WEDNESDAY Evening Post associated with Finance and Commerce. v. 1- No.
  1-20, July 18, 1928-Nov. 28, 1928// Shanghai, 1928-.

## Law and International Relations

BULLETIN on China's Foreign Relations [and Public Events in the Far East]
  [v. 1]-3, no. 1; Oct. 1931-Jan. 1935. Nanking [1931-35]// Vol. 1, no. 1-11
  published by the faculty of the University of Nanking; v. 1, no. 12-v. 3, no.1
  by the Foreign relations association (v. 1, no. 12-v. 2 under its earlier name,
  International relations club).
CHINA. Ministry of Foreign Affairs. Information Bulletin no. 1- Nanking, [1933-
  34.
CHINA Institute of International Affairs. [Publications] [Shanghai] 1939-40//.
The CHINA Law Review. v. 1- Apr. 1922- Shanghai, [1922- "Published by
  the Comparative law school of China, law department of Soochow university."
The CHINESE Administrator. v. 1, no. 1-3; Jan./Mar.-July/Sept. 1935. Shang-
  hai, China United Press [1935]//.
CHINESE Association for the United Nations. Newsletter. [Monthly] v. 1- (1951- )
  Taipei, 1951-.
The CHINESE Social and Political Science Review. v. 1-24. Peking, 1916-41//.
INSTITUTE of Social Research, Peking. Bulletin. [no.] 1-7; Dec. 1928-Dec. 1933.
  Peiping, 1928-33.
The POLITICAL Review. Published by the Political department of the Headquar-
  ters of the National Revolutionary Army. v. 1- June 6, 1927- Canton, 1927-//.
SHANGHAI. UNIVERSITÉ L'AURORE. Mélanges juridiques. t. 1- Paris, Re-
  cueil Sirey, 1946- .
The YENCHING Journal of Social Studies. v. 1- June 1938-49. Peking, Yen-
  ching University [1938-49] Suspended between Aug. 1941-Aug. 1948.

## Religion

ANNUAIRES des missions catholiques de Chine. 1901- Changhai, Bureau sino-
  logiqe de Zi-ka-wei, 1901-22; Sér. 1, 1901-22 "Annuaire de l'Observatoire
  de Zi-ka-wei." Sér. 2, 1922-32 "Missions, seminars, écoles en Chine,"
  1933-47 "Annuaires des missions catholiques de Chine." Sér. 3, 1948-49
  "Annuaire de l'église catholique."

BULLETIN catholique de Pékin. Pékin, Impr. des Lazaristes du Pé-t'ang, 1914-194?

CATHOLIC CHURCH IN CHINA. Synodal Commission. Collectanea Commissionis Synodalis. v. 1-19. Maius 1928-47. Peking, 1928-47. Issues for 1925-28 have caption title: Dossiers de la Commission synodale. Digest of the Synodal Commission.

CHINA Bulletin. v. 1-  New York, Far Eastern Joint Office, National Council of the Churches of Christ in U. S. A. 1952-.

CHINA INLAND MISSION. Miscellaneous publications. No. 1-  London, 1940-.

CHINA Missionary Bulletin. v. 1-2, n. s. v. 1-4. Hong Kong, Catholic Truth Society, 1948-53. Supersedes in part Collectanea commissionis synodalis. 1948-49 as Chinese Missionary.

CHINA Sunday School Journal. v. 1-  Shanghai, China Sunday School Union, 1913-34//.

CHINA'S millions. v. 1-17, 1875-92; n. s. v. 1-78, 1893-1952. London, China Inland Mission, 1875-1952//. Its North American ed. 1893-  Continued as The Millions beginning with v. 78, no. 6, June. 1952.

CHINESE Christian Monitor. v. 1-2. Nov. 15, 1926-June 15, 1927. New York, First Chinese Presbyterian Church, 1926-27.

The CHINESE Recorder. [Monthly] Foochow, Printed by Rozario, Marcel and Co., 1868-72; Shanghai, American Presbyterian Mission Press [etc.] 1874-1941. Supersedes the Missionary recorder. Publication suspended from June 1872 to December 1873, inclusive. From June 1870 to January 1912 title reads: The Chinese recorder and missionary journal.

FAR EAST; a magazine devoted to the conversion of China. v. 1-  Omaha, Neb. 1876-.

The MILLIONS. [Philadelphia] China Inland Mission, 1952-.

Les MISSIONS de Chine et du Japon. Année 1-  Pékin, Impr. des Lazaristes, 1916-  Editor: J. M. Planchat.

PROTESTANT Episcopal Church in the U. S. A. Hankow (Missionary district) Newsletter. Hankow.

VISVA-BHARATI annals. v. 1- Santiniketan, 1945-.

WEST CHINA Missionary News. [Monthly] 1899-1926? [Chengtu] West China Missions Advisory Board, 1899-1926.

## Education and Psychology

ACADEMIA SINICA. National Research Institute of Psychology, Peking. Contributions. v. 1-  Peiping [etc., 1932-.

——. Monographs of the National research institute of psychology, Academia sinica. no. 1-  ; Mar. 1932-  Peiping, National research institute of psychology [1932-.

CANTON University Forum published by the Canton University. v. 1 (no. 1-8); Jan. 10-Apr. 25, 1938. [Canton, 1938]//.

CATHOLIC University of Peking. Bulletin. No. 1-9. Peking, 1926-34.

CHINA. Board of Trustees for Administration of Boxer Indemnity Funds remitted by the British Government. Report. [Nanking? 1931-194-?

CHINA Call. v. 1-  Rolla, Mo., Chinese Students Association of the South, 1941-.

CHINA Christian Educational Association. Bulletin. No. 1-20. Shanghai, 1924-28.

CHINA Foundation for the Promotion of Education and Culture. Report. 1st-1925/26-  Peking, 1926-.

CHINESE Christian Student. v. 1-  New York [Chinese Students' Christian Assn. in North America] 1925-47//.

CHINA INSTITUTE IN AMERICA. Occasional Bulletin. v. 1-9. New York, 1926-36//.

——. China Institute Bulletin. v. 1-  New York, [1936-47//.

——. China and America; a chronicle of cultural relations. v. 1-2, no. 3; Mar. 1948-June 1949// [New York] 1948-49.

The CHINESE Journal of Psychology. v. 1; Sept. 1936-June 1937. [ Peiping, 1936-
    37]//.
CHINESE NATIONAL ASSOCIATION FOR THE ADVANCEMENT OF EDUCATION,
    Peking. Bulletin on Chinese Education. v. 1-4. Shanghai, Commercial Press,
    1922-26//.
CHINESE Student. v. 1-2, No. 5 (Dec. 1935-June 1938) Chicago, 1935-38//.
CHINESE Student; Far Eastern magazine. v. 1-3, no. 6; Nov. 1937-summer
    1941. [New York] Chinese students association of America [etc., 1937-.
The CHINESE Students' Monthly. 1905-28. [New Haven] Chinese Students' Alli-
    ance of Eastern States, 1905-28.
COMITÉ interuniversitaire sino-belge. Bulletin annuel. Bruxelles, 1931-37.
FU Jen Magazine. [Bi-monthly] v. 1-18. Mar./Apr. 1932-June 1949. Peking,
    Catholic University press, 1932-34; Techny, Ill., 1935-49.
FU Jen News-letter (Catholic University of Peking) no. 1-12; Mar. 1931-Feb.
    1932. Peking, Catholic University Press, 1931-32.
SHANGHAI. Université l'Aurore. Bulletin. no. 1-19, 1909-19, s2, no. 1-40,
    1919-40, s3, v. 1-9, 1940-48. Shanghai, 1909-48//. no. 1-12 as its Bulletin
    de littérature et de droit.
UNITED BOARD FOR CHRISTIAN COLLEGES IN CHINA. Annual report. [New
    York] 1943-51.
U. S. Dept. of State. Division of Cultural Cooperation. News notes for Chinese
    Students. Nov. 1942-Apr. 1945. Washington, 1942-45.

## Literature

L'AMI; revue bi-mensuelle. v. 1,   Pékin, Université de Yenching, 1937-38.
CHINESE Literature. autumn 1951-date. [Peking, Foreign Languages Press]
    1951-.
CONTEMPORARY Scene; a play quarterly. v. 1-  New York, China Aid Coun-
    cil in cooperation with the Cultural Department of the American League for
    Peace and Democracy, 1938-.
FOLKLORE Studies. v. 1-  1942-  [annual] [Peking] Catholic University, 1942-.
LEAVES from a Western Garden; a magazine devoted to the Orient. Edited by
    Helen B. Chapin. [Quarterly] v. 1-(no. 1-4); Jan. -Oct. 1938. [Mills College,
    Calif., 1938].
LECTURES chinoises. No. 1-  Édités par André d'Hormon. Peking, [Centre
    Franco-Chinois d'Études sinologiques] 1945-  Peiping 1, Jan. 1945//.

## Art

AMSTERDAM. RIJKSMUSEUM.   Bulletin of the Society of Friends of Asiatic
    Art. Amsterdam, 1953-.
ARS Orientalis; the Arts of Islam and the East. v. 1-  [Washington] 1954-  Issued
    by Freer Gallery of Art, Smithsonian Institution and Fine Arts Dept., Univer-
    sity of Michigan.
ARTIBUS Asiae. 1925/26-  Hellerau-Dresden, Avalun-Verlag [1925-.
ARTS asiatiques. t. 1-  Paris, Presses univeritaires de France, 1954-  Super-
    sedes Revue des Arts Asiatiques.
BULLETIN of Eastern art. No. 1-  1940-  July/Aug. 1941. Tokyo, The Society
    of Friends of Eastern Art, 1940-41.
CHINESE ART SOCIETY OF AMERICA. Archives. [v.]1-  [New York] 1945/46-.
EASTERN Art. v. 1-3; July 1928-31. Philadelphia, College Art Association,
    c 1928-31//. Vol. 1, quarterly (July 1928-Apr. 1929); v. 2-3, annual (1930-
    31).
FAR EASTERN Ceramic Bulletin. no. 1- [Quarterly] [Ann Arbor?] Far East-
    ern Ceramic Group, 1948-.
JAHRBUCH der Asiatischen Kunst. 1-2. Leipzig, 1924-1925//.

ORIENT Art. v. 1-4. 1948-51; n. s. 1955-  London, 1948-51; 1955-  .
ORIENTAL CERAMIC SOCIETY. London. Transactions. 1921/22-  London, 1922-  .
OSTASIATISCHE Zeitschrift. Beiträge zur Kenntnis der Kultur und Kunst des Fernen Ostens. 1. -  Jahrg.; apr. 1912-43. Berlin, Oesterheld und co., 1912-43.
PARIS. MUSÉE GUIMET. Annales. Bibliothèque d'études. t. 1-  Paris, 1892-19-  .
――――. Bulletin archéologique. fasc. 1-2. Paris, 1921//.
REVUE des arts asiatiques. 1-  1924-39. Paris, Librairie des arts et voyages, 1924-39//.
YEAR Book of Oriental Art and Culture. 1924/25. London, E. Benn, 1925-//
Editor: Arthur Waley.

### Library Science and Bibliography

BULLETIN of Far Eastern Bibliography. v. 1-5; Feb. 1936-40. Washington, D. C., Committees on Far Eastern Studies, American Council of Learned Societies, 1936-40//. Continued in Far Eastern Quarterly.
PEKING. NATIONAL LIBRARY. The Metropolitan Library Record. v. 1, no. 1-4; Oct. 1928-July 1929. Peiping, Metropolitan Library, 1928-29//.
――――. Annual report, 1926/27-1938/39. Peking, 1927-28; Peiping, 1929-39//.
PHILOBIBLON; a Review of Chinese Publications. v. [1]-II. Nanking, National Central Library, 1946-48//.
QUARTERLY Bulletin of Chinese Bibliography. [Combined ed. ] v. 1, 1934-v. 4, 1937. Shanghai, Chinese National Committee on Intellectual Cooperation, 1934-37.
――――. English ed. v. 1-4, n. s. v. 1-8. Shanghai, etc. Chinese National Committee on Intellectual Cooperation and the National Library of Peiping, 1934-37, 1940-48//.
SCRIPTA SINICA. v. 1-2. Pékin, Centre franco-chinois d'études sinologiques, 1945-46//.

### General Science

ACADEMIA SINICA. Science Record. v. 1-5. Chungking, Nanking and Peking, 1942-52//.
――――. Scientia Sinica. v. 1-  Peking, 1952-  v. 1-3, no. 2 as Acta Scientia Sinica.
ACTA Brevia Sinensia. no. 1-2. Chungking, 1943-44//.
AMOY. UNIVERSITY. Collected Papers in Science and Engineering. v. 1-2. Changting, National University of Amoy, 1943-44//.
――――. Natural Science Bulletin. Amoy, Science College, University of Amoy, 1934-  .
CHINA Science Service. (Monthly). Chungking, Sino-American Cultural Service, 1944-46//.
CHINESE ASSOCIATION FOR THE ADVANCEMENT OF SCIENCE. The Transactions. vol. 9-10. Shanghai, 1947-48//.
――――. Bulletin. v. 1-  Taipei, 1953-  .
HANGCHOW. NATIONAL UNIVERSITY OF CHEKIANG. Science Reports. v. 1-Hangchow, 1933? -  .
NANKING. NATIONAL CENTRAL UNIVERSITY. Science Reports. Ser. A: Physical Sciences, 1930-36? Nanking, 1930-36//.
NYSTROM INSTITUTE FOR SCIENTIFIC RESEARCH IN SHANSI. Contributions. 1-8. Peking, 1922-24//.
PEKING, NATIONAL UNIVERSITY. Science Quarterly. v. 1-5; Oct. 1929-Sept. 1935. Peiping, College of Science, National University of Peking, 1929-35//.

Superseded by its Science reports.
――. The Science Reports. v. 1-        Peiping, College of Science, National University of Peking, 1936-37//. Supersedes its Science quarterly.
――. Acta Scientiarum Naturalium. Universitatis Pekinensis. v. 1-        Peking, 1955-  .
PEKING. NATIONAL TSING HUA UNIVERSITY. The Science Reports of National Tsing Hua University. Series A: Mathematical and physical sciences. v. 1-Apr. 1931-48. Peiping, 1931-48//.
PEKING. UNIVERSITÉ FRANCO-CHINOISE. Faculté des sciences. Bulletin. 1-3. [Peiping] 1934-36//.
SCIENCE and Technology in China. [Bi-monthly] v. 1-2. [Nanking] Natural Science Society of China, 1948-49//. Supersedes Acta brevia sinensia.
SCIENCE SOCIETY OF CHINA. The Transactions of the Science Society of China. v. 1-8. Shanghai, Science Society of China [1922-35//.
――. Memoirs. v. 1-9. Shanghai, Science Society of China, 1924-32//.
SHANGHAI. UNIVERSITÉ L'AURORE. Bulletin des sciences. v. 1-17. Zi-ka-wei, Changhai, 1920-29//.

## Mathematics, Physics and Chemistry

ACADEMIA SINICA. National Research Institute of Chemistry, Shanghai. Contributions from the National Research Institute of Chemistry, Academia Sinica. Research paper no. 1-        Shanghai, 1934-37//.
――. Memoirs. v. 1-10. Shanghai, 1930-33//.
ACADEMIA SINICA. National Research Institute of Physics, Shanghai. Scientific Papers. v. 1-        Shanghai, 1930-37//.
ACTA CHIMICA SINICA. v. 19-        Peking, Chinese Chemical Society, 1952-Supersedes the Journal of Chinese Chemical Society.
ACTA MATHEMATICA SINICA. v. 1-        Peking, Chinese Mathematical Society, 1951-  .
ACTA PHYSICA SINICA. v. 8-        Peking, Chinese Physical Society, 1952-  .
CHINESE CHEMICAL SOCIETY. Journal. v. 1-18. Peking, 1933-51//. Suspended 1937-39. Superseded by Acta Chimica Sinica.
――. Series 11, v. 1-        Taipei, 1954-  .
――. Chemistry. v. 1-        Taipei, 1954.
CHINESE MATHEMATICAL SOCIETY. Journal. v. 1-        Shanghai, 1936-37//.
CHINESE PHYSICAL SOCIETY. Chinese Journal of Physics. v. 1-7. Shanghai, 1933-49//.
NATIONAL ACADEMY OF PEIPING. Institute of Chemistry. Contributions. v. 1-2, no. 9; Jan. 1934-Oct. 1936. Peiping, 1934-36//.
SHANGHAI SCIENCE INSTITUTE. Journal. Section 1. Mathematics, astronomy, physics, geophysics, chemistry and allied sciences. v. 1-        Shanghai, 1933-40// n. s. v. 1-Aug. 1941 - ?

## Astronomy and Meteorology

ACADEMIA SINICA. National Research Institute of Astronomy, Nanking. Reprint series. v. 1-        Nanking, 1930-36//.
ACADEMIA SINICA. National Research Institute of Meteorology, Nanking. Annual Report. v. 1-7. Nanking, 1928-34//.
――. Memoirs, v. 1-14. Nanking, 1929-46//.
ACTA ASTRONOMICA SINICA. v. 1-        Nanking, Chinese Astronomical Society, 1953-  .
ACTA GEOPHYSICA SINICA. v. 1-        Peking, Chinese Geophysical Society, 1952-  .
ACTA METEOROLOGICA SINICA. v. 21-        Peking, Chinese Meteorological Society, 1950-  . Supersedes the Meteorological Magazine.

CANTON. LINGNAN UNIVERSITY. Freeman Meteorological Observatory. Daily
    Meteorological Record. [Canton, 1919-26//.
JOURNAL of the Chinese Geophysical Society. v. 1-4. Nanking, 1948-51//.
ZI-KA-WEI. Observatoire. Revue mensuelle. v. 1-18. Zi-ka-wei, Changhai,
    1913-30//.

## Biology

ACADEMIA SINICA. National Institute of Zoology and Botany, Nanking. Mem-
    oirs of the National Institute of Zoology and Botany, Academia Sinica. Zoolog-
    ical series. no. 1-       Nanking, 1937-   .
ACTA Experimentali Biologica Sinica. v. 1-      Shanghai, Science Press, 1952-  .
ACTA Hydrobiologica Sinica. v. 1-      Peking?, Institute of Marine Biology, Aca-
    demia Sinica, 1956-   .
ACTA Microbiologica Sinica. v. 1-      Peking, Chinese Microbiological Society,
    1953-   .
The AMOY Marine Biological Bulletin. v. 1-      Amoy, Marine Biological Sta-
    tion, University of Amoy, [1936-37//.
CHINESE Journal of Experimental Biology. v. 1-5. Shanghai, 1936-40//.
FOOCHOW. FUKIEN CHRISTIAN UNIVERSITY. Proceedings of the Natural His-
    tory Society of Fukien Christian University, Foochow, v. 1-      Shanghai,
    1928-30//.
MARINE BIOLOGICAL ASSOCIATION OF CHINA. Annual Report. [Peking?]
    1932-33//.
NANKING. NATIONAL CENTRAL UNIVERSITY. Science Reports. Ser. B. Bio-
    logical Sciences; 1930-36? Nanking, 1930-36?//.
PEKING. FAN MEMORIAL INSTITUTE OF BIOLOGY. Annual Report. Peiping,
    The Institute, 1929-36//.
PEKING. NATIONAL TSING HUA UNIVERSITY. The Science Reports of National
    Tsing Hua University. Series B: Biological and psychological sciences. v. 1-
    [Peiping] 1931-48//.
PEKING. YENCHING UNIVERSITY. Bulletin of the Department of Biology of
    Yenching University. v. 1; Jan. -July 1930. Peping, Pub. by the Department
    of Biology, Yenching University [1930]. Combined in September, 1930, with
    the Bulletin of the Peking society of natural history to form one publication
    entitled Peking natural history bulletin, issued jointly by the society and the
    department.
PEKING Natural History Bulletin. v. 1-      1926/27-      [Peiping, Published by
    the Peking Society of Natural History and the Department of Biology, Yen-
    ching University, 1927-      Title varies: 1926/27-1929/30 (v. 1-4) Peking
    society of natural history bulletin. 1930/31-      (v. 5-  ) Peking natural
    history bulletin.
SCIENCE SOCIETY OF CHINA. Biological Laboratory. Contributions from the
    Biological Laboratory of the Science Society of China. v. 1-5. Nanking, The
    Society, 1925-29//.
SHANGHAI. ST. JOHN'S UNIVERSITY. Biological bulletin. No. 1-      Shanghai,
    1931-   .
SHANGHAI SCIENCE INSTITUTE. Journal. Section III. Systematic and morpho-
    logical biology (systematics, ecology, anatomy, histology, embryology) and
    pharmacognosy. v. 1-4; May 1933-July 1940. Shanghai, 1933-48//.
──────. Section IV. Experimental biology and medicine. v. 1-5; Oct. 1932-Mar.
    1941. Shanghai, 1932-41//.
SINENSIA; contributions from the Metropolitan Museum of Natural History, Aca-
    demia Sinica. v. 1-      Nanking, Metropolitan Museum of Natural History,
    Academia Sinica [1929-30//.
SINENSIA; Special Bulletin of the Metropolitan Museum of Natural History, Aca-
    demia Sinica. no. 1-  ; Dec. 1930//  Nanking, 1930//.

## Botany

ACADEMIA SINICA. Institute of Botany. Botanical Bulletin of Academia Sinica.
  v. 1-2. [Shanghai] 1947-48//.
ACTA Botanica Sinica. v. 1-    Peking, Chinese Botanical Society, 1952-  .
ACTA Phytopathologica Sinica. v. 1-    Peking, Chinese Society of Plant Pathol-
  ogy, 1955-  .
ACTA Phytotaxonomia Sinica. v. 1-    Peking, Institute of Botany, Academia
  Sinica, 1952-  .
CHINESE BOTANICAL SOCIETY. Bulletin. v. 1-3. Peiping, 1935-37//.
NATIONAL ACADEMY OF PEIPING. Institut de botanique. Contributions. v. 1-
  6, 1931-36//.
NORTHWEST China Botanical Survey. Contributions, v. 1-    Wukung, 1939-  .
PEKING. FAN MEMORIAL INSTITUTE OF BIOLOGY. Bulletin. Botanical series.
  v. 1-10. Peiping, The Institute, 1929-41//.
SHANGHAI. MUSÉE HEUDE. Notes de botanique chinoise. No. 1-8. October 31,
  1931-48. Changhai, 1931-48//.
SUNYATSENIA. v. 1-7. Canton and Hong Kong, 1930-48//. Suspended 1931-32.

## Zoology

ACTA Entomologica Sinica, v. 1-    Peking, Chinese Entomological Society,
  1952-  .
ACTA Zoologica Sinica. v. 1-    Peking, Chinese Zoological Society, 1949-  .
CHEKIANG. BUREAU OF ENTOMOLOGY. Miscellaneous publication. No. 1-
  Hangchow, 1930-?
————. Year Book. no. 1-    Hangchow, 1931-?
CHINESE Journal of Zoology. v. 1-3. 1935-37. Nanking, Zoological Society of
  China, 1935-37//.
ENTOMOLOGIA et ars. v. 1-    Wukung, Institutum entomologium Choni, 1946-
FISHERIES EXPERIMENT STATION, Canton. Contributions. no. 1-8. Canton,
  1932-  .
SHANGHAI. MUSÉE HEUDE. Fichier entomologique chinois. sér. 1. Changhai,
  194-
————. Notes d'entomologie chinoise. fasc. 1-10. Mars 1929-Dec. 7, 1937.
  Changhai, 1929-37.
————. Notes d'herpétologie. no. 1-    Changhai, 1943-  .
————. Notes de malacologie. no. 1-    Changhai, 194-
————. Notes de mammalogie. no. 1-    Changhai, 1943-  .
————. Notes d'ornithologie. no. 1-    Changhai, 1943-  .

## Geography and Ethnology

ACADEMIA SINICA. Institute of Ethnology. Bulletin. v. 1-    Taipei, 1955-  .
ACTA Geographica Sinica, v. 18-    Peking, Geographical Society of China,
  1952-  . Supersedes the Journal of the Geographical Society of China.
GEOGRAPHICAL SOCIETY OF CHINA. Journal. v. 1-5. Nanking, 1934-38//.
WEST CHINA BORDER RESEARCH SOCIETY. Journal of the West China Border
  Research Society. 1922/23-    Chengtu [1923-45//.

## Geology and Paleontology

ACADEMIA SINICA. National Research Institute of Geology. Shanghai. Memoirs.
  no. 1-    Shanghai, 1928-36//.
————. Monograph[s] of the National Research Institute of Geology. Series A.
  v. 1-4. [Nanking] 1930-34//.
————. Contributions. no. 1-    Shanghai, 1931-?

ACTA Geological Sinica. no. 29-      Peking, Geological Society of China, 1951- .
    Supersedes the Bulletin of Geological Society of China.
ACTA Palaeontologica Sinica. v. 1-      Peking, Chinese Palaeontological Society,
    1953-  .
CHINA. Geological Survey. Bulletin no. 1-37. July, 1919-      Peking, 1919-48//.
──────, Memoirs. Series A-     [Peking] 1920-  .
──────, Memoirs. Series B. Peking, 1919-  .
──────. Special Report. no. 1-7. Peking [1921-45. no. 1-2 as General statement
    of the mining industry.
──────. Cartographic records. no. 1-4. Pehpei, Chungking, The National Geo-
    logical Survey of China, 1943-46//.
──────, Palaeontologia Sinica. Ser. A[-D] Peking, Geological Survey of China,
    1922-48//.
──────. Soil bulletin. no. 1-24. Peiping [etc.] 1931-45//.
──────. Special soil publication. Ser. A. No. 1- ; Ser. B. No. 1-      Peiping,
    1934-  .
──────. Chiufeng Seismic Station. Seismological Bulletin, no. 1-      Peiping,
    1930-  .
──────, Sin Yuan Fuel Laboratory. Contributions from the Sin Yuan Fuel Labora-
    tory No. 1-23. Peiping, 1930-37//.
CHINA. National Resources Commission. Mineral Exploration Bureau. Contri-
    butions to Economic Geology. No. 1-      Kueiyang, 1944-  .
CHINA INSTITUTION OF MINING AND METALLURGY. Bulletin. v. 1-3.  Pe-
    king, China Institution of Mining and Metallurgy [1922-24//.
GEOBIOLOGIA. [Annual] v. 1-2. Peking, Institut de géobiologie, 1943-45//.
GEOLOGICAL SOCIETY OF CHINA. Bulletin of the Geological Society of China.
    v. 1-28. Peking, The Society, 1922-48//.
HUNAN, Geological Survey. Bulletin 1-      Changsha, 1927-  .
──────. Memoir. Ser. A, v. 1-      Changsha, 1934-  .
KIANGSI. Geological Survey. Bulletin. No. 1-7. Nanch'ang and Kanhsien, 1939-
    42//.
──────, Geological memoirs. Ser. A. No. 1-      Nanchang, 1936-  . [Ser. B. in
    Chinese].
KWANGTUNG, Geological Survey. Annual Report of the Geological Survey of
    Kwangtung and Kwangsi. Hongkong, 1928-  .
──────, Palaeontological Memoir, v. 1-      Canton, 1930-  .
──────, Special publication no. 1-      Canton, 1929-  .
──────. Geological Bulletin. N. 1-3. Pingshih, 1943-45//.
PEKING. NATIONAL TSING HUA UNIVERSITY. The Science Reports of National
    Tsing Hua University. Series C: Geological, Geographical and Meteorologi-
    cal Sciences. v. 1-      Peiping, 1936-37; 1947-49//.
SHANGHAI SCIENCE INSTITUTE. Journal. Section II. Geology, palaeontology,
    mineralogy, and petrology. v.  -3, no. 2. Shanghai, 1933-40//.
VERTEBRATA PALASIATICA. v. 1-      Peking, Laboratory of Vertebrate Pale-
    ontology, Academia Sinica, 1957-  .


Medicine and Public Health

ACTA Anatomia Sinica. v. 1-      Peking, Chinese Anatomical Society, 1956-  .
ACTA Nutrimenta Sinica. v. 1-      Peking, Chinese Physiological Society, 1956- .
ACTA Pharmaceutica Sinica. v. 1-      Peking, Chinese Pharmaceutical Associa-
    tion, 1953-  .
ACTA Physiologica Sinica. v. 18-      Peking, Chinese Physiological Society,
    1953-  . Supersedes the Chinese Journal of Physiology.
BULLETIN medical franco-chinois. Peking, 1921-  .
CHINA. Central Epidemic Prevention Bureau. see China. Epidemic Prevention
    Bureau.

CHINA. CENTRAL FIELD HEALTH STATION. Report of the Central Field
    Health Station. 1st-        Apr. 1931/Dec. 1933-      Nanking, 1934-    .
CHINA. EPIDEMIC PREVENTION BUREAU. Monthly returns (by province) of
    the prevalence of communicable diseases in China. Peking, 1925-    .
CHINA. NATIONAL DEFENCE MEDICAL CENTRE. Bulletin. Shanghai, 1947-
    49//.
CHINA MEDICAL BOARD OF NEW YORK. Report. 1954/55-      New York,
    1955-    .
CHINA Medical Journal. v. 1-45. Shanghai, China Medical Missionary Associa-
    tion, ı887-1931//. Continued as Chinese Medical Journal. Title varies: v. 1-
    21, no. 3, as China Medical Missionary Journal.
CHINESE Journal of Medical History. v. 1-2. Shanghai, Chinese Medical His-
    tory Society, 1947-48//.
CHINESE Journal of Nutrition. v. 1-      Anshun, Kweichow, 1946-47//.
CHINESE Journal of Physiology. v. 1-17. Jan. 1927-41. [Peking] Chinese Physi-
    ological Society, 1927-41; 1948-49//. Superseded by Acta Physiologica Sini-
    ca.
———. Report series. No. 1-2, July 1928-32. Peiping, Chinese Physiological
    Society, 1928-32//.
CHINESE MEDICAL ASSOCIATION. Special report series. no. 1-      Shanghai,
    1934-    .
———. Council on Christian Medical Work. News letter v. 1-      Shanghai, 1950-
    Supersedes the English ed. of the Council's Bulletin.
———. Council on Medical Missions. Occasional leaflets, v. 1-8 (No. 1-33); De-
    cember 1932-October 1940. Shanghai, 1932-40//.
CHINESE Medical Journal. v. 46-      Peiping, Chinese Medical Association,
    1932-    . In Jan. 1932 the Chinese Medical Journal absorbed the National
    Medical Journal of China (English ed.) and continued under the above title.
———. Chengtu ed. v. 61A-63A, no. 5. Chengtu, Chinese Medical Association,
    1942-45//.
———. Free China ed. Taipei, Chinese Medical Association, 195-
CHINESE PHYSIOLOGICAL SOCIETY. Chengtu Branch. Proceedings. v. 1-3.
    Chengtu, 1943-45//.
FENCHOW, SHANSI. Harwood Memorial Hospital for Men. Annual report of the
    Fenchow hospitals consisting of the Harwood Memorial Hospital for Men, the
    Kate Ford Whitman Hospital for Women, the Scudder Children's Ward, 1925-
    Fenchow, 1925-    .
The LEPER Quarterly. v. 1-      Shanghai, 1927-43//.
The NATIONAL Medical Journal of China. v. 1-17, Nov. 1915-31. Shanghai
    [etc.] National Medical Association of China, 1915-31//. Merged into Chi-
    nese Medical Journal.
PEKING UNION MEDICAL COLLEGE. Dept. of Pharmacology. Collected Pa-
    pers, 1-6. Peking, 1920-25//. v. 1, no. 1-3 as Contributions.
———. Dept. of Physiology. Contributions. v. 1-6, n. s. v. 1-12. Peking, 1921-
    26, 1927-38//.
———. Hospital. Annual Report of the Superintendent. Peiping [192-1941?
RED CROSS. China. Red Cross Society of China. Report of the Shanghai Inter-
    national Red Cross, October, 1937-March 31, 1939. [Shanghai, Shanghai
    International Committee of the Red Cross Society of China, 1939]//.
ROCKEFELLER FOUNDATION. China Medical Board. Annual Report. 1st-1-12,
    1914/15-1953-54.  New York, 1916-54//. Continued by the Board's report
    1954/55.
SHANGHAI. Henry Lester Institute of Medical Research. Annual Report, 1934-
    Shanghai, 1935-    .
———. Public Health Dept. Report of Commissioner of Public Health. Shanghai,
    Kelly and Walsh, 1923-27//?
———. Université l'Aurore. Bulletin Medical. no. 1-24, oct. 1928-nov/dec

1938, t. 4-14, 1939-49. Zi-ka-wei, Changhai, 1928-49//. no. 1-3 issed as
Supplement medical to Bulletin de l'Université l'Aurore, no. 16, 18-19.
TSINAN. Cheeloo University, College of Medicine. Bulletin, 1948-     Tsinan,
1948 .
——. Cheeloo University, Hospital. Report. Tsinan, 1933- .
——. Leper Hospital. A report dating from July 1, 1926 to July 31, 1932.
Tsinan, 1932.
TUNG-CHI medizinische Monatsschrift. [1.]-     Jahrg.; [Shanghai, 1925-  ].
WUCHANG. Church General Hospital. Report, 1919- .


## Agriculture and Forestry

ACTA Agriculturae Sinica. v. 1-     Peking, Chinese Agricultural Society,
1950- .
ACTA Pedologica Sinica. v. 1-     Peking, Chinese Society for the Study of Soils,
1953- .
CHINA. National Agricultural Research Bureau. Crop Reports. v. 1-7. Nanking
and Chungking, 1933-39//.
——. Agricultura Serica; contributions from the National Agricultural Research
Bureau. v. 1-     Nanking, 1934- .
——. Miscellaneous Publication no. 1-8. Nanking [1934-38//].
——. Special Publication no. 1-20. Nanking [1934-38//].
CHINA. National Forestry Research Bureau. Technical bulletin No. 1-     Nan-
king, 1948-49//.
CHINESE Agricultural News-Letter, v. 1-3, February 1944-February 1946.
Washington, Office of the resident representative of the Ministry of Agricul-
ture and Forestry of the Chinese Government, 1944-46//.
CHINESE Journal of Scientific Agriculture v. 1-2. Chungking, Ministry of Agri-
culture and Forestry, 1943-44//.
FORESTRY Science. v. 1-     Peking, Chinese Forestry Society, 1957- .
LINGNAN Agricultural Journal. v. 1-2, no. 4. Canton, 1934-36//.
LINGNAN Agricultural Review     see   Lingnan Science Journal
LINGNAN Science Journal. v. 1-20. Canton, Lingnan University, 1922-42//.
v. 1-4 as Lingnan Agricultural Review. Suspended publication with v. 20, no.
214, Aug. 1942.
NANKING. UNIVERSITY. College of Agriculture and Forestry. Economic Facts.
no. 1-     Sept. 1936-46//.
——. Special report. Nanking, 193-.
UNITED NATIONS. Food and Agriculture Organization. Annual progress and
program report on food and agriculture for China, 1947-48. Washington,
1948-49//.


## Engineering

ACADEMIA SINICA. National Research Institute of Engineering, Shanghai. Mem-
oirs. no. 1-     Shanghai, 1930- .
——. Report of the National Ceramic Laboratory, 1st-     Shanghai, 1930- .
ACTA Focalia Sinica. v. 1-     Shanghai, Science Press, 1956- .
ACTA Mechanica Sinica. v. 1-     Peking, Chinese Dynamics Society, 1957- .
ACTA Metallurgica Sinica. v. 1-     Peking, Chinese Metallurgical Society,
1956- .
ASSOCIATION OF CHINESE AND AMERICAN ENGINEERS, Peking. Journal of
the Association of Chinese and American Engineers. Peking, 1920-37//.
1926-27 as Oriental Engineer.
C. N. A. C. Monthly Bulletin. v. 1, no. 1-7; May-Dec. 1948//. [n. p.].
C. I. E. journal. [Semiannual] [New York] Chinese Institute of Engineers, A-

merica Section. 1943-44//.

CHINESE Journal of Civil Engineering. v. 1-      Peking, Chinese Society of Civil Engineers, 1954-  .

CHINESE Journal of Mechanical Engineering. v. 1-      Peking, Chinese Society of Mechanical Engineers, 1954-  .

ORIENTAL Motor. v. 1-4, no. 13. Shanghai, 1919-24//.

PEKING. NATIONAL TSING HUA UNIVERSITY. The Engineering Reports of the National Tsing Hua University. v. 1-4. Peiping, 1945-50//.

QUARTERLY Review of Chinese Railways. v. 1-2, no. 1. July 1, 1936-July 1937. Nanking, Institute of Railway Economics, 1936-37//.

## Manchuria

CONTEMPORARY Manchuria; a bi-monthly review of Manchuria. v. 1-5. [Dairen, Manchuria] South Manchuria Railway Company [1937-41//.

EASTERN Asia, an illustrated quarterly. v. 1-      [Tokyo, South Manchuria Railway Company, 1940-

HERALD OF ASIA. Library of contemporary history. Tokyo, Herald Press [pref. 1931-           8 v.

———. Bibliothèque d'histoire contemporaine. Tokyo, Herald Press, 1931- 8 v.

HSINKING. CENTRAL NATIONAL MUSEUM OF MANCHOUKUO. Bulletin. no. 1-2. Sept. 1939-Nov. 1940. [Hsinking, 1939-40//.

HSINKING. INSTITUTE OF SCIENTIFIC RESEARCH OF MANCHOUKUO. Reports of the Institute of Scientific Research, Manchoukuo. v. 1-4. [Hshinching, Institute of Scientific Research of Manchoukuo, 1936-40//.

LIGHT of Manchuria, the monthly organ of the Manchuria Enlightening Society. No. 1-25. Dairen, 1920-23//. Superseded by Manchuria Daily News. Monthly supplement, The Manchurian Month.

MAMCHOUKUO Current Topics. no. 1-4. June 1940-Oct. 1940. [Hsinking] Manchoukuo Press [1940//.

MANCHOUKUO in 1940-41; annual publication of Manchuria Daily News. Hsinking [1940-41//.

MANCHURIA. Council Board. Intelligence Office. First report on the plots to disturb N. Manchuria. Ch'angchun, 1932. 23 p. plates.

———. Dept. of Foreign Affairs. Information bulletin no. 1-224? Hsinking, 1934?-40//.

———. Dept. of Foreign Affairs. Publications. Series no. 1-4. Hsinking, Manchuria [1932-33//.

———. Foreign Office. Manchoukuo today. no. 1-10. Hsinking, 1940//.

MANCHURIA Daily News. Manchuria; semi-monthly publication of the Manchuria Daily News. v. 1-4. Dairen, 1936-41//.

———. Manchurian Month; monthly supplement of Manchuria Daily News. no. 1-152. Dairen, 1922-36.

MANCHURIA RESEARCH SOCIETY. Review. v. 1-2. Harbin, 1926-28//.

MUKDEN. MANCHURIAN SCIENCE MUSEUM. Bulletin. [no.] 1. Mukden, Educational Institute, South Manchuria Ry. Co., 1937//.

SCIENTIFIC EXPEDITION TO MANCHOUKUO, 1st, 1933. Report of the first Scientific expedition to Manchoukuo under the leadership of Shigeyasu Tokunaga, June-October 1933. [Tokyo? 1934-

## Tibet

GRAND ST. BERNARD Thibet. 1. -      Fribourg, 1946-  .

HIMALAYAN Journal; records of the Himalayan Club. v. 1-      Oxford [etc. ]

Clarendon Press, 1929-  .
"URUSVATI," HIMALAYAN RESEARCH INSTITUTE. Annual report of Urusvati,
    Himalayan Research Institute of Roerich Museum, 1929/30-   New York,
    Roerich Museum Press, 1931-  .
——, Journal of Urusvati, Himalayan Research Institute of Roerich Museum.
    v. 1-3. Naggar, Kulu, Punjab. 1931-33//.

## Taiwan

ACTA Geologica Taiwanica. v. 1-    Taipei, National Taiwan University, 1947-  .
CHINESE-AMERICAN Economic Cooperation. [Monthly] v. 1-2, no. 5; Jan. 1952-
    May 1953. Taipei, U. S. Mutual Security Agency Mission to China, 1952-
    53//.
The CHINESE Review of Tropical Medicine, v. 1-    Taipei, Institute of Tropi-
    cal Medicine, National Taiwan University, 1948-  .
FORMOSAN Science. v. 1-    Taipei, Formosan Association for the Advance-
    ment of Science, 1947-  .
JOINT COMMISSION ON RURAL RECONSTRUCTION IN CHINA (U. S. and China).
    Economic Digest Series. no. 1-    Taipeh, 1952-  .
NEW Taiwan Monthly. Aug. 1946-Mar. 1947. [Taipei, Stanway Cheng].
OCEANOGRAPHICA Sinica. v. 1-    February, 1953. Taipei, 1953-  .
TAIWAN AGRICULTURAL AND FORESTRY CORPORATION. Statistical Year
    Book, 1946-51—
TAIWAN. Agricultural Research Institute. Agricultural Research v. 1-    Tai-
    pei, 1950-  .
——, Bulletin, 195-    Taipei, 195-.
TAIWAN. Bank of Taiwan. Taiwan Financial Statistics Monthly. v. 1-    Taipei,
    1952-  .
TAIWAN. Department of Agriculture and Forestry. Bureau of Inspection and
    Quarantine. Summary of Inspection and Quarantine Statistics. 1-    Tai-
    pei, 1954-  .
TAIWAN. Fisheries Research Institute. Fish culture report No. 1-    Taipei,
    1954-  .
TAIWAN. Forest Research Institute. Bulletin No. 1-    Taipei, 1947-  .
TAIWAN. Geological Survey. Bulletin No. 1-    Taipei, Dec. 1947-  .
TAIWAN. Industrial Development Commission. Industry of Free China [Monthly]
    v. 1-    Taipei, 1954-  .
TAIWAN. Malaria Research Institute. Annual report. 1st-    Ch'ao-chow, Tai-
    wan, 195-.
TAIWAN. Oceanographical Institute. Bulletin. no. 1-5. Taipei, 1946-49//.
TAIWAN. Provincial Health Administration. Report on health activities in Tai-
    wan province. Taipei, 1947/53-  .
——. Maternal and child health welfare demonstration project. [Report] Tai-
    pei, 1952/54-  .
——, Taiwan V-D control program. Taipei, 1953-  .
——. Malaria control program in Taiwan province. annual report    Taipei,
    1953/54-  .
——. Brief Report, 1953/54 -  .
TAIWAN. Sugar Corporation. Taiwan sugar v. 1-    Taipei, 1954-  .
TAIWAN. Taipei Hydraulic Laboratory. Research Bulletin, 1952-    Taipei,
    1952-  .
TAIWAN. Taiwan Museum. Quarterly Journal. v. 1-    Taipei, 1948-  .
TAIWAN. Tea Experiment Station. Memoirs v. 1-    Taipei, 1954-  .
TAIWAN Production Statistics Monthly. v. 1-    Taipei, Ministry of Economic
    Affairs and Bank of Taiwan, 1956-  .
TAIWANIA. v. 1-    Taipei, Laboratory of Systematic Botany, National Taiwan
    University, 1948.

## Other

ACTA Psychologica Sinica. v. 1-    Peking, Chinese Psychological Society,
  1956-  .
CHINA Clipper Monthly v. 1-    New York, China Stamp Society, 1936-  .
CHINA INTERNATIONAL FAMINE RELIEF COMMISSION. Famine Commission
  Bulletin. v. 1-14. Peking, China International Famine Relief Commission
  [1923-36//.
CHINA Stamp Monthly. v. 1, no. 1-2. Shanghai, 1939-40//.
CHINESE PHILATELIC SOCIETY. Philatelic Bulletin. v. 1-3. Shanghai, 1923-
  27//.
———. Monthly. v. 1-    Shanghai, 1928-  .
NANKING INTERNATIONAL RELIEF COMMITTEE. Report. Nov. 1937/Apr.
  1939. [Shanghai, 1939//.
NUMISMATIC SOCIETY OF CHINA. Bulletin. no. 1-    [Shanghai, 1937-
OPIUM, a world problem; published quarterly by the National Anti-opium Asso-
  ciation of China. v. 1-2. Shanghai [1927-29//.
The SHANGHAI Spectator. [Weekly] v. 1-    [Shanghai, Shanghai Spectator, 1931-

## APPENDIX II: ADDENDA

### General

AMERICAN INSTITUTE OF PACIFIC RELATIONS. China; a selected list of references. New York, 1957. 23 l.

BOL'SHAIA SOVETSKAIA ENTSIKLOPEDIIA. China, eine Grossmacht im Wandel der Jahrtausende; Abriss der Geschichte, Wirtschaft und Kultur mit 4 mehrfarbigen und 8 einfarbigen Karten, sowie 19 Bildtafeln, 33 Bildern und einem ausführlichen Register. [Ins Deutsche übertragen von einem Übersetzerkollektiv] Berlin, Verlag Kultur und Fortschritt, 1957. 464 p. illus., ports., maps (4 fold. col.) ''Китай. Aus: Grosse Sowjet-Enzyklopädie, 2. Ausg., Moskau, 1953, Bd. 21, S. 167-312; ergänzt bis Ende 1956.''

BOWMAN ISAIAH, 1878-1950. Problem of China. Translated by Chang Chi-yun, 張其昀 . Taipei, China Culture Pub. Foundation, 1953. 10 p. (Pamphlets on Chinese affairs).

COLUMBIA UNIVERSITY. EAST ASIATIC LIBRARY. Columbia University masters' essays and doctoral dissertations on Asia, 1875-1956. New York, 1957. 96 p. [Mimeographed].

HINTON, HAROLD C. 1924-    Major topics on China and Japan; a handbook for teachers. Edited by Harold C. Hinton and Marius B. Jansen. [New York] Institute of Pacific Relations, 1957. 326 p. illus.

KYOTO. UNIVERSITY. RESEARCH INSTITUTE OF HUMANISTIC SCIENCE. Silver jubilee volume of the Zinbun-kagaku-kenkyusyo, Kyoto University. Kyoto, 1954. xv, 603 p. illus. plates.

NOACK, LUTZ. Neues China; eine empfehlende Bibliographie. Leipzig, Verlag für Buch-und Bibliothekswesen, 1957. 71 p. (Sonderbibliographien d. deutschen Bücherei, 9).

REVUE BIBLIOGRAPHIQUE DE SINOLOGIE. [annual] Edited by P. van der Loon. 1955- Paris, Mouton. 1957-

### Description and Travel

BERTRAM, JAMES M. Return to China. London, Heinemann [1957] 251 p. illus.

BIDSTRUP, HERLUF. Chinareise. Eindrücke und Zeichnungen von einer Reise durch China vom Februar bis zum April 1955. Die Übersetsung aus dem Dänischen besorgte Ellen Schou. Dresden, Verlag der Kunst, 1957. 1 v. (unpaged) Danish ed.: Kina rejse. København, Forlaget Tiden, 1956.

BROWN, HOMER G. New China as we saw it by Homer G. Brown and Muriel J. Brown. St. Marys, Ontario, 1957. 27 p. illus.

CHINA PICTORIAL. China. [Edited by China Pictorial. Peking, Foreign Languages Press, 1954-55.] 2 v. (chiefly illus., part col.)

FREE CHINA REVIEW. To hell and back. Taiwan, China Cultural Service, 1956. 62 p.

GIGON, FERNAND, 1908-    Chine, cette éternité. Texte et photos de Fernand Gigon. Neuchâtel, La Baconnière [1957] 149 p. illus. (Collection ''Espaces'').

KIESLING, GERHARD. China [von] Gerhard Kiesling [und] Bernt von Kügelgen. Berlin, Verlag Neues Leben, 1957. 62 p., 148 p. of illus. (part col.) col. fold. map (inserted).

KINMOND, WILLIAM. No dogs in China; a report on China today. New York, T. Nelson [1957] London, Oxford University Press; Toronto, University of Toronto Press, 1958. 211 p. illus.

KRAUSZ, GEORG. Kreuz und quer durch China; aus Reisetagebüchern. Berlin, Verlag Volk und Welt, 1957. 225 p. illus.

LUNDKVIST, ARTUR, 1906-  Der verwandelte Drache; eine Reise durch das neue China. [Aus dem Schwedischen übertragen von Otto Schwede] Leipzig, Brockhaus, 1956. 305 p. illus.

MINNEY, RUBEIGH JAMES, 1895-  Next stop--Peking; record of a 16,000 mile journey through Russia, Siberia, and China. London, G. Newnes [1957] 192 p. illus.

PEACE CONFERENCE OF THE ASIAN AND PACIFIC REGIONS. Peking, 1952. What we saw in China by 15 Americans. New York, Weekly Guardian Associates, 1952? 64 p. illus.

PEKING. [Peking, Peking Press] 1956. 1 v. (unpaged, chiefly illus.).

PIERSON-PIÉRARD, MARIANNE. La Chine à bâtons rompus. Photos de Serge Creuz. Courtrai, J. Vermaut [1957] 187 p. illus.

POLO, MARCO. 1254-1323? The travels of Marco Polo. Introd. by Thomas Yoseloff. New York, Fine Editions Press [1956] 359 p.

——. Le livre de Marco Polo, le divisement du monde. Text intégral remis en francais moderne et commenté par Albert t'Serstevens. Paris, Club des editeurs, 1957. 520 p. illus. (Hommes et faites de l'Histoire, 8).

RENOVANZ, PAUL. Tee, Seide, Porzellan. Leipzig, Brockhaus, 1957. 359 p. illus.

SCHMID, PETER, 1912-  China, Reich der neuen Mitte. Frankfurt am Main, S. Fischer [1957] 205 p. illus.

——. Voyage en Chine. Traduit de l'Allemand par Henry Daussy. Paris, Horizons de France, 1957. 160 p. illus.

SEKINO, TADASHI, 1868-1935. Jehol; the most glorious and monumental relics, by Tadashi Sekino and Takuichi Takeshima. Tokyo, Zauho Press, 1937. 28, 254 p.

## Atlases and Gazeteers

CHINA. General Staff. Symbols used on Chinese General Staff maps, 1:10,000; 1:25,000; 1:50,000 [translated by the Army Map Service, Corps of Engineers, U. S. Army, Washington, Army Map Service, 1943. 1v. (unpaged) illus.

CHINA. Geological Survey. Explanation to the geological map of China, scale 1: 1,000,000. Peking-Tsinan sheet, by H. C. T'an, 譚錫疇. Peking, Geological Survey of China 1924. cover-title, 46 p. 74 p., tables, 2 fold. diagr.

——. Explanation to the geological map of China. Scale 1:1,000,000. Taiyuan-Yulin sheet, by C. C. Wang, 王竹泉. Peking, Geological Survey of China, 1926. cover-title, 50, [134] p. incl. tables. 2 fold. plates.

——. Explanation to the geological map of China; scale 1:1,000,000. Nanking-Kaifeng sheet, by C. Li, 李捷. Peiping, Geological Survey of China, 1929. 27 p. 2, 2, 76 p. fold. plates.

The CHINA provincial atlas and geography; the provinces and outer territories of China (including the newly-formed provinces) with key map, contents and index. Shanghai, North-China Daily News and Herald. [1934] [5]-60 p. illus. (incl. maps).

FANG, J. T., 方俊. Map projections. Peiping, Geological Survey of China, 1934. 128 p. incl illus., tables, diagrs. (1 fold.) (China. Geological Survey. Geological memoirs, ser. B, no. 6).

GILES, LIONEL, 1875-1958. Glossary of Chinese topographical terms. [London, Geographical Section, General Staff, War Office] 1943. 29 p.

GT. BRIT. ROYAL AIR FORCE. AIR COMMAND, SOUTHEAST ASIA. China; gazetteer of place names. [Place names included taken from map sheets of

the 1/million Carte Internationale series] Produced by Air Command, S. E. A.,
   War Room. n. p., 1944. 61 l.
HUDSON, GEOFFREY FRANCIS, 1903-    An explanatory atlas of the Far East,
   [2d ed.] by G. F. Hudson and Marthe Rajchman, with a foreword by Sir Arthur
   Salter. London, Faber and Faber, [1942] 143 p. illus. maps.
HUMMEL, SIEGBERT. Namenkarte von Tibet. Kopenhagen, Munksgaard, [195-]
   [2] p., fold. map.
JAPAN. Ministry of Foreign Affairs. Gazetteer of Chinese geographic names.
   Reprint ed. Washington. Military Intelligence Division, 1945.  v, 663 p.
KAO, CHONG-RWEN, 高鍾潤 1914-    The derivation of Chinese place names.
   [Bloomongton, Ill., 1952] 12 p.
NIHON CHIMEI DAI JITEN. Formosan place names. Excerpts from: Nippon chi-
   mei daijiten, by Sawada. [Tokyo, Nihon shobō, 1938] facsim.: 60 l.
PATTEN, ROBERT M, 1919-    A gazetteer of China and Manchuria, arranged
   alphabetically. [Berkely, Calif.] c1949. ii, 102 l.
RAJCHMAN, MARTHE. A new atlas of China, land, air and sea routes; descrip-
   tive text by the staff of Asia magazine, with an introduction by H. E. Yarnell.
   New York, Published for Asia magazine. John Day, [1941] 24 p. illus. (maps).
SHABAD, THEODORE. China's changing map; a political and economic geogra-
   phy of the Chinese People's Republic. Maps by Vaughn S. Gray. New York,
   F. A. Praeger [1956] x, 295 p. maps.
——. Chinas neues Gesicht. Eine wirtschaftspolitische Geographie der chines-
   ischen Volksrepublik. Aus dem Amerikanisch ins Dt. übertragen von Karl
   Krüger. Berlin, Safari Verlag, 1957. 290 p. maps.
TAGUCHI, MINORU. Les noms des lieux habités par les Chinois en Mandchourie.
   Paris, Jouve, 1931. 108 p.
U. S. Army. Far East Command. Manual of conventional symbols and glossaries
   on Japanese maps of northeast Asia areas; Manchuria, Eastern Siberia, Mon-
   golia, and North China. Advance ed. [Tokyo?] Office of the Engineer, General
   Headquarters, Far East Command, 1947. 89 p. illus.
U. S. Army Map Service. Symbols appearing on original Chinese maps, scales,
   1:10,000, 1:25,000, 1:50,000. 2d ed. AMS 2. [Washington] 1944. 22 p. illus.
——. Cartographic notes on large scale maps of China. Washington, D. C.,
   1945. 18 p. maps (3 fold, 2 col.) diagrs, tables.
——. Gazetteer to maps of Formosa (Taiwan) map series AMS L792, scale 1:
   50,000. Washington, 1945. viii, 184 p. 2 col. maps (1 fold.).
——. Gazetteer to maps of China proper, southwest. Map series AMS L582,
   1:250,000. 1st ed., July 1947. Washington, Army Map Service [1947] vi,
   442 p. fold. map.
——. Gazetteer to maps of China Proper, southeast. Map series AMS L581,
   1:250,000. 1st ed., June 1948. Washington [1949] v, 1113 p. fold. col. map.
——. Gazetteer to AMS 1:250,000 maps of Manchuria (AMS series L542) Wash-
   ington, 1955. iv, 228 p. fold. map.
——. Gazetteer to AMS 1:50,000 and 1:250,000 maps of Taiwan (Formosa)
   (series L 792 and L 594) Washington, 1955. vi, 128 p. 2 fold. maps.
U. S. Board on Geographical Names. Guide to geographical names in China.
   Washington, 1944. cover-title, 230 p. (Its Special publication, 24).
——. Gazetteer of Chinese place names based on the index to V. K. Ting atlas.
   Compiled by the United States Board on geographical names. June, 1944.
   Washington [1944] lxxix, 229 p.
——. Place names in Manchuria. Washington, D. C., 1945. 40 p.
——. Directions for the treatment of geographical names in Manchuria. Re-
   vised, January 2, 1945. [Washington, 1945] 56 numb. l. (Its Special pub-
   lication, 6).
——. Place names in Sinkiang. [Washington] 1945. 27 p. (Decision list, 4513).
——. Cumulative list of place names in Mongolia, decision list no. 4517, Oct-
   ober 1945. Washington, D. C. 1946. 24 p.

————. Preliminary NIS gazetteer China. Official standard names prepared in
the division of geography, Department of the Interior. Washington, Central
Intelligence Agency, 1952. 3 v.

————. Decisions on names in China. Washington, 1952. 95 p. (Decision list,
5201).

U. S. Dept. of State. Office of Intelligence Research. Map analysis of Manchuria.
Washington, Dept. of State, Office of Intelligence Coordination and Liaison,
1946. vi, 117 p. fold. col. maps. (Its [R and A] no. 3042).

U. S. Embassy. China. A gazetteer of place names in Formosa (Taiwan), compiled by Charles H. Pletcher, third secretary and vice consul. [Taipei],
1951] 115 l.

U. S. Hydrographic Office. Gazetteer to maps and charts of Formosa(Taiwan)
map series AMS L593, 1:250,000 (First Edition), U. S. Hydrographic Office
navigational charts and miscellaneous sources. Comp. jointly by the Hydrographic Off., U. S. Navy and Army Map Service, Corps of Engineers, U. S.
Army. Washington, Army Map Service, 1944. ix, 139 p. fold. col. map.

————. Gazetteer (No. 15) China coast, December 1945. Washington, Govt.
Print. Off., 1945. vi, 364 p. illus. (map) (H. O. Publ. No. 895).

U. S. Library of Congress. Map Division. A supplementary key to accompany
the V. K. Ting atlas of China (edition of 1934) comp. by L. W. Wadsworth.
Washington, 1949. 22 l. maps.

U. S. Navy. Pacific Fleet and Pacific Ocean Areas. Gazetteer of standard place
names, China coast and the lower reaches of the Ch'ang Chiang (Yangtze)
river [n. p.] 1945. cover-title, v, 125 p. illus. (map) (Its Cincpac-Cincpoa
bulletin no. 74-45). ————Corrections and additions to Gazetteer of standard
place names, China coast and the lower reaches of the Ch'ang Chiang (Yangtze)
river. Supplement to Cincpac-Cincpoa bulletin no. 74-75. [n. p.] 1945. cover-
title, 14, [2] p. (Its Cincpac-Cincpoa bulletin, no. 165-45).

U. S. Office of Censorship. Vocabulary of Chinese place names. Washington,
Library of Chief Cable Censor, 1943. 45 l.

U. S. Office of Coordinator of Information. Research and Analysis Branch. Far
Eastern Section. Glossary of place names of Hainan Island. [Washington]
1942. 6 l. [R and A no. 647].

U. S. Office of Geography. Hong Kong, Macao, Sinkiang, Taiwan, and Tibet;
official standard names approved by the United States Board on Geographic
Names. Washington, Govt. Print. Off., 1955. [vi], 390 p. (U. S. Board
on Geographic Names. Gazetteer, 5).

————. China; official standard names approved by the U. S. Board on Geographic
Names. Washington, Govt. Print. Off., 1956. 2 v. (6, vii, 979 p.) (U. S.
Board on Geographic Names. Gazetteer, 22).

U. S. War Dept. Japanese readings for Chinese place names, arranged by Japanese readings. Washington, Govt. Print. Off., 1945. xlvii, 520 p. map.
(Its War Department technical manual TM 30-488).

## History

BODDE, DERK, 1909-   China's cultural tradition, what and whither?  New
York, Rinehart [1957] 90 p. illus. (Source problems in world civilization).

CHANG, CARSUN, 張嘉森, 1886-   China and Gandhian India. Edited by Kalidas
Nag. Allahabad, Indo-Chinese Literature Publications; Calcutta, Book Co.
[1956]. 318 p.

CHANG, CH'I-YÜN, 張其昀, 1901-   . The essence of Chinese culture 中國
文化要義 . [Taipei, China News Press, 1957] 504 p. illus.

COMMEAUX, CHARLES. De K'ang Hi à K'ien Long; l'âge d'or des Ts'ing (1662-
1796) Paris, Société d'Édition "Les Belles Lettres" 1957. 181 [3] p. (Lyons.
Université. Annales. 3. série, 29).

DEBON, GÜNTHER, 1921-   Chinesische Geisteswelt von Konfucius bis Mao Tse-

tung. Text ausgewahlt und eingeleitet von Günther Debon und Werner Speiser.
Baden-Baden, Holle [1957] 340 p. (Geist d. Morgenlandes).

FRANKE, WOLFGANG, 1912-   Das Jahrhundert der Chinesischen Revolution,
1851-1949. München, R. Oldenbourg, 1957. 299 p. map.

GREGORY, JOHN STRADBROKE. British attitudes and policy toward the Taiping rebellion in China, 1850-1864. London, 1956? 547 l. Thesis--School
of Oriental and African Studies, University of London.

KLEMANN, FRIEDRICH. Europäer und Ostasiaten; die Verschiedenheit ihres
Intellekts. München, E. Reinhardt, 1957. 258 p.

KO, PYŎNG-IK, 高炳翊 , 1924-   Zur Werttheorie in der chinesischen Historio-
graphie auf Grund des Shih-t'ung des Liu Chih-Chi (661-721) 劉知幾 . [Mün-
chen] 1956. 223 l. Diss. --Munich Univ.

LIEBERMAN, SAMUAL. Contact between Rome and China. Ann Arbor, University Microfilms, 1953. (University Microfilms, Ann Arbor, Mich. Publication
No. 6662) ix, 337 l.

LOU, KAN-JOU, 陸侃如 . Histoire sociale de l'époque Tcheou. Paris, L. Rodstein, 1935. 200 p. Thèse--Univ. de Paris.

MICHAUD, PAUL M, 1927-   The rebellion of the Yellow Turbans in China, A.
D. 184. Chicago [Library, Dept. of Photographic Reproduction, University
of Chicago] 1957. Microfilm copy (positive) of typescript. Collation of the
original: 114 l. illus. Thesis--University of Chicago.

PRINCETON UNIVERSITY. Library. East and West: Europe's discovery of China
and China's response to Europe, 1511-1839; a check-list of the exhibition in
the Princeton University Library, February 15-April 30, 1957, compiled by
Howard C. Rice, Jr., Shih-kang Tung 童世綱 [and] Frederick W. Mote.
Princeton, N. J., 1957. xi, 94 l.

SCHULTE-UFFELAGE, HELMUT, 1929-   Das Keng-shen wai-shih, 權衡
庚申外史 , eine Quelle zur späten Mongolenzeit. [München] 1955. 200 l.
maps. Typescript (carbon copy) Diss. --Munich Univ.

TSIEN, TSUEN-HSUIN, 錢存訓 , 1909-   The pre-printing records of China;
a study of the development of early Chinese inscriptions and books. Chicago
[Dept. of Photographic Reproduction, University of Chicago Library] 1957.
Microfilm copy (positive) of typescript. Collation of the original: 302 l. illus.
Thesis--University of Chicago.

WELCH, WINDON CHANDLER. Chinese-American calendar for the 40th through
the 89th year of the Chinese Republic, February 6, 1951 to January 23, 2001.
Rev. Washington, Administrative Division, Immigration and Naturalization
Service, 1957. v. 50 p. (U. S. Immigration and Naturalization Service.
[Publication] M-113).


Politics and Government


Free China


CHIANG, KAI-SHEK, 1886-   Selected speeches and messages in 1956. [Taipei?
1957] 94 p.

------. Selected speeches and messages in 1957. Taipei, 1957. 53 p.

CHINA CULTURAL SERVICE. Free China on the march. Taipei, 1957. 118 p.

CROZIER, BRAIN. I was wrong about Free China. London, Friends of Free
China Association, 1957. 14 p.

FOREIGN reviews on President Chiang's book: Soviet Russia in China. Taipei,
Free China review, 1957. 76 p.

OGDEN, SIR ALWYNE, 1889-   Resurgent China. London, Friends of Free
China Association, 1957. 24 p.

SOONG, MAYLING,蔣宋美齡, 1897-   Selected speeches. Taipei, Govt. Information Off., 1957. 73 p.

THE WEEK, Ankara. Turkey presents Free China. [Ankara, 1955?] 1 v. (unpaged) illus.

## Communist China

CHINA CULTURAL SERVICE. Red terror on the mainland. Rev. ed.  Taipei,
1957.  292 p.

DUPLICITY of Mao's "bloom-contend"policy. Taipei, Free China review, 1957.
112 p. illus.

HYDE, DOUGLAS ARNOLD, 1911-   The mind behind new China. London, Phoenix House [1956]  36 p. (A Background book).

LIAO, KAI-LUNG, 廖蓋隆 . Kurze Geschichte des chinesischen Volksbefreiung-
skrieges. [Übersetzung aus dem Chinesischen: Liselotte Pötz und Gottfried
Spies] Berlin, Deutscher Verlag der Wissenschaften, 1957.  198 p. illus.

MAO, TSE-TUNG, 毛澤東 , 1893-   . The People's Political Council; its past
work and present talks, by Mao Tse-tung [and others] and the present internal
and international situation and the achievements of the Fourth Session of the
People's Political Council, a report by Wang Ming [ 陳紹禹 ] Chungking, 1940.
55 p. (New China Information Committee, Bull. 11.

————. Rectify the Party's style in work. Peking, Foreign Languages Press,
1955.  29 p.

————. Die Lehre von den Widersprüchen. Gekurzte und redigierte Fassung seiner Rede vom 27. Februar 1957. Wiesbaden, Hessische Landeszentrale f.
Heimatdienst, 1957.  44 p. (Hessische Landeszentrale f. Heimatdienst. Son-
derdruckreihe, 9).

————. Über die richtige Lösung von Widersprüchen im Volke [von] Mao Tse-tung.
Entscheidende Siege des Sozialismus in China [von] Tschou En-lai. Berlin,
Dietz, 1957.  95 p.

MIF, PAVEL ALEKSANDROVICH, 1901-  Die Kommunistische Partei Chinas
im Kampfe um die Befreiung des chinesischen Volkes. [Die Übertragung aus
dem Russischen redigierte J. Biefang] Moskau, Verlagsgenossenschaft ausländischer Arbeiter in der UdSSR, 1937.  110 p.

O'DWYER, GREG. The truth about conditions in Communist China.  London,
Friends of Free China Association, 1957.  35 p. (Friend of Free China pamphlet, 6).

PEOPLE'S democracy in China; editorials from the Cominform journal and
"Pravda." Bombay, People's Pub. House [1950?] 16 p.

RICKETT, ALLYN, 1921-   Prisoners of liberation [by] Allyn and Adele Rickett.
[1st ed.] New York, Cameron Associates, 1957.  288 p.

SCHENKE, WOLF. Neue Weltmacht China. Hamburg, Holsten-Verlag, 1957.
319 p. illus. maps.

SNOW, EDGAR, 1905-   Random notes on Red China (1936-1945)  Cambridge,
Chinese Economic and Political Studies, Harvard University; distributed by
Harvard University Press, 1957.  148 p. (Harvard University. Chinese Eco-
nomic and Political Studies. Special series).

TÊNG, HSIAO-P'ING, 鄧小平, 1900-   Report on the Rectification campaign,
delivered at the Third Plenary Session, enlarged, of the Eighth Central Committee of the Communist Party of China on September 23, 1957. Peking,
Foreign Languages Press, 1957.  58 p.

UNION RESEARCH INSTITUTE. Communist China, 1956. Kowloon, Hong Kong
[1957] xl, 236 p. (Communist China problem research series, EC 18).

U. S. Joint Publications Research Service. Political theory and ideology in Communist China. NY-31/1- July 19, 1957- irregular. (Its JPRS/NY report).

————. Mass organizations in Communist China. NY-4/1- July 19, 1957- irregular. (Its JPRS/NY report).

————. Non-technical education in Communist China. NY-3/1- July 26, 1957-
    irregular. (Its JPRS/NY report).
————. Manpower in Communist China. NY-54/1- Oct. 7, 1957- irregular. (Its
    JPRS/NY report).
————. Wages in Communist China. NY-53/1- Dec. 5, 1957- (Its JPRS/NY report).
————. Domestic trade in Communist China. NY-8/1- Dec. 6, 1957- (Its JPRS/
    NY report).
————. Health and sanitation in Communist China. NY-33/1- Dec. 17, 1957 (Its
    JPRS/NY report).
————. Textile industry in Communist China. NY-51/1- Dec. 31, 1957- irregular.
    (Its JPRS/NY report).
WANG, LI-MING, 王力明 . Communist China to-day. Kowloon, H. K., Union
    Press [1957] 101 p.
WEI, HENRY, 韋文趏 , 1909-    Courts and police in Communist China to 1952.
    Produced under contract no. AF 33 (038)-25075. Lackland Air Force Base,
    Tex., Air Force Personnel and Training Research Center, Air Research and
    Development Command, 1955. xi, 63 p. map. ([U. S.] Human Resources Re-
    search Institute. Research memorandum no. 44).

## Foreign Relations

CHINA. (People's Republic of China, 1949-  ) Die Verträge der Volksrepublik
    China mit anderen Staaten. Frankfurt a M., A. Metzner Verlag, c1957.
    105 p. (Hamburg. Institut für Asienkunde. Schriften, Bd. 1).
CHINA VIEWPOINTS. Peking's people's diplomacy. Hong Kong, China View-
    points, 1957?    20 p.
————. Report on Hungary: the Hungarian revolution as presented to the Chinese
    public. Hong Kong, China Viewpoints, 1957.  69 p.
CHOU, EN-LAI, 1898-    Report on foreign affairs at the 33rd session of the
    Central People's Government Council. [Peking, 1954] 11 p. "Supplement
    to 'People's China,' September 1, 1954."
DASGUPTA, DHIRENDRANATH. With Nehru in China.  Calcutta, National Book
    Agency [1955] 148 p. illus., ports.
HENDERSON, H. W. Why Communist China should not be admitted to the United
    Nations; with an address by the Hon. Dr. T. F. Tsiang.  London, Friends of
    Free China Association, 1957.  35 p.
KOHL, MICHAEL. Die Vertretung Chinas im internationalen Verkehr.  Berlin,
    Deutscher Zentralverlag, 1957.  99 p. (Deutsches Institut für Rechtswissen-
    schaft. Schriftenreihe Völkerrecht, Heft 3).
MEZERIK, AVRAHM A., 1901-    ed. Representation of China in the United Na-
    tions.  New York, International Review Service, 1957.  28 p.
THOMSON, JOHN SEABURY, 1921-    The government of the International Set-
    tlement at Shanghai; a study of the politics of an international area.  Ann Ar-
    bor, University Microfilms, 1953.  [University Microfilms, Ann Arbor, Mich.
    Publication no. 6722]  413 l.
U. S. Treaties, etc., 1953-    (Eisenhower) Parcel post. Agreement between
    the United States of America and China signed at Taipei July 30, 1957, and at
    Washington August 19, 1957. [Washington, Govt. Print. Off., 1957] 12 p.
    (Treaties and other international acts series, 3941)
WHITING, ALLEN SUESS, 1926-    Contradictions in the Moscow-Peking axis.
    Santa Monica, Calif., Rand Corp., 1957.  vii, 60 p. (Rand Corporation. Re-
    search memorandum, RM-1992).

## Economic Conditions

BUILDING a new life, stories about China's reconstruction.  Peking, Foreign
    Languages Press, 1955.  163 p. illus.

CH'EN, JACK, 陳伊範 . New earth; how the peasants in one Chinese county solved the problem of poverty. Peking, New World Press [1957] 255 p. illus.

CHENG, CHO-YUAN, 鄭竹園 . Income and standard of living in mainland China.
v. 1. Kowloon, H. K., Union Research Institute, 1957. 166 p.

CH'IAO, SHU-FAN, 焦樹藩 . The oil pressing industry in Hopei province. Peiping, Yu Lien Press, 1934. 59 p. (Yenching series on Chinese industry and
trade, 3).

CHINESE FEDERATION OF LABOR. The objectives and achievement of the Chinese Federation of Labor. Taipei, 1957. 48 p.

CHU, FU-SUNG, 朱撫松 1915-   Price and commodity control in wartime China. Chungking, Chinese Ministry of Information, 1943. 35 p. (China Handbook ser. 16).

FRANCE. Centre national du commerce extérieur. Démocraties populaires: Bul-
garie, Hongrie, Pologne, Roumanie, Tchécoslovaquie, U. R. S. S., République
populaire de Chine. Paris, 1956. 103 p. (Its Cahiers de documentation).

MISSION des économistes belges en République populaire de Chine. Rapport col-
lectif. Bruxelles, Association Belgique-Chine, 1957. [20] p.

ONG, SHAO-ER, 翁紹耳 , 1917-   Agrarian reform in Communist China. [Los
Angeles] University of Southern California, Dept. of Asiatic Studies, 1952.
123 l. diagr. (Studies in Chinese Communism, ser. 1, no. 2).

TAIRE, LUCIAN. Shanghai episode; the end of Western commerce in Shanghai.
Hong Kong, Rainbow Press [1957] 111 p. illus.

U. S. Congress. Senate. Committee on Interior and Insular Affairs. Relationships of river and related water resource development programs of United
States, Soviet Russia, and (Red) China. [Report of Michael W. Straus, committee consultant] Memorandum of the chairman to members of the Senate
Committee on Interior and Insular Affairs. Washington, Govt. Print. Off.,
1957. iii, 26 p. tables.

YANG, HSIEN-TONG, 楊顯東 . Wartime contton industry control in Free China,
a voluntary report. Chungking, 1945. Microfilm copy (negative) of typescript.
Collation of the original: 30 l. diagrs., tables.

## Social Conditions

AVENARIUS, G. G. The Chinese guilds; brief sketch of their history. With colour
printed signs representing different lines of trade. Harbin, Manchuria Research Society [1928] 78 p.; 19 p. illus.

BODARD, LUCIEN. La Chine de la douceur. Paris, Gallimard [1957] 336 p.
illus. (L'Air du temps).

COMBER, LEON. An introduction to Chinese secret societies in Malaya. [Sing-
apore] D. Moore [1957;label: distributed by the Institute of Pacific Relations,
N. Y.] 77 p. illus.

LUKER, PHILIP. Change for China. Hong Kong, China Viewpoints, 1956. 54 p.
illus.

## Philosophy and Religion

CHAO, P'U-CH'U, 趙樸初 . Buddhism in China. Peking, Chinese Buddhist Association, 1957. 55 p. illus.

CHINESE ISLAMIC ASSOCIATION. Chinese Moslems. [Peking, Foreign Languages
Press] 1955. 1 v. (chiefly col. illus.).

CHOW, P. BONAVENTURA SHAN-MOU, 周善謀 , 1923-   Ethica Confucii. Köhn,
1957. 136 p. Diss.--Univ. Köhn.

FA-HSIEN, 法顯 fl. 388-414. A record of the Buddhist countries, translated from
the Chinese by Li Yung-hsi, 李永熙 . Peking, Chinese Buddhist Association,
1957. 93 p. map.

LIEBENTHAL, WALTER, 1886-   Festschrift. Edited by K. Roy. Santiniketan,

1957.　xi, 294 p. plates. (Sino-Indian studies, 3-4).

SIH, PAUL K. T., 薛光前 , 1909-　Chinese culture and Christianity; selected works of Paul K. T. Sih. Compiled and published by China Culture Pub. Foundation. Taipei, 1957.　194 p.

SUN TSE, 孫子 . Ssun-ds'. Traktat über die Kriegskunst.Übers aus dem Altchinesisch ins Russ. u. Anm. von Oberstlt. J. I. Sidorenko. Mit einem Einleitung von J. A. Rasin. Aus dem Russisch ins Dt übertr. von Ina Balcerowiak. Berlin, Verlag des Ministeriums für nationale Verteidigung, 1957.　154 p.

SUZUKI, DAISETZ TEITARO, 1870-　Die Zen-Lehre vom Nicht-Bewusstsein (Zen doctrine of no-mind) Die Bedeutung des Sutra von Hui-neng (Wei-lang). Übers. von Emma von Pelet. München-Planegg, O. W. Barth, 1957.　147 p.

———. Der Weg zur Ehleuchtung; Die Übung des Koan als Mittel, Satori zu verwirklichen oder Erleuchtung zu erlangen. Übers. von Fritz Kraus. Baden-Baden, Holle [c1957] 232 p.

WALDSCHMIDT, ERNST, 1897-　Kusum Mittal, Dogmatische Bogriffsreihen im älteren Buddhismus. 1. Fragmente des Dasottarasutra aus Zentralasiatischen Sanskrit-Handschriften. Berlin, Akademie-Verlag, 1957.　129 p. (Veröffentlichungen des Instituts für Orientforschung der Dt. Akademie der Wissenschaften zu Berlin. Fasc. 34).

YANG, I-FAN. 楊一帆 . Islam in China.　Hong Kong, Union Press [1957] 83 p.

YUNG HSI, 融熙 Abbot. The commentary on Formless Gāthā　無相頌講話 . Translated by Chou Hsiang Kuang 周祥光 . Allahabad, Indo-Chinese Literature Publications, 1956.　92 p.

## Foreign Missions

BURGESS, ALAN. The small woman. London, Evans Bros. [1957] 221 p. illus.

———. The same; New York, E. P. Dutton, 1957.　256 p.

FOSTER, JOHN. 1898-　Chinese realities. London, Edinburgh House Press, 1928.　240 p. diagr.

MCROBERTS, DUNCAN, 1912-　Pleading China. Grand Rapids, Mich., Zondervan Pub. House [1946] 141 p. plates, ports.

MEISTER, HANS. Arzt in China. Bilder aus der ärztlichen Mission. Stuttgart, Evang. Missionsverlag; Basel, Basler Missionsbuchhandlung, 1957.　16 p. (Von Fernen Ufern, 47).

THOMPSON, PHYLLIS. King of the Lisu. Illustrated by Carolyn Canfield. London, China Inland Mission; agents: Lutterworth Press [1956] 63 p. illus.

WATSON, BERNARD, 1906-　Olive in China. Illus. by James Moss. London, Salvationist Pub. and Supplies [1957] 105 p. illus.

## Language

ELEMENTARGRAMMATIK des Neuchinesischen. Deutsche Fassung des grammatischen Lehrbuches der Universität Peking. Ju fa giau sai 語法教材 . Übers. und bearb. von Martin Piasek. Leipzig, O. Harrassowitz, 1957. 287 p

POPPE, NIKOLAÎ NIKOLAEVICH, 1897-　Studia Altaica. Festschrift für Nicholas Poppe zum 60. Geburststag. Wiesbaden, O. Harrasowitz, 1957.　230 p. plates. (Ural-Altaische Bibliothek, 5).

U. S. Army Language School, Monterey, Calif. Chinese Mandarin: newspaper Chinese. Presidio of Monterey, 1957-58 [v. 1, 1958] 4 v.

WANG, LIEN-TSENG, 王聯曾 . Un dictionnaire phonologique des T'ang: "le Tsie yun corrigé et complété" de Wang jen-hiu 王仁昫刊謬補闕切韻 . Leiden, E. J. Brill, 1957.　51-150 p. Reprinted trom T'oung Pao 45:1-3 1957.

## Literature

CHINA VIEWPOINTS. The role of literature in Communist China. Hong Kong,

[1956]  19 p.

CHU, SU-CHÊN, 朱素臣 . Fifteen strings of cash; a Kunchü opera. Original
libretto by Chu Su-chên, rev. by Chou Chuan-ying and others; final version
by Chen Sze, 陳思 . [Translated by Yang Hsien-yi and Gladys Yang] Peking,
Foreign Languages Press, 1957.  84 p. illus.

[CHÜ YÜAN] 屈原 ca. 343-ca. 277 B. C. Die neun Gesänge 九歌. Eine Studie über
Schamanismus im Alten China von Arthur Waley. Aus dem Englischen übertr.
von Franziska Meister. Hamburg, Schröder, 1957.  98 p.

ERDBERG, OSKAR. Die drei Grundsätze des Mister Kung, und andere chinesische
Novellen. Berechtigte Übersetzung aus dem Russischen von Anna S. Kulischer.
Wien, Verlag für Literatur und Politik [1932]  188 p. Russian ed.: Kitaiekije
nowelly.

HUANG, SUNG-K'ANG, 黃松康 . Lu Hsün and the new culture movement of modern China. Amsterdam, Djambatan, 1957.  x, 158 p.

SHANG, CHUNG-I, 尚仲衣 , 1902-   A method of selecting foreign stories for
the American elementary schools: applied to the evaluation of stories translated by the author from the Chinese folk literature. New York, Teachers
College, Columbia University, 1929.  46 p. (Teachers college, Columbia
university. Contributions to education, 398).

THANNER, JOSEF. Liebesgeschichten aus China. Von den Liebe der schönen
Er Tu Meh, 二度梅 . München, Kellermann, 1957.  238 p.

TIEN, HAN, 田漢 . The white snake, a Peking opera. [Translated by Yang
Hsien-yi and Gladys Yang] Peking, Foreign Languages Press, 1957.  79 p.
illus.

YANG, CHIA-LO, 楊家駱 , ed. Brief synopses of the seven great series of Chinese classical writings: 73 works, 1736 volumes. [Translated by Pan Chia-lin.
Taipei, World Book Co., 1956] 35 p.; 13 p. (His Presentation of Chinese
classical writings, v. 1).

## Novels

BAUMANN, HANS, 1914-   Steppensöhne; vom Sieg über Dschingis-Khan. Reutlingen, Ensslin and Laiblin [1954]  285 p. illus.
——. Sons of the steppe, the story of how the conqueror Genghis Khan was overcome. London, Oxford University Press, 1957.  273 p. illus.

BEATON-JONES, CYNON, 1921-   The adventures of So Hi; illustrated by John
Ward. London, J. Barrie, 1951.  150 p. illus.
——. The same; New York, Vanguard Press [1956] 178 p. illus.
——. So Hi and the white horse. Illustrated by John Ward. New York, Van-
guard Press [1957] 120 p. illus.

CHAO, SHU-LI, 趙樹理 . Sanliwan village. Peking, Foreign Languages Press,
1957.  275 p.

CONSTEN, HERMANN, 1878-   Mysterien im Lande der Götter und lebenden
Buddhas; mit 9 Bildtafeln und einem farbigen Einbandbilde. Berlin, Vossische
Buchhandlung [c1925]  250 [1] p., 1 l. front. (port.) plates (part col.) (Pan-
bücherei eines freien lesebundes, III).

FOLK tales from China, first series. [Translated by Chang Su-chu. Illus. by
Chang Ta-yu. Peking, Foreign Languages Press, 1957.  146 p.

HOMEWARD journey and other stories, by contemporary Chinese writers. Peking, Foreign Languages Press, 1957. 234 p.

[HSI yu chi] 西遊記 Si yeou ki; ou, le voyage en Occident. Traduit de chinois
par Louis Avenol. Paris, Éditions du Seuill [1957] 2 v. illus.

[HSING shih hêng yen] 醒世恆言 Das chinesische Dekameron. [Aus dem Chinesischen von Johanna Herzfeldt] Rudolstadt, Greifenverlag, 195-.  345 p.

HUELSENBECK, RICHARD, 1892-   China fritzt Menschen, Roman. Frankfurt
a M., Ullstein Taschenbücher-Verlag, 1957.  221 p. (Ullstein Bücher, 160)
[1. Aufl. Zürich, Füssli, 1930,  347 p. ].

HUNG lo mêng 紅樓夢 . Le rêve dans le Pavillon Rouge. Traduit du chinois
   par Franz Kuhn. Version française établié par Armel Guerne. Paris, Guy
   Le Prat, 1957 . 344 p. front. illus.
ORLOWSKI, AXEL VON. Chinas letzte Kaiserin; Sittenverfall des chinesischen
   Kaiserreiches, Roman. Nach zeitgenössischen Quellenwerken und Memoiren
   frei bearb. Berlin, Deutsche Buchvertriebs- und Verlagsgesellschaft. [1957]
   350 p.
PATERSON, NEIL. Wettfahrt nach China. [The China run] Biographie einer Ur-
   grossmutter. Ins Deutsche übertragen von N. H. Reimers. München, Langen/
   Müller [1957] 71 p. (Langen-Müllers kleine Geschenkbücher, 68).
SHEN, YEN-PING, 沈雁冰 , 1896-    Midnight [by] Mao Tun [pseud. Translation
   by Hsu Meng-hsiung 許孟雄 ] Peking, Foreign Languages Press, 1957. 524
   p. illus.
SMITH, MABEL WALN. Springtime in Shanghai. London, Harrap, 1957. 216 p.
   illus.
SNEIDER, VERN J. A pail of oysters. New York, Putnam [1953] 311 p.
YEN, WEN-CHING, 嚴文井 . A strange journey (story) adapted by Chang Tsai-
   hsueh, 張再學 . [Translated by Yu Fan-chin.] Peking, Foreign Languages
   Press, 1957. 66 p. illus.

### Juvenile Literature

CHIANG, YEE, 1903-    The story of Ming. Middlesex, Eng., Penguin Books,
   1945. 30 p. illus. (Puffin Picture books).
JUDSON, CLARA (INGRAM), 1879-    Sun Yat-sen; illus. by Alexander Key.
   Evanston, Ill., Row, Peterson, c1953. 36 p. (Real People, 8).
MEINCK, WILLI. Die seltsamen Abenteuer des Marco Polo. Textill. von Hans
   Mau. 2. Aufl. Berlin, Kinderbuchverlag, 1956. 305 p.
———. Die seltsamen Reisen des Marco Polo. Textill. von Hans Mau. Berlin,
   Kinderbuchverlag, 1957. 417 p.
WEDDING, ALEX. Das eiserne Büffelchen; ein Jugendroman aus dem heutigen
   China. Mit Illustrationen von Kurt Zimmermann. [2., verb. Aufl.] Berlin,
   Verlag Neues Leben, 1953 [c1952] 407 p. illus.

### Art

BEARDSLEY, RICHARD KING, 1918-    Bibliographic materials in the Japanese
   language on Far Eastern archeology and ethnology [by] Richard K. Beardsley,
   with John B. Cornell and Edward Norbeck. Ann Arbor, University of Michigan Press, 1950. vi, 74 p. (University of Michigan. Center for Japanese
   Studies. Bibliographical series, 3).
CHINA VIEWPOINTS. Mei hsu; new art in China. Hong Kong, China Viewpoints,
   1957. 45 p. illus.
CHRISTENSEN, ERWIN OTTOMAR, 1890-    Chinese porcelains of the Widener
   collection. Washington, National Gallery of Art, 1947. 39 p. illus. (National gallery of art handbook, 2).
DESIGNS on Chinese opera costumes    中國·戲曲服裝圖案 , edited by the Research studio of the Northeast Drama Institute. Designs reproduced by Lu
   Hua 魯華 and Ma Chiang 馬強 . Peking, People's Art Pub. House, 1957.
   1 v., in portfolio (chiefly illus.) German ed.: Chinesische Theaterkostüme
   zusammengestellt vom Studio des Theaterinstituts nordostchinas. Kopiert
   von Lu Hua and Ma Tschiang. Peking, Volks Verlag für Kunst, 1957. i v. in
   portfolio (chiefly illus.).
DEXEL, THOMAS, 1890-    Chinesisches Steinzeug. Darmstadt, F. Schneekluth
   [1957] 34 p. 20 plates, map. (Wohnkunst und Hausrat, einst und jetzt, Bd. 30).
PELERZI, E. Les grottes de Loung-men. Shanghai, Oriental Press, 1923. 99
   p. illus.

SELECTED Chinese paper-cuts. [Peking, Guozi Shudian, 195-] [1] l., 17 mounted illus. (part col.)

SHEK, KAI-NUNG, 戚開儂 . Sketches of Christ from a Chinese brush, from the brush of Shek Kai-nung (Johnny Shek) in collaboration with Olaf K. Skinsnes. [Minneapolis, Augsburg Pub. House, 1956] 79 p. illus.

VANDERSTAPPEN, HARRIE A., 1921-    Investigation into the status of Chinese painters at the early Ming court and the existence of a painting academy.  Chicago [Library, Dept. of Photographic Reproduction, University of Chicago] 1955.  Microfilm copy (positive) of typescript.  Collation of the original, iv, 100 l.  Thesis--University of Chicago.

VICTORIA AND ALBERT MUSEUM, South Kensington. Chinese porcelain of the Ch'ing Dynasty. London, H. M. Stationery Off., 1957. 1 v. (unpaged, chiefly illus.).

WEDDING, ALEX. Leuchtende Schätze aus der Werkstatt Jung Pao-dsai. Berlin, Holz, 1957. 50 double pages.

YAMANAKA AND CO. Exhibition of early Chinese bronzes. New York, Yamanaka and Co., 1925. Cover-title, 14 p. photos.

## Science and Technology

CHANG, CALVIN C.,張長昌 [Chang Ch'ang-ch'ang] English-Chinese automotive nomenclature, compiled and edited by Calvin C. Chang; reviewed by John K. J. Kang, 康國涇 , George B Fraumann. Indianapolis, Marmon-Herrington Co. [1943] 236 [2] p.

CHINA (People's Republic of China, 1949-    ) Ministry of Railways. The construction of the Wu-han Yangtze river bridge. Peking, People's Railroad Press, 1957. 175 p. illus. tables.

DAVID, ARMAND, 1826-1900. Abbé David's diary: being an account of the French naturalist's journeys and observations in China in the years 1866-1869; tr. and ed. by Helen M. Fox. Cambridge, Harvard Univ. Press, 1949. xxxii, 302 p. col. illus.

GRESSITT, J. LINSLEY. The California Academy-Lingnan Dawn-Redwood Expedition. San Francisco, The Academy, 1953. 25-58 p. illus. (Proceedings of the California Academy of Sciences, 4th ser., 28:2).

[HSIA, YUNG-P'ING] 夏永平  comp. A glossary of structural engineering terms. [Tientsin, Civil engineering faculty of the School of Industry and Commerce, 1940] cover-title. 50, [2] p.

HSU, YIN-CHI, 徐蔭祺 , comp. Directory of Chinese biologists. Soochow, Biological Supply Service, Soochow University, 1934. 162 p.

HU, HSEN-HSU,胡先驌 . 1894-    The silva of China; a description of the trees which grow naturally in China. Peiping, Fan Memorial institute of biology and the National Forestry Research Bureau, Ministry of Agriculture and Forestry, 1948. 1 v. plates.

IKLE, FRED C. The growth of China's scientific and technical manpower. Santa Monica, Calif., Rand Corp., 1957. iii, 74 l. diagrs. (Rand Corporation. Research memorandum RM-1893).

KLAUTKE, PAUL. Nutzpflanzen und Nutztiere Chinas. Hannover, Hahnsche Buchhandlung, 1922. 159, [1] p. illus. (Weltwirtschaftliche Abhandlungen, v. bd.).

KURTÉN, BJÖRN. The Chinese hipparion fauna; a quantitative survey with comments on the ecology of the machairodonts and hyaenids and the taxonomy of the gazelles. Helsingfors, 1952. 82 p. illus., map, diagrs. (Societas Scientiarum Fennica. Commentationes biologicae, xiii, 4).

———. Age groups in fossil mammals, a preliminary report. [Helsingfors, 1953] 6 p. diagrs. (Societatis Scientiarum Fennica. Commentationes biologicae, xiii, 13).

LICENT, ÉMILE. Hoang ho--Pai ho. Comptes rendus de dix années (1914-1923) de séjour et d'exploration dans le bassin du Fleuve Jaune, du Pai ho et des autres tributaires du golfe du Pei Tcheu ly. Tientsin, La Librairie française, 1924. 4 v. illus., plates, plans. and atlas.

——. Dix années (1914-1923) de séjours et d'exploration dans le basin du Fleuve Jaune, du Pai ho et des autres tributaires du golfe du Pei tcheu ly. Album des photographies de l'atlas. (reimpression) Tientsin, Mission de Sien Hsien, 1933. 383 p. of illus.

——. Bibliographie critique du Musée Hoang ho Pai ho de Tientsin, 1914-1933. Tientsin, Mission de Sien Hsien, 1934. 27 p. (Publications du Musée Hoang ho Pai ho, 30).

——. Hoang ho—Paiho. Comptes-rendus de onze années (1923-1933) de séjour et d'exploration dans le bassin du fleuve Jaune, du Pai ho et des autres tributaires du golfe du Pei Tcheu ly. Tientsin, Mission de Sienhsien, 1935-36. 4 v. in 3. illus., plates (part fold.) and atlas (3 l., illus., maps) (Publications du Musée Hoang ho Paiho--no. 38).

——. Vingt deux années d'exploration dans le Nord de la Chine, en Mandchourie, en Mongolie et au Bas-Tibet (1914-1935). Tientsin, Musée Hoang ho Pai ho de Tientsin, 1935. 42 p. illus. ports. fold. map. (Publications du Musée Hoang ho Pai ho, 39).

MELL, RUDOLF, 1878-    Ein Biolog erlebt China.  Berlin-Frohnau, Condor Verlag, 1947. 237 p.

ROYAL ASIATIC SOCIETY OF GREAT BRITAIN AND IRELAND. North China Branch, Shanghai. China's natural history; a guide to the Shanghai Museum (R.A.S.) by Arthur de Carle Sowerby. Lepidoptera, by S. Josefsen-Bernier. Shanghai, Royal Asiatic Society, North China Branch, 1936. 108 p. col. front., illus (incl. plans) plates (part col.) ports.

SHANGHAI.MUSÉE HEUDE.  Le 70e anniversaire du Musée Heude, 1868-1938, par O. Piel.  Shanghai, 1939.  39 p.

SOWERBY, ARTHUR DE CARLE, 1885-1954. The natural history of China. (In Smithsonian institution. Annual report. 1923. Washington, 1925. p. 351-368). ''Reprinted from the Journal of the North China Branch of the Royal Asiatic society, vol. liii, 1922.''

——. A naturalist's note-book in China. Illustrated with numerous photographs and one hundred and eight sketches by the author. Shanghai, North-China Daily News and Herald, 1925. 17-270 p. illus., plates.

SOWERBY, RICHARD RAINE, 1886-    Sowerby of China: Arthur de Carle Sowerby, F.R.G.S.. F.Z.S. Kendal [Eng.] Printed by T. Wilson, 1956. 58 p. illus.

SUN, YÜN-CHU, 孫雲鑄, 1897-    The upper Cambrian trilobite-faunas of North China. Peiping, Geological Survey of China, 1935. [5]-93 p.; 3 p. incl. illus., tables, plates. (China. Geological survey. Palaeontologia sinica, ser. B, vol. vii, fasc. 2).

T'ANG, P'EI-SUNG, 湯佩松 , 1903-    Green thraldom, essays of a Chinese biologist. With an introd. by Joseph Needham. London, G. Allen and Unwin [1949] 127 p. port.

T'IEN, CH'I-CH'IUNG, 田奇瓗 , 1899-    Reports on the tin and arsenic deposits of Tanshanwo, Taishunlung and Hsianghualing, Hunan, by C. C. Tien, H. C. Wang and H. C. Hsiu 粟顯倓 . Changsha, 1931. 20, [52] p., 1 l. illus., x plates (incl. 4 fold. maps; 1 col.) (Hunan. Geological survey. Bulletin 11. Econ. geology 8).

WANG, KUNG-PIN, 王恭斌 , 1919-    Controlling factors in the future development of the Chinese coal industry. New York, King's Crown Press, 1947. 231 p. diagrs. maps.

## Miscellaneous

AUDEMARD, LOUIS, 1865-1955. Les jonques chinoises. Rotterdam, 1957- v. illus., port., fold. map. (Publicaties van het Museum voor Landen Volken-

kunde en het Maritiem Museum "Prins Hendrik," 5; Museum voor Land-en
Volkenkunde, Publicatie 4; Maritiem Museum "Prins Hendrik," Publicatie 3).

CHOAIN, JEAN. La voie rationelle de la médecine chinoise. Lille, Société
lilloise d'éditions et de librairie, 1957. 505 p. illus. (part col.).

GILES, LIONEL, 1875-1958. Six centuries at Tunhuang; a short account of the
Stein collection of Chinese mss. in the British Museum. London, China Society, 1944. 50 p. facsims. (China Society Sinological series, 2 ).

GRANET, MARCEL, 1884-1940. Fêtes et chansons ancienne de la Chine. 2. éd.
Paris, E. Leroux, 1929. 301, [1] p.

————. Festivals and songs of ancient China. Translated from the French by E. D.
Edwards. New York, E. P. Dutton; London, Routledge, 1932. ix, 281 p.
(The Broadway oriental library).

GULIK, ROBERT HANS VAN, 1910-    Hayagrîva; the mantrayânic aspect of
horse-cult in China and Japan. Leiden, E. J. Brill, 1935. 103 p., 1 l. illus.,
plates (Internationales archiv für ethnographie, supplement zu bd. xxxiii ).

HAO, TE-YUAN, 郝德元. An analysis of certain learning difficulties of Chinese
students in New York City. Ann Arbor, University Microfilms [1955] (University Microfilms, Ann Arbor, Mich. Publication no. 12218) Microfilm
copy of typescript. Collation of the original: xiv, 332 l. maps, tables. Thesis-
New York University.

HEWAT, ELIZABETH GLENDINNING KIRKWOOD. China: back to the wall. [Lec-
ture] 5th February, 1944. Bombay, National War Front, 1944. 12 p. (Studies in international relationship, 4 ).

MÉDARD, JULES HENRI, 1883-    Au pays de Si-wang-mou, Ta-ts'in 大秦西王
母 province romaine en Asie. Pékin, Impr. de la Politique de Pékin, 1936.
38 p. (Collection de la "Politique de Pékin").

WEI, YUNG-CHING, 魏永清. A plan for the preparation of secondary school
teachers in Hopei Province, China. New York, 1943. 150 l. (Columbia University. Teachers College Ed. D. report).

WHITAKER, URBAN GEORGE, 1924-    Americans and Chinese political problems, 1912-23. Ann Arbor, University Microfilms [1954] ([University Microfilms, Ann Arbor, Mich.] Publication no. 10,018) Microfilm copy (positive) of typescript. Collation of the original: iv, 415 l. Thesis-University of
Washington.

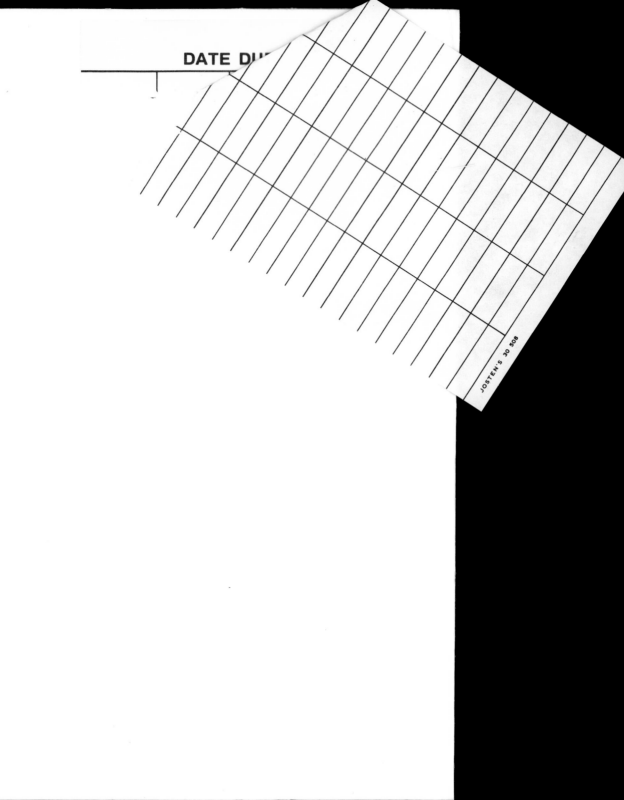

**DATE DUE**

JOSTEN'S 30 508